PRENTICE HALL
ADVANCED
ALGEBRA

Prentice Hall dedicates
this mathematics program
to all mathematics educators
and their students.

PRENTICE HALL
Needham, Massachusetts
Upper Saddle River, New Jersey
Glenview, Illinois

A U T H O R S

Allan Bellman

Sadie Chavis Bragg

Suzanne H. Chapin

Theodore J. Gardella

Bettye C. Hall

William G. Handlin, Sr.

Edward Manfre

Geometry Authors

Laurie E. Bass   Art Johnson

Basia Rinesmith Hall   Dorothy F. Wood

Contributing Author

Simone W. Bess

ADVANCED ALGEBRA

TOOLS FOR A CHANGING WORLD

$$y = a(x - h)^2 + k$$

Authors, Algebra & Advanced Algebra

Allan Bellman
Blake High School
Silver Spring, Maryland

Sadie Chavis Bragg, Ed.D.
Borough of Manhattan
Community College
The City University of New York
New York, New York

Suzanne H. Chapin, Ed.D.
Boston University
Boston, Massachusetts

Theodore J. Gardella
Formerly, Bloomfield Hills Public Schools
Bloomfield Hills, Michigan

Bettye C. Hall
Mathematics Consultant
Houston, Texas

William G. Handlin, Sr.
Spring Woods High School
Houston, Texas

Edward Manfre
Mathematics Consultant
Albuquerque, New Mexico

Authors, Geometry

Laurie E. Bass
The Fieldston School
Riverdale, New York

Basia Rinesmith Hall
East District
Houston Independent School District
Houston, Texas

Art Johnson, Ed.D.
Nashua High School
Nashua, New Hampshire

Dorothy F. Wood
Formerly, Kern High School District
Bakersfield, California

Contributing Author
Simone W. Bess, Ed.D.
University of Cincinnati
College of Education
Cincinnati, Ohio

PRENTICE HALL

ISBN: 0-13-050183-2

1 2 3 4 5 6 7 8 9 10   04 03 02 01 00

R E V I E W E R S

Series Reviewers

James Gates, Ed.D.
Executive Director Emeritus, National Council of Teachers of Mathematics, Reston, Virginia

Vinetta Jones, Ph.D.
National Director, EQUITY 2000, The College Board, New York, New York

Advanced Algebra

Eleanor Boehner
Methacton High School
Norristown, Pennsylvania

Laura Price Cobb
Dallas Public Schools
Dallas, Texas

William Earl, Ed.D.
Formerly Mathematics
 Education Specialist
Utah State Office of Education
Salt Lake City, Utah

Robin Levine Rubinstein
Shorewood High School
Shoreline, Washington

Algebra

John J. Brady III
Hume-Fogg High School
Nashville, Tennessee

Elias P. Rodriguez
Leander Junior High School
Leander, Texas

Dorothy S. Strong, Ed.D.
Chicago Public Schools
Chicago, Illinois

Art W. Wilson, Ed.D.
Abraham Lincoln High School
Denver, Colorado

Geometry

Sandra Argüelles Daire
Miami Senior High School
Miami, Florida

Priscilla P. Donkle
South Central High School
Union Mills, Indiana

Tom Muchlinski, Ph.D.
Wayzata High School
Plymouth, Minnesota

Bonnie Walker
Texas ASCD
Houston, Texas

Karen Doyle Walton, Ed.D.
Allentown College of
 Saint Francis de Sales
Center Valley, Pennsylvania

Staff Credits

The people who made up the *Advanced Algebra* team—representing editorial, design, marketing, page production, editorial services, production, manufacturing, technology, electronic publishing, and advertising and promotion—and their managers are listed below. Bold type denotes core team members.

Barbara A. Bertell, Bruce Bond, Judith D. Buice, Kathy Carter, Todd Christy, Linda M. Coffey, Noralie V. Cox, Sheila DeFazio, Edward de Leon, Christine Deliee, Gabriella Della Corte, Robert G. Dunn, Frederick Fellows, Barbara Flockhart, Patricia Fromkin, Elizabeth Good, David Graham, Maria Green, Bridget A. Hadley, Kerri Hoar, Joanne Hudson, Vanessa Hunnibell, Albert S. Jacobson, Mimi Jigarjian, Linda D. Johnson, Russell Lappa, Ann M. McSweeney, **Eve Melnechuk**, Cindy A. Noftle, **Caroline M. Power**, **Roger E. Powers**, Robin Santel, Martha G. Smith, Kira Thaler, **Christina Trinchero,** Stuart Wallace, Jeff Weidenaar, Pearl B. Weinstein, Joe Will, **Mary Jane Wolfe, Stewart Wood**

We would like to give special thanks to our National Math Consultants, Ann F. Bell and Brenda Underwood, for all their help in developing this program.

Advanced Algebra Contents

Models, Functions, and Permutations

Connections and Applications

. . . and More!

Step by Step

Chapter Project

Determining Whether Practice Affects Performance

CHAPTER 2

Linear Relationships and Functions

Connections and Applications

. . . and More!

ASSESSMENT

Chapter Project

Time Squeeze
Comparing Team and Individual Productivity

CHAPTER

3

Matrices

 Connections

. . . and More!

Chapter Project *Munching Microbes*
Writing Matrices to Analyze Ecological Data

CHAPTER 4

Linear Systems

Connections and Applications

Chapter Project **Hot Hot Hot!**
Using Systems to Make Production Decisions

Quadratic Equations and Functions

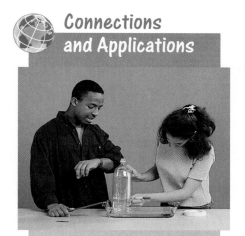

Connections and Applications

. . . and More!

Chapter Project **On Target**
Analyzing the Mathematics of Archery

Polynomials and Polynomial Functions

Connections and Applications

. . . and More!

Connections and Applications

. . . and More!

Chapter Project   *Aging Artifacts*
Determining the Age of Objects

Rational Functions

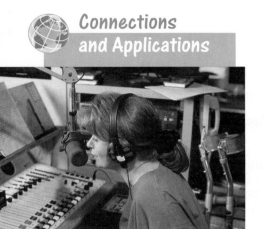

**Connections
and Applications**

. . . and More!

Chapter Project **Under Pressure**
Comparing Depth and Pressure Under Water

Periodic Functions and Trigonometry

Connections and Applications

. . . and More!

Chapter Project **The Wave of the Future**
Analyzing the Effects of Tidal Power

CHAPTER 10

Quadratic Relations

Connections
and Applications

Design 461
Solar Energy 467
Earth Science 470
Architecture 479
Geometry 483
Air Traffic Control 490
History 496

...and More!

Chapter Project **About Face!**
Using Conic Sections to Draw Clown Faces

More Probability and Statistics

Connections and Applications

Chapter Project *On the Move*
Creating a Survey to Investigate Transportation

Sequences and Series

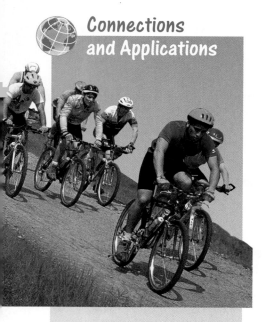

Connections and Applications

ASSESSMENT

Chapter Project **Get the Picture**
Designing Pages of a Book

To the Student

Students like you helped Prentice Hall develop this program. They identified tools you can use to help you learn now in this course and beyond. In this special "To the Student" section and throughout this program, you will find the **tools you need to help you succeed.** We'd like to hear how these tools work for you. Write us at Prentice Hall Mathematics, 160 Gould Street, Needham, MA 02194 or visit us at http://www.phschool.com.

"...Instead of problem after problem of pointless numbers, we should have a chance to think and to truly understand what we are doing. I personally think that we all should be taught this way."

Chris, Grade 9
Carson City, NV

"...I learn mathematics best when I draw a diagram or make a graph that helps show what the problem is that I will solve."

Amy, Grade 11
Columbia, SC

"...I like to review what I learn as I go, rather than cramming the night before a test."

Ali, Grade 10
St. Paul, MN

LEARN About Learning!

What comes to your mind when you hear the word **style**? Maybe it's hair style, or style of dress, or walking style. Have you ever thought about your learning style? Just like your hair or your clothes or your walk, everybody has a learning style that they like best because it works best for them. Look around you now. What do you see? Different styles ... some like yours, some different from yours. That's the way it is with learning styles, too.

What's Your Best Learning Style?

I understand math concepts best when I...

- ❏ A. Read about them.
- ❏ B. Look at and make illustrations, graphs, and charts that show them.
- ❏ C. Draw sketches or handle manipulatives to explore them.
- ❏ D. Listen to someone explain them.

When I study, I learn more when I...

- ❏ A. Review my notes and the textbook.
- ❏ B. Study any graphs, charts, diagrams, or other illustrations.
- ❏ C. Write ideas on note cards; then study the ideas.
- ❏ D. Explain what I know to another person.

When I collaborate with a group, I am most comfortable when I...

- ❏ A. Take notes.
- ❏ B. Make visuals for display.
- ❏ C. Demonstrate what I know to others.
- ❏ D. Give presentations to other groups or the whole class.

Look for a pattern in your responses.
"A" responses suggest that you learn best by reading;
"B" responses indicate a visual learning style;
"C" responses suggest a tactile, or hands-on, learning style;
"D" responses signal that you probably learn best by listening and talking about what you are learning.

Having a preferred learning style does not limit you to using just that one. Most people learn by using a combination of learning styles. You'll be amazed by the ways that knowing more about yourself and how you learn will help you be successful — not only successful in mathematics, but successful in all your subject areas. When you know how you learn best, you will be well equipped to enter the work place.

Use this chart to help you strengthen your different learning styles.

Learning Style	Learning Tips
Learning by *reading*	✳ Schedule time to read each day. ✳ Carry a book or magazine to read during wait time. ✳ Read what you like to read—it's OK not to finish a book.
Learning by using *visual* cues	✳ Visualize a problem situation. ✳ Graph solutions to problems. ✳ Let technology, such as computers and calculators, help you.
Learning by using *hands-on* exploration	✳ Make sketches when solving a problem. ✳ Use objects to help you solve problems. ✳ Rely on technology as a tool for exploration and discovery.
Learning by *listening and talking*	✳ Volunteer to give presentations. ✳ Explain your ideas to a friend. ✳ Listen intently to what others are saying.

Most important, believe in yourself and your ability to learn!

What you do now...

Learn best by using a particular learning style . . .

What you do in this course...

Example 1
Example 2

Relating to the Real World 🌐

What you do in the workplace...

Choose a career that you enjoy because it is natural for you.

Help Teamwork Work for YOU!

Each of us works with other people on teams throughout our lives. What's your job? Your job on a team, that is. Maybe you play center on your basketball team, maybe you count votes for your school elections, perhaps you help decorate the gym for a school function, or maybe you help make scenery for a community play. From relay races to doing your part of the job in the workplace, teamwork is required for success.

TEAMWORK CHECKLIST

☑ **Break apart the large task into smaller tasks, which become the responsibility of individual group members.**

☑ **Treat the differences in group members as a benefit.**

☑ **Try to listen attentively when others speak.**

☑ **Stay focused on the task at hand and the goal to be accomplished.**

☑ **Vary the tasks you do in each group and participate.**

☑ **Recognize your own and others' learning styles.**

☑ **Offer your ideas and suggestions.**

☑ **Be socially responsible and act in a respectful way.**

What you do now....	What you do in this course...	What you do in the workplace...
Play on a team, decorate the gym, or perform in the band . . .	WORK TOGETHER	Collaborate with coworkers on projects.

It's All COMMUNICATION

We communicate in songs. We communicate in letters. We communicate with our body movements. We communicate on the phone. We communicate in cyberspace. It's all talking about ideas and sharing what you know. It's the same in mathematics — we communicate by reading, writing, talking, and listening. Whether we are working together on a project or studying with a friend for a test, we are communicating.

Ways to Communicate What You Know and Are Able to Do

✔ Explain to others how you solve a problem.

✔ Listen carefully to others.

✔ Use mathematical language in your writing in other subjects.

✔ Pay attention to the headings in textbooks — they are signposts that help you.

✔ Think about videos and audiotapes as ways to communicate mathematical ideas.

✔ Be on the lookout for mathematics when you read, watch television, or see a movie.

✔ Communicate with others by using bulletin boards and chat rooms on the Internet.

What you do now...

Teach a young relative a sport . . .

What you do in this course...

THINK AND DISCUSS

What you do in the workplace...

Written and verbal communication at work.

Solving PROBLEMS — a SKILL You USE Every DAY

Problem solving is a skill — a skill that you probably use without even knowing it. When you think critically in social studies to draw conclusions about pollution and its stress on the environment, or when a mechanic listens to symptoms of trouble and logically determines the cause, you are both using a mathematical problem-solving skill. Problem solving also involves logical reasoning, wise decision making, and reflecting on your solutions.

Tips for Problem Solving

Recognize that there is more than one way to solve most problems.

When solving a word problem, read it, decide what to do, make a plan, look back at the problem, and revise your answer.

Experiment with various solution methods.

Understand that it is just as important to know how to solve a problem as it is to actually solve it.

Be aware of times you are using mathematics to solve problems that do not involve computation, such as when you reason to make a wise decision.

What you do now...	What you do in this course...	What you do in the workplace...
Make decisions based on changing conditions, such as weather . . .	PROBLEM SOLVING	*Synchronize the timing of traffic lights to enhance traffic flow.*

Studying for the **TEST** Whatever It May Be

SATs, ACTs, chapter tests, and weekly quizzes — they all test what you know and are able to do. Have you ever thought about **how** you can take these tests to your advantage? You are evaluated now in your classes and you will be evaluated when you hold a job.

Pointers for Gaining Points

◆ Study as you progress through a chapter, instead of cramming for a test.

◆ Recognize when you are lost and seek help before a test.

◆ Review important graphs and other visuals when studying for a test, then picture them in your mind.

◆ Study for a test with a friend or study group.

◆ Take a practice test.

◆ Think of mnemonic devices to help you, such as Please Excuse My Dear Aunt Sally, which is one way to remember order of operations (parentheses, exponents, multiply, divide, add, subtract).

◆ Reread test questions before answering them.

◆ Check to see if your answer is reasonable.

◆ Think positively and visualize yourself doing well on the test.

◆ Relax during the test … there is nothing there that you have not seen before.

What you do now...	What you do in this course...	What you do in the workplace...
Study notes in preparation for tests and quizzes . . .	**SELF ASSESSMENT** How am I doing?	Prepare for and participate in a job interview.
	Exercises ON YOUR OWN	
	Exercises CHECKPOINT	

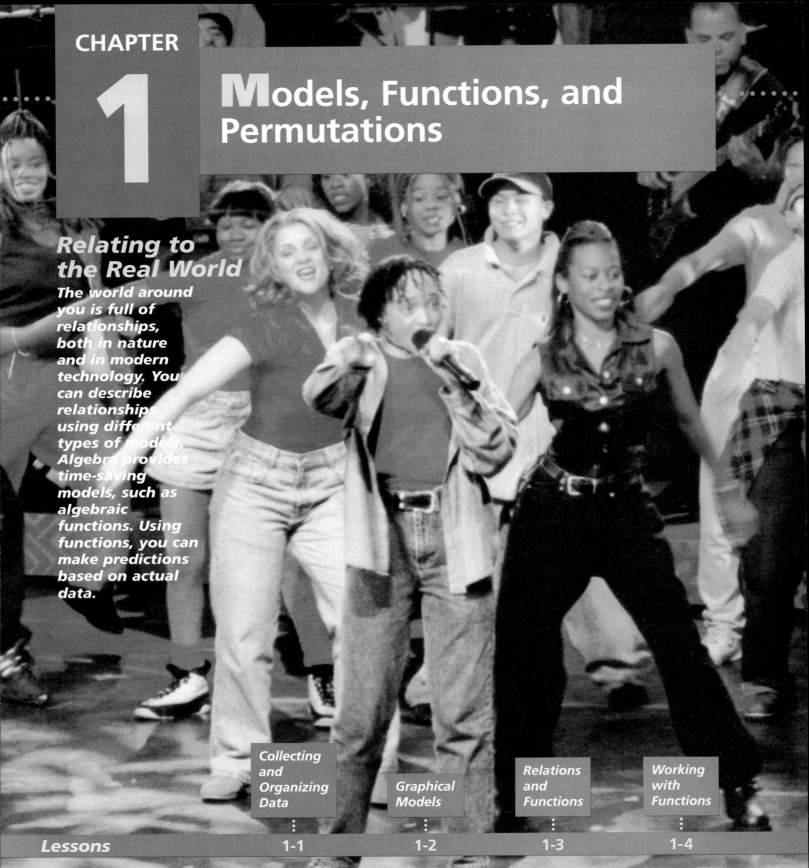

CHAPTER 1

Models, Functions, and Permutations

Relating to the Real World

The world around you is full of relationships, both in nature and in modern technology. You can describe relationships using different types of models. Algebra provides time-saving models, such as algebraic functions. Using functions, you can make predictions based on actual data.

Collecting and Organizing Data

Graphical Models

Relations and Functions

Working with Functions

Lessons

1-1

1-2

1-3

1-4

STEP BY STEP

Does the amount of time you spend practicing something affect your final performance? Does the number of times you complete a puzzle affect how quickly you can finish it? Behavioral scientists and psychologists analyze how people learn.

As you work through this chapter, you will collect and record data on learning. You will use scatter plots and graphs to display and analyze relationships in the data you gather. Then you will summarize your findings and make predictions.

To help you complete the project:

▼ **p. 10** *Find Out by Observing*
▼ **p. 25** *Find Out by Doing*
▼ **p. 31** *Find Out by Graphing*
▼ **p. 50** *Finishing the Project*

Vertical and Horizontal Translations

Counting Methods and Permutations

Real Numbers

1-5   1-6   1-7

What You'll Learn

- Organizing data in tables, matrices, and graphs

...And Why

To analyze relationships and calculate data totals

1-1 Collecting and Organizing Data

WORK TOGETHER

Are height and shoe size related? Try this activity to find out.

- Write your height and shoe size on a piece of paper. Collect and put the pieces of paper from the class in a box.

- Work with several classmates. Have your group pick six pieces of paper, record the data, and place the pieces of paper back in the box.

1. Graph the data on your own individual scatter plot. Plot shoe size on the horizontal axis and height on the vertical axis.

2. Describe the relationship between height and shoe size suggested by your graph.

3. *Discussion* Compare the graphs drawn by the members of your group. How are they similar? How are they different?

4. *Statistics* Do you think your group's data represent the students in your school? Explain. How could you improve the sample?

QUICK REVIEW

A *scatter plot* is a graph that relates data from two different sets by plotting the data as ordered pairs. You can use a scatter plot to determine a relationship between two sets of data.

For more practice on descriptive statistics, see the Skills Handbook page 678.

Using Scatter Plots

Two sets of data are related if the values of a variable representing one set depend on the values of a variable for another set.

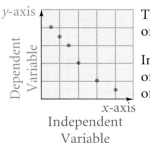

The value of y depends on the value of x.

In this case, as the value of x increases, the value of y decreases.

Example 1 **Relating to the Real World**

Consumer Issues A magazine rates notebook computers. In the ratings, what relationship exists between the price of each computer and its performance index?

Price/Performance Index of Notebook Computers

Brand	Price	Index
A	$3000	89
B	$2600	98
C	$3200	98
D	$2900	99
E	$3900	101
F	$4700	110
G	$5100	113
H	$4700	144
I	$7000	164

Source: PC Magazine

A scatter plot helps you see the relationship between two sets of numbers. You want to see how the performance index is related to the price.

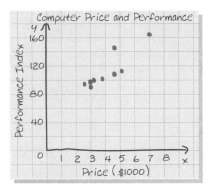

In general, as the price of the computer increases, so does its performance index.

QUICK REVIEW

A *correlation* is a mutual relationship or connection. Correlations can be positive, negative, or nonexistent.

Relationships can also be expressed in terms of correlation.

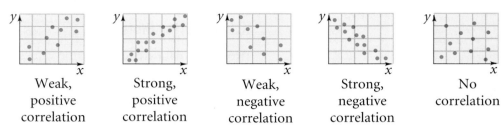

| Weak, positive correlation | Strong, positive correlation | Weak, negative correlation | Strong, negative correlation | No correlation |

5. Compare the weak and strong correlations. Describe the difference between them. Compare the positive and negative correlations. Describe the difference between them.

6. Describe the type of correlation between the cost of a notebook computer and its performance index.

7. **Estimation** Estimate what performance index to expect for a $6000 notebook computer.

8. **Critical Thinking** Do you think the relationship you found in Example 1 would apply to all types of computers? Explain.

Using Spreadsheets and Matrices

Graphs are created using information found in tables. A computer spreadsheet program is a table that not only displays numbers but adds, subtracts, multiplies, or divides them. You enter the data and write a formula. The spreadsheet does the computation.

TECHNOLOGY HINT

A spreadsheet allows you to enter formulas in cells so that calculations can be done automatically.

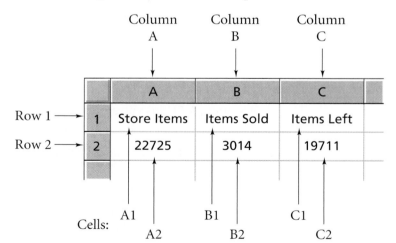

- Type information in cells A1, B1, and C1.

- Enter data in cells A2 and B2.

- Type the formula =A2−B2 in cell C2. The answer appears in C2.

Example 2 **Relating to the Real World** ┄┄┄┄┄┄┄┄┄┄┄┄┄

Retailing This spreadsheet shows the number and types of books sold by a book store during August. Determine how many books of each type were sold that month.

	A	B	C	D	E	
1	August	Novels	Biographies	Science Fiction	Other Nonfiction	
2	1st wk	175	100	93	100	
3	2nd wk	154	93	81	104	
4	3rd wk	201	110	114	103	
5	4th wk	180	92	100	110	

To find out how many books of each type were sold during August, add the entries in each column except A. Record the information in row 6.

Novels: In cell B6, enter the formula $=B2+B3+B4+B5$. The spreadsheet adds 175, 154, 201, and 180, and the sum 710 appears.

Biographies: In C6, enter $=C2+C3+C4+C5$. ⟶ 395

Science Fiction: In D6, enter $=D2+D3+D4+D5$. ⟶ 388

Other Nonfiction: In E6, enter $=E2+E3+E4+E5$. ⟶ 417

6	Totals	710	395	388	417	

9. Describe how you would find the total number of books sold each week. Write the formula you would use.

Another type of table you can use to organize and work with data is a matrix. A **matrix** (plural: matrices) is a rectangular array of numbers arranged in rows and columns. Matrices are represented by a capital letter and written within brackets.

The **dimensions of a matrix** are the numbers of rows and columns. For example, you can display the second row of Example 2 as a 1×4 (read "one by four") matrix since it has one row and four columns.

$$
\begin{array}{cccc}
\text{Novels} & \text{Biographies} & \text{Science Fiction} & \text{Other Nonfiction} \\
\downarrow & \downarrow & \downarrow & \downarrow
\end{array}
$$

$$
\text{1st Wk} \longrightarrow \begin{bmatrix} 175 & 100 & 93 & 100 \end{bmatrix}
$$

10. What are the dimensions of each matrix?

a. $\begin{bmatrix} -4 & 1 & -3 \end{bmatrix}$
b. $\begin{bmatrix} 4 & 6 & 5 \\ 2 & -3 & -7 \\ 1 & 0 & 8 \end{bmatrix}$
c. $\begin{bmatrix} 1 & 0 \\ 2 & -4 \\ 6 & 5 \end{bmatrix}$

Each number in a matrix is an **element** of the matrix. An element of a matrix is identified by its position, given by the row and column numbers. For example, a_{13} is the element in row 1 and column 3.

Example 3   Relating to the Real World

Education The table shows data about technology in public schools in a recent year. Display the data as a 3×4 matrix.

Type of School	Videodisk Players	Modems	Networks	CD-ROMs
Elementary	12,326	14,782	11,155	16,816
Junior High	4,672	5,393	4,425	6,170
Senior High	5,805	8,620	8,042	9,063

Source: *Quality Education Data, Inc.*

$$T = \begin{bmatrix} 12{,}326 & 14{,}782 & 11{,}155 & 16{,}816 \\ 4{,}672 & 5{,}393 & 4{,}425 & 6{,}170 \\ 5{,}805 & 8{,}620 & 8{,}042 & 9{,}063 \end{bmatrix}$$

11. What is element t_{32} of matrix T?

Exercises   ON YOUR OWN

Classify each scatter plot as showing *positive*, *negative*, or *no correlation*. If possible, state whether the relationship is strong or weak.

1.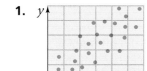

2.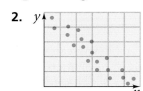

3.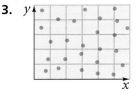

4. Use the matrix at the right.
   a. What are the dimensions of the matrix?
   b. What is element a_{31}?
   c. Determine the percent of people 60 or older who change channels during commercials.

5. How would you define an $m \times n$ matrix?

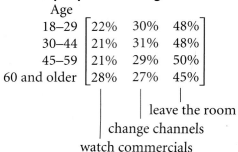

What do people do during commercials?

Age
$$\begin{array}{l} \text{18–29} \\ \text{30–44} \\ \text{45–59} \\ \text{60 and older} \end{array} \begin{bmatrix} 22\% & 30\% & 48\% \\ 21\% & 31\% & 48\% \\ 21\% & 29\% & 50\% \\ 28\% & 27\% & 45\% \end{bmatrix}$$

leave the room
change channels
watch commercials

6. Classify the shoes shown in order from tallest person to shortest person.

7. a. Describe the relationship between the amount of time a volleyball player is in a game and the number of points the player scores.
  b. How could you collect data to verify your answer to part (a)?
  c. How would you display the data collected?

Construct scatter plots to display the data in the tables below. Be sure to label both axes. Describe any correlation.

8.

Year	Consumer Price Index
1985	107.6
1986	109.6
1987	113.6
1988	118.3
1989	124.0
1990	130.7
1991	136.2
1992	140.3
1993	144.5
1994	148.2
1995	152.4

Source: *U.S. Bureau of Labor Statistics*

9.

School Year Ending	Total Expenditures for Education ($ millions)
1986	269,485
1987	291,974
1988	313,375
1989	346,883
1990	381,228
1991	412,652
1992	434,102
1993	458,048
1994	486,100
1995	508,600

Source: *U.S. Dept. of Education*

10.

City and Latitude		Average Sept. Temperature (°F)
Charlotte	35.2° N	82
Chicago	41.9° N	76
Dallas	32.8° N	90
Indianapolis	39.7° N	78
Kansas City	39.3° N	79
Memphis	35.1° N	84
Minneapolis	45.0° N	71
Pittsburgh	40.4° N	75
San Diego	32.7° N	77
Seattle	47.5° N	69
Washington	38.9° N	80

Source: *National Oceanic and Atmospheric Administration*

11. Your principal conducted a study. The data have been displayed in the four tables shown at the right.
  a. Use the information in the tables to create four 2 × 2 matrices displaying the given information for students from grades 9–12.
  b. How many males in the school have part-time jobs?
  c. How many females in the school have part-time jobs?
  d. What percent of the students with part-time jobs are female?

9th Grade	Has Part-time Job	No Part-time Job
Males	5	95
Females	15	90

10th Grade	Has Part-time Job	No Part-time Job
Males	35	65
Females	30	55

11th Grade	Has Part-time Job	No Part-time Job
Males	65	35
Females	75	30

12th Grade	Has Part-time Job	No Part-time Job
Males	70	25
Females	65	45

12. Open-ended Choose a data set from the lesson and display it another way.

13. Writing Choose two ways of displaying data. Describe the advantages and disadvantages of each.

14. Spreadsheet The spreadsheet shows the values of the merchandise sold for the last four years at Bob's House of Fashion.

	A	B	C	D	
1	Year	Shirts	Pants	Sweaters	
2	1993	$2500	$1250	$1200	
3	1994	$3000	$1550	$1300	
4	1995	$3250	$270	$900	
5	1996	$4000	$2300	$1600	

a. What does the number in cell C4 represent?
b. Which cell shows the value of the shirts that were sold in 1995?
c. What formula would you use to find the total sales for 1995?
d. Calculate the value of all the shirts sold from 1993 to 1996.

Chapter Project **Find Out by Observing**

Work in pairs. Time each other as you solve a puzzle or maze. Take turns until you have each completed the puzzle or maze five times. (Don't watch each other's solutions!) Time other people solving your puzzle or maze five times. Organize all the trials and times in a table. Summarize your results. What effect does repetition have on solving time? How would more repetitions affect the time?

Exercises   MIXED REVIEW

Simplify each expression.

15. $16 + 4 \cdot 2 \div 10$

16. $25 - 10^2 + 150 \div 3$

17. $1.25 \div 0.5 + 7.5 - 115$

18. $9 - (8 - 3)^2 \div 2$

19. $5 + \left(\frac{3}{4}\right)^2 \cdot \frac{8}{15} - 2$

20. $12 + ((-6)^2 - 4^2)^2 - 7$

21. Aviation In 1995, a Concorde set the around-the-world record time for a passenger jet at 31 h, 27 min, 49 s. Six refueling stops took a total of 8 h, 48 min, 8 s. What percent of the time was spent in the air?

22. You are buying lunch for your family. You get two turkey sandwiches for $3.50 each, a cheese sandwich for $2.50, and two yogurts for $1 each. You also buy 3 cartons of milk for $.50 each and 2 cans of juice for $1 each. How much did you spend in all?

Getting Ready for Lesson 1-2

23. Troy baby-sits for neighbors. His fees are shown in the table.
  a. Graph the relationship between hours worked and fee. What do you notice?
  b. Draw a line that best shows the trend in the data. How much should he charge for working $\frac{1}{2}$ h? 5 h? $1\frac{1}{2}$ h?

Hours Worked	1	2	3	4
Fee	$2.50	$5.00	$8.00	$10.00

Math Toolbox

The Slope of a Line

Before Lesson 1-2

The average rate of change between points $P_1(x_1, y_1)$ and $P_2(x_2, y_2)$ is the **slope** of $\overline{P_1P_2}$. It is found using the ratio below.

$$m = \frac{\text{vertical change}}{\text{horizontal change}} \quad \text{or} \quad \frac{y_2 - y_1}{x_2 - x_1}$$

At the right, the slope of $\overline{PQ}$ is $\frac{QM}{PM}$ and the slope of $\overline{QR}$ is $\frac{RN}{QN}$. These two ratios are equal because they involve corresponding sides of the similar triangles PQM and QRN.

By similar reasoning, the slopes found from any two pairs of points on a line are equal. This number is the **slope of the line.**

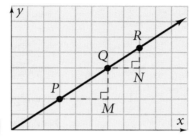

Example 1

Find the slope of the line that contains the points $(3, 2)$ and $(9, 6)$.

Identify $(3, 2)$ as (x_1, y_1) and $(9, 6)$ as (x_2, y_2). [Or, you could have used $(3, 2)$ as (x_2, y_2) and $(9, 6)$ as (x_1, y_1).]

$$m = \frac{y_2 - y_1}{x_2 - x_1} = \frac{6 - 2}{9 - 3} = \frac{4}{6} = \frac{2}{3}$$

The slope of the line that contains $(3, 2)$ and $(9, 6)$ is $\frac{2}{3}$.

Example 2

Find the slope of the line $y = -3x - 7$.

Choose two convenient values for x and substitute to find the y-values.

If $x = 1$, $y = -3(1) - 7 = -10$. If $x = 0$, $y = -3(0) - 7 = -7$.

$$m = \frac{-7 - (-10)}{0 - 1} = \frac{3}{-1} = -3$$

Find the slope of the line that contains each pair of points.

1. $P(6, 2)$ and $Q(4, 1)$

2. $A(0, 0)$ and $B(5, -4)$

3. $G(-1, 5)$ and $H(4, -3)$

Find the slope of each line.

4. $y = -4x + 12$

5. $y = 7x - 1$

6. $y = \frac{1}{2}x$

7. $y = -\frac{2}{3}x + 1$

8. $3y = x - \frac{1}{2}$

9. $-2y = 6x + 2$

10. $3y - 2x = 1$

11. $-2y + 8x - 5 = 0$

12. Writing Compare the slope of a line that rises as you move to the right with the slope of one that falls as you move to the right.

What You'll Learn

- Representing data graphically

...And Why

To make reasonable predictions about sports events

What You'll Need

- six books
- scale
- graph paper
- clear plastic ruler

TECHNOLOGY HINT

You can use a graphing calculator to display the scatter plot.

For more practice on the coordinate plane, see the Skills Handbook page 668.

1-2 Graphical Models

WORK TOGETHER

Work with a partner.

1. Place one of your textbooks on a scale. Record the weight in a table like the one below.

Number of Pages	▦	▦	▦	▦	▦	▦
Weight (oz)	▦	▦	▦	▦	▦	▦

2. Weigh another book and record its weight.

3. Weigh four other books and complete your table.

4. a. Construct a scatter plot for the data in your table.
   b. Describe any relationship you see between the number of pages in a book and its weight.
   c. Draw a trend line that seems to best fit the points on your scatter plot. Describe the trend in the data.
   d. Do all points on the scatter plot appear to fit the trend line?
   e. **Predict** the weight of a book with 1000 pages; with 250 pages.

5. Will everyone in the class have the same line for the book experiment? Why or why not?

A *mathematical model* can be an equation, a graph, a set of ordered pairs, or a table of values.

Number of Subscribers to Cable TV (1980 to 1994)

Year	Number of Subscribers
1980	17.5 million
1985	35.5 million
1986	38.2 million
1987	41.2 million
1988	44.2 million
1989	47.5 million
1990	50.5 million
1991	52.6 million
1992	54.3 million
1993	56.2 million
1994	58.5 million

Source: *Paul Kagan Associates*

THINK AND DISCUSS

The trend line you drew in the Work Together activity is a mathematical model. It shows the relationship between the number of pages and the weight of each book. You can use trend lines to make predictions.

Example 1 **Relating to the Real World**

Media The table at the left shows the number of cable subscribers from 1980 to 1994. Draw a line that models how the number of subscribers relates to time. Use your model to predict the number of cable television subscribers in the year 2000.

Draw a scatter plot from the data in the table.

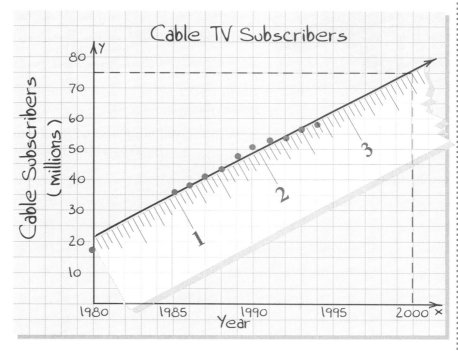

Use a clear plastic ruler to draw the line that best fits the points.

The model predicts that cable television will have 75 million subscribers in the year 2000.

6. Describe the correlation between the year and the number of cable television subscribers.

7. Explain why the year was graphed as the independent variable.

8. **Critical Thinking** What would cause the slope of the trend line to increase? to decrease? Give an example of each.

Example 2   **Relating to the Real World**

Sports Find a trend line that models the relationship between the year of the Boston Marathon and the winning time (in minutes) for the women's wheelchair division.

Year	Time (min)	Year	Time (min)
1977	229	1989	110
1980	169	1990	103
1982	133	1991	103
1984	177	1992	97
1985	125	1993	95
1986	129	1994	94
1987	140	1995	101
1988	131	1996	113

Source: *Sports 'n Spokes Magazine*

Create a scatter plot to show the correlation. Draw the line that seems to best fit the data.

Who? Jean Driscoll from Illinois has won the women's wheelchair division of the Boston Marathon more times than any male or female runner. The race covers more than 26 mi.

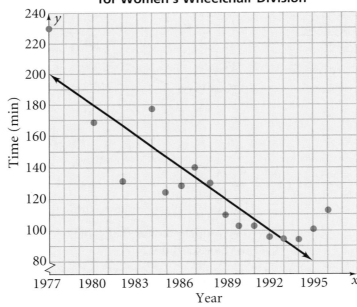

Winning Time of the Boston Marathon for Women's Wheelchair Division

9. Is the trend shown above likely to continue? Explain.

When you can draw a line through or close to the points of a graph, the relationship is linear.

Not all sets of data are best represented with a line.

Example 3 **Relating to the Real World**

Construction The table at the left shows the number of new apartments completed in the years from 1980 to 1993. Draw a scatter plot to show the correlation.

Number of New U.S. Apartments Completed (1980 to 1993)

Year	Number of Apartments
1980	196,100
1981	135,300
1982	117,000
1983	191,500
1984	313,200
1985	365,200
1986	407,600
1987	345,600
1988	284,500
1989	247,800
1990	214,300
1991	165,300
1992	110,200
1993	77,200

Source: *U.S. Bureau of the Census*

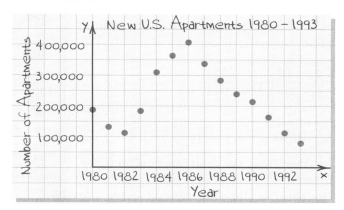

Looking at the scatter plot, you can see that it would be difficult to place a trend line on the graph. These data do not show a linear correlation.

10. Describe the correlation, if any, between the year and the number of new apartments built.

11. **Statistical Reasoning** Using the graph, could you predict the number of apartments that would be built in 2010? Explain.

12. Suppose the data set for Example 3 had only included the years 1986–1993. Describe the resulting correlation.

Exercises   **ON YOUR OWN**

Draw a trend line for each scatter plot.

1.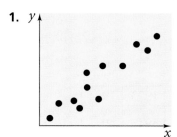

2.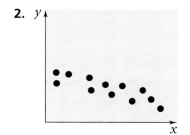

3.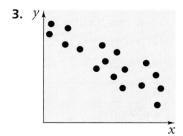

4. **Standardized Test Prep** Which relationship is most likely to be linear?
  A. age in years and height in inches
  B. weight in pounds and height in inches
  C. age in years and age in months
  D. age in years and weight in pounds
  E. weight in pounds and shoe size

5. Economics Use the data at the right.
  a. Draw a scatter plot to show the total sales of products in the United States between 1980 and 1993. Draw a trend line to model the relationship.
  b. **Critical Thinking** Does your model give a good prediction for total sales in 1994? 1995? 2005? Explain.
  c. Use the model to predict the sales this year.

6. a. Use the table below. Draw a scatter plot and a trend line to model a relationship between x and y.

x	1.0	2.0	3.0	4.0	5.0	6.0	7.0
y	0.0	1.0	1.5	7.0	7.0	8.0	12.0

  b. Predict the value of y if $x = 10$.
  c. Predict the value of x at which $y = 14$.

Year	Total Sales (billions)
1980	$328
1985	$424
1986	$432
1987	$459
1988	$496
1989	$523
1990	$542
1991	$538
1992	$559
1993	$592

Source: *U.S. Bureau of the Census*

7. Social Studies The table shows per capita (person) revenue and expenditure for selected states from a recent year.
  a. Show the data on a scatter plot. Draw a trend line.
  b. If a state collected revenue of $2000 per person, how much would you expect it to spend per person?
  c. Nebraska spent $2304 per person during that year. According to your model, how much did it collect in taxes per person?
  d. In that same year, Alaska collected $10,303 per person in taxes and spent $8253 per person. Does this information follow the trend? Explain.

8. a. Health Draw a scatter plot of the data shown below and a trend line to model the relationship.

State	Per Capita Revenue ($)	Per Capita Expenditure ($)
Connecticut	3359	3228
Delaware	3625	3321
Georgia	2039	2037
Hawaii	4151	4365
Missouri	1974	1875
Nevada	2305	2280
Oklahoma	2250	2183
Texas	1980	1948
Washington	2774	2879

Source: *U.S. Bureau of the Census*

Year	1980	1985	1989	1990	1991	1992	1993	1994
Red Meat Eaten Per Capita (lb)	126.4	124.9	115.9	112.3	111.9	114.1	112.1	114.8

Source: *U.S. Dept. of Agriculture*

  b. Does your model suggest that the amount of red meat Americans eat each year is decreasing linearly? Explain.
  c. How much red meat do you think the average American will eat in the year 2000?

9. Social Studies The table below shows data from the state of Arizona.

Year	1970	1980	1985	1987	1988	1989	1990	1991	1992	1993	1994
Population (thousands)	1775	2718	3184	3437	3535	3622	3665	3747	3835	3945	4075

Source: *U.S. Bureau of the Census*

  a. Draw a scatter plot. Describe the correlation, if any.
  b. Is a line a reasonable model for the trend in these data?
  c. **Predict** the population of Arizona in 2005.

10. Data Analysis Is the population of a state related to the number of licensed drivers in that state? The statistics from a recent year are at the right.
  a. Which variable should be the independent variable?
  b. Draw a scatter plot.
  c. Draw a trend line.
  d. The population of Oregon was approximately 3 million in a recent year. About how many licensed drivers lived in Oregon that year?
  e. **Writing** Is the relationship between population and number of licensed drivers a strong relationship? Explain.

11. Geography The map shows the distance by air in miles and travel time in minutes between Cleveland and eight other cities. Use this information to develop a model for the time it would take to fly different distances. According to your model, how long would it take to fly to a city 1000 mi away?

State	Population (millions)	Licensed Drivers (millions)
Texas	17.7	11.4
California	30.9	20.1
Maryland	4.9	3.2
Florida	13.5	10.6
Michigan	9.4	6.5
Georgia	6.8	4.6
New York	18.1	10.4
Illinois	11.6	7.4
Tennessee	5.0	3.5
New Mexico	1.6	1.1
Montana	0.8	0.6
Pennsylvania	12.0	8.0

Source: *Highway Statistics*

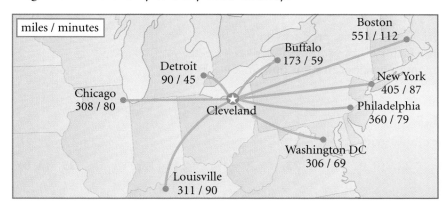

12. Health Care The number of female doctors practicing in the United States from 1970 through 1993 is shown in the table below.

Year	1970	1980	1985	1989	1990	1992	1993
Number of Female Doctors	21,400	48,700	74,800	90,700	96,100	110,100	117,200

Source: *American Medical Association*

  a. Use the data to **predict** the number of female doctors in 2010.
  b. Do you think the relationship you used to **predict** the number is a strong one? How confident are you of your prediction?
  c. **Critical Thinking** Suppose in 50 years someone updates the table and then looks at a scatter plot of the data. Do you think the model will be linear? Explain.

13. Open-ended Describe two sets of data that you would expect to have weak negative correlations. Describe two sets of data that you would expect to have strong positive correlations.

14. **Health** A medical handbook allows physicians to compare the height of a child to an average height. This information is given in table form.

Age	8	9	10	11	12	13	14	15
Height (cm)	127.0	132.0	137.1	142.2	147.3	152.4	157.5	162.2

   a. Show the data on a scatter plot. Draw a trend line.
   b. **Estimate** the average height of a 16-year-old.
   c. Brian's height was recorded each year on a door frame at his home. For the ages in the chart, his heights were 124, 126, 128, 132, 138, 146, 157, and 168 cm. Plot Brian's growth pattern and write a sentence comparing it to the average heights. Estimate how old Brian was when he matched the average height.

Exercises   MIXED REVIEW

Find each percent of increase or decrease.

15. 14 in. to 12 in.   **16.** 98 lb to 100 lb   **17.** 5 km to 6 km   **18.** 1.6 cm to 1.2 cm

19. **Factory Work** A factory in York, Pennsylvania, produces 460 motorcycles per day. Assume the factory is in production 7 days a week and 52 weeks a year. How many motorcycles can it produce in a week? in a year?

Getting Ready for Lesson 1-3
Graph the ordered pairs on a coordinate grid.

20. $(-4, -8)$ **21.** $(3, 6)$ **22.** $(0, 0)$ **23.** $(-2, -4)$ **24.** $(1, 2)$ **25.** $(4, 8)$

Exercises   CHECKPOINT

   1. a. Make a scatter plot of the data at the right.
      b. Describe the correlation, if any.
      c. Draw a trend line.
      d. **Predict** how many seeds per ounce an herb would have if it cost $14/oz.

Write the indicated element of each matrix.

2. $\begin{bmatrix} 4 & 8 \\ 1 & 7 \end{bmatrix}$; a_{12} **3.** $\begin{bmatrix} -5 & 9 \\ 2 & -4 \end{bmatrix}$; a_{21}

4. **Open-ended** Describe two sets of data that have a strong negative correlation.

Herbs

	Price / oz	Number of seeds / oz
basil	$ 3.50	20,000
cumin	$ 2.50	8,800
dill	$ 8.00	20,000
lavender	$10.00	25,000
oregano	$24.00	140,000
sage	$ 6.00	3,400
thyme	$29.00	125,000

Finding a Line of Best Fit

After Lesson 1-2

You can use your graphing calculator to display data sets, draw scatter plots, and draw a line to fit the data. The line is called the linear regression line. The LinReg feature on your calculator fits data to the model $y = ax + b$. It also displays the correlation coefficient, r.

Example

The table shows the number of bicycles produced in the United States from 1989 to 1993. Enter the given data on your calculator. Draw a scatter plot of the data and draw a line of best fit.

Clear any existing lists. Press STAT 4 2nd L1 ›
2nd L2 › ... 2nd L6 ENTER. Clear any equations you may have by pressing Y= . For each equation, press CLEAR and use ▼ to move to the next equation.

Year	Number of Bicycles Produced (millions)
1989	5.3
1990	6.0
1991	7.3
1992	7.4
1993	8.0

Source: *Bicycle Manufacturers Association of America, Inc.*

L1	L2	L3
89	5.3	
90	6	
91	7.3	
92	7.4	
93	8	
------	------	

L2(6)=

```
LinReg
 y=ax+b
 a=.68
 b=-55.08
 r=.9674876685
```

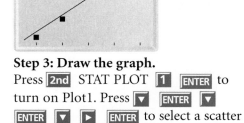

Step 1: Enter data.
Press STAT ENTER.
Enter the x-values in List 1 and the y-values in List 2.

Step 2: Find a line of best fit.
Press STAT ► 5 ENTER to select LinReg(ax+b).
Press Y= VARS 5 ► ►
7 to enter the equation to Y₁.

Step 3: Draw the graph.
Press 2nd STAT PLOT 1 ENTER to turn on Plot1. Press ▼ ENTER ▼
ENTER ▼ ► ENTER to select a scatter plot using L1 and L2. Then press ZOOM
9 to get the scatter plot and the line of best fit.

Find a line of best fit for each set of data.

1. $\{(-5, 6.3), (-4, 5.6), (-3, 4.8), (-2, 3.1), (-1, 2.5), (0, 1.0), (1, -1.4)\}$

2.

Year	1988	1989	1990	1991	1992	1993	1994
National Health Expenditures (billions of dollars)	562.3	623.9	696.6	755.6	820.3	884.2	949.4

Source: *U.S. Health Care Financing Administration*

3. Writing Describe the advantages of using a graphing calculator to draw the line of best fit.

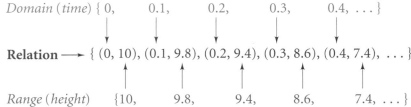
What You'll Learn

- Defining and using relations and functions
- Deciding whether a relation is a function

...And Why

To describe and analyze the path of a falling object

1-3 **R**elations and Functions

Defining Relations and Functions

Suppose you drop an object from 10 ft above the ground and record its height at regular intervals. You will produce a set of ordered pairs, like the one below.

Domain (time) { 0,   0.1,   0.2,   0.3,   0.4, . . . }

Relation ⟶ { (0, 10), (0.1, 9.8), (0.2, 9.4), (0.3, 8.6), (0.4, 7.4), . . . }

Range (height)   {10,   9.8,   9.4,   8.6,   7.4, . . . }

A **relation** is a set of ordered pairs. The **domain** is the set of all first numbers in each pair, or the x-values. The **range** is the set of all second numbers in each pair, or the y-values.

1. Which set, domain or range, consists of values for the dependent variable?

2. Using the equation $y = 2x + 3$, complete the following table.

x	3	4	5	6	7	8
y	9					

3. Write the values from your table as a set of ordered pairs.

4. Graph the ordered pairs on a coordinate grid.

5. If $y = 2x + 3$, how many y-values would correspond to any given x-value?

You have just represented the relation $y = 2x + 3$ in three different ways. You have completed a table, written a set of ordered pairs, and made a graph. Another way to show a relation is to use a *mapping diagram*.

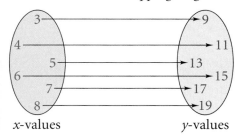

This diagram maps the x-values onto the y-values.

x-values y-values

When each element of the domain has only one element associated with it in the range, the relation is called a **function.**

Example 1 **Relating to the Real World** 🌐

Physics The equation $h = 10 - 16t^2$ expresses the relationship between the height h of an object (dropped from 10 ft) at time t since you dropped it. (See picture above.) Is this relation a function?

You can represent the relation by graphing the equation.

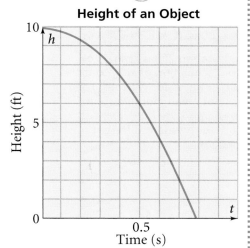

Height of an Object

The ball is at only one height above the ground at any given time. Every vertical line will intersect the graph in at most one place. This relation is a function.

QUICK REVIEW

To determine whether a relation is a function you can use the *vertical line test*. If every vertical line intersects the graph in at most one place, then the relation is a function.

6. Critical Thinking Why is the domain of the function restricted to positive values of t?

7. Define the domain for the function that models the height of the dropped ball in Example 1.

Example 2

Which of the following relations are functions?

a. $y = 2x + 7$

b.

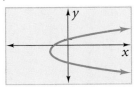

a. This is a function because each value of x will produce only one value of y.

b. This is not a function. Some vertical lines will intersect the graph in two places.

8. Try This Do these ordered pairs belong to a function? How do you know? $\{(1, 4), (2, 6), (3, 5), (1, 2), (5, 5), (7, 2)\}$

Function Notation

You can think of a function as a machine that performs an operation (or a series of operations) on the input to produce an output.

QUICK REVIEW

The notation $f(x)$ is read "f of x" or "a function of x." $f(x)$ is another name for y. (Note: $f(x)$ does not mean multiplication.) You can also use $g(x)$, $h(x)$, and so on, to represent different functions.

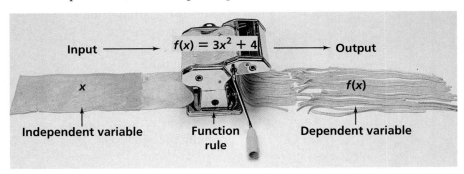

9. List, in order, the operations the machine performs.

GRAPHING CALCULATOR HINT

You can use the Function option of the Y-VARS menu to evaluate functions.

The $f(x)$ notation is called function notation. When the value of the independent variable is 3, $f(3)$ represents the value of the function.

Example 3

Evaluate $f(-2)$ if $f(x) = -5x + 7$.

$$f(x) = -5x + 7$$
$$f(-2) = -5(-2) + 7 \quad \longleftarrow \text{Substitute } -2 \text{ for } x.$$
$$= 10 + 7 \quad \longleftarrow \text{Simplify.}$$
$$= 17$$

The value of $f(-2)$ is 17.

An equation that describes a function, such as that in Example 3, can be written in one of two ways: as $f(x) = -5x + 7$, or as $y = -5x + 7$.

10. Try This Evaluate $f(4)$ if $f(x) = x^2 + 2x - 5$.

11. Graphing Calculator Use your calculator to evaluate $g(4)$ if $g(x) = 2x^2 + 3x - 1$.

Sometimes you may need to evaluate a function for a domain value that contains a variable.

Example 4

Evaluate $f(t + 1)$ if $f(x) = 2x - 5$.

$$f(x) = 2x - 5$$
$$f(t + 1) = 2(t + 1) - 5 \quad \longleftarrow \text{Substitute } t + 1 \text{ for } x.$$
$$= 2t + 2 - 5 \quad \longleftarrow \text{Use the distributive property.}$$
$$= 2t - 3$$

If $f(x) = 2x - 5$, then $f(t + 1) = 2t - 3$.

12. Try This Evaluate $h(2t)$ if $h(x) = 5x - 2$.

13. Explain why you would not use a graphing calculator to evaluate the function in Example 4.

Exercises   ON YOUR OWN

Use the vertical line test to determine if each of the following represents a function.

1.
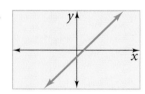

2.
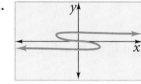

3.
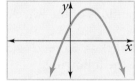

Determine if each relation is a function.

4. $\{(1, 1), (1, 2), (2, 3), (3, 4), (4, 5)\}$

5. $\{(1, 1), (2, 1), (3, 1), (4, 1), (5, 1)\}$

6. $\{(1, 1), (2, 4), (3, 9), (4, 16), (5, 25)\}$

7. $\{(1, 2), (2, 3), (3, 4), (4, 3), (3, 2)\}$

 8. (Row 1 contains the x-values.)

	A	B	C	D	E	F
1	−6	−5	−4	−3	−2	−1
2	−0.17	−0.2	−0.25	−0.33	−0.5	−1

9. (Row 1 contains the x-values.)

	A	B	C	D	E	F
1	−3	−2	−1	0	1	2
2	1	0	1	0	1	0

10. Which of the following relations are functions? Sketch a graph of those that are.
   a. *Geometry* the number of sides in a regular polygon and the measure of one of its central angles
   b. *Science* the length of time after a bowl of soup was removed from the stove and its temperature
   c. the month a student was born and the distance that same student lives from school

11. Does the diagram at the right illustrate a function? Why or why not?

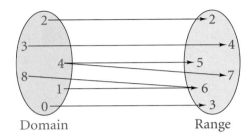

Domain   Range

12. *Writing* Explain why pricing in a grocery store should be described as a function.

Geometry **Complete each equation to show the relationship between the area (or surface area) *A* of the figure and its labeled parts.**

13. $A(s) = ?$

14. $A(r) = ?$

15. $A(s) = ?$

16. Suppose you are on a Ferris wheel. Draw a graph to show a function relationship between your height above the ground and time for three revolutions of the wheel.

**Suppose $f(x) = 3x + 7, g(x) = -x + 8,$ and $h(x) = x^2 + 3x - 1.$
Evaluate the following.**

17. $f(-4)$ **18.** $g(7)$ **19.** $h(-2)$ **20.** $f(2) + h(1)$ **21.** $-2f(1)$

22. $\dfrac{f(1)}{g(3)}$ **23.** $g(3) + h(1)$ **24.** $f(x + 2)$ **25.** $3f(2)$ **26.** $h(0) - 3$

27. $f(t - 2) + g(-4)$ **28.** $f(0) - g(0) + h(0)$ **29.** $g(3x) + h(-1)$ **30.** $h(x + 1) + g(1)$

Open-ended **Write a story to represent each graph. Identify any functions you describe in your story.**

31.

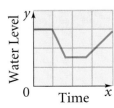

32.

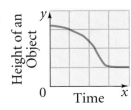

33.

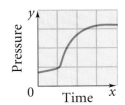

34. Research Draw a graph to show the relationship between the weight of a letter and the cost of postage. Is it a graph of a function? Explain.

Chapter Project

Find Out by Doing

Work in a group.

- Make a list of at least a dozen words.
- Give group members 10 s to study the list. Then have them write down items they can recall. Record the number of correct items.
- Give group members an additional 10 s to study the list again. Have them write down items and record the results.
- Repeat the procedure two more times.
- Describe any correlation you see in the data.

Exercises   M I X E D   R E V I E W

Find each percent of increase or decrease.

35. 60 lb to 63 lb   **36.** 4 in. to 3.5 in.   **37.** 6 ft to 2 ft

38. 9 m to 10 m   **39.** 1 gal to 1.5 gal   **40.** 2 km to 1.5 km

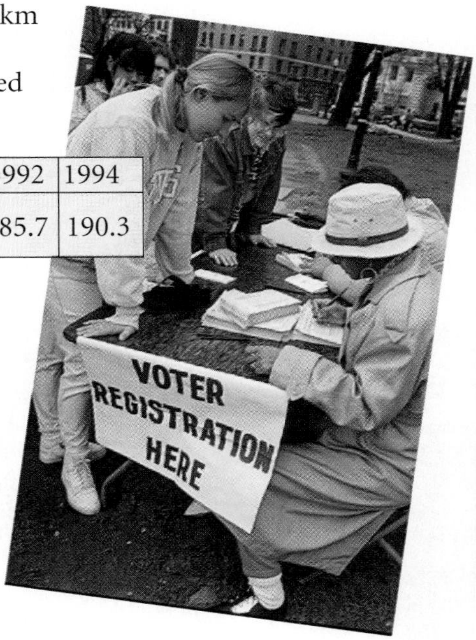

41. Data Analysis The table shows the voting-age population of the United States from 1980 to 1994.

Year	1980	1982	1984	1986	1988	1990	1992	1994
Voting-age Population (millions)	157.1	165.5	170.0	173.9	178.1	182.1	185.7	190.3

Source: *U.S. Bureau of the Census*

   a. Which is the dependent variable? the independent variable?
   b. Choose appropriate scales and draw a scatter plot of the data.
   c. Describe any correlation you see.

Getting Ready for Lesson 1-4

Use the graph at the right. Read the value of *y* for each value of *x*.

42. 2   **43.** -3

44. 0   **45.** 3

46. -2 **47.** 1

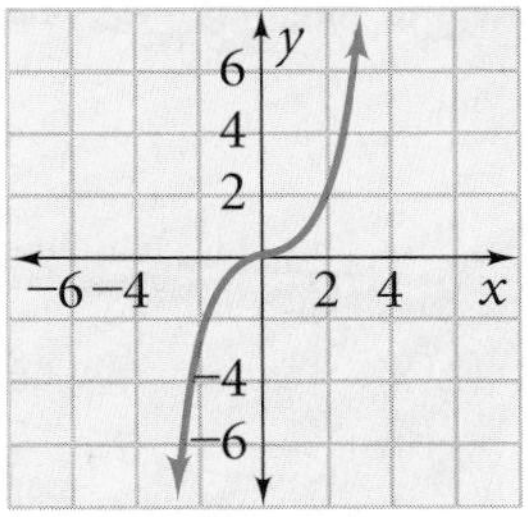

What You'll Learn

- Combining functions
- Adding functions

...And Why

To determine the better deal when using a combination of discounts and coupons

1-4 **W**orking with Functions

WORK TOGETHER

Which is the better deal? Do you take a 20% discount on an item first and then use a coupon? Or do you use the coupon and then take a 20% discount? Does the order matter? Answer the questions below and find out.

1. You want to get an oil change for your car at Scott's Auto Clinic. It normally costs $24, but you work there and receive a 20% employee discount. How much will the oil change cost you?

2. You have a coupon for $4 off. How much will you pay for the oil change if you take the employee discount and then subtract the coupon?

3. How much will you pay if you subtract the coupon and then take the employee discount?

4. Compare the final cost of the oil change from Questions 2 and 3. Does the order matter? Explain.

THINK AND DISCUSS

Composite Functions

In the Work Together, you found that the order in which you did the steps made a difference. The order in which you apply two functions also makes a difference.

This diagram shows what happens when you apply one function $g(x)$ after another function $f(x)$.

The output from the first function becomes the input for the second function.

5. What operation does the function $g(x)$ perform on its input?

6. If the input for $f(x)$ is $x = 3$, what is the output from $g(x)$?

7. Suppose you reverse the order of the functions, so that x represents the input of $g(x)$ first. What would be the final output? Draw a diagram to represent this combination of functions.

When you combine two functions as in the diagram above, you are forming their **composite.** This is written as $g(f(x))$ and is read "g of f of x." This process is known as the composition of functions.

Composite of two functions

$$g(f(x))$$

① Evaluate the inner function $f(x)$ first.

② Then use your answer as the input of the outer function $g(x)$.

> **Example 1**
>
> If $f(x) = x - 2$ and $g(x) = x^2$, evaluate $g(f(-5))$.
>
> Find $f(-5)$ first.
>
> $f(x) = x - 2$
> $f(-5) = (-5) - 2$ ←—Substitute -5 for x.
> $\qquad = -7$ ←—The first output becomes the second input.
>
> Then find $g(-7)$.
>
> $g(x) = x^2$
> $g(-7) = (-7)^2$ ←—Substitute -7 for x.
> $\qquad = 49$ ←—Second output
>
> Therefore, $g(f(-5)) = 49$.

8. Try This Evaluate $f(g(-5))$ for the functions in Example 1. What do you notice?

9. Let $f(x) = 5x - 1$ and $g(x) = 2x$. Evaluate $g(f(-1))$ and $f(g(-1))$.

10. Let $f(x) = x^2 - 4$ and $g(x) = 3x$. Explain why $g(f(x)) = 3x^2 - 12$.

11. Is the composition of functions commutative? Explain.

Example 2 Relating to the Real World

Sales A store offers a 10% discount sale on its $25 jeans. You also have a coupon worth $5 off any item. How much would you pay for the jeans if the clerk applied the coupon first and then applied the discount?

Define Let x represent the original price.

Relate $f(x) = x - 5$ ⟵ the price with $5 off
$g(x) = x - 0.1x$, or $0.9x$ ⟵ the price with the 10% discount

Since the clerk applied the $5 coupon before the discount, first find $f(25)$.

Write $f(25) = 25 - 5$

$f(25) = 20$ ⟵ the price with the coupon
$g(f(25)) = g(20)$ ⟵ Now apply $g(x)$ to this price.
$= 0.9(20)$
$= 18$

You will pay $18 for the jeans.

12. What price would you pay for the jeans if the clerk applied the 10% discount first and then subtracted the coupon?

13. Which is the better deal for you? for the owner of the store? Does the order matter?

14. Try This You eat at Armand's during the early-bird hours. The price of your meal is $14, but you pay for part of it with a $2 coupon. How much will you pay if the restaurant cashier subtracts your coupon before giving you the early-bird discount?

Operations with Functions

Functions can be combined using other rules as well. You can add, subtract, multiply, and divide two functions.

Example 3

Let $f(x) = 3x + 8$ and $g(x) = 2x - 12$. Find $f(x) + g(x)$.

$f(x) = 3x + 8$ and $g(x) = 2x - 12$

$f(x) + g(x) = (3x + 8) + (2x - 12)$ ⟵ Substitute the expressions.

$= 3x + 2x + 8 - 12$ ⟵ Use the associative and commutative properties.

$= (3 + 2)x + 8 - 12$ ⟵ Use the distributive property.

$= 5x - 4$ ⟵ arithmetic

15. Try This If $f(x) = 3x + 8$ and $g(x) = 2x - 12$, find $f(x) - g(x)$.

16. Suppose $f(x) = -2x + 7$. Find $3(f(9x))$.

17. If $f(x) = 9x$ and $g(x) = 3x$, find $f(x) \cdot g(x)$ and $f(x) \div g(x)$.

Use each diagram to find $g(f(3))$, $g(f(-2))$, and a rule for $g(f(x))$.

1.

$f(x) = 2x$ $g(x) = x + 3$

2.

$f(x) = x^2$ $g(x) = |x + 5|$

Evaluate. Let $g(x) = 2x$ and $h(x) = x^2 + 4$.

3. $h(g(1))$ **4.** $h(g(-5))$ **5.** $h(g(-2))$ **6.** $g(h(-2))$ **7.** $g(h(0))$

8. $g(h(-1))$ **9.** $h(g(3))$ **10.** $h(g(-4))$ **11.** $g(h(-5))$ **12.** $h(g(10))$

Evaluate. Let $f(x) = x^2$ and $g(x) = x - 3$.

13. $g(f(1))$ **14.** $f(g(1))$ **15.** $g(f(-2))$ **16.** $f(g(-2))$ **17.** $g(f(0))$

18. $f(g(0))$ **19.** $g(f(3.5))$ **20.** $f(g(3.5))$ **21.** $f\left(g\left(\frac{1}{2}\right)\right)$ **22.** $g\left(f\left(\frac{1}{2}\right)\right)$

23. $f\left(g\left(-\frac{1}{2}\right)\right)$ **24.** $f(g(c))$ **25.** $g(f(c))$ **26.** $f(g(-a))$ **27.** $g(f(-a))$

28. Evaluate $g(f(3))$, when $f(x) = 2x$ and $g(x) = x + 1$. Explain what you do first and why.

29. Sales A car dealer offers a 10% discount off the list price x for any car on the lot. At the same time, the manufacturer offers a $2000 rebate for each purchase of its cars.
   a. Write a function $f(x)$ to represent the price after the discount.
   b. Write a function $g(x)$ to represent the price after the $2000 rebate.
   c. Suppose the list price of a car is $18,000. Use a composite function to find the price of the car if the discount is applied before the rebate.

30. Economics International companies must often compute their costs in many currencies. At one time in 1995, the function $f(x) = 0.71x$ represented the number of U.S. dollars in a Singapore dollar. The function $g(x) = 7.75x$ was used to convert U.S. dollars to Mexican pesos. Find the value in Mexican pesos of an item costing 15 Singapore dollars.

Evaluate. Let $g(x) = 3x + 2$ and $f(x) = \frac{x - 2}{3}$.

31. $f(g(1))$ **32.** $g(f(-4))$ **33.** $f(g(0))$ **34.** $g(f(2))$ **35.** $g(f(-3))$

36. $f(g(3))$ **37.** $f(g(a))$ **38.** $g(f(a))$ **39.** $f(g(-b))$ **40.** $g(f(-b))$

41. Writing A salesperson earns a 3% bonus on weekly sales over $5000.

$$g(x) = 0.03x$$
$$h(x) = x - 5000$$

   a. Explain what each function above represents.
   b. Which composition, $h(g(x))$ or $g(h(x))$, represents the weekly bonus? Explain.

42. Geometry You toss a pebble into a pool of water and watch the circular ripples radiate outward. You find that the function $r(t) = 12.5t$ describes the radius of the first circle r in inches after t seconds. The function $A(r) = \pi r^2$ describes the area A of the circle.

   a. Find $A(r(t))$ when $t = 2$. Then interpret your answer.

   b. Find the area of the circle after 4 s.

43. a. Technology Suppose $f(x) = 3x$ and $g(x) = x^2 + 3$. Look at the spreadsheet below. Column A contains values for x. What do columns B and C represent?

   b. Complete columns B and C.

   c. Write the function rule for $f(g(x))$.

   d. Complete column D for $f(g(x))$.

   e. Write the function rule for $g(f(x))$.

   f. Complete column E for $g(f(x))$.

	A	B	C	D	E
1		=3*A1	=A1^2+3	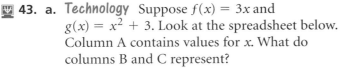	
2	0				
3	5				
4	10				

44. Education Suppose your teacher offers to give the whole class a bonus if everyone passes the next math test. The teacher says she will (1) give a 10-point bonus and (2) increase everyone's grade by 9% of their score.

   a. Let x represent the original test scores. Write statements (1) and (2) as the functions $f(x)$ and $g(x)$, respectively.

   b. Explain the meaning of $f(g(x))$. Evaluate $f(g(75))$.

   c. Explain the meaning of $g(f(x))$. Evaluate $g(f(75))$.

   d. Does $g(f(x)) = f(g(x))$?

Write a function rule for $g(f(x))$ and for $f(g(x))$.

45. $f(x) = 3x$, $g(x) = x^2$

46. $f(x) = x + 3$, $g(x) = x - 5$

47. $f(x) = 3x^2 + 2$, $g(x) = 2x$

48. $f(x) = \frac{x - 2}{3}$, $g(x) = 3x + 2$

49. $f(x) = -x - 7$, $g(x) = 4x$

50. $f(x) = \frac{x + 5}{2}$, $g(x) = x^2$

Evaluate each expression. Let $f(x) = 3x + 5$ and $g(x) = x^2$.

51. $f(2) + g(2)$

52. $3f(-2)$

53. $f(1) \cdot g(1)$

54. $g(-3) + 5$

55. $\dfrac{f(5)}{g(5)}$

Write and simplify a function rule for $h(x)$. Let $f(x) = 2x + 5$ and $g(x) = x^2 - 3x + 2$.

56. $h(x) = f(x) + g(x)$

57. $h(x) = 4f(x)$

58. $h(x) = 3f(x) - 2$

59. $h(x) = g(x) - f(x)$

60. $h(x) = -2g(x) + f(x)$

61. $h(x) = f(x) - g(x) + 10$

62. Business You have invented a brush to use as a hose attachment for washing cars. The function $C(x) = 1000 + 3x$ represents your cost in dollars to produce x brushes. The function $I(x) = 29.95x$ represents the income in dollars from selling x brushes.

   a. Write and simplify a profit function $P(x) = I(x) - C(x)$.

   b. Find $P(300)$, the profit earned when you make and sell 300 brushes.

63. Open-ended Write a function rule that approximates each value.

   a. The amount you save is a percent of what you earn. (You choose the percent.)

   b. The amount you earn depends on how many hours you work. (You choose the hourly wage.)

   c. Write and simplify a composite function that expresses your savings as a function of the number of hours you work. Interpret your results.

Chapter Project .... **Find Out by Graphing**

> Create scatter plots of the data you collected for the Find Out activities on pages 10 and 25. Describe any correlations suggested by the scatter plots. Does a line seem to fit your data? What would happen to a line of best fit after several more trials?

Exercises   M I X E D   R E V I E W

Determine if each relation is a function.

64. $\{(3, 5), (6, 1), (0, -4), (7, 1)\}$

65. $\{(4, 7), (3, 6), (-4, 7), (-3, 5)\}$

66. $\{(1, 4), (4, 2), (-4, 6), (1, 3)\}$

67. $\{(9, -5), (5, 9), (-5, -9), (9, 5)\}$

68. $\{(0, 1), (2, 0), (-4, 0), (0, 0)\}$

69. $\{(6, 2), (7, 1), (9, -3), (3, 10)\}$

Getting Ready for Lesson 1–5

70. Complete the table. Then graph the function $f(x) = (x - 1)^2$ by plotting the points and connecting them with a smooth curve.

x	-2	-1	0	1	2	3	4
$f(x) = (x - 1)^2$	9	▪	▪	▪	▪	▪	▪

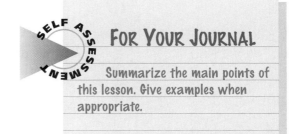

FOR YOUR JOURNAL

Summarize the main points of this lesson. Give examples when appropriate.

What You'll Learn

- Analyzing vertical and horizontal translations of a function

...And Why

To solve problems involving textile designs

1-5 Vertical and Horizontal Translations

GRAPHING CALCULATOR HINT

The Table feature on your graphing calculator provides a good way to study these graphs.

WORK TOGETHER

Use a graphing calculator to answer these questions. Discuss your results with others in your group.

1. Graph the functions $y = x$, $y = x + 1$, $y = x - 1$, and $y = x + 3$ on the same screen.

2. Compare the four graphs. Describe the effect of adding or subtracting a constant to the function $y = x$.

3. Graph $y = x^2$, $y = x^2 + 2$, $y = x^2 - 2$, and $y = x^2 + 3$ on the same screen.

4. Compare the four graphs. Describe the effect of adding or subtracting a constant to the function $y = x^2$.

THINK AND DISCUSS

Shifting Graphs Vertically

The graphs in the Work Together are translations of the graphs of $y = x$ and $y = x^2$. A **translation** shifts a graph either horizontally, vertically, or both. It results in a graph of the same shape and size in a different position.

Let k be a positive real number. To graph the functions $y = x + k$, $y = x^2 + k$, and $y = |x| + k$, shift the graph up k units. To graph the functions $y = x - k$, $y = x^2 - k$, and $y = |x| - k$, shift the graph down k units.

QUICK REVIEW

Remember that the absolute value of a number is its distance from 0 on the number line.
$|a| = a$ if $a \geq 0$
$|a| = -a$ if $a < 0$

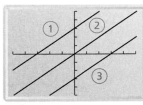
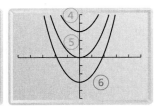
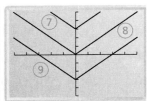

(1) $y = x + k$ (4) $y = x^2 + k$ (7) $y = |x| + k$
(2) $y = x$ (5) $y = x^2$ (8) $y = |x|$
(3) $y = x - k$ (6) $y = x^2 - k$ (9) $y = |x| - k$

A family of functions is a group of equations that share common characteristics. The graphs of the first three equations above are lines, the graphs of the second three equations are parabolas, and the graphs of the last three equations are absolute-value graphs.

The photograph above would illustrate a translation if the bottom escalator could be moved up 1, 2, and 3 units.

Example 1

Without using graphing technology, graph each function.

a. $y = x + 2$

b. $y = x^2 - 3$

a. $y = x + k,\ k = 2$

b. $y = x^2 + k,\ k = -3$

The graph of $y = x + 2$ is the graph of $y = x$ shifted *up* 2 units.

The graph of $y = x^2 - 3$ is the graph of $y = x^2$ shifted *down* 3 units.

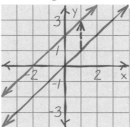

5. **Try This** Graph the function $y = |x| - 1$.

6. **Try This** Graph the function $y = x^2 + 1$.

Shifting Graphs Horizontally

7. **Graphing Calculator** Graph the functions $y = x^2$ and $y = (x + 1)^2$ on the same screen. How are the graphs alike? How are they different?

8. Describe the translation of the graph of $y = x^2$ that gives you the graph of $y = (x + 1)^2$.

Let h be a positive real number. To graph the functions $y = (x + h)^2$ and $y = (x - h)^2$, shift the graph of $y = x^2$ to the left or to the right respectively.

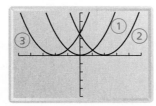

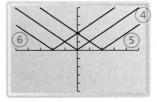

The graph of $y = (x - h)^2$ is the graph of $y = x^2$ shifted h units to the *right*.

The graph of $y = |x - h|$ is the graph of $y = |x|$ shifted h units to the *right*.

The graph of $y = (x + h)^2$ is the graph of $y = x^2$ shifted h units to the *left*.

The graph of $y = |x + h|$ is the graph of $y = |x|$ shifted h units to the *left*.

9. **Try This** Graph the function $y = (x - 4)^2$.

10. **Try This** Graph the function $y = |x + 3|$.

Example 2

Each graph is a translation of $y = x^2$ or $y = |x|$. Write the equation of each graph.

a.

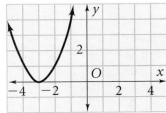

b.

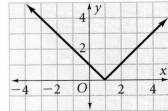

a. This is the graph of $y = x^2$ shifted 3 units to the left. It is the graph of $y = (x + 3)^2$.

b. This is the graph of $y = |x|$ shifted 1 unit to the right. It is the graph of $y = |x - 1|$.

Vertical and horizontal translations can be combined to produce diagonal translations.

Example 3   **Relating to the Real World**

Textile Designs   A Nigerian textile design is shown below. Describe a possible translation of Figures A and B in the design.

Nigeria

What? Historically, both women and men crafted Nigerian textiles. As in most of the world, however, hand-woven garments are now a semi-luxury item. They compete with inexpensive machine-woven fabrics and luxury imported fabrics.

Source: *African Textiles*

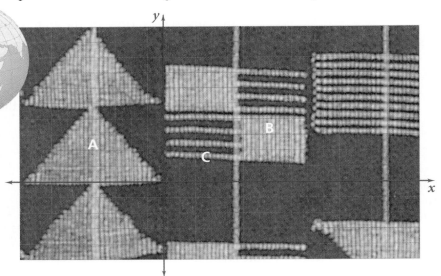

A translation of Figure A:
5 units up or
5 units down

A translation of Figure B:
about 5 units left and
about 3 units up

11. Describe how to translate Figure C to complete the design above.

Example 4 ·············

Graph each function.

a. $f(x) = (x + 2)^2 - 3$ **b.** $f(x) = |x - 3| + 1$

a. $f(x) = (x + h)^2 + k$
    $h = 2 \longrightarrow$ 2 units *left*;
    $k = -3 \longrightarrow$ 3 units *down*

b. $f(x) = |x - h| + k$
    $h = 3 \longrightarrow$ 3 units *right*;
    $k = 1 \longrightarrow$ 1 unit *up*

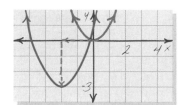
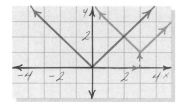

12. Try This Graph the function $f(x) = |x + 5| - 3$.

Summary of Vertical and Horizontal Translations

If k and h are positive numbers and $f(x)$ is a function, then

$f(x) + k$ shifts $f(x)$ up k units; $f(x) - k$ shifts $f(x)$ down k units;

$f(x + h)$ shifts $f(x)$ left h units; $f(x - h)$ shifts $f(x)$ right h units.

Exercises   **O N   Y O U R   O W N**

Without using graphing technology, graph each function.

1. $y = x + 3$ **2.** $y = x^2 + 6$ **3.** $y = |x| + 2$ **4.** $y = (x - 6)^2$

5. $y = |x - 4|$ **6.** $y = x - 3$ **7.** $y = x^2 - 5$ **8.** $y = |x| - 6$

9. $y = (x + 4)^2$ **10.** $y = |x + 5|$ **11.** $y = (x - 5)^2 + 1$ **12.** $y = |x + 2| - 3$

13. Roberta is playing with a yo-yo.

  a. Sketch a graph of $h(t)$ that shows the height h of the yo-yo above the floor over time t. At $t = 0$, the yo-yo leaves her hand.

  b. *Critical Thinking* Should your graph be that of a function? Explain.

  c. Roberta gets on the stage to show her yo-yo ability. Describe the translation of the graph of $h(t)$ that represents the height of the yo-yo above the auditorium floor.

  d. *Standardized Test Prep* The stage is 5 ft above the floor. Choose a function $g(t)$ that represents the height of the yo-yo above the auditorium floor when Roberta is on stage.

    A. $g(t) = h(t + 5)$ **B.** $g(t) = h(t - 5)$
    C. $g(t) = h(t) + 5$ **D.** $g(t) = h(t) - 5$

Describe several possible translations for each figure.

14.

15.

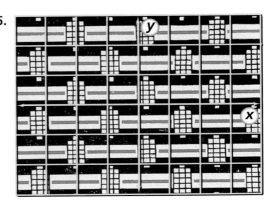

16. Write an equation of the graph at the right. Express your equation in terms of $f(x) = |x|$.

17. Open-ended Draw a figure in the first quadrant. Use a translation to move your figure into the third quadrant. Describe your translation.

18. Writing Explain why applying a vertical translation and then a horizontal translation produces the same result as the reverse order of operations.

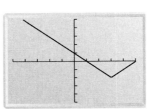

Xmin=−5   Ymin=−5
Xmax=5   Ymax=5
Xscl=1   Yscl=1

Describe the vertical and/or horizontal translations of the graphs of $f(x) = x^2$ or $f(x) = |x|$. Then graph each function.

19. $f(x) = (x - 5)^2$

20. $f(x) = x^2 - 5$

21. $f(x) = (x - 5)^2 + 3$

22. $f(x) = |x - 5| + 3$

23. $f(x) = |x| + 1$

24. $f(x) = |x + 1|$

25. $f(x) = (x - 1)^2 + 5$

26. $f(x) = (x + 3)^2$

27. $f(x) = |x - 3| - 6$

28. $f(x) = |x + 4| - 2$

29. $f(x) = (x - 6)^2$

30. $f(x) = (x + 2)^2 + 5$

Write the equation of each translation of the graphs of $y = x$, $y = x^2$, or $y = |x|$. Assume that the x- and y-scales range from −5 to 5.

31.

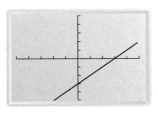

32.

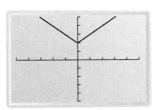

33.

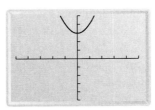

34.

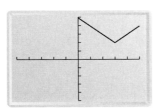

35.

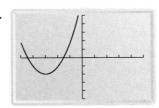

36.

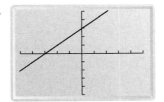

37. Compare the graph at the right to the one in Example 2 on page 14. Describe the transformation that this graph represents. Why do you think graphs like this one are often used when dealing with years?

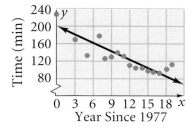

38. Graphing Calculator The graph of each function below is a translation of the graph of $f(x) = x^2$. Graph the function. Write the equation of the function in the form $f(x) = (x - h)^2 + k$.
  a. $f(x) = x^2 - 4x + 5$ **b.** $f(x) = x^2 - 6x + 5$

39. Use the graph of the function $y = s(x)$, at the right. Sketch the graph of each function below.
  a. $y = s(x + 1)$ **b.** $y = s(x) - 2$ **c.** $y = s(x + 2) + 1$

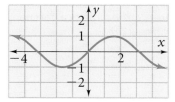

40. Data Analysis Suppose you plot data with years as the independent variable. What type of translation are you making when you start with $x = 0$ rather than a year such as 1992?

Exercises   MIXED REVIEW

Open-ended Draw a scatter plot with the given correlation.

41. strong, positive correlation   **42.** no correlation   **43.** weak, negative correlation

44. Marine Life Keiko, the whale that starred in a recent movie, moved into a new outdoor pool. It is a rectangular prism 25 ft deep. The surface is 150 ft by 75 ft. Find its volume.

Getting Ready for Lesson 1-6
Simplify each expression.

45. $8 \cdot 7 \cdot 6 \cdot 5$ **46.** $5 \cdot 4 \cdot 3 \cdot 2 \cdot 1$ **47.** $10 \cdot 9 \cdot 8$ **48.** $6 \cdot 5 \cdot 4 \cdot 3$

Exercises   CHECKPOINT

Suppose $f(x) = 2x + 5$, $g(x) = x^2 - 3x$, and $h(x) = -3x - 4$. **Evaluate.**

1. $f(8)$ **2.** $h(-5)$ **3.** $g(6) + 2h(-1)$ **4.** $f(3 - x)$

5. $f(h(1))$ **6.** $2f(0) - 3g(-2)$ **7.** $g(h(4))$ **8.** $g(x + 9)$

9. Writing Explain how to add two functions. Include an example.

Graph each function.

10. $y = x - 5$ **11.** $y = (x + 2)^2 - 9$ **12.** $y = |x + 1| + 4$ **13.** $y = x^2 - 4$

14. Standardized Test Prep The graph of $y = x^2$ is shifted down 5 units and right 4 units. What is the equation of the new graph?
  A. $y = (x + 4)^2 + 5$ **B.** $y = (x + 4)^2 - 5$ **C.** $y = (x - 4)^2 + 5$
  D. $y = (x - 4)^2 - 5$ **E.** none of the above

1-6 Counting Methods and Permutations

What You'll Learn

• Using basic counting methods

• Finding permutations

...And Why

To find the number of different products a company can market

THINK AND DISCUSS

Using Basic Counting Methods

To increase the visibility of their products, manufacturers want more shelf space in stores. One way to get shelf space is to market several varieties of the same product. For example, one company markets shampoo in four different formulas and two different sizes.

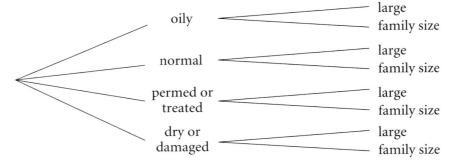

Each path of the tree diagram represents a different product. The company has eight products to display.

The tree diagram also illustrates an important counting method.

Multiplication Counting Principle

If there are *m* ways to make a first selection and *n* ways to make a second selection, there are $m \times n$ ways to make the two selections.

Example: For 4 formulas of shampoo and 2 sizes, the number of different products is $4 \cdot 2 = 8$.

You can also apply the multiplication counting principle when there are more than two selections to be made.

Example 1　**Relating to the Real World** ··············

Marketing　A company markets toothpaste in three flavors (plain, mint, and cool gel), two formulas (regular and tartar control), and four sizes. How many different products does it make?

$3 \cdot 2 \cdot 4 = 24$　← Use the multiplication counting principle.

The company makes 24 different products.

1. **Try This** A sandwich shop offers three types of bread, four different meats, and seven toppings for sandwiches. How many different sandwiches can be made using one bread, one meat, and one topping?

Counting Permutations

A **permutation** is an arrangement of items in a particular order. The letters N, O, and W can be arranged in six permutations.

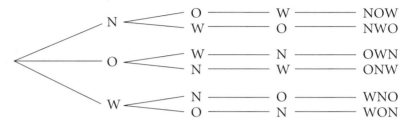

Using the multiplication counting principle, there are three ways to select the first letter in an arrangement, two ways to select the second letter, and only one way to select the final letter. So there are $3 \cdot 2 \cdot 1 = 6$ ways to arrange the three letters.

You can write the multiplication $3 \cdot 2 \cdot 1$ using the notation 3!, read *three factorial*. For any positive integer n, $n! = n(n - 1) \cdot \ldots \cdot 3 \cdot 2 \cdot 1$.

Example 2

GRAPHING CALCULATOR HINT

On most graphing calculators, the factorial function is located in the Probability menu of the MATH feature.

In how many different orders can ten dogs line up to be groomed?

Since there are ten ways to select the first dog in line, nine ways to select the next dog, and so on, the total number of permutations is 10!.

$$10! = 3,628,800 \longleftarrow \text{Use a calculator.}$$

The ten dogs can line up in 3,628,800 different orders.

39

Some permutations do not use all the items available in a set. You can still use the multiplication counting principle for these problems. You can also use factorial notation.

Suppose only four of the ten dogs line up.

Method 1: Use the multiplication counting principle. Only four selections are made.

$$10 \cdot 9 \cdot 8 \cdot 7 = 5040$$

Method 2: Use factorial notation. Only four selections are made.

$$\frac{10!}{6!} = \frac{10 \cdot 9 \cdot 8 \cdot 7 \cdot \cancel{6} \cdot \cancel{5} \cdot \cancel{4} \cdot \cancel{3} \cdot \cancel{2} \cdot \cancel{1}}{\cancel{6} \cdot \cancel{5} \cdot \cancel{4} \cdot \cancel{3} \cdot \cancel{2} \cdot \cancel{1}} \quad \longleftarrow \quad \text{Divide by 6! to remove all factors after the first four.}$$

$$= 5040$$

Although factorial notation seems longer, using a calculator can save time.

2. a. Simplify $12 \cdot 11 \cdot 10 \cdot 9 \cdot 8 \cdot 7 \cdot 6 \cdot 5$.

    b. Use a calculator to simplify $\frac{12!}{4!}$.

3. Write a fraction with factorials to find the product $15 \cdot 14 \cdot 13 \cdot 12$. **Verify** your work.

Example 3

Seven bands are entered in a contest. First, second, and third place will be given to the top three bands. How many arrangements of first, second, and third place are possible with seven bands?

Method 1: Use the multiplication counting principle.
$$7 \cdot 6 \cdot 5 = 210$$

Method 2: Use factorial notation.
$$\frac{7!}{4!} = 210$$

There are 210 ways that three bands in a field of seven can finish in first, second, and third place.

You can write the number of permutations of 7 items arranged 3 items at a time as $_7P_3$. The relationship between permutations and factorials can be summarized with a formula.

Number of Permutations

The number of permutations of n items of a set arranged r items at a time is $_nP_r$.
$$_nP_r = \frac{n!}{(n-r)!} \text{ for } 1 \le r \le n$$
Example: $_7P_3 = \frac{7!}{(7-3)!} = \frac{7!}{4!} = 210$

4. a. *Critical Thinking* Suppose you want to arrange 6 trophies on a shelf, selecting from your collection of 15 trophies. Explain why the denominator in the formula for $_{15}P_6$ should be $(15-6)!$.
   b. Use factorials to evaluate $_{15}P_6$.
   c. Verify your work by multiplying six factors to evaluate $_{15}P_6$.

GRAPHING CALCULATOR HINT
Use the $_nP_r$ option on the Probability menu to evaluate permutations.

5. *Calculator* Many calculators have a feature to evaluate permutations in one step. Use a calculator to evaluate $_{20}P_5$.

6. Try This Evaluate each expression.
   a. $_7P_5$ **b.** $_{12}P_1$ **c.** $_8P_4$ **d.** $_{100}P_3$

7. a. Use a calculator to find the value of $0!$.
   b. Use two different methods to evaluate $_4P_4$.

8. *Critical Thinking* Use a tree diagram or the multiplication counting principle to explain why $_4P_3$ and $_4P_4$ are equal.

Exercises   ON YOUR OWN

Evaluate each expression.

1. $5!$	**2.** $10!$	**3.** $1!$	**4.** $13!$	**5.** $_8P_1$	**6.** $_8P_2$
7. $_8P_3$	**8.** $_8P_4$	**9.** $_3P_2$	**10.** $_5P_4$	**11.** $_9P_6$	**12.** $_5P_3$

13. The prom committee has four sites available for the banquet and three sites for the dance. How many arrangements are possible for the banquet and dance?

14. *Auto Mechanics* Auto mechanics advise that tires on a car should be rotated every 6000 miles.
   a. In how many ways can four tires be arranged on a car?
   b. If the spare tire is included, how many arrangements are possible?

15. Fifteen students ask to visit the admissions representative from Rice University. In how many ways can ten time slots be assigned?

16. **Advertising** Use the ad and the telephone keypad at the right. How many seven-number arrangements can be made using the last seven numbers of this phone number?

Call 1-555-DIAL VSW
for information on
Video Sales Worldwide.

17. **Discrete Math** A consumer magazine rates televisions by identifying two levels of price, five levels of repair frequency, three levels of features, and two levels of picture quality. How many different ratings are possible?

18. **a.** If your teacher could arrange the chapters of this book in any order, how many arrangements would be possible?
    b. How many arrangements would be possible if your teacher covered all but three chapters?

Suppose a and b are positive integers. Decide whether each statement is true or false. If true, explain why. If not true, give a counterexample.

19. $a! + b! = b! + a!$

20. $a!(b!c!) = (a!b!)c!$

21. $(a + b)! = a! + b!$

22. $(ab)! = a!b!$

23. $(a!)! = (a!)^2$

24. $(a!)^b = a^{(b!)}$

25. **Writing** In how many ways is it possible to arrange the two numbers a and b in an ordered pair? Explain why such a pair is called an ordered pair.

26. Each line in the ▭MODE▭ screen of a graphing calculator shows two or more choices. In how many different ways can you set the mode of this calculator?

```
Normal  Sci  Eng
Float   0123456789
Radian  Degree
Func  Par  Pol  Seq
Connected  Dot
Sequential  Simul
Full Screen  Split
```

27. **a.** **Calculator** Find a number n for which entering $n!$ in your calculator causes overflow error.
    b. Use *Guess and Test* to find the greatest integer n for which your calculator will evaluate $n!$. Before you start, estimate how many guesses it should take you to do this.

28. **Discrete Math** Suppose a car door lock has a five-button keypad. Each of the buttons includes two digits. How many different five-button patterns are possible? (*Hint:* Each button can be used more than once.)

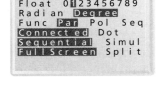

The entry code 21914 uses the same button sequence as the code 11023.

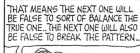

29. Refer to the cartoon above.
  a. How many different sets of answers are possible if the test includes eleven true/false questions?
  b. Do you agree with the last statement in the last part of the cartoon? **Justify** your response.

30. **Open-ended** Describe a counting situation that can be solved using each technique.
  a. the multiplication counting principle
  b. a single factorial
  c. the permutation formula

Exercises   MIXED REVIEW

Use the vertical line test to determine whether each relation is a function.

31.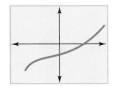

32.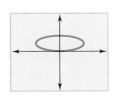

33.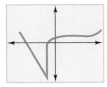

34. a. You have a part-time job washing cars. You earn $5/h. Write an equation to model your earnings.
  b. Graph your equation.
  c. If you earned $32.50 last week, how many hours did you work?
  d. How many hours will you have to work to buy a telephone that costs $48?

Getting Ready for Lesson 1-7

Solve each equation. Graph each solution on a number line.

35. $x - 6 = 32$ **36.** $3x + 4x = -49$

37. $4x^2 = 36$ **38.** $5x = 48$

39. $\frac{2}{3}x = 7$ **40.** $0.6x = 4.2$

41. $\frac{3}{4}x = 1\frac{9}{16}$ **42.** $0.8x - 0.2x = 10$

FOR YOUR JOURNAL

Summarize the difference between applying the multiplication counting principle and using permutations.

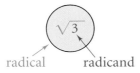

- Reviewing types of numbers
- Solving equations using irrational numbers

...And Why

To investigate car accidents

What You'll Need

- graph paper
- ruler
- protractor

PROBLEM SOLVING HINT

Look Back If you know the lengths of two sides of a right triangle, you can find the length of the third by using the Pythagorean theorem.

$$c^2 = a^2 + b^2$$

QUICK REVIEW

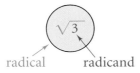

radical   radicand

If the radicand is not a perfect square, its square root is an *irrational number*.

1-7 Real Numbers

WORK TOGETHER

Accident investigators can tell how fast a car was traveling by measuring its skid marks. One formula they often use involves square roots. A number n is a square root of x if $n^2 = x$. To estimate a square root of a number, you can use the Pythagorean theorem to construct lengths of $\sqrt{2}$, $\sqrt{3}$, and so on.

1. Use the Pythagorean theorem to calculate *PB*, *PC*, *PD*, and so on in the diagram below.

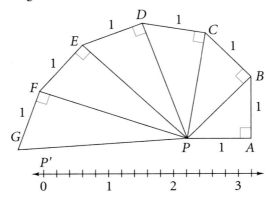

2. Copy the number line above on a sheet of paper. Mark point B' so that $PB = P'B'$. Similarly mark points C', D', and so on on your number line.

3. Estimate the decimal coordinate of B', C', D', and so on. Copy and complete the table below.

Leg 1	1	$\sqrt{2}$	■	■	■	■
Leg 2	1	1	1	1	1	1
Hypotenuse	$\sqrt{2} \approx ?$	■	■	■	■	■

4. Evaluate each square root in the table using your calculator. Does the calculator give you exact answers? How do you know?

THINK AND DISCUSS

Subsets of the Real Numbers

Rational numbers can be written as a ratio of two integers.
Irrational numbers cannot be written as a ratio of two integers. Rational and irrational numbers make up the set of **real numbers** and can be assigned to points on the number line.

The set of real numbers has many subsets, as shown below. In real life, you need to know which set of numbers makes sense in a given situation.

Real Numbers

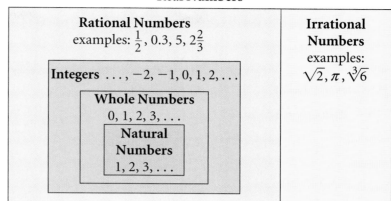

| Rational Numbers examples: $\frac{1}{2}$, 0.3, 5, $2\frac{2}{3}$ | Irrational Numbers examples: $\sqrt{2}, \pi, \sqrt[3]{6}$ |

Integers ..., $-2, -1, 0, 1, 2, ...$

Whole Numbers
0, 1, 2, 3, ...

Natural Numbers
1, 2, 3, ...

5. If a number is in the set of rational numbers, is it necessarily a real number? an integer? an irrational number?

6. Is the set of whole numbers a subset of the set of real numbers? of the set of natural numbers?

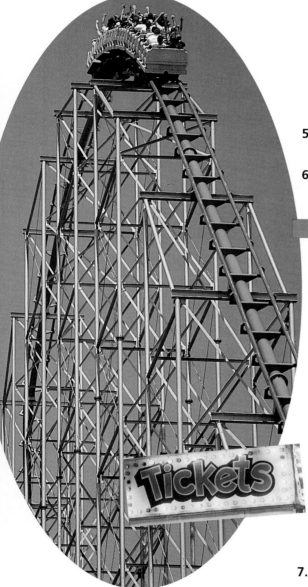

Example 1   **Relating to the Real World**

Entertainment Amusement parks use many mathematical relationships involving variables. Which set of numbers best describes the values for each variable?

a. the cost C in dollars of admission for n people
b. the maximum speed s in meters per second on a roller coaster of height h in meters

$$\left(\text{Use the formula } s = \frac{1200}{\sqrt{h}}.\right)$$

c. the park's profit (or loss) P in dollars for each week w of the year

a. The cost C of admission will be a rational number (such as $7.25), and the number n of people will be a whole number.

b. The height h will usually be measured in rational numbers. Since the speed s is calculated using a formula with a radical, it will be a real number.

c. The week number w will be the first 52 natural numbers, and the profit (or loss) P will be a rational number.

7. Try This Which set of numbers would best describe the values for the distance d traveled by a plane and its flight time t?

Example 2

Simplify each square root. Then decide if the number is rational or irrational.

a. $\sqrt{625}$ **b.** $\sqrt{12}$ **c.** $\sqrt{\dfrac{3}{25}}$

a. $\sqrt{625} = 25$
Since 25 is a whole number, it is rational.

b. $\sqrt{12} = \sqrt{4 \cdot 3}$
$\phantom{\sqrt{12}} = \sqrt{4}\,\sqrt{3}$ ← 3 is not a perfect square; it must
$\phantom{\sqrt{12}} = 2\sqrt{3}$ remain under the radical.
$2\sqrt{3}$ is irrational.

c. $\sqrt{\dfrac{3}{25}} = \dfrac{\sqrt{3}}{\sqrt{25}} = \dfrac{\sqrt{3}}{5}$

$\dfrac{\sqrt{3}}{5}$ is irrational.

> ### QUICK REVIEW
>
> **Properties of Square Roots**
> $\sqrt{ab} = \sqrt{a} \cdot \sqrt{b}$ and
>
> $\sqrt{\dfrac{a}{b}} = \dfrac{\sqrt{a}}{\sqrt{b}}$
>
> but $\sqrt{a + b} \neq \sqrt{a} + \sqrt{b}$.

8. Try This Decide whether $\sqrt{\dfrac{25}{36}}$ is rational or irrational.

Solving Equations with Irrational Numbers

Skid marks can be used to determine how fast a car was traveling when the brakes were applied. The speed s in meters per second is determined from the length d in meters of the skid marks. Use the formula $s = \sqrt{15d}$.

9. Which set of numbers best describes the values for each variable in the formula? Explain.

10. Why is the the information from Question 9 important? Can d be a negative number?

11. *Critical Thinking* For the situation and formula above, which is the independent variable? Explain.

12. Consider your answer to Question 11. Describe a situation in which the other variable would be the independent one.

Example 3   **Relating to the Real World** · · · · · · · · ·

Accident Investigation   A car left a 30-m skid mark. Use the formula $s = \sqrt{15d}$. Find the car's speed in meters per second when the brakes were applied.

$$s = \sqrt{15d}$$
$$= \sqrt{15(30)} \quad \longleftarrow \text{Substitute 30 for } d.$$
$$= \sqrt{15(15)(2)}$$
$$\approx 21.2$$

The car was traveling about 21.2 m/s.

13. Write the speed found in Example 3 as an exact answer.

14. Try This Suppose a skid mark is 32 m long. How fast was the car traveling in meters per second?

Example 4 ·

PROBLEM SOLVING HINT

To solve an equation such as $x^2 = 4$, give all possible answers (both square roots). Be sure to check both answers.

The *principal square root,* or the positive square root only, of 4 (written $\sqrt{4}$) is 2.

Solve $3x^2 + 5 = 20$. Then check the solution(s).

$$3x^2 + 5 = 20$$
$$3x^2 = 15 \qquad \longleftarrow \text{Subtract 5 from both sides.}$$
$$x^2 = 5 \qquad \longleftarrow \text{Divide both sides by 3.}$$
$$x = \sqrt{5} \text{ or } x = -\sqrt{5} \longleftarrow \text{Find the square root of both sides.}$$

The solutions are $x = \sqrt{5}$ and $x = -\sqrt{5}$.

Check: $3(\sqrt{5})^2 + 5 = 20$ and $3(-\sqrt{5})^2 + 5 = 20$. ✔

The symbol $\pm$ is used to indicate both a positive and negative value. In Example 4 above you could have written the solutions as $x = \pm\sqrt{5}$.

15. Try This Solve and check: $21x^2 - 17 = 9x^2 + 7$.

Exercises   **ON YOUR OWN**

Classify each expression as rational or irrational.

1. $-\frac{1}{3}$ **2.** $\frac{1}{2}$ **3.** $\sqrt{7}$ **4.** 52   **5.** 2π **6.** 4.1

7. $\sqrt{\dfrac{1}{4}}$ **8.** $\sqrt{64}$ **9.** $\sqrt{\dfrac{\pi}{2}}$ **10.** $\sqrt{\dfrac{8}{2}}$ **11.** $\sqrt{130}$ **12.** $\sqrt{\dfrac{45}{20}}$

13. Physics   The formula $t = \dfrac{\sqrt{d}}{4}$ describes the time t in seconds it takes for an object to fall d feet. Suppose a ball is dropped from a height of 12 ft. Approximate the time it takes to fall to the ground.

14. Critical Thinking   For what values of d does the formula $t = \dfrac{\sqrt{d}}{4}$ give an exact value for t? When is an approximation necessary?

15. Photography The time-lapse photos show the crown that forms when a drop of milk falls into a liquid. The photos were taken at 0.01-s intervals.

    a. Describe how the height h of the crown changes as the time t changes.

    b. Identify the independent and dependent variables. Which set of numbers best describes the values for each variable?

Evaluate each expression.

16. $5\sqrt{12x}$ for $x = 3$ **17.** $10\sqrt{35x}$ for $x = 5$ **18.** $-6\sqrt{2x}$ for $x = 18$

Solve each equation for x. Simplify your answers. What type of number is each answer?

19. $3x + 11 = 41$ **20.** $x^2 = 36$ **21.** $6x^2 = 216$ **22.** $4x + 7 = 3x - 18$

23. $6x = x + 15$ **24.** $7x^2 + 3 = 31$ **25.** $2x^2 + 8 = 58$ **26.** $3x^2 - 7 = 10$

27. $12x + 3 = 2x - 7$ **28.** $x^2 = 60$ **29.** $3x^2 - 1 = 95$ **30.** $3x^2 + 1 = 7x^2 - 1$

31. Research Use a driver's handbook. Find tables of speeds and stopping distances. Compare the stopping distance for several speeds to the length of the skid marks created. Are the distances in the table the same as the length of the skid marks? Explain.

Determine the dependent and independent variables. Which set of numbers best describes the value of each variable? Explain.

32. Entertainment on a Ferris wheel, your height h in feet above the ground; the time t in seconds since the ride started

33. Science the volume V of ice in a glass; the time t in seconds since the ice was removed from the freezer

34. Nature the number n of times a cricket chirps; the outdoor temperature T in tenths of a degree

35. Economics the year y; the median selling price p for a house that year

36. Open-ended Describe two sets of data that are related by a function rule. Which set of numbers best describes the data in each set?

37. Writing The word "rational" stems from the word "ratio." Explain the connection between the two terms.

38. Physics The formula $p = 2\pi\sqrt{\dfrac{L}{9.81}}$ shows the relationship between the period p of a pendulum's swing in seconds and the length L of the pendulum in meters. What is the period of the pendulum shown? Is your answer exact? Explain.

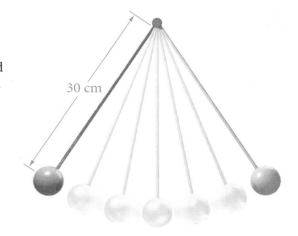

30 cm

39. Standardized Test Prep Which statements are true?
   I. Some integers are natural numbers.
   II. All whole numbers are rational numbers.
   III. All real numbers are rational or irrational.
   A. I only   **B.** II only   **C.** II and III only
   D. I, II, and III   **E.** None

Exercises   **M I X E D R E V I E W**

Graph each function.

40. $f(x) = (x + 3)^2 - 5$ **41.** $f(x) = (x - 1)^2 + 4$

42. $f(x) = |x - 5|$ **43.** $f(x) = |x + 2| - 6$

44. Science Absolute zero is approximately $-459.7°$F. The temperature of cosmic background radiation, found throughout space, is approximately $4.9°$F above absolute zero. Determine this temperature in degrees Fahrenheit. Indicate the values on a number line.

SELF ASSESSMENT

PORTFOLIO

Select two items from your work for this chapter. Consider:
• a diagram, graph, or chart
• a journal entry
• something that interested you.
Explain each selection.

Algebra at Work

Wildlife Biologist

Wildlife biologists can model changes in an animal population. An animal population increases rapidly when conditions are good. However, as the number of animals increases, the food supplies decrease. Hunger and disease then lower the population.

Wildlife biologists take a special interest in extremes of animal populations. If the population of one

species becomes too large, it may reduce the population of another species. A continuing decrease may result in an endangered or extinct species.

Mini Project: Find and graph the population of your favorite wild animal over the last ten years. Is your animal population well represented by a linear model? Explain your reasoning.

Finishing the Chapter Project

STEP BY STEP

Find Out activities on pages 10, 25, and 31 should help you to complete your project. Present your project for this chapter as a visual display. For each experiment you have conducted, you should show a table of data, a scatter plot of the data including a line of best fit, and a paragraph analyzing what happened. Your presentation should discuss any correlations and lines of best fit you have found and any conclusions you have drawn.

Reflect and Revise

Show your project to an adult and review your work together. Are your tables, graphs, and other work clear and easy to follow? Have you included all the necessary information? How can you change your work to avoid misunderstandings? How appealing is your display? Make any revisions necessary to improve your work.

Follow Up

Suppose you conducted your experiments with a group of adults. How would you expect the results to differ from your original results? Why? Try one of your experiments with adults. Show a graphical comparison between the results of your original experiment and the results of the new one.

For More Information

Brink, Susan. "Smart Moves: New Research Suggests that Folks from 8 to 80 Can Shape Up Their Brains with Aerobic Exercise." *U.S. News & World Report* (May 1995): 76–81.

Rubin, Don. *Brainstorms.* New York: Harper & Row, 1988.

Shortz, Will, ed. *Games Magazine Big Book of Games.* New York: Workman Publishing, 1984.

Key Terms

composite (p. 27)
dimensions of a matrix (p. 7)
domain (p. 20)
element (p. 8)
function (p. 20)
irrational numbers (p. 44)
mathematical model (p. 13)
matrix (p. 7)

multiplication counting
  principle (p. 38)
permutation (p. 39)
range (p. 20)
rational numbers (p. 44)
real numbers (p. 44)
relation (p. 20)
translation (p. 32)

How am I doing?

- State three ideas from this chapter that you think are important. Explain your choices.
- Explain the different ways you can describe mathematical relationships.

SELF ASSESSMENT

Collecting and Organizing Data   1-1

A scatter plot can show if a relationship exists between two sets of data. A correlation, if it exists, may be positive or negative, and strong or weak.

A **matrix** is a rectangular array of numbers. The **dimensions of a matrix** are the numbers of rows and columns. You can use spreadsheets and matrices to analyze data.

The matrix shows the number of baskets three players scored this year.

1. How many points has Tamika made?

2. How many three-point shots has Tran made?

3. What percent of Johanna's points were from free throws?

Free throws Two-pt. baskets Three-pt. baskets

$$\begin{array}{c} \text{Tamika} \\ \text{Johanna} \\ \text{Tran} \end{array} \begin{bmatrix} 22 & 30 & 48 \\ 21 & 31 & 48 \\ 21 & 29 & 50 \end{bmatrix}$$

Graphical Models   1-2

You can use different **mathematical models**, such as scatter plots, sets of ordered pairs, or tables of values, to show relationships between sets of data. You can use these models to make predictions about points that are not part of the data set. Data can be nonlinear as well as linear.

4. Data Analysis The table shows the number of cellular telephone users from 1989 through 1995.
  a. Draw a scatter plot of the data.   **b.** Describe any correlation.
  c. Draw a trend line.   **d.** **Predict** the number of cellular telephone users in 2005.

Cellular Telephone Users 1989–1995

Year	1989	1990	1991	1992	1993	1994	1995
Number of Cellular Phone Users (millions)	3.51	5.28	7.56	11.03	16.01	24.13	33.79

Source: *The Cellular Telecommunications Industry Association*

A **relation** is a set of ordered pairs. The **domain** is the set of first numbers in the pairs. The **range** is the set of second numbers in the pairs. When each element of the domain has only one element of the range associated with it, the relation is a **function**. You can write a function using the notation $f(x)$, called function notation.

Determine whether each relation is a function.

5. $\{(0, -3), (2, 1), (8, 3), (-1, 3)\}$

6. $\{(-4, 7), (5, 4), (7, 3), (9, 4), (3, 4)\}$

7. $\{(5, 0), (8, 1), (1, 3), (5, 2), (3, 8)\}$

8. $\{(10, 2), (-10, 2), (6, 4), (5, 3), (-6, 7)\}$

9. Standardized Test Prep Which point could not be part of a function that includes $(5, 4), (8, -1), (7, 3), (0, 5),$ and $(10, -2)$?

    A. $(6, 4)$ **B.** $(10, 1)$ **C.** $(11, -1)$ **D.** $(9, 3)$ **E.** $(-8, -2)$

When you put functions together, you form their **composite**. Apply the inner function first; then apply the outer function. You can add, subtract, multiply, or divide two functions.

If $f(x) = x^2 - 2$, $g(x) = 4x + 1$, and $h(x) = -x + 3$, evaluate the following.

10. $g(h(4))$ **11.** $f(g(-1))$ **12.** $h(f(5))$ **13.** $g(f(-2))$

14. $f(7) + h(6)$ **15.** $f(h(t))$ **16.** $g(h(t))$ **17.** $f(3) - h(3)$

A **translation** of a function moves the function vertically, horizontally, or both. However, its graph is the same size and shape as the original function.

If k and h are positive numbers and $f(x)$ is a function, then

    $f(x) + k$ shifts $f(x)$ up k units; $f(x) - k$ shifts $f(x)$ down k units;

    $f(x + h)$ shifts $f(x)$ left h units; $f(x - h)$ shifts $f(x)$ right h units.

Describe the translations of $y = x^2$ or $y = |x|$. Then sketch the graph of the function.

18. $f(x) = (x + 2)^2$ **19.** $f(x) = (x + 7)^2 - 4$ **20.** $f(x) = |x| - 8$

21. $f(x) = |x - 5|$ **22.** $f(x) = x^2 + 1$ **23.** $f(x) = |x - 3| + 3$

24. Open-ended Write the equation of a function whose graph is an absolute-value function. Then write the equation of the function after shifting 2 units down and 5 units to the right.

If there are m ways to make a first selection and n ways to make a second selection, there are $m \times n$ ways to make both selections. This is the **multiplication counting principle**.

A **permutation** is an arrangement of items in a particular order. The number of permutations of n items of a set arranged r items at a time is as follows.

$$_nP_r = \frac{n!}{(n-r)!} \text{ for } 1 \le r \le n$$

Evaluate each expression.

25. $6!$ **26.** $_5P_1$ **27.** $8!$ **28.** $_9P_2$ **29.** $_6P_3$ **30.** $_4P_2$

31. Writing Explain when the number of permutations of n objects equals n.

The **real numbers** include all the rational and irrational numbers. Different sets of numbers are reasonable to use in different contexts.

Classify each expression as rational or irrational.

32. $\sqrt{25}$ **33.** 5.1212 **34.** $\sqrt{37}$ **35.** 8.1π **36.** 79 **37.** $\frac{5}{7}$

38. -40 **39.** $\sqrt{121}$ **40.** $12\frac{7}{8}$ **41.** $\sqrt{200}$ **42.** -7π **43.** 5.172

Evaluate each expression.

44. $8\sqrt{7x}$ for $x = 49$ **45.** $-5\sqrt{12x}$ for $x = 3$ **46.** $10\sqrt{24x}$ for $x = 2$

47. $-6\sqrt{5x}$ for $x = 15$ **48.** $3\sqrt{10x}$ for $x = 6$ **49.** $3\sqrt{6x}$ for $x = 12$

Getting Ready for..▶ CHAPTER 2

List all the possible outcomes of each situation.

50. choosing a digit at random **51.** rolling a 6-sided number cube

52. choosing a day of the week at random **53.** tossing a coin

Simplify each expression.

54. $\frac{4-3}{8-2}$ **55.** $\frac{3-(-1)}{8-0}$ **56.** $\frac{-7-3}{9-10}$

57. $\frac{-4-(-1)}{-7-3}$ **58.** $\frac{9-0}{7-(-5)}$ **59.** $\frac{-4-2}{15-3}$

The spreadsheet shows the number and types of items sold by a school store during Semester 1.

	A	B	C	D
1	Month	Pens	Pencils	Markers
2	September	250	300	100
3	October	200	150	80
4	November	100	180	70
5	December	150	120	20

1. Write a spreadsheet formula that computes how many pens were sold. Find the number of pencils and markers sold.

2. Write a spreadsheet formula that computes how many items were sold in October. Use your formula to find the number of items sold in the other months.

3. Write two ways to find the total items sold during Semester 1. Do they give the same answer?

Describe each correlation.

4.

5.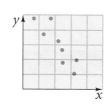

6. **Writing** Explain the differences between a strong and a weak correlation. Include a scatter plot of each.

Determine if each relation is a function.

7. $\{(0, 0), (1, -1), (2, -4), (3, -9), (4, -16)\}$

8. $\{(2, -6), (2, -2), (2, 0), (2, 3), (2, 7)\}$

9. $\{(2, 2), (1, 1), (0, 0), (1, -1), (2, -2)\}$

10. $\{(3, 2), (4, 3), (5, 4), (6, 5), (7, 6)\}$

11. **Open-ended** Sketch a graph of a relation that is not a function.

Suppose $f(x) = 2x - 5, g(x) = -3x - 1$, and $h(x) = 2x^2 + x - 7$. Evaluate the following.

12. $f(3)$

13. $f(1) + g(2)$

14. $g(0)$

15. $g(2) - f(0)$

16. $h(-1) - g(3)$

17. $h(-4)$

18. $f(g(2))$

19. $g(f(3))$

20. $g(h(-1))$

21. $f(t) + g(t)$

22. $g(f(t))$

Describe the translations of $y = x^2$ or $y = |x|$. Then sketch the graph of each function.

23. $y = (x - 2)^2 + 6$

24. $y = |x - 1| - 5$

25. $y = |x + 4| + 3$

26. $y = (x + 1)^2 - 4$

Describe several possible translations.

27.

28.

Evaluate.

29. $7!$

30. $_8P_3$

31. $3!$

32. $_5P_4$

Classify each expression as rational or irrational.

33. 81%

34. $\sqrt{120}$

35. -5.823

36. 7π

37. **Standardized Test Prep** Which set(s) of numbers belong(s) to the set of real numbers?
    I. rational numbers
    II. integers
    III. whole numbers
    IV. irrational numbers
    A. I only
    B. II only
    C. IV only
    D. II and III
    E. I, II, III, and IV

For Exercises 1–9, choose the correct letter.

1. Which scatter plot has a strong negative correlation?

A.

B.

C.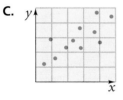

D.

E. none of the above

2. What is the equation of the function found by shifting the function $y = x^2$ up 3 units and left 4 units?

A. $y = (x - 3)^2 - 4$ **B.** $y = (x + 4)^2 + 3$
C. $y = (x - 4)^2 + 3$ **D.** $y = (x + 3)^2 - 4$
E. $y = (x + 4)^2 - 3$

3. Which relations are functions?

I. **II.**

III. 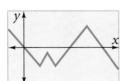 **IV.**

A. I and II **B.** II and III **C.** III and IV
D. I and IV **E.** I and III

4. Which phrase could not describe $\sqrt{625}$?
A. whole number **B.** irrational number
C. integer **D.** rational number
E. natural number

5. Which expression has the greatest value?
A. 4! **B.** $_7P_2$ **C.** $_6P_3$ **D.** $_4P_1$ **E.** 3!

6. Let $f(x) = 4x - 1$ and $g(x) = 2x^2$. What is the function rule for $h(x) = g(f(x + 1))$?
A. $h(x) = 8x^2 - 1$
B. $h(x) = 32x^2 + 48x + 18$
C. $h(x) = 32x^2 - 16x + 2$
D. $h(x) = 8x^2 + 16x + 3$
E. none of the above

7. Which number is irrational?
A. $\sqrt{1000}$ **B.** $1.2121\ldots$ **C.** $\frac{4}{7}$
D. 956.1 **E.** $\sqrt{400}$

Compare the boxed quantity in Column A with the boxed quantity in Column B. Choose the best answer.

A. The quantity in Column A is greater.
B. The quantity in Column B is greater.
C. The two quantities are equal.
D. The relationship cannot be determined on the basis of the information supplied.

Column A	Column B
$f(x) = -2x + 5$ and $g(x) = x^2 + 4x - 1$	

8. $f(g(5))$ | $g(f(5))$

9. $_8P_6$ | 48

Find each answer.

10. **Civics** How many president and vice-president pairs could be elected from a field of 16 candidates?

11. **Writing** Explain why the vertical line test determines whether a graph is that of a function. Include an example.

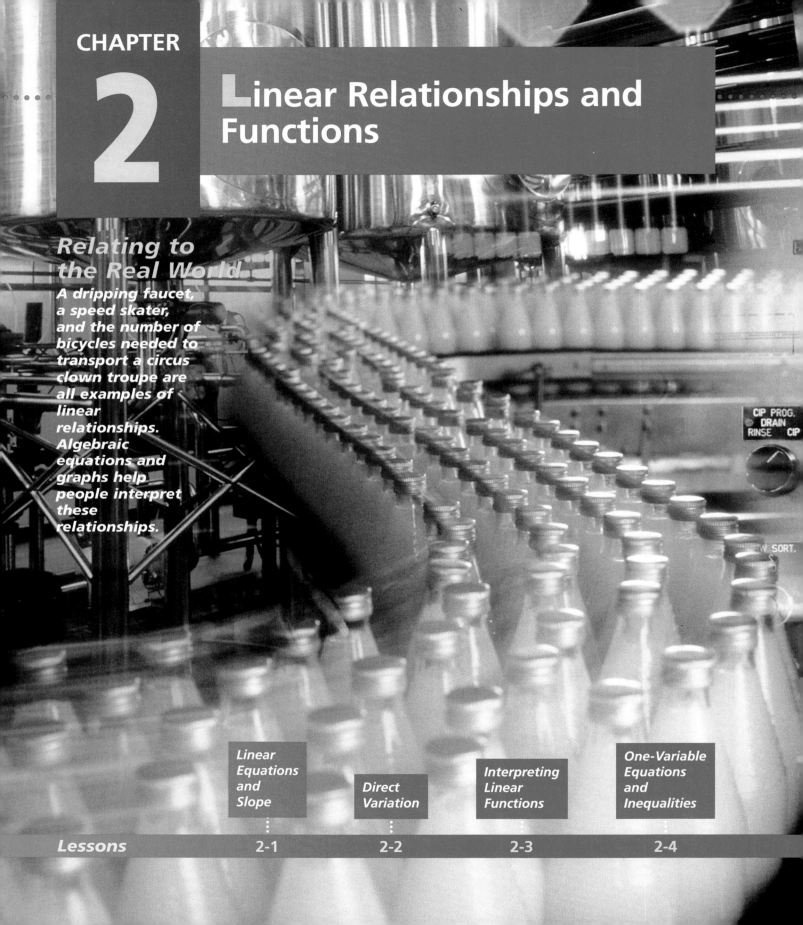

Relating to the Real World

A dripping faucet, a speed skater, and the number of bicycles needed to transport a circus clown troupe are all examples of linear relationships. Algebraic equations and graphs help people interpret these relationships.

CIP PROG.
DRAIN
RINSE   CIP

W SORT.

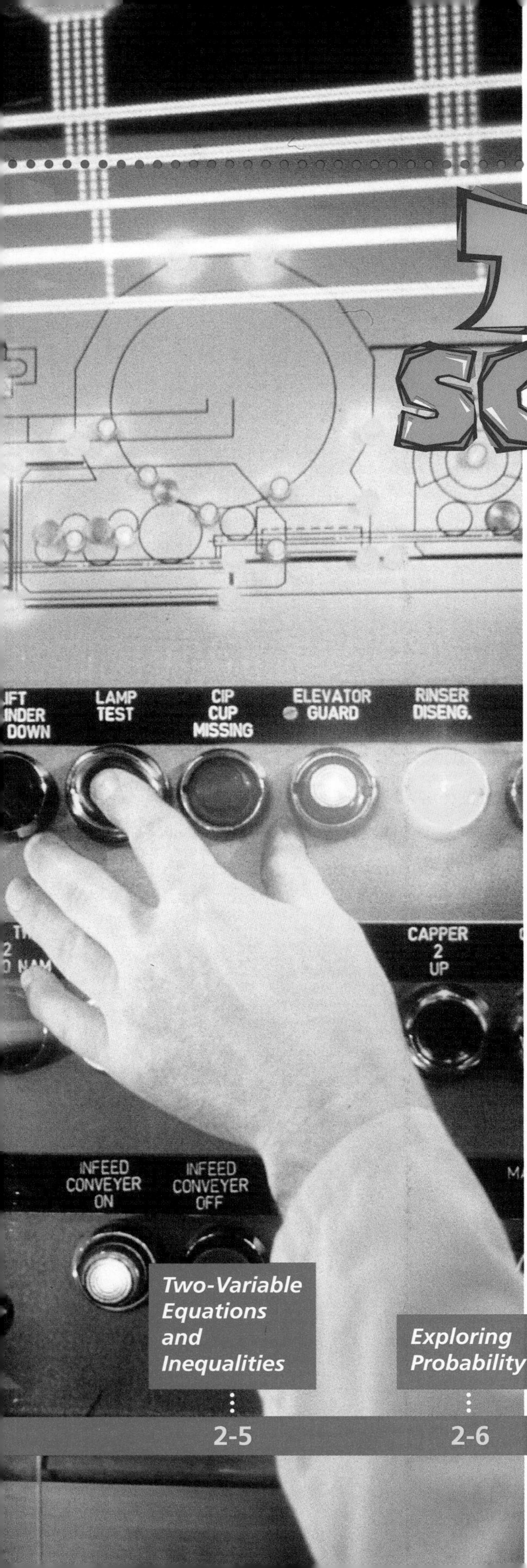

TIME SQUEEZE

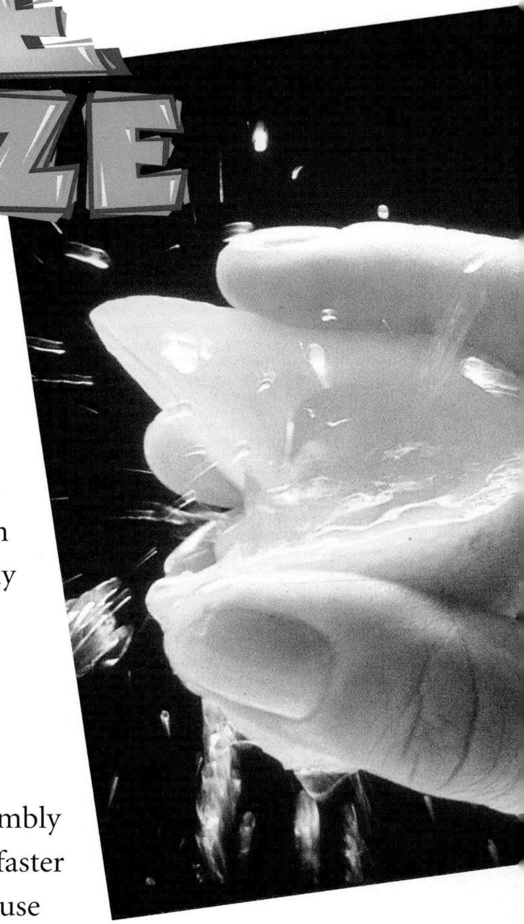

How long do you think it would take you to fill 1200 juice bottles by hand? Modern machines in factories can fill up to 1200 bottles per minute. Modern mass production depends on assembly lines that use highly specialized machines and production techniques.

As you work through the chapter, you will apply mathematics to analyze assembly line production so that it is faster and more efficient. You will use graphs and equations to help you make decisions about how to improve it. You will describe your methods and conclusions in a presentation to the class.

To help you complete the project:

▼ **p. 63** *Find Out by Investigating*
▼ **p. 68** *Find Out by Graphing*
▼ **p. 80** *Find Out by Analyzing*
▼ **p. 94** *Finishing the Project*

Two-Variable Equations and Inequalities

Exploring Probability

2-5

2-6

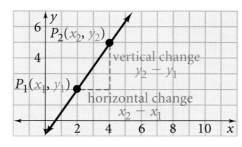
2-1 Linear Equations and Slope

What You'll Learn
• Defining and interpreting slope
• Using the slope-intercept form to write equations

...And Why

To solve problems involving sports

WORK TOGETHER

Work with a partner.

1. Make three tables similar to the one below or use a spreadsheet to calculate values for the equations $y = x - 4$, $y = 2x - 1$, and $y = 5x + 3$. Use the domain $\{-5, -2, 0, 1, 5\}$.

x	$y = x - 4$	Change in x	Change in y	$\dfrac{\text{Change in } y}{\text{Change in } x}$
-5	-9	—	—	—
-2	-6	$-2 -(-5) = 3$	$-6 -(-9) = \blacksquare$	$\frac{3}{3} = 1$
0	$\blacksquare$	$0 - (-2) = \blacksquare$	$\blacksquare$	$\frac{2}{2} = \blacksquare$
1	$\blacksquare$	$\blacksquare$	$\blacksquare$	$\blacksquare$
5	$\blacksquare$	$\blacksquare$	$\blacksquare$	$\blacksquare$

2. Compare the coefficients of x from each equation in Question 1 to the answers in the last row of each table. What do you notice?

3. Compare the three tables. How are the results alike? How are they different?

4. Graph the three equations from Question 1 on the same set of axes. Describe each graph. Which graph is the steepest? Which graph is the least steep?

THINK AND DISCUSS

Determining the Slope of a Line

The graph of a **linear equation** is a line. Since the graphs of the equations in the Work Together are lines, the equations are linear equations.

QUICK REVIEW

When you use the slope formula, define either point as P_1 or P_2.

The **slope** of a line is a measure of its steepness. You can use the coordinates of any two points on a line to find the slope of that line. The slope is the ratio of the vertical change to the horizontal change.

$$\text{slope} = \frac{\text{vertical change (rise)}}{\text{horizontal change (run)}}$$

$$= \frac{y_2 - y_1}{x_2 - x_1}, (x_2 - x_1 \neq 0)$$

Example 1   Relating to the Real World

Sports The graph below shows the results from a 500-m speed skating race. The slope of each line represents the average speed $\left(\frac{\text{distance}}{\text{time}}\right)$ for that skater. Find the slope of the line representing the average speed of Skater 1. Interpret the meaning of the slope.

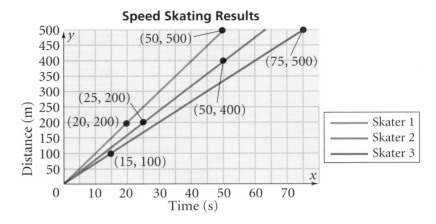

Speed Skating Results

(50, 500)
(75, 500)
(25, 200)
(50, 400)
(20, 200)
(15, 100)

Skater 1
Skater 2
Skater 3

Who? Bonnie Blair of the United States won the 500-m speed skating event at the winter Olympics in 1988, 1992, and 1994.

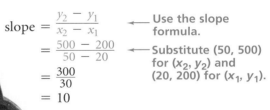

slope $= \dfrac{y_2 - y_1}{x_2 - x_1}$ ◂——— Use the slope formula.

$= \dfrac{500 - 200}{50 - 20}$ ◂——— Substitute (50, 500) for (x_2, y_2) and (20, 200) for (x_1, y_1).

$= \dfrac{300}{30}$

$= 10$

The slope of the line representing the average speed of Skater 1 is 10. Skater 1 is moving at a rate of 10 m/s.

5. **Try This** Find the slopes of the lines representing Skaters 2 and 3.

6. **a.** Who won the race? How can you tell by looking at the graph?
   b. How does the slope indicate who wins the race?

7. A line passes through $(-2, 4)$ and $(6, 7)$. Find the slope of the line.

2-1 Linear Equations and Slope   **59**

Using the Slope-Intercept Form of a Line

The **y-intercept** of a line is the point at which it crosses the y-axis. It is also the y-coordinate of this point.

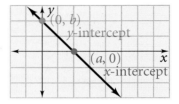

The **x-intercept** of a line is the point at which it crosses the x-axis. It is also the x-coordinate of this point.

8. a. The equation of a line is $y = x - 4$. What is the value of x when $y = 0$? What is the value of y when $x = 0$?

 b. What are the x- and y-intercepts of the line in part (a)?

Linear equations written in the form $y = mx + b$, such as those in the Work Together, are in **slope-intercept form.**

$$y = mx + b$$

slope y-intercept

For example, the equation $y = x - 4$ has a slope of 1 (the coefficient of x) and a y-intercept of -4 (the constant term).

9. Write each equation in slope-intercept form. Then identify the slope and the y-intercept of each line.

 a. $2x + y = 7$ **b.** $3x + 5y = -10$

10. Write an equation for the line that has slope -9 and y-intercept 5.

11. Explain how to graph a line using only its slope and y-intercept. **Verify** your explanation by graphing the line that has a y-intercept of -3 and a slope of $\frac{1}{2}$.

You can write the equation of a line when you know the slope and a point on the line.

> ### Example 2
>
> Write an equation of the line with slope $-\frac{1}{2}$ through the point $(8, -1)$.
>
> $y = mx + b$ ⟵ Use the slope-intercept form.
>
> $y = -\frac{1}{2}x + b$ ⟵ Substitute $-\frac{1}{2}$ for m.
>
> $(-1) = -\frac{1}{2}(8) + b$ ⟵ Substitute $(8, -1)$ for (x, y).
>
> $-1 = -4 + b$
>
> $3 = b$ ⟵ Solve for b.
>
> Since $m = -\frac{1}{2}$ and $b = 3$, an equation is $y = -\frac{1}{2}x + 3$. ■

12. Try This Write an equation of the line with slope $\frac{2}{5}$ through the point $(-2, 3)$.

A function whose graph forms a line is a **linear function.** For every *x*-value there is only one *y*-value.

The slopes of horizontal, vertical, perpendicular, and parallel lines have special properties.

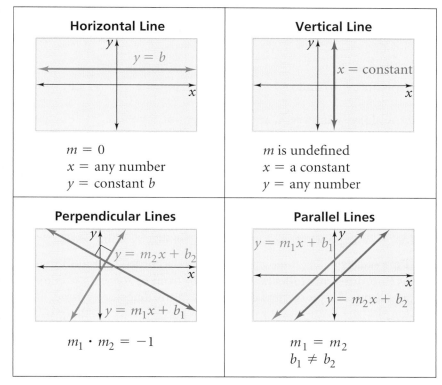

Horizontal Line	Vertical Line
$y = b$	$x = \text{constant}$
$m = 0$ $x = $ any number $y = $ constant b	m is undefined $x = $ a constant $y = $ any number
Perpendicular Lines	**Parallel Lines**
$y = m_2x + b_2$ $y = m_1x + b_1$	$y = m_1x + b_1$ $y = m_2x + b_2$
$m_1 \cdot m_2 = -1$	$m_1 = m_2$ $b_1 \neq b_2$

13. Draw the graph of a horizontal line. Identify two points on the line. **Verify** that the slope of the line is 0.

14. **Critical Thinking** Write the equation of a vertical line. Is the equation a linear equation? Does the equation define a linear function? **Justify** your reasoning.

15. **Critical Thinking** Draw the graph of a vertical line. Use the coordinates of two points to explain why the slope of a vertical line is undefined.

16. Draw the graph of two lines that are perpendicular to each other. Find their slopes. **Verify** that the product of the slopes is -1.

17. **a. Open-ended** Write equations of three lines that have the same *y*-intercepts but different slopes. Graph the lines. How are the graphs alike? How are they different?

    b. Write the equations of three lines that have the same slope but different *y*-intercepts. Graph the lines. How are the graphs alike? How are they different?

Can you find horizontal, vertical, perpendicular, and parallel lines in this bridge?

GRAPHING CALCULATOR HINT

Entering $Y_1 = 2X + \{1,2,3\}$ draws three lines with the same slope.

Find the slope of each line.

1.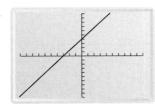

2.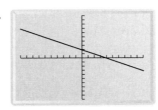

3.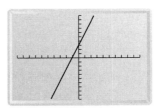

4. contains $(1, 6)$ and $(8, -1)$ **5.** contains $(-3, 9)$ and $(0, 3)$ **6.** contains $(0, 0)$ and $(2, 6)$

Find the slope, y-intercept, and x-intercept of each line.

7. $y = \frac{2}{3}x + 4$ **8.** $y = -0.8x - 5$ **9.** $y = 7$ **10.** $y = -x + 7$

11. $y = -\frac{5}{2}x + \frac{17}{2}$ **12.** $y = -\frac{5}{6}x + \frac{91}{3}$ **13.** $y = -\frac{3}{5}x - \frac{12}{5}$ **14.** $x = -3$

15. Writing Explain how you would graph a line if you knew only its slope and a point on the line. Then use your method to graph each line.
  a. $m = 2$; point $(1, 3)$ **b.** $m = -3$; point $(3, 1)$ **c.** $m = 0$; point $(-5, 1)$

16. Data Analysis The following plots were recorded by a motion detector as four different students walked away from or toward the detector one at a time. The plots show distance from the detector vs. time.

I. 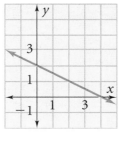 **II.** 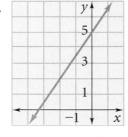 **III.** 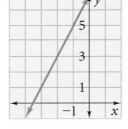 **IV.**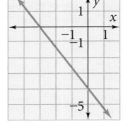

  a. Which student(s) walked at a constant rate? Which student(s) did not? **Justify** your reasoning.
  b. Which student(s) walked away from the motion detector?
  c. Which student started the farthest from the motion detector?

Write an equation of each line.

17.   **18.**   **19.**   **20.**

21. $m = -4$; contains $(2, 5)$ **22.** $m = \frac{1}{3}$; contains $(0, -4)$ **23.** $m = 2$; contains $(-2, 10)$

24. $m = 3$; contains $(1, 5)$ **25.** $m = -2$; contains $(-1, 6)$ **26.** $m = -\frac{3}{5}$; contains $(-4, 0)$

27. a. Geometry Sketch the graph of $y = 3x + 1$.

   b. On the same coordinate plane, sketch the line through point (2, 10) that is parallel to the first line. Write its equation.

28. Open-ended Write a story about each graph. Describe what the graph models and how you interpret the slopes of the lines.

   a.    **b.**

Use the information given to graph each line.

29. $m = 2$; contains $(1, 3)$

30. $m = 3$; contains $(4, 1)$

31. $m = -\frac{3}{5}$; contains $(-2, 5)$

32. $m = -\frac{3}{2}$; contains $(1, -4)$

33. $m = -4$; contains $(0, -1)$

34. $m = -\frac{5}{6}$; contains $(-4, 0)$

35. $m = -\frac{3}{8}$; contains $(2, -6)$

36. $m = 0$; contains $(-5, -1)$

37. m undefined; contains $(1, 3)$

Chapter Project   **Find Out by Investigating**

Work in a group. Think of a process your group could perform in an assembly line. Gather the materials. Have each person perform the entire process once. Record each time. Find the average time needed to perform the process once. Time more people. If necessary, revise your average.

Now break the procedure down into separate tasks. Assign each person in your group a task, and time how long the procedure takes. Does the average time differ? Compare your results with those of other groups.

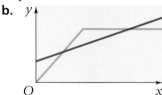

Exercises   M I X E D   R E V I E W

38. Fabric Design A fabric designer makes a 60% commission for works sold in a textile studio. The studio receives the other 40%. How much does the studio receive for selling a bolt of fabric that costs $15.65? How much does the designer receive?

Evaluate each composition. Let $f(x) = x^2 + 3$ and $g(x) = 8 - x$.

39. $f(g(2))$ **40.** $g(f(-1))$ **41.** $f(g(0))$ **42.** $g(f(-2))$

Getting Ready for Lesson 2-2

Solve each equation for y.

43. $5y = 35$ **44.** $12y = 3x$ **45.** $12y = 5x$ **46.** $\frac{3}{4}y = 15$ **47.** $0.9y = 27x$

What You'll Learn

- Writing and interpreting direct variation equations

...And Why

To determine the rate at which water is wasted

What You'll Need

- watch, clock, or timer with a second hand
- graph paper

2-2 Direct Variation

WORK TOGETHER

Work in pairs.

- Have one person watch the time while the other person counts the number of times his or her heart beats in 10 seconds. Record the data in a table.

- Repeat the process for 20, 30, 40, 50, and 60 seconds. Graph the set of ordered pairs. Draw a trend line for the data.

- Switch roles and repeat the procedure.

  1. How close is each set of data points to its corresponding trend line?

  2. For each trend line, identify the range for the domain {10, 20, 30, 40, 50, 60}.

  3. Find the slope of each trend line.

  4. Find the y-intercept of each trend line.

THINK AND DISCUSS

If a relationship can be expressed in the form $y = kx$, the two variables are said to *vary directly* or to *be proportional*. The value of k shows the constant rate of change of the dependent variable and is the **constant of variation.**

A **direct variation** is a linear function that can be written in the form $y = kx$, where $k \neq 0$.

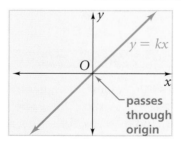

Since the y-intercept of any direct variation is 0, the slope-intercept form of its equation ($y = mx + b$) becomes $y = mx$. In other words, the constant of variation k has the same value as the slope (m) of its line.

5. Solve each equation for y. Do x and y vary directly? If so, identify the constant of variation.

   a. $7y = 2x$ **b.** $3y + 4x = 8$ **c.** $y - 7.5x = 0$

6. Critical Thinking What can you conclude about the x- and y-intercepts of any direct variation?

You can use a direct variation to model the situation in each photograph.

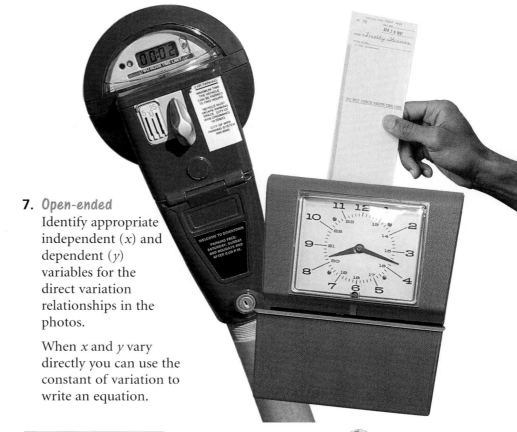

7. Open-ended Identify appropriate independent (x) and dependent (y) variables for the direct variation relationships in the photos.

When x and y vary directly you can use the constant of variation to write an equation.

Relating to the Real World 🌐 ·········

Water Conservation Suppose a dripping faucet wastes a cup of water if it drips for three minutes. The amount of water wasted varies directly with the amount of time the faucet drips. Find the constant of variation k. Then write an equation to model the direct variation.

Define t = time in minutes a faucet drips
w = number of cups of water wasted

Relate

water wasted	varies directly	with time

Write w = k · t

$w = kt$
$(1) = k(3)$ ◄— Substitute 3 for t and 1 for w.
$\frac{1}{3} = k$ ◄— Solve for k.

The constant of variation k is $\frac{1}{3}$. The equation $w = \frac{1}{3}t$ models the direct variation.

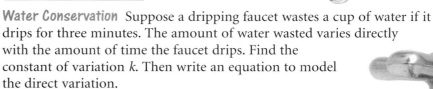

8. Use the equation in the example to find how many cups of water you waste when the faucet drips for 7 min.

9. Try This Identify the slope of each direct variation.
   a. $y = 7x$ **b.** $y = -\frac{1}{3}x$ **c.** $y = 7.5x$

You can use dimensional analysis to rewrite rates in other units, such as a snail's pace of $\frac{3 \text{ ft}}{1 \text{ h}}$.

$$\frac{3 \text{ ft}}{1 \text{ h}} \cdot \frac{24 \text{ h}}{1 \text{ day}} \cdot \frac{12 \text{ in.}}{1 \text{ ft}} = \frac{864 \text{ in.}}{1 \text{ day}} \quad \longleftarrow \quad \text{Cancel equivalent units in the numerator and denominator.}$$

10. Multiply to find the missing value. $\frac{1 \text{ c}}{3 \text{ min}} \cdot \frac{1 \text{ min}}{60 \text{ s}} = \blacksquare$ How did you know what units to use for your answer?

11. Use the constant of variation in the water conservation example to find the number of cups wasted if the faucet is left dripping for one week (7 days) without stopping.

The diagram illustrates the relationships among linear equations, linear equations in function form, and direct variations.

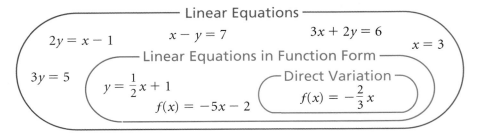

12. Is a direct variation always a linear function?

13. Under what circumstances, if any, would a linear function be a direct variation?

Exercises   ON YOUR OWN

Identify the slope of each direct variation.

1. $y = 5x$ **2.** $y = -2x$ **3.** $y = 7x$ **4.** $y = -3x$

5. $y = 10x$ **6.** $y = x$ **7.** $y = \frac{3}{4}x$ **8.** $y = 6.5x$

9. Automobiles You drive a car 392 mi on one tank of gas. The tank holds 14 gal. The number of miles traveled varies directly with the number of gallons of gas you use.
   a. Write an equation that relates miles traveled to gallons of gas used.
   b. Suppose you only have enough money to get 3.7 gal of gas. How far can you drive before refueling?
   c. Over the past year you drove 11,700 mi. About how many gallons of gas did you use?
   d. Suppose gasoline costs $1.43/gal. Find the cost per mile.

10. Writing Describe how to tell whether a graph represents a direct variation or not.

Health and Fitness **Use information from the chart.**

11. Write an equation of a direct variation that relates calories burned while bicycling at 12 mi/h to a person's weight. About how many calories would a 115-lb person burn while bicycling at 12 mi/h for an hour?

12. About how many calories would a 180-lb person burn while playing 1 h of tennis?

13. How many calories would you burn if you walked at 2 mi/h for 1 h? (*Hint:* You might want to graph the data from the table and draw a trend line.)

14. No calories are burned when no work is done. Your answer from Exercise 13 can be considered to be a data point (time, calories burned). Another data point in this set would be (0, 0). Use these two data points to write an equation relating calories burned to time when you walk at 2 mi/h.

15. Suppose you participated in a 10-mi walk to raise money for a charity and walked at a constant 2 mi/h. How many calories would you burn? How would your answer change if the walk was 7.25 mi?

Write the equation of a direct variation that passes through the given point.

16. $(1, 2)$ 17. $(-3, -7)$

18. $(2, -9)$ 19. $(-0.1, 50)$

20. Open-ended Give a real-world example of a direct variation. Write and graph its equation.

21. Environment Suppose you work on a tree farm and you need to find the height of each tree. You know that the length of an object's shadow varies directly with its height and that at noon, a person 6 ft tall casts a shadow 2 ft 2 in. long.
   a. Find the constant of variation.
   b. Write an equation to calculate the height of the tree.
   c. Find the height of a tree with a shadow 8 ft 4 in. long.

Calories Burned During One Hour of Exercise			
Activity	Rate	For a 100-lb Person	For a 150-lb Person
Bicycling	12 mi/h	270	410
Jogging	7 mi/h	610	920
Swimming	25 yd/min	185	275
Tennis	–	265	400
Walking	2 mi/h	160	240

Source: American Heart Association

Multiply to find the missing value. Include units in your answer.

22. $\dfrac{12 \text{ blocks}}{1 \text{ h}} \cdot \dfrac{1 \text{ mi}}{8 \text{ blocks}} = \blacksquare$

23. $20 \text{ yd} \cdot \dfrac{3 \text{ ft}}{1 \text{ yd}} = \blacksquare$

24. $3 \text{ gal} \cdot \dfrac{4 \text{ qt}}{1 \text{ gal}} \cdot \dfrac{2 \text{ pt}}{1 \text{ qt}} = \blacksquare$

25. $4 \text{ cm} \cdot \dfrac{1 \text{ m}}{100 \text{ cm}} \cdot \dfrac{1 \text{ km}}{1000 \text{ m}} = \blacksquare$

26. $\dfrac{100 \text{ ft}}{1 \text{ s}} \cdot \dfrac{12 \text{ in.}}{1 \text{ ft}} \cdot \dfrac{60 \text{ s}}{1 \text{ min}} \cdot \dfrac{60 \text{ min}}{1 \text{ h}} = \blacksquare$

27. $\dfrac{55 \text{ mi}}{1 \text{ h}} \cdot \dfrac{5280 \text{ ft}}{1 \text{ mi}} \cdot \dfrac{1 \text{ h}}{60 \text{ min}} \cdot \dfrac{1 \text{ min}}{60 \text{ s}} = \blacksquare$

28. Critical Thinking Suppose you use the origin to test whether a linear equation is a direct variation. Does this method work? **Verify** your answer with an example.

29. If z varies directly with the product of x and y ($z = kxy$), then z is said to vary jointly with x and y.

  a. The area of a triangle varies jointly with its base and height. What is the constant of variation?
  b. Suppose q varies jointly with v and s, and $q = 24$ when $v = 2$ and $s = 3$. Find q when $v = 4$ and $s = 2$.
  c. Suppose z varies jointly with x and y, and x varies directly with w. Show that z varies jointly with w and y.

Chapter Project **Find Out by Graphing**

A juice bottling machine fills 1200 bottles per minute. Graph the number of bottles filled versus the time in minutes the machine runs. Is this model a direct variation? If so, what is the constant of variation?

Exercises   M I X E D   R E V I E W

Evaluate each expression.

30. $_{10}P_6$ **31.** $8!$ **32.** $_6P_3$ **33.** $12!$ **34.** $_8P_5$ **35.** $4!$

36. Probability A store carries blue jeans and khakis in slim fit, regular fit, and relaxed fit. Make a tree diagram of the different kinds of pants.

Getting Ready for Lesson 2-3

37. Graph the ordered pairs $(0, 6)$, $(1, 5.4)$, $(2, 4.8)$ and connect the points. If the pattern continues, what range would you predict for $\{3, 4, 5\}$?

Algebra at Work

Miniaturist

People who make a career out of designing and creating miniature models of an actual object are called *miniaturists*. Miniaturists apply direct variations to reproduce realistic models of items such as doll houses, stores, displays, or scenes. Common scales used to create miniatures are the following.
• the one-inch scale (1 in. : 1 ft, or 1 : 12)
• the half-inch scale (0.5 in. : 1 ft or 1 : 24)
• the quarter-inch scale (0.25 in. : 1 ft or 1 : 48)

Mini Project: Identify an object and measure it. Give its dimensions and the dimensions of a miniature of the object using a common scale.

What You'll Learn

- Writing linear equations in slope-intercept and standard forms
- Making predictions regarding linear functions

...And Why

To make wise consumer decisions

2-3 Interpreting Linear Functions

THINK AND DISCUSS

Writing Linear Equations

You have written linear equations using slope-intercept form. You should also be able to find the equation of a line given two points on the line.

Example 1 **Relating to the Real World**

Science A candle is 6 in. tall after burning for 1 h. After 3 h, it is $5\frac{1}{2}$ in. tall. Write an equation to model the height y of the candle at time x.

Step 1: Identify the data points $(3, \frac{11}{2})$ and $(1, 6)$ as (x_1, y_1) and (x_2, y_2).

Step 2: Find the slope of the line.

$$m = \frac{y_2 - y_1}{x_2 - x_1}$$

$$m = \frac{6 - \frac{11}{2}}{1 - 3} \longleftarrow \text{Substitute.}$$

$$m = \frac{\frac{1}{2}}{-2} \longleftarrow \text{Simplify.}$$

$$m = -\frac{1}{4}$$

Step 3: Use the slope-intercept form to find the y-intercept.

Since both points are on the line, each satisfies the equation of the line. Substitute one of the points into the equation.

$$y = mx + b$$
$$y = -\frac{1}{4}x + b \longleftarrow \text{Substitute } -\frac{1}{4} \text{ for } m.$$
$$6 = -\frac{1}{4}(1) + b \longleftarrow \text{Substitute (1, 6) for } (x, y).$$
$$6 = -\frac{1}{4} + b$$
$$6\frac{1}{4} = b \longleftarrow \text{Solve for } b.$$

 GRAPHING CALCULATOR HINT

You can use a graphing calculator to find the equation of a line given two points. Input the coordinates of points into two lists, and then use the LinReg feature.

The equation of the line that models the height of the candle is $y = -\frac{1}{4}x + 6\frac{1}{4}$.

1. In Example 1, what does the slope $-\frac{1}{4}$ represent? What does the value $6\frac{1}{4}$ represent?

2. Using the information from Example 1, **predict** when the candle will be 4 in. tall. Explain how you made your prediction.

3. For Example 1, what are realistic values for the domain and range?

4. **Try This** Write the equation of each line.
   a. passes through the points $(-1, 3)$ and $(3, -5)$
   b. contains the point $(2, 5)$ and has a y-intercept of -1

The **standard form** of an equation of a line is $ax + by = c$ where a, b, and c are integers. Notice that x and y are on the same side of the equal sign.

5. a. Rewrite the equation from Example 1 in standard form.
   b. List the steps you used for part (a) in order.

6. Write each linear equation in standard form.
   a. $y = 2x + 7$ b. $-4y + x = -12$ c. $x + y - 1 = 0$

Determining Linear Functions from Data

You can often model data with a linear function. Determining how closely the data points fit the linear function will indicate whether the model is reasonable.

Example 2   **Relating to the Real World**

Automobiles In 1997, Lalia considered buying a 1991 car with an asking price of $1400. She researched prices for various years of the same model and recorded the data in the table.

Model Year	1992	1993	1994	1995	1996
Price	$2100	$3050	$4180	$4595	$5825

a. Graph the data. Decide if a linear model is reasonable.
b. Determine a fair price for the car. Is the asking price reasonable?

a. Let x be the year the car was made. (Use 6 for 1996, etc.) Let y be the price of the car.

   Graph the data.

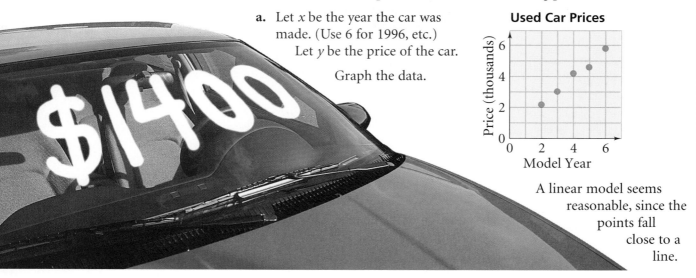

Used Car Prices

A linear model seems reasonable, since the points fall close to a line.

You can use the LinReg feature to generate a line of best fit.

b. Draw a trend line.

Used Car Prices

One possible linear model is $y = 0.9x + 0.5$.

A fair price would be the value of y for $x = 1$, or about $1200.

The asking price of $1400 is reasonable, although slightly high.

7. Critical Thinking Do you think you could use this model to **predict** the price of a 9-year-old car today? Explain.

8. Critical Thinking Under what conditions would the asking price of the car differ greatly from the price the model predicts?

Exercises   O N   Y O U R   O W N

Write each linear equation in standard form.

1. $y = 6x - 5$

2. $-9x = 2y + 3$

3. $-x + 5y - 4 = 0$

4. $x - 2y = 0$

5. $y - 4 = x + 2$

6. $-x = y - 13$

7. $y = \frac{1}{2}x + 1$

8. $7y + 6x = 12$

Write an equation of the line through the given points. Then graph each equation.

9. $(6, -2)$ and $(4, 8)$

10. $(-5, -3)$ and $(-8, 12)$

11. $(6, -1)$ and $(-4, -7)$

12. $(0, -6)$ and $(9, -12)$

13. $(-10, -4)$ and $(-2, -7)$

14. $(15, 0)$ and $(0, -15)$

15. $(-1, 7)$ and $(6, 4)$

16. $(18, 3)$ and $(0, -3)$

17. $(4, 4)$ and $(5, -8)$

18. Entertainment Ali is trying to decide whether to get his local cable service or just rent movies from the local video store. Basic cable service has a monthly fee of $29.95. The local video store charges $2.95 per movie ($x$).
   a. Write an equation to model the cost y of the cable service for one month.
   b. Write a second equation to model the cost y of renting x movies from the local video store. What is the slope? the y-intercept?
   c. Open-ended Ali now rents 8–12 movies each month. Graph the two equations from parts (a) and (b). Interpret the graph. Use your interpretation to make a recommendation to Ali.

19. Math in the Media You are making and selling tarps. The ad shows the prices of the sizes you currently make.

  a. Create a scatter plot showing the relationship between the cost and the area of the tarp. Which variable is the independent variable?

  b. Use your scatter plot to develop a model relating the area of the tarp to its cost.

  c. How good a model do you feel you have? Explain.

  d. Is $7.00 a reasonable price for a tarp that is 10 ft by 15 ft? Explain.

  e. Using your model and the prices in the table, which size tarp varies the most from the price you predicted? How large is the discrepancy between your model and the selling price?

TARPS

5 X 7 ft........$1.39	18 x 20 ft....$14.39
6 X 8 ft........$1.99	15 x 30 ft....$17.99
8 X 10 ft......$3.19	20 x 30 ft....$23.99
10 X 12 ft.....$4.79	20 x 40 ft....$31.99
12 x 16 ft.....$7.69	25 x 45 ft....$44.99
10 x 20 ft.....$7.99	30 x 50 ft....$59.99
16 x 20 ft....$12.79	30 x 60 ft....$71.99

ON SALE! ANY SIZE!

Write an equation of the line containing each pair of points.

20. $(-1, 3)$ and $(3, -5)$

21. $(6, 1)$ and $(-2, 2)$

22. $(5, 3)$ and $(8, 12)$

23. $(6, 2)$ and $(4, 8)$

24. $(4, 2)$ and $(6, 5)$

25. $(-1, 5)$ and $(-3, -2)$

26. $(-8, 7)$ and $(-5, 9)$

27. $(-4, 0)$ and $(-7, -9)$

28. $(-6, -1)$ and $(-3, -2)$

29. $(5, -2)$ and $(-6, 8)$

30. $(-12, -5)$ and $(-11, -9)$

31. $(0, -10)$ and $(-8, -14)$

32. Health The table shows the relationship between calories and fat in fast-food hamburgers.

  a. Develop a model for the relationship between calories and fat.

  b. A hamburger not on this list has 330 calories. About how much fat would you expect it to have?

  c. Are these estimates reasonable: 10g of fat for a 200-calorie hamburger? 36 g of fat for a 660-calorie hamburger? Explain. How do these amounts compare with what the model predicts.

Hamburger									
	A	**B**	**C**	**D**	**E**	**F**	**G**	**H**	**I**
Calories	720	530	510	500	305	410	440	320	598
Fat (grams)	46	30	27	26	13	20	25	13	26

Source: *The Fat Counter*

33. Writing Suppose a linear function models a data set. Explain how to predict where a new data point might fall.

34. Geometry Write the equation of the perpendicular bisector of the segment with endpoints $(-3, 5)$ and $(7, 1)$.

35. a. Research Find a data set that you think is linear.

  b. Graph the data and draw a trend line or a line of best fit.

  c. Write an equation for the trend line in slope-intercept form. What do the slope and the *y*-intercept tell you about the data?

36. Standardized Test Prep Which equation is *not* an equation for the line passing through the points $(1, -3)$ and $(-5, 2)$?

A. $y = -\frac{5}{6}x + -\frac{13}{6}$ **B.** $6y + 5x = -13$ **C.** $\frac{5}{6}x + y = -\frac{13}{6}$

D. $-5x + 13 = -6y$ **E.** $5x + 6y + 13 = 0$

Exercises   MIXED REVIEW

Find the range of each function when the domain is $\{-3, -1, 0, 1.5, 4\}$.

37. $f(x) = 2x - 1$ **38.** $y = x^2 + 3$ **39.** $g(x) = \dfrac{x - 4}{2}$ **40.** $y = 9 - 2x$

41. Track Paula Ivan of Romania holds the women's world record for running the mile. Her time was 4 min 15.61 s.
   a. Find Paula's rate in feet per second. How far did she run in 100 s?
   b. Write an equation that relates the distance she ran to time. Use feet and seconds as the units.
   c. Calculate Paula's speed in miles per hour.

FOR YOUR JOURNAL

In your own words, describe what this lesson enables you to do. Provide examples in your explanation.

Getting Ready for Lesson 2-4

Solve each equation for *x*. Graph each solution on a number line.

42. $5x + 8 = 0$ **43.** $0.5x - 4 = -8$

44. $-4x - 7 = -3x$ **45.** $-x - 20 = -5x + 9$

Exercises   CHECKPOINT

Find the *x*- and *y*-intercepts of each line.

   1. $x - 3y = 9$ **2.** $y = 7x + 5$ **3.** $y = 6x$ **4.** $-4x + y = 10$

Write the equation of each line in slope-intercept form.

   5. $2x - y = 9$ **6.** $4x = 2 + y$ **7.** $5y = 3x - 10$ **8.** $4x + 6y = 12$

9. a. Entertainment A group of friends is going to the movies. Each ticket is $7.00. Write a function to model the relationship between total cost *c* and number of friends *f*.
   b. Describe the graph of this function.
   c. Could the domain include negative numbers? Could it include fractions? Explain.

10. Standardized Test Prep Which line is perpendicular to $3x + 2y = 6$?

   A. $4x - 6y = 3$ **B.** $y = -\frac{3}{2}x + 4$ **C.** $2x + 3y = 12$

   D. $y = -\frac{2}{3}x - 7$ **E.** $y = \frac{3}{2}x + 1$

Exploration

Piecewise Functions

After Lesson 2-3

A **piecewise function** has different rules for different parts of its domain.

Example 1

Write a piecewise function to represent the graph at the right. There are three sections on the graph, so there will be three parts to the function.

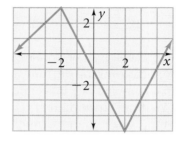

When $x \leq -2$, the function is $f(x) = x + 5$. When $-2 < x \leq 2$, the function is $f(x) = -2x - 1$. When $x > 2$, the function is $f(x) = 2x - 9$.

The piecewise function is $f(x) = \begin{cases} x + 5, \text{ if } x \leq -2 \\ -2x - 1, \text{ if } -2 < x \leq 2 \\ 2x - 9, \text{ if } x > 2 \end{cases}$.

Some piecewise functions are **step functions.** Their graphs look like the steps of a staircase. One step function is the greatest integer function $f(x) = [x]$, where $[x]$ means the greatest integer less than or equal to x.

Example 2

Graph the function $f(x) = [x]$.

Step 1: Choose an interval bounded by two consecutive integers. Make a table of values for the interval $0 \leq x \leq 1$.

x	0	0.25	0.5	0.75	1
$f(x)$	0	0	0	0	1

Each section of the graph starts and ends at the same y-value. The left-hand point of each "step" is a closed circle. The right-hand point is an open circle.

Step 2: Graph the function.

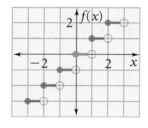

Use a closed circle for included endpoints; use open circles for excluded endpoints.

Graph each piecewise function.

1. $y = [x] + 2$

2. $f(x) = 3[x]$

3. $y = \begin{cases} x + 4, \text{ if } x \leq -2 \\ -x, \text{ if } x > -2 \end{cases}$

4. $f(x) = \begin{cases} -2x + 1, \text{ if } x < 3 \\ x - 8, \text{ if } x \geq 3 \end{cases}$

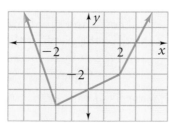

5. Write a piecewise function to represent the graph at the right.

6. **Writing** Explain how to graph a step function.

What You'll Learn
- Solving one-variable equations and inequalities
- Solving absolute-value equations and inequalities

...And Why
To solve problems involving shopping

What You'll Need
- graphing calculator

2-4 One-Variable Equations and Inequalities

WORK TOGETHER

Geometer the magician asks spectators to think of a number and perform certain operations on it. When he hears a result, he guesses the original number. One set of operations he uses is listed below. Have each person in your group follow these steps:

- Select a number and add 1 to it.
  - Multiply the new number by the number of diagonals in a square.
    - Add the number of sides in a triangle.
      - Subtract the number of sides in a trapezoid.
    - Multiply by the number of sides in a pentagon.

1. How does Geometer know the original number? (*Hint:* Look for a pattern in your group's results.)

2. Suppose one result is 1405. Let x represent the original number. Write mathematical expressions for each step listed. Solve an equation to find the original number.

3. Open-ended Make up your own sequence of operations.

THINK AND DISCUSS

Solving and Graphing Equations and Inequalities

Any value of the variable that makes an equation or an inequality true is a **solution.** Solving an inequality is similar to solving an equation. Solutions to equations and inequalities using one variable can be graphed on a number line. Here are some examples.

$$x = -2 \qquad x > -2 \qquad x \leq -2$$

$x = -2$	$x > -2$	$x \leq -2$
$-3\,-2\,-1\ \ 0\ \ 1$	$-3\,-2\,-1\ \ 0\ \ 1$	$-3\,-2\,-1\ \ 0\ \ 1$
includes -2	includes only values greater than -2	includes -2 and all values less than -2

4. Graph each equation or inequality.
  a. $x \geq -7$ **b.** $x \neq 5$ **c.** $4 \leq x < 10$

You can solve some equations by inspection or by using the *Guess and Test* method. Others require an algebraic or a graphing method.

QUICK REVIEW

Example 1

QUICK REVIEW

To solve equations, you use the associative, commutative, identity, inverse, and distributive properties, page 682.

Solve $6x + 2(3 - x) = 7x + 1$. Then check your answer.

Method 1: Use algebraic properties to get the variable by itself on one side of the equation.

$$6x + 2(3 - x) = 7x + 1$$
$$6x + 6 - 2x = 7x + 1 \quad \longleftarrow \text{Use the distributive property.}$$
$$4x + 6 = 7x + 1 \quad \longleftarrow \text{Combine like terms.}$$
$$6 = 3x + 1 \quad \longleftarrow \text{Subtract } 4x \text{ from each side.}$$
$$5 = 3x \quad \longleftarrow \text{Subtract 1 from each side.}$$
$$\frac{5}{3} = x \quad \longleftarrow \text{Divide each side by 3.}$$

GRAPHING CALCULATOR HINT

Some graphing calculators have an Intersect option. You can use it to find the coordinates of the point of intersection of two lines.

Method 2: Use a graphing calculator.

Enter one side of the equation as Y1 and the other side as Y2.

Find a suitable viewing window.

Press **2nd** Calc **5**. Then press **ENTER** three times to find the x-coordinate of the point of intersection.

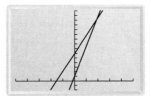

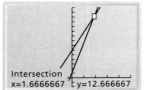

Xmin=–5   Ymin=–2
Xmax=5   Ymax=15
Xscl=1   Yscl=1

The x-coordinate of the point of intersection is $1.\overline{6}$, or $1\frac{2}{3}$.

Check: Substitute $1\frac{2}{3}$ or $\frac{5}{3}$ for x in the original equation.

$$6\left(\frac{5}{3}\right) + 2\left(3 - \frac{5}{3}\right) \stackrel{?}{=} 7\left(\frac{5}{3}\right) + 1$$
$$\frac{30}{3} + 6 - \frac{10}{3} \stackrel{?}{=} \frac{35}{3} + 1$$
$$\frac{(30 + 18 - 10)}{3} \stackrel{?}{=} \frac{(35 + 3)}{3}$$
$$\frac{38}{3} = \frac{38}{3} ✔$$

For more practice solving equations, see the Skills Handbook, page 669.

5. Try This Solve each equation. Check each answer.
   a. $3x + 1 = 16$
   b. $10x + 4 = 8 - 2x$
   c. $2(x - 3) = 4x$
   d. $4x - 5(x - 2) = 9x - 14$

You can solve inequalities with one variable in a similar manner.

Example 2 **Relating to the Real World**

Shopping Jeanine has $20 and is going shopping to buy three scarves and as many pairs of earrings as possible. How many pairs of earrings can she buy?

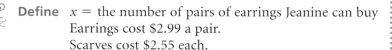

Define x = the number of pairs of earrings Jeanine can buy
Earrings cost $2.99 a pair.
Scarves cost $2.55 each.

Relate	The cost of 3 scarves	plus	x pairs of earrings	is less than or equal to	$20.
Write	2.55(3)	+	2.99x	≤	20

$$2.55(3) + 2.99x \leq 20$$
$$7.65 + 2.99x \leq 20 \quad \longleftarrow \text{Simplify.}$$
$$2.99x \leq 12.35 \quad \longleftarrow \text{Subtract 7.65 from both sides.}$$
$$x \leq 4.13 \quad \longleftarrow \text{Divide both sides by 2.99.}$$

Jeanine can buy at most four pairs of earrings. ■

6. Try This Solve $5x - 3(x + 4) > 10$.

Solving and Graphing Absolute-Value Equations and Inequalities

An absolute value equation such as $|x - 6| = 10$ has two solutions, since the expression $x - 6$ can equal 10 or -10.

Example 3

Solve and graph the equation $|x - 6| = 10$.

$$|x - 6| = 10 \quad \longleftarrow \text{The value of the expression } x - 6 \text{ is 10 or } -10.$$
$$x - 6 = 10 \text{ or } x - 6 = -10 \quad \longleftarrow \text{Write two equations.}$$
$$x = 16 \text{ or } \qquad x = -4 \quad \longleftarrow \text{Solve each equation.}$$

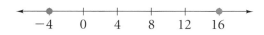

■

7. Try This Solve and graph each equation. Check each answer.

    a. $|x| - 5 = 7$ **b.** $|x + 5| = 7$ **c.** $|x - 7| = 5$

You can solve simple absolute-value inequalities by graphing the solutions.

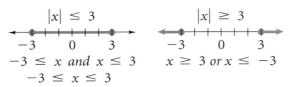

$|x| \leq 3$ $|x| \geq 3$

$-3 \leq x$ and $x \leq 3$ $x \geq 3$ or $x \leq -3$

$-3 \leq x \leq 3$

8. Why is the word *or* used in the solution of $|x| \geq 3$ above?

Sometimes you need to rewrite an absolute-value inequality as two inequalities. Then you can solve each inequality algebraically.

Example 4

Solve each inequality. Graph the solutions on a number line.

a. $|x + 4| \leq 7$ **b.** $|2x - 1| + 2 > 5$

a. $|x + 4| \leq 7$

$x + 4 \leq 7$ ⟵ Write two inequalities. ⟶ $x + 4 \geq -7$

$x \leq 3$ ⟵ Solve each inequality. ⟶ $x \geq -11$

The solutions $-11 \leq x \leq 3$ are all numbers that are greater than or equal to -11 *and* less than or equal to 3.

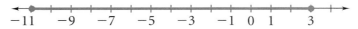

b. $|2x - 1| + 2 > 5$

$|2x - 1| > 3$ ⟵ Subtract 2 from each side.

$2x - 1 > 3$ ⟵ Write two inequalities. ⟶ $2x - 1 < -3$

$2x > 4$ $2x < -2$

$x > 2$ ⟵ Solve each inequality. ⟶ $x < -1$

The solutions $x > 2$ or $x < -1$ are all numbers greater than 2 *or* less than -1.

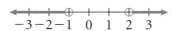

9. Try This Solve each inequality. Graph the solutions on a number line.

    a. $|x + 7| < 5$ **b.** $2|x + 8| \leq 4$ **c.** $|x - 6| - 7 \geq 5$

Exercises ON YOUR OWN

Use pencil and paper to solve each equation or inequality.

  1. $2x + 10 < 34$ **2.** $13 - 5x = 48$ **3.** $t + 1.6 \leq 4.8$ **4.** $32.6 = 2.6x + 2.2$

5. $3x + 7.35 = 14.26$ **6.** $11x - 5 = 4x$ **7.** $3(m - 5) = 17$ **8.** $1.3t + 4 = 2.7t$

9. Health Insurance An insurance company reimburses a customer for 80% of her medical expenses over $500. Let x represent her total expenses. Find her expenses if she receives $360 from the company.

10. Refer to the cartoon. Write the steps used to solve each equation. Then write your own rhyming equation.

11. Open-ended Write a one-variable equation that has more than one solution.

12. Writing Explain how the principles of solving an equation can be applied to solving an inequality.

13. Physical Science For a given hot-air balloon, subtract the weight w it can carry from 1540 lb. This difference must be at least 920 lb. To determine the maximum weight the balloon can carry, write and solve the inequality.

SHAKESPEARE'S BRIEF FLING WITH MATH: EVERYTHING HAD TO RHYME

$30 = 3N$
$N = 10$
$X - 4 = 7$
$X = 11$

Use pencil and paper to solve each equation or inequality.

14. $24 - \frac{x}{3} = 6$ **15.** $\frac{4}{3}s + 4 \geq 12$ **16.** $\frac{2}{3}x > 12$ **17.** $\frac{4}{5}x - 7 = 16$

18. $7t \leq 13$ **19.** $x + 32 \leq 16$ **20.** $3x - 5 > x + 7$ **21.** $3x + 1 = 5x - 3$

Solve each equation or inequality. Graph the solutions on a number line.

22. $|1.2x + 8| = 16$ **23.** $25 < |x - 16|$ **24.** $|2x + 4| \leq 8$ **25.** $|3x - 7| > 14$

26. $|10 - 8x| \geq 6$ **27.** $|10 + 3(2x - 1)| \leq 1$ **28.** $|13x - 2(3x + 1)| \leq 8$

29. Communication Tyler has cellular phone service. He has the Flex Plan and uses his phone during peak hours. He can only afford $40 a month in cellular phone charges.
  a. Write an inequality to express the number of minutes a month (m) he can use his phone and stay under his $40 limit.
  b. Solve and graph the inequality you wrote in part (a).
  c. Suppose Tyler changes to the Security Plan. Now how many minutes a month can he use his phone and stay under his $40 limit? Under what conditions would Tyler want to change to this plan?

Flex Plan		Security Plan	
Monthly Access per Phone	Peak Rate	Monthly Access per Phone	Peak Rate
$24.95	$.39/min	$19.95	$.75/min

Write an inequality for each graph.

30.
$$\begin{array}{c} \longleftrightarrow \\ -3\,-2\,-1\ \ 0\ \ 1\ \ 2\ \ 3 \end{array}$$

31.
$$\begin{array}{c} \longleftrightarrow \\ -3\,-2\,-1\ \ 0\ \ 1\ \ 2\ \ 3 \end{array}$$

32.
$$\begin{array}{c} \longleftrightarrow \\ -3\,-2\,-1\ \ 0\ \ 1\ \ 2\ \ 3 \end{array}$$

33.
$$\begin{array}{c} \longleftrightarrow \\ -3\,-2\,-1\ \ 0\ \ 1\ \ 2\ \ 3 \end{array}$$

34. Real Estate Nadia earns $450 per week managing a real estate office plus a 1.5% commission when she sells a house.
   a. Let x represent her sales for the month. Write an expression for her total monthly income. (Use $4\frac{1}{3}$ weeks in a month.)
   b. Suppose one month Nadia sold a house for $80,000. How much did she earn that month?
   c. Next month Nadia would like to earn at least $4000. Find the total sales she must make next month to meet her goal.

35. Graphs on the number line can be described with *interval notation*.
   Examples:

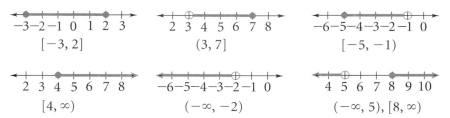

$[-3, 2]$ (3, 7] $[-5, -1)$

$[4, \infty)$ $(-\infty, -2)$ $(-\infty, 5), [8, \infty)$

Chapter Project ▼ **Find Out by Analyzing**

Suppose you manage a juice factory. One of your machines fills 850 bottles per minute. Each day it takes 30 min to get the machine started after an hour for maintenance. Graph the number of bottles filled as a function of time that the machine runs. Find the domain, range, and y-intercept of the graph. Interpret these numbers. Write an equation for your graph.

   a. Use interval notation to describe the graphs in Exercises 30–33.
   b. Solve each *compound inequality* and use interval notation to describe the solutions.
      I. $4 < 2x < 10$ **II.** $4 \le x + 2 \le 10$
      III. $5 < 2x + 5 \le 7$ **IV.** $3x > -6$ or $2 - x > 6$
   c. Solve each absolute-value inequality and use interval notation to describe the solutions.
      I. $|2x + 4| \le 4$ **II.** $|3x - 6| > 9$ **III.** $|5 - 4x| \ge 6$ **IV.** $|5 - 2x| < 3$

Exercises   M I X E D   R E V I E W

Simplify each expression, and classify it as rational or irrational.

36. $4\sqrt{10x}$ for $x = 5$ **37.** $-7\sqrt{27x}$ for $x = 3$ **38.** $-2\sqrt{12x}$ for $x = 9$ **39.** $9\sqrt{4x}$ for $x = 10$

40. Data Analysis The table shows the daily and Sunday circulations of some newspapers, in hundred thousands.
   a. Make a scatter plot of the data.
   b. Describe any correlation and draw a trend line.
   c. Find an equation to model the relationship.
   d. **Predict** the Sunday circulation of a newspaper with a daily circulation of 700,000.

Newspaper	Daily	Sunday
Chicago Tribune	6.9	11.1
The Boston Globe	5.0	8.1
The New York Times	12.3	18.1
The Washington Post	8.6	11.7
San Francisco Chronicle	5.6	7.2
The Dallas Morning News	5.3	8.3

Getting Ready for Lesson 2-5

Substitute the given value into $4x - y = -7$. Solve for the remaining variable.

41. $y = 19$ **42.** $y = -5$ **43.** $y = 17$ **44.** $x = 4$ **45.** $x = -3$ **46.** $x = 2y$

What You'll Learn

- Solving and graphing equations and inequalities having two variables
- Graphing absolute-value equations having two variables

...And Why

To make decisions about transportation options

What You'll Need

- graph paper
- three different colored pens or pencils
- graphing calculator

2-5 Two-Variable Equations and Inequalities

W O R K   T O G E T H E R

Graph the line $y = 2x + 3$ on graph paper.

1. **a.** Plot the points on your graph. Make all points above the line one color, all points below the line a second color, and all points on the line a third color.
   $(-2, -3), (-2, -1), (-1, -1), (-1, 5), (0, 4), (0, 5), (1, 6), (2, 3), (2, 7)$
   b. Classify each of the points above as *on the line, above the line,* or *below the line.*

2. Are all the points that satisfy the inequality $y > 2x + 3$ *above, below,* or *on* the line?

3. Are all the points that satisfy the equation $y = 2x + 3$ *above, below,* or *on* the line?

4. Without drawing it, describe the graph of $y \geq 5x + 1$. Relate your description to the graph of $y = 5x + 1$.

T H I N K   A N D   D I S C U S S

Graphing Linear Inequalities

The graph of a **linear inequality** is a region of the coordinate plane that is bounded by a line. To graph an inequality involving two variables, first graph the boundary line. Then decide which side of the line contains solutions and whether the boundary line is included.

$$y > \frac{1}{2}x - 1$$

To satisfy the inequality, *y*-values must be *greater* than those on the boundary line. ➤

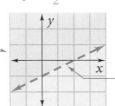

A *dashed* boundary line indicates that it is not part of the solution.

$$2x + 3y \leq 6$$

A *solid* boundary line indicates that the line is a part of the solution. ➤

Choose a test point above or below the boundary line. The test point (0, 0) satisfies the inequality. Shade the region containing (0, 0).

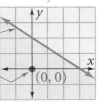

Example 1 Relating to the Real World ·············

Entertainment At least 35 performers of the Big Tent Circus are in the grand finale. Some are piled into cars, while others are balanced on bicycles. Seven performers are in a car; five performers are balanced on each bicycle. Draw a graph showing all the possible combinations of cars and bicycles that could be used in the finale.

Define $x =$ the number of cars
$y =$ the number of bicycles

	the number of performers in cars	plus	the number of performers on bicycles	is greater than or equal to	35
Relate					
Write	$7x$	$+$	$5y$	$\geq$	35

Step 1: Find two points on the boundary line. Use the points to graph the boundary line.

When $y = 0, 7x + 5(0) = 35.$ When $x = 0, 7(0) + 5y = 35.$
$7x = 35$ $5y = 35$
$x = 5$ $y = 7$

Graph the points $(5, 0)$ and $(0, 7)$. Since the inequality includes *equal*, use a solid boundary line.

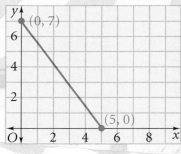

Step 2: Test the point $(0, 0)$. Since $7(0) + 5(0) < 35$, shade the region on the other side of the line from $(0, 0)$

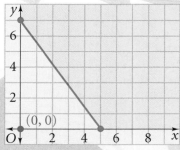

All ordered pairs with whole-number coordinates that are in the shaded area represent a combination of cars x and bicycles y that could be used in the grand finale.

5. For Example 1, determine the minimum number of bicycles that will be needed if three cars are available. Then determine three other possible combinations of bicycles and cars.

6. Give the domain and range for Example 1. **Justify** your reasoning.

7. Graph each inequality.
   a. $4x + 2y \le 4$ b. $y \ge 3x$ c. $\frac{x}{3} < -y + 2$

Graphing Two-Variable Absolute-Value Equations

The graphs of absolute-value equations involving two variables look like angles.

Example 2

Graph $y = |2x + 4| - 3$.

Method 1: Evaluate the function for several values of x. Begin with $x = -5$.

$$y = |2x + 4| - 3$$
$$= |2(-5) + 4| - 3 \quad \longleftarrow \text{Substitute.}$$
$$= |-6| - 3 \quad \longleftarrow \text{Simplify.}$$
$$= 6 - 3$$
$$= 3$$

Choose several other x-values. Record the results in a table of values. Graph the ordered pairs and connect them.

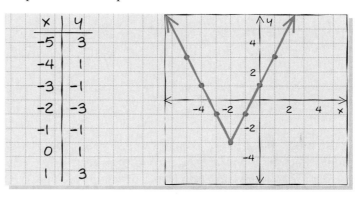

Method 2: Use a graphing calculator.

Use the absolute value key. Graph the equation $Y_1 = \text{abs}(2X + 4) - 3$.

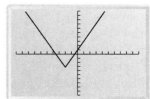

8. **Try This** Graph $y = 3 - \left|\frac{x}{2}\right|$.

Write an inequality for each graph. In each case, the equation for the boundary line is given.

1. $y = -x - 2$

2. $5x + 3y = 9$

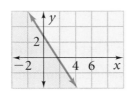

3. $x = -3$

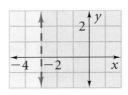

4. $2y - 3x = 4$

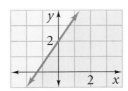

5. Cooking The time it takes to roast a chicken depends on how much the chicken weighs. Allow at least 20 min per pound for a chicken weighing up to six pounds. Allow at least 15 min per pound for a chicken weighing more than six pounds.
   a. Write two inequalities to represent the time it takes to roast a chicken.
   b. Choose one of the inequalities you wrote in part (a). Choose an appropriate domain. Graph the inequality.

6. a. Graph the equations $y = \left|\frac{1}{2}x - 6\right| + 3$ and $y = -\left|\frac{1}{2}x + 6\right| - 3$ on the same set of axes.
   b. Writing Describe the similarities and differences in the graphs.

Graph each equation or inequality on a coordinate plane.

7. $y = |4x + 2|$

8. $y = |-3x + 5|$

9. $y = |4 - 2x|$

10. $y > 2x + 1$

11. $y = \left|-\frac{1}{4}x - 1\right|$

12. $5x - 2y \geq -10$

13. $y = |3x - 6| + 1$

14. $y = \left|\frac{5}{2}x - 2\right|$

15. $y = \left|\frac{3}{2}x + 2\right|$

16. $2x - 5y < -10$

17. $\frac{3}{4}x + \frac{2}{3}y \geq \frac{5}{2}$

18. $y = -|x - 3|$

19. $3(x - 2) + 2y \leq 6$

20. $y = |2x + 6|$

21. $y = 2|x + 2| - 3$

22. $y < 3$

23. $x \leq 0$

24. $0.5x + 1.2y > 6$

25. $-3x + 4y > -6$

26. $\frac{1}{2}x + \frac{2}{3}y \geq 1$

27. Business To raise funds, the junior class plans to sell frozen yogurt cones and sundaes. Each treat contains one scoop of yogurt.
   a. Write an expression to represent the number of scoops of yogurt used in making c cones and s sundaes.
   b. You have enough yogurt for 200 scoops. Write an inequality to represent all the possible combinations of cones and sundaes.
   c. Graph the inequality. Is the point (20, 50) a solution?
   d. On your graph, find the point representing 60 cones and as many sundaes as possible. What does the s-value of this point represent?

28. Writing When you graph an inequality, you can often use the point (0, 0) to test which side of the boundary line to shade. Describe a situation in which you could *not* use (0, 0) as a test point.

29. Open-ended Write an inequality that has $(10, 15)$, $(-10, 20)$, $(-20, -25)$, and $(25, -10)$ as solutions.

30. Standardized Test Prep Which point(s) are solutions of $5x + 3y \geq 2$?

I. $(0, 0)$ **II.** $(-1, 0)$ and $\left(0, -\frac{2}{3}\right)$ **III.** $\left(0, \frac{2}{3}\right)$ and $\left(1, -\frac{2}{3}\right)$

A. I only   **B.** II only   **C.** III only   **D.** I and II   **E.** II and III

Exercises   MIXED REVIEW

Evaluate each composition. Let $f(x) = |x - 2|$ and $g(x) = 2x + 5$.

31. $f(g(2))$ **32.** $g(f(2))$ **33.** $g(f(1))$

34. $f(g(-3))$ **35.** $g(f(-4))$ **36.** $f(g(-1))$

37. A tutor earns \$8 per hour. Write a function to model the tutor's earnings after h hours. What kind of function is this?

FOR YOUR JOURNAL

Describe the similarities and differences between graphing an equation and an inequality on a coordinate plane.

Getting Ready for Lesson 2-6

Probability List all the possible outcomes of each action.

38. tossing a coin   **39.** tossing three coins

40. picking a random letter of the alphabet   **41.** rolling a number cube numbered 1–6 on its sides

---

Exercises   CHECKPOINT

Solve each equation or inequality.

1. $\frac{3}{4}x - \frac{1}{4} = 2$ **2.** $7t \leq 3t + 22$

3. $-2m = 3(m - 5)$ **4.** $2c + 5 > 7c$

Graph each equation or inequality.

5. $y = 3x + 4$ **6.** $y < -x + 6$

7. $y = |9 - 2x|$ **8.** $y \geq \frac{1}{2}x + 1$

9. Weather At least 300 tornadoes occur in the United States each year. Write an inequality to model the number of tornadoes that could occur in the next x years. Describe the domain and range of the relation.

10. Open-ended Write an absolute-value equation that has 8 as one solution.

11. Writing Explain when you would graph solutions of an equation or inequality on a number line and when you would graph solutions on a coordinate plane.

Parametric Equations

After Lesson 2-5

Sometimes you need to determine the position of an object over time. Equations expressing the horizontal distance x and the vertical distance y as functions of time t are examples of **parametric equations**.

Example

At the 1996 Olympics, Muhammed Ali transferred the Olympic flame to a cord, and the flame traveled along the cord to light the Olympic torch. The equations $x(t) = 3t$ and $y(t) = 4t + 3$ model the path such a flame might take, where t is time in seconds and x and y are distances in feet.

Graph the equations and interpret the position of the flame at time $t = 3$.

Step 1: Before entering the equations, press the MODE key and change the function mode to *parametric*.

```
Normal Sci Eng
Float 0123456789
Radian Degree
Func Par Pol Seq
Connected Dot
Sequential Simul
FullScreen Split
```

Step 2: Enter the equations. (When you press the Y= key, you will see a list of pairs of equations.)

```
X₁ₜ=3T
Y₁ₜ=4T+3
X₂ₜ=■
Y₂ₜ=
X₃ₜ=
Y₃ₜ=
X₄ₜ=
Y₄ₜ=
```

Step 3: Set the window values as shown.

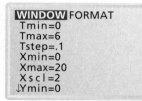

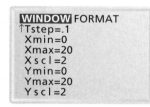

Step 4: Graph the equations. Press TRACE to find x and y values for $t = 3$.

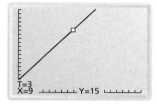

After three seconds, the flame has moved 9 ft horizontally and 15 ft vertically.

Graph each pair of parametric equations. Use the standard window with the t-values at the right. Find the values of x and y at time $t = 3$.

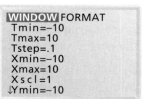

1. $x(t) = t$
$y(t) = -t + 6$

2. $x(t) = -3t$
$y(t) = t - 6$

3. $x(t) = |t - 2|$
$y(t) = t + 2$

4. Writing Write a story about the graph of $x(t) = 3t$ and $y(t) = 10t$. Interpret the x- and y-values at times $t = 0$, $t = 5$, and $t = -2$.

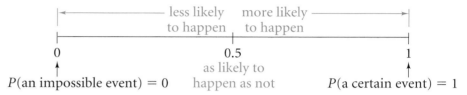

What You'll Learn
• Finding
  experimental
  probability
• Finding and using
  theoretical
  probability

...And Why
To predict the probability of
inheriting a genetic trait

What You'll Need
• index card

2-6 Exploring Probability

THINK AND DISCUSS

Experimental Probability

Probability measures how likely it is that some event, or outcome, will happen. Probability is always a number from 0 through 1.

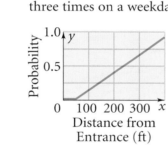

less likely   more likely
to happen   to happen

0   0.5   1
                      as likely to
$P(\text{an impossible event}) = 0$ happen as not $P(\text{a certain event}) = 1$

Refer to the graphs below. They show the probability of finding a parking space versus the distance from the parking space to the mall entrance at three times on a weekday.

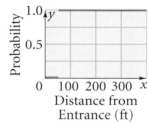 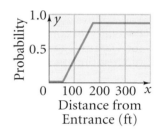

Distance from
Entrance (ft)

Distance from
Entrance (ft)

Distance from
Entrance (ft)

1. Find the domain and range of each graph.

2. a. Which graph most likely represents the probability of finding a parking space at noon? at 8 P.M.? at 3 A.M.? **Justify** your reasoning.

   b. Estimate the probability that you will find a parking space at noon if you are 200 ft from the entrance. Estimate the probability that you will find a parking space at 3 A.M. if you are 100 ft from the entrance.

   c. When are your chances of finding a parking place the greatest—noon, 8 P.M., or 3 A.M.?

2-6 Exploring Probability   **87**

When you gather data from observations, you can calculate an **experimental probability.** Each observation is an *experiment* or a *trial*.

Experimental Probability

Probability of an event $=\dfrac{\text{number of times an event happens}}{\text{number of times the experiment is done}}$

Example: Suppose a baseball player gets a base hit 21 times in 60 at bats. Then $P(\text{base hit}) = \frac{21}{60} \approx 0.35$ or 35%.

When actual trials are difficult to conduct, you can find experimental probabilities by using a **simulation,** or model.

Example 1   Relating to the Real World

Meteorology Suppose weather forecast models predict an 80% chance of rain for each of the next four days. Find the probability of four consecutive days of rain.

GRAPHING CALCULATOR HINT

You can use a graphing calculator or computer software to generate random numbers.

Step 1: Define how the simulation will be done.

- Use numbers from a random number table.

Random Number Table			
30656	17894	52324	18481
36872	86497	67619	97558
02673	97595	11772	44834
26038	76572	12236	63429

- Let 1, 2, 3, 4, 5, 6, 7, and 8 represent rain. Let 9 and 0 represent no rain. ← *80% of the numbers must represent rain.*
- Since the simulation is for four days, list the numbers in groups of four.
- Look at twenty groups.

Step 2: Conduct the simulation.

3065 <u>6178</u> 9452 <u>3241</u> <u>8481</u> <u>3687</u> <u>2864</u> 9767 6199 <u>7558</u>
0267 3975 9511 <u>7724</u> 4834 2603 <u>8765</u> <u>7212</u> <u>2366</u> 3429

Each underlined group shows four consecutive days of rain. Each of the other groups contains at least one day of no rain.

Step 3: Interpret the simulation.

Since 11 of the 20 groups represent four days of rain,
$P(\text{four consecutive days of rain}) = \frac{11}{20} = 55\%$.

3. In Example 1, could you use any two numbers from 0 to 9 to represent *no rain*? **Justify** your reasoning.

4. Use the random number table on page 92 to conduct 20 more trials for Example 1. What experimental probability do you get?

5. The probability of four consecutive days of rain is actually about 41%. Combine your results from Question 4 with the results of several classmates. How does increasing the number of trials affect the results?

Theoretical Probability

Some real-world situations have equally likely outcomes. In genetics, when a parent has both a dominant and a recessive gene, the parent is equally likely to contribute either type of gene to the child. When outcomes are equally likely, you can find probabilities without conducting trials.

Fold your hands so your fingers interlace. Do you naturally place your left thumb or right thumb on top? Placing your left thumb on top is a dominant genetic trait.

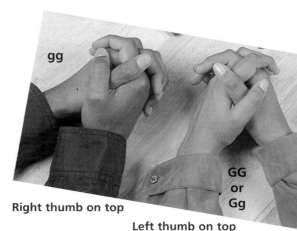

Right thumb on top

gg

GG or Gg

Left thumb on top

Let G represent the gene for the left thumb on top. Let g represent the gene for the right thumb on top. The genes are written as GG, Gg, or gg.

| Example 2 | Relating to the Real World |

Biology What is the probability that a child of parents each having the mixed gene pair Gg will naturally place his or her left thumb on top?

Make a chart.

		Gene from Mother	
		G	g
Gene from Father	G	GG	Gg
	g	Gg	gg

There are four possible outcomes. Each outcome is equally likely.

Three out of four outcomes contain the dominant gene G. The probability that the child will place his or her left thumb on top is $\frac{3}{4}$.

In Example 2 there are four possible outcomes. The set of all possible outcomes is called the **sample space.**

6. a. For Example 2, list the sample space.
   b. Find P(the child will inherit the gene pair Gg).
   c. Find P(the child will place his or her right thumb on top).

It is not always possible to run a simulation to determine the probability of an event occurring. Then you apply theoretical probability.

Theoretical Probability

A sample space has n outcomes, each of which is equally likely to happen, and an event A occurs in m of these outcomes. Then the **theoretical probability** $P(A) = \dfrac{\text{number of favorable outcomes}}{\text{number of possible outcomes}}$, or $\dfrac{m}{n}$.

Example: The probability of randomly choosing an even number from the set of numbers $\{1, 2, 4, 5, 7, 10\}$ is $\frac{3}{6}$ or $\frac{1}{2}$.

You can assume that situations such as choosing a number at random, rolling a number cube, or tossing a coin involve equally likely outcomes.

7. Suppose you roll a number cube marked with integers from 1 to 6. Find each probability.
   a. $P(5)$ **b.** P(an even number)
   c. P(a number less than 5)   **d.** $P(8)$

Sometimes you can use areas to find probability.

Example 3 ···

Suppose a dart lands somewhere on the dartboard. Find the probability of scoring at least ten points.

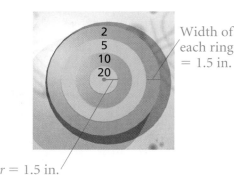

2
5
10
20

Width of each ring = 1.5 in.

r = 1.5 in.

P(scoring 10 or 20 points)

$= \dfrac{\text{area of the two inner circles}}{\text{area of the dartboard}}$

$= \dfrac{\pi(2r)^2}{\pi(4r)^2}$

$= \dfrac{\pi(2 \times 1.5)^2}{\pi(4 \times 1.5)^2}$

$= \dfrac{9}{36}$

The probability of scoring at least ten points is $\frac{9}{36}$, or $\frac{1}{4}$.

8. Try This Use the dartboard from Example 3. Find each probability.
   a. P(scoring 20 points)   **b.** P(scoring exactly 5 points)

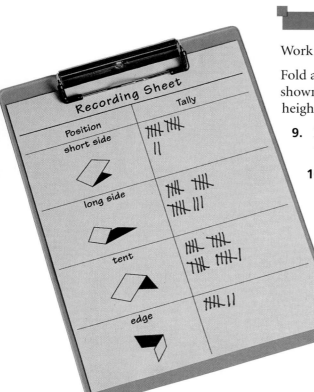

Recording Sheet

Position	Tally
short side	卌 卌 ‖
long side	卌 卌 卌 卌 ‖
tent	卌 卌 卌 卌 ‖
edge	卌 ‖

Work with a partner.

Fold an index card slightly off center, as shown. When you drop the card from a height of several feet, how will it land?

9. Drop the card 50 times. Record the number of times the card lands in each position on your recording sheet.

10. In what percent of the 50 drops does the card land on its short side? Find the percents for the other positions.

11. In what position is the card most likely to land? In what position is it least likely to land?

12. Suppose that you drop the card another 20 times. Use your answers to Question 10 to **predict** how many times it will land in each position.

13. **a.** Drop the card another 20 times. Record your results.
    b. Compare the results with your predictions from Question 12. Are they close? How could you improve your predictions?

Suppose a number is selected at random from the sample space {1, 2, 3, 4, 5, 6, 7, 8, 9}. Find each probability.

1. P(the number is a multiple of 3)   2. P(the number is less than 5)

3. P(the number is prime)   4. P(the number is even)

5. **Sports** Find the probability that a baseball thrown at random within the batter's strike zone will be "high and inside." This is one of the harder pitches to hit!

6. **Biology** Suppose a child has a father with the gene pair gg and a mother with Gg. Find the probability that the child will naturally place her left thumb on top when she interlaces her fingers.

7. The common interpretation of Murphy's Law is "If something can go wrong, it will." Assume that Murphy's Law applies, and estimate each probability as either 0 or 1.
   a. P(your dog chews up your homework after you've finished it)
   b. P(you finish your homework in study hall)

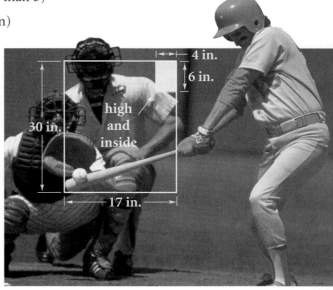

Use the sample space at the right. Find each probability.

8. *P*(the sum is 2)

9. *P*(the sum is 7)

10. *P*(the sum is 8)

11. *P*(the product is 12)

12. *P*(the cubes show equal numbers)

13. *P*(at least one cube shows a 3)

14. *P*(the sum is 14)

15. *P*(the sum is an integer)

Sample Space for Two Number Cubes					
(1, 1)	(1, 2)	(1, 3)	(1, 4)	(1, 5)	(1, 6)
(2, 1)	(2, 2)	(2, 3)	(2, 4)	(2, 5)	(2, 6)
(3, 1)	(3, 2)	(3, 3)	(3, 4)	(3, 5)	(3, 6)
(4, 1)	(4, 2)	(4, 3)	(4, 4)	(4, 5)	(4, 6)
(5, 1)	(5, 2)	(5, 3)	(5, 4)	(5, 5)	(5, 6)
(6, 1)	(6, 2)	(6, 3)	(6, 4)	(6, 5)	(6, 6)

16. Suppose you open this textbook somewhere in the middle and look at the number of the right-hand page. Find each probability.
   a. *P*(page number is even)   **b.** *P*(page number is odd)
   c. *P*(page number ends in 1)   **d.** *P*(page number begins with a 1)

Suppose a dart lands at random on each dartboard. Find the probability that the dart will land in the purple region.

17.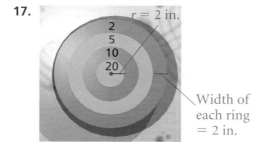

18.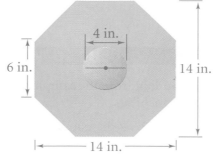

19.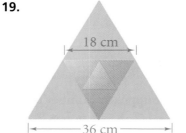

20. Use the random number table to find the experimental probability that the outcome of a coin toss is heads.
   a. Which numbers will represent which outcomes? Explain.
   b. Simulate 50 trials, and draw a conclusion based on your data.

21. Suppose the probability that a carton of eggs will contain at least one broken egg is $\frac{1}{3}$. Use a simulation of 20 trials to find the probability that the next three cartons will contain only unbroken eggs. (*Hint:* Use nine digits from the random number table to represent the condition of the carton. Discard the tenth digit.)

22. Writing Explain what you would need to know to determine the theoretical probability that a five-digit postal ZIP code ends in 1.

Random Number Table			
31504	51648	40613	79321
80927	42404	15594	84675
68591	34178	00460	31754
49676	58733	00884	85400
72294	22551	22547	86066
93114	85211	07790	20890
21339	09414	51549	13843
18407	87043	34990	16214
46849	11390	01322	82656
45950	37521	77417	84932

23. Language In a recent year, 31.8 million residents of the United States spoke a language other than English as their primary language. (This is your sample space.) Use the table to find each probability.
   a. P(a U.S. resident whose primary language is not English speaks primarily Spanish)
   b. P(a U.S. resident whose primary language is not English speaks primarily Chinese)
   c. P(a U.S. resident whose primary language is not English speaks primarily Tagalog)

24. Suppose you choose a two-digit number at random. What is the probability that its square root is an integer?

25. Open-ended Use a telephone book. Select 50 telephone numbers at random and record the first three digits (the "exchange") of each number. **Summarize** your results using probability statements.

26. a. Graphing Calculator Graph the functions $y = 5$ and $y = -2$. Use the standard window.
   b. Use areas to approximate the probability that a randomly selected point on the screen falls above the line $y = 5$; below the line $y = -2$; between the lines $y = 5$ and $y = -2$. (*Hint:* Use square units.)
   c. Geometry Graph the function $y = x$ in addition to the functions from part (a). Approximate the probability that a randomly selected point on the screen falls in the triangle formed by the y-axis, the line $y = 5$, and the line $y = x$. (*Hint:* What kind of triangle is it?)

U.S. Residents Whose Primary Language Is Not English

Language	Number (in millions)
Spanish	17.3
French	1.7
German	1.5
Italian	1.3
Chinese	1.2
Tagalog	0.8
44 Others	8.0

Exercises   MIXED REVIEW

Write a function that translates the given function in the given direction.

27. $y = x^2$; right 6, up 2

28. $y = x$; down 5

29. $y = |x|$; left 1, up 3

Simplify each expression.

30. $25 - 10^2 + 150 \div 3$

31. $1.25 \div 0.5 + 7.5 - 115$

32. $5 + \left(\frac{3}{4}\right)^2 \cdot \frac{8}{15} - 2$

33. $12 + [(-6)^2 - 4^2]^2 - 7$

34. Economics In one month, an index measuring the number of help-wanted advertisements rose from 126 to 131. Find its percent of increase.

35. Shopping You have a coupon for $10 off on a piece of clothing. When you arrive, all items are on sale for 20% off. Does it make a difference whether you get the discount or use the coupon first? Explain.

PORTFOLIO

SELF ASSESSMENT

For your portfolio, select one or two items from your work that you think best show the things you learned or did in this chapter. Explain why you have included each selection.

Finishing the Chapter Project

TIME SQUEEZE

Find Out questions on pages 63, 68, and 80 should help you complete your project. Your group should prepare an oral presentation for the class describing how you devised, analyzed, and improved your assembly line. Demonstrate how your assembly line works and explain your analysis of each task in the assembly line. Make charts and graphs showing how you collected and analyzed your data.

Reflect and Revise

Before giving your presentation to the class, meet with another group. Have the group perform the tasks in your assembly line. Explain the improvements you have made and ask for their comments and suggestions. You may want to make further improvements based on their ideas before planning your final presentation.

Follow Up

Investigate the career possibilities in the field of quality control. Find out what education and training are necessary to become a quality control engineer. If possible, interview someone in this field to find out what types of tasks are performed daily.

For More Information

Deming, W. Edwards. "Making Things Right." *Statistics: A Guide to the Unknown.* San Francisco: Holden-Day, 1981.

Moore, David S., "Statistical Process Control." *For All Practical Purposes.* New York: W. H. Freeman, 1988.

Key Terms

constant of variation (p. 64)
direct variation (p. 64)
experimental probability (p. 88)
linear equation (p. 58)
linear inequality (p. 81)
linear function (p. 61)
sample space (p. 90)
simulation (p. 88)

slope (p. 58)
slope-intercept form (p. 60)
solution (p. 75)
standard form (p. 70)
theoretical probability (p. 90)
x-intercept (p. 60)
y-intercept (p. 60)

How am I doing?

- State three ideas from this chapter that you think are important. Explain your choices.
- Describe what you can tell about the graph of a linear function from its equation.

Linear Equations and Slope
2-1

The graph of a **linear equation** forms a line. The **x-intercept** is the point where the line crosses the x-axis. The **y-intercept** is the point where it crosses the y-axis.

The **slope** of a line is the measure of the steepness of a line.

$$\text{slope} = \frac{\text{vertical change}}{\text{horizontal change}} = \frac{y_2 - y_1}{x_2 - x_1}$$

The **slope-intercept form** of a linear equation is $y = mx + b$, where m is the slope and b is the y-intercept.

The slope of a horizontal line is 0. The slope of a vertical line is undefined. Parallel lines have the same slope. The product of the slopes of a pair of perpendicular lines is -1.

You can write the equation of a line when you know the slope and a point on the line. Substitute the coordinates of the point and the slope into the slope-intercept form and solve for the y-intercept.

Find the slope and x- and y-intercepts of each line.

1. $y = 3x - 8$ **2.** $y = -x + 5$ **3.** $y = x$ **4.** $x = 4$

Write an equation of each line.

5. $m = 2$; contains $(1, 3)$ **6.** $m = -3$; contains $(4, 0)$ **7.** $m = \frac{1}{2}$; contains $(-5, 2)$

8. Open-ended Write the equation of a line that has undefined slope. Then write the equation of a line perpendicular to the first line.

9. Standardized Test Prep Which lines are parallel?

    I. $y = -2x + 1$ **II.** $y = \frac{1}{2}x - 4$ **III.** $y = -\frac{1}{2}x + 5$ **IV.** $y = 3 - 2x$

    A. I and II   **B.** I and III   **C.** II and III   **D.** II and IV   **E.** I and IV

Direct Variation

A **direct variation** is a linear equation that can be written in the form $y = kx$, where $k \neq 0$. The variable k is the **constant of variation**. The constant of variation has the same value as the slope of its line. You can use the constant of variation to write equations.

Identify the slope for each direct variation.

10. $y = 4x$

11. $y = \frac{1}{2}x$

12. $3y = 6x$

13. $y = -0.65x$

Write an equation of a direct variation that includes the given point.

14. $(3, 5)$

15. $(-1, 6)$

16. $(7, -3)$

17. $(-4, -8)$

18. Writing Describe the difference between a linear function that is a direct variation and one that is not. Include an example of each.

Interpreting Linear Functions

You can write the equation of a line when you know two points on the line. Find the slope. Then substitute the coordinates of one of the points and the slope into the slope-intercept form. Solve for the y-intercept.

The **standard form** of an equation of a line is $ax + by = c$, where a, b, and c are integers.

Write each linear equation in standard form.

19. $y = 3x + 1$

20. $2x = y - 4$

21. $x - y = \frac{3}{4}$

Write an equation of the line through the given points.

22. $(2, 3)$ and $(3, 5)$

23. $(9, -5)$ and $(6, 0)$

24. $(-1, 4)$ and $(-7, -2)$

One-Variable Equations and Inequalities

Any value for the variable that makes an equation or inequality true is a **solution**. Some equations and inequalities have no solution and some have many. Using a number line, you can graph the solution(s) of an equation or inequality that has one variable.

You can solve equations by inspection, *Guess and Test*, using algebra, or graphing.

Solve each equation or inequality.

25. $2x - 5 = 17$

26. $3x < 56$

27. $x - 7 \geq 12$

28. $3x = 4x - 5$

29. $8 - \frac{1}{2}x = 3$

30. $5x + 2 \leq 27$

31. $0.1x + 1 = 1.2x - 3$

32. $4 - x > 12$

33. A book club gives three books for the price of two after you buy six. If you pay for 14 books through the club, how many will you get in all?

A **linear inequality** describes a region of the coordinate plane that has a boundary line. To graph an inequality involving two variables, first graph the boundary line. Then decide which side of the line contains solutions. Points on a dashed boundary line are not solutions. Points on a solid boundary line are solutions.

Graph each equation or inequality.

34. $y \geq -2$ **35.** $y = 4x + 1$ **36.** $y \leq -x - 5$ **37.** $y = |2x + 1|$

38. *Open-ended* Write an inequality with a solid boundary line that only has solutions below the *x*-axis.

Exploring Probability 2-6

Probability is a ratio between 0 and 1 that measures how likely an event, or outcome, is to happen. The set of all possible outcomes is the **sample space**.

When you gather data from observations, you can calculate an **experimental probability.** When observing trials is difficult, you can find **experimental probabilities** using a **simulation**, or model.

$$P(\text{event}) = \frac{\text{number of times an event happens}}{\text{number of times the experiment is done}}$$

If a sample space has n outcomes, each of which is equally likely to happen, and an event A occurs in m of these outcomes, $P(A) = \frac{m}{n}$.

Suppose a number is selected at random from the sample space $\{-3, -2, -1, 0, 1, 2, 3, 4\}$. Find each probability.

39. P(the number is positive)   **40.** P(the number is less than 2)   **41.** P(the number is odd)

42. P(the number is greater than 3)   **43.** P(the number is even)   **44.** P(the number is negative)

45. *Telephones* Until the 1990s, all area codes had a 0 or 1 as the middle digit. What is the probability that an area code was all odd numbers?

Getting Ready for.. ▶ CHAPTER 3

What is the size of each matrix?

46. $\begin{bmatrix} 1 & 6 & -3 \\ 0 & -4 & 2 \end{bmatrix}$ **47.** $\begin{bmatrix} 21 & 23 & 19 & 17 \\ 16 & 26 & 38 & 41 \\ 31 & 27 & 27 & 23 \\ 19 & 20 & 18 & 54 \end{bmatrix}$ **48.** $\begin{bmatrix} 7 & 10 \\ -1 & 4 \\ -7 & 9 \\ 3 & 2 \end{bmatrix}$

49. *Open-ended* Write a matrix that has 1 row and 4 columns.

Find the slope and the *x*- and *y*-intercepts of each line.

1.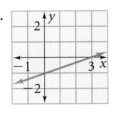

2.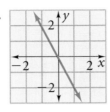

3.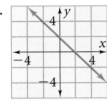

4.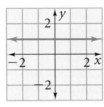

Solve each equation for *y*. Do *x* and *y* vary directly? If so, identify the constant of variation.

5. $4x = 5y$

6. $2y = 4x - 9$

7. $2x + 3y = 6$

8. $3x - 1 = 7y - 1$

9. Writing Explain how you can find the constant of variation if you know one point of a direct variation.

Write each linear equation in slope-intercept form.

10. $y = 3x + 1$

11. $4x = 2y - 8$

12. $x = -2y - 7$

13. $y - x = 10$

Use the information given to write the equation of each line.

14. contains $(-2, 0)$ and $(4, 1)$

15. $m = -1$; contains $(3, -5)$

16. $m = \frac{3}{2}$; contains $(-1, 0)$

17. contains $(-3, -5)$ and $(3, -7)$

18. Open-ended Write the equations of two lines that are parallel.

Solve each equation or inequality.

19. $x - 15 = 27$

20. $3x + 1 \leq 10$

21. $-2x = x + 33$

22. $\frac{1}{2}x - 5 > \frac{3}{2}x$

Graph each equation or inequality.

23. $y \leq 2x - 5$

24. $2y < 3x$

25. $y = 3x + 4$

26. $y = |1 - x| - 2$

27. $y > 8 - x$

28. $y \geq x + 7$

29. $y = |5x - 3| + 1$

30. $y = 5 - x$

31. Standardized Test Prep Which point(s) solve(s) the inequality $y < 2x + 3$?

   I. $(0, 2)$ **II.** $(-1, 1)$ **III.** $(2, 0)$

   A. I only   **B.** II only   **C.** I and III

   D. II and III   **E.** I, II, and III

Write a function to represent each graph.

32.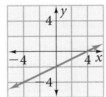

33.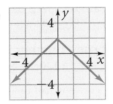

Suppose a number is selected at random from the sample space {5, 6, 7, 8, 9, 10, 11, 12, 13, 14}. Find each probability.

34. $P(\text{greater than } 10)$

35. $P(\text{less than } 7)$

36. $P(\text{integer})$

37. $P(\text{multiple of } 3)$

38. Weather A weather forecaster predicts a 60% chance of rain Saturday and Sunday. Use the random number table to simulate 20 trials to find the probability that it will *not* rain all weekend.

Random Number Table					
26038	76572	12236	63429	02673	97495
11772	44834	36872	86497	67619	97558

For Exercises 1–11, choose the correct letter.

1. What is the y-intercept of the line with equation $y = \frac{1}{2}x + 1$?

   A. 1 **B.** -2 **C.** $-\frac{1}{2}$
   D. 0 **E.** -1

2. Which equation shifts $y = x^2$ left 2 units and up 4 units?

   A. $y = (x - 2)^2 + 4$ **B.** $y = (x + 2)^2 + 4$
   C. $y = (x + 2)^2 - 4$ **D.** $y = (x - 4)^2 + 2$
   E. $y = (x + 4)^2 - 2$

3. Which equation(s) is (are) in standard form?

   I. $x - y = 7$ **II.** $y = 3x - 1$
   III. $x = 4y + 2$ **IV.** $5x + 2y = 10$
   A. I only **B.** IV only **C.** I and II
   D. II and III **E.** I and IV

4. Which is *not* a function?

   A. $f(x) = 4x - 7$ **B.** $g(x) = |5 - x|$
   C. $y = 8$ **D.** $x = -7$
   E. $h(x) = (x - 1)^2 + 4$

5. What is the equation of the line that contains the points $(1, -4)$ and $(-5, 5)$?

   A. $y = \frac{4}{9}x - \frac{32}{9}$ **B.** $y = \frac{3}{2}x - \frac{11}{2}$
   C. $y = -\frac{3}{2}x - \frac{5}{2}$ **D.** $y = \frac{1}{6}x - \frac{23}{6}$
   E. $y = -4x$

6. Which is the graph of an absolute value function?

   A.   **B.**

   C. **D.**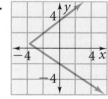

   E. none of the above

7. Which line is perpendicular to $y = 2x - 4$?

   A. $y = -2x + 5$ **B.** $y = x - 3$
   C. $y = \frac{1}{2}x + 7$ **D.** $y = -\frac{1}{2}x - 8$
   E. none of the above

8. If $f(x) = 3x + 1$ and $g(x) = 4 - x$, which has the least value?

   A. $f(g(2))$ **B.** $g(f(2))$ **C.** $f(f(2))$
   D. $g(g(-2))$ **E.** $g(g(2))$

9. Which line contains the point $(3, 4)$?

   A. $y = 3x - 4$ **B.** $y = 4x + 3$
   C. $x + y = 7$ **D.** $y = x + 7$
   E. none of the above

Compare the boxed quantity in Column A with the boxed quantity in Column B. Choose the best answer.

   A. The quantity in Column A is greater.
   B. The quantity in Column B is greater.
   C. The two quantities are equal.
   D. The relationship cannot be determined on the basis of the information supplied.

Column A	Column B
10. the x-intercept of $3x + 4y = 12$	the y-intercept of $3x + 4y = 12$
11. the slope of $y = 3x - 4$	the slope of $2y - 6x = 7$

Find each answer.

12. **Open-ended** Describe two sets of data that have a negative correlation.

13. **Critical Thinking** What point is contained in every direct variation?

14. Use the spinner at the right to find each probability.

    a. $P(A)$
    b. $P(B)$
    c. $P(C)$

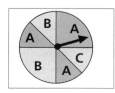

CHAPTER
3
Matrices

Relating to the Real World

People in almost every field use data on a regular basis. One way to organize data concisely is in a matrix. Because you can add, subtract, and multiply matrices, you can use them to obtain additional information and draw conclusions.

Organizing Data Into Matrices

Adding and Subtracting Matrices

Matrix Multiplication

Geometric Transformations with Matrices

Lessons   3-1   3-2   3-3   3-4

Munching Microbes

Oil spills and chemical contamination of groundwater are some of the hazards of the modern age. The field of bioremediation uses bacteria that occur naturally in the environment to decompose hazardous wastes.

As you work through the chapter, you will organize data from a bioremediation project. You will manipulate the data and use the results to draw conclusions and make predictions. Then you will research other bioremediation projects. Finally, you will summarize and display your findings.

To help you complete the project:

Networks

Identity and Inverse Matrices

3-5

3-6

What You'll Learn

- Organizing data into matrices

...And Why

To organize energy production and consumption data

QUICK REVIEW

A *matrix* is a rectangular array of numbers arranged in rows and columns. A 3 × 4 matrix has three rows and four columns.

3-1 Organizing Data into Matrices

THINK AND DISCUSS

Organizing Statistical Data

Successful businesses must track great amounts of data in order to plan the best use of their resources. They use matrices to organize and compare statistical data. Graphs are a good source of statistical data.

Example 1 **Relating to the Real World**

Energy Energy can be measured in kilowatt-hours. Write a matrix to represent the graphed data.

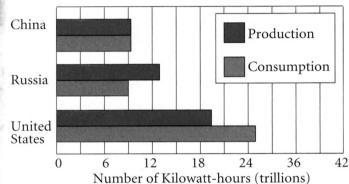

Annual Energy Production and Consumption

Source: *Energy Information Administration, International Energy Database*

Let each row represent a country and each column represent production and consumption levels. Estimate the values from the graph.

$$\begin{array}{c} \\ \text{China} \\ \text{Russia} \\ \text{United States} \end{array} \begin{array}{cc} \text{Production} & \text{Consumption} \\ \left[\begin{array}{cc} 9.5 & 9.5 \\ 13 & 9 \\ 19 & 25 \end{array} \right. & \left. \begin{array}{c} \\ \\ \end{array} \right] \end{array}$$

1. Explain how you could modify the matrix to include data from additional countries.

2. Rewrite the matrix as a 2 × 3 matrix. Label the rows and columns.

3. **Critical Thinking** Explain the difference between a $c \times d$ matrix and a $d \times c$ matrix.

You can also use matrices to present data from tables. Since you often refer to individual matrix elements, it is convenient to name the matrix.

Example 2 **Relating to the Real World**

Gymnastics Write a matrix G to represent the information from the table.

Olympic Gymnastics Trials Results, Day 2

Gymnast	Vault	Uneven Bars	Balance Beam	Floor Exercise
Amanda Borden	9.625	9.787	9.862	9.787
Amy Chow	9.800	9.825	9.275	9.712
Dominique Dawes	9.850	9.950	9.825	9.612
Jaycie Phelps	9.737	9.825	9.287	9.712
Kerri Strug	9.950	9.700	9.825	9.925

Source: *USA Today*

When? The ancient Greeks and Romans practiced an early form of gymnastics during the days of the ancient Olympic Games (776 B.C. to A.D. 393). Gymnastics as we know it today was first taught in Germany in 1776.

Source: *Guinness Book of Records*

You can use a matrix that has 5 rows and 4 columns (a 5 × 4 matrix).

$$G = \begin{bmatrix} 9.625 & 9.787 & 9.862 & 9.787 \\ 9.800 & 9.825 & 9.275 & 9.712 \\ 9.850 & 9.950 & 9.825 & 9.612 \\ 9.737 & 9.825 & 9.287 & 9.712 \\ 9.950 & 9.700 & 9.825 & 9.925 \end{bmatrix}$$

Each column represents a different event.

Each row represents a different gymnast.

You identify a matrix element by its position. Write the row number first and then the column number.

$$A = \begin{bmatrix} a_{11} & a_{12} & a_{13} \\ a_{21} & a_{22} & a_{23} \\ a_{31} & a_{32} & a_{33} \end{bmatrix}$$

The element in the first row and the third column is a_{13}.

4. Find g_{32} from matrix G in Example 2. What does this element represent?

Evaluating Equal Matrices

Two matrices are **equal matrices** if and only if they have the same dimensions and their corresponding elements are equal.

$$A = \begin{bmatrix} -0.75 & \frac{1}{5} \\ \frac{1}{2} & -2 \end{bmatrix}$$

Both *A* and *B* have two rows and two columns. Their corresponding elements are equal.

$$B = \begin{bmatrix} -\frac{3}{4} & 0.2 \\ 0.5 & -2 \end{bmatrix}$$

5. Are matrices *S* and *T* below equal? **Justify** your response.

$$S = \begin{bmatrix} 3 & 4 \\ 0 & -2 \end{bmatrix} \qquad T = \begin{bmatrix} -1 & 9 \\ 0 & 2 \end{bmatrix}$$

You can use the definition of equal matrices to solve equations.

Example 3

Solve the equation $\begin{bmatrix} 2x - 5 & 4 \\ 3 & 3y + 12 \end{bmatrix} = \begin{bmatrix} 25 & 4 \\ 3 & y + 18 \end{bmatrix}$ for *x* and *y*.

$$\begin{bmatrix} 2x - 5 & 4 \\ 3 & 3y + 12 \end{bmatrix} = \begin{bmatrix} 25 & 4 \\ 3 & y + 18 \end{bmatrix}$$

$2x - 5 = 25$	$3y + 12 = y + 18$
$2x = 30$	$2y = 6$
$x = 15$	$y = 3$

Since the two matrices are equal, their corresponding elements are equal.

The solutions are $x = 15$ and $y = 3$.

6. Try This Solve $\begin{bmatrix} x + 8 & -5 \\ 3 & -y \end{bmatrix} = \begin{bmatrix} 38 & -5 \\ 3 & 4y - 10 \end{bmatrix}$ for *x* and *y*.

7. Critical Thinking Solve $\begin{bmatrix} 3x & x + y & x - y \end{bmatrix} = \begin{bmatrix} -9 & 4 & -10 \end{bmatrix}$ for *x* and *y*.

Exercises   ON YOUR OWN

State the dimensions of each matrix.

1. $\begin{bmatrix} 4 & -2 & 2 \\ 1 & 4 & 1 \\ 0 & 5 & -7 \end{bmatrix}$
2. $\begin{bmatrix} 1 \\ -9 \\ 5 \end{bmatrix}$
3. $\begin{bmatrix} 2 & \sqrt{5} \end{bmatrix}$
4. $\begin{bmatrix} 3 & 2 & 1 \\ 2 & 0 & -3 \end{bmatrix}$

Decide if each pair of matrices is *equal* or *not*. Justify your response.

5. $\begin{bmatrix} 4 \\ -6 \\ 8 \end{bmatrix}, \begin{bmatrix} \sqrt{16} & -6 & 64 \end{bmatrix}$
6. $\begin{bmatrix} -2 & 3 \\ 5 & 0 \end{bmatrix}, \begin{bmatrix} 2(-1) & 2(1.5) \\ 2(2.5) & 2(0) \end{bmatrix}$
7. $\begin{bmatrix} 2 & 3 \\ 4 & -2 \\ -3 & -4 \end{bmatrix}, \begin{bmatrix} 2 & 3 & 4 \\ -2 & -3 & -4 \end{bmatrix}$

State the dimensions of each matrix. Identify the indicated element.

8. $\begin{bmatrix} 4 & 6 & 5 \\ 2 & -3 & -7 \\ 1 & 0 & 9 \end{bmatrix}$; a_{23}

9. $\begin{bmatrix} -4 & 1 & -3 \\ 2 & 1 & 0 \end{bmatrix}$; a_{12}

10. $\begin{bmatrix} 1 & 1 & 1 \\ 1 & 0 & 0 \\ 1 & 0 & 0 \\ 0 & 0 & 1 \end{bmatrix}$; a_{32}

Use the table below for Exercises 11–13.

U.S. Households with Televisions (in millions)

Type	1980	1982	1984	1987	1990	1993
Color	82	85	88	93	96	98
Black & White	51	47	43	36	31	20

Source: *Nielsen Media Research*

11. Display the data in a matrix with rows indicating type of television and columns indicating years. Identify a_{23} and tell what it represents.

12. Display the data in a matrix with rows indicating years and columns indicating type of television. Identify a_{41} and tell what it represents.

13. State the dimensions of the matrices in Exercises 11 and 12.

14. **Geography** The chart at the right indicates road mileage between some cities.
 a. Complete the chart. How is it possible for you to do this?
 b. Create a mileage matrix for the data.

City	Amarillo	Dallas	El Paso	Houston	Laredo
Amarillo	—	367	412	604	676
Dallas	▪	—	610	237	427
El Paso	▪	▪	—	746	608
Houston	▪	▪	▪	—	355
Laredo	▪	▪	▪	▪	—

Source: *AAA Road Atlas*

15. **Open-ended** Find some data you could display in a matrix. Write a matrix for the data. Label the rows and columns.

16. **Standardized Test Prep** Which of the following pairs of expressions satisfies $\begin{bmatrix} 2x & x - y \end{bmatrix} = \begin{bmatrix} a & b \end{bmatrix}$?
 A. $x = 2a$
   $y = 0.5a - b$
 B. $x = 0.5a$
   $y = 0.5a + b$
 C. $x = 0.5a$
   $y = 0.5a - b$
 D. $x = 2a$
   $y = 0.5a + b$

Solve each equation for each variable.

17. $\begin{bmatrix} 2x - 5 & 3 \\ 5 & 2t + 10 \end{bmatrix} = \begin{bmatrix} 12 & 3 \\ 5 & 4t + 19 \end{bmatrix}$

18. $\begin{bmatrix} x^2 & 4 \\ -2 & y^2 \end{bmatrix} = \begin{bmatrix} 9 & 4 \\ -2 & 5y \end{bmatrix}$

19. $\begin{bmatrix} 2 & 4 \\ 8 & -12 \end{bmatrix} = \begin{bmatrix} 4x - 6 & -10t + 5x \\ 4x & -15t - 1.5x \end{bmatrix}$

20. $\begin{bmatrix} 2x + 4 & y - 5 \\ z + 6 & 2t - 5 \end{bmatrix} = \begin{bmatrix} 4 & 2y - 2 \\ 4 & 4t + 15 \end{bmatrix}$

21. $\begin{bmatrix} 4b + 2 & -3 & 4d \\ -4a & 2 & 3 \\ 2f - 1 & -14 & 1 \end{bmatrix} = \begin{bmatrix} 11 & 2c - 1 & 0 \\ -8 & 2 & 3 \\ 0 & 3e - 2 & 1 \end{bmatrix}$

22. $\begin{bmatrix} 4c & 2 - d & 5 \\ -3 & -1 & 2 \\ 0 & -10 & 15 \end{bmatrix} = \begin{bmatrix} 2c + 5 & 4d & g \\ -3 & h & f - g \\ 0 & -4c & 15 \end{bmatrix}$

23. Music The graph shows sales figures for August at a music store.

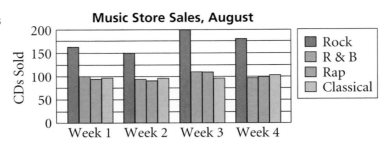

Music Store Sales, August

a. **Estimation** Record the data in a table.

b. Show the data in a matrix. What do the columns represent? the rows?

24. Transportation Costs A computer accessory company makes computer carrying cases at four plants, in Atlanta, Boston, Chicago, and Denver. Represent the data in a matrix. Label the rows and columns.

Transportation Costs

Atlanta to Boston $19
Atlanta to Chicago $12
Atlanta to Denver $23
Boston to Atlanta $19
Boston to Chicago $10
Boston to Denver $21
Chicago to Atlanta $12
Chicago to Boston $10
Chicago to Denver $15
Denver to Atlanta $23
Denver to Boston $21
Denver to Chicago $15

25. Writing Describe the information you must provide to make a matrix containing numerical data meaningful.

Chapter Project

Find Out by Organizing

The table shows data from an above-ground biotreatment project. Scientists analyzed five samples from the same soil for the presence of hazardous components of petroleum products. They found benzene (B), toluene (T), ethylbenzene (E), and xylenes (X). Present the data in four matrices. Choose an element from each matrix and tell what it represents.

Component Levels in Soil (mg/kg)

Sample	B	T	E	X
1	0.06	0.95	0.9	18.5
2	0.06	1.05	0.73	13.5
3	0.35	6	5.6	49
4	0.22	0.19	2	19.5
5	0.11	0.82	2.5	26

Exercises   MIXED REVIEW

Find the constant of variation for a direct variation that includes the given point.

26. $(2, 4)$ **27.** $(-1, 7)$ **28.** $(-4, -10)$ **29.** $(3, 5)$ **30.** $\left(\frac{1}{2}, 9\right)$ **31.** $(6, -2)$

32. Probability In the United States, 326,083 babies are born each month. Of these, 52,891 are the third born. What is the probability that a baby is the third child in a family?

Getting Ready for Lesson 3-2

Simplify the elements of each matrix.

33. $\begin{bmatrix} 3+1 & 4+9 \\ -2+0 & 5+7 \end{bmatrix}$

34. $\begin{bmatrix} 8-4 & -5-1 \\ 9-1 & 6-9 \end{bmatrix}$

FOR YOUR JOURNAL

SELF ASSESSMENT

List some advantages of using a matrix to organize data instead of a table or spreadsheet.

Entering and Transposing Matrices

Before Lesson 3-2

You can use a graphing calculator to work with matrices. First, you need to know how to enter a matrix into the calculator.

Example 1

Enter matrix A into your graphing calculator. Press MATRX ▶ ▶ ENTER 3 ENTER 2 ENTER. Enter the elements one row at a time, pressing ENTER after each element. Then press 2nd QUIT to return to the main screen.

$$A = \begin{bmatrix} -3 & 4 \\ 7 & -5 \\ 0 & -2 \end{bmatrix}$$

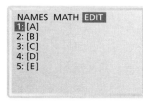
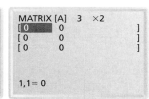
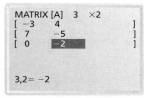

You may want to change a matrix so that its rows and columns are reversed. Call this new matrix A^T (read "A transpose").

Example 2

Transpose matrix A. Press MATRX 1 to choose the matrix. Then press MATRX ▶ 2 for the transpose command. Press ENTER to view A^T.

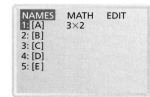
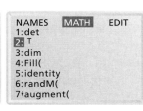
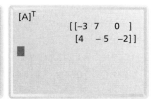

Use your graphing calculator to enter each matrix. Transpose the matrix, and write the new matrix.

1. $\begin{bmatrix} 0 & -3 \\ 5 & -7 \end{bmatrix}$
   2. $\begin{bmatrix} 3 & 5 & -7 \\ 0 & -2 & 0 \end{bmatrix}$
   3. $\begin{bmatrix} 3 \\ 5 \end{bmatrix}$
   4. $\begin{bmatrix} 4 & 6 & 5 & 2 \\ -2 & 9 & 0 & -4 \end{bmatrix}$

5. $\begin{bmatrix} 3 & 5 & -8 \end{bmatrix}$
   6. $\begin{bmatrix} 17 & 8 \\ 0 & 3 \\ -5 & 2 \end{bmatrix}$
   7. $\begin{bmatrix} 8 \\ 4 \\ -3 \end{bmatrix}$
   8. $\begin{bmatrix} -9 & 6 & 4 & -3 \end{bmatrix}$

9. Writing Compare the dimensions of the matrices in Exercises 1–8 to those of the corresponding transposed matrices.

3-2 **A**dding and Subtracting Matrices

What You'll Learn
- Adding and subtracting matrices
- Solving matrix equations

...And Why
To compile a new data set from existing data sets

What You'll Need
- graphing calculator

WORK TOGETHER

Statistics Work with a partner. Use the information in the table.

Mean SAT Scores

Year	Verbal		Math	
	Male	Female	Male	Female
1992	428	419	499	456
1993	428	420	502	457
1994	425	421	501	460
1995	429	426	503	463

Source: *College Entrance Examination Board*

1. **a.** Find the combined mean SAT score for males for each year in the table.
   b. Find the combined mean SAT score for females for each year in the table.

2. **a.** Write a matrix to represent the mean Verbal SAT scores for males and females. Label the matrix and its rows and columns.
   b. State the dimensions of the matrix.

3. **a.** Write a matrix to represent the mean Math SAT scores for males and females. Label the matrix and its rows and columns.
   b. State the dimensions of the matrix.

4. Consider your answers to Question 1 and the matrices you wrote in Questions 2 and 3. Write a third matrix to represent the combined mean SAT scores for males and females. Label the matrix and its rows and columns. State the dimensions of the matrix.

5. Use your observations and any patterns you see to formulate a method for adding matrices.

THINK AND DISCUSS

Adding and Subtracting Matrices

QUICK REVIEW

Corresponding elements are in the same position in each matrix.

Sometimes you want to add or subtract matrices to get new information. You perform **matrix addition** by adding corresponding elements. You subtract matrices by subtracting corresponding elements.

Example 1 **Relating to the Real World**

Sports The modern pentathlon is a grueling one-day competition. The athletes from each country compete in each of five events: target shooting, fencing, swimming, horseback riding, and cross-country running. Find the total score for the U.S. team for each event.

World Championship Trials Results – U.S. Team

Event	Scott Christie	Mike Gostigian	James Gregory
Shoot	1156	1036	1024
Fence	816	816	678
Swim	1188	1280	1296
Ride	889	826	1070
Run	1168	1210	1270

Source: *U.S. Modern Pentathlon Association*

Write three 5 × 1 matrices. Then add the matrices.

$$
\begin{array}{l}
\text{Shoot} \\
\text{Fence} \\
\text{Swim} \\
\text{Ride} \\
\text{Run}
\end{array}
\quad
M = \begin{bmatrix} 1156 \\ 816 \\ 1188 \\ 889 \\ 1168 \end{bmatrix}
\quad
S = \begin{bmatrix} 1036 \\ 816 \\ 1280 \\ 826 \\ 1210 \end{bmatrix}
\quad
J = \begin{bmatrix} 1024 \\ 678 \\ 1296 \\ 1070 \\ 1270 \end{bmatrix}
$$

$$
M + S + J = \begin{bmatrix} 1156 \\ 816 \\ 1188 \\ 889 \\ 1168 \end{bmatrix} + \begin{bmatrix} 1036 \\ 816 \\ 1280 \\ 826 \\ 1210 \end{bmatrix} + \begin{bmatrix} 1024 \\ 678 \\ 1296 \\ 1070 \\ 1270 \end{bmatrix}
$$

$$
= \begin{bmatrix} 1156 + 1036 + 1024 \\ 816 + 816 + 678 \\ 1188 + 1280 + 1296 \\ 889 + 826 + 1070 \\ 1168 + 1210 + 1270 \end{bmatrix}
$$

$$
= \begin{bmatrix} 3216 \\ 2310 \\ 3764 \\ 2785 \\ 3648 \end{bmatrix}
$$

The United States scored a total of 3216 points in target shooting, 2310 points in fencing, 3764 points in swimming, 2785 points in horseback riding, and 3648 points in cross-country running.

6. Try This Add $\begin{bmatrix} 1 & -2 & 0 \\ 3 & -5 & 7 \end{bmatrix}$ and $\begin{bmatrix} 3 & 9 & -3 \\ -9 & 6 & 12 \end{bmatrix}$.

7. Explain why you can add matrices only if they have the same dimensions.

8. **a.** Use matrix addition to **verify** that the equation is true.

$$\begin{bmatrix} 2 & -3 \\ 10 & 11 \\ -4 & 6 \end{bmatrix} + \begin{bmatrix} 3 & -7 \\ 6 & 2 \\ 5 & 0 \end{bmatrix} = \begin{bmatrix} 3 & -7 \\ 6 & 2 \\ 5 & 0 \end{bmatrix} + \begin{bmatrix} 2 & -3 \\ 10 & 11 \\ -4 & 6 \end{bmatrix}$$

   b. Is matrix addition commutative? Explain your response, and give an example.

9. Find $\begin{bmatrix} 6 & -9 & 7 \\ -2 & 1 & 8 \end{bmatrix} - \begin{bmatrix} -4 & 3 & 0 \\ 6 & 5 & 10 \end{bmatrix}$.

You can use your graphing calculator to add or subtract matrices.

Example 2

Graphing Calculator Use matrices A, B, and C. Find each sum or difference.

$$A = \begin{bmatrix} 0 & -4 & 0.5 \\ 2 & -1 & 0 \end{bmatrix} \quad B = \begin{bmatrix} 1.5 & 0 & -3 \\ -2 & 0 & 0 \end{bmatrix} \quad C = \begin{bmatrix} 1.5 & -4 & -2.5 \\ 0 & -1 & 0 \end{bmatrix}$$

a. $B - C$ **b.** $A + (B - C)$

a.
```
[B]–[C]
        [ [0   4  –.5]
          [–2  1  0 ] ]
```

b.
```
[A]+( [B]–[C] )
           [ [0 0 0]
             [0 0 0] ]
```

---

10. Try This Use your graphing calculator to find each sum or difference.

   a. $\begin{bmatrix} -12 & 24 \\ -3 & 5 \\ -1 & 10 \end{bmatrix} - \begin{bmatrix} -3 & 1 \\ 2 & -4 \\ -1 & 5 \end{bmatrix}$ **b.** $\begin{bmatrix} -12 & 24 \\ -3 & 5 \\ -1 & 10 \end{bmatrix} + \begin{bmatrix} -3 & 1 \\ 2 & -4 \\ -1 & 5 \end{bmatrix}$

11. How is subtracting matrices similar to adding matrices? Explain.

12. Is matrix subtraction commutative? **Justify** your reasoning.

Solving Matrix Equations

A **matrix equation** is an equation in which the variable is a matrix. You can use the addition and subtraction properties of equality to solve matrix equations. For any matrices A, B, and C, if $A = B$, then $A + C = B + C$ and $A - C = B - C$.

Example 3

Solve $X - \begin{bmatrix} 1 & 1 \\ 3 & 2 \end{bmatrix} = \begin{bmatrix} 0 & 1 \\ 8 & 9 \end{bmatrix}$ for the matrix X.

$$X - \begin{bmatrix} 1 & 1 \\ 3 & 2 \end{bmatrix} = \begin{bmatrix} 0 & 1 \\ 8 & 9 \end{bmatrix}$$

$$X = \begin{bmatrix} 0 & 1 \\ 8 & 9 \end{bmatrix} + \begin{bmatrix} 1 & 1 \\ 3 & 2 \end{bmatrix} \quad \longleftarrow \text{Add } \begin{bmatrix} 1 & 1 \\ 3 & 2 \end{bmatrix} \text{ to each side of the equation.}$$

$$X = \begin{bmatrix} 1 & 2 \\ 11 & 11 \end{bmatrix}$$

13. Try This Solve $X + \begin{bmatrix} -1 & 0 \\ 2 & 5 \end{bmatrix} = \begin{bmatrix} 10 & 7 \\ -4 & 4 \end{bmatrix}$.

Exercises ON YOUR OWN

Mental Math Find each sum or difference.

1. $\begin{bmatrix} 2 & -3 & 4 \\ 5 & 6 & -7 \end{bmatrix} + \begin{bmatrix} 0 & 0 & 0 \\ 0 & 0 & 0 \end{bmatrix}$

2. $\begin{bmatrix} 5 & 4 & 3 \\ 1 & -2 & 6 \end{bmatrix} - \begin{bmatrix} 1 & 1 & 1 \\ 1 & 1 & 1 \end{bmatrix}$

3. $\begin{bmatrix} 2 & 1 & 2 \\ 1 & 2 & 1 \end{bmatrix} - \begin{bmatrix} 2 & 3 & 2 \\ 3 & 2 & 3 \end{bmatrix}$

4. $\begin{bmatrix} 6 & -3 \\ -7 & 2 \end{bmatrix} + \begin{bmatrix} -6 & 3 \\ 7 & -2 \end{bmatrix}$

5. $\begin{bmatrix} 1 & 3 \\ 4 & 0 \end{bmatrix} + \begin{bmatrix} 0 & 5 \\ -1 & 2 \end{bmatrix} + \begin{bmatrix} 0 & -5 \\ 1 & -2 \end{bmatrix}$

6. $\begin{bmatrix} 0.5 & 9.5 \\ -3.5 & 5.5 \end{bmatrix} - \begin{bmatrix} 0.5 & 9.5 \\ -3.5 & 5.5 \end{bmatrix}$

7. Manufacturing The table shows the number of beach balls produced at two plants and production levels for one shift. Plant 1 has two shifts per day; Plant 2 has three.
a. Write matrices to represent one day's total output at each plant.
b. Use the results from part (a). Find the difference between production totals at the plants. Which produces more 3-color plastic balls? more 1-color rubber balls?

Beach Ball Production per Shift

	Plant 1		Plant 2	
	Plastic	Rubber	Plastic	Rubber
1-Color	500	700	400	1200
3-Color	1300	1900	600	1600

Use mental math or paper and pencil to find each sum or difference.

8. $\begin{bmatrix} 1 & 2 \\ -3 & 1 \end{bmatrix} + \begin{bmatrix} -1 & 5 \\ 2 & 0 \end{bmatrix}$

9. $\begin{bmatrix} -4 & 2 \\ 9 & -5 \end{bmatrix} - \begin{bmatrix} 2 & 8 \\ 4 & 1 \end{bmatrix}$

10. $\begin{bmatrix} 3 & 6 & 4 \\ -1 & 1 & 0 \end{bmatrix} + \begin{bmatrix} 2 & 3 & -5 \\ 1 & 2 & -1 \end{bmatrix}$

11. $\begin{bmatrix} 3 & 2 & -5 \\ 6 & 1 & 0 \end{bmatrix} + \begin{bmatrix} 0 & -2 & 6 \\ -5 & 5 & -6 \end{bmatrix}$

12. $\begin{bmatrix} 6 & -9 & 0 \\ -8 & 5 & 7 \end{bmatrix} - \begin{bmatrix} -2 & -4 & 1 \\ 3 & 11 & 10 \end{bmatrix}$

13. $\begin{bmatrix} 9 & -7 & 8 \\ 6 & -3 & -4 \end{bmatrix} - \begin{bmatrix} 10 & -5 & 2 \\ 4 & 1 & -9 \end{bmatrix}$

14. The table indicates whether each store sells (1) or does not sell (0) various sizes of bags of dog or cat food.

Size	Store A		Store B		Store C	
	Cat Food	Dog Food	Cat Food	Dog Food	Cat Food	Dog Food
5 lb	0	0	0	0	1	1
10 lb	1	1	0	0	1	1
25 lb	1	1	0	0	0	0
50 lb	1	0	1	1	0	0

a. Write three 4 × 2 matrices to represent the availability of each product at each store.

b. Write one 4 × 2 matrix to represent the total availability of each product.

15. **Open-ended** Describe a situation that would require adding or subtracting information stored in matrices.

Choose Use mental math, paper and pencil, or a graphing calculator to find each sum or difference.

16. $\begin{bmatrix} -2 & 0 & 0 \\ 1 & -4 & 5 \\ 7 & 0 & -10 \end{bmatrix} - \begin{bmatrix} 1 & 2 & 0 \\ 3 & -4 & 5 \\ 7 & 0 & -2 \end{bmatrix}$

17. $\begin{bmatrix} -9 & 1 & 6 \\ -5 & 0 & -9 \\ 2 & -2 & 3 \end{bmatrix} + \begin{bmatrix} 8 & 0 & 4 \\ 5 & -6 & 7 \\ -2 & 2 & -1 \end{bmatrix}$

18. $\begin{bmatrix} 1 & 3 \\ 2 & 4 \\ 6 & 7 \end{bmatrix} + \begin{bmatrix} 0 & 2 \\ -3 & 6 \\ -5 & 7 \end{bmatrix} - \begin{bmatrix} 7 & 5 \\ 3 & -2 \\ 3 & 4 \end{bmatrix}$

19. $\begin{bmatrix} 1 & 0 \\ 0 & 0 \\ 0 & 1 \end{bmatrix} - \begin{bmatrix} 0 & 1 \\ 0 & 1 \\ 1 & 0 \end{bmatrix} - \begin{bmatrix} 1 & 1 \\ 0 & 0 \\ 1 & 1 \end{bmatrix}$

Graphing Calculator Use matrices A, B, C, and D. Find each sum or difference if possible. If not possible, give a reason.

$A = \begin{bmatrix} 1 & \frac{1}{2} & 4 & 5 \\ 2 & \frac{3}{5} & 8 & 9 \end{bmatrix}$ $B = \begin{bmatrix} 1 & -2 \\ 0.33 & 4 \\ -7 & 0.15 \end{bmatrix}$ $C = \begin{bmatrix} 3 & 44 \\ 1 & 0 \\ 14 & 23.3 \end{bmatrix}$ $D = \begin{bmatrix} -2 & -4 & \frac{7}{8} & \frac{11}{2} \\ 3 & 2 & -1 & -\frac{10}{11} \end{bmatrix}$

20. $A + D$ **21.** $D - A$ **22.** $C + B$ **23.** $B - C$ **24.** $D + A$

25. $A + B$ **26.** $A - D$ **27.** $B + C$ **28.** $A + B + C$ **29.** $A + (C - D)$

30. **Data Analysis** Use the information in the printout.
   a. Put the data into two matrices. Label each matrix.
   b. Use matrix addition to find the number of people who participated in each activity.
   c. Use matrix subtraction to find the difference between the numbers of males and females participating in each activity.
   d. **Research** **Analyze** one activity. Explain the differences in participation and give examples.

U.S. Participation in Selected Leisure Activities (in millions)	
Movies:	Male, 53.4; Female, 57.1
Exercise Program:	Male, 54.3; Female, 57.1
Sports Events:	Male, 39.2; Female, 29
Gardening:	Male, 40.9; Female, 60

Source: *U.S. National Endowment for the Arts*

Solve each matrix equation for X.

31. $\begin{bmatrix} 1 & 2 & -3 \\ 2 & 1 & 3 \end{bmatrix} + X = \begin{bmatrix} 5 & 1 & 8 \\ -6 & 0 & 5 \end{bmatrix}$

32. $\begin{bmatrix} 1 & 2 \\ 2 & 1 \\ -3 & 4 \end{bmatrix} + X = \begin{bmatrix} 5 & -6 \\ 1 & 0 \\ 8 & 5 \end{bmatrix}$

33. $X - \begin{bmatrix} 4 & 12 \\ 75 & -1 \end{bmatrix} = \begin{bmatrix} 5 & 50 \\ 50 & -10 \end{bmatrix}$

34. $\begin{bmatrix} 2 & 1 & -1 \\ 0 & 2 & 1 \end{bmatrix} - X = \begin{bmatrix} 11 & 3 & -13 \\ 15 & -9 & 8 \end{bmatrix}$

35. $X - \begin{bmatrix} 1 & 7 \\ 3 & -2 \\ 0 & 1 \end{bmatrix} = \begin{bmatrix} 1 & 7 \\ 3 & -2 \\ 0 & 1 \end{bmatrix}$

36. $-X + \begin{bmatrix} 3 & 2 & 1 \\ 0 & 5 & 9 \\ 12 & 8 & -3 \end{bmatrix} = \begin{bmatrix} -5 & 0 & 0 \\ 2 & 0 & 2 \\ 0 & 5 & -3 \end{bmatrix}$

37. $X + \begin{bmatrix} 12 & 5 \\ 17 & 28 \\ -3 & 2 \end{bmatrix} = \begin{bmatrix} 14 & 20 \\ -5 & 0 \\ 3 & -19 \end{bmatrix}$

38. $\begin{bmatrix} 0 & 0 & 0 \\ 2 & 4 & -24 \end{bmatrix} = X - \begin{bmatrix} 13 & 24 & 5 \\ -6 & -17 & 1 \end{bmatrix}$

39. Writing Suppose A and B are two matrices with the same dimensions.
   a. Explain how to find $A + B$ and $A - B$.
   b. Explain how to find a matrix A' such that $A + A'$ gives you a matrix with all elements equal to 0.

Chapter Project

Find Out by Calculating

Use the matrices you wrote for the Find Out question on page 106. Find the combined amount of benzene, toluene, ethylbenzene, and xylenes in mg/kg for each soil sample.

After 12 months of bioremediation, the levels of each component dropped to < 0.05 mg/kg for each soil sample. Use matrices to calculate by how much the level of each component for each sample dropped (minimum amount).

Exercises   M I X E D   R E V I E W

Find the slope and y-intercept of each function.

40. $y = 2x - 6$ **41.** $3y = 6 + 2x$ **42.** $-x - 2y = 12$ **43.** $y = 5x$

44. Probability Make a tree diagram to show the kinds of T-shirts a store sells. T-shirts are available in five colors: black, navy blue, white, hot pink, and teal. They are available in medium, large, and extra-large sizes.

Getting Ready for Lesson 3-3

Find each sum.

45. $\begin{bmatrix} 3 & 5 \\ 2 & 8 \end{bmatrix} + \begin{bmatrix} 3 & 5 \\ 2 & 8 \end{bmatrix} + \begin{bmatrix} 3 & 5 \\ 2 & 8 \end{bmatrix}$

46. $\begin{bmatrix} -4 \\ 7 \end{bmatrix} + \begin{bmatrix} -4 \\ 7 \end{bmatrix} + \begin{bmatrix} -4 \\ 7 \end{bmatrix} + \begin{bmatrix} -4 \\ 7 \end{bmatrix} + \begin{bmatrix} -4 \\ 7 \end{bmatrix}$

What You'll Learn

- Multiplying matrices

...And Why

To solve problems involving food and transportation

What You'll Need

- graphing calculator

3-3 Matrix Multiplication

Work with a partner. Use the data in the table.

	Lunch 1	Lunch 2	Lunch 3
Cost per Lunch	$2.50	$1.75	$2.00
Number Sold	50	100	75

1. How much money did the cafeteria make selling Lunch 1? Lunch 2? Lunch 3?

2. **a.** How much did the cafeteria make selling all three lunches?
   b. Explain how you used the data in the table to find your answer.

3. **a.** Write a 1×3 matrix to represent the cost of the lunches.
   b. Write a 3×1 matrix to represent the number of lunches sold.
   c. Writing Use the words *row*, *column*, and *element*. Describe a procedure for using your matrices to find how much money the cafeteria received from selling all three lunches.

THINK AND DISCUSS

Multiplying by a Scalar

You can multiply a matrix by a number called a **scalar.** To perform scalar multiplication, multiply every element in the matrix by the scalar.

Example 1 **Relating to the Real World**

Food Use the price list at the left. The school cafeteria plans to raise the cost of each beverage to one and a half times the current cost. How much will each beverage cost?

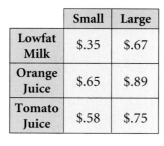

	Small	Large
Lowfat Milk	$.35	$.67
Orange Juice	$.65	$.89
Tomato Juice	$.58	$.75

— Multiply each element by 1.5.

$$1.5 \begin{bmatrix} 0.35 & 0.67 \\ 0.65 & 0.89 \\ 0.58 & 0.75 \end{bmatrix} = \begin{bmatrix} 1.5(0.35) & 1.5(0.67) \\ 1.5(0.65) & 1.5(0.89) \\ 1.5(0.58) & 1.5(0.75) \end{bmatrix}$$

$$\approx \begin{bmatrix} 0.53 & 1.00 \\ 0.98 & 1.34 \\ 0.87 & 1.13 \end{bmatrix}$$

Milk will cost $.53 and $1.00. Orange juice will cost $.98 and $1.34. Tomato juice will cost $.87 and $1.13.

4. Try This Find $-3\begin{bmatrix} 15 & -12 & 10 & 0 \\ 20 & -10 & 7 & 0 \end{bmatrix}$.

Multiplying Matrices

You can also multiply two matrices. To perform **matrix multiplication,** multiply the elements of each row of the first matrix by the elements of each column of the second matrix. Add the products.

Example 2

Find the product of $A = \begin{bmatrix} 0 & 3 \\ -1 & -4 \\ 1 & 2 \end{bmatrix}$ and $B = \begin{bmatrix} 4 & 0 \\ -2 & 1 \end{bmatrix}$.

Multiply a_{11} and b_{11}. Then multiply a_{12} and b_{21}. Add the products.

$$\begin{bmatrix} 0 & 3 \\ -1 & -4 \\ 1 & 2 \end{bmatrix}\begin{bmatrix} 4 & 0 \\ -2 & 1 \end{bmatrix} = \begin{bmatrix} ? & \blacksquare \\ \blacksquare & \blacksquare \\ \blacksquare & \blacksquare \end{bmatrix}$$
$\qquad (0)(4) + (3)(-2) = -6$

The result is the element in the first row, first column.

Repeat with the rest of the rows and columns.

$$\begin{bmatrix} 0 & 3 \\ -1 & -4 \\ 1 & 2 \end{bmatrix}\begin{bmatrix} 4 & 0 \\ -2 & 1 \end{bmatrix} = \begin{bmatrix} -6 & ? \\ \blacksquare & \blacksquare \\ \blacksquare & \blacksquare \end{bmatrix}$$
$\qquad (0)(0) + (3)(1) = 3$

$$\begin{bmatrix} 0 & 3 \\ -1 & -4 \\ 1 & 2 \end{bmatrix}\begin{bmatrix} 4 & 0 \\ -2 & 1 \end{bmatrix} = \begin{bmatrix} -6 & 3 \\ ? & \blacksquare \\ \blacksquare & \blacksquare \end{bmatrix}$$
$\qquad (-1)(4) + (-4)(-2) = 4$

$$\begin{bmatrix} 0 & 3 \\ -1 & -4 \\ 1 & 2 \end{bmatrix}\begin{bmatrix} 4 & 0 \\ -2 & 1 \end{bmatrix} = \begin{bmatrix} -6 & 3 \\ 4 & ? \\ \blacksquare & \blacksquare \end{bmatrix}$$
$\qquad (-1)(0) + (-4)(1) = -4$

$$\begin{bmatrix} 0 & 3 \\ -1 & -4 \\ 1 & 2 \end{bmatrix}\begin{bmatrix} 4 & 0 \\ -2 & 1 \end{bmatrix} = \begin{bmatrix} -6 & 3 \\ 4 & -4 \\ ? & \blacksquare \end{bmatrix}$$
$\qquad (1)(4) + (2)(-2) = 0$

$$\begin{bmatrix} 0 & 3 \\ -1 & -4 \\ 1 & 2 \end{bmatrix}\begin{bmatrix} 4 & 0 \\ -2 & 1 \end{bmatrix} = \begin{bmatrix} -6 & 3 \\ 4 & -4 \\ 0 & ? \end{bmatrix}$$
$\qquad (1)(0) + (2)(1) = 2$

The product of $\begin{bmatrix} 0 & 3 \\ -1 & -4 \\ 1 & 2 \end{bmatrix}$ and $\begin{bmatrix} 4 & 0 \\ -2 & 1 \end{bmatrix}$ is $\begin{bmatrix} -6 & 3 \\ 4 & -4 \\ 0 & 2 \end{bmatrix}$.

5. Describe the pattern of the shaded rows and columns.

6. Try This Find the product of $\begin{bmatrix} -1 & 0 \\ 3 & -4 \end{bmatrix}$ and $\begin{bmatrix} -3 & 3 \\ 5 & 0 \end{bmatrix}$.

7. a. In Example 2, what are the dimensions of the original matrices? What are the dimensions of the product matrix?

   b. *Critical Thinking* How do the dimensions of the product matrix compare to the dimensions of the original matrices?

Matrix Multiplication

If matrix A is an $m \times n$ matrix and matrix B is an $n \times p$ matrix, then the product matrix AB is an $m \times p$ matrix.

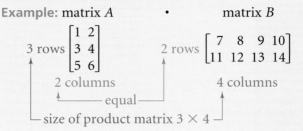

Example: matrix A • matrix B

3 rows $\begin{bmatrix} 1 & 2 \\ 3 & 4 \\ 5 & 6 \end{bmatrix}$ 2 rows $\begin{bmatrix} 7 & 8 & 9 & 10 \\ 11 & 12 & 13 & 14 \end{bmatrix}$

2 columns   4 columns

— equal —

size of product matrix 3×4

A product matrix is defined if the number of *columns* in the first matrix equals the number of *rows* in the second matrix.

Example 3

Let $G = \begin{bmatrix} 2 & 3 \\ -1 & 8 \\ 4 & 0 \end{bmatrix}$ and $H = \begin{bmatrix} 8 & 0 \\ 2 & -5 \end{bmatrix}$. Determine whether products GH

and HG are *defined* or *undefined*.

Find the dimensions of each defined product matrix.

$$\begin{array}{ccc} GH & \quad a & HG \\ (3 \times 2)(2 \times 2) \rightarrow 3 \times 2 & \quad & (2 \times 2)(3 \times 2) \end{array}$$

equal   product matrix   *not* equal

Product GH is defined and is a 3×2 matrix. Product HG is undefined, because the number of columns of H is not equal to the number of rows of G.

8. Let $R = \begin{bmatrix} 4 & -2 \\ 5 & -4 \end{bmatrix}$ and $S = \begin{bmatrix} 8 & 0 & -1 & 0 \\ 2 & -5 & 1 & 8 \end{bmatrix}$.

   a. **Try This** Determine whether products RS and SR are *defined* or *undefined*.

   b. Find each defined product.

9. *Critical Thinking* Suppose A is a 2×3 matrix and B is a 3×2 matrix. Are AB and BA equal? Explain your reasoning.

You can use a graphing calculator to multiply matrices and solve problems involving real-world data.

Example 4 **Relating to the Real World**

Transportation Use the data in the table and the graph. How many males and how many females commute to school by each method of transportation?

Students in School

	Males	Females
9th Grade	110	105
10th Grade	100	95
11th Grade	95	90
12th Grade	95	89

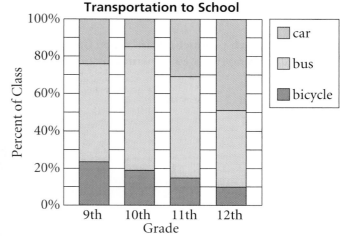

Transportation to School

□ car
□ bus
■ bicycle

$$A = \begin{array}{c} \\ \text{bicycle} \\ \text{bus} \\ \text{car} \end{array} \begin{array}{cccc} \text{9th} & \text{10th} & \text{11th} & \text{12th} \\ \left[\begin{array}{cccc} 0.23 & 0.19 & 0.15 & 0.10 \\ 0.53 & 0.66 & 0.54 & 0.41 \\ 0.24 & 0.15 & 0.31 & 0.49 \end{array} \right] \end{array} \qquad B = \begin{array}{c} \\ \text{9th} \\ \text{10th} \\ \text{11th} \\ \text{12th} \end{array} \begin{array}{cc} \text{M} & \text{F} \\ \left[\begin{array}{cc} 110 & 105 \\ 100 & 95 \\ 95 & 90 \\ 95 & 89 \end{array} \right] \end{array}$$

Matrix A represents transportation by grade; matrix B represents grade by gender. So, the product AB represents transportation by gender.

Use a graphing calculator. Enter both matrices and multiply them.

GRAPHING CALCULATOR HINT

Use the MATRX and ENTER keys to retrieve each matrix.

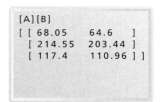

```
[A][B]
[ [ 68.05      64.6    ]
  [ 214.55    203.44 ]
  [ 117.4     110.96 ] ]
```

About 68 males and 65 females commute by bicycle. About 215 males and 203 females commute by bus. About 117 males and 111 females commute by car.

10. How could you check that the answer to Example 4 is reasonable?

11. a. Graphing Calculator Try to find the product BA for the data in Example 4. What error message do you see on the screen?
   b. Explain in your own words what the error message means.

Mental Math Find each product.

1. $\begin{bmatrix} 1 & 0 \\ 0 & -1 \end{bmatrix}\begin{bmatrix} -1 & 0 \\ 0 & -1 \end{bmatrix}$

2. $\begin{bmatrix} 1 & 1 & 1 \\ 0 & 1 & 0 \\ 0 & 1 & 1 \end{bmatrix}\begin{bmatrix} 1 & 1 & 1 \\ 0 & 1 & 0 \\ 0 & 1 & 1 \end{bmatrix}$

3. $\begin{bmatrix} -1 & 0 \\ 0 & -1 \end{bmatrix}\begin{bmatrix} -1 & 0 & 1 \\ 0 & -1 & 1 \end{bmatrix}$

4. $2\begin{bmatrix} -1 & 4 \\ 2 & 5 \end{bmatrix}$

5. $-3\begin{bmatrix} 6 & -3 \\ -7 & 4 \end{bmatrix}$

6. $-1\begin{bmatrix} 9 & -7 & -4 \\ -8 & -2 & 3 \end{bmatrix}$

Find the dimensions of each product matrix. Then find each product, if possible. If the product is not defined, explain why not.

7. $\begin{bmatrix} 1 & 0 & -5 \\ 2 & -1 & 6 \end{bmatrix}\begin{bmatrix} 2 & 4 & -2 \\ 0 & 10 & 4 \\ 0 & 1 & -7 \end{bmatrix}$

8. $\begin{bmatrix} 0 & 7 & k & 5 \\ 0 & 6 & 0 & 5 \end{bmatrix}\begin{bmatrix} 9 & -1 & 3 & 0 \\ 7 & 0 & 7 & 0 \end{bmatrix}$

9. $\begin{bmatrix} w & x \\ y & z \end{bmatrix}\begin{bmatrix} 9 & -7 \\ 3 & 1 \end{bmatrix}$

10. $\begin{bmatrix} 1.0 \\ 0.25 \\ -0.5 \end{bmatrix}\begin{bmatrix} 80 & 75 \\ 42 & 67 \\ 91 & 80 \end{bmatrix}$

11. $\begin{bmatrix} 1 & 0 & 0 \\ 1 & 0 & -2 \\ 0 & 0 & 2 \\ -1 & 0 & 1 \end{bmatrix}\begin{bmatrix} a & 0 & b & 0 \\ 0 & c & 0 & d \\ e & 0 & 0 & f \end{bmatrix}$

12. $\begin{bmatrix} -9 & 6 & 3 & 0 \\ -1 & 6 & -3 & 9 \end{bmatrix}\begin{bmatrix} -4 & 2 \\ -2 & 4 \end{bmatrix}$

Multiply.

13. $4\begin{bmatrix} 2 & 4 & -2 \\ 0 & 10 & 4 \\ 0 & 1 & -7 \end{bmatrix}$

14. $-1\begin{bmatrix} 7.5 & 6.2 & 4.0 \\ 6.7 & 8.2 & 0 \end{bmatrix}$

15. $0.5\begin{bmatrix} 3 & 14 \\ 7 & -4 \end{bmatrix}$

16. $100\begin{bmatrix} 80 & 75 \\ 42 & 67 \\ 91 & 80 \end{bmatrix}$

17. $-6\begin{bmatrix} 5 & -1 & 0 \\ 2 & 2 & -1 \\ 7 & 0 & 5 \\ -1 & 4 & 0 \end{bmatrix}$

18. $\frac{1}{4}\begin{bmatrix} 4 & 0 & -3 & 1 \\ 12 & 16 & 6 & -4 \\ 0 & -2 & 5 & 8 \end{bmatrix}$

19. Use the matrices below.

I. $\begin{bmatrix} 1 & 0 \\ 0 & 1 \end{bmatrix}\begin{bmatrix} 2 & -3 \\ 4 & 5 \end{bmatrix}$

II. $\begin{bmatrix} 1 & 0 \\ 0 & 1 \end{bmatrix}\begin{bmatrix} -3 & 3 \\ 3 & -3 \end{bmatrix}$

III. $\begin{bmatrix} 10 & 2 \\ -1 & 9 \end{bmatrix}\begin{bmatrix} 1 & 0 \\ 0 & 1 \end{bmatrix}$

   a. What matrix factor appears in I, II, and III?
   b. Find each product.
   c. Compare each product to its factors. What do you notice? What property does this illustrate?

20. Writing Refer to the cartoon. An *algorithm* is a step-by-step description of a calculation rule. What is the algorithm for matrix multiplication?

21. Let $A = \begin{bmatrix} 1 & 3 \\ -3 & 5 \end{bmatrix}$, $B = \begin{bmatrix} 3 & 0 \\ 7 & -2 \end{bmatrix}$, and $C = \begin{bmatrix} 1 & -5 \\ -5 & 8 \end{bmatrix}$.
   a. Find $A(BC)$ and $(AB)C$.
   b. Do you think multiplication of 2×2 matrices is associative? Explain. **Verify** your **conjecture** with another example.

OFF THE MARK

...THUS, THE ALGORITHM FOR MULTIPLYING TWO MATRICES WITH THE LEAST NUMBER OF COMPUTATIONS IS... CARL, YOU'RE DRIFTING!

For Exercises 22 and 23, write a pair of matrices that satisfies the given condition.

22. *AB* is defined but *BA* is not.

23. Both *AB* and *BA* are defined but $AB \neq BA$.

24. Floral Design A florist creates three special floral arrangements. One uses three lilies. The second uses three lilies and four carnations. The third type uses four daisies and three carnations. Lilies cost $2.15 each, carnations $.90 each, and daisies $1.30 each.

   a. Write a matrix to represent the number of each type of flower in each arrangement.

   b. Write a matrix to represent the cost of each type of flower.

   c. Find the matrix representing the cost of each type of arrangement.

25. Entertainment Use the data below. Write a matrix that represents the income from the play each day.

Ticket Prices by Location

	Orchestra	Main	Balcony
Ticket Price	$7.00	$6.00	$5.00

Number of Tickets Sold

Location	Thursday	Friday	Saturday
Orchestra	150	130	160
Main	125	130	175
Balcony	60	52	80

Use matrix multiplication and equal matrices to find *x* and *y*.

26. $\begin{bmatrix} 0 & -1 \\ 2 & 0 \end{bmatrix} \begin{bmatrix} x & 3 \\ -3 & 2y \end{bmatrix} = \begin{bmatrix} 3 & -6 \\ -4 & 6 \end{bmatrix}$

27. $\begin{bmatrix} x & -2 \\ 1 & 0 \end{bmatrix} \begin{bmatrix} 3 & -2 \\ 1 & y \end{bmatrix} = \begin{bmatrix} 4 & -14 \\ 3 & -2 \end{bmatrix}$

28. $\begin{bmatrix} 2x & 1 \\ 2 & 0 \end{bmatrix} \begin{bmatrix} 1 & 3 \\ 2 & -y \end{bmatrix} = \begin{bmatrix} -4 & -9 \\ 2 & 6 \end{bmatrix}$

29. $\begin{bmatrix} 2 & 1 \\ x & 2y \end{bmatrix} \begin{bmatrix} 1 & 4 \\ -2 & 3 \end{bmatrix} = \begin{bmatrix} 0 & 11 \\ -13 & 14 \end{bmatrix}$

Graphing Calculator **Find each product, if possible. If not possible, write *product undefined*.**

30. $\begin{bmatrix} 4 & -2 & -5 \\ -1 & 1 & 0 \end{bmatrix} \begin{bmatrix} 1 & 5 & 0 \\ 0 & 3 & -1 \\ 0 & 4 & 1 \end{bmatrix}$

31. $\begin{bmatrix} 3 & -2 & 0 & 4 \\ 4 & -2 & -3 & 4 \end{bmatrix} \begin{bmatrix} 0 & 1 & 1 \\ 0 & -1 & 0 \end{bmatrix}$

32. $\begin{bmatrix} 1.5 & 2.5 \\ 0.5 & 1.0 \end{bmatrix} \begin{bmatrix} 6 & 5 \\ 3 & 1 \end{bmatrix}$

33. $\begin{bmatrix} 3 & 2 & 1 & 0 \\ 0 & 2 & 5 & 1 \end{bmatrix} \begin{bmatrix} 0.15 & 0.20 \\ 0.60 & 0.35 \end{bmatrix}$

34. $\begin{bmatrix} 11 \\ 14 \end{bmatrix} \begin{bmatrix} 3.75 & 6.45 & 2.49 \end{bmatrix}$

35. $\begin{bmatrix} 0.35 \\ 0.99 \end{bmatrix} \begin{bmatrix} 6 & 13 \\ 10 & 4 \end{bmatrix}$

36. $\begin{bmatrix} 5 & 7 & 0 \\ -\frac{4}{5} & 3 & 6 \\ 0 & -\frac{2}{3} & 4 \end{bmatrix} \begin{bmatrix} 2 & -1 \\ 1 & 1 \\ 0 & -1 \end{bmatrix}$

37. $\begin{bmatrix} 0 & -1 & 3 \\ 0 & -5 & 2 \\ 0 & 0 & 2 \\ 1 & 0 & -3 \end{bmatrix} \begin{bmatrix} -1.5 & 4.3 & 0 \\ 1.6 & -2.2 & 1.8 \\ 1 & 0 & -1.2 \end{bmatrix}$

38. $\begin{bmatrix} 11 \\ 15 \\ \frac{9}{11} \end{bmatrix} \begin{bmatrix} 0.35 & 5 \\ 2.5 & 1.5 \\ 4.3 & 6.6 \end{bmatrix}$

39. Standardized Test Prep Which product equals $\begin{bmatrix} 10 & 6 \\ 16 & 10 \end{bmatrix}$?

   A. $\begin{bmatrix} 1 & 2 \\ 3 & 4 \end{bmatrix} \begin{bmatrix} 4 & 3 \\ 2 & 1 \end{bmatrix}$

   B. $\begin{bmatrix} 1 & 2 \\ 3 & 4 \end{bmatrix} \begin{bmatrix} 4 & 2 \\ 3 & 1 \end{bmatrix}$

   C. $\begin{bmatrix} 1 & 3 \\ 2 & 4 \end{bmatrix} \begin{bmatrix} 4 & 3 \\ 2 & 1 \end{bmatrix}$

   D. $\begin{bmatrix} 4 & 3 \\ 2 & 1 \end{bmatrix} \begin{bmatrix} 1 & 2 \\ 3 & 4 \end{bmatrix}$

Use matrices *A*, *B*, *C*, and *D* below. Find each product, if possible. If not possible, write *product undefined*.

$$A = \begin{bmatrix} 3 & 0 \\ 1 & 7 \\ 4 & 2 \end{bmatrix} \qquad B = \begin{bmatrix} 7 & 8 & 15 \\ 3 & 5 & -6 \end{bmatrix} \qquad C = \begin{bmatrix} 3 & 5 & 9 \\ -1 & -2 & 4 \\ 0 & 6 & 0 \end{bmatrix} \qquad D = \begin{bmatrix} -5 & 6 \\ -4 & 0 \\ -1 & -3 \end{bmatrix}$$

40. $2B$ **41.** $-3A$ **42.** $\frac{1}{2}C$ **43.** $-1.5B$ **44.** BD **45.** DB

46. AC **47.** CA **48.** AD **49.** DA **50.** CD **51.** DC

Exercises   MIXED REVIEW

Graph each inequality.

52. $y < 4x - 1$ **53.** $y \le -3x + 8$ **54.** $y \ge |2x + 5| - 3$

55. a. Probability The town has a drawing for 50 summer jobs. If 150 students apply, including you, what are the odds that you will get one of the jobs?
    b. What is the probability that you will get one of the jobs?
    c. If you and a friend both apply, what is the probability that you will both get jobs?

Getting Ready for Lesson 3-4

Without using graphing technology, graph each function and its translation. Write the new function.

56. $y = x^2 + 2$;   **57.** $f(x) = x^2$;   **58.** $g(x) = |x|$;   **59.** $y = x$;
     left 4   up 5   right 3   down 2

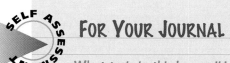

SELF ASSESSMENT

FOR YOUR JOURNAL

What topic in this lesson did you find the most difficult? What can you do to understand this topic better?

Exercises   CHECKPOINT

State the dimensions of each matrix. Identify the indicated element.

1. $\begin{bmatrix} 5 & 2 \\ -8 & 3 \\ 10 & 1 \end{bmatrix}$; a_{32} **2.** $\begin{bmatrix} 9 & 1 & 7 \\ 6 & -2 & 4 \end{bmatrix}$; a_{22} **3.** $\begin{bmatrix} 8 & 1 & 5 \\ 9 & 4 & 2 \\ 7 & 0 & 3 \end{bmatrix}$; a_{13}

Use matrices *A*, *B*, *C*, and *D* below. Perform each operation.

$$A = \begin{bmatrix} 3 & 1 \\ 5 & 7 \end{bmatrix} \qquad B = \begin{bmatrix} 4 & 6 \\ 1 & 0 \end{bmatrix} \qquad C = \begin{bmatrix} -5 & 3 \\ 1 & 9 \end{bmatrix} \qquad D = \begin{bmatrix} 1.5 & 2 \\ 9 & -6 \end{bmatrix}$$

4. $A + C$ **5.** $B - A$ **6.** $3D$ **7.** CD **8.** BA **9.** $C(DB)$

10. Writing How do you decide if two matrices can be multiplied?

11. Open-ended Write a matrix equation for which the solution is $\begin{bmatrix} 12 & 7 & -3 & 8 \\ 9 & 0 & -11 & 1 \end{bmatrix}$.

Geometric Transformations

Before Lesson 3-4

Geometric patterns, such as geese flying south for the winter and tiles on a plane surface, can be described using geometric transformations. A **transformation** is a change made to a figure. There are four types.

A **translation** slides a figure a given distance and direction without changing its size or shape.

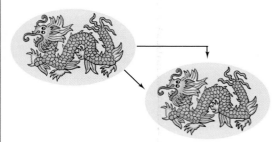

A **rotation** turns a figure through a given angle about a point called its center.

A **reflection** flips a figure over a given line called its *axis of symmetry*.

A **dilation** enlarges or shrinks a figure by a given *scale factor*.

Describe each transformation from the black figure to the red figure as a *translation*, *rotation*, *reflection*, **or** *dilation*.

1.
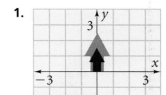

2.
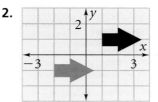

3.
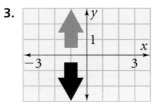

4.
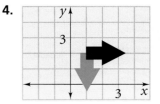

5. a. Open-ended List the coordinates of the vertices of one figure above. List the coordinates of its image.

b. Writing Make a **conjecture** about how the coordinates of the figure relate to the coordinates of its image. Use examples to **verify** your conjecture.

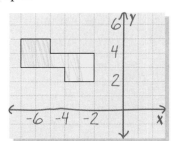

What You'll Learn

- Representing translations and dilations with matrices

...And Why

To create computer art

What You'll Need

- graph paper

3-4 Geometric Transformations with Matrices

WORK TOGETHER

Geometry In Chapter 1 you used vertical and horizontal translations to graph functions. A *translation* shifts a graph without changing its size or shape. Work with a partner. Use graph paper.

1. Draw the figure on a coordinate grid as shown.

2. Translate the figure 4 units right and 6 units down. Label the new figure.

3. Identify the coordinates of the vertices of the original figure and the new figure.

4. How does the translation *4 units right and 6 units down* relate the coordinates of the new figure to the original figure?

5. Without graphing, identify the coordinates of the figure that results from a translation of the original figure 10 units right and 3 units up.

6. **Critical Thinking** What translations of the original figure will result in a tessellation?

7. **Open-ended** Design another simple figure that will tessellate the plane. Describe the translations needed to fill the plane.

QUICK REVIEW

A *tessellation* is a repeating pattern of figures that completely covers a plane without gaps or overlaps.

Representing Translations with Matrices

You can write the vertices of a figure as a matrix. For example, the matrix below represents the vertices of figure *ABCD*.

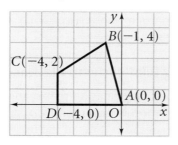

$$\begin{array}{c}\text{x-coordinate} \\ \text{y-coordinate}\end{array} \begin{array}{cccc} A & B & C & D \\ \left[\begin{array}{cccc} 0 & -1 & -4 & -4 \\ 0 & 4 & 2 & 0 \end{array}\right]\end{array}$$

8. **Try This** Write the ordered pairs in matrix form.
   a. $G(2, 3), H(0, 1), I(-3, 6), J(7, 4)$ **b.** $A(12, 9), B(15, 4), C(20, 6)$

A **transformation** is a change made to a figure. The transformed figure is called the **image.** The original figure is called the **preimage.** A translation is one type of transformation. You can use matrix addition to translate all the points of a figure in one step.

Example 1

Geometry Quadrilateral *ABCD* above has vertices $A(0, 0)$, $B(-1, 4)$, $C(-4, 2)$, and $D(-4, 0)$. Use a matrix to find the vertices of the image translated 6 units right and 2 units down. Then graph *ABCD* and its image *A'B'C'D'*.

vertices of the quadrilateral	translation matrix	vertices of the image

Add 6 to each *x*-coordinate.

$$\begin{array}{cccc} A & B & C & D \\ \left[\begin{array}{cccc} 0 & -1 & -4 & -4 \\ 0 & 4 & 2 & 0 \end{array}\right]\end{array} + \left[\begin{array}{cccc} 6 & 6 & 6 & 6 \\ -2 & -2 & -2 & -2 \end{array}\right] = \begin{array}{cccc} A' & B' & C' & D' \\ \left[\begin{array}{cccc} 6 & 5 & 2 & 2 \\ -2 & 2 & 0 & -2 \end{array}\right]\end{array}$$

Subtract 2 from each *y*-coordinate.

The vertices of the image are $A'(6, -2)$, $B'(5, 2)$, $C'(2, 0)$, and $D'(2, -2)$.

Graph both quadrilaterals.

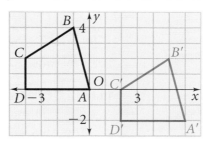

9. **Critical Thinking** Explain how to translate quadrilateral $A'B'C'D'$ from Example 1 so that its image is quadrilateral $ABCD$.

10. **a.** What matrix would you use to translate the vertices of a pentagon 3 units left and 2 units up?

   b. **Try This** Use your answer to part (a) to translate the pentagon with vertices $(0, -5)$, $(-1, -1)$, $(-5, 0)$, $(1, 3)$, and $(4, 0)$. Find the coordinates of the vertices of the image. Graph the preimage and the image.

Representing Dilations with Matrices

A **dilation** is a transformation that changes the size of a figure. When the center of the dilation is the origin, you can use scalar multiplication to find the coordinates of the vertices of the image. All dilations in this book will be centered at the origin.

Example 2   **Relating to the Real World**

Computer Art An artist sends you a photo electronically. Increase the dimensions of the photo by a factor of 1.2. Find the coordinates of the vertices of the enlargement.

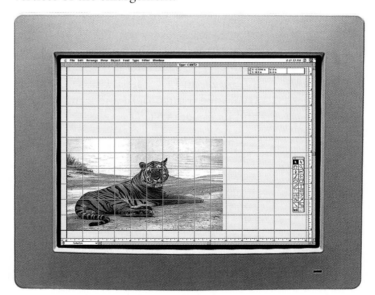

Write a matrix to represent the coordinates of the vertices.

$$1.2\begin{bmatrix} 0 & 0 & 9.75 & 9.75 \\ 0 & 5.875 & 5.875 & 0 \end{bmatrix} = \begin{bmatrix} 0 & 0 & 11.7 & 11.7 \\ 0 & 7.05 & 7.05 & 0 \end{bmatrix} \longleftarrow \text{Multiply.}$$

The new coordinates are $(0, 0)$, $(0, 7.05)$, $(11.7, 7.05)$, and $(11.7, 0)$. ▪

11. **Try This** The coordinates of the vertices of figure ABC are $A(-5, 0)$, $B(8, -1)$, and $C(4, 5)$. Find the coordinates of each image under the following dilations. Then graph each pair of figures.
   a. 4   **b.** $\frac{1}{5}$ **c.** -1.5

Write the vertices of each figure in matrix form.

1. $A(1, -3)$, $B(1, 1)$, $C(5, 1)$, $D(5, -3)$

2. $G(0, 0)$, $H(4, 4)$, $I(4, -4)$, $J(8, 0)$

3. $J(-10, 2)$, $K(-16, a)$, $L(12, -5)$

4. $R(9, 3)$, $S(3, 6)$, $T(3, 3)$, $U(6, -3)$

5. $A(5, -y)$, $B(1, 9)$, $C(4, y)$, $D(x, 0)$, $E(6, 7)$

6. $E(-1, -5)$, $F(-10, -d)$, $G(-3, c)$

**Each matrix represents vertices of a polygon. Translate each figure
5 units left and 1 unit up. Express your answer as a matrix.**

7. $\begin{bmatrix} -3 & -3 & 2 & 2 \\ -2 & -4 & -2 & -4 \end{bmatrix}$

8. $\begin{bmatrix} 2 & 4 & 6 & 8 & 8 & 6 & 4 & 2 \\ 2 & 0 & 0 & 2 & 4 & 6 & 6 & 4 \end{bmatrix}$

9. $\begin{bmatrix} -3 & 0 & 3 & 0 \\ -9 & -6 & -9 & -12 \end{bmatrix}$

**For Exercises 10–13, use $\triangle ABC$ at the right. Find the coordinates of the
image under each transformation.**

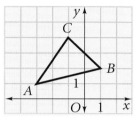

10. a dilation four times
the original size

11. a translation 2 units left and 3
units down

12. a dilation half the original size

13. a translation 1 unit right and 7 units up

14. Writing Explain why you might want to represent a geometric
transformation as a matrix.

15. Geometry Create a tessellation based on the quadrilateral $\begin{bmatrix} 0 & -3 & -5 & 0 \\ 1 & 3 & -1 & -1 \end{bmatrix}$.

Translate using $\begin{bmatrix} 5 & 5 & 5 & 5 \\ 2 & 2 & 2 & 2 \end{bmatrix}$ and $\begin{bmatrix} 3 & 3 & 3 & 3 \\ -4 & -4 & -4 & -4 \end{bmatrix}$.

16. Find $\begin{bmatrix} -3 & 0 \\ 0 & -3 \end{bmatrix}\begin{bmatrix} 1 & -2 & 4 \\ 1 & -1 & 2 \end{bmatrix}$ and $-3\begin{bmatrix} 1 & -2 & 4 \\ 1 & -1 & 2 \end{bmatrix}$. What do you
notice about the products?

17. Architecture Use the pattern of tiles shown.
  a. Copy the graph. Mark scales on the axes so
  that the dimensions of the square tiles are 1
  unit by 1 unit.
  b. Write a matrix for the translation of tile
  $ABCD$ to tile $A'B'C'D'$. What are the
  coordinates of the vertices of the preimage
  and the image?
  c. A dark blue tile is 6 units right and 6 units
  down from tile $ABCD$. Write a matrix to
  represent the coordinates of the vertices of
  this tile.
  d. A tile has vertices at $(-6, 9)$, $(-6, 8)$,
  $(-7, 9)$, and $(-7, 8)$. What translation of
  tile $ABCD$ results in these coordinates?

Use matrices to represent the vertices of graph *f* and graph *g*.

18.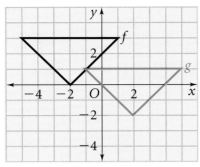

19.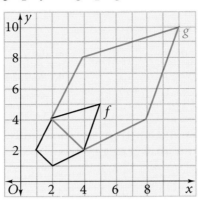

20.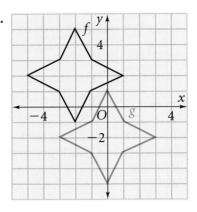

21. **Art** Use the butterfly graph at the right. Translate it 5 units right and 2 units down. Sketch the image.

22. **Open-ended** Create a design by making several transformations of a shape. Identify the shape you started with and record the transformations you made along the way.

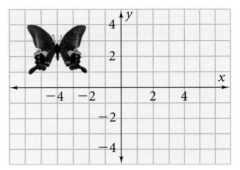

23. **a.** Graph $\begin{bmatrix} 9 & 10 & 6 \\ 1 & -3 & -2 \end{bmatrix}$ and $2\begin{bmatrix} 9 & 10 & 6 \\ 1 & -3 & -2 \end{bmatrix}$.

 b. Compare the graphs in part (a). **Generalize** how a dilation changes a graph.

24. Suppose the matrix $\begin{bmatrix} x \\ y \end{bmatrix}$ represents points on the graph $y = x^2$.

 a. Complete the table. Sketch the graph.

x	-3	-2	-1	0	1	2	3
y	■	■	■	■	■	■	■

 b. **Critical Thinking** What does the matrix addition $\begin{bmatrix} x \\ y \end{bmatrix} + \begin{bmatrix} -1 \\ 2 \end{bmatrix}$ represent? Show your answer on the graph in part (a).

Graph each triangle and its translation on the same coordinate plane.

25. $\begin{bmatrix} 0 & 2 & 3 \\ 0 & 0 & 5 \end{bmatrix}$; 3 units right, 4 units down

26. $\begin{bmatrix} -5 & 3 & 4 \\ 5 & 1 & -4 \end{bmatrix}$; 2 units left, 5 units up

Graph each figure and its image after the given dilation on the same coordinate plane.

27. $\begin{bmatrix} 0 & 2 & 5 & 8 \\ 0 & 4 & 5 & 1 \end{bmatrix}$; 2

28. $\begin{bmatrix} -7 & -3 & 4 \\ -5 & 4 & 0 \end{bmatrix}$; 0.5

29. $\begin{bmatrix} 10 & 0 & 10 \\ 5 & 0 & -5 \end{bmatrix}$; 0.8

30. $\begin{bmatrix} -10 & -5 & 0 & 5 & 10 \\ 8 & 16 & 20 & 16 & 8 \end{bmatrix}$; $\frac{1}{4}$

31. $\begin{bmatrix} -1 & -2 & 0 & 1 \\ -1 & 0 & 0 & -1 \end{bmatrix}$; 7.5

32. $\begin{bmatrix} -8 & 2 & 3 & 1 & -2 \\ 6 & 4 & 0 & -4 & 0 \end{bmatrix}$; 1.5

33. a. Data Analysis Make a scatter plot of the data at the right.
   b. Describe any trends you see.
   c. If the data look linear, draw a line of best fit.
   d. **Predict** how many visitors there would be to a state with 300,000 acres of national park land.

National Parks

State	Acres (1000s)	Visitors (millions)
Alabama	50	6.3
California	1323	67.3
Hawaii	25	19.2
Illinois	403	38.6
Michigan	264	21.2
Minnesota	231	7.9
Texas	501	24.4

Source: *National Association of State Park Directors*

Use $f(x)$, $g(x)$, and $h(x)$. Write and simplify each function rule.

$$f(x) = 4x^2 \qquad g(x) = \tfrac{1}{2}x + 7 \qquad h(x) = |-2x + 4|$$

34. $f(g(x))$

35. $g(f(x))$

36. $h(g(x))$

37. $h(g(f(x)))$

38. $f(g(x)) + h(x)$

39. $h(x) - f(x)$

40. $g(x) + g(x)$

41. $g(f(x)) - h(x)$

Getting Ready for Lesson 3-5

Find each product.

42. $\begin{bmatrix} 0 & 1 & 1 \\ 0 & 1 & 0 \\ 1 & 0 & 1 \end{bmatrix} \begin{bmatrix} 0 & 1 & 1 \\ 0 & 1 & 0 \\ 1 & 0 & 1 \end{bmatrix}$

43. $\begin{bmatrix} 1 & 1 & 0 \\ 1 & 0 & 1 \\ 0 & 0 & 1 \end{bmatrix} \begin{bmatrix} 1 & 1 & 0 \\ 1 & 0 & 1 \\ 0 & 0 & 1 \end{bmatrix}$

A Point in Time

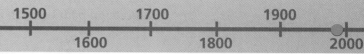

1500 — 1600 — 1700 — 1800 — 1900 — 2000

Education Through Art

An artist who paints murals usually creates a sketch (often on a computer) and then uses a dilation of the sketch for the actual mural. Judith Francisca Baca is a muralist who uses her talents to promote and educate others about her Mexican American heritage. In a project completed in the summer of **1996,** she directed 215 teenagers over five summers. Computers allowed the students to experiment with their images. The result was six 8 ft-by-9 ft panels illustrating the history of Los Angeles.

Another of her famous murals is the Great Wall of Los Angeles (pictured at right). It is half a mile long and represents California's multicultural history since prehistoric times.

3-5   Networks

What You'll Learn
- Drawing and interpreting finite graphs
- Drawing and interpreting directed graphs

...And Why

To plan routes for city streets

What You'll Need
- graph paper
- graphing calculator

WORK TOGETHER

City Planning Work with a partner to plan and design a town.

1. **a.** Make a list of the five most important places or buildings for the town.
   b. On a sheet of graph paper, draw a map of the town. Mark each building and include roads to get from place to place.
   c. Make a table that indicates which pairs of locations you can travel between without going through other locations.

THINK AND DISCUSS

Drawing and Interpreting Finite Graphs

A **finite graph** is a set of points connected by paths. The points are called **vertices.** You can use a matrix to describe a finite graph.

Example 1

Present the information from the finite graph in a matrix. Use a 1 to indicate a path between two vertices or one vertex and itself. Use a 0 to indicate no path between two vertices or one vertex and itself.

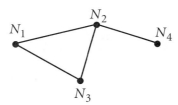

$$A = \begin{array}{c} \\ N_1 \\ N_2 \\ N_3 \\ N_4 \end{array} \begin{array}{c} \begin{array}{cccc} N_1 & N_2 & N_3 & N_4 \end{array} \\ \begin{bmatrix} 0 & 1 & 1 & 0 \\ 1 & 0 & 1 & 1 \\ 1 & 1 & 0 & 0 \\ 0 & 1 & 0 & 0 \end{bmatrix} \end{array}$$

2. **Critical Thinking** What do the zeros along the main diagonal of matrix A represent?

3. What does the zero in position a_{41} indicate? Explain.

4. Try This Construct a matrix for each finite graph.

a.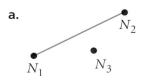

b.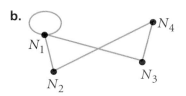

Drawing and Interpreting Directed Graphs

Directed graphs are finite graphs that indicate the direction of a path.

Example 2   **Relating to the Real World**

City Planning The directed graph indicates the one-way and two-way streets that connect the fire department (F), the school (S), the hospital (H), and an apartment building (A). Write a matrix of the information.

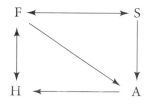

To ⟶ F S A H

$$C = \begin{array}{c} \text{From} \rightarrow F \\ S \\ A \\ H \end{array} \begin{bmatrix} 0 & 1 & 1 & 1 \\ 1 & 0 & 1 & 0 \\ 0 & 0 & 0 & 1 \\ 1 & 0 & 0 & 0 \end{bmatrix}$$

There is a path from S to A.

5. a. In the directed graph, what does the arrow from the apartments to the hospital mean?
  b. How is this shown in the matrix?

6. a. In Example 2, what does the value c_{13} represent?
  b. How is this shown in the directed graph?

7. Try This Write a matrix C for the directed graph at the right.

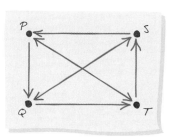

You can use a matrix to write a directed graph.

Example 4   **Relating to the Real World**

Air Travel Draw a directed graph to represent the data in the airline route matrix.

	To Orlando	To Philadelphia	To Seattle
From Orlando	0	1	1
From Philadelphia	1	0	1
From Seattle	0	1	0

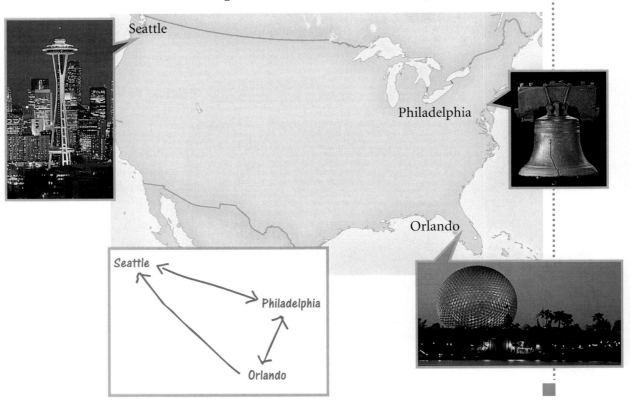

8. **Try This** Draw a directed graph to represent the data in each matrix.

a.

	A	B	C
A	1	0	0
B	0	0	1
C	1	1	1

b.

	P	Q	R	S
P	1	1	1	1
Q	0	0	1	0
R	1	1	0	1
S	0	1	1	1

9. Which matrix represents the directed graph at the right?

A.

	L	M	N
L	1	1	1
M	0	0	1
N	1	0	0

B.

	L	M	N
L	1	0	1
M	1	0	0
N	1	1	0

Write a matrix for each finite graph.

1.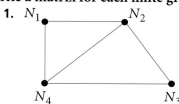

2.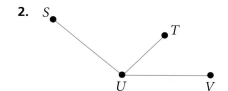

3.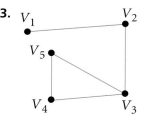

Draw a directed graph to represent the information in each matrix.

4.
$$
\begin{array}{c}
 & \begin{array}{cccc} J & K & L & M \end{array} \\
\begin{array}{c} J \\ K \\ L \\ M \end{array} &
\left[\begin{array}{cccc}
0 & 0 & 0 & 1 \\
0 & 0 & 1 & 1 \\
0 & 1 & 0 & 1 \\
1 & 1 & 1 & 0
\end{array}\right]
\end{array}
$$

5.
$$
\begin{array}{c}
 & \begin{array}{cccc} A & B & C & D \end{array} \\
\begin{array}{c} A \\ B \\ C \\ D \end{array} &
\left[\begin{array}{cccc}
0 & 0 & 1 & 1 \\
1 & 1 & 0 & 0 \\
0 & 1 & 0 & 1 \\
1 & 0 & 1 & 0
\end{array}\right]
\end{array}
$$

6.
$$
\begin{array}{c}
 & \begin{array}{cccc} N_1 & N_2 & N_3 & N_4 \end{array} \\
\begin{array}{c} N_1 \\ N_2 \\ N_3 \\ N_4 \end{array} &
\left[\begin{array}{cccc}
1 & 1 & 1 & 1 \\
0 & 0 & 1 & 1 \\
1 & 0 & 0 & 0 \\
0 & 0 & 1 & 0
\end{array}\right]
\end{array}
$$

7.
$$
\begin{array}{c}
 & \begin{array}{cccc} V & W & X & Y \end{array} \\
\begin{array}{c} V \\ W \\ X \\ Y \end{array} &
\left[\begin{array}{cccc}
0 & 1 & 1 & 0 \\
1 & 0 & 0 & 1 \\
1 & 0 & 0 & 1 \\
0 & 1 & 1 & 0
\end{array}\right]
\end{array}
$$

Write a matrix for each directed graph.

8.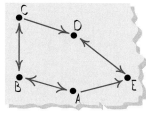

9.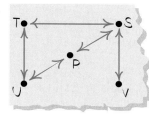

10.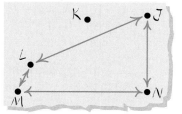

11.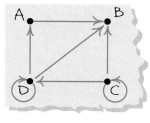

12.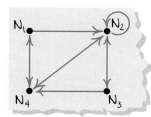

13.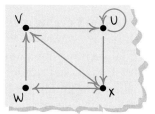

14. **Geography** Use the bus route map. Write a matrix *A* that indicates the routes between cities.

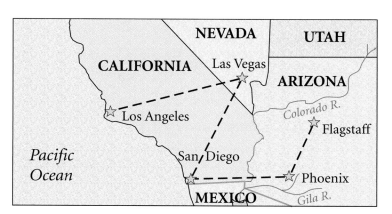

15. Match each matrix with its directed graph.

a.
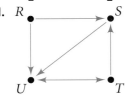
$$\begin{array}{c} & R \quad S \quad T \quad U \\ \begin{matrix} R \\ S \\ T \\ U \end{matrix} & \begin{bmatrix} 0 & 1 & 0 & 1 \\ 0 & 0 & 1 & 1 \\ 0 & 1 & 0 & 1 \\ 1 & 1 & 0 & 0 \end{bmatrix} \end{array}$$

b.
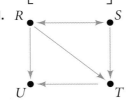
$$\begin{array}{c} & R \quad S \quad T \quad U \\ \begin{matrix} R \\ S \\ T \\ U \end{matrix} & \begin{bmatrix} 0 & 1 & 1 & 1 \\ 1 & 0 & 1 & 0 \\ 0 & 0 & 0 & 1 \\ 0 & 0 & 0 & 0 \end{bmatrix} \end{array}$$

c.
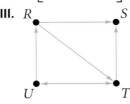
$$\begin{array}{c} & R \quad S \quad T \quad U \\ \begin{matrix} R \\ S \\ T \\ U \end{matrix} & \begin{bmatrix} 0 & 1 & 0 & 1 \\ 0 & 0 & 0 & 1 \\ 0 & 1 & 0 & 1 \\ 0 & 0 & 1 & 0 \end{bmatrix} \end{array}$$

d.
$$\begin{array}{c} & R \quad S \quad T \quad U \\ \begin{matrix} R \\ S \\ T \\ U \end{matrix} & \begin{bmatrix} 0 & 1 & 1 & 0 \\ 0 & 0 & 0 & 0 \\ 0 & 1 & 0 & 1 \\ 1 & 0 & 1 & 0 \end{bmatrix} \end{array}$$

I.   II.   III.   IV.

16. Communications Scientists A, B, and C communicate by fax if they have each other's fax numbers. They communicate by electronic mail if they have each other's e-mail addresses. Matrix E models the scientists' possible e-mail matrix, and matrix F models their possible fax matrix.

$$E = \begin{array}{c} & \begin{matrix} \text{To} & \text{To} & \text{To} \\ A & B & C \end{matrix} \\ \begin{matrix} \text{From } A \\ \text{From } B \\ \text{From } C \end{matrix} & \begin{bmatrix} 1 & 1 & 0 \\ 1 & 1 & 1 \\ 0 & 1 & 1 \end{bmatrix} \end{array} \qquad F = \begin{array}{c} & \begin{matrix} \text{To} & \text{To} & \text{To} \\ A & B & C \end{matrix} \\ \begin{matrix} \text{From } A \\ \text{From } B \\ \text{From } C \end{matrix} & \begin{bmatrix} 0 & 0 & 0 \\ 1 & 0 & 1 \\ 0 & 1 & 0 \end{bmatrix} \end{array}$$

a. Draw directed graphs for each matrix.
b. Analyze the values along the main diagonals of E and F.
c. Critical Thinking Calculate $E + F$. What does the matrix model? Explain.

17. Crystal and Enrique each live near a train station. The train stops near both houses. Vanessa drives a car and has permission to drive to Crystal and Enrique's houses. Enrique can go by bus to Vanessa's house but Crystal cannot get to Vanessa's house by bus. Draw a directed graph indicating the travel options. Then write a matrix to represent the information.

18. Write a matrix to represent the finite graph at the right.

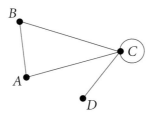

19. Alice and Becky live on River Drive East, at the intersections of Memorial Bridge and Benjamin Bridge, respectively. Carl and David live on River Drive West, at the intersections of Benjamin Bridge and Memorial Bridge, respectively. River Drive East is a one-way street running east. River Drive West is one-way running west. Both bridges are two-way. Draw a directed graph indicating road travel between the houses. Then write a matrix to represent the information.

20. Data Analysis The table shows median U.S. household income for
several years.
   a. Draw a scatter plot. Describe the correlation, if any.
   b. Draw a trend line to model the relationship.

21. a. Jobs You make $4.50/h mowing lawns. How much will you make
if you mow lawns for 4 h this weekend?
   b. Write a function to model your earnings after h hours of mowing
lawns. What kind of function is it?
   c. Suppose you want to buy a $60 jacket with the money you earn.
How many hours would you have to work?

Year	U.S. Median Income (thousands)
1975	32
1979	33.9
1983	32.1
1987	35
1991	33.8
1995	34.1

Source: *U.S. Bureau of the Census*

Solve each equation.

22. $5x + 3 = 7x - 10$ **23.** $x^3 = 169x$ **24.** $27 - x = -2x + 27$ **25.** $23x = 42$

Getting Ready for Lesson 3-6

Find $a_{11}a_{22} - a_{12}a_{21}$ for each matrix.

26. $A = \begin{bmatrix} 3 & 1 \\ 9 & 7 \end{bmatrix}$ **27.** $A = \begin{bmatrix} -5 & 0 \\ 8 & 1 \end{bmatrix}$ **28.** $A = \begin{bmatrix} 8 & -2 \\ 1.5 & 3 \end{bmatrix}$ **29.** $A = \begin{bmatrix} 0 & 1 \\ 0.5 & 4 \end{bmatrix}$

Use $\triangle ABC$ with coordinates $A(3, 4)$, $B(5, -2)$, and $C(-1, -1)$. Find the
coordinates of the image under each transformation.

   1. dilation size 5   **2.** translation 2 units right, 3 units down   **3.** dilation size $\frac{1}{2}$

Write a matrix for each directed graph.

4. 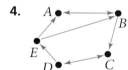   **5.** 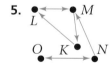   **6.** 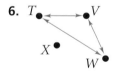   **7.**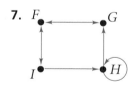

8. Standardized Test Prep The matrix of which finite graph has the least
number of 1's?

A. 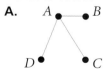   **B.** 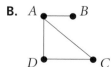   **C.** 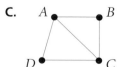   **D.**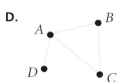

   E. It cannot be determined from the information given.

Matrices and Determinants

Before Lesson 3-6

A **square matrix** is a matrix with the same number of columns as rows. Every square matrix with real number elements has a real number associated with it called its **determinant.**

Write $\quad\quad\quad\quad\quad$ Read $\quad\quad\quad\quad\quad$ Evaluate

$$A = \begin{bmatrix} a & b \\ c & d \end{bmatrix} \quad \det A = \begin{vmatrix} a & b \\ c & d \end{vmatrix} \quad \text{the determinant of } A \quad \begin{vmatrix} a & b \\ c & d \end{vmatrix} = ad - bc$$

Example 1

Evaluate $\begin{vmatrix} -3 & 4 \\ 2 & -5 \end{vmatrix}$.

$\begin{vmatrix} -3 & 4 \\ 2 & -5 \end{vmatrix} = (-3)(-5) - (4)(2) = 7 \quad \longleftarrow$ **Multiply and simplify.**

Example 2

Enter matrix A into your graphing calculator. Use the **MATRX** submenus to evaluate its determinant.

$$A = \begin{bmatrix} 1 & 7 & 2 \\ -1 & 1 & -2 \\ 1 & 1 & 1 \end{bmatrix}$$

```
NAMES MATH EDIT
1:det
2: T
3:dim
4:Fill(
5:identity
6:randM(
7↓augment(
```

```
NAMES MATH EDIT
1: [A]   3×3
2: [B]
3: [C]
4: [D]
5: [E]
```

```
det [A]
                    -8
■
```

Use pencil and paper or a graphing calculator to evaluate each determinant.

1. $\begin{bmatrix} 2 & -3 \\ 3 & -2 \end{bmatrix}$ $\quad$ **2.** $\begin{bmatrix} a & 0 \\ 0 & a \end{bmatrix}$ $\quad$ **3.** $\begin{bmatrix} a & b \\ b & a \end{bmatrix}$ $\quad$ **4.** $\begin{bmatrix} 4 & 2 \\ 4 & 2 \end{bmatrix}$

5. $\begin{bmatrix} 1 & 0 & 0 \\ 0 & 1 & 0 \\ 0 & 0 & 1 \end{bmatrix}$ $\quad$ **6.** $\begin{bmatrix} 0 & -2 & -3 \\ 1 & 2 & 4 \\ -2 & 0 & 1 \end{bmatrix}$ $\quad$ **7.** $\begin{bmatrix} 13 & 21 & 11 \\ -2 & 4 & -1 \\ 17 & -2 & 0 \end{bmatrix}$ $\quad$ **8.** $\begin{bmatrix} 12.2 & 13.3 & 9 \\ 1 & -4 & -17 \\ 21.4 & -15 & 0 \end{bmatrix}$

Writing Evaluate the determinants of each pair of matrices. Describe any patterns you see.

9. 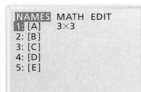 $F = \begin{bmatrix} 4 & 0 \\ 2 & 6 \end{bmatrix}$, $G = \begin{bmatrix} 4 & 2 \\ 0 & 6 \end{bmatrix}$ $\quad\quad$ **10.** 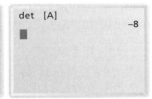 $M = \begin{bmatrix} -2 & 3 \\ -2 & 3 \end{bmatrix}$, $N = \begin{bmatrix} 4 & 10 \\ 4 & 10 \end{bmatrix}$

What You'll Learn
- Finding and using inverse matrices
- Using inverse matrices to solve matrix equations

...And Why
To decode messages encoded using a matrix

What You'll Need
- graphing calculator

3-6 Identity and Inverse Matrices

WORK TOGETHER

Work with a partner.

1. Find each product.

   a. $\begin{bmatrix} -5 & 6 \\ 4 & 2 \end{bmatrix}\begin{bmatrix} 1 & 0 \\ 0 & 1 \end{bmatrix}$

   b. $\begin{bmatrix} 1 & 0 \\ 0 & 1 \end{bmatrix}\begin{bmatrix} -5 & 6 \\ 4 & 2 \end{bmatrix}$

   c. $\begin{bmatrix} 3 & 4 & 1 \\ -2 & 0 & 2 \\ 1 & 5 & 3 \end{bmatrix}\begin{bmatrix} 1 & 0 & 0 \\ 0 & 1 & 0 \\ 0 & 0 & 1 \end{bmatrix}$

   d. $\begin{bmatrix} 1 & 0 & 0 \\ 0 & 1 & 0 \\ 0 & 0 & 1 \end{bmatrix}\begin{bmatrix} 3 & 4 & 1 \\ -2 & 0 & 2 \\ 1 & 5 & 3 \end{bmatrix}$

2. **Patterns** Describe any patterns you see in your answers to Question 1.

3. **Graphing Calculator** **Predict** the product. **Verify** your prediction.

$$\begin{bmatrix} 2 & 3 & -2 & 4 \\ 1 & 2 & 3 & 0 \\ -1 & -2 & 1 & 4 \\ 5 & 2 & 3 & 0 \end{bmatrix}\begin{bmatrix} 1 & 0 & 0 & 0 \\ 0 & 1 & 0 & 0 \\ 0 & 0 & 1 & 0 \\ 0 & 0 & 0 & 1 \end{bmatrix}$$

4. Find each product.

   a. $\begin{bmatrix} 3 & 5 \\ 1 & 2 \end{bmatrix}\begin{bmatrix} 2 & -5 \\ -1 & 3 \end{bmatrix}$

   b. $\begin{bmatrix} 2 & -5 \\ -1 & 3 \end{bmatrix}\begin{bmatrix} 3 & 5 \\ 1 & 2 \end{bmatrix}$

   c. $\begin{bmatrix} 1 & 5 & -1 \\ 1 & 0 & -1 \\ 1 & 0 & 0 \end{bmatrix}\begin{bmatrix} 0 & 0 & 1 \\ 0.2 & -0.2 & 0 \\ 0 & -1 & 1 \end{bmatrix}$

   d. $\begin{bmatrix} 0 & 0 & 1 \\ 0.2 & -0.2 & 0 \\ 0 & -1 & 1 \end{bmatrix}\begin{bmatrix} 1 & 5 & -1 \\ 1 & 0 & -1 \\ 1 & 0 & 0 \end{bmatrix}$

5. **Patterns** Describe any patterns you see in your answers to Question 4.

6. **Critical Thinking** How are your answers to Questions 1 and 4 related?

THINK AND DISCUSS

Finding the Inverse of a 2 × 2 Matrix

A **square matrix** is a matrix with the same number of columns as rows. The square $n \times n$ matrix with 1's along its main diagonal and 0's elsewhere is the **identity matrix** for multiplication. You write the identity matrix as I.

$$I_{2\times 2} = \begin{bmatrix} 1 & 0 \\ 0 & 1 \end{bmatrix} \qquad I_{3\times 3} = \begin{bmatrix} 1 & 0 & 0 \\ 0 & 1 & 0 \\ 0 & 0 & 1 \end{bmatrix}$$

Suppose A is a square matrix and X is another square matrix such that $AX = I$. Then X is the **inverse matrix** of A. You write the inverse matrix of A as A^{-1}. So, $AA^{-1} = I$ and $A^{-1}A = I$.

Not all square matrices have inverses. The following test will help you find out if a 2 × 2 matrix has an inverse. It will also help you find the inverse, if it exists.

The Inverse of a 2 × 2 Matrix

Suppose $A = \begin{bmatrix} a & b \\ c & d \end{bmatrix}$. If $ad - bc \neq 0$, then A has an inverse.

If $ad - bc \neq 0$, then $A^{-1} = \dfrac{1}{ad - bc} \begin{bmatrix} d & -b \\ -c & a \end{bmatrix}$.

Example: $A = \begin{bmatrix} -1 & 0 \\ 8 & -2 \end{bmatrix}$

$ad - bc = (-1)(-2) - (0)(8) = 2$

$A^{-1} = \dfrac{1}{2} \begin{bmatrix} -2 & 0 \\ -8 & -1 \end{bmatrix} = \begin{bmatrix} -1 & 0 \\ -4 & -0.5 \end{bmatrix}$

7. a. Does $B = \begin{bmatrix} 1 & 2 \\ 3 & 4 \end{bmatrix}$ have an inverse? **Justify** your response.

b. Does $C = \begin{bmatrix} 6 & 8 \\ -3 & -4 \end{bmatrix}$ have an inverse? **Justify** your response.

Example 1

Determine whether each matrix has an inverse. If an inverse matrix exists, find it.

a. $M = \begin{bmatrix} -2 & 2 \\ 5 & -4 \end{bmatrix}$ **b.** $N = \begin{bmatrix} 3 & 9 \\ 2 & 6 \end{bmatrix}$

a. $M = \begin{bmatrix} -2 & 2 \\ 5 & -4 \end{bmatrix}$

$ad - bc = (-2)(-4) - (2)(5)$ ←— Calculate $ad - bc$.

$\quad\quad\quad = -2$ ←— Since $ad - bc \neq 0$, the inverse of *M* exists.

$M^{-1} = \dfrac{1}{-2} \begin{bmatrix} -4 & -2 \\ -5 & -2 \end{bmatrix}$

$\quad\quad = \begin{bmatrix} 2 & 1 \\ 2.5 & 1 \end{bmatrix}$

b. $N = \begin{bmatrix} 3 & 9 \\ 2 & 6 \end{bmatrix}$

$ad - bc = (3)(6) - (9)(2)$ ←— Calculate $ad - bc$.

$\quad\quad\quad = 0$

Since $ad - bc = 0$, the inverse of N does not exist.

8. Multiply to **verify** that $\begin{bmatrix} 2 & 1 \\ 2.5 & 1 \end{bmatrix}$ is the inverse of $\begin{bmatrix} -2 & 2 \\ 5 & -4 \end{bmatrix}$.

What? Around the fifth century B.C., the Spartans developed an encoding device. They wrapped a strip of parchment around a stick and wrote across it. The unrolled parchment could not be deciphered unless it was wrapped around another stick with exactly the same dimensions!

Source: *More Joy of Mathematics*

A	1	N	14
B	2	O	15
C	3	P	16
D	4	Q	17
E	5	R	18
F	6	S	19
G	7	T	20
H	8	U	21
I	9	V	22
J	10	W	23
K	11	X	24
L	12	Y	25
M	13	Z	26

9. Try This Determine whether each matrix has an inverse. If an inverse matrix exists, find it.

a. $\begin{bmatrix} 2 & 4 \\ 1 & 3 \end{bmatrix}$
b. $\begin{bmatrix} 0.5 & 2.3 \\ 3 & 7.2 \end{bmatrix}$

You can use any matrix with an inverse to encode a message. Use the inverse matrix to decode it. Using the table at the left, the message **GO TEAM** written as 2×1 matrices becomes the list of numbers below.

$$\begin{matrix} \mathbf{G} \\ \mathbf{O} \end{matrix}\begin{bmatrix} 7 \\ 15 \end{bmatrix} \qquad \begin{matrix} \mathbf{T} \\ \mathbf{E} \end{matrix}\begin{bmatrix} 20 \\ 5 \end{bmatrix} \qquad \begin{matrix} \mathbf{A} \\ \mathbf{M} \end{matrix}\begin{bmatrix} 1 \\ 13 \end{bmatrix}$$

When you use matrix multiplication to apply a matrix such as $E = \begin{bmatrix} 6 & 2 \\ 2 & 1 \end{bmatrix}$ to the list of letters, the message becomes these matrices.

$$\begin{bmatrix} 72 \\ 29 \end{bmatrix} \qquad \begin{bmatrix} 130 \\ 45 \end{bmatrix} \qquad \begin{bmatrix} 32 \\ 15 \end{bmatrix}$$

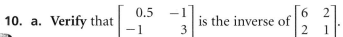

Example 2   **Relating to the Real World**

Cryptography Find the decoding matrix E^{-1}, if it exists.

$$E = \begin{bmatrix} 6 & 2 \\ 2 & 1 \end{bmatrix}$$

$(6)(1) - (2)(2) = 2$ ← Since $ad - bc \neq 0$, E^{-1} exists.

$$E^{-1} = \frac{1}{2}\begin{bmatrix} 1 & -2 \\ -2 & 6 \end{bmatrix} = \begin{bmatrix} 0.5 & -1 \\ -1 & 3 \end{bmatrix}$$

10. a. Verify that $\begin{bmatrix} 0.5 & -1 \\ -1 & 3 \end{bmatrix}$ is the inverse of $\begin{bmatrix} 6 & 2 \\ 2 & 1 \end{bmatrix}$.

b. Use E^{-1} and matrix multiplication to decode.

$$\begin{bmatrix} 124 \\ 43 \end{bmatrix} \qquad \begin{bmatrix} 92 \\ 32 \end{bmatrix} \qquad \begin{bmatrix} 58 \\ 21 \end{bmatrix} \qquad \begin{bmatrix} 104 \\ 40 \end{bmatrix}$$

c. Write the message.

The photographs show different types of decoding machines used around the 1940s.

Using Inverse Matrices to Solve Matrix Equations

You can use inverse matrices to solve matrix equations.

If A, B, and X are matrices such that $AX = B$, and matrix A has an inverse, then you can multiply each side of the equation by A^{-1} to find X.

$$AX = B$$
$$(A^{-1}A)X = A^{-1}B$$
$$(I)X = A^{-1}B$$
$$X = A^{-1}B$$

Example 3

Solve each equation for X.

a. $\begin{bmatrix} 0 & -4 \\ 0 & -1 \end{bmatrix} X = \begin{bmatrix} 0 \\ 4 \end{bmatrix}$

b. $\begin{bmatrix} 0 & 0 & 2 \\ 1 & 3 & -2 \\ 1 & -2 & 1 \end{bmatrix} X = \begin{bmatrix} 6 \\ -11 \\ 8 \end{bmatrix}$

a. $\begin{bmatrix} 0 & -4 \\ 0 & -1 \end{bmatrix} X = \begin{bmatrix} 0 \\ 4 \end{bmatrix}$ ⟵ Let $A = \begin{bmatrix} 0 & -4 \\ 0 & -1 \end{bmatrix}$.

To solve the equation, find the inverse of A.

$ad - bc = (0)(-1) - (-4)(0)$ ⟵ Determine if A^{-1} exists.
$= 0$ ⟵ A^{-1} does not exist.

The matrix A^{-1} does not exist, so the equation cannot be solved.

b. $\begin{bmatrix} 0 & 0 & 2 \\ 1 & 3 & -2 \\ 1 & -2 & 1 \end{bmatrix} X = \begin{bmatrix} 6 \\ -11 \\ 8 \end{bmatrix}$ ⟵ Let $C = \begin{bmatrix} 0 & 0 & 2 \\ 1 & 3 & -2 \\ 1 & -2 & 1 \end{bmatrix}$.

Use a graphing calculator to find the inverse of matrix C.

If it exists, multiply C^{-1} by $\begin{bmatrix} 6 \\ -11 \\ 8 \end{bmatrix}$ (matrix D).

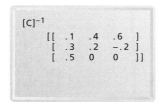

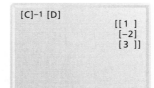

$X = \begin{bmatrix} 1 \\ -2 \\ 3 \end{bmatrix}$

11. Use matrix multiplication to **verify** that C and C^{-1} are inverses.

12. Try This Solve $\begin{bmatrix} 12 & 7 \\ 5 & 3 \end{bmatrix} X = \begin{bmatrix} 2 & -1 \\ 3 & 2 \end{bmatrix}$ for X. Check your work.

Use paper and pencil to find the inverse of each 2×2 matrix, if it exists. If it does not exist, write *no inverse*.

1. $\begin{bmatrix} 2 & -1 \\ 1 & 0 \end{bmatrix}$
2. $\begin{bmatrix} 2 & 3 \\ 1 & 1 \end{bmatrix}$
3. $\begin{bmatrix} 2 & 3 \\ 2 & 4 \end{bmatrix}$
4. $\begin{bmatrix} 1 & 3 \\ 2 & 0 \end{bmatrix}$

5. $\begin{bmatrix} 6 & -8 \\ -3 & 4 \end{bmatrix}$
6. $\begin{bmatrix} 4 & 8 \\ -3 & -2 \end{bmatrix}$
7. $\begin{bmatrix} -1.5 & 3 \\ 2.5 & -0.5 \end{bmatrix}$
8. $\begin{bmatrix} 1 & -2 \\ 3 & 0 \end{bmatrix}$

9. $\begin{bmatrix} 2 & 6 \\ 7 & 1 \end{bmatrix}$
10. $\begin{bmatrix} -4 & 2 \\ -6 & 3 \end{bmatrix}$
11. $\begin{bmatrix} -6 & 3 \\ 9 & -2 \end{bmatrix}$
12. $\begin{bmatrix} 13 & -3 \\ 17 & 3 \end{bmatrix}$

Solve each matrix equation for X.

13. $\begin{bmatrix} 5 & -3 \\ 4 & -2 \end{bmatrix} X = \begin{bmatrix} 5 \\ 10 \end{bmatrix}$

14. $\begin{bmatrix} 1 & 0 \\ 0 & 1 \end{bmatrix} X = \begin{bmatrix} -13 \\ 17 \end{bmatrix}$

15. $\begin{bmatrix} 7 & -5 \\ 6 & 5 \end{bmatrix} X = \begin{bmatrix} 61 \\ -22 \end{bmatrix}$

16. $\begin{bmatrix} \frac{1}{2} & \frac{1}{3} \\ \frac{1}{4} & \frac{1}{3} \end{bmatrix} X = \begin{bmatrix} 20 \\ 18 \end{bmatrix}$

17. $\begin{bmatrix} 4 & 7 \\ 1 & 2 \end{bmatrix} X + \begin{bmatrix} 2 & 7 \\ -3 & 4 \end{bmatrix} = \begin{bmatrix} 6 & 2 \\ -2 & 3 \end{bmatrix}$

18. $\begin{bmatrix} 1 & 9 \\ 6 & -6 \end{bmatrix} = \begin{bmatrix} -7 & -9 \\ 4 & 5 \end{bmatrix} X + \begin{bmatrix} 3 & 4 \\ 4 & -3 \end{bmatrix}$

Cryptography Refer to the alphabet table. **(a)** Find the decoding matrix E^{-1}. **(b)** Decode each encoded message.

19. $E = \begin{bmatrix} 24 & 23 \\ 26 & 25 \end{bmatrix}; \begin{bmatrix} 814 \\ 884 \end{bmatrix} \begin{bmatrix} 777 \\ 843 \end{bmatrix} \begin{bmatrix} 492 \\ 534 \end{bmatrix} \begin{bmatrix} 1153 \\ 1251 \end{bmatrix}$
$\begin{bmatrix} 783 \\ 849 \end{bmatrix} \begin{bmatrix} 472 \\ 512 \end{bmatrix} \begin{bmatrix} 606 \\ 658 \end{bmatrix} \begin{bmatrix} 772 \\ 838 \end{bmatrix}$

20. $E = \begin{bmatrix} -4 & -3 \\ 3 & 2 \end{bmatrix}; \begin{bmatrix} -134 \\ 94 \end{bmatrix} \begin{bmatrix} -85 \\ 59 \end{bmatrix} \begin{bmatrix} -96 \\ 70 \end{bmatrix} \begin{bmatrix} -132 \\ 96 \end{bmatrix} \begin{bmatrix} -93 \\ 66 \end{bmatrix}$

21. $E = \begin{bmatrix} 3 & 3 \\ 3 & 4 \end{bmatrix}; \begin{bmatrix} 93 \\ 115 \end{bmatrix} \begin{bmatrix} 87 \\ 93 \end{bmatrix} \begin{bmatrix} 138 \\ 160 \end{bmatrix} \begin{bmatrix} 57 \\ 68 \end{bmatrix} \begin{bmatrix} 132 \\ 154 \end{bmatrix} \begin{bmatrix} 108 \\ 121 \end{bmatrix} \begin{bmatrix} 48 \\ 52 \end{bmatrix}$

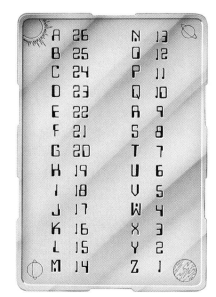

22. Graphing Calculator Kate and Fred, members of the Hopewell High School math club, have decided to share messages in code. They use the alphabet table at the right.
   a. Kate has lost her encoding matrix. Luckily, she remembers that the decoding matrix is
   $$E^{-1} = \begin{bmatrix} 1 & -1 & 0 \\ 0 & 1 & -1 \\ 0 & 0 & 1 \end{bmatrix}.$$ Compute E to find the encoding matrix.
   b. Use your answer to part (a) to encode the message **HI FRED**.

23. Critical Thinking Which of the following matrices could be used to encode messages? **Justify** your reasoning.

a. $\begin{bmatrix} -4 & 6 \\ 2 & -3 \end{bmatrix}$
b. $\begin{bmatrix} 0 & 2 \\ -3 & 1 \end{bmatrix}$
c. $\begin{bmatrix} 1 & 0 \\ 0 & 1 \end{bmatrix}$
d. $\begin{bmatrix} 0 & 1 \\ 1 & 0 \end{bmatrix}$

Graphing Calculator Verify that each matrix has no inverse.

24. $\begin{bmatrix} 1 & 0 & 1 \\ 0 & 1 & 0 \\ 1 & 0 & 1 \end{bmatrix}$
25. $\begin{bmatrix} 0 & 1 & 0 \\ 1 & 0 & 1 \\ 0 & 1 & 0 \end{bmatrix}$
26. $\begin{bmatrix} 0 & 1 & 0 \\ 0 & 1 & 0 \\ 1 & 1 & 1 \end{bmatrix}$

Graphing Calculator Find the inverse of each 3 × 3 matrix, if it exists. If it does not exist, write *no inverse*.

27. $\begin{bmatrix} 0 & -1 & 2 \\ 1 & 1 & -1 \\ 2 & 0 & 3 \end{bmatrix}$
28. $\begin{bmatrix} -2 & 1 & -1 \\ 2 & 0 & 4 \\ 0 & 2 & 5 \end{bmatrix}$
29. $\begin{bmatrix} 2 & 0 & -1 \\ -1 & -1 & 1 \\ 3 & 2 & 0 \end{bmatrix}$

30. $\begin{bmatrix} 0 & 0 & 2 \\ 1 & 4 & -2 \\ 3 & -2 & 1 \end{bmatrix}$
31. $\begin{bmatrix} 1 & 2 & 6 \\ 1 & -1 & 0 \\ 1 & 0 & 2 \end{bmatrix}$
32. $\begin{bmatrix} -17 & 1 & 13 \\ 5 & -3 & 0 \\ 9 & 1 & 0.5 \end{bmatrix}$

Graphing Calculator Solve each matrix equation for *X*.

33. $\begin{bmatrix} 1 & 1 & 1 \\ 1 & -4 & 3 \\ 1 & 6 & 2 \end{bmatrix} X = \begin{bmatrix} 16 \\ 42 \\ 14 \end{bmatrix}$
34. $\begin{bmatrix} 5 & 1 & -4 \\ 2 & -3 & -5 \\ 7 & 2 & -6 \end{bmatrix} X = \begin{bmatrix} 5 \\ 2 \\ 5 \end{bmatrix}$

35. $\begin{bmatrix} 6 & 10 & -13 \\ 4 & -2 & 7 \\ 0 & 9 & -8 \end{bmatrix} X = \begin{bmatrix} 84 \\ 18 \\ 56 \end{bmatrix}$
36. $\begin{bmatrix} 13.2 & 14 & 21 \\ 7 & -1 & -3 \\ 45.5 & 8 & -9 \end{bmatrix} X = \begin{bmatrix} 1 \\ 1 \\ 1 \end{bmatrix}$

37. Coordinate Geometry Use the diagram at the right and the matrix $T = \begin{bmatrix} 1 & -1 \\ -1 & 2 \end{bmatrix}$.

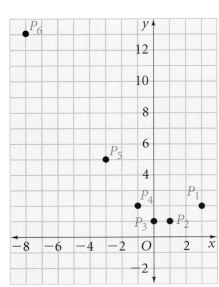

a. Find the product $\begin{bmatrix} 1 & -1 \\ -1 & 2 \end{bmatrix}\begin{bmatrix} 0 \\ 1 \end{bmatrix}$. The coordinates of what point are represented by this product matrix?

b. Find the product $\begin{bmatrix} 1 & -1 \\ -1 & 2 \end{bmatrix}\begin{bmatrix} -1 \\ 2 \end{bmatrix}$. The coordinates of what point are represented by this product matrix?

c. Find T^{-1}.

d. Multiply the matrix for T^{-1} by $\begin{bmatrix} 1 \\ 1 \end{bmatrix}$. The coordinates of what point are represented by this product matrix?

38. Writing Suppose $A = \begin{bmatrix} a & b \\ c & d \end{bmatrix}$ has an inverse. In your own words, describe how to switch or change the elements of *A* to write A^{-1}.

39. a. Open-ended Make an alphabet table (different from the ones in the text) in which each letter is assigned a unique integer from 1 to 26.

   b. Create a 2 × 2 or 3 × 3 encoding matrix. Calculate its inverse.

   c. Make and encode messages of your own. Give your message and your decoding matrix to a friend to decode.

   d. Writing Describe to a friend unfamiliar with codes how to decode the messages.

40. Standardized Test Prep Given that $a > 1$, which of the following matrices will *not* have an inverse?

   A. $\begin{bmatrix} a + 1 & a \\ a & a - 1 \end{bmatrix}$ **B.** $\begin{bmatrix} a + 1 & a + 1 \\ a - 1 & a - 1 \end{bmatrix}$ **C.** $\begin{bmatrix} a + 1 & a \\ a & a + 1 \end{bmatrix}$

   D. $\begin{bmatrix} a + 1 & a - 1 \\ a - 1 & a + 1 \end{bmatrix}$ **E.** $\begin{bmatrix} a - 1 & a \\ a & a - 1 \end{bmatrix}$

41. Critical Thinking For what values of a, b, c, and d will $A = \begin{bmatrix} a & b \\ c & d \end{bmatrix}$ be its own inverse?

Chapter Project    **Find Out by Researching**

Research a hazardous waste clean-up that includes bioremediation. How large is the site? What treatment methods other than bioremediation are being used, if any? Write a few paragraphs summarizing your research. Include data from the site, if possible.

Exercises   **MIXED REVIEW**

Suppose a number is selected at random from the sample space {1, 3, 5, 7, 9}. Find each probability.

42. P(the number is prime)

43. P(the number is greater than 3)

44. Probability How many different 3-person committees can be chosen from a 16-student board?

45. Cryptography Use the encoding matrix and the method on page 137 to encode the message below. Use the inverse matrix to check your work.

"A mind is a terrible thing to waste."

Munching Microbes

Find Out questions on pages 106, 113, and 141 should help you complete your project. You should prepare a presentation for the class describing some aspect of a bioremediation project. Your presentation could be a graph or chart analyzing bioremediation data or a poster advertising a bioremediation project.

Reflect and Revise

Ask a classmate to review your project with you. After you have seen each other's presentations, decide if your work is complete, clear, and convincing. Make sure that you have included all supporting material from your work on the project. Check that the information you have presented is accurate. You may want to make some changes based on your meeting.

Follow Up

Bioremediation is a fairly new field. You can do more research into the field by contacting the United States Department of the Interior. You can also get more information by using the Internet or from one of the resources listed below.

For More Information

U.S. Environmental Protection Agency. *Bioremediation Case Study Collection: 1991 Augmentation of the Alternative Treatment Technology Information Center (ATTIC).* Washington, D.C.: Office of Research and Development, 1993.

The Toxic Substances Hydrology Program
U.S. Geological Survey, 412 National Center, Reston, Virginia 22092.

Key Terms

adjacent (p. 128)
arcs (p. 128)
dilation (p. 124)
directed graphs (p. 129)
edges (p. 128)
equal matrices (p. 104)
finite graph (p. 128)
identity matrix (p. 135)
image (p. 123)

inverse matrix (p. 135)
matrix addition (p. 108)
matrix equation (p. 110)
matrix multiplication (p. 115)
preimage (p. 123)
scalar (p. 114)
square matrix (p. 143)
transformation (p. 123)
vertices (p. 128)

How am I doing?

- State three ideas from this chapter that you think are important. Explain your choices.
- Explain how you can do different matrix operations.

SELF ASSESSMENT

Organizing Data Into Matrices   3-1

You can organize data from graphs and tables in matrices. A matrix element is identified by its position, row number first and then column number.

Two matrices are **equal** if and only if they have the same dimensions and their corresponding elements are equal.

State the dimensions of each matrix. Identify the indicated element.

1. $\begin{bmatrix} 5 & 8 & -7 \\ 1 & 11 & 3 \end{bmatrix}$; a_{13}

2. $\begin{bmatrix} 3 & 1 \\ -5 & 0 \\ 7 & 6 \end{bmatrix}$; a_{21}

3. $\begin{bmatrix} 5 & 1 & -2 \\ 4 & -7 & 12 \\ 0 & 78 & 3 \end{bmatrix}$; a_{23}

4. $\begin{bmatrix} 54 & -27 \\ 91 & 134 \end{bmatrix}$; a_{11}

Solve each equation for each variable.

5. $\begin{bmatrix} x-5 & 9 \\ 4 & t+2 \end{bmatrix} = \begin{bmatrix} -7 & w+1 \\ 8-r & 1 \end{bmatrix}$

6. $\begin{bmatrix} -4+t & 2y \\ r & w+4 \end{bmatrix} = \begin{bmatrix} 2t & 3y-11 \\ -2r+12 & 9 \end{bmatrix}$

Adding and Subtracting Matrices   3-2

You perform **matrix addition** or subtraction by adding or subtracting corresponding elements. A **matrix equation** is an equation in which the variable is a matrix. You can use addition and subtraction properties of equality to solve matrix equations.

Solve each matrix equation for matrix X.

7. $\begin{bmatrix} 7 & -1 \\ 0 & 8 \end{bmatrix} + X = \begin{bmatrix} 4 & 9 \\ -3 & 11 \end{bmatrix}$

8. $\begin{bmatrix} 21 & 50 \\ -31 & 26 \end{bmatrix} - X = \begin{bmatrix} 71 & -21 \\ -38 & 10 \end{bmatrix}$

9. $X - \begin{bmatrix} -7 & 13 & 5 \\ 31 & 0 & -4 \end{bmatrix} = \begin{bmatrix} 9 & -5 & 8 \\ 2 & 0 & -3 \end{bmatrix}$

10. $X + \begin{bmatrix} 0.3 & 5.1 \\ -2.7 & 6.4 \end{bmatrix} = \begin{bmatrix} -8.5 & 1.6 \\ 4.3 & -9.2 \end{bmatrix}$

Matrix Multiplication

You perform **scalar** multiplication by multiplying every element in the matrix by the same number.

You can do **matrix multiplication** on matrices A and B when the number of columns in the first matrix equals the number of rows in the second matrix. Multiply the elements of each row of the first matrix by the elements of each column of the second matrix. Add the products. The result is an element of the product matrix.

Find each product.

11. $5\begin{bmatrix} 6 & 1 & 0 & 8 \\ -4 & 3 & 7 & 11 \end{bmatrix}$

12. $\begin{bmatrix} 5 & 1 \\ 9 & 4 \end{bmatrix}\begin{bmatrix} 0 & 3 \\ -5 & 1 \end{bmatrix}$

13. $\begin{bmatrix} 3 & -1 & 5 \\ -4 & 0 & 2 \end{bmatrix}\begin{bmatrix} 5 & 2 \\ -1 & 7 \\ -8 & 0 \end{bmatrix}$

14. Standardized Test Prep For which pair(s) of matrices can you find the product AB?

I. $A = \begin{bmatrix} 1.2 & 4.7 \\ -5.9 & 9.3 \end{bmatrix}$; $B = \begin{bmatrix} -7.1 \\ 6.8 \end{bmatrix}$

II. $A = \begin{bmatrix} -23 & 56 \\ 1 & 17 \end{bmatrix}$; $B = \begin{bmatrix} 8 & 41 \\ 39 & -72 \end{bmatrix}$

III. $A = \begin{bmatrix} 2 \\ -5 \\ 3 \end{bmatrix}$; $B = \begin{bmatrix} 6 & -7 & 1 & -1 \\ 0 & 5 & 18 & 2 \end{bmatrix}$

IV. $A = \begin{bmatrix} 5 & 6 \\ -9 & 18 \\ 3 & 21 \end{bmatrix}$; $B = \begin{bmatrix} 4 & -5 & 1 \\ 0 & 7 & 11 \end{bmatrix}$

A. I only   **B.** II only   **C.** I and IV only   **D.** II and III   **E.** I, II, and IV

Geometric Transformations with Matrices

A **transformation** is a change made to a figure. The original figure is the **preimage** and the transformed figure is the **image.** A translation shifts a graph without changing its size or shape. A **dilation** changes the size of a figure. You can use matrix addition to translate a figure and scalar multiplication to dilate a figure.

Write the vertices of each figure in matrix form.

15. $K(1, 0), L(8, -1), M(5, 3), N(2, 7), O(0, 1)$

16. $W(-2, -3), X(-4, 0), Y(-3, 8), Z(0, 7)$

Find the image of $\triangle ABC$ with vertices $A(3, 1)$, $B(-2, 0)$, and $C(1, 5)$ under each transformation.

17. translation left 5, up 2

18. dilation of size 5

19. translation right 2, down 4

Networks

A **finite graph** is a set of **vertices** connected by paths. **Directed graphs** indicate the direction of a path. You can use the information from a directed graph or a finite graph to write a matrix, or use a matrix to draw a directed graph.

For each finite graph, or directed graph, write a matrix.

20.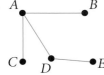

21.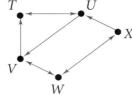

22.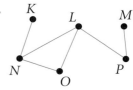

Draw a directed graph to represent each matrix.

23.
$$\begin{array}{c}\ A\ \ B\ \ C \\ \begin{array}{c}A\\B\\C\end{array}\begin{bmatrix}1 & 0 & 1\\1 & 1 & 0\\1 & 1 & 0\end{bmatrix}\end{array}$$

24.
$$\begin{array}{c}\ K\ \ L\ \ M \\ \begin{array}{c}K\\L\\M\end{array}\begin{bmatrix}0 & 0 & 1\\0 & 1 & 1\\1 & 0 & 0\end{bmatrix}\end{array}$$

25.
$$\begin{array}{c}\ P\ \ Q\ \ R \\ \begin{array}{c}P\\Q\\R\end{array}\begin{bmatrix}1 & 0 & 0\\0 & 0 & 1\\1 & 1 & 1\end{bmatrix}\end{array}$$

Identity and Inverse Matrices   3-6

A **square matrix** is a matrix with the same number of columns as rows. The square $n \times n$ matrix with 1's along its main diagonal and 0's elsewhere is the **identity matrix** for multiplication, I. If A is a square matrix and X is another square matrix such that $AX = I$, then X is the **inverse** of A, A^{-1}.

$$I_{2\times 2} = \begin{bmatrix}1 & 0\\0 & 1\end{bmatrix}$$

If $A = \begin{bmatrix}a & b\\c & d\end{bmatrix}$ and $ad - bc \neq 0$, then $A^{-1} = \dfrac{1}{ad - bc}\begin{bmatrix}d & -b\\-c & a\end{bmatrix}$.

$$I_{3\times 3} = \begin{bmatrix}1 & 0 & 0\\0 & 1 & 0\\0 & 0 & 1\end{bmatrix}$$

Find the inverse of each matrix. If it does not exist, write *no inverse*.

26. $\begin{bmatrix}6 & 1\\0 & 4\end{bmatrix}$

27. $\begin{bmatrix}5 & -2\\10 & -4\end{bmatrix}$

28. $\begin{bmatrix}10 & 1\\8 & 5\end{bmatrix}$

29. $\begin{bmatrix}1 & 0 & 2\\-1 & 0 & 1\\-1 & -2 & 0\end{bmatrix}$

Use inverses to solve each equation.

30. $\begin{bmatrix}3 & 5\\6 & 2\end{bmatrix}X = \begin{bmatrix}-2 & 6\\4 & 12\end{bmatrix}$

31. $\begin{bmatrix}-6 & 0\\7 & 1\end{bmatrix}X = \begin{bmatrix}-12 & -6\\17 & 9\end{bmatrix}$

32. $\begin{bmatrix}5 & -1\\1 & -4\end{bmatrix}X = \begin{bmatrix}13 & -3\\-16 & 7\end{bmatrix}$

33. a. *Open-ended* Write a 2 × 2 matrix and its inverse.
   b. Use your matrix and the alphabet table on p. 139 to encode the message YOU DON'T HAVE TO USE A CALCULATOR. (*Hint:* Use a zero as the final matrix element.)

Getting Ready for..▶ CHAPTER

4

Graph each inequality.

34. $y \leq 2x + 1$ **35.** $y > |x + 4|$ **36.** $y < x - 4$ **37.** $y \geq |3x| - 2$

Graph each pair of linear equations on the same set of axes.

38. $y = -x + 2$; $y = x - 4$ **39.** $y = x + 4$; $y = -3x + 2$ **40.** $y = \frac{1}{2}x - 5$; $y = x + 1$

1. **History** The table shows the years of each presidency, the number of presidential vetoes, and the number of Congressional overrides.

President	Years	Vetoes	Overrides
Kennedy	3	21	9
Johnson	5	30	0
Nixon	5.5	43	7
Ford	2.5	66	12
Carter	4	31	2
Reagan	8	78	9
Bush	4	46	1

Source: *USA Today*

  a. Display the data in a matrix whose rows indicate the data for each President. State the dimensions of the matrix.
  b. Find and identify a_{32}.

2. **Standardized Test Prep** Which matrices are equal to $\begin{bmatrix} 3 & -7 & 1.2 \\ 4 & 0 & -2 \end{bmatrix}$?

  I. $\begin{bmatrix} \frac{6}{2} & -7 & \frac{6}{5} \\ 2^2 & 0 & \frac{-4}{2} \end{bmatrix}$

  II. $\begin{bmatrix} 2+1 & -4-3 & 2-0.8 \\ 7-3 & 4-4 & 1-3 \end{bmatrix}$

  III. $\begin{bmatrix} \sqrt{9} & -(6+1) & 8^0+0.2 \\ \sqrt{16} & 3^2-9 & -\sqrt{4} \end{bmatrix}$

  A. I only **B.** I and II only **C.** I and III only
  D. II and III only **E.** I, II, and III

Find each sum or difference.

3. $\begin{bmatrix} 4 & 7 \\ -2 & 1 \end{bmatrix} - \begin{bmatrix} -9 & 3 \\ 6 & 0 \end{bmatrix}$

4. $\begin{bmatrix} 4 & -5 & 1 \\ 10 & 7 & 4 \\ 21 & -9 & -6 \end{bmatrix} + \begin{bmatrix} -7 & -10 & 4 \\ 17 & 0 & 3 \\ -2 & -6 & 1 \end{bmatrix}$

5. $\begin{bmatrix} 0.3 & 5.1 \\ -6.3 & 1.9 \end{bmatrix} - \begin{bmatrix} 7.2 & -9.8 \\ 2.6 & -3.1 \end{bmatrix}$

6. **Writing** Explain how to determine if two matrices can be multiplied and what the size of the product matrix will be.

7. **Open-ended** Write a matrix that has no inverse.

Find each product.

8. $\begin{bmatrix} 2 & 6 \\ 1 & 0 \end{bmatrix} \begin{bmatrix} -1 & 5 \\ 3 & 1 \end{bmatrix}$

9. $-2 \begin{bmatrix} -8 & 5 & -1 \\ 0 & 9 & 7 \end{bmatrix}$

10. $\begin{bmatrix} 0 & 3 \\ -4 & 9 \end{bmatrix} \begin{bmatrix} -4 & 6 & 1 & 3 \\ 9 & -8 & 10 & 7 \end{bmatrix}$

$\triangle ABC$ **has vertices** $A(2, -1)$, $B(4, 3)$, **and** $C(1, 5)$. **Find its image after each transformation.**

11. a translation right 2 units and down 4 units

12. a dilation three times the original size

13. a translation left 5 units and up 3 units

Find the inverse of each matrix if it exists.

14. $\begin{bmatrix} 3 & 8 \\ -7 & 10 \end{bmatrix}$

15. $\begin{bmatrix} 0 & -5 \\ 9 & 6 \end{bmatrix}$

16. $\begin{bmatrix} -8 & 4 & -11 \\ 5 & 2 & 9 \\ -5 & 6 & 2 \end{bmatrix}$

17. $\begin{bmatrix} 4 & 1 & -2 \\ 8 & 11 & 3 \\ -7 & 10 & -1 \end{bmatrix}$

Solve each matrix equation.

18. $\begin{bmatrix} 3 & -8 \\ 10 & 5 \end{bmatrix} - X = \begin{bmatrix} 2 & 8 \\ -1 & 12 \end{bmatrix}$

19. $X + \begin{bmatrix} 2 & 5 & -11 \\ 6 & -4 & 13 \end{bmatrix} = \begin{bmatrix} -6 & 9 & 21 \\ -9 & -5 & 3 \end{bmatrix}$

20. $\begin{bmatrix} 3 & 2 \\ -1 & 5 \end{bmatrix} X = \begin{bmatrix} -10 & -11 \\ 26 & -36 \end{bmatrix}$

For each directed graph, write a matrix A.

21.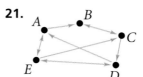

22.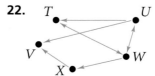

For Exercises 1–9, choose the correct letter.

1. Find the product $\begin{bmatrix} 3 & 1 \\ -4 & 0 \end{bmatrix}\begin{bmatrix} -2 & 5 \\ 1 & 6 \end{bmatrix}$.

   A. $\begin{bmatrix} -26 & -2 \\ -21 & 1 \end{bmatrix}$ B. $\begin{bmatrix} -1 & 9 \\ 8 & -4 \end{bmatrix}$ C. $\begin{bmatrix} 1 & 6 \\ -3 & 6 \end{bmatrix}$

   D. $\begin{bmatrix} -5 & 21 \\ 8 & -20 \end{bmatrix}$ E. none of the above

2. Which equation could represent the linear relationship of data having a negative correlation?
   A. $y = 3x + 1$ B. $2x + y = 4$
   C. $x - y = -8$ D. $y = x - 5$
   E. none of the above

3. Which equation has the solution $\begin{bmatrix} 1 & -2 & 0 \\ -5 & 4 & 7 \end{bmatrix}$?

   A. $X - \begin{bmatrix} 3 & 7 & 4 \\ 8 & -6 & 1 \end{bmatrix} = \begin{bmatrix} 2 & -5 & 4 \\ -3 & 2 & 6 \end{bmatrix}$

   B. $\begin{bmatrix} 0 & -6 & 5 \\ 2 & -1 & 9 \end{bmatrix} + X = \begin{bmatrix} 1 & 4 & 5 \\ -3 & 3 & -2 \end{bmatrix}$

   C. $\begin{bmatrix} 10 & -8 & 12 \\ 4 & 0 & 5 \end{bmatrix} - \begin{bmatrix} -9 & -6 & 12 \\ -1 & -4 & -2 \end{bmatrix} = X$

   D. $\begin{bmatrix} 7 & -2 & -3 \\ 0 & 1 & 8 \end{bmatrix} - X = \begin{bmatrix} 8 & -4 & -3 \\ -5 & 5 & 15 \end{bmatrix}$

   E. none of the above

4. Which outcome has the greatest probability for one roll of a number cube?
   A. an even number B. a factor of 6
   C. a prime number D. a rational number
   E. a negative number

5. Which matrix would represent $\begin{bmatrix} -1 & 4 & 5 \\ 0 & 7 & 2 \end{bmatrix}$ after a translation 7 units left and 2 units up?

   A. $\begin{bmatrix} 6 & 11 & 12 \\ 2 & 9 & 4 \end{bmatrix}$ B. $\begin{bmatrix} 6 & 11 & 12 \\ -2 & 5 & 0 \end{bmatrix}$

   C. $\begin{bmatrix} -8 & -3 & -2 \\ -2 & 5 & 0 \end{bmatrix}$ D. $\begin{bmatrix} 1 & 6 & 7 \\ -7 & 0 & -5 \end{bmatrix}$

   E. $\begin{bmatrix} -8 & -3 & -2 \\ 2 & 9 & 4 \end{bmatrix}$

6. Which inequality does *not* include $(-3, 2)$ as a solution?
   A. $y \le 4x + 7$ B. $y \ge |x| - 1$
   C. $y < -2x - 3$ D. $y \le |2x + 1|$
   E. $y > x + 2$

7. For $f(x) = 4x - 3$ and $g(x) = |2x| + 3$, which has the greatest value?
   A. $f(g(2))$ B. $f(4)$ C. $g(f(3))$
   D. $g(4)$ E. $f(g(-5))$

Compare the boxed quantity in Column A with that in Column B. Choose the best answer.

A. The quantity in Column A is greater.
B. The quantity in Column B is greater.
C. The two quantities are equal.
D. The relationship cannot be determined on the basis of the information supplied.

Column A	Column B

$$A = \begin{bmatrix} 4 & 1 & 9 \\ -5 & 3 & 2 \\ 7 & -4 & 1 \end{bmatrix}$$

8. a_{13} a_{31}

9. the slope of $y = 2x - 7$ the y-intercept of $y = -x + 2$

Find each answer.

10. Draw a directed graph to represent the information in the matrix.

$$\begin{array}{c} \\ A \\ B \\ C \\ D \end{array} \begin{array}{c} A\ \ B\ \ C\ \ D \\ \begin{bmatrix} 0 & 1 & 1 & 0 \\ 1 & 1 & 1 & 0 \\ 0 & 1 & 0 & 0 \\ 1 & 0 & 0 & 1 \end{bmatrix} \end{array}$$

11. **Open-ended** Write the equations of a line parallel to and a line perpendicular to $y = 2x - 5$.

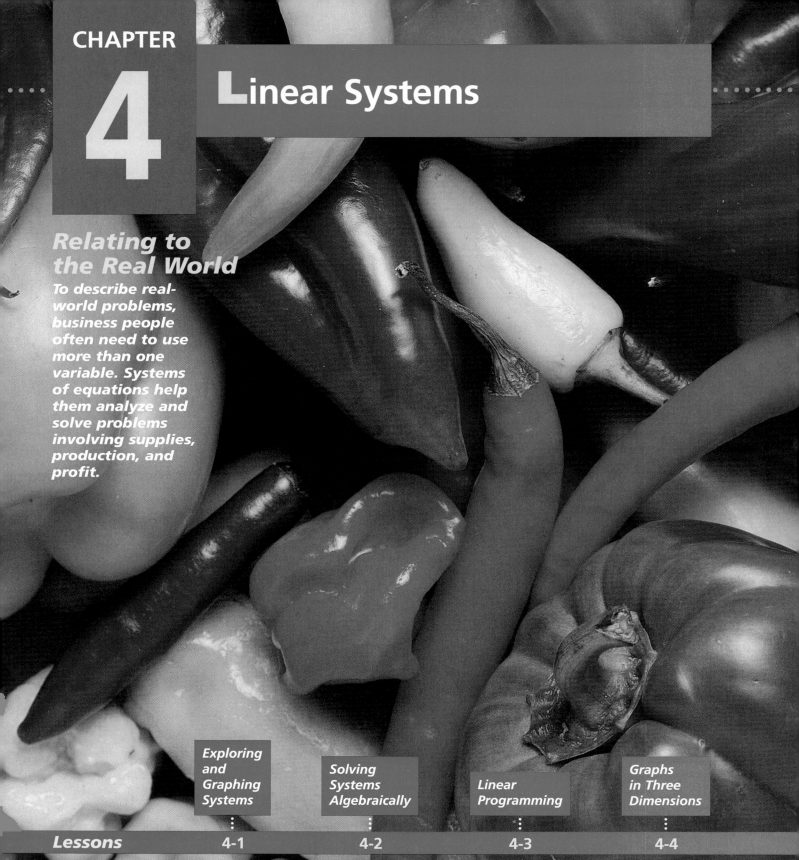

CHAPTER

4

Linear Systems

Relating to the Real World

To describe real-world problems, business people often need to use more than one variable. Systems of equations help them analyze and solve problems involving supplies, production, and profit.

Exploring and Graphing Systems	Solving Systems Algebraically	Linear Programming	Graphs in Three Dimensions

Lessons	4-1	4-2	4-3	4-4

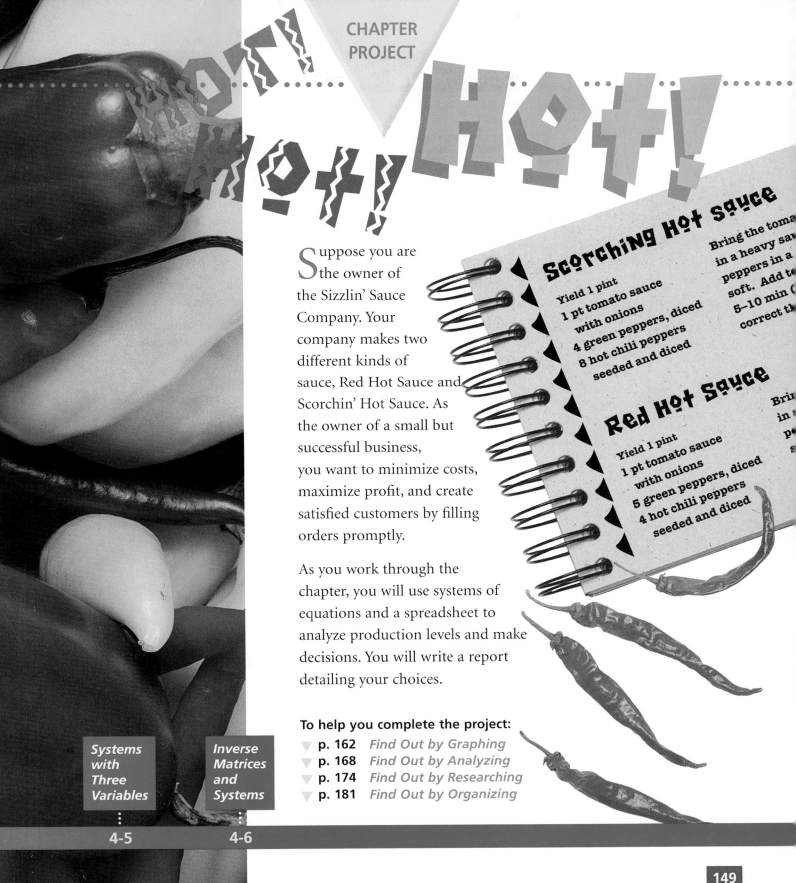

HOT! HOT! HOT! HOT!

Suppose you are the owner of the Sizzlin' Sauce Company. Your company makes two different kinds of sauce, Red Hot Sauce and Scorchin' Hot Sauce. As the owner of a small but successful business, you want to minimize costs, maximize profit, and create satisfied customers by filling orders promptly.

As you work through the chapter, you will use systems of equations and a spreadsheet to analyze production levels and make decisions. You will write a report detailing your choices.

Scorching Hot Sauce

Yield 1 pint
1 pt tomato sauce with onions
4 green peppers, diced
8 hot chili peppers seeded and diced

Bring the toma in a heavy sa peppers in a soft. Add t 5–10 min (correct th

Red Hot Sauce

Yield 1 pint
1 pt tomato sauce with onions
5 green peppers, diced
4 hot chili peppers seeded and diced

Brin in t pe s

To help you complete the project:

Systems with Three Variables

Inverse Matrices and Systems

4-5

4-6

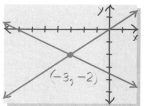

What You'll Learn

- Solving a system by graphing
- Graphing systems of inequalities

...And Why

To use linear systems to analyze sports trends and to make business decisions

What You'll Need

- graphing calculator

QUICK REVIEW

A line whose equation is $y = mx + b$ has slope m and y-intercept b.

4-1 Exploring and Graphing Systems

THINK AND DISCUSS

Systems of Equations

A **system of equations** is a set of two or more equations using the same variables. In a **linear system,** the graph of each equation is a line.

Brackets are sometimes used to keep the equations of a system together. $\longrightarrow$ $\begin{cases} y = x + 3 \\ y = -2x + 3 \end{cases}$

1. Examine the slopes and y-intercepts of the linear equations in the system above. Will the graphs of these equations intersect? If so, where?

A **solution of a system of equations** is a set of values for the variables that makes each equation true. Graphically, each point of intersection represents a solution.

With some systems, you must first write the equations in a form that makes graphing them easier.

Example 1

Solve the system $\begin{cases} x + 2y = -7 \\ 2x - 3y = 0 \end{cases}$ by graphing.

First, solve each equation for y.

$$x + 2y = -7 \qquad\qquad 2x - 3y = 0$$
$$2y = -x - 7 \qquad\qquad -3y = -2x$$
$$y = -\tfrac{1}{2}x - \tfrac{7}{2} \qquad\qquad y = \tfrac{2}{3}x$$

Graph the equations and find the intersection.

$(-3, -2)$

The solution is $(-3, -2)$.

PROBLEM SOLVING

Look Back Explain how to graph the system of equations using a graphing calculator.

---

2. **Verify** that $(-3, -2)$ is the solution by showing that the values $x = -3$ and $y = -2$ make each equation in the original system true.

3. **Try This** Solve the system $\begin{cases} 4x - y = 6 \\ 5x - 3y = 4 \end{cases}$ by graphing.

Example 2 **Relating to the Real World**

Sports Some sportswriters think women's track records may surpass men's in the near future. Use the data in the table to find linear models for men's and women's times for the Olympic 100-m dash. Predict when women's Olympic winning times might be faster than men's.

Winning Times in the Olympic 100-M Dash

Years Since 1960	Men's Time (sec)	Women's Time (sec)
0	10.2	11
4	10	11.4
8	9.9	11
12	10.14	11.07
16	10.06	11.08
20	10.25	11.06
24	9.99	10.97
28	9.92	10.54
32	9.96	10.82

Let x represent the number of years since 1960. Let y represent the winning time in seconds. Use the LinReg feature of a graphing calculator to find linear models for the times.

Men's time: $y = -0.0038x + 10.1073$
Women's time: $y = -0.0140x + 11.2180$

Graph each model. Use the intersect feature from the CALC menu. The two lines meet at about (108.9, 9.7).

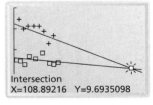

Intersection
X=108.89216 Y=9.6935098

The models predict that the times for women and men will be equal in about 109 years from 1960, in 2069. If the trends in the data continue, women may run faster than men by the 2072 Olympics.

4. Use the models in Example 2 to predict the winning times for the Olympics in 2004; in 2024.

QUICK REVIEW

Interpolation uses a model to make predictions within the range of given data; *extrapolation* predicts results outside that range.

5. **a.** Do the models in Example 2 appear to be good fits? Explain.
   b. Are the models being used to interpolate or to extrapolate?
   c. What running times do the models predict for the year 2100?
   d. *Critical Thinking* Do you think these models are good for extrapolation? Explain.

6. Try This Solve each system by graphing. **Verify** your solutions by showing that each equation is true.

a. $\begin{cases} y = 2x + 3 \\ y = -x + 9 \end{cases}$ **b.** $\begin{cases} y = -4x \\ 3x - 2y = 11 \end{cases}$ **c.** $\begin{cases} 3x + 2y = -6 \\ x - y = -2 \end{cases}$

Systems of Inequalities

QUICK REVIEW

Use a dashed boundary with $>$ and $<$. Use a solid boundary with $\leq$ and $\geq$. To decide which side of the boundary to shade, use a test point or solve the inequality for y.

Just as you have systems of equations, you can have systems of inequalities.

$y < 4$ $y \geq |x - 3|$ $\begin{cases} y \geq |x - 3| \\ y < 4 \end{cases}$

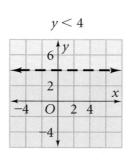 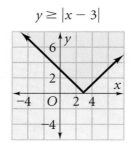 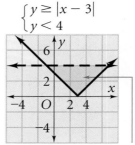

Solutions are found in the overlapping region.

7. a. Verify that $(3, 2)$ is a solution of the system. (Show that each inequality is true for the given values of x and y.)
  b. Is $(3, 4)$ a solution to the system? Explain.

Example 3

QUICK REVIEW

When you multiply or divide each side of an inequality by the same negative number, reverse the direction of the inequality symbol.

Graph the following system of inequalities. $\begin{cases} x - 2y < 2 \\ y \leq \frac{1}{2}x - 2 \end{cases}$

$x - 2y < 2$ ⟵ Solve the first inequality for y.
$\quad -2y < -x + 2$
$\qquad y > \frac{1}{2}x - 1$ ⟵ Reverse the direction of the inequality symbol.

$y > \frac{1}{2}x - 1$
Use a dashed boundary.
Shade above.
slope $= \frac{1}{2}$
y-intercept $= -1$

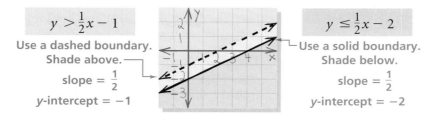

$y \leq \frac{1}{2}x - 2$
Use a solid boundary.
Shade below.
slope $= \frac{1}{2}$
y-intercept $= -2$

Since the shaded regions do not overlap, the system has no solution. ∎

For more practice with graphing inequalities, see Skills Handbook page 671.

8. Try This Graph each system of inequalities. Indicate any region containing solutions.

a. $\begin{cases} y < 2x \\ y \geq -x + 3 \end{cases}$ **b.** $\begin{cases} x + 2y \leq 10 \\ x + y \geq 3 \end{cases}$ **c.** $\begin{cases} |x| < 2 \\ 3x - 4y < 12 \end{cases}$

Suppose your group must choose a company to manufacture a product you have designed. Use the graphs below to choose company A or company B.

9. a. Which company has the greater growth in productivity?
   b. When was the productivity of the two companies equal? How is this shown on the graph?

10. a. Are the production costs of the two companies ever equal?
   b. Which company has consistently lower production costs?

11. What does the third graph tell about each company's sales?

12. Which company would your group recommend? Explain.

13. Complete the table for the graph of a system of two linear equations.

Description of Graph	Number of Solutions	Equal Slopes? (yes/no)	Same y-intercepts? (yes/no)
parallel lines	▪	▪	▪
intersecting lines	▪	▪	could be either
same line	▪	▪	▪

14. Use slopes and y-intercepts to describe the graph of each system. Tell how many solutions it has.

a. $\begin{cases} y = 2x + 1 \\ y = 2x + 3 \end{cases}$
b. $\begin{cases} y = 2x + 3 \\ -4x + 2y = 6 \end{cases}$
c. $\begin{cases} x - y = 5 \\ y + 3 = 2x \end{cases}$

15. The notation $\{(x, y)\mid y = 2x + 3\}$ is read as "the set of ordered pairs x, y such that $y = 2x + 3$." It describes the solutions for one of the systems in Question 14. Which one? Explain.

Describe the graph of each system and tell how many solutions it has.

1. $\begin{cases} y = x + 2 \\ y = -2x + 6 \end{cases}$
2. $\begin{cases} y = 5x - 3.5 \\ 10x - 2y = 7 \end{cases}$
3. $\begin{cases} 3a + b = 7 \\ 3a + b = 5 \end{cases}$
4. $\begin{cases} p = -3n + 1 \\ p = 3n + 1 \end{cases}$

5. a. Advertising The spreadsheet shows the monthly income and expenses for a new business. Find a linear model for monthly income and a linear model for monthly expenses.

b. Use the models to estimate the first month in which income will exceed expenses.

6. Writing Summarize the possible relationships for the *y*-intercepts, slopes, and number of solutions in a system of two linear equations using two variables.

	A	B	C
1	Month	Income	Expenses
2	Feb	8000	35000
3	Mar	12000	33000
4	Apr	13000	34000
5	May	18000	32000
6	Jun	20000	31000

Solve each system by graphing.

7. $\begin{cases} y = x - 2 \\ y = -2x + 7 \end{cases}$

8. $\begin{cases} x = -3 \\ y = 5 \end{cases}$

9. $\begin{cases} y = -x + 3 \\ y = \frac{3}{2}x - 2 \end{cases}$

10. $\begin{cases} r = s \\ s - 5r = 0 \end{cases}$

11. $\begin{cases} y = 3x + 1 \\ 6x - 2y = -2 \end{cases}$

12. $\begin{cases} 3a + 6b = 14 \\ a + 2b = 3 \end{cases}$

13. $\begin{cases} 3g + h = 5 \\ g - h = 7 \end{cases}$

14. $\begin{cases} 15x + 20y = 35 \\ 5x - 15y = 55 \end{cases}$

Graph each system of inequalities.

15. $\begin{cases} y > -2 \\ x < 1 \end{cases}$

16. $\begin{cases} y > x - 5 \\ 3x + y < -2 \end{cases}$

17. $\begin{cases} y \leq 3 \\ y \leq \frac{2}{5}x + 1 \end{cases}$

18. $\begin{cases} c \geq |d - 3| \\ c < \frac{1}{2}d + 3 \end{cases}$

19. Direct Mail The Stamoses are mailing advertising flyers to their customers. Helena addresses 6 flyers/min and has already done 80. Demitri addresses 4 flyers/min and has already done 100. When will they have addressed an equal number of flyers?

Open-Ended **Write a second equation for each system so that the system will have the given number of solutions.**

20. one solution
$\begin{cases} y = -3x + 2 \\ \underline{\quad ? \quad} \end{cases}$

21. no solution
$\begin{cases} 5x + 2y = 10 \\ \underline{\quad ? \quad} \end{cases}$

22. infinitely many solutions
$\begin{cases} \frac{x}{4} + \frac{y}{3} = 1 \\ \underline{\quad ? \quad} \end{cases}$

23. no solution
$\begin{cases} y = -4x - 6 \\ \underline{\quad ? \quad} \end{cases}$

24. infinitely many solutions
$\begin{cases} 8x + 3y = 24 \\ \underline{\quad ? \quad} \end{cases}$

25. one solution
$\begin{cases} \frac{x}{5} + \frac{y}{6} = 2 \\ \underline{\quad ? \quad} \end{cases}$

In Exercises 26–31, identify a system using two of the inequalities A, B, and C. The given ordered pair must be a solution of the system.

A. $x + y \leq 2$

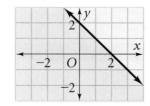

B. $y \leq \frac{3}{2}x - 1$

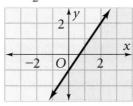

C. $y > -\frac{1}{3}x - 2$

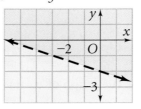

26. $(0, 0)$
27. $(-2, -5)$
28. $(2, 2)$
29. $(-2, 0)$
30. $(0, -2)$
31. $(-15, 15)$

Geometry Write a system of inequalities to describe each shaded figure. Check your work by testing several points.

32.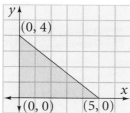

33.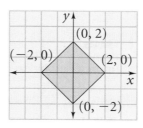

34.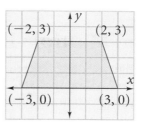

35.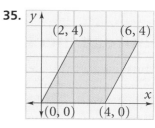

36. Research You can get prints made from photographic film either by mail or at local stores. Find out prices for rolls of 12, 24, and 36 prints from two different places. Graph your results. Which place is less expensive? Are the prices ever equal? Explain.

37. Standardized Test Prep Which system describes the graph at the right?

A. $\begin{cases} y < x \\ x + y \geq 4 \end{cases}$

B. $\begin{cases} y \leq x \\ y \leq -x - 4 \end{cases}$

C. $\begin{cases} y > x \\ x + y > 4 \end{cases}$

D. $\begin{cases} y < x \\ x + y \leq 4 \end{cases}$

E. $\begin{cases} y \geq x \\ y < x + 4 \end{cases}$

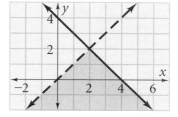

38. Critical Thinking How many students receive each grade?
- Each student receives a grade of A, B, C, or D.
- There are equal numbers of As, Cs, and Ds.
- The number of Bs exceeds the total number of all other grades.
- There are at least twelve students.
- Fewer than ten students receive grades of A or B.

Exercises   MIXED REVIEW

Perform each matrix operation.

39. $\begin{bmatrix} 2 & 6 \\ -3 & 0 \end{bmatrix}\begin{bmatrix} 8 \\ -4 \end{bmatrix}$

40. $5\begin{bmatrix} 1 & -6.1 & 0.8 \\ 2.9 & -3.1 & -1.2 \end{bmatrix}$

41. Newspapers One ton (2000 lb) equals about 600 copies of *The New York Times* Sunday edition or about 5350 copies of *USA Today.* About how much does one copy of each newspaper weigh?

Getting Ready for Lesson 4-2

Solve each equation for y.

42. $y - 4x = 5$

43. $3x - y = 4$

44. $6x + 3y = 15$

45. $5x - 2y = -6$

46. $\frac{y}{2} + \frac{x}{5} = 3$

47. $0.5x - 0.8y = 7$

Spreadsheets and Multiple Equations

Before Lesson 4-2

Imagine that you are 21 and have your first credit card. Suppose you buy an electronic keyboard and sound system for $500 and say "charge it!" When you get your monthly statement, you find your first payment is only $25! The minimum payment is either 5% of your balance or $15, whichever is greater. Interest is calculated at 1.8% per month. How much will you pay?

Example

You can examine the situation described above with a spreadsheet. Write cell formulas for row 3 of the spreadsheet.

	A	B	C	D	E	F	G
1	Month	Balance	Interest	Payment	New Balance	Total Interest	Total Payment
2	1	$500.00	$9.00	$25.00	$484.00	$9.00	$25.00
3	2	$484.00	$8.71	$24.20	$468.51	$17.71	$49.20
4	3	$468.51	$8.43	$23.43	$453.52	$26.15	$72.63

Month	$A3 = A2 + 1$	← Increase the month by 1.
Balance	$B3 = E2$	← Balance from the previous month
Interest	$C3 = B3 * 0.018$	← 1.8% of the month's balance
Payment	$D3 = B3 * 0.05$	← 5% of the month's balance
New Balance	$E3 = B3 + C3 - D3$	← Add the interest; subtract the payment.
Total Interest	$F3 = F2 + C3$	← Add the month's interest to the previous total.
Total Payment	$G3 = G2 + D3$	← Add the month's payment to the previous total.

1. Create a spreadsheet for the situation in the Example.
   a. In which month will the minimum payment first be $15?
   b. After how many months will the balance reach zero?
   c. What is the total interest paid?
   d. How many payments are required to reduce the balance to $400?
   e. Use substitution to rewrite the right side of $E3 = B3 + C3 - D3$ in terms of B3.

2. Create a new spreadsheet for an account that charges 14.9% annual interest. Use a minimum payment of 10% or $20, whichever is greater. What is the total interest paid?

3. **Writing** Why is it better to pay off a credit card debt than just pay the minimum payment each month?

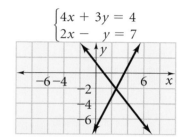

What You'll Learn

- Using substitution to solve a system of equations
- Using elimination to solve a system of equations

...And Why

To solve problems involving expenses and income

4-2 Solving Systems Algebraically

THINK AND DISCUSS

Solving Systems Using Substitution

Not every system can be solved easily by graphing.

$$\begin{cases} 4x + 3y = 4 \\ 2x - y = 7 \end{cases}$$

1. **Estimation** Use the graph to estimate the solution to the system at the right.

2. Check your estimate by substituting the x- and y-values into each equation. What do you learn about the solution?

Although you can graph each line easily, the exact point of intersection is not obvious. The process of substitution helps you find the solution precisely.

Example 1

Solve the system $\begin{cases} 4x + 3y = 4 \\ 2x - y = 7 \end{cases}$ using substitution.

$$\begin{aligned} 2x - y &= 7 \\ -y &= 7 - 2x \\ y &= 2x - 7 \end{aligned}$$

⟵ Solve for one of the variables. Solving the second equation for y is easiest.

$$\begin{aligned} 4x + 3y &= 4 \\ 4x + 3(2x - 7) &= 4 \\ 4x + 6x - 21 &= 4 \\ 10x &= 25 \\ x &= 2.5 \end{aligned}$$

⟵ Substitute the expression for y into the first equation. Then solve for x.

$$\begin{aligned} y &= 2x - 7 \\ y &= 2(2.5) - 7 \\ y &= -2 \end{aligned}$$

⟵ Substitute the value of x into one of the equations. Then solve for y.

The solution is $(2.5, -2)$.

3. **a.** Solve the system in Example 1 by solving the first equation for x. Then substitute the expression for x into the second equation.
   b. Compare your solution to the one given. Which process is easier? Why?

4. **a.** What are the coefficients of x and y in Example 1?
   b. Which variable has a coefficient of 1 or −1?
   c. **Critical Thinking** How do these coefficients help you identify the simplest way to substitute?

5. Try This Solve each system using substitution. **Verify** the solution in each equation.

a. $\begin{cases} 2x - 3y = 6 \\ x + y = -12 \end{cases}$ b. $\begin{cases} 3x - y = 0 \\ 4x + 3y = 26 \end{cases}$ c. $\begin{cases} 7x + 2y = -8 \\ 8y = 4x \end{cases}$

Example 2   Relating to the Real World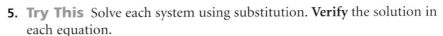

Art The school Art Club wants each member to have a tie-dyed shirt.

Hand-dyed Shirts

$7.49 per shirt

4 large pots at $9.95 each

$15 for dye (up to 50 shirts)

Ready-made Shirts

$12.99 per shirt

For how many shirts is hand-dyeing shirts less expensive than buying ready-made shirts?

Define Let n represent the number of shirts.
Let r represent the cost of ready-made shirts.
Let d represent the cost of hand-dyed shirts.

Relate $r = 12.99n$
$d = 7.49n + 4(9.95) + 15$
$d < r$

Write
$$d < r \quad \longleftarrow \text{Substitute the}$$
$$7.49n + 4(9.95) + 15 < 12.99n \quad \text{expressions for } d \text{ and } r.$$
$$7.49n + 54.80 < 12.99n \quad \longleftarrow \text{Solve for } n.$$
$$54.80 < 5.5n$$
$$9.96 < n \quad \longleftarrow \text{Round your answer.}$$

For 10 or more shirts, hand-dyeing shirts is less expensive.

6. Find the cost of each method for exactly 10 shirts.

7. Solve Example 2 by graphing. What do the coordinates of the point of intersection represent?

Solving Systems Using Elimination

In solving a system, you can eliminate a variable if like terms have opposite or the same coefficients.

QUICK REVIEW

The *Addition Property of Equality* states that when equal quantities (or the same number) are added to each side of an equation, the results are equal.

Apply the Addition Property of Equality to add the equations below.

$$\begin{array}{rcr} 4x - 2y &=& 7 \\ x + 2y &=& 3 \\ \hline 5x &=& 10 \end{array}$$

8. **a.** Finish solving the system above. Write your solution as an ordered pair.

   b. Verify your solution by testing the ordered pair in both equations.

9. **Try This** Solve each system using elimination.

   a. $\begin{cases} 3x + y = -9 \\ -3x - 2y = 12 \end{cases}$ **b.** $\begin{cases} x - y = -2 \\ x + y = 10 \end{cases}$ **c.** $\begin{cases} 2x + 3y = 2 \\ 4x - 3y = 1 \end{cases}$

You can use subtraction as well as addition to eliminate a variable.

Example 3   **Relating to the Real World**

Advertising An ad for a health club offers a two-month membership for $100 or a six-month membership for $200. The memberships include an initiation fee. Find the monthly charge and the initiation fee if the fee is the same for both memberships.

Define   Let m represent the monthly charge.
            Let f represent the initiation fee.

Relate $2m + f = 100$ ← two-month membership cost
            $6m + f = 200$ ← six-month membership cost

Write   You can eliminate the variable f by subtracting the equations.

$$\begin{array}{rcr} 2m + f &=& 100 \\ 6m + f &=& 200 \\ \hline -4m &=& -100 \end{array}$$ ← Solve for m.
$$m = 25$$

$$\begin{aligned} 2m + f &= 100 \\ 2(25) + f &= 100 \\ f &= 50 \end{aligned}$$ ← Substitute into one of the equations to find the initiation fee.

The memberships cost $25 a month, with a $50 initiation fee.

10. *Critical Thinking* Do you think the six-month health club membership in Example 3 is a bargain? Explain your reasoning.

11. **Try This** Suppose a three-hour computer class costs $115. A five-hour computer class offered by the same company costs $185. Both classes include the same laboratory fee. Write a system of two equations. Determine the hourly cost and the fee.

Often you must multiply one or both equations in a system to create opposite coefficients. Then you can add to eliminate a variable.

Example 4

Solve the system $\begin{cases} 3x + 7y = 15 \\ 5x + 2y = -4 \end{cases}$ using elimination.

① $\begin{cases} 3x + 7y = 15 \\ 5x + 2y = -4 \end{cases}$ ② $\Rightarrow$

$$
\begin{array}{rl}
6x + 14y = 30 & \longleftarrow \text{Multiply ① by 2.} \\
-35x - 14y = 28 & \longleftarrow \text{Multiply ② by } -7. \\
\hline
-29x \qquad\quad = 58 & \longleftarrow \text{Add the equations.} \\
x = -2 &
\end{array}
$$

$$
\begin{array}{rl}
3x + 7y = 15 & \longleftarrow \text{Substitute the value} \\
3(-2) + 7y = 15 & \text{of } x \text{ into either} \\
7y = 21 & \text{original equation.} \\
y = 3 & \text{Solve for } y.
\end{array}
$$

The solution is $(-2, 3)$.

12. Explain how to solve the system in Example 4 by eliminating x.

13. Try This Solve each system using elimination.

a. $\begin{cases} 2m + 3n = 12 \\ 5m - n = 13 \end{cases}$ b. $\begin{cases} 3x - 5y = 26 \\ -2x - 3y = -11 \end{cases}$ c. $\begin{cases} 5a + 2b = 0 \\ -3a + 2b = 16 \end{cases}$

The equations in Example 4 are **independent** because they represent two different lines. They are **consistent** because they have at least one solution. Sometimes a system can be dependent or inconsistent:

Solve: $\begin{cases} 4x - 2y = 6 \\ y = 2x - 3 \end{cases}$

$$4x - 2(2x - 3) = 6$$
$$4x - 4x + 6 = 6$$
$$6 = 6$$

When you get an equation that is always true, the system has an infinite number of solutions: $\{(x, y) \mid y = 2x - 3\}$. The graphs of both equations are the same line. The equations are **dependent**.

Solve: $\begin{cases} 2x - 3y = 18 \\ 2x - 3y = 6 \end{cases}$

$$\overline{0 = 12}$$

When you get an equation that is always false, the system has no solution. The graphs are parallel lines. The equations are **inconsistent**.

Exercises   ON YOUR OWN

Solve each system using substitution.

1. $\begin{cases} 3c + 2d = 2 \\ d = 4 \end{cases}$

2. $\begin{cases} 4x + 2y = 7 \\ y = 5x \end{cases}$

3. $\begin{cases} 4p + 2q = 8 \\ q = 2p + 1 \end{cases}$

4. $\begin{cases} x + 12y = 68 \\ x = 8y - 12 \end{cases}$

5. $\begin{cases} x + 3y = 7 \\ 2x - 4y = 24 \end{cases}$

6. $\begin{cases} 3a + b = 3 \\ 2a - 5b = -15 \end{cases}$

7. $\begin{cases} t = 2r + 3 \\ 5r - 4t = 6 \end{cases}$

8. $\begin{cases} x + 6y = 2 \\ 5x + 4y = 36 \end{cases}$

9. Write and solve a system of equations to help Sam and Silo find the correct mathematical answer.

Sam and Silo *by dumas*

Solve each system using elimination. Identify each pair of equations as consistent or inconsistent and as dependent or independent.

10. $\begin{cases} x + y = 12 \\ x - y = 2 \end{cases}$

11. $\begin{cases} x + 2y = 10 \\ x + y = 6 \end{cases}$

12. $\begin{cases} 2w + 5y = -24 \\ 3w - 5y = 14 \end{cases}$

13. $\begin{cases} 3u + 3v = 15 \\ -2u + 3v = -5 \end{cases}$

14. $\begin{cases} 2a + 3b = 12 \\ 5a - b = 13 \end{cases}$

15. $\begin{cases} 6x - 2y = 11 \\ -9x + 3y = 16 \end{cases}$

16. $\begin{cases} 9a - 3d = 3 \\ -3a + d = -1 \end{cases}$

17. $\begin{cases} 20x + 5y = 120 \\ 10x + 7.5y = 80 \end{cases}$

18. Transportation A youth group with 26 members is going skiing. Each of the five chaperones will drive a van or a sedan. The vans can seat 7 people, and the sedans can seat 5 people. How many of each type of vehicle could transport everyone to the ski area in one trip?

19. Open-ended Write a system you would solve using elimination. Solve and graph your system.

20. Writing Explain how you decide whether to use substitution or elimination to solve a system.

21. Communications The ads at the right show what two companies charge for Internet access.
 a. Write a system of equations to represent the cost *c* for *t* hours of access in one month from each company.
 b. For how many hours of use will both companies charge the same amount?
 c. If you used the Internet about 20 h per month, which company would be the most resonable choice? Why?

Solve each system. Choose an appropriate method.

22. $\begin{cases} y = \frac{2}{3}x - 3 \\ 2x - 3y = 9 \end{cases}$

23. $\begin{cases} v = 9t + 300 \\ v = 7t + 400 \end{cases}$

24. $\begin{cases} 0.02a - 1.5b = 4 \\ 0.5b - 0.02a = 1.8 \end{cases}$

25. $\begin{cases} 0.03x + 0.02y = -1 \\ 0.02x + 0.05y = 14 \end{cases}$

26. $\begin{cases} 2m = -4n - 4 \\ 3m + 5n = -3 \end{cases}$

27. $\begin{cases} 5x + y = 0 \\ 5x + 2y = 30 \end{cases}$

28. $\begin{cases} 0.25p + 0.1q = 4 \\ p + q = 31 \end{cases}$

29. $\begin{cases} 80x + 60y = 85 \\ 100x - 40y = 20 \end{cases}$

30. $\begin{cases} \frac{1}{2}x - \frac{1}{3}y = 10 \\ x + y = 120 \end{cases}$

31. $\begin{cases} \frac{x}{3} + \frac{4y}{3} = 300 \\ 3x - 4y = 300 \end{cases}$

32. $\begin{cases} 4.7w + 0.2y = 13.4 \\ y - 10w = 0 \end{cases}$

33. $\begin{cases} 2x + 3y = 0 \\ 7x = 3(2y + 3) + 2 \end{cases}$

34. Entertainment A theater production costs $40,000 plus $2800 per performance. A sold-out performance brings in $3675. How many sold-out performances will it take to break even?

35. Weather The equation $F = \frac{9}{5}C + 32$ relates temperatures on the Celsius and Fahrenheit scales. Does any temperature have the same number reading on both scales?

Equivalent Temperatures

Celsius	35°	5°	-55°
Fahrenheit	95°	41°	-67°

Chapter Project **Find Out by Graphing**

....

To fill an order for Sizzlin' Sauce sauces, you bought 1050 green peppers and 1200 hot chili peppers. Write and graph a system of inequalities to represent how many pints of each kind of sauce you can make. (Refer to the recipes on page 149.) How many peppers will you have left using various solutions?

....

Exercises   MIXED REVIEW

Solve each equation.

36. $\frac{1}{3} = \frac{4}{3}x - 3$

37. $3(x - 2) = -18$

38. $5x + 13 = 2x - 8$

39. $-2x + 8 = 0$

40. a. Biology Elephants gain an average of 1.5 lb/day their first two years and then 1 lb/day after this until age 20. Write an equation to model this pattern.

b. On December 30, 1992, the elephant Juliette was born weighing 198 lb 3 oz. How much would you expect her to weigh now?

Getting Ready for Lesson 4-3

Graph each inequality.

41. $y \leq \frac{1}{2}x + 4$

42. $x + y < 4$

43. $3x - 2y \leq 8$

44. $y > 7 - 2x$

FOR YOUR JOURNAL

Summarize the methods of solving systems of equations and inequalities with two variables.

What You'll Learn

• Solving linear programming problems

...And Why

To help plan a fund raiser

What You'll Need

• graphing calculator

4-3 Linear Programming

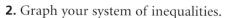
W O R K   T O G E T H E R

Music Suppose you want to buy a number of tapes and CDs. You can afford up to 10 tapes or 7 CDs. You want at least 4 CDs and at least 10 h of recorded music. Each tape holds about 45 min of music and each CD holds about an hour.

1. Write a system of inequalities to model this situation.

    Let x represent the number of tapes purchased.
    Let y represent the number of CDs purchased.

2. Graph your system of inequalities.

3. Does each ordered pair satisfy the system you have graphed? Explain.
    a. $(4, 7)$ b. $(6, 5)$ c. $(8, 6)$ d. $(10, 4)$

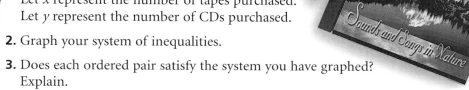
T H I N K   A N D   D I S C U S S

Solutions to the system of inequalities in the Work Together represent ways you can buy tapes and CDs within the conditions. You may also want to control how much you spend.

4. Suppose each tape costs $8 and each CD costs $12. Find the cost of buying each combination of tapes and CDs from the table at the left.

Tapes	CDs	Total Cost
x	y	C
7	7	■
10	5	■
13	3	■
6	6	■
9	4	■
12	2	■
8	7	■
11	5	■

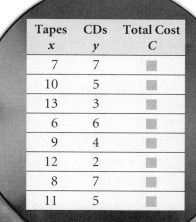

5. The red line on the graph at the right contains several points that represent a cost of $140. What cost do the points on the blue line represent? What cost do the points on the green line represent?

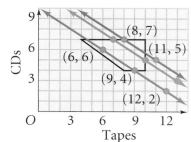

6. Suppose your goal is to spend as little as possible while meeting all the conditions in the Work Together. Find the combination of tapes and CDs with the lowest cost.

7. **Critical Thinking** Why do you think the lowest cost occurs at a vertex of the shaded region?

How? The name linear programming did not come from the fact that computer programs are used to solve many linear programming problems. Linear programming provides a plan, or a *program*, based on linear equations. This plan makes the most efficient use of resources, keeps costs to a minimum, or maximizes profit.

Linear programming identifies conditions that make a quantity as large or as small as possible. This quantity is expressed as the **objective function.** Limits on the variables in the function are called **restrictions.**

8. Find some restrictions in the Work Together.

9. Write a formula for the cost C of x tapes and y CDs from Question 4. This is the objective function.

Example 1

Use linear programming. Find the values of x and y that maximize and minimize the objective function $P = 3x + 2y$.

Restrictions $\begin{cases} y \geq \frac{3}{2}x - 3 \\ y \leq -x + 7 \\ x \geq 0, y \geq 0 \end{cases}$

Step 1:
Graph the restrictions.

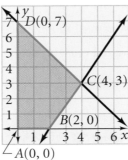

Step 2:
Find coordinates for each vertex.

Vertex
$A(0, 0)$
$B(2, 0)$
$C(4, 3)$
$D(0, 7)$

Step 3:
Evaluate P at each vertex.

$P = 3x + 2y$
$P = 3(0) + 2(0) = 0$
$P = 3(2) + 2(0) = 6$
$P = 3(4) + 2(3) = 18$
$P = 3(0) + 2(7) = 14$

The maximum value of 18 occurs when $x = 4$ and $y = 3$.
The minimum value of 0 occurs when $x = 0$ and $y = 0$.

GRAPHING CALCULATOR HINT

Use a graphing calculator to graph the restrictions and to find the coordinates of each vertex.

10. What system of two equations should you solve to find the coordinates of point C?

11. **Critical Thinking** Copy the graph in Example 1. Add a graph of the objective function, using a convenient value for P. For example, graph $12 = 3x + 2y$. How does graphing the objective function help you find the vertices at which the maximum and minimum values occur?

12. **a.** Write a 1×2 matrix containing the coefficients of the objective function.
    b. Write a 2×4 matrix of the coordinates of the vertices.
    c. Multiply the matrices you wrote. What does the product represent?

13. **a.** Change the objective function to $P = 2x + 3y$. Use the same restrictions. Find the maximum value and where it occurs.
    b. Does the minimum value change? Explain.

In many linear programming problems, you must write inequalities for the restrictions and write the objective function.

164 Chapter 4 Linear Systems

Example 2 **Relating to the Real World**

Fund Raising Suppose you order cases of Mixed Nuts and Roasted Peanuts to raise money for your marching band uniforms. You can order no more than a total of 500 cans and packages and spend no more than $600. How can you maximize your profit?

Mixed Nuts
12 cans per case

You pay ...... $24 per case
Sell at .... $3.50 per can

$18 profit per case!

Roasted Peanuts
20 packages per case

You pay ...... $15 per case
Sell at ... $1.50 per package

$15 profit per case!

Define Let x represent the number of cases of Mixed Nuts ordered.
Let y represent the number of cases of Roasted Peanuts ordered.
Let P represent the total profit.

Relate Organize the information in a table.

	Mixed Nuts	Roasted Peanuts	Totals	
Number of Cases	x	y		
Number of Units	$12x$	$20y$	500	← restriction
Cost	$24x$	$15y$	600	← restriction
Profit	$18x$	$15y$	$18x + 15y$	← objective

Write Write the restrictions. Then simplify them.

$$\begin{cases} 12x + 20y \le 500 \\ 24x + 15y \le 600 \\ x \ge 0, y \ge 0 \end{cases} \Longrightarrow \begin{cases} 3x + 5y \le 125 \\ 8x + 5y \le 200 \\ x \ge 0, y \ge 0 \end{cases}$$

← You cannot order a negative number of cases.

Write the objective function. $P = 18x + 15y$

Step 1:
Graph the restrictions.

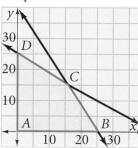

Step 2:
Find coordinates for each vertex.

Vertex
$A(0, 0)$
$B(25, 0)$
$C(15, 16)$
$D(0, 25)$

Step 3:
Evaluate P at each vertex.

$P = 18x + 15y$
$P = 18(0) + 15(0) = 0$
$P = 18(25) + 15(0) = 450$
$P = 18(15) + 15(16) = 510$
$P = 18(0) + 15(25) = 375$

The maximum profit will be $510. It occurs when you order 15 cases of Mixed Nuts and 16 cases of Roasted Peanuts.

Some marching bands raise money to travel to band festivals, like the Battle of the Flowers Festival held in San Antonio, Texas.

14. Suppose you sell the Mixed Nuts for $4.25 per can. Find the new profit formula. What order would yield the maximum profit?

In Example 2, you can only order a whole number of cases. When a vertex does not have whole-number coordinates, the solution may be nearby in the shaded region.

15. a. Use the restrictions to **verify** that $(23\frac{1}{3}, 13\frac{1}{3})$ are the coordinates of point Q.
  b. Verify that point Q yields the minimum cost for the objective function $C = 6x + 9y$.
  c. How should you round the coordinates of point Q to stay within the shaded region? What whole-number values of x and y give you the lowest cost?

Restrictions

$$\begin{cases} x + 2y \geq 50 \\ 2x + y \geq 60 \\ x \geq 0, y \geq 0 \end{cases}$$

Graph

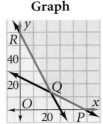

16. Try This A game arcade gives away prize packs. Pack A consists of 5 game tokens and 2 pizzas. The cost to the arcade is $5.25. Pack B contains 15 tokens and 1 pizza. The cost is $5.75. The arcade gives away at least 30 packs, at least 300 tokens, and at most 60 pizzas.
  a. Copy and complete the table.
  b. How many of each pack should the arcade give away to minimize its cost?

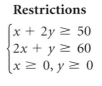

	Pack A	Pack B	Totals
Number of Packs	x	y	30
Number of Tokens	$5x$	■	■
Number of Pizzas	■	■	■
Cost	■	■	■

Exercises   ON YOUR OWN

Find the values of x and y that maximize or minimize the objective function on each graph.

1.

$D(0, 6)$
$C(4, 2)$
$A(0, 0)$ $B(5, 0)$

Maximum for
$P = 3x + 2y$

2.

$D(0, 500)$
$C(400, 300)$
$A(0, 0)$ $B(600, 0)$

Maximum for
$P = 7x + 4y$

3.

$R(0, 16)$
$Q(6, 8)$
$P(30, 0)$

Minimum for
$C = 2x + 3y$

4.

$R(0, 40)$
$Q(10, 20)$
$P(50, 0)$

Minimum for
$C = 0.25x + 0.75y$

5. Writing Explain why solving a system of equations is a necessary skill in the linear programming process.

Use linear programming. Find the values of x and y that maximize or minimize the objective function.

6. $\begin{cases} x \le 5 \\ y \le 4 \\ x \ge 0, y \ge 0 \end{cases}$

Maximum for
$P = 3x + 2y$

7. $\begin{cases} x \le 5 \\ y \le 4 \\ x \ge 0, y \ge 0 \end{cases}$

Minimum for
$P = 3x + 2y$

8. $\begin{cases} x + y \ge 8 \\ y \ge 5 \\ x \ge 0 \end{cases}$

Minimum for
$C = 3x + 2y$

9. $\begin{cases} x + y \le 8 \\ 2x + y \le 10 \\ x \ge 0, y \ge 0 \end{cases}$

Maximum for
$N = 100x + 40y$

10. $\begin{cases} 2 \le x \le 6 \\ 1 \le y \le 5 \\ x + y \le 8 \end{cases}$

Maximum for
$P = 3x + 2y$

11. $\begin{cases} x + 2y \ge 8 \\ x \ge 2 \\ y \ge 0 \end{cases}$

Minimum for
$C = x + 3y$

12. $\begin{cases} 2x + y \le 300 \\ x + y \le 200 \\ x \ge 0, y \ge 0 \end{cases}$

Maximum for
$P = x + 2y$

13. $\begin{cases} 5x + y \ge 10 \\ x + y \ge 6 \\ x + 4y \ge 12 \\ x \ge 0, y \ge 0 \end{cases}$

Minimum for
$C = 10x + 200y$

14. Business A concession stand makes $.85 on each regular hot dog and $1.33 on each foot-long hot dog. On a typical Saturday, it sells between 25 and 40 regular hot dogs and between 30 and 50 foot-longs. The total sales have never exceeded 80 hot dogs. How many of each type should be prepared to maximize profit?

15. Forestry Teams formed from 30 forest rangers and 16 trainees are planting trees. An experienced team consisting of two rangers can plant 500 trees per week. A training team consisting of one ranger and two trainees can plant 200 trees per week.

	Experienced Teams	Training Teams	Totals
Number of Teams	x	y	
Number of Rangers	$2x$	y	30
Number of Trainees	0	$2y$	16
Number of Trees Planted	$500x$	$200y$	$500x + 200y$

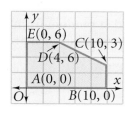

a. How many of each type of team should be formed to maximize the number of trees planted? How many trainees are used in this solution? How many trees are planted?

b. Find a solution that uses all the trainees. How many trees will be planted in this case?

16. Critical Thinking Sometimes two corners of a graph both yield the maximum profit. In this case, many other points may also yield the maximum profit. Evaluate the profit function $P = x + 2y$ for the graph shown. Find four points that yield the maximum profit.

17. Commercial Art Four artists and three writers create two types of greeting cards. Each art card requires four hours of art and two hours of writing. Each sonnet card takes two hours of art and six hours of writing. Each employee can work up to 40 h/wk. The company makes a profit of $2000 on each art card and $1000 on each sonnet card. How many of each card should be created and sold each week to maximize profit?

18. Open-ended Write a system of restrictions that form a trapezoid. Write an objective function and evaluate it at each vertex.

19. Environment Trees in urban areas help keep air fresh by absorbing carbon dioxide. A city has $2100 and 45,000 ft² of land to plant spruce and maple trees. How many of each tree should the city plant to maximize carbon dioxide absorption?

Facts for a Single Tree

	Spruce Tree	Maple Tree
Cost to Plant	$30	$40
Area Required	600 ft²	900 ft²
Carbon Dioxide Absorption	650 lb/yr	300 lb/yr

Source: *Auburn University and Anderson & Associates*

20. Standardized Test Prep Which point gives the maximum value for $N = 4x + 3y$ and lies within the system of restrictions at the right?

$$\begin{cases} x \leq 7 \\ x + y \leq 10 \\ x \geq 0, y \geq 0 \end{cases}$$

A. $(0, 0)$ **B.** $(10, 0)$ **C.** $(7, 0)$ **D.** $(7, 3)$ **E.** $(0, 10)$

Chapter Project

Find Out by Analyzing

Suppose you make $1.20/pt profit on Red Hot Sauce and $1.00/pt profit on Scorchin' Hot Sauce. Use the restrictions from the Find Out question on page 162 to decide how much of each sauce you should make and sell to maximize profit.

Exercises   MIXED REVIEW

Suppose a number is selected at random from the sample space consisting of whole numbers from 1 to 100. Find each probability.

21. P(the number is a multiple of 10)

22. P(the number consists of two digits)

23. P(the number is even)

24. P(the number is less than 61)

25. Data Analysis Use the data below.

A Survey of Paperback Books: How Long and How Much?

Pages	326	450	246	427	208	339	367	445	404	465	378	256
Price ($)	7.50	7.99	6.99	7.99	6.99	7.95	7.50	7.95	7.95	7.99	7.99	6.99

a. Make a scatter plot of the data.
b. What scales did you use for the axes?
c. What kind of correlation do you see?
d. Find an equation for the line of best fit.
e. What price would you predict for a paperback book containing 100 pages?

Getting Ready for Lesson 4-4

Find the *x*- and *y*-intercepts of each line.

26. $y = 2x + 6$ **27.** $2x + 9y = 36$ **28.** $3x - 8y = -24$ **29.** $4x - 5y = 40$

Exercises   CHECKPOINT

Solve each system of equations.

1. $\begin{cases} 3x + 2y = 6 \\ x - 2y = 10 \end{cases}$ **2.** $\begin{cases} 4x + 7y = 28 \\ y = 2x - 14 \end{cases}$ **3.** $\begin{cases} 7x - 2y = 20 \\ 6y = 3 \end{cases}$ **4.** $\begin{cases} 4x + 5y = -12 \\ 3x - 4y = 22 \end{cases}$

5. Open-ended Write and solve three systems of equations. Solve one system by graphing, one using substitution, and one using elimination.

6. Smart Shopping A regular model refrigerator costs $489 and has an estimated annual operating cost of $84. An energy-saving model costs $599, with an estimated annual cost of $61.
a. When will the costs to buy and operate each model be equal?
b. If the expected life of a refrigerator is 12 yr, which model would you buy? Explain.

7. Standardized Test Prep Solve the system at the right. Then compare the quantities in Column A and Column B. $\begin{cases} x - 2y = 11 \\ 5x + 4y = 27 \end{cases}$

Column A	Column B
$5x$	35

A. The quantity in Column A is greater.
B. The quantity in Column B is greater.
C. The quantities are equal.
D. The relationship cannot be determined from the information given.

8. Agriculture A farmer has 400 acres and $45,000 available to grow corn and soybeans. Use the cost and profit information to decide how many acres of each crop will maximize profit.

Cost and Profit for Corn and Soybeans

	Corn	Soybeans
Number of Acres	x	y
Cost	$100x$	$150y$
Profit	$60x$	$75y$

What You'll Learn

- Graphing points in three dimensions
- Graphing equations in three dimensions

...And Why

To describe locations in computer-assisted designs

4-4 **G**raphs in Three Dimensions

THINK AND DISCUSS

Graphing Points in Three Dimensions

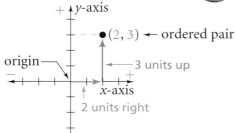

1. Describe how you could get from point A to point B moving along the grid shown.

2. Is there more than one way to move from A to B? If possible, list your moves using a different order.

To describe positions in space, you need a *three-dimensional* coordinate system. Of the many ways to do this, graphic designers often use one based on three perpendicular number lines.

Points in a Plane

$+$ y-axis

$(2, 3)$ ← ordered pair

origin

3 units up

x-axis

2 units right

Points in Space

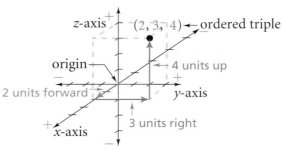

z-axis $(2, 3, 4)$ ← ordered triple

origin

4 units up

2 units forward

y-axis

3 units right

x-axis

3. **a.** The coordinates $(2, 3, 4)$ are described as "2 units forward, 3 units right, and 4 units up." How would you describe the coordinates $(-3, 5, -2)$?

b. **Open-ended** Write coordinates for a point partially described as "backward, left, and up."

Example 1 Relating to the Real World

Product Design Computers are used to design three-dimensional objects like the bicycle helmet shown below. The designer views the object from different perspectives. Give coordinates for *A*, *B*, *C*, and *D* in the diagram.

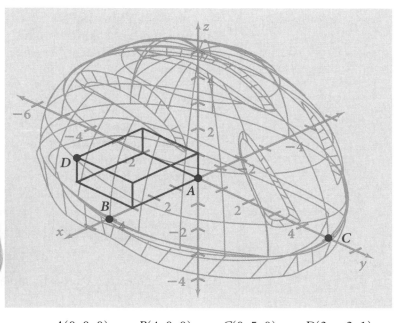

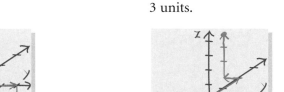

$A(0, 0, 0)$ $B(4, 0, 0)$ $C(0, 5, 0)$ $D(3, -2, 1)$

4. Does the point $(-3, 2, 4)$ lie inside or outside the helmet? Explain.

Example 2

Graph each point in coordinate space.

a. $(0, 3, -2)$ **b.** $(-2, -1, 3)$

a. First sketch the axes. Then move right 3 units and down 2 units.

b. Sketch the axes. Move back 2 units, left 1 unit, and up 3 units.

5. Try This Graph each point in coordinate space.
  a. $(0, -4, -2)$ **b.** $(-1, 1, 3)$ **c.** $(3, -5, 2)$ **d.** $(3, 3, -3)$

6. Identify the axis on which each point lies. Describe the direction it represents.
   a. $(0, 0, -9)$ **b.** $(0, -5, 0)$ **c.** $(0, 4, 0)$ **d.** $(7, 0, 0)$

Graphing Equations in Three Dimensions

A graph of an equation is a picture of all the solutions to the equation. In two dimensions, the graph of $3x - 2y = 6$ is a line. In three dimensions, the graph of $3x - 2y + z = 6$ is a plane.

A point at which the plane intersects one of the axes of a coordinate system is called an **intercept.** A line that passes through two intercepts is called a *trace*.

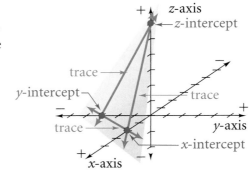

Example 3

Graph $2x + 3y + 4z = 12$. Use intercepts and traces.

Step 1: Find each intercept by replacing two variables with 0.

$$2x + 3y + 4z = 12$$
$$2x + 3(0) + 4(0) = 12 \longleftarrow \text{To find the } x\text{-intercept replace}$$
$$2x = 12 \qquad y \text{ and } z \text{ with zero.}$$
$$x = 6 \longleftarrow \text{The } x\text{-intercept is 6.}$$
$$2(0) + 3y + 4(0) = 12 \longleftarrow \text{Replace } x \text{ and } z \text{ with zero.}$$
$$3y = 12$$
$$y = 4 \longleftarrow \text{The } y\text{-intercept is 4.}$$
$$2(0) + 3(0) + 4z = 12 \longleftarrow \text{Replace } x \text{ and } y \text{ with zero.}$$
$$4z = 12$$
$$z = 3 \longleftarrow \text{The } z\text{-intercept is 3.}$$

Step 2:
Graph the intercepts.

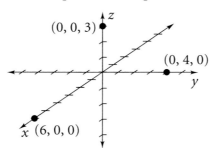

Step 3:
Draw the traces. Shade the plane.

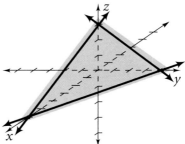

Each point on the plane represents a solution to $2x + 3y + 4z = 12$.

7. **a. Verify** that $(1, 2, 1)$ is a solution of $2x + 3y + 4z = 12$.
   b. Open-ended Find another solution for the equation. Does it lie on the plane shown in Example 3? Explain.

8. **Try This** Graph each equation.
   a. $x + y + z = 5$ **b.** $2x - y + 3z = 6$ **c.** $x + 2y - z = -4$

State the coordinates of each point in the diagram.

1. A 2. B 3. C

4. D 5. E 6. F

Describe the location of each point in coordinate space. Use *forward* or *back, left* or *right, up* or *down*, with units.

7. $(-1, 5, 0)$ 8. $(3, -3, -4)$

9. $(2, 0, 5)$ 10. $(-4, -7, -1)$

Graph each point.

11. $(5, 0, -2)$ 12. $(0, 0, 4)$

13. $(10, -2, -5)$ 14. $(-1, -1, -1)$

15. $(-4, -5, 3)$ 16. $(25, 40, -30)$

17. $(1, 1, 0)$ 18. $(0, -2, 2)$

19. **Standardized Test Prep** Which point does *not* lie on the graph of $2x + 3y - z = 12$?
    A. $(6, 0, 0)$ **B.** $(3, 3, 3)$ **C.** $(0, 4, 0)$
    D. $(1, 1, 7)$ **E.** $(2, 3, 1)$

20. **Writing** While visiting friends in New York, Consuela went to a concert. Explain how her ticket represents a point in a three-dimensional coordinate system.

21. **a. Party Planning** You have \$20 to spend on party decorations. Balloons are \$.05 each, streamers are \$.25 each, and noisemakers are \$.40 each. Write and graph an equation for the number of decorations you can buy. Use three variables.
    b. Open-ended Find two solutions for your equation.

Graph each equation. Use intercepts and traces.

22. $x + y + 2z = 4$ 23. $2x - y - 5z = 10$ 24. $2x + 6y + z = 6$

25. $3x - 6y - 2z = -12$ 26. $x - y - 4z = 8$ 27. $50x + 25y + 100z = 200$

Geography Use the map to identify the geographic feature found at each location.

28. latitude 3° S
longitude 37° E
elevation 19,340 ft

29. latitude 23° N
longitude 5° E
elevation 9,573 ft

30. latitude 25° S
longitude 6° E
elevation −3,072 ft

31. latitude 15° N
longitude 18° W
elevation 0 ft

32. latitude 30° N
longitude 27° E
elevation −440 ft

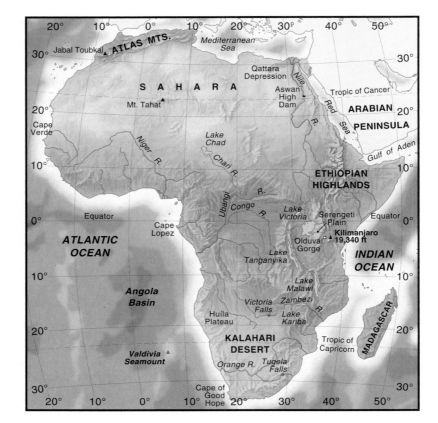

Chapter Project .... **Find Out by Researching**

Find the cost to produce 1 pt of each type of sauce found on page 149. Visit a local grocery store to estimate the cost of each ingredient. Remember that buying in large quantities can save you money. What selling price will you set for each sauce to maintain your profit?

Exercises   MIXED REVIEW

Graph each function.

33. $y = 5x - 8$ 34. $y = |x| - 4$ 35. $y = -2x + 5$ 36. $y = |x + 6|$

37. **a.** Graph the function $f(x) = 3x^2 - 1$.
    b. Shift the graph right five units and down two units.
    c. What is the minimum point of the new function?

Getting Ready for Lesson 4-5

Solve each system of equations.

38. $\begin{cases} 2x + 5y = 17 \\ -4x + 3y = 5 \end{cases}$ 39. $\begin{cases} x + 2y = 0 \\ 3x - 2y = -16 \end{cases}$

FOR YOUR JOURNAL

Describe several methods used to locate positions in the real world. Give examples.

- Using elimination to solve systems with three variables
- Using substitution to solve systems with three variables

...And Why

To make decisions involving money management

4-5 Systems with Three Variables

THINK AND DISCUSS

Elimination With Three Variables

Systems of equations with three variables can be represented as three-dimensional graphs such as those in Lesson 4-4. The graph of any equation of the form $Ax + By + Cz = D$ is a plane. In a system of these equations, the number of solutions depends on how the planes intersect.

No solution
No point lies in all three planes.

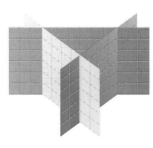 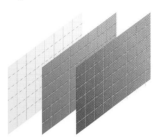

You can use technology to solve a system with three variables. The student has entered the equation $z = 2x + 3y - 15$.

One solution
The planes intersect at one common point.

An infinite number of solutions
The planes intersect at all the points along a common line.

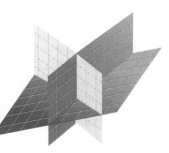

When the solution for a system of equations with three variables is one point, it can be written in the form (x, y, z).

1. Show that $(1, 2, -1)$ is a solution of each equation in the system below.

$$\begin{cases} 2x + y - z = 5 \\ 3x - y + 2z = -1 \\ x - y - z = 0 \end{cases}$$

To solve a system of equations with three variables, begin by eliminating one of the variables. It is easiest to eliminate a variable that has opposite coefficients.

Example 1

Solve the following system using elimination.

① $\quad x - 3y + 3z = -4$
② $\begin{cases} 2x + 3y - z = 15 \end{cases}$
③ $\quad 4x - 3y - z = 19$

Step 1: Pair the equations to eliminate y, since y already has opposite coefficients.

① $\begin{cases} x - 3y + 3z = -4 \\ 2x + 3y - z = 15 \end{cases}$
②

② $\begin{cases} 2x + 3y - z = 15 \\ 4x - 3y - z = 19 \end{cases}$
③

④ $\quad 3x + 2z = 11$

⑤ $\quad 6x - 2z = 34$

Step 2: Write the two new equations as a system. Solve for x and z.

④ $\begin{cases} 3x + 2z = 11 \\ 6x - 2z = 34 \end{cases}$
⑤

$9x = 45$
$x = 5$ ◀— **Partial solutions** —▶

④ $\quad 3x + 2z = 11$
$3(5) + 2z = 11$
$2z = -4$
$z = -2$

Step 3: Substitute values for x and z into one of the original equations (①, ②, or ③). Solve for y.

①

$x - 3y + 3z = -4$
$(5) - 3y + 3(-2) = -4$
$5 - 3y - 6 = -4$
$-3y = -3$
$y = 1$ ◀— **Partial solution**

The solution of the system is $(5, 1, -2)$.

You can apply the process used in Example 1 to *any* system of three equations with three variables. Begin by working with the equations in pairs. You will use one of the equations twice. Often you must multiply to create opposite coefficients.

2. By what number should you multiply the second equation in each system to eliminate y?

a. $\begin{cases} 3x + 3y - z = 5 \\ 2x - y + 2z = 9 \\ x + 3y - 4z = 1 \end{cases}$

b. $\begin{cases} x + 2y + z = -3 \\ 2x + y - z = 3 \\ 3x + 2y - 5z = 11 \end{cases}$

Example 2

Solve the following system using elimination.

① $\quad 2x + y - z = 5$
② $\begin{cases} x + 4y + 2z = 16 \end{cases}$
③ $\quad 15x + 6y - 2z = 12$

Step 1: Pair the equations to eliminate z.

① $\begin{cases} 2x + y - z = 5 \\ x + 4y + 2z = 16 \end{cases}$

$\quad \begin{aligned} 4x + 2y - 2z &= 10 \quad \longleftarrow \times 2 \\ x + 4y + 2z &= 16 \end{aligned}$

④ $5x + 6y \qquad = 26$

② $\begin{cases} x + 4y + 2z = 16 \\ 15x + 6y - 2z = 12 \end{cases}$

⑤ $\quad 16x + 10y \qquad = 28$

Step 2: Write the two new equations as a system. Solve for x and y.

④ $\begin{cases} 5x + 6y = 26 \\ 16x + 10y = 28 \end{cases}$

$\begin{aligned} 25x + 30y &= 130 \quad \longleftarrow \times 5 \\ -48x - 30y &= -84 \quad \longleftarrow \times -3 \\ \hline -23x \qquad &= 46 \\ x &= -2 \end{aligned}$

④ $\qquad 5x + 6y = 26$
$\qquad 5(-2) + 6y = 26$
$\qquad 6y = 36$
$\qquad y = 6$

Step 3: Substitute values for x and y into one of the original equations (①, ②, or ③). Solve for z.

① $\qquad 2x + y - z = 5$
$\qquad 2(-2) + 6 - z = 5$
$\qquad -4 + 6 - z = 5$
$\qquad -z = 3$
$\qquad z = -3$

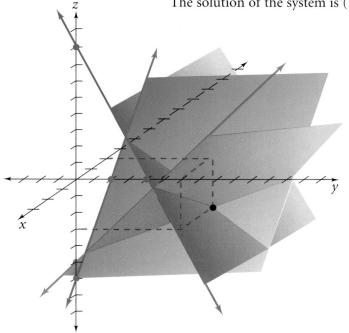

The solution of the system is $(-2, 6, -3)$.

The graph at the left illustrates the solution to Example 2. Each equation in the system represents a "tilted" plane. The three planes intersect at the point $(-2, 6, -3)$.

3. When you solve a system using elimination, why is it important in Step 1 to eliminate the *same* variable from each pair of equations you use?

4. Try This Solve each system using elimination.

a. $\begin{cases} 4a - b + c = 3 \\ a + 2b + c = 0 \\ 3a + 7b - 3c = 6 \end{cases}$

b. $\begin{cases} x + 4y - 5z = -7 \\ 3x + 2y + 3z = 7 \\ 2x + y + 5z = 8 \end{cases}$

Substitution With Three Variables

Sometimes you can use substitution early in the process to save time.

Example 3   **Relating to the Real World**

Money Management   Suppose you have saved $3200 from a part-time job. You can invest your savings in a growth fund, an income fund, and a money market fund. You estimate the return rates at 10%, 7%, and 5% per year, respectively. To increase your return, you decide to put twice as much money in the growth fund as in the money market fund. How should you invest the $3200 to get a return of $250 after 1 year?

Define   Let g, i, and m represent the amounts invested in each account (growth fund, income fund, and money market fund).

Relate   ① $g + i + m = 3200$ ⟵ The total amount available is $3200.
         ② $g = 2m$ ⟵ The growth amount should be twice the money market amount.

     ③ $0.10g$ $+$ $0.07i$ $+$ $0.05m$ $=$ 250

     ↑   ↑   ↑   ↑

    10% of the $+$ 7% of the $+$ 5% of the money $=$ total
   growth amount   income amount   market amount   return

Write   **Step 1:**   Substitute using equation ②. Replace g with $2m$ in ① and ③. Simplify.

     ① $g + i + m = 3200$ ③ $0.10g + 0.07i + 0.05m = 250$
         $2m + i + m = 3200$ $0.10(2m) + 0.07i + 0.05m = 250$
     ④ $3m + i \quad\;\; = 3200$ ⑤ $0.25m + 0.07i \quad\quad\;\; = 250$

Step 2:   Write the two new equations as a system. Solve.

   ④ $\begin{cases} 3m + \quad\;\; i = 3200 \\ 0.25m + 0.07i = 250 \end{cases}$ ⑤ $\Rightarrow$ $\begin{cases} 3m + \quad\quad\; i = 3200 \\ 3m + 0.84i = 3000 \end{cases}$ ⟵ Subtract.

                                           $0.16i = 200$
                                              $i = 1250$

       ④ $3m + i = 3200$
       $3m + 1250 = 3200$
             $3m = 1950$
               $m = 650$

Step 3:   Substitute into ② to find g.

     ② $g = 2m$
        $g = 2(650)$
        $g = 1300$

You should invest $1300 in the growth fund, $1250 in the income fund, and $650 in the money market fund to get a return of $250.

The systems of equations in this book contain the same number of equations as variables (for example, three equations with three variables). In solving such a system, you can sometimes get an equation that is always *false*. In this case, the system is inconsistent and has no solution.

If you get an equation that is always *true*, the system contains dependent equations. So long as the system does not also contain inconsistent equations, there will be an infinite number of solutions.

5. Classify each system as inconsistent or dependent.

a. $\begin{cases} x + 2y - 4z = 7 \\ x - y + z = 5 \\ 2x + y - 3z = 6 \end{cases}$

b. $\begin{cases} x + 2y - 4z = 7 \\ x - y + z = 5 \\ 2x + y - 3z = 12 \end{cases}$

Exercises ON YOUR OWN

Solve each system using elimination.

1. $\begin{cases} 2x - y + z = -2 \\ x + 3y - z = 10 \\ x + 2z = -8 \end{cases}$

2. $\begin{cases} a + b + c = -3 \\ 3b - c = 4 \\ 2a - b - 2c = -5 \end{cases}$

3. $\begin{cases} 6q - r + 2s = 8 \\ 2q + 3r - s = -9 \\ 4q + 2r + 5s = 1 \end{cases}$

4. $\begin{cases} x + 2y = 2 \\ 2x + 3y - z = -9 \\ 4x + 2y + 5z = 1 \end{cases}$

5. $\begin{cases} 3x + 2y - z = 17.8 \\ x - 3y + 2z = 7.9 \\ 2x + y - 3z = 3.9 \end{cases}$

6. $\begin{cases} 4A + 2U + I = 2 \\ 5A - 3U + 2I = 17 \\ A - 5U = 3 \end{cases}$

7. **Sports** A stadium has 49,000 seats. Seats cost $25 in Section A, $20 in Section B, and $15 in Section C. The number of seats in Section A equals the total of Sections B and C. Suppose the stadium takes in $1,052,000 from each sold-out event. How many seats does each section hold?

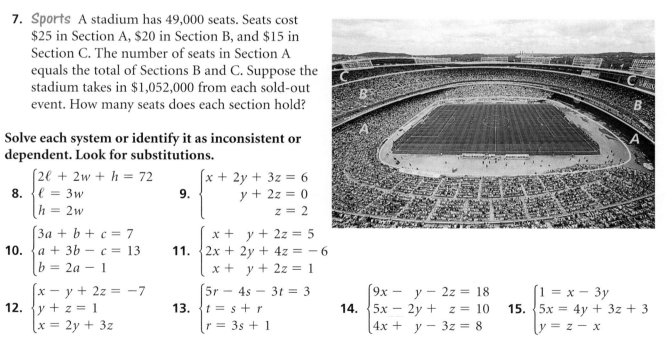

Solve each system or identify it as inconsistent or dependent. Look for substitutions.

8. $\begin{cases} 2\ell + 2w + h = 72 \\ \ell = 3w \\ h = 2w \end{cases}$

9. $\begin{cases} x + 2y + 3z = 6 \\ y + 2z = 0 \\ z = 2 \end{cases}$

10. $\begin{cases} 3a + b + c = 7 \\ a + 3b - c = 13 \\ b = 2a - 1 \end{cases}$

11. $\begin{cases} x + y + 2z = 5 \\ 2x + 2y + 4z = -6 \\ x + y + 2z = 1 \end{cases}$

12. $\begin{cases} x - y + 2z = -7 \\ y + z = 1 \\ x = 2y + 3z \end{cases}$

13. $\begin{cases} 5r - 4s - 3t = 3 \\ t = s + r \\ r = 3s + 1 \end{cases}$

14. $\begin{cases} 9x - y - 2z = 18 \\ 5x - 2y + z = 10 \\ 4x + y - 3z = 8 \end{cases}$

15. $\begin{cases} 1 = x - 3y \\ 5x = 4y + 3z + 3 \\ y = z - x \end{cases}$

16. **Writing** In a system with three variables, how do you decide if early substitution may save time? Give examples.

17. Geometry Write and solve a system of three equations. Find the measure of each labeled angle in the regular five-pointed star.

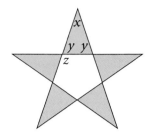

QUICK REVIEW

Sum of angles in a triangle: 180
Sum of supplements: 180
Sum of angles in a pentagon: 540

18. Finance A company places $1,000,000 in three different accounts. It places part in short-term notes paying 4.5% per year, twice as much in government bonds paying 5%, and the rest in utility bonds paying 4%. The income after one year is $45,500. How much did the company place in each account?

Tell how many solutions each system has.

19.

20.

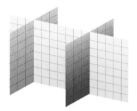

21.

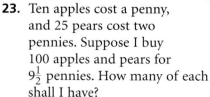

History Exercises 22 and 23 appeared in the book *Algebraical Problems*, published in 1824. Write and solve a system for each problem.

22. A fish was caught whose tail weighed 9 lb. Its head weighed as much as its tail plus half its body. Its body weighed as much as its head and tail. What did the fish weigh?

23. Ten apples cost a penny, and 25 pears cost two pennies. Suppose I buy 100 apples and pears for $9\frac{1}{2}$ pennies. How many of each shall I have?

24. Open-ended Write your own system having three variables. Begin by choosing the solution. Then write three equations that are true for your solution. Use elimination and substitution to solve the system and **verify** your work.

Find Out by Organizing

You can sell your sauce to a supermarket chain, a local grocery, and a specialty store. The supermarket chain will buy 288 pt at a time, every eight weeks. The grocery will buy 60 pt every four weeks and the specialty store will buy 24 pt each week.

• How much sauce should you produce each week to fill these orders? (Consider that you want to produce the same amount each week.)

• Design a spreadsheet to track your stock of sauce after each week. Use cell formulas.

Exercises   M I X E D   R E V I E W

Evaluate each expression for $f(x) = x^2 - x + 3$ and $g(x) = -4x - 2$.

25. $f(g(2))$ **26.** $5f(1) + 3g(-1)$ **27.** $g(f(-3))$

28. a. Construction Each inch of snow places 1.3 lb on each square foot of roof. Write a function rule to describe this relationship.

b. After a blizzard, some buildings had 20 in. of snow on them. How many pounds were on each square foot of roof?

c. Research How many pounds must roofs be able to carry to meet your local building codes?

Getting Ready for Lesson 4-6

Find the inverse of each matrix.

29. $\begin{bmatrix} 2 & 3 \\ 5 & 8 \end{bmatrix}$ **30.** $\begin{bmatrix} 1 & -1 \\ 0 & 2 \end{bmatrix}$ **31.** $\begin{bmatrix} 3 & 4 \\ -2 & -1 \end{bmatrix}$ **32.** $\begin{bmatrix} 1 & 0 & 3 \\ 0 & 1 & -3 \\ 2 & 2 & -1 \end{bmatrix}$

Exercises   C H E C K P O I N T

Graph each equation. Use traces and intercepts.

1. $3x + 2y + z = 6$ **2.** $x - y + z = 4$ **3.** $2x + y + z = 4$ **4.** $10x - 20y + 30z = 60$

Solve each system.

5. $\begin{cases} 3x + y - z = 6 \\ y + z = 7 \\ x - y + 2z = 11 \end{cases}$ **6.** $\begin{cases} x - y - z = -9 \\ 3x + y + 2z = 12 \\ x = y - 2z \end{cases}$ **7.** $\begin{cases} -x + 2y + z = 0 \\ y = -2x + 3 \\ z = 3x \end{cases}$

8. Writing Compare solving systems with three variables to solving systems with two variables. What are the similarities and differences?

Augmented Matrices

After Lesson 4-5

Remember your study of matrices in Chapter 3. An *augmented matrix* contains the coefficients and constants from a system of equations. You can use an augmented matrix to solve a system of equations. Each row of the matrix represents an equation.

System of Equations   **Augmented Matrix**

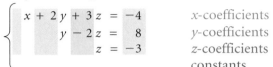 x-coefficients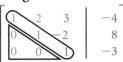
$\begin{cases} x + 2y + 3z = -4 \\ \quad\quad y - 2z = 8 \\ \quad\quad\quad\quad z = -3 \end{cases}$ y-coefficients
                                             z-coefficients
                                             constants

The augmented matrix contains an entry of zero for any term missing in the system. With its zero entries, the system shown above can easily be solved. To get the necessary zeros and ones, you can multiply a row by a constant, add rows, switch rows, or a combination of these steps.

Example

Solve the system represented by $\begin{bmatrix} 1 & 2 & | & -1 \\ 2 & 5 & | & -4 \end{bmatrix}$.

Step 1: Enter the augmented matrix as Matrix [A]. Return to the home screen with `2nd` `QUIT`.

```
MATRIX [A] 2 X 3
[   1    2    -1   ]
[   2    5    -4   ]
```

Step 2: To replace the highlighted entry 2 with 0, multiply row 1 by -2 and add to row 2.

`MATRX` `▶` `ALPHA` `A` ⟵ Access the *multiply and add* command.

-2 `›` `MATRX` `1` `›` 1 `›` 2 `ENTER` ⟵ Multiply row 1 by -2 add to row 2.

```
*row + ( -2, [A], 1, 2
        [[ 1 2 -1 ]
         [ 0 1 -2 ]]
```

Step 3: The second row of the display represents $y = -2$. Substitute $y = -2$ into the first equation $x + 2y = -1$. Therefore, $x + 2(-2) = -1$ and $x = 3$. The solution is $(3, -2)$

Some newer calculators perform the changes in one step. Enter the equations $2x + 3y - z = 11$, $3x - 2y + 4z = 10$, and $x + 4y - 2z = 8$ as an augmented matrix. Then press `MATRX` `▶` `ALPHA` `B` `MATRX` `1` `ENTER`. The solution shown at the right is $x = 4$, $y = 1$, and $z = 0$.

```
rref ( [A] )
        [[ 1 0 0 4 ]
         [ 0 1 0 1 ]
         [ 0 0 1 0 ]]
```

Solve the system represented by each augmented matrix.

1. $\begin{bmatrix} 1 & 1 & | & -10 \\ -1 & 1 & | & 20 \end{bmatrix}$
 2. $\begin{bmatrix} 1 & 2 & | & 7 \\ 2 & 3 & | & 12 \end{bmatrix}$
 3. $\begin{bmatrix} 2 & 1 & | & 7 \\ -2 & 5 & | & -1 \end{bmatrix}$
 4. $\begin{bmatrix} 1 & 1 & 0 & | & 2 \\ 0 & 1 & 1 & | & 17 \\ 1 & 0 & 1 & | & 5 \end{bmatrix}$

5. Writing Compare the method used in the example to solving a system using elimination. How are the methods related?

Inverse Matrices and Systems

What You'll Learn

- Solving systems of equations using inverse matrices
- Comparing methods used to solve systems

...And Why

To solve problems in marketing

What You'll Need

- graphing calculator

THINK AND DISCUSS

A matrix equation can represent an entire system of equations.

System of Equations

$$\begin{cases} x + 2y = 5 \\ 3x + 5y = 14 \end{cases}$$

Matrix Equation

$$\begin{bmatrix} 1 & 2 \\ 3 & 5 \end{bmatrix}\begin{bmatrix} x \\ y \end{bmatrix} = \begin{bmatrix} 5 \\ 14 \end{bmatrix}$$

1. Compare the two ways of writing a system. In the matrix equation, where are the coefficients of x and y? the variables? the constants?

Each matrix in an equation of the form $AX = B$ has a name.

coefficient matrix A **variable matrix** X **constant matrix** B

$$\begin{bmatrix} 1 & 2 \\ 3 & 5 \end{bmatrix} \qquad \cdot \qquad \begin{bmatrix} x \\ y \end{bmatrix} \qquad = \qquad \begin{bmatrix} 5 \\ 14 \end{bmatrix}$$

2. **a.** Find the matrix product $\begin{bmatrix} 1 & 2 \\ 3 & 5 \end{bmatrix}\begin{bmatrix} x \\ y \end{bmatrix}$.

   b. The product you have written must equal the matrix $\begin{bmatrix} 5 \\ 14 \end{bmatrix}$.

   Explain how the matrix equation represents the system of equations.

As you did in Chapter 3, you can find the inverse for the coefficient matrix. Then you can quickly solve systems having many variables.

Example 1

Solve the system $\begin{cases} 2x + y + 3z = 1 \\ 5x + y - 2z = 8 \\ x - y - 9z = 5 \end{cases}$ using an inverse matrix.

Write the system as a matrix equation. $\begin{bmatrix} 2 & 1 & 3 \\ 5 & 1 & -2 \\ 1 & -1 & -9 \end{bmatrix}\begin{bmatrix} x \\ y \\ z \end{bmatrix} = \begin{bmatrix} 1 \\ 8 \\ 5 \end{bmatrix}$

Use a graphing calculator. Enter $A = \begin{bmatrix} 2 & 1 & 3 \\ 5 & 1 & -2 \\ 1 & -1 & -9 \end{bmatrix}$ and $B = \begin{bmatrix} 1 \\ 8 \\ 5 \end{bmatrix}$.

Then, calculate $A^{-1}B$.

$\begin{bmatrix} x \\ y \\ z \end{bmatrix} = \begin{bmatrix} 4 \\ -10 \\ 1 \end{bmatrix}$ The solution is $(4, -10, 1)$.

```
[A]⁻¹[B]
            [[ 4 ]
             [-10]
             [1  ]]
```

3. **Verify** the solution in Example 1 in each equation of the system.

Profits Soar as Jewelry Company Drops Prices

Classy Rings Corporation announced a huge increase in earnings in the fiscal year just ended. CEO Martin Wood gave credit to a new marketing strategy. "We lowered the prices," said Wood, "and we've been able to sell a lot more merchandise."

Over the last fifteen years, Classy Rings Corporation has grown from a ~~op in Wood's garage to~~ ~~ti-million-dollar retailer~~ ~~cialized segment of the~~ ~~et.~~

There are many business applications for systems of equations. In the following example, you will use the formula

cost + margin = sales.

Margin includes operating expenses (such as employees' salaries) and profit.

Margin

Original cost

} Sales

Example 2   **Relating to the Real World**

Sales of Class Rings

Year	Selling Price	Number Sold
First	$295	300
Second	$129	3000

Math in the Media By dropping the selling price of a class ring nearly $170, Classy Rings' margin increased $42,000. Find the original cost of one ring and the margin for each year.

Define Let x represent the cost to produce one ring.
Let y represent the margin for the first year.

Relate Then $y + 42{,}000$ represents the margin for the second year.

	cost	**+**	**margin**	**=**	**sales**
For 1995:	$300x$	+	y	=	$300 \cdot 295$
For 1996:	$3000x$	+	$(y + 42{,}000)$	=	$3000 \cdot 129$

Write Simplify the system. Write it as a matrix equation.

$$\begin{cases} 300x + y = 88{,}500 \\ 3000x + y = 345{,}000 \end{cases} \Rightarrow \begin{bmatrix} 300 & 1 \\ 3000 & 1 \end{bmatrix}\begin{bmatrix} x \\ y \end{bmatrix} = \begin{bmatrix} 88{,}500 \\ 345{,}000 \end{bmatrix}$$

Use a graphing calculator.

Enter $A = \begin{bmatrix} 300 & 1 \\ 3000 & 1 \end{bmatrix}$ and $B = \begin{bmatrix} 88{,}500 \\ 345{,}000 \end{bmatrix}$.

Calculate $A^{-1}B$.

$$\begin{bmatrix} x \\ y \end{bmatrix} = \begin{bmatrix} 95 \\ 60{,}000 \end{bmatrix}$$

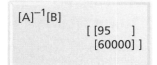

```
[A]⁻¹[B]
           [ [95    ]
            [60000] ]
```

The company's cost to produce one ring is about $95. The margin on the sale of rings the first year was about $60,000. For the second year, it was $60,000 plus $42,000, or about $102,000.

The inverse of $\begin{bmatrix} a & b \\ c & d \end{bmatrix}$

is $\dfrac{1}{ad - bc}\begin{bmatrix} d & -b \\ -c & a \end{bmatrix}$. The

matrix $\begin{bmatrix} a & b \\ c & d \end{bmatrix}$ has no inverse

when $ad - bc = 0$.

4. **Try This** Solve each system. Use an inverse matrix.

a. $\begin{cases} 5a + 3b = 7 \\ 3a + 2b = 5 \end{cases}$

b. $\begin{cases} x + y + z = 2 \\ 2x + y = 5 \\ x + 3y - 3z = 14 \end{cases}$

When the coefficient matrix of a system has an inverse, the system has exactly one solution. Similarly, when the coefficient matrix does *not* have an inverse, the system does *not* have a unique solution. In this case, the system either has no solution or has an infinite number of solutions.

5. Write the coefficient matrix for each system. Use it to determine if the system has exactly one solution.

a. $\begin{cases} x + y = 3 \\ x - y = 7 \end{cases}$

b. $\begin{cases} x + 2y = 5 \\ 2x + 4y = 8 \end{cases}$

c. $\begin{cases} x - 3y = 4 \\ -4x + 12y = -16 \end{cases}$

6. *Critical Thinking* Solve each system in Question 5. Use an alternate method when the coefficient matrix has no inverse.

7. *Graphing Calculator* How does your calculator indicate that a system does not have exactly one solution?

In this chapter, you have learned many methods of solving systems of linear equations. Some strengths of the most common methods are listed below.

Graphing	• useful for showing trends and relationships • helpful in linear programming • efficient with a graphing calculator
Substitution	• able to reduce the number of variables quickly
Elimination	• applicable to any system • efficient with two variables • best method (without technology) for three variables
Inverse matrices	• limited to systems with one solution • efficient with a graphing calculator

WORK TOGETHER

Work with a partner. Discuss how to solve each system. Then solve. Use each method at least once.

8. $\begin{cases} 3x + 5y = 1 \\ 2x - y = -8 \end{cases}$

9. $\begin{cases} y = 2000 - 65x \\ y = 500 + 55x \end{cases}$

10. $\begin{cases} 3x + 2y = 16 \\ y = 5 \end{cases}$

11. $\begin{cases} x - y + z = 0 \\ x - 2y - z = 5 \\ 2x - y + 2z = 8 \end{cases}$

12. $\begin{cases} x + 3y - z = 2 \\ x + 2z = 8 \\ 2y - z = 1 \end{cases}$

13. $\begin{cases} x + 2y + z = 4 \\ y = x - 3 \\ z = 2x \end{cases}$

Write each system as a matrix equation.

1. $\begin{cases} x + y = 5 \\ x - 2y = -4 \end{cases}$

2. $\begin{cases} y = 3x - 7 \\ x = 2 \end{cases}$

3. $\begin{cases} 3a + 5b = 0 \\ a + b = 2 \end{cases}$

4. $\begin{cases} r - s + t = 150 \\ 2r + t = 425 \\ s + 3t = 0 \end{cases}$

Solve each matrix equation. If the coefficient matrix has no inverse, write
no unique solution.

5. $\begin{bmatrix} 1 & 1 \\ 1 & 2 \end{bmatrix} \begin{bmatrix} x \\ y \end{bmatrix} = \begin{bmatrix} 8 \\ 10 \end{bmatrix}$

6. $\begin{bmatrix} 2 & -3 \\ -4 & 6 \end{bmatrix} \begin{bmatrix} a \\ b \end{bmatrix} = \begin{bmatrix} 1 \\ -2 \end{bmatrix}$

7. $\begin{bmatrix} 2 & 1 \\ 4 & 3 \end{bmatrix} \begin{bmatrix} x \\ y \end{bmatrix} = \begin{bmatrix} 10 \\ -2 \end{bmatrix}$

8. $\begin{bmatrix} 3 & 2 \\ -2 & -1 \end{bmatrix} \begin{bmatrix} m \\ n \end{bmatrix} = \begin{bmatrix} 2 \\ -3 \end{bmatrix}$

9. $\begin{bmatrix} 10 & 5 \\ 5 & 10 \end{bmatrix} \begin{bmatrix} c \\ d \end{bmatrix} = \begin{bmatrix} -30 \\ 45 \end{bmatrix}$

10. $\begin{bmatrix} 1 & 1 \\ 3 & 3 \end{bmatrix} \begin{bmatrix} x \\ y \end{bmatrix} = \begin{bmatrix} -4 \\ 3 \end{bmatrix}$

11. **Open-ended** Complete each system for the given number of solutions.

   a. infinitely many solutions

$\begin{cases} x + y = 7 \\ 2x + 2y = \blacksquare \end{cases}$

   b. one solution

$\begin{cases} x + y + z = 7 \\ y + z = \blacksquare \\ z = \blacksquare \end{cases}$

   c. no solution

$\begin{cases} x + y + z = 7 \\ y + z = \blacksquare \\ y + z = \blacksquare \end{cases}$

12. **Writing** Suppose you want to fill nine 1-lb tins with a holiday mix. You plan to mix almonds at $2.45/lb, peanuts at $1.85/lb, and raisins at $.80/lb. You have $15 and want to use twice as much nuts as raisins by weight. How much of each ingredient should you buy?

$\begin{cases} x + y + z = 9 \\ 2.45x + 1.85y + 0.8z = 15 \\ x + y = 2z \end{cases}$

   a. Explain how each equation in the system at the right relates to the problem. What does each variable represent?

   b. Solve the system using two different methods. Do you prefer one method over the other? Explain.

Solve each system. Use an inverse matrix.

13. $\begin{cases} x + 3y = 5 \\ x + 4y = 6 \end{cases}$

14. $\begin{cases} p - 3q = -1 \\ -5p + 16q = 5 \end{cases}$

15. $\begin{cases} 300x - y = 130 \\ 200x + y = 120 \end{cases}$

16. $\begin{cases} x + y + z = 4 \\ 4x + 5y = 3 \\ y - 3z = -10 \end{cases}$

17. $\begin{cases} -9a + 3b + c = 6 \\ 10a + b - c = 3 \\ 5a + 9b - 2c = 5 \end{cases}$

18. $\begin{cases} a + b + c + d = 7 \\ 2a - b + c - d = -10 \\ a + b - 2c + d = 16 \\ -a + b - c + 2d = 15 \end{cases}$

19. **Tea Time** When hot and cold liquids are mixed, the formula $T = \dfrac{ah + bc}{a + b}$ is used to find the temperature of the mixture. If hot tea and cold milk are mixed in a 9 : 1 ratio, the temperature becomes 117°F. If the tea : milk ratio is 2 : 1, the temperature becomes 96°F. Find the initial temperatures of the tea and milk.

T temperature of the mixture
h hot liquid temperature
c cold liquid temperature
a and b represent the amounts of hot and cold liquid in the ratio $a : b$.

20. Marketing Photographer Kieron Williams offers several packages of school photos. Each package includes the same base price and a cost for each print. Write and solve a system of four equations. Find the base price and the cost of a single print for each size.

Photo Packages

	Pack A	Pack B	Pack C	Pack D
Minis	15	20	30	30
5x7's	1	2	3	4
8x10's	1	1	2	3
Only!	$25.95	$29.95	$39.45	$44.95

21. A high school requires each student in grades 10, 11, and 12 to take a physical education elective for one trimester each year. Use the data to determine the number of students in each grade.

When Do Students Take Physical Education Electives?
(Percent of Each Grade Enrolled Each Trimester)

Trimester	Tenth Grade	Eleventh Grade	Twelfth Grade	Total Students Enrolled
1	40%	35%	30%	424
2	40%	30%	30%	404
3	20%	35%	40%	377

Solve each system. Use the method suggested.

22. $\begin{cases} 20x + 5y = 240 \\ y = 20x \end{cases}$
substitution

23. $\begin{cases} 20x + 5y = 145 \\ 30x - 5y = 125 \end{cases}$
elimination

24. $\begin{cases} x + 3y = 22 \\ 3x + 2y = 10 \end{cases}$
elimination

25. $\begin{cases} y = \frac{2}{3}x - 3 \\ y = -x + 7 \end{cases}$
graphing

26. $\begin{cases} 3x + 2y = 10 \\ 8x - 3y = 16 \end{cases}$
inverse matrix

27. $\begin{cases} 9y + 2z = 18 \\ 3x + 2y + z = 5 \\ x - y = -1 \end{cases}$
inverse matrix

Solve each problem. Use an appropriate method.

28. Catering Paella is a classic Spanish fiesta dish. A caterer combines the ingredients so the resulting paella weighs 18 lb, costs $29.50, and supplies 850 g of protein. How much rice, chicken, and shellfish did she use?

29. Entertainment A reggae group has $350,000 in start-up costs, plus expenses of $25,000 per performance. Each sold-out performance brings in revenue of $36,250. When will there be a $100,000 profit?

30. Geometry A rectangle is twice as long as it is wide. The perimeter is 840 ft. Find the dimensions of the rectangle.

Nutrition Chart

Food	Cost/lb	Protein/lb
Chicken	$1.50	100 g
Rice	$0.40	20 g
Shellfish	$6.00	50 g

Perform each matrix operation.

31. $\begin{bmatrix} 5 & -3 \\ 4 & 11 \end{bmatrix} + \begin{bmatrix} 4 & 0 \\ -9 & 1 \end{bmatrix}$ **32.** $\begin{bmatrix} 2 & -3 \end{bmatrix} \begin{bmatrix} 3 & -2 & 4 & 1 \\ 2 & 0 & -3 & 2 \end{bmatrix}$ **33.** $\begin{bmatrix} 3 & 10 \\ 1 & 5 \end{bmatrix} \begin{bmatrix} -7 & 2 \\ 8 & 4 \end{bmatrix}$

34. **a.** Agriculture You have 1000 acres of wheat and expect to harvest 47 bushels per acre. How much will it cost to harvest your crop?
   b. How much will it cost to move the crop to a warehouse?
   c. You are able to sell your wheat for $3 per bushel. How much do you make after harvesting and transportation costs?

Harvester Rates	Transport Rates
$12 per acre + $.12 per bushel for each bushel over 20 bushels per acre	$.12 per bushel to warehouse

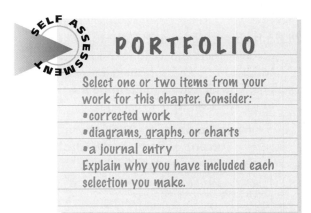

Algebra at Work

Radiologist

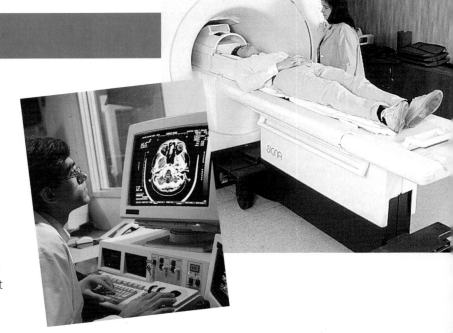

Radiologists are medical doctors who use X-rays, sound waves, and other means to diagnose and treat disease. Among the radiologist's most powerful diagnostic devices is the CT (computerized tomography) scan. The patient lies on a table inside the X-ray equipment. As the equipment rotates, X-rays are beamed through the patient's body from different angles. Images are recorded and fed into a computer.

The computer uses a three-dimensional coordinate system to record information. When the radiologist requests a picture, the computer produces a TV image of a cross-section of the patient's body.

Mini Project: Sketch and describe a three-dimensional coordinate system for a human head. Tell where the origin is, describe the units, and estimate the coordinates of several parts of the head.

Cramer's Rule

After Lesson 4-6

You can solve systems of linear equations using determinants and a pattern called Cramer's Rule. The *determinant* of the matrix $\begin{bmatrix} a & b \\ c & d \end{bmatrix} = ad - bc$.

Example

Use Cramer's Rule to solve the system $\begin{cases} 3x + 2y = 0 \\ x - y = -5 \end{cases}$.

First, write the coefficient matrix C of the system. $C = \begin{bmatrix} 3 & 2 \\ 1 & -1 \end{bmatrix}$

Form the matrices C_x and C_y by replacing one column of C with the constant terms from the system. For example, to form C_x replace the column of x-coefficients in C with the column of constants.

$C_x = \begin{bmatrix} 0 & 2 \\ -5 & -1 \end{bmatrix}$ $C_y = \begin{bmatrix} 3 & 0 \\ 1 & -5 \end{bmatrix}$

Now find the determinants for C, C_x, and C_y.

$$\det C = \det \begin{bmatrix} 3 & 2 \\ 1 & -1 \end{bmatrix} = (3)(-1) - (2)(1) = -3 - 2 = -5$$

$$\det C_x = \det \begin{bmatrix} 0 & 2 \\ -5 & -1 \end{bmatrix} = (0)(-1) - (2)(-5) = 10 \quad \det C_y = \det \begin{bmatrix} 3 & 0 \\ 1 & -5 \end{bmatrix} = (3)(-5) - (0)(1) = -15$$

Cramer's Rule gives the solution by using the following formulas.

$$x = \frac{\det C_x}{\det C} = \frac{10}{-5} = -2 \qquad\qquad y = \frac{\det C_y}{\det C} = \frac{-15}{-5} = 3$$

The solution for the system is $(-2, 3)$.

Find the determinant of each matrix. (To use a graphing calculator, first enter the matrix as matrix A, then press MATRX ▶ 1 MATRX 1 ENTER **.)**

1. $\begin{bmatrix} -3 & 4 \\ 2 & -5 \end{bmatrix}$

2. $\begin{bmatrix} 2 & -2 \\ 5 & 4 \end{bmatrix}$

3. $\begin{bmatrix} 2 & -2 & 3 \\ 4 & 1 & -1 \\ 1 & 2 & -1 \end{bmatrix}$

4. $\begin{bmatrix} 3 & -1 & -4 \\ 5 & 0 & -1 \\ 2 & 2 & 0 \end{bmatrix}$

Solve each system using Cramer's Rule.

5. $\begin{cases} 3x + y = 5 \\ 2x + 3y = 8 \end{cases}$

6. $\begin{cases} 2x + 7y = 1 \\ 3x - 4y = 16 \end{cases}$

7. $\begin{cases} 2x + y = 4 \\ 3x - y = 6 \end{cases}$

8. $\begin{cases} -1.2x - 0.3y = 2.1 \\ -0.2x + 0.8y = 4.6 \end{cases}$

9. **Writing** List some advantages and disadvantages of using Cramer's Rule to solve a system.

Finishing the Chapter Project

HOT! HOT! HOT!

Scorching Hot Sauce
Yield 1 pint
1 pt tomato sauce
with onions
4 green peppers, diced
8 hot chili peppers
seeded and diced

Bring the tomato sauce to
in a heavy sauce pan. Sa
peppers in a nonstick s
soft. Add to tomato s
5–10 min (until thi
correct the season

Red Hot Sauce
Yield 1 pint
1 pt tomato sauce
with onions
5 green peppers, diced
4 hot chili peppers
seeded and diced

Bring the
in a hea
peppe
soft
5–
c

Find Out questions on pages 162, 168, 174, and
181 should help you to complete your project. Your
report should include your analysis of the cost of
producing Sizzlin' Sauces. Include your profit analysis
and production spreadsheet. Illustrate your reasoning
and decisions with graphs.

Reflect and Revise

Present your analysis to a small group of classmates. After you
have heard their analyses and presented your own, decide if your
work is complete, clear, and convincing. If needed, make changes
to improve your presentation.

Follow Up

Are there other expenses you could expect in addition to those
you have already considered? Estimate them. Modify your
recommendations if necessary.

For More Information

Bacon, Mark S. *Do-It-Yourself Direct Marketing: Secrets for Small
Business.* New York: John Wiley & Sons, 1992.

Berle, Gustav. *The Instant Business Plan Book: 12 Quick-and-Easy Steps
to a Profitable Business.* Santa Maria, California: Puma, 1994.

DeGeorge, Gail and Stephanie Anderson Forest. "Reinventing the
Store: How smart retailers are changing the way we shop."
Business Week (November 27, 1995): 84–88.

The Market for Ethnic Foods: A Consumer Attitude and Behavior Study.
Washington, D.C.: The Association, 1989.

Key Terms

coefficient matrix (p. 183)
consistent equations (p. 160)
constant matrix (p. 183)
dependent equations (p. 160)
inconsistent equations
  (p. 160)
independent equations
  (p. 160)
intercept (p. 172)

linear programming (p. 164)
linear system (p. 150)
objective function (p. 164)
restrictions (p. 164)
solution of a system of
  equations (p. 150)
system of equations (p. 150)
variable matrix (p. 183)

How am I doing?

- State three ideas from this chapter that you think are important. Explain your choices.
- Describe different ways you can solve systems having two or three variables.

Exploring and Graphing Systems   4-1

A **system of equations** is a set of two or more equations using the same variables. In a **linear system,** the graph of each equation is a line. A **solution of a system** is a set of values for the variables that makes each equation true. You can find solutions of a system by graphing each equation and finding the point of intersection.

You can solve a system of inequalities by graphing each inequality. Then find the region that has the solutions of all the inequalities in the system.

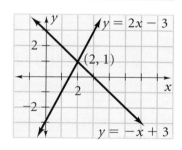

Solve each system by graphing.

1. $\begin{cases} y = 3x - 2 \\ y = -2x + 8 \end{cases}$

2. $\begin{cases} y < -x + 1 \\ y \geq \frac{3}{4}x - 6 \end{cases}$

3. $\begin{cases} 4x - y = 6 \\ -2x + 3y = 12 \end{cases}$

4. $\begin{cases} x + y \leq 4 \\ y < 6 \end{cases}$

5. **Writing** Describe the similarities and differences in solving a system of equations and a system of inequalities.

Solving Systems Algebraically   4-2

When you solve a system using substitution, solve one equation for one variable. Then substitute the expression into the second equation.

You can eliminate a variable by adding or subtracting the equations if one variable has opposite coefficients. You may have to multiply one or both equations by a number to make opposite coefficients.

Solve each system using substitution or elimination.

6. $\begin{cases} 3x + 5y = 10 \\ y = -4 \end{cases}$

7. $\begin{cases} 2x + y = 13 \\ x - y = -4 \end{cases}$

8. $\begin{cases} 4x + 3y = 12 \\ x - 5y = -20 \end{cases}$

9. $\begin{cases} 8x + y = 17 \\ x + 4y = 37 \end{cases}$

Linear Programming

Linear programming identifies conditions that make the **objective function** as large or as small as possible. Limits on the variables for the function are **restrictions**.

To use linear programming, graph the restrictions. Then find the maximum or minimum value of the objective function within the restrictions.

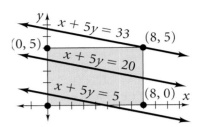

Use linear programming. Find the values of x and y that maximize or minimize the objective function.

10. $\begin{cases} x \leq 8 \\ y \leq 5 \\ x \geq 0, y \geq 0 \end{cases}$
Minimum for
$C = x + 5y$

11. $\begin{cases} 4 \leq x \leq 8 \\ 3 \leq y \\ x + y \leq 12 \end{cases}$
Maximum for
$P = 3x + 2y$

12. $\begin{cases} x \geq 2 \\ y \geq 0 \\ 3x + 2y \geq 12 \end{cases}$
Minimum for
$C = 4x + y$

13. $\begin{cases} 3x + 2y \leq 12 \\ x + y \leq 5 \\ x \geq 0, y \geq 0 \end{cases}$
Maximum for
$P = 3x + 5y$

14. Open-ended Write a system of restrictions that form a triangle. Write an objective function and evaluate it at each vertex. At which vertex does the objective function have its maximum value?

Graphs in Three Dimensions

You can use three perpendicular axes to graph equations in three variables. The graph of an equation of the form $Ax + By + Cz = D$ is a plane. The plane intersects one of the axes of the coordinate system at an **intercept**. A line through two intercepts is a trace.

Give a description of where each point lies. Then graph the point.

15. $(0, 2, 0)$ **16.** $(2, 3, 0)$ **17.** $(1, 0, 4)$ **18.** $(1, 3, -1)$

Graph each equation. Use intercepts and traces.

19. $2x + 6y + 3z = 18$ **20.** $-10x + 4y + 5z = -20$ **21.** $3x - y + 3z = 9$

22. $x - 2y + z = 4$ **23.** $20x - 70y - 50z = 100$ **24.** $-x + 3y - 2z = 6$

25. Standardized Test Prep Which point does *not* lie on the graph of $2x + y - 4z = 16$?

  A. $(0, 16, 0)$ **B.** $(10, 4, 2)$ **C.** $(3, 2, -2)$ **D.** $(4, 4, 1)$ **E.** $(2, 4, -2)$

Systems with Three Variables

In a system of equations of the form $Ax + By + Cz = D$, the number of solutions depends on how the planes intersect. There can be no solution, one solution, or an infinite number of solutions.

You can use elimination and substitution to solve systems of equations with three variables. Work with the equations in pairs.

In a system of equations, if equations simplify to an equation that is always false, the equations are inconsistent. If equations simplify to an equation that is always true, the equations are dependent.

Solve each system. Look for substitutions to shorten your work.

26. $\begin{cases} 2x + y - z = 5 \\ 3x + 2y + z = -1 \\ x + 5y + 2z = 6 \end{cases}$

27. $\begin{cases} x + y + z = 3 \\ 2y - 3z = -7 \\ z = 1 \end{cases}$

28. $\begin{cases} 3x + 7y + 2z = 8 \\ -3x + 5y - z = 13 \\ 3x - y - 2z = 4 \end{cases}$

29. $\begin{cases} x + y + z = 10 \\ 2x - y + z = 2 \\ -x + 2y - z = 5 \end{cases}$

30. $\begin{cases} a + 2b + c = 14 \\ b = c + 1 \\ a = -3c + 6 \end{cases}$

31. $\begin{cases} 3r + s - 2t = 22 \\ r + 5s + t = 4 \\ r = -3t \end{cases}$

Inverse Matrices and Systems 4-6

You can write a system of equations as a matrix equation. When a matrix equation is in the form $AX = B$, A is the **coefficient matrix**, X is the **variable matrix**, and B is the **constant matrix**. To solve $AX = B$, find the inverse of matrix A and use the equation $X = A^{-1}B$.

When the coefficient matrix has no inverse, the system either has no solution or an infinite number of solutions. In this case, you must use another method to solve the system.

32. A club of 17 students is going on a canoe trip. They also have five chaperones, one for each canoe. Some canoes hold five people, some hold four people. How many of each kind of canoe should they rent?

Solve each system. If possible, use an inverse matrix.

33. $\begin{cases} x - y = 3 \\ 2x - y = -1 \end{cases}$

34. $\begin{bmatrix} 4 & 1 \\ 2 & 1 \end{bmatrix}\begin{bmatrix} x \\ y \end{bmatrix} = \begin{bmatrix} 10 \\ 6 \end{bmatrix}$

35. $\begin{cases} 4x + 5y = 7 \\ x + 2y = 3 \end{cases}$

36. $\begin{bmatrix} 1 & 2 \\ 3 & -1 \end{bmatrix}\begin{bmatrix} x \\ y \end{bmatrix} = \begin{bmatrix} -4 \\ 9 \end{bmatrix}$

37. $\begin{cases} x + 2y = 15 \\ 2x + 4y = 30 \end{cases}$

38. $\begin{cases} 2x - y = 15 \\ x + 3y = -17 \end{cases}$

Getting Ready for.. ▶ CHAPTER

5

Graph each function.

39. $y = x^2$

40. $y = x^2 - 4$

41. $y = x^2 + 3$

42. $y = (x - 3)^2$

43. $y = -(x + 2)^2$

44. $y = \frac{1}{2}x^2$

45. $y = -x^2 + 1$

46. $y = 5x^2 - 3x - 2$

Evaluate each function for $x = -2, 0, 3,$ and 5.

47. $y = 2x^2$

48. $y = -x^2 - x$

49. $y = x^2 + 2x - 3$

50. $y = 4x^2 - x + 2$

Solve each system. State which method you use.

1. $\begin{cases} y = 5x - 2 \\ y = x + 4 \end{cases}$
2. $\begin{cases} y \geq x + 3 \\ y < -x - 1 \end{cases}$

3. $\begin{cases} y \leq 7 \\ y \leq x + 1 \end{cases}$
4. $\begin{cases} 3x + 2y = 9 \\ x + y = 4 \end{cases}$

5. $\begin{cases} x - y + z = 0 \\ 3x - 2y + 6z = 9 \\ -x + y - 2z = -2 \end{cases}$
6. $\begin{cases} 2x + y + z = 8 \\ x + 2y - z = -5 \\ z = 2x - y \end{cases}$

7. $\begin{cases} x + y + z = 9 \\ 4x + 3y - z = -6 \\ -x - y + 2z = 21 \end{cases}$
8. $\begin{cases} x + 2y + z = -1 \\ 4x - y - z = -1 \\ 2z = -3y \end{cases}$

9. **Writing** List the four methods of solving systems of linear equations. When is it most useful to use each method?

Use linear programming. Find the values of x and y that maximize or minimize the objective function.

10. $\begin{cases} x \leq 6 \\ y \leq 5 \\ x \geq 0, y \geq 0 \end{cases}$
    Maximum for
    $P = 2x + y$

11. $\begin{cases} x + y \leq 8 \\ x + 2y \geq 6 \\ x \geq 0, y \geq 0 \end{cases}$
    Minimum for
    $C = x + 3y$

12. **Sales** A pizza shop makes $1.50 on each small pizza and $2.15 on each large pizza. On a typical Friday, it sells from 70 to 90 small pizzas and from 100 to 140 large pizzas. The total sales have never exceeded 210 pizzas. How many of each size of pizza must be sold to maximize profit?

13. **Open-ended** Write a system of restrictions that form a parallelogram.

Graph each point.

14. $(0, 5, 0)$ 15. $(-1, 0, 0)$ 16. $(1, 0, 4)$

17. $(3, 0, -1)$ 18. $(1, 4, -1)$ 19. $(2, -2, 3)$

Graph each equation. Use intercepts and traces.

20. $x + y + z = 6$ 21. $2x - 3y + z = 6$

22. $-2x + y - 5z = 10$ 23. $x - y + 2z = 8$

24. You are going to buy decorations for a party. You can spend no more than $24. Regular balloons cost $.06, mylar balloons cost $.48, and streamers cost $.08 each. Write an inequality that models this situation.

Solve each system of equations using a matrix equation.

25. $\begin{cases} 2x - y = 5 \\ x + 4y = 7 \end{cases}$
26. $\begin{cases} 4x + 5y = 20 \\ 7x - y = 11 \end{cases}$

27. $\begin{cases} -3x + 2y = 10 \\ 2x + 3y = 12 \end{cases}$
28. $\begin{cases} x + 5y = 10 \\ 3x - y = 8 \end{cases}$

29. $\begin{cases} x - y = 7 \\ 4x + y = 38 \end{cases}$
30. $\begin{cases} -2x + 7y = 19 \\ x + 3y = 10 \end{cases}$

31. **Standardized Test Prep** How many solutions can a system with two linear equations have?
    I. 0   **II.** 1   **III.** infinitely many
    A. I only   **B.** II only   **C.** I or II
    D. II and III   **E.** I, II, and III

Write a system of equations to solve each problem. State which method you use.

32. A company had $50,000 to invest in three funds. After one year it had $54,500. The growth fund returned 12%, the income fund returned 8%, and the money market fund returned 5%. The company invested twice as much in the income fund as in the money market fund. How much did it invest in each fund?

33. Sharnell can make a weekly salary of $200 plus 15% commission on sales at the Radio Barn or a weekly salary of $300 plus 10% commission on sales at Woofer, Etc. For what amount of sales do these two jobs pay the same?

For Exercises 1–12, choose the correct letter.

1. Which point is not a solution of the following system?
$$\begin{cases} x + y \leq 4 \\ 2x - y \geq -3 \end{cases}$$
   A. $(1, 1)$ **B.** $(0, 3)$ **C.** $(-5, -1)$
   D. $(3, 0)$ **E.** $(2, 2)$

2. What is the probability of rolling a 1 and a 6 if you roll two number cubes?
   A. $\frac{1}{6}$ **B.** $\frac{1}{12}$ **C.** $\frac{1}{3}$
   D. $\frac{1}{36}$ **E.** none of the above

3. Which lines are perpendicular to $y = 3x - 8$?
   I. $y = \frac{1}{3}x - 1$ **II.** $y = -\frac{1}{3}x + 1$
   III. $y = 3x + 2$ **IV.** $y = 6x + 3$
   A. I only   **B.** II only   **C.** I and II
   D. II and IV   **E.** I and III

4. What is the inverse of $\begin{bmatrix} 2 & 3 \\ -1 & -1 \end{bmatrix}$?
   A. $\begin{bmatrix} 1 & 3 \\ -1 & -2 \end{bmatrix}$ **B.** $\begin{bmatrix} 1 & -3 \\ 1 & -2 \end{bmatrix}$ **C.** $\begin{bmatrix} -1 & 3 \\ -1 & 2 \end{bmatrix}$
   D. $\begin{bmatrix} -1 & -3 \\ 1 & 2 \end{bmatrix}$ **E.** none of the above

5. Simplify $\begin{bmatrix} 3 & 7 & -2 \\ 0 & 10 & 5 \end{bmatrix} + \begin{bmatrix} 6 & -8 & 1 \\ 9 & -4 & 11 \end{bmatrix}$.
   A. $\begin{bmatrix} 9 & -1 & -1 \\ 9 & 6 & 16 \end{bmatrix}$ **B.** $\begin{bmatrix} 9 & 15 & -1 \\ 9 & 6 & 16 \end{bmatrix}$
   C. $\begin{bmatrix} 9 & 15 & -3 \\ 9 & 6 & 16 \end{bmatrix}$ **D.** $\begin{bmatrix} -3 & 1 & -3 \\ -9 & 14 & -6 \end{bmatrix}$
   E. none of the above

6. When $f(x) = x^2$ and $g(x) = -2x - 5$, what is the value of $f(g(-3))$?
   A. 3   **B.** 259   **C.** 12
   D. 363   **E.** none of the above

7. A scatter plot has a positive correlation. Which equation could model the data?
   A. $-y = 4x - 2$ **B.** $2x + 3y = 6$
   C. $y = 3x - 8$ **D.** $y = -6x + 8$
   E. none of the above

8. At which vertex is the objective function $C = 3x + y$ maximized?
   A. $(0, 0)$ **B.** $(6, 0)$ **C.** $(2, 6)$
   D. $(3, 5)$ **E.** $(0, 5)$

9. Which number is irrational?
   A. 8.12   **B.** $\sqrt{121}$ **C.** 25
   D. $\sqrt{35}$ **E.** none of the above

10. Which point is a solution of $y > x^2 + 5$?
    A. $(2, 10)$ **B.** $(1, 6)$ **C.** $(0, 4)$
    D. $(-1, 4)$ **E.** $(-3, 0)$

Compare the quantity in Column A with that in Column B. Choose the best answer.

   A. The quantity in Column A is greater.
   B. The quantity in Column B is greater.
   C. The two quantities are equal.
   D. The relationship cannot be determined on the basis of the information supplied.

Column A	Column B
11. $\frac{6!}{2!}$	$\frac{9!}{7!}$
12. the slope of $2x + 3y = 6$	the y-intercept of $3x + 2y = 4$

Find each answer.

13. **Open-ended** Draw a mapping diagram of a relation that is not a function.

14. A dietitian prepares a meal with three foods.

Food	Protein	Fat	Carbohydrates
A	2 g/oz	3 g/oz	4 g/oz
B	3 g/oz	3 g/oz	1 g/oz
C	3 g/oz	3 g/oz	2 g/oz

The meal should have 24 g of protein, 27 g of fat, and 20 g of carbohydrates. How many ounces of each food should be used?

5 Quadratic Equations and Functions

Relating to the Real World

Falling objects—everything from skydivers to arrows shot from bows—are affected by gravity. The distance an object travels is modeled by a quadratic function. Graphing quadratic functions and solving related equations can help you solve many problems related to the paths of falling objects.

Modeling Data with Quadratic Functions

Properties of Parabolas

Comparing Vertex and Standard Forms

Inverses and Square Root Functions

Quadratic Equations

| Lessons | 5-1 | 5-2 | 5-3 | 5-4 | 5-5 |

ON TARGET

A rchery has its roots in prehistoric times. Cave drawings in Spain, France, and North Africa show hunters using bows and arrows. In the Far East, people made bows by gluing wood, bone, and animal tendons together. Early Native Americans also used bows and arrows. After the introduction of firearms, archery became a recreational sport. In 1988 at the Olympic Games in Barcelona, it was an archer who lit the Olympic flame. As you work through the chapter, you will research topics such as how archers choose their arrows and how technology has changed the sport. You may want to finish your project by making a display or other presentation.

To help you complete the project:

▼ **p. 210** *Find Out by Graphing*
▼ **p. 215** *Find Out by Analyzing*
▼ **p. 233** *Find Out by Modeling*
▼ **p. 239** *Find Out by Researching*
▼ **p. 246** *Finishing the Project*

Complex Numbers	Completing the Square	The Quadratic Formula
5-6	5-7	5-8

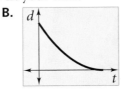

What You'll Learn

- Recognizing and using quadratic functions
- Deciding whether to use a linear or a quadratic model

...And Why

To describe nonlinear data, such as temperatures

What You'll Need

- two-liter plastic bottle
- masking tape
- nail
- ruler
- digital watch
- water
- pan or basin
- graph paper
- graphing calculator

5-1 Modeling Data with Quadratic Functions

W O R K   T O G E T H E R

Science Do this experiment in groups. Assign the roles of timer and marker to members of your group.

Setting Up Place a strip of masking tape along the length of the bottle. Make a hole near its base using a nail.

Getting Ready Mark the level of the hole on the tape. Label this mark 0. Place tape over the hole. Fill the bottle with water and mark the water level on the tape.

Collecting the Data Remove the tape from the hole and let the water escape. Every ten seconds, mark the level of the water. Continue marking until the water level reaches 0.

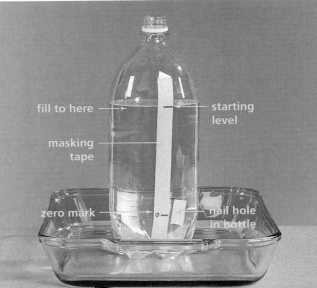

Time (s)	Water Level (mm)
0	
10	
20	
30	
40	
⋮	⋮

1. Measure the distance from 0 to each mark. Make a table like the one at the left for your data.

2. **a.** Graph your data.
   b. Add a trend line to your graph. Do the data appear to be linear?

3. Which curve seems to fit your data more closely? Sketch a curve to fit your data.

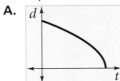

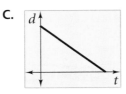

Quadratic Functions

Nonlinear data, such as the data you gathered in the Work Together, can sometimes be modeled by a quadratic function. A **quadratic function** is one that can be written in the form $f(x) = ax^2 + bx + c$, where $a \neq 0$.

$$f(x) = ax^2 + bx + c \leftarrow \textbf{standard form}$$

$$\begin{array}{ccc}
\uparrow & \uparrow & \uparrow \\
\text{quadratic} & \text{linear} & \text{constant} \\
\text{term} & \text{term} & \text{term}
\end{array}$$

The graph of a quadratic function is a **parabola.**

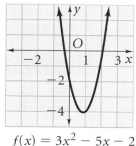

$$f(x) = 3x^2 - 5x - 2$$

4. Which points are on the graph of the function $f(x) = 3x^2 - 5x - 2$?
   a. $(1, -4)$ **b.** $(2, 0)$ **c.** $(0, 2)$ **d.** $(-3, 40)$

The greatest exponent of a variable in a quadratic function is two. A function is linear if the greatest exponent of a variable is one.

Example 1 ···

Tell whether the function $y = (2x + 3)(x - 4)$ is linear or quadratic.

Begin by rewriting the function in standard form. Multiply the binomials using the FOIL method.

$$y = (2x + 3)(x - 4)$$

with labels: First, Last, Inner, Outer

$$= 2x^2 - 8x + 3x - 12 \quad \leftarrow \text{Multiply.}$$
$$= 2x^2 - 5x - 12 \quad \leftarrow \text{Combine like terms.}$$

Since this function has an x^2 term, it is quadratic.

5. Try This Tell whether each function is linear or quadratic.
   a. $y = (x - 3)(x + 2)$ **b.** $f(x) = x(x + 3)$
   c. $f(x) = (x^2 + 5x) - x^2$ **d.** $y = (x - 5)^2$

Modeling Data

Gatlinburg Average High Temperatures

Month	Temperature
Feb	52°F
Apr	72°F
Jun	84°F
Aug	86°F
Oct	71°F
Dec	52°F

Source: *USA Today Weather Almanac*

In Lesson 1-3, you found a linear model with a trend line or a line of best fit. Some data can be modeled better with a quadratic function.

6. Weather The scatter plot shows the average high temperature in Gatlinburg, Tennessee, for each month listed in the table (January = 1, and so on). Why would a linear model not be useful?

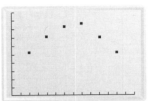

Xmin=0   Ymin=0
Xmax=14   Ymax=100
Xscl=1   Yscl=10

The data appear to fit the shape of a parabola that opens downward. You can use a quadratic equation to model the data.

To find a quadratic model, you can either solve a system of equations or use the quadratic regression feature of a graphing calculator.

Example 2 · Relating to the Real World

Weather Use the data in the table to find a quadratic model for the average monthly high temperature in Gatlinburg.

You need to find an equation of the form $y = ax^2 + bx + c$. Let x represent the month of the year and y represent the temperature in degrees Fahrenheit.

Method 1: Solving a System of Equations

From the table, you know six points that should be on the graph. Choose three points. Substitute their coordinates into the equation $y = ax^2 + bx + c$ to form a system of three linear equations.

For more practice evaluating expressions, see the Skills Handbook page 666.

$$y = ax^2 + bx + c$$
$$52 = a(2)^2 + b(2) + c \quad \longleftarrow \text{Use the point (2, 52).}$$
$$84 = a(6)^2 + b(6) + c \quad \longleftarrow \text{Use the point (6, 84).}$$
$$71 = a(10)^2 + b(10) + c \quad \longleftarrow \text{Use the point (10, 71).}$$

In which month(s) would you be most likely to see this temperature in Gatlinburg?

Simplify these equations. Then solve them using one of the methods of Chapter 4. The solution is $a \approx -1.41$, $b = 19.25$, and $c \approx 19.13$.

Substitute the values of a, b, and c into the general equation. A quadratic model is $y = -1.41x^2 + 19.25x + 19.13$.

Method 2: Using the Quadratic Regression Feature
- Clear all statistical lists from your graphing calculator.
- Using the STAT feature, enter the data in the table. Enter the number of each month in one list and the corresponding temperature in another.
- Choose the QuadReg option. The following screen should appear.

QuadReg
$y=ax^2+bx+c$
$a=-1.352678571$
$b=18.92321429$
$c=19.1$

Rounding the a and b values to the nearest hundredth, you find that a quadratic model that approximates the temperature data is $y = -1.35x^2 + 18.92x + 19.1$.

7. Use each quadratic model from Example 2. **Predict** the average high temperature in Gatlinburg in September. How close are your two results?

8. **a.** Find an equation to model the data on page 200 using the first three sets of month and temperature data.
   b. Use the equation you found in part (a) to predict the average high temperature in Gatlinburg in September.
   c. *Critical Thinking* The average high temperature in Gatlinburg in September is 81°F. What conclusions can you make about selecting data if you are not using all the data to find a model?

Exercises ON YOUR OWN

Tell whether each graph could be that of a quadratic function.

1.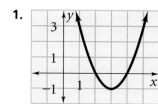
2.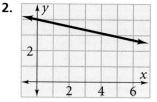
3.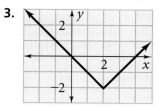
4.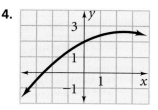

Multiply.

5. $(x + 4)(x - 7)$ 6. $(2b - 1)(b - 1)$ 7. $(x + 3)^2$ 8. $(z - 8)(z + 8)$

9. $(3t + 10)(2t + 1)$ 10. $(7r - 6)^2$ 11. $(2w - 9)^2$ 12. $(5y + 4)(5y - 6)$

13. $(8x + b)(7x - b)$ 14. $(2x + 5y)(3x + 9y)$ 15. $w(w - 4)(w - 2)$ 16. $2p(-p + 1)(p + 1)$

17. Modeling The table shows possible data from the Work Together experiment.

Elapsed Time	Water Level
0 s	120 mm
10 s	100 mm
20 s	83 mm
30 s	66 mm
40 s	50 mm
50 s	37 mm
60 s	28 mm

   a. Find a linear model for the data.
   b. Find a quadratic model for the data.
   c. Graph the data and each model. Which appears to be a better fit? Explain.

18. Open-ended Find a quadratic model for your own Work Together data.

19. Writing When is a quadratic function a better model than a linear function? Illustrate your answer with an example.

Tell whether each function is linear or quadratic.

20. $y = x + 4$ **21.** $f(x) = x^2 - 7$ **22.** $g(x) = -7x$

23. $y = 3(x - 1)^2 + 4$ **24.** $f(x) = \frac{1}{2}(4x + 10)$ **25.** $y = 3x(x - 2)$

26. $h(x) = (3x)(2x)$ **27.** $g(x) = (2x + 5)^2$ **28.** $y = (x - 2)(x + 5)$

29. $f(x) = -x(x - 4) + x^2$ **30.** $y = 2x - (3x - 5)$ **31.** $y = (2x + 1)(x - 4)$

32. a. Geometry Copy and complete the table below. It shows the total number of segments that can be drawn among x points, no three of which are collinear.

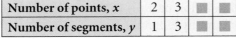

Number of points, x	2	3	■	■
Number of segments, y	1	3	■	■

   b. Write a quadratic model for the data.
   c. Predict the number of segments that can be drawn among ten points.

33. a. Copy and complete the two tables below. In the last row, write the difference between the consecutive y-values.

Table 1

x	0	1	2	3	4	5
$y = 2x$	0	2	4	6	8	10
Difference	2	2	■	■	■	

Table 2

x	0	1	2	3	4	5
$y = 2x^2$	0	2	8	18	32	50
Difference	2	6	■	■	■	

   b. Which function is quadratic?
   c. What pattern do you see in the last row of Table 1? of Table 2?
   d. Make tables of values for the functions $y = -x + 4$ and $y = -x^2 + 4$. Use the same x-values as in part (a). Do you see the same patterns as in part (c)?
   e. Write a **conjecture** about how the y-values of a data set can help you predict whether a linear or a quadratic function will be a better model.

34. a. Postage Find a quadratic model and a linear model for the data.

Price of a First-Class Stamp (1 oz)

Year (58 = 1958)	58	63	68	71	74	78	81	83	88	95
Cost (in cents)	4	5	6	8	10	15	18	22	25	32

Source: *U.S. Postal Service*

b. Which model represents the data better? Explain.
c. Estimate when first-class postage was 29¢.
d. Predict when first-class postage will be 50¢.

35. Critical Thinking What is the minimum number of data pairs needed to find a quadratic model for a data set?

Find an equation for each set of data.

36.

x	−1	0	1	2	3
f(x)	5	3	1	−1	−3

37.

x	−1	0	1	2	3
f(x)	−1	0	3	8	15

38.

x	−1	0	1	2	3
f(x)	17	20	17	8	−7

39. a. Communications Find a quadratic model for the data about television viewing habits in the United States.

Percent of Households Watching the Top-Rated Television Show

Season Ending In	1984	1985	1988	1990	1992	1994
Rating (%)	25.7	33.8	27.8	23.4	21.7	21.9

Source: *Nielsen Media Research*

b. Estimation Estimate the rating of the top-rated television show in 1998; in 2004.
c. Research Find the rating of the top-rated television show for a year since 1995. Compare it with the prediction from your model.

Exercises   MIXED REVIEW

Solve each equation.

40. $3x - 4 = -25$ **41.** $2r + 7 = 5r - 1$ **42.** $\frac{3}{4}z = \frac{1}{2}z - 3$ **43.** $\frac{x-2}{3} = 8$

44. Air Travel Traveling with the wind, a plane flew 4000 km in 5 h. Against the wind, the plane only flew 3000 km in the same amount of time. Find the speed of the plane in calm air and the speed of the wind.

Getting Ready for Lesson 5-2

Describe the translation of the function $y = x^2$.

45. $y = (x - 3)^2$ **46.** $y = (x + 2)^2 - 7$ **47.** $y = x^2 + 9$ **48.** $y = (x - 6)^2 + 4$

Comparing Models

After Lesson 5-1

You can have more than one model for a set of data. You can determine which is a better model by analyzing the differences between the y-values of the data and the y-values of each model. The differences are called *residuals*. The better model will have residuals that are closer to zero.

Example

The calculator screen shows the graphs of two models, $y = 224.88x - 1896$ and $y = 3.58x^2 + 46.13x - 108.5$, for the data below.

Mobile Homes in the United States

Year (0 = 1950)	10	20	30	40
Number (1000s)	767	2074	4663	7400

Xmin=0 Ymin=0
Xmax=50 Ymax=7500
Xscl=5 Yscl=1500

To find out which model fits the data better, use these steps.

Step 1: Use the $\boxed{\text{STAT}}$ feature to enter the data in L_1 and L_2. Enter the linear model as Y_1 and the quadratic model as Y_2.

Step 2: To find the residuals of the linear model and store the differences in L_3, press $\boxed{\text{2nd}}$ L_2 $\boxed{-}$ $\boxed{\text{2nd}}$ Y-vars $\boxed{1}$ $\boxed{1}$ $\boxed{(}$ $\boxed{\text{2nd}}$ L_1 $\boxed{)}$ $\boxed{\text{STO}\blacktriangleright}$ $\boxed{\text{2nd}}$ L_3 $\boxed{\text{ENTER}}$.

Step 3: Find the residuals of the quadratic model. Store the differences in L_4.

Step 4: Compare the residuals in L_3 and L_4. The values in L_4 are closer to 0, so the quadratic model is the better fit.

L2	L3	L4
767	414.2	56.2
2074	−527.6	−172.1
4663	−187.4	165.6
7400	300.8	−64.7
------	-------	------

L4(5)=

Writing For each set of data, which model is the better fit? Justify your reasoning.

1. Use the data at the right and the models $y = 3.08x + 0.12$ and $y = 0.19x^2 - 1.37x + 9.59$.

Money Spent on Personal Technology in U.S.

Year (0 = 1970)	0	10	20	21	22	23
Billions of Dollars	8.8	17.6	54.1	62.2	70.4	83.7

2. Use the data at the right and the models $y = 0.25x + 32.21$ and $y = -0.01x^2 + 0.43x + 31.66$.

Fishing Licenses Sold

Year (0 = 1970)	0	5	10	15	20
Millions Sold	31.1	34.9	35.2	35.7	37.0

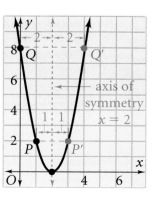
What You'll Learn

- Finding the minimum or maximum value of a quadratic function
- Graphing a parabola in vertex form

...And Why

To find an equation that models the cables of a suspension bridge

5-2 Properties of Parabolas

THINK AND DISCUSS

Comparing Parabolas

Objects that are tossed into the air, such as the oranges in the photo, follow a parabolic path.

1. Use the graph on the photo below. The scale is in inches. What is the greatest height the oranges reach?

The function $y = -0.35x^2 + 50$ models the parabola. You can use the equation to find the highest point of the parabola.

2. **a.** Make a table of values for $y = -0.35x^2 + 50$. Which value of x seems to make y greatest? What is the maximum value for y?
   b. How do your answers to Questions 1 and 2a compare?

The highest (or lowest) point of a parabola that is the graph of a function is its **vertex.** It is the point at which the function has its maximum (or minimum) value.

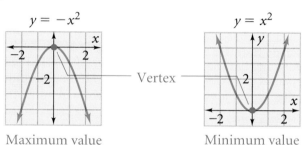

$y = -x^2$ — Maximum value

$y = x^2$ — Minimum value

Vertex

The **axis of symmetry** divides a parabola into two parts that are mirror images. Each point of the parabola has a corresponding point on its mirror image. Two corresponding points are the same distance from the axis of symmetry.

3. **a.** Use the graph at the right. Give the coordinates of the vertex.

   b. What point corresponds to $Q'(4, 8)$? to $P(1, 2)$?

All parabolas have the same basic shape. The width of a parabola changes as the coefficient of the quadratic term (x^2) changes. Consider the graphs at the right.

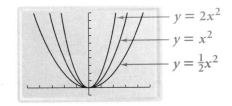

$y = 2x^2$
$y = x^2$
$y = \frac{1}{2}x^2$

4. a. Identify the coefficient of each quadratic term.

b. How does increasing the value of a coefficient affect the graph of a quadratic function?

5. a. **Graphing Calculator** Graph the parabolas $y = -\frac{1}{3}x^2$, $y = -x^2$, and $y = -3x^2$.

b. Complete this statement: As the absolute value of the coefficient of the quadratic term increases, the graph of a function becomes (wider, narrower).

The function that models a parabola that has a vertex at $(0, 0)$ is $y = ax^2$. To find an equation of the function, use the coordinates of a point other than the vertex.

Example 1   **Relating to the Real World** ···················

Civil Engineering   Each tower of the Verrazano-Narrows Bridge rises about 650 ft above the center of the roadbed. The length of the main span is 4260 ft. Find the equation of the parabola that could model its main cables. Assume that the vertex of the parabola is at the origin.

Start by drawing a diagram.

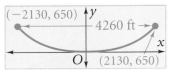

$(-2130, 650)$ y
4260 ft
x
O $(2130, 650)$

Since $(2130, 650)$ is on the graph, substitute the values into $y = ax^2$.

$$y = ax^2$$
$$650 = a(2130)^2$$
$$\frac{650}{2130^2} = a$$
$$a \approx 0.00014$$

An equation describing the shape formed by the cables is $y = 0.00014x^2$.

The Verrazano-Narrows Bridge in New York City has the longest span of any suspension bridge in the United States.

Translating Parabolas

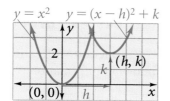

$y = x^2 \quad y = (x - h)^2 + k$

(h, k)

$(0, 0)$

Not every parabola has its vertex at the origin. An equation of the form $y = a(x - h)^2 + k$, called the **vertex form,** is a translation of $y = ax^2$.

Recall from Chapter 1 that when h and k are positive, the translation moves the graph h units right and k units up. When h is negative, the graph shifts left. When k is negative, the graph shifts down.

You can use the vertex form to write the equation of a translated parabola.

Example 2

Write the equation of the translated parabola.

The vertex has moved 3 units to the right and 4 units up from the origin. So use the equation for a translation, $y = a(x - h)^2 + k$. Then solve for a.

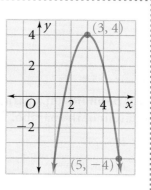

$$y = a(x - h)^2 + k$$
$$y = a(x - 3)^2 + 4 \quad \longleftarrow h = 3, k = 4$$
$$-4 = a(5 - 3)^2 + 4 \quad \longleftarrow \text{Substitute (5, −4).}$$
$$-8 = 4a \quad \longleftarrow \text{Simplify.}$$
$$-2 = a \quad \longleftarrow \text{Solve for } a.$$

The equation of the parabola is $y = -2(x - 3)^2 + 4$.

You can use the properties of parabolas to graph quadratic functions.

Example 3

Sketch the graph of $y = -\frac{1}{2}(x - 2)^2 + 3$.

■ Plot the vertex, (2, 3). Draw the axis of symmetry, $x = 2$.

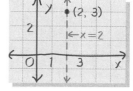

■ Find another point.
For $x = 0$, $y = 1$. Plot (0, 1).

■ Plot the reflection of (0, 1).

■ Sketch a curve through the three points.

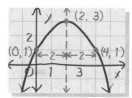

6. **a.** Find the coordinates of the vertex and the equation of the axis of symmetry for the graph of $y = -2(x - 5)^2 - 1$.
   b. Try This Sketch the graph of the equation in part (a).

The properties of parabolas are summarized below.

Properties of Parabolas Written in Vertex Form

An equation of the form $y = a(x - h)^2 + k$ is a function written in vertex form. The vertex form gives you the following information.

- The vertex is (h, k) and the axis of symmetry is the line $x = h$.
- The parabola opens up when a is positive and opens down when a is negative.
- If $|a| < 1$, the graph will be wider than the graph of $y = x^2$; if $|a| > 1$, the graph will be narrower.

Exercises   ON YOUR OWN

Each point lies on a parabola that has its vertex at the origin. Write the equation of the parabola. Tell whether the graph opens up or down.

1. $P(3, 2)$ **2.** $Q(-1, 6)$ **3.** $R(2, -1)$ **4.** $A(4, -8)$

5. $B(-3, 1)$ **6.** $C(5, -2)$ **7.** $F(8, -12)$ **8.** $G(-6, -2)$

Write the equation of each parabola in vertex form.

9.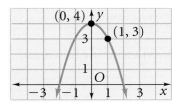

10.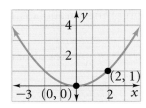

11.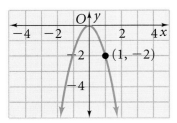

12.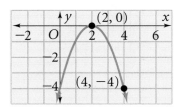

13.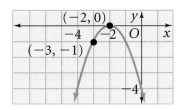

14.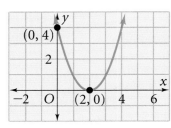

15.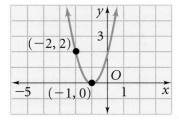

16.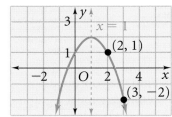

17.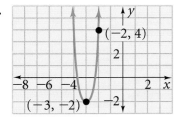

Sketch the graph of each equation. Label the coordinates of each vertex.

18. $y = (x + 3)^2$

19. $y = (x - 2)^2$

20. $y = -(x + 1)^2$

21. $y = -x^2 + 3$

22. $y = -5x^2 + 3$

23. $y = (x + 4)^2 + 1$

24. $y = 3(x - 2)^2 + 4$

25. $y = -4(x + 3)^2$

26. $y = -2(x + 1)^2 - 4$

27. $y = (x + 2)^2 - 3$

28. $y = (x - 2)^2 - 3$

29. $y = 2x^2 + 3$

30. $y = 0.5(x - 2)^2 - 5$

31. $y = \frac{1}{4}(x - 12)^2$

32. $y = -(x + 1)^2 + 11$

33. a. Technology Determine the axes of symmetry for the parabolas defined by the spreadsheet values at the right.
  b. How could you use the spreadsheet columns to verify that the axes of symmetry are correct?
  c. Write equations in vertex form that model the data. Check that the axes of symmetry are correct.

	A	B
1	X1	Y1
2	1	-35
3	2	-15
4	3	-3
5	4	1
6	5	-3

	A	B
1	X2	Y2
2	1	10
3	2	2
4	3	2
5	4	10
6	5	26

34. Open-ended Write the equation of a function whose graph is a parabola with an axis of symmetry of $x = -2$.

35. a. Geometry You throw a ball over a 5-ft fence. The ball clears the fence but without much room to spare. The ball lands 10 ft from the fence. Using the fence as the axis of symmetry, write an equation that approximates the path of the ball. (Let the origin be where the fence meets the ground.)
  b. Is the equation you wrote in part (a) in vertex form? Why or why not?

36. Business The Brick Oven Bakery sells more loaves of bread when it reduces its price, but then its profits change. The function $y = -100(x - 1.75)^2 + 300$ models the bakery's profits, in dollars, where x is the price of a loaf of bread in dollars. The bakery wants to maximize its profits.
  a. What is the domain of the function? Can x ever be negative? Explain.
  b. Find the daily profit for selling the bread at $2.00 per loaf; at $1.25 per loaf.
  c. What price should the bakery charge to maximize its profits?
  d. What is the maximum profit?

37. Writing Describe the steps you would use to sketch the graph of $y = -2(x - 3)^2 + 4$.

Sketch each parabola using the given information. Write its equation in vertex form.

38. vertex $(0, 0)$; point $(2, 10)$ **39.** vertex $(0, 0)$; point $(-2, 10)$ **40.** vertex $(0, 0)$; point $(2, -5)$

41. vertex $(3, 6)$; y-intercept of 2   **42.** vertex $(-3, 6)$; point $(1, -2)$ **43.** vertex $(-2, 6)$; x-intercept of 2

44. vertex $(-1, 4)$; y-intercept of 3   **45.** vertex $(0, 5)$; point $(1, -2)$ **46.** vertex $(8, -3)$; x-intercept of 5

Chapter Project   **Find Out by Graphing**

An archer releases an arrow at shoulder height. Measure the distance from the floor to your shoulder when you are standing. Suppose you release an arrow and it hits the target at a point 5 ft above the ground. Sketch a possible parabolic path of your arrow's flight using this information.

Archery is one of only a few sports in which athletes using wheelchairs can compete with other athletes. Measure the distance from the floor to your shoulder while you are sitting in a chair. Sketch the possible path of an arrow released by someone using a wheelchair. Describe the similarities and differences between your two sketches.

Exercises   M I X E D   R E V I E W

Graph each inequality. Use a coordinate grid.

47. $y < 5x - 1$ **48.** $y > 2x + 7$ **49.** $3x - 2y \leq 12$ **50.** $5x + 4y \geq 20$

51. $3y \leq 15x - 12$ **52.** $-y \geq 4x - 6$ **53.** $-2x - 3y < 30$ **54.** $0.5x + 0.4y > 2$

55. a. Museums The Smithsonian Institution has a traveling exhibit of popular items. The exhibit requires 3 million ft^3 of space, including 100,000 ft^2 of floor space. How tall must the ceilings be?

    b. The exhibit also requires a constant temperature of 70°F, plus or minus 3°. Write an inequality to model this temperature T.

Getting Ready for Lesson 5-3

Rewrite each equation without parentheses.

56. $y = (x + 1)^2 + 4$ **57.** $y = 2(x - 5)^2$

58. $y = -(x - 3)^2 + 6$ **59.** $y = -3(x - 7)^2$

60. $y = 7(x + 4)^2$ **61.** $y = (x - 6)^2 + 10$

62. $y = -5(x - 5)^2$ **63.** $y = -(x + 4)^2 + 10$

SELF ASSESSMENT

FOR YOUR JOURNAL

In your own words, summarize the properties of parabolas. List the advantages of having an equation written in vertex form when sketching its graph.

What You'll Learn

- Finding the vertex of a function written in standard form
- Writing equations in vertex and standard forms

...And Why

To find the maximum area of objects such as picture frames

What You'll Need

- graphing calculator

5-3 Comparing Vertex and Standard Forms

WORK TOGETHER

Work in groups of four.

1. a. Graphing Calculator Have each person in your group graph a pair of the following equations on the same calculator screen.

$y = ax^2 + bx + c$ (standard form)	a	b	$y = a(x - h)^2 + k$ (vertex form)	h
$y = x^2 - 4x + 4$	▧	▧	$y = (x - 2)^2$	▧
$y = x^2 + 6x + 8$	▧	▧	$y = (x + 3)^2 - 1$	▧
$y = -3x^2 - 12x - 8$	▧	▧	$y = -3(x + 2)^2 + 4$	▧
$y = 2x^2 + 12x + 19$	▧	▧	$y = 2(x + 3)^2 + 1$	▧

b. What do you notice about the graphs of each pair of equations?

c. What is true of each pair of equations?

2. a. Patterns Copy and complete the table above.

b. Look at the values of b and h in the first two pairs of equations. Write a formula to show the relationship between b and h.

c. Use the last two pairs of equations to extend your formula to show the relationship among a, b, and h.

THINK AND DISCUSS

In the Work Together, you investigated how to locate the vertex of the graph of a quadratic function. When the equation of the function is written in standard form, the x-coordinate of the vertex is $-\frac{b}{2a}$. To find the y-coordinate, you substitute the value of the x-coordinate for x in the equation and simplify.

Example 1

Write the function $y = 2x^2 + 10x + 7$ in vertex form.

x-coordinate $= -\dfrac{b}{2a}$ ← Use $-\frac{b}{2a}$ to find the x-coordinate.

$= -\dfrac{10}{2(2)}$ ← Substitute for a and b.

$= -2.5$

y-coordinate $= 2(-2.5)^2 + 10(-2.5) + 7$ ← Substitute -2.5 for x in

$= -5.5$ the original equation.

The vertex form of the function is $y = 2(x + 2.5)^2 - 5.5$.

3. **a.** What is the relationship between the axis of symmetry and the vertex of a parabola?

   b. For the graph of $y = ax^2 + bx + c$, what is the equation of the axis of symmetry?

   c. What is the equation of the axis of symmetry of the graph of $y = 2x^2 + 10x + 7$?

4. **Try This** Write $y = -3x^2 + 12x + 5$ in vertex form. Then graph the function.

You can use the vertex of a parabola to maximize or minimize area.

Example 2   **Relating to the Real World**

Woodworking As a graduation gift for a friend, you plan to frame a collage of pictures. You have a 9-ft strip of wood for the frame. What dimensions of the frame give you the maximum area for the collage?

Use the perimeter formula to find an expression for the length of the frame in terms of the width.

$$108 = 2(\text{length} + w) \quad \longleftarrow P = 9 \text{ ft} = 108 \text{ in.}$$
$$\text{length} = 54 - w \quad \longleftarrow \text{Simplify and solve for length.}$$

Write the equation for the area of the frame.

$$A = (54 - w)(w) \quad \longleftarrow \text{Substitute for length and width.}$$
$$= -w^2 + 54w \quad \longleftarrow \text{Simplify.}$$

The maximum area occurs when $w = -\frac{b}{2a} = -\frac{54}{2(-1)} = 27$.

Since length $= 54 - w$, the maximum area for the frame occurs when the length and the width of the frame are both 27 in.

5. What is the maximum area of the collage in Example 2?

6. **a.** What is the best name for the geometric shape that gives the maximum area for the frame in Example 2?

   b. *Critical Thinking* Do you think this shape will always give the maximum area for a rectangular shape of a given perimeter? **Justify** your answer.

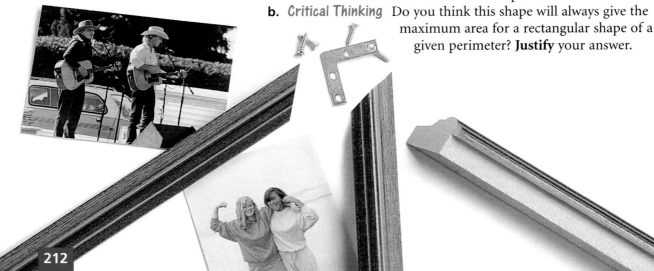

You have changed the equation of a function from standard form to vertex form. You can also change an equation from vertex form to standard form.

Example 3

Write $y = 3(x - 1)^2 + 12$ in standard form.

$y = 3(x - 1)^2 + 12$
$y = 3(x^2 - 2x + 1) + 12$ ←— Find $(x - 1)(x - 1)$.
$y = 3x^2 - 6x + 3 + 12$ ←— Use the distributive property.
$y = 3x^2 - 6x + 15$ ←— Simplify.

7. **Critical Thinking** Both the vertex form and the standard form give information about a function. What are the advantages of using each form to graph a function?

 Exercises ON YOUR OWN

Match each equation with its graph.

1. $y = x^2 + 4x + 1$ 2. $y = -x^2 - 4x + 1$ 3. $y = -\frac{1}{2}x^2 - 2x + 1$ 4. $y = 2x^2 + 4x + 1$
A. 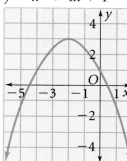   B. 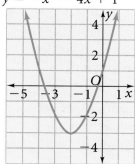   C. 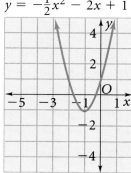   D.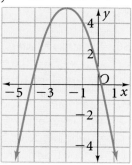

5. **Writing** Explain how you matched $y = -x^2 - 4x + 1$ with its graph in the exercises above.

6. **a. Graphing Calculator** Graph $y = (x - 3)(x + 2)$. What points on the graph can you determine from the equation?
   b. Write the equation in part (a) in standard form and in vertex form.

State whether each equation is written in vertex form. If it is not, write it in vertex form.

7. $y = x^2 - 4x + 6$ 8. $y = x^2 + 2x + 5$ 9. $y = 6x^2 - 10$

10. $f(x) = -2x^2 + 35$ 11. $y = -8x^2$ 12. $f(x) = -5x^2 + 12$

13. $y = 4x^2 + 7x$ 14. $f(x) = 2x^2 + x$ 15. $y = -3x^2 - 2x + 1$

16. $y = 2x^2 - 5x + 12$ 17. $f(x) = \frac{9}{4}x^2$ 18. $y = -2x^2 + 8x + 3$

19. **Landscape Design** A town is planning a child-care facility. It wants to fence in a rectangular playground using one of the walls of a building. What is the largest playground that can be fenced in using 100 ft of donated fencing?

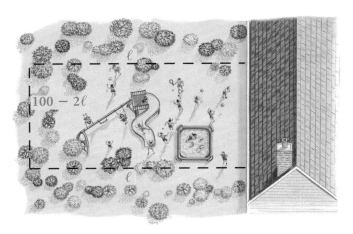

20. **Critical Thinking** Describe a situation in which you might want to maximize the area of a figure that has a given perimeter.

Write the equation of each quadratic function in standard form.

21. $y = (x - 1)^2 + 2$

22. $y = (x + 3)^2 - 4$

23. $f(x) = 2(x - 2)^2 + 5$

24. $f(x) = 3(x + 5)^2 - 8$

25. $f(x) = -(x - 7)^2 + 10$

26. $y = -4(x + 8)^2 - 6$

27. $y = (5x + 6)^2 - 9$

28. $f(x) = -(3x - 4)^2 + 6$

29. $y = -2x(x + 7) + 8x$

Sketch the graph of each equation. Label the maximum or minimum point and the axis of symmetry.

30. $y = x^2 + 2x - 7$

31. $y = x^2 - 4x - 5$

32. $f(x) = 3x^2 + 1$

33. $f(x) = -x^2 - 8x - 9$

34. $y = -8x^2 - 5$

35. $f(x) = -6x^2 - 12x - 1$

36. **Critical Thinking** The equation of one of the graphs at the right is $y = x^2 - 8x + 18$. Write the equation of the other graph in standard form.

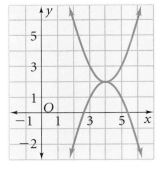

37. **Economics** A rock club's profit from booking local bands depends on the ticket price. Using past receipts, the owners find that the profit p can be modeled by the function $p = -15t^2 + 600t + 50$, where t represents the ticket price in dollars.
    a. What price gives the maximum profit?
    b. What is the maximum profit?
    c. **Open-ended** What is the most you would pay to see your favorite local band? How much profit would the club owner make using this ticket price?

38. **History** In the Indus Valley of South Asia, the Harappan civilization built one of the first cities around 2500 B.C. The Harappans built rectangular houses that had open courtyards in the center, surrounded by solid brick walls.
    a. You plan to build a model of a Harappan house. For the outer walls you plan to use 2400 bricks. The walls of the model are 10 bricks high and 1 brick deep. Draw several possible floor plans.
    b. Find the dimensions of the floor plan that give the model the maximum area.

The archaeological remains of the Harappan city Mohenjo Daro show the thick walls that were built to keep out the hot sun.

39. The graph of the function $y = 2x^2 - 6x + c$ has a vertex at $(3, 5)$. What is the value of c?

40. The graph of the function $y = ax^2 + bx + 8$ has a vertex at $(2, -4)$. What are the values of a and b?

 Chapter Project · · · · **Find Out by Analyzing**

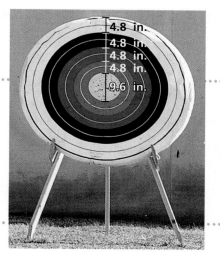

4.8 in.
4.8 in.
4.8 in.
4.8 in.
9.6 in.

If an arrow randomly hits a target, you can find the probability that it will hit a given area by comparing this area to the total area of the target. Suppose an arrow randomly hits the target shown. Find the probability that the arrow will hit the following.

• the bull's-eye (yellow area)

• the red area

• the black or white area

• any area except the blue area

Exercises   MIXED REVIEW

41. Data Analysis The table shows the number of cable television subscribers in each year.

Year	1980	1985	1990	1991	1992	1993	1994	1995
Subscribers (millions)	17.7	39.9	54.9	55.8	57.2	58.8	60.5	61.0

Source: *National Cable Television Association*

a. Find a linear model for the data.
b. Find a quadratic model for the data.
c. Use each model. Predict the number of cable subscribers in the year 2005; in the year 2012.
d. Which model do you think is more reasonable? Explain.

Write the equation of each line.

42. contains $(0, 3)$ and $(5, 0)$ **43.** contains $(-2, 5)$ and $(3, -1)$ **44.** has slope $\frac{1}{2}$; contains $(3, -2)$

Getting Ready for Lesson 5-4

Graph each pair of functions on the same coordinate plane.

45. $y = x - 6$
$y = x + 6$

46. $y = \frac{x - 7}{2}$
$y = 2x + 7$

47. $y = 3x - 1$
$y = \frac{x + 1}{3}$

48. $y = 0.5x + 1$
$y = 2x - 2$

49. $y = -3x$
$y = -\frac{1}{3}x$

50. $y = \frac{x + 4}{5}$
$y = 5x - 4$

Finding x-intercepts

After Lesson 5-3

In Chapter 2, you found the x-intercepts of a function using the intersection of the function and the x-axis. Here are two more methods.

Example

Find the x-intercepts of $y = x^2 - 5x + 2$ using a graphing calculator.

Method 1: Zoom: Trace

Step 1

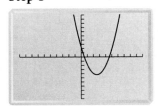

Enter $y = x^2 - 5x + 2$.
Press ZOOM , then
select **6:ZStandard**.

Step 2

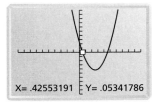

X= .42553191 ⋮ Y= .05341786

Use TRACE . Move the
cursor until the y-value is
as close to zero as possible.

Step 3

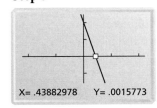

X= .43882978   Y= .0015773

To enlarge the view press ZOOM .
Select **2:Zoom In.** Then press
ENTER . Repeat as necessary.

Method 2: Calc: Root

Step 1

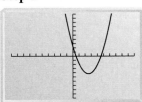

Enter $y = x^2 - 5x + 2$.
Use the CALC feature.
Select **2:Root**.

Step 2

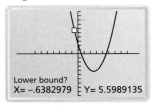

Lower bound?
X= −.6382979 ⋮ Y= 5.5989135

Move the cursor to the
left of one root. Press
ENTER .

Step 3

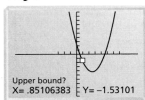

Upper bound?
X= .85106383 ⋮ Y= −1.53101

Move the cursor to the
right of the root. Press
ENTER .

Step 4

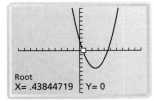

Root
X= .43844719 ⋮ Y= 0

Press ENTER to show
the root.

To find the second intercept, repeat the steps shown. The roots are about
0.44 and 4.56.

Find the x-intercepts of each function. Where necessary, round to the nearest hundredth.

1. $y = x^2 - 6x - 7$

2. $y = 2x^2 + x - 9$

3. $y = -x^2 + 2x + 4$

4. $y = -x^2 + 3x + 5$

5. $y = 0.5x^2 - x - 3$

6. $y = -2.25x^2 - x + 8$

7. Writing Which method for finding the x-intercepts do you prefer? Why?

What You'll Learn

- Finding the inverse of a function
- Using square root functions

...And Why

To find the size of a television screen

5-4   Inverses and Square Root Functions

WORK TOGETHER

Did you know that the length of an icicle and its diameter are related?

1. The function $\ell = 11d - 0.5$ can approximate the length ℓ in inches of an icicle when you know its diameter d in inches at the widest point.
   a. The diameter of an icicle at its widest point is 5 cm. Find its length.
   b. Explain the steps you used to find the length in part (a).

2. a. The length of an icicle is 27 cm. Find its widest diameter.
   b. Explain the steps you used to find the diameter in part (a).

THINK AND DISCUSS

The Inverse of a Function

The steps you used to find the diameter of an icicle when you knew its length are similar to the ones you use to find the *inverse of a function*. Consider the functions $f(x) = 2x - 8$ and $g(x) = \frac{x + 8}{2}$.

$f(x) = 2x - 8$	Input 6	→	Multiply by 2	→	Subtract 8	→	Output 4
	Output 6	←	Divide by 2	←	Add 8	←	Input 4	$g(x) = \frac{x + 8}{2}$

The functions $f(x) = 2x - 8$ and $g(x) = \frac{x + 8}{2}$ are inverses because one function *undoes* the other.

3. a. Graph $f(x) = 2x - 8$ and $g(x) = \frac{x + 8}{2}$ on the same coordinate axes.

    b. Find three points on the graph of $f(x)$.

    c. Reverse the coordinates of each point and then graph the new points. What do you notice?

If the graph of a function contains a point (a, b), then the graph of the **inverse of a function** contains the point (b, a). So to graph the inverse of a linear function, reverse the ordered pairs of the function.

Example 1

Graph the function $y = \frac{x - 4}{2}$ and its inverse. Then write the equation of the inverse.

- Graph the original function.

- Find two points on the graph.
  Two points on $y = \frac{x - 4}{2}$ are $(4, 0)$ and $(0, -2)$.

- Reverse the order of the coordinates of these points and plot them.
  $(4, 0) \longrightarrow (0, 4)$
  $(0, -2) \longrightarrow (-2, 0)$

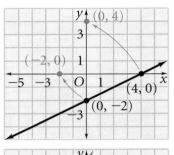

- Draw the line through the two new points.

To write the equation, find the slope and the y-intercept on the graph. The slope is 2 and the y-intercept is 4.

The equation of the inverse is $y = 2x + 4$.

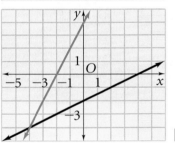

Another way to find the inverse of a function is to interchange the variables. For a function in x and y, interchange x and y. Then solve for y. If a function uses $f(x)$ notation, substitute y for $f(x)$.

Example 2

Find the inverse of $f(x) = x^2 + 3$.

$$f(x) = x^2 + 3$$
$$y = x^2 + 3 \quad \longleftarrow \text{Substitute } y \text{ for } f(x).$$
$$x = y^2 + 3 \quad \longleftarrow \text{Interchange } x \text{ and } y.$$
$$x - 3 = y^2 \quad \longleftarrow \text{Solve for } y.$$
$$\pm\sqrt{x - 3} = y \quad \longleftarrow \text{Find the square root of each side.}$$

The inverse of $f(x) = x^2 + 3$ is $y = \pm\sqrt{x - 3}$.

At the right are the graphs of $y = x^2 + 3$ and its inverse, $y = \pm\sqrt{x - 3}$. As you can see, the inverse of a function may not be a function. The inverse of the parabola graphed by $y = x^2 + 3$ is a parabola that opens to the right. This is not a function because there are two y-values for some x-values.

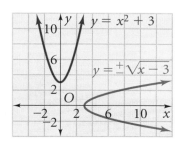

4. **a.** What is the equation of the inverse of $y = x^2 + 3$ for $x \geq 0$?
   b. Is the inverse a function?

5. **a.** What is the equation of the inverse of $y = x^2 + 3$ for $x \leq 0$?
   b. Is the inverse a function?

Square Root Functions

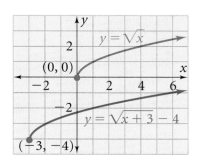

The equation $y = \sqrt{x}$ is a **square root function.** The graph of this function starts at $(0, 0)$. Since the function is defined only for zero and positive values of x, its domain is $x \geq 0$. The range is $y \geq 0$ because these are the values of the function for the given domain.

The graph of the square root function $y = \sqrt{x - h} + k$ is a translation of $y = \sqrt{x}$. Translating $y = \sqrt{x}$ three units to the left and four units down results in the graph of $y = \sqrt{x - (-3)} - 4$ or $y = \sqrt{x + 3} - 4$.

> ### Example 3
>
> Graph $y = \sqrt{x - 4} - 2$ and state the domain and range of the function.
>
> Translate $y = \sqrt{x}$ four units right and two units down.
>
>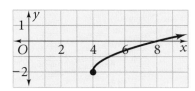
>
> The graph shows that the domain is $x \geq 4$ and the range is $y \geq -2$. ◼

6. **a.** At what point does the graph start in Example 3?
   b. What is the relationship between the point at which the graph starts and the domain and range?

7. **a.** **Try This** Graph $y = \sqrt{x - 2} + 1$ and $y = -\sqrt{x - 2} + 1$.
   b. State the domain and range of each function.

8. The graph of $y = \sqrt{x}$ is translated five units to the right and two units down. Write the equation of the translated function.

You can use a square root function to model real-world situations.

Example 4   Relating to the Real World

Electronics The size of a television screen is the length of the screen's diagonal d in inches. The equation $d = \sqrt{2A}$ estimates the length of a diagonal of a television screen with area A. Suppose you want to buy a new television that has twice the screen area of your old television, which has an area of 100 in.^{2}. What size screen should you buy?

The new screen will have an area of $2 \cdot 100$ in.^{2} or 200 in.^{2}.

Method 1: Using substitution

$$
\begin{aligned}
d &= \sqrt{2A} \quad \longleftarrow \text{Use the square root function.} \\
&= \sqrt{2(200)} \quad \longleftarrow \text{Substitute 200 for } A. \\
&= \sqrt{400} = 20
\end{aligned}
$$

Method 2: Using a graphing calculator

Enter $y = \sqrt{2x}$. Set your window values for $0 \le x \le 250$ and $0 \le y \le 25$.

Press **2nd** CALC **1** to find the y-value when $x = 200$.

You should buy a 20-in. screen.

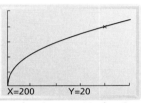

```
X=200          Y=20
Xmin=0         Ymin=0
Xmax=250       Ymax=25
Xscl=50        Yscl=5
```

Exercises   ON YOUR OWN

Graph the given function and its inverse on the same coordinate axes. Write an equation for the inverse.

1. $y = \frac{1}{2}x$

2. $y = \frac{x + 1}{3}$

3. $y = 5x + 3$

4. $y = \frac{3}{2}x - 2$

Write the equation of the inverse of each function.

5. $y = 3x$

6. $y = x - 5$

7. $y = \frac{x + 5}{3}$

8. $y = 6x + 2$

9. $y = \frac{1}{3}x^2$

10. $y = x^2 - 4$

11. $y = (x - 2)^2 + 3$

12. $y = -3$

13. Agriculture Center-pivot watering systems can irrigate from 1 to 130 acres of cropland. The length ℓ in feet of rotating pipe needed to irrigate A acres is given by the function $\ell = 117.75\sqrt{A}$.
   a. Graph the equation on your calculator. Make a sketch of the graph
   b. Find the length of pipe needed to irrigate 40, 80, and 130 acres.

14. Writing Describe the steps you would use to find the inverse of a linear function. Include an example.

15. Circus The time t in seconds for a trapeze artist's swing to complete one full cycle is given by the function $t = 1.11\sqrt{\ell}$, where ℓ is the length of the rope in feet. How long is a full cycle if the ropes are 15 feet long? 30 feet long?

16. Two functions are inverses if $f(g(x)) = x$ and $g(f(x)) = x$. Use the functions $f(x) = 3x - 2$ and $g(x) = \frac{x + 2}{3}$.
  a. Find $g(f(4))$, $g(f(0))$, and $g(f(a))$.
  b. Find $f(g(7))$, $f(g(1))$, and $f(g(b))$.
  c. Are $f(x)$ and $g(x)$ inverse functions? Explain.

Graph each square root function. State its domain and range.

17. $y = \sqrt{x - 2}$ **18.** $y = \sqrt{x + 2}$ **19.** $y = \sqrt{x} + 3$ **20.** $y = \sqrt{x} - 3$

21. $y = -\sqrt{x - 1}$ **22.** $y = -\sqrt{x} + 2$ **23.** $y = \sqrt{x - 4} + 2$ **24.** $y = -\sqrt{x + 3} - 2$

25. a. Math in the Media Write a function that will give the sale price y for an original price x for the items in the advertisement at the right.
  b. Find the inverse of the function you wrote in part (a).
  c. Writing What does the function you wrote in part (b) represent?

Sketch each graph and its inverse. Then write the equation of each graph and its inverse.

26. 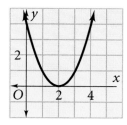   **27.** 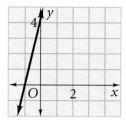   **28.** 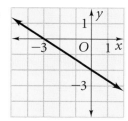   **29.**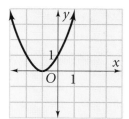

Exercises   MIXED REVIEW

Solve each system.

30. $\begin{cases} x - y = -2 \\ 3x + y = 6 \end{cases}$ **31.** $\begin{cases} 2x + y = -1x \\ -2y = -18 \end{cases}$ **32.** $\begin{cases} 4x + 3y = 15 \\ x - y = -5 \end{cases}$ **33.** $\begin{cases} 3x + 4y = 11 \\ 2x + 3y = 6 \end{cases}$

34. Theater The stage production of *The Phantom of the Opera* uses 550 lb of dry ice per show, or 114.8 tons per year. About how many performances are put on each week?

Getting Ready for Lesson 5-5

Multiply.

35. $(x + 5)(x + 5)$ **36.** $(x + 6)(x + 4)$ **37.** $(x + 12)(x - 12)$ **38.** $(x + 10)(x - 7)$

39. $(x - 9)(x + 7)$ **40.** $(x - 5)(x - 8)$ **41.** $(x - 10)(x - 6)$ **42.** $(x + 8)(x + 11)$

Exercises   CHECKPOINT

Tell whether each function is linear or quadratic.

1. $f(x) = (x - 3)(x + 1)$ **2.** $g(x) = \frac{3}{4}(x + 8)$ **3.** $h(x) = 5x(x - 4)$ **4.** $y = 7x - (x + 1)$

Graph each quadratic function.

5. $y = (x - 4)^2$ **6.** $y = 2x^2 - 5x$ **7.** $y = (x + 8)^2 - 3$ **8.** $y = -(x^2 + 2) - 7$

9. Open-ended Write the equation of a parabola with its vertex at $(3, 2)$. Name the axis of symmetry and two corresponding points.

Write the inverse of each function.

10. $y = 3x - 7$ **11.** $y = x^2 - 4$ **12.** $y = \frac{x + 1}{2}$ **13.** $y = (x + 3)^2 - 4$

Algebra at Work

Landscape Architect

Landscape architects create outdoor environments for parks, office buildings, and homes. They plan needed plantings, walls, staircases, pools, and walkways.

When planning decorative fountains for pools, architects need to predict the parabolic path of a spray. The height and distance of the spray depend on the speed of the water and the angle at which it exits a pipe. Basic principles of physics help architects model the spray. By making adjustments to the model, they can plan the effect they want before building a fountain. Landscape architects blend ideas from art, science, and nature in their work. They need training in all three areas before they begin their careers.

Mini Project: Using graph paper, sketch several parabolas for a fountain design. Then write their equations.

Factoring Quadratic Expressions

Before Lesson 5-5

To factor $x^2 + bx + c$, find two factors of c that have the sum b.

Example 1

Factor $x^2 - 10x - 24$.

Factors of -24	$\longrightarrow$	1 and -24	2 and -12	3 and -8	4 and -6
Sum of Factors	$\longrightarrow$	-23	-10		

-10 $\longleftarrow$ Stop when you find -10.

$x^2 - 10x - 24 = (x + 2)(x - 12)$

To factor $ax^2 + bx + c$, use factors of a and c. Find the combination that gives you bx.

Example 2

Factor $5x^2 + 7x - 6$.

Factors of 5 and -6.	Use the factors to write binomials.	Find the combination that gives you $7x$.
1 5 1 -6	$(\boxed{1}x + \boxed{1})(\boxed{5}x + \boxed{-6})$	$-6x + 5x = -1x$
-1 -5 -6 1	$(\boxed{1}x + \boxed{-6})(\boxed{5}x + \boxed{1})$	$1x - 30x = -29x$
2 -3	$(\boxed{1}x + \boxed{2})(\boxed{5}x + \boxed{(-3)})$	$-3x + 10x = 7x$

Stop when you find $7x$.

$5x^2 + 7x - 6 = (1x + 2)(5x - 3)$ or $(x + 2)(5x - 3)$

Watch for common factors and "perfect squares."

Example 3

Factor each quadratic expression.

a. $4x^3 - 100x$
$4x(x^2 - 25)$ $\longleftarrow$ Use the distributive property to factor out $4x$.
$4x(x + 5)(x - 5)$ $\longleftarrow$ Factor $x^2 - 25$, a difference of perfect squares.

b. $3x^2 + 6x + 3$
$3(x^2 + 2x + 1)$ $\longleftarrow$ Factor out 3.
$3(x + 1)(x + 1)$ $\longleftarrow$ Factor $x^2 + 2x + 1$, a perfect-square trinomial.

Factor each quadratic expression.

1. $x^2 + 4x + 4$

2. $x^2 + 6x + 8$

3. $2x^2 + x - 15$

4. $3x^2 + 5x - 12$

5. $4x^2 - 15x + 9$

6. $5x^2 + 15x$

7. $25x^2 - 144$

8. $x^2 - 14x - 32$

9. $9x^2 - 12x + 4$

10. $6x^2 + x - 12$

11. $8x^2 - 18$

12. $6x^2 + 14x - 12$

13. Writing Describe how to factor $4x^4 + 24x^3 + 32x^2$.

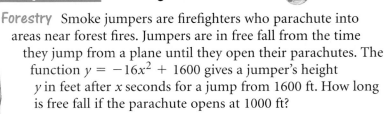
What You'll Learn

- Solving quadratic equations by factoring, finding square roots, and graphing

...And Why

To investigate golden rectangles

What You'll Need

- graphing calculator

5-5 **Q**uadratic Equations

THINK AND DISCUSS

One way to solve a quadratic equation is to factor and use the Zero-Product Property.

> ### Zero-Product Property
>
> For all real numbers a and b, if $ab = 0$, then $a = 0$ or $b = 0$.
>
> Example: $(x + 3)(x - 7) = 0$
> $(x + 3) = 0$ or $(x - 7) = 0$

To solve by factoring, first write an equation in standard form, $ax^2 + bx + c = 0$.

Example 1

Solve $x^2 + x = 6$ by factoring.

$$x^2 + x = 6$$
$$x^2 + x - 6 = 0 \quad \longleftarrow \text{ Write in standard form.}$$
$$(x + 3)(x - 2) = 0 \quad \longleftarrow \text{ Factor.}$$
$$x + 3 = 0 \text{ or } x - 2 = 0 \quad \longleftarrow \text{ Use the zero-product property.}$$
$$x = -3 \text{ or } x = 2 \quad \longleftarrow \text{ Solve for } x.$$

The solutions are -3 and 2.

1. **Try This** Solve each equation by factoring.
   a. $x^2 + 7x - 18 = 0$
   b. $2x^2 - 11x + 15 = 0$

You can solve quadratic equations by finding square roots. You can use this method to solve quadratic equations, which you can write in the form $ax^2 = c$.

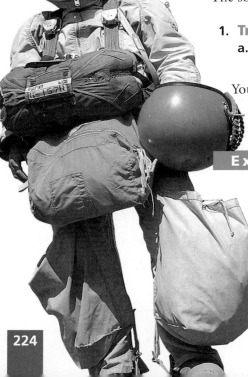

Example 2 Relating to the Real World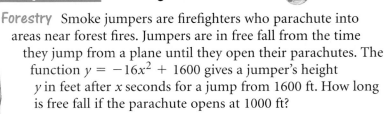

Forestry Smoke jumpers are firefighters who parachute into areas near forest fires. Jumpers are in free fall from the time they jump from a plane until they open their parachutes. The function $y = -16x^2 + 1600$ gives a jumper's height y in feet after x seconds for a jump from 1600 ft. How long is free fall if the parachute opens at 1000 ft?

$$y = -16x^2 + 1600$$
$$1000 = -16x^2 + 1600 \quad \longleftarrow \text{Substitute 1000 for } y.$$
$$-600 = -16x^2 \quad\quad \longleftarrow \text{Solve for } x.$$
$$37.5 = x^2$$
$$\pm 6.1 \approx x \quad \longleftarrow \text{Find the square root of each side of the equation.}$$

The jumper is in free fall for about 6.1 s.

2. Try This Solve $5x^2 = 180$ using square roots. Then solve $5x^2 - 180 = 0$ by factoring. Which method do you prefer? Explain.

Another way you can solve the quadratic equation $ax^2 + bx + c = 0$ is by graphing its related quadratic function $y = ax^2 + bx + c$. The x-intercepts are the solutions of the equation (also called the **zeros** of the function) because they are the values of x for which $y = 0$.

Example 3   **Relating to the Real World**

Art   A *golden rectangle* has special properties. You can divide it into a square and a second rectangle that is similar to the first one. The ratio of the longer side to the shorter side of a golden rectangle is the *golden ratio*. Use the figure at the right to find the golden ratio.

Rectangle A

Rectangle B

$x - 1$ 1

x

1

Define $x = $ longer side of rectangle A
$x - 1 = $ shorter side of rectangle B

Relate $\dfrac{\text{longer side of } A}{\text{shorter side of } A} = \dfrac{\text{longer side of } B}{\text{shorter side of } B}$

Write $\dfrac{x}{1} = \dfrac{1}{x - 1}$

$x^2 - x = 1 \quad \longleftarrow$ Use cross products.

$x^2 - x - 1 = 0 \quad \longleftarrow$ Write in standard form.

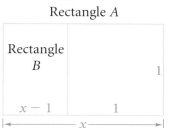

Graph the related function $y = x^2 - x - 1$. Use the CALC feature to find the positive root.

The ratio is about 1.62 : 1.

Root
X= 1.618034   Y= 0

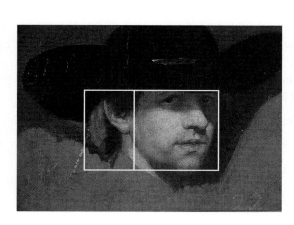

3. Why does the negative root not apply to the situation in Example 3?

4. **Try This** Use a graphing calculator to solve each equation. When necessary, round your answers to the nearest tenth.
   a. $x^2 + 6x + 5 = 0$
   b. $3x^2 + 5x - 12 = 8$

WORK TOGETHER

Work with a partner.

5. Write each equation in factored form. Then write the solutions of the equation.

Quadratic Equation	Factored Form	Solutions
$x^2 + 3x - 10 = 0$	$(x + \blacksquare)(x + \blacksquare) = 0$	$\blacksquare , \blacksquare$
$x^2 - 2x - 8 = 0$	$(x + \blacksquare)(x + \blacksquare) = 0$	$\blacksquare , \blacksquare$
$3x^2 - 7x - 20 = 0$	$(3x + \blacksquare)(x + \blacksquare) = 0$	$\blacksquare , \blacksquare$
$6x^2 + x - 2 = 0$	$(2x + \blacksquare)(3x + \blacksquare) = 0$	$\blacksquare , \blacksquare$

6. **Graphing Calculator** Graph the related function for each equation in Question 5. Then use the x-intercepts to find the solutions.

7. Which method for solving a quadratic equation do you prefer for equations that can be factored? Explain.

Exercises   ON YOUR OWN

Solve each equation by factoring.

1. $x^2 + 6x + 8 = 0$
2. $x^2 + 18 = 9x$
3. $x^2 - 2x = 3$
4. $x^2 + 8x = 0$
5. $2x^2 + 6x = -4$
6. $3x^2 = 16x + 12$

7. **Physics** A smoke jumper jumps from a plane that is 1700 ft above the ground. The function $y = -16x^2 + 1700$ gives a jumper's height y in feet after x seconds.
   a. How long is the jumper in free fall if the parachute opens at 1000 ft?
   b. How long is the jumper in free fall if the parachute opens at 940 ft?

Solve each equation by graphing. When necessary, round your answers to the nearest tenth.

8. $x^2 + 5x + 4 = 0$
9. $x^2 - 7x = -12$
10. $2x^2 - x = 3$
11. $6x^2 = -19x - 15$
12. $3x^2 - 5x - 4 = 0$
13. $5x^2 - 7x - 3 = 8$
14. $6x^2 + 31x = 12$
15. $1 = 4x^2 + 3x$
16. $\frac{1}{2}x^2 - x = 8$

Choose Solve each equation by finding square roots, by graphing, or by factoring. When necessary, round your answers to the nearest tenth.

17. $5x^2 = 80$

18. $x^2 + 6x + 5 = 45$

19. $x^2 - 11x + 24 = 0$

20. $x^2 + 4x = 0$

21. $12x^2 - 154 = 0$

22. $6x^2 + 4x = 0$

23. $2x^2 - 5x - 3 = 0$

24. $x^2 + 2x = 6 - 6x$

25. $6x^2 + 13x + 6 = 0$

26. $3x^2 + 7x = 9$

27. $x^2 = 8x - 7$

28. $2x^2 + 8x = 5x + 20$

29. a. Verify that the Ming painting below is a golden rectangle.
  b. What element in the painting divides it into a square and another golden rectangle?

Critical Thinking The graphs of each pair of functions intersect. Find their points of intersection without using a calculator.

30. $y = x^2$
$y = -\frac{1}{2}x^2 + \frac{3}{2}x + 3$

31. $y = x^2 - 2$
$y = 3x^2 - 4x - 2$

32. $y = -x^2 + x + 4$
$y = 2x^2 - 6$

33. Writing Explain how you found the intersections in Exercises 30–32.

34. Science The period of a pendulum is the time it takes a pendulum to swing back and forth. The function $\ell = 0.81t^2$ relates the length ℓ in feet of a pendulum to the time t in seconds that the pendulum takes to swing back and forth.
  a. Find the period of a pendulum that is 2.5 ft long.
  b. The convention center in Portland, Oregon, has the longest pendulum in the world. The pendulum's length is 90 ft. Find the period of the pendulum.

35. Discrete Math Find the possible values of x and y.
$$\begin{bmatrix} x & 2 \\ 3 & y \end{bmatrix}^2 = \begin{bmatrix} 22 & 10 \\ 15 & \blacksquare \end{bmatrix}$$

36. Gardening You want to expand the garden at the right by planting a border of flowers. The border will have the same width around the entire garden. The flowers you bought will fill an area of 276 ft^2. How wide should the border be?

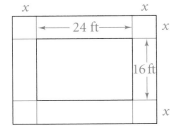

37. a. A parabola has a vertex at $(-3, 5)$. It passes through $(-4, 6)$. Write an equation of the function that graphs the parabola.
b. What are the x-values of the function when $y = 8$?

38. Open-ended Write an equation in standard form that you can solve by factoring and one that you cannot solve by factoring.

For each exercise, write a quadratic equation for which the given numbers are the solutions.

39. 3 and 5

40. -3 and 2

41. -1 and -6

42. $\frac{1}{2}$ and $\frac{2}{3}$

43. Standardized Test Prep Which set of conditions for the function $y = ax^2 + bx + c$ is contradictory?
A. two x-intercepts, vertex below the x-axis, $a > 0$
B. one x-intercept, vertex on the x-axis
C. two x-intercepts, vertex below the x-axis, $a < 0$
D. no x-intercepts, vertex above the x-axis, $a > 0$

Exercises   M I X E D   R E V I E W

Write the equation of each line, given its slope and one of its points.

44. slope 4; $(7, 3)$

45. slope -5; $(0, 2)$

46. slope $\frac{3}{4}$; $(-6, 2)$

47. slope $-\frac{1}{2}$; $(8, -3)$

48. Insurance For the winter of 1995–1996, Boston's Logan Airport bought a snow insurance policy for $300,000. For each inch of snow above 44 in., the airport collected $50,000. The maximum amount the insurance company would pay was $2 million.
a. Write a function that relates the amount of snow to the amount of money paid by the insurance company.
b. After how many inches of snow fell was the airport able to collect the cost of the policy? to collect the maximum amount?

Getting Ready for Lesson 5-6
Simplify each expression.

49. $\sqrt{3^2 + 4^2}$

50. $\sqrt{(-2)^2 + 8^2}$

51. $\sqrt{5^2 + (-12)^2}$

52. $\sqrt{6^2 + 10^2}$

53. $\sqrt{(-7)^2 + 9^2}$

54. $\sqrt{15^2 + 25^2}$

55. $\sqrt{x^2 + x^2}$

56. $\sqrt{(3x)^2 + (4x)^2}$

SELF ASSESSMENT

FOR YOUR JOURNAL

Make sketches of three objects that look as if they may be golden rectangles, such as windows, doors, desktops, and so on. Measure their dimensions and determine whether they are golden rectangles or not.

5-6 Complex Numbers

What You'll Learn

• Identifying and graphing complex numbers

• Adding, subtracting, and multiplying complex numbers

...And Why

To graph sets of numbers in the complex plane

THINK AND DISCUSS

Identifying Complex Numbers

When you learned to count, you used *natural numbers,* 1, 2, 3 and so on. As you have grown, your number system has grown to include other types of numbers. Now you use *real numbers,* which include rational numbers (integers and the ratios they form) and irrational numbers (like π and $\sqrt{2}$). Next, your number system will expand to include numbers like $\sqrt{-2}$.

The imaginary number *i* is defined as $\sqrt{-1}$, with the property that $\sqrt{-a} = i\sqrt{a}$ for any positive real number *a*. This means that $i^2 = -1$ and $(\sqrt{-2})^2 = -2$ (not 2). Other imaginary numbers are $-5i$, $i\sqrt{2}$ and $2 + 3i$. An **imaginary number** has the form $a + bi$, where $b \neq 0$.

Example 1

Simplify each number, using the imaginary number *i.*

a. $\sqrt{-4}$ **b.** $\sqrt{-8}$

a. $\sqrt{-4} = \sqrt{4 \cdot -1} = 2i$ **b.** $\sqrt{-8} = \sqrt{8 \cdot -1} = 2\sqrt{2}i$ or $2i\sqrt{2}$ ■

1. Try This Simplify each number using the imaginary number *i.*

a. $\sqrt{-9}$ **b.** $\sqrt{-12}$ **c.** $\sqrt{-16}$

A **complex number** is a number that can be written in the form $a + bi$, where *a* and *b* are real numbers (including 0).

The diagram shows the sets of numbers that are part of the complex number system and examples of each set.

Complex Numbers

$$a \; + \; bi$$

↑ real part   ↑ imaginary part

Complex Numbers: $-4i$, $2i\sqrt{2}$, $3 + 2i$, -5, $-\sqrt{3}$, 0, $\sqrt{5}$, $\frac{8}{3}$, 9		
Real Numbers: -5, $-\sqrt{3}$, 0, $\sqrt{5}$, $\frac{8}{3}$, 9		**Imaginary Numbers:**
Rational Numbers: -5, 0, $\frac{8}{3}$, 9	**Irrational Numbers:**	$-4i$
Integers: -5, 0, 9	$-\sqrt{3}$	$3 + 2i$
Whole Numbers: 0, 9	$\sqrt{5}$	$2i\sqrt{2}$
Natural Numbers: 9		

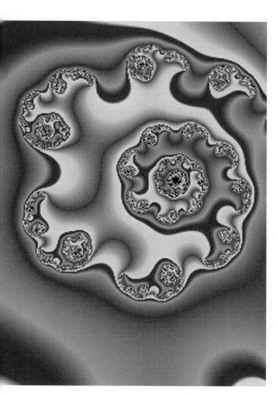

This computer-generated image is part of a *fractal.* Images such as this are created using complex numbers.

You can represent a complex number geometrically on the complex number plane. You find the real part of the number on the horizontal axis and the imaginary part of the number on the vertical axis. You graph $3 - 4i$ the same way you would graph the point $(3, -4)$ on the coordinate plane.

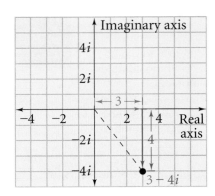

QUICK REVIEW

The Pythagorean theorem:
$c^2 = a^2 + b^2$
So, $c = \sqrt{a^2 + b^2}$.

The absolute value of a real number is its distance from zero on a number line. Similarly, the **absolute value of a complex number** is its distance from the origin on the complex number plane, which you can find using the Pythagorean theorem. In general, $|a + bi| = \sqrt{a^2 + b^2}$.

Example 2

a. Find $|5i|$.   **b.** Find $|3 - 4i|$.

a. $5i$ is 5 units from the origin on the imaginary axis. So, $|5i| = 5$

b. $|3 - 4i| = \sqrt{3^2 + (-4)^2}$
$= \sqrt{9 + 16} = 5$

2. **Try This** Find $|6 - 4i|$.

If the sum of two complex numbers is 0, then each number is the **additive inverse** of the other

3. Find the additive inverse of each number.
    a. $2i$ **b.** $-2 + 5i$ **c.** $a + bi$

Operations with Complex Numbers

To add or subtract complex numbers, combine the real parts and the imaginary parts separately.

Example 3

Simplify the expression $(5 + 7i) + (-2 + 6i)$.

$(5 + 7i) + (-2 + 6i) = 5 + (-2) + 7i + 6i$
$= 3 + 13i$ ← Simplify.

4. **Try This** Simplify $(8 + 3i) - (2 + 4i)$.

For two imaginary numbers bi and ci, $(bi)(ci) = bc(i^2) = bc(-1) = -bc$. Multiply two imaginary numbers of the form $a + bi$ by using the procedure for multiplying binomials.

Example 4

a. Multiply $(5i)(-4i)$.

b. Multiply $(2 + 3i)(-3 + 5i)$.

a. $(5i)(-4i) = -20i^2$
$$= -20(-1) \quad \longleftarrow \text{Substitute } -1 \text{ for } i^2.$$
$$= 20 \quad \longleftarrow \text{Multiply.}$$

b. $(2 + 3i)(-3 + 5i)$
$$= -6 + 10i - 9i + 15i^2 \quad \longleftarrow \text{Multiply the binomials.}$$
$$= -6 + 10i - 9i + 15(-1) \quad \longleftarrow \text{Substitute } -1 \text{ for } i^2.$$
$$= -21 + i \quad \longleftarrow \text{Simplify.}$$

5. Try This Simplify each expression.

a. $(12i)(7i)$ **b.** $(6 - 5i)(4 - 3i)$ **c.** $(4 - 9i)(4 + 9i)$

You can now solve quadratic equations using complex numbers.

Example 5

Solve the equation $4k^2 + 100 = 0$.

$$4k^2 + 100 = 0 \quad \longleftarrow \text{Solve for } k^2.$$
$$4k^2 = -100$$
$$k^2 = -25$$
$$k = \pm\sqrt{-25} \text{ or } \pm 5i \quad \longleftarrow \text{Find the square root of each side.}$$

The solutions are $5i$ and $-5i$.

6. Try This Solve each equation.

a. $3t^2 + 48 = 0$ **b.** $5x^2 = -150$

Julia sets A different Julia set is graphed for each value of *c*.

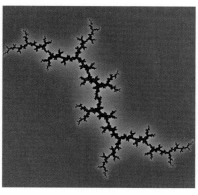

$c = i$

$c = 0.383 + 0.211i$

Fractals are self-similar designs. Functions that generate fractals like the ones at the left have the form $f(z) = z^2 + c$, where *c* is a complex number. The points on the graph are the output values. To find points, use 0 as the first input value, then use each output value as the next input value.

Example 6   Relating to the Real World

Fractals Find the first three output values for $f(z) = z^2 + i$.

Use $z = 0$ as the first input value.

$$f(0) = 0^2 + i \qquad\qquad f(i) = i^2 + i$$
$$= i \quad \longleftarrow \text{first output} \qquad = -1 + i \quad \longleftarrow \text{second output}$$

$$f(-1 + i) = (-1 + i)^2 + i$$
$$= [(-1)^2 + (-1)(i) + (-1)(i) + (i)^2] + i$$
$$= (1 - 2i - 1) + i$$
$$= -i \quad \longleftarrow \text{third output}$$

The first three output values are i, $-1 + i$, and $-i$.

Simplify each expression.

1. i^2 **2.** i^3 **3.** i^4 **4.** i^5 **5.** i^6 **6.** i^7

7. Patterns Describe any patterns you see in the answers to Exercises 1–6.

Simplify each expression using the imaginary number *i*.

8. $\sqrt{-16}$ **9.** $\sqrt{-32}$ **10.** $3\sqrt{-9}$ **11.** $-\sqrt{-100}$ **12.** $\sqrt{-72}$

13. a. Name the complex number represented by each point on the graph at the right. Then find its absolute value.
    b. Find the additive inverse of each number.

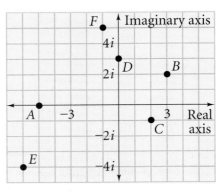

Simplify each expression.

14. $(2 + i) + (-3 + 4i)$ **15.** $(4 + 3i) + (6 - 7i)$

16. $(10 + 3i) + (2 + 5i)$ **17.** $(8i)(4i)(-9i)$

18. $(8 - i) - (-3 + 4i)$ **19.** $2i(5 - 3i)$

20. $-5(1 + 2i) + 3i(3 - 4i)$ **21.** $(3 + 2i)(4 + i)$

22. $(-2 + 3i)(6 + 5i)$ **23.** $(1 - 2i)(-3 - 5i)$

Solve each equation.

24. $x^2 + 25 = 0$ **25.** $2x^2 + 1 = 0$ **26.** $3s^2 + 2 = 66$

27. $x^2 = -7$ **28.** $x^2 + 36 = 0$ **29.** $-5x^2 + 3 = 0$

30. $x^2 + 16 = -49$ **31.** $t^2 - 30 = -79$ **32.** $3x^2 + 1 = x^2 - 1$

33. Critical Thinking Graph $1 + 3i$ and $6 + 2i$. Also graph their sum. Draw the quadrilateral that has these three points and the origin as vertices. Repeat with other complex numbers. What do you notice?

34. Writing In reality, is it possible for Mr. Milde's average to be an imaginary number? Explain.

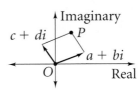

ROBOTMAN by Jim Meddick

Find the first three output values of each fractal-generating function. Use $z = 0$ as the first input value.

35. $f(z) = z^2 - 1$

36. $f(z) = z^2 + 1 - i$

37. a. Open-ended Name eight complex numbers that have absolute values of 10. Plot them in the complex number plane.
   b. Patterns What is the geometric figure that contains *all* the points that have absolute values of 10?

38. a. Copy and complete the table.
   b. Number pairs such as p and q in the table are *complex conjugates*. Describe at least three patterns you see in conjugate pairs.
   c. Plot each pair of conjugates. How are the points of each complex conjugate pair related?
   d. True or false: The conjugate of an additive inverse is equal to the additive inverse of the conjugate. Explain your answer.

Values of p and q	$p + q$	$p \cdot q$	$\lvert p \rvert$	$\lvert q \rvert$
$p = 1 + 2i, q = 1 - 2i$	▪	▪	▪	▪
$p = 3 - i, q = 3 + i$	▪	▪	▪	▪
$p = -6 + 8i, q = -6 - 8i$	▪	▪	▪	▪

Two complex numbers $a + bi$ and $c + di$ are equal when $a = c$ and $b = d$. Solve each equation for x and y.

39. $2x + 3yi = -14 + 9i$

40. $3x + 19i = 16 - 8yi$

41. $-14 - 3i = 2x + yi$

Chapter Project **Find Out by Modeling**

Archers want to use arrows that do not bend easily. The table shows how the weight of an arrow affects its *spine*, or the distance the center of the arrow bends when a certain constant weight is attached. Graph the data in the table. Is a linear model or a quadratic model a better fit? Explain.

Weight (in grains)	140	150	170	175	205
Spine (in inches)	1.4	1.25	0.93	0.78	0.43

Exercises   M I X E D   R E V I E W

Graph each point in coordinate space.

42. $(0, 0, -4)$ **43.** $(3, -1, 0)$ **44.** $(-6, 2, 4)$ **45.** $(6, 0, 0)$ **46.** $(0, 2, 0)$ **47.** $(-4, 3, -2)$

48. Real Estate A developer will receive $3,800,000 for selling all the units listed. How many units of each type are for sale?

ONLY 50 UNITS LEFT!

2-bedroom units-**$70,000**

3-bedroom units-**$95,000**

Getting Ready for Lesson 5-7
Multiply.

49. $(x + 1)(x + 1)$ **50.** $(x - 3)(x - 3)$

51. $(x + 6)(x + 6)$ **52.** $(2x - 1)(2x - 1)$

5-7 Completing the Square

What You'll Learn
- Solving quadratic equations by completing the square
- Rewriting quadratic equations in vertex form

...And Why

To find the maximum profit from a business

What You'll Need
- algebra tiles
- graphing calculator

WORK TOGETHER

Work in groups.

1. **a.** Use tiles or draw a diagram. Copy the model below.
   b. Add unit tiles until you have a complete square. How many tiles did you add?
   c. Write an expression to represent each of the following:
   (1) the sum of the areas of the tiles and (2) the length times the width of the completed square.
   d. How do the six x-tiles in the model relate to the length of the sides of the completed square? to the number of unit tiles used?

$$x^2 + 6x + \blacksquare$$

2. Suppose the expression $x^2 + 8x + \blacksquare$ can also be modeled by a complete square of tiles.
   a. Draw a diagram or use tiles to find the missing value.
   b. What is the coefficient of x in the expression?
   c. *Critical Thinking* How can you use the coefficient of x to find the length of the completed square?

THINK AND DISCUSS

Solving Quadratic Equations by Completing the Square

When you square a binomial, the result is a **perfect-square trinomial.**

Binomial Squared	Perfect-Square Trinomial
$(x + 5)^2 \longrightarrow$	$x^2 + 2(5)x + 5^2 = x^2 + 10x + 25$
$(x - 4)^2 \longrightarrow$	$x^2 + 2(-4)x + (-4)^2 = x^2 - 8x + 16$
$\left(x + \frac{b}{2}\right)^2 \longrightarrow$	$x^2 + 2\left(\frac{b}{2}\right)x + \left(\frac{b}{2}\right)^2 = x^2 + bx + \left(\frac{b}{2}\right)^2$

From the last trinomial, you can see the relationship between the coefficient of the x-term and the last term of a perfect-square trinomial. The last term equals the square of half the coefficient of the middle term.

The process of finding the last term of a perfect-square trinomial is called **completing the square.**

3. Try This Find the missing value to complete the square.
  a. $x^2 + 2x + \blacksquare$ **b.** $x^2 - 12x + \blacksquare$ **c.** $x^2 + 3x + \blacksquare$

4. Explain why $x^2 + 3x + 9$ is not a perfect square.

You can solve any quadratic equation by completing the square. You will first find a perfect-square trinomial and then write the trinomial as a binomial squared. Keep the following relationship in mind.

$$x^2 + bx + \left(\frac{b}{2}\right)^2 = \left(x + \frac{b}{2}\right)^2$$

Example 1

Solve $x^2 = 8x - 36$.

$$x^2 - 8x = -36 \quad \longleftarrow \text{Write the equation with all terms containing } x \text{ on one side.}$$

$$x^2 + (2)(-4)x + (-4)^2 = -36 + (-4)^2 \quad \longleftarrow \begin{array}{l}\text{Complete the square.}\\ \text{Add } (-4)^2 \text{ to each side.}\end{array}$$

$$(x - 4)^2 = -20 \quad \longleftarrow \begin{array}{l}\text{Write the trinomial as a}\\ \text{binomial squared.}\end{array}$$

$$x - 4 = \pm\sqrt{-20} \quad \longleftarrow \begin{array}{l}\text{Find the square root of}\\ \text{each side.}\end{array}$$

$$x = 4 \pm 2i\sqrt{5} \quad \longleftarrow \text{Solve for } x \text{ and simplify.}$$

The solutions are $4 + 2i\sqrt{5}$ and $4 - 2i\sqrt{5}$.

To solve an equation that has an x^2 coefficient that is not 1, divide both sides of the equation by the coefficient first.

Example 2

Solve $5x^2 = 6x + 8$.

$$x^2 = \frac{6}{5}x + \frac{8}{5} \quad \longleftarrow \text{Divide both sides by 5.}$$

$$x^2 - \frac{6}{5}x = \frac{8}{5} \quad \longleftarrow \begin{array}{l}\text{Write the equation with terms}\\ \text{containing } x \text{ on one side.}\end{array}$$

$$x^2 + 2\left(-\frac{3}{5}\right)x + \left(-\frac{3}{5}\right)^2 = \frac{8}{5} + \left(-\frac{3}{5}\right)^2 \quad \longleftarrow \begin{array}{l}\text{Complete the square.}\\ \text{Add } \left(-\frac{3}{5}\right)^2 \text{ to each side.}\end{array}$$

$$\left(x - \frac{3}{5}\right)^2 = \frac{49}{25} \quad \longleftarrow \begin{array}{l}\text{Write as the square of}\\ \text{a binomial.}\end{array}$$

$$x - \frac{3}{5} = \pm\sqrt{\frac{49}{25}} \quad \longleftarrow \begin{array}{l}\text{Find the square root of}\\ \text{each side.}\end{array}$$

$$x = \frac{3}{5} \pm \left(\frac{7}{5}\right) \quad \longleftarrow \text{Solve for } x.$$

$$= 2 \text{ or } -\frac{4}{5} \quad \longleftarrow \text{Simplify.}$$

The solutions are 2 and $-\frac{4}{5}$.

5. Try This Solve each quadratic equation by completing the square.
   a. $2x^2 + x = 6$ **b.** $2x^2 = 3x - 4$

6. a. Graphing Calculator Graph the related functions of the equations in Exercise 5.
   b. Can you solve both equations using the calculator? Explain.

Rewriting a Quadratic Equation in Vertex Form

In Lesson 5-3 you wrote the equations of quadratic functions by first finding the x-coordinate of the vertex using $-\frac{b}{2a}$. Then you substituted for x to find the y-coordinate of the vertex. Another way to transform these equations is to complete the square.

When you work with only one side of an equation, remember to keep the equality true.

$$y = x^2 + 6x + 2 \text{ is equivalent to } y = x^2 + 6x + 9 + 2 - 9.$$

When you add 9 to the right side of the equation, you must also remember to subtract 9 to keep the equality true.

Example 3   **Relating to the Real World**

Manufacturing The daily profit P of a small clothing factory depends on the price d at which each dress is sold. The function $P = -d^2 + 120d - 2000$ models the daily profit. Write the function in vertex form. Use it to find the price that yields the maximum daily profit and the amount of the maximum profit.

$$P = -d^2 + 120d - 2000$$
$$= -(d^2 - 120d) - 2000$$
$$= -[d^2 - 120d + (-60)^2] - 2000 + (-60)^2 \quad \longleftarrow \text{Complete the square.}$$

$$\underbrace{-(-60)^2} \qquad \qquad + (-60)^2$$

$$= -(d - 60)^2 - 2000 + 3600 \quad \longleftarrow \text{Write the trinomial as a binomial squared.}$$
$$= -(d - 60)^2 + 1600 \quad \longleftarrow \text{vertex form}$$

The vertex is at (60, 1600). A price of \$60 per dress gives the maximum daily profit of \$1600.

7. How do you know that the vertex represents a maximum point?

8. Use the function in Example 3 to find the profit when the price is \$59 per dress and \$61 per dress.

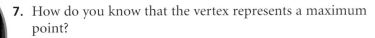

Complete each square. Then rewrite each perfect-square trinomial as the square of a binomial.

1. $n^2 + 18n + $ ▨

2. $k^2 - k + $ ▨

3. $x^2 - 24x + $ ▨

4. $x^2 + 20x + $ ▨

5. $m^2 - 3m + $ ▨

6. $x^2 + 4x + $ ▨

7. Open-ended Write an expression with an x^2-term and an x-term. Draw a diagram or use tiles to complete the square. Then write your perfect-square trinomial as the square of a binomial.

8. Writing Why is $x^2 + 6x - 9$ not a perfect-square trinomial?

Solve each quadratic equation by completing the square.

9. $x^2 - 3x = 28$

10. $x^2 - 3x = 4$

11. $6x - 3x^2 = -12$

12. $-d^2 - 2d = 5$

13. $x^2 + 6x + 41 = 0$

14. $t^2 - 2t = -2$

15. $w^2 - 8w - 9 = 0$

16. $t^2 + 4 = 0$

17. $2p^2 = 6p - 20$

18. $3x^2 - 12x + 7 = 0$

19. $t^2 + 6t = -22$

20. $4c^2 + 10c = -7$

21. Standardized Test Prep What is the vertex of the quadratic function $y = -3x^2 + 12x - 9$?

    A. $(-2, 3)$ **B.** $(2, -3)$ **C.** $(1, 2)$ **D.** $(2, 1)$ **E.** $(2, 3)$

22. Sports The height of a punted football can be modeled by the quadratic function $h = -0.01x^2 + 1.18x + 2$. The horizontal distance in feet from the point of impact is x, and h is the height of the ball in feet.

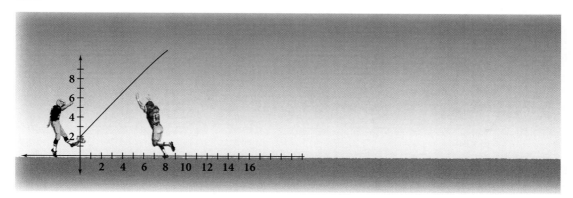

   a. Find the vertex of the graph of the function by completing the square.

   b. What was the maximum height of this punt?

   c. The nearest defensive player from the point of impact is 5 ft away. How high must he get his hand to block the punt?

   d. Critical Thinking The linear equation $h = 1.13x + 2$ could model the path of the football shown in the graph. Why is this not a good model for the path of the football?

23. An electronics company has a new line of portable radios with CD players. Their research suggests that the daily sales s for the new product can be modeled by $s = -p^2 + 120p + 1400$, where p is the price of each unit.
  a. Find the vertex of the function by completing the square.
  b. What is the maximum daily sales total for the new product?
  c. What price should the company charge to make this profit?

Rewrite each equation in vertex form. Then sketch the graph.

24. $y = x^2 + 4x - 7$

25. $y = -x^2 + 4x - 1$

26. $y = -2x^2 + 6x + 1$

27. $y = \frac{1}{2}x^2 - 5x + 12$

28. $y = -\frac{1}{5}x^2 + \frac{4}{5}x + \frac{11}{5}$

29. $y = x^2 + 4x + 1$

30. $y = -4x^2 - 5x + 3$

31. $y = 2x^2 - 8x + 1$

32. $y = -x^2 - 2x + 3$

33. Geometry The table shows some possible dimensions of rectangles with perimeters of 100 units. Complete the table.

Width	1	2	3	4	5	6	7	8	9
Length	49	48							
Area	49								

  a. Plot the points (width, area). Find a model for the data set.
  b. Find another point in the data set and use it to **verify** your model.
  c. What is a reasonable domain for this function? Explain.
  d. Find the maximum possible area. Find its dimensions.
  e. Find an equation for area in terms of width without using the table. Do you get the same equation as in part (a)? Why or why not?

34. Architecture The shape of the Gateway Arch in St. Louis is a *catenary* curve, which closely resembles a parabola. The function $y = -\frac{2}{315}x^2 + 4x$ closely models the shape of the arch, where y is the height in feet and x is the horizontal distance from the base of the left side of the arch in feet.
  a. Graphing Calculator Graph the function and find its vertex.
  b. According to the model, what is the maximum height of the arch? What is the width of the arch at the base?
  c. Research What is the definition of a catenary curve?

Chapter Project · Find Out by Researching

Research the new styles of archery that use three-dimensional targets or moving video targets. Create one of these targets using readily available materials or a computer program.

Exercises · MIXED REVIEW

35. Your expenses and income for decorating T-shirts are at the right.
   a. Suppose you sold ten T-shirts. Would you have a profit or a loss? Explain.
   b. How many T-shirts must you sell to break even?

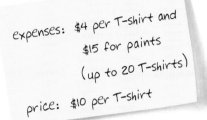

expenses: $4 per T-shirt and $15 for paints (up to 20 T-shirts)

price: $10 per T-shirt

Perform each matrix operation.

36. $8 \cdot \begin{bmatrix} 4 & -16 \\ 18 & 12 \end{bmatrix}$

37. $\begin{bmatrix} 7 & 2 \\ 1 & -4 \end{bmatrix} \cdot \begin{bmatrix} 0 & 5 \\ -3 & 6 \end{bmatrix}$

38. $\begin{bmatrix} 8 & 3 \\ -7 & 10 \end{bmatrix} - \begin{bmatrix} 0 & -5 \\ 11 & 3 \end{bmatrix}$

39. $\begin{bmatrix} 1 & -2 \\ 0 & 4 \end{bmatrix} \cdot \begin{bmatrix} 5 & 9 & -7 \\ 1 & 8 & 2 \end{bmatrix}$

Getting Ready for Lesson 5-8

Evaluate the expression $b^2 - 4ac$ for the given values.

40. $a = 1, b = 6, c = 3$
41. $a = -5, b = 2, c = 4$
42. $a = 3, b = -6, c = 7$
43. $a = 2, b = 3, c = -10$

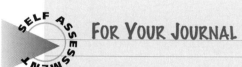

FOR YOUR JOURNAL

When would you use "completing the square" to solve a quadratic equation? Provide at least two examples of quadratic equations that you would solve by completing the square.

Exercises · CHECKPOINT

Solve each quadratic equation.

1. $(x - 3)(x + 8) = 0$
2. $x^2 - 2x + 1 = 0$
3. $2x^2 + x - 6 = 0$
4. $x(x + 4) = 0$

Graph each number on the complex plane and find its absolute value.

5. $5 - 2i$
6. $5 + 6i$
7. $9 - i$
8. $7 + 4i$

9. Standardized Test Prep What does i^{32} equal?
   A. i **B.** $-i$ **C.** 1 **D.** -1 **E.** none of the above

Rewrite each equation in vertex form.

10. $y = x^2 + x - 3$
11. $y = -x^2 + 2x - 1$
12. $y = \frac{1}{2}x^2 + 5x + 4$
13. $y = x^2 + 7x + 2$

14. Writing Describe how you would find the vertex of a parabola from a quadratic equation written in standard form.

What You'll Learn

- Solving quadratic equations using the quadratic formula
- Determining types of solutions using the discriminant

...And Why

To solve business and manufacturing problems

What You'll Need

- graphing calculator

T H I N K   A N D   D I S C U S S

Using the Quadratic Formula

You can derive a formula for solving quadratic equations by completing the square. Below is the equation $2x^2 + 6x + 1 = 0$. Next to it is the general form of a quadratic equation, $ax^2 + bx + c = 0$. Both are solved for x.

$$2x^2 + 6x + 1 = 0 \qquad\qquad ax^2 + bx + c = 0$$

$$x^2 + \frac{6}{2}x + \frac{1}{2} = 0 \qquad\qquad x^2 + \frac{b}{a}x + \frac{c}{a} = 0$$

$$x^2 + 3x = -\frac{1}{2} \qquad\qquad x^2 + \frac{b}{a}x = -\frac{c}{a}$$

$$x^2 + 2\left(\frac{3}{2}\right)x + \left(\frac{3}{2}\right)^2 = \left(\frac{3}{2}\right)^2 - \frac{1}{2} \qquad x^2 + 2\left(\frac{b}{2a}\right)x + \left(\frac{b}{2a}\right)^2 = \left(\frac{b}{2a}\right)^2 - \frac{c}{a}$$

$$\left(x + \frac{3}{2}\right)^2 = \frac{9}{4} - \frac{2}{4} \qquad\qquad \left(x + \frac{b}{2a}\right)^2 = \frac{b^2}{4a^2} - \frac{c}{a}$$

$$\left(x + \frac{3}{2}\right)^2 = \frac{7}{4} \qquad\qquad \left(x + \frac{b}{2a}\right)^2 = \frac{b^2 - 4ac}{4a^2}$$

$$x + \frac{3}{2} = \pm\sqrt{\frac{7}{4}} \qquad\qquad x + \frac{b}{2a} = \pm\sqrt{\frac{b^2 - 4ac}{4a^2}}$$

$$x = -\frac{3}{2} \pm \frac{\sqrt{7}}{2} \qquad\qquad x = -\frac{b}{2a} \pm \frac{\sqrt{b^2 - 4ac}}{2a}$$

$$x = \frac{-3 \pm \sqrt{7}}{2} \qquad\qquad x = \frac{-b \pm \sqrt{b^2 - 4ac}}{2a}$$

Quadratic Formula

A quadratic equation written in standard form $ax^2 + bx + c = 0$ can be solved using the **quadratic formula.**

$$x = \frac{-b \pm \sqrt{b^2 - 4ac}}{2a}$$

QUICK REVIEW

You can divide any golden rectangle into a square and a smaller, similar rectangle.

In Lesson 5-5, you found an approximate value for the golden ratio by graphing the related function for the equation $x^2 - x - 1 = 0$. You can now use the quadratic formula to find an exact value for the golden ratio.

Example 1

The golden ratio is the ratio of the longer side to the shorter side of a golden rectangle. Solve the equation $x^2 - x - 1 = 0$ for x to find the exact value of the golden ratio.

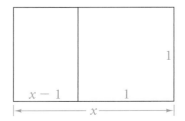

$$x^2 - x - 1 = 0$$

$a = 1, b = -1, c = -1$ ← Find the values of a, b, and c.

$$x = \frac{-b \pm \sqrt{b^2 - 4ac}}{2a}$$ ← Use the quadratic formula.

$$= \frac{-(-1) \pm \sqrt{(-1)^2 - 4(1)(-1)}}{2(1)}$$ ← Substitute for a, b, and c.

$$= \frac{1 \pm \sqrt{5}}{2}$$ ← Simplify.

The golden ratio is $\frac{1 + \sqrt{5}}{2}$: 1 or simply $\frac{1 + \sqrt{5}}{2}$.

1. Why is $\frac{1 + \sqrt{5}}{2}$ the only solution used to write the golden ratio?

2. Find a decimal value for the golden ratio. Round your answer to the nearest hundredth.

3. **Try This** Use the quadratic formula to solve each equation. Find the exact solutions. Then approximate any radical solutions. Round to the nearest hundredth.

   a. $4x^2 = 8x - 3$ **b.** $x^2 + 4x = 41$

The quadratic formula will also give you complex solutions that you cannot find by graphing or factoring.

Example 2

Solve $2x^2 = -6x - 7$ using the quadratic formula.

$2x^2 + 6x + 7 = 0$ ← Write in standard form.

$a = 2, b = 6, c = 7$ ← Find the values of a, b, and c.

$$x = \frac{-(6) \pm \sqrt{(6)^2 - 4(2)(7)}}{2(2)}$$ ← Substitute into the quadratic formula.

$$= \frac{-6 \pm \sqrt{36 - 56}}{4}$$ ← Simplify.

$$= \frac{-6 \pm \sqrt{-20}}{4}$$

$$= \frac{-6 \pm 2i\sqrt{5}}{4}$$

$$= -\frac{3}{2} + \frac{i\sqrt{5}}{2} \text{ or } -\frac{3}{2} - \frac{i\sqrt{5}}{2}$$

The solutions are $-\frac{3}{2} + \frac{i\sqrt{5}}{2}$ and $-\frac{3}{2} - \frac{i\sqrt{5}}{2}$.

4. **Try This** Solve $-2x^2 = 4x + 3$ using the quadratic formula.

5. **a.** *Graphing Calculator* Graph the related quadratic function of $-2x^2 = 4x + 3$.

   b. Explain why you cannot use the graph to find the solution(s) of the equation in Question 4.

The golden ratio occurs in nature as well as in art. In sunflowers, the ratio of the number of clockwise spirals to the number of counterclockwise spirals approximates the golden ratio.

Using the Discriminant

Quadratic equations with real-number coefficients can have real or imaginary solutions (or roots). You can determine the type and number of solutions using the **discriminant,** the value of the expression $b^2 - 4ac$.

$$x = \frac{-b \pm \sqrt{b^2 - 4ac}}{2a} \quad \longleftarrow \text{discriminant}$$

The table below shows the relationship between the value of a discriminant and the solutions of a quadratic equation and the graph of the related function.

Value of the Discriminant	Type and Number of Solutions for $ax^2 + bx + c = 0$	Examples of Graphs of Related Functions $y = ax^2 + bx + c$
$b^2 - 4ac > 0$	two real solutions	two x-intercepts
$b^2 - 4ac = 0$	one real solution	one x-intercept
$b^2 - 4ac < 0$	no real solution; two imaginary solutions	no x-intercept

You can use the discriminant of an equation to solve real-world problems.

Example 3   **Relating to the Real World**

Field Hockey A scoop is a field-hockey pass that propels the ball from the ground into the air. Suppose a player makes a scoop that releases the ball with an upward velocity of 34 ft /s. The function $h = -16t^2 + 34t$ models the height h in feet of the ball at time t in seconds. Will the ball ever reach a height of 20 ft? If so, how many seconds will it take?

$$h = -16t^2 + 34t$$
$$20 = -16t^2 + 34t \quad \longleftarrow \text{Substitute 20 for } h.$$
$$0 = -16t^2 + 34t - 20 \quad \longleftarrow \text{Write the equation in standard form.}$$

Evaluate the discriminant.

$$b^2 - 4ac = (34)^2 - 4(-16)(-20) \quad \longleftarrow a = -16, b = 34, \text{ and } c = -20$$
$$= 1156 - 1280 \quad \longleftarrow \text{Simplify.}$$
$$= -124$$

Since the discriminant is negative, the equation $20 = -16t^2 + 34t$ has no real solutions. The ball will not reach a height of 20 ft.

6. Will the ball ever reach a height of 15 ft? If so, how many seconds will it take?

7. **Try This** Determine the type and number of solutions of each equation.
   a. $x^2 + 6x + 8 = 0$ b. $x^2 + 6x + 9 = 0$ c. $x^2 + 6x + 10 = 0$

You are now familiar with five methods of solving quadratic equations: finding square roots, factoring, graphing, using the quadratic formula, and completing the square. For $ax^2 = c$, finding square roots works. The discriminant can help you decide how to solve equations that have an x-term.

Discriminant	Methods for Solving
positive square number	factoring, graphing, quadratic formula, or completing the square
positive nonsquare number	for approximate solutions: graphing, quadratic formula, or completing the square for exact solutions: quadratic formula or completing the square
zero	factoring, graphing, quadratic formula, or completing the square
negative	quadratic formula or completing the square

8. **Try This** Tell which method you would use to solve each equation and why you would choose that method.
   a. $x^2 - 7x + 10 = 0$ b. $4x^2 - 28 = 0$ c. $x^2 - 4x + 8 = 0$

Solve each equation using the quadratic formula.

1. $2x^2 + 8x + 12 = 0$
2. $3x^2 + 2x - 1 = 0$
3. $-x^2 + 5x - 7 = 0$
4. $x^2 - 4x + 3 = 0$
5. $x^2 = 3x - 1$
6. $x^2 = 2x - 5$
7. $9x^2 + 12x - 5 = 0$
8. $x(x - 5) = -4$
9. $x^2 - 6x + 11 = 0$
10. $x^2 + 6x - 5 = 0$
11. $x^2 - 2x + 3 = 0$
12. $x^2 + 10x = -25$

13. a. The area of a rectangle is 36 in.^{2}. The perimeter of the rectangle is 36 in. Write an equation using one variable to find the dimensions of the rectangle.
  b. Find the dimensions of the rectangle to the nearest tenth of an inch.

14. Writing Describe how the value of the discriminant affects the type of solutions a quadratic equation has.

Evaluate the discriminant of each equation. Tell how many solutions each equation has and whether the solutions are real or imaginary.

15. $x^2 + 4x + 5 = 0$ **16.** $x^2 - 4x - 5 = 0$ **17.** $4x^2 + 20x + 25 = 0$

18. $2x^2 + x + 28 = 0$ **19.** $2x^2 + 7x - 15 = 0$ **20.** $6x^2 - 2x + 5 = 0$

21. $2x^2 + 7x = -6$ **22.** $x^2 - 12x + 36 = 0$ **23.** $x^2 = 8x - 16$

24. Critical Thinking Determine the value(s) of k for which $3x^2 + kx + 12 = 0$ has each type of solution.
  a. exactly one real solution   **b.** two real solutions   **c.** two imaginary solutions

25. Physics The equation $h = 80t - 16t^2$ models the height h an object propelled straight up from the ground reaches in t seconds.
  a. Will the object ever reach a height of 90 ft?
  b. Graphing Calculator Verify your answer to part (a) with a graph.
  c. For what values of t will the object will be in the air?

26. Critical Thinking Explain why a quadratic equation with real coefficients cannot have exactly one imaginary solution.

Without graphing, tell how many x-intercepts each function has.

27. $y = -2x^2 + 3x - 1$ **28.** $y = 0.25x^2 + 2x + 4$ **29.** $y = x^2 + 3x + 5$

30. $y = -x^2 + 3x + 10$ **31.** $y = 3x^2 - 10x + 6$ **32.** $y = 10x^2 + 13x - 3$

33. $y = -3x^2 - 4x - 6$ **34.** $y = x^2 + 5 - 3(x + 1)$ **35.** $y = x^2 + x + 1$

36. Open-ended Find a value of k such that $x^2 + kx + 4 = 0$ has each of the following types of solutions.
  a. one real solution   **b.** two real solutions   **c.** two imaginary solutions

37. Use the discriminant to match each function with its graph.
  a. $y = x^2 - 4x + 2$ **b.** $y = x^2 - 4x + 4$ **c.** $y = x^2 - 4x + 6$

  I. 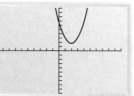   **II.** 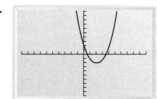   **III.**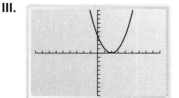

38. a. Geometry Write an equation to find the dimensions of a square
that has the same area as the circle at the right.

b. Find the length of a side of the square to the nearest hundredth.

10 cm

39. Air Pollution The function $y = 0.09x^2 - 4.10x + 115.96$ models the
number of metric tons y (in millions) of carbon monoxide emissions
released into the air in the United States since 1980. In the function, y
represents the amount of carbon monoxide released in a year, and
$x = 0$ represents the year 1980.

a. How can you use a graph to estimate the year in which fewer than
100 million metric tons of carbon monoxide were released into the
air?

b. How can you use the quadratic formula to estimate the year in
which fewer than 100 million metric tons of carbon monoxide were
released into the air?

c. Which method do you prefer? Why?

40. Standardized Test Prep Which equation has $-3 \pm 5i$ as its solutions?

A. $x^2 - 3x = 2$ **B.** $x^2 - 3x = 1$ **C.** $x^2 + 3x = 2$

D. $x^2 + 3x = 4$ **E.** $x^2 + 6x = -34$

Choose **Solve each equation using any method you have studied. When
necessary, round real solutions to the nearest hundredth. For imaginary
solutions, write the exact solutions.**

41. $x^2 = 11x - 10$ **42.** $5x^2 = 210x$ **43.** $4x^2 + 4x = 3$

44. $2x^2 + 4x = 10$ **45.** $x^2 - 2x + 2 = 0$ **46.** $x^2 - 3x - 8 = 0$

47. $-3x^2 + 147 = 0$ **48.** $x^2 + 8x = 4$ **49.** $x^2 = 6x - 11$

Exercises MIXED REVIEW

Graph each equation.

50. $y = 5x - 2$ **51.** $y = 2x^2 - x + 4$

52. $y = |x - 4| + 3$ **53.** $y = -x + 7$

54. $y = \sqrt{x} + 1$ **55.** $y = -(x + 3)^2$

56. Skating The Elfstedentocht, or 11-City Race, loops
124 mi through the Netherlands. The race is only
held in years when the ice is frozen deep enough for
safe skating.

a. In the 1963 race, 69 out of 9294 skaters finished the
race. What percent finished?

b. The record for the course is 6 h 46 min. How fast is
this in miles per hour?

SELF ASSESSMENT

PORTFOLIO

Select one or two items from your
work for this chapter. Here are
some possibilities.
• a journal entry
• corrected work
• an explanation or definition
Explain why you have included each
selection you make.

On Target

Find Out questions on pages 210, 215, 233, and 239 should help you to complete your project. Present your project for this chapter as a visual display, a short theatrical play, or, if equipment is available, as a videotape.

Reflect and Revise

Present your information to a small group of classmates. After you have seen each others' presentations, decide if your work is complete, clear, and convincing. If needed, make changes to improve your presentation.

Follow Up

Interview an archer. Find out about techniques archers use to increase the range and accuracy of a shot.

For More Information

Archery Shooters Association (ASA)
P.O. Box 5078
Old Valdosta Highway
Nashville, GA 31639

National Archery Association (NAA)
One Olympic Plaza
Colorado Springs, CO 80909

National Field Archery Association (NFAA)
31407 Outer Highway 10
Redlands, CA 92373

Key Terms

absolute value of a complex number (p. 230)

additive inverse of a complex number (p. 230)

axis of symmetry (p. 205)

completing the square (p. 235)

complex number (p. 229)

discriminant (p. 242)

imaginary number (p. 229)

inverse of a function (p. 218)

parabola (p. 199)

perfect-square trinomial (p. 234)

quadratic formula (p. 240)

quadratic function (p. 199)

square root function (p. 219)

standard form (p. 199, 240)

vertex of a parabola (p. 205)

vertex form (p. 207)

zero product property (p. 224)

zeros of a function (p. 225)

How am I doing?

- State three ideas from this chapter that you think are important. Explain your choices.
  - Describe the forms that you can use to write a quadratic function.

SELF ASSESSMENT

Modeling Data with Quadratic Functions   5-1

A **quadratic function** in **standard form** is written $f(x) = ax^2 + bx + c$. The graph of a quadratic function is a **parabola**.

You can find a quadratic model for a data set by solving three equations for a, b, and c, or by using the quadratic regression feature of a graphing calculator.

1. **a.** Recreation Use the data at the right. Find a quadratic model for the attendance at women's college basketball games from 1987–1993.
   b. Use your model to **predict** in what year attendance will first reach 5,000,000.

Attendance at Women's College Basketball Games

Year	Attendance (thousands)
1987	2156
1988	2325
1989	2502
1990	2777
1991	3013
1992	3397
1993	4193

Source: *National Collegiate Athletic Association*

Properties of Parabolas   5-2

The **vertex** of a parabola is the point at which the function has its maximum or minimum value. The **axis of symmetry** of a parabola is a vertical line through its vertex.

A quadratic function can be written in **vertex form,** $y = a(x - h)^2 + k$. The vertex of its graph is (h, k) and the axis of symmetry is the line $x = h$. If $a > 0$, then the parabola opens up. If $a < 0$, it opens down.

Sketch the graph of each equation.

2. $y = (x - 5)^2$ **3.** $y = -x^2 + 7$ **4.** $y = 2(x + 1)^2 - 4$ **5.** $y = -2(x - 2)^2 + 1$

Comparing Vertex Form and Standard Form
5-3

The x-coordinate of the vertex of the graph of $y = ax^2 + bx + c$ is $-\frac{b}{2a}$. You can use the x-coordinate to find the y-coordinate. Then you can write the function in vertex form.

Find the vertex of the graph of each function. Then write the function in vertex form.

6. $y = x^2 + x - 12$ **7.** $y = -\frac{1}{2}x^2 + 5$ **8.** $y = 2x^2 + 8x - 3$ **9.** $y = -x^2 + 2x + 2$

Inverses and Square Root Functions
5-4

You can find the **inverse of a function** by reversing the coordinates in each ordered pair of the function. The inverse of the quadratic function $y = x^2$ results in the two functions $y = \sqrt{x}$ and $y = -\sqrt{x}$. The graph of the inverse is a parabola that opens to the right.

Find the inverse of each function.

10. $y = 3x - 2$ **11.** $y = x^2 - 7$ **12.** $y = 2x^2 + 6$ **13.** $y = \frac{1}{8}x^2 + 1$

Quadratic Equations
5-5

You can solve some quadratic equations by factoring and using the **zero product property.** You can solve some quadratic equations by finding the square root of each side, or by finding the x-intercepts of the related quadratic function. The x-intercepts of a function are called the *zeros* of the function.

Solve each equation.

14. $x^2 + 2x - 8 = 0$ **15.** $x^2 - 3x - 4 = 0$ **16.** $3x^2 - 14x + 8 = 0$ **17.** $x^2 - 7x = 0$

18. Writing Which method would you use to solve $x^2 - 5x + 6 = 0$? Explain.

Complex Numbers
5-6

The imaginary number i is defined as $\sqrt{-1}$. An **imaginary number** has the form $a + bi$ where a and b are real numbers and $b \neq 0$.

A **complex number** is also of the form $a + bi$, but b can be 0. This means that a real number is also a complex number.

The **absolute value of a complex number** is its distance from the origin when it is graphed in the complex plane. If two complex numbers have sum 0, each is the **additive inverse** of the other.

Simplify each expression. Then give the additive inverse and absolute value of each result.

19. $(3 + 4i) - (7 - 2i)$ **20.** $(5 - i)(9 + 6i)$ **21.** $(3 + 8i) + (5 - 2i)$ **22.** $(4 + 6i)(2 + i)$

23. Standardized Test Prep Which complex number has absolute value 10?

   A. $1 - 10i$ **B.** $6 - 8i$ **C.** $10 + i$ **D.** $4 + 6i$ **E.** $7 - 3i$

Completing the Square   5-7

When a binomial is squared, the result is a **perfect-square trinomial.** You can solve any quadratic equation by completing the square. Keep the following relationship in mind.

$$x^2 + bx + \left(\frac{b}{2}\right)^2 = \left(x + \frac{b}{2}\right)^2$$

Solve each quadratic equation by completing the square.

24. $x^2 + 3x = -25$ **25.** $x^2 - 2x + 4 = 0$ **26.** $-x^2 + x - 7 = 0$ **27.** $2x^2 + 3x = 8$

The Quadratic Formula   5-8

You can solve any quadratic equation using the **quadratic formula.**

If $ax^2 + bx + c = 0$, then $x = \dfrac{-b \pm \sqrt{b^2 - 4ac}}{2a}$.

When a quadratic equation is in standard form, the discriminant $b^2 - 4ac$ determines the number and type of solutions the equation has.

If $b^2 - 4ac > 0$, the equation has two real solutions.
If $b^2 - 4ac = 0$, the equation has one real solution.
If $b^2 - 4ac < 0$, the equation has no real solutions and
                     two imaginary solutions.

Solve each equation using the quadratic formula.

28. $4x^2 - x - 3 = 0$ **29.** $x^2 = 6x - 2$ **30.** $-2x^2 + 7x = 10$ **31.** $x^2 + 4 = 6x$

32. Open-ended Write the equation of a parabola that has two imaginary solutions.

Getting Ready for .... ▶ CHAPTER

6

Evaluate each expression for $a = 3$, $b = 2$, and $c = -1$.

33. $4a^2b$ **34.** $5b^2c^2$ **35.** $a^b + c^b$ **36.** $5c^2 - 4a^2$

Simplify each expression.

37. $4 \cdot 10^2$ **38.** $5.1 \cdot 10^4$ **39.** $0.06 \cdot 10^3$ **40.** $8.05 \cdot 10^6$

Graph each set of data. Then write an equation for each set of data.

1.

x	$f(x)$
-1	-1
0	-3
1	-1
2	5
3	15
4	29

2.

x	$f(x)$
-1	-11
0	-7
1	-3
2	1
3	5
4	9

Sketch a graph of the parabola with the given vertex and additional point.

3. vertex $(0, 0)$; point $(-3, 3)$

4. vertex $(1, 5)$; point $(2, 11)$

Graph each quadratic function. Label the coordinates of the vertex.

5. $y = x^2 - 7$

6. $y = x^2 + 2x + 6$

7. $y = -x^2 + 5x - 3$

8. $y = -\frac{1}{2}x^2 - 8$

9. **Standardized Test Prep** The graph of which function has an axis of symmetry at $x = 3$?
    I. $y = 2(x - 3)^2$ **II.** $y = x^2 - 6x + 9$
    III. $y = x^2 + 3x + 6$ **IV.** $y = 4(x + 3)^2$
    A. I only   **B.** II only   **C.** IV only
    D. I and II   **E.** I, II, and III

Find the inverse of each function.

10. $y = 4x + 1$

11. $y = \frac{2}{3}x - 6$

12. $y = x^2 - 10$

13. $y = (x + 2)^2 - 3$

14. **Open-ended** Write the equation of a function for which the graph of its inverse is a parabola.

Simplify each expression.

15. $(4 - i) + (5 - 9i)$ 16. $(2 + 3i)(8 - 5i)$

17. $(-3 + 2i) - (6 + i)$ 18. $(7 - 4i)(10 - 2i)$

Graph each number on the complex plane and find its absolute value.

19. $7 - 2i$ 20. $8i$ 21. $4 + 8i$

22. 5 23. $6 - 4i$ 24. $-2 + 3i$

25. **Writing** Compare graphing a number on the complex plane to graphing a point on the coordinate plane. How are they similar? How are they different?

Solve each quadratic equation.

26. $x^2 - 25 = 0$

27. $x^2 + 5x - 24 = 0$

28. $x^2 + 8x - 9 = 0$

29. $3x^2 - 21x + 30 = 0$

Write each function in vertex form. Sketch the parabola and label its vertex.

30. $y = x^2 - 6x + 5$

31. $y = -x^2 + 8x - 10$

32. $y = 2x^2 - 3x + 1$

33. $y = -\frac{1}{2}x^2 + 4x - 9$

Evaluate the discriminant of each equation. How many real solutions does each have?

34. $x^2 + 6x - 7 = 0$

35. $3x^2 - x + 3 = 0$

36. $-2x^2 - 4x + 1 = 0$

37. $-x^2 + 6x - 9 = 0$

38. Find the maximum area you can enclose in two rectangular pens of equal size using 120 ft of fencing. The pens have one side in common.

For Exercises 1–10, choose the correct letter.

1. What is the solution of the system below?
$$\begin{cases} x + y - z = 5 \\ 2x - y + z = -2 \\ -x + 2y + 2z = 3 \end{cases}$$
   A. $2, 1, -2$ **B.** $-1, 4, 4$
   C. $1, 3, -1$ **D.** $0, 9, 4$
   E. There is no solution.

2. In which quadrant(s) is the graph of
   $y = |x - 3| + 1$?
   I. quadrant I   **II.** quadrant II
   III. quadrant III   **IV.** quadrant IV
   A. I and II   **B.** II and III   **C.** III and IV
   D. I and IV   **E.** I, II, III, and IV

3. Which equation has roots at 6 and -2?
   A. $x^2 - 4x - 12 = 0$
   B. $x^2 + 8x + 12 = 0$
   C. $x^2 - 8x + 12 = 0$
   D. $x^2 + 4x - 12 = 0$
   E. $x^2 + 8x - 12 = 0$

4. Which expressions have the same value as $5!$?
   I. $\dfrac{8!}{336}$ **II.** $\dfrac{7!}{3!}$
   III. $3! + 2!$ **IV.** 120
   A. I and II   **B.** II and III   **C.** III and IV
   D. I and IV   **E.** I, II, and IV

5. Which point is *not* a solution of
   $y < x^2 - 2x + 5$?
   A. $(-2, 10)$ **B.** $(3, 2)$ **C.** $(1, -4)$
   D. $(0, 3)$ **E.** $(-1, 8)$

6. Find the product. $\begin{bmatrix} 2 & -1 & 4 \\ 7 & 0 & 3 \end{bmatrix} \begin{bmatrix} 5 & 2 \\ -4 & -3 \\ 9 & 1 \end{bmatrix}$

   A. $\begin{bmatrix} 24 & -5 & 26 \\ -29 & 4 & -25 \\ 25 & -9 & 39 \end{bmatrix}$ **B.** $\begin{bmatrix} 50 & 11 \\ 62 & 17 \end{bmatrix}$

   C. $\begin{bmatrix} 42 & 13 \\ 78 & 13 \end{bmatrix}$ **D.** $\begin{bmatrix} 39 & 2 & 23 \\ -34 & -3 & -24 \\ 65 & 1 & 31 \end{bmatrix}$

   E. The matrices cannot be multiplied.

7. If $f(x) = |2x + 3|$ and $g(x) = -x^2 + 8$, which has the greatest value?
   A. $f(3)$ **B.** $g(3)$ **C.** $g(-3)$
   D. $f(g(3))$ **E.** $g(f(3))$

8. Which vertex minimizes the objective function
   $C = 3x + y$?
   A. $(1, 3)$ **B.** $(0, 5)$ **C.** $(5, 5)$
   D. $(2, 7)$ **E.** $(2, 1)$

Compare the boxed quantity in Column A with the boxed quantity in Column B. Choose the best answer.

A. The quantity in Column A is greater.
B. The quantity in Column B is greater.
C. The two quantities are equal.
D. The relationship cannot be determined on the basis of the information supplied.

	Column A	Column B
9.	the distance of $4 - 3i$ from the origin	the distance of $5 + 2i$ from the origin

$$\begin{bmatrix} 4 & -2 & 7 \\ 10 & -12 & 3 \end{bmatrix}$$

10.	a_{12}	a_{21}

Find each answer.

11. *Open-ended* Write a system of three linear equations. Find the solution. Describe the solution geometrically.

12. Graph $(3, 4, 1)$ in coordinate space.

13. Find the inverse of the matrix. $\begin{bmatrix} 3 & -7 \\ 1 & 6 \end{bmatrix}$

14. Draw a tree diagram for tossing two coins and rolling a number cube.

Polynomials and Polynomial Functions

Relating to the Real World

Many relationships in design and manufacturing require more accurate models than linear or quadratic functions provide. Polynomials offer a way to model and work with curves and to work more easily in three dimensions.

CURVES BY DESIGN

A continuous curve can be approximated by the graph of a polynomial. This fact is central to modern car design. Scale models are first shaped by a designer. Even such apparently minor parts of the design as door handles are included in models.

When the modeling process is complete, every curve in the design becomes an equation that is adjusted by the designer on a computer. Minor changes can be made through slight changes in an equation. When the design has been finalized, the information is used to produce dies and molds to manufacture the car.

To help you complete the project:

Dividing Polynomials	Combinations	The Binomial Theorem
6-5	6-6	6-7

Properties of Exponents

Before Lesson 6-1

Exponents are used to indicate powers. Their properties are listed below. Assume throughout your work that no denominator is equal to zero.

- $a^n = \underset{\substack{n \text{ factors of } a}}{a \cdot a \cdot a \cdot \ldots \cdot a}$
- $a^0 = 1 \ (a \neq 0)$
- $a^m \cdot a^n = a^{m+n}$
- $\dfrac{a^m}{a^n} = a^{m-n}$
- $a^{-n} = \dfrac{1}{a^n}$
- $(a^m)^n = a^{mn}$
- $(ab)^n = a^n b^n$
- $\left(\dfrac{a}{b}\right)^n = \dfrac{a^n}{b^n}$

Example

Simplify and rewrite each expression using only positive exponents.

a. $(7a^2)(-2a^{-5})$

b. $(-2x^{-1}y^2)^3$

c. $\dfrac{2ab^5c^2}{a^3bc^2}$

a. $(7a^2)(-2a^{-5})$

$= 7(-2)a^{2+(-5)}$

$= -14a^{-3}$

$= \dfrac{-14}{a^3}$

b. $(-2x^{-1}y^2)^3$

$= (-2)^3(x^{-1})^3(y^2)^3$

$= -8x^{-3}y^6$

$= \dfrac{-8y^6}{x^3}$

c. $\dfrac{2ab^5c^2}{a^3bc^2}$

$= 2a^{1-3}b^{5-1}c^{2-2}$

$= 2a^{-2}b^4c^0$

$= \dfrac{2b^4}{a^2}$

Simplify each expression. Use only positive exponents.

1. $(3a^2)(4a^6)$

2. $(-4x^2)(-2x^{-2})$

3. $(4x^3y^5)^2$

4. $(2x^{-5}y^4)^3$

5. $\dfrac{8a^5}{2a^2}$

6. $\dfrac{6x^7y^5}{3x^{-1}}$

7. $\dfrac{(4x^2)^0}{2xy^5}$

8. $\left(\dfrac{3x^2}{2}\right)^2$

9. $(-6m^2n^2)(3mn)$

10. $(3x^4y^5)^{-3}$

11. $\dfrac{(2r^{-1}s^2t^0)^{-2}}{2rs}$

12. $x^5(2x)^3$

13. $\dfrac{x^4x^{-2}}{x^{-5}}$

14. $\dfrac{(12x^2y^6)^2}{8x^4y^7}$

15. $(4p^2q)(p^2q^3)$

16. $\dfrac{4x^3}{2x}$

17. $(p^2q)^{-2}$

18. $\dfrac{-15x^4}{3x}$

19. $\dfrac{r^2s^3t^4}{r^2s^4t^{-4}}$

20. $\dfrac{xy^2}{2} \cdot \dfrac{6x}{y^2}$

21. $(s^2t)^3(st)$

22. $(3x^{-3}y^{-2})^{-2}$

23. $(h^4k^5)^0$

24. $\dfrac{s^2t^3}{r} \cdot \dfrac{sr^3}{t}$

25. Writing Write a numerical example for each property of exponents shown above. Which properties could be called *distributive* properties for exponents? Explain.

6-1 Power Functions and Their Inverses

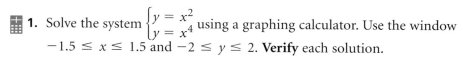

What You'll Learn

- Exploring graphs of power functions
- Using exponents for radicals
- Using powers and roots to solve equations

...And Why

To explore the relationship between the circumference and weight of fruit

What You'll Need

- graphing calculator
- graph paper

QUICK REVIEW

A graph has *line symmetry* if you can fold the graph along a line of symmetry and match the halves exactly.

WORK TOGETHER

1. Solve the system $\begin{cases} y = x^2 \\ y = x^4 \end{cases}$ using a graphing calculator. Use the window $-1.5 \leq x \leq 1.5$ and $-2 \leq y \leq 2$. **Verify** each solution.

2. The table at the right shows $y_1 = x^2$ and $y_2 = x^4$. For which x-values in the table is $x^2 < x^4$? For which x-values is $x^2 > x^4$?

X	Y1	Y2
-1.2	1.44	2.0736
-.8	.64	.4096
-.4	.16	.0256
0	0	0
.4	.16	.0256
.8	.64	.4096
1.2	1.44	2.0736

Y1=1.44

3. Use your graph or a similar table to find *all* the solutions of each inequality.
   a. $x^2 < x^4$ b. $x^2 > x^4$

4. Do the graphs of $y = x^2$ and $y = x^4$ each have line symmetry? If so, for what line? Use specific points to **justify** your answer.

5. For what values of x is $x^6 < x^4$ true? Sketch the graph of $y = x^6$. Use your graphing calculator to **verify** your answer.

THINK AND DISCUSS

Exploring Power Functions and Their Inverses

Functions like $y = x^4$ and $w = 0.0084C^3$ are power functions. A **power function** has the form $y = ax^n$, with $a \neq 0$ and n a positive integer.

Example 1   Relating to the Real World

Shipping The formula $w = 0.0084C^3$ uses the circumference C of an orange (in inches) to estimate its shipping weight w (in ounces). **Estimate** the weight of an orange whose circumference is 9 in.

$$w = 0.0084C^3$$
$$= 0.0084(9)^3 \longleftarrow \text{Replace } C \text{ with 9.}$$
$$= 6.1236$$

An orange with a circumference of 9 in. will weigh about 6.1 oz.

6. a. **Try This** Estimate the shipping weights of oranges with circumferences of 10 in. and 11 in.
   b. Find the percent difference between the circumferences of the two oranges. (Compare the larger to the smaller.) Show the process you use.
   c. Find the percent difference between the weights of the two oranges.

In the Work Together activity you explored functions with even exponents. Power functions with odd exponents also have special properties.

7. **a.** The table at the right shows $y = x^3$. In which quadrants does the graph appear?

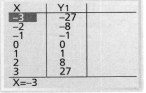

b. Complete each pair of points on the graph: $(4, 64)$ and $(-4, \blacksquare)$; $(-0.5, -0.125)$ and $(\blacksquare, 0.125)$.

c. Suppose the point (a, b) lies on the graph of $y = x^3$. Which of the following points will also lie on the graph?

   I. $(a, -b)$ **II.** $(-a, b)$ **III.** $(-a, -b)$

QUICK REVIEW

A graph has *point symmetry* if there is a half-turn (a rotation of 180°) that maps the graph onto itself.

8. Graph $y = x^3$. Does the graph have point symmetry? If so, around what point?

Power functions are the simplest examples of even and odd functions. **Even functions** have the y-axis as a line of symmetry. **Odd functions** have the origin as a point of symmetry. However, not all functions are even or odd.

9. Graph each function. Describe its symmetry. Tell whether it is *even*, *odd*, or *neither*.

   a. $y = x^5$ **b.** $y = |x|$ **c.** $y = 2x + 3$ **d.** $y = 2x^4$

10. Critical Thinking What relationship exists between the exponent of a power function and the symmetry of its graph?

What is the inverse of a power function? To *undo* squaring, you find a square root. Similarly, you can use a cube root to undo $y = x^3$ or a fourth root to undo $y = x^4$. For example, since $2^3 = 8$, the cube root of 8 is 2.

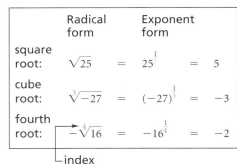

You can use a radical symbol or a rational exponent to indicate roots. In radical form, the **index** indicates the root that you want. the index becomes the denominator in the exponent form, as shown in the chart at the left.

The number 16 has two real square roots, since $4^2 = 16$ and $(-4)^2 = 16$. The positive root is called the **principal root.** The radical form and the exponent form always indicate the principal root.

11. Find the value of each root.

   a. $144^{\frac{1}{2}}$ **b.** $(-125)^{\frac{1}{3}}$ **c.** $-81^{\frac{1}{4}}$ **d.** $1000^{\frac{1}{3}}$

12. What exponent would you use to indicate the fifth root of 32?

The properties of exponents found on page 254 can be applied to rational number exponents:

$$25^{\frac{3}{2}} = 25^{(3 \cdot \frac{1}{2})} = (25^3)^{\frac{1}{2}} = \sqrt{25^3}$$
$$25^{\frac{3}{2}} = 25^{(\frac{1}{2} \cdot 3)} = (25^{\frac{1}{2}})^3 = (\sqrt{25})^3$$

For more practice with exponents, see Skills Handbook page 672.

These properties lead to the following definition of **rational exponent**:

$$b^{\frac{m}{n}} = \sqrt[n]{b^m} = (\sqrt[n]{b})^m$$ for any nonzero real number b and any integers m and n, with $n > 1$, except when $b < 0$ and n is even.

13. Simplify each expression.

    a. $8^{\frac{2}{3}}$ **b.** $4^{\frac{3}{2}}$ **c.** $\left(5^{\frac{3}{4}}\right)^{\frac{4}{3}}$ **d.** $243^{\frac{4}{5}}$

QUICK REVIEW

If (a, b) is on the graph of a function, then (b, a) is on the graph of its inverse. When a vertical line intersects a graph in two places, it is not a function.

By looking at graphs of power functions and their inverses (which are not necessarily functions), you can tell how many real roots a number will have.

Power function	**Inverse**	
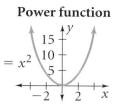	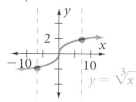	Positive numbers have two real square roots. Negative numbers have none.
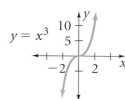	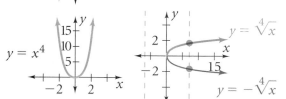	All real numbers have one real cube root.
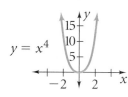	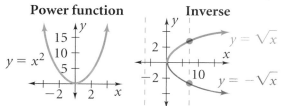	Positive numbers have two real fourth roots. Negative numbers have none.

14. According to the graph, how many square roots does zero have?

Example 2   **Relating to the Real World**

Zoology The radical function $h(x) = 0.4\sqrt[3]{x}$ is an approximation of the height h in meters of a female giraffe using her weight x in kilograms. Find the heights of female giraffes with weights of 500 kg and 545 kg.

Evaluate $h(x)$ for both weights.

$$h(500) = 0.4\sqrt[3]{500} \approx 3.17 \text{ m}$$

$$h(545) = 0.4\sqrt[3]{545} \approx 3.27 \text{ m}$$

The heights are approximately 3.17 m and 3.27 m.

Using Powers and Roots

You can use powers and roots to find inverses and to solve equations.

Example 3

Find the inverse of the power function $y = 2x^4$.

$$y = 2x^4 \qquad \longleftarrow \text{Note that } y \geq 0.$$
$$x = 2y^4 \qquad \longleftarrow \text{Reverse input and output variables.}$$
$$\frac{x}{2} = y^4 \qquad \longleftarrow \text{Solve for } y.$$
$$\left(\frac{x}{2}\right)^{\frac{1}{4}} = (y^4)^{\frac{1}{4}} \qquad \longleftarrow \text{Find the fourth root of each side.}$$
$$\pm \left(\frac{x}{2}\right)^{\frac{1}{4}} = y \qquad \longleftarrow \text{When } x > 0, \text{ there are two fourth roots.}$$

The inverse of $y = 2x^4$ is $y = \pm\sqrt[4]{\dfrac{x}{2}}$.

15. Is the inverse of $y = 2x^4$ a function? Why or why not?

When you raise each side of an equation to an even power, an extraneous solution can occur. An **extraneous solution** satisfies the later equations in your work, but it does not make the original equation true.

$$\sqrt{x} = -3$$
$$(\sqrt{x})^2 = (-3)^2 \qquad \longleftarrow \text{Square each side.}$$
$$x = 9 \qquad \longleftarrow 9 \text{ seems to be a solution.}$$

Check 9 in the original equation.

$$\sqrt{9} \stackrel{?}{=} -3$$
$$3 \neq -3$$

To eliminate extraneous solutions, you should check each possible solution in the original equation.

Example 4

Solve $\sqrt{x} = x - 6$. Discard any extraneous solutions.

$$\sqrt{x} = x - 6$$
$$(\sqrt{x})^2 = (x - 6)^2 \qquad \longleftarrow \text{Square each side.}$$
$$x = x^2 - 12x + 36$$
$$0 = x^2 - 13x + 36$$
$$0 = (x - 4)(x - 9)$$
$$x = 4 \text{ or } x = 9 \qquad \longleftarrow \text{There are two possible solutions.}$$

Check each possible solution:
$$\begin{array}{ll} \sqrt{x} = x - 6 & \sqrt{x} = x - 6 \\ \sqrt{4} \stackrel{?}{=} 4 - 6 & \sqrt{9} \stackrel{?}{=} 9 - 6 \\ 2 \neq -2 & 3 = 3 \end{array}$$

Since 4 does not make the original equation true, it is an extraneous solution. The only solution for $\sqrt{x} = x - 6$ is 9.

Evaluate each expression. Use mental math when possible.

1. $\sqrt[4]{16}$ **2.** $-\sqrt[4]{81}$ **3.** $\sqrt[3]{125}$ **4.** $\sqrt[3]{-64}$ **5.** $\sqrt[7]{-1}$ **6.** $-\sqrt[3]{8}$

7. $27^{\frac{1}{3}}$ **8.** $144^{\frac{1}{2}}$ **9.** $-\left(25^{\frac{1}{2}}\right)$ **10.** $(-8)^{\frac{1}{3}}$ **11.** $1^{\frac{1}{5}}$ **12.** $\sqrt[4]{7^4}$

13. a. Complete: $25^{\frac{3}{2}} = \left(25^{\frac{1}{2}}\right)^3 = \blacksquare^3 = \blacksquare$

     b. Use a calculator to **verify** your answers in part (a).

Simplify each expression.

14. 16^0 **15.** $16^{\frac{1}{4}}$ **16.** $16^{\frac{2}{4}}$ **17.** $16^{\frac{3}{4}}$ **18.** 16^1 **19.** $16^{\frac{5}{4}}$

20. $8^{\frac{2}{3}}$ **21.** $(-125)^{\frac{2}{3}}$ **22.** $36^{\frac{3}{2}}$ **23.** $729^{\frac{1}{6}}$ **24.** $729^{\frac{5}{6}}$ **25.** $625^{\frac{3}{4}}$

26. $(a^3)^{\frac{1}{3}}$ **27.** $\left(x^{\frac{1}{4}}\right)^4$ **28.** $8^{\frac{1}{2}} \cdot 8^{\frac{1}{2}}$ **29.** $10{,}000^{\frac{1}{4}}$ **30.** $(-1)^{\frac{1}{3}}$ **31.** $\sqrt[6]{0}$

Graph each function. Tell whether it is *odd*, *even*, or *neither*.

32. $y = x^3$ **33.** $y = x^3 + 2$ **34.** $f(x) = x^4$

35. $g(x) = (x + 2)^4$ **36.** $y = (x - 1)^3$ **37.** $g(x) = -x^4$

38. $y = (x + 2)^4 - 3$ **39.** $y = (x - 1)^3 + 2$ **40.** $y = -x^3$

41. $f(x) = -x^4 + 3$ **42.** $y = \sqrt[4]{x}$ **43.** $f(x) = -\sqrt[4]{x}$

QUICK REVIEW

If h and k are positive numbers and $f(x)$ is a function, then

• $f(x) + k$ shifts $f(x)$ up k units
• $f(x) - k$ shifts $f(x)$ down k units
• $f(x + h)$ shifts $f(x)$ left h units
• $f(x - h)$ shifts $f(x)$ right h units

Find the inverse of each function. Graph the function and its inverse on the same coordinate system.

44. $y = \frac{1}{3}x^3$ **45.** $y = 2x^4$ **46.** $y = 2\sqrt[4]{x}$ **47.** $y = \frac{\sqrt[3]{x}}{3}$

48. $y = 1.2x^4$ **49.** $y = (x - 2)^3$ **50.** $y = \frac{1}{3}x^4$ **51.** $y = 1.5x^3 + 1$

52. Suppose $f(x) = x^3$ and $g(x) = x^{\frac{1}{3}}$. Find each value.

     a. $f(g(8))$ **b.** $f(g(343))$ **c.** $g(f(-3))$ **d.** $g\left(f\left(\frac{1}{2}\right)\right)$ **e.** $f(g(0))$

53. a. *Shipping* The formula $w = 0.008C^3$ models the weight w in ounces for a cantaloupe having a circumference of C inches. Estimate the weight of a cantaloupe whose circumference is 20 in.

     b. Solve the equation $w = 0.008C^3$ for C.

     c. Find the circumference of a cantaloupe weighing 49 oz.

54. *Open-ended* Write a power function whose graph lies in Quadrant II and Quadrant IV.

259

55. Geometry Revolve a circle about a line such as the purple line in the diagram at the right. The surface that results is called a *torus*, or donut. Its volume V is given by $V = 2\pi^2 Rr^2$.

  a. Suppose $R = 3r$. **Verify** that $V = 6\pi^2 r^3$.

  b. Find V if $R = 3r$ and $r = 0.5$ in., 1.5 in., and 3.0 in. Give your answers to one decimal place.

  c. Critical Thinking What must be true of R and r if the torus has a hole in it?

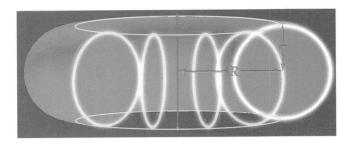

56. Writing Explain why the expression $(-64)^{\frac{1}{2}}$ does not represent a real number, but the expression $(-64)^{\frac{1}{3}}$ does.

Calculator **Find each root to the nearest hundredth.**

57. $\sqrt{10}$ **58.** $\sqrt[3]{10}$ **59.** $\sqrt[4]{10}$ **60.** $\sqrt[5]{10}$ **61.** $\sqrt[10]{10}$ **62.** $\sqrt[100]{10}$

63. $0.5^{\frac{1}{2}}$ **64.** $0.5^{\frac{1}{3}}$ **65.** $0.5^{\frac{1}{4}}$ **66.** $0.5^{\frac{1}{5}}$ **67.** $0.5^{\frac{1}{10}}$ **68.** $0.5^{\frac{1}{100}}$

Solve each equation. Discard any extraneous solutions.

69. $\sqrt[3]{x-1} = 2$

70. $2x^4 - 1 = 161$

71. $\sqrt{2x - 4} = -3$

72. $\sqrt{x-3} = x - 5$

73. $2x^3 - 1 = 249$

74. $x^{\frac{1}{2}} - 3 = 8$

75. $x^2 + 5 = 9$

76. $x^3 + 5 = 9$

77. $x^{\frac{1}{4}} + 2 = 0$

78. $\sqrt{x+7} = x + 1$

79. $\sqrt{x+4} = \sqrt{3x}$

80. $\sqrt[3]{3x+1} = -5$

81. Critical Thinking Describe the graph of $f(x) = ax^n$ given each set of conditions placed on a and n. Use technology to verify your results.

  a. n is an even integer and $a > 0$.
  b. n is an even integer and $a < 0$.
  c. n is an odd integer and $a > 0$.
  d. n is an odd integer and $a < 0$.

Exercises   MIXED REVIEW

Solve each quadratic equation using the quadratic formula. Round answers to the nearest tenth.

82. $x^2 - 4x + 1 = 0$

83. $3x^2 + 2x - 7 = x^2$

84. $-x^2 + 2x - 10 = 0$

85. You are making pizzas. A small pizza has six slices and takes 10 min to bake. A large pizza has ten slices and takes 12 min to bake. The oven will hold either two small pizzas or one large pizza. How can you maximize the number of slices you make in an hour?

Getting Ready for Lesson 6-2

Graph each function. Find the x-intercept(s) of each graph.

86. $y = 2x - 6$

87. $f(x) = x^2 - 4x + 3$

88. $g(x) = \sqrt{x-1}$

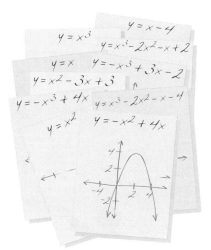

6-2 Polynomial Functions

What You'll Learn

- Describing graphs of polynomial functions
- Fitting polynomial models to data

...And Why

To estimate the number of answering machines sold in a year

What You'll Need

- graphing calculator
- index cards

WORK TOGETHER

Work in groups. Each group needs a graphing calculator and ten index cards.

1. Graph each equation listed at the right. Sketch each graph on a separate card. Label each graph with its equation.

2. Sort the graphs into groups based on their shapes.

3. How are the graphs of the linear equations alike?

4. How are the graphs of the quadratic equations alike?

5. How are the graphs of the remaining equations alike? How are they different?

6. **a.** Estimate the *x*-intercept(s) of each graph. Write them on each card.
   b. What do you notice about the number of *x*-intercepts of each graph and the greatest exponent found in its equation?

THINK AND DISCUSS

Exploring Polynomial Functions

When you add or subtract various power functions and constants, you get a **polynomial function.** The functions in the Work Together activity are all polynomial functions, like $P(x)$ below.

Polynomial Function

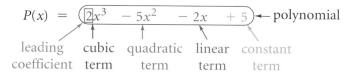

$$P(x) = \boxed{2}x^3 - 5x^2 - 2x + 5 \leftarrow \text{polynomial}$$

leading coefficient — cubic term — quadratic term — linear term — constant term

The exponent in a term determines the **degree** of that term. The terms in the polynomial shown above are in descending order by degree. This order is called **standard form.** In standard form, all like terms have been combined.

For more practice with polynomials, see Skills Handbook page 673.

7. Write each polynomial function in standard form.
   a. $f(x) = 3x - 6x + 5$
   b. $y = 3x^3 + x^2 - 4x + 2x^3$

You can describe or classify a polynomial in standard form by the number of terms it contains or by its highest degree.

Polynomial	Degree	Name Using Degree	Number of Terms	Name Using Number of Terms
6	0	constant	1	monomial
$x + 3$	1	linear	2	binomial
$3x^2$	2	quadratic	1	monomial
$2x^3 - 5x^2 - 3$	3	cubic	3	trinomial

8. Classify each polynomial by number of terms and by degree.
   a. $5x^2 - 7x$ b. $-10x^3$ c. $x^2 + 3x - 2$

The **end behavior** of a graph describes the far left and far right portions of the graph. For polynomial functions, there are four types of end behavior— *up and up, down and down, down and up,* and *up and down.*

These are semaphore signals that resemble three of the four end behaviors. Which end behavior is not illustrated?

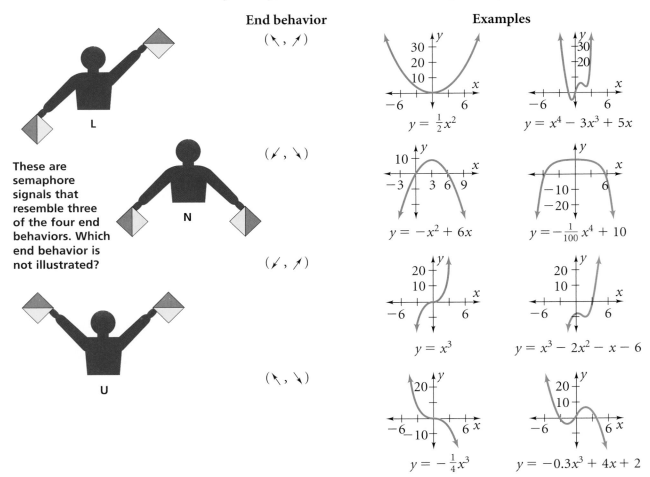

For each polynomial function shown above, the end behavior is determined by the term of the polynomial that has the highest degree.

9. a. *Graphing Calculator* Graph $y = x^3$, $y = x^3 - 2x^2 - x - 6$, and $y = 4x^3 - 3x$. Use a standard viewing window.

b. Change the window to $-20 \le x \le 20$ and $-7000 \le y \le 7000$. Graph the equations from part (a) again. What do you notice?

10. Find a graph from the Work Together activity to illustrate each type of end behavior.

a. $(\nwarrow, \nearrow)$ **b.** $(\nwarrow, \searrow)$ **c.** $(\swarrow, \nearrow)$ **d.** $(\swarrow, \searrow)$

Between the two ends of its graph, a polynomial function of degree n will always have exactly one y-intercept and up to n x-intercepts. You can use either a table or a graph to describe end behavior and estimate intercepts.

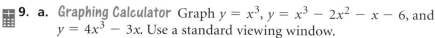

Example 1

Describe the end behavior and estimate the x- and y-intercepts for the function $y = x^3 - 3x^2 + x - 2$.

Method 1: Make and interpret a table of values.

x	-10	-3	-2	-1	0	1	2	3	4	10
y	-1312	-59	-24	-7	-2	-3	-4	1	18	708

Since the far left values of y are negative and the far right values are positive, the end behavior is $(\swarrow, \nearrow)$. The y-intercept is -2. Since y-values change from negative to positive when x is between 2 and 3, there is an x-intercept between 2 and 3.

Method 2: Use a graphing calculator.

Graph the function.   Use `TRACE` to find the y-intercept.   Use `TRACE` and `ZOOM` to estimate the x-intercept.

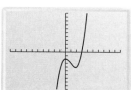

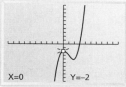

The end behavior is $(\swarrow, \nearrow)$.   The y-intercept is -2.   The x-intercept is about 2.9.

GRAPHING CALCULATOR HINT

You can also use the Root or Zero option of the CALC feature to find x-intercepts.

11. Find the degree of the function in Example 1. Is the leading coefficient *positive* or *negative*? How can you tell the end behavior from this information?

12. a. Find $f(0)$ for the function $f(x) = 2x^3 - 4x^2 + 6x - 8$.

b. What is the relationship between the y-intercept of a polynomial function and the constant term of the polynomial?

13. Try This Describe the end behavior and estimate the x- and y-intercepts for each function.

    a. $y = x^3 - 4x$ **b.** $y = x^4 + 3x^2 - 4$ **c.** $f(x) = -x$

Modeling Data with a Polynomial Function

You already have used lines and parabolas to model data. Sometimes you can fit data more closely by using polynomials of degree three or more.

linear model   **quadratic model**   **cubic model**

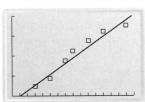 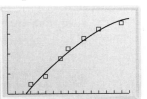 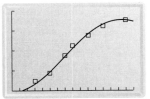

Finding a close fit is helpful when you are trying to estimate values between known data points. The data shown above are used in the next example.

Example 2   **Relating to the Real World**

Communications The table shows the number of answering machines sold in several years. Find a cubic function to model the data. Use it to estimate sales in 1994.

Years since 1980	3	5	7	8	10	12	15
Answering Machines Sold (in millions)	2.0	4.2	8.8	11.1	13.8	16.0	17.7

Source: *Electronic Industries*

Enter the data. To find the best-fitting cubic model, use the CubicReg option found in the [STAT] feature.

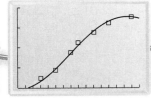

CubicReg
y=ax3+bx2+cx+d
a=−.0100941752
b=.2009019257
c=.5230827394
d=−1.395852173

The cubic function
$$f(x) = -0.0101x^3 + 0.201x^2 + 0.523x - 1.40$$
models the data. To estimate sales in 1994, you can use [TABLE] or [TRACE] to find that $f(14) \approx 17.6$. According to this model, about 17.6 million answering machines were sold in 1994.

14. Estimate the number of answering machines sold in 1989.

15. a. The best fit line for the data from Example 2 has the equation $y = 1.40x - 1.46$. Use it to estimate sales in 1989 and 1994.
   b. Data Analysis The actual sales of answering machines were 12.5 million in 1989 and 17.6 million in 1994. Why do you think the cubic model gives better estimates than the linear model?
   c. Critical Thinking Which model would you use to estimate sales in 1999? Explain.

Exercises   O N   Y O U R   O W N

Write each polynomial function in standard form. Then classify it by number of terms and by degree.

1. $y = 7x + 3x + 5$

2. $f(x) = 5 - 3x$

3. $n = 2m^2 - 3 + 7m$

4. $y = -x^3 + x^4 + x$

5. $q = -4p + 3p + 2p^2$

6. $f(a) = 5a^2 + 3a^3 + 1$

7. $f(x) = 7x^3 - 10x^3 + x^3$

8. $y = 4x + 5x^2 + 8$

9. $g(x) = x^3 - x^4 + 2x^3$

Choose the correct description for the end behavior of each function.

A. $(\nwarrow, \nearrow)$ **B.** $(\nwarrow, \searrow)$ **C.** $(\swarrow, \nearrow)$ **D.** $(\swarrow, \searrow)$

10. $y = 4x^3$

11. $g(t) = -t^2 + t$

12. $y = -x + 4$

13. $f(x) = \frac{1}{2}x^4 - 2$

14. $f(x) = -2x^3 + 3x$

15. $y = 3x + 2$

16. $g(x) = x^6$

17. $y = 3x^5 - 4x^4$

Find the y-intercept of each polynomial function.

18. $f(n) = 3n - 1$

19. $g(x) = x^2 + 5x + 6$

20. $y = x^3 + 3x$

21. $y = 4x^4 - x^2 + 2$

For each table, describe the end behavior and find the x- and y-intercepts. Sketch the graph. Estimate when needed.

22.

x	−2.5	−2	−1.5	−1	−0.5	0	0.5	1	1.5	2	2.5
y	−5.6	0	2.6	3	1.9	0	−1.9	−3	−2.6	0	5.6

23.

x	−4	−3	−2	−1	0	1	2	3	4	5	6
y	98	42	10	−4	−6	−2	2	0	−14	−46	−102

24.

x	−6	−5	−4	−3	−2	−1	0	1	2	3	4	5
y	−70	−25	−2	5	2	−5	−10	−7	10	47	110	205

25. Standardized Test Prep Which of the following cannot be the number of intersection points of a horizontal line and the graph of a cubic function?

  A. 0   **B.** 1   **C.** 2   **D.** 3   **E.** none of the above

26. Health Care The data below indicate that the life expectancy for residents of the United States has been increasing.

Life Expectancy (in years)

Year of Birth	Males	Females
1970	67.1	74.1
1980	70.0	77.4
1990	71.8	78.8
2000	73.2	80.2
2010	74.5	81.3

Source: *U.S. Bureau of the Census*

  a. Find a cubic polynomial to model the life expectancy for males; for females.
  b. Estimate the life expectancy of a girl born in 1999.
  c. Estimate your own life expectancy.
  d. Estimate the life expectancy of a boy born when you are 24.

Graph each function. Describe the end behavior and find the *x*- and *y*-intercepts. Estimate to the nearest tenth when needed.

27. $y = x^3 + 6x^2 - x - 6$ **28.** $f(x) = x^4 - 5x^3$ **29.** $f(a) = -a^2 + 4a - 4$

30. $y = x^3 - 8x$ **31.** $g(x) = x^3 - x^2 - 12x$ **32.** $y = x^3 - 4x^2 + x + 6$

33. $f(x) = x^4 + 15x^2 - 16$ **34.** $y = x^4 - 4x^3 - 4x^2 + 16x$ **35.** $y = x^3 - 8$

36. $g(x) = x^4 - x^2$ **37.** $y = x^3 - 4x^2 + 2x + 1$ **38.** $y = -2t^3 - 3t^2 + 8t + 12$

39. Packaging Design The diagram at the right shows a cologne bottle that consists of a cylindrical base and a hemispherical top.
  a. Write an expression for the volume of the cylinder.
  b. Write an expression for the volume of the hemispherical top.
  c. Write a polynomial to represent the total volume.

40. Writing Explain why cubic functions are useful for interpolating between known data points. Why are they often not reliable for extrapolating from data?

41. Open-Ended Write a third-degree polynomial function. Make a table of values and a graph. Describe the end behavior and find the *x* and *y*-intercepts.

42. Geometry Use $V = \frac{\pi h}{3}(r^2 + rs + s^2)$ to find the volume of the truncated cone at the right. Express your answer in scientific notation with the appropriate number of significant digits.

43. Critical Thinking Is the function $y = x^3 + 2x$ an *odd* function, an *even* function, or *neither*? Explain.

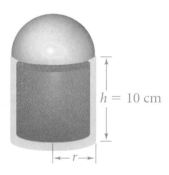

$h = 10$ cm

$s = 3.8 \times 10^2$ cm

$h = 3.5 \times 10^2$ cm

$r = 5.6 \times 10^2$ cm

Find Out by Graphing

A hood section of a new car is modeled by the equation $y = 0.00143x^4 + 0.00166x^3 - 0.236x^2 + 1.53x + 0.739$. The graph of this polynomial equation is shown at the right. Use a graphing calculator to fine-tune the equation. Keep the same window but change the equation. Pretend you are the designer and produce a curve with a shape more pleasing to your eye!

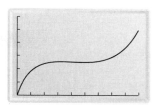

Exercises   MIXED REVIEW

Evaluate.

44. $6!$ **45.** $_8P_2$ **46.** $5!$ **47.** $3!$ **48.** $_7P_6$ **49.** $_9P_4$

50. Sales The sales for a computer company can be modeled by a linear function. When it sells 20 computers, the company earns $40,000. For 50 computers, the company earns $100,000. How much will the company earn if it sells 125 computers?

Getting Ready for Lesson 6-3

Use the distributive property to simplify each expression.

51. $3x^3(2x - 4)$ **52.** $-3x(-2x^2 + 4x - 1)$ **53.** $(x - 3)(x + 2)$

Exercises   CHECKPOINT

Find the inverse of each function. Graph each function and its inverse on the same coordinate plane.

1. $y = 5x^4$ **2.** $y = 2\sqrt[3]{x}$ **3.** $y = (x + 1)^3$ **4.** $y = 2x^4 - 6$

Write each polynomial function in standard form. Then classify it by the number of terms and by degree.

5. $n = 6m^4 - m + 4m^2$ **6.** $f(t) = 2t + 5t^3 - 9$ **7.** $f(r) = 10 + 6r + r^2 + r$

8. Writing Describe the characteristics of even and odd functions. Include an example of each.

9. Standardized Test Prep What is the end behavior of the function $f(x) = 4x^6 + x^3$?
    A. increases to the left and right   **B.** increases to the left and decreases to the right
    C. decreases to the left and increases to the right   **D.** decreases to the left and right
    E. cannot be determined from the information given

Polynomials and Linear Factors

What You'll Learn

- Analyzing the factored form of a polynomial
- Writing a polynomial function from its zeros
- Analyzing multiple zeros and factors

...And Why

To determine a realistic domain for the volume of a piece of luggage

What You'll Need

- graphing calculator

T H I N K   A N D   D I S C U S S

The Factored Form of a Polynomial

Sometimes, it is more useful to work with polynomials in **factored form.**

The factored form of $x^3 + 6x^2 + 11x + 6$ is $(x + 1)(x + 2)(x + 3)$.

  1. How could you verify that $x + 1$, $x + 2$, and $x + 3$ are the factors of $x^3 + 6x^2 + 11x + 6$?

Consider this function for volume: $V = $ (length)(width)(depth). Each dimension is a linear term, or *linear factor*, of the polynomial function.

Example 1   Relating to the Real World

 Travel Several popular models of carry-on luggage have a length 10 in. greater than their depth. To comply with federal regulations, the sum of the length, width, and depth may not exceed 40 in.

  a. Graph the function relating volume V to depth x. Find the x-intercepts of the function. What do they represent?
  b. Describe a realistic domain for the function.
  c. What is the maximum possible volume of the piece of luggage?

x

x + 10

a. Define Let x represent the depth and let $x + 10$ represent the length. Since the sum of the dimensions cannot exceed 40 in., the expression for width will be $40 - (\text{depth} + \text{length})$.

Relate Volume $=$ (depth) $\cdot$ (length) $\cdot$ (width)

Write $V(x) \;=\; x \;\cdot\; (x + 10) \cdot (40 - (x + (x + 10)))$

$= x\,(x + 10)(30 - 2x)$ ←——Simplify.

Graph the function for volume.

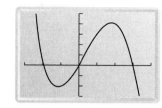

Xmin=–15
Xmax=20
Xscl=5
Ymin=–1500
Ymax=2500
Yscl=500

The x-intercepts of the function are 0, -10, and 15. These values of x produce a volume of zero.

b. The function has values over the set of all real numbers x. Since x represents the depth of the luggage, $x > 0$. Since the volume must be positive, $x < 15$. A realistic domain is $0 < x < 15$.

⊞ GRAPHING CALCULATOR HINT

To find a maximum value, use the Maximum option of the CALC feature.

c. The maximum volume must occur when $0 < x < 15$. Use a graphing calculator to find the highest value of $V(x)$ that occurs within that domain. A volume of approximately 2052 in.^{3} occurs when the depth is about 8.9 in.

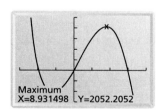

Maximum
X=8.931498 Y=2052.2052

2. a. Find the length and width of the piece of luggage with maximum volume.

   b. Verify that these dimensions produce a volume of 2052 in.^{3}.

3. Compare the x-intercepts to the factors of the polynomial. What do you notice?

The maximum value you found in Example 1 is *not* the greatest value of the function. It *is* the greatest y-value when you consider only nearby points on the graph. It is called a **relative maximum.** Similarly, a **relative minimum** is the least y-value on a graph among nearby points.

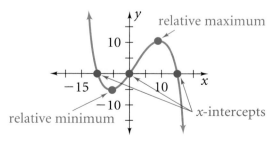

Recall that the x-intercepts of a function are called *zeros* because the value of the function is zero at the x-intercepts.

Factors and Zeros of a Polynomial Function

QUICK REVIEW

The *zero product property* says that when a product equals zero, at least one of its factors must equal zero.

If a polynomial function is in factored form, you can use the *zero product property* to find values that will make the function equal zero.

4. Suppose $f(x) = (x - 1)(x + 2)(x - 4)$. For which values of x will $f(x) = 0$? (Find all the correct choices.)

   I. 1   **II.** 2   **III.** -2 **IV.** 0   **V.** 4   **VI.** -4

You can also reverse this process and write linear factors when you know the zeros. This relationship is called the **factor theorem.**

For a proof of the factor theorem, see Additional Topics page 625.

Factor Theorem

The expression $x - a$ is a linear factor of a polynomial if and only if the value a is a zero of the related polynomial function.

Example: Consider the polynomial function $y = x^2 + 3x - 4$. Since the value 1 makes the function equal zero, $x - 1$ is a factor of the polynomial.

Example 2

a. Determine the zeros of the function $y = (x - 2)(x + 1)(x + 3)$.
b. Graph the function and locate the zeros on the graph.

a. There is a zero for each linear factor:

   $x - 2$ $x + 1$ $x + 3$ ←factors
      2   -1 -3 ←Each linear factor determines a zero.

The zeros of the function are 2, -1, and -3.

b. Graph the function. Use the TABLE feature to locate the zeros.

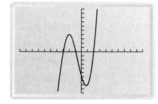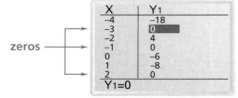

The factor theorem helps relate four key concepts about polynomials. These ideas are equivalent—that is, if you know one of them, you know them all!

① -4 is a solution of $x^2 + 3x - 4 = 0$.
② -4 is an x-intercept of $y = x^2 + 3x - 4$.
③ -4 is a zero of $y = x^2 + 3x - 4$.
④ $x + 4$ is a factor of $x^2 + 3x - 4$.

5. **Open-Ended** Write four equivalent statements about one of the solutions of the equation $x^2 - 4x + 3 = 0$.

When a linear factor in a polynomial is repeated, the zero is repeated. A repeated zero is called a **multiple zero.**

Example 3 ....

Write a polynomial function in standard form with zeros at -2, 3, and 3.

$$-2 \quad\quad 3 \quad\quad 3 \quad\longleftarrow \text{zeros}$$
$$\downarrow \quad\quad \downarrow \quad\quad \downarrow$$

$$
\begin{aligned}
f(x) &= (x + 2)(x - 3)(x - 3) &&\longleftarrow \text{Write a linear factor for each zero.} \\
&= (x + 2)(x^2 - 6x + 9) &&\longleftarrow \text{Multiply } (x - 3) \text{ and } (x - 3). \\
&= x(x^2 - 6x + 9) + 2(x^2 - 6x + 9) &&\longleftarrow \text{Distribute.} \\
&= x^3 - 6x^2 + 9x + 2x^2 - 12x + 18 \\
&= x^3 - 4x^2 - 3x + 18 &&\longleftarrow \text{Simplify.}
\end{aligned}
$$

The function $f(x) = x^3 - 4x^2 - 3x + 18$ has zeros at -2, 3, and 3.

6. Graph the function in example 3. What are its x-intercepts?

While the function in Example 3 has three zeros, it has only two *distinct* zeros: -2 and 3. You can describe the zero 3 as having a **multiplicity** of 2.

7. Match each function with the correct description of its zeros.
   I. 1, 2 (multiplicity 2)   **II.** 1 (multiplicity 2), 2
   a. $y = (x - 1)^2(x - 2)$ **b.** $y = (x - 1)(x - 2)^2$

8. **Try This** Write a polynomial function in standard form with the given zeros.
   a. $-1, 0, 4$ **b.** $-2, -2, 5$

Exercises   ON YOUR OWN

1. **Geometry** A box has length $2x + 1$ units, width $x + 4$ units, and height $x + 3$ units. If you build the box using x^3, x^2, x, and unit (1) blocks, how many of each will you need?

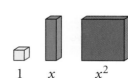 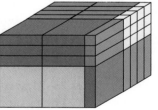

$$1 \quad\quad x \quad\quad x^2 \quad\quad x^3$$

2. **Geometry** A rectangular box is $2x + 3$ units long, $2x - 3$ units wide, and $3x$ units high. Express its volume as a polynomial.

3. **Critical Thinking** If a polynomial function has a zero at $x = -2a$, find one factor of the polynomial.

For each function, determine the zeros and their multiplicity.

4. $y = (x - 1)(x + 2)$ 5. $y = (x + 2)^2(x - 9)$ 6. $y = (x + 3)^3$

7. $y = x(x - 1)^3$ 8. $y = (x + 3)(x - 1)^2$ 9. $y = x^3$

Graph each function. Determine its zeros and their multiplicity.

10. $y = (x + 1)(x - 2)(x - 3)$ **11.** $y = (x - 4)^2$ **12.** $y = (x - 2)(x + 2)$

13. $y = (x + 1)^2(x - 1)(x - 2)$ **14.** $y = (x - 2)^2(x - 1)$ **15.** $y = x(x + 2)^2$

16. Standardized Test Prep Which of the following, when multiplied by
$(x - 1)$, will give a cubic polynomial having three terms ?
A. $(x - 1)^2$ **B.** $x^2 - x$ **C.** $x^2 - 1$ **D.** $x - 1$

17. Critical Thinking How can you find where the graph of a polynomial
function crosses the y-axis without graphing it?

Write each polynomial function in standard form.

18. $y = (x + 3)(x - 2)$ **19.** $y = (x + 3)(x + 4)(x + 5)$ **20.** $y = (x - 3)^2(x - 1)$

21. $y = x(x + 2)^2$ **22.** $y = x(x + 5)^2$ **23.** $y = x(x - 1)(x + 1)$

24. Coordinate Geometry The diagram at the right shows a rectangular
region, one of whose corners is on the graph of $y = -x^2 + 2x + 4$.
a. Write a polynomial function in standard form for
the area A of the rectangular region.
b. Find the area of the rectangular region if $x = 2\frac{1}{2}$.

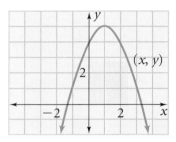

25. Open-ended Write a polynomial function with all of the following
features: it has three distinct zeros; one of the zeros is 1; another zero
has a multiplicity of 2.

26. Writing Explain how the graph of a polynomial function
can help you factor the polynomial.

27. Woodworking A cabinetmaker began his work with a
block of wood as shown. Using power tools, he hollowed
out the center of the block.
a. Express the volume of the original block and the
volume of the hole as polynomials in standard form.
b. Write a polynomial for the volume of the wood
remaining.

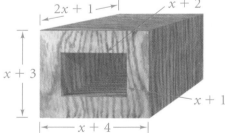

**For Exercises 28–31, write a polynomial function to describe
each volume. Then graph your function to solve each problem.**

28. Geometry Suppose a 2-in. slice is cut from one face of
the cheese block as shown. The remaining solid has a
volume of 224 in.^{3}. Find the dimensions of the original
block.

29. Geometry The width of a box is 2 m less than the length. The height is
1 m less than the length. Find the length of the box when its volume is
60 m^3.

30. Metalwork A metalworker wants to make an open box from a sheet of metal. It will be formed by cutting equal squares from each corner as shown. Find the maximum volume that can be contained by the box and the size x of the square cuts that produce this volume.

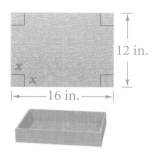

12 in.

16 in.

31. A storage company needs a storage box that has twice the volume of its largest box. Its largest box is 5 ft long, 4 ft wide, and 3 ft high. The new box must be formed by increasing each dimension by the same amount. Find the increase in each dimension.

Write a polynomial function in standard form with the given zeros.

32. $1, -1$

33. $0, 1, 2$

34. $-4, -1, 3$

35. $2, 2, 0$

36. $5, 6, 7$

37. $-2, 0, 1$

38. $0, 0, 2$

39. $3, 3, 3$

Exercises   MIXED REVIEW

Perform the indicated operations.

40. $\begin{bmatrix} -1 & 2 & 0 \\ -2 & 1 & -3 \end{bmatrix} \begin{bmatrix} -1 & 2 \\ -2 & 0 \\ -2 & 1 \end{bmatrix}$

41. $12 \cdot \begin{bmatrix} 1 & 2 \\ 3 & 4 \end{bmatrix}$

42. $\begin{bmatrix} 2 & 7 \\ 1 & 4 \end{bmatrix} \begin{bmatrix} 4 & -7 \\ -1 & 2 \end{bmatrix}$

43. Writing What is the difference between a relation and a function?

44. Solve the system by graphing. $\begin{cases} 2x + y = 8 \\ x - 3y = -3 \end{cases}$

45. a. Health You begin a training program by walking two miles every day. During the first week the walk takes you 40 min/day. Each week after that, you reduce your time by one minute. Write a formula to model this relationship.

   b. Critical Thinking Can you continue to improve at this rate? Explain.

Getting Ready for Lesson 6-4

Factor each expression.

46. $x^2 - 9$

47. $x^2 + 3x - 18$

48. $x^2 - 7x + 10$

49. $x^3 - 4x$

SELF ASSESSMENT

FOR YOUR JOURNAL

Describe the relationships among the terms zero, linear factor, and x-intercept with regard to polynomials and polynomial functions.

6-4 Solving Polynomial Equations

What You'll Learn

- Solving polynomial equations by factoring
- Solving polynomial equations by graphing

...And Why

To find interest rates related to savings

What You'll Need

- graphing calculator

QUICK REVIEW

If savings increase by 5%, the growth factor is 1.05.

THINK AND DISCUSS

Solving Equations by Graphing

You can solve a polynomial equation by using the **TRACE**, **ZOOM**, **TABLE**, or **CALC** feature of a graphing calculator. Options such as Intersect, Root, or Zero will help you to locate solutions.

Example 1   Relating to the Real World

Savings Suppose you save $900 one summer working at a camp. The next two summers you save $1300 and $1500. You can use the polynomial $900x^3 + 1300x^2 + 1500x$ to represent your savings after three years, where x represents the growth factor due to interest earned. The annual interest rate equals $x - 1$. Find the interest rate needed so you will have $4000 after three years.

Write an equation: Savings after three years   equals $4000.

$$900x^3 + 1300x^2 + 1500x = 4000$$

Graph $y_1 = 900x^3 + 1300x^2 + 1500x$ and $y_2 = 4000$. The window $-5 \le x \le 5$ by $-4000 \le y \le 10{,}000$ shows that the graphs intersect at only one point.

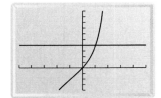

Use the Intersect option of the **CALC** feature. When $x \approx 1.043$, $y \approx 4000$. So, when $x = 1.043$, the polynomial $900x^3 + 1300x^2 + 1500x$ has a value of about 4000.

Since $x = 1.043$, the interest rate $x - 1$ is 0.043, or 4.3%.

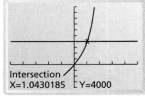

Intersection
X=1.0430185   Y=4000

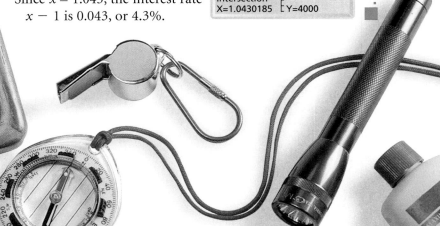

1. **a.** The table shows values of
$y_1 = 900x^3 + 1300x^2 + 1500x$.
How much money will you have if no
interest is earned ($x = 1$)?
   b. How much will 3% interest yield?
   c. What interest rate yields $4122.60?

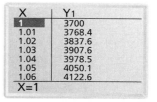

X	Y₁
1	3700
1.01	3768.4
1.02	3837.6
1.03	3907.6
1.04	3978.5
1.05	4050.1
1.06	4122.6

X=1

2. By changing the table increment to 0.001,
you can "zoom in" on the interest rate
needed to yield $4100. Estimate this rate.

X	Y₁
1.053	4071.8
1.054	4079
1.055	4086.2
1.056	4093.5
1.057	4100.8
1.058	4108
1.059	4115.3

X=1.053

GRAPHING CALCULATOR HINT

When one side of an
equation is zero, use the
Root or Zero option found
in the CALC feature.

3. **Try This** Graph and solve each equation.
   a. $x^3 - 2x^2 + 3 = 0$
   b. $x^3 + 3x^2 - x = 3$

Solving Equations by Factoring

Sometimes you can solve a polynomial equation by factoring. When you
factor a polynomial, you change its form from a sum (or difference) to a
product.

Standard Form	**Factored Form**
$x^2 - 4x - 12$	$(x + 2)(x - 6)$
$3x^3 - 12x$	$3x(x - 2)(x + 2)$
$3x^2 + 5x + 2$	$(3x + 2)(x + 1)$
$x^3 + 6x^2 + 11x + 6$	$(x + 1)(x + 2)(x + 3)$

4. Use these two methods to show that the forms above are equivalent.
   a. Graph $y_1 = 3x^2 + 5x + 2$ and $y_2 = (3x + 2)(x + 1)$. What do you
   notice about the graphs?
   b. Multiply and simplify the expression $(3x + 2)(x + 1)$.

You can solve some polynomial equations by factoring and using the zero
product property, just as you did with quadratic equations in Chapter 5.

Example 2

Solve $3x^3 + 6x^2 - 9x = 0$ by factoring.

$3x^3 + 6x^2 - 9x = 0$
$3x(x^2 + 2x - 3) = 0$ ⟵ Factor out the GCF: $3x$.
$3x(x + 3)(x - 1) = 0$ ⟵ Factor $x^2 + 2x - 3$.
$x = 0, x = -3, x = 1$ ⟵ Use the factor theorem.

The solutions are 0, −3, and 1.

PROBLEM SOLVING

Look Back Examine the
graph of the function
$y = 3x^3 + 6x^2 - 9x$. How
are the zeros of the
function related to the
solutions of the equation?

5. Verify that 0, −3, and 1 are solutions by testing each one in the original
equation.

6. **Try This** Solve $4x^3 - 16x^2 - 20x = 0$ by factoring.

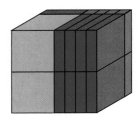

7. You can use the graph of a polynomial function to help find the factors.
   a. Graph $y = 2x^3 + 10x^2 + 8x$. What are its zeros?
   b. Factor $2x^3 + 10x^2 + 8x$.
   c. Describe two methods you could use to solve $2x^3 + 10x^2 + 8x = 0$. Which method do you prefer? Why?

Sometimes you do not have to completely factor a polynomial equation to solve it. Whenever you find a quadratic factor, you can use the quadratic formula.

Example 3

Solve $12x^3 + 14x^2 = 10x$.

$$12x^3 + 14x^2 = 10x$$
$$12x^3 + 14x^2 - 10x = 0 \qquad \longleftarrow \text{Set one side equal to zero.}$$
$$2x(6x^2 + 7x - 5) = 0 \qquad \longleftarrow \text{Factor.}$$
$$2x = 0 \ \text{ or } \ 6x^2 + 7x - 5 = 0 \qquad \longleftarrow \text{Use the zero product property.}$$
$$x = \frac{-b \pm \sqrt{b^2 - 4ac}}{2a} \qquad \longleftarrow \text{Use the quadratic formula.}$$
$$= \frac{-7 \pm \sqrt{7^2 - 4(6)(-5)}}{2(6)}$$
$$= \frac{-7 \pm \sqrt{169}}{12}$$
$$= \frac{-7 \pm 13}{12}$$
$$= \frac{6}{12} \ \text{ or } -\frac{20}{12}$$
$$x = 0 \ \text{ or } \ x = \frac{1}{2} \ \text{ or } \ x = -\frac{5}{3}$$

The solutions are 0, $\frac{1}{2}$, and $-\frac{5}{3}$.

8. **Verify** each solution in Example 3 by showing that it makes the original equation true.

9. **Try This** Solve each equation. When necessary, round your answers to the nearest hundredth.
   a. $2x^3 = 3x - 5x^2$ b. $a^3 - a^2 - 3a = 0$

10. You can use the zeros $-\frac{5}{3}$ and $\frac{1}{2}$ of $y = 6x^2 + 7x - 5$ to write $6x^2 + 7x - 5$ in factored form.
    a. Complete the equation. $6x^2 + 7x - 5 = \blacksquare\left(x^2 + \frac{7}{6}x - \frac{5}{6}\right)$
    b. Multiply $\left(x + \frac{5}{3}\right)$ and $\left(x - \frac{1}{2}\right)$.
    c. Use your work to write $6x^2 + 7x - 5$ in factored form as $\blacksquare(x + \blacksquare)(x - \blacksquare)$.
    d. Show that the factored form in part (c) is equivalent to $(3x + 5)(2x - 1)$.

11. The polynomial function $y = 4x^2 - 12x - 7$ has $-\frac{1}{2}$ and $\frac{7}{2}$ as its zeros. Write the polynomial in factored form.

Solve each equation. When necessary, round your answers to the nearest hundredth.

1. $4z^3 - 16z^2 + 12z = 0$

2. $3x^3 - 6x^2 - 9x = 0$

3. $4x^3 - 8x^2 + 4x = 0$

4. $6y^2 = 48y$

5. $12x^3 - 60x^2 + 75x = 0$

6. $2x^3 + 5x^2 = 7x$

7. $4c^3 = 4c^2 + 3c$

8. $2a^4 - 5a^3 - 3a^2 = 0$

9. $x^2 - 8x + 7 = 0$

10. $x^3 - 6x^2 + 6x = 0$

11. $x^3 + 3x^2 + 2x = 0$

12. $x^3 + 13x = 10x^2$

13. $2y^3 = 5y^2 + 12y$

14. $2d^4 + 18d^3 = 0$

15. $2x^4 - 14x^3 + 12x^2 = 0$

16. Discrete Math The product of three consecutive integers $n - 1$, n, and $n + 1$ is 210. Write and solve an equation to find the numbers.

Match each equation in Exercises 17–22 with its graph.

A.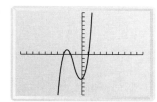

B.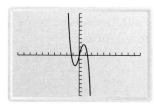

C.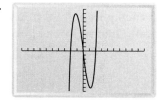

D.

E.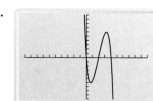

F.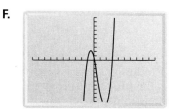

17. $y = -x^3 + 4x$

18. $y = (x - 1)(x + 2)(x + 3)$

19. $y = 2x^3 - 4x^2 - 6x$

20. $y = -2x(x^2 - 6x + 8)$

21. $y = 3x(x - 2)(x + 2)$

22. $y = -3x^3 + 5x$

23. Writing From the large cube whose edges are a units long, you cut a smaller cube whose edges are three units long. Explain how the diagram illustrates the following.
$a^3 - 27 = (a - 3)(a^2 + 3a + 9)$

24. Geometry The volume V of a container is modeled by the function $V(x) = x^3 - 3x^2 - 4x$. Let x represent the width, $x + 1$ the length, and $x - 4$ the height. If the container has a volume of 70 ft^3, find its dimensions.

25. Savings The polynomial $1600x^3 + 1200x^2 + 800x$ represents Devone's savings from a summer job after three years. The annual interest rate equals $x - 1$. Find the interest rate needed so he will have $4000 after three years.

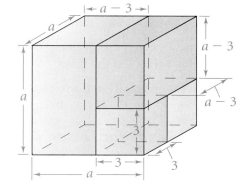

26. Design The chamber in each container shown at the right consists of a cylinder on top of a hemisphere. Each chamber holds 500 cm³. Find the radius of each chamber.

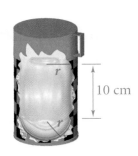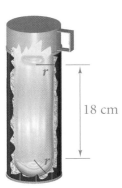

10 cm

18 cm

27. Open-ended To solve a polynomial equation, you can use one or more of the following methods: graphing, factoring, the quadratic formula. Write and solve an equation to illustrate each method.

Solve each equation by graphing. When necessary, round your answer to the nearest tenth.

28. $x^3 + 3x^2 - 4x - 12 = 0$

29. $w^3 - 5w^2 + 3w + 9 = 0$

30. $t^3 - t^2 - 6t - 4 = 0$

31. $x^3 - 4x^2 - 7x + 10 = 0$

32. $x^4 + 2x^3 - 7x^2 - 8x = -12$

33. $x^4 + x^3 = 4x^2 + 4x - 5$

Graph each polynomial function. Use the graph to find the zeros of the function. Then write the polynomial in factored form.

34. $y = x^3 - 2x^2 - 5x + 6$

35. $y = 2x^2 - 5x + 2$

36. $y = 2x^2 + 3x - 5$

37. $y = x^3 + 2x^2 - 11x - 12$

38. $y = x^4 - 10x^2 + 9$

39. $y = x^3 - 3x^2 + 4$

Chapter Project **Find Out by Analyzing**

Research the design of a car or another object that has curved parts. On graph paper, sketch a curve of the object you chose to research. Label four points that you think would help identify the curve. Find the cubic function that fits these four points. Use the equation $y = ax^3 + bx^2 + cx + d$. Solve for the variables a, b, c, and d using a 4×4 inverse matrix.

Exercises   M I X E D   R E V I E W

40. Write an equation for the line that passes through $(-2, 3)$ and is parallel to the graph of $3x + 4y = 5$.

41. Solve each equation for n.

a. $5n^2 + 8n = -5$ **b.** $n^2 - 1 = -37$ **c.** $2n + \frac{7}{2} = \frac{n}{2} - 9$ **d.** $5|n - 3| = 2$

Getting Ready for Lesson 6-5

42. Divide 7222 by 46.

43. Divide $49x^5$ by $7x^2$.

44. Explain the following: $\frac{\text{dividend}}{\text{divisor}} = \text{quotient} + \frac{\text{remainder}}{\text{divisor}}$.

45. Explain the following: dividend $= $ quotient $\times$ divisor $+$ remainder.

What You'll Learn
- Dividing polynomials
- Finding all the zeros of a polynomial function

...And Why
To find imaginary solutions of polynomial equations

What You'll Need
- graphing calculator

IMAGINE A NUMBER . . .

$\sqrt{-1}$

6-5 Dividing Polynomials

WORK TOGETHER

The zeros of a polynomial function are not always real numbers. In this activity you will find some imaginary numbers that make polynomials equal zero. Recall that $\sqrt{-1}$ is represented by i, $i^2 = -1$, and $i^3 = -i$.

1. Graph the function $f(x) = 2x^3 + 4x^2 + 2x + 4$. Find its real zero.

2. Evaluate $f(i)$ and $f(-i)$. What are the three zeros of $f(x)$?

3. The function $g(x) = x^3 - x^2 + 4x - 4$ can be factored as $(x - 1)(x^2 + 4)$. Use the factor theorem and the quadratic formula to find three zeros for this function.

THINK AND DISCUSS

Using Long Division

You can use polynomial long division to help find imaginary zeros. When you divide a polynomial by one of its factors, you get another factor. To divide, you follow the procedure used to divide whole numbers.

Example 1

Divide $x^2 + 3x - 12$ by $x - 2$.

Set up as a division problem.

$$\begin{array}{r} x \\ x - 2 \overline{)x^2 + 3x - 12} \\ \underline{x^2 - 2x} \\ 5x - 12 \end{array}$$

← Divide: $\frac{x^2}{x} = x$.

← Multiply: $x(x - 2) = x^2 - 2x$.

← Subtract: $(x^2 + 3x) - (x^2 - 2x) = 5x$. Bring down −12.

Repeat the process of dividing, multiplying, and subtracting.

$$\begin{array}{r} x + 5 \\ x - 2 \overline{)x^2 + 3x - 12} \\ \underline{x^2 - 2x} \\ 5x - 12 \\ \underline{5x - 10} \\ -2 \end{array}$$

← Divide: $\frac{5x}{x} = 5$.

← Multiply: $5(x - 2) = 5x - 10$.

← Subtract: The remainder is −2.

The quotient is $x + 5$ with a remainder of -2.

4. **Verify** the result in Example 1 by finding $(x + 5)(x - 2)$. Then add the remainder -2.

5. Try This Divide.

    a. $x + 2 \overline{)x^2 + 5x + 6}$
               b. $x - 8 \overline{)2x^2 - 19x + 24}$

When a numerical division has a remainder of zero, the divisor and quotient are both factors of the dividend.

$$\begin{array}{r} 7 \\ \hline 8)\overline{56} \\ 56 \\ \hline 0 \end{array}$$ ←—7 and 8 are factors of 56.

The same is true of polynomial division. When a polynomial division has no remainder, you have factored the polynomial.

6. Based on your work in Question 5, factor each polynomial.

    a. $x^2 + 5x + 6$
               b. $2x^2 - 19x + 24$

7. a. Divide $x^3 - 8x^2 + x + 42$ by $x - 3$.

    b. *Critical Thinking* Explain how to find three linear factors of $x^3 - 8x^2 + x + 42$.

Using Synthetic Division

When you are dividing by a linear factor, you can use a simplified process known as **synthetic division.** In synthetic division, you omit all variables and exponents. Also, by reversing the sign of the divisor, you can add throughout the process rather than subtracting.

Example 2

Use synthetic division to divide $x^3 - 13x + 12$ by $x + 4$.

Step 1: Reverse the sign of the divisor. Use 0 as a place holder for any missing term.

    Write $x + 4 \overline{)x^3 + 0x^2 - 13x + 12}$ ←—Insert $0x^2$.

    as $\underline{-4|}$ 1   0 -13 12.

Step 2: Bring down the first coefficient.

    $\underline{-4|}$ 1   0 -13 12   ←—Bring down the 1.
                                        This begins the quotient.
        1

Step 3: Multiply the first coefficient by the divisor. Write the result under the next coefficient. Add.

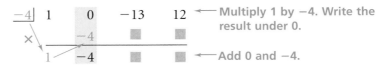

    $\underline{-4|}$ 1   0 -13 12   ←—Multiply 1 by -4. Write the
                                  result under 0.
     × -4
        1   -4 ←—Add 0 and -4.

Step 4: Repeat the steps of multiplying and adding.

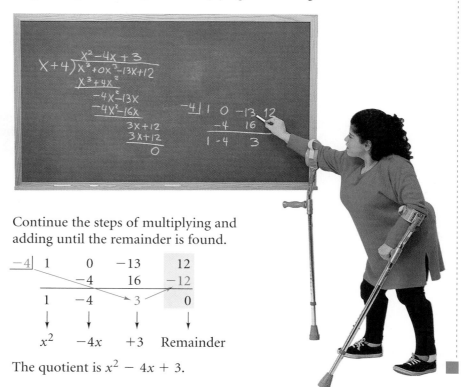

Continue the steps of multiplying and adding until the remainder is found.

$$
\begin{array}{r|rrrr}
-4 & 1 & 0 & -13 & 12 \\
 & & -4 & 16 & -12 \\
\hline
 & 1 & -4 & 3 & 0
\end{array}
$$

$$x^2 \quad -4x \quad +3 \quad \text{Remainder}$$

The quotient is $x^2 - 4x + 3$.

8. How do you know that 1, the first coefficient of the quotient, is the coefficient of x^2?

9. Find $(x + 4)(x^2 - 4x + 3)$ to **verify** the quotient in Example 2.

10. **Critical Thinking** If $x + 4$ is a factor of $x^3 - 13x + 12$, explain why -4 is a solution of $x^3 - 13x + 12 = 0$.

11. a. **Try This** Use synthetic division: $(x^3 - 2x^2 - 5x + 6) \div (x + 2)$.
    b. Use part (a) to factor $x^3 - 2x^2 - 5x + 6$.

12. When a polynomial division has a nonzero remainder, the remainder is related to the value of a polynomial function.
    a. Use synthetic division for $(x^3 + 4x^2 + x - 6) \div (x + 1)$.
    b. If $f(x) = x^3 + 4x^2 + x - 6$, find $f(-1)$.
    c. How is the remainder in part (a) related to the value $f(-1)$ in part (b)?
    d. **Critical Thinking** Suppose you want to find $f(2)$. What divisor should you use in synthetic division? **Verify** your answer.

The relationship explored in Question 12 is called the Remainder Theorem. For more work with this theorem, see Additional Topics page 624.

For more work with the Fundamental Theorem of Algebra, see Additional Topics page 628.

The **Fundamental Theorem of Algebra** states that a polynomial function of degree n has exactly n zeros. Some of these zeros may be imaginary numbers and some may be multiple zeros. Using a graphing calculator, the factor theorem, polynomial division, and the quadratic formula, you often can find all the zeros.

Example 3

Find all the zeros of $f(x) = x^3 + x^2 - x + 2$.

Graph the function. Since a cubic polynomial is involved, you should expect to find three zeros.

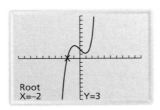

Root
X=-2   Y=3

←── The function has a zero at $x = -2$. By the factor theorem, $x + 2$ is a factor of $x^3 + x^2 - x + 2$.

To find the other zeros, divide the polynomial by the factor $x + 2$.

$$\underline{-2|}\ \ \begin{array}{cccc} 1 & 1 & -1 & 2 \\ & -2 & 2 & -2 \\ \hline 1 & -1 & 1 & 0 \end{array}$$

$$\downarrow \quad \downarrow \quad \downarrow$$

$$1x^2 \ -1x \ +1$$

The quotient is $x^2 - x + 1$. Since $y = x^2 - x + 1$ has no real zeros, use the quadratic formula to solve the related quadratic equation $x^2 - x + 1 = 0$.

$$x = \frac{-b \pm \sqrt{b^2 - 4ac}}{2a}$$

$$= \frac{-(-1) \pm \sqrt{(-1)^2 - 4(1)(1)}}{2(1)}$$ ←── Substitute 1 for a, -1 for b, and 1 for c.

$$= \frac{1 \pm \sqrt{-3}}{2}$$

$$= \frac{1 \pm i\sqrt{3}}{2}$$

The polynomial function $f(x) = x^3 + x^2 - x + 2$ has one real zero at $x = -2$ and two imaginary zeros at $x = \frac{1 + i\sqrt{3}}{2}$ and $x = \frac{1 - i\sqrt{3}}{2}$. ■

PROBLEM SOLVING HINT

To see whether a quadratic function has any real zeros, graph it on your graphing calculator.

Another tool for finding zeros is the Rational Root Theorem, found on page 626.

13. Try This Find all the zeros of each function.

a. $y = x^3 - 2x^2 + 4x - 8$ b. $f(x) = x^3 - x^2 - 4$

Exercises   ON YOUR OWN

Use polynomial long division.

1. $(x^2 - 3x - 40) \div (x + 5)$

2. $x + 4\overline{)3x^2 + 7x - 20}$

3. $x - 1\overline{)x^3 + 3x^2 - x + 2}$

4. $(2x^3 - 3x^2 - 18x - 8) \div (x - 4)$

5. $3x + 1\overline{)9x^3 - 18x^2 - x + 2}$

6. $(9x^2 - 21x - 20) \div (x - 1)$

7. Writing Explain why a polynomial of degree n, divided by a polynomial of degree 1, yields a quotient of degree $n - 1$ and a remainder that is a constant.

Use synthetic division.

8. $(x^3 + 3x^2 - x - 3) \div (x - 1)$

9. $(x^3 - 4x^2 + 6x - 4) \div (x - 2)$

10. $(x^4 - 5x^2 + 4x + 12) \div (x + 2)$

11. $(x^3 - 3x^2 - 5x - 25) \div (x - 5)$

12. $(2x^3 + 4x^2 - 10x - 9) \div (x - 3)$

13. $(2x^4 + 6x^3 + 5x^2 - 45) \div (x + 3)$

14. $(x^3 - 2x^2 - 5x + 6) \div (x - 1)$

15. $(-2x^3 + 5x^2 - x + 2) \div (x + 2)$

16. Patterns Divide. Look for patterns in your answers.
   a. $(x^2 - 1) \div (x - 1)$
   b. $(x^3 - 1) \div (x - 1)$
   c. $(x^4 - 1) \div (x - 1)$
   d. Based on the patterns in parts (a–c), factor $x^5 - 1$.

17. Patterns Divide. Look for patterns in your answers.
   a. $(x^3 + 1) \div (x + 1)$
   b. $(x^5 + 1) \div (x + 1)$
   c. $(x^7 + 1) \div (x + 1)$
   d. Based on the patterns in parts (a–c), factor $x^9 + 1$.

18. a. Graph $y = x^2 + 1$. Does $y = x^2 + 1$ have any real zeros?
   b. Explain why $x^2 + 1$ cannot be factored using real numbers.

One zero is given for each function. Find all the other zeros (both real and imaginary). Give exact answers.

19. $f(x) = x^3 - x^2 - 6x$; zero at $x = -2$

20. $y = 3x^3 + 10x^2 - x - 12$; zero at $x = 1$

21. $g(x) = x^3 - 4x^2 + 2x + 1$; zero at $x = 1$

22. $y = x^3 + 4x^2 + x - 6$; zero at $x = -3$

23. $y = 2x^3 + x^2 + 1$; zero at $x = -1$

24. $f(x) = x^3 - 3x^2 + x - 3$; zero at $x = 3$

Find all the real zeros of each function. Use a graphing calculator or paper and pencil. When necessary, round to the nearest hundredth.

25. $g(x) = x^3 - 5x^2 + 5x - 4$

26. $f(x) = x^4 - 6x^2 + 8$

27. $f(x) = x^4 - 3x^2 - 4$

28. $y = x^3 - 3x^2 - 9x$

29. Open-ended Write a polynomial function in the form $y = x^3 + ax$. (Choose a value for a.) Identify the shape of the graph and find its zeros.

30. Critical Thinking Suppose a cubic function has real-number coefficients. Can it have three imaginary zeros? Explain.

31. A polynomial $P(x)$ is divided by a binomial $x - a$. The remainder is zero. What conclusion can you draw? Explain.

32. Geometry The volume of a footlocker can be expressed in terms of the length of its sides as $V(x) = x^3 + x^2 - 6x$. The height is represented as $x - 2$. Write expressions for the locker's length and width.

33. Rodriguez represented the product of three numbers as $x^3 - x^2 - 2x$. If he used x and $x + 1$ as two of the factors, find the third factor.

34. Critical Thinking Suppose 3, -1, and 4 are solutions of a cubic polynomial equation. Sketch a graph of the related cubic function. Could there be more than one graph?

Chapter Project

Find Out by Graphing

Use the sketch you made in the Find Out activity on page 278. Identify and label ten points. Do you think the function that best fits these points will be more accurate than the function you found through four points? Explain your reasoning. Then find the new function using a graphing calculator and the QuadReg feature.

Exercises   MIXED REVIEW

Determine the number of x-intercepts of each function. Verify each answer by drawing a graph.

35. $y = 3x^2 + x - 6$ **36.** $y = 5x^2 - 9$ **37.** $y = -x^2 + 2x - 8$ **38.** $y = \frac{1}{2}x^2 + 3$

39. Write a matrix for the directed graph at the right.

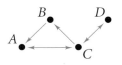

Getting Ready for Lesson 6-6
Simplify each expression.

40. $_5P_1$ **41.** $7!$ **42.** $_7P_2$ **43.** $5!$ **44.** $8!$ **45.** $_4P_3$

Exercises   CHECKPOINT

For each function, determine the zeros and their multiplicity.

1. $y = (x - 2)^2(x + 1)$ **2.** $y = (2x + 1)(x - 4)$ **3.** $y = x^3(x - 3)(x + 1)^2$

Solve each equation.

4. $6x^3 - 3x^2 - 9x = 0$ **5.** $x^4 - 5x^2 + 4 = 0$ **6.** $4x^3 - 4x^2 + 5x = 0$

Divide.

7. $(x^3 + 3x^2 + 3x + 1) \div (x + 1)$ **8.** $x - 2 \overline{) 2x^3 - 7x^2 + 7x - 2}$

9. Open-ended Write a polynomial function with at least three negative-valued zeros, with one of the zeros having multiplicity 2.

6-6 Combinations

What You'll Learn

• Finding combinations

...And Why

To find the number of possible ways to choose flags for a flag corps

What You'll Need

• graphing calculator

T H I N K   A N D   D I S C U S S

Suppose your school's flag corps is selecting three sets of flags out of all the flags the school owns to use during a marching band competition.

In a situation like this, the *order* in which the flags are chosen does not matter. This kind of selection is called a **combination.**

Example 1   **Relating to the Real World**

Band The flag corps uses three sets of flags during the band show. In how many ways can it choose three flags from the five flags shown?

purple

gold

white

blue

red

List the combinations:

PGB PGR PGW ←— All the combinations containing *purple.*
　　PBR PBW
　　　　PRW

　　GBR GBW ←— With *purple* removed, all the
　　　　GRW 　　combinations containing *gold.*

　　　　BRW ←— With *purple* and *gold* removed, all the
　　　　　　 combinations containing *blue.*

There are ten different ways to choose three flags for the band show.

1. Suppose the flag corps uses only two flags in the show. List all the combinations of two flags chosen from the five flags.

2. **Try This** How many different combinations of three flags will there be if you add a turquoise flag to the original five choices?

When you are finding combinations of a few objects, you can make a list. However, with high numbers making a list can be time-consuming. You can use a mathematical formula to find the number of possible combinations.

Number of Combinations

The number of combinations of n objects of a set chosen r objects at a time is given by the following formula.

$$_nC_r = \frac{n!}{r!(n-r)!} \text{ for } 0 \leq r \leq n$$

Example: $_5C_3 = \frac{5!}{3!(5-3)!} = \frac{5!}{3! \cdot 2!} = \frac{120}{6 \cdot 2} = \frac{120}{12} = 10$

3. **Critical Thinking** Why must the variable r have a value greater than or equal to zero and less than or equal to n?

Example 2

Evaluate $_{12}C_3$.

Method I:

$_{12}C_3 = \frac{12!}{3!(12-3)!}$ ← Use the formula $_nC_r = \frac{n!}{r!(n-r)!}$.

$= \frac{12!}{3!9!}$ ← Evaluate the factorials.

$= \frac{12 \cdot 11 \cdot 10 \cdot 9 \cdot 8 \cdot 7 \cdot 6 \cdot 5 \cdot 4 \cdot 3 \cdot 2 \cdot 1}{3 \cdot 2 \cdot 1 \cdot 9 \cdot 8 \cdot 7 \cdot 6 \cdot 5 \cdot 4 \cdot 3 \cdot 2 \cdot 1}$ ← Simplify.

$= \frac{12 \cdot 11 \cdot 10}{3 \cdot 2 \cdot 1}$

$= 220$

Method II:

$_{12}C_3 = \frac{12!}{3!(12-3)!}$ ← Use the formula.

$= \frac{12!}{3! \cdot 9!}$

$= 220$ ← Use a calculator.

4. Evaluate $_6C_2$ and $_6C_4$. Explain why they are equal.

5. **Try This** How many ways can you choose five of ten friends?

6. **a.** Evaluate $0!$ using a calculator.
   b. Evaluate $_3C_3$.
   c. Suppose there are three open seats on a town council. Only three candidates are running for those seats. How many ways are there to vote for three people? two people? one person? none?

7. **a.** Evaluate $_5C_3$ and $_5P_3$.
   b. Which is greater: the number of ways to *choose* 3 items out of 5 or the number of ways to *choose and arrange in order* 3 items out of 5?

Many calculators have a feature to evaluate combinations.

Example 3 **Relating to the Real World**

Literature A reading list for a course in world literature has 20 books on it. How many ways are there to choose four books to read?

Define 20 books chosen 4 at a time

Relate   20   C   4

Write $_{20}C_4 =$

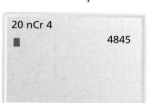

20 nCr 4

　　　　　　4845

⟵ Use the $_nC_r$ feature on a calculator.

There are 4845 different ways to choose four books to read.

8. **Try This** Evaluate each expression.
   a. $_6C_4$ **b.** $_8C_2$ **c.** $_{10}C_5$ **d.** $_{25}C_7$

9. Suppose the *order* in which you read the four books in Example 3 matters. Find the number of permutations of four books selected from 20.

Example 4 **Relating to the Real World**

Civics There are ten candidates running for three seats in the student government. You may vote for up to three people. In how many ways can you vote for three or fewer candidates?

You may vote for 3 people, 2 people, 1 person, or none.

$$_{10}C_3 \qquad _{10}C_2 \qquad _{10}C_1 \qquad _{10}C_0$$
$$120 \qquad 45 \qquad 10 \qquad 1$$

To find the total number of ways you can vote, find $120 + 45 + 10 + 1$. There are 176 ways to cast your ballot.

Tell whether each situation involves a combination or a permutation.

1. 12 books arranged on a shelf

2. 4 books pulled at random from a shelf

3. 3 flavors of juice selected from a variety pack

4. 5 runners crossing the finish line

Evaluate each expression.

5. $8!$

6. $5!3!$

7. $\frac{12!}{6!}$

8. $5(4!)$

9. $\frac{10!}{7!3!}$

10. $_6C_2$

11. $_8C_5$

12. $_4C_4$

13. $_4P_4$

14. $_8P_5$

15. $3(_5C_4)$

16. $\frac{15!}{10!5!}$

17. $_9P_7$

18. $_6P_2$

19. $_7C_3$

20. $_6C_2 + _6C_3$

21. $\frac{_7C_4}{_9C_4}$

22. $\frac{_{50}C_5}{_{50}C_{10}}$

23. a. Geometry Eight points lie on a circle. How many triangles can you make using three of the points as vertices?
  b. How many pentagons can you make using five points as vertices?
  c. **Analyze** why your answers to parts (a) and (b) should be the same.

24. Open-ended Write and solve a problem involving a combination.

25. Food Preparation The students at a culinary arts school are learning to prepare seven different items. In how many ways can you place each order?
  a. two items   **b.** three items
  c. four items   **d.** five items

26. a. How many ways are there to choose three flags from a collection of seven different flags?
  b. Once a set of three flags is chosen, in how many different orders can the set be arranged?
  c. Writing Suppose you want to arrange three objects from a group of seven. Explain how you can use the relationship $_7C_3 \cdot 3!$ to create the permutation formula.

Discrete Math **In Exercises 27–30, state whether each situation involves a combination or a permutation. Then solve.**

27. How many different starting teams of 11 players can be chosen from a soccer squad of 16?

28. How many different nine-player batting orders can be chosen from a baseball squad of 16?

29. Suppose you find seven articles related to the topic of your research paper. In how many ways can you choose five of the articles to read?

30. For a band camp, you can choose two or three roommates from a group of 25 friends. In how many ways can you do this?

31. a. Discrete Math The graph at the right shows the function $y = {_x}C_2$. Use it to graph the function $y = {_x}C_{x-2}$.
   b. Critical Thinking Explain why the graph isn't a continuous function.

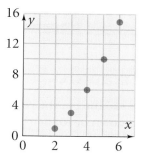

Use paper and pencil, a calculator, or mental math to evaluate each expression.

32. ${_4}C_3$ **33.** $\frac{1}{3}({_{10}}C_5)$ **34.** $\frac{{_{25}}C_2}{{_{50}}C_2}$ **35.** $\frac{{_6}C_2}{3}$

How many combinations of four objects can you make from each set?

36. $\{0, 1, 2, 3, 4, 5, 6, 7, 8, 9\}$

37. 300 people in a union

38. 25 baseball cards

39. a rose, a daisy, a peony, a daffodil, and a tulip

40. Data Analysis The circle graph at the right shows the results of 40 responses to a survey.
   a. How many people said they squeeze the toothpaste from the middle of the tube?
   b. Use your answer to part (a). Find the number of possible combinations of five people who squeeze toothpaste from the middle of the tube.
   c. Suppose five people are chosen at random from all the people who responded to the survey. How many combinations of five people are possible?
   d. Probability What is the probability that the five people selected at random will all squeeze toothpaste from the middle of the tube?

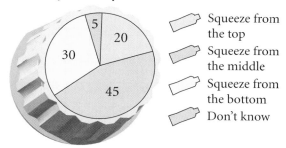

**Toothpaste Survey Results
(Percents)**

Squeeze from the top

Squeeze from the middle

Squeeze from the bottom

Don't know

Exercises   MIXED REVIEW

Graph each equation.

41. $y = 5x - 2$ **42.** $y < 4x + 1$ **43.** $y = |x - 3|$ **44.** $y = x^2 + x - 2$

Solve for x.

45. $2x^2 + 5x = 12$ **46.** $3|2x - 5| > 15$

47. $3a - 2x = 5x + 9a$ **48.** $x - 5 = 2x + 7$

49. You can tutor students after school 3 h/wk for $9/h. Another job is packing groceries 5 h/wk for $5/h. How long would it take you to make $130 at each job?

Getting Ready for Lesson 6-7
Find each product.

50. $(x - 5)^2$ **51.** $(3x + 5y)^2$ **52.** $(x + 1)^3$

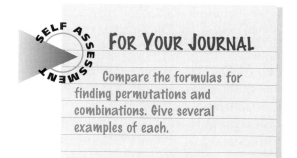

SELF ASSESSMENT

FOR YOUR JOURNAL

Compare the formulas for finding permutations and combinations. Give several examples of each.

Pascal's Triangle

Before Lesson 6-7

Suppose you are standing at the corner of the grid (point $A1$). You are allowed to travel down or to the right only. The only way you can get to $A2$ is by traveling down one unit. You can get to $B1$ by traveling to the right one unit. The number of ways you can get to points $A2$, $B1$, and $B2$ is written next to each point.

You are here.

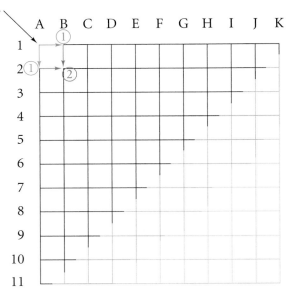

1. The number 2 is written next to point $B2$. What are the two different ways you can get from $A1$ to $B2$?

2. Copy the grid. Travel only down or to the right. In how many ways can you get from $A1$ to $A3$? from $A1$ to $C2$?

3. Mark the number of ways you can get to each point from point $A1$.

4. **Patterns** Describe any patterns you see in the numbers on the grid.

5. **a.** Make a copy of your completed grid. Color the numbers that are multiples of 2. (You may need to extend the grid to see a pattern.)
   b. **Research** The pattern you see in part (a) is called the Sierpinski triangle. Find another way to describe how to obtain this pattern.

6. **Writing** The completed grid is called Pascal's triangle. Turn your copy of the grid so that $A1$ is at the top. Explain why the grid is called a triangle.

What You'll Learn

- Using Pascal's triangle
- Using the binomial theorem
- Finding probabilities

...And Why

To find probabilities when there are two possible outcomes

The numbers in Pascal's triangle also describe how many balls are in each section of this probability machine.

6-7 The Binomial Theorem

WORK TOGETHER

1. Write $(x + y)^2$ as a polynomial in standard form.

2. Write $(x + y)^3$ and $(x + y)^4$ as polynomials in standard form.

3. For Questions 1 and 2, compare the number of terms you get with the power used. What do you notice?

4. **Patterns** What patterns do you see in the terms of your answers to Questions 1 and 2? in the exponents? in the coefficients?

THINK AND DISCUSS

Binomial Expansion and Pascal's Triangle

To **expand** a binomial being raised to a power, you multiply and write the result as a polynomial in standard form. The table below shows part of **Pascal's triangle,** which contains the coefficients of the expansion.

Coefficients of an Expansion (Pascal's Triangle)

$(a + b)^0$						1					
$(a + b)^1$					1		1				
$(a + b)^2$				1		2		1			
$(a + b)^3$			1		3		3		1		
$(a + b)^4$		1		4		6		4		1	
$(a + b)^5$	▦		▦		▦		▦		▦		▦

5. Compare the values in Pascal's triangle with the coefficients in each expansion from the Work Together. What do you notice?

6. **Patterns** Explain how you can use addition to find each row of Pascal's triangle from the previous row.

7. **a.** Without multiplying, predict the powers of x and y for each term of $(x + y)^5$.
   b. Write the next row of Pascal's triangle.
   c. Expand $(a + b)^5$.

8. **Patterns** Compare the second coefficient in each row to the power of $a + b$ for that row. What is the second coefficient in the expansion of $(a + b)^{10}$?

9. Based on the patterns you have seen, what are the first two terms in the expansion of $(a + b)^{10}$?

Pascal's Triangle

$$1$$
$$1 \quad 1$$
$$1 \quad 2 \quad 1$$
$$1 \quad 3 \quad 3 \quad 1$$
$$1 \quad 4 \quad 6 \quad 4 \quad 1$$
$$1 \quad 5 \quad 10 \quad 10 \quad 5 \quad 1$$
$$1 \quad 6 \quad 15 \quad 20 \quad 15 \quad 6 \quad 1$$
$$1 \quad 7 \quad 21 \quad 35 \quad 35 \quad 21 \quad 7 \quad 1$$
$$1 \quad 8 \quad 28 \quad 56 \quad 70 \quad 56 \quad 28 \quad 8 \quad 1$$

Each row of Pascal's triangle contains coefficients for the expansion of $(a + b)^n$. For example, when $n = 6$, use the row that begins with 1   6 . . . .

Example 1

Use Pascal's triangle to expand $(a + b)^6$.

Use the row that has 6 as its second number.

The exponents for a begin with 6 and decrease.

$$1a^6b^0 + 6a^5b^1 + 15a^4b^2 + 20a^3b^3 + 15a^2b^4 + 6a^1b^5 + 1a^0b^6$$

The exponents for b begin with 0 and increase.

In simplest form, the expansion is
$a^6 + 6a^5b + 15a^4b^2 + 20a^3b^3 + 15a^2b^4 + 6ab^5 + b^6$.

When? The earliest known version of Pascal's triangle was developed in the third century B.C. by the Indian mathematician Halayudha. The Chinese knew of the triangle in A.D. 1100. Later in the twelfth century, it also appeared in *The Luminous Book on Arithmetic*, by As-Samaw'al ibn-Yahya al'Mighribi. The triangle has been named for Blaise Pascal (1623–1662), a French mathematician.

10. Try This Use Pascal's triangle to expand $(a + b)^8$.

Sometimes the terms of the binomial have coefficients other than one. The expansion to standard form is still based on the pattern for $(a + b)^n$.

Example 2

Use Pascal's triangle to expand $(x - 2)^3$.

First, write the pattern for raising a binomial to the third power.

$$1 \quad 3 \quad 3 \quad 1 \qquad \leftarrow \text{coefficients from Pascal's triangle}$$

$$(a + b)^3 = a^3 + 3a^2b + 3ab^2 + b^3$$

Since $(x - 2)^3 = (x + (-2))^3$, replace a with x and b with -2.

$$(x + (-2))^3 = x^3 + 3x^2(-2) + 3x(-2)^2 + (-2)^3$$
$$= x^3 - 6x^2 + 12x - 8$$

The expansion of $(x - 2)^3$ is $x^3 - 6x^2 + 12x - 8$.

11. Try This Use Pascal's triangle to expand $(x - 2)^4$.

12. Evaluate each combination. Look for a pattern in your answers.
   a. $_5C_0$ **b.** $_5C_1$ **c.** $_5C_2$ **d.** $_5C_3$ **e.** $_5C_4$ **f.** $_5C_5$

13. Critical Thinking Explain how to use combinations to find the coefficients of $(a + b)^5$.

14. Suppose $_8C_3x^5y^3$ is a term of a binomial expansion. Write the next term.

The Binomial Theorem

All the patterns you have seen are summarized in the **binomial theorem.** Notice that the sequence of exponents for a is decreasing, while the sequence for b is increasing.

> ### Binomial Theorem
>
> For every positive integer n, $(a + b)^n =$
> $${}_nC_0a^n + {}_nC_1a^{n-1}b + {}_nC_2a^{n-2}b^2 + \ldots + {}_nC_{n-1}ab^{n-1} + {}_nC_nb^n.$$
> **Example:**
> $$(a + b)^4 = {}_4C_0a^4 + {}_4C_1a^3b + {}_4C_2a^2b^2 + {}_4C_3ab^3 + {}_4C_4b^4$$
> $$= a^4 + 4a^3b + 6a^2b^2 + 4ab^3 + b^4$$

15. Try This Use the binomial theorem to expand each binomial.

    a. $(v + w)^9$ **b.** $(g + h)^4$ **c.** $(c - 2)^5$

You can use the binomial theorem to solve some probability problems. Suppose an event has a probability of success p and a probability of failure q. Each term in the expansion of $(p + q)^n$ represents a probability. For example, ${}_{10}C_2p^8q^2$ represents the probability of eight successes in ten trials.

Example 3   Relating to the Real World

Probability Mark Price has held a National Basketball Association career record for free throws. He has attempted more than 2000 free throws and made 90% of them. If his probability of success on any single shot is 0.9, find the probability that he will make exactly 6 out of 10 consecutive shots.

Since you want 6 successes (and 4 failures), use the term containing p^6q^4. This term has the coefficient ${}_{10}C_4$.

Probability (6 out of 10 baskets)

$$= {}_{10}C_4p^6q^4$$
$$= \frac{10!}{4! \cdot 6!} \cdot (0.9)^6(0.1)^4 \quad \begin{array}{l}\text{The probability } p \text{ of success} = 0.9.\\ \longleftarrow\text{The probability } q \text{ of failure} = 0.1.\end{array}$$
$$= 0.011160261 \quad \longleftarrow\text{Use a calculator.}$$

Mark Price has about a 1% chance of making exactly 6 out of 10 free throws.

16. a. Try This Find the probability that Mark Price will make exactly 9 out of 10 free throw attempts.

    b. Find the probability that he will make 10 out of 10 attempts.

State the number of terms in each expansion and give the first two terms.

1. $(d + e)^{12}$　　**2.** $(x - y)^2$　　**3.** $(a + b)^4$　　**4.** $(x - y)^7$　　**5.** $(a + b)^3$

Use Pascal's triangle to expand each binomial.

6. $(x - y)^5$　　**7.** $(a - b)^6$　　**8.** $(x + y)^4$　　**9.** $(x - 3)^3$　　**10.** $(a + 3b)^4$

11. In the expansion of $(m + n)^9$, one of the terms contains m^3.
　　a. What is the exponent of n in this term?
　　b. What is the coefficient of this term?

12. The term $126c^4d^5$ appears in the expansion of $(c + d)^n$. Find n.

13. The coefficient of the second term in the expansion of $(r + s)^n$ is 7.
　　Find the value of n, and write the complete term.

Use the binomial theorem to expand each binomial.

14. $(x + y)^4$　　**15.** $(s - t)^2$　　**16.** $(w + 1)^5$　　**17.** $(x - 1)^6$　　**18.** $(4 - x)^3$

19. $(x - y)^4$　　**20.** $(3x - y)^4$　　**21.** $(x^2 + y^2)^2$　　**22.** $(2x + 3y)^3$　　**23.** $(x + y)^7$

24. a. Expand $(1 + i)^4$. Simplify your expression by replacing i^2 with -1,
　　　i^3 with $-i$, and i^4 with 1. The expression should simplify to a
　　　negative real number.
　　b. Verify that $1 - i$ is a fourth root of -4 by repeating the process in
　　　part (a) for $(1 - i)^4$.

25. Verify that $-1 + \sqrt{3}i$ is a cube root of 8 by expanding
　　$(-1 + \sqrt{3}i)^3$.

26. Probability A coin is tossed ten times. The probability of heads on
　　each toss is 0.5. Write the term in the expansion of
　　$(h + t)^{10}$ for each outcome described. Then evaluate it.
　　a. exactly 5 heads　　　**b.** exactly 6 heads　　　　**c.** exactly 7 heads

27. Meteorology Based on the long-range forecast at the
　　right, find the probability that it will rain on exactly
　　three out of the four days.

28. Research Use the current winning percentage of a
　　local sports team as its probability of success. Find
　　the probability that the team will win three games
　　in a row.

29. Writing Explain why the terms of $(a - 4)^6$ have
　　alternating positive and negative signs.

30. Open-ended Write a probability problem for
　　which $_5C_3(0.5)^2(0.5)^3$ is the solution.

4　 THE HERALD

*It looks like it will be a long, wet
holiday weekend!*

Friday: 80% chance of rain
Saturday: 80% chance of rain
Sunday: 80% chance of rain
Monday: 80% chance of rain

31. Geometry A cube has sides of length s. Suppose each of the dimensions of the cube is increased by 0.5.
a. Write a binomial expression for the volume of the new cube.
b. Expand the binomial.

Graph each function and find its x-intercepts.

32. $y = -6x^2 + 5$ **33.** $y = 0.1x^3 - 3x$

34. $y = x^2 - 3x + 5$ **35.** $y = x^3 - 3x^2 - 10x$

36. Business Juanita Perez plans to open a restaurant. She needs an initial investment of $90,000. Weekly costs will be about $8200. If the weekly revenue is $8900, in how many weeks will she break even?

37. Standardized Test Prep Which best approximates the distance in miles between Birmingham and Denver?
A. 1.3×10^{-5} **B.** 1.3×10^{-2} **C.** 1.3×10^0
D. 1.3×10^3 **E.** 1.3×10^7

PORTFOLIO

For your portfolio, select one or two items from your work for this chapter. Here are some possibilities.
• best work
• work you found challenging
• part of your project
Explain why you have included each selection you make.

Algebra at Work

Quality Control Engineer

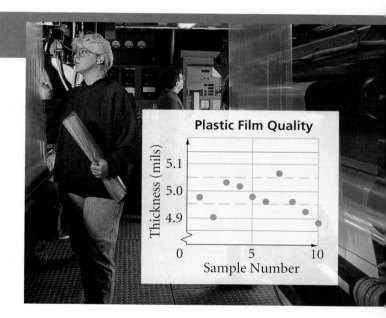

Quality control engineers establish procedures for assuring that products meet minimum standards of quality such as length or purity. Each product is sampled regularly. Data relating to each standard are graphed on a chart like the one shown. It records the thickness of plastic film in thousandths of an inch (mils).

All samples must fall within the limiting parameters indicated by the red lines. Quality is further controlled by requiring that a significant portion of the samples, say 60%, fall within the middle third of the limiting parameters (broken lines).

Mini Project: Suppose the thickness of the plastic film is measured six times. Assume that the quality goals are being met (all samples measure within 0.15 mils of 5.0 and 60% measure within 0.05 mils). Find the probability that at least three of the measurements fall within the middle third of the acceptable thickness range.

Finishing the Chapter Project

CURVES BY DESIGN

Find Out questions on pages 267, 278, and 284 should help you to complete your project. Make a poster to display the sketch and graphs you have completed for the object you have designed. On the poster, include your research about the design.

Reflect and Revise

Before completing your poster, check your equations for correctness, your graph designs for neatness, and your written work for clarity. Is your poster eye-catching, exciting, and appealing as well as correct in content? Show your work to at least one adult and one classmate. Discuss improvements you could make.

Follow Up

Interview someone who uses a computer-assisted design (CAD) program at work. If possible, arrange to have a demonstration of the program. Find out what skills, education, or experience helped the person successfully enter the field of computer-assisted design.

For More Information

How Things Work: Structures. Alexandria, Virginia: Time-Life Books, 1991.

Janicki, Edward. *Cars Detroit Never Built: Fifty Years of American Experimental Cars.* New York: Sterling Publishing Company, 1990.

Understanding Computers: Transportation. Alexandria, Virginia: Time-Life Books, 1988.

Key Terms

binomial theorem (p. 293)
combination (p. 285)
degree (p. 261)
end behavior (p. 262)
even functions (p. 256)
expand (p. 291)
extraneous solution (p. 258)
factor theorem (p. 270)
factored form (p. 268)
Fundamental Theorem of
   Algebra (p. 281)
index (p. 256)

multiple zeros (p. 271)
multiplicity (p. 271)
odd functions (p. 256)
Pascal's triangle (p. 291)
polynomial function (p. 261)
power function (p. 255)
principal root (p. 256)
relative maximum (p. 269)
relative minimum (p. 269)
standard form (p. 261)
synthetic division (p. 280)

How am I doing?

- State three ideas from this chapter that you think are important. Explain your choices.

SELF ASSESSMENT

- Describe the graphs of polynomials with different degrees.

Power Functions and Their Inverses

6-1

A **power function** has the form $y = ax^n$, with $a \neq 0$ and n a positive integer. **Even functions** have the y-axis as a line of symmetry. **Odd functions** have the origin as a point of symmetry. Power functions are even or odd.

The inverse of a power function involves finding a root. The **index** of the radical sign indicates the kind of root.

When you work with radical equations, check for **extraneous solutions.** These satisfy later equations but do not make the original equation true.

Simplify each expression.

1. $100^{\frac{1}{2}}$ **2.** 13^0 **3.** $49^{\frac{3}{2}}$ **4.** $27^{\frac{2}{3}}$ **5.** $32^{\frac{2}{5}}$ **6.** $(a^4)^{\frac{1}{4}}$

Find the inverse of each function. Graph the function and its inverse on the same coordinate system.

7. $y = x^4$ **8.** $y = 3\sqrt[4]{x}$ **9.** $y = 3.1x^3$

Solve each equation. Find and discard any extraneous roots.

10. $\sqrt[3]{x + 2} = -4$ **11.** $\sqrt{x - 4} = x - 6$ **12.** $x^{\frac{1}{2}} + 2 = 5$

13. Open-ended Write the rule of a function that is odd.

14. a. Geometry The volume of a sphere is given by the formula
    $V = \frac{4}{3}\pi r^3$. Find the volume if $r = 4$ in.
  b. Solve the formula in part (a) for r.
  c. Find the radius of a sphere of volume 100 in.^{3}.

A **polynomial function** is the sum of various power functions and constants. The exponent in a term is the **degree** of that term. When the terms of a polynomial are in descending order by degree, it is in **standard form.** You can classify a polynomial in standard form by the number of terms it has or by its highest degree.

The **end behavior** of a graph describes the far left and far right portions of the graph. The end behavior is determined by the term of the polynomial that has the highest degree. A polynomial function of degree n will have one y-intercept and up to n x-intercepts.

Graph each function. Find the x- and y-intercepts. Estimate to the nearest tenth when needed.

15. $f(x) = -x^3 + 2x - 4$

16. $h(x) = x^3 + x^2 - 6x$

17. $f(x) = x^4 - x^3 - 2x^2 + 1$

18. Standardized Test Prep What is the end behavior of the function $g(x) = 3x^5 - 7x^3 + 4x^2 - 8x + 1$?

A. $(\nwarrow, \nearrow)$ **B.** $(\nwarrow, \searrow)$ **C.** $(\swarrow, \nearrow)$ **D.** $(\swarrow, \searrow)$ **E.** none of the above

When you consider only nearby points on a graph, the greatest y-value is a **relative maximum.** The least y-value is a **relative minimum.**

You can write polynomials in standard form or in **factored form.** The **factor theorem** states that the expression $x - a$ is a linear factor of a polynomial if and only if a is a zero of the related polynomial function. When a linear factor is repeated, it represents a **multiple zero.** If the factor appears twice, the zero has **multiplicity** of 2.

For each function, determine the zeros and their multiplicity.

19. $y = (x - 1)(x + 3)^2$

20. $y = x^3(x + 7)(x - 2)$

21. $y = (x - 5)^2(x + 1)$

Write a polynomial function in standard form with the given zeros.

22. $2, -3$

23. $0, 5, -2$

24. $2, 4, 4$

You can solve polynomial equations by graphing or by factoring. Sometimes you can use the quadratic formula.

Solve each equation. Round your answers to the nearest tenth when necessary.

25. $x^3 - 5x^2 + 4x = 0$

26. $4t^6 - t^4 = 0$

27. $x^3 - 4x^2 + 5 = 0$

28. $x^3 = 2x^2 + 8x$

29. $x^3 = 9x$

30. $x^3 - 2x^2 - 5x = 0$

Dividing Polynomials

6-5

The **Fundamental Theorem of Algebra** states that a polynomial function of degree n has exactly n zeros. Some zeros may be imaginary numbers and some may be multiple zeros.

You can divide a polynomial by one of its factors to find other factors. When you divide by a linear factor, you can simplify this division by omitting the variables and exponents. This is called **synthetic division.**

Use synthetic division.

31. $(x^3 - 2x^2 - 3x) \div (x + 1)$

32. $(x^4 + 4x^3 + 2x^2 + 9x + 4) \div (x + 4)$

33. $(2x^4 - x^3 - 6x^2 - 2x + 4) \div (x - 2)$

34. $(3x^3 - 10x^2 + 8x - 15) \div (x - 3)$

Combinations

6-6

In a **combination,** the order of selection does not matter. The number of combinations of n objects of a set chosen r objects at a time is $_nC_r = \frac{n!}{r!(n - r)!}$ for $0 \le r \le n$.

Simplify each expression.

35. $_5C_2$ **36.** $_5C_3$ **37.** $_9C_8$ **38.** $_{11}C_1$ **39.** $_8C_4$ **40.** $_7C_5$

41. How many different ways can you choose 5 baseball cards from 16?

The Binomial Theorem

6-7

You can expand a binomial being raised to a power by using the coefficients in **Pascal's triangle.**

The **binomial theorem** states that for every positive integer n, $(a + b)^n = {}_nC_0a^n + {}_nC_1a^{n-1}b^1 + {}_nC_2a^{n-2}b^2 + \ldots + {}_nC_{n-1}ab^{n-1} + {}_nC_nb^n$.
You can use the binomial theorem to find probabilities.

Use the binomial theorem to expand each binomial.

42. $(x - y)^3$ **43.** $(q + 1)^5$ **44.** $(2x + y)^2$ **45.** $(t - 3w)^3$

46. Writing Do you prefer to expand binomials using Pascal's triangle or the binomial theorem? Include your reasons.

Getting Ready for..

CHAPTER 7

Evaluate each expression.

47. 2^x for $x = 3$

48. 4^{x+1} for $x = 1$

49. 2^{3x+4} for $x = -1$

50. 3^x3^{x-2} for $x = 2$

51. $\left(\frac{1}{2}\right)^x$ for $x = 0$

52. 2^x for $x = -2$

Find the inverse of each function. Graph the function and its inverse on the same coordinate system.

1. $y = \frac{1}{2}x^4$

2. $y = (x + 1)^3$

3. $y = (x + 1)^2 - 3$

4. $y = \sqrt{x + 5}$

5. Writing Describe the characteristics of odd functions and even functions. Give an example of each.

Solve each equation. Discard any extraneous solutions.

6. $\sqrt[3]{x + 4} = 3$

7. $2x^2 + 4 = 22$

8. $\sqrt{x + 2} = x + 2$

9. $x^{\frac{1}{4}} = 1$

Write each polynomial function in standard form. Then classify it by number of terms and by degree.

10. $f(x) = 3x^2 - 7x^4 + 9 - x^4$

11. $f(x) = 11x^2 + 8x - 3x^2$

12. $f(x) = 2x(x - 3)(x + 2)$

Graph each function. Describe the end behavior and find the x- and y-intercepts. Estimate to the nearest tenth when needed.

13. $f(x) = x^4 + 3x^3 - 1$

14. $f(x) = -x^6 - x^3 + 2$

15. $f(x) = -x^3 - x^2 + x$

16. $f(x) = x^3 - 3x^2 + 2$

17. Open-ended Write a function that has the end behavior $(\nwarrow, \searrow)$.

Write a polynomial function in standard form with the following zeros.

18. $1, 2, 5$

19. $-2, 0, 1$

20. $-4, -4, -4$

21. $-1, 1, 1$

Solve each equation. Give an exact answer or round your answer to the nearest tenth.

22. $(x - 3)(x^2 + 3x - 4) = 0$

23. $(x + 2)(x^2 + 5x + 1) = 0$

24. $x^3 - 2x^2 + x = 0$

25. $x^3 + 3x^2 - 5x - 4 = 0$

Use polynomial long division.

26. $(x^2 + 3x - 4) \div (x - 1)$

27. $(x^3 + 7x^2 - 5x - 6) \div (x + 2)$

28. Standardized Test Prep Which binomials are factors of $x^4 + 2x^3 - 3x^2 - 4x + 4$?

  I. $x + 2$ **II.** $x - 1$ **III.** $x + 1$

  A. I only   **B.** II only   **C.** I and II

  D. II and III   **E.** I, II, and III

Evaluate each expression.

29. $6!$ **30.** $\frac{6!}{4!2!}$ **31.** $_7C_3$ **32.** $_5P_2$

33. $_9C_4$ **34.** $_7P_4$ **35.** $_{11}P_9$ **36.** $_9C_8$

Decide whether each problem is a combination or a permutation. Then solve.

37. How many ways are there to select five actors from a troupe of nine?

38. How many different three-student study groups can be formed from a class of 15?

39. Five apartments are for rent. In how many different orders can you view the apartments?

Use the binomial theorem to expand each binomial.

40. $(x + z)^5$

41. $(1 - 2t)^4$

42. A weighted coin has $P(\text{heads}) = \frac{2}{5}$. The coin is tossed seven times. Evaluate the term in the expansion of $(a + b)^7$ that expresses the probability of getting exactly three heads.

For Exercises 1–11, choose the correct letter.

1. Which function shifts the graph of $y = x^2$ right 5 units and down 1 unit?
   A. $y = (x - 5)^2 - 1$ **B.** $y = (x + 5)^2 + 1$
   C. $y = (x - 1)^2 - 5$ **D.** $y = (x + 1)^2 + 5$
   E. $y = (x + 5)^2 + 1$

2. At which point is the cost function $C = 3x + y$ minimized?
   A. $(3, 1)$ **B.** $(1, 0)$ **C.** $(0, 1)$
   D. $(3, 4)$ **E.** $(2, 1)$

3. Identify the zero(s) of the polynomial function $y = x^3 - 4x^2 + x + 6$.
   I. 1   **II.** 2   **III.** 3
   A. I only   **B.** II only   **C.** I and II
   D. II and III   **E.** I, II, and III

4. What is the solution of this matrix equation?
$$\begin{bmatrix} 1 & 0 & 2 \\ 3 & 1 & 1 \\ -5 & 4 & 0 \end{bmatrix} X = \begin{bmatrix} 0 & -1 & 20 \\ -2 & 2 & 27 \\ 22 & -5 & -22 \end{bmatrix}$$
   A. $\begin{bmatrix} 1 & 3 & -2 \\ -1 & 0 & 1 \\ 7 & 2 & 7 \end{bmatrix}$ **B.** $\begin{bmatrix} -2 & 1 & 6 \\ 3 & 0 & 2 \\ 1 & -1 & 7 \end{bmatrix}$
   C. $\begin{bmatrix} -2 & 3 & 1 \\ 1 & 0 & 1 \\ 6 & 2 & 7 \end{bmatrix}$ **D.** $\begin{bmatrix} -2 & 0 & 7 \\ 3 & 1 & -1 \\ 1 & 2 & 6 \end{bmatrix}$
   E. There is no solution.

5. Which relation is not a function?
   A. $y = 3\sqrt{x} - 1$ **B.** $y = |x - 7|$
   C. $y = 3x^5 - 4$ **D.** $y = \pm 3x$
   E. $y = 3x^4 - x^3 - 4x^2 + 7x - 10$

6. Which point is a solution of the system below?
$$\begin{cases} y \le 2x + 3 \\ y > |x + 1| \\ y < -x + 4 \end{cases}$$
   I. $(0, 2)$ **II.** $(1, -3)$ **III.** $(-1, 4)$
   A. I only   **B.** II only   **C.** I and II
   D. II and III   **E.** I, II, and III

7. What is the discriminant of $2x^2 - 5x + 4 = 0$?
   A. $(-5)^2 - 4(2)(4)$ **B.** $-5^2 - 4(2)(4)$
   C. $(-5)^2 + 4(2)(4)$ **D.** $-5^2 + 4(2)(4)$
   E. none of the above

8. Which line is perpendicular to $y = 2x + 1$?
   A. $y = \frac{1}{2}x + 7$ **B.** $x + 2y = 4$
   C. $y = -2x - 5$ **D.** $x - 2y = 10$
   E. $2x + y = 11$

9. What is the end behavior of the function $f(x) = 5x^4 - 3x^3 + x - 2$?
   A. $(\nwarrow, \nearrow)$ **B.** $(\nwarrow, \searrow)$ **C.** $(\swarrow, \nearrow)$
   D. $(\swarrow, \searrow)$ **E.** none of the above

Compare the boxed quantity in Column A with the boxed quantity in Column B. Choose the best answer.

   A. The quantity in Column A is greater.
   B. The quantity in Column B is greater.
   C. The two quantities are equal.
   D. The relationship cannot be determined on the basis of the information supplied.

Column A	Column B
10. sum of the roots of $x^2 + 4x + 3 = 0$	degree of $2x^4 - 3x^2$
11. $_8C_2$	$_8P_2$

Find each answer.

12. *Open-ended* Use a coordinate plane to graph a polygon. Then use matrices to find the image of the polygon after a dilation of $\frac{2}{3}$ with its center at the origin.

13. An employer selects 4 out of 30 workers as employees of the month.
   a. Is this a combination or a permutation? Explain.
   b. How many different selections are possible?

Exponential and Logarithmic Functions

Relating to the Real World

Radioactive decay and bacteria growth can be modeled using exponential functions. To solve problems involving exponential growth and decay, you need to know how to use exponential functions and their inverses, logarithmic functions.

Aging Artifacts

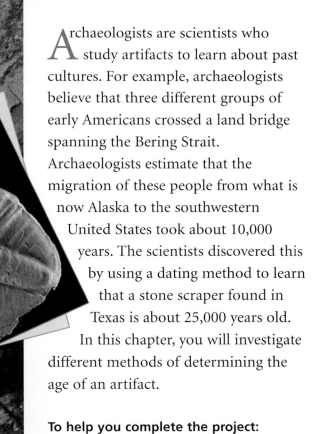

$\mathbf{A}$rchaeologists are scientists who study artifacts to learn about past cultures. For example, archaeologists believe that three different groups of early Americans crossed a land bridge spanning the Bering Strait. Archaeologists estimate that the migration of these people from what is now Alaska to the southwestern United States took about 10,000 years. The scientists discovered this by using a dating method to learn that a stone scraper found in Texas is about 25,000 years old.

In this chapter, you will investigate different methods of determining the age of an artifact.

To help you complete the project:
▼ **p. 310** *Find Out by Researching*
▼ **p. 323** *Find Out by Analyzing*
▼ **p. 340** *Find Out by Calculating*
▼ **p. 342** *Finishing the Project*

Exponential and Logarithmic Equations

Natural Logarithms

7-5

7-6

What You'll Learn

• Modeling exponential growth and decay

...And Why

To solve problems involving population growth

What You'll Need

• graph paper
• graphing calculator

7-1

Exploring Exponential Models

WORK TOGETHER

The National Collegiate Athletic Association (NCAA) holds an annual basketball tournament. The nation's top 64 teams in Division I are invited to play each spring. When a team loses, it is out of the tournament.

1. Work with a partner to determine how many teams are left in the tournament after the first round of basketball games.

2. **a.** Copy, complete, and extend the table until only one team is left.

After Round x	Number of Teams Left in Tournament (y)
0	64
1	■
2	■

   b. How many rounds of games must be played?

3. Graph the points from your table on graph paper.

4. Does the graph represent a linear function? Explain.

5. How does the number of teams left in each round compare to the number of teams in the previous round?

GRAPHING CALCULATOR HINT

You can use STAT lists on a graphing calculator to graph the ordered pairs in your table.

The NCAA is an association of colleges, universities, organizations and individuals devoted to the proper administration of intercollegiate athletics.

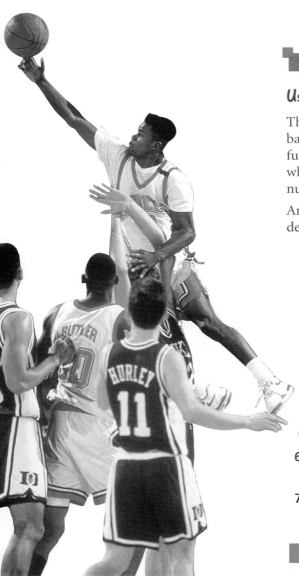

Using Exponential Functions

The function that represents the number of teams remaining in the NCAA basketball tournament after each round is an example of an exponential function. The standard form of an **exponential function** is $y = ab^x$, where a is a constant, $a \neq 0$, b is the base, $b > 0$ and $b \neq 1$, and x is a real number.

An exponential function with $a > 0$ can be used to model either growth or decay, depending on the value of b.

Exponential Growth	Exponential Decay
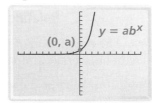	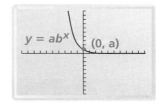
growth factor $b > 1$	decay factor $b < 1$

When $b > 1$, the function models exponential growth, and b is the **growth factor.** When $0 < b < 1$, the function models exponential decay, and b is the **decay factor.**

6. How does the growth factor affect the value of y in an exponential function?

7. For the function $y = b^x$, choose a value of b between 0 and 1. Demonstrate that as x increases, the value of the function decreases.

Example 1

Graphing Calculator Graph the function $y = 64\left(\frac{1}{2}\right)^x$. Explain whether the function models exponential growth or exponential decay.

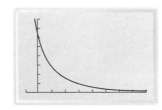

Xmin=−1   Ymin=0
Xmax=8   Ymax=80
Xscl=1   Yscl=10

The y-values decrease as the x-values increase, so the function models exponential decay. Notice that $b = \frac{1}{2}$, which is between 0 and 1.

8. Compare the graph of $y = 64\left(\frac{1}{2}\right)^x$ to the graph you created in the Work Together. How are the graphs alike? How are they different?

9. a. Evaluate the function $y = 64\left(\frac{1}{2}\right)^x$ for $x = 0, 1, 2, 3, 4, 5,$ and 6.

   b. Patterns Describe any patterns you notice in the data.

10. Try This Use a graphing calculator to graph the function $y = 5(2)^x$. Does this function model exponential growth or decay? **Justify** your answer.

Modeling Growth or Decay

You can use exponential functions to model the way that certain populations increase or decrease over time. Increasing populations can be modeled by exponential growth functions.

Example 2	Relating to the Real World

For practice with percents, see Skills Handbook page 662.

Social Studies The population of the United States in 1994 was about 260 million, with an average annual rate of increase of about 0.7%.

   a. What is the growth factor for the United States population?

   b. Suppose this rate of growth continues. Write an equation that models the future growth of the United States population.

   a. After one year the population would be $260 + 260(0.7\%)$ million.

$$260 + 260(0.7\%)$$
$$= 260 + 260(0.007) \quad \longleftarrow \text{0.7\% = 0.007}$$
$$= 260(1 + 0.007) \quad \longleftarrow \text{distributive property}$$
$$= 260(1.007) \quad \longleftarrow \text{Simplify.}$$

The growth factor is 1.007.

   b. To write the equation, find a and b.

      Define x = number of years after 1994
                  y = the population (in millions)

      Relate   The population increases exponentially.

      Write $y = ab^x$
                 $y = 260(1.007)^x \quad \longleftarrow a = 260, b = 1.007$

The equation $y = 260(1.007)^x$ models the future growth of the United States population. ■

11. Try This Use the equation from Example 2 to **predict** the United States population in the year 2001 to the nearest million.

12. Critical Thinking Using the model from Example 2, when will the United States population be closest to 289 million?

Depreciation is the decline in an item's value resulting from age and/or wear. When an item loses about the same percent of its value each year, you can use an exponential function to model the depreciation.

Example 3   **Relating to the Real World**

Car Dealer A car dealer provides the exponential decay graph shown at the right.

Expected Decrease in Value of Minivan

Value in $ (y-axis: 5,000; 10,000; 15,000; 20,000)
Year Since Purchase (x-axis: 0 1 2 3 4)

a. Estimate the percent decrease in the value of the minivan in the first year.

b. Estimate the depreciated value of the minivan after six years.

a. The initial value of the minivan is $20,000. After one year, the value of the van is about $17,000.

$$\text{percent decrease} = \frac{\text{initial value} - \text{final value}}{\text{initial value}}$$
$$= \frac{20,000 - 17,000}{20,000}$$
$$= \frac{3,000}{20,000}$$
$$= 0.15$$

The value decreases, or depreciates, 15% in the first year.

b. Use $y = ab^x$ to estimate the value of the minivan after 6 years.

Define x = number of years
          y = value of the minivan

Relate   The initial value a is $20,000.
          The decay factor b is $1 - 0.15$ or 0.85.

Write $y = ab^x$
        $y = 20,000(0.85)^x$ ← $a = 20,000, b = 0.85$
           $= 20,000(0.85)^6$ ← Substitute 6 for x.
           ≈ 7542.9903125 ← Use a calculator.

The minivan's value after six years will be about $7500.

For more practice with exponents, see Skills Handbook page 672.

13. At this rate, what will be the value of the minivan after ten years?

14. Graphing Calculator Use the [TRACE] feature to determine when the minivan will first be worth less than $2000.

15. Open-ended List five other items that might depreciate exponentially.

Identify each function as modeling either exponential growth or exponential decay. What is the function's percent increase or decrease?

1. $y = 1298(1.63)^x$ **2.** $y = 0.65(1.3)^x$ **3.** $f(x) = 2(0.65)^x$ **4.** $s(t) = 0.8\left(\frac{1}{8}\right)^t$

5. $y = 12(1.7)^x$ **6.** $y = 5(6)^x$ **7.** $y = 16\left(\frac{1}{4}\right)^x$ **8.** $y = \frac{5}{6}(0.45)^x$

9. Social Studies The table shows information about the population of the four largest cities in the world in 1994.

Rank in 1994	City	1994 Population	Average Annual Growth Rate
1	Tokyo, Japan	26,518,000	1.4%
2	New York City, U.S.	16,271,000	0.3%
3	São Paulo, Brazil	16,110,000	2.0%
4	Mexico City, Mexico	15,525,000	0.7%

Source: *United Nations, Department for Economic and Social Information and Policy Analysis*

  a. Suppose these rates of growth continue. Write equations that model the future growth of each city.

  b. Use your equations to **predict** the population of each city in 2004. Does the ranking change?

10. Analyze the graph at the right to determine which of the following functions the graph represents. Explain your reasoning.

  A. $y = \left(\frac{1}{3}\right)2^x$ **B.** $y = 2\left(\frac{1}{3}\right)^x$ **C.** $y = -2(3)^x$

11. Economics Suppose you want to buy a car that costs $11,800. The expected depreciation of the car is 20% per year. You take out a four-year loan to pay for the car. How much will the car be worth after you have paid off the loan in four years?

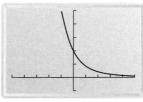

Xmin=–5   Ymin=–1
Xmax=5   Ymax=5
Xscl=1   Yscl=1

Graphing Calculator **Graph each function. Explain whether the function models exponential growth or exponential decay.**

12. $y = 100(0.5)^x$ **13.** $f(x) = 2^x$ **14.** $y = 1000(1.04)^x$ **15.** $f(x) = 200(0.85)^x$

16. Open-ended Write an exponential growth or decay problem for each function in Exercises 12–15.

17. Business On their federal income tax returns, many self-employed individuals can depreciate the value of the business equipment they purchase. Suppose a computer valued at $6500 depreciates at a rate of 14.3% per year. After how many years is the value of the computer less than $2000?

18. Technology Design a spreadsheet that you could use to find the value of a car every year for 15 years.

Write an exponential function to model each situation. Find the value of the function after five years.

19. A population of 250 frogs increases at an annual rate of 22%.

20. A stock priced at $35 increases at a rate of 7.5% per year.

21. A $17,500 delivery van depreciates 11% each year.

22. A population of 115 cougars decreases 1.25% each year.

23. Wildlife Suppose the population of a certain endangered species decreases at a rate of 3.5% per year. You have counted 80 of these animals in the habitat you are studying.
 a. Predict the number of animals that will remain after ten years.
 b. At this rate, after how many years will the population first drop below 15 animals?

24. Economics The 1994 gross domestic product and the real growth rate for several countries are given in the table.
 a. Describe how you would represent a negative growth rate in terms of an exponential model.
 b. Write an equation for each country to describe the change in the gross domestic product.
 c. Suppose this real growth rate continues. If possible use a calculator, spreadsheet, or table on a graphing calculator. Determine the gross domestic product in 2000 and 2005 for each country.
 d. Suppose this real growth rate continues. What do you think the gross domestic product will be for each of these countries in 2015? Use a graphing calculator to check your answer.

Country	1994 Gross Domestic Product (in billions)	1994 Real Growth Rate
Armenia	$ 8.1	−2%
Canada	$639.8	4.5%
Colombia	$172.4	5.7%
New Zealand	$ 56.4	6.2%

Source: *CIA World Factbook 1995*

25. Standardized Test Prep Which function best models the data in the table?

x	0	1	2	3
y	4.00	5.20	6.76	8.79

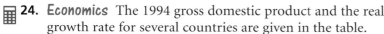

A. $y = x^2 + \frac{1}{2}x + 4$ **B.** $y = 4(1.3)^x$ **C.** $y = 1.6x + 4$ **D.** $y = \frac{1}{2x}$

26. Suppose you are buying a new car. You want the car that will be worth the most after five years. Of the three choices listed at the right, which car should you buy?

27. Research Find the rate of depreciation for several models of cars. Write an exponential function for each.

Car	Original Price	Expected Depreciation
1	$ 12,455	10%
2	$ 15,320	12%
3	$ 17,005	15%

Find Out by Researching ·

Archaeologists use items left behind by ancient humans to study ancient cultures. They date and interpret the items to tell the history of the people. Methods of dating archaeological artifacts include archaeomagnetism, obsidian hydration, radiocarbon dating, and tree-ring dating. Write a paragraph about each method, describing the principles on which each method is based.

Exercises   M I X E D   R E V I E W

Solve each system of equations.

28. $\begin{cases} 3x + y - z = -4 \\ -2x + 4y + 3z = -2 \\ x - 2y + z = 11 \end{cases}$ **29.** $\begin{cases} x + y + z = 7 \\ 3x + 2y - z = 6 \\ -x - y + 3z = 1 \end{cases}$ **30.** $\begin{cases} x + 2y + z = -2 \\ 3x - 3y - z = 6 \\ 2x + y + 4z = 5 \end{cases}$

31. a. Data Analysis The table below shows the average amount of taxes paid and charitable gifts given for people in different tax brackets in a recent year. Make a scatter plot of the data.

Taxes	$2,815	$3,367	$4,421	$6,260	$9,773	$22,086
Gifts	$1,392	$1,536	$1,716	$2,315	$3,420	$ 8,372

  b. Is there a correlation in the data? If so, what kind?
  c. If there is a correlation, write a linear function to model the data. Then use your model to **predict** how much a person who paid $6500 in taxes would have given in charitable gifts.

Getting Ready for Lesson 7-2

32. Graphing Calculator Use your graphing calculator to evaluate $\sqrt{2}$ and $2^{\frac{1}{2}}$.
  a. Compare your answers. What do you notice?
  b. How do you think the values of $\sqrt{3}$ and $3^{\frac{1}{2}}$ are related? Use your graphing calculator to check your answer.
  c. Graph the equation $y = 2^x$ on your graphing calculator. Use the CALC feature to evaluate $y = 2^{\frac{1}{2}}$.

Use the formula for simple interest, $I = Prt$. Find each missing value.

33. $I = \blacksquare, P = \$550, r = 3\%, t = 2\text{yr}$

34. $I = \$75, P = \$625, r = 2\%, t = \blacksquare$

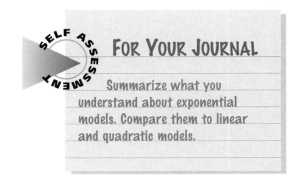

FOR YOUR JOURNAL

Summarize what you understand about exponential models. Compare them to linear and quadratic models.

Fitting Exponential Curves to Data

After Lesson 7-1

In previous chapters you learned to fit lines and quadratic curves to sets of data. Some data sets are better modeled by exponential functions. You can use your graphing calculator to fit an exponential curve to data and find the exponential function.

Cooling Coffee

Time (min)	°F Above Room Temperature
0	135
5	100
10	74
15	55
20	41
25	30
30	22
35	17
40	12
45	9
50	7
55	5
60	4

Example

The table shows the number of degrees above room temperature of a cup of coffee after x minutes of cooling. Use a graphing calculator to graph the data. Find the best-fitting exponential function.

Step 1: Press `STAT` `ENTER` to enter the data in lists.

Step 2: Press `2nd` [STAT PLOT] to plot the points.

Step 3: Find the equation for the best-fitting exponential function. Press `STAT` `▶` `ALPHA` [A] `ENTER` to get the ExpReg feature.

```
ExpReg
 y=a*b^x
 a=133.4584506
 b=.942405561
 r=-.9997925841
```

Step 4: Graph the function. Press `Y=` `CLEAR` `VARS` `5` `▶` `▶` `7` to enter the ExpReg results. Press `GRAPH` to display the data and the function together. Adjust the viewing window. Pressing `ZOOM` `9` `ENTER` will automatically adjust the window.

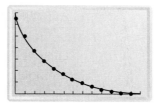

```
WINDOW FORMAT
Xmin=0
Xmax=65
Xscl=5
Ymin=0
Ymax=140
Yscl=20
```

Use a graphing calculator to find the exponential function that best fits each set of data. Graph each function.

1.

x	−4	−3	−2	−1	0	1	2
y	100	50	25	12.5	6.25	3.125	1.5625

2.

x	0	1	2	3	4	5
y	2	2.4	2.88	3.46	4.15	5

3.

x	0	1	2	3	4	5	6
y	0.3	1.2	4.8	19.2	76.8	307.2	1228.8

4.

x	−10	−9	−8	−7	−6	−5
y	0.03	0.07	0.14	0.27	0.55	1.09

5. **Writing** In the example above, the function appears to level off. Explain why this happens.

6. Explain how you could decide whether an exponential model is a better fit than a linear model.

7-2 Exponential Functions

What You'll Learn

• Graphing exponential functions

• Identifying the role of constants in $y = ab^{kx}$

• Using e as a base

...And Why

To compute continuously compounded interest

What You'll Need

• graphing calculator

QUICK REVIEW

When a bank pays interest on both the principal and the interest an account has already earned, the bank is paying *compound interest*.

For practice with formulas, see Skills Handbook page 666.

WORK TOGETHER

The **compound interest formula** for the amount *A* in an account is given below.

rate of interest

$$A = P\left(1 + \frac{r}{n}\right)^{nt} \longleftarrow \text{time in years}$$

principal   number of times per year the interest is compounded

CURRENT INVESTMENT OFFERINGS

	RATE	YIELD
7-31 Day Certificate	6.80%	
32-89 Day Certificate	7.10%	
90-179 Day Certificate	7.30%	
6 Month Certificate	7.55%	
1 Year Certificate	7.70%	7.93%
2 Year Certificate	7.75%	7.98%
30 Month Certificate	7.85%	8.08%
3 Year Certificate	8.00%	8.24%
4 Year Certificate	8.00%	8.24%
5 Year Certificate	8.00%	8.24%
6 Year Certificate	8.00%	8.24%
7 Year Certificate	8.00%	8.24%

Ask Us For Current Jumbo CD Rates

1. Copy the table below. Use a calculator to help you complete the table. See what happens when a principal of $1000 is invested at a rate of 10% for one year and *n* gets greater and greater.

Number of Times Compounded per Year (*n*)	$P\left(1 + \frac{r}{n}\right)^{nt}$	Value of *A*
Annually (1)	$1000\left(1 + \frac{0.1}{1}\right)^1$	$1100
Semi-annually (2)	▪	▪
Quarterly (4)	▪	▪
Monthly (12)	▪	▪
Daily (365)	▪	▪
Hourly (8760)	▪	▪
By the Minute (525,600)	▪	▪

2. Describe what happens as *n* gets greater and greater.

3. What would happen if *P* changed? Give several examples to support your answer.

4. What would happen if *t* changed? Give several examples to support your answer.

Graphing Exponential Functions

The compound interest formula, $A = P\left(1 + \frac{r}{n}\right)^{nt}$, is in the general form of an exponential function, $y = ab^{kx}$. You have seen some of the effects of changing one of the values in this formula. You can also use graphs to study the effect of different values of a, b, and k on this function.

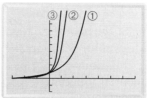

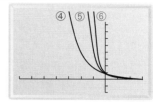

① $y = 2^x$ ④ $y = \left(\frac{1}{2}\right)^x$

② $y = 4^x$ ⑤ $y = \left(\frac{1}{4}\right)^x$

③ $y = 7^x$ ⑥ $y = \left(\frac{1}{7}\right)^x$

5. a. Graphing Calculator On the same axes, graph $y = 10(2)^x$, $y = 6(2)^x$, and $y = 2(2)^x$. Sketch and describe your results.

   b. Clear your screen. On the same axes, graph $y = 2^{4x}$, $y = 2^{3x}$, $y = 2^{2x}$, and $y = 2^x$. Sketch and describe your results.

6. Writing Describe the effect of different values of a, b, and k on the function $y = ab^{kx}$.

If you know the base of an exponential function and the coordinates of one point on the graph of the function, you can write an equation to describe the function.

Example 1

Write an equation to describe the exponential function of the form $y = ab^x$ with base 2 whose graph passes through the point $(3, 4)$. Graph the equation.

Since the graph passes through the point $(3, 4)$, $y = 4$ when $x = 3$.

$y = ab^x$ ⟵ exponential function
$4 = a \cdot 2^3$ ⟵ Substitute.
$\frac{4}{8} = a$ ⟵ Solve for a.
$a = \frac{1}{2}$ ⟵ Simplify.

The equation is $y = \frac{1}{2} \cdot 2^x$. The graph is shown at the right.

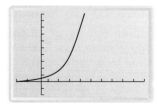

Xmin=−2   Ymin=−2
Xmax=10   Ymax=10
Xscl=1   Yscl=1

7. Try This Write an equation to describe the exponential function $y = ab^x$ with base 4 and whose graph passes through the point $(2, 3)$.

The **half-life** of a radioactive substance is the time it takes for half of the material to decay or decompose.

Example 2 **Relating to the Real World**

What? Technetium-99*m* is a radioactive substance that is widely used to diagnose thyroid, brain, liver, and kidney diseases.

Hospital Work Suppose a hospital prepares a 100-mg supply of technetium-99*m*, which has a half-life of 6 hours.

a. Make a table showing the amount of technetium-99*m* remaining at the end of each 6-hour interval for 36 hours.
b. Write the equation to describe the exponential function.
c. Use the function to find the amount after 75 hours.

Number of 6-h Half-lives	Technetium-99*m* Present (mg)
0	100
1	50
2	25
3	12.5
4	6.25
5	3.125
6	1.5625

a. The amount of technetium-99*m* is reduced by one half every 6 hours, as shown in the table.

b. The initial amount of technetium-99*m* is 100 mg. The decay factor is 0.5. Let y represent the amount after x half-lives have occurred.

$$y = ab^x$$
$$y = 100(0.5)^x \quad \longleftarrow \text{Substitute 100 for } a \text{ and 0.5 for } b.$$

The exponential decay function is $y = 100(0.5)^x$.

c. $x = 75 \div 6 \quad \longleftarrow \text{Find the number of half-lives.}$
   $= 12.5$
   $y = 100(0.5)^x$
   $= 100(0.5)^{12.5} \quad \longleftarrow \text{Substitute 12.5 for } x.$
   $\approx 0.017 \quad \longleftarrow \text{Simplify.}$

The amount of technetium-99*m* remaining after 75 hours is about 0.017 mg.

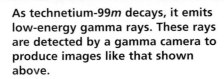

As technetium-99*m* decays, it emits low-energy gamma rays. These rays are detected by a gamma camera to produce images like that shown above.

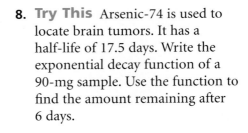

8. **Try This** Arsenic-74 is used to locate brain tumors. It has a half-life of 17.5 days. Write the exponential decay function of a 90-mg sample. Use the function to find the amount remaining after 6 days.

The Number "e"

When interest is compounded continuously, the formula can be simplified using the number e.

9. Use your calculator to evaluate the expression $\left(1 + \frac{1}{n}\right)^n$ for $n = 2, 8, 32, 128$, and 512. Display your results in a table.

10. What do you think will happen as n continues to increase?

11. **Calculator** Find the key labeled e or e^x on your calculator. Find the value of e. How does this value compare with your results from Question 9?

The formula for **continuously compounded interest** is $A = Pe^{rt}$.

Example 3 **Relating to the Real World**

Investment Suppose you invest $1050 at an annual interest rate of 5.5% compounded continuously. Find the amount you will have in the account after five years.

$A = Pe^{rt}$
$\quad = 1050 \cdot e^{0.055(5)}$ ← Substitute 1050 for P, 0.055 for r, and 5 for t.
$\quad = 1050 \cdot e^{0.275}$
$\quad \approx 1050(1.31653)$ ← Evaluate $e^{0.275}$ on your calculator.
$\quad \approx 1382.357$

You will have about $1382.36 in the account after five years.

---

12. **Estimation** How long will you need to leave the money in this account in order to double your initial investment of $1050?

13. **Try This** Suppose you invest $1300 at an annual interest rate of 4.3% compounded continuously. Find the amount you will have in the account after three years.

14. **Open-ended** Choose a principal, an interest rate, and a number of years. Calculate the amount in the account using both the compound interest formula and the continuously compounded interest formula.

Exercises   ON YOUR OWN

Graphing Calculator Graph each exponential function using a graphing calculator. Sketch your results.

1. $y = 4^x$

2. $y = \left(\frac{1}{2}\right)^x$

3. $y = 6^x + 3$

4. $y = 10^{x+2}$

5. $y = 2^{-x}$

6. $y = -3^{x+4}$

7. $y = -\left(\frac{1}{3}\right)^x$

8. $y = 20(0.234)^x$

9. $y = 3.25(5)^x$

10. $y = 0.3(0.2)^x$

11. $y = 120(3.5)^x$

12. $y = 4^{5x}$

13. $y = 6^{-2x}$

14. $y = -(0.3)^x$

15. $y = 12^x$

Write an equation to describe the exponential function of the form
$y = ab^x$ **with the given base whose graph passes through the given point.**

16. base 7, (2, 122.5)

17. base 0.6, (2, 1.8)

18. base $\frac{1}{2}$, (−2, 12)

19. base 2, (6, 32)

Use your calculator to evaluate each expression to four decimal places.

20. e^2

21. e^3

22. $5e^6$

23. $3e^7$

24. e^{10}

25. $\frac{1}{e^5}$

26. $\frac{4}{e^6}$

27. $\frac{3}{2e}$

28. $\left(\frac{5}{4}\right)e^{\frac{1}{2}}$

29. e^e

30. Writing Explain the meaning of negative growth.

31. Suppose that the value of a certain machine used in a manufacturing industry has an annual decay factor of 0.75. If the machine is worth $10,000 after 5 yr, what was the original value of the machine?

32. Social Studies The population of Karachi, Pakistan, was about 8 million in 1991. The annual growth factor at that time was 1.039.
 a. What is the projected population for the year 2010?
 b. What is the projected annual rate of increase?
 c. When will the population reach 10 million?

33. Find the value of a for which the graph of $y = ab^x$ is a horizontal line.

34. Open-ended Write two exponential functions, one showing growth and one showing decay. Graph them on the same axes.

35. Investment How long would it take to double your principal at an interest rate of 8% compounded continuously?

36. a. Chemistry The formula $L = Be^{-0.0001t}$ gives the amount L, in micrograms, of a certain radioactive substance remaining after t years of decay. The initial amount of the radioactive substance is B. Use the formula to complete the table.
 b. Patterns Do you see a pattern in the data in the last column? If so, describe the pattern.

Initial Amount of Substance (B)	Years (t)	Remaining Amount of Substance (L)
10,000	5	■
7,500	5	■
6,000	5	■
5,000	5	■
2,500	5	■
2,000	5	■

37. World Population The world population, about 5.63 billion in 1994, is said to be growing at a rate of 2% per year.
 a. Write an exponential equation to describe such growth.
 b. Describe the population growth that occurs every 35 yr.
 c. Describe the growth in half the time referred to in part (b).

38. Medicine Calcium-47 is used for scanning bones for suspected disorders. It has a half-life of 113 hours. Write the exponential decay function for a 105-mg sample. Use the function to find the amount of calcium-47 left after 350 hours.

39. Oceanography The intensity of sunlight decreases as you descend in the ocean. If the intensity of sunlight at the surface of the ocean is I, then the percent of I that reaches a depth of x feet is given by the function $y = 20 \cdot 0.975^x$. (The model is accurate for depths of 20 to 600 feet.)

a. Find the percent of sunlight found 50 ft below sea level.

b. The world record for an unaided deep-sea dive is 351 ft. Find the percent of sunlight at that depth.

40. What is the y-intercept of $y = ab^x$?

Exercises   MIXED REVIEW

Describe the end behavior of each polynomial function.

41. $y = x^3 - 4x + 1$ **42.** $y = 3x^2 + 6x - 2$ **43.** $y = -x^5 + x^3 - x$ **44.** $y = -5x^4 - x^3$

45. Graph the plane $x + y + 2z = 4$. Find the x-, y-, and z-intercepts.

Getting Ready for Lesson 7-3

Graph each function and its inverse on a coordinate plane.

46. $y = 5x$ **47.** $y = 2x^2$ **48.** $y = -x^3$ **49.** $y = \frac{1}{2}x$

Exercises   CHECKPOINT

Identify each function as exponential growth or decay. What is the function's percent increase or decrease?

1. $y = 15(1.45)^x$ **2.** $y = 0.32(0.99)^x$ **3.** $y = 0.1(1.7)^x$ **4.** $y = 7.3(0.8)^x$

Graph each exponential function.

5. $y = 3^x$ **6.** $y = 2^x + 1$ **7.** $y = \left(\frac{1}{3}\right)^x$ **8.** $y = 4^x - 5$

9. Open-ended Describe a situation that would be modeled by exponential growth.

10. Chemistry A radioactive element has a half-life of 30 hours. Write the exponential decay function for a 100-mg sample. Use the function to find the amount of the element remaining after 100 hours.

What You'll Learn

- Using logarithmic notation
- Evaluating logarithmic expressions
- Graphing logarithmic functions

...And Why

To solve problems involving pH values

What You'll Need

- scientific or graphing calculator

7-3 Logarithmic Functions as Inverses

WORK TOGETHER

1. Using the exponential function $y = 10^x$, complete the table below.

x	0	1	2	3	4	5	6	7
y								

2. For each unit increase in x, describe the corresponding increase in y.

3. Describe the increase in y if x increases by 1.5; by 0.5.

THINK AND DISCUSS

Writing and Evaluating Logarithmic Expressions

The *magnitude* of an earthquake is a measure of the amount of energy released. The Richter scale measures the magnitude of earthquakes by using exponents. An earthquake of magnitude 5 releases about 30 times as much energy as an earthquake of magnitude 4.

4. Compare the energy released in the 1985 Mexican earthquake and the 1989 San Francisco earthquake, registering 8.1 and 7.1, respectively, on the Richter scale.

The Richter Scale

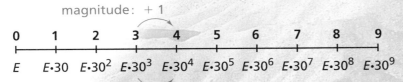

Seismology is the study of earthquakes. The San Andreas fault emerges from the Pacific Ocean and stretches from Southern California to the Northern Coast.

The exponents used in the Richter scale are called logarithms, or logs. The **logarithm** of a positive number y to the base b is defined as follows.

$$\log_b y = x \text{ if } y = b^x \text{ (read } \log_b y \text{ as } log \ base \ b \ of \ y)$$

The base b in the exponential expression b^x is the same as the base b in the logarithm. In both cases, $b > 0$ and $b \neq 1$. Also, the exponent x in b^x is the logarithm in the equation $\log_b y = x$.

5. The equation $\log_4 4^3 = 3$ illustrates that a logarithm is an exponent written in a different form. Evaluate each logarithm.
   a. $\log_5 5^2$ b. $\log_2 2^5$ c. $\log_b b^3$

Example 1

Write $5^2 = 25$ in logarithmic form.

$25 = 5^2$

$\quad y = b^x$ ←— exponential function
$\quad x = \log_b y$ ←— corresponding logarithmic function
$\quad 2 = \log_5 25$ ←— Substitute 2 for x, 5 for b, and 25 for y.

The logarithmic form of $5^2 = 25$ is $\log_5 25 = 2$.

6. **Try This** Write $\left(\frac{1}{2}\right)^3 = \frac{1}{8}$ in logarithmic form.

7. **Try This** Write $\log_2 64 = 6$ in exponential form.

To evaluate logarithms, you can write them in exponential form.

Example 2

Evaluate $\log_8 16$.

Let $x = \log_8 16$.

$\quad x = \log_8 16$ ←— logarithmic form
$\quad 16 = 8^x$ ←— exponential form
$\quad 2^4 = (2^3)^x$ ←— Write both sides with base 2.
$\quad 2^4 = 2^{3x}$
$\quad 4 = 3x$ ←— Set the exponents equal to each other.
$\quad \frac{4}{3} = x$ ←— Solve for x.

So $\log_8 16 = \frac{4}{3}$.

8. **Try This** Evaluate $\log_5 125$.

9. To evaluate $\log_2 16$, ask yourself "What power of 2 is equal to 16?" What question would you ask to evaluate $\log_3 27$? $\log_{10} 100$? Evaluate each logarithm.

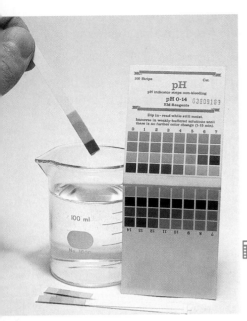

10. What is the value of $\log_2 1$? $\log_3 1$? $\log_5 1$? In general, what is the value of $\log_b 1$?

11. What is the value of $\log_2 2$? $\log_4 4$? $\log_5 5$? In general, what is the value of $\log_b b$?

12. Explain why the base b in $y = \log_b x$ cannot equal 1.

The pH level of a substance describes the relative acidity of the substance. It is computed using a logarithm with base 10, called a **common logarithm**. You can write a common logarithm, $\log_{10} y$, as $\log y$.

| **Example 3** | **Relating to the Real World** |

Chemistry The $[H^+]$ of lemon juice is $1 \times 10^{-2.2}$ while the $[H^+]$ of milk is 2.5×10^{-7}. Which is a better conductor of electricity, lemon juice or milk?

 pH = $-\log [H^+]$ where $[H^+]$ is the concentration of hydrogen ions in a substance. The pH scale ranges from 0 to 14. A pH level of 7 is neutral. A level greater than 7 is basic, and a level less than 7 is acidic. The more acidic a substance, the better it will conduct an electric current.

lemon juice	milk
pH = $-\log[H^+]$	pH = $-\log[H^+]$
$= -\log 10^{-2.2}$	$= -\log (2.5 \times 10^{-7.0})$ ← Use your calculator.
$= -(-2.2)$	$= -(-6.6)$
$= 2.2$	$= 6.6$

The pH level of lemon juice is 2.2. The pH level of milk is 6.6. Lemon juice is more acidic than milk. Therefore, lemon juice is the better conductor.

13. **Try This** Find the pH level of sea water if its $[H^+]$ is about 3.2×10^{-9}.

Graphing Logarithmic Functions

The graph below shows the functions $y = 10^x$ and $y = \log x$.

CALCULATOR HINT

The LOG key on your calculator represents $\log_{10}$.

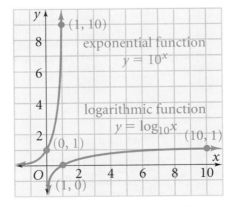

14. **a.** Verify that the point (2, 100) lies on the graph of $y = 10^x$.
    b. Does the point (100, 2) lie on the graph of $y = \log x$? Explain.

15. a. Find another pair of points in the form (a, b) and (b, a) that lie on the graphs of these two functions.

   b. Use your answers to Exercises 14 and 15a to complete the sentence: The functions $y = 10^x$ and $y = \log x$ are ___?___ of each other.

16. What is the inverse of the function $y = 3^x$? $y = 5^x$? $y = b^x$?

Since logarithmic functions are the inverses of exponential functions, their graphs are reflections of one another over the line $y = x$.

Example 4

Use the properties of inverse functions to graph $y = \log_2 x$.

The function $y = \log_2 x$ is the inverse of $y = 2^x$. First, graph the function $y = 2^x$.

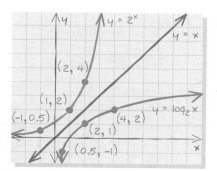

← Draw the line $y = x$.

← Choose two or three points on the graph of $y = 2^x$. Reverse the coordinates and plot the new points.

GRAPHING CALCULATOR HINT

Use the TABLE feature to find the coordinates of points on the original function.

17. Try This Graph the functions $y = \log_3 x$ and $y = \log_4 x$.

18. Graphing Calculator Graph the functions $y = \log x$ and $y = 10^x$. Use a viewing window that shows both graphs on the same screen. In what quadrants does each graph appear?

Exercises ON YOUR OWN

Write each equation in logarithmic form.

1. $3^2 = 9$

2. $4^2 = 16$

3. $8^2 = 64$

4. $5^3 = 125$

5. $6^4 = 1296$

6. $7^3 = 343$

7. $\left(\frac{1}{2}\right)^{-2} = 4$

8. $8^{-\frac{2}{3}} = \frac{1}{4}$

9. $\left(\frac{1}{3}\right)^3 = \frac{1}{27}$

10. $10^{-2} = 0.01$

11. $6^{\frac{3}{2}} = 6\sqrt{6}$

12. $5^{-3} = \frac{1}{125}$

13. Writing Your younger sister has not yet studied algebra. Write a paragraph to her explaining logarithms.

14. The $\left[H^+\right]$ of lime juice is about 1.26×10^{-2}. Find its pH.

15. Open-ended Write a logarithmic function of the form $y = \log_b x$. Find its inverse function. Graph both functions on one set of axes.

Write each equation in exponential form.

16. $\log_2 128 = 7$

17. $\log_3 6561 = 8$

18. $\log_4 64 = 3$

19. $\log_7 16807 = 5$

20. $\log 100 = 2$

21. $\log_2 8 = 3$

22. $\log_3 \frac{1}{9} = -2$

23. $\log 0.0001 = -4$

24. $\log_4 1 = 0$

25. $\log_2 \frac{1}{8} = -3$

26. $\log_6 6 = 1$

27. $\log_3 \frac{1}{243} = -5$

28. The table shows the $[H^+]$ for some common foods. List the foods in order of ascending pH.

Food	Apples	Bananas	Carrots	Peas	Spinach	Tuna	Water
$[H^+]$	8×10^{-4}	2.5×10^{-5}	8×10^{-6}	8×10^{-7}	4×10^{-6}	1×10^{-6}	1×10^{-7}

Evaluate each logarithm.

29. $\log_2 4$

30. $\log_{49} 7$

31. $\log_4 16$

32. $\log_2 8$

33. $\log_5 25$

34. $\log_8 8$

35. $\log_2 2^5$

36. $\log_{\frac{1}{2}} \frac{1}{2}$

37. $\log_4 2$

38. $\log 0.01$

39. $\log_9 \frac{1}{3}$

40. $\log 10{,}000$

41. Photographer The aperture setting of a camera is called the *f*-stop. This controls the amount of light that hits the film. Each larger *f*-stop setting allows twice as much light to enter as the preceding one. Let p represent the fraction of normal sunny-day light. The formula $n = \log_2 \frac{1}{p}$ allows a photographer to calculate through how many settings n she should move to accommodate for less light.

aperture setting

exposure setting

a. A particular brand of film suggests an *f*-stop of *f*/11 for an exposure time of $\frac{1}{60}$ s on a normal sunny day. Through how many settings should a photographer move when the light is only one-eighth as bright as a normal sunny day?

b. If she moves the setting five places from *f*/11, what fraction of sunny-day light is she accommodating?

42. Match each function with the graph of its inverse.

   a. $y = \log_3 x$

   b. $y = \log_2 4x$

   c. $y = \log_{\frac{1}{2}} x$

I.

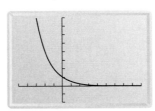

II.

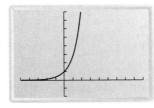

III.

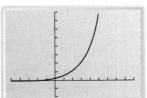

43. Seismology The Alaskan earthquake of 1964 measured 9.2 on the Richter scale. It was about 150 times as strong as the San Francisco earthquake of 1906. Estimate the magnitude of the 1906 earthquake.

44. The pH of maple syrup is about 6.7. Find its $[H^+]$.

Graph each logarithmic function.

45. $y = \log_2 x$ **46.** $y = \log_3 x$ **47.** $y = \log_4 x$ **48.** $y = \log_5 x$

49. *Science* Humans can hear a wide range of sound intensities, as shown in the table. Sound intensity is a measure of the amount of energy produced by the source of the sound. The intensity level (loudness) of a sound depends on the sound intensity and also on the distance between the source and the person hearing the sound. The intensity level measured in decibels (dB) is defined by the following equation.

$$\text{Intensity level} = 10 \log \frac{I}{I_0}$$

The intensity of the sound is I, and I_0 is the intensity of a barely audible sound. Complete the table.

Type of Sound	Intensity (W/m²)	Intensity Level (dB)
Pain-producing	1	120
Jackhammer	10^{-2}	■
Busy street	10^{-5}	■
Conversation	10^{-6}	■
Whisper	10^{-10}	■
Rustle of leaves	10^{-11}	■
Barely audible sound	10^{-12}	0

50. Match each function with its inverse.

a. $y = \log_{\frac{1}{4}} x$ **b.** $y = \log_4 x$ **c.** $y = -\log_4 x$ **d.** $y = -\log_{\frac{1}{4}} x$

I. $y = 4^x$ **II.** $y = \left(\frac{1}{4}\right)^{-x}$ **III.** $y = \left(\frac{1}{4}\right)^x$ **IV.** $y = 4^{-x}$

Chapter Project *Find Out by Analyzing*

One method of dating artifacts is called radiocarbon dating. The objects listed were discovered near Kit Carson, Colorado.

Use the formula $t = 1.904 \times 10^4 \times \log \frac{13.7}{R}$. Let t represent the age of the object in years and R represent the number of beta emissions per minute per gram of carbon in the object. Calculate the age of each object. What is unusual about the data? How might you account for this?

Object	Mass of Carbon (g)	Beta Emissions per Minute
Buffalo bone	400	1640 ± 30
Bone fragment	15	61.5 ± 1.5
Pottery shard	25	342 ± 7
Charcoal	10	41.0 ± 1.3
Spear shaft	250	1020 ± 30

Exercises   MIXED REVIEW

Write a polynomial function in standard form with the given zeros.

51. $x = 0, 1,$ and 4 **52.** $x = -2, -1,$ and 3 **53.** $x = 5, 0,$ and 2

54. *Probability* You have three pairs of blue jeans, one pair of shorts, four white T-shirts, and two blue T-shirts. What is the probability you will wear blue jeans and a blue T-shirt if you choose an outfit at random?

Getting Ready for Lesson 7-4

Simplify each expression.

55. $\log_2 4 + \log_2 8$ **56.** $\log_3 9 - \log_3 27$ **57.** $\log_2 16 \div \log_2 64$ **58.** $\log_3 27 \cdot \log_3 9$

Graphing Inverses

After Lesson 7-3

You can use a graphing calculator to graph inverses of functions as well as the functions themselves.

Example

Graph the inverse of $y = -x^2 + 3$.

Step 1: Press **2nd** [DRAW] **8** to access the draw inverse feature.

Step 2: Enter the function. Press **ENTER** to graph the inverse.

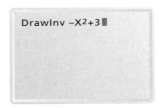

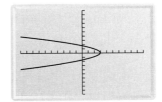

Step 3: Press **2nd** [DRAW] **1** **ENTER** to clear the graph of the inverse.

1. Match each function with the graph of its inverse.

   a. $y = -|x|$ **b.** $y = -|x - 2|$ **c.** $y = -\left|\frac{x}{5}\right|$

   I. 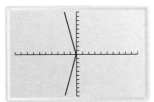   **II.** 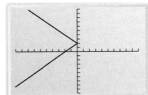   **III.**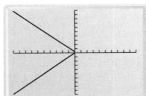

Graph the inverse of each function. Sketch each graph. Remember to clear the screen after each graph.

2. $f(x) = -|2x|$ 3. $y = -(2^x)$ 4. $g(x) = 5 \log x$ 5. $y = x^3 + 2x^2 + x + 1$

6. $y = \frac{x^2 - 2}{6}$ 7. $h(x) = \frac{x}{3}$ 8. $s(x) = -3 + 3e^x$ 9. $t(x) = x^2 + x + 1$

10. **a.** Critical Thinking **Predict** the graph of the inverse of $y = \sqrt{x^2}$.
    b. Graph the inverse. Sketch the graph.
    c. Writing Compare the graph of the inverse with your prediction. What might account for any differences you found? **Generalize** your findings by comparing other square root graphs and their inverses.

Properties of Logarithms

What You'll Learn

- Condensing and expanding logarithmic expressions
- Applying properties of logarithms

...And Why

To solve problems involving sound intensity

What You'll Need

- graphing calculator

WORK TOGETHER

1. Work with a partner. Use your calculator to complete the table below.

x	1	2	3	4	5	6	7	8	9	10	15	20
$\log x$	■	■	■	■	■	■	■	■	■	■	■	■

2. Use your table to complete each pair of statements. What do you notice?
   a. $\log 3 + \log 5 = $ ■ and $\log (3 \cdot 5) = $ ■
   b. $\log 1 + \log 6 = $ ■ and $\log (1 \cdot 6) = $ ■
   c. $\log 10 + \log 2 = $ ■ and $\log (10 \cdot 2) = $ ■

3. **Generalize** Complete the statement: $\log M + \log N = $ ■.

4. a. **Critical Thinking** Make a **conjecture** about how you could rewrite the expression $\log \frac{M}{N}$ using the expressions $\log M$ and $\log N$.
   b. Use your calculator to **verify** your conjecture for several values of M and N.

GRAPHING CALCULATOR HINT

These range values will give you a clear picture of the functions in Question 5.

Xmin = −2	Ymin = −3
Xmax = 10	Ymax = 3
Xscl = 1	Yscl = 1

5. **Graphing Calculator** Graph each pair of functions on the same set of axes. What do you notice?
   a. $y = \log x^3$ and $y = 3 \log x$ b. $y = \log x^{-1}$ and $y = (-1)\log x$

6. Use your graphs to help you complete the statement: $\log M^k = $ ■.

7. Explain how you could use this result to evaluate $\log 1000$.

THINK AND DISCUSS

Rewriting Logarithmic Expressions

The properties of logarithms are summarized below. You can use these properties to rewrite logarithmic expressions.

Properties of Logarithms

For any positive numbers M, N, and b, $b \neq 1$, each of the following statements is true.

$$\log_b MN = \log_b M + \log_b N \qquad \textbf{Product Property}$$

$$\log_b \frac{M}{N} = \log_b M - \log_b N \qquad \textbf{Quotient Property}$$

$$\log_b M^k = k \log_b M \qquad \textbf{Power Property}$$

8. Compare the properties of logarithms to the properties of exponents.

You can write the sum or difference of logarithms (having the same bases) as a single logarithm.

Example 1

Write each logarithmic expression as a single logarithm.

a. $\log_3 20 - \log_3 4$
b. $3 \log_2 x + \log_2 y$

a. $\log_3 20 - \log_3 4 = \log_3 \frac{20}{4}$ ← Quotient Property
$\qquad\qquad\qquad\quad = \log_3 5$ ← Simplify.

b. $3 \log_2 x + \log_2 y = \log_2 x^3 + \log_2 y$ ← Power Property
$\qquad\qquad\qquad\quad = \log_2 (x^3 y)$ ← Product Property

So, $\log_3 20 - \log_3 4 = \log_3 5$ and $3 \log_2 x + \log_2 y = \log_2 (x^3 y)$. ■

9. Try This Write each expression as a single logarithm.
  a. $\log_2 9 - \log_2 3$
  b. $3 \log 2 + \log 4 - \log 16$
  c. $\log 8 - 2 \log 2 + \log 3$

10. Critical Thinking Can you write $\log_3 6 + \log_2 5$ as a single logarithm? Explain.

You can sometimes write a single logarithm as a sum or difference of two or more logarithms.

Example 2

Expand each logarithm.

a. $\log_5 \frac{x}{y}$ **b.** $\log 3r^4$

a. $\log_5 \frac{x}{y} = \log_5 x - \log_5 y$ ← Quotient Property

b. $\log 3r^4 = \log 3 + \log r^4$ ← Product Property
$\qquad\qquad\;\; = \log 3 + 4 \log r$ ← Power Property

So, $\log_5 \frac{x}{y} = \log_5 x - \log_5 y$ and $\log 3r^4 = \log 3 + 4 \log r$. ■

11. Open-ended Write $\log 150$ as a sum or difference of two logarithms.

12. Critical Thinking Can you expand $\log_3 (2x + 1)$? Explain.

13. Writing If you knew the values of $\log 2$ and $\log 5$, how could you evaluate $\log 20$ without using a calculator?

14. Try This Expand each logarithm.
  a. $\log_2 7b$ **b.** $\log \left(\frac{y}{3}\right)^2$ **c.** $\log_7 a^3 b^4$

Applying the Properties of Logarithms

The intensity of a sound is a measure of the energy carried by the sound wave. The greater the intensity of a sound, the louder it seems. This apparent loudness, or intensity level, L, is measured in decibels. It is given by the formula $L = 10 \log \frac{I}{I_0}$. The intensity of the sound in watts per square meters (W/m^2) is I. The lowest-intensity sound an average human ear can detect is I_0.

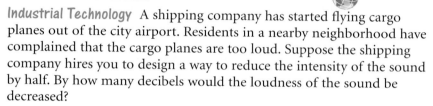

Example 3   Relating to the Real World

Industrial Technology A shipping company has started flying cargo planes out of the city airport. Residents in a nearby neighborhood have complained that the cargo planes are too loud. Suppose the shipping company hires you to design a way to reduce the intensity of the sound by half. By how many decibels would the loudness of the sound be decreased?

Define $L_1 = $ present loudness;
$L_2 = $ reduced loudness

Relate The decrease in loudness is given by $L_1 - L_2$, where the reduced intensity is one-half the present intensity.

Write $L_1 = 10 \log \frac{I}{I_0}, L_2 = 10 \log \frac{0.5I}{I_0}$

$$L_1 - L_2 = 10 \log \frac{I}{I_0} - 10 \log \frac{0.5I}{I_0}$$

$$= 10 \log \frac{I}{I_0} - 10 \log \left(0.5 \cdot \frac{I}{I_0}\right)$$

$$= 10 \log \frac{I}{I_0} - 10 \left(\log 0.5 + \log \frac{I}{I_0}\right) \quad \longleftarrow \text{Product Property}$$

$$= 10 \log \frac{I}{I_0} - 10 \log 0.5 - 10 \log \frac{I}{I_0}$$

$$= -10 \log 0.5 \quad \longleftarrow \text{Combine like terms.}$$

$$\approx 3.01$$

The decrease in loudness would be about three decibels.

15. Try This Suppose the shipping company wants you to reduce the sound intensity to 25% of the original intensity. By how many decibels would the loudness be reduced?

State the property or properties used to rewrite each expression.

1. $\log 4 + \log 5 = \log 20$

2. $\log z^2 = 2 \log z$

3. $\log_3 32 - \log_3 8 = \log_3 4$

4. $\log \sqrt[3]{3x} = \frac{1}{3} \log 3x$

5. $2 \log_2 m - 4 \log_2 n = \log_2 \frac{m^2}{n^4}$

6. $\log_6 \sqrt[n]{x^p} = \frac{p}{n} \log_6 x$

7. $8 \log 2 - 2 \log 8 = \log 4$

8. $3 \log_b 4 - \log_b 8 = \log_b 8$

9. $\log_5 12 - \log_5 6 = \log_5 2$

10. Open-ended Use the properties of logarithms to rewrite log 64 in four different ways.

11. Manufacturing Suppose you work for a vacuum cleaner manufacturer. You helped design new components that reduce the sound intensity of a certain model from 10^{-4} W/m^2 to 6.31×10^{-6} W/m^2. By what percent do these new components reduce the vacuum cleaner's loudness? (Use $I_0 = 10^{-12}$ W/m^2.)

Write each logarithmic expression as a single logarithm.

12. $\log 7 + \log 2$

13. $\log_2 27 - \log_2 9$

14. $\frac{1}{2} \log_4 t - \log_4 s$

15. $5 \log 3 + \log 4$

16. $\log 5 + \log 8 - 2 \log 2$

17. $\log a + 3 \log b$

18. $4 \log m - \log n$

19. $\frac{1}{2}(\log_7 x + \log_7 y) - 3 \log_7 z$

20. $\log x + \log y + \log z$

21. $7 \log r - \log s + \log t$

22. $\log \frac{a}{4} + \log \frac{b}{3} - \log \frac{z}{2}$

23. $\frac{1}{4} \log_6 5 + \frac{1}{4} \log_6 x$

Expand each logarithm.

24. $\log_5 \frac{r}{s}$

25. $\log x^3 y^5$

26. $\log_3 7(2x - 3)^2$

27. $\log \frac{a^2 b^3}{c^4}$

28. $\log 3m^4 n^{-2}$

29. $\log_4 5\sqrt{x}$

30. $\log_7 22xyz$

31. $\log (2(x + 1))^3$

32. $\log_2 \left(\frac{5a}{b^2}\right)$

33. $\log_4 (4mn)^5$

34. $\log_3 (2x)^2$

35. $\log \sqrt{\frac{2x}{y}}$

36. Writing Explain why $\log (5 \cdot 2) \neq \log 5 \cdot \log 2$.

37. Construction Worker Suppose you are a worker on a road construction job. Your team is blasting rock to make way for a roadbed. One explosion has an intensity of 1.65×10^{-2} W/m^2. What is the loudness of the sound in decibels? (Use $I_0 = 10^{-12}$ W/m^2.)

Use the properties of logarithms to evaluate each expression.

38. $\log_2 4 - \log_2 16$

39. $\log_5 5 - \log_5 125$

40. $3 \log_2 2 - \log_2 4$

41. $\log 1 + \log 100$

42. $5 \log_3 3 - \log_3 9$

43. $\log_6 4 + \log_6 9$

44. $2 \log_8 4 - \frac{1}{3} \log_8 8$

45. $\log_3 81 - \log_3 27$

46. $\log_3 3 - 5 \log_3 3$

Assume that $\log 4 \approx 0.6021$, $\log 5 \approx 0.6990$, and $\log 6 \approx 0.7782$. Use the properties of logarithms to evaluate each expression. Do not use your calculator. Round your answers to the nearest thousandth.

47. $\log 20$

48. $\log 24$

49. $\log 16$

50. $\log 0.8$

51. $\log 1.25$

52. $\log 30$

53. $\log 125$

54. $\log 1.5$

55. $\log \frac{1}{36}$

56. $\log \frac{1}{4}$

57. $\log 36$

58. $\log \frac{1}{25}$

59. Since $y = \log_b x$ and $y = b^x$ are inverse functions, $\log_b b^x = x$. Use this property, and the "one-line proof" shown below of the product property of logarithms, to help you prove the quotient and power properties.

$$\log_b MN = \log_b(b^{\log_b M} b^{\log_b N}) = \log_b b^{\log_b M + \log_b N} = \log_b M + \log_b N$$

Write *true* or *false* for each statement. Justify your answer.

60. $\log_2 4 + \log_2 8 = 5$

61. $\log_5 16 - \log_3 2 = \log_5 8$

62. $\log_3 8 = 3 \log_3 2$

63. $\log_3 \frac{x}{y} = \frac{\log_3 x}{\log_3 y}$

64. $\frac{\log_b x}{\log_b y} = \log_b x - \log_b y$

65. $\log(x + 2) = \frac{\log x}{\log 2}$

66. $\log x - 4 \log y = \log \frac{x}{y^4}$

67. $\log_3 \frac{3}{2} = \frac{1}{2} \log_3 3$

68. $\frac{1}{2} \log_4 t - \log_4 s = \log_4 \frac{\sqrt{t}}{s}$

69. Standardized Test Prep Which expression has the greatest value when $m = 4$ and $n = 3$?

A. $3 \log m - 2 \log n$ **B.** $\log 3m - \log 2n$ **C.** $2 \log n - 3 \log m$

D. $\log 2m - \log 3n$ **E.** $\log n^3 - \log m^2$

Exercises   MIXED REVIEW

Find the inverse of each function.

70. $y = 3x^2 - 1$

71. $y = 5x + 7$

72. $y = 2x^3 + 10$

73. $y = -x^2 + 5$

74. Coordinate Geometry A rectangle has vertices at $(0, 3)$, $(0, 5)$, $(4, 5)$, and $(4, 3)$. Find the coordinates of the vertices of the image of the rectangle after a translation 7 units left and 2 units down.

Getting Ready for Lesson 7-5

Simplify each expression.

75. $4^{\frac{1}{2}}$

76. $27^{\frac{2}{3}}$

77. $\left(\frac{1}{9}\right)^{-\frac{1}{2}}$

78. $16^{\frac{3}{4}}$

79. $125^{-\frac{2}{3}}$

80. $16^{\frac{1}{4}}$

7-5 Exponential and Logarithmic Equations

What You'll Learn

- Solving equations with exponents
- Using logarithms to solve exponential equations
- Using exponents to solve logarithmic equations

...And Why

To solve problems related to storms

What You'll Need

- graphing calculator

For practice with literal equations, see Skills Handbook page 666.

WORK TOGETHER

Biology The formula $F = km^{\frac{2}{3}}$ describes the amount of food F, in kilograms, that a mammal must eat daily. (In this formula, k is a constant of variation that depends upon the species, and m is the mass of the animal.)

Work with a partner. For a large elephant, $F = 145$ kg and $k = 0.421$.

1. **Estimation** Substitute these values for F and k into the given formula. Estimate the value of $m^{\frac{2}{3}}$.

2. Estimate the value of m. (Use a calculator to find a value of m for which $m^{\frac{2}{3}}$ is near your estimate from Question 1.)

3. How could you solve the equation $F = km^{\frac{2}{3}}$ for $m^{\frac{2}{3}}$? Describe the result if each side of the equation is then raised to the $\frac{3}{2}$ power.

4. Solve the equation to find the typical body mass of a large elephant. How does this result compare with your estimate from Question 2?

5. For a raccoon, $F = 2$ kg and $k = 0.431$. Find the typical body mass of a raccoon in kilograms.

THINK AND DISCUSS

Solving Equations Containing Exponents or Radicals

To solve equations in the form $x^a = c$, where the variable is raised to a power, you can either use the properties of exponents or use radicals. When the variable occurs in a radicand, the equation is a **radical equation.**

Example 1

Solve $4 + x^{\frac{3}{2}} = 31$.

$4 + x^{\frac{3}{2}} = 31$

$x^{\frac{3}{2}} = 27$ ⟵ Subtract 4 from each side.

$\left(x^{\frac{3}{2}}\right)^{\frac{2}{3}} = (27)^{\frac{2}{3}}$ ⟵ Raise each side to the $\frac{2}{3}$ power.

$x^1 = 27^{\frac{2}{3}}$ ⟵ Multiply exponents.

$x = \left(27^{\frac{1}{3}}\right)^2$ ⟵ Use the property $(a^m)^n = a^{mn}$.

$x = 3^2$ ⟵ Simplify.

$x = 9$

The solution is 9.

For practice with radicals, see Skills Handbook page 675.

PROBLEM SOLVING

Look Back What is the meaning of $x^{\frac{1}{3}}$?

6. Try This Solve $3y^{\frac{4}{3}} = 768$ by using exponents.

7. Writing Suppose you are solving an equation containing exponents. You find that $x^{\frac{5}{3}} = k$. Describe how to solve for x.

8. Suppose you are solving a radical equation. You find that $\sqrt[6]{10y} = 3$. What is the next step?

9. a. Try This Solve $\sqrt{7x} - 4 = 0$. Check your answer.
   b. Critical Thinking Why is it important to check the possible solutions?

You can use this method to solve problems involving exponents.

Example 2 **Relating to the Real World** 🌐

Weather Meteorologists use the formula $D^3 = 216T^2$ to describe the size and duration of storms, such as tornadoes, thunderstorms, hurricanes, and cyclones. In the formula, D is the diameter of the storm in miles and T is the duration, or the number of hours the storm lasts. If the diameter of a thunderstorm is 12 mi, about how long would this storm last?

Define T represents how long the thunderstorm lasts.

Relate The diameter of the storm is related to the duration of the storm.

Write $D^3 = 216T^2$

$(12)^3 = 216T^2$ ⟵ Substitute $D = 12$

$1728 = 216T^2$ ⟵ Simplify.

$8 = T^2$ ⟵ Divide each side by 216.

$\sqrt{8} = T$ ⟵ Take the square root of each side.

$2.8 \approx T$ ⟵ Use a calculator.

The thunderstorm would last about 2.8 hours.

10. **Try This** Suppose a hurricane lasts for six days. Estimate the diameter of the storm.

11. **Research** Find out about a storm that occurred in your area, including how long it lasted. Estimate the diameter of the storm.

Solving Exponential or Logarithmic Equations

An equation in the form $a = b^{cx}$, where the exponent includes a variable, is called an **exponential equation.** You can solve exponential equations by taking the logarithm of each side.

Example 3

Solve $7^{3x} = 20$.

$$7^{3x} = 20$$
$$\log 7^{3x} = \log 20 \qquad \longleftarrow \text{Take the common logarithm of each side.}$$
$$3x \log 7 = \log 20 \qquad \longleftarrow \text{Use the power property of logarithms.}$$
$$x = \frac{\log 20}{3 \log 7} \qquad \longleftarrow \text{Divide each side by 3 log 7.}$$
$$x \approx 0.513 \qquad \longleftarrow \text{Use a calculator.}$$

The solution is about 0.513.

12. **Try This** Solve each equation.

 a. $3^x = 4$ **b.** $6^{2x} = 21$ **c.** $3^{x+4} = 101$

To evaluate a logarithm with any base, you can use the **change of base formula.**

Change of Base Formula

For any positive numbers M, b, and c, with $b \neq 1$ and $c \neq 1$:

$$\log_b M = \frac{\log_c M}{\log_c b}$$

Example: $\log_3 5 = \dfrac{\log_{10} 5}{\log_{10} 3} \approx \dfrac{0.6990}{0.4771} \approx 1.465$

13. Test that the change of base formula gives the same result for any positive value of c (except 1) by evaluating $\log_8 32$ for $c = 10$ and $c = 2$.

GRAPHING CALCULATOR HINT

Try these range values when graphing $y = \log_3 x$.

Xmin = −2   Ymin = −3
Xmax = 10   Ymax = 4
Xscl = 1   Yscl = 1

14. **Graphing Calculator** Use the change of base formula and a graphing calculator to graph $y = \log_3 x$. What base did you choose? Why?

If the base of the exponent in an equation is not 10, you can also use the change of base formula to solve the equation. Example 4 shows that you can begin by using any convenient base logarithm. Then use the change of base formula to help evaluate the logarithm.

Example 4

Solve $6^{2x} = 1500$.

Method 1: $\log_6 6^{2x} = \log_6 1500$ ◀── Take the logarithm of each side.

$\qquad 2x = \log_6 1500$ ◀── Simplify.

$\qquad 2x = \dfrac{\log 1500}{\log 6}$ ◀── Use the Change of Base Formula.

$\qquad 2x \approx 4.0816$ ◀── Use a calculator.

$\qquad x \approx 2.0408$ ◀── Divide each side by 2.

Method 2: Graph the equations $y = 6^{2x}$ and $y = 1500$. Use the intersect option on the CALC menu to find the point of intersection.

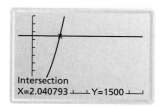

Intersection
X=2.040793   Y=1500

The solution is $x \approx 2.041$.

15. What base was used to evaluate $\log_6 1500$ when applying the change of base formula?

16. Try This Solve $7^{3x} = 9$. Check the solution in the original equation.

When equations include logarithmic expressions, use the properties of logarithms to simplify expressions before solving.

Example 5

Solve each logarithmic equation.

a. $\log (3x + 1) = 5$ **b.** $2 \log x - \log 3 = 2$

a. $\log (3x + 1) = 5$

$\qquad 3x + 1 = 10^5$ ◀── Write in exponential form.

$\qquad 3x + 1 = 100,000$

$\qquad\qquad x = 33,333$ ◀── Solve for x.

The solution is 33,333.

b. $2 \log x - \log 3 = 2$

$\qquad \log \left(\dfrac{x^2}{3}\right) = 2$ ◀── Write as a single logarithm.

$\qquad \dfrac{x^2}{3} = 10^2$ ◀── Write in exponential form.

$\qquad x^2 = 3(100)$

$\qquad x = \pm 10\sqrt{3},$ or about ± 17.32.

The solution is about 17.32.

17. Why was the negative solution ignored in Example 5, part (b)?

18. Try This Solve each equation.
     a. $\log (7 - 2x) = -1$ **b.** $\log 6 - \log 3x = -2$

Mental Math Solve each equation.

1. $x^3 = 8$

2. $\sqrt{x} = 4$

3. $5\sqrt{2} = \sqrt{x}$

4. $2^x = \frac{1}{2}$

5. $3^x = 27$

6. $x^2 = 49$

7. $\sqrt[3]{x} = 5$

8. $9^x = 3$

9. **Meteorology** Use the formula $D^3 = 216T^2$ from Example 2. Find what happens to the duration of a storm if its diameter is doubled.

10. **Open-ended** Write an exponential equation and solve it.

Solve each equation. Check each solution.

11. $x^{\frac{2}{3}} = 25$

12. $y^{\frac{3}{4}} - 5 = 1$

13. $z^{\frac{2}{5}} = 32$

14. $q^{\frac{3}{2}} = 64$

15. $3x^{\frac{3}{2}} = 27$

16. $5c^{\frac{5}{4}} = 81$

17. $7w^{\frac{5}{6}} = 2$

18. $2 + 8r^{\frac{5}{3}} = 26$

19. **Biology** Find the typical body mass of a mouse if $F = 0.12$ kg and $k = 1.243$. Use the formula from the Work Together.

Solve and check each equation.

20. $\sqrt[3]{y^4} = 16$

21. $3 + \sqrt[3]{x} = 20$

22. $6 - \sqrt[5]{w} = 12$

23. $-3 + 2\sqrt[4]{x^3} = 33$

24. $\sqrt[7]{g^2} - 12 = 5$

25. $8 + 10^x = 1008$

26. $5 - 3^x = -40$

27. $7^x - 2 = 252$

28. $9^{2y} = 66$

29. $14^{x+1} = 36$

30. $12^{y-2} = 20$

31. $25^{2x+1} = 144$

32. **Graphing Calculator** The function $y = 200(1.04)^x$ models the first-grade population y of an elementary school x years after the year 2000.
    a. Graph the function on your graphing calculator. Adjust the viewing window.
    b. **Estimation** Study the graphing calculator screen to estimate when the first-grade population will reach 250.
    c. **Writing** How could you use a graphing calculator to **predict** when the population will reach 325? How could you **verify** this prediction?

33. **Geometry** Some raindrops are spheres. Suppose the radius of a spherical raindrop decreases by 0.02 mm due to evaporation as it falls. If the volume of the drop is now 7 mm³, what was the original radius of the raindrop?

QUICK REVIEW

The volume V of a sphere with radius r is given by the formula $V = \frac{4}{3}\pi r^3$.

34. **Standardized Test Prep** Which number is the solution to $\log 5 + \log x = 1$?
    A. $\frac{1}{2}$ B. 0.5   C. 2   D. $\sqrt{5}$ E. 5

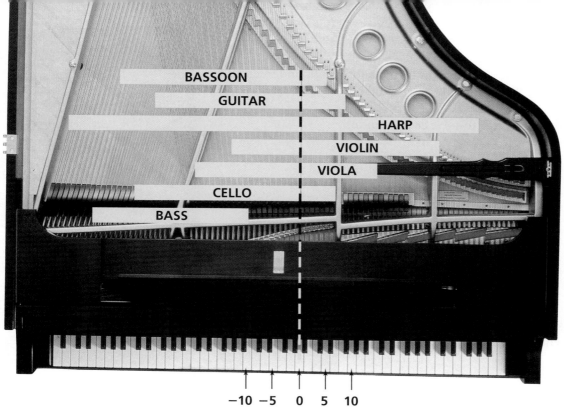

-10 -5   0   5   10

35. Music The pitch, or frequency, of a piano note is related to its position on the keyboard by the function $F(n) = 440 \cdot 2^{\frac{n}{12}}$. The frequency of the sound wave F is given in cycles per second, and n is the number of piano keys above or below Concert A, as shown. If $n = 0$ at Concert A, which of the instruments shown in the diagram can sound notes of the given frequency?

   a. 587   **b.** 123   **c.** 1480   **d.** 2093

Solve each logarithmic equation.

36. $\log 2x = -1$ **37.** $2 \log x = -1$ **38.** $\log 6x - 3 = -4$

39. $\log x - \log 3 = 8$ **40.** $\log 2x + \log x = 11$ **41.** $3 \log x - \log 6 + \log 2.4 = 9$

Use the change of base formula to evaluate each logarithm.

42. $\log_2 7$ **43.** $\log_5 510$ **44.** $\log_3 33$ **45.** $\log_4 1.116$ **46.** $\log_{12} 0.085$

47. Consider the equation $2^{\frac{x}{3}} = 80$.
   a. Solve the equation by taking the logarithm in base 2 of each side.
   b. Solve the equation by taking the logarithm in base 10 of each side.
   c. Compare your results in parts (a) and (b). Which method do you prefer? Why?

48. Consider the equation $a^x = b$.
   a. Solve the equation by using log base c.
   b. Solve the equation by using log base a.
   c. Use your results in parts (a) and (b) to **justify** the Change of Base Formula.

49. Use the cartoon at the right and the formula for compound interest. How long has the $50 been in the piggy bank?

BY MY CALCULATIONS, AT 8% INTEREST, COMPOUNDED QUARTERLY, I SHOULD HAVE $74.30! COOL!

Use your graphing calculator to solve each equation.

50. $4^{7x} = 250$

51. $5^{3x} = 500$

52. $2^{3x} = 172$

53. $1.5^x = 356$

54. $8^x = 444$

55. $14^{9x} = 146$

56. $3^{7x} = 120$

57. $7^{5x} = 3000$

58. $3^{2x} = 196$

59. $3.7^x = 372$

60. $6^x = 4565$

61. $11^{6x} = 786$

Exercises   M I X E D   R E V I E W

62. Probability Your principal randomly assigns 3 students from a class of 20 to serve on a committee. How many different combinations are there?

Simplify each expression.

63. $5!$

64. $_5P_2$

65. $_7C_3$

66. $\frac{6!}{3!}$

67. $_9C_4$

68. $_6P_1$

Getting Ready for Lesson 7-6

Use your calculator to evaluate each expression.

69. e^5

70. $2e^3$

71. e^{-2}

72. $\frac{1}{e}$

73. $0.5e^2$

74. $4.2e$

Exercises   C H E C K P O I N T

Evaluate each logarithm.

1. $\log_3 81$

2. $\log_6 36$

3. $\log_{36} 6$

4. $\log 0.001$

Expand each logarithm.

5. $\log_2 x^2 y^5$

6. $\log \frac{s^3}{5}$

7. $\log_5 (3xy)^2$

8. $\log_6 4\sqrt{x}$

Solve and check each equation.

9. $x^{\frac{2}{3}} = 64$

10. $\log 5x = 2$

11. $7 - 2^x = -1$

12. $3 \log x = 9$

13. Writing Explain how to use the change of base formula to rewrite $\log_2 10$ as a logarithmic expression with base 3.

14. Standardized Test Prep Which expression has the greatest value?

A. 2^3 **B.** $\log_2 3$ **C.** $\log_3 2$ **D.** 3^2 **E.** $\log 2$

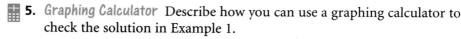

What You'll Learn

- Relating natural logarithms to the function $y = e^x$
- Solving equations using natural logarithms

...And Why

To find the speed at which a rocket will attain a stable orbit

What You'll Need

- graphing calculator

7-6 Natural Logarithms

T H I N K   A N D   D I S C U S S

In Lesson 7-2, you found that the number $e \approx 2.71828\ldots$ could be used as a base for exponents. The function $y = e^x$ has an inverse, called the **natural logarithmic function,** $y = \log_e x$. This function is usually written $y = \ln x$, read *y equals the natural logarithm of x.*

1. Calculator Use your calculator to find ln 5, ln 3, and ln 15. Use the "LN" key on your calculator. How are your answers related to each other?

2. Writing The properties of common logarithms also apply to natural logarithms. Restate the Product Property, the Quotient Property, and the Power Property in terms of natural logarithms.

The graphs below show the two functions on the same screen.

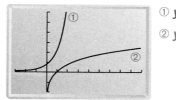

① $y = e^x$

② $y = \ln x$

3. Verify that the functions are inverse functions.

4. a. Simplify $\ln e^x$.
   b. Simplify $e^{\ln x}$. (*Hint:* Evaluate $e^{\ln x}$ for several positive values of x.)

Example 1

Use natural logarithms to solve $8e^{2x} = 20$.

$$8e^{2x} = 20$$
$$e^{2x} = \frac{20}{8} \quad \longleftarrow \text{Divide each side by 8.}$$
$$\ln e^{2x} = \ln 2.5 \quad \longleftarrow \text{Take the natural logarithm of each side.}$$
$$2x = \ln 2.5 \quad \longleftarrow \text{Simplify.}$$
$$x = \frac{\ln 2.5}{2} \quad \longleftarrow \text{Divide each side by 2.}$$
$$x \approx 0.458 \quad \longleftarrow \text{Use your calculator.}$$

The solution is $x \approx 0.458$.

5. Graphing Calculator Describe how you can use a graphing calculator to check the solution in Example 1.

6. Explain why $\ln e = 1$.

Natural logarithms were invented because they simplify the expression of many relationships in the physical world.

Example 2   Relating to the Real World

Space A rocket can attain a stable orbit 300 km above Earth if it reaches a velocity of 7.7 km/s. The formula for the maximum velocity v of a rocket is given by $v = -0.0098t + c \ln R$. (The rocket engines fire for t seconds and the velocity of the exhaust is c km/s. The ratio of the mass of the rocket with fuel to its mass without fuel is R.) Suppose a rocket used to propel a spacecraft has a mass ratio of about 25, an exhaust velocity of 2.8 km/s, and a firing time of 100 s. Can this rocket attain a stable orbit?

In this case, $R \approx 25$, $c = 2.8$, and $t = 100$. Use the formula $v = -0.0098t + c \ln R$ to find v.

$$v = -0.0098t + c \ln R$$
$$= -0.0098(100) + 2.8 \ln 25$$
$$\approx -0.98 + 2.8(3.219)$$
$$\approx 8.0$$

This velocity is more than the 7.7 km/s needed for a stable orbit. The orbit can be attained.

7. **Try This** Find the velocity of a rocket with a mass ratio of about 15, an exhaust velocity of 2.1 km/s, and a firing time of 30 s. Can this rocket achieve a stable orbit 300 km above Earth?

Example 3

Solve $\ln (3x + 5) = 4$.

$$\ln (3x + 5) = 4$$

$3x + 5 = e^4$ ←— Rewrite in exponential form.

$3x = e^4 - 5$ ←— Subtract 5 from each side.

$x = \dfrac{e^4 - 5}{3}$ ←— Divide each side by 3.

$x \approx 16.53$ ←— Use a calculator.

The solution is about 16.53.

8. **Try This** Solve each equation.

   a. $e^{\frac{2x}{5}} + 7.2 = 9.1$ b. $-5 + \ln \left(\dfrac{x + 2}{3}\right) = 7$

Exercises   ON YOUR OWN

Solve each equation.

1. $\ln x = 0.1$ 2. $e^x = 18$ 3. $\ln (3x - 9) = 21$

4. $e^{2x} = 10$ 5. $e^{x+1} = 30$ 6. $\ln (4x - 1) = 36$

7. $e^{\frac{x}{5}} + 4 = 7$ 8. $2 \ln e^x = 10$ 9. $e^{2x} = 12$

Evaluate each natural logarithm without a calculator.

10. $\ln e$ 11. $\ln e^2$ 12. $\ln e^{10}$ 13. $\ln e^{100}$

14. **Investing** Suppose you invest $500 in a savings account that pays 5% interest compounded continuously. You make no additional deposits or withdrawals. Copy and complete the table at the right, using the formula for continuously compounded interest, $A = Pe^{rt}$. Find how long it would take for your money to increase to each given amount.

Amount (A)	Time (years)
$600	
$700	
$800	
$900	
$1000	
$1100	
$1200	
$1300	

15. Use your table from Exercise 14 to predict when the amount in your account will triple. Then use the formula to check your prediction.

16. **Space** Use the formula for the maximum velocity of a rocket from Example 2 to find the mass ratio of a rocket with an exhaust velocity of 3.1 km/s, a firing time of 50 s, and a maximum velocity of 6.9 km/s.

17. The formula $P = 40e^{\frac{-t}{300}}$ gives the power output, P, in watts, of a satellite after t days. How long has the satellite been operating if its output is 15 W?

Solve each equation. Use properties of logarithms to simplify each.
(Use the quadratic formula when necessary.)

18. $\ln(x + 1) + \ln x = 1$

19. $\ln x - \ln(x - 1) = 2$

20. $\ln 6 + \ln x - \ln 2 = 3$

21. $\ln(y + 5) + \ln(y - 1) = 3$

22. $\ln x + \ln 3 = 6$

23. $4 \ln y - \ln 3 = 5$

24. The function $U(t) = 1.31e^{0.548t}$ describes how the number of Internet users, in millions, increased exponentially from 1990 to 1995. Let t represent the time, in years, since 1990.
  a. What was the first year in which there were 13 million Internet users?
  b. How many years did it take for the number of users to double since 1990?
  c. Solve the equation $U = 1.31e^{0.548t}$ for t.
  d. **Writing** Explain how to use your equation from part (c) to verify your answers to parts (a) and (b). What results do you get?

25. **Physics** Newton's Law of Cooling is given by the function $T(t) = T_r + (T_i - T_r)e^{kt}$. The temperature of a heated substance t minutes after it has been removed from a heat source is $T(t)$. The substance's initial temperature is T_i, k is a constant for that substance, and T_r is room temperature.
  a. Suppose the initial surface temperature of a beef roast is 236°F and room temperature is 72°F. If $k = -0.041$, how long will it take for this roast to cool to 100°F?
  b. **Graphing Calculator** Write and graph an equation that you can use to check your answer to part (a).
  c. Use your graph from part (b) to complete the table at the right.

Temperature (°F)	225	200	175	150	125	100	75
Minutes Later	■	■	■	■	■	■	■

26. **Open-ended** Write a real-life problem that you can answer by using Newton's Law of Cooling. Then answer it.

Chapter Project **Find Out by Calculating**

Radiocarbon dating is a method of using information about the half-life of an isotope to determine the age of an object. The half-life of carbon-14 is 5730 ± 40 yr. An axe handle has 42 g of carbon-14 and is believed to be about 19,040 yr old. Explain how an archaeologist could use the formula found on page 323 to find the beta emission rate of the axe handle.

27. Fishing A bass's weight in ounces can be related to its length in inches by the equation $w(l) = 0.012l^3$. What would you expect the length of a 40-oz bass to be?

Write a matrix for each graph.

28.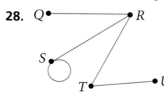

29.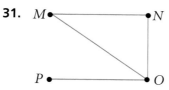

30.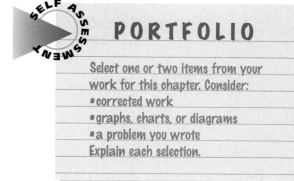

31.

PORTFOLIO

Select one or two items from your work for this chapter. Consider:
- corrected work
- graphs, charts, or diagrams
- a problem you wrote

Explain each selection.

A Point in Time

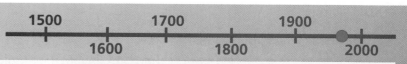

A Test of Time

The first moon landing, on July 20, **1969**, gave scientists a unique opportunity to test their theories about the moon's geological history using actual lunar materials. When *Apollo 11* astronauts Neil Armstrong and Edwin "Buzz" Aldrin, Jr. returned to Earth, they brought with them a sample of rocks, shown at the right, taken from the moon's Sea of Tranquillity.

A logarithmic function was used to date the rocks. Radioactive rubidium-87 decays into stable strontium-87 at a fixed rate. The ratio *r* of the two isotopes in a sample can be measured and assigned a time *T*, in years. Use the equation $T = -h\frac{\ln(r + 1)}{\ln 0.5}$, where *h* is the half-life of rubidium-87, 4.7×10^{10} yr. For the lunar sample, *r* was measured at 0.0588, giving an approximate age of 3.87 billion years. One conclusion was that the moon has a thick crust that for the past three to four billion years has prevented volcanic eruptions from burying old rocks.

Finishing the Chapter Project

Aging Artifacts

Find Out questions on pages 310, 323, and 340 should help you to complete your project. Present your project for this chapter as a visual display. Your display could include photographs or sketches of archaeological dig sites and items that have been discovered at similar sites.

Reflect and Revise

Show your display to a small group of classmates. Is your information presented in a clear and interesting way? Are your calculations correct? Make any necessary changes and improvements before presenting your project to your class.

Follow Up

Find out if there are any archaeological digs going on in your area. If possible, arrange to visit one. Interview some of people working on the dig.

For More Information

Archaeological Institute of America (AIA)
656 Beacon St.
Boston, MA 02215

Southeast Archeological Center (SAC)
National Park Service
2035 E. Paul Dirac Drive, Box 7
Johnson Building, Suite 120
Tallahassee, FL 32310

Society for American Archaeology (SAA)
900 Second Street NE #12
Washington, D.C. 20002-3557

Institute of Egyptian Art and Archaeology
University of Memphis
Campus Box 526545
Memphis, TN 38152

Key Terms

change of base formula (p. 332)
common logarithm (p. 320)
compound interest formula
   (p. 312)
continuously compounded
   interest (p. 315)
decay factor (p. 305)
exponential decay (p. 305)

exponential equation (p. 332)
exponential function (p. 305)
growth factor (p. 305)
half-life (p. 314)
logarithm (p. 319)
natural logarithmic function
   (p. 337)
radical equation (p. 330)

How am I doing?

- State three ideas from this chapter that you think are important. Explain your choices.
- List the properties of exponential and logarithmic functions.

Exploring Exponential Models
7-1

The standard form of an **exponential function** is $y = ab^x$, where x is a real number, $a \neq 0$, $b > 0$, and $b \neq 1$. When $b > 1$, the function models exponential growth, and b is the **growth factor**. When $0 < b < 1$, the function models exponential decay, and b is the **decay factor**.

Identify each function as modeling either exponential growth or exponential decay. What is the function's percent increase or decrease?

  1. $y = 12(1.45)^x$ **2.** $y = 4.1(0.12)^x$ **3.** $y = 0.2(3.8)^x$ **4.** $y = 3(0.4)^x$

Write an exponential function to model each situation. Find the value of each function after five years.

  5. A home worth \$150,000 appreciates 1% each year.

  6. A \$12,500 car depreciates 9% each year.

  7. A baseball card worth \$50 increases 3% in value each year.

Exponential Functions
7-2

The **compound interest formula** is $A = P\left(1 + \frac{r}{n}\right)^{nt}$, where P is the principal, r is the rate, t is the time in years, and n is the number of times per year the interest is compounded. The formula for **continuously compounded interest** is $A = Pe^{rt}$.

The **half-life** of a substance is the time it takes for half of the material to decay or decompose.

Write an equation to describe the exponential function of the form $y = ab^x$ with the given base whose graph passes through the given point.

  8. base 3, (1, 3)   **9.** base 8, (2, 8)   **10.** base 2, (−2, 1)

If $y = b^x$, then $\log_b y = x$. The logarithmic function is the inverse of the exponential function. The graphs of the functions are reflections of one another over the line $y = x$. When $b = 10$, the logarithm is called a **common logarithm**, which you can write as $\log y$.

Write each equation in logarithmic form.

11. $6^2 = 36$ **12.** $2^{-3} = \frac{1}{8}$ **13.** $3^3 = 27$ **14.** $10^{-3} = 0.001$

Write each equation in exponential form.

15. $\log_2 64 = 6$ **16.** $\log_3 \frac{1}{9} = -2$ **17.** $\log 0.000\,01 = -5$ **18.** $\log_2 1 = 0$

Graph each logarithmic function.

19. $y = \log_4 x$ **20.** $y = \log x$ **21.** $y = \log_2 x$ **22.** $y = \log_8 x$

23. An earthquake measured 5.6 on the Richter scale. An aftershock measured 4.8. The energy released in the earthquake was how many times as great as the energy released in the aftershock?

24. Standardized Test Prep Which expression has the same value as $\log_2 4$?

   A. $\log_4 2$ **B.** $\log_2 1$ **C.** $\log 2$ **D.** $\log_3 9$ **E.** $\log 4$

Properties of Logarithms

For any positive numbers, M, N, and b, $b \neq 1$, each of the following statements is true.

- $\log_b MN = \log_b M + \log_b N$ Product Property
- $\log_b \frac{M}{N} = \log_b M - \log_b N$ Quotient Property
- $\log_b M^x = x \log_b M$ Power Property

To condense a logarithmic expression, you rewrite it as a single logarithm. To expand a logarithmic expression, you rewrite it as a sum or difference of two or more logarithms.

Write each logarithmic expression as a single logarithm.

25. $\log 8 + \log 3$ **26.** $\log_2 5 - \log_2 3$ **27.** $4 \log_3 x + \log_3 7$ **28.** $\log z - \log y$

Expand each logarithmic expression.

29. $\log_4 x^2 y^3$ **30.** $\log 4s^4 t$ **31.** $\log_3 2\sqrt{x}$ **32.** $\log \left(\frac{x}{3}\right)^2$

33. Open-ended Write two logarithmic expressions with the same base. Then find their sum.

34. Critical Thinking Can you write $\log_x 10 + \log_{2x} 5$ as a single logarithm? Explain.

Exponential and Logarithmic Equations

You can solve equations in the form $x^a = c$, where the variable is raised to a power, by using the properties of exponents or by using radicals. An equation in the form $a = b^{cx}$, where the exponent includes a variable, is an **exponential equation**. You can solve exponential equations by taking the logarithm of each side.

Choose a method to solve each equation. Check each solution.

35. $x^{\frac{3}{4}} = 27$ **36.** $9^x = 27$ **37.** $5^x = 33$ **38.** $5 - x^{\frac{1}{3}} = 4$

Solve each logarithmic equation.

39. $\log 3x = 1$ **40.** $\log_2 4x = 5$ **41.** $3 \log x - \log 2x = 2$ **42.** $2 \log_3 x = 54$

43. Open-ended Write a logarithmic equation that has a solution of 6.

44. Weather Find the diameter of a storm that lasts 2 hours. Use the formula $D^3 = 216T^2$, where D is the diameter of the storm and T is its duration in hours.

Natural Logarithms

The inverse of the function $y = e^x$ is the **natural logarithmic function** $y = \ln x$. Equations with natural logarithmic expressions are solved similarly to equations that contain expressions with common logarithms. Natural logarithms are useful because many relationships in the physical world depend on them.

Solve each equation.

45. $e^{3x} = 12$ **46.** $\ln x + \ln (x + 1) = 2$ **47.** $2 \ln x + 3 \ln 2 = 5$

48. $\ln 4 - \ln x = 10$ **49.** $4e^{(x-1)} = 64$ **50.** $3 \ln x + \ln 5 = 7$

51. Writing Describe the differences and similarities between the graphs of $y = \ln x$ and $y = \log x$.

Getting Ready for..▶ CHAPTER

8

Find the constant of variation for each direct variation.

52. $y = 3x$ **53.** $y = \frac{1}{2}x$ **54.** $y = 0.56x$ **55.** $y = -2x$

Factor each polynomial.

56. $x^2 + 3x + 2$ **57.** $x^2 - 5x + 6$ **58.** $x^3 - 2x^2 - x$ **59.** $x^2 - 9$

Simplify each expression.

60. $\frac{1}{2} + \frac{3}{4}$ **61.** $\frac{2}{5} - \frac{1}{3}$ **62.** $\frac{4}{5} \cdot \frac{10}{12}$ **63.** $\frac{2}{3} \div \frac{1}{6}$

Graph each function.

1. $y = 3(0.25)^x$ **2.** $f(x) = \frac{1}{2}(6)^x$

3. $y = 0.1(10)^x$ **4.** $f(x) = 100(2)^x$

5. **Writing** Explain how you can tell whether an exponential function models exponential growth or exponential decay. Include an example of each.

Write an equation to describe the exponential function of the form $y = ab^x$, with the given base whose graph passes through the given point.

6. base 3, $(2, 3)$ **7.** base 5, $(1, 10)$

8. base 4, $(-1, 1)$ **9.** base 2, $(0, 3)$

10. base 6, $(2, 18)$ **11.** base 0.5 $(2, 0.75)$

12. **Investment** You put $1500 into an account earning 7% interest compounded continuously. How long will it be until you have $2000 in your account?

Evaluate each logarithm.

13. $\log_2 8$ **14.** $\log_7 7$ **15.** $\log_5 25$

16. $\log_3 27$ **17.** $\log_{11} 1$ **18.** $\log_4 256$

19. **Seismology** How many times as strong is an earthquake measuring 5.2 on the Richter scale compared to one measuring 3.0?

Graph each logarithmic function.

20. $y = \log_8 x$ **21.** $y = \log_3 x$

22. $y = \log_6 x$ **23.** $y = \log_9 x$

Write each logarithmic expression as a single logarithm.

24. $\log 9 + \log 4$ **25.** $\log_3 6 - 2\log_3 4$

26. $3\log a - 2\log b$ **27.** $\log_2 4 + 3\log_2 9$

Expand each logarithm.

28. $\log_4 r^2 t$ **29.** $\log_2 (x + 1)^2$

30. $\log_7 \frac{a}{b}$ **31.** $\log 3x^3 y^2$

Use the properties of logarithms to evaluate each expression.

32. $\log_3 27 - \log_3 9$ **33.** $2\log_2 64 + \log_2 2$

34. $-\log_4 \frac{1}{16} - \log_4 64$ **35.** $2\log 5 + \log 40$

36. **Open-ended** Write two logarithmic expressions. Which one has the greater value? Explain.

Solve each equation. Check each solution.

37. $x^{\frac{3}{4}} = 81$ **38.** $3q^{\frac{3}{2}} = 24$

39. $\log 4x = 3$ **40.** $2\log x = -4$

Use the change of base formula to rewrite each expression using common logarithms.

41. $\log_3 16$ **42.** $\log_2 10$ **43.** $\log_7 8$

44. **Standardized Test Prep** Which expression is greatest when $x = 4$?

  A. e^x **B.** $\ln (x - 4)$ **C.** $3\ln x$

  D. $\frac{1}{3}\ln 2x$ **E.** $x\ln 3$

Solve each equation.

45. $\ln (x - 2) + \ln x = 1$

46. $\ln (x + 1) + \ln (x - 1) = 4$

47. $\ln x + \ln (2x - 1) = 7$

48. $3\ln x - \ln 2 = 4$

49. **Physics** Sea water absorbs light. In some locations, this relationship is modeled by $\ln I = \ln I_0 - 0.014d$. The intensity of the light in the atmosphere is I_0, and I is the intensity at a depth of d cm. At what depth will the intensity of the light in the water be 25% of the light in the atmosphere?

For Exercises 1–10, choose the correct letter.

1. What can you tell about the roots of
$3x^2 + 4x - 1 = 0$ using the discriminant?
  A. There are two real roots.
  B. There are two imaginary roots.
  C. There is one real and one imaginary root.
  D. There are no roots.
  E. You cannot tell anything about the roots.

2. Which expression(s) is/are equivalent to
$\log a - 3 \log b$?
  I. $\log ab^3$ **II.** $\log \dfrac{a}{b^3}$
  III. $\log a - \log b^3$ **IV.** $\log (ab)^3$
  A. I and II   **B.** II and III   **C.** III and IV
  D. I and IV   **E.** II, III, and IV

3. What is the factored form of $2x^3 + 5x^2 - 12x$?
  A. $x(2x - 3)(x + 4)$ **B.** $(2x^2 - 3)(x + 4)$
  C. $x(2x + 4)(x - 3)$ **D.** $(2x - 4)(x + 3)$
  E. $(2x + 4)(x^2 - 3)$

4. Which is the graph of an exponential function?
  A. 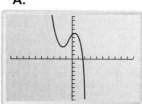   **B.**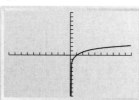

  C. 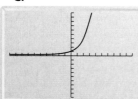   **D.**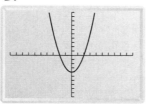

  E. none of them

5. Which point is *not* a solution of the system
$\begin{cases} x - y > 3 \\ 2x + y \geq 5 \end{cases}$?
  A. $(3, 0)$ **B.** $(4, -1)$ **C.** $(6, 1)$
  D. $(10, -2)$ **E.** $(9, 4)$

6. How is the graph of $y = (x - 4)^2 + 1$ shifted
from the graph of $y = x^2$?
  A. right 4, up 1   **B.** left 4, down 1
  C. right 1, down 4   **D.** left 1, up 4
  E. right 4, down 1

7. What is the inverse of $\begin{bmatrix} 3 & -5 \\ 1 & 4 \end{bmatrix}$?
  A. $\begin{bmatrix} 4 & 5 \\ -1 & 3 \end{bmatrix}$ **B.** $\begin{bmatrix} -2 & 5 \\ -1 & -3 \end{bmatrix}$
  C. $\begin{bmatrix} -3 & 5 \\ -1 & -4 \end{bmatrix}$ **D.** $\dfrac{1}{17}\begin{bmatrix} 4 & 5 \\ -1 & 3 \end{bmatrix}$
  E. The matrix has no inverse.

8. Which function has growth factor 1.25?
  A. $y = 1.25x$ **B.** $y = 4.1(1.25)^x$
  C. $y = 1.25(3.7)^x$ **D.** $y = 1.25(0.9)^x$
  E. $y = 3x^{1.25}$

Compare the boxed quantity in Column A with the boxed quantity in Column B. Choose the best answer.

  A. The quantity in Column A is greater.
  B. The quantity in Column B is greater.
  C. The two quantities are equal.
  D. The relationship cannot be determined on the basis of the information supplied.

Column A	Column B
9. e^2	$2 \ln e$
10. $\log_3 2$	$\log_2 3$

Find each answer.

11. **Writing** Explain the difference between common and natural logarithms.

12. **Investment** You put $1000 in an account earning 5.5% interest compounded continuously. How much will be in the account after four years?

Rational Functions

Relating to the Real World

Two quantities can vary so that as one increases, the other decreases. For example, as the length of a taut string increases, its pitch (in vibrations per second) when plucked decreases. Relationships such as these can be modeled by a function of the form $y = \frac{k}{x}$.

UNDER PRESSURE

S cuba diving helps marine scientists explore the underwater frontier. It is also a popular sport. But to dive safely, divers must understand that water pressure at depths of even 30 or 40 feet can be very dangerous.

Modern scuba-diving equipment allows divers to stay under water for long periods of time. But the depth and length of dives are limited by the amount of pressure that the human body can tolerate. You will use mathematics to explore safety questions in scuba-diving, Then you will design a poster or brochure about scuba-diving safety.

To help you complete the project:

Solving Rational Equations	*Probability of Multiple Events*
8-6	8-7

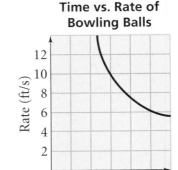

What You'll Learn

8-1

Exploring Inverse Variation

• Identifying and solving inverse variations

...And Why

To solve problems involving heart rates and illumination

QUICK REVIEW

Rate = $\frac{distance}{time}$ or

distance = rate · time or

$d = r \cdot t$.

WORK TOGETHER

Work with a partner.

Suppose a bowling ball travels at a constant speed in a straight line down a bowling lane. You can find its speed (or rate) *r* by measuring the time *t* in seconds that it takes the ball to travel the distance *d* to the pins.

1. Refer to the graph at the right. Copy and complete the table below.

Speed of Bowling Balls Down a 60-ft Lane

Time (s)	Speed (ft/s)
t	*s*
5	■
6	■
8	■
9	■
11	■

Time vs. Rate of Bowling Balls

(graph: Rate (ft/s) vs. Time (s); a decreasing curve)

2. Describe the relationship between the time taken and the rate of the ball.

3. What quantity remains constant?

4. Write an equation to find the rate *r* in ft/s of each ball in the table.

Identifying Inverse Variation

In the Work Together you used the equation $r = \frac{d}{t}$. An equation in two variables of the form $y = \frac{k}{x}$ or $xy = k$, where $k \neq 0$, is an **inverse variation.** The **constant of variation** is k.

You can identify direct and inverse variations by examining data. In a direct variation, y increases as x increases. In an inverse variation, y decreases as x increases.

Example 1

Identify the relationship among the data in each table as a *direct variation* or an *inverse variation*. Then write an equation to model the data.

a.

x	0.5	2	6
y	1.5	6	18

b.

x	0.2	0.6	1.2
y	12	4	2

a. As x increases, y increases. Check that the data vary directly by calculating the ratio $\frac{y}{x}$ for each data pair.

$$\frac{1.5}{0.5} = 3 \qquad \frac{6}{2} = 3 \qquad \frac{18}{6} = 3$$

The ratio $\frac{y}{x}$ is constant, so x varies directly with y, and $k = 3$. The equation is $y = 3x$.

b. As x increases, y decreases. Check that the data vary inversely by calculating the product xy for each data pair.

$$(0.2)(12) = 2.4 \qquad (0.6)(4) = 2.4 \qquad (1.2)(2) = 2.4$$

The product xy is constant, so x varies inversely with y, and $k = 2.4$. The equation is $xy = 2.4$.

5. **Try This** Identify each relationship as a *direct variation* or an *inverse variation*. Then write an equation to model the data.

a.

x	1.2	1.4	1.6
y	18	21	24

b.

x	0.8	0.6	0.4
y	0.9	1.2	1.8

6. Kelly described the data at the right as varying inversely. Was she correct? Explain.

x	1	2	3
y	0.5	0.25	0.125

7. Each point is from a model for inverse variation. Find each constant of variation.

   a. $(3, 7)$ b. $(2.5, 1.5)$ c. $\left(15, \frac{1}{3}\right)$

8. Each pair of points is from a model for inverse variation. Find the missing value.

    a. $\left(\frac{2}{3}, \frac{1}{4}\right)$ and $\left(\frac{1}{2}, y\right)$ **b.** $(10, 12)$ and $(x, 5)$

Modeling Inverse Variation

You can use data pairs to write a model for the relationship.

 Example 2   **Relating to the Real World** 🌐 ....

Zoology The heart rates and life spans of most mammals are inversely related. Write an equation to model this inverse variation. Use your equation to find the average life span of a cat (heart rate 126 beats/min).

Define r = heart rate (beats/min)
                 s = life span (min)
                 k = constant of variation (beats)

Relate   Heart rate times life span is a constant.

Write r × s = k

Use the formula $rs = k$, the data in the table, and a calculator to find k.

$(634)(1{,}576{,}800) \approx 1{,}000{,}000{,}000$
$(158)(6{,}307{,}200) \approx 1{,}000{,}000{,}000$
$(76)(13{,}140{,}000) \approx 1{,}000{,}000{,}000$
$(63)(15{,}768{,}000) \approx 1{,}000{,}000{,}000$

So, k is about 1,000,000,000.

Animal	Heart rate (beats/min)	Life span (min)
Mouse	634	1,576,800
Rabbit	158	6,307,200
Lion	76	13,140,000
Horse	63	15,768,000

Source: *The Handy Science Answer Book*

       $rs = 1{,}000{,}000{,}000$ ←— Substitute 1,000,000,000 for k.

The equation $rs = 1{,}000{,}000{,}000$ models the relationship between heart rate and life span. The number of heartbeats k is approximately the same for most mammals (not including humans).

Next, find the average life span of a cat.

         $rs = 1{,}000{,}000{,}000$
   $(126)s = 1{,}000{,}000{,}000$ ←— Substitute 126 for r.
           $s = \dfrac{1{,}000{,}000{,}000}{126}$ ←— Solve for s.
            $\approx 8{,}000{,}000$ ←— Use a calculator.

A cat's life span is 8 million minutes (about 15.2 years).

9. **Try This** A squirrel's heart rate is 190 beats per minute. Find its average life span.

10. An elephant's life span is about 70 years. Find its average heart rate.

Sometimes a variable y varies inversely with the square of another variable x. Then $y = \frac{k}{x^2}$ or $x^2 y = k$. For example, the amount of light falling on an object varies inversely with the square of the distance between the object and the light source.

Example 3	**Relating to the Real World**

Light The equation $E = \frac{53.2}{d^2}$ models the amount of light E provided by a 50-watt light bulb, where E (measured in lux) depends on the distance d (in meters) from the bulb, for $d \geq 1$. Sketch a graph showing how the amount of light changes as you move away from the bulb.

Use the equation to complete the table.

Distance d (m)	Amount of Light E (1ux)
1.0	53.2
1.5	23.6
3.0	5.9
5.0	2.1

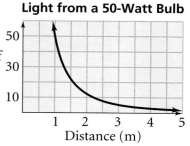

Light from a 50-Watt Bulb

Plot the ordered pairs and sketch a curve.

11. **a.** Use the graph to find the amount of light 2 m from the bulb.
   b. *Critical Thinking* If the distance is doubled, is the amount of light reduced by one-half? Explain.

Copy and complete each table using the given equation.

1.

x	y
6	■
5	■
■	2
1.5	■
■	2.5

$xy = 6$

2.

x	y
0.2	■
■	3.2
■	1
4	■
2	■

$xy = 1.6$

3.

x	y
■	16
■	6.4
4	■
■	1
0.2	■

$xy = 32$

4.

x	y
$\frac{1}{4}$	■
$\frac{1}{2}$	■
■	1
■	2

$xy = \frac{1}{8}$

Each point is from an inverse variation. Find each constant of variation.

5. $(6, 3)$ 　　　　6. $(8, 12)$ 　　　　7. $(0.9, 4)$ 　　　8. $\left(\frac{1}{2}, 6\right)$ 　　　　9. $(0.3, 7)$ 　　　10. $\left(\frac{3}{8}, \frac{2}{3}\right)$

11. At a family gathering, 36 people will be seated at tables of the same size. The number of tables t varies inversely with the number n of people at each table. Write an equation to model this relationship.

Identify the data in each table as a *direct variation* or an *inverse variation*. Then write an equation to model the data.

12.

x	y
3	15
8	40
10	50
22	110
45	225

13.

x	y
3	14
5	8.4
7	6
10.5	4
21	2

14.

x	y
7	$\frac{1}{7}$
3	$\frac{1}{3}$
1	1
$\frac{1}{5}$	5

15.

x	y
0.125	0.25
0.5	1
2	4
3.5	7
11	22

16. a. Technology The spreadsheet shows data that could be modeled by an equation of the form $PV = k$. Estimate the value of k.
b. Estimate P when $V = 62$.

17. Standardized Test Prep Which set of data does not model an inverse variation?
A. $x_1 = 1.0; y_1 = 10.0$
$x_2 = 2.0; y_2 = 5.0$
B. $x_1 = 2.5; y_1 = 5.0$
$x_2 = 5.0; y_2 = 2.5$
C. $x_1 = 3.0; y_1 = 4.0$
$x_2 = 2.0; y_2 = 6.0$
D. $x_1 = 2.5; y_1 = 5.0$
$x_2 = 5.2; y_2 = 2.5$
E. none of the above

	A	B
1	P	V
2	140.00	100
3	147.30	95
4	155.60	90
5	164.70	85
6	175.00	80

Each point is from an inverse variation. Write an equation to model the data.

18. $(1, 11)$
19. $(13, 100)$
20. $(1, 1)$
21. $(28, 2)$
22. $(12, 37)$
23. $(4, 21)$
24. $(15, 9)$
25. $(2, 6.3)$
26. $(1.2, 3)$
27. $(2.5, 100)$

28. Construction A concrete supplier sells premixed concrete in 300-ft³ truckloads. The area A that the concrete will cover is inversely proportional to the depth d of the concrete.
a. Write a model for the relationship between the area and the depth of the poured concrete.
b. What area will the concrete cover if it is poured to a depth of $\frac{1}{2}$ ft? 1 ft? 1.5 ft?
c. When the concrete is poured into a circular area, the depth of the concrete is inversely proportional to the square of the radius r. Write a model for this relationship.

29. In the formula $h = \frac{2A}{b}$, h varies directly with A and inversely with b. This is an example of *combined variation*.
a. Suppose z varies directly with x and inversely with y, and $z = 15$ when $x = 6$ and $y = 2$. Find z when $x = 8$ and $y = 4$.
b. The force of gravity g on a rocket varies directly with its mass m and inversely with the square of its distance d from Earth. Write a model for this combined variation.
c. Writing The Formula $V = \frac{1}{3}Bh$ shows joint variation. Explain how this formula can be written to show combined variation.

30. Critical Thinking Suppose that (x_1, y_1) and (x_2, y_2) both satisfy $xy = k$. Show that $\frac{x_1}{x_2} = \frac{y_2}{y_1}$.

31. Mechanics Gear A drives gear B. Gear A has a teeth and speed r_A in rpm (revolutions per minute). Gear B has b teeth and speed r_B. Let $ar_A = br_B$. Gear A has 60 teeth and speed 5400 rpm. Gear B has 45 teeth. Find the speed, in revolutions per minute, of gear B.

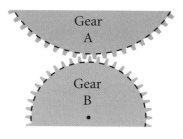

Gear A

Gear B

32. Light The equation $E = \frac{129.6}{d^2}$ models the amount of light provided by a 100-W light bulb. Graph the relationship. Find the amount of light falling on a book that is 1.5 m from the bulb.

Each pair of points is from an inverse variation. Find the missing value.

33. $(3, 7)$ and $(8, y)$ **34.** $(8.3, 7.1)$ and $(4, y)$ **35.** $(4, 6)$ and $(x, 3)$ **36.** $(12, 2)$ and $(24, y)$

Chapter Project   **Find Out by Graphing**

Scuba divers must learn about pressure under water. At the water's surface, air exerts 1 atmosphere (atm) of pressure. Under water, the pressure increases. The pressure P (atm) varies with depth d (ft) according to the equation $P = \frac{d}{33} + 1$. Boyle's Law states that the volume V of air varies inversely with the pressure P. If you hold your breath, the volume of air in your lungs increases as you ascend. If you have 4 qt of air in your lungs at a depth of 66 ft ($P = 3$ atm), the air will expand to 6 qt when you reach 33 ft, where $P = 2$ atm.

• Using the data in the example above, make a table and graph to show how the volume of air in your lungs varies with depth.

• Make a table and graph to show how the volume of air in your lungs varies with pressure.

Exercises   **MIXED REVIEW**

Evaluate each function at $x = 3$.

37. $y = 5x - 1$ **38.** $y = 2^x$ **39.** $y = |-x - 4| + 1$

40. Zoology Tiger sharks can have 10 to 80 offspring in a brood. Suppose an aquarium has three breeding pairs of tiger sharks, and each pair has one brood per year. What are the least and greatest numbers of offspring the tiger sharks could have in a year?

Getting Ready for Lesson 8-2

Evaluate each function for $x = -4, -3, -2, -1, 0, 1, 2, 3,$ and 4.

41. $y = \frac{2}{x}$ **42.** $y = \frac{1}{x + 2}$ **43.** $y = \frac{2}{x - 2}$

FOR YOUR JOURNAL

Think of real-world examples of direct variation and inverse variation. Describe each situation and write an equation to model each.

Graphing Rational Functions

Before Lesson 8-2

You can use your graphing calculator to graph rational functions.

Example

Graph the function $y = \frac{1}{2x - 5} - 3$.

Step 1: Press the MODE key. Scroll down to highlight the word "Dot." Then press ENTER.

Step 2: Enter the function. Use parentheses to enter the denominator accurately.

Step 3: Graph the function.

```
Normal Sci Eng
Float 0123456789
Radian Degree
Func Par Pol Seq
Connected Dot
Sequential Simul
FullScreen Split
```

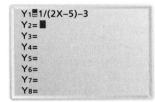

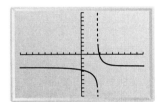

Graphing Calculator **Use a graphing calculator to graph each function. Then sketch the graph.**

1. $y = \frac{7}{x}$

2. $y = \frac{3}{x + 4} - 2$

3. $y = \frac{x + 2}{(x + 1)(x + 3)}$

4. $y = \frac{4x + 1}{x - 3}$

5. $y = \frac{2}{x - 2}$

6. $y = \frac{1}{x + 2} + 3$

7. $y = \frac{2x}{x + 3}$

8. $y = \frac{x^2}{x^2 - 5}$

9. $y = \frac{20}{x^2 + 5}$

10. $y = \frac{1}{x - 3} - 6$

11. $y = \frac{10}{x^2 - 5x - 10}$

12. $y = \frac{x}{x^2 - 1}$

13. a. Graphing Calculator Graph $y = \frac{1}{x}$. Sketch the graph.
   b. Examine both negative and positive values of x. Describe what happens to the y-values as x approaches zero.
   c. What happens to the y-values as x increases? as x decreases?

14. a. Graphing Calculator Change the mode on your graphing calculator to "Connected." Graph the function from the example. Sketch the graph.
   b. Press the TRACE key and trace the function. What happens between $x \approx 2.3$ and $x \approx 2.6$?
   c. Critical Thinking How does your graph differ from the graph in the example? Explain the differences.

What You'll Learn

- Identifying asymptotes and graphing inverse variations
- Using graphs of inverse variations

...And Why

To solve problems involving musical pitch

What You'll Need

- graphing calculator

8-2 Graphing Inverse Variations

WORK TOGETHER

Work in groups of four.

1. **a.** Have each person in your group make a table of values for one of the functions $y = \frac{k}{x}$, $k = 1, 4, 9$, or 16. Include several nonzero values of x between -1 and 1.

   b. Graph each function. Do the graphs ever cross the x-axis? the y-axis? Use the equations of the functions to **justify** your answer.

2. Describe what happens to each graph as $|x|$ decreases. What happens as $|x|$ increases?

3. **a.** Add the line $y = x$ to each graph. Find the coordinates of the points of intersection. Compare the coordinates and the value of k. How are they related?

   b. **Predict** the coordinates of the points of intersection of $y = x$ and $y = \frac{25}{x}$. **Verify** your prediction by graphing.

4. Compare the graphs of the four functions from Question 1. How are they alike? How are they different?

THINK AND DISCUSS

Using Graphs of Inverse Variations

The graph at the right shows the function $y = \frac{5}{x}$. Notice that the graph has two parts. Each part is called a **branch**.

The **asymptotes** of a graph are lines the graph approaches. The graph of $y = \frac{5}{x}$ gets closer and closer to the x-axis as x approaches $\pm\infty$ (infinity). The graph gets closer and closer to the y-axis as x approaches zero.

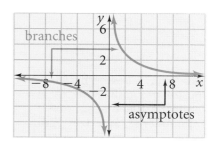

A function must be defined for all values of its domain. Since $y = \frac{5}{x}$ is not defined for $x = 0$, zero is not included in its domain. Its domain is all real numbers except zero.

5. What is the equation of the vertical asymptote of the graph of $y = \frac{5}{x}$? What is the equation of the horizontal asymptote?

6. a. Graphing Calculator Graph $y = \frac{1}{x}$. Sketch the graph. Clear your screen and graph $y = \frac{-1}{x}$. Sketch the graph. Compare the two sketches. How does the negative sign affect the graph? Describe the asymptotes of the two graphs.

b. Graph $y = \frac{1}{x^2}$. Sketch the graph. Compare the sketch with the graph of $y = \frac{1}{x}$ from part (a). How does squaring x affect the graph? Describe the asymptotes of the two graphs.

You can use graphs of inverse variations to solve problems.

> **Example 1**   **Relating to the Real World**

Music A musical pitch is measured in vibrations per second, or Hertz (Hz). The pitch y produced by a panpipe varies inversely with the length of the pipe x, measured in feet. The equation $y = \frac{564}{x}$ models the inverse variation. Find the length of the pipe that produces a pitch of 277 Hz.

Graph the functions $y = \frac{564}{x}$ and $y = 277$ on the same screen. Use the CALC feature to find the point of intersection.

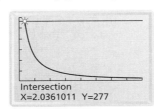

Intersection
X=2.0361011 Y=277

Xmin=0   Ymin=–75
Xmax=40   Ymax=300
Xscl=5   Yscl=50

The pipe should be about 2.0 ft long.

7. Try This Pitches of 247 Hz, 311 Hz, and 370 Hz form a musical chord. Find the length of pipe that will produce each pitch.

8. The asymptotes of $y = \frac{564}{x}$ are $x = 0$ and $y = 0$. Explain why this makes sense in terms of the panpipe.

Inca Son is a Boston-based musical group that specializes in the music and dance of Latin America, especially Peru. The musicians make their own instruments, including their panpipes.

PERU

Graphing Translations of Inverse Variations

The graphs at the right show the functions
$y = \frac{4}{x}$, $y = \frac{4}{x} + 2$, and $y = \frac{4}{x} - 4$.

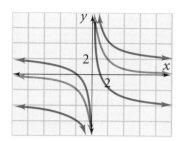

9. What is the vertical asymptote of each graph? the horizontal asymptote?

10. How are the graphs of $y = \frac{4}{x}$ and $y = \frac{4}{x} + c$ related?

The graphs at the right show the functions
$y = \frac{4}{x}$, $y = \frac{4}{x - 2}$, and $y = \frac{4}{x + 4}$.

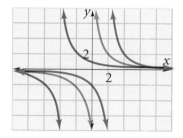

11. What is the vertical asymptote of each graph? the horizontal asymptote?

12. How are the graphs of $y = \frac{4}{x}$ and $y = \frac{4}{x - b}$ related?

Translations of Inverse Variations

The graph of $y = \frac{k}{x - b} + c$ is a translation of $y = \frac{k}{x}$ that has moved b units horizontally and c units vertically. It has a vertical asymptote at $x = b$ and a horizontal asymptote at $y = c$.

Example: $y = \frac{4}{x + 2} - 3$ translates $y = \frac{4}{x}$ two units left and three units down. It has a vertical asymptote at $x = -2$ and a horizontal asymptote at $y = -3$.

You can use the asymptotes to graph translations of inverse variations.

Example 2

Sketch the graph of $y = \frac{1}{x - 2} - 3$.

Identify the asymptotes.

   horizontal asymptote: $y = -3$
   vertical asymptote: $x = 2$

Draw the asymptotes on the graph.

The graph of $y = \frac{1}{x}$ contains the points $(1, 1)$ and $(-1, -1)$. Translate these points 2 units to the right and 3 units down to $(3, -2)$ and $(1, -4)$. Draw the branches through these points.

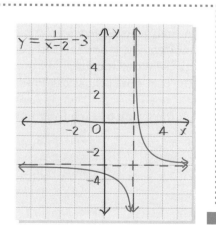

13. Without graphing, find the vertical and horizontal asymptotes of the graph of each function.

a. $y = \frac{2}{x} + 8$ **b.** $y = \frac{5}{x + 10}$ **c.** $y = -\frac{1}{x - 3} + 5$

14. Try This Sketch the graph of $y = -\frac{1}{x + 7} - 3$.

You can use what you know about asymptotes and translations of inverse variations to write equations.

Example 3

Write an equation for a translation of $y = \frac{5}{x}$ that has asymptotes at $x = -2$ and $y = 3$.

$y = \frac{5}{x - b} + c$ ⟵ Use the general form of a translation.

$\quad = \frac{5}{x - (-2)} + 3$ ⟵ Substitute −2 for *b* and 3 for *c*.

$\quad = \frac{5}{x + 2} + 3$ ⟵ Simplify.

An equation for the translation is $y = \frac{5}{x + 2} + 3$.

---

15. Graphing Calculator Graph the solution from Example 3 to **verify** that it has asymptotes at $x = -2$ and $y = 3$.

Exercises   ON YOUR OWN

Identify the vertical and horizontal asymptotes of each graph.

1.
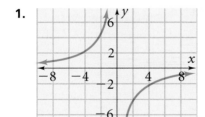

2.
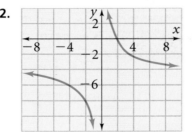

3.
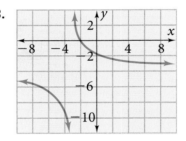

4. A high school spends $750 each year on student academic achievement awards. The amount spent per award depends on how many awards are given. Write and graph a function of the number *a* of awards given and the cost *c* of each award. Find the asymptotes.

Sketch the graph of each function.

5. $y = \frac{3}{x}$ **6.** $y = -\frac{5}{x}$ **7.** $y = \frac{1}{x} - 3$ **8.** $y = -\frac{6}{x^2} + 4$

9. $y = \frac{2}{x + 2}$ **10.** $y = -\frac{1}{x - 1}$ **11.** $y = \frac{1}{x + 6} + 1$ **12.** $y = -\frac{5}{x - 2} - 4$

13. Meteorology The function $p = \frac{69.1}{a + 2.3}$ relates atmospheric pressure p in inches of mercury to altitude a in miles.

   a. Graphing Calculator Graph the function.

   b. The photo shows various altitudes on Earth. Find the atmospheric pressure at each altitude. (*Hint:* 1 mi = 5280 ft.)

   c. Is there an altitude at which the atmospheric pressure is 0 in. of mercury? Use your graph to **justify** your reasoning.

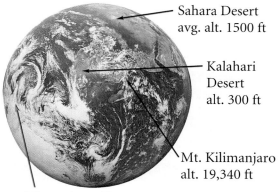

Sahara Desert avg. alt. 1500 ft

Kalahari Desert alt. 300 ft

Mt. Kilimanjaro alt. 19,340 ft

Vinson Massif alt. 16,860 ft

Write the equation for a translation of $y = \frac{4}{x}$ with the given asymptotes.

14. $x = 2; y = 0$ **15.** $x = -3; y = -1$

16. $x = 0; y = 10$ **17.** $x = 1; y = -1$

18. a. Automobiles Suppose you drive an average of 10,000 mi each year. Your gasoline mileage (mi/gal) varies inversely with the number of gallons of gasoline you use during the year. Write and graph a model for your average mileage m in terms of the gallons g of gasoline used.

   b. After you begin driving on the highway more often, you use 50 gal less per year. Write and graph a new model to include this information.

   c. Calculate your old and new mileage assuming that you originally used 400 gal of gasoline per year.

Graphing Calculator **Graph each pair of functions. Find the point(s) of intersection.**

19. $y = \frac{6}{x - 2}; y = 6$ **20.** $y = -\frac{2}{x^2}; y = -10$ **21.** $y = \frac{1}{x - 3} - 6; y = 6.2$

22. $y = \frac{3}{x + 1}; y = -4$ **23.** $y = -\frac{1}{x - 4}; y = 4.2$ **24.** $y = \frac{4}{x^2} + 2; y = 9$

Choose **Use paper and pencil or a graphing calculator. First explain how the graph of $y = \frac{1}{x}$ is translated. Then graph each function.**

25. $y = \frac{1}{x} + 2.5$ **26.** $y = \frac{1}{x - 3} + 3$ **27.** $y = \frac{1}{x + 4} - 3$ **28.** $y = \frac{1}{x + 5} - 7$

Write the equation for the translation of each function with the given asymptotes. Then graph each function.

29. $y = -\frac{5}{x}$; asymptotes $y = 3, x = -2$ **30.** $y = -\frac{1}{x^2}$; asymptotes $y = -2, x = 0$

31. Writing Explain how knowing the asymptotes of a translation of $y = \frac{k}{x}$ can help you to graph the function. Include an example.

32. Open-ended Write an equation for a horizontal translation of $y = \frac{2}{x}$. Then write an equation for a vertical translation of $y = \frac{2}{x}$. Identify the horizontal and vertical asymptotes of the graph of each function.

33. Standardized Test Prep Which function has $x = 2.5$ and $y = 4$ as the asymptotes of its graph?

   A. $y = \frac{4}{x - 2.5} - 4$ **B.** $y = -\frac{4}{x + 2.5} + 4$ **C.** $y = -\frac{4}{x + 2.5} - 4$ **D.** $y = \frac{4}{x - 2.5} + 4$

Exercises   M I X E D   R E V I E W

Write each equation in vertex form.

34. $y = x^2 + 3x - 1$ **35.** $y = 2x^2 - x + 7$ **36.** $y = x^2 + 8$ **37.** $y = -x^2 - 5x$

38. Probability A student took a survey of how many books students had in their backpacks. The results are at the right. Using the data, find the probability that the next student will have three books in his or her backpack.

How many books are in your pack?

| 3 | 1 | 2 | 0 | 2 | 4 | 0 | 5 | 3 | 2 | 1 | 2 | 6 | 1 | 3 | 2 |
| 4 | 0 | 3 | 1 | 3 | 2 | 1 | 2 | 3 | 4 | 2 | 3 | 2 | 1 | 0 | 3 |

Getting Ready for Lesson 8-3
Find the vertical asymptote of each function.

39. $y = \frac{3}{x}$ **40.** $y = \frac{4}{x + 1}$ **41.** $y = \frac{8}{x - 5} + 2$ **42.** $y = \frac{9}{x^2 - 1}$

Algebra at Work

Economist

A major concern of economists is the relationship between the supply of a product and public demand for the product. The supply curve shows that the number of units n a retailer has in supply will increase as the price of the item p increases. The demand curve shows that the number of units sold will decrease as p increases. The curves cross at a *market equilibrium point,* which establishes a stable *equilibrium price* that meets both supply and demand requirements. By solving the system of supply and demand curves, you can find the equilibrium price.

Mini Project: Use technology to graph the supply curve $n = \frac{p}{5 - p}$ and the demand curve $n = -\frac{3p - 24}{p - 2}$. Sketch the graph. Estimate the equilibrium price.

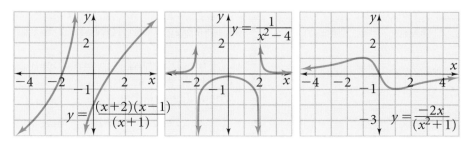
What You'll Learn

- Identifying and classifying discontinuities of rational functions
- Identifying behavior near asymptotes

...And Why

To find the average cost of producing computer games

What You'll Need

- graphing calculator

About 275,000 acres of land in Texas are dedicated to growing peanuts. In 1996, Texas ranked second in the nation in peanut production, producing 577,500,000 lb of peanuts.

8-3 Rational Functions and Their Graphs

WORK TOGETHER

How many pounds of peanuts do you think you ate last year?

Work with a partner to answer the questions.

1. Use the table at the right. What was the average peanut consumption per person in the United States in 1993? How did you find this average?

You can use the data in the table to model the average U.S. peanut consumption per person between 1970 and 1993.

Year	U.S. Peanut Consumption (millions of pounds)	U.S. Population (millions)
1970	1118	203.3
1980	1087	226.5
1985	1499	237.9
1990	1492	248.7
1991	1639	252.1
1992	1581	255.0
1993	1547	257.8

2. **Graphing Calculator** Let $x = 0$ represent 1970.
   a. Input the data into three lists. Find a cubic function $f(x)$ to model the annual consumption of peanuts.
   b. Find a linear function $g(x)$ to model the U.S. population since 1970.
   c. Write a function $h(x)$ to model the the average peanut consumption in the U.S. since 1970. $\left(Hint: h(x) = \dfrac{f(x)}{g(x)}.\right)$
   d. Graph the function you wrote in part(c). Use the graph to estimate the number of pounds of peanuts you ate last year.

THINK AND DISCUSS

Properties of Rational Functions

A function that is the quotient of two polynomials, such as $h(x)$ in the Work Together, is a **rational function.** The graphs of some rational functions are shown below.

$$y = \frac{(x+2)(x-1)}{(x+1)}$$

$$y = \frac{1}{x^2-4}$$

$$y = \frac{-2x}{(x^2+1)}$$

The graph of any polynomial function is a **continuous** curve. It has no jumps, breaks, or holes in it. The graph of a rational function may be **discontinuous.** A rational function is discontinuous at the real values of x for which the rational expression is undefined.

3. Look at the graphs on page 363. Which are continuous? Which are discontinuous?

4. A rational expression is undefined if the denominator is zero. For what value of x is the expression $\frac{1}{x-4}$ undefined?

Example 1

Classify each function as continuous or discontinuous. If discontinuous, give the value(s) of x for which the function is undefined.

a. $y = \frac{-x+1}{x^2+1}$ **b.** $y = \frac{1}{x^2+2x+1}$

a. The function $y = \frac{-x+1}{x^2+1}$ is undefined at the value(s) of x for which $x^2 + 1$ equals zero.

$$x^2 + 1 = 0 \qquad \longleftarrow \text{Set the denominator equal to zero.}$$
$$x^2 = -1$$
$$x = \pm\sqrt{-1} \qquad \longleftarrow \text{Solve for } x.$$

Since $\sqrt{-1}$ is not a real number, there is no real value of x for which the function $y = \frac{-x+1}{x^2+1}$ is undefined. It is continuous.

b. The function $y = \frac{1}{x^2+2x+1}$ is undefined at the value(s) of x for which $x^2 + 2x + 1 = 0$.

$$x^2 + 2x + 1 = 0 \qquad \longleftarrow \text{Set the denominator equal to zero.}$$
$$(x+1)(x+1) = 0 \qquad \longleftarrow \text{Factor.}$$
$$x + 1 = 0$$
$$x = -1 \qquad \longleftarrow \text{Solve for } x.$$

The function $y = \frac{1}{x^2+2x+1}$ is discontinuous at $x = -1$. ■

5. Try This Classify each function as continuous or discontinuous. If discontinuous, give the value(s) of x for which the function is undefined.

a. $y = \frac{1}{x^2-16}$ **b.** $y = \frac{x^2-1}{x^2+3}$ **c.** $y = \frac{x+1}{x^2+2x-6}$

Properties of Rational Functions

• The function $f(x) = \frac{g(x)}{h(x)}$ is discontinuous if $h(x) = 0$. If $g(x)$ and $h(x)$ have no common factors, then $f(x)$ has a vertical asymptote when $h(x) = 0$.

• $f(x)$ has, at most, one horizontal asymptote.

Graphing Rational Functions

You can easily graph rational functions using your graphing calculator.

Example 2   **Relating to the Real World**

Computer Games The CD-ROMs for a computer game can be produced for $.25 each. The development cost is $124,000. The first 100 discs are samples and will not be sold.

a. Write a function $c(x)$ for the average cost of a saleable disc. Graph the function.

b. Find the average cost if 2000 discs are produced; if 12,800 discs are produced.

a. Write a function for the average cost.

Define x = number of CD-ROMs produced
$c(x)$ = average cost of one saleable disc

Relate   Average cost = $\dfrac{\text{production cost of } x \text{ discs} + \text{development cost}}{\text{number of saleable discs}}$

Write $c(x) = \dfrac{0.25x + 124{,}000}{x - 100}$

The function $c(x) = \dfrac{0.25x + 124{,}000}{x - 100}$ represents the average cost of a saleable disc.

Graph the function
$y = \dfrac{0.25x + 124{,}000}{x - 100}$
on your graphing calculator.
Adjust the viewing window.

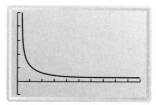

Xmin=0	Ymin=-50
Xmax=13000	Ymax=500
Xscl=5000	Yscl=100

b. Use the CALC feature to evaluate the function at $x = 2000$ and at $x = 12{,}800$.

If 2000 discs are produced, the average cost will be about $65.53.
If 12,800 discs are produced, the average cost will be about $10.02. ∎

6. Critical Thinking How could you find the number of discs that must be produced to bring the average cost under $2?

7. What is the vertical asymptote of the function in Example 2? the horizontal asymptote?

To sketch the graph of a rational function by hand, it is helpful to know the vertical and horizontal asymptotes and the behavior of the function as it gets closer to the asymptotes.

Example 3

Sketch the graph of $y = \frac{3x + 5}{x - 2}$.

Step 1: Find the vertical asymptotes.

The function $y = \frac{3x + 5}{x - 2}$ is undefined at $x = 2$. The line $x = 2$ is a vertical asymptote. Show this asymptote on your graph.

Step 2: Find any horizontal asymptote by first dividing the polynomials.

$$
\begin{array}{r}
3 \\
x - 2 \overline{)3x + 5} \\
\underline{3x - 6} \\
11
\end{array}
$$

The function $y = \frac{3x + 5}{x - 2}$ can be written as $y = \frac{11}{x - 2} + 3$.
It is a translation of $y = \frac{11}{x}$ and has a horizontal asymptote at $y = 3$.
Show this asymptote on your graph.

Step 3: See what happens as x approaches $\pm \infty$. Evaluate the function for various values of x. (Use a calculator.)

x	-1000	-100	-10	-3	0	3	10	100	1000
y	2.989	2.892	2.083	0.8	-2.5	14	4.375	3.112	3.011

As $|x|$ increases, the function approaches the horizontal asymptote $y = 3$. When $x < 2$, the function is below the horizontal asymptote; when $x > 2$, the function is above the horizontal asymptote.

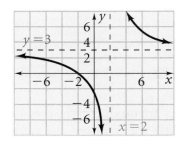

8. **Try This** Sketch the graph of $y = \frac{4x - 2}{x + 3}$.

9. **Graphing Calculator** Graph the functions $y = \frac{(x - 2)(x + 2)}{x - 2}$ and $y = x + 2$. Evaluate each function at $x = 2$. Explain your results.

Rational functions that have a common linear factor in the numerator and denominator have a **removable discontinuity,** or **hole,** in their graphs.

Classify each function as continuous or discontinuous. If discontinuous, give the value(s) of x for which the function is undefined.

1. $y = \dfrac{3}{x + 2}$

2. $y = \dfrac{x + 5}{x + 5}$

3. $y = \dfrac{x(x + 2)}{x^2 + 2}$

4. $y = \dfrac{(x + 3)(x - 2)}{(x - 2)(x + 1)}$

5. $y = \dfrac{x + 3}{(2x + 3)(x - 1)}$

6. $y = \dfrac{4x}{x^3 - 6x}$

7. $y = \dfrac{3}{x - 2}$

8. $y = \dfrac{x + 5}{x^2 + 9}$

9. $y = \dfrac{2x^2 + 5}{x^2 - 2x}$

10. $y = \dfrac{3x - 3}{x^2 - 1}$

11. $y = \dfrac{x^2 - 4}{3x - 6}$

12. $y = \dfrac{x^2 + 4x + 3}{-2x^2 + 6x - 7}$

13. Patterns Look for a pattern in the sequence of shells below.

   a. Write a model for the number of purple shells $P(n)$ at each step n.
   b. Write a model for the number of brown shells $B(n)$ at each step n.
   c. Write a model for the ratio of $P(n)$ to $B(n)$. Use it to predict the ratio of purple shells to brown in the next figure. **Verify** your work.

14. Basketball Raima plays basketball for her high school. She has made 21 of her last 30 free throws—an average of 70%. To model what her percentage will be if she makes x more consecutive free throws, use the function $y = \dfrac{21 + x}{30 + x}$.
   a. Graph the function.
   b. Estimation Use the graph to estimate how many consecutive free throws she needs to raise her percentage to 75%; to 90%.

Find the vertical asymptotes, if any, of each rational function.

15.

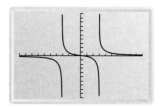

16.

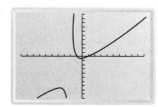

17.

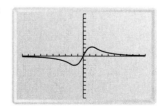

18. Writing Describe the conditions that will produce a rational function that has no vertical asymptotes.

19. **Math in the Media** The graph at the right compares the average wages for production workers and the minimum wage as enacted by Congress for the years from 1947 to 1995.

a. **Statistics** The graph shows that the minimum wage has not increased at the same rate as the average wage. Is it reasonable to expect the two numbers to be equal for each year? Explain.

b. The author may have expected the minimum wage to stay at a constant fraction of the average wage (such as half). If each trend is modeled by a polynomial, what type of function would model their ratio?

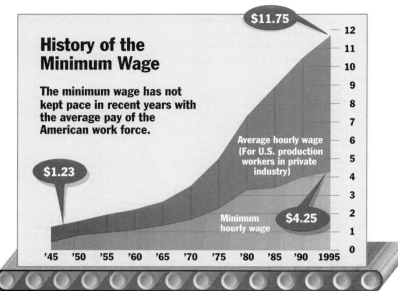

History of the Minimum Wage

The minimum wage has not kept pace in recent years with the average pay of the American work force.

$11.75

$1.23

Average hourly wage (For U.S. production workers in private industry)

Minimum hourly wage

$4.25

'45 '50 '55 '60 '65 '70 '75 '80 '85 '90 1995

Sources: *Associated Press; U.S. Bureau of Labor Statistics*

c. The function $A(x) = (-7.33 \times 10^{-6})x^4 + (5.14 \times 10^{-4})x^3 - 0.004x^2 + 0.04x + 1.61$ approximately models the average wage, where x represents the number of years since 1950. The function $M(x) = 0.0014x^2 + 0.025x + 0.67$ models the minimum wage. Write a model for the ratio of these two functions.

Find the vertical asymptotes of each of the following functions.

20. $y = \dfrac{1}{x + 2}$

21. $y = \dfrac{x + 2}{x + 3}$

22. $y = \dfrac{x}{x - 4}$

23. $y = \dfrac{5x + 3}{x - 2}$

24. $y = \dfrac{4x^2 + 3x + 1}{x^2 - x - 1}$

25. $y = \dfrac{-x^2 + x}{x^2 - 2}$

Sketch the graph of each rational function.

26. $y = \dfrac{1}{x - 1}$

27. $y = \dfrac{x + 4}{x - 4}$

28. $y = \dfrac{x(x + 1)}{x + 1}$

29. $y = \dfrac{2x + 3}{x - 5}$

30. $y = \dfrac{x^2 + 6x + 9}{x + 3}$

31. $y = \dfrac{4x^2 - 100}{2x^2 + x - 15}$

32. $y = \dfrac{x + 6}{(x - 2)(x + 3)}$

33. $y = \dfrac{3x}{(x + 2)^2}$

34. $y = -\dfrac{x}{(x - 1)^2}$

35. **Statistics** The president of XYZ Company earns $200,000 a year. Each of her x employees earns $20,000 a year.

a. Write a function that models the average salary of all employees of XYZ.

b. **Estimation** Graph the function. Use the graph to estimate the average salary at XYZ Company if it has 3 employees; if it has 30 employees.

c. **Critical Thinking** Is the average salary the best measure of the workers' pay? Explain. What other measure could you use?

Chapter Project *Find Out by Writing*

In the Find Out by Graphing on page 355, you found that the volume of air in a diver's lungs could more than double as the diver resurfaces. This expansion can cause the membranes of the lungs to rupture. Divers must learn to exhale properly while ascending.

- If you fill your lungs with 4 qt of air at a depth of 66 ft, how many quarts of air will you need to exhale during your ascent to still have 4 qt of air in your lungs when you reach the surface?

- Write an explanation of why beginning divers are told "Don't hold your breath!" Refer to your tables and graphs.

Exercises MIXED REVIEW

Identify each function as exponential growth or decay, and find the growth or decay factor.

36. $y = 3 \cdot 4^x$

37. $y = 0.1 \cdot 2^x$

38. $y = 5 \cdot (0.8)^x$

39. $y = 3 \cdot \left(\frac{1}{2}\right)^x$

40. Geometry The lengths of two sides of a square are $(x^2 + 6x)$ in. and $(2x^2 - 7)$ in. What is the area of the square?

Getting Ready for Lesson 8-4

Simplify each expression.

41. $\frac{1}{2} \cdot \frac{4}{7}$

42. $\frac{3}{8} \div \frac{2}{15}$

43. $\frac{2}{10} \cdot \frac{18}{16}$

44. $\frac{6}{9} \div \frac{15}{20}$

Exercises CHECKPOINT

Each point belongs to a relationship that varies inversely. Write an equation to model the inverse variation.

1. $(4, 3)$

2. $(8, 1)$

3. $(10, 2)$

4. $\left(\frac{1}{3}, 12\right)$

5. $(5, 1.4)$

6. $\left(\frac{1}{4}, \frac{3}{8}\right)$

Graph each function.

7. $y = \frac{1}{x} - 4$

8. $y = \frac{x - 2}{x + 1}$

9. $y = \frac{1}{x - 5}$

10. $y = \frac{x(x + 4)}{(x - 2)(x + 2)}$

11. Open-ended Write an equation for a function that has an asymptote at $x = 8$ and another equation for one that has a removable discontinuity at $x = 8$.

12. Standardized Test Prep Which function translates the graph of $y = \frac{1}{x}$ right three units and down five units?

A. $y = \frac{1}{x - 3} + 5$

B. $y = \frac{1}{x + 3} - 5$

C. $y = \frac{1}{x - 5} + 3$

D. $y = \frac{1}{x - 3} - 5$

E. $y = \frac{1}{x + 5} - 3$

What You'll Learn
- Simplifying rational expressions
- Multiplying and dividing rational expressions

...And Why

To compare designs for submersibles

8-4 Rational Expressions

THINK AND DISCUSS

Simplifying Rational Expressions

Submersibles are underwater laboratories that scientists use to study the ocean floor. Some submersibles can descend to a depth of 20,000 ft. At that depth, the pressure of the water on the submersible is about 722 lb/in.^{2}.

When designing submersibles, oceanographers try to minimize the surface area of the craft (because of the water pressure) and maximize the work space, or volume. They use ratios to compare these numbers.

Example 1   **Relating to the Real World**

Oceanography   Find the ratio of the surface area to the volume of a cylindrical submersible with height and radius equal to c.

Use the formulas for surface area and volume of a cylinder.

$$\text{Surface Area} = 2\pi rh + 2\pi r^2$$
$$\text{Volume} = \pi r^2 h$$

$$\frac{\text{Surface Area}}{\text{Volume}} = \frac{2\pi rh + 2\pi r^2}{\pi r^2 h} \quad \longleftarrow \text{Write a ratio.}$$

$$= \frac{2\pi c(c) + 2\pi c^2}{\pi c^2(c)} \quad \longleftarrow \text{Substitute } c \text{ for } h \text{ and } r.$$

$$= \frac{2\pi c^2 + 2\pi c^2}{\pi c^3} \quad \longleftarrow \text{Simplify.}$$

$$= \frac{4\pi c^2}{\pi c^3} \quad \longleftarrow \text{Combine like terms.}$$

$$= \frac{4}{c} \quad \longleftarrow \text{Simplify.}$$

The ratio of the surface area to the volume is 4 : c.

These photographs show what happens to a plastic foam cup during a descent to the ocean floor in the unpressurized part of a submersible.

1. a. *Open-ended*   Suppose you were building a cylindrical submersible with its height equal to its radius. What size radius would you use? Explain.
  b. *Critical Thinking*   Consider the parameters of Example 1 and your answer to part (a). How would you change the design to make a better submersible? **Justify** your answer.
  c. Why might an engineer want a large submersible? a small submersible?

2. **a. Geometry** The formula for the surface area of a sphere is $A = 4\pi r^2$. The volume of a sphere is $V = \frac{4}{3}\pi r^3$. Find the ratio of surface area to volume for a spherical submersible with radius c.

b. Critical Thinking For a given radius, which shape would make a better submersible, a cylinder (with height = radius) or a sphere? **Justify** your reasoning by using the ratios and giving examples.

A rational expression is in **simplest form** when its numerator and denominator are polynomials that have no common divisors.

In simplest form	Not in simplest form
$\dfrac{x}{x-1}$ $\dfrac{2}{x^2+3}$	$\dfrac{x}{x^2}$ $\dfrac{\frac{1}{x}}{x+1}$ $\dfrac{2(x-3)}{3(x-3)}$

You can simplify some expressions by dividing out common factors.

Example 2

Simplify $\dfrac{x^2 + 10x + 25}{x^2 + 9x + 20}$.

$$\frac{x^2 + 10x + 25}{x^2 + 9x + 20} = \frac{(x+5)(x+5)}{(x+4)(x+5)}$$ ← Factor the polynomials.

$$= \frac{(x+5)\cancel{(x+5)}}{(x+4)\cancel{(x+5)}}$$ ← Divide out common factors.

$$= \frac{x+5}{x+4}$$

The simplified expression is $\dfrac{x+5}{x+4}$ for $x \neq -4$ or -5.

3. **Critical Thinking** Why does the solution for Example 2 exclude $x = -4$? Why does it exclude $x = -5$?

4. **Try This** Simplify each expression.

   a. $\dfrac{-27x^3 y}{9x^4 y}$ **b.** $\dfrac{6 - 3x}{x^2 - 5x + 6}$ **c.** $\dfrac{2x^2 - 3x - 2}{x^2 - 5x + 6}$

Multiplying and Dividing Rational Expressions

You can use what you know about simplifying rational expressions when you multiply and divide them.

Example 3

Multiply $\dfrac{2x^2 + 7x + 3}{x - 4}$ and $\dfrac{x^2 - 16}{x^2 + 8x + 15}$.

$\dfrac{2x^2 + 7x + 3}{x - 4} \cdot \dfrac{x^2 - 16}{x^2 + 8x + 15}$

$= \dfrac{(2x + 1)(x + 3)}{x - 4} \cdot \dfrac{(x - 4)(x + 4)}{(x + 3)(x + 5)}$ ⟵ Factor.

$= \dfrac{(2x + 1)\cancel{(x + 3)}}{\cancel{x - 4}} \cdot \dfrac{\cancel{(x - 4)}(x + 4)}{\cancel{(x + 3)}(x + 5)}$ ⟵ Divide out common factors.

$= \dfrac{(2x + 1)(x + 4)}{x + 5}$

$= \dfrac{2x^2 + 9x + 4}{x + 5}$ ⟵ Multiply.

The product is $\dfrac{2x^2 + 9x + 4}{x + 5}$.

5. For which value(s) of x is the product in Example 3 not defined? **Justify** your reasoning.

6. **Try This** Multiply $\dfrac{a^2 - 4}{a^2 - 1}$ and $\dfrac{a + 1}{a^2 + 2a}$.

To divide rational expressions, remember to multiply by the reciprocal of the divisor, just as you did when dividing rational numbers.

Example 4

Divide $\dfrac{4 - x}{(3x + 2)(x - 2)}$ by $\dfrac{5(x - 4)}{(x - 2)(7y - 5)}$.

$\dfrac{4 - x}{(3x + 2)(x - 2)} \div \dfrac{5(x - 4)}{(x - 2)(7y - 5)}$

$= \dfrac{-(x - 4)}{(3x + 2)(x - 2)} \cdot \dfrac{(x - 2)(7y - 5)}{5(x - 4)}$ ⟵ Multiply by the reciprocal.

$= \dfrac{-\cancel{(x - 4)}}{(3x + 2)\cancel{(x - 2)}} \cdot \dfrac{\cancel{(x - 2)}(7y - 5)}{5\cancel{(x - 4)}}$ ⟵ Divide out common factors.

$= \dfrac{-1}{3x + 2} \cdot \dfrac{7y - 5}{5}$

$= \dfrac{-7y + 5}{15x + 10}$ ⟵ Multiply.

The quotient is $\dfrac{-7y + 5}{15x + 10}$.

7. For which values of x is the quotient in Example 4 not defined? **Justify** your answer.

8. **Try This** Divide $\dfrac{a^2 + 2a - 15}{a^2 - 16}$ by $\dfrac{a + 1}{3a - 12}$.

Simplify each rational expression.

1. $\dfrac{2x}{4x^2 - 2x}$

2. $\dfrac{6c^2 + 9c}{3c}$

3. $\dfrac{b^2 - 1}{b - 1}$

4. $\dfrac{z^2 - 49}{z + 7}$

5. $\dfrac{3x^2}{6x^2 - 3x}$

6. $\dfrac{2x + 10}{x^2 + 10x + 25}$

7. $\dfrac{y^2 - 49}{y^2 - 14y + 49}$

8. $\dfrac{x^2 + 8x + 16}{x^2 - 2x - 24}$

9. $\dfrac{x^2 - 5x - 24}{x^2 - 7x - 30}$

10. $\dfrac{x^2 + 2x - 3}{x^2 + 6x + 9}$

11. $\dfrac{5t^3 - 45t}{5t}$

12. $\dfrac{2y^2 + 8y - 24}{2y^2 - 8y + 8}$

13. Industry A fuel tank will have a circular base. The fuel tank can be either cylindrical or hemispherical (half a sphere). To keep construction costs down, the architects want to minimize the ratio of surface area to volume.
   a. Write and simplify an expression that compares the surface area of the hemisphere and its base with radius t to its volume.
   b. Write and simplify an expression that compares the surface area of the cylinder of height and diameter $2t$ to its volume.
   c. Based on your answers to parts (a) and (b), which design would you recommend to the architects? Explain.

14. Writing How can you tell whether a rational expression is in simplest form? Include an example with your explanation.

15. Open-ended Write three rational expressions that simplify to $\dfrac{x}{x + 1}$.

16. Standardized Test Prep Which of the expressions below always has a positive value? Assume that $x \neq 0$, 1, or -1.

   A. $x\left(\dfrac{1}{x - 1}\right) \div (x - 1)$

   B. $\dfrac{1}{x - 1} \div (x - 1)\left(\dfrac{1}{x}\right)$

   C. $\dfrac{x - 1}{x^2} \div (x^2 - 1)\left(\dfrac{1}{x^2}\right)$

   D. $\left(\dfrac{x^2 - 1}{x}\right)\left(\dfrac{x^2 - 1}{(x - 1)^2}\right) \div \dfrac{1}{x^2}$

   E. $\dfrac{1}{x^2 - 1} \div x^2\left(\dfrac{1}{x^2 - 1}\right)$

17. Physics The acceleration of an object is a measure of how much its speed changes in a given period of time.

$$\text{acceleration} = \frac{\text{final speed} - \text{initial speed}}{\text{time}}$$

Suppose you are riding a bicycle at a speed of 3 m/s. You step hard on the pedals and increase your speed to 6 m/s in 2 s.
   a. Identify your initial speed, your final speed, and the time.
   b. Write an expression for your acceleration. Evaluate the expression. Write your answer in m/s^2.
   c. A sedan can go from 0 to 60 mi/h in about 10 s. What is the acceleration? Write your answer in m/s^2. (*Hints:* 1 mi $\approx$ 1609 m; 1 h = 3600 s.)
   d. Research Find out how quickly a car of your choice can go from 0 to 60 mi/h. Calculate the acceleration. Write your answer in m/s^2.

18. a. Critical Thinking Simplify $\dfrac{(2x^n)^2 - 1}{2x^n - 1}$, where x is an integer and n is a positive integer. (*Hint:* Factor the numerator).

   b. Use the result from part (a) to show that the value of the given expression is always an odd integer.

19. Electrical Circuits *Electrical resistance* is a measure of how a conducting path reacts to electrical current. The total resistance R (in ohms) of a string of eight party lights is given by

$$R = \dfrac{1}{\dfrac{1}{R_1} + \dfrac{1}{R_2} + \dfrac{1}{R_3} + \cdots + \dfrac{1}{R_8}}.$$

   a. Suppose each light in the string has a resistance of x ohms. Write and simplify an expression for the total resistance of the string.

   b. Suppose each light in the string has a resistance of $x + 1$ ohms. Write and simplify a new expression for the total resistance.

Multiply or divide. Write the result in simplest form.

20. $\dfrac{a + 3}{a^2 + a - 12} \div \dfrac{a^2 - 9}{a^2 + 7a + 12}$

21. $\dfrac{b^2 - 25}{(b + 5)^2} \div \dfrac{2b - 10}{4b + 20}$

22. $\dfrac{6x^3 - 6x^2}{x^4 + 5x^3} \div \dfrac{3x^2 - 15x + 12}{2x^2 + 2x - 40}$

23. $\dfrac{2x^2 - 6x}{x^2 + 18x + 81} \cdot \dfrac{9x + 81}{x^2 - 9}$

24. $\dfrac{x^2 - x - 2}{2x^2 - 5x + 2} \div \dfrac{x^2 - x - 12}{2x^2 + 5x - 3}$

25. $\dfrac{2x^2 + 5x + 2}{4x^2 - 1} \cdot \dfrac{2x^2 + x - 1}{x^2 + x - 2}$

Divide to simplify each complex fraction.

Sample: $\dfrac{\frac{a}{b}}{\frac{c}{d}} = \dfrac{a}{b} \div \dfrac{c}{d} = \dfrac{a}{b} \cdot \dfrac{d}{c} = \dfrac{ad}{bc}$

26. $\dfrac{\frac{8x^2y}{x + 1}}{\frac{6xy^2}{x + 1}}$

27. $\dfrac{\frac{3a^3b^3}{a - b}}{\frac{4ab}{b - a}}$

28. $\dfrac{\frac{3(f + g)}{5f^3g^2}}{\frac{-2f - 2g}{10}}$

29. $\dfrac{\frac{9m + 6n}{m^2n^2}}{\frac{12m + 8n}{5m^2}}$

Exercises   MIXED REVIEW

Each pair of points belongs to a direct variation. Find the missing value.

30. $(4, 2)$ and $(x, 1)$

31. $(9, 3)$ and $(27, x)$

32. $(5.5, x)$ and $(11, 2)$

33. $(x, 7)$ and $(3, 49)$

34. a. Pets About 8% of all travelers in the United States take their pets with them on vacation. This translates to about five million pets on vacation. About how many people travel annually?

   b. Dogs are the most popular animal traveling companions. About 6.2% of travelers bring their dogs. How many dogs go on vacation?

   c. Only 0.1% of travelers bring their birds. How many birds travel?

Getting Ready for Lesson 8-5
Simplify.

35. $\dfrac{3}{4} + \dfrac{2}{3}$

36. $\dfrac{2}{5} - \dfrac{3}{4}$

37. $\dfrac{1}{2} + \dfrac{5}{8}$

38. $\dfrac{6}{11} - \dfrac{3}{7}$

39. $-\dfrac{1}{3} + \dfrac{2}{9}$

40. $-\dfrac{4}{5} - \dfrac{3}{8}$

Exploration

Using Conjugates in Division

After Lesson 8-4

Expressions like $3 + \sqrt{2}$ and $3 - \sqrt{2}$ are *conjugates* of each other. When you multiply conjugates, the product is a difference of squares.

$$(3 + \sqrt{2})(3 - \sqrt{2}) = 3^2 - (\sqrt{2})^2 \qquad (3 + 2i)(3 - 2i) = 3^2 - (2i)^2$$
$$= 9 - 2 \qquad\qquad\qquad = 9 - (-4)$$
$$= 7 \qquad\qquad\qquad = 13$$

You can use conjugates to divide by an imaginary number or by an expression of either form $a + \sqrt{b}$ or $a - \sqrt{b}$.

Example

Simplify each quotient so the denominator is a rational number.

a. $\dfrac{1}{2 - i}$

$$= \dfrac{1}{2 - i} \cdot \dfrac{2 + i}{2 + i}$$

Multiply the numerator and the denominator by the conjugate of the denominator.

$$= \dfrac{2 + i}{2^2 - i^2}$$

$$= \dfrac{2 + i}{4 - (-1)}$$

$$= \dfrac{2 + i}{5} \text{ or } \dfrac{2}{5} + \dfrac{1}{5}i$$

The denominator has been *rationalized*.

b. $\dfrac{5}{4 + \sqrt{3}}$

$$= \dfrac{5}{4 + \sqrt{3}} \cdot \dfrac{4 - \sqrt{3}}{4 - \sqrt{3}}$$

$$= \dfrac{5(4 - \sqrt{3})}{4^2 - (\sqrt{3})^2}$$

$$= \dfrac{5(4 - \sqrt{3})}{16 - (3)}$$

$$= \dfrac{20 - 5\sqrt{3}}{13}$$

Simplify each expression.

1. $\dfrac{2}{3 + \sqrt{2}}$

2. $\dfrac{4}{3 - \sqrt{3}}$

3. $\dfrac{1}{3 + i}$

4. $\dfrac{2}{4 - 2i}$

5. $\dfrac{\sqrt{2}}{1 - i}$

6. $\dfrac{5}{2 + \sqrt{7}}$

7. $\dfrac{5}{3 + i}$

8. $\dfrac{\sqrt{5}}{4 - \sqrt{5}}$

9. $\dfrac{2i}{2 - i}$

10. $\dfrac{i}{1 - \sqrt{7}}$

11. a. Use a calculator to **verify** that $\dfrac{1}{2 + \sqrt{3}} = 2 - \sqrt{3}$.
  b. Demonstrate that $2 - \sqrt{3}$ is the reciprocal of $2 + \sqrt{3}$.
  c. Open-ended Find another pair of conjugates that are also reciprocals of each other.

12. a. Multiply $(x + i)$ and $(x - i)$.
  b. Use part (a) to factor $x^2 + 4$ as the product of two binomials.

13. Writing Without using a calculator, evaluate the expressions $\dfrac{1}{3 - \sqrt{7}}$ and $\dfrac{3 + \sqrt{7}}{2}$. (*Hint:* $\sqrt{7} \approx 2.65$.) Why do you think the expression $\dfrac{3 + \sqrt{7}}{2}$ is considered "simpler" than $\dfrac{1}{3 - \sqrt{7}}$? How do you think calculators have affected which expression could be called "simpler"?

What You'll Learn

• Adding and subtracting rational expressions

...And Why

To calculate the focal length of a camera lens

8-5 Adding and Subtracting Rational Expressions

WORK TOGETHER

Work with a partner.

1. Add. Simplify where possible.

a. $\dfrac{2}{x} + \dfrac{3}{x}$ b. $\dfrac{4}{3x} + \dfrac{2}{3x}$ c. $\dfrac{3c}{2c - 1} + \dfrac{5c + 1}{2c - 1}$

2. Subtract. Simplify where possible.

a. $\dfrac{4}{c} - \dfrac{4}{c}$ b. $\dfrac{3}{2x} - \dfrac{6}{2x}$ c. $\dfrac{5c}{4c + 1} - \dfrac{c + 1}{4c + 1}$

3. Explain the steps you followed in Questions 1 and 2.

4. How are adding and subtracting rational expressions similar to adding and subtracting fractions?

THINK AND DISCUSS

To produce a clear photograph, light rays must be focused on the film. The focal length of a camera lens is the distance between the lens and the point at which it focuses rays of light. A camera lens must be adjusted according to how far the subject is from the camera. When you adjust the focus, you change the distance from the lens to the film.

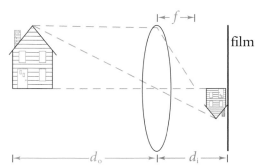

The *lens equation* is
$$\frac{1}{f} = \frac{1}{d_i} + \frac{1}{d_o},$$
where f is the focal length of the lens, d_i represents the distance from the lens to the film, and d_o is the distance from the lens to the object.

Example 1   **Relating to the Real World**

Photography Suppose an object is 15 cm from a camera lens. When the object, seen through the lens, is in focus, the lens is 10 cm from the film. Find the focal length of the lens.

$$\frac{1}{f} = \frac{1}{d_i} + \frac{1}{d_o}$$ ← Use the lens equation.

$$\frac{1}{f} = \frac{1}{10} + \frac{1}{15}$$ ← Substitute 10 for d_i and 15 for d_o.

$$= \frac{3}{30} + \frac{2}{30}$$ ← Write equivalent expressions with the least common denominator.

$$= \frac{3 + 2}{30}$$ ← Write as a single fraction.

$$= \frac{5}{30}$$ ← Add the numerators.

$$= \frac{1}{6}$$ ← Simplify.

If $\frac{1}{f} = \frac{1}{6}$, then $f = 6$. The focal length of the lens is 6 cm. ■

5. **Try This** Suppose an object is 20 cm from a camera lens. When the object is properly focused, the lens is 5 cm from the film. Find the focal length of the lens.

In the Work Together, you added and subtracted rational expressions with the same (common) denominator. To add or subtract rational expressions with different denominators, you must write each expression with a common denominator. It is easiest to use the least common denominator (LCD). To do this, find the least common multiple of the denominators.

Example 2

Find the least common multiple of $4x^2 - 36$ and $6x^2 + 36x + 54$.

Step 1: Find the prime factors of each expression.

$4x^2 - 36 = 4(x^2 - 9) = (2)(2)(x - 3)(x + 3)$

$6x^2 + 36x + 54 = 6(x^2 + 6x + 9) = (2)(3)(x + 3)(x + 3)$

Step 2: Write each prime factor the greatest number of times it appears in either expression. Simplify where possible.

$(2)(2)(3)(x - 3)(x + 3)(x + 3) = 12(x - 3)(x + 3)^2$

The least common multiple of $4x^2 - 36$ and $6x^2 + 36x + 54$ is $12(x - 3)(x + 3)^2$. ■

6. **Try This** Find the least common multiple of each pair of expressions.
   a. $3x^2 - 9x - 30$ and $6x + 30$
   b. $5x^2 + 15x + 10$ and $2x^2 - 8$

Example 3

Simplify $\dfrac{1}{x^2 + 5x + 4} + \dfrac{5x}{3x + 3}$.

$\dfrac{1}{x^2 + 5x + 4} + \dfrac{5x}{3x + 3}$

$= \dfrac{1}{(x + 1)(x + 4)} + \dfrac{5x}{3(x + 1)}$ ← Factor the denominators.

$= \dfrac{3}{3(x + 1)(x + 4)} + \dfrac{5x(x + 4)}{3(x + 1)(x + 4)}$ ← Write equivalent expressions with the LCD.

$= \dfrac{3 + 5x(x + 4)}{3(x + 1)(x + 4)}$ ← Add.

$= \dfrac{5x^2 + 20x + 3}{3(x + 1)(x + 4)}$ ← Simplify the numerator.

The sum of $\dfrac{1}{x^2 + 5x + 4}$ and $\dfrac{5x}{3x + 3}$ is $\dfrac{5x^2 + 20x + 3}{3(x + 1)(x + 4)}$.

7. Explain why the LCD in Example 3 is *not* $3(x + 4)(x + 1)(x + 1)$.

8. Try This Simplify $\dfrac{1}{x^2 - 4x - 12} + \dfrac{3x}{4x + 8}$.

Example 4

Simplify $\dfrac{7y}{5y^2 - 125} - \dfrac{4}{3y + 15}$.

$\dfrac{7y}{5y^2 - 125} - \dfrac{4}{3y + 15}$

$= \dfrac{7y}{5(y + 5)(y - 5)} - \dfrac{4}{3(y + 5)}$ ← Factor the denominators.

$= \dfrac{(3)(7y)}{(3)(5)(y + 5)(y - 5)} - \dfrac{(4)(5)(y - 5)}{(3)(5)(y + 5)(y - 5)}$ ← Write equivalent expressions.

$= \dfrac{(3)(7y) - (4)(5)(y - 5)}{(3)(5)(y + 5)(y - 5)}$ ← Subtract.

$= \dfrac{y + 100}{15(y + 5)(y - 5)}$ ← Simplify.

The difference between $\dfrac{7y}{5y^2 - 125}$ and $\dfrac{4}{3y + 15}$ is $\dfrac{y + 100}{15(y + 15)(y - 5)}$.

9. Try This Simplify each expression.

a. $\dfrac{-2}{3x^2 + 36x + 105} - \dfrac{3x}{6x + 15}$

b. $\dfrac{x}{3x^2 - 9x + 6} - \dfrac{2x + 1}{3x^2 + 3x - 6}$

Exercises   ON YOUR OWN

Simplify each expression.

1. $\dfrac{1}{2x} + \dfrac{1}{2x}$

2. $\dfrac{d - 3}{2d + 1} - \dfrac{d - 1}{2d + 1}$

3. $\dfrac{c + 2}{c^2} + \dfrac{c}{c^2}$

4. $\dfrac{-2}{x} - \dfrac{1}{x}$

5. $\dfrac{3g + 1}{3g} + \dfrac{-1}{3g}$

6. $\dfrac{-5y}{2y - 1} - \dfrac{y + 3}{2y - 1}$

Find the least common multiple of each pair of polynomials.

7. $(2x - 3)(x + 1)$ and $(2x - 3)(x + 2)$

8. $9(x + 2)(2x - 1)$ and $3(x + 2)$

9. $x^2 - 1$ and $x + 1$

10. $x^2 - 1$ and $x^2 + 2x + 1$

11. $(x - 2)(x + 3)$ and $10(x + 3)^2$

12. $12x^2 - 6x + 126$ and $18x - 63$

13. $5y^2 - 80$ and $y + 4$

14. $x^2 - 3x - 10$ and $2x + 10$

Find the LCD of each pair of fractions.

15. $\frac{1}{3t}; \frac{1}{5t^2}$

16. $\frac{x}{2}; \frac{3x}{8}$

17. $\frac{4}{3h^2}; \frac{2h}{h^3}$

18. $\frac{2k}{k^7}; \frac{7}{k^{15}}$

19. $\frac{4}{y + 2}; \frac{3}{y - 1}$

20. $\frac{z}{2z + 1}; \frac{1}{z}$

21. $\frac{1}{k + 2}; \frac{3k}{k^2 - 4}$

22. $\frac{5}{y - 2}; \frac{y + 2}{2y + 3}$

Add or subtract. Simplify where possible.

23. $\frac{3}{4x} - \frac{2}{x^2}$

24. $\frac{3}{x + 1} + \frac{x}{x - 1}$

25. $\frac{2x}{x^2 - 1} - \frac{1}{x^2}$

26. $\frac{4}{x^2 - 9} + \frac{7}{x + 3}$

27. $\frac{x + 2}{x - 1} - \frac{x - 3}{2x + 1}$

28. $\frac{5x}{x^2 - x - 6} - \frac{4}{x^2 + 4x + 4}$

29. $\frac{x}{2x^2 - x} + \frac{1}{2x}$

30. $3x + \frac{x^2 + 5x}{x^2 - 2}$

31. Open-ended Write two rational expressions with a sum of $\frac{x - 2}{x + 4}$.

32. Writing Explain how factoring is used when adding or subtracting rational expressions. Include an example in your explanation.

33. Electricity The total resistance R for a parallel circuit with three bulbs is

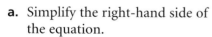

$$R = \frac{1}{\frac{1}{R_1} + \frac{1}{R_2} + \frac{1}{R_3}}.$$

   a. Simplify the right-hand side of the equation.
   b. Find the total resistance R of the parallel circuit at the right.

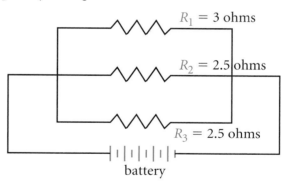

$R_1 = 3$ ohms

$R_2 = 2.5$ ohms

$R_3 = 2.5$ ohms

battery

34. Physics A magnifying glass focuses on type the same way the lens of a camera focuses on an object. Use the lens equation $\frac{1}{f} = \frac{1}{d_i} + \frac{1}{d_o}$, where d_i is the distance from the lens to your eye and d_o is the distance from the lens to the page of type.
   a. Suppose that, when the type is in focus, the magnifying glass is 8 cm from the page and 6 cm from your eye. Find the focal length of the magnifying glass.
   b. Suppose that, when the type is in focus, the magnifying glass is x cm from the page and $(2x + 1)$ cm from your eye. Find the focal length of the magnifying glass.

35. Standardized Test Prep Which graphing calculator display represents

the function $y = \dfrac{x}{x+1} + \dfrac{1}{x-1}$?

A.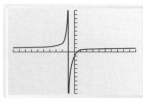

B.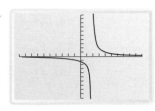

C.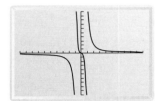

D.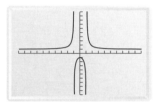

E.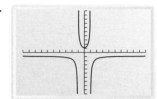

Chapter Project **Find Out by Solving**

A popular size of scuba-diving tank is 71.2 ft³. The 71.2 ft³ is the volume that the compressed air inside the tank would occupy at a normal surface pressure of 1 atm. The air in the tank is at a pressure of about 2250 lb/in.², so the tank itself can have a volume much less than 71.2 ft³.

• How large does the tank need to be to hold 71.2 ft³? (*Hint:* Use Boyle's Law: $PV = k$. Remember that 1 atm = 14.7 lb/in.².)

Exercises   M I X E D   R E V I E W

Find each sum or difference.

36. $\begin{bmatrix} 0.4 & -5.2 \\ 3.4 & -1.7 \end{bmatrix} - \begin{bmatrix} -3.1 & -4.8 \\ -3.9 & 1.5 \end{bmatrix}$ **37.** $\begin{bmatrix} 12 & -21 \\ -10 & 17 \end{bmatrix} - \begin{bmatrix} 32 & -15 \\ 23 & 14 \end{bmatrix}$ **38.** $\begin{bmatrix} 5 & 3 \\ -9 & 1 \end{bmatrix} + \begin{bmatrix} -3 & 6 \\ 0 & 7 \end{bmatrix}$

39. a. Biology Two robins have four eggs in each clutch. They have three clutches each year. Each chick can mate the spring after it hatches. Write a function to model the maximum number of descendants of the original robins that will hatch during year *n*.

   b. How many years would it take for the original pair to have 60 descendants?

Getting Ready for Lesson 8-6

Solve each proportion.

40. $\dfrac{3}{4} = \dfrac{x}{16}$ **41.** $\dfrac{2}{5} = \dfrac{3}{x}$ **42.** $\dfrac{x}{2} = \dfrac{5}{8}$ **43.** $\dfrac{6}{x} = \dfrac{3}{7}$

What You'll Learn

- Solving rational equations

...And Why

To solve cost-per-unit problems

8-6 Solving Rational Equations

WORK TOGETHER

Does 2 = 1? Justin seems to think so!

Work with a partner. Study Justin's "proof" below.

$$a = b$$
$$a^2 = b^2$$
$$a^2 = ab$$
$$a^2 - b^2 = ab - b^2$$
$$(a - b)(a + b) = b(a - b)$$
$$\frac{(a - b)(a + b)}{a - b} = \frac{b(a - b)}{a - b}$$
$$a + b = b$$
$$b + b = b$$
$$2b = b$$
$$2 = 1$$

1. a. Describe each step of Justin's proof.
   b. **Critical Thinking** Which step leads to this incorrect conclusion? Explain. (*Hint:* $a - b = 0$.)
   c. Why is it important that you check all solutions to an equation?
2. a. **Justify** each step of the solution to $\frac{1}{x^2} = \frac{2}{x}$.

$$\frac{1}{x^2} = \frac{2}{x}$$
$$2x^2 = x$$
$$2x^2 - x = 0$$
$$x(2x - 1) = 0$$
$$x = 0 \text{ or } 2x - 1 = 0$$
$$x = 0 \text{ or } \tfrac{1}{2}$$

   b. Check each solution. What do you notice? Explain.

THINK AND DISCUSS

You can use many properties of fractions to solve rational equations. For example, if two rational expressions are equal, you can solve the equation as you would a proportion, using cross products.

If $\frac{a}{b} = \frac{c}{d}$ ($b, d \neq 0$), then, by cross-multiplication, $ad = bc$.

Example 1

Solve $\frac{5}{2x - 2} = \frac{15}{x^2 - 1}$. Check each solution.

$$\frac{5}{2x - 2} = \frac{15}{x^2 - 1}$$

$5(x^2 - 1) = 15(2x - 2)$ ⟵ Cross multiply.

$5x^2 - 5 = 30x - 30$

$5x^2 - 30x + 25 = 0$ ⟵ Write in standard form.

$x^2 - 6x + 5 = 0$ ⟵ Divide each side by 5.

$(x - 1)(x - 5) = 0$ ⟵ Factor.

$x = 1 \text{ or } x = 5$

When $x = 1$, both denominators above are zero. The original equation is undefined at $x = 1$. So, $x = 1$ is not a solution.

Check: $\frac{5}{2x - 2} = \frac{15}{x^2 - 1}$

$\frac{5}{2(5) - 2} = \frac{15}{5^2 - 1}$ ⟵ Substitute 5 for x.

$\frac{5}{8} = \frac{5}{8}$ ✔

The fractions are equivalent, so $x = 5$.

3. Try This Solve each equation. Check each solution.

a. $\dfrac{-4}{5(x + 2)} = \dfrac{3}{x + 2}$

b. $\dfrac{-2}{x^2 - 2} = \dfrac{2}{x - 3}$

When an equation has a sum or difference of two rational expressions, you can use the least common denominator (LCD) to simplify the problem.

Example 2

Solve $\frac{1}{2x} - \frac{2}{5x} = \frac{1}{2}$.

The least common multiple of the denominators ($2x$, $5x$, and 2) is $10x$.

$$\frac{1}{2x} - \frac{2}{5x} = \frac{1}{2}$$

$10x\left(\dfrac{1}{2x} - \dfrac{2}{5x}\right) = 10x\left(\dfrac{1}{2}\right)$ ⟵ Multiply each side by $10x$.

$\dfrac{10x}{2x} - \dfrac{10x(2)}{5x} = \dfrac{10x}{2}$ ⟵ Distribute.

$\dfrac{^5\cancel{10x}}{_1\cancel{2x}} - \dfrac{^2\cancel{10x}(2)}{_1\cancel{5x}} = \dfrac{^5\cancel{10x}}{\cancel{2}_1}$ ⟵ Divide out common factors.

$5 - 4 = 5x$ ⟵ Simplify.

$x = \dfrac{1}{5}$

The solution is $x = \frac{1}{5}$.

4. Try This Solve each equation.

a. $\dfrac{4}{x} - \dfrac{3}{x + 1} = 1$

b. $\dfrac{1}{x - 2} + \dfrac{-3x}{x^2 - 4} = 6$

Example 3   Relating to the Real World

Business Your company makes ecology posters. The office expenses are $54,000 a year. The materials for each poster cost $.28. The company can produce and sell twice as many posters next year as this year. This will reduce the per-poster cost by $1.80. How many posters are you producing this year?

Define x = number of posters produced this year
         $2x$ = number of posters produced next year
         $0.28x + 54{,}000$ = total cost this year
         $0.28(2x) + 54{,}000$ = total cost next year

Relate $\dfrac{\text{per-poster cost}}{\text{this year}} - \dfrac{\text{per-poster cost}}{\text{next year}} = \$1.80$

Write $\dfrac{0.28x + 54{,}000}{x} - \dfrac{0.28(2x) + 54{,}000}{2x} = 1.80$

The LCD is $2x$.

$$(2x)\dfrac{0.28x + 54{,}000}{x} - (2x)\dfrac{0.28(2x) + 54{,}000}{2x} = (2x)1.80 \qquad \longleftarrow \text{Multiply.}$$
$$(0.56x + 108{,}000) - (0.56x + 54{,}000) = 3.6x \qquad \longleftarrow \text{Simplify.}$$
$$0.56x + 108{,}000 - 0.56x - 54{,}000 = 3.6x$$
$$108{,}000 - 54{,}000 = 3.6x$$
$$54{,}000 = 3.6x$$
$$15{,}000 = x \qquad \longleftarrow \text{Solve for } x.$$

You are producing 15,000 posters this year.

Once you know how to solve rational equations, you can solve problems about rates of production.

Example 4 **Relating to the Real World**

Business Suppose Tran can stuff envelopes three times as fast as his friend Georgia. They have to stuff 5000 envelopes for a fund-raiser. Working together, Tran and Georgia can complete the job in four hours. How long would it take each of them if they worked alone?

Define

	Time (hr)	Rate (envelopes per hour)
Tran	x	$\dfrac{5000}{x}$
Georgia	$3x$	$\dfrac{5000}{3x}$
Combined	4	$\dfrac{5000}{4} = 1250$

Relate   Tran's rate + Georgia's rate = combined rate

Write $\dfrac{5000}{x}$ + $\dfrac{5000}{3x}$ =   1250

$3x\left(\dfrac{5000}{x} + \dfrac{5000}{3x}\right) = 3x(1250)$ ⟵ Multiply each side by 3x.

$\dfrac{(3x)(5000)}{x} + \dfrac{(3x)(5000)}{3x} = 3x(1250)$

$15{,}000 + 5{,}000 = 3750x$ ⟵ Simplify.

$20{,}000 = 3750x$

$5.33 \approx x$ ⟵ Divide each side by 3750.

Tran could stuff 5000 envelopes in about 5.33 h. Georgia could stuff 5000 envelopes in 3(5.33) or about 16 h.

5. **Try This** Suppose Maria can stuff envelopes twice as fast as her friend Paco. Together, they can stuff 6750 envelopes in 4.5 h. How long would it take each of them working alone?

6. *Critical Thinking* Explain why the equation $\dfrac{x}{x-2} = \dfrac{1}{2} + \dfrac{2}{x-2}$ has no solution.

Exercises   **O N   Y O U R   O W N**

Solve each equation. Check your solutions.

1. $\dfrac{x}{5} = \dfrac{x+3}{8}$

2. $\dfrac{3}{x} = \dfrac{12}{x+7}$

3. $\dfrac{8}{x} = \dfrac{6}{2x-2}$

4. $\dfrac{1}{4} - x = \dfrac{x}{8}$

5. $\dfrac{2}{x-1} = \dfrac{x+4}{3}$

6. $\dfrac{1}{x} + \dfrac{1}{2} = \dfrac{x+4}{2x}$

7. $\dfrac{3}{x+1} = \dfrac{1}{x^2+1}$

8. $\dfrac{1}{x} - \dfrac{1}{3} = \dfrac{6}{x^2}$

9. $\dfrac{4}{2x-3} = \dfrac{x}{5}$

10. $\dfrac{5}{2x-2} = \dfrac{15}{x^2-1}$

11. $\dfrac{10}{6x+7} = \dfrac{6}{2x+9}$

12. $\dfrac{2}{3x-5} = \dfrac{4}{x-15}$

13. **Woodworking** A tapered cylinder is made by decreasing the radius of a rod continuously as you move from one end to the other. The rate at which it tapers is the *taper per foot.* You can calculate the taper per foot using the formula below.

$$T = \frac{24(R - r)}{L}$$

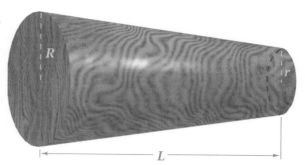

The lengths R, r, and L are measured in inches.
   a. Solve this equation for L.
   b. Find L if $R = 4$ in., $r = 3$ in., and $T = 0.75, 0.85$ and 0.95.

Solve each equation.

14. $\frac{3}{2x} - \frac{5}{3x} = 2$

15. $\frac{5x}{4} - \frac{3}{x} = \frac{1}{4}$

16. $\frac{2}{y} + \frac{1}{2} = \frac{5}{2y}$

17. $x + \frac{6}{x} = -5$

18. $\frac{15}{x} + \frac{9x - 7}{x + 2} = 9$

19. $\frac{2}{x + 2} - \frac{1}{x} = \frac{-4}{x(x + 2)}$

20. $\frac{1}{b + 1} + \frac{1}{b - 1} = \frac{2}{b^2 - 1}$

21. $c - \frac{c}{3} + \frac{c}{5} = 26$

22. $\frac{2}{x - 3} - \frac{4}{x + 3} = \frac{8}{x^2 - 9}$

23. $\frac{1}{8} + \frac{5x}{x + 2} = \frac{5}{2}$

24. $\frac{1}{x - 5} = \frac{x}{x^2 - 25}$

25. $\frac{k}{k + 1} + \frac{k}{k - 2} = 2$

26. **Test Scores** On the first four tests of the term your average is 84%. You think you can score 96% on each of the remaining tests. How many consecutive test scores of 96% would you need to bring your average up to 90% for the term?

Solve each equation for the given variable.

27. $m = \frac{2E}{V^2}$; E

28. $\frac{c}{E} - \frac{1}{mc} = 0$; E

29. $\frac{m}{F} = \frac{1}{a}$; F

30. $\frac{1}{c} - \frac{c}{a^2 - b^2} = 0$; c

31. $\frac{\ell}{T^2} = \frac{g}{4\pi^2}$; T

32. $\frac{q}{m} = \frac{2V}{B^2 r^2}$; B

33. **Open-ended** Write a rational equation that has the same solution as the question in the cartoon.

34. For some numbers A and B,
    $$\frac{18x - 1}{x^2 + x - 6} = \frac{A}{x - 2} + \frac{B}{x + 3}.$$

   a. Simplify the equation to an equivalent linear equation.
   b. **Critical Thinking** Write a system of linear equations in A and B by using the coefficients of the linear terms and the remaining constants. Solve for A and B.

35. Anita and Fran have volunteered to contact every member of their organization by phone to inform them of an upcoming event. Fran can complete the calls in 6 days if she works alone. Anita can complete them in 4 days. How long will it take them working together?

The Family Circus *by Bil Keane*

4-25

"What's 129 divided by 4?"

36. Travel A plane flies from New York to Chicago (≈ 700 miles) at a speed of 360 mi/h.
   a. The speed s of the plane is given by $\frac{d}{t}$ where d represents the distance and t is the time. Solve the equation $s = \frac{d}{t}$ for t.
   b. Find the time for the trip.
   c. On the return trip from Chicago to New York, a tailwind helps the plane move faster. Write an expression for the speed of the plane on the return trip. Let x represent the speed of the tail wind.
   d. The total flying time for the round trip is 3.5 h. Write a rational equation for the sum of the flying times. Find the speed x of the tail wind.

37. Field Trip You are planning a school field trip to a local theater. It costs $60 to rent the bus. Each theater ticket costs $5.50.
   a. Write a function $c(x)$ to represent the cost per student if x students sign up.
   b. How many students must sign up if the cost is to be no more than $10 per student?

38. Manufacturing The average hourly wage $H(x)$ of workers in the manufacturing industries is modeled by the function $H(x) = \frac{16.24x}{0.062x + 39.42}$, where x represents the number of years since 1970.
   a. In what year does the model predict that wages will be $25/h for manufacturing workers?
   b. **Critical Thinking** Do you think that your prediction is reasonable? Explain your answer.

39. Fuel Economy Suppose you drive an average of 15,000 mi per year, and your car gets 24 miles per gallon. Suppose gasoline costs $1.50 a gallon.
   a. How much money per year do you spend on gasoline?
   b. You plan to trade in your car for one that gets x more miles per gallon. Write an expression to represent the new yearly cost.
   c. Write an expression to represent your savings.
   d. Suppose you save $187.50 a year with the new car. How many miles per gallon does the new car get?

40. Landscape Designer Suppose you want to double the area of the patio shown at the right. Find the increase x of both the length and the width of the patio.

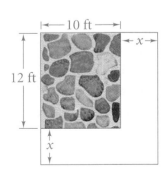

41. Open-ended Write a rational equation that has the following.
   a. one solution   **b.** two solutions   **c.** no real solution

The rate at which a scuba diver uses air in the tank depends on many factors, such as the diver's age and lung capacity. Another important factor is the depth of the dive.

A scuba diver continues to breathe normally while descending. Every time the diver inhales, the tank delivers enough air to inflate the diver's lungs. This means that the amount of air delivered by the tank must increase with the depth in order to withstand the increasing pressure. At greater depths, the diver uses the air in the tank more quickly. The amount of time the air will last is inversely proportional to the pressure at the depth of the dive.

- Suppose a tank has enough air to last 60 min at the surface. How long will it last at a depth of 99 ft? (The pressure is 4 atm, or 4 times as great.) Make a table showing how long the air will last at 10 ft, 20 ft, 33 ft, 40 ft, 50 ft, and 66 ft.

Exercises   M I X E D   R E V I E W

Find the inverse of each function.

42. $y = 3^x$
43. $y = 5(x - 3)^2$
44. $y = 8x^4 + 3$
45. $y = 5^x + 2$

46. *Coordinate Geometry* A quadrilateral has vertices at $A(5, 2)$, $B(8, 1)$, $C(9, 5)$, and $D(6, 6)$. Use matrices to find the image of the vertices of the quadrilateral after translating it left 3 units and down 2 units.

Getting Ready for Lesson 8-7
Find each probability for one roll of a standard number cube.

47. $P(4)$
48. $P(\text{odd number})$
49. $P(\text{prime number})$
50. $P(\text{not a } 5)$

Exercises   C H E C K P O I N T

Simplify each expression.

1. $\dfrac{6x^2 - 3x}{2x^2 + 5x - 3}$
2. $\dfrac{2x + 5}{x - 4} \cdot \dfrac{x^2 - 16}{x + 4}$
3. $\dfrac{3x}{x^2 + 3x + 2} - \dfrac{5}{x + 2}$
4. $\dfrac{4x^2}{6x - 2} \div \dfrac{x}{9x^2 - 1}$

Solve each equation.

5. $\dfrac{3}{x} = 4x + 1$
6. $\dfrac{5}{x - 1} = \dfrac{4}{x}$
7. $\dfrac{x}{6} + \dfrac{x}{3} = 16$
8. $8 = \dfrac{2x + 7}{x - 1}$

9. *Writing* Explain how you can have an extraneous solution to a rational equation. Include an example of an equation with an extraneous solution.

8-7 Probability of Multiple Events

What You'll Learn

• Identifying
  independent and
  mutually exclusive
  events

• Finding probabilities
  of multiple events

...And Why

To solve problems about radio
show call-ins

What You'll Need

• 2 number cubes

QUICK REVIEW

Probability of an event
$= \dfrac{\text{number of desired outcomes}}{\text{number of possible outcomes}}$

W O R K   T O G E T H E R

Work with a partner to analyze the game "Primarily Odd."

Partner A: Roll two standard number cubes. If the
sum is either odd *or* a prime number, score a point.

Partner B: Roll two standard number cubes. If the
sum is both odd *and* a prime number, score a point.

Alternate turns rolling the number cubes.

1. **a.** List all the possible outcomes of rolling two number cubes.
   b. How many outcomes result in an odd sum? Calculate the
      probability of getting an odd sum.
   c. How many outcomes result in a prime sum? Calculate the
      probability of getting a prime sum.

2. **Predict** which partner is more likely to score points in "Primarily
   Odd." **Justify** your reasoning.

3. Play the game with your partner. Take 10 turns each. Keep track of
   each player's score. How do your results compare with the prediction
   you made in Question 2?

T H I N K   A N D   D I S C U S S

Finding P(A and B)

When the occurrence of one event affects the probability of a second event,
the two events are **dependent.** When the occurrence of one event does *not*
affect the probability of a second event, the two events are **independent.**

4. Classify each pair of events as *dependent* or *independent*.
   a. Roll a number cube. Then toss a coin.
   b. Pick a flower from a garden. Then pick another flower from the
      same garden.
   c. Select a marble from a bag of marbles. Replace it. Select another
      marble from the bag.

You multiply to find the probability of two independent events occurring.

> ### Probability of *A* and *B*
> ....
> If *A* and *B* are independent events, then $P(A \text{ and } B) = P(A) \cdot P(B)$.
> **Example:** If $P(A) = \frac{1}{2}$, $P(B) = \frac{1}{3}$, then $P(A \text{ and } B) = \frac{1}{2} \cdot \frac{1}{3} = \frac{1}{6}$

WKW Radio Statistics

Hour	Calls Received That Hour
7:00 A.M.	125
3:00 P.M.	200

Example 1 **Relating to the Real World**

Radio Suppose your favorite radio station is running a promotional campaign. Each hour, four randomly selected callers get to make two song selections each. You call the station after 7:00 A.M. and again after 3:00 P.M. What is the probability that you will be one of the four callers both times you call?

Define Event A = you are one of the four callers after 7:00 A.M.
Event B = you are one of the four callers after 3:00 P.M.

$$P(A) = \frac{4}{125}$$
$$P(B) = \frac{4}{200}$$

Relate probability is probability times probability
of A and B of A of B

Write $P(A \text{ and } B) = \quad P(A) \quad \cdot \quad P(B)$
$P(A \text{ and } B) = \frac{4}{125} \cdot \frac{4}{200}$

$\qquad\qquad = \frac{16}{25,000}$ ⟵ **Multiply.**

$\qquad\qquad = \frac{2}{3125}$ ⟵ **Simplify.**

The probability of being one of the four randomly selected callers both times you call is $\frac{2}{3125}$.

5. **Try This** Suppose the radio station changes the promotional campaign. Now they take five randomly selected callers each hour.
   a. Find the probability that you will be one of the five callers after 7 A.M.; after 3 P.M.
   b. Find the probability that you will be one of the five callers both times you call.

Finding P(A or B)

When two events cannot happen at the same time, the events are **mutually exclusive.** Rolling a 5 and rolling a number less than 3 on a number cube are mutually exclusive events, because a number cannot be 5 and less than 3 at the same time.

QUICK REVIEW

If A and B are mutually exclusive events, then
P(A and B) = 0.

6. Are the events mutually exclusive? Explain.
a. on a number cube: rolling a 2; rolling a 3
b. on a number cube: rolling an even number; rolling a multiple of 3

You need to determine whether event A and event B are mutually exclusive before you find the probability of A or B.

Probability of A or B

If A and B are mutually exclusive events, then

$$P(A \text{ or } B) = P(A) + P(B).$$

If A and B are not mutually exclusive events, then

$$P(A \text{ or } B) = P(A) + P(B) - P(A \text{ and } B).$$

For many games, a player must rely on his or her knowledge of probability to find a winning strategy.

Example 2 Relating to the Real World

Games Suppose you are playing a game with five number cubes. You roll the cubes and may keep any of the numbers rolled. You can roll the other cubes one or two more times. After two rolls, you have kept the numbers shown below. On the final roll of the remaining cube, you want to roll a 1 or a 6 to complete the sequence. Find $P(1 \text{ or } 6)$.

Since you cannot roll one number cube and get both a 1 and a 6, these events are mutually exclusive.

$$
\begin{aligned}
P(1 \text{ or } 6) &= P(1) + P(6) \quad \longleftarrow \text{ Use the } P(A \text{ or } B) \text{ rule for} \\
&= \tfrac{1}{6} + \tfrac{1}{6} \qquad\qquad\quad \text{mutually exclusive events.} \\
&= \tfrac{2}{6} \\
&= \tfrac{1}{3}
\end{aligned}
$$

The probability of rolling a 1 or a 6 is $\tfrac{1}{3}$.

7. Try This Suppose after two rolls you have kept four number cubes, showing two 3's and two 4's. What is the probability that you will roll a 3 or a 4 with your remaining cube?

When two events are *not* mutually exclusive, you need to subtract the probability of the common outcomes.

| Example 3 | **Relating to the Real World** |

Nutrition Suppose you reach into the fruit bowl and select a piece of fruit at random. What is the probability that the piece of fruit is an apple or green?

P(apple or green)

$= P$(apple) $+ P$(green) $- P$(apple and green) ⟵ not mutually exclusive events

$= \frac{5}{9} + \frac{3}{9} - \frac{2}{9}$

$= \frac{6}{9}$

≈ 0.667, or 66.7%

The probability of picking a piece of fruit that is an apple or green is $\frac{2}{3}$, or approximately 66.7%.

8. Try This C and D are not mutually exclusive events. Copy and complete the table to find each missing probability.

$P(C)$	$P(D)$	$P(C$ and $D)$	$P(C$ or $D)$
$\frac{4}{9}$	$\frac{4}{9}$	■	$\frac{5}{9}$
$\frac{1}{2}$	$\frac{1}{3}$	$\frac{1}{4}$	■
$\frac{2}{3}$	$\frac{3}{5}$	■	$\frac{13}{15}$
$\frac{3}{7}$	$\frac{1}{4}$	$\frac{1}{8}$	■

Exercises ON YOUR OWN

State whether the events are *dependent* or *independent*.

1. a month is randomly selected; a number from 1 to 30 is randomly selected

2. a month is randomly selected; a day of that month is randomly selected

3. a letter of the alphabet is randomly selected; one of the remaining letters is randomly selected

4. the color of a car is randomly selected; the type of transmission is randomly selected

Q and R are independent events. Find the missing probability.

5. $P(Q) = \frac{1}{4}$, $P(R) = \frac{2}{3}$. Find $P(Q$ and $R)$.

6. $P(Q) = \frac{12}{17}$, $P(R) = \frac{3}{8}$. Find $P(Q$ and $R)$.

7. $P(Q) = \frac{7}{11}$, $P(Q$ and $R) = \frac{6}{11}$. Find $P(R)$.

8. $P(R) = \frac{1}{3}$, $P(Q$ and $R) = \frac{2}{x}$. Find $P(Q)$.

Statistics The graph at the right shows the types of jobs held by people in the United States. Find each probability.

9. a person is in a service occupation

10. a person is in service or support

11. a person is not in farming, fishing, or forestry

12. a person is neither an operator nor a laborer nor in precision production

13. Suppose you select a number from 1 to 100 at random.
   a. What is the probability that you select a multiple of 5? a multiple of 4? a multiple of 3? Are these events mutually exclusive? Explain.
   b. What is the probability that you select a multiple of 5 and 4? a multiple of 5 and 3? a multiple of 4 and 3?
   c. What is the probability that you select a multiple of 5, 4 and 3?

U.S. Employment, by Occupation

Source: *U.S. Bureau of Labor Statistics*

Two standard number cubes are tossed. State whether or not the events are mutually exclusive. Then find $P(A)$, $P(B)$, and $P(A \text{ or } B)$.

14. the sum is a prime number; the sum is less than 4

15. the numbers are equal; the sum is odd

16. the product is greater than 20; the product is a multiple of 3

S and T are mutually exclusive events. Find each probability.

17. $P(S) = \frac{5}{8}$, $P(T) = \frac{1}{8}$. Find $P(S \text{ and } T)$ and $P(S \text{ or } T)$.

18. $P(S) = \frac{3}{5}$, $P(T) = \frac{1}{3}$. Find $P(S \text{ and } T)$ and $P(S \text{ or } T)$.

19. $P(S) = \frac{1}{10}$, $P(S \text{ or } T) = \frac{1}{2}$. Find $P(T)$.   **20.** $P(T) = \frac{3}{x}$, $P(S \text{ or } T) = \frac{6}{x}$. Find $P(S)$.

21. A multiple-choice test has four choices for each answer.
   a. What is the probability that a random guess on a question will yield the correct answer?
   b. You need to make a random guess on three of the ten test questions. What is the probability that you will answer all three correctly?

22. H and J are not mutually exclusive events. Copy and complete the table to find each missing probability.

$P(H)$	$P(J)$	$P(H \text{ and } J)$	$P(H \text{ or } J)$
$\frac{7}{11}$	$\frac{3}{11}$		$\frac{9}{11}$
$\frac{1}{2}$		$\frac{1}{4}$	$\frac{2}{3}$
	$\frac{2}{5}$	$\frac{1}{5}$	$\frac{2}{3}$
$\frac{2}{x}$	$\frac{3}{2x}$	$\frac{1}{x}$	

23. Suppose you have five books in your book bag. Three are novels, one is a biography, and one is a poetry book. Today you grab one out of your bag without looking and return it later. Tomorrow you do the same thing. What is the probability that you grab a novel both days?

24. *Open-ended* Describe two events that are not mutually exclusive. Estimate the probability of both events occurring.

One student from each school at the right is chosen at random to be on a committee. Find each probability.

25. a junior from School A and a senior from School B

26. two juniors

27. an underclassman (freshman or sophomore) from School A and a senior from School B

School A

Freshman	Sophomore	Junior	Senior
30%	27%	25%	18%

School B

Freshman	Sophomore	Junior	Senior
28%	28%	24%	20%

28. *Critical Thinking* Tatyana and Samuel each have $x + 2$ pens in the pocket of their backpacks.
  a. Tatyana has 2 blue pens. Find the probability that she pulls out a blue pen at random.
  b. Samuel has $x - 3$ blue pens. Find the probability that he pulls out a blue pen at random.
  c. Find the probability that both Tatyana and Samuel pull out blue pens at random.
  d. Find the probability that either Tatyana or Samuel pulls out a blue pen at random.

Exercises **MIXED REVIEW**

Find the inverse of each matrix. If the matrix has no inverse, write *no inverse*.

29. $\begin{bmatrix} 6 & 1 & -3 \\ 2 & 0 & 1 \\ -1 & 1 & 0 \end{bmatrix}$ **30.** $\begin{bmatrix} -2 & 3 & 1 \\ -3 & 1 & -1 \end{bmatrix}$ **31.** $\begin{bmatrix} 5 & 8 \\ 3 & 1 \end{bmatrix}$

32. *Social Studies* About half of U.S. adults trace their family tree as a part-time hobby. Of those, 94% have discussed family history with relatives, 57% have written a family history or created a family tree, and 45% have visited an ancestral home or country.
  a. In a group of 35 adults, about how many trace their family tree?
  b. Use your answer to part (a). About how many have discussed family history with relatives? About how many have visited an ancestral home or country?

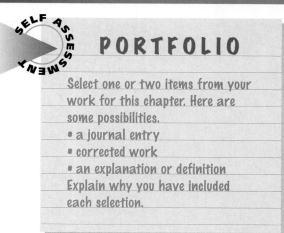

Finishing the Chapter Project

UNDER PRESSURE

Find Out questions on pages 355, 369, 380, and 387 should help you complete your project. Design a poster or brochure explaining what you learned about scuba-diving safety in this chapter. Use graphs, tables, and examples to support your conclusions.

Reflect and Revise

Work with a classmate to review your poster or brochure. Check that your graphs and examples are correct and that your explanations are clear. If you are unsure about something, you may want to refer to a book on scuba diving. Several good ones are listed below.

Discuss your poster or brochure with an adult who works in the area of sports safety, such as a lifeguard, coach, physical education teacher, or recreation director. Ask for their suggestions for improvements.

Follow Up

What other safety issues must scuba divers consider? Ask a scuba diver or refer to the books below to find other things a scuba diver must consider to dive safely.

For More Information

Balder, A.P. *The Complete Manual of Skin Diving.* New York: Macmillan, 1968.

Culliney, John L. and Edward S. Crockett. *Exploring Underwater.* San Francisco: Sierra Club Books, 1980.

Marcante, Duilio. *This Is Diving.* Dobbs Ferry, New York: Sheriday House, 1976.

Smith, Robert W., ed. *The New Science of Skin and Scuba Diving,* Sixth Edition. Piscataway, New Jersey: New Century Publishers, 1985.

Key Terms

asymptote (p. 357)
branch (p. 357)
constant of variation (p. 351)
continuous (p. 364)
dependent (p. 388)
discontinuous (p. 364)
hole (p. 366)

independent (p. 388)
inverse variation (p. 351)
mutually exclusive (p. 390)
rational function (p. 363)
removable discontinuity
    (p. 366)
simplest form (p. 371)

How am I doing?

- State three ideas from this chapter that you think are important. Explain your choices.
  - Describe what you can tell about the graph of a rational function without graphing it.

Exploring Inverse Variation   8-1

An equation in two variables of the form $y = \frac{k}{x}$ or $xy = k$, where $k \neq 0$, is an **inverse variation.** The **constant of variation** is k.

Each point is from a model for inverse variation. Find each constant of variation.

1. $(4, 1)$ **2.** $\left(7, \frac{1}{2}\right)$ **3.** $(9, 6)$ **4.** $(4, 6)$ **5.** $(0.2, 4)$

6. a. Exercise You buy a year's membership at a gym for $200. Each time you go, the average cost per visit decreases. Write a function to model this relationship.

b. A visitor's pass for a day is $10. How many times do you have to go to the gym to make membership the better deal?

Graphing Inverse Variations   8-2

The graph of an inverse variation has two parts. Each part is called a **branch.** The **asymptotes** of a graph are lines the graph approaches. For a vertical asymptote $x = k$, k is not included in the domain of the function.

The graph of $y = \frac{k}{x - b} + c$ is a translation of $y = \frac{k}{x}$ that has moved b units horizontally and c units vertically. It has a vertical asymptote at $x = b$ and a horizontal asymptote at $y = c$.

Write the equation for a translation of $y = \frac{4}{x}$ with the given asymptotes.

7. $x = 0, y = 3$ **8.** $x = -1, y = 0$ **9.** $x = 2, y = 2$ **10.** $x = -3, y = -4$

Graph each function.

11. $y = \frac{1}{x}$ **12.** $y = -\frac{2}{x^2}$ **13.** $y = -\frac{1}{x} - 4$ **14.** $y = \frac{3}{x - 2} + 1$

The graph of any polynomial function is a **continuous** curve. The graph of a rational function may be **discontinuous.** A rational function is discontinuous at the values of x for which the rational expression is undefined.

- The function $f(x) = \frac{g(x)}{h(x)}$ is discontinuous if $h(x) = 0$. If $g(x)$ and $h(x)$ have no common factors, then $f(x)$ has a vertical asymptote when $h(x) = 0$.

- $f(x)$ has, at most, one horizontal asymptote.

Rational functions that have a common linear factor in the numerator and denominator have a **removable discontinuity**, or **hole,** in their graphs.

Classify each function as continuous or discontinuous. If discontinuous, give the value(s) of x for which the function is undefined.

15. $y = \frac{5}{x + 7}$
16. $y = \frac{x - 1}{(x + 2)(x - 1)}$
17. $y = \frac{3x}{x^2 - x}$

Sketch the graph of each rational function.

18. $y = \frac{1}{x + 3}$
19. $y = \frac{x(x - 2)}{x - 2}$
20. $y = \frac{x}{(x + 1)(x - 1)}$

21. Standardized Test Prep Which function has a removable discontinuity at $x = 3$?

A. $y = \frac{1}{x + 3}$ **B.** $y = \frac{3}{x - 1}$ **C.** $y = \frac{x - 3}{x - 3}$ **D.** $y = \frac{3}{x - 3}$ **E.** $y = \frac{x + 3}{x - 5}$

A rational expression is in **simplest form** when its numerator and denominator are polynomials that have no common divisors.

Simplify each rational expression.

22. $\frac{x^2 + 3x - 10}{x^2 + x - 6}$
23. $\frac{x^2 - 2x - 24}{x^2 + 7x + 12} \cdot \frac{x^2 - 1}{x - 6}$
24. $\frac{4x^2 - 2x}{x^2 + 5x + 4} \div \frac{2x}{x^2 + 2x + 1}$

25. Open-ended Write two rational expressions that simplify to $\frac{x}{x - 2}$.

To add or subtract rational expressions, write each expression with the least common denominator.

Add or subtract. Simplify where possible.

26. $\frac{2}{3x} + \frac{3}{x^2}$
27. $\frac{x - 3}{x + 2} - \frac{2x - 1}{x - 3}$
28. $\frac{3x}{x^2 - 4} + \frac{6}{x + 2}$

29. $\frac{1}{x^2 - 1} - \frac{2}{x^2 + 3x + 2}$
30. $\frac{x}{x^2 - 5x + 6} + \frac{2}{3x - 6}$
31. $\frac{x - 3}{2x + 4} - \frac{x - 4}{2x + 4}$

If two rational expressions are equal, you can solve the equation using cross-products.

When an equation has a sum or a difference of two rational expressions, you can use the least common denominator to simplify the problem.

Solve each equation. Check your solutions.

32. $\dfrac{1}{x} = \dfrac{5}{x - 4}$

33. $\dfrac{2}{x + 3} - \dfrac{1}{x} = \dfrac{-6}{x(x + 3)}$

34. $\dfrac{1}{2} + \dfrac{x}{6} = \dfrac{18}{x}$

35. $\dfrac{6}{x} = x - 1$

When the occurrence of one event affects the probability of a second event, the two events are **dependent.** When the occurrence of one event does not affect the probability of a second event, the two events are **independent.**

When two events cannot happen at the same time, the events are **mutually exclusive.**

If A and B are independent, then $P(A \text{ and } B) = P(A) \cdot P(B)$.

If A and B are mutually exclusive, then $P(A \text{ or } B) = P(A) + P(B)$.

If A and B are not mutually exclusive, then $P(A \text{ or } B) = P(A) + P(B) - P(A \text{ and } B)$.

Find the probability for one roll of a standard number cube.

36. a 5 or a 6

37. an even number or a number > 4

38. an odd number or a number ≤ 5

Suppose you roll two standard number cubes. Find each probability.

39. a 5 and a 6 (in either order)

40. the sum is odd or less than 7

41. the sum is 11

42. Writing Explain the difference between independent events and mutually exclusive events. Include an example of each.

Getting Ready for ·· ▶ **CHAPTER 9**

Find the missing length.

43.

44.

45.

46.

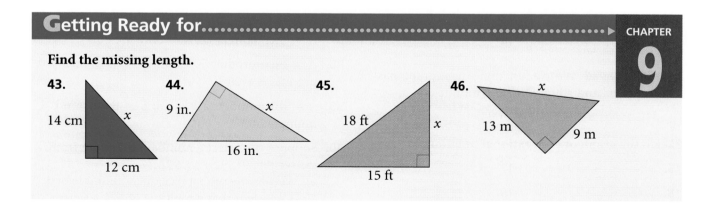

Each point is from a model for inverse variation. Find each constant of variation.

1. $(2, -8)$ **2.** $(0.2, 3)$ **3.** $\left(\frac{1}{3}, \frac{1}{5}\right)$

4. Standardized Test Prep Which inverse variation has the greatest constant of variation?

A. $xy = 3$ **B.** $y = \frac{4}{x}$ **C.** $2x = \frac{5}{y}$

D. $3xy = 10$ **E.** $4y = \frac{12}{x}$

Identify the data as a *direct variation* or an *inverse variation*. Write an equation to model the data.

5.

x	y
2	6
5	15
7	21
11	33
15	45

6.

x	y
3	4
2	6
1	12
4	3
6	2

Write the equation for a translation of $y = \frac{7}{x}$ with the given asymptotes.

7. $x = 1; y = 2$ **8.** $x = -1; y = 0$

9. $x = 0; y = 3$ **10.** $x = -3; y = -2$

Classify each function as *continuous* or *discontinuous*. If discontinuous, give the value(s) of x for which the function is undefined.

11. $y = \frac{x + 1}{x - 1}$ **12.** $y = \frac{x + 3}{x + 3}$

13. $y = \frac{x - 2}{(x + 1)(x - 2)}$ **14.** $y = \frac{2x}{x^2 + 4}$

15. Open-ended Write a function whose graph has a vertical and a horizontal asymptote and a removable discontinuity.

Sketch the graph of each rational function.

16. $y = \frac{1}{x + 2} - 3$ **17.** $y = \frac{5}{x - 2} + 1$

18. $y = \frac{x}{x + 2}$ **19.** $y = \frac{2x - 1}{3x + 2}$

20. $y = \frac{x + 5}{x - 5}$ **21.** $y = \frac{x + 2}{(x + 2)(x - 3)}$

Simplify each rational expression.

22. $\frac{x^2 + 7x + 12}{x^2 - 9}$

23. $\frac{x^2 y}{3x(x - 1)} \cdot \frac{x(y + 2)}{y(x - 1)}$

24. $\frac{(x + 3)(2x - 1)}{x(x + 4)} \div \frac{(-x - 3)(2x + 1)}{x}$

Find the least common multiple of each pair of polynomials.

25. $4(x + 2)$ and $3(x - 2)(x + 1)$

26. $3x + 5$ and $9x^2 - 25$

27. $5(x + 3)(x + 1)$ and $2(x + 1)(x - 3)$

Add, subtract, or multiply. Simplify.

28. $\frac{(x + 2)}{(x - 3)(x + 1)} + \frac{(x - 1)(x + 2)}{(x - 3)}$

29. $\frac{x^2 - 1}{(x - 2)(3x - 1)} - \frac{x + 1}{x + 3}$

30. $\frac{x(x + 4)(x - 1)}{(x - 2)} \cdot \frac{3x - 6}{x + 4}$

Solve each equation. Check your solutions.

31. $\frac{x}{2} = \frac{x + 1}{4}$ **32.** $\frac{3}{x - 1} = \frac{4}{3x + 2}$

33. $\frac{3x}{x + 1} = 0$ **34.** $\frac{3}{x + 1} = \frac{1}{x^2 - 1}$

35. $\frac{1}{x} + \frac{1}{3} = \frac{6}{x^2}$ **36.** $\frac{1}{x} + \frac{x}{x + 2} = 1$

Two standard number cubes are rolled. State whether the events are mutually exclusive. Then find $P(A \text{ or } B)$.

37. $A = $ their sum is 12; $B = $ both are odd

38. $A = $ their product is less than 15; $B = $ their product is even

39. $A = $ the numbers are equal; $B = $ their sum is a multiple of 3

40. Suppose you select a number at random from the set $\{90, 91, 92, \ldots, 99\}$.
   a. What is the probability that a multiple of 3 is selected? that a multiple of 4 is selected?
   b. Writing Are these two events mutually exclusive? Explain.

For Exercises 1–11, choose the correct letter.

1. What are the asymptotes of $y = \frac{3}{x-1} + 4$?
   A. $x = 1, y = 4$ B. $x = 3, y = 4$
   C. $x = -1, y = -4$ D. $x = -3, y = -4$
   E. $x = -4, y = -1$

2. Solve the system $\begin{cases} 2x + 3y - z = -2 \\ x - 4y + 2z = 18 \\ 5x + y - 6z = 11 \end{cases}$.
   A. $x = 3, y = 1, z = 2$
   B. $x = -3, y = 2, z = -1$
   C. $x = 4, y = -3, z = 1$
   D. $x = 2, y = -4, z = 3$
   E. $x = -1, y = 3, z = 2$

3. Which are zeros of the function $y = x^2 - 2x$?
   I. 0   II. 1   III. 2   IV. 3
   A. I and II   B. II and IV   C. I and III
   D. III and IV   E. I, III, and IV

4. Which function is greatest at $x = 3$?
   A. $y = 2^x$ B. $y = x^3 - 2x^2$
   C. $y = x^2 - 3x + 6$ D. $y = 5x - 1$
   E. $y = |8 - x|$

5. You toss two number cubes. Which probability is greatest?
   A. P(an even and an odd)
   B. P(one is prime and the sum is odd)
   C. P(the sum is even and the product is a multiple of 5)
   D. P("doubles" and the product is odd)
   E. P(the sum is greater than 9 and one is less than 4)

6. Which function is an example of a direct variation?
   A. $y = 7x$ B. $xy = 4$
   C. $y = 3x - 9$ D. $y = \frac{2}{x}$
   E. $y = x^2 + 5$

7. Which of the following points are solutions of $y < x^2 + x - 1$?
   I. $(-1, -4)$ II. $(2, 5)$ III. $(-3, 4)$
   A. I only   B. II only   C. I and II
   D. I and III   E. I, II, and III

8. What is $\log \frac{x^2 y^3}{z^6}$ in expanded form?
   A. $\log x^2 - \log y^3 + \log z^6$
   B. $\log x^2 + \log y^3 + \log z^6$
   C. $2 \log x + 3 \log y - 6 \log z$
   D. $2 \log x + 3 \log y + 6 \log z$
   E. $\log x + \log y - \log z$

9. Add $\frac{x+2}{3(x-1)} + \frac{x+4}{x-2}$.
   A. $\frac{2x^2 + 3x - 8}{3(x-1)(x-2)}$ B. $\frac{(x+2)(x+4)}{3(x-1)(x-2)}$
   C. $\frac{x^2 + 6x + 16}{3(x-1)(x-2)}$ D. $\frac{2x+6}{3(x-1)(x-2)}$
   E. $\frac{4x^2 + 9x - 16}{3(x-1)(x-2)}$

Compare the boxed quantity in Column A with the boxed quantity in Column B. Choose the best answer.

   A. The quantity in Column A is greater.
   B. The quantity in Column B is greater.
   C. The two quantities are equal.
   D. The relationship cannot be determined on the basis of the information supplied.

Column A	Column B
10. $\log_a a$	$\log_a 1$
11. $_7C_2$	$_7C_5$

Find each answer.

12. *Open-ended* Write two 3×2 matrices. Then find their sum.

13. Solve $3^x = 7$.

14. Write $y = x^2 - 4x + 1$ in vertex form.

15. Find the inverse of the matrix $\begin{bmatrix} 6 & -2 \\ 11 & 3 \end{bmatrix}$.

Periodic Functions and Trigonometry

Relating to the Real World

Phenomena that repeat over time, such as the phases of the moon, sound waves from a tuning fork, and the rhythms of the human heartbeat, are called periodic. Quantifying data from such a sequence of events yields a periodic function. Studying the characteristics of these functions allows you to interpret the data knowledgeably.

The Wave of the Future

The ebb and flow of the ocean tides contain tremendous amounts of energy. For centuries this energy has been used to run tidal mills. In the last few decades, utility companies have explored ways to use this energy to generate electricity.

The tides vary greatly, but in predictable, repetitive ways that can be utilized. Tides are periodic, as are the functions in this chapter.

To determine where a tidal power plant might be feasible, accurate predictions of the tides are essential. In this chapter, you will consider how tides are modeled and how the periodic nature of tides creates special problems in the design of tidal power plants. Then you will summarize what you have learned and discuss whether you think tidal power plants will be a practical source of electricity in the future.

Right Triangles and Trigonometric Ratios

9-6

Oblique Triangles

9-7

To help you complete the project:

▼ **p. 408** *Find Out by Estimating*
▼ **p. 428** *Find Out by Modeling*
▼ **p. 448** *Find Out by Researching*
▼ **p. 450** *Finishing the Project*

What You'll Learn

- Recognizing periodic graphs and their features

...And Why

To make predictions about cyclic events such as sound waves

What You'll Need

- graph paper

40 ft

5 ft

9-1 Exploring Periodic Data

W O R K   T O G E T H E R

Work with a partner.

You and a friend are the last people seated on a Ferris wheel. Once the ride begins, the wheel moves at a constant speed. It takes 36 seconds to complete one revolution.

1. a. When the ride starts, how high above the ground are you?
   b. At what height are you after 9 s? after 18 s? after 27 s?
   c. At what height are you after 126 s? How many revolutions have you made?
   d. **Predict** where you will be after 3 min.

2. Sketch a graph showing the relationship between your height above the ground and the time since the ride began. Use $0 \leq t \leq 144$ for the domain, where $t = 0$ is the time when the ride started.

3. Critical Thinking   How far have you traveled after one revolution of the wheel? after 144 s?

A **periodic function** repeats a pattern of *y*-values (outputs) at regular intervals. One complete pattern is called a **cycle** . A cycle may begin at any point on the graph.

A Periodic Function

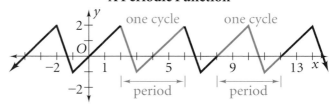

The **period** of a function is the horizontal length of one cycle. The period in the graph shown above is 4.

Example 1

Tell whether each function is periodic. If it is, find the period.

a.

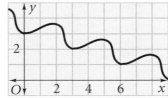

b.

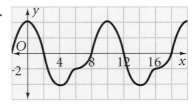

a. While the graph shows similar curves, the *y*-values from one section do not repeat in other sections. The function is not periodic.

b. The pattern of *y*-values in one section is repeated exactly in other sections. The function is periodic.

Find points at the beginning and end of one cycle.

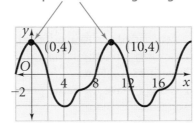

$f(0) = 4$ $f(10) = 4$

$10 - 0 = 10$ ← Subtract the *x*-values.

The pattern in the graph repeats every 10 units, so the period is 10. ∎

4. Use the function shown in part (b) of Example 1. Find $f(4)$ and $f(14)$. **Predict** the value of $f(24)$.

5. Examine your graph from the Work Together on page 402. Does it represent a periodic function? If so, find the period.

The **amplitude** of a periodic function is half the difference between the maximum and minimum values of the function.

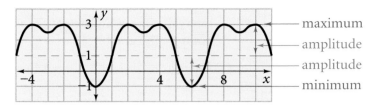

maximum
amplitude
amplitude
minimum

Example 2

Use the graph. Find the amplitude of the function.

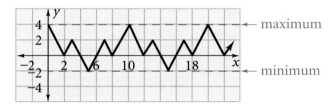

maximum

minimum

amplitude $= \frac{1}{2}$ (maximum value $-$ minimum value)

$\qquad = \frac{1}{2}[(4 - (-2)]$

$\qquad = \frac{1}{2}(6)$

$\qquad = 3$

The amplitude of the function is 3.

6. Complete each statement with x or y.
  a. You use ▨-values to compute the amplitude of a function.
  b. You use ▨-values to compute the period of a function.

7. Find the amplitude of your graph from the Work Together.

8. A second Ferris wheel is half as tall as the one in the Work Together. It also takes 36 seconds for one revolution. A function $g(t)$ relates the time t the ride lasts to a rider's distance $g(t)$ above the ground.
  a. Does $g(t)$ have the same amplitude as the function in the Work Together? Explain.
  b. Does $g(t)$ have the same period as the function in the Work Together? Explain.

9. Try This Find the period and the amplitude of each function below.

  a.
  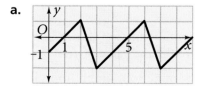

  b.
  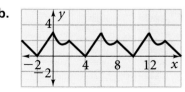

What? Sound is produced by periodic changes in air pressure, called *sound waves*. A sound wave with a period of 0.0045 s will produce the pitch A on a musical scale.

Example 3 **Relating to the Real World**

Music The oscilloscope at the right shows the graph of a pure tone produced by a tuning fork. Find the period and the amplitude of the sound wave.

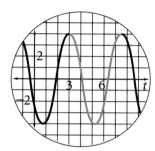

1 unit on the *t*-axis = 0.001 s

One cycle of the sound wave occurs between 0.003 s and 0.0075 s, so the period of the sound wave is 0.0075 − 0.003, or 0.0045 s.

$$\text{amplitude} = \tfrac{1}{2}[4 - (-4)] \quad \overset{\text{maximum value}}{\underset{\text{minimum value}}{}}$$

$$= \tfrac{1}{2}(8)$$

$$= 4$$

The amplitude of the function is 4.

10. Sketch the graph of a sound wave with a period of 0.004 s and an amplitude of 2.

Exercises **O N   Y O U R   O W N**

Find the period and amplitude of each function.

1.
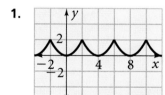

2.
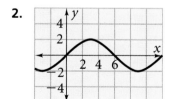

3.
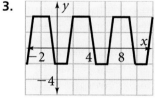

4.
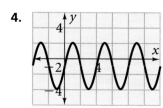

5.
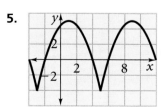

6.
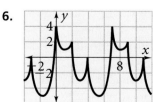

7. Standardized Test Prep Which graph is *not* the graph of a periodic function?

I.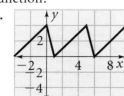
II.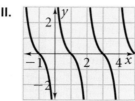
III.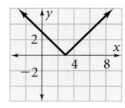
IV.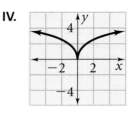

A. I only   **B.** II only   **C.** III and IV   **D.** I and II   **E.** I, II, and IV

8. Writing Describe a periodic function in your own words. Include an example.

9. Open-ended Sketch the graph of a periodic function that has a period of 3 and an amplitude of 2.

10. Suppose f is a periodic function. The period of f is 5 and $f(1) = 2$. Find $f(6)$; $f(11)$; $f(-4)$.

11. Suppose f is a periodic function. The period of f is 24, $f(3) = 67$, and $f(8) = 70$. Find each function value.
   a. $f(27)$ **b.** $f(80)$ **c.** $f(-16)$ **d.** $f(51)$

Writing Can each situation described below be modeled with a periodic function? Explain.

12. the average monthly temperature in your community, recorded every month for two years

13. the population of your community, recorded every year for the last 50 years

14. the number of cars per hour that pass through an intersection near where you live, recorded for two consecutive workdays

Health Use the graph below for Exercises 15 and 16.

15. A person's pulse rate is the number of times his heart beats in one minute. Each cycle in the graph represents one heartbeat. Find the pulse rate.

16. An electrocardiogram (EKG or ECG) measures the electrical activity of a person's heart in millivolts over time.
   a. What is the period of the EKG shown?
   b. What is the amplitude of the EKG?
   c. **Research** Why do doctors use EKGs?

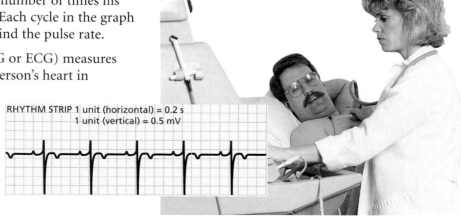

RHYTHM STRIP 1 unit (horizontal) = 0.2 s
1 unit (vertical) = 0.5 mV

17. **Motion** You are sitting on a pier watching the waves when you notice a bottle in the water. The bottle bobs so that it is between 2.5 ft and 4.5 ft below the pier. You know you can reach 3 ft below the pier. Suppose the bottle reaches its highest point every 5 s.

  a. Sketch a graph of the bottle's distance below the pier for 15 s. Assume that at $t = 0$, the bottle is closest to the pier.
  b. Find the period and the amplitude of the function.
  c. **Estimation** Use your graph to estimate the length of time the bottle is within reach during each cycle.

Find the maximum, minimum, and period of each periodic function. Then copy the graph and sketch two more cycles.

18.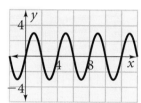

19.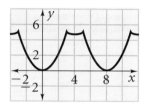

20.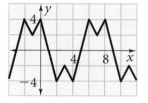

Language Arts **Functions that repeat over time are common in everyday life. The English language has many words that stand for common periods of time. State the period of time that each term indicates.**

21. annual   22. biweekly   23. quarterly   24. hourly   25. circadian

26. **Calendar** A day—the time it takes for Earth to rotate from one noon to the next—is a basic measure of time. A solar year—the time it takes for Earth to revolve once around the sun—is about 365.2422 days. We try to keep our calendar year in step with the solar year.
  a. If every calendar year has 365 days, by how many days would the calendar year and the solar year differ after 100 years? Why is it important for the difference to be zero?
  b. If every fourth year has an extra "leap" day added, by how many days would the two systems differ after 100 years?
  c. If every hundred years the "leap" day is omitted, by how many days would the two systems differ after 100 years? 1000 years?
  d. **Research** What is the pattern of leap days in our current calendar? How long does it take to complete one cycle in the pattern?

27. a. **Block Scheduling** A *block* schedule for seven classes (labeled A through G) is shown at the right. One complete cycle takes 3 days. How many times does each class meet during one cycle?
  b. **Open-ended** Make a block schedule for your school. What is the period of your schedule?

	8:00–9:15	9:20–10:35	10:40–11:55*	12:00–1:15	1:20–2:35
Day 1	A	B	C	D	E
Day 2	F	G	C	A	B
Day 3	D	E	C	F	G

* includes a 25-minute lunch

Find Out by Estimating

You can use a periodic function to approximate the cycle of the tides. Every day at many locations around the world, people record the height of the tide above a level called *mean low water.* The table shows possible data at two locations. Estimate the period and amplitude of the function that models the tide cycle at each location.

Location 1		Location 2	
Time	Tide Height (feet)	Time	Tide Height (feet)
11:30 A.M.	0.6	4:46 P.M.	−2.4
5:42 P.M.	4.8	10:59 P.M.	3.3
11:55 P.M.	0.6	5:11 A.M.	−2.4
6:07 A.M.	4.8	11:24 A.M.	3.3

Exercises   MIXED REVIEW

Solve each system by graphing.

28. $\begin{cases} x - 3y = 6 \\ 2x - y = 12 \end{cases}$

29. $\begin{cases} y \leq 4x + 1 \\ y > 5 - 2x \end{cases}$

30. $\begin{cases} y < 4x \\ y > 3x \end{cases}$

31. $\begin{cases} y = |x + 3| \\ y = 1 - x \end{cases}$

32. Find all the zeros of the polynomial function $y = x^3 - x^2 - 2x$.

Getting Ready for Lesson 9-2

For each measure, draw an angle with its vertex at the origin of the coordinate plane. Use the positive *x*-axis as one ray of the angle.

33. 90°   **34.** 45°   **35.** 30°   **36.** 150°   **37.** 135°   **38.** 120°

A Point in Time

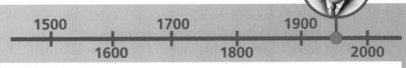

Otis Boykin

To human beings, the most important periodic function in nature is the rhythm of the human heart. About once per second, a nerve in the heart's right atrium generates an electrical signal. This causes the heart to contract and force blood through the body, sustaining the functions of life. Until the invention of the pacemaker, thousands of people suffered from a malfunctioning nerve that caused their hearts to beat erratically, or even to stop altogether.

In **1958**, doctors placed the first battery-powered regulator for the human heartbeat—the pacemaker—in a patient. The creator of the device's control unit was Otis Boykin. Boykin, an inventor from Dallas, Texas, began his distinguished career testing automatic airplane controls. Today, thanks to Otis Boykin's contribution to the pacemaker, more than a million people worldwide are able to enjoy the normal rhythms of the human heart.

What You'll Learn

- Sketching angles in standard position
- Finding the coordinates of points on the unit circle

...And Why

To solve problems involving an ancient calendar

What You'll Need

- graph paper
- ruler
- protractor
- compass

CALCULATOR HINT

When you work with degrees, set your calculator to Degree mode.

Connections 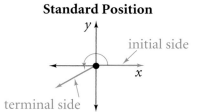 **History . . . and more**

9-2 The Unit Circle

WORK TOGETHER

Work with a partner.

- Use a compass. Construct a circle with a radius of 1 unit on the coordinate plane. Place the center of the circle at the origin.

- Use a protractor. Draw an angle of 30°. Place one ray along the positive *x*-axis. Place the other ray in Quadrant I. Label the point where the second ray intersects the circle $P(x, y)$.

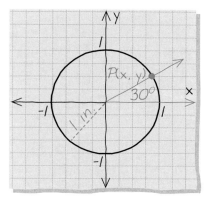

1. Identify the methods you could use to find the coordinates of *P*.

2. Choose one method and find the values of *x* and *y*. Express the coordinates in decimal form.

3. **Calculator** Find the values of cos 30° (read *cosine of 30 degrees*) and sin 30° (read *sine of 30 degrees*). Compare these values to the values you found in Question 2.

4. **a.** Repeat the steps above using an angle of 45°. What are the coordinates of the new point *P*?
   b. Find cos 45° and sin 45° using your calculator. How do these values compare to those you found in part (a)?
   c. Make a **conjecture** about the relationship between the coordinates of a point *P* on the circle and the values of the sine and cosine of the angle containing *P*.

THINK AND DISCUSS

Working with Angles in Standard Position

An angle is in **standard position** when the vertex is at the origin and one ray is on the positive *x*-axis. The ray on the *x*-axis is the **initial side** of the angle; the other ray is the **terminal side** of the angle.

Standard Position

To measure an angle in standard position, find the amount of rotation from the initial side to the terminal side. The angle shown measures 200° (20° more than a straight angle of 180°).

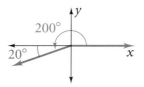

You can use the symbol θ (the Greek letter *theta*) for the measure of an angle in standard position. The measure is positive when the rotation from the initial side to the terminal side is in the *counterclockwise* direction. The measure is negative when the rotation is *clockwise*.

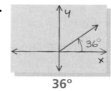 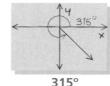 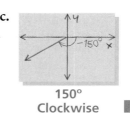

Example 1

Sketch each angle in standard position.
a. 36°   b. 315°   c. −150°

a.

b.

c.

| 36° | 315° | 150° |
| Counterclockwise | Counterclockwise | Clockwise |

5. **Try This** Sketch each angle in standard position.
   a. 135°   b. −320°   c. 180°

6. A full rotation contains 360 degrees. How many degrees are in one quarter of a rotation? half of a rotation? three quarters of a rotation?

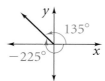

Two angles in standard position are **coterminal** if they have the same terminal side. For example, angles that have measures 135° and −225° are coterminal.

The Aztec calendar stone shows 20 divisions for the 20 days in each month of the Aztec year. The angle marks the passage of 11 days.

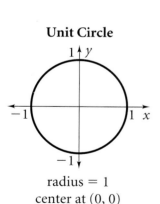

Example 2	**Relating to the Real World**

History Find the measures of two coterminal angles that coincide with the angle shown in the photograph.

The terminal side of the angle is $\frac{11}{20}$ of a full rotation from the initial side.

$$\frac{11}{20} \cdot 360° = 198°$$

To find a coterminal angle, subtract one full rotation.

$$198° - 360° = -162°$$

Two coterminal angle measures for the angle in the photo are 198° and −162°.

7. Find another angle coterminal with 198° by adding one full rotation.

8. **a.** Are angles with measures of −40° and 680° coterminal? Explain.
   b. **Generalize** how the measures of two coterminal angles are related.

9. **Try This** Find the measure of an angle between 0° and 360° that is coterminal with the given angle.
   a. −245°   **b.** 385°   **c.** −215°

Using the Unit Circle

Unit Circle

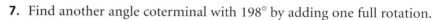

radius = 1
center at (0, 0)

The **unit circle** has a radius of 1 unit and has its center at the origin. Points on the unit circle are related to periodic functions.

Cosine and Sine of Angles

Suppose an angle in standard position has measure θ. The **cosine of θ** (cos θ) is the x-coordinate of the point at which the terminal side of the angle intersects the unit circle. The **sine of θ** (sin θ) is the y-coordinate.

Example: cos 60° = 0.5
sin 60° ≈ 0.87

$P(\cos 60°, \sin 60°)$

60°

The coordinates of the point at which the terminal side of a 60° angle intersects the unit circle are about (0.5, 0.87).

9-2 The Unit Circle   **411**

Notice that 0.87 is an *approximate* value of sin 60°. For some angles, you can use right triangles to find the *exact* coordinates.

Example 3

Find the exact values of $\cos(-120°)$ and $\sin(-120°)$.

Step 1: Sketch an angle of $-120°$ in standard position. Sketch a unit circle.

Step 2: Sketch a right triangle. Place the hypotenuse on the terminal side of the angle. Place one leg on the *x*-axis. (The other leg will be parallel to the *y*-axis.)

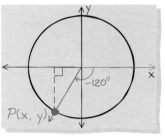

x-coordinate = cos (−120°)
y-coordinate = sin (−120°)

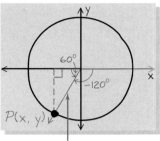

The triangle contains angles of 30°, 60°, and 90°.

Step 3: Find the length of each side of the triangle.

Step 3: Find the length of each side of the triangle.

$\text{hypotenuse} = 1$ ← The hypotenuse is a radius of the unit circle.

$\text{short leg} = \frac{1}{2}$ ← The short leg is $\frac{1}{2}$ the hypotenuse.

$\text{long leg} = \frac{1}{2}\sqrt{3}$ or $\frac{\sqrt{3}}{2}$ ← The long leg is $\sqrt{3}$ times the short leg.

Since the point lies in Quadrant III, both coordinates are negative. The *x*-axis contains the short leg, so $\cos(-120°) = -\frac{1}{2}$. $\sin(-120°) = -\frac{\sqrt{3}}{2}$. ■

QUICK REVIEW

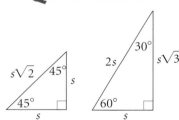

10. a. **Calculator** Find the decimal equivalents of $-\frac{1}{2}$ and $-\frac{\sqrt{3}}{2}$.
    b. Use a calculator to find $\cos(-120°)$ and $\sin(-120°)$. How do these values compare to the exact values found in Example 3?

11. a. **Try This** Find the exact values of cos 135° and sin 135°. Use properties of a 45°- 45°- 90° triangle.
    b. **Verify** your work. Use a calculator to find cos 135° and sin 135°.

12. **Try This** Find the exact values of cos 150° and sin 150°.

Exercises   ON YOUR OWN

Sketch each angle in standard position.

1. 40°
2. 255°
3. −130°
4. −85°
5. −270°

6. 125°
7. −425°
8. 160°
9. 213°
10. −57°

Find the exact coordinates of the point at which the terminal side of each angle intersects the unit circle.

11.

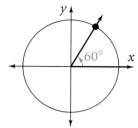

12.

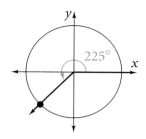

13.

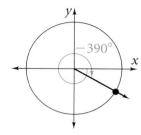

Sketch each angle in standard position. Use a right triangle to find exact values of the cosine and the sine of the angle.

14. $240°$ **15.** $-30°$ **16.** $45°$

17. $120°$ **18.** $330°$ **19.** $-225°$

20. Navigation When navigators locate an object, they measure in a clockwise direction from due north. The measure of the angle is called the *bearing*. Suppose a lighthouse's bearing is $110°$ from a ship.
   a. Sketch the diagram shown at the right on coordinate axes. Place north along the positive y-axis.
   b. Express the location of the lighthouse in terms of an angle in standard position.

Find the measure of an angle between 0° and 360° that is coterminal with the given angle.

21. $500°$ **22.** $-210°$ **23.** $415°$ **24.** $-180°$ **25.** $-359°$

Open-ended **Find a positive and a negative coterminal angle for the given angle.**

26. $225°$ **27.** $45°$ **28.** $-125°$ **29.** $-675°$ **30.** $400°$

31. Copy and complete the chart at the right. **Summarize** how the quadrant in which the terminal side of an angle lies affects the sign of the sine and cosine of that angle.

32. Writing Explain how to find the sine and cosine of angles with measures of $0°$, $90°$, $180°$, $270°$, and $360°$ without using a calculator.

33. a. Use a calculator to find the value of each expression: $\cos 40°$; $\cos 400°$; $\cos (-320°)$.
   b. *Critical Thinking* Explain why the values you found in part (a) are identical.

Quadrant II	y	Quadrant I
cos θ is ▦		cos θ is +
sin θ is ▦		sin θ is +
Quadrant III		Quadrant IV
cos θ is ▦		cos θ is ▦
sin θ is ▦		sin θ is ▦

34. Design Navaho sand paintings
like the one at the right have
many lines of symmetry. Suppose
point *A* is on a unit circle.
Estimate the coordinates of *A*.

35. Open-ended Find the measures
of four angles in standard
position that have a sine of 0.5.
(*Hint:* Use right triangles.)

Calculator For each angle θ, find the values
of $\cos \theta$ and $\sin \theta$. Round your answers to
the nearest hundredth.

36. $0°$ **37.** $10°$ **38.** $20°$ **39.** $30°$

40. $40°$ **41.** $50°$ **42.** $60°$ **43.** $70°$

44. $80°$ **45.** $90°$ **46.** $370°$ **47.** $-280°$

Exercises   MIXED REVIEW

Evaluate each logarithm.

48. $\log_4 16$ **49.** $\log_7 \frac{1}{49}$ **50.** $\log_9 27$

51. a. Agriculture Plot the data shown in the table
below. Enter the year as an *x*-value, using $x = 0$
for 1950. Enter the number of cows as a *y*-value.

b. Does a *quadratic* model or an *exponential* model
provide the better fit for the given data? Explain.

c. Write an equation to model the number of cows
in the United States over time.

d. Predict how many dairy cows there will be in the
United States in the year 2000.

Dairy Cows in the United States

Year	1950	1960	1970	1980	1985	1990	1995
Cows (in thousands)	23,853	19,527	13,303	10,758	10,311	10,153	9,532

Source: U.S. Department of Agriculture

Getting Ready for Lesson 9-3
**Find the circumference of a circle with the given radius. Round your
answers to the nearest tenth.**

52. 4 in.   **53.** 70 m   **54.** 8 mi   **55.** 3.4 ft   **56.** 5 mm

9-3 Radian Measure

What You'll Learn

- Using radian measure for angles
- Relating radians to the lengths of arcs in a circle

...And Why

To solve problems involving satellite motion

What You'll Need

- cylinder
- ruler
- string
- protractor

WORK TOGETHER

In the past, you have used degrees to measure angles. When angles are used in periodic functions, they are often measured in larger units called *radians*.

1. Measure the diameter of a cylinder and calculate its radius. On a piece of string, mark off a "number line" with each unit equal to the radius. Mark at least seven units.

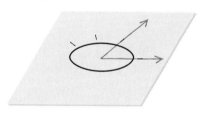

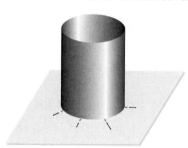

2. Wrap the string around the cylinder. How many "radius units" are needed to go around the cylinder one time?

3. Use the end of the cylinder to draw a circle on a sheet of paper. Keep the cylinder in place and wrap the string around it on the paper. Mark an arc of the circle equal to one "radius unit" of length.

4. Remove the cylinder and string. Use paper folding to locate the center of the circle. (Fold the circle onto itself and crease the paper along a diameter. Repeat to get a second diameter.) Draw a central angle that intercepts one "radius unit" of arc.

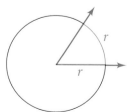

5. Use a protractor to measure the angle in Question 4 in degrees.

THINK AND DISCUSS

Using Radian Measure

A **radian** is the measure of a central angle that intercepts an arc equal in length to the radius of the circle. Like degrees, radians measure the amount of rotation from the initial side to the terminal side of an angle.

6. **Critical Thinking** The formula $C = 2\pi r$ relates the circumference of a circle C to its radius r. *Exactly* how many radians (radius units) are in a $360°$ angle? Explain.

QUICK REVIEW

A *central angle* is an angle whose vertex is at the center of a circle. The *intercepted arc* is the portion of the circle whose endpoints are on the sides of the angle and whose remaining points lie in the interior of the angle.

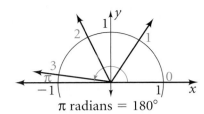

$\pi \text{ radians} = 180°$

The diagram at the left shows that a rotation of 180° is equivalent to π radians.

7. Find the number of degrees in one radian by dividing 180 by π. How does your answer compare to the measurement you made in Question 5?

8. Use the proportion $\dfrac{\blacksquare°}{180°} = \dfrac{\blacksquare \text{ radians}}{\pi \text{ radians}}$ to find the number of radians in 10°.

You can always use a proportion to convert degrees and radians. However, the method shown in the next example is usually faster.

Example 1

a. Find the radian measure of an angle of 60°.

b. Find the degree measure of an angle of $-\dfrac{3\pi}{4}$ radians.

a. $60° \cdot \dfrac{\pi \text{ radians}}{180°} = \dfrac{\pi}{3}$ radians   ◄— Multiply by $\dfrac{\pi \text{ radians}}{180°}$.

≈ 1.05 radians

b. $-\dfrac{3\pi \text{ radians}}{4} \cdot \dfrac{180°}{\pi \text{ radians}} = -135°$ ◄— Multiply by $\dfrac{180°}{\pi \text{ radians}}$.

You can express the *exact* radian measure for many angles in terms of π.

9. **Try This** Write each degree measure in radians. (Express radian measures in terms of π and round to the nearest hundredth.)

  a. 225°   b. −150°   c. 270°

10. **Try This** Write each radian measure in degrees.

  a. $\dfrac{\pi}{2}$ radians   b. $\dfrac{5\pi}{6}$ radians   c. 2 radians

Example 2

Find the exact values of cos ($\dfrac{\pi}{4}$ radians) and sin ($\dfrac{\pi}{4}$ radians).

$\dfrac{\pi}{4} \cdot \dfrac{180}{\pi} = 45°$ ◄— Convert radians to degrees.

Draw the angle. Complete a 45°- 45°- 90° triangle. Since the hypotenuse has length 1, the legs are each $\dfrac{\sqrt{2}}{2}$.

Thus, cos ($\dfrac{\pi}{4}$ radians) = $\dfrac{\sqrt{2}}{2}$

and sin ($\dfrac{\pi}{4}$ radians) = $\dfrac{\sqrt{2}}{2}$.

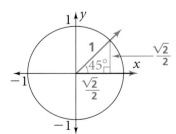

GRAPHING CALCULATOR HINT

Use the MODE feature to select the Radian option when an angle is measured in radians.

11. Use a calculator to find cos ($\dfrac{\pi}{4}$ radians) and sin ($\dfrac{\pi}{4}$ radians). How do these values compare to the coordinates found in Example 2?

12. Explain how to use mental math to convert $\dfrac{\pi}{4}$ radians into degrees. *Hint:* Begin with the relationship π radians = 180°.

Finding the Length of an Arc

Suppose you know the radius r of a circle and the measure θ (in radians) of a central angle. Then you can find the length s of the intercepted arc by using the formula $s = r\theta$.

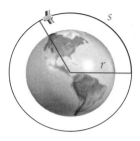

Example 3   **Relating to the Real World**

Space A weather satellite in a circular orbit around Earth completes one orbit every 3 h. The radius of Earth is about 6400 km, and the satellite is positioned 2600 km above Earth. How far does the satellite travel in 1 h?

Since one complete rotation (orbit) takes 3 h, the satellite completes $\frac{1}{3}$ of a rotation in 1 h.

Define s = distance traveled in 1 h ⟵ length of an arc
$r = 6400 + 2600 = 9000$ ⟵ measure of the radius from Earth's center
$\theta = \frac{1}{3} \cdot 2\pi = \frac{2\pi}{3}$ ⟵ radian measure for $\frac{1}{3}$ of a rotation

Relate   distance traveled = length of intercepted arc

Write
$$s = r\theta$$
$$= 9000\left(\frac{2\pi}{3}\right)$$
$$\approx 18849.55592 \quad \longleftarrow \text{Use a calculator.}$$

The satellite travels about 19,000 km in 1 hour.

---

13. How far does the satellite travel during each orbit of Earth?

14. Find the length of the arc intercepted by each angle.

   a. $\angle AOB$ **b.** $\angle COD$
   c. $\angle AOC$ **d.** $\angle AOD$

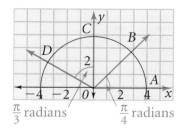

1. Copy and complete the diagram at the right. Fill in the missing measures in radians or degrees.

Write each measure in radians. Express the answer in terms of π and round to the nearest hundredth.

2. $-300°$ **3.** $150°$ **4.** $-60°$

5. $-90°$ **6.** $160°$ **7.** $20°$

Write each measure in degrees. When necessary, round your answer to the nearest degree.

8. 3π radians   **9.** $\frac{11\pi}{10}$ radians   **10.** $-\frac{2\pi}{3}$ radians

11. -3 radians   **12.** 1.57 radians   **13.** 4.71 radians

14. **Space** A geostationary satellite is positioned 35,800 km above Earth. It takes 24 h to complete one orbit. What distance does the satellite travel in 1 h?

15. **Open-ended** Measure the radius of a bicycle wheel or the wheel on a car. (Make sure you measure to the outside of the tire.) Find the number of radians through which a point on the tire turns when the wheel has moved a distance of 12 ft.

16. **Writing** Two angles are measured in radians. Explain how you can tell whether the angles are coterminal without rewriting their measures in degrees.

17. a. **Calculator** Evaluate, to seven decimal places, the first three terms of Jason's expression in the cartoon below. Then evaluate the first four terms. Which is more accurate as an estimate of cos 60°?

   b. Jason's expression can be used to find the cosine of any angle after you know its radian measure. **Generalize** his expression by substituting x for $\frac{\pi}{3}$.

   c. Use the general formula to estimate cos $(\frac{\pi}{10}$ radians$)$ to the nearest thousandth. How many degrees are in this angle?

FOX TROT by Bill Amend

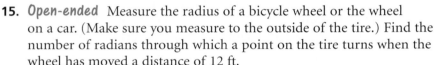

Find the length of each arc.

18.

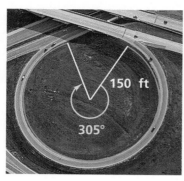

150 ft

305°

19.

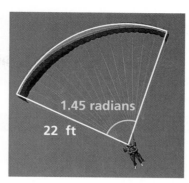

1.45 radians

22 ft

20.

255°

24 in.

Draw angles in standard position with the given measures. Then find the exact values of the cosine and sine of the angle.

21. $\frac{7\pi}{4}$ radians   **22.** $-\frac{2\pi}{3}$ radians   **23.** $\frac{5\pi}{2}$ radians   **24.** -2π radians   **25.** $\frac{7\pi}{6}$ radians

Calculator The measure θ of an angle in standard position is given. Find the values of $\cos \theta$ and $\sin \theta$. Round to the nearest hundredth.

26. $\frac{\pi}{5}$ radians   **27.** $\frac{4\pi}{5}$ radians   **28.** $\frac{6\pi}{5}$ radians   **29.** $\frac{9\pi}{5}$ radians   **30.** $\frac{3\pi}{10}$ radians

31. a. Geometry Draw a unit circle on the coordinate plane. Then draw five angles in standard position with the measures given in Exercises 26–30.
  b. For each angle, complete a right triangle. Place the hypotenuse along the terminal side (from the origin to the unit circle). Place one leg along the x-axis. The other leg will be parallel to the y-axis.
  c. Critical Thinking Are the five triangles congruent? Justify your answer by using values of $\sin \theta$ and $\cos \theta$ from Exercises 26–30.

32. Use the proportion $\frac{\text{measure of central angle}}{\text{measure of one complete rotation}} = \frac{\text{length of arc}}{\text{circumference}}$ to **justify** the formula $s = r\theta$. Use θ for the central angle measure and s for the arc length. Measure the rotation in radians.

33. Geography The 24 lines of longitude that approximate the 24 standard time zones are equally spaced around the equator.
  a. Suppose you use 24 central angles to divide a circle into 24 equal arcs. Express the measure of each angle in degrees and in radians.
  b. The radius of the equator is about 3960 mi. About how wide is each time zone at the equator?
  c. The radius of the Arctic Circle is about 1580 mi. About how wide is each time zone at the Arctic Circle?

34. Technology A student wanted to rewrite $\frac{9\pi}{4}$ radians as degrees. The screen at the right shows the student's calculations. Was the method successful? **Justify** your answer.

```
9*π/4*360/2*π
    3997.189782
```

35. Cars Suppose a windshield wiper arm has a length of 22 in. and rotates through an angle of 110°. What distance does the tip of the wiper travel as it moves once across the windshield?

Solve each equation.

36. $x^3 - 6x^2 + 3x = 0$

37. $2 \log 3 - \log x = 1$

38. $|2x - 9| + 6 = 14$

39. Write the equation of a line perpendicular to $3x - y = 12$ through $(-1, 4)$.

Getting Ready for Lesson 9-4

Use the periodic function shown in the graph. Find the value(s) of each of the following.

40. the period

41. the domain

42. the amplitude

43. the range

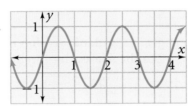

Find the period and amplitude of each periodic function.

1.

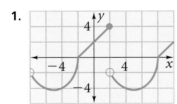

2.

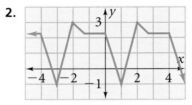

3.

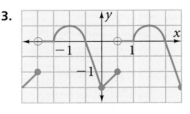

Convert each angle measure into its equivalent in radians or degrees.

4. 30°   **5.** −180°   **6.** 36°   **7.** $\frac{\pi}{3}$ radians   **8.** $-\frac{3\pi}{4}$ radians   **9.** $\frac{\pi}{8}$ radians

Find the exact value of sin θ and cos θ for an angle in standard position with the given measure θ.

10. 90°   **11.** −45°   **12.** 210°   **13.** π radians   **14.** $\frac{3\pi}{4}$ radians   **15.** $\frac{4\pi}{3}$ radians

16. Open-ended Write the radian measure for three coterminal angles.

17. Standardized Test Prep An angle of 120° is in standard position. What are the coordinates of the point at which the terminal side intersects the unit circle?

A. $\left(\frac{1}{2}, \frac{\sqrt{3}}{2}\right)$ **B.** $\left(-\frac{1}{2}, -\frac{\sqrt{3}}{2}\right)$ **C.** $\left(-\frac{\sqrt{3}}{2}, \frac{1}{2}\right)$ **D.** $\left(-\frac{1}{2}, \frac{\sqrt{3}}{2}\right)$ **E.** $\left(-\frac{\sqrt{3}}{2}, -\frac{1}{2}\right)$

Graphing Trigonometric Functions

Before Lesson 9-4

You can use a graphing calculator to graph trigonometric functions in radians or degrees.

Example 1

Compare the graphs of $y = \cos x$ from $-360°$ to $360°$ and from -2π to 2π radians.

Step 1: Press $\boxed{\text{MODE}}$ to change the mode to degrees. Adjust the window values. Graph the function.

Step 2: Change the mode to radians. Graph the function.

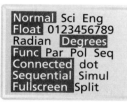
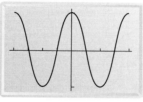
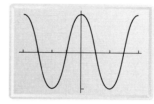

Xmin = –360   Ymin = –1.2
Xmax = 360   Ymax = 1.2
Xscl = 90   Yscl = 1

Xmin = –2π   Ymin = –1.2
Xmax = 2π   Ymax = 1.2
Xscl = π/2   Yscl = 1

The graphs are identical. The function has a period of $360°$ or 2π radians.

Example 2

Graph the function $y = \sin x$. Find $\sin 30°$ and $\sin 150°$.

Step 1: Change the mode to degrees. Adjust the window values.

Step 2: Graph the function. Use the $\boxed{\text{TRACE}}$ key to find the y-values when $x = 30$ and $x = 150$.

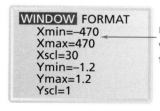

Use these values to trace easily.

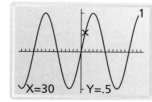
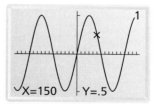

The graph shows that $\sin 30° = 0.5$ and $\sin 150° = 0.5$.

Use appropriate window values to identify the period of each function in radians and in degrees. Then evaluate each function at $90°$.

1. $y = \cos x$ **2.** $y = \sin x$ **3.** $y = \sin 3x$ **4.** $y = \cos (x + 30)$

5. Writing Graph $y = \sin x$ and $y = \cos x$ in the same window. Compare the graphs. How are they similar? How are they different?

What You'll Learn

• Identifying properties of the sine function

• Writing equations for sine functions

• Graphing sine curves

...And Why

To model light waves and other periodic waves

What You'll Need

• graphing calculator

9-4 The Sine Function

THINK AND DISCUSS

Writing Equations for Sine Functions

The sine function, $y = \sin\theta$, matches the measure θ of an angle in standard position with the y-coordinate of a point on the unit circle. This point is where the terminal side of the angle intersects the unit circle.

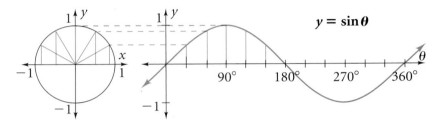

1. **a.** For what value of θ does the graph of $y = \sin\theta$ reach the maximum value of 1?

   b. Extend the graph to include angle measures from 360° to 720°. Will the graph reach the maximum value of 1 again? If so, where?

   c. Is the sine function a periodic function? Explain.

The sine function can also be graphed in radians. In the unit circle, you can show radian measures along the circle as lengths of arcs. In the graphs below, the points for 1, 2, and 3 radians are marked on the unit circle and on the θ-axis.

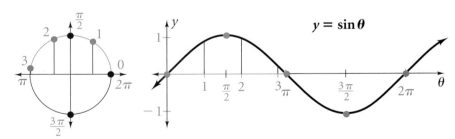

As you have seen, an angle measure θ can be expressed in degrees or in radians. In this book, when no unit is mentioned you should use radians.

2. **Estimate** each value from the graph above: sin 1; sin 2; sin 3; sin π. **Verify** your estimates with a calculator.

3. Use the two graphs of $y = \sin\theta$ shown above.
   a. Find the amplitude of the sine function.
   b. Express the period of the sine function in degrees and in radians.
   c. What are the domain and range of the sine function?

The graph of a sine function is called a *sine curve*. By varying the period, you get many sine curves. The graphs below show three equations in the form $y = \sin b\theta$. For each graph, the θ-axis shows values from 0 to 2π.

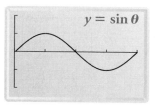

$$y = \sin \theta$$

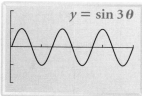

$$y = \sin 3\theta$$

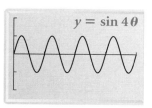

$$y = \sin 4\theta$$

4. How many cycles occur in each graph?

In the graph of $y = \sin b\theta$, b represents the number of cycles in the interval from 0 to 2π. Using this information, you can find a formula relating the period of a sine curve to its equation.

number of cycles from 0 to 2π · length of one cycle $= 2\pi$

$\downarrow$ $\downarrow$

$\quad b \qquad\qquad\cdot\qquad$ period $\quad = 2\pi$

$\qquad\qquad\qquad\qquad\qquad$ period $\quad = \dfrac{2\pi}{b}$

Example 1 **Relating to the Real World**

Optics Light waves can be modeled by sine functions. The graphs below model each of the colors red, blue and yellow. Find the period of the sine curve representing blue. Then write the equation.

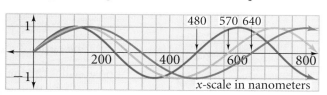

x-scale in nanometers

As you can tell from the graph, one cycle is completed in 480 nanometers. So, the period is 480. To write the equation, first find b.

$$\text{period} = \frac{2\pi}{b}$$

$$480 = \frac{2\pi}{b} \qquad\longleftarrow \text{Multiply each side by } \frac{b}{480}.$$

$$b = \frac{2\pi}{480}$$

$$\approx 0.013$$

Use the form $y = \sin b\theta$. The equation for blue light is $y = \sin 0.013\theta$.

5. Try This Write equations for the sine curves that model the red and yellow light waves in Example 1.

6. **Technology** The graphing calculator screens below show several graphs of $y = a \sin \theta$. How does the value of a affect the amplitude of a sine curve? How does it affect the position of the curve?

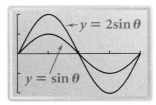 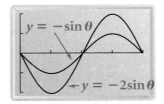

Sine Functions

Suppose $y = a \sin b\theta$, with $a \neq 0$, $b > 0$, and θ in radians.
- $|a|$ is the amplitude of the function.
- b is the number of cycles in the interval from 0 to 2π.
- $\dfrac{2\pi}{b}$ is the period of the function.

7. How many cycles does the function $y = \frac{1}{2} \sin \frac{1}{2}\theta$ have in the interval from 0 to 2π? What are the amplitude and period of this function?

Graphing Sine Functions

You can use five points equally spaced through one cycle to sketch a sine curve. For $a > 0$, this five-point pattern is *zero–max–zero–min–zero*.

Example 2

Sketch one cycle of a sine curve with amplitude 2 and period 4π.

Choose scales for the y-axis and the θ-axis that are about equal ($\pi \approx 3$ units). On the θ-axis, mark one period (4π).

To find the equal spacing through one cycle, divide the period into fourths.

Since the amplitude is 2, the maximum is 2 and the minimum is -2.

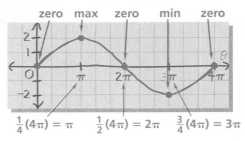

$\frac{1}{4}(4\pi) = \pi$ $\frac{1}{2}(4\pi) = 2\pi$ $\frac{3}{4}(4\pi) = 3\pi$

Plot the five points and sketch the curve.

8. **Critical Thinking** Use the form $y = a \sin b\theta$. Write an equation with $a > 0$ for the sine curve in Example 2.

9. Use the formula $period = \frac{2\pi}{b}$ to find the period of each sine function.

    a. $y = 1.5 \sin 2\theta$ **b.** $y = 3 \sin \frac{\pi}{2}\theta$

10. **Try This** Sketch one cycle of each sine curve.

    a. $y = 1.5 \sin 2\theta$ **b.** amplitude 3; period 4; $a > 0$

For more work with graphing sine curves, see Additional Topics in Trigonometry, p. 604.

11. **a.** Describe the five-point pattern of a sine curve when $a < 0$. *Hint:* Examine the graphs in Question 6.

    b. Graph $y = -0.5 \sin 3\theta$.

You can use the graph of a sine function to solve equations.

Example 3

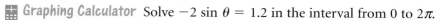

Graphing Calculator Solve $-2 \sin \theta = 1.2$ in the interval from 0 to 2π.

GRAPHING CALCULATOR HINT

When you use the Intersect feature and there is more than one point of intersection, move the cursor close to the desired point after the prompt "Guess?" appears.

Use x for θ. Graph the equations $y = -2 \sin x$ and $y = 1.2$ on the same screen.

Use the [TRACE] or Intersect feature to find the points at which the two graphs intersect.

The graph shows two solutions in the interval from 0 to 2π. They are $\theta \approx 3.79$ and $\theta \approx 5.64$.

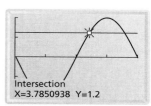

Intersection
X=3.7850938 Y=1.2

Xmin=0   Ymin=-2.1
Xmax=2π   Ymax=2.1
Xscl=π/2   Yscl=1

12. Solve $-2 \sin \theta = 1.2$ in the interval $2\pi \le \theta \le 4\pi$. How are these solutions related to the solutions in Example 3?

Exercises   ON YOUR OWN

How many cycles does each sine function have in the interval from 0 to 2π? Find the amplitude and period of each function.

1.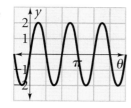

2.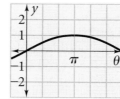

3.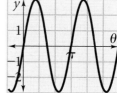

4. $y = \sin \theta$ **5.** $y = \sin 5\theta$ **6.** $y = \sin \pi\theta$

7. $y = 3 \sin \theta$ **8.** $y = -5 \sin \theta$ **9.** $y = -5 \sin 2\pi\theta$

10. **Writing** Suppose the independent variable θ is measured in degrees. Restate the properties of the sine function $y = a \sin b\theta$ found on page 424 in terms of degrees. Which properties are affected by the conversion to degrees?

Write an equation of the sine function in each graph.

11.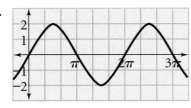

12.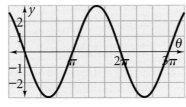

13.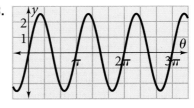

14.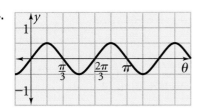

15.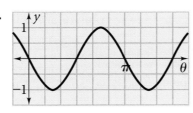

16.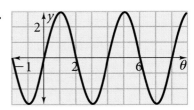

Sketch one cycle of each sine curve. Assume that $a > 0$. Write an equation for each graph.

17. amplitude 1, period $\frac{2\pi}{3}$

18. amplitude $\frac{1}{3}$, period π

19. amplitude 4, period 4π

20. amplitude 3, period 2π

21. amplitude 1, period 2

22. amplitude 1.5, period 3

🖩 **Graphing Calculator** **Solve each equation in the interval from 0 to 2π. Round your answers to the nearest hundredth.**

23. $\sin \theta = 0.6$

24. $-3 \sin 2\theta = 1.5$

25. $\sin \pi\theta = 1$

26. $\sin \theta = -0.8$

27. $3 \sin \frac{\theta}{2} = 1$

28. $\sin \pi\theta = 0.4$

29. Electricity One type of generator consists of a rotating magnetic field surrounded by stationary coils. The voltages produced by the generator can be modeled by sine curves. Suppose three coils are placed symmetrically around a magnetic field. The graph below shows the voltages produced in each coil.
  a. Find the amplitude and period of each sine curve.
  b. Write an equation for the graph that models the voltage produced by coil A.
🖩 **c.** One of the graphs has the equation $y = 4 \sin\left(\theta - \frac{2\pi}{3}\right)$. Use what you know about transformations in the coordinate plane to **predict** whether this is the equation for coil B or coil C. Then check your prediction using a graphing calculator.

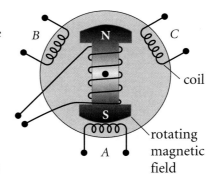

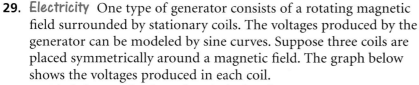

Sketch one cycle of each sine function.

30. $y = 2 \sin \theta$

31. $y = 4 \sin \frac{1}{2}\theta$

32. $y = \frac{1}{2} \sin 2\theta$

33. $y = \sin 3\theta$

34. $y = \sin 5\theta$

35. $y = 2 \sin \pi\theta$

36. $y = -4 \sin \frac{1}{2}\theta$

37. $y = -\sin \frac{\pi}{2}\theta$

38. $y = -2 \sin 2\pi\theta$

39. a. Graphing Calculator Graph the functions $y = 3 \sin \theta$ and $y = -3 \sin \theta$ on the same screen. How are the two graphs related?
   b. Graph the functions $y = \sin 3\theta$ and $y = \sin(-3\theta)$ on the same screen. How are the two graphs related?
   c. Writing How does the graph of $y = a \sin b\theta$ change when a is replaced with its opposite? How does the graph change when b is replaced with its opposite?

40. Astronomy Sunrise and sunset are when someone at sea level would see the uppermost edge of the sun on the horizon. In Houston at the spring equinox (March 21), there are 12 h 9 min of sunlight. Throughout the year, the variation from 12 h 9 min of sunlight can be modeled by a sine function. For example, the longest day (June 21) has 1 h 55 min more sunlight than at the equinox. The shortest day (December 21) has 1 h 55 min less sunlight.

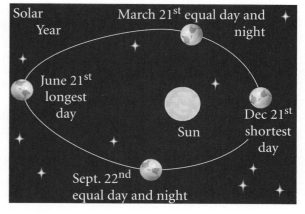

Solar Year   March 21st equal day and night

June 21st longest day

Dec 21st shortest day

Sun

Sept. 22nd equal day and night

   a. Define the independent and dependent variables for a function that models the variation in hours of sunlight in Houston.
   b. What are the amplitude and period of the function?
   c. Write a function that relates the number of days away from the spring equinox to the variation in hours of sunlight in Houston.
   d. Estimation Use your function from part (c). In Houston, about how many fewer hours of sunlight does Valentine's Day (February 14) have than March 21?
   e. Research Find out the number of hours of sunlight in your area on June 21 and on December 21. Develop a sunlight model from your data. Use your model to **predict** the number of hours of sunlight you will have one week from now.

Sound For sound waves, the period and the frequency of a pitch are reciprocals of each other.

$$\text{period} = \frac{\text{seconds}}{\text{cycle}} \qquad \text{frequency} = \frac{\text{cycles}}{\text{second}}$$

Write an equation for each pitch. Let $\theta = $ time in seconds. Use $a = 1$.

41. the lowest pitch easily heard by humans: 30 cycles per second

42. the lowest pitch known to be heard by elephants: 15 cycles per second

43. the highest pitch known to be heard by bats: 120,000 cycles per second

44. Open-ended Write the equations of three sine functions with the same amplitude that have periods of 2, 3, and 4. Then sketch all three graphs on the same coordinate axes.

45. Standardized Test Prep Which function has a period of $\frac{\pi}{2}$ and an amplitude of 3?

A. $y = 3 \sin \frac{\pi\theta}{2}$ **B.** $y = -6 \sin 4\theta$ **C.** $y = -3 \sin 4\theta$ **D.** $y = 6 \sin \frac{\theta}{2}$ **E.** $y = 3 \sin \frac{\theta}{2}$

Chapter Project

Find Out by Modeling

The range of the tides is affected by the relative positions of the sun and the moon. During the new moon and the full moon, the highest high tides and the lowest low tides occur. During the first and third quarters of the lunar month, the lowest high tides and the highest low tides occur. Throughout the month, the tidal range gradually increases and decreases between the minimum and maximum values of the range.

• Sketch a graph of a tidal range as a function of time, showing what you think the shape of a tidal cycle might look like for one month. On your graph, indicate where you think each phase of the moon occurs.

• Research how the phases of the moon and the forces that control the tides are related. Include an illustration with your explanation.

Exercises   MIXED REVIEW

Simplify each expression.

46. $\log 4 - 2 \log 6$ **47.** $\frac{x}{x-1} + \frac{x}{2}$ **48.** $\frac{x^4 - 2x^3}{x-2}$ **49.** $e^{x+4}e^{3x}$

50. Government The U. S. House of Representatives has 435 members. The number of representatives from each state is proportional to the state's population, based on a census taken every ten years. In the 1990 census, the population of the United States was about 249 million. The population of Texas was 17 million. Based on this census, how many representatives should Texas have?

Getting Ready for Lesson 9-5

Find the x-coordinate of each point on the unit circle at the right.

51. A **52.** B

53. C **54.** D

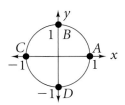

SELF ASSESSMENT

FOR YOUR JOURNAL

Describe how you would solve an inequality of the form $a \sin b\theta \le k$. How is it like solving the related equation? Include an example and solve it.

What You'll Learn

- Graphing and writing cosine functions
- Graphing tangent functions

...And Why

To solve problems involving wave motion

What You'll Need

- graphing calculator

9-5 The Cosine and Tangent Functions

Graphing and Writing Cosine Functions

The cosine function, $y = \cos \theta$, matches the measure θ of an angle in standard position with the x-coordinate of a point on the unit circle. This point is where the terminal side of the angle intersects the unit circle.

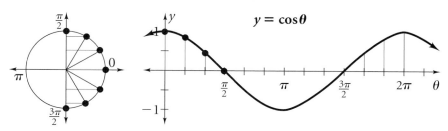

$$y = \cos\theta$$

1. Use the graph shown above to find the domain, period, range, and amplitude of the cosine function.

2. Look at the cycle of the cosine function that occurs in the interval from 0 to 2π. Where in the cycle does the maximum value occur? the minimum? the zeros?

3. Use the graphs below. How are the graphs of the sine and cosine functions alike? How are they different?

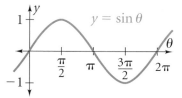

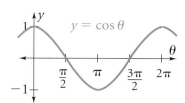

Cosine Functions

Suppose $y = a \cos b\theta$, with $a \neq 0$, $b > 0$, and θ in radians.

- $|a|$ is the amplitude of the function.

- b is the number of cycles in the interval from 0 to 2π.

- $\frac{2\pi}{b}$ is the period of the function.

To graph a cosine function, locate five points equally spaced through one cycle. For $a > 0$, this five-point pattern is *max - zero - min - zero - max*.

Example 1

Sketch the graph of $y = 1.5 \cos 2\theta$ in the interval from 0 to 2π.

Since $b = 2$, the graph will have two full cycles in the interval from 0 to 2π. Mark one period, which is $\frac{2\pi}{2}$, or π.

Choose scales for axes that are about equal ($\frac{\pi}{3} \approx 1$).

Divide the period into fourths.

Plot five points for the first cycle. Use 1.5 for the maximum and −1.5 for the minimum. Repeat the pattern for the second cycle.

max zero min zero max

Sketch the curve.

4. a. **Graphing Calculator** Graph the equations $y = \cos x$ and $y = -\cos x$ on the same axes. Compare the graphs.
   b. **Critical Thinking** Describe the five-point pattern used to graph $y = a \cos b\theta$ when $a < 0$.

5. **Try This** Sketch each cosine curve in the interval from 0 to 2π.
   a. $y = 3 \cos \theta$ b. $y = -2 \cos 2\theta$ c. $y = \frac{1}{2} \cos \pi\theta$

Waves of water show periodic motion. Away from the shore, individual water molecules return to their initial position after a wave passes. Their height can be modeled by a cosine function.

wave direction ——→

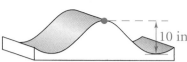

10 in.

Particle is at the crest
of the wave.

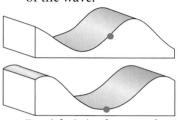

Particle is in the trough
of the wave.

For more work with solving
trigonometric equations,
see page 614.

Example 2   Relating to the Real World ·········

Wave Motion The figures at the left show the vertical motion of a water
particle as a wave moves by. If 10-in. waves occur every 4 s, write an
equation that models the height of the water particle as it moves from
crest to crest.

Use the form $y = a \cos b\theta$. Find values for a and b.

$$a = \frac{10}{2} \quad \longleftarrow \text{amplitude} = \frac{\text{maximum} - \text{minimum}}{2}$$
$$= 5$$
$$\text{period} = \frac{2\pi}{b}$$
$$4 = \frac{2\pi}{b} \quad \longleftarrow \text{Multiply each side by } \frac{b}{4}.$$
$$b = \frac{2\pi}{4}$$
$$= \frac{\pi}{2}$$

The equation for the height of the water particle is $y = 5 \cos \frac{\pi}{2}\theta$. ■

6. Try This Write a cosine function for each description. Choose $a > 0$.
 a. amplitude 4, period 6π **b.** amplitude 2.5, period 8

7. a. Graph the equation from Example 2.
 b. The independent variable θ represents time (in seconds). Find four
 times at which the particle is at the crest of a wave.
 c. For how many seconds during each cycle is the particle above the
 line $y = 0$? below $y = 0$?

You can see from your graph in Question 7 that the height of the water
particle varies around an average height represented by $y = 0$. The next
Example shows how to find out when the particle is exactly 3 inches above
the average height. The variable t represents time in seconds.

Example 3 ·······························

Graphing Calculator Solve $5 \cos \frac{\pi}{2}t = 3$ in the interval from 0 to 8 s.

Graph the equations $y = 3$ and
$y = 5 \cos \frac{\pi}{2}t$ on the same screen.
Use the Intersect feature.

The graph shows four solutions.
They are $t \approx 0.6, 3.4, 4.6,$ and
7.4 s.

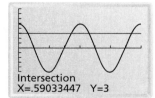

Xmin=0
Xmax=8
Xscl=1
Ymin=−8
Ymax=8
Yscl=1

Intersection
X=.59033447   Y=3

8. When is the particle described by the equation in Example 3 *less* than
 3 in. above the average height? Use the interval from 0 to 8 s.

9. Try This Find all solutions in the interval from 0 to 2π.
 a. $3 \cos 2t = -2$ **b.** $8 \cos \frac{\pi}{3}t = 5$

Graphing Tangent Functions

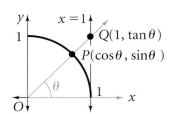

The terminal side of θ intersects the line $x = 1$ at Q.

Sine and cosine are related to the coordinates of a point on the unit circle. Tangent relates to a point on a line *tangent* to the unit circle. The **tangent** of an angle θ in standard position is the y-coordinate of the point at which the line containing the terminal side of the angle intersects the line $x = 1$.

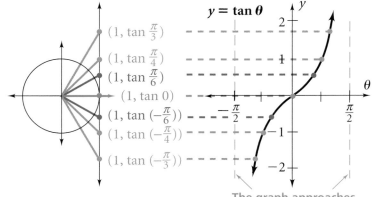

The graph approaches two vertical asymptotes.

10. Use the graph above to find each value. **Verify** your answers with a calculator.
   a. $\tan\left(-\frac{\pi}{4}\right)$ **b.** $\tan 0$ **c.** $\tan\frac{\pi}{4}$

11. a. *Critical Thinking* Explain why the terminal side of an angle with measure $\frac{\pi}{2}$ *does not intersect* the tangent line.
   b. Use a calculator to find the value of tan 1.53, tan 1.56, and tan 1.57. Why do these values increase as the angle measures approach $\frac{\pi}{2}$?
   c. Use a calculator to find $\tan\frac{\pi}{2}$. Explain the result.

The graph above shows one cycle of the tangent function, $y = \tan\theta$. Since the period is π, the asymptote that occurs at $\theta = \frac{\pi}{2}$ is repeated every π units.

You can use asymptotes and three points to sketch one cycle of a tangent curve. As with sine and cosine, the five elements are equally spaced through one cycle. Use the pattern *asymptote - −1 - zero - 1 - asymptote.*

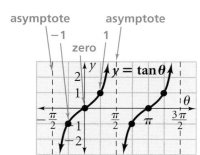

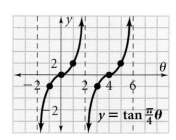

12. What is the period of each function in the graphs shown above?

Tangent Functions

Suppose $y = \tan b\theta$, with $b > 0$ and θ in radians.

- $\frac{\pi}{b}$ is the period of the function.
- One cycle occurs in the interval from $-\frac{\pi}{2b}$ to $\frac{\pi}{2b}$.
- There are vertical asymptotes at each end of the cycle.

The next Example shows how to use the period, amplitude, and points to graph a tangent function.

Example 4

Sketch two cycles of the graph of $y = \tan \pi\theta$.

$\text{period} = \frac{\pi}{b}$

$\quad\quad\quad = \frac{\pi}{\pi} = 1$

One cycle occurs in the interval from $-\frac{1}{2}$ to $\frac{1}{2}$.

Asymptotes occur every 1 unit, at $\theta = -\frac{1}{2}, \frac{1}{2}$, and $\frac{3}{2}$.

Sketch the asymptotes. Plot three points in each cycle. Sketch the curve.

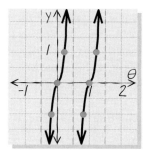

13. **Try This** Sketch the graph of each tangent curve from 0 to π.

   a. $y = \tan 3\theta$ **b.** $y = \tan \frac{\pi}{2}\theta$

Exercises   ON YOUR OWN

Identify the period and amplitude for each function.

1. $y = 3 \cos \theta$ **2.** $y = \cos 2t$ **3.** $y = 2 \cos \frac{1}{2}t$ **4.** $y = \frac{1}{3} \cos \frac{\theta}{2}$

5. $y = 3 \cos \frac{\theta}{3}$ **6.** $y = \frac{1}{2} \sin 3\theta$ **7.** $y = 0.7 \cos \pi t$ **8.** $y = 16 \sin \frac{3\pi}{2}t$

Identify the period and tell where two asymptotes occur for each function.

9. $y = \tan 5\theta$ **10.** $y = \tan \frac{3\theta}{2}$ **11.** $y = \tan 4\theta$ **12.** $y = \tan \frac{2}{3\pi}\theta$

Sketch the graph of each function in the interval from 0 to 2π.

13. $y = \cos 2\theta$ **14.** $y = -3 \cos \theta$ **15.** $y = -\cos 3t$ **16.** $y = \sin \frac{\pi}{2}\theta$

17. $y = \tan \theta$ **18.** $y = \tan 2\theta$ **19.** $y = \tan \frac{2\pi}{3}\theta$ **20.** $y = -5 \sin t$

21. Recreation Suppose a friend gives you a push on a large swing. Your friend starts by pulling you backward six feet and letting go.

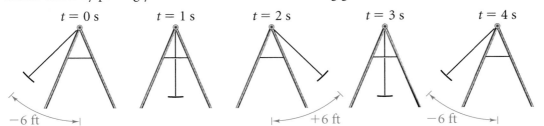

$t = 0$ s $t = 1$ s $t = 2$ s $t = 3$ s $t = 4$ s

−6 ft   +6 ft   −6 ft

   a. How many seconds does it take to complete one cycle in the motion of the swing? What is the amplitude of the motion?

   b. Modeling Suppose you maintain the rate and amplitude of your swinging. Express your arc distance from the resting point of the swing as a function of time. Use a cosine function.

   c. Graph your function. In the interval from 0 s to 10 s, how many times do you pass the resting point of the swing?

   d. Write an equation to find the times in the first 10 s that you are exactly 3 ft forward (of the resting point) in your swing.

   e. Writing Suppose you jump from the swing 13.5 s after you start. Will you land in the puddle? **Justify** your answer.

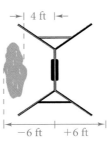

4 ft

−6 ft   +6 ft

Solve each equation in the interval from 0 to 2π.

22. $\cos 2t = \frac{1}{2}$ **23.** $20 \cos t = -8$ **24.** $6 \tan 2\theta = 1$ **25.** $-2 \cos \pi\theta = 0.3$

26. $\tan \theta = 2$ **27.** $\tan \theta = -2$ **28.** $3 \cos \frac{t}{3} = 2$ **29.** $\cos \frac{1}{4}\theta = 1$

Write an equation of a cosine or tangent function for each graph.

30.

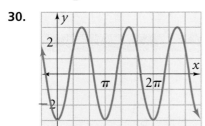

31.

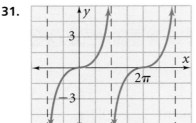

32.

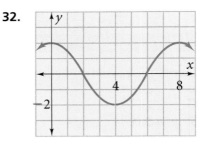

Write a cosine function for each description. Assume that $a > 0$.

33. amplitude 5, period 3π **34.** amplitude 2, period π **35.** amplitude π, period 2

36. a. Graph $y = \cos \theta$ and $y = \cos\left(\theta - \frac{\pi}{2}\right)$ in the interval from 0 to 2π. What translation of the graph of $y = \cos \theta$ produces the graph of $y = \cos\left(\theta - \frac{\pi}{2}\right)$?

   b. Graph $y = \cos\left(\theta - \frac{\pi}{2}\right)$ and $y = \sin \theta$ in the interval from 0 to 2π. What do you notice?

37. Math in the Media The newspaper clipping at the right shows the times for high tide and low tide in Annapolis, Maryland. The markings on the side of a local pier showed a high tide of 7 ft and a low tide of 4 ft on the previous day.

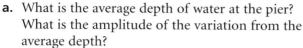

THE ANNAPOLIS HERALD

High Tide—4:03 A.M.
High Tide—4:25 P.M.
Low Tide—10:14 A.M.
Low Tide—10:36 P.M.

   a. What is the average depth of water at the pier? What is the amplitude of the variation from the average depth?

   b. How long is one cycle of the tide?

   c. Write a cosine function that models the relationship between the depth of water and the time of day. Use $y = 0$ to represent the average depth of water. Use $t = 0$ to represent the time 4:03 A.M.

   d. *Critical Thinking* Suppose your boat needs at least 5 ft of water to come or go to the pier. At what time(s) could you come and go?

38. Geometry Use the drawing at the right and similar triangles. Justify the statement that $\tan \theta = \frac{\sin \theta}{\cos \theta}$.

39. Critical Thinking Graph $y = \tan x$, $y = a \tan x$ (with $a > 0$), and $y = a \tan x$ (with $a < 0$). Recall the pattern of five elements for graphing a tangent function: *asymptote - −1 - zero - 1 - asymptote*. How does the value of a affect this pattern?

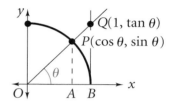

40. Biology A helix is a three-dimensional spiral. The coiled strands of DNA and the edges of twisted crepe paper are examples of helixes. In the diagram, the y-coordinate of each edge illustrates a cosine function. Write an equation for the y-coordinate of one edge.

Exercises   MIXED REVIEW

Graph each variation. State whether it is direct or inverse.

41. $y = 4x$ **42.** $xy = 8$ **43.** $\frac{y}{x} = 5$

44. Probability You are rolling a number cube. What is the probability of rolling a factor of 6?

Getting Ready for Lesson 9-6

Find the ratio of the length of the leg opposite $\angle A$ to the length of the leg adjacent to $\angle A$.

45.

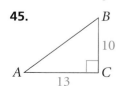

46.

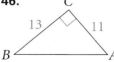

47.

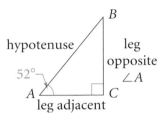
9-6 **R**ight Triangles and Trigonometric Ratios

What You'll Learn

• Evaluating trigonometric ratios and inverse trigonometric ratios

• Using trigonometric ratios to find missing measures of right triangles

...And Why

To solve construction problems by using trigonometric ratios

What You'll Need

• metric ruler

• protractor

W O R K   T O G E T H E R

Draw three right triangles, each having an acute angle of 52°. Make the hypotenuse of the first triangle 10 cm long, and make the other two hypotenuses differ by at least 5 cm. Label the triangles 1, 2, and 3.

Copy the table below. In each triangle that you drew, measure the lengths of the hypotenuse, the leg opposite the 52° angle, and the leg adjacent to the 52° angle.

Record your measurements. Then calculate the three ratios for each triangle.

Triangle	Hyp. (cm)	Leg opp. ∠*A* (cm)	Leg adj. to ∠*A* (cm)	opp. hyp.	adj. hyp.	opp. adj.
1	10	7.9	6.2	0.79	0.62	1.28
2	■	■	■	■	■	■
3	■	■	■	■	■	■

1. **Patterns** What patterns do you see in the last three columns of the table? Check your results with others.

2. Make a **conjecture** about these ratios for all right triangles that have an acute angle of 52°.

3. **Critical Thinking** In the photograph of the pyramid, $\frac{\text{length of leg opposite } \angle A}{\text{length of leg adjacent to } \angle A} = \frac{h}{b} \approx 1.28$. Notice that this ratio equals the ratio for triangle 1 in the table above. Make a **conjecture** about the size of angle *A*.

Using the Sine, Cosine, and Tangent Ratios

The three ratios you calculated in the Work Together are the **trigonometric ratios** for a right triangle. These ratios do not depend on the size of the right triangle. They depend only on the size of the acute angles in the triangle. In a right triangle that has an acute $\angle A$, the ratios are defined as follows.

$$\sin A = \frac{\text{length of leg opposite } \angle A}{\text{length of hypotenuse}} = \frac{a}{c}$$

$$\cos A = \frac{\text{length of leg adjacent to } \angle A}{\text{length of hypotenuse}} = \frac{b}{c}$$

$$\tan A = \frac{\text{length of leg opposite } \angle A}{\text{length of leg adjacent to } \angle A} = \frac{a}{b}$$

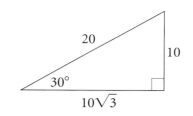

Example 1

Use this right triangle to find the exact values of the trigonometric ratios sin 30°, cos 30°, and tan 30°.

$$\sin 30° = \frac{10}{20} = \frac{1}{2}$$

$$\cos 30° = \frac{10\sqrt{3}}{20} = \frac{\sqrt{3}}{2}$$

$$\tan 30° = \frac{10}{10\sqrt{3}} = \frac{1}{\sqrt{3}}$$

Who? In the second century B.C., the Greek mathematician and astronomer Hipparchus compiled a table for finding the lengths of chords cut off by central angles of a circle. This table (the equivalent of a table of sines) became the basis for modern trigonometry.

4. **Try This** Use the triangle in Example 1 to find the exact values of sin 60°, cos 60°, and tan 60°.

The definition of sine using the unit circle is equivalent to the definition using a right triangle.

Sin θ Using the Unit Circle

$$\sin \theta = y\text{-coordinate of } P$$
$$= PQ$$

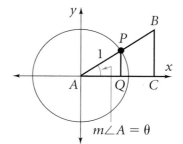

$$m\angle A = \theta$$

Sin A Using a Right Triangle

$$\sin A = \frac{\text{length of leg opposite } \angle A}{\text{length of hypotenuse}}$$
$$= \frac{BC}{AB}$$

Since $\triangle APQ$ and $\triangle ABC$ are similar triangles, $\frac{PQ}{PA} = \frac{BC}{AB}$.

So, $\sin \theta = PQ = \frac{PQ}{1} = \frac{PQ}{PA} = \frac{BC}{AB} = \sin A$.

5. Show that cos A defined as a ratio equals cos θ using the unit circle.

Example 2

In $\triangle ABC$, $\angle C$ is a right angle and $\sin A = \frac{5}{13}$. Find $\cos A$, $\tan A$, and $\sin B$ in fraction and in decimal form.

QUICK REVIEW

Geometry The Pythagorean theorem states that in a right triangle, the square of the length of the hypotenuse is equal to the sum of the squares of the lengths of the legs.

For more practice using the Pythagorean theorem, see the Skills Handbook page 676.

Step 1: Draw a diagram.

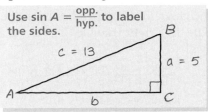

Use $\sin A = \frac{\text{opp.}}{\text{hyp.}}$ to label the sides.

$c = 13$
$a = 5$

Step 2: Use the Pythagorean theorem to find b.

$$c^2 = a^2 + b^2$$
$$13^2 = 5^2 + b^2$$
$$169 = 25 + b^2$$
$$144 = b^2$$
$$b = 12$$

Step 3: Calculate the ratios.

$$\cos A = \frac{\text{length of leg adjacent to } \angle A}{\text{length of hypotenuse}} = \frac{b}{c} = \frac{12}{13} \approx 0.9231$$

$$\tan A = \frac{\text{length of leg opposite } \angle A}{\text{length of leg adjacent to } \angle A} = \frac{a}{b} = \frac{5}{12} \approx 0.4167$$

$$\sin B = \frac{\text{length of leg opposite } \angle B}{\text{length of hypotenuse}} = \frac{b}{c} = \frac{12}{13} \approx 0.9231$$

6. **Try This** In $\triangle DEF$, $\angle D$ is a right angle and $\tan E = \frac{3}{4}$. Draw a diagram and find $\sin E$ and $\tan F$ in fraction and in decimal form.

If you are given the measures of an acute angle and a side of a right triangle, you can find the length of another side of the triangle.

Example 3   Relating to the Real World

Construction Park planners would like to build a bridge across a creek. Surveyors have determined that from 5 ft above the ground the angle of elevation to the top of a 8-ft pole on the opposite side of the creek is 5°. Find the length of the bridge to the nearest foot.

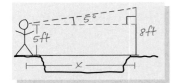

In the right triangle, the length of the leg opposite the 5° angle is $8 - 5$, or 3 ft. You need to find the length of the leg adjacent to the 5° angle. Use the tangent ratio.

$\tan 5° = \frac{3}{x}$ ← Multiply each side by $\frac{x}{\tan 5°}$

$x = \frac{3}{\tan 5°}$ ← Use a calculator in degree mode to find $\tan 5°$.

$= \frac{3}{0.0875}$

≈ 34.29

The bridge will be about 34 ft long.

7. **Try This** Find the length of the bridge in Example 3 by using the 85° angle in the right triangle instead of the 5° angle.

8. Using the given information in Example 3, which trigonometric ratio would you use to find the length of the hypotenuse? Explain.

Finding Angles with Trigonometric Ratios

You can use trigonometric ratios to find the measures of angles in a right triangle. In the diagram, $\sin A = \frac{3}{5}$.

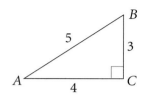

The notation $\sin^{-1}\frac{3}{5}$ represents *the angle whose sine is $\frac{3}{5}$.*

9. Use $\sin^{-1}$ notation to represent the angle whose sine is $\frac{4}{5}$.

10. Express $\tan^{-1}\frac{4}{3} = B$ as a statement about $\tan B$.

11. Use a calculator to find each angle measure in degrees.

   a. $\tan^{-1}\sqrt{3}$ **b.** $\sin^{-1}\frac{\sqrt{2}}{2}$ **c.** $\cos^{-1}\frac{\sqrt{3}}{2}$

12. **a.** Use a calculator to find $\tan 36.87°$.
    b. Find $\tan^{-1} 0.75$

While the notation $\tan^{-1} x$ means the measure of an angle whose tangent is x, $\tan^{-1} x$ is usually read *inverse tangent of x.* Note that $^{-1}$ is a symbol for inverse. It is not an exponent.

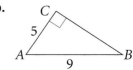

On many calculators you press **2nd** **TAN** to use the $\tan^{-1}$ function.

Example 4

In $\triangle DEF$, $\angle D$ is a right angle, $f = 12$, and $e = 5$. Find $m\angle F$ to the nearest tenth of a degree.

Step 1: Draw a diagram.

```
     E
     |\
     | \
  12 |  \    ← Side f is opposite ∠F.
     |   \
     |____\
   F   5  D   ← Side e is opposite ∠E.
```

Step 2: Use a tangent ratio.

$$\tan F = \frac{12}{5} = 2.4$$
$$m\angle F = \tan^{-1} 2.4$$
$$\approx 67.38°$$

To the nearest tenth of a degree, $m\angle F$ is 67.4°.

13. **Try This** Use a trigonometric ratio to find $m\angle A$ in each triangle.

   a.
```
   B
   |\
   | \  10
 4 |  \
   |___\
   C    A
```

   b.
```
      C
     /|
    / |
 5 /  
  /___
 A  9  B
```

14. **a.** In Example 4, use the Pythagorean theorem to find EF.
    b. Use a trigonometric ratio to find EF.

Example 5 Relating to the Real World

Construction The bridge in Example 3 will be 12 in. above ground level. A 10-ft ramp will be built between the ground and the bridge. What angle will the ramp make with the ground, to the nearest tenth of a degree?

Let θ = the measure of the angle the ramp makes with the ground.

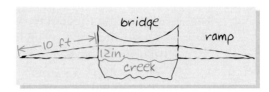

You know the length of the leg opposite the angle you need to find. You know the length of the hypotenuse. So, use the sine ratio.

$\sin \theta = \frac{1}{10}$ ← Rewrite 12 in. as 1 ft

$\sin \theta = 0.1$

$\quad \theta = \sin^{-1} 0.1$

$\quad\quad \approx 5.7°$

The angle between the ramp and the ground will be about 5.7°.

For more work with trigonometric ratios, see page 608.

15. Try This In $\triangle DEF$, $\angle F$ is a right angle, $d = 7$, and $f = 10$. Draw a diagram and find the remaining side length and angle measures. Round to the nearest tenth.

Exercises ON YOUR OWN

Find each value to the nearest tenth. Use the diagram at the right.

1. $\sin A$ **2.** $\cos A$ **3.** $\cos B$

4. $\tan B$ **5.** $m\angle A$ **6.** $m\angle B$

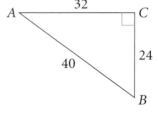

7. In $\triangle GHI$, $\angle H$ is a right angle, $GH = 40$, and $\cos G = \frac{40}{41}$. Draw a diagram and find HI.

8. *Indirect measurement* The tallest flagpole in the world was built in San Francisco in 1915.

   a. When the angle of elevation of the sun was 55°, the length of the shadow cast by this flagpole was 210 ft. Find the height of the flagpole to the nearest foot.

   b. What was the length of the shadow when the angle of elevation of the sun was 34°?

   c. *Writing* What do you need to assume about the flagpole and the shadow to solve these problems? Why?

Find each angle measure to the nearest tenth of a degree.

9. $\cos^{-1}\frac{\sqrt{2}}{2}$

10. $\tan^{-1}0.3333$

11. $\sin^{-1}\frac{3}{4}$

12. $\tan^{-1}\sqrt{3}$

13. $\sin^{-1}0.335$

14. $\cos^{-1}0.992$

15 $\tan^{-1}3.552$

16. $\sin^{-1}0.052$

Sketch a right triangle with θ as the measure of one acute angle. Find the other two trigonometric ratios of θ.

17. $\sin\theta = \frac{3}{8}$

18. $\cos\theta = \frac{7}{20}$

19. $\cos\theta = \frac{1}{5}$

20. $\tan\theta = \frac{24}{7}$

21. Ballooning From a hot-air balloon 3000 ft above the ground, you see a clearing whose angle of depression is 19.5°. What is your horizontal distance from the clearing? Round to the nearest foot.

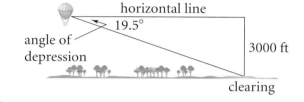

In $\triangle ABC$, $\angle C$ is a right angle. Two measures are given. Find the remaining sides and angles. Round to the nearest tenth.

22. $m\angle A = 52°$, $c = 10$

23. $a = 7$, $b = 10$

24. $m\angle A = 34.2°$, $b = 5.7$

25. $b = 8$, $c = 17$

26. $m\angle B = 17.2°$, $b = 8.3$

27. $m\angle B = 8.3°$, $c = 20$

28. a. In $\triangle DEF$, h is the length of an altitude. Find h to the nearest tenth.
   b. If $DF = 10.8$, find the area of $\triangle DEF$ to the nearest tenth.
   c. Find the area of $\triangle RST$ to the nearest tenth.

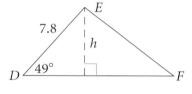
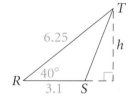

29. Open-ended If $\sin\theta = \frac{1}{2}$, describe a method you could use to find all the angles between 0° and 360° that satisfy this equation.

30. Baseball The bases on a baseball diamond form a square, 90 ft on a side. The pitcher's plate is about 62 ft from the back corner of home plate.
   a. About how far is the pitcher's plate from second base?
   b. A line drive is 10 ft high when it passes over the third baseman, who is 100 ft from home plate. At what angle did the ball leave the bat? (Assume the ball is 4 ft above the ground when it is hit.)

31. Geometry A regular pentagon is inscribed in a circle of radius 10 cm.
a. Find the measure of $\angle C$.
b. Find the length of the diagonal *PS*. Hint: First find *RS*.
c. Find the measure of $\angle CQS$. Then find the length of a side of the pentagon.

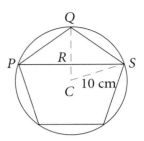

32. a. Technology Test the $\cos^{-1}$ feature on your calculator. What happens if you try to find $\cos^{-1} x$ for values of x between -1 and 0? What happens for $x < -1$? for $x > 1$?
b. Use the graph of $y = \cos x$ to explain your results in part (a).
c. Test the $\tan^{-1}$ feature on your calculator. Can you find $\tan^{-1} x$ for any value of x? What angles does $\tan^{-1} x$ represent? Is this the same as for $\cos^{-1} x$?

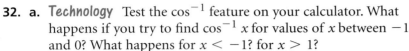

Exercises   MIXED REVIEW

Graph each function.

33. $y = 2|3 - x| + 1$ **34.** $y = -(x + 4)^2 + 5$ **35.** $y = \frac{1}{2x} - 1$

36. a. You put $750 into an account that earns 6% interest compounded continuously. How much will be in the account after two years?
b. How much would be in the account after two years if you added $250 at the end of the first year?

Getting Ready for Lesson 9-7

Find the cosine of each angle to the nearest hundredth.

37. $34°$ **38.** $89°$ **39.** $115°$ **40.** $150°$

Exercises   CHECKPOINT

Sketch the graph of each function in the interval from 0 to 2π.

1. $y = 4 \cos \theta$ **2.** $y = \frac{2}{3} \sin 3\theta$ **3.** $y = -2 \cos \pi t$ **4.** $y = \tan 2\theta$

Write a sine function for each description. Choose $a > 0$.

5. amplitude $\frac{3}{2}$, period 2π **6.** amplitude 0.8, period $\frac{\pi}{4}$ **7.** amplitude 1, period 2

8. In $\triangle ABC$, $\angle C$ is a right angle and $\tan A = \frac{12}{5}$. Find $\sin A$, $\cos A$, and $m\angle A$.

9. Writing Compare the range of values of y in the function $y = \tan \theta$ with the range of values of y in the function $y = \cos \theta$.

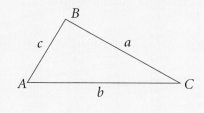

What You'll Learn

- Using the Law of Cosines to find the measures of the sides or angles of a triangle
- Using the Law of Sines to find the measures of the sides or angles of a triangle

...And Why

To determine the length of a leg of a triangular race course

9-7 Oblique Triangles

T H I N K   A N D   D I S C U S S

Using the Law of Cosines

Trigonometric ratios can be used to solve problems involving *oblique triangles*—triangles that do not contain right angles.

1. **Patterns** Each of the triangles below has sides of lengths 3 and 4. When the included angle, $\angle A$, is a right angle, $a = \sqrt{4^2 + 3^2} = 5$. What are the possible values of a when $\angle A$ is smaller than a right angle? when $\angle A$ is larger than a right angle?

  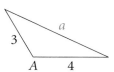

The Law of Cosines relates the length of a side of any triangle to the measure of the angle opposite that side.

Law of Cosines

In $\triangle ABC$, let a, b, and c represent the lengths of the sides opposite $\angle A$, $\angle B$, and $\angle C$, respectively. Then:

$$a^2 = b^2 + c^2 - 2bc \cos A$$
$$b^2 = a^2 + c^2 - 2ac \cos B$$
$$c^2 = a^2 + b^2 - 2ab \cos C$$

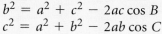

You can use the Law of Cosines to find missing parts of any triangle when you know the measures of

- two sides and the angle between them, or
- all three sides.

The course for each America's Cup sailboat race is laid out with much care. The expected wind speeds, roughness of the seas, and the capabilities of the boats must be considered.

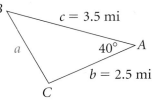
Example 1   Relating to the Real World

Sailing A racing committee wants to lay
out a triangular course with a 40° angle
between two sides of 3.5 mi and 2.5 mi.
What will be the length of the third side?

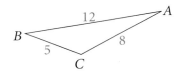

Choose the form of the Law of Cosines
that has a^2 on one side.

$a^2 = b^2 + c^2 - 2bc \cos A$
$a^2 = 2.5^2 + 3.5^2 - 2(2.5)(3.5) \cos 40°$ ⟵ Substitute.
$\quad \approx 6.25 + 12.25 - 17.5(0.7660)$ ⟵ Use a calculator.
$\quad \approx 5.095$
$\quad a \approx 2.3$ ⟵ Find the principal square root.

The third side of the triangular course will be about 2.3 mi long. ■

2. **Critical Thinking** How would a change if the racing committee decided
to make $\angle A$ a larger acute angle? an obtuse angle?

Example 2

Find the measure of $\angle C$ in the triangle at
the right. Round to the nearest tenth.

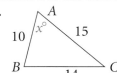

PROBLEM SOLVING

Look Back Why is the
cosine of 133.4° negative?

Choose the form of the Law of Cosines
that contains $\angle C$.

$c^2 = a^2 + b^2 - 2ab \cos C$
$12^2 = 5^2 + 8^2 - 2(5)(8) \cos C$ ⟵ Substitute.
$144 = 25 + 64 - 80 \cos C$ ⟵ Combine like terms.
$55 = -80 \cos C$ ⟵ Divide each side by −80.
$-\dfrac{55}{80} = \cos C$
$m\angle C \approx \cos^{-1}\left(-\dfrac{55}{80}\right)$ ⟵ Use $\cos^{-1}$ to find the angle whose cosine is $-\dfrac{55}{80}$.
$\quad \approx 133.4°$ ■

3. Which form of the Law of Cosines would you use to find $m\angle A$?

4. **Try This** In each triangle, find the measure x to the nearest tenth.

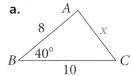

a.

b.

Using the Law of Sines

The Law of Sines relates the lengths of the sides of any triangle to the sines
of the angles opposite them.

For proofs of the Law of Sines and the Law of Cosines, see page 622.

Law of Sines

In $\triangle ABC$, let a, b, and c represent the lengths of the sides opposite $\angle A$, $\angle B$, and $\angle C$, respectively.

Then $\dfrac{\sin A}{a} = \dfrac{\sin B}{b} = \dfrac{\sin C}{c}$.

You can use the Law of Sines to find missing parts of any triangle when you know the measures of

▪ two angles and any side, or

▪ two sides and the angle opposite one of them.

Surveyors can use the Law of Sines to measure the height of a mountain indirectly.

Example 3   **Relating to the Real World**

Civil Engineering A surveyor locates points A and B at the same elevation and 3950 ft apart. At A, the angle of elevation to the summit of the mountain is 18°. At B, the angle of elevation is 31°.

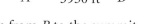

a. Find BC, the distance from B to the summit.
b. Find CD, the height of the mountain.

a. First, find $m\angle ABC$ and $m\angle ACB$.

$$m\angle ABC = 180° - 31° = 149°$$
$$m\angle ACB = 180° - 18° - 149° = 13°$$

Now use the Law of Sines in $\triangle ABC$. Write a proportion that includes the side you know, AB, and the side you want, BC.

$$\frac{\sin A}{BC} = \frac{\sin C}{AB}$$
$$\frac{\sin 18°}{BC} = \frac{\sin 13°}{3950} \qquad \longleftarrow \text{Substitute.}$$
$$BC = \frac{3950 \sin 18°}{\sin 13°} \qquad \longleftarrow \text{Solve for } BC.$$
$$BC \approx 5426 \text{ ft}$$

b. In right $\triangle BCD$, you know BC and $m\angle B$. Use the sine ratio.

$$\sin 31° \approx \frac{CD}{5426}$$
$$CD \approx 5426 \sin 31°$$
$$\approx 2795 \text{ ft}$$

The summit is about 2795 ft higher than points A and B.

Surveyors have measured the height of Mount Everest since 1852. Their measurements have ranged from 28,990 ft to 29,141 ft. Today, radar signals from orbiting satellites are used to measure heights more accurately.

5. Try This Draw a diagram and find the indicated part of each triangle.
  a. In $\triangle ABC$, $m\angle A = 40°$, $m\angle B = 60°$, and $a = 8$. Find b.
  b. In $\triangle RST$, $m\angle T = 97.5°$, $t = 80$, and $r = 75$. Find $m\angle R$.

Exercises   ON YOUR OWN

Use the Law of Cosines. Find the measure x to the nearest tenth.

1.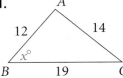

2.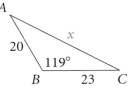

3.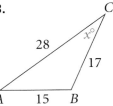

4.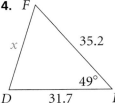

Use the Law of Sines. Find the measure x to the nearest tenth.

5.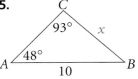

6.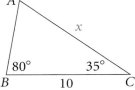

7.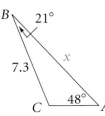

8.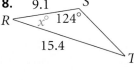

For each triangle, write the correct form of the Law of Cosines or the Law of Sines to solve for the measure in red. Use only the information given in blue.

9.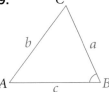

10.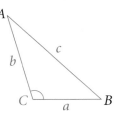

11.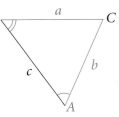

12.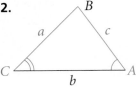

13. Softball A softball diamond is a square that measures 60 ft on a side. The pitcher's mound is 46 ft from home plate. How far is the pitcher from third base?

14. The distance from point A to the top of the hill is 2760 ft. The angle of elevation from A to the base of the tower is 28° and the angle of elevation from A to the top of the tower is 32°.
  a. Find the measures of $\angle 1$ and $\angle 2$.
  b. Find the height of the tower.

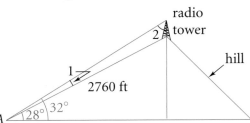

15. Forestry A forest ranger in an observation tower sights a fire 39° east of north. A ranger in a tower 10 miles due east of the first tower sights the fire at 42° west of north. How far is the fire from each tower?

16. a. Open-ended Sketch a triangle. Specify three of its measures so that you can use the Law of Sines to find the remaining measures.

   b. Sketch another triangle. Specify three of its measures so that you can use the Law of Cosines to find the remaining measures.

   c. Solve for the remaining measures of each of your triangles.

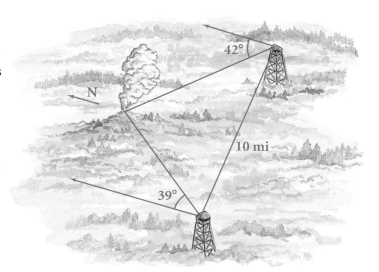

Find the remaining sides and angles in each triangle. Round to the nearest tenth.

17.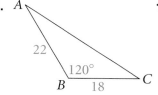

18.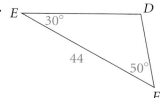

19.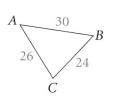

20.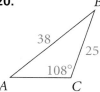

21.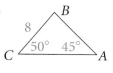

22.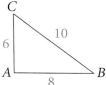

23.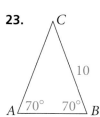

24.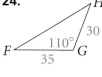

25. Navigation A pilot is flying from city A to city B, which is 85 mi due north. After flying 20 mi, the pilot must change course and fly 10° east of north to avoid a cloud bank.

   a. If the pilot remains on this course for 20 mi, how far will the plane be from city B?

   b. How many degrees will the pilot have to turn to the left to fly directly to city B? How many degrees from due north is this course?

26. a. In $\triangle ABC$, $a = 8$, $b = 15$, and $c = 17$. Find $m\angle C$.

   b. Suppose $a = 8$, $b = 15$, and $c = 18$. Will $\angle C$ be acute or obtuse? **Verify** your answer.

27. Writing Suppose you know the measures of all three angles of a triangle. Can you use the Law of Cosines or the Law of Sines to find the length of a side? Explain.

28. a. Find the length of the altitude to $\overline{PQ}$ in the triangle at the right.
   b. Find the area of $\triangle PQR$.

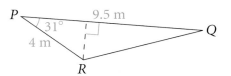

29. Writing Does the Law of Cosines apply to a right triangle? That is, does $c^2 = a^2 + b^2 - 2ab \cos C$ when $\angle C$ is a right angle? Justify your answer.

Chapter Project *Find Out by Researching*

To harness tidal power, a dam is built across the narrow neck of a bay where there is a large difference between high and low tide. Power is generated with both the incoming and outgoing tides, as water flows through the dam. However, near the times of high and low tide, other sources of energy must be used to supplement tidal power.

- How does the periodic nature of tides explain why tidal power is not a steady source of energy?
- Find out in what parts of the world it is practical to harness tidal power.
- How do utility companies that use tidal power provide energy when their customers need it?

Exercises   M I X E D   R E V I E W

Sketch the graph of the data in each table. Write a function to model each set of data, and find the *x*- and *y*-intercepts.

30.

x	y
−3	−13.5
−2	−4
−1	−0.5
0	0
1	0.5
2	4
3	13.5

31.

x	y
−3	5
−2	0
−1	−3
0	−4
1	−3
2	0
3	5

32.

x	y
−3	−2
−2	0
−1	2
0	4
1	6
2	8
3	10

33. Gardening You have a 150-ft^2 garden. You are going to plant tomato and squash plants. Tomato plants need 4 ft^2 of space and produce about 10 lb of tomatoes. Squash plants need 9 ft^2 of space and produce about 15 lb of squash. You want about the same number of pounds of each vegetable. How many of each vegetable should you plant?

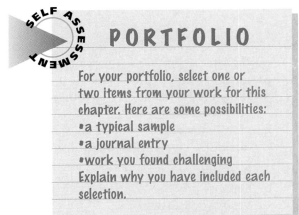

PORTFOLIO

For your portfolio, select one or two items from your work for this chapter. Here are some possibilities:
- a typical sample
- a journal entry
- work you found challenging

Explain why you have included each selection.

The Law of Sines with Two Triangles

After Lesson 9-7

The triangles at the right have one pair of congruent angles and two pairs of congruent sides. But the triangles are not congruent. Notice that the congruent angles are opposite one of the congruent sides. So, when you know the measures of two sides of a triangle and one of the opposite angles, there may be two triangles with those measurements. You can use the Law of Sines to find the other measures for both triangles.

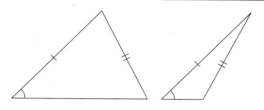

Example

In each $\triangle ABC$, $m\angle A = 35°$, $a = 11$, $b = 15$. Find $m\angle B$.

$\dfrac{\sin A}{a} = \dfrac{\sin B}{b}$ ◄——Use the Law of Sines.

$\dfrac{\sin 35°}{11} = \dfrac{\sin B}{15}$ ◄——Substitute values.

$\sin B = \dfrac{15 \sin 35°}{11}$ ◄——Solve for sin B.

$\sin B \approx 0.7821$

$m\angle B = \sin^{-1} 0.7821$ ◄——Solve for $m\angle B$.

$m\angle B \approx 51°$

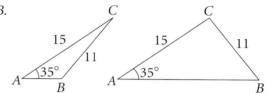

The calculator gives only an acute angle value for $m\angle B$, but there is also an obtuse angle. Its measure is $180° - 51°$, or $129°$.

Because there are two possible angle measures for $\angle B$, there are two triangles that satisfy the given conditions. In one triangle the angle measures are about 35°, 51°, and 94°. In the other, the angle measures are about 35°, 129°, and 16°.

In each $\triangle ABC$, find the measures for $\angle B$ and $\angle C$ that satisfy the given conditions. Draw diagrams to help you decide whether two triangles are possible. Remember that a triangle can have only one obtuse angle.

1. $m\angle A = 62°$, $a = 30$, and $b = 32$

2. $m\angle A = 16°$, $a = 12$, and $b = 37.5$

3. $m\angle A = 48°$, $a = 93$, and $b = 125$

4. $m\angle A = 112°$, $a = 16.5$, and $b = 5.4$

5. $m\angle A = 23.6°$, $a = 9.8$, and $b = 17$

6. $m\angle A = 155°$, $a = 12.5$, and $b = 8.4$

7. Writing Sometimes two different triangles can have the same measures for two sides and an angle opposite one of the sides. Describe conditions when those measures determine only one triangle.

Finishing the Chapter Project

The Wave of the Future

Find Out questions on pages 408, 428, and 448 should help you complete your project. Write a brief paper describing how the tides can be harnessed to create electrical power. Discuss what you think are the advantages and disadvantages of tidal power. Based on your research and analysis, do you think tidal power plants are a practical source of electricity for the future? Support your conclusions.

Reflect and Revise

Find someone in your class whose conclusion about tidal power is different from yours. Read each other's papers. Discuss your differences of opinion. Have you changed your mind about your conclusions? If necessary, do further research and revise your paper.

Follow Up

Research other factors that affect the cycle of the tides, such as the changing distances of the moon and sun from Earth. Describe these in terms of periodic functions, if possible.

For More Information

Arnold, Guy. *Facts on Water, Wind, and Solar Power.* New York: Franklin Watts, 1990.

Douglas, John H. *The Future World of Energy.* Grolier Incorporated, 1984.

Goldin, Augusta. *Oceans of Energy.* New York: Harcourt Brace Javanovich, 1980.

Wylie, Francis, E. *Tides and the Pull of the Moon.* Brattleboro, Vermont: The Stephen Greene Press, 1979.

Key Terms

amplitude (p. 404)
cosine of θ (p. 411)
coterminal (p. 410)
cycle (p. 403)
initial side (p. 409)
Law of Cosines (p. 443)
Law of Sines (p. 445)
period (p. 403)

periodic function (p. 403)
radian (p. 415)
sine of θ (p. 411)
standard position (p. 409)
tangent of θ (p. 432)
terminal side (p. 409)
trigonometric ratios (p. 437)
unit circle (p. 411)

How am I doing?

- State three ideas from this chapter that you think are important. Explain your choices.
- Describe the features of periodic functions.

SELF ASSESSMENT

Exploring Periodic Data   9-1

A **periodic function** repeats a pattern of y-values at regular intervals. One complete pattern is called a **cycle.** A cycle may begin at any point on the graph. The **period** of a function is the length of one cycle.

The **amplitude** of a function is half the difference between its maximum and minimum values.

Use the function $f(x)$ shown at the right.

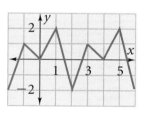

1. Graph the next two cycles of this function.

2. What is the period of the function? What is its amplitude?

3. State three values of x for which $f(x) = 2$.

The Unit Circle   9-2

An angle is in **standard position** when the vertex is at the origin and one ray is on the positive x-axis. The ray on the x-axis is the **initial side** of the angle; the other ray is the **terminal side** of the angle. Two angles in standard position are **coterminal** if they have the same terminal side.

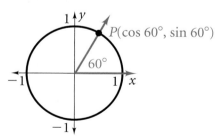

The **unit circle** has a radius of 1 unit and has its center at the origin. The **cosine of θ** (cos θ) is the x-coordinate of the point at which the terminal side of the angle intersects the unit circle. The **sine of θ** (sin θ) is the y-coordinate.

Sketch each angle in standard position. Then find the exact values of the cosine and the sine of the angle.

4. $45°$ 5. $90°$ 6. $-30°$ 7. $120°$ 8. $180°$ 9. $315°$

A **radian** is the measure of a central angle that intercepts an arc equal in length to a radius of the circle.

To convert degrees to radians, multiply by $\frac{\pi \text{ radians}}{180°}$. To convert radians to degrees, multiply by $\frac{180°}{\pi \text{ radians}}$.

When the measure of an angle θ is in radians and r is the radius, the length s of the intercepted arc is $s = r\theta$.

Write each measure in radians. Express each answer in terms of π.

10. $60°$ **11.** $-45°$ **12.** $180°$ **13.** $-270°$ **14.** $450°$ **15.** $-720°$

Rewrite each measure in degrees.

16. 2π **17.** $\frac{5\pi}{6}$ **18.** $-\frac{3\pi}{4}$ **19.** $\frac{12\pi}{5}$ **20.** $-\frac{10\pi}{3}$ **21.** -3π

22. Standardized Test Prep Which pair of angles is coterminal?

     A. $\frac{3\pi}{4}$ and $-\frac{3\pi}{4}$ **B.** $90°$ and $270°$ **C.** $\frac{5\pi}{3}$ and $\frac{2\pi}{3}$ **D.** π and $-\pi$ **E.** none of these

The table below summarizes information about sine functions and cosine functions.

	Sine Functions	Cosine Functions
Equation	$y = a \sin b\theta$	$y = a \cos b\theta$
Amplitude	$|a|$	$|a|$
Number of Cycles	b cycles from 0 to 2π	b cycles from 0 to 2π
Period	$\frac{2\pi}{b}$	$\frac{2\pi}{b}$

The **tangent** of an angle θ in standard position is the y-coordinate of the point where the terminal side of the angle intersects the tangent line $x = 1$. Tangent functions in the form $y = \tan b\theta$ have a period of $\frac{\pi}{b}$.

Sketch the graph of each function in the interval from 0 to 2π.

23. $y = -\sin 3\theta$ **24.** $y = 2 \cos \frac{\pi}{2}t$ **25.** $y = \tan \frac{1}{2}t$ **26.** $y = 3 \sin \theta$

Graphing Calculator Solve each equation in the interval from 0 to 2π.

27. $\cos \theta = -0.7$ **28.** $\tan 0.5t = 3$ **29.** $\sin \frac{\pi}{3}\theta = 0.25$ **30.** $3 \sin 4\theta = -2$

31. Write an equation of a sine function that has amplitude 4 and period 0.5π. Choose $a > 0$.

You can use a right triangle to find the sine, cosine, and tangent of an acute angle.

$$\sin A = \frac{\text{length of leg opposite } \angle A}{\text{length of hypotenuse}} \qquad \cos A = \frac{\text{length of leg adjacent to } \angle A}{\text{length of hypotenuse}} \qquad \tan A = \frac{\text{length of leg opposite } \angle A}{\text{length of leg adjacent to } \angle A}$$

$\text{Sin}^{-1}x$ represents the measure of the angle whose sine is x. $\text{Sin}^{-1}x$ is usually read *inverse sine of x*.

In $\triangle ABC$, $\angle C$ is a right angle. Two measures are given. Find the remaining sides and angles. When necessary, round to the nearest tenth.

32. $a = 4$, $b = 3$ **33.** $m\angle A = 34°$, $c = 12$ **34.** $m\angle B = 64°$, $b = 15$

35. Writing You know that the sine of one angle of a right triangle is $\frac{11}{15}$. Explain how to find the cosine and tangent of this angle.

You can use the **Law of Cosines** to find the missing measures of a triangle when you know the measures of three sides, or two sides and the angle between them.

Law of Cosines

$$a^2 = b^2 + c^2 - 2bc \cos A$$
$$b^2 = a^2 + c^2 - 2ac \cos B$$
$$c^2 = a^2 + b^2 - 2ab \cos C$$

You can use the **Law of Sines** to find the missing measures of a triangle when you know the measures of two angles and any side, or two sides and the angle opposite one of them.

Law of Sines

$$\frac{\sin A}{a} = \frac{\sin B}{b} = \frac{\sin C}{c}$$

$\triangle ABC$ is oblique. Find the remaining measures of each triangle. Round answers to the nearest hundredth.

36. $m\angle A = 60°$, $b = 10$, $c = 9$ **37.** $m\angle B = 25°$, $m\angle C = 58°$, $a = 3$

38. Open-ended Sketch an oblique triangle. Give three of its measures, including one side. Find the remaining measures.

Getting Ready for..

CHAPTER

10

Graph each quadratic function.

39. $y = 4x^2 + 3$ **40.** $y = 2(x - 1)^2 + 5$ **41.** $y = \frac{1}{2}(x + 2)^2 - 4$

Solve each system of equations.

42. $\begin{cases} y = 2x - 1 \\ y = 3x + 1 \end{cases}$ **43.** $\begin{cases} y = 4x - 3 \\ y = 9 - x \end{cases}$ **44.** $\begin{cases} x + y = 2 \\ 2x - 3y = 6 \end{cases}$

Does each graph illustrate a periodic function? Explain why or why not.

1.

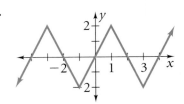

2.

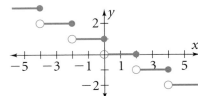

Find a positive and a negative coterminal angle for each given angle.

3. 32°   **4.** −229°   **5.** 315°

Write each measure in radians. Express the answer in terms of π.

6. −225°   **7.** 120°   **8.** 600°

Write each measure in degrees. When necessary, round your answer to the nearest degree.

9. $\frac{5\pi}{6}$ **10.** −2.5π   **11.** 0.8

12. Writing Explain how to write radian measures as degree measures. Include an example.

Calculator **Evaluate each expression. When necessary, round to the nearest tenth.**

13. sin 34°   **14.** cos 102°

15. $\tan^{-1} 2.75$ **16.** $\sin^{-1} 0.5$

Sketch the graph of each function in the interval from 0 to 2π.

17. $y = \sin 2x$ **18.** $y = 2 \cos x$

19. $y = \tan\frac{1}{3}\theta$ **20.** $y = -3 \sin 2\theta$

21. $y = -\cos \pi\theta$ **22.** $y = \tan \frac{\pi}{3}\theta$

Find the exact value of each expression.

23. sin 120°   **24.** tan 225°

25. $\cos \frac{\pi}{3}$ **26.** sin 3π

27. Standardized Test Prep Which curve has period 3?
A. $y = \sin 3\theta$ **B.** $y = \cos \frac{\pi}{3}\theta$
C. $y = \tan \frac{\pi}{3}\theta$ **D.** $y = \frac{1}{3}\cos \theta$
E. $y = 3 \sin \theta$

Use the right triangle below. Find each value to the nearest hundredth.

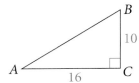

28. sin A   **29.** tan B   **30.** m∠A

31. a. Open-ended Sketch a right △ABC where sin A is greater than cos A. Label the measures of the angles.
  b. What is the range of m∠A such that sin A > cos A ?

Find the altitude to $\overline{AB}$ in each triangle.

32.   **33.**

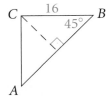

Find the remaining measures of each triangle.

34.   **35.**

For Exercises 1–9, choose the correct letter.

1. Which polynomial has $(x - 1)$ as a factor?
  A. $x^2 + 3x + 2$ **B.** $x^2 + 2x + 1$
  C. $x^3 - x^2 - x + 1$ **D.** $x^3 - 3x - 2$
  E. $x^3 + 5x^2 + 4x$

2. Which point(s) are on the unit circle?
  I. $\left(\frac{1}{2}, \frac{\sqrt{3}}{2}\right)$ **II.** $\left(\frac{\sqrt{2}}{2}, -\frac{\sqrt{2}}{2}\right)$
  III. $\left(-\frac{\sqrt{2}}{2}, -\frac{1}{2}\right)$ **IV.** $\left(\frac{\sqrt{3}}{2}, -\frac{1}{2}\right)$
  A. I and II **B.** II and III **C.** III and IV
  D. I and IV **E.** I, II, and IV

3. The Law of Sines cannot be used with one of these triangles. Which one?
  A.
  B.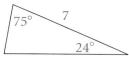
  C.
  D.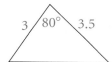
  E.

4. What is the amplitude of $y = -4 \sin \frac{1}{2}x$?
  A. 4 **B.** $\frac{1}{2}$ **C.** 4π
  D. -4 **E.** 1

5. Which function does not have a vertical asymptote?
  A. $y = \frac{2}{x - 3}$ **B.** $y = \frac{4x^2}{x^3 - 1}$
  C. $y = -\cos x$ **D.** $y = \tan 2x$
  E. $y = \begin{cases} \frac{3}{x}, \text{if } x < 6 \\ x - 5.5, \text{if } x \geq 6 \end{cases}$

6. Rewrite $3 \log x - 2 \log 2x$ as a single logarithmic expression.
  A. $-\log x$ **B.** $\log (-x)$
  C. $\log \frac{3}{4}$ **D.** $\log \frac{x}{4}$
  E. $\log \frac{x}{2}$

7. Write $\frac{5\pi}{6}$ radians in degrees.
  A. $300°$ **B.** $170°$ **C.** $30°$
  D. $80°$ **E.** $150°$

Compare the boxed quantity in Column A to the boxed quantity in Column B. Choose the best answer.
  A. The quantity in Column A is greater.
  B. The quantity in Column B is greater.
  C. The two quantities are equal.
  D. The relationship cannot be determined on the basis of the information supplied.

Column A	Column B
8. $\sin \frac{\pi}{2}$	$\cos \frac{\pi}{2}$

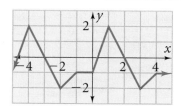

9. the period	the amplitude

Find each answer.

10. *Open-ended* Sketch a periodic function with period 7.

11. *Physics* A pendulum is 18 in. long. It swings through an angle of $\frac{3\pi}{4}$ radians. How far does the tip of the pendulum travel in one swing? Round your answer to the nearest inch.

Relating to the Real World

Quadratic relations are everywhere. Practical applications of parabolas, circles, ellipses, and hyperbolas can be found in headlights, mirrors, lenses, radar, planetary orbits, architecture, marine biology, and navigation.

About Face!

When was the last time you were entertained by a clown? Most of us have seen clowns at a circus, a party, or in a street show. Many cultures enjoy the art of clowning. Clowns can depict many emotions depending on their dress and makeup.

As you work through the project for this chapter, you will use graphs of quadratic relations to create designs for clown faces. You will try to capture specific emotions in your designs. Along with your classmates, you will organize a display of your work.

To help you complete the project:

▼ **p. 470** *Find Out by Graphing*
▼ **p. 475** *Find Out by Creating*
▼ **p. 483** *Find Out by Analyzing*
▼ **p. 498** *Finishing the Project*

Hyperbolas
10-5

Translating Conic Sections
10-6

10-1 Exploring Conic Sections

WORK TOGETHER

Work with a partner to see the ways that a plane can slice a cone.

1. a. Begin with two circular areas, each four inches in diameter. Cut each circular area in half. Roll each half into a cone and secure it with tape.

b. Trace the templates below onto a sheet of paper. Cut them out and label each one.

c. Make a fourth template for a circle. Use any coin of any size to draw the circle.

d. Fit each template around the cones so that the template stays flat, like a plane. The ellipse is shown at the left. Sketch each result.

Parabola

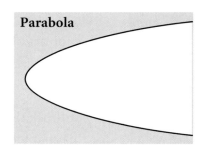

Ellipse

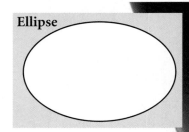

Hyperbola

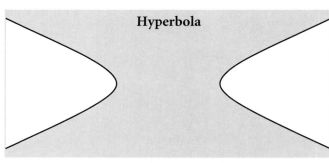

2. a. The template for a hyperbola has two parts. Which photograph at the right shows a plane intersecting a double cone to form a hyperbola?

b. Suppose you tried to fit your other three templates around a double cone. Would the results change? Explain.

3. a. Fold the template for each curve so that two halves coincide. In how many ways can you do this for each of the four templates?

b. How many axes of symmetry does each template have?

A

Graphing Equations of Conic Sections

Each of the curves from the Work Together activity—circle, ellipse, parabola, and hyperbola—is a conic section. A **conic section** is formed by the intersection of a plane and a double cone.

You can use symmetry to help graph each conic section.

4. Recall that the graph of a quadratic function is a parabola.
   a. What are some of the properties of the graph of $y = 2x^2$?
   b. What are the domain and range of this function?

Example 1

The face of a clock can be modeled by the equation $x^2 + y^2 = 25$. Graph the equation. Describe the graph and its lines of symmetry.

Make a table of values. Then plot the points and connect them with a smooth curve. Some points on the graph are shown in the table.

x	-5	-4	-3	0	3	4	5
y	0	± 3	± 4	± 5	± 4	± 3	0

⟵ Since x is squared, both -4 and 4 can be used.

⟵ Since y is squared, both 3 and -3 can be used.

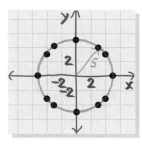

The graph is a circle of radius 5. Its center is at the origin. Every line through the center is a line of symmetry.

5. a. Explain why there is no point on the graph in Example 1 with an x-coordinate of 6.
   b. What are the domain and range of the graph?
   c. Does the graph represent a function? Explain.

6. a. **Graphing Calculator** Graph the functions $y = \sqrt{25 - x^2}$ and $y = -\sqrt{25 - x^2}$ on the same screen. Use the Zoom feature to choose a square window. How does this graph compare to the graph in Example 1?
   b. Explain how to get the equations in part (a) from $x^2 + y^2 = 25$.

7. Try This Graph the equations $x^2 + y^2 = 9$ and $x^2 + y^2 = 4$. What are the centers and radii of these graphs?

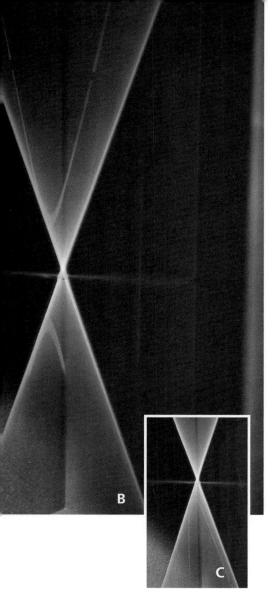

B

C

The photographs show a double cone of illuminated smoke being intersected by a rotating laser.

D

Example 2

Graph the equation $9x^2 + 16y^2 = 144$. Describe the graph and its lines of symmetry.

Find the y-intercepts by replacing x with 0.

x	-4	-3	0	3	4
y	0	± 2.6	± 3	± 2.0	0

Find the x-intercepts by replacing y with 0.

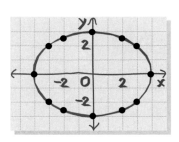

The graph is an ellipse. Its center is at the origin. It has two lines of symmetry, the x-axis and the y-axis.

8. In Example 2, how far are the x-intercepts from the center of the ellipse? How far are the y-intercepts? Describe how an ellipse differs from a circle.

9. The point $(1, 2.9)$ is on the graph in Example 2. Use symmetry to find three other points on the ellipse.

10. **Predict** what the graph of $16x^2 + 9y^2 = 144$ would look like. Then graph the equation. Compare it with the graph in Example 2.

11. **Try This** Graph the equation $2x^2 + y^2 = 18$. Describe the graph and give the coordinates of the x- and y-intercepts.

Example 3

Graph the equation $x^2 - y^2 = 9$. Describe the graph and its lines of symmetry.

PROBLEM SOLVING

Look Back Why is the y-value undefined when $x = -2, -1, 0, 1,$ or 2?

x	-5	-4	-3	-2	-1	0	1	2	3	4	5
y	± 4	± 2.6	0	$-$	$-$	$-$	$-$	$-$	0	± 2.6	± 4

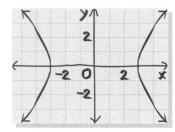

The graph is a hyperbola that consists of two branches. Its center is at the origin. It has two lines of symmetry, the x-axis and the y-axis.

12. **a.** What are the domain and range of this graph?
    b. Does the graph represent a function? Explain.

13. **a.** *Critical Thinking* What two lines does each branch of this hyperbola get very close to?
    b. What are these types of lines called?

14. **a.** **Try This** Graph the equation $2x^2 - y^2 = 18$.
    b. In what ways is the graph similar to and different from the graph in Question 11?

A moiré pattern can occur in printing four-color photographs when the dot patterns on the separate color plates are misaligned. In which photo do the plates need adjusting?

Identifying Conic Sections

You will study conic sections in detail later in this chapter. However, by studying the graphs of the conic sections in this chapter, you can match equations with their corresponding graphs.

Example 4   **Relating to the Real World** ·············

Design Moiré patterns are formed when two patterns, such as an array of dots or lines, overlap to produce a third, unintended, pattern. Moiré patterns cause problems for printers and video technicians. Describe each unintended pattern. Match it with a possible equation.

a. 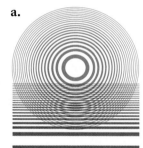   b. 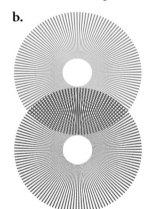   c.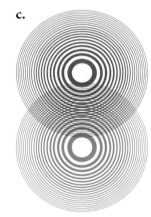

Equations: $x^2 - y^2 = 1$, $x^2 + y^2 = 16$, and $9x^2 + 25y^2 = 225$

a. Ellipse. The equation $9x^2 + 25y^2 = 225$ represents a conic section with two sets of intercepts, $(\pm 5, 0)$ and $(0, \pm 3)$. Since the intercepts are not equidistant from the center, it models an ellipse.

b. Hyperbola. The equation $x^2 - y^2 = 1$ represents a conic section with one set of intercepts, $(\pm 1, 0)$, so it must model a hyperbola.

c. Circle. The equation $x^2 + y^2 = 16$ represents a conic section with two sets of intercepts, $(\pm 4, 0)$ and $(0, \pm 4)$. Since each intercept is 4 units from the center, it models a circle.

Identify the center and the *x*- and *y*-intercepts for each ellipse. Give the domain and range of each graph.

1.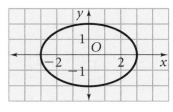

2.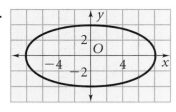

3.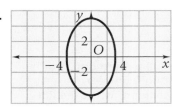

📇 **Graphing Calculator** **Identify the center and intercepts of the hyperbola on each graphing calculator screen. Give the domain and range of each graph. Assume each Xscl and Yscl = 1.**

4.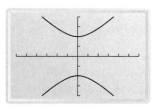

5.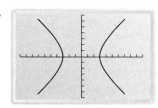

6.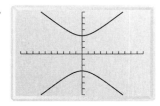

Graph each equation. Describe each graph and its lines of symmetry. Give the domain and range for each graph.

7. $3y^2 - x^2 = 25$

8. $2x^2 + y^2 = 36$

9. $x^2 + y^2 = 16$

10. $4x^2 + 4y^2 - 20 = 0$

11. $4x^2 + 25y^2 = 100$

12. $25x^2 + 16y^2 - 320 = 0$

13. $3y^2 - x^2 = 9$

14. $x^2 - y^2 + 1 = 0$

15. $x^2 - 2y^2 = 4$

Graph each circle so that its center is at the origin. Then write its equation.

16. radius 6

17. radius $\frac{1}{2}$

18. diameter 8

19. diameter 2.5

20. Light The light emitted from a lamp with a shade forms a shadow on the wall. Explain how you could turn the lamp in relation to the wall so that the shadow cast by the shade forms each of the following conic sections.
a. hyperbola   **b.** parabola
c. ellipse   **d.** circle

21. Open-ended Describe any other figures you can imagine that can be formed by the intersection of a plane and other shapes.

22. *Sound* When an airplane flies faster than the speed of sound, it creates a pressure disturbance in the air. This cone-shaped disturbance is heard by people on the ground as a sonic boom. Describe the shape of the path along which the sonic boom is heard at any given time when the plane is cruising overhead.

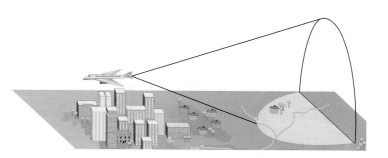

23. a. *Writing* Describe the relationship between the center of a circle and the circle's axes of symmetry.

    b. Make a **conjecture** about where the center of an ellipse or a hyperbola is located in relation to its axes of symmetry. **Verify** your conjecture with an example of each.

Mental Math **The given point is on the graph of the given equation. Find at least one more point on the graph.**

24. $(2, -4); y^2 = 8x$

25. $(-\sqrt{2}, 1); x^2 + y^2 = 3$

26. $(2, 2\sqrt{2}); x^2 + 4y^2 = 36$

27. $(-2, 0); 9x^2 + 9y^2 - 36 = 0$

28. $(-3, -\sqrt{51}); 6y^2 - 9x^2 - 225 = 0$

29. $(0, \sqrt{7}); x^2 + 2y^2 = 14$

30. a. Graph the equation $xy = 16$. Use both positive and negative values for x.

    b. Which conic section does the equation appear to model?

    c. Identify any intercepts and lines of symmetry.

    d. Does your graph represent a function? If so, rewrite the equation in function form.

31. The sharpened portion of the pencil at the right meets each painted side in a curved path. Describe the curve and **justify** your reasoning.

Exercises   M I X E D   R E V I E W

Solve each equation.

32. $\sin \theta = \frac{1}{2}$

33. $x^2 + x = 4x - 2$

34. $x = \frac{3}{1 - x}$

35. $\log_4 x = 3$

36. *Coordinate Geometry* A quadrilateral has vertices $A(3, 5)$, $B(-2, 1)$, $C(0, -3)$, and $D(6, 1)$. Use matrices to find the vertices of the image of the quadrilateral after a translation 5 units left and 1 unit down.

Getting Ready for Lesson 10-2
Graph each function.

37. $y = x^2 - 4$

38. $y = (x + 1)^2 + 2$

39. $y = (x - 4)^2 + 1$

40. $y = 3x^2$

Graphing Relations

After Lesson 10-1

Your graphing calculator can graph relations that are not functions.

Example

Graph the ellipse $\frac{x^2}{16} + \frac{y^2}{9} = 1$.

Step 1: Solve the equation for y.

$$\frac{x^2}{16} + \frac{y^2}{9} = 1$$

$$\frac{y^2}{9} = 1 - \frac{x^2}{16}$$

$$y^2 = 9\left(1 - \frac{x^2}{16}\right)$$

$$y = \pm\, 3\sqrt{\left(1 - \frac{x^2}{16}\right)} \quad\longleftarrow\quad \text{The expression } 9\left(1 - \frac{x^2}{16}\right) \text{ has both a positive and a negative square root.}$$

Step 2: Enter the two square roots as Y_1 and Y_2.

Step 3: Select a square window. The window shown below allows integer values to be graphed.

Step 4: Graph.

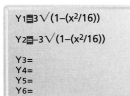

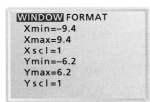

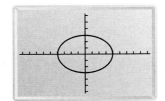

Graph each conic section.

1. $x^2 + y^2 = 25$

2. $4x^2 + y^2 = 16$

3. $9x^2 - 16y^2 = 144$

4. $x^2 - y^2 = 3$

5. $\frac{x^2}{4} + \frac{y^2}{9} = 1$

6. $\frac{x^2}{4} - \frac{y^2}{9} = 1$

7. $\frac{x^2}{9} + \frac{y^2}{9} = 1$

8. $x^2 + \frac{y^2}{4} = 16$

9. a. Graph the functions $y = \sqrt{\frac{81}{4} - x^2}$ and $y = -\sqrt{\frac{81}{4} - x^2}$.

    b. Use TRACE to estimate the x-intercepts.

    c. Use 2nd CALC 1 for $x = 0$ to find the y-intercepts.

    d. Adjust the window to $-9.3 \le x \le 9.5$. **Verify** the x-intercepts.

    e. What conic section does the graph represent?

10. Graph each conic section. Find the x- and y-intercepts.

    a. $4x^2 + y^2 = 25$ **b.** $x^2 + y^2 = 30$ **c.** $9x^2 - 4y^2 = 72$ **d.** $x = y^2 - 5.3$

11. Writing Explain how to use a graphing calculator to graph the relation $x = |y - 3|$.

What You'll Learn

- Writing and graphing the equation of a parabola

- Using the properties of a parabola to solve problems

...And Why

To design a solar collector

What You'll Need

- ruled paper
- ruler

10-2 Parabolas

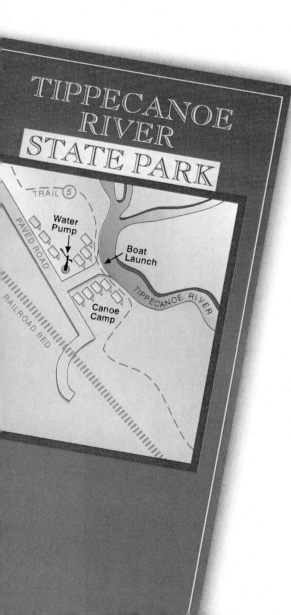

W O R K   T O G E T H E R

Suppose you and your friends are on a canoe trip along the Tippecanoe River in Indiana. You want a campsite that is the same distance from a water pump as it is from the river's edge. Using a sheet of ruled paper, make a model to determine all the possible campsite locations.

Step 1:

- Draw a horizontal line ℓ near the bottom of the page to represent the river's edge. Number the lines above it.

- Mark the location P of the pump as shown, three ruled lines above the river.

- Draw a line perpendicular to ℓ through P. Label this line "axis of symmetry." Find the point on the axis of symmetry that lies exactly halfway between P and ℓ.

Step 2: Now find other points that are the same distance from the pump P and the river ℓ.

- Measure the distance d from line 2 to ℓ. Locate two points on line 2 that are d units from P. (There will be one on each side of the axis of symmetry.) Mark them.

- Measure the distance e from line 3 to ℓ. Find two points on line 3 that are e units from P and mark them. Continue marking points in a similar way using lines 4, 5, 6, ...

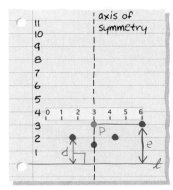

1. Connect the points of your model with a smooth curve. What kind of curve have you drawn?

2. **Critical Thinking** How would your curve change if the pump were closer to the river? farther away from the river?

3. What point is closest to the pump and the river? What is this called?

Writing the Equation of a Parabola

A parabola is the set of all points in a plane that are the same distance from a fixed line and a fixed point not on the line. The fixed point is the **focus.** The fixed line is the **directrix.** The line through the focus perpendicular to the directrix is the axis of symmetry.

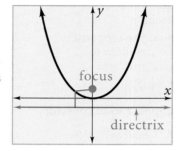

Example 1

Write the equation whose graph is the set of all points in the plane that are equidistant from the point $F(0, 3)$ and the line $y = -3$.

You need to find all points $P(x, y)$ such that FP and the distance from P to the given line are equal.

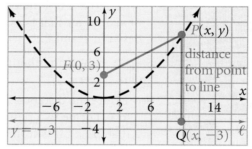

QUICK REVIEW

The distance between the points $P_1(x_1, y_1)$ and $P_2(x_2, y_2)$ can be found using the formula:

$d = \sqrt{(x_2 - x_1)^2 + (y_2 - y_1)^2}$

$$FP = PQ$$
$$\sqrt{(x - 0)^2 + (y - 3)^2} = \sqrt{(x - x)^2 + (y - (-3))^2}$$
$$x^2 + (y - 3)^2 = 0^2 + (y + 3)^2 \quad \longleftarrow \text{Square each side.}$$
$$x^2 + y^2 - 6y + 9 = y^2 + 6y + 9 \quad \longleftarrow \text{Expand } (y - 3)^2 \text{ and } (y + 3)^2.$$
$$x^2 = 12y$$
$$y = \frac{1}{12}x^2$$

The equation of the set of points equidistant from the point $F(0, 3)$ and the line $y = -3$ is $y = \frac{1}{12}x^2$.

For more practice with the distance formula, see Skills Handbook page 676.

4. What is the equation of the axis of symmetry of this parabola?

5. What are the coordinates of the vertex? How do you know?

6. How far is the vertex from the focus? from the directrix?

7. **Try This** Write the equation of the set of all points in the plane that are equidistant from the point $F(2, 0)$ and the line $x = -2$.

In the equation $y = \frac{1}{12}x^2$, the denominator 12 is four times the distance from the vertex to the focus, 3. Suppose c is the distance from the vertex to the focus of a parabola represented by $y = ax^2$ or $x = ay^2$. Then $a = \frac{1}{4c}$.

8. Verify that $a = \frac{1}{4c}$ for the parabola in Question 7.

Example 2   Relating to the Real World

Solar Energy In some solar collectors, a mirror with a parabolic cross section is used to concentrate sunlight on the pipe, which is located at the focus of the mirror.

a. Suppose the pipe is located 6 in. from the vertex of the mirror. Write an equation of the parabola to model the cross section of the mirror.

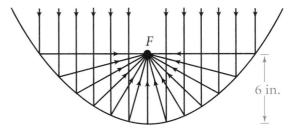

b. The amount of light collected by the mirror is directly proportional to its width. Using this mirror, the pipe receives 30 times more sunlight than it would without the mirror. Suppose the diameter of the pipe is 1 in. What must the width of the mirror be?

a. Since the distance from the vertex to the focus is 6 in., $c = 6$. Now find the value of a.

$$a = \frac{1}{4c}$$
$$= \frac{1}{4(6)}$$
$$= \frac{1}{24}$$

The equation of the parabola is $y = \frac{1}{24}x^2$.

b. The width of the mirror must be 30 times the diameter of the pipe, or 30 in.

Parabolic solar mirrors are used to heat water in Chasa, Tibet.

The world's largest solar energy complex, located in the Mojave Desert, uses thousands of parabolic mirrors. The mirrors gather the heat, which produces steam to drive the generators.

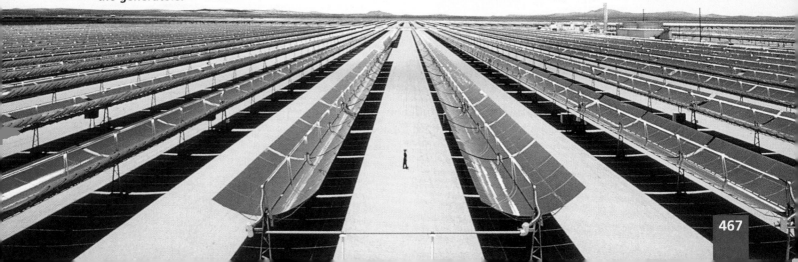

Graphing Parabolas

You saw in Chapters 5 and 6 that a parabola can open up, down, to the left, or to the right.

For $y = ax^2$:

If $a > 0$, then
- the parabola opens up;
- the focus is at $(0, c)$;
- the directrix is $y = -c$.

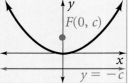

If $a < 0$, then
- the parabola opens down;
- the focus is at $(0, -c)$;
- the directrix is $y = c$.

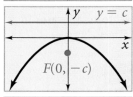

For $x = ay^2$:

If $a > 0$, then
- the parabola opens to the right;
- the focus is at $(c, 0)$;
- the directrix is $x = -c$.

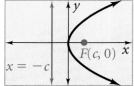

If $a < 0$, then
- the parabola opens to the left;
- the focus is at $(-c, 0)$;
- the directrix is $x = c$.

For all of the parabolas above, $|a| = \frac{1}{4c}$.

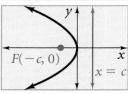

Example 3

Identify the focus and directrix of the graph of the equation $x = -\frac{1}{16}y^2$. Then graph the parabola.

The parabola is of the form $x = ay^2$, so its vertex is at the origin and it has a horizontal axis of symmetry. Since $a < 0$, the parabola opens to the left.

$$|a| = \frac{1}{4c}$$
$$\left|-\frac{1}{16}\right| = \frac{1}{4c} \quad \longleftarrow \text{ Substitute } -\frac{1}{16} \text{ for } a.$$
$$4c = 16 \quad \longleftarrow \text{ Solve for } c.$$
$$c = 4$$

The focus is at $(-4, 0)$.

The equation of the directrix is $x = 4$.

Locate two more points on the parabola. Select values for y, such as ± 4. Then two other points on the graph are $(-1, 4)$ and $(-1, -4)$.

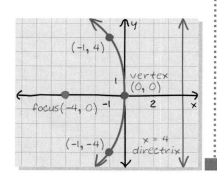

Tell whether the parabola opens up, down, left, or right.

1. $y = \frac{1}{2}x^2$ **2.** $x = \frac{1}{2}y^2$ **3.** $x^2 + 4y = 0$ **4.** $-9x - 27y^2 = 0$

5. Optics A cross section of a flashlight reflector is a parabola. The bulb is located at the focus of the parabola. Use the properties of parabolas to explain the advantages of this design.

6. Writing Explain how to find the distance from the focus to the directrix for the parabola $x = 2y^2$.

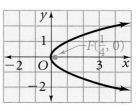

Use the information in each graph to write the equation for the parabola shown.

7.
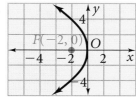

8.
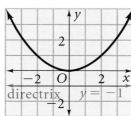

9.

Identify the focus and directrix of each parabola. Then graph the parabola.

10. $y = \frac{1}{8}x^2$ **11.** $x = \frac{1}{24}y^2$ **12.** $y = -\frac{1}{8}x^2$ **13.** $-8x = y^2$

14. $x = \frac{1}{12}y^2$ **15.** $y^2 - 25x = 0$ **16.** $x^2 = 4y$ **17.** $x^2 = -4y$

Write the equation of each parabola with its vertex at the origin.

18. focus at $(6, 0)$ **19.** focus at $(0, -4)$ **20.** directrix $x = -3$ **21.** directrix $y = 5$

22. You and your family are looking for a new home in the neighborhood shown on the map. Your parents can catch a bus anywhere on W. First Street to get to work. You must walk to school each morning. The best location would be somewhere that is the same distance from W. First Street as it is to your school.
   a. Show that the corner of E. First Street and Second Avenue N. is one possible location.
   b. Describe the set of all possible locations that satisfy the condition geometrically.
   c. Critical Thinking Would all these points realistically be just as long a walk for you as for your parents? Explain.

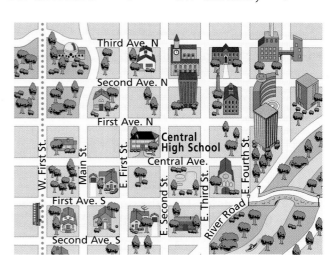

23. Earth Science A tsunami is an ocean wave that results from an undersea earthquake. In deep water, the waves are small but move at high speeds. When they reach shallower water, their height increases and their speed decreases. The equation $d = \frac{1}{10}s^2$ relates the depth d of the ocean (in meters) to the speed s at which the waves travel (in m/s). Graph the parabola that models this equation.

24. Open-ended Write three equations for parabolas that open to the left. Give the focus and directrix of each parabola.

25. Modeling Draw a cross section of a parabolic mirror modeled by the equation $y = 0.0023x^2$.

26. a. What part of a parabola is modeled by the function $y = -\sqrt{x}$?
  b. State the domain and range for the function in part (a).

Chapter Project .... **Find Out by Graphing**

Design a clown face using only graphs (or parts of graphs) of parabolas. When you have a design you like, record the equations you use, including any restrictions on the domain or range of each.

Give the equations for your clown face to two classmates. Ask them to sketch the face from the equations. Compare their sketches with yours. Check your equations to resolve any differences among the graphs.

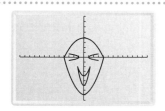

Exercises   MIXED REVIEW

How many x-intercepts does each function have?

27. $y = 5x^2 + 6x - 2$ **28.** $y = -2x^2$ **29.** $y = 3x^2 - 9x + 8$ **30.** $y = x^2 - 4x + 1$

31. Banking You deposit $600 of your summer earnings in an account earning 6% interest compounded annually. How much will be in the account after 4 years?

Getting Ready for Lesson 10-3
Coordinate Geometry Find the coordinates of three points that are the given distance from the given point.

32. 3; $(0, 0)$ **33.** 5; $(-2, 3)$

34. 8; $(4, 1)$ **35.** 10; $(-4, -5)$

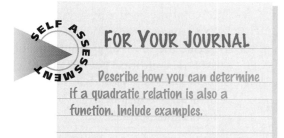

SELF ASSESSMENT **FOR YOUR JOURNAL**

Describe how you can determine if a quadratic relation is also a function. Include examples.

10-3 Circles

What You'll Learn

• Writing and graphing the equation of a circle

• Finding the center and radius of a circle

...And Why

To solve problems about landscaping and mechanics that involve circles

What You'll Need

• graph paper

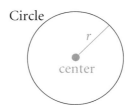

Many cultures use circular dwellings to maximize volume for a given surface area. The examples shown are (from top to bottom) from Canada, Mongolia, and Mali.

THINK AND DISCUSS

Writing Equations of Circles

A circular region that encloses the same area as a rectangular region has a smaller perimeter. For a given area, a circular home would require less material than a rectangular one of the same height.

1. Describe how you could use a stake and a long piece of rope to mark the perimeter of a circular home that will be 20 ft across.

This method for constructing a circle is related to the definition of a circle.

A **circle** is the set of all points in a plane at a distance r from a given point, called the **center.** The distance r is the **radius** of the circle.

Circle

r

center

If r represents the radius of a circle with its center at the origin, then the equation of the circle can be written in the form $x^2 + y^2 = r^2$.

2. Open-ended Let $P(x, y)$ be any point on this circle. **Choose** a method for proving that $x^2 + y^2 = r^2$.

Not every circle has its center at the origin. You can use the distance formula to find an equation of a circle that has its center at the point (h, k) and radius r.

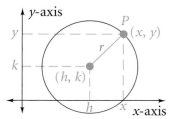

Let (x, y) be any point on the circle. The distance from (h, k) to (x, y) is the radius.

$d = \sqrt{(x_2 - x_1)^2 + (y_2 - y_1)^2}$ ← distance formula

$r = \sqrt{(x - h)^2 + (y - k)^2}$ ← Substitute r for d, (h, k) for (x_1, y_1) and (x, y) for (x_2, y_2).

$r^2 = (x - h)^2 + (y - k)^2$ ← Square both sides.

The equation of the circle with center (h, k) and radius r is

$$(x - h)^2 + (y - k)^2 = r^2.$$

This form of the equation is called the **standard form,** or center-radius form, of the equation of a circle.

3. What is the simplified form of this equation if the center is $(0, 0)$?

Example 1   **Relating to the Real World**

Landscaping A tree in your garden has a ring of flowers. Each flower is four feet from the center of the tree trunk. You draw a coordinate grid to model your yard. The tree trunk is located at $(-4, 3)$. Write an equation that models the ring of flowers.

$(x - h)^2 + (y - k)^2 = r^2$ ← equation of a circle

$(x - (-4))^2 + (y - 3)^2 = 4^2$ ← Substitute -4 for h, 3 for k, and 4 for r.

$(x + 4)^2 + (y - 3)^2 = 16$ ← Simplify.

The equation of the ring of flowers is $(x + 4)^2 + (y - 3)^2 = 16$. ■

4. Try This Write the equation of the circle whose center is at $(5, -3)$ and whose radius is 5.

5. Critical Thinking Can a circle have a radius of -5? **Justify** your answer.

The graph of the equation $(x - h)^2 + (y - k)^2 = r^2$ is a translation of the graph of the equation $x^2 + y^2 = r^2$. When h and k are positive, the graph is moved h units right and k units up.

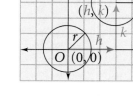

6. Writing Suppose h is positive, and k is negative. Explain how the graph of $x^2 + y^2 = r^2$ would be affected.

7. Describe the translation that gives you the equation $(x + 2)^2 + (y - 5)^2 = 1$.

Using the Center and Radius to Graph a Circle

Example 2

Find the center and radius of the circle $(x + 6)^2 + (y - 7)^2 = 25$. Draw the graph.

Compare the equation to the form
$(x - h)^2 + (y - k)^2 = r^2$.

$(x + 6)^2 + (y - 7)^2 = 25$
$-h = 6 \qquad k = 7 \qquad r^2 = 25$
$\quad h = -6 \qquad\qquad\quad r = 5$

The center is $(-6, 7)$ and the radius is 5.

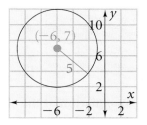

8. Try This Find the center and radius of the circle whose equation is $(x - 16)^2 + (y + 9)^2 = 144$. Draw the graph.

Example 3   **Relating to the Real World**

Machinery The diagram shows four gears in a motor assembly. Gear B rotates 8 times for each rotation of Gear A. Gears B and C share the same shaft, with their centers at the origin. The radius of Gear C is 6 times the radius of Gear B. The radius of Gear D is $\frac{1}{3}$ the radius of Gear C. Write the equation of the circle that represents each gear.

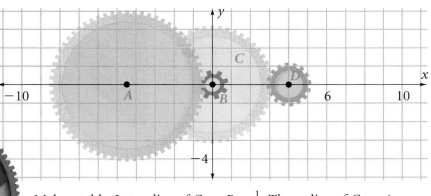

Gears help to change the rate of rotation of different parts of a machine. The gears shown above are part of a machine used in the textile industry.

Make a table. Let radius of Gear $B = \frac{1}{2}$. The radius of Gear A must be 8 times the radius of Gear B, or 4.

Gear	(h, k)	r	Equation
A	$(-4\frac{1}{2}, 0)$	4	$(x + \frac{9}{2})^2 + y^2 = 16$
B	$(0, 0)$	$\frac{1}{2}$	$x^2 + y^2 = \frac{1}{4}$
C	$(0, 0)$	3	$x^2 + y^2 = 9$
D	$(4, 0)$	1	$(x - 4)^2 + y^2 = 1$

9. For each rotation of Gear A, how many times does Gear D rotate?

Graphing Calculator **Write an equation in standard form for each circle.
Assume Xscl and Yscl = 1.**

1.

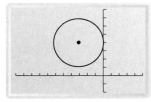

2.

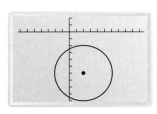

3.

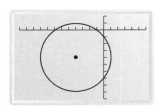

**Write an equation of the circle with the given center and radius.
Then graph the circle.**

4. center $(0, 0)$; radius 10

5. center $(-4, -6)$; radius 7

6. center $(2, 3)$; radius 4.5

7. center $(-6, 10)$; radius 1

8. center $(0, 0)$; radius $\frac{1}{2}$

9. center $(-1.5, -3)$; radius 2

10. center $(-3, 0)$; radius 8

11. center $(-2, 11)$; radius 5

12. center $(0, -1)$; radius 12

13. Recreation Suppose your community is
planning to build an in-ground circular
fountain. Use the picture at the right to
write the equation of the fountain.

14. Standardized Test Prep Which circle has a
radius of 4 and center at $(2, -3)$?
 A. $(x - 2)^2 + (y - 3)^2 = 16$
 B. $(x - 2)^2 + (y + 3)^2 = 16$
 C. $(x - 2)^2 + (y + 3)^2 = 4$
 D. $(x + 2)^2 + (y - 3)^2 = 4$
 E. $(x + 2)^2 + (y + 3)^2 = 16$

C(24, 22)

10

15. What translation of the circle $x^2 + y^2 = 8$
gives you the circle $(x + 7)^2 + (y - 7)^2 = 8$?
 A. 7 right, 7 down   **B.** 7 left, 7 down   **C.** 7 right, 8 up   **D.** 7 right, 7 up   **E.** 7 left, 7 up

Find the center and radius of each circle.

16. $(x - 3)^2 + (y - 1)^2 = 36$

17. $(x + 3)^2 + (y - 5)^2 = 38$

18. $x^2 + y^2 = 14$

19. $x^2 + (y - 4)^2 = 11$

20. $x^2 + (y + 3)^2 = 25$

21. $(x - 6)^2 + y^2 = 64$

22. $(x - 1)^2 + (y + 3)^2 = 16$

23. $(x + 3)^2 + (y - 9)^2 = 49$

24. $(x + 5)^2 + y^2 = 18$

Graphing Calculator **Graph each pair of functions. Identify the conic
section represented by the graph. Then write its equation.**

25. $y = \sqrt{36 - x^2}$
 $y = -\sqrt{36 - x^2}$

26. $y = 3 + \sqrt{16 - (x - 4)^2}$
 $y = 3 - \sqrt{16 - (x - 4)^2}$

27. $y = -2 + \sqrt{x - 3}$
 $y = -2 - \sqrt{x - 3}$

28. Design A three-dimensional computer program uses coordinates to locate points in the image. Suppose you are designing an image that has a light source at $(5, 6, 7)$. The light illuminates everything inside a cone, including a circular region with radius 3 on the floor. Give the equation of the circle. (*Hint:* Use only two variables.)

29. a. Writing Explain why $x^2 + y^2 = 0$ does not represent a circle.
　　b. Critical Thinking What does the equation represent?

30. Open-ended Write two functions that together represent a circle.

31. The table gives the diameters of four planets.
　　a. Use a center of $(0, 0)$ to graph the size of each planet. Use your graphs to compare the sizes of the planets.
　　b. Write an equation of the circular cross section through the center of each planet.

Planet	Diameter (miles)
Earth	7926
Mars	4222
Mercury	3031
Pluto	1430

Source: *The Cambridge Factfinder*

Use the given information to write an equation for each circle.

32. radius 7; center $(-6, 13)$

33. diameter 22; translated 4 units right and 2 units up

34. center $(-2, 7.5)$; circumference 3π

35. area 78.54; center $(5, -3)$

36. radius 4; center: $(16, y)$; passing through $(20, 15)$

37. translation of the circle $(x - 1)^2 + (y + 3)^2 = 36$, 2 units left and 4 units down

Chapter Project **Find Out by Creating**

Design several clown faces using graphs (or parts of graphs) of conic sections. Each face should convey a different emotion, such as anger, sadness, joy, or surprise. For each face, record the equations you use, including any restrictions.

Exercises MIXED REVIEW

Graph each function. Include any asymptotes.

38. $y = \cos \theta$　　　**39.** $y = |x - 2| + 1$　　**40.** $y = \dfrac{5}{x} - 2$　　　**41.** $y = \sqrt{x}$

42. The Richter scale describes the magnitude of earthquakes. An increase of 1 unit on the Richter scale indicates that the amount of energy released has increased by a factor of about 30. How many times as much energy is released by an earthquake measuring 7.1 on the Richter scale as by one measuring 5.5?

Find the distance between each pair of points.

43. $(10, 0)$ and $(-10, 0)$ **44.** $(0, 4)$ and $(0, -4)$ **45.** $(-7, 0)$ and $(7, 0)$ **46.** $(0, -2)$ and $(0, 2)$

Exercises   CHECKPOINT

Identify the focus and directrix of each parabola. Then graph the parabola.

1. $y = 3x^2$ **2.** $x = \frac{1}{2}y^2$ **3.** $x = 3y^2$ **4.** $y = -\frac{1}{6}x^2$

Write an equation in standard form of the circle with the given center and radius.

5. $(0, 0)$; radius 5   **6.** $(1, 3)$; radius 2   **7.** $(-6, -3)$; radius 8   **8.** $(2, -5)$; radius 7

9. Open-ended Write the equation of a circle that does not intersect the x-axis.

10. Critical Thinking Which conic sections are also intersections of a plane and a cylinder?

A Point in Time

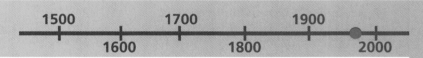

Finding the Titanic

In 1985 a French-American team used historical records to narrow the site of the 1912 sinking of the *Titanic* to a 150-square-mile target zone southeast of Newfoundland.

Research vessels systematically combed the area with deep-search sonar. Transmitters aboard each ship sent out powerful spherical sound waves. Each wave reflected off any object in a half-mile-wide strip of ocean floor and returned to a receiver. The receiver then converted the echo to a picture of the object and calculated its depth. Two months after the search began, the *Titanic* was discovered lying in two sections at a depth of some 13,000 feet. The ship has since been visited by deep-sea vessels and has been photographed extensively.

Note: drawing not to scale

At 882.5 feet in length, the steamship *Titanic* was the largest passenger liner ever built. The "unsinkable" ship left England in 1912 on its maiden voyage. The *Titanic* struck an iceberg and sank. More than 1500 people died.

Exploration

Using Parametric Forms

After Lesson 10-3

The graphing calculator program below uses parametric forms to graph a circle. To enter the program on your calculator, begin with the PRGM New menu and name your program CIRCLE.

Note that you find the Disp, Prompt, and DispGraph features in the PRGM I/O menu; X_{1T} and Y_{1T} in the Y-VARS Parametric menu; Param (Par) and Radian under MODE ; and Tmin, Tmax, and Tstep in the VARS Window menu. Use ALPHA keys to enter all words, quotation marks, and the variables H, K, R, and T.

```
PROGRAM:CIRCLE
:Disp "CENTER (H, K)"
:Disp "RADIUS R"

:Prompt H,K,R
:"Rcos T+H"→X1T
:"Rsin T+K"→Y1T
```

```
PROGRAM:CIRCLE
:█Rsin T+K"→Y1T
:Param
:Radian
:0→Tmin
:2π→Tmax
:.05→Tstep
:DispGraph
```

The next screens show the program being run for a circle with its center at (−2, 3) and a radius of 5. First, enter appropriate square window values. Then choose the program from the PRGM Exec menu.

```
WINDOW FORMAT
Xmin=-12
Xmax=12
Xscl=1
Ymin=-8
Ymax=8
Yscl=1
```

```
prgmCIRCLE
CENTER (H, K)
RADIUS R
H=?-2
K=?3
R=?5█
```

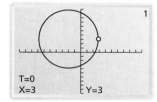

```
T=0
X=3      Y=3
```

Note that you can trace to find the coordinates of points on the circle.

Use your program to graph each circle. Use an appropriate square window for each graph.

1. center (0, 2), radius 4

2. center (5, −2), radius 5

3. center (−1, 3), radius 8

4. $(x - 2)^2 + (y + 1)^2 = 25$

5. $(x + 4)^2 + (y - 3)^2 = 100$

6. $x^2 + (y + 2)^2 = 49$

7. Open-ended Use trace to find four points in Quadrant III that lie on the circle described by the equation $(x + 5)^2 + (y - 2)^2 = 16$.

8. Writing Describe how to change your program to work in degrees, plotting a point every 5° of rotation.

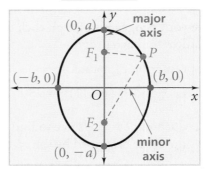
What You'll Learn

- Writing the equation of an ellipse
- Finding the foci of an ellipse

...And Why

To find the equation of the elliptical opening of the Transonic Tunnel

10-4 **E**llipses

WORK TOGETHER

1. **a.** Find the *x*- and *y*-intercepts of the relation $\frac{x^2}{16} + \frac{y^2}{16} = 1$.
    b. Plot the points on a set of axes. Graph four other points that satisfy the equation above. Connect them. What shape have you formed?
    c. What are the coordinates of the center of your shape?

2. Now find the *x*- and *y*-intercepts of $\frac{x^2}{16} + \frac{y^2}{9} = 1$ and plot them on a second set of axes. Plot four or five other points that satisfy the equation. Compare the two graphs. What do you notice?

3. **Analyze** the relationship between the equation and the intercepts.

4. Find the *x*- and *y*-intercepts of the relation $\frac{x^2}{9} + \frac{y^2}{16} = 1$. **Predict** what the graph will look like. **Verify** your prediction.

THINK AND DISCUSS

Writing the Equation of an Ellipse

An **ellipse** is a set of points *P* in a plane such that the sum of the distances from *P* to two fixed points F_1 and F_2 is a given constant, *k*.

$$PF_1 + PF_2 = k$$

Each fixed point *F* is a **focus** (plural: *foci*) of the ellipse. The **major axis** is the segment that contains the foci and has its endpoints on the ellipse. These endpoints are **vertices.** The midpoint of the major axis is the **center** of the ellipse. The **minor axis** is perpendicular to the major axis at the center. The endpoints of the minor axis are **co-vertices.**

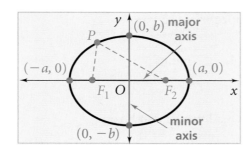

$$\frac{x^2}{a^2} + \frac{y^2}{b^2} = 1$$

major axis: horizontal
vertices: $(\pm a, 0)$
co-vertices: $(0, \pm b)$

Standard forms of the
←——equation of an ellipse——→
a > b
center at the origin

$$\frac{x^2}{b^2} + \frac{y^2}{a^2} = 1$$

major axis: vertical
vertices: $(0, \pm a)$
co-vertices: $(\pm b, 0)$

The Transonic Tunnel at NASA
Langley Research Center,
Virginia, is used to study the
dynamics of air flow. The guide
vanes in the elliptical opening
allow a smooth flow of air
through the passageways.

5. What is the length of each axis of each ellipse shown on page 478?

You can write the equation of an ellipse whose center is at the origin, if you know the x- and y-intercepts.

shown on page 478

Example 1 **Relating to the Real World**

Architecture The elliptical opening of the Transonic Tunnel is 82 ft wide and 58 ft high. Find an equation of the ellipse.

Imagine a large coordinate grid placed over the elliptical opening. Since the widest part of the ellipse is horizontal and the width is 82 ft, place the vertices at $(\pm41, 0)$. Similarly, place the co-vertices at $(0, \pm29)$.

Thus $a = 41$, $b = 29$, $a^2 = 1681$, and $b^2 = 841$.

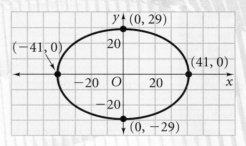

$$\frac{x^2}{a^2} + \frac{y^2}{b^2} = 1 \quad \leftarrow \text{ standard form for an ellipse with a horizontal major axis}$$

$$\frac{x^2}{1681} + \frac{y^2}{841} = 1 \quad \leftarrow \text{Substitute 1681 for } a^2 \text{ and 841 for } b^2.$$

An equation of the ellipse is $\frac{x^2}{1681} + \frac{y^2}{841} = 1$.

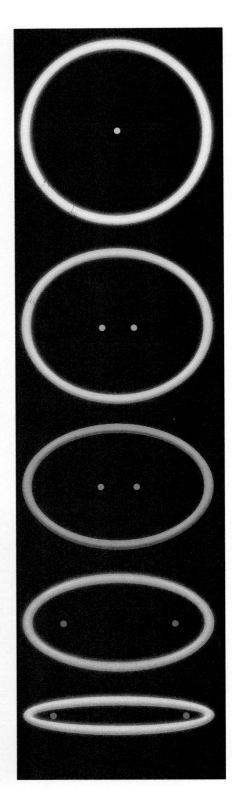

6. Name the coordinates of the center of the ellipse in Example 1.

7. Try This Find an equation of an ellipse that is 12 units wide and 30 units high.

Finding the Foci of an Ellipse

The foci are important points in an ellipse. For example, in Earth's orbit around the sun, the sun is at a focus, not at the center.

The foci of an ellipse are always on the major axis and are c units from the center.

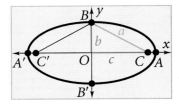

There is an important and useful relationship among a, b, and c.

$$c^2 = a^2 - b^2$$

8. Critical Thinking How can you identify the major axis of an ellipse if you know the coordinates of the foci?

Example 2

Find the foci of the ellipse with the equation $25x^2 + 9y^2 = 225$. Graph the ellipse.

$25x^2 + 9y^2 = 225$

$\dfrac{x^2}{9} + \dfrac{y^2}{25} = 1$ ◄——— Divide each side by 225.

Since $25 > 9$ and 25 is with y^2, the major axis is vertical, $a^2 = 25$, and $b^2 = 9$.

$c^2 = a^2 - b^2$
$\quad = 25 - 9$ ◄——— Substitute 25 for a^2
$\quad = 16$ $\qquad$ and 9 for b^2.
$\quad c = 4$

The major axis is vertical, so the coordinates of the foci are $(0, \pm c)$. The foci are the points $(0, 4)$ and $(0, -4)$.

The vertices are $(0, 5)$ and $(0, -5)$. The co-vertices are $(3, 0)$ and $(-3, 0)$.

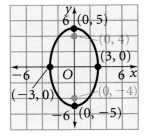

9. Try This Find the foci of the ellipse with equation $x^2 + 9y^2 = 9$. Graph the ellipse.

You can use the relationship among a, b, and c to write the equation of an ellipse.

Example 3

Write an equation of the ellipse with foci at $(\pm 7, 0)$ and co-vertices at $(0, \pm 6)$.

Since the foci have coordinates $(\pm 7, 0)$, the major axis of the ellipse is horizontal. The equation is in the form $\frac{x^2}{a^2} + \frac{y^2}{b^2} = 1$.

Since $c = 7$ and $b = 6$, $c^2 = 49$ and $b^2 = 36$.

$$c^2 = a^2 - b^2$$
$$49 = a^2 - 36$$
$$a^2 = 49 + 36$$
$$a^2 = 85$$
$$\frac{x^2}{85} + \frac{y^2}{36} = 1 \quad \longleftarrow \text{Substitute 85 for } a^2 \text{ and 36 for } b^2.$$

An equation of the ellipse is $\frac{x^2}{85} + \frac{y^2}{36} = 1$.

10. What is the length of each axis? How do you know?

Exercises ON YOUR OWN

Find the equation of each ellipse whose height and width are given. Assume the center of each is $(0, 0)$.

1. height 32 ft; width 16 ft

2. height 20 ft; width 12 ft

3. height 10 units; width 7 units

4. height 14 units; width 28 units

5. height 8 ft; width 2 ft

6. height 15 ft; width 32 ft

7. height 40 units; width 60 units

8. height 5 units; width 2 units

9. height 108 ft; width 54 ft

10. Draw an ellipse by placing two tacks in a piece of graph paper laid over a piece of cardboard. Tie the ends of a piece of string in a knot and place it around the tacks. With your pencil keeping the string taut, draw around the tacks. Mark the center of your ellipse $(0, 0)$ and draw the x- and y-axes.

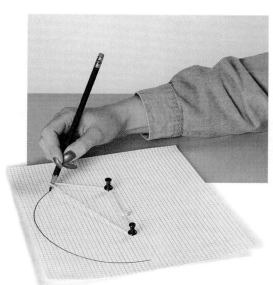

a. Where are the vertices and co-vertices of your ellipse?

b. Where are the foci?

c. Write the equation of your ellipse.

11. Find the coordinates of the foci of the Transonic Tunnel in Example 1.

12. Writing Suppose the foci of an ellipse are near the center of the ellipse. Will the shape of the ellipse be nearly a circle? Explain.

Find the foci of each ellipse whose equation is given. Graph each ellipse.

13. $\dfrac{x^2}{100} + \dfrac{y^2}{36} = 1$

14. $\dfrac{x^2}{64} + \dfrac{y^2}{100} = 1$

15. $\dfrac{x^2}{81} + \dfrac{y^2}{49} = 1$

16. $\dfrac{x^2}{9} + \dfrac{y^2}{25} = 1$

17. $3x^2 + y^2 = 9$

18. $\dfrac{x^2}{225} + \dfrac{y^2}{144} = 1$

19. $\dfrac{x^2}{256} + \dfrac{y^2}{121} = 1$

20. $\dfrac{x^2}{4} + \dfrac{y^2}{9} = 1$

21. $x^2 + 4y^2 = 16$

22. The *eccentricity* of an ellipse is a measure of how nearly circular it is. It is defined as $\frac{c}{a}$, where c is the distance from the center to a focus and a is the distance from the center to a vertex.
  a. Find the eccentricity of an ellipse whose foci are $(\pm9, 0)$ and whose vertices are $(\pm10, 0)$. Sketch the graph.
  b. Find the eccentricity of an ellipse whose foci are $(\pm1, 0)$ and whose vertices are $(\pm10, 0)$. Sketch the graph.
  c. Describe the shape of an ellipse whose eccentricity is close to 0.
  d. Describe the shape of an ellipse whose eccentricity is close to 1.

Write the equation of each ellipse whose foci and co-vertices are given.

23. foci $(\pm6, 0)$, co-vertices $(0, \pm8)$

24. foci $(0, \pm8)$, co-vertices $(\pm8, 0)$

25. foci $(\pm5, 0)$, co-vertices $(0, \pm8)$

26. foci $(0, \pm4)$, co-vertices $(\pm2, 0)$

27. foci $(\pm14, 0)$, co-vertices $(0, \pm7)$

28. foci $(\pm17, 0)$, co-vertices $(0, \pm15)$

Write the equation of each ellipse whose graph is shown.

29.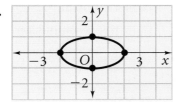

30.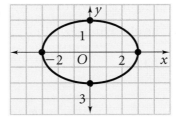

31.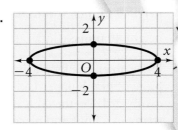

32.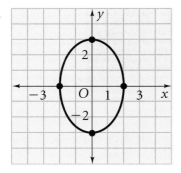

33.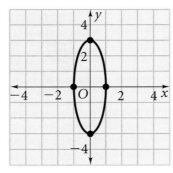

34.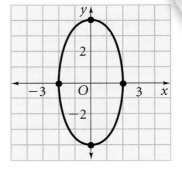

35. Astronomy The planets in our solar system move around the sun in elliptical orbits, with the sun at a focus. Assume the major axis is horizontal.

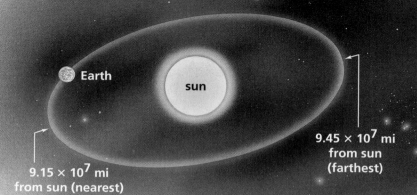

Earth

sun

9.45×10^7 mi from sun (farthest)

9.15×10^7 mi from sun (nearest)

    a. Find the distance from the sun to the other focus.

    b. What is the eccentricity of the orbit? (*Hint:* First find *a*.)

    c. Write an equation of Earth's orbit.

36. Writing The area of a circle is πr^2. The area of an ellipse is πab. Explain the connection.

37. Find the equation of the ellipse whose foci are on the *x*-axis, whose major axis is 9 units long, whose minor axis is 4 units long, and whose center is at the origin.

38. Open-ended Find a design that uses ellipses. Place a coordinate grid over the design and write an equation of the ellipse.

39. Acoustics In "whispering galleries" a sound made at one focus can be clearly heard at the other focus, even though very little can be heard in between. Suppose an elliptical room measures 320 ft long and 150 ft wide. How far would the listener have to be from the source of the sound in order to hear it?

Chapter Project **Find Out by Analyzing**

> For each person in your class, collect measurements for the distance *h* from the top of the head to the chin and the distance *w* across the face at the eyes. Analyze the data to design an elliptical outline for a clown face that will fit the "average" student. Record the equation you use. How well does your ellipse fit your own face? Do you think an ellipse is a good approximation for the shape of a human face? Why or why not?

Exercises   **MIXED REVIEW**

Solve each equation.

40. $3x = 5x - 18$ **41.** $x^2 + 5x = -4$ **42.** $6x^2 - x = x^3$ **43.** $3^x = 12$

44. Geometry What is the area of a rectangle with sides $x + 5$ and $x + 3$?

Getting Ready for Lesson 10-5

Graph each inverse variation.

45. $y = \dfrac{3}{x}$ **46.** $xy = 12$ **47.** $y = -4 \cdot \dfrac{1}{x}$ **48.** $xy = -6$

What You'll Learn

10-5 **H**yperbolas

- Graphing hyperbolas
- Finding the foci of a hyperbola

...And Why

To find the equation of the hyperbolic path of *Voyager 2* around Saturn

W O R K   T O G E T H E R

Work in groups of two or three.

1. The diagram below shows the shape of a hyperbola. Measure the distances to the nearest millimeter to complete the table.

2. What is the relationship between the distances from the foci to any point on the hyperbola?

Distance	P_1	P_2	P_3	...
Distance from F_1	▣	▣	▣	▣
Distance from F_2	▣	▣	▣	▣
$\lvert PF_1 - PF_2 \rvert$	▣	▣	▣	▣

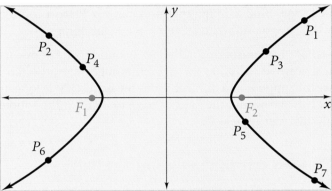

Voyager 1 and *Voyager 2* were launched from Cape Canaveral, Florida in the summer of 1977. Both spacecraft used Jupiter's gravity field to be thrust toward Saturn. Between them, *Voyager 1* and *Voyager 2* explored the outer planets of our solar system.

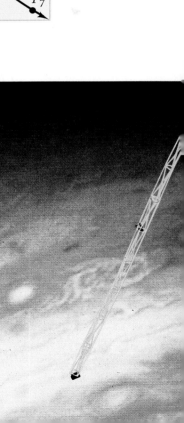

Graphing Hyperbolas Centered at the Origin

Hyperbolas play an important role in navigating, locating objects under water, and locating electronically-tagged animals. The two spacecraft *Voyager 1* and *Voyager 2* followed hyperbolic paths around the planets.

A **hyperbola** is a set of points P in a plane such that the difference between the distances from P to the foci F_1 and F_2 is a given constant, k.

$$\left| PF_1 - PF_2 \right| = k$$

The segment that lies on the line containing the foci and has endpoints on the hyperbola is the **transverse axis**. These endponts are the **vertices** of the hyperbola. The midpoint of this segment is the **center** of the hyperbola.

Standard form of the equation of a hyperbola with a horizontal transverse axis. $\longrightarrow \quad \dfrac{x^2}{a^2} - \dfrac{y^2}{b^2} = 1$

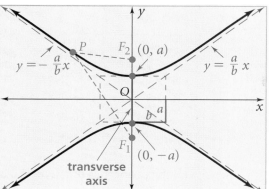

vertices: $(\pm a, 0)$
asymptotes: $y = \pm \dfrac{b}{a}x$
x-intercepts: $\pm a$
y-intercepts: none

Standard form of the equation of a hyperbola with a vertical transverse axis. $\longrightarrow \quad \dfrac{y^2}{a^2} - \dfrac{x^2}{b^2} = 1$

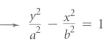

vertices: $(0, \pm a)$
asymptotes: $y = \pm \dfrac{a}{b}x$
x-intercepts: none
y-intercepts: $\pm a$

3. **Critical Thinking** What is the length of the transverse axis of each hyperbola shown above?

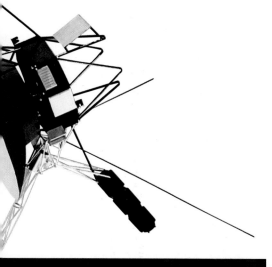

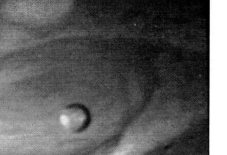

To graph a hyperbola, use the standard form of the equation to find the values of a and b. You can use these values to find and graph the vertices, to draw the *central rectangle*, and to draw the asymptotes as shown on page 485. Then draw the branches of the hyperbola through the vertices so that they approach the asymptotes.

Example 1

Graph the hyperbola whose equation is $9x^2 - 25y^2 = 225$.

Rewrite the equation in standard form.

$$9x^2 - 25y^2 = 225$$

$$\frac{x^2}{25} - \frac{y^2}{9} = 1 \quad \longleftarrow \text{Divide each side by 225 and simplify.}$$

The equation is of the form $\frac{x^2}{a^2} - \frac{y^2}{b^2} = 1$, so the transverse axis is horizontal. Since $a^2 = 25$ and $b^2 = 9$, $a = 5$ and $b = 3$.

Step 1: Locate the vertices. Since the transverse axis is horizontal, the vertices lie on the x-axis. The coordinates are $(\pm a, 0)$ or $(\pm 5, 0)$.

Step 2: Use the values of a and b to draw the central rectangle. The lengths of its sides are $2a$ and $2b$, or 10 and 6.

Step 3: Draw the asymptotes. The equations of the asymptotes are $y = \pm\frac{b}{a}x$ or $y = \pm\frac{3}{5}x$. (Notice that the asymptotes contain the diagonals of the central rectangle.)

Step 4: Sketch the branches of the hyperbola through the vertices so they approach the asymptotes.

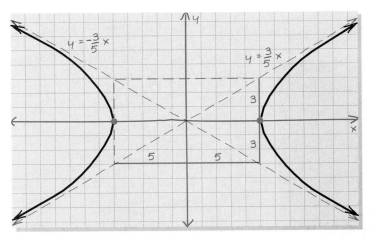

4. List all the properties of a hyperbola that allow you to draw its graph.

5. **Try This** Graph the hyperbola whose equation is $\frac{y^2}{16} - \frac{x^2}{4} = 1$.

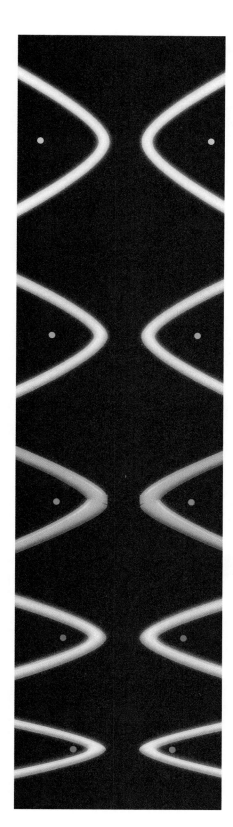

Finding the Foci of a Hyperbola

Let the coordinates of the foci be $(\pm c, 0)$ if the transverse axis is horizontal or $(0, \pm c)$ if it is vertical.

The distance between the foci, $2c$, is also the length of the diagonal of the central rectangle.

You can find the value of c using the Pythagorean theorem.

$$c^2 = a^2 + b^2$$

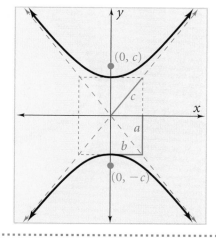

Example 2

Find the foci of the hyperbola $\dfrac{x^2}{36} - \dfrac{y^2}{4} = 1$. Draw the graph.

The equation is in the form $\dfrac{x^2}{a^2} - \dfrac{y^2}{b^2} = 1$, so the transverse axis is horizontal. The foci will be at $(\pm c, 0)$.

$a^2 = 36$ and $b^2 = 4$

$$\begin{aligned}
c^2 &= a^2 + b^2 \quad \longleftarrow \text{ Substitute 36 for } a^2 \text{ and 4 for } b^2. \\
&= 36 + 4 \\
&= 40 \\
c &= \sqrt{40} \approx 6.3 \quad \longleftarrow \text{ Find the square root of each side.}
\end{aligned}$$

The foci of $\dfrac{x^2}{36} - \dfrac{y^2}{4} = 1$ are approximately $(-6.3, 0)$ and $(6.3, 0)$. The vertices $(\pm a, 0)$ are $(6, 0)$ and $(-6, 0)$.

The asymptotes are the lines $y = \pm \dfrac{b}{a}x = \pm \dfrac{2}{6}x$, or $y = \pm \dfrac{1}{3}x$.

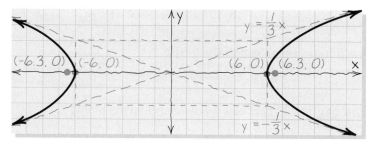

6. **Try This** Find the foci of the hyperbola $\dfrac{x^2}{25} - \dfrac{y^2}{9} = 1$. Draw the graph.

Example 3   Relating to the Real World

Space As a spacecraft approaches a planet, the gravitational pull of the planet changes the spacecraft's path from a straight line to one branch of a hyperbola. Find an equation that models the path of *Voyager 2* around Saturn, given that $a = 332{,}965$ km and $c = 492{,}788.2$ km.

Assume that the center of the hyperbola is at the origin and that the transverse axis is horizontal.

$$c^2 = a^2 + b^2$$
$$(492{,}788.2)^2 = (332{,}965)^2 + b^2$$
$$2.428 \times 10^{11} = 1.109 \times 10^{11} + b^2 \quad \longleftarrow \text{Use a calculator.}$$
$$b^2 = 2.428 \times 10^{11} - 1.109 \times 10^{11}$$
$$= 1.319 \times 10^{11}$$

$b^2 = 1.319 \times 10^{11}$. The equation will be in the form $\dfrac{x^2}{a^2} - \dfrac{y^2}{b^2} = 1$.

$$\frac{x^2}{1.109 \times 10^{11}} - \frac{y^2}{1.319 \times 10^{11}} = 1 \quad \longleftarrow \begin{array}{l}\text{Substitute for}\\ a^2 \text{ and } b^2.\end{array}$$

For practice with scientific notation, see Skills Handbook page 674.

The hyperbolic path that *Voyager 2* took around Saturn can be modeled by the following equation.

$$\frac{x^2}{1.109 \times 10^{11}} - \frac{y^2}{1.319 \times 10^{11}} = 1$$

7. Try This Find an equation that models the path of *Voyager 2* around Jupiter given that $a = 2{,}184{,}140$ km and $c = 2{,}904{,}906.2$ km.

Exercises   ON YOUR OWN

Graph each hyperbola.

1. $\dfrac{x^2}{16} - \dfrac{y^2}{4} = 1$ **2.** $\dfrac{y^2}{169} - \dfrac{x^2}{16} = 1$ **3.** $25x^2 - 16y^2 = 400$ **4.** $\dfrac{x^2}{25} - \dfrac{y^2}{36} = 1$

Find the foci of each hyperbola. Sketch the graph.

5. $\dfrac{y^2}{81} - \dfrac{x^2}{16} = 1$ **6.** $\dfrac{y^2}{49} - \dfrac{x^2}{64} = 1$ **7.** $\dfrac{x^2}{121} - \dfrac{y^2}{144} = 1$ **8.** $\dfrac{x^2}{64} - \dfrac{y^2}{36} = 1$

9. Research Find out how hyperbolas are used in marine biology.

Graphing Calculator Solve each equation for *y*. Graph each relation on your graphing calculator. Use the TRACE feature to locate the vertices.

10. $x^2 - 2y^2 = 4$ **11.** $x^2 - y^2 = 1$ **12.** $3x^2 - y^2 = 2$ **13.** $y^2 - 2x^2 = 8$

14. Math in the Media Refer to the article at the right and the table below.

	Jupiter	Saturn
a	1,092,356 km	166,152 km
c	1,441,909.92 km	219,320.64 km

a. Write an equation of the path taken by *Voyager 1* around Jupiter.

b. Write an equation of the path taken by *Voyager 1* around Saturn.

Jupiter Bound: *Voyager* on its Way...

Voyager 1 was launched by NASA in September 1977. Its purpose was to explore the outer planets of our solar system. The path taken by *Voyager 1* depended on the planet that happened to be closest.

15. Open-ended Choose two points on an axis to be the vertices of a hyperbola. Chose two other points on the same axis to be the foci. Write the equation of your hyperbola and draw its graph.

16. Writing Describe the similarities and differences between hyperbolas and ellipses.

Write the equation of each hyperbola from the given information. Graph each hyperbola. Place the center of each hyperbola at the origin of the coordinate plane.

17. transverse axis is vertical and is 9 units; central rectangle is 9 units by 4 units

18. perimeter of central rectangle is 16 units; vertices at $(0, 3)$, $(0, -3)$

19. (distance from the center of a hyperbola to a focus)$^2 = 96$; endpoints of the transverse axis at $(-\sqrt{32}, 0)$ and $(\sqrt{32}, 0)$

20. one focus located at $(\sqrt{5}, 0)$; one vertex at $(-2, 0)$

Write the equation of each hyperbola in standard form. Sketch the graph.

21. $64x^2 - 36y^2 = 2304$ **22.** $x^2 - 4y^2 = 4$ **23.** $144y^2 - 25x^2 = 3600$

24. $16x^2 - 20y^2 = 560$ **25.** $9y^2 - 49x^2 = 441$ **26.** $5x^2 - 12y^2 = 120$

27. Graphing Calculator The function $y = \sqrt{x^2 - 9}$ represents part of a hyperbola. The tables at the right show the coordinates of several points on the graph.

a. Explain why "ERROR" appears for some entries.

b. Describe the relationship between the x- and y-coordinates as x gets larger.

c. Do you think that the x- and y-coordinates will ever be equal? Explain.

d. Make a **conjecture** about the equations for the asymptotes of this hyperbola. **Verify** your conjecture by drawing the complete graph.

X	Y1
0	ERROR
1	ERROR
2	ERROR
3	0
4	2.6458
5	4
6	5.1962
X=0	

X	Y1
10	9.5394
20	19.774
30	29.85
40	39.887
50	49.91
60	59.925
70	69.936
X=10	

28. Air Traffic Control Suppose you are the pilot of a plane on a hyperbolic flight path. You receive radio signals sent simultaneously from two different airports, 48 km apart. Your instrument panel tells you that the signal from Airport 1 always comes in 100 μs (microseconds) before the signal from Airport 2.

   a. To which airport are you closer?

   b. If the signals travel at a rate of 300 m/μs, what is the difference in distances from you to each airport? What is the focal constant (k) of your plane's hyperbolic path?

   c. Write the equation of your flight path. (*Hint:* $k = 2a$)

   d. Draw the hyperbola. Which branch represents the flight path?

Exercises   MIXED REVIEW

Solve each matrix equation.

29. $\begin{bmatrix} 7 & 3 & -5 \\ 1 & 4 & 0 \end{bmatrix} - X = \begin{bmatrix} 8 & -1 & 11 \\ 6 & 2 & -5 \end{bmatrix}$

30. $\begin{bmatrix} 3 & -4 \\ 0 & 8 \end{bmatrix} X = \begin{bmatrix} -5 & 19 \\ 16 & -8 \end{bmatrix}$

31. Sports Your baseball team has 18 players. What is the probability that you will bat second if all players have an equal likelihood of going to bat?

Getting Ready for Lesson 10-6

Describe how each function is shifted from $y = x^2$.

32. $y = x^2 - 6$ **33.** $y = (x + 1)^2$

34. $y = x^2 + 7$ **35.** $y = (x - 2)^2 + 1$

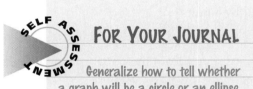

SELF ASSESSMENT

FOR YOUR JOURNAL

Generalize how to tell whether a graph will be a circle or an ellipse based on its eccentricity.

Exercises   CHECKPOINT

Write an equation of each ellipse with the given foci and co-vertices.

1. foci $(\pm 3, 0)$
   co-vertices $(0, \pm 4)$

2. foci $(0, \pm 2)$
   co-vertices $(\pm 5, 0)$

3. foci $(0, \pm 7)$
   co-vertices $(\pm 10, 0)$

Find the foci of each hyperbola. Sketch the graph.

4. $\frac{x^2}{16} - \frac{y^2}{49} = 1$

5. $\frac{y^2}{25} - \frac{x^2}{64} = 1$

6. $\frac{x^2}{4} - \frac{y^2}{81} = 1$

7. $\frac{y^2}{100} - \frac{x^2}{36} = 1$

8. Writing Explain how you can shift a hyperbola right 3 units and down 5 units.

9. Standardized Test Prep Which conic section always passes the vertical-line test?

   A. parabola   **B.** circle   **C.** ellipse   **D.** hyperbola   **E.** none of the above

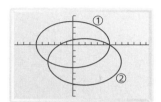
What You'll Learn

- Translating conic sections

- Writing and identifying the equation of a translated conic section

...And Why

To locate a ship using the Loran navigation system

What You'll Need

- graph paper

The Loran system of navigation allows precise navigation of ships.

10-6 Translating Conic Sections

WORK TOGETHER

Work with a partner.

1. Examine the calculator screen at the right. Describe the relationship between the two ellipses. How are they similar? How are they different?

2. The equation of ellipse ① is $\frac{x^2}{36} + \frac{y^2}{16} = 1$. Use what you know about translations to write the equation of ellipse ②.

Xmin=−9.870967   Ymin=−9
Xmax=12.870967   Ymax=6
Xscl=1   Yscl=1

3. The graph at the right shows the hyperbola whose equation is $\frac{x^2}{9} - \frac{y^2}{4} = 1$. Write the equation of the hyperbola that has been shifted four units left and one unit up.

Xmin=−12   Ymin=−8.2021276
Xmax=12.870967   Ymax=8.2021276
Xscl=1   Yscl=1

Writing Equations of Translated Conic Sections

The graph of each conic section can be translated horizontally and vertically.

Conic Section	Standard Form of Equation	
parabola	vertex $(0, 0)$ $y = ax^2$ $x = ay^2$	vertex (h, k) $y - k = a(x - h)^2$ or $y = a(x - h)^2 + k$ $x - h = a(y - k)^2$ or $x = a(y - k)^2 + h$
circle	center $(0, 0)$ $x^2 + y^2 = r^2$	center (h, k) $(x - h)^2 + (y - k)^2 = r^2$
ellipse	center $(0, 0)$ $\dfrac{x^2}{a^2} + \dfrac{y^2}{b^2} = 1$ $\dfrac{x^2}{b^2} + \dfrac{y^2}{a^2} = 1$	center (h, k) $\dfrac{(x - h)^2}{a^2} + \dfrac{(y - k)^2}{b^2} = 1$ $\dfrac{(x - h)^2}{b^2} + \dfrac{(y - k)^2}{a^2} = 1$
hyperbola	center $(0, 0)$ $\dfrac{x^2}{a^2} - \dfrac{y^2}{b^2} = 1$ $\dfrac{y^2}{a^2} - \dfrac{x^2}{b^2} = 1$	center (h, k) $\dfrac{(x - h)^2}{a^2} - \dfrac{(y - k)^2}{b^2} = 1$ $\dfrac{(y - k)^2}{a^2} - \dfrac{(x - h)^2}{b^2} = 1$

4. How does the translation of an ellipse or hyperbola from center $(0, 0)$ to center (h, k) affect the coordinates of the vertices and foci?

5. How does the translation of an ellipse affect the length of its major and minor axes? **Justify** your answer.

Example 1

Write the equation of each conic section.

a. ellipse with center $(-3, -2)$; vertical major axis of length 8; minor axis of length 6

b. hyperbola with vertices $(0, 1)$ and $(6, 1)$ and foci $(-1, 1)$ and $(7, 1)$

a. length of major axis $2a$; length of minor axis $2b$
  $2a = 8$ so $a = 4$; $2b = 6$ so $b = 3$

Since the center is $(-3, -2)$, $h = -3$ and $k = -2$.

The major axis is vertical, so the equation will have the following form.

$$\frac{(x - h)^2}{b^2} + \frac{(y - k)^2}{a^2} = 1$$

$$\frac{(x - (-3))^2}{3^2} + \frac{(y - (-2))^2}{4^2} = 1 \quad \longleftarrow \text{ Substitute.}$$

The equation of the ellipse is $\dfrac{(x + 3)^2}{9} + \dfrac{(y + 2)^2}{16} = 1$.

b. Draw a sketch. The center is the midpoint of the line joining the vertices. Its coordinates are (3, 1).

The distance between the vertices is $2a$ and the distance between the foci is $2c$.

$2a = 6$ so $a = 3$; $2c = 8$ so $c = 4$

Find b^2 using the relationship $c^2 = a^2 + b^2$.

$c^2 = a^2 + b^2$
$16 = 9 + b^2$
$b^2 = 7$

The transverse axis is horizontal, so the equation will have the form $\dfrac{(x - h)^2}{a^2} - \dfrac{(y - k)^2}{b^2} = 1$.

The equation of the hyperbola is $\dfrac{(x - 3)^2}{9} - \dfrac{(y - 1)^2}{7} = 1$.

Some ships navigate using Loran. The ship's equipment calculates the difference between the arrival times of simultaneously broadcast radio signals. This difference indicates how much closer the ship is to one transmitter than to the other. This difference locates it on a red hyperbola. The process is repeated using a second pair of transmitters to locate the ship on a blue hyperbola.

Example 2 Relating to the Real World

Navigation All points on hyperbola #25800 are 48 mi closer to one transmitter than the other. Find the equation of this hyperbola. (The transmitters, at the foci, are 200 mi apart and are located at $(0, 0)$ and $(0, 200)$.)

Since $2c = 200$, $c = 100$. The center of the hyperbola is at $(100, 0)$.

Calculate a by finding the difference in the distances from the vertex at $(a + 100, 0)$ to the two foci.

$48 = (a + 100) - (200 - (a + 100))$
$\quad = 2a$
$24 = a$

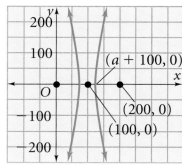

Use the relationship $c^2 = a^2 + b^2$ to find $b = 97$.

The equation of the hyperbola is
$\dfrac{(x - 100)^2}{24^2} - \dfrac{y^2}{97^2}$ or $\dfrac{(x - 100)^2}{576} - \dfrac{y^2}{9409} = 1$.

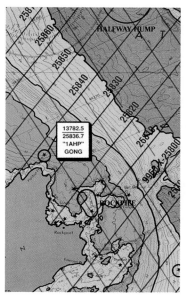

Loran stands for long range navigation. It uses simultaneously broadcast radio signals from three transmitters to locate a ship's position at the intersection of a red and a blue hyperbola.

Identifying Translated Conic Sections

An equation in the form $Ax^2 + Bxy + Cy^2 + Dx + Ey + F = 0$ represents a conic section. To determine which conic section the equation represents, write the equation in standard form by completing the square for the x- and y-terms.

Example 3

Identify the conic section with equation $4x^2 + y^2 - 24x + 6y + 9 = 0$. If it is a parabola, give its vertex. If it is a circle, give its center and radius. If it is an ellipse or a hyperbola, give its center and foci. Sketch the graph.

Complete the square for the x- and y-terms to write the equation in standard form.

PROBLEM SOLVING HINT

How do you find the missing terms when you complete the square?

$$4x^2 + y^2 - 24x + 6y + 9 = 0$$
$$4x^2 - 24x + y^2 + 6y = -9 \quad \longleftarrow \text{Group the } x\text{- and } y\text{-terms.}$$
$$4(x^2 - 6x + ?) + (y^2 + 6y + ?) = -9 \quad \longleftarrow \text{Factor.}$$
$$4(x^2 - 6x + 9) + (y^2 + 6y + 9) = -9 + 36 + 9$$
$$4(x - 3)^2 + (y + 3)^2 = 36$$
$$\frac{4(x - 3)^2}{36} + \frac{(y + 3)^2}{36} = 1 \quad \longleftarrow \text{Divide each side by 36.}$$
$$\frac{(x - 3)^2}{9} + \frac{(y + 3)^2}{36} = 1 \quad \longleftarrow \text{Simplify.}$$

The equation represents an ellipse. The center is $(3, -3)$. The major axis is vertical.

$b^2 = 9$ so $b = 3$; $a^2 = 36$ so $a = 6$

$c^2 = a^2 - b^2$
$\quad = 36 - 9$
$\quad = 27$
$c = 3\sqrt{3}$

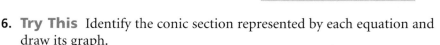

The foci are at $(3, 3\sqrt{3})$ and $(3, -3\sqrt{3})$.

6. **Try This** Identify the conic section represented by each equation and draw its graph.
   a. $x^2 + 14x - 4y + 29 = 0$ **b.** $x^2 + y^2 - 12x + 4y = 8$

7. **Writing** Describe the translation that would produce the equation $x^2 - 2y^2 + 6x - 7 = 0$.

8. **Critical Thinking** Identify the shape of the graph that results in each case using the equation $Ax^2 + Bxy + Cy^2 + Dx + Ey + F = 0$.
   a. $A = C = D = E = 0; B \neq 0; F \neq 0$
   b. $A = B = C = 0; D \neq 0; E \neq 0; F \neq 0$

Identify each quadratic relation as a parabola, a circle, an ellipse, or a hyperbola.

1. $x^2 - 8x - y + 19 = 0$

2. $x^2 + y^2 + 12x = 45$

3. $3x^2 + 6x + y^2 - 6y = -3$

4. $x^2 + y^2 - 2x + 6y = 3$

5. $y^2 - x^2 + 6x - 4y = 6$

6. $x^2 - 4y^2 - 2x - 8y = 7$

Write each equation in standard form and graph it.

7. $x^2 + y^2 + 14y = -13$

8. $y^2 - 2x - 4y = -10$

9. $4x^2 + 9y^2 + 16x - 54y = -61$

10. $x^2 - y^2 + 6x + 10y = 17$

11. $x^2 - 2x - 4y^2 = 15$

12. $x^2 + y^2 + 8x - 10y = -16$

13. Writing Describe how the translation of a hyperbola affects the equations of its asymptotes.

Write an equation of each conic section and sketch its graph.

14. circle with center at $(-6, 9)$ and radius 9

15. ellipse with center at $(3, 2)$, vertices at $(9, 2)$, $(-3, 2)$, and co-vertices at $(3, 5)$, and $(3, -1)$

16. parabola with vertex at $(2, -3)$ and focus at $(2, 5)$

17. hyperbola with center at $(6, -3)$, one focus at $(6, 0)$, and one vertex at $(6, -1)$

The graph of each equation is to be translated 3 units right and 5 units up. Write each new equation.

18. $(x - 5)^2 + (y + 3)^2 = 4$

19. $\dfrac{(x - 3)^2}{64} + \dfrac{(y + 3)^2}{36} = 1$

20. $y = 4x^2$

21. Standardized Test Prep Which conic section is represented by the equation $x^2 + 4y^2 - 2x - 15 = 0$?
   A. a parabola   **B.** a circle   **C.** an ellipse   **D.** a hyperbola

22. Open-ended On a graphing calculator, create a design using three translated quadratic relations.

Graphing Calculator Graph each pair of functions. Identify the conic section represented by the graph and write its equation in standard form.

23. $y = \sqrt{36 - 4x^2}$
$y = -\sqrt{36 - 4x^2}$

24. $y = \sqrt{4x^2 - 36}$
$y = -\sqrt{4x^2 - 36}$

25. $y = \sqrt{4x^2 + 36}$
$y = -\sqrt{4x^2 + 36}$

26. $y = \sqrt{36 - x^2}$
$y = -\sqrt{36 - x^2}$

27. $y = 0.5\sqrt{36 - x^2}$
$y = -0.5\sqrt{36 - x^2}$

28. $y = \sqrt{x - 4}$
$y = -\sqrt{x - 4}$

29. History Some symbols of the writing system of the Ejagham, people who lived in Nigeria and Cameroon, are shown. The symbol for marriage consists of two parabolic shapes. Reproduce this symbol on a graphing calculator. What equations did you use?

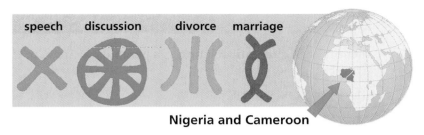

speech   discussion   divorce   marriage

Nigeria and Cameroon

30. Astronomy The data for the elliptical orbits of three planets are given in millions of kilometers. The sun is at one focus. The other focus is on the positive x-axis.

Planet	a	b
Earth	149.60	149.58
Mars	227.9	226.9
Mercury	57.9	56.6

a. Write an equation for each orbit and draw the curves on your graphing calculator. (Remember to adjust the viewing window.)

b. Critical Thinking Which orbit is most circular? **Justify** your reasoning.

Write the equation of each graph.

31.

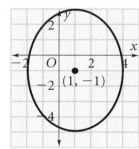

32.

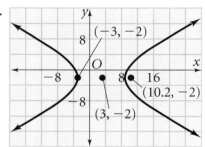

33.

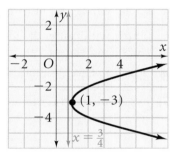

Find each product.

34. $-1 \begin{bmatrix} 0 & 1 & 2 \\ 1 & 0 & 4 \end{bmatrix}$

35. $-2 \begin{bmatrix} -1 & 0 & -2 \\ 0 & -1 & 3 \end{bmatrix}$

36. $2 \begin{bmatrix} 1 & 0 & -1 \\ 0 & -1 & -1 \end{bmatrix}$

37. $1.5 \begin{bmatrix} 0 & 1 & 0 \\ -1 & 0 & 4 \end{bmatrix}$

38. Health When the temperature and humidity are high, it is unsafe to exercise. The following system of inequalities gives the temperature and humidity combinations that are unsafe, where x is the percent humidity and y is the temperature in °F. Graph the system of inequalities.

$4x - 3y < 70$
$x + y > 160$

PORTFOLIO

SELF ASSESSMENT

For your portfolio, select one or two items from your work for this chapter. Here are some possibilities.
• diagrams, graphs, or charts
• work you found challenging
• cooperative work
Explain why you have included each selection.

Nonlinear Systems

After Lesson 10-6

Example

Graphing Calculator A circle has the equation $(x - 3)^2 + (y - 5)^2 = 25$.
A parabola with the equation $y = 2(x + 1)^2 - 3$ intersects the circle at two
points. Graph the system and locate the points of intersection.

Step 1: Solve each equation
for y. Enter your results on the $\boxed{Y=}$
screen on your graphing
calculator.

> Y₁=5+√(25–(X–3)²) ◄—— top half of the circle
> Y₂=5–√(25–(X–3)²) ◄—— bottom half of the circle
> Y₃=2(X+1)²–3 ◄—— parabola
> Y₄=
> Y₅=
> Y₆=

Step 2: Press $\boxed{\text{GRAPH}}$ to see
the curves. Choose an
appropriate square window.
Use the CALC feature to locate
the points of intersection.

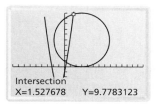

Intersection
X=1.527678   Y=9.7783123

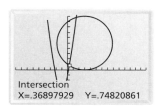

Intersection
X=.36897929   Y=.74820861

The parabola intersects the circle at $(1.53, 9.78)$ and $(0.37, 0.75)$.

Graph each system and find the points of intersection.

1. $\begin{cases} y = (x + 1)^2 - 2 \\ \dfrac{x^2}{25} + \dfrac{y^2}{9} = 1 \end{cases}$

2. $\begin{cases} x^2 + y^2 = 16 \\ 3x - 2y = 6 \end{cases}$

3. $\begin{cases} 16x^2 + 9y^2 = 144 \\ 25x^2 - 4y^2 = 100 \end{cases}$

4. $\begin{cases} x^2 - y^2 = 1 \\ 2x - y = 4 \end{cases}$

5. $\begin{cases} (x - 4)^2 + y^2 = 25 \\ (x + 4)^2 + y^2 = 25 \end{cases}$

6. $\begin{cases} \dfrac{x^2}{25} - \dfrac{y^2}{9} = 1 \\ \dfrac{x^2}{25} + \dfrac{y^2}{9} = 1 \end{cases}$

7. Suppose you solve a system algebraically and one or more of the
   numbers in the ordered pairs of the solution is an imaginary number.
   What can you conclude about its graph?

8. **Open-ended** Graph a nonlinear system that has three solutions.

9. **Writing** Describe two other methods of solving nonlinear systems. Use
   the two methods to solve Exercises 4 and 5. What are the advantages
   and disadvantages of each method?

Finishing the Chapter Project

Find Out activities on pages 470, 475, and 483 should
help you to complete your project. Plan a class
exhibit of your clown face designs and descriptions.
Learn about your classmates' designs so you can
explain them to visitors. Invite other classes to tour
the exhibit.

Reflect and Revise

Work in a small group. Have other members of your group evaluate
your clown faces and written explanation. Are the calculations correct
and the explanation clear? Will your presentation be understandable and
interesting to the visitors who come to view the exhibit? Discuss ideas for
revision with your group.

Follow Up

Make a clown face using one of your designs. For ideas about how to
make faces, consult your art teacher or a book on clowning such as
one of the ones listed below.

For More Information

Stoltzenburg, Mark. *Clown for Circus and Stage.* New York: Sterling
    Publishing, 1981.

Fife, Bruce et al. *Creative Clowning.* Texas: Java Publishing, 1988.

The Clown Hall of Fame & Research Center, Inc. 114 North Third St.
    Delavan, WI 53115 (414) 728–9075

10 Wrap Up

Key Terms

center (p. 471)
circle (p. 471)
conic section (p. 459)
co-vertices (p. 478)
directrix (p. 466)
ellipse (p. 478)
focus (pp. 466, 478, 485)

hyperbola (p. 485)
major axis (p. 478)
minor axis (p. 478)
radius (p. 471)
standard form (p. 472)
transverse axis (p. 485)
vertices (pp. 478, 485)

How am I doing?

SELF ASSESSMENT

- State three ideas from this chapter that you think are important. Explain your choices.
- Describe the features of different conic sections.

Exploring Conic Sections   10-1

A **conic section** is formed by the intersection of a plane and a double cone. The four conic sections are circles, ellipses, parabolas, and hyperbolas.

Use symmetry to graph each equation. Identify the conic section and its intercepts. Give the domain and range for each graph.

1. $\dfrac{x^2}{49} + \dfrac{y^2}{121} = 1$ **2.** $x^2 + y^2 = 4$ **3.** $\dfrac{x^2}{25} - \dfrac{y^2}{4} = 1$ **4.** $x = 2y^2 + 5$

Parabolas   10-2

A parabola is the set of all points in a plane that are the same distance from a fixed point (the **focus**) and a line (the **directrix**). If $|c|$ is the distance from the vertex to the focus of a parabola $y = ax^2$, then $a = \dfrac{1}{4c}$.

Identify the focus and directrix of each parabola. Then graph the parabola.

Equation	Coefficient	Direction	Focus	Directrix
$y = ax^2$	$a > 0$	opens up	$(0, c)$	$y = -c$
	$a < 0$	opens down	$(0, -c)$	$y = c$
$x = ay^2$	$a > 0$	opens right	$(c, 0)$	$x = -c$
	$a < 0$	opens left	$(-c, 0)$	$x = c$

5. $y = 5x^2$ **6.** $x = 2y^2$ **7.** $y = -x^2$ **8.** $x = -\dfrac{1}{8}y^2$

9. Open-ended Write the equation of a parabola that does not intersect the y-axis.

Circles   10-3

A **circle** is the set of all points in a plane a given distance from a given point (the **center**). The equation in **standard form** of a circle that has a center at (h, k) and **radius** r is $(x - h)^2 + (y - k)^2 = r^2$.

**Write an equation in standard form of the circle with the given center
and radius. Then graph the circle.**

10. center $(0, 0)$; radius 4   **11.** center $(8, 1)$; radius 5   **12.** center $(-3, 2)$; radius 10

13. Writing Explain how you can write an equation of a circle in standard
form when you know the center and the circumference.

An **ellipse** is the set of all points in a plane such that the sum of the
distances from any point to two fixed points is constant. Each fixed point is
a **focus** of the ellipse.

The **major axis** of an ellipse is the segment that contains the
foci and has its endpoints on the ellipse. These endpoints are
vertices. The **minor axis** is perpendicular to the major axis at
its midpoint. Its endpoints are **co-vertices**.

The foci of an ellipse are on the major axis c units from
the center, and $c^2 = a^2 - b^2$.

	$\dfrac{x^2}{a^2} + \dfrac{y^2}{b^2} = 1$	$\dfrac{x^2}{b^2} + \dfrac{y^2}{a^2} = 1$
Vertices	$(\pm a, 0)$	$(0, \pm a)$
Co-vertices	$(0, \pm b)$	$(\pm b, 0)$
Foci	$(\pm c, 0)$	$(0, \pm c)$

Write the equation of each ellipse whose foci and co-vertices are given.

14. foci $(\pm 1, 0)$; co-vertices $(0, \pm 4)$ **15.** foci $(0, \pm 2)$; co-vertices $(\pm 5, 0)$

16. foci $(0, \pm 1)$; co-vertices $(\pm 3, 0)$ **17.** foci $(\pm 2, 0)$; co-vertices $(0, \pm 6)$

18. Write the equation of an ellipse centered at the origin with height 8
units and width 16 units.

19. Standardized Test Prep What are the foci of $\dfrac{x^2}{64} + \dfrac{y^2}{36} = 1$?

A. $(0, \pm 10)$ **B.** $(\pm 2\sqrt{7}, 0)$ **C.** $(\pm 10, 0)$ **D.** $(0, \pm 2\sqrt{7})$ **E.** $(\pm 8, 0)$

A **hyperbola** is the set of all points in a plane such that the
difference of the distance from any point to two fixed points
is constant. Each fixed point is a focus of the hyperbola.

Each branch of a hyperbola intersects the **transverse axis**
at a **vertex**. Each branch approaches the two asymptotes.
You can locate the asymptotes by using the central
rectangle, which has dimensions $2a$ and $2b$.

The foci of a hyperbola lie on the line containing the
transverse axis. The foci are c units from the center,
with $c^2 = a^2 + b^2$.

	$\dfrac{x^2}{a^2} - \dfrac{y^2}{b^2} = 1$	$\dfrac{y^2}{a^2} - \dfrac{x^2}{b^2} = 1$
Vertices	$(\pm a, 0)$	$(0, \pm a)$
x-intercepts	$\pm a$	none
y-intercepts	none	$\pm a$
Transverse axis	horizontal	vertical
Asymptotes	$y = \pm \dfrac{b}{a} x$	$y = \pm \dfrac{a}{b} x$
Foci	$(\pm c, 0)$	$(0, \pm c)$

Find the foci of each hyperbola. Sketch the graph.

20. $\dfrac{x^2}{36} - \dfrac{y^2}{225} = 1$ **21.** $\dfrac{y^2}{400} - \dfrac{x^2}{169} = 1$ **22.** $\dfrac{x^2}{121} - \dfrac{y^2}{81} = 1$ **23.** $\dfrac{y^2}{100} - \dfrac{x^2}{9} = 1$

24. Write the equation of a hyperbola with its center at the origin and the following characteristics: the transverse axis is horizontal and is 16 units, one focus is located at $(\sqrt{89}, 0)$.

Translating Conic Sections

You can translate conic sections horizontally and vertically.

Conic Section	Standard Form of Equation	
parabola	vertex $(0, 0)$ $y = ax^2$ $x = ay^2$	vertex (h, k) $y - k = a(x - h)^2$ or $y = a(x - h)^2 + k$ $x - h = a(y - k)^2$ or $x = a(y - k)^2 + h$
circle	center $(0, 0)$ $x^2 + y^2 = r^2$	center (h, k) $(x - h)^2 + (y - k)^2 = r^2$
ellipse	center $(0, 0)$ $\frac{x^2}{a^2} + \frac{y^2}{b^2} = 1$ $\frac{x^2}{b^2} + \frac{y^2}{a^2} = 1$	center (h, k) $\frac{(x - h)^2}{a^2} + \frac{(y - k)^2}{b^2} = 1$ $\frac{(x - h)^2}{b^2} + \frac{(y - k)^2}{a^2} = 1$
hyperbola	center $(0, 0)$ $\frac{x^2}{a^2} - \frac{y^2}{b^2} = 1$ $\frac{y^2}{a^2} - \frac{x^2}{b^2} = 1$	center (h, k) $\frac{(x - h)^2}{a^2} - \frac{(y - k)^2}{b^2} = 1$ $\frac{(y - k)^2}{a^2} - \frac{(x - h)^2}{b^2} = 1$

An equation in the form $Ax^2 + Bxy + Cy^2 + Dx + Ey + F = 0$ represents a conic section. To determine which conic section the equation represents, rewrite the equation in standard form.

Identify each conic section.

25. $-x^2 + y^2 + 4y - 16 = 0$

26. $x^2 + y^2 + 3x - 4y - 9 = 0$

27. $3x^2 - 4y^2 + 12x + 8y - 4 = 0$

28. $2x^2 + 3y^2 - 4x + 12y - 20 = 0$

29. Writing Compare the standard forms of an ellipse and a hyperbola.

Getting Ready for..

CHAPTER 11

Find each probability for two tosses of a number cube.

30. $P(4 \text{ and } 3)$

31. $P(\text{two odd numbers})$

32. $P(5 \text{ and } 1)$

33. $P(\text{two integers})$

Put each set in numerical order. Find the middle data point and the most frequent data point(s) in each set.

34. 1 0 2 2 1 3 0 1 1 0 1

35. 19 12 11 18 11 14 19 20 19

36. 32 27 35 30 31 29 31 33 28

37. 5 4 1 5 3 6 3 3 7 2 1 5 8

Identify the center and vertices of each ellipse or hyperbola. Write its equation and give its domain and range.

1.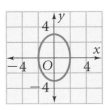

2.

3.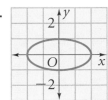

4.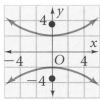

5. Writing Explain how you can tell what kind of conic section a quadratic equation describes without graphing it.

Tell whether each parabola opens up, down, left, or right.

6. $y = 3x^2$

7. $x = -2y^2$

8. $x + 5y^2 = 0$

9. $9x^2 - 2y = 0$

Write the equation of each parabola with its vertex at the origin.

10. focus at $(0, -2)$

11. focus at $(3, 0)$

12. directrix $x = 7$

13. directrix $y = -1$

Find the radius and center of each circle. Then sketch its graph.

14. $(x - 2)^2 + (y - 3)^2 = 36$

15. $(x + 5)^2 + (y + 8)^2 = 100$

16. $(x - 1)^2 + (y + 7)^2 = 81$

17. $(x + 4)^2 + (y - 10)^2 = 121$

18. Open-ended Write the equation of a circle with a diameter of 10.

Find the equation of each ellipse whose height and width are given. Assume the center of each is $(0, 0)$.

19. height 10 units; width 16 units

20. height 2 units; width 12 units

21. height 9 units; width 5 units

22. height 8 units; width 3 units

Find the foci of each ellipse whose equation is given. Graph each ellipse.

23. $\frac{x^2}{81} + \frac{y^2}{36} = 1$

24. $\frac{x^2}{25} + \frac{y^2}{121} = 1$

25. $x^2 + \frac{y^2}{49} = 1$

26. $4x^2 + y^2 = 4$

27. Critical Thinking What shape is an ellipse whose height and width are equal?

Find the foci of each hyperbola. Sketch the graph.

28. $\frac{x^2}{144} - \frac{y^2}{100} = 1$

29. $\frac{y^2}{169} - \frac{x^2}{400} = 1$

30. $\frac{x^2}{64} - \frac{y^2}{4} = 1$

31. $y^2 - \frac{x^2}{225} = 1$

32. Open-ended Write the equation of a hyperbola whose transverse axis is on the x-axis.

The graph of each equation is to be translated 2 units left and 7 units up. Write each new equation.

33. $\frac{x^2}{9} - \frac{y^2}{16} = 1$

34. $\frac{x^2}{4} + \frac{y^2}{25} = 1$

35. $x^2 = \frac{1}{2}y^2 + 1$

36. $x^2 + y^2 = 4$

37. Standardized Test Prep Which quadratic relation is an ellipse?
   A. $3y^2 - x - 6y + 5 = 0$
   B. $x^2 + y^2 - 4x - 6y + 4 = 0$
   C. $4x^2 + y^2 - 16x - 6y + 9 = 0$
   D. $4x^2 - y^2 - 16x + 6y - 9 = 0$
   E. none of them

For Exercises 1–12, choose the correct letter.

1. Which polynomial has roots $-3, 0, 1,$ and 2?
  A. $x^4 - 7x^2 + 6x$
  B. $x^4 - 6x^3 + 11x^2 - 6x$
  C. $x^4 - 4x^3 + x^2 - 6x$
  D. $x^4 - 7x^2 - 6$
  E. $x^4 + 6x^3 + 11x^2 + 6x$

2. Which function has a constant of variation 6?
  I. $2xy = 12$ **II.** $3y = \frac{18}{x}$
  III. $2x + 3y = 6$ **IV.** $y = 6x - 1$
  A. I only   B. IV only   C. I and II
  D. II and IV   E. I and III

3. Which matrix is a 2×3 matrix?
  A. $\begin{bmatrix} 3 & 4 & 2 \\ 1 & 0 & 3 \end{bmatrix}$ B. $\begin{bmatrix} 2 & 2 \\ 3 & 3 \end{bmatrix}$
  C. $\begin{bmatrix} 5 & 1 \\ 0 & 2 \\ 3 & 4 \end{bmatrix}$ D. $\begin{bmatrix} 2 & 2 & 2 \\ 2 & 2 & 3 \\ 2 & 3 & 3 \end{bmatrix}$
  E. none of the above

4. Which parabola has focus $(3, 0)$ and directrix $x = -3$?
  A. $y = \frac{1}{12}x^2$ B. $y = -\frac{1}{3}x^2$ C. $x = \frac{1}{12}y^2$
  D. $x = \frac{1}{3}y^2$ E. $y = \frac{1}{3}x^2$

5. Which events are dependent?
  I. spinning a spinner three times
  II. picking three students from a class
  III. tossing two coins and a number cube
  A. I only   B. II only   C. III only
  D. I and III   E. I, II, and III

6. Which point lies on the x-axis?
  A. $(0, 1, 0)$ B. $(0, 0, 3)$ C. $(-2, 0, 1)$
  D. $(5, -3, 0)$ E. none of the above

7. Which hyperbola has asymptotes $y = \pm\frac{3}{4}x$?
  A. $\frac{x^2}{9} - \frac{y^2}{16} = 1$ B. $\frac{y^2}{3} - \frac{x^2}{4} = 1$
  C. $\frac{y^2}{16} - \frac{x^2}{9} = 1$ D. $\frac{x^2}{16} - \frac{y^2}{9} = 1$
  E. none of the above

8. What is the vertical asymptote of $y = \frac{5}{x - 2}$?
  A. $y = 2$ B. $x = -1$ C. $y = -1$
  D. $x = 2$ E. $x = -5$

9. For $f(x) = x^2 - 1$ and $g(x) = |2x + 3|$, which has the greatest value?
  A. $f(g(3))$ B. $g(f(2))$ C. $g(f(-1))$
  D. $f(g(-5))$ E. $g(10)$

10. Which is *not* a solution of $y < -2x^2 + 5$?
  A. $(0, 1)$ B. $(-2, 0)$ C. $(1, -7)$
  D. $(2, -4)$ E. none of the above

Compare the boxed quantity in Column A with the boxed quantity in Column B. Choose the best answer.
  A. The quantity in Column A is greater.
  B. The quantity in Column B is greater.
  C. The two quantities are equal.
  D. The relationship cannot be determined on the basis of the information supplied.

Column A	Column B
11. $\sin \theta$	$\cos \theta$
12. the length of the radius of $(x - 3)^2 + (y - 1)^2 = 34$	the length of the radius of $(x - 4)^2 + (y + 2)^2 = 48$

13. *Open-ended* Write an equation of an ellipse whose minor axis is on the x-axis.

14. *Writing* What can you tell about a parabola written in standard form without graphing it?

15. *Money* Suppose you deposit $750 in an account that earns 4% annual interest compounded continuously. How much will be in the account after one year? after five years?

16. Express $\frac{5\pi}{9}$ radians in degrees. Round your answer to the nearest tenth.

More Probability and Statistics

Relating to the Real World

A manufacturer analyzes data about product sales to look for trends. Then the manufacturer can make improvements that consumers want. Airline companies analyze their schedules in order to make changes that meet market demands. These are just two ways that probability and statistics can be used to help people.

	Probability Distributions	Conditional Probability	Analyzing Data	Standard Deviation	Working with Samples
Lessons	11-1	11-2	11-3	11-4	11-5

On the Move

Surveys show that many people list
traffic as one of their top problems. Creative
people in the transportation industry are
designing faster, safer, less
expensive, and environmentally
cleaner ways to get around. In
Curitiba, Brazil, a highly efficient
bus system uses design features of
a modern subway to move people
faster and more smoothly.

As you work through the chapter,
you will identify a transportation
problem. Then you will design a
new product or service to solve this
problem. Finally, you will conduct a survey to
decide whether your product or service is
practical and marketable.

To help you complete the project:

▼ **p. 517** *Find Out by Interviewing*
▼ **p. 525** *Find Out by Analyzing*
▼ **p. 531** *Find Out by Creating*
▼ **p. 551** *Find Out by Interviewing*
▼ **p. 552** *Finishing the Project*

**Binomial
Distributions**

**Normal
Distributions**

11-6

11-7

What You'll Learn

• Making a probability distribution

• Using a probability distribution to conduct a simulation

...And Why

To determine how many customers will have to wait in line at a checkout counter

WORK TOGETHER

Work in groups of four to six.

1. How long does it take you to get ready for school in the morning? On a slip of paper, estimate your time to the nearest five minutes. Make a table to tally the times for your group.

Time to Get Ready	Number of People
<15 min	
15 min	
20 min	1
25 min	11
30 min	
35 min	1
40 min	1

2. What is the probability that a person in your group takes 25 minutes to get ready for school?

3. Combine your group's data with the data from the other groups in your class. Make a table that reflects the data for the class.

4. Based on the data for your class, **predict** how long it will take an average high school student to get ready for school.

THINK AND DISCUSS

Making a Probability Distribution

You can organize data in a **frequency table** that lists each outcome in a sample space and the number of times it occurs. Then you can use the frequencies to calculate experimental probabilities based on the data.

Example 1 **Relating to the Real World**

Social Science Use the frequency table below. Choose an elderly person at random who lives alone. Find the probability that he or she will have contact with his or her children more than once a week.

Contact between Children and Elderly Who Live Alone

How Often Contact Is Made	Number of Elderly
7 times/wk	680
2–6 times/wk	276
1 time/wk	236
Less than 1 time/wk	199
Total	1391

Source: *Statistical Handbook on the American Family*

Find the experimental probability for the first two outcomes in the table.

$P(\text{contact 7 times/wk}) = \frac{680}{1391} \approx 0.489$ ◄——— These probabilities represent contact more than one time/wk.

$P(\text{contact 2–6 times/wk}) = \frac{276}{1391} \approx 0.198$ ◄—

The probability of contact more than once a week is $0.489 + 0.198$, or 0.687.

5. In a sample of 100 elderly people who live alone, **predict** how many will have contact with their children more than once a week.

6. Are the outcomes given in this frequency table equally likely? **Justify** your reasoning.

Probabilities over a continuous range of outcomes are called *cumulative* probabilities.

7. a. Try This Find $P(\text{contact once a week or more})$.
   b. Explain why you use addition to find cumulative probabilities.

A **probability distribution** is a function that tells the probability of each outcome in a sample space. You can use either a table or a graph to show a probability distribution.

One Roll of a Number Cube

Outcome	1	2	3	4	5	6
Probability	$\frac{1}{6}$	$\frac{1}{6}$	$\frac{1}{6}$	$\frac{1}{6}$	$\frac{1}{6}$	$\frac{1}{6}$

◄—— Each outcome is equally likely.

The Sum of Two Number Cubes

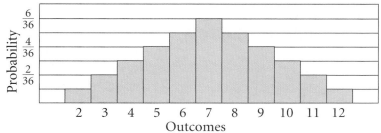

For more practice with graphs of data, see Skills Handbook page 677.

8. Graph the probability distribution for one roll of a number cube.

9. Make a table of the distribution for the sum of two number cubes.

10. Find the sum of the probabilities in each distribution shown above. What is the sum of the probabilities for any sample space?

11. Use the probability distribution for the sum of two number cubes.
   a. Describe the independent and dependent variables.
   b. What is the range of this function?

A situation may be described by more than one sample space. In that case, each sample space has its own probability distribution.

Some agriculturists experiment to grow different types of corn. Some hybrid varieties are shown below.

Example 2 **Relating to the Real World**

Genetics Graph the probability distribution for each sample space. Use the information in the chart below.

Inherited Gene Pairs From Two Hybrid Corn Plants

		Parent Plant	
		G	w
Parent Plant	G	GG	Gw
	w	Gw	ww

← four equally likely outcomes

GG = dominant gene pair (green plant)
Gw = hybrid gene pair (green plant)
ww = recessive gene pair (white plant)

a. {GG, Gw, ww}   **b.** {green, white}

a.

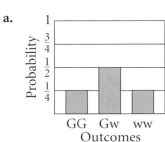

b.

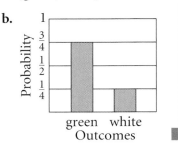

12. Compare the probability distributions for each sample space. How are they related?

13. *Critical Thinking* Which probability distribution from Example 2 would be more useful to a farmer who must avoid raising white corn plants? Why?

A sample space must contain mutually exclusive events. The sum of probabilities for the events in a sample space must be 1.

14. Explain why each set cannot be a sample space for Example 2.
a. {GG, ww}   **b.** {green plant, Gw, white plant}

Using a Probability Distribution

You can design a simulation based on a probability distribution. First, use the probabilities to assign numbers to each outcome in the sample space. For example, if $P(\text{outcome}) = 0.15$, assign 15 out of 100 numbers to that outcome. Then you can conduct trials by generating random numbers.

Example 3 Relating to the Real World

Market Research At a certain store, the number of customers *c* who arrive at the checkout counters each minute varies according to the distribution below.

Number of Customers Each Minute

c	0	1	2	3	4	5	6
P(c)	0.15	0.24	0.28	0.17	0.09	0.05	0.02

Use random numbers to simulate the number of customers over a ten-minute period.

Step 1: Define how the simulation will be done. Assign numbers from 1 to 100 to each outcome (number of customers), based on its probability. Use cumulative probabilities to help you assign the numbers.

Outcome	Probability	Cumulative Probability	Assigned Numbers
0	0.15	0.15	01 – 15
1	0.24	0.39	16 – 39
2	0.28	0.67	40 – 67
3	0.17	0.84	68 – 84
4	0.09	0.93	85 – 93
5	0.05	0.98	94 – 98
6	0.02	1.00	99 – 100

Since *P*(0) = 0.15, assign 15 numbers to this outcome.

There are 17 numbers from 68 to 84.

Step 2: Conduct the simulation. Model a ten-minute period by generating ten random numbers from 1 to 100.

minute ⟶	1st	2nd	3rd	4th	5th	6th	7th	8th	9th	10th
random numbers ⟶	81	29	83	93	18	9	40	97	47	16
number of customers ⟶	3	1	3	4	1	0	2	5	2	1

The random number 9 is assigned to the outcome 0 customers.

Step 3: Interpret the simulation. Based on this simulation, a total of 22 customers would arrive at checkout counters over a ten-minute period. ▪

15. Suppose you use pairs of digits from a random number table to select numbers from 1 to 100. What number should the digits 00 represent?

16. *Critical Thinking* Suppose you are the manager for the store mentioned in Example 3. Use the simulation to decide how many checkout counters to open during the given time period. (Assume it takes one minute to serve each customer.)

17. **Try This** Conduct a simulation of 20 trials for Example 3.

⊞ **GRAPHING CALCULATOR HINT**

On some calculators you can use the command int(100*rand) + 1 to generate random numbers from 1 to 100. Using the MATH feature, you will find the int option under the NUM menu and the rand option under the PRB menu.

Suppose you roll a number cube marked with integers from 1 to 6. Tell whether each set represents a sample space for the outcomes. Explain.

1. {1, 2, 3, 4, 5, 6}

2. {greater than 3, less than 3}

3. {even, prime}

Use the probability distribution below to find each probability.

Number of Letters in Response to Editorials

n	0	1	2	3	4	5	6 or more
$P(n)$	0.10	0.15	0.28	0.19	0.17	0.08	0.03

4. P(0, 1, or 2 letters)

5. P(at least 3 letters)

6. P(at most 4 letters)

7. P(5 or more letters)

8. P(3–5 letters)

9. P(less than 5 letters)

10. Sometimes a probability distribution is shown as a circle graph.
   a. Describe the independent and dependent variables in the distribution shown at the right.
   b. Present the distribution as a bar graph (as in Example 2).
   c. Find P(the tank is at least half full when a person buys gas)

How Full Is the Tank When People Buy Gas?

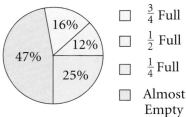

☐ $\frac{3}{4}$ Full

☐ $\frac{1}{2}$ Full

☐ $\frac{1}{4}$ Full

☐ Almost Empty

Source: *The First Really Important Survey of American Habits*

11. **Standardized Test Prep** Each function is defined for a sample space of {1, 2, 3, 4}. Which function represents a probability distribution?
   A. $P(1) = 0.4$, $P(2) = -0.2$, $P(3) = 0.4$, $P(4) = 0.4$
   B. $P(1) = 0.2$, $P(2) = 0.2$, $P(3) = 0.3$, $P(4) = 0.3$
   C. $P(1) = \frac{1}{3}$, $P(2) = \frac{1}{4}$, $P(3) = \frac{1}{4}$, $P(4) = \frac{1}{4}$
   D. $P(1) = 0.1$, $P(2) = 0$, $P(3) = 0.1$, $P(4) = 0.5$

12. Use the spinner shown at the right. Make a probability distribution for the sample space {red, green, blue, yellow}.

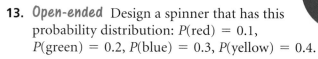

13. **Open-ended** Design a spinner that has this probability distribution: P(red) = 0.1, P(green) = 0.2, P(blue) = 0.3, P(yellow) = 0.4.

14. a. Make a table showing the probability distribution for weather in Dayton.
   b. Describe the independent and dependent variables.
   c. Find the probability that a day in Dayton will include rain or snow.

15. a. **Research** Find weather data for a city near you. Make a probability distribution in graph form.
   b. Explain why a circle graph is an appropriate form to use.

Weather Conditions in Dayton, Ohio

Type of Weather	Number of Days Per Year
Clear	82
Partly Cloudy	118
Mostly Cloudy (no precipitation)	34
Rain	75
Light Snow (< 1.5 in.)	45
Snow (≥ 1.5 in.)	11
Total	365

Source: *The USA Today Weather Almanac*

Graph the probability distribution described by each function. Use a bar graph.

16. $P(x) = \frac{x}{10}$ for $x = 1, 2, 3,$ and 4

17. $P(x) = \frac{2x + 1}{15}$ for $x = 1, 2,$ and 3

18. a. Modeling Design and conduct a simulation for the number of 911 emergency calls over a 24-hour period in a certain town.
  b. If there are two response teams available, and each response takes about an hour, how many callers in your simulation have to wait?
  c. Find P(caller will have to wait) for your simulation.

19. Writing In a simulation, how do equally likely outcomes help you represent the probability distribution?

Suppose you roll two number cubes. Find the probability distribution for each sample space.

20. {the sum of the two cubes is an even number, the sum is an odd number}

21. {both cubes are even, both cubes are odd, one cube is even and the other is odd}

22. {both cubes show 6, exactly one cube shows 6, neither cube shows 6}

23. the sample space containing all possible products of the two cubes

24. Research Construct a probability distribution for the types of television shows broadcast in your area during prime time (8 P.M. to 11 P.M.). You will need to decide which networks to include and what categories to use in your sample space (situation comedy, sports, news, and so on). Use half-hour time blocks.

Probability Distribution for Number of 911 Calls Each Hour

c	P(c)
0	0.21
1	0.30
2	0.18
3	0.13
4	0.09
5	0.05
6	0.03
7	0.01

Exercises   M I X E D   R E V I E W

Solve each equation.

25. $\sin \theta = \frac{1}{2} \ (0° \leq \theta < 360°)$

26. $\frac{3}{x} - \frac{4}{x - 1} = 11$

27. $\log_2 3 = c$

28. Coordinate Geometry Write the equation of a circle centered at $(4, -5)$ with radius 7.

Getting Ready for Lesson 11-2

A spinner has four equal sections that are red, blue, green, and yellow. Suppose you spin twice. Find each probability.

29. P(red, then yellow)

30. P(not yellow, then green)

31. P(not blue, then not red)

32. P(red, then not red)

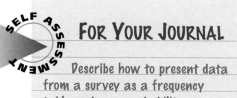

FOR YOUR JOURNAL

Describe how to present data from a survey as a frequency table and as a probability distribution.

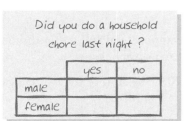
What You'll Learn

11-2 Conditional Probability

- Finding conditional probabilities
- Using formulas and tree diagrams

...And Why

To find probabilities associated with recycling and airline travel

---

WORK TOGETHER

Did you do a household chore last night?

1. **Data Collection** Conduct a survey of your class. Each of you should answer the question on a slip of paper and write whether you are male or female.

2. Have one student record the class results in a table like the one shown.

3. Suppose a person from your class is chosen at random. Use the table to find each probability.
   a. *P*(the person is male)
   b. *P*(the person did a chore)
   c. *P*(the person is male and did a chore)

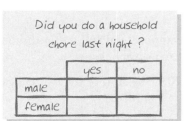

Did you do a household chore last night?

	yes	no
male		
female		

THINK AND DISCUSS

Finding Conditional Probabilities

The table below shows the results for one class.

What is the probability that a person did a chore, *given that the person is male?* The condition *the person is male* limits the sample space to 15 possible outcomes, of which 7 are favorable (did a chore). So the probability is $\frac{7}{15}$.

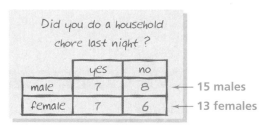

Did you do a household chore last night?

	yes	no	
male	7	8	← 15 males
female	7	6	← 13 females

4. Use the data for the class shown above. Find the probability that a person did a chore, given that the person is female.

When a probability contains a condition that may limit the sample space, it is called a **conditional probability.** You can write a conditional probability using the notation $P(B \mid A)$, read *the probability of event B, given event A.*

5. Use the data for your class to find each probability.
   a. *P*(did a chore | female)   b. *P*(male | did a chore)

Municipal Waste Collected in the United States
(millions of tons)

	Paper	Aluminum	Glass	Plastic	Other
Recycled	26.5	1.1	3.0	0.7	13.7
Not Recycled	51.3	1.9	10.7	19.3	78.7

Source: *Franklin Associates, Ltd.*

Example 1   **Relating to the Real World**

Environment Each year Americans recycle more and more material through municipal waste collections. Use the information shown above, based on a recent year, to find each probability.

a. *P*(recycled | aluminum)   b. *P*(paper | recycled)

a. The given condition *aluminum* limits the sample space to 1.1 + 1.9, or 3.0 million tons. Of these, 1.1 million were recycled. Therefore, *P*(recycled | aluminum) = $\frac{1.1}{3.0}$, or 0.367.

   The probability that aluminum collected was recycled is about 37%.

b. The given condition limits the sample space to *recycled* waste. A favorable outcome is recycled paper.

$$P(\text{paper} \mid \text{recycled}) = \frac{26.5}{26.5 + 1.1 + 3.0 + 0.7 + 13.7}$$
$$= \frac{26.5}{45.0}$$
$$\approx 0.589$$

   The probability that recycled waste was paper is about 59%.

6. **Try This** Find each probability.
   a. *P*(paper | not recycled)   b. *P*(recycled | plastic)

7. **Critical Thinking** Of all the types of waste collected, which type is most likely to be recycled? Which type is least likely to be recycled? **Justify** your answers.

8. **Open-ended** Use the data from Example 1 to write and evaluate your own conditional probability.

Using Formulas and Tree Diagrams

Results from a poll are shown in the frequency table at the right.

Suppose one of the people polled is chosen at random. Let F = *a female is chosen* and D = *the person pours shampoo directly onto the head.*

Applying Shampoo

	Directly Onto Head	Into Hand First
Male	2	18
Female	6	24

9. a. Find $P(F) \cdot P(D)$ and $P(F \text{ and } D)$.
   b. Are events F and D independent? Explain.
   c. Find $P(F) \cdot P(D \mid F)$. What do you notice?

The results of Question 9 suggest that $P(A \text{ and } B) = P(A) \cdot P(B \mid A)$. This multiplication pattern applies to *any* events A and B, whether or not they are independent. This equation contains a formula for conditional probability.

Conditional Probability Formula

For any two events A and B from a sample space, with $P(A) \neq 0$:

$$P(B \mid A) = \frac{P(A \text{ and } B)}{P(A)}$$

Example: Suppose you roll a number cube marked with integers from 1 to 6. Let M = *the number is prime* and let E = *the number is even.*

$$P(M \mid E) = \frac{P(E \text{ and } M)}{P(E)} = \frac{\frac{1}{6}}{\frac{3}{6}} = \frac{1}{3}$$

QUICK REVIEW

The only number that is even and prime is 2.

Notice that, with the formula, you can calculate a conditional probability from other probabilities.

Example 2

Travel Suppose that 80% of an airline's flights depart on schedule. Suppose also that 72% of its flights depart and arrive on schedule. Find the probability that a flight arrives on time, given that it departs on time.

Use the formula $P(B \mid A) = \frac{P(A \text{ and } B)}{P(A)}$.

$P(\text{arrives on time} \mid \text{departs on time})$ ← Substitute *arrives on time* for B.
← Substitute *departs on time* for A.

$= \dfrac{P(\text{departs on time and arrives on time})}{P(\text{departs on time})}$

$= \dfrac{0.72}{0.80} = 0.9$

The probability that a flight arrives on time, given that it departs on time, is 90%.

You can also use tree diagrams to help you solve problems involving conditional probabilities.

A student in Buffalo, New York, made the following observations:

- When a snowfall is heavy ($\geq$ 6 in.), schools are closed 80% of the time.
- When a snowfall is light ($<$ 6 in.), schools are closed 30% of the time.
- 40% of the snowfalls are heavy.

To organize these probabilities in a tree diagram, use H (heavy snowfall), L (light snowfall), C (schools closed), and O (schools open).

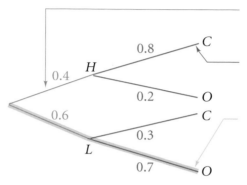

Each first branch represents a simple probability. $P(H) = 0.4$

Each second branch represents a conditional probability. $P(C|H) = 0.8$

The highlighted path represents $P(L \text{ and } O)$.
$$P(L \text{ and } O) = P(L) \cdot P(O|L)$$
$$= 0.6 \cdot 0.7$$
$$= 0.42$$

10. What probability is represented by each branch?
   a. the branch labeled 0.6   **b.** the branch labeled 0.3

11. Find each probability in the diagram shown above.
   a. $P(H)$ **b.** $P(O \mid H)$ **c.** $P(O \mid L)$

12. Find $P(L \text{ and } C)$ by using the path labeled 0.6 and 0.3.

Example 3

Use the tree diagram above to find the probability that Buffalo schools will be closed because of snow.

The path containing H and C and the path containing L and C both represent schools closed for snow. Find the probability for each path. Then add.

$P(H \text{ and } C)$
$= P(H) \cdot P(C|H)$
$= 0.4 \cdot 0.8$
$= 0.32$

$P(L \text{ and } C)$
$= P(L) \cdot P(C \mid L)$
$= 0.6 \cdot 0.3$
$= 0.18$

The probability that Buffalo schools will be closed because of snow is $0.32 + 0.18$, or 50%.

13. a. What is the probability that Buffalo schools will be open despite snow?
   b. Verify your answer to part (a) by using the tree diagram above.

Jobs **The table contains information about 90 applicants for a job. Suppose an applicant is chosen at random. Find each probability.**

1. P(applicant has a diploma)

2. P(applicant has experience)

3. P(applicant has a diploma and experience)

4. the probability that the applicant has experience, given that the applicant has a diploma

5. the probability that the applicant has experience, given that the applicant has no diploma

Characteristics of Job Applicants

		Has High School Diploma	
		Yes	No
Has Experience	Yes	54	5
	No	27	4

6. Writing In Exercises 1–5, are having a diploma and having experience independent events? **Justify** your answer.

7. Education Use the frequency table at the right to find each probability. Let M and F represent male and female recipients, and let A, B, and V represent associate's, bachelor's, and advanced degrees, respectively.
  a. $P(F)$ **b.** $P(B)$
  c. $P(F \text{ and } B)$ **d.** $P(F \mid B)$
  e. $P(M \mid V)$ **f.** $P(V \mid M)$

Projected Number of Degree Recipients in 2004 (in thousands)

Degree	Male	Female
Associate's	218	334
Bachelor's	572	676
Advanced	223	261

Source: *U.S. National Center for Education Statistics*

8. Let S, C, W, and R represent sunny, cloudy, windy and rainy weather, respectively. Use probability notation to describe each event.
  a. the chance of rainy weather
  b. the chance of rainy weather if it is windy
  c. the chance of windy weather if it is sunny
  d. the chance of sunny and windy weather

9. Suppose A and B are independent events, with $P(A) = 0.60$ and $P(B) = 0.25$. Find each probability.
  a. $P(A \text{ and } B)$ **b.** $P(A \mid B)$
  c. What do you notice about $P(A)$ and $P(A \mid B)$?
  d. Critical Thinking A "common sense" way to describe A and B as independent events is that *the occurrence of B has no effect on the probability of A.* Which two probabilities in this exercise illustrate this relationship? Explain.

10. Medicine The tree diagram at the right shows probabilities concerning a disease and a medical test used to detect it. Find each probability.
  a. $P(D)$ **b.** $P(P \mid D)$
  c. $P(D \text{ and } P)$ **d.** $P(H \text{ and } P)$
  e. the probability that a person chosen at random will test positive for the disease

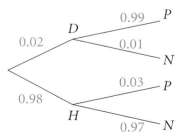

D = person has the disease
H = person is healthy
P = person tests positive
N = person tests negative

11. Writing Explain which branches of the tree diagram at the right represent conditional probabilities. Give specific examples.

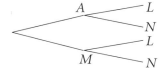

12. Open-ended Estimate probabilities for each branch of the tree diagram at the right for your city or town. Then find $P(L)$.

A = adult (21 or older)
M = minor (under 21)
L = licensed driver
N = not licensed to drive

13. A football team has a 70% chance of winning when it doesn't snow, but only a 40% chance of winning when it snows. Suppose there is a 50% chance of snow. Find the probability that the team will win.

14. Critical Thinking Sixty percent of a company's sales representatives have completed training seminars. Of these, 80% have had increased sales. Overall, 56% of the representatives (whether trained or not) have had increased sales. Use a tree diagram to find the probability of increased sales, given that a representative has not been trained.

Chapter Project **Find Out by Interviewing**

Conduct a survey to identify a transportation problem in your community.

• Choose the group of people you want to survey.

• Design the survey. Before you write questions, decide what data you want to collect. You can collect data about types of transportation people use, how far or how often they use each type, and how satisfied they are.

• Test the survey on a few people to make sure the questions are clear. Revise it if necessary.

• Collect the data.

Exercises   MIXED REVIEW

Write each expression as a polynomial in standard form.

15. $x^2(x - 3)(x + 1)$ **16.** $(x - 2)^3$ **17.** $x(x + 4)(x + 3)^2$

18. The number of students in one school is growing by 2% per year. Write an exponential function to model this relationship.

Getting Ready for Lesson 11-3

Put the members of each data set in order from smallest to largest. Then find the middle value.

19. 0.2   0.3   0.6   1.2   0.7   0.9   0.8   **20.** 11   23   15   17   21   18   20   21

Comparing Conditional Probabilities

After Lesson 11-2

You can use the tree diagram at the right to find conditional probabilities like $P(P \mid D) = 0.99$. Scientists also look at $P(H \mid P)$, the probability of a "false positive" test. Since this probability is not found on a branch in the diagram, you must use the formula for conditional probability.

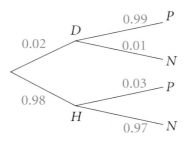

D = person has the disease
H = person is healthy
P = person tests positive
N = person tests negative

Example   Relating to the Real World

Medicine   Use the tree diagram above to find $P(H \mid P)$.

$P(H \mid P) = \dfrac{P(H \text{ and } P)}{P(P)}$

Find $P(H \text{ and } P)$ and $P(P)$.

$\begin{aligned} P(H \text{ and } P) &= 0.98 \cdot 0.03 \\ &= 0.0294 \end{aligned}$
$\qquad$
$\begin{aligned} P(P) &= P(D \text{ and } P) \text{ or } P(H \text{ and } P) \\ &= 0.02 \cdot 0.99 + 0.98 \cdot 0.03 \\ &= 0.0492 \end{aligned}$

So $\begin{aligned} P(H \mid P) &= \dfrac{P(H \text{ and } P)}{P(P)} \\ &= \dfrac{0.0294}{0.0492} \\ &\approx 0.597 \end{aligned}$

About 60% of the people who test positive do not actually have the disease.

1. Use the tree diagram in the Example to find each probability.
   a. $P(D \mid P)$
   b. $P(N \mid D)$
   c. $P(D \mid N)$

Use the tree diagram relating to snowfall and school closings at the right to find each probability.

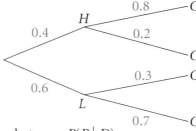

H = heavy snowfall
L = light snowfall
C = schools closed
O = school open

2. $P(C \mid H)$
3. $P(H \mid C)$
4. $P(L \mid C)$
5. $P(O \mid L)$
6. $P(L \mid O)$
7. $P(H \mid O)$

8. **Writing**   Explain the difference in meaning between $P(P \mid D)$ and $P(D \mid P)$ in the Example. Compare $P(P \mid D)$ and $P(D \mid P)$. Is the test in the Example as useful as you might expect? Explain.

What You'll Learn

- Calculating measures of central tendency
- Drawing and interpreting box-and-whisker plots

...And Why

To draw conclusions from statistical data about water temperatures

What You'll Need

- graphing calculator

For more practice with statistics, see Skills Handbook page 678.

11-3 Analyzing Data

THINK AND DISCUSS

Calculating Measures of Central Tendency

Statistics is the study of data analysis and interpretation. The *mean*, the *median*, and the *mode* are central values that help describe a set of data. They are called **measures of central tendency.**

Measures of Central Tendency

Measure	Definition	Example (using {1, 2, 2, 3, 5, 5})
mean	$\frac{\text{sum of the data values}}{\text{number of data values}}$	$\frac{1+2+2+3+5+5}{6} = \frac{18}{6} = 3$
median	middle value *or* mean of the two middle values	$\frac{2+3}{2} = 2.5$
mode	most frequently occurring value(s)	2 and 5

- You can use the symbol $\bar{x}$, read *x bar,* to designate the mean.

- To find the median, arrange the data in increasing or decreasing order.

- If no value occurs more frequently than any other, there is no mode.

You can use a graphing calculator to calculate statistical information quickly, or when the data set is large and calculations are complicated.

Gulf of Mexico Water Temperatures (°F)

Location	J	F	M	A	M	J	J	A	S	O	N	D
Pensacola	56	58	63	71	78	84	85	86	82	74	65	58
St. Petersburg	62	64	68	74	80	84	86	86	84	78	70	64
Naples	66	66	71	77	82	86	87	87	86	81	73	68
Key West	71	72	75	78	82	85	87	87	86	82	76	72

Example 1 **Relating to the Real World** ·······

Oceanography Find the mean, the median, and the mode of all the water temperatures for the Gulf of Mexico in the table below.

Gulf of Mexico Water Temperatures (°F)

Location	J	F	M	A	M	J	J	A	S	O	N	D
Pensacola	56	58	63	71	78	84	85	86	82	74	65	58
St. Petersburg	62	64	68	74	80	84	86	86	84	78	70	64
Naples	66	66	71	77	82	86	87	87	86	81	73	68
Key West	71	72	75	78	82	85	87	87	86	82	76	72

Step 1: Use the **STAT** feature to enter the data into your graphing calculator as L1.

Step 2: Use the List feature to access the Math menu. Find the mean.

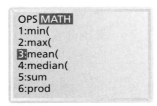
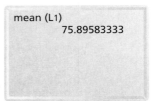

Step 3: Return to the same menu to find the median.

```
OPS MATH
1:min(
2:max(
3:mean(
4:median(
5:sum
6:prod
```

```
mean (L1)
            75.89583333
median (L1)
                  77.5
```

Step 4: Use the StatPlot feature to access Plot 1. Choose the histogram, L1, and Frequency 1 options. Then enter an appropriate viewing window.

```
Plot1
On Off
Type:  ⠠⠄  ⤳  ⠒⠒  ▟▙
Xlist:  L1 L2 L3 L4 L5 L6
Freq: 1 L1 L2 L3 L4 L5 L6
```

```
Window Format
Xmin=50
Xmax=90
Xscl=1
Ymin=−2
Ymax=8
Yscl=1
```

Step 5: Graph the data. Use TRACE to move the cursor to the highest point of the graph.

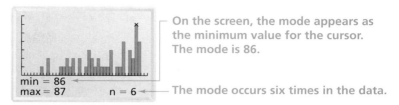

On the screen, the mode appears as the minimum value for the cursor. The mode is 86.

min = 86
max = 87   n = 6 — The mode occurs six times in the data.

The mean temperature is about 75.9°F, the median is 77.5°F, and the mode is 86°F.

1. Which measure—the mean, the median, or the mode—do you think most accurately represents the "average" water temperature of the Gulf of Mexico along the Florida coast? **Justify** your reasoning.

2. **Try This** Find the mean, the median, and the modes of the 12 temperature readings from St. Petersburg. Use the data on page 520.

3. *Critical Thinking* For each data set, determine which is greater, the *mean* or the *median*. **Justify** your answer.
   a. 10   10   10   12   12   20   b. 20   19   18   18   11

Using Box-and-Whisker Plots

When data are arranged in increasing order, the median divides the data into two equal parts. You can use the median of each of these parts to divide the data further into four equal parts. The values separating these parts are called **quartiles.** Quartiles are shown below for the 12 water temperatures for Pensacola.

median of lower part (Q_1) = 60.5   median of upper part (Q_3) = 83

56   58   58 │ 63   65   71 ↓ 74   78   82 │ 84   85   86

median of data set (Q_2) = 72.5

The values Q_1, Q_2, and Q_3 are the first, second, and third quartiles. A **box-and-whisker plot** uses quartiles to form a center box and whiskers.

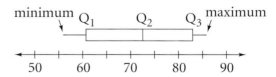

4. What percent of the data falls in the "box" of a box-and-whisker plot? What percent falls in each whisker?

Example 2

Graphing Calculator Find the quartiles of the water temperature data from Example 1 using a box-and-whisker plot.

Use the StatPlot feature and select a box-and-whisker plot. Use Ymin = 0, Ymax = 1, and appropriate *x*-values. Press **GRAPH**.

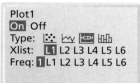 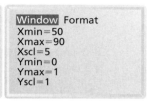 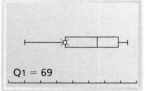

Use **TRACE** to find the quartile values. They are $Q_1 = 69$, $Q_2 = 77.5$, and $Q_3 = 84.5$.

An **outlier** is an item of data with a substantially different value from the rest of the items in the data set. Sometimes an outlier is an important part of the data. At other times it can represent a false reading. When you are sure an outlier is erroneous, you may remove it from the data set.

5. a. Identify the outlier in the following data set.

56   64   73   59   98   65   59

b. Find the mean, the median, and the mode of the data.

c. Remove the outlier and recalculate the mean, the median, and the mode. What effect does removing the outlier have on each measure of central tendency?

6. a. Suppose the data in Question 5 represents measures of water temperature at seven locations on a large lake. How would you treat the outlier? Explain.

b. Suppose the data in Question 5 represents the number of customers in a small restaurant each night during one week. How would you treat the outlier? Explain.

Exercises   ON YOUR OWN

Find the mean, median, and mode for each data set.

1. 100   95   99   55   89   92   97   95   90

2. 2.4   4.3   5.5   3.7   3.9   2.8   5.4   2.8

3. 475   499   402   407   405   480   422

4. 14   17   20   15   13   17   14   13   20   15

5. 1057   1120   1025   1103   1090   1199   1200

6. 17.1   12.8   13.8   19.1   15.3   17.9   12.8

7. 18   15   17   15   15   17   18   9   12   17   9

8. 6283   5700   6381   6275   5700   5896

9. 17.8   16.3   19.1   15.9   16.3   18.5   15.2   19.1

10. 672.5   800.9   732.1   818.2   603.7   556.3

DILBERT by Scott Adams

Panel 1: MY MARKET RESEARCH INDICATES THAT 50% OF YOUR CUSTOMERS ARE ABOVE THE MEDIAN AGE.

Panel 2: BUT THE SHOCKING DISCOVERY WAS THAT 50% WERE BELOW THE MEDIAN AGE.

Panel 3: WHAT PERCENT ARE EXACTLY THE MEDIAN AGE? / I'M PROPOSING TO STUDY THAT IN PHASE TWO.

11. a. What percent of the customers in the cartoon above are exactly the median age?
  b. Must an item from a data set fall exactly at the median? Explain.
  c. Can the company do anything about the shocking discovery? Why or why not?

12. Open-ended Find a data set in your local newspaper. Calculate the mean, median, and mode of the data. Decide which measure best represents the data set, and explain your decision.

Make a box-and-whisker plot for each data set. Use a graphing calculator, paper and pencil, or mental math.

13. 49 58 62 64 67 77 80

14. 57.5 49.2 22.2 52.1 99.9 51.7

15. 1020 1045 1033 1005 1017 1050

16. 12 11 15 12 19 20 19

Identify the outlier of each data set. Then describe how its value affects the mean of the data.

17. 3.4 4.5 2.3 5.9 9.8 3.3 2.1 4.4

18. 17 21 19 10 15 19 14 0

19. Weather The table at the right shows various high temperature readings for one day on the island of Maui, Hawaii.
  a. Find the mean and the median of the data.
  b. Which measure from part (a) more accurately represents the high temperature on Maui on that day? **Justify** your reasoning.

20. a. Research Find the per capita (per person) taxes paid by residents of each state to the Federal government.
  b. Compute the mean, the median, and the mode of the per capita taxes.
  c. Compare the amount residents of your state pay with the measures of central tendency from part (b). **Justify** any conclusions you make.
  d. Find the quartiles of the data from part (a). Make a box-and-whisker plot of the data.

High Temperatures on Maui

Location	Temperature
Kahului	88°F
Kihei	85°F
Lahaina	86°F
Hana	82°F
Haleakala	66°F
Kula	75°F

21. **Meteorology** In 1995, 80 tornadoes hit the state of Oklahoma. Seven of these were classified F2 or F3 ("strong" tornadoes).
   a. Make a box-and-whisker plot of the data.
   b. Identify the outlier. Remove it from the data set and make a revised box-and-whisker plot.
   c. **Writing** How does the removal of the outlier affect the box-and-whisker plot? How does it affect the median of the data set?

Some Oklahoma Tornadoes

Date	Length (miles)	Intensity
4/17/95	2	F2
4/17/95	4.5	F2
4/17/95	7	F2
5/7/95	34	F3
5/7/95	6	F2
6/8/95	5	F2
6/9/95	5.25	F2

Source: *National Weather Service*

22. **Geology** The table below shows the number of major earthquakes (magnitude 7.0 or greater) throughout the world in the ten-year period from 1985 through 1994.

Year	1985	1986	1987	1988	1989	1990	1991	1992	1993	1994
Earthquakes	14	6	11	8	7	13	11	23	14	14

   a. Find the mode of the data.
   b. Calculate the mean and median annual number of earthquakes.
   c. Identify the outlier of the data. Remove it from the data and recalculate the mean and median. How does the outlier affect the mean and median of the data?
   d. **Technology** Compare the box-and-whisker plots at the right. One shows the data above. The other shows worldwide earthquake data from 1900 to 1994. What conclusions can you draw about recent earthquakes? **Justify** your reasoning.

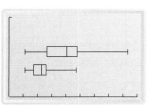

Xmin = 0   Ymin = 0
Xmax = 45   Ymax = 1
Xscl = 5   Yscl = 1

23. a. **Data Analysis** How does a presidential election in the United States affect the voter turnout rate in elections for the House of Representatives? Make a box-and-whisker plot for the data from each of the three types of election shown in the table below.

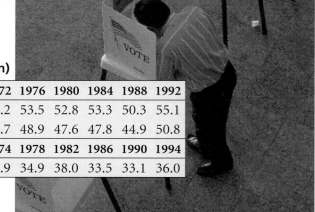

Voter Turnout (in Percent of Voting-Age Population)

Presidential Year	1956	1960	1964	1968	1972	1976	1980	1984	1988	1992
Voting for President	59.3	62.8	61.9	60.9	55.2	53.5	52.8	53.3	50.3	55.1
Voting for Representatives	55.9	58.5	57.8	55.1	50.7	48.9	47.6	47.8	44.9	50.8
Non-Presidential Year	1958	1962	1966	1970	1974	1978	1982	1986	1990	1994
Voting for Representatives	43.0	45.4	45.4	43.5	35.9	34.9	38.0	33.5	33.1	36.0

Source: *U.S. Bureau of the Census*

   b. **Writing** Use your box-and-whisker plots to describe any effect that you see.

Chapter Project

Find Out by Analyzing

Organize the data you gathered in the survey in the Find Out activity on page 517. Make graphs of the data. Calculate summary statistics. Use your graphs and summary statistics to analyze the data. List problems or issues revealed by your data.

Exercises   M I X E D   R E V I E W

Find the inverse of each function.

24. $y = x^2 - 7$ **25.** $y = 3^x$ **26.** $y = \dfrac{7}{4 - x}$ **27.** $y = \dfrac{8}{x^2}$

28. Banking Suppose you deposited $500 in an account the day you finished eighth grade. Suppose the account pays 4% annual interest, compounded continuously. How much will you have when you finish twelfth grade?

Getting Ready for Lesson 11-4

Simplify each expression. Round your answers to the nearest hundredth.

29. $\frac{1}{3}\left[(2 - 6)^2 + (7 - 6)^2 + (8 - 6)^2\right]$ **30.** $\sqrt{\frac{1}{2}\left[(4 - 3)^2 + (5 - 3)^2\right]}$

Exercises   C H E C K P O I N T

Each function is defined for a sample space of $\{4, 5, 6, 7\}$. Decide if the function represents a probability distribution. Explain your answer.

1. $P(4) = 1, P(5) = 0.2, P(6) = 0.1, P(7) = 0.1$ **2.** $P(4) = \frac{1}{5}, P(5) = \frac{1}{2}, P(6) = \frac{1}{5}, P(7) = \frac{1}{10}$

Use the results of the survey at the right to find each probability.

3. $P(\text{teacher} \mid \text{yes})$ **4.** $P(\text{no} \mid \text{teacher})$

5. $P(\text{student} \mid \text{no})$ **6.** $P(\text{yes} \mid \text{student})$

Find the mean, median, and mode of each data set.

7. 7 4 9 3 5 4 4 7 9 10 3 1 8

8. 1.2 2.1 4.6 2.5 9.7 6.2 2.6 2.4 3.1 3.8

9. Writing How does an outlier affect the mean, median, and mode of a data set? Explain.

10. Open-ended Write a data set that includes an outlier. Make a box-and-whisker plot of your data set with and without the outlier.

Did You Eat Breakfast Today?

	Yes	No
Teachers	12	20
Students	45	23

What You'll Learn

- Determining standard deviation

...And Why

To describe sets of data

What You'll Need

- graphing calculator

11-4 Standard Deviation

WORK TOGETHER

1. Find the mean, the median, and the mode of each set of data. Are the sets the same? Explain.

Set 1:	77	78	79	80	80	81	82	83
Set 2:	20	60	70	80	80	90	100	140
Set 3:	50	60	70	80	80	90	100	110
Set 4:	20	30	40	80	80	120	130	140

2. Find the difference between the greatest value and the least value in each set of data. What do these differences tell you about the sets of data?

3. Find the quartiles of each set of data. For each set, half of the data lie between Q_1 and Q_3. The value $Q_3 - Q_1$ gives you an idea of how the data are spread out. Find $Q_3 - Q_1$ for each set of data. How do these values compare?

4. a. Summarize the similarities and differences among the four sets in terms of central tendency and spread. Which is the most spread-out set? Which is the least? Explain.

   b. Make box-and-whisker plots of the four sets of data. Do the graphs support your conclusions from part (a)?

THINK AND DISCUSS

Statisticians use several **measures of variation** to describe how the data in a data set are spread out.

Measures of Variation

Measure	Definition
range	greatest value − least value
interquartile range	$Q_3 - Q_1$
standard deviation	measure of how each data value in the set varies from the mean

5. a. Can the variation, or spread, in two sets of data be different, even though they have the same range? Give an example.

   b. Can the variation in two sets of data be different, even though they have the same interquartile range? Give an example.

The Greek letter *sigma*, σ, represents standard deviation. Use the following procedure to calculate the standard deviation.

Procedure for Finding Standard Deviation

- Find the mean of the data set, $\bar{x}$.
- Find the difference between each data value and the mean.
- Square each difference.
- Find the average (mean) of these squares.
- Take the square root of the average. This is the standard deviation.

Example 1 Relating to the Real World

Energy Use the data in the table to find the standard deviation in electric energy used for the five days shown.

**Electric Energy Usage for Selected Days
in Megawatt-hours (MWh)**

Day	1	2	3	4	5
Energy Used	48.0	53.2	52.3	46.6	49.9

First, find the mean of the data.

$$\bar{x} = \frac{48.0 + 53.2 + 52.3 + 46.6 + 49.9}{5} = 50.0$$

Organize the next steps in a table.

x	$\bar{x}$	$x - \bar{x}$	$(x - \bar{x})^2$
48.0	50.0	−2.0	4.00
53.2	50.0	3.2	10.24
52.3	50.0	2.3	5.29
46.6	50.0	−3.4	11.56
49.9	50.0	−0.1	0.01
		Sum:	31.1

Now calculate the standard deviation.

average of squares $= \dfrac{\text{sum}}{5}$

$$= \frac{31.1}{5}$$

$$= 6.22$$

$$\sigma = \sqrt{6.22}$$

$$\approx 2.5$$

The standard deviation of the data is about 2.5 MWh.

6. Try This Find the standard deviation for data set 3 from the Work Together on page 526.

7. Critical Thinking The other three data sets on page 526 have standard deviations of 43.9, 32.0 and 1.9. Match each data set with its standard deviation.

Standard deviation is like a custom-made measuring stick for the variation in a set of data. A low standard deviation (compared to actual data values) indicates that the data are clustered tightly around the mean. As the data become more spread out, the standard deviation increases.

Electrical power companies use standard deviation to prepare for days of peak demand.

Example 2   Relating to the Real World

Graphing Calculator Find the mean and the standard deviation of the data for the daily energy demand in a small town.

Daily Energy Demand During August (in MWh)

Sun	Mon	Tues	Wed	Thurs	Fri	Sat
		53	52	47	50	39
33	40	41	44	47	49	43
39	47	49	54	53	46	36
33	45	45	42	43	39	33
33	40	40	41	42		

Step 1: Use the STAT feature to enter the data as L1.

Step 2: Use the CALC menu of the STAT feature to access the 1-Var Stats option. Request L1 and press ENTER.

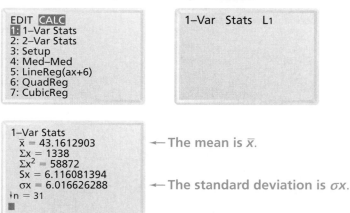

The mean of the daily energy usage is about 43.2 MWh. The standard deviation is about 6.0 MWh.

To see how the power company uses standard deviation, first draw a number line showing the mean of 43.2. Then mark off intervals of 6.0 on either side of the mean.

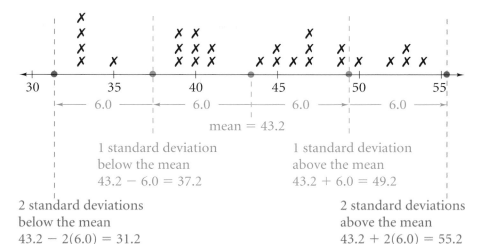

1 standard deviation below the mean
43.2 − 6.0 = 37.2

1 standard deviation above the mean
43.2 + 6.0 = 49.2

2 standard deviations below the mean
43.2 − 2(6.0) = 31.2

2 standard deviations above the mean
43.2 + 2(6.0) = 55.2

The graph also shows the original data. The power company can expect that the daily demand on most days will fall within two standard deviations of the mean.

Example 3   **Relating to the Real World**

Energy   Use the mean, 43.2, and standard deviation, 6.0, from the energy demand data in Example 2. Within how many standard deviations of the mean is a demand of 38.5 mWh? of 53.0 MWh?

Since the mean is 43.2 and one standard deviation below the mean is 37.2, 38.5 is within one standard deviation below the mean.

Since 53 < 55.2, but 53 ≮ 49.2, 53 is within two standard deviations above the mean.

8. **Try This**   In May, the mean daily energy demand is 35.8 MWh, with a standard deviation of 3.5 MWh. The power company prepares for any demand within three standard deviations of the mean. Are they prepared for a demand of 48 MWh? Explain.

Exercises   ON YOUR OWN

Find the mean, the range, and the interquartile range for each data set.

1. 3   4   5   5   6   6   7   7   8

2. 20   34   56   67   78   91   125

3. 25   30   35   40   45   50

4. 25   36   37   38   39   50

5. 1724   1786   1670   1760   1300

6. 187   190   345   456   732   891   879   324

Find the standard deviation for each data set.

7. 78   90   456   673   111   381   21

8. 13   15   17   18   12   21   10

9. 52   63   54   70   66

10. 121   240   179   208   157

11. 1   0   17   12   15   9   11   15

12. 350   480   610   230   720   590

Find the standard deviation for each data set. Use the standard deviations to compare the data sets.

13. fastest recorded speeds of various cats (mi/h):   30   70   50
fastest recorded speeds of various birds (mi/h): 217   55   200

14. the number of buttons on selected outfits: 11   5   12   8   3   12
the number of pockets in the same outfits: 5   5   5   2   2   5

15. **Statistics** The bar graph shows the number of movies 50 people saw during the month of May.
   a. Find the mean number of movies viewed by the 50 people. *Hint:* First add the number of movies viewed by *each* of the 50 people.
   b. Calculate the standard deviation of the data.

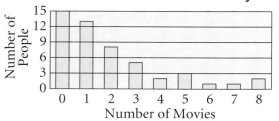

Number of Movies Seen in May

16. a. Find the mean and the standard deviation for daily power usage during ten days in June.

   51.8   53.6   54.7   51.9   49.3
   52.0   53.5   51.2   60.7   59.3

   b. How many items in the data set fall within one standard deviation of the mean? within two standard deviations? within three standard deviations?

17. **Earnings** The table below shows the median weekly earnings of union and nonunion workers in various occupations.
   a. Find the mean and the range of the data for union workers and for nonunion workers.
   b. Calculate the standard deviation for each set of data.
   c. Within how many standard deviations of the mean is a weekly salary of $600 for union workers? for nonunion workers?
   d. **Writing** Compare the values you calculated for union and nonunion workers in parts (a) through (c). **Analyze** the meaning of any differences you find. Discuss your conclusions.

Workers' Median Weekly Earnings, 1994

Occupation	Union	Nonunion
Managerial & professional	$768	$628
Precision craft & repair	$672	$458
Technical sales & support	$518	$407
Fabricators & laborers	$514	$327
Service occupations	$483	$268
Farming, forestry & fishing	$416	$273

Source: *U.S. Bureau of Labor Statistics*

Income Use the chart at the right for Exercises 18–20.

18. Calculate the mean income for each year.

19. Writing Use the range of the data for each year to describe how farm income varied from 1992 to 1993.

20. Calculate the standard deviation for each year. In which year did farm income cluster more around the mean?

21. Open-ended Create two sets of data with the same mean but whose standard deviations differ by at least five points. Calculate the mean and standard deviation of each set of data.

Farm Income in Midwestern States (millions of dollars)

State	1992	1993
Iowa	10,409	10,001
Kansas	7,170	7,363
Minnesota	7,023	6,574
Missouri	4,174	4,053
North Dakota	2,984	2,933
Nebraska	8,783	8,909
South Dakota	3,157	3,320

Source: *U.S. Department of Agriculture*

Chapter Project **Find Out by Creating**

Suppose the members of your survey population are potential customers for your business. What problem seems the most important to the people you surveyed? Invent a product or service that could solve this problem. Be sure your idea is practical. Make a drawing, scale model, or written description of your new transportation product or service. Include a price or charge that you think is appropriate.

Exercises MIXED REVIEW

Simplify each expression.

22. $(4 - i) + (5 - 4i)$ **23.** $(3 + 2i) - (2 + 8i)$ **24.** $(1 - 2i) + 7i$ **25.** $5 - (9 - 3i)$

26. 3^{-2} **27.** $4^{\frac{1}{2}}$ **28.** $8^{\frac{2}{3}}$ **29.** $(x^3)^{\frac{1}{3}}$

30. $\log 100$ **31.** $\log_2 8$ **32.** $\log_3 \left(\frac{1}{9}\right)$ **33.** $\log_4 (4^x)$

34. You are setting up wires to steady a young tree. Two 8-ft wires will go from a protective collar on the tree 6 ft up the trunk to the ground. At what angle will the wires meet the ground?

Getting Ready for Lesson 11-5

Simplify each expression.

35. $\dfrac{1}{\sqrt{4}}$ **36.** $-\dfrac{1}{\sqrt{9}}$ **37.** $\dfrac{1}{\sqrt{36}}$

38. $-\dfrac{1}{\sqrt{121}}$ **39.** $\dfrac{1}{\sqrt{50}}$ **40.** $-\dfrac{1}{\sqrt{81}}$

SELF ASSESSMENT

FOR YOUR JOURNAL

Compare a box-and-whisker plot and standard deviation. What information does each one contain about variation found in data?

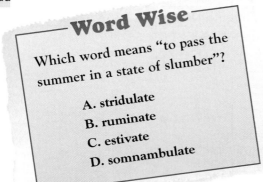

What You'll Learn

- Finding sample proportions
- Finding the margin of error

...And Why

To predict whether a political candidate can be confident of her lead

11-5 **W**orking With Samples

WORK TOGETHER

1. Write your answer to the question at the left below. After everyone has written an answer, find the correct response.

2. Ask ten classmates what their response was. What percent of your sample chose the correct answer?

3. Compare your sample results with those of others. Compile a list of sample results from everyone in your class. Does each sample show the same result? Explain.

4. How did the class as a whole do? Find the percent of correct answers in the entire class. Do you expect this percent to be the same as in your sample? Why or why not?

Word Wise

Which word means "to pass the summer in a state of slumber"?

A. stridulate
B. ruminate
C. estivate
D. somnambulate

THINK AND DISCUSS

Sampling Without Bias

Suppose you want to know what percent of all teenagers recognize the word meaning "to pass the summer in a state of slumber." Since it is too costly and time consuming to ask every teenager, use a sample. A **sample** contains information from only part of a population.

For any sample, you can find a sample proportion. Suppose an event occurs x times in a sample of size n. The **sample proportion** is the ratio $\frac{x}{n}$.

5. In a sample of 350 teenagers, 294 have never made a snow sculpture. Find the sample proportion for those who have never made a snow sculpture. Express your answer as a decimal and as a percent.

6. **Critical Thinking** A sample proportion provides an estimate for the percent of an entire population that favors an event. Is a sample proportion an *experimental* or a *theoretical* probability? Explain.

QUICK REVIEW

When some part of a population is overrepresented or underrepresented in a sample, the sample is *biased*.

As you saw in the Work Together, samples vary in how accurately they reflect the entire population. In a **random sample,** each member of the population is equally likely to be chosen for the sample. A random sample can help avoid bias in gathering data.

7. Suppose the 350 teenagers in Question 5 all live in Florida. What is wrong with this sample? Explain.

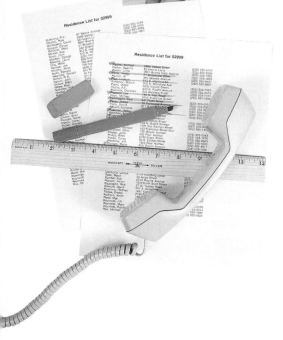

Example 1 **Relating to the Real World**

Community Access News The staff of a news program wants to find out what percent of the population in the program's viewing area favors a school dress code. Identify any bias in each sampling method.

a. Viewers are invited to call and express their preference.
b. A reporter interviews people on the street near the local high school.
c. During the program, 300 people are randomly selected from the viewing area. Then each person is contacted.

a. The people who call in may over- or underrepresent some views. For example, a group favoring the new dress code might encourage its members to call. This is a *self-selected* sample.

b. This is a *convenience* sample, since it is convenient for the reporter to stay in one place. Because the location is near the school, students may be overrepresented in the sample and bias the results.

c. This sampling method contains the least bias. It is a random sample. ■

Exploring Sample Size

What effect does the size of a sample have on its reliability?

With a small sample size, you are likely to get a wide range of sample proportions. For example, in some samples, no one will recognize the word meaning "to pass the summer in a state of slumber." In other samples, everyone will recognize it.

With larger sample sizes, you are less likely to have a sample containing an "all or nothing" result. The graphs on the next page compare results of small versus large sample sizes.

11-5 Working With Samples   **533**

Distributions of Sample Proportions

5 People per Sample

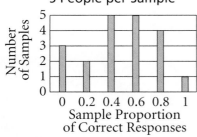

10 People per Sample

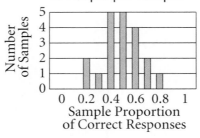

20 People per Sample

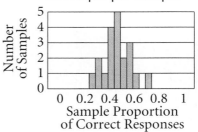

8. a. What is the range for the sample proportions in each graph?

b. *Critical Thinking* Without calculating, which distribution appears to have the lowest standard deviation? Explain.

What? The only way to know a true population proportion is to poll every person in the population. Such a poll is no longer a sample, it is a *census*. The first census of the United States was conducted in 1790.

A sample proportion should be reported with an estimate of error, called the **margin of error.** The margin of error is based on the standard deviation in graphs like those above. The greater the sample size, the lower the margin of error.

Suppose a poll reports that 56% of voters favor candidate *B*, with a margin of error of ±3%.

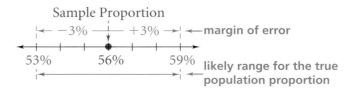

Margin of Error Formula

When a random sample of size n is taken from a large population, the sample proportion has a margin of error of approximately $\pm\frac{1}{\sqrt{n}}$.

Example: For a sample size of 400, the margin of error is about
$$\pm\frac{1}{\sqrt{400}} = \pm\frac{1}{20} = \pm0.05 = \pm5\%.$$

9. Find the margin of error for a sample size of 100.

> ### Example 2   Relating to the Real World
>
> *Public Opinion* A poll of 637 taxpayers finds that 29% say their tax returns are difficult to prepare.
>
> **a.** Find the margin of error for this sample.
> **b.** Use the margin of error to find an interval that is likely to contain the true population proportion.

a. Since $n = 637$, the margin of error is about
$$\pm \frac{1}{\sqrt{637}} \approx \pm \frac{1}{25.239} \approx \pm 0.0396 \approx \pm 4\%.$$

b. The margin of error forms an interval with the sample proportion at its midpoint.

Sample Proportion

$$\vert\!\!\leftarrow -4\% \xrightarrow{} +4\% \rightarrow\!\!\vert$$

25%   29%   33%

The proportion of taxpayers who say their returns are difficult to prepare is likely to be between 25% and 33%.

10. Try This For each poll, find (a) the sample proportion, (b) the margin of error, and (c) an interval likely to contain the true population proportion.
  a. In a poll of 400 students, 216 have never ridden a ferry.
  b. In a poll of 1085 voters, 564 favor Candidate A.

Example 3

What sample size will produce a margin of error of $\pm 3\%$?

Use the margin of error formula, substituting 0.03 for the margin of error.

$$\frac{1}{\sqrt{n}} = 0.03$$
$$\sqrt{n} = \frac{1}{0.03} \quad \longleftarrow \text{Write the reciprocal of each side.}$$
$$\sqrt{n} \approx 33.33$$
$$n \approx 1111$$

A sample size of 1111 will produce a 3% margin of error.

11. Conjecture How will the margin of error be affected if you double the sample size?

Exercises   ON YOUR OWN

Express each sample proportion as a percent.

1. Out of 1150 insurance applicants, 837 have no citations on their driving record.

2. Out of 60 shoppers, 27 prefer generic brands when available.

3. Out of 580 households, 532 own a color television set.

Find the margin of error for the sample proportion, given a sample of size *n*.

4. $n = 200$ **5.** $n = 400$ **6.** $n = 800$ **7.** $n = 1000$ **8.** $n = 1200$

Identify any bias in each sampling method. When appropriate, suggest a method more likely to produce a random sample.

9. *Store Manager* A grocery store wants to find the proportion of shoppers who use reduced-price coupons. The manager interviews every shopper who enters the greeting card aisle.

10. A maintenance crew wants to estimate how many of 3000 air filters in an office building need replacing. The crew randomly examines five filters on each floor of the building.

11. The student government wants to find out how many students have after-school jobs. A pollster interviews randomly selected students as they board buses at the end of the school day.

12. *Open-ended* Suppose you want to find out the proportion of students at your school who plan to attend college. What question would you ask? Describe the sampling method you would use. Identify any bias in your method.

Find the sample size that produces the given margin of error.

13. $\pm 10\%$ 　 14. $\pm 6\%$ 　 15. $\pm 5\%$ 　 16. $\pm 4\%$ 　 17. $\pm 2\%$

An event occurs x times in a sample of size n. Find its sample proportion and margin of error.

18. $x = 50$ $n = 100$ 　 19. $x = 96$ $n = 900$ 　 20. $x = 20$ $n = 64$ 　 21. $x = 100$ $n = 250$ 　 22. $x = 175$ $n = 500$

23. *Standardized Test Prep* Which sample size will produce a margin of error of $\pm 1\%$?
　 A. 100 　 **B.** 500 　 **C.** 1000 　 **D.** 5000 　 **E.** 10,000

24. For each situation, find an interval likely to contain the true population proportion.
　 a. Of 750 teenagers polled, 59% think boys and girls are portrayed as equals on television.
　 b. Of 400 teenagers surveyed, 62% plan to stay in their community.
　 c. Of 1017 people polled, 85% say that music is important.

25. *Writing* Write a news article stating the sample proportion and margin of error for the poll results shown at the right.

26. **a.** *Critical Thinking* Suppose it costs $20 to interview each person for a survey. Find the cost to obtain a $\pm 3\%$ margin of error.
　 b. Find the cost to obtain a $\pm 2\%$ margin of error. Why do you think polls with lower margins of error are rare?

27. **a.** *Election Polls* A poll of 150 voters shows Ms. Tsossie leading her opponent 56% to 44%. Should Ms. Tsossie be concerned? Explain.
　 b. A poll of 600 voters shows Ms. Tsossie leading 55% to 45%. Should she be more or less confident with this result? Explain.

Do you save more than 5% of your income?

yes: 370　　no: 583

For each sample, find (a) the sample proportion, (b) the margin of error, and (c) an interval likely to contain the true population proportion.

28. In a random sample of 408 grocery shoppers, 258 prefer one large trip per week over several smaller ones.

29. Of 500 teenagers surveyed, 460 would like to see adults do more to solve drug problems in their community.

30. In a certain region, 23 out of 325 deer ticks were carriers of Lyme disease.

31. Of 420 full-time workers surveyed, 283 took at least two weeks of vacation last year.

Exercises   MIXED REVIEW

Open-ended **Write the equation of the given conic section with the given characteristics.**

32. a circle with center at $(4, -7)$

33. a parabola with axis of symmetry $x = 2$

34. an ellipse with the major axis 8 units long

35. a hyperbola with an asymptote at $y = -1$

36. A small pizza uses half the cheese and two-thirds the dough of a large pizza. You have enough dough to make 12 small pizzas and enough cheese for 14 small pizzas. If small pizzas sell for $8 and large pizzas sell for $13, how many of each should you make to maximize income?

Getting Ready for Lesson 11-6
Use the binomial theorem to expand each binomial.

37. $(x + 2)^3$
38. $(w + 1)^4$
39. $(m + n)^3$
40. $(t - s)^4$

Exercises   CHECKPOINT

Calculate the mean, median, mode, range, and standard deviation for each set of data.

1. 25 29 34 34 36 45
2. 12 9 10 11 14 10
3. 1 5 2 1 4 1 3 2

4. *Purchasing* In a poll of 683 randomly selected car owners, 235 paid cash for their first car. Find (a) the sample proportion, (b) the margin of error, and (c) an interval likely to contain the true population proportion.

5. *Standardized Test Prep* Which data set has the lowest mean?
   - **A.** 10 11 12 13 15
   - **B.** 8 10 15 17 18
   - **C.** 0 1 19 20 23
   - **D.** 5 14 14 16 19
   - **E.** 2 3 5 9 37

What You'll Learn

- Finding binomial probabilities
- Using binomial distributions

...And Why

To find the probability of suitable launch weather for a hot-air balloon.

What You'll Need

- graphing calculator

PROBLEM SOLVING HINT

You can use a coin, a number cube, or random numbers to conduct a simulation.

11-6 Binomial Distributions

1. With a partner, examine the situations described in the list below. What do the situations printed in green have in common?

> receive a numerical grade
> receive a pass/fail grade
> wear soccer, running, basketball or street shoes
> wear shoes with cleats or no cleats
> guess on a matching test
> guess on a true/false test

2. Suppose you guess each answer on a ten-question true/false test. Are you likely to get 70% or more right?
   a. Design and conduct a simulation for this situation.
   b. Gather the results of the simulations from your class. Make a frequency table of the scores.
   c. Find P(70% or more right).

Finding Binomial Probabilities

Several of the situations described above are binomial experiments. A **binomial experiment** has three important features:

- The situation involves repeated trials.

- Each trial has two possible outcomes (success or failure).

- The probability of success is constant throughout the trials. (The trials are independent.)

3. Suppose that you guess on three questions of a multiple choice test. Each question has five choices, with one correct choice.
   a. Describe a trial for this situation. How many trials are there?
   b. Describe a success. What is the probability of success on any single trial?

4. Which situations in the Work Together are binomial experiments?

   Binomial experiments occur in a wide variety of situations. You can use a tree diagram to analyze binomial probabilities.

Example 1 **Relating to the Real World** ·············

Merchandising As part of a promotion, a store is giving away scratch-off cards. Half the cards will reveal a prize; the other half will not. Suppose you have three cards. Find the probability that two of the three cards will reveal a prize.

Each card represents a trial with a probability of success equal to $\frac{1}{2}$. The tree diagram for three trials shows eight possible outcomes. Each path in the diagram represents a probability of $\frac{1}{2} \cdot \frac{1}{2} \cdot \frac{1}{2} = \frac{1}{8}$.

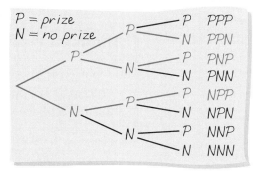

Three of the paths represent two prizes, so $P(\text{two prizes}) = \frac{3}{8}$. ■

5. Use the tree diagram from Example 1 to find each probability.
   a. $P(\text{all three cards will reveal a prize})$
   b. $P(\text{exactly one of the three cards will reveal a prize})$
   c. $P(\text{none of the three cards will reveal a prize})$
   d. Find the sum of the probabilities for three, two, one, and no prizes.

Suppose only 40% of the game cards reveal a prize. Then the probability of success on each trial is reduced to 0.4 and the probability of failure is 0.6. The tree diagram below shows the probabilities along each path.

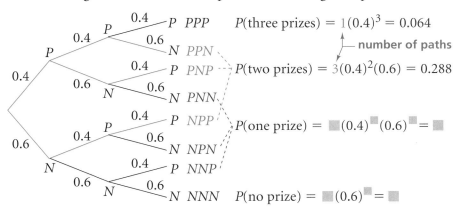

6. **a.** Use the tree diagram to find the probability of receiving one prize.
   b. Find the probability of receiving no prize.
   c. **Verify** your work by adding the probabilities for three, two, one, and no prizes. What answer should you get?

$$_nC_r = \frac{n!}{r!(n-r)!}$$

7. **a.** Evaluate $_3C_0$, $_3C_1$, $_3C_2$, and $_3C_3$.
   b. **Critical Thinking** How are your answers to part (a) related to the number of paths in a tree diagram for three trials?

8. Suppose 30% of the game cards reveal prizes. Which expression represents the probability of getting two prizes with five cards?
   A. $_5C_2(0.3)^3(0.7)^2$ **B.** $_5C_2(0.3)^2(0.7)^3$ **C.** $_5C_3(0.3)^3(0.7)^2$

9. **Verify** your choice in Question 8 by evaluating the expression. You should get 0.3087.

The relationships you have seen are summarized in the following formula.

Binomial Probability

Suppose you have repeated independent trials, each with a probability of success p and a probability of failure q (with $p + q = 1$). Then the probability of x successes in n trials is:
$$_nC_x p^x q^{n-x}.$$

10. Evaluate each expression.
    a. $_4C_3(0.5)^3(0.5)$ **b.** $_3C_3(0.2)^3(0.8)$

Example 2   **Relating to the Real World**

Battery Life A calculator contains four batteries. With normal use, each battery has a 90% chance of lasting for one year. What is the probability that all four batteries will last a year?

Relate   This is a binomial experiment. There are four batteries. Each battery may succeed or fail. The probability of success is 0.9 for each battery.

Define   Let $n = 4$.
                $p = 0.9$
                $q = 0.1$
                $x = 4$

(4 nCr 4)*0.9^4*0.1^0
.6561

Write $_nC_x p^x q^{n-x} = {_4C_4}(0.9)^4(0.1)^0$
                          $= (1)(0.9)^4(1)$
                          $= 0.6561$

The probability of all four batteries lasting one year is about 66%.

11. Find the probability that exactly three of the four batteries will last a year.

12. **Try This** Find the probability of x successes in n trials for the given probability of success p on each trial.
    a. $x = 2$, $n = 5$, $p = 0.25$ **b.** $x = 8$, $n = 10$, $p = 0.7$

Using a Binomial Distribution

QUICK REVIEW

You can use combinations or Pascal's triangle to find the coefficients in a binomial expansion.

To find the full probability distribution for a binomial experiment, expand the binomial $(p + q)^n$. For example, suppose you guess on a five-choice multiple choice test. For four questions, $n = 4$, $p = 0.2$, and $q = 0.8$.

$$
\begin{array}{ccccccccc}
& & 4\text{ correct} & & 3\text{ correct} & & 2\text{ correct} & & 1\text{ correct} & & 0\text{ correct} \\
(p + q)^4 & = & 1p^4 & + & 4p^3q & + & 6p^2q^2 & + & 4pq^3 & + & 1q^4 \\
& = & (0.2)^4 & + & 4(0.2)^3(0.8) & + & 6(0.2)^2(0.8)^2 & + & 4(0.2)(0.8)^3 & + & (0.8)^4 \\
& = & 0.0016 & + & 0.0256 & + & 0.1536 & + & 0.4096 & + & 0.4096
\end{array}
$$

Of course, you can display a binomial distribution as a graph.

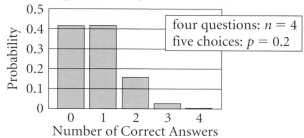

Guessing on a Multiple-Choice Test

four questions: $n = 4$
five choices: $p = 0.2$

13. **a.** Find the probability that you will get at least two correct answers. Use the probability distribution shown above.
    b. What should be the sum of all the probabilities shown in the graph above? **Verify** your answer and explain why it is correct.

Example 3   **Relating to the Real World**

Recreation A balloonist hopes to launch a hot-air balloon on one of the next three mornings. For each morning, there is a 40% chance of suitable weather. What is the probability that there will be at least one morning with suitable weather?

Use the expansion for $(p + q)^n$, with $n = 3$, $p = 0.4$, and $q = 0.6$.

$$
\begin{array}{ccccccc}
& 3\text{ successes} & & 2\text{ successes} & & 1\text{ success} & & 0\text{ successes} \\
(p + q)^3 = & 1p^3 & + & 3p^2q & + & 3pq^2 & + & 1q^3 \\
= & (0.4)^3 & + & 3(0.4)^2(0.6) & + & 3(0.4)(0.6)^2 & + & (0.6)^3 \\
= & 0.064 & + & 0.288 & + & 0.432 & + & 0.216
\end{array}
$$

The probability of at least one morning with suitable weather is $0.064 + 0.288 + 0.432$, or 0.784.

14. The complement of an event consists of all the outcomes in a sample space not in the event. Explain how to solve Example 3 by using the complement of the event *at least one morning has suitable weather*.

For each situation, (a) describe a trial and a success, (b) tell how many trials there are, and (c) identify the probability of success on each trial. Then solve the problem.

1. On a true/false test, you guess the answers to five questions. Find the probability that you answer three questions correctly.

2. A poll shows that 40% of the voters favor a bond issue to finance park improvements. Suppose ten voters are selected at random. Find the probability that exactly four of them will vote in favor of it.

3. A plant production line has a 90% probability of not having a breakdown during an eight-hour shift. Find the probability that three successive shifts will not have a breakdown.

Suppose you guess on a true/false test. Find each probability.

4. P(1 correct in 2 guesses)

5. P(2 correct in 4 guesses)

6. P(3 correct in 6 guesses)

7. P(4 correct in 6 guesses)

8. P(5 correct in 6 guesses)

9. P(6 correct in 6 guesses)

Find the probability of x successes in n trials for the given probability of success p on each trial.

10. $x = 3, n = 8, p = 0.3$

11. $x = 4, n = 8, p = 0.3$

12. $x = 5, n = 8, p = 0.3$

13. $x = 5, n = 10, p = 0.5$

14. $x = 5, n = 10, p = 0.3$

15. $x = 5, n = 10, p = 0.1$

16. **Standardized Test Prep** A survey shows that 60% of the adults in a community floss their teeth every day. Which probability has the greatest value?
   A. P(exactly 5 of the 10 people floss every day)
   B. P(exactly 6 of the 10 people floss every day)
   C. P(at least 7 of the 10 people floss every day)
   D. P(at most 4 of the 10 people floss every day)

17. **Marketing** A fruit company claims that 90% of the pineapples it ships will be ripe within four days of receipt. A case of 12 pineapples is shipped.
   a. Find each probability.
      I. All 12 are ripe within four days.
      II. At least 11 are ripe within four days.
      III. No more than 10 are ripe within four days.
   b. You receive the case, and fewer than 11 are ripe within four days. Should you complain to the company? Explain your answer using probabilities.

18. **Writing** Explain how a *binomial experiment* and a *binomial expansion* are related.

19. Genetics About 13% of the general population is left-handed. At a school with an average class size of 30, each classroom contains four left-handed desks. Does this seem adequate? **Justify** your answer.

20. Sociology A study shows that 50% of the families in a community watch television during dinner. Suppose you randomly select 10 families from this population. Find each probability.
  a. $P(5$ of the 10 families watch television during dinner$)$
  b. $P(6$ of the 10 families watch television during dinner$)$
  c. $P(\text{at least } 5$ of the 10 families watch television during dinner$)$

21. Graphing Calculator Enter the binomial probability formula shown. Set the window and table values. (To get integer values of x, your window may vary.)

```
Y1 ▄ (6 nCr X)*0.5^X*
0.5^(6−X)
Y2 =
Y3 =
Y4 =
Y5 =
Y6 =
Y7 =
```

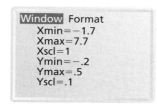

```
Window Format
Xmin=−1.7
Xmax=7.7
Xscl=1
Ymin=−.2
Ymax=.5
Yscl=.1
```

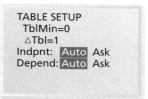

```
TABLE SETUP
TblMin=0
△Tbl=1
Indpnt: Auto Ask
Depend: Auto Ask
```

  a. Examine the graph of $y = {}_6C_x(0.5)^x(0.5)^{6-x}$. Describe any symmetry you see in the graph.
  b. **Verify** the symmetry by displaying values of the function in table form.
  c. Change the graph to $y = {}_6C_x(0.6)^x(0.4)^{6-x}$. Does this graph have any symmetry?

Use the binomial expansion of $(p + q)^n$ to calculate and graph each binomial distribution.

22. $n = 5, p = 0.3$ **23.** $n = 5, p = 0.5$ **24.** $n = 5, p = 0.9$

25. Statistics A multiple-choice test has ten questions. Each question has five choices, with only one correct.
  a. Statisticians consider a *rare event* to have less than a 5% chance of occurring. According to this standard, what grades would be rare on this test if you guess? **Justify** your answer.
  b. Design and conduct a simulation to model this situation. Gather results of simulations from your classmates. Do these results confirm the grades you identified as rare in part (a)? Explain.

26. Quality Control A company claims that 99% of its cereal boxes have at least as much cereal by weight as the amount stated on the box.
  a. At a quality control checkpoint, one out of ten boxes checked at random falls short of its stated weight. What is the probability of this happening due to chance variation in box weights?
  b. Suppose three of ten boxes fail to have the claimed weight. What would you conclude? Why?

27. Open-ended Describe a binomial experiment that can be solved using the expression $_7C_6(0.6)^6(0.4)$.

Exercises   **MIXED REVIEW**

Solve each quadratic equation.

28. $x^2 - 2x + 15 = 0$ **29.** $2x^2 = x^2 + 9x$ **30.** $4x^2 = 5x + 1$ **31.** $x^2 - 6x = 7$

32. $6x^2 + 54 = 0$ **33.** $3x^2 = 12x - 7$ **34.** $x^2 + 8x = -65$ **35.** $-x^2 - 5x = 0$

36. Construction Work The resale value of an earthmover bought for $600,000 is $s = 600{,}000e^{-0.2t}$, where t is time in years. What is the resale value of the earthmover after one year? after three years?

Getting Ready for Lesson 11-7

Find the numbers that are one and two standard deviations above and below the given mean.

37. $\bar{x} = 12$; $\sigma = 2$ **38.** $\bar{x} = 33.1$; $\sigma = 1.2$ **39.** $\bar{x} = 17.5$; $\sigma = 0.9$ **40.** $\bar{x} = 22$; $\sigma = 1.7$

Algebra at Work

Market Researcher

When questions arise about consumer products or services, a market researcher gathers statistical information to help answer the questions. The information a market researcher collects and analyzes helps companies improve their products and make decisions about their customer base. Quantitative research allows a market researcher to analyze data from a large population of potential customers. Marketing strategies for gathering information include the following:

- mail surveys
- telephone surveys
- focus groups
- in-person interviews

Market researchers collect the *raw data* from these studies and analyze the data as a group or subgroup to create summaries of market facts and trends.

Mini Project: Gather data to analyze the student population at your school. Data collected could include grade level, gender, sports, hobbies, teams, or languages. Write a profile of the students in your school. Include summary statistics.

Area Under a Curve

Before Lesson 11-7

You can use a graphing calculator to find the area under a curve. For example, the graph of the function $f(x) = \frac{1}{\sqrt{2\pi}} e^{-\frac{x^2}{2}}$ is a *normal curve* used to describe probability distributions. To find the area between this curve, the x-axis, and the lines $x = -2$ and $x = 2$, use the steps shown below.

Step 1: Input the equation for the standard normal curve. Adjust the window values.

```
Y1 = 1/√(2π)*e^−(X²/2)
Y2 =
Y3 =
Y4 =
Y5 =
Y6 =
Y7 =
```

```
Window Format
Xmin=−4.7
Xmax=4.7
Xscl=1
Ymin=−.2
Ymax=.5
Yscl=.1
```

Step 2: Press **2nd** CALC **7** to access the $\int f(x)\,dx$ feature. Move the cursor until the lower limit is $x = -2$. Press **ENTER**. Move the cursor until the upper limit is $x = 2$. Press **ENTER**.

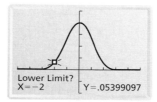

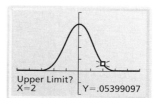

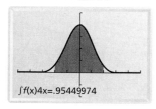

The area under the curve between $x = -2$ and $x = 2$ is about 0.95.

Use the function and graph shown above. Evaluate the area under the curve for each set of limits.

1. $-1 \le x \le 1$
2. $-1.5 \le x \le 1.5$
3. $-0.5 \le x \le 0.5$
4. $-4.7 \le x \le 4.7$

5. $0 \le x < 2$
6. $-2.5 \le x \le 0$
7. $0.1 \le x \le 0.9$
8. $-2.9 \le x \le -1.1$

9. a. Evaluate the area under the curve for $-2 \le x \le 0$ and $0 \le x \le 2$.
   b. Compare your answers to part (a). Make a **conjecture** about the symmetry of the graph of the function.
   c. Test your **conjecture** by evaluating two other pairs of limits.

10. The entire area under the curve is 1 unit. About what *percent* of the area falls between $x = -1$ and $x = 1$?

11. Writing Explain how to use a graphing calculator to find the area of the triangle formed by the x-axis, the y-axis, and the line $y = -x + 4$.

Connections 🌐 Biology . . . and more

11-7 Normal Distributions

What You'll Learn
- Using a normal curve to describe data distribution
- Using a normal distribution to find probabilities

...And Why

To describe variability in the jaws of great white sharks

What You'll Need
- graphing calculator

THINK AND DISCUSS

Using a Curve to Describe Data Distribution

The graph of birth weights shows that there is a pattern to babies' weights. Suppose you weighed 100 babies. Their weights would most likely fall in a pattern similar to the one in the graph below. That's because birth weights are *normally distributed*.

A **normal distribution** shows data that vary randomly from the mean in the pattern of a bell-shaped curve. This curve is called a *normal curve*.

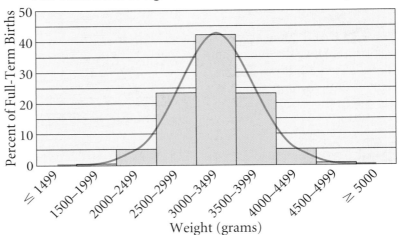

Full-Term Birth Weight Distribution for a Given Population

1. **a.** About what percent of babies in the population weigh between 2500 and 3999 g?
   b. Suppose the survey included data on 250 babies. About how many would you expect to weigh 2500–3999 g?

2. **a.** **Estimate** the percent of babies weighing 3000–3249 g by taking half the percent for 3000–3499 g.
   b. The mean of the data is 3250 g, and the standard deviation is about 500 g. **Estimate** the percent of babies whose birth weights are within one standard deviation of the mean.

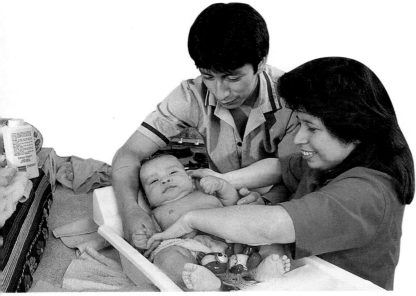

Every normal curve has a symmetrical "bell" shape. When outcomes are normally distributed, you can sketch the graph of the distribution.

Example 1 **Relating to the Real World**

Biology In a population of great white sharks, jaw widths are normally distributed. Survey results reveal a mean jaw width of 15.7 in., with a standard deviation of 2.8 in. Sketch a normal curve showing the jaw widths at one, two, and three standard deviations from the mean.

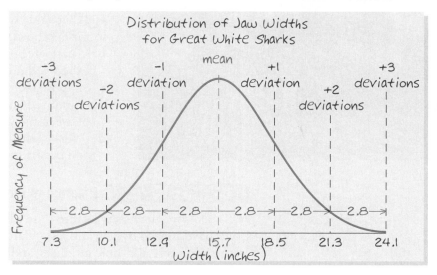

3. **Try This** Suppose the mean in Example 1 is 15.4 in. with a standard deviation of 3.1 in. Sketch a normal curve showing the jaw widths at one, two, and three standard deviations from the mean.

Using Normal Curves

When you show a distribution as a bar graph, the height of the bar for each outcome indicates the probability. For a normal curve, however, the area between the curve and the *x*-axis represents the probability.

The **standard normal curve** is a normal distribution centered on the *y*-axis. The mean of the standard normal curve is 0. The standard deviation is 1.

The Standard Normal Curve

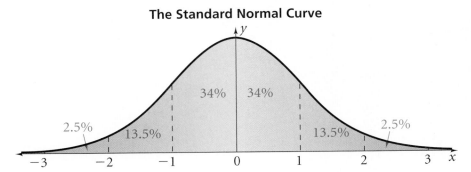

Every normal curve contains the same percent distribution. When a data set is normally distributed, about 68% of the data fall within one standard deviation of the mean. About 95% of the data fall within two standard deviations of the mean.

JEFFY LEARNS ABOUT STANDARD DEVIATION.

4. A survey asks *How much time do you spend at meals in one week?* Suppose the responses are normally distributed. The mean is 13 h, and the standard deviation is 3 h.
   a. What value is one standard deviation below the mean? above the mean?
   b. What percent of the responses would you expect to find between the values 10 and 16?
   c. Suppose there are 100 responses to the survey question. How many would you expect to find between the values 10 and 16?
   d. *Critical Thinking* How many responses would you expect to find between the values 7 and 19?

| Example 2 | Relating to the Real World |

Education In a university lecture class with 174 students, the final exam scores have a mean of 68.5 and a standard deviation of 7.3. The grades on the exams are all whole numbers, and the grade pattern follows a normal curve.

a. Find the number of students who receive grades between one and two standard deviations above the mean.
b. Find the number of students who receive grades of 61 or below.

a. Use the normal curve.

Distribution of Final Exam Scores

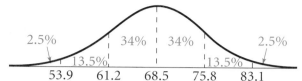

2.5%   34%   34%   2.5%
13.5%   13.5%
53.9   61.2   68.5   75.8   83.1

About 13.5% of the students receive grades between one and two standard deviations above the mean. Calculate the number of students that corresponds to 13.5%.

$$0.135(174) = 23.49$$

About 23 or 24 students receive grades between one and two standard deviations above the mean.

b. Use the normal curve from part (a). A grade of 61 is about one standard deviation below the mean. Calculate the percent of grades at least one standard deviation below the mean.

$$13.5\% + 2.5\% = 16\%$$

Calculate the number of students.

$$0.16(174) = 27.84$$

About 28 students receive grades of 61 or below.

5. How do you know that about 28 students receive grades of 76 or higher?

6. Suppose there are 140 students in the class. About how many would receive grades between 69 and 75?

Exercises   ON YOUR OWN

A set of data with a mean of 62 and a standard deviation of 5.7 is normally distributed. Find each value.

1. +1 standard deviation from the mean

2. −2 standard deviations from the mean

3. +3 standard deviations from the mean

4. −1 standard deviation from the mean

Sketch a normal curve for each distribution. Label the *x*-axis values at one, two, and three standard deviations from the mean.

5. mean = 45; standard deviation = 5

6. mean = 45; standard deviation = 10

7. Writing In a class of 25 students, Ahleem received a grade of 100. The grades were distributed normally, with a mean of 78 and a standard deviation of 5. Do you think his grade is an outlier? Explain.

8. **Biology** The graph shows the result of a survey on men's heights.
   a. About what percent of men aged 25 to 34 are 69–71 inches tall?
   b. Suppose the survey included data on 100 men. About how many would you expect to be 69–71 inches tall?
   c. Suppose the survey included data on 250 men. About how many would you expect to be 69–71 inches tall?
   d. The mean of the data is 70, and the standard deviation is 2.5. About what percent of men are within one standard deviation of the mean in height? What percent are within two standard deviations of the mean?

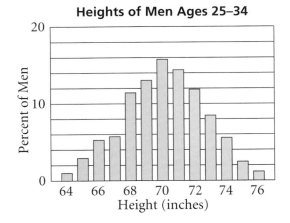

Heights of Men Ages 25–34

A set of data has a normal distribution with a mean of 50 and a standard deviation of 8. Find the percent of data within each interval.

9. between 42 and 58
10. greater than 58
11. less than 58
12. less than 42
13. between 34 and 58
14. between 34 and 42

15. The table shows the number of earthquakes worldwide in 1994.
    a. Draw a histogram to represent the data.
    b. Does the histogram approximate a normal curve? Explain.

Worldwide Earthquakes in 1994

Magnitude	0.1–0.9	1.0–1.9	2.0–2.9	3.0–3.9	4.0–4.9	5.0–5.9	6.0–6.9	7.0–7.9	8.0–8.9
Number	17	779	5369	5000	4544	1542	161	13	2

16. **Education** A college entrance exam has two parts: mathematical and verbal. The scores for each part are normally distributed with a mean of 500 and a standard deviation of 100.
    a. What is the probability that a student's score on one part is between 400 and 500?
    b. What is the probability that a student's score on one part is 700 or above?
    c. Susanna's math score and verbal score were both more than one standard deviation above the mean but less than two standard deviations above the mean. What was the range of her possible *combined* score?

17. A data set is normally distributed with a mean of 76 and a standard deviation of 7.2.
    a. Draw a normal curve to represent the distribution of the data set. Identify and label each standard deviation.
    b. What percent of the data fall between 68.8 and 90.4?

18. Critical Thinking Jake and Elena took the same standardized test, but with different groups of students. They each received a score of 87. In Jake's group, $\bar{x} = 80$ and $\sigma = 6$. In Elena's group, $\bar{x} = 76$ and $\sigma = 4$. Did either student score in the top 10% of his or her group? Explain.

19. Open-ended Use an almanac to find a data set that appears to be distributed normally. Make a histogram of the data. Then sketch a normal curve over your graph.

20. Graphing Calculator Use the area feature and the equation for the standard normal curve, $y = \dfrac{1}{\sqrt{2\pi}} e^{-\frac{x^2}{2}}$. Find the area for each set of limits.
   a. within one standard deviation of the mean
   b. within two standard deviations of the mean
   c. within 1.5 standard deviations of the mean

Chapter Project

Find Out by Interviewing

Conduct a market survey for the transportation product or service you invented. In a series of interviews, identify your potential customers, what they want the product to do, and what changes they would like for the product.

Graph the data. Analyze your results. Should your business market this new product or service? If so, what changes should you make first, if any? Be sure you can defend your marketing decisions on the basis of the data you collected.

Exercises   MIXED REVIEW

Write the equation of each conic section.

21.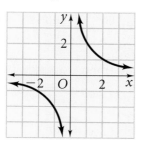

22.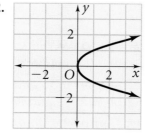

23. a. A cable company charges $30/month plus $3.50 for each movie. Write and graph a function to model the cost of viewing x movies in a month.
   b. A second cable company charges $7 per movie. When is it cheaper to use the second company?

PORTFOLIO

SELF ASSESSMENT

Select one or two items from your work for this chapter. Consider:
• part of your project
• work you found challenging
• corrected work
Explain why you have included each selection.

Finishing the Chapter Project

On the Move

Questions on pages 517, 525, 531, and 551 should help you complete your project. Prepare a presentation that unveils the new product or service you invented and describes the results of your surveys. Present it to your classmates. Then discuss with them the marketing decision you made on the basis of your survey. Do they agree with your decision?

Reflect and Revise

Before giving a presentation, review your analysis of the market survey. Are your graphs clear and correct? If you are using summary statistics, have they been calculated correctly? Are your decisions and conclusions supported by the data? Practice your presentation in front of at least two people before presenting it to the class. Ask for suggestions for improvement.

Follow Up

Market research plays an important role in many business decisions. Find out about some of the survey techniques used by market researchers.

For More Information

Breen, George, and A.B. Blankenship. *Do-It-Yourself Marketing Research*. New York: McGraw Hill Publishing Company, 1989.

Carlson, Daniel. *At Road's End: Transportation and Land Use Choices for Communities*. Washington, D.C.: Island Press, 1995.

Hawkes, Nigel. *New Technology: Transportation on Land and Sea*. New York: Twenty-First Century Books, 1994.

Sudman, Seymour, and Norman M. Bradburn. *Asking Questions: A Practical Guide to Questionnaire Design*. San Francisco: Jossey-Bass Publishers, 1989.

Key Terms

binomial experiment (p. 538)
binomial probability (p. 540)
box-and-whisker plot (p. 521)
conditional probability (p. 512)
frequency table (p. 506)
interquartile range (p. 526)
margin of error (p. 534)
mean (p. 519)
measures of central tendency (p. 519)
measures of variation (p. 526)
median (p. 519)

mode (p. 519)
normal distribution (p. 546)
outlier (p. 522)
probability distribution (p. 507)
quartile (p. 521)
random sample (p. 532)
range (p. 526)
sample (p. 532)
sample proportion (p. 532)
standard deviation (p. 526)
standard normal curve (p. 548)

How am I doing?

- State three ideas from this chapter that you think are important. Explain your choices.
- Expain what you can tell about a data set if you know its measures of central tendency and variation.

SELF ASSESSMENT

Probability Distributions

11-1

A **probability distribution** is a function that tells the probability of each outcome in a sample space. You can show a probability distribution as a table or a graph. You can also organize outcomes in a **frequency table.**

Each function is defined for the sample space {red, green, blue, purple}. Explain whether the function represents a probability distribution or not.

1. $P(\text{red}) = 0.3$, $P(\text{green}) = -0.1$, $P(\text{blue}) = 0.4$, $P(\text{purple}) = 0.4$

2. $P(\text{red}) = 0.5$, $P(\text{green}) = 0.2$, $P(\text{blue}) = 0.1$, $P(\text{purple}) = 0.2$

3. **Open-ended** Write two sample spaces for rolling one number cube.

Conditional Probability

11-2

A **conditional probability** contains a condition that may limit the sample space. You can use the notation $P(B \mid A)$, read *the probability of event B, given event A.* You can find conditional probability from a table, a tree diagram, or by using the conditional probability formula.

For any two events A and B, $P(B \mid A) = \frac{P(A \text{ and } B)}{P(A)}$.

Use the tree diagram at the right to find each probability.

4. $P(\text{have one sibling})$
5. $P(\text{have own room} \mid \text{only child})$
6. $P(\text{have own room})$
7. $P(\text{share a room} \mid \text{have one sibling})$

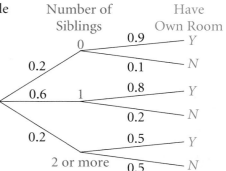

Number of Siblings		Have Own Room
0	0.9	Y
	0.1	N
1	0.8	Y
	0.2	N
2 or more	0.5	Y
	0.5	N

0.2, 0.6, 0.2

Analyzing Data

You can use **measures of central tendency** to analyze data.

The mean, $\bar{x}$, is the sum of the data values divided by the number of data values.	The **median** is the middle value of a data set in numerical order. If the set has an even number of values, the median is the mean of the middle two values.	The **mode** is the most frequently occurring value in a data set. There can be more than one mode or no mode.

An **outlier** is an item of data with a substantially different value from the rest of the items in the data set.

Quartiles divide a sorted data set into four equal parts. The first quartile is the median of the lower half of the set. The second quartile is the median of the whole set. The third quartile is the median of the upper half of the set.

Find the mean, median, and mode of each data set.

8. 12   15   16   12   11   13   12   19   14   10   **9.** 5.2   6.4   4.3   3.7   5.9   6.1   5.0   4.1   3.9

10. Writing What can you tell about two data sets that have the same mean but different medians?

Standard Deviation

You can use **measures of variation** to describe how data are spread out.

The **range** is the difference between the greatest and the least value of a data set.	The **interquartile range** is the difference between the third and first quartiles of a data set.	The **standard deviation** shows how each data value varies from the mean.

To find the standard deviation, (1) find the mean, (2) find the difference between each data value and the mean, (3) square each difference, (4) find the mean of the squares, and (5) take the square root of this mean.

Calculate the mean, range, interquartile range, and standard deviation of each data set.

11. 4   5   6   7   7   8   8   9   10   11   **12.** 99   101   127   356   453   475

13. Standardized Test Prep Which is greatest for the following data?
   3   4   5   5   5   5   6   7   8   9
   A. mean   **B.** standard deviation   **C.** median   **D.** range   **E.** mode

Working with Samples

A **sample** contains part of the information from a population. When an event occurs x times in n trials, the **sample proportion** is the ratio $\frac{x}{n}$.

In a **random sample**, each member of the population is equally likely to be chosen for the sample.

When a random sample of size n is taken from a large population, the sample proportion has a **margin of error** of approximately $\pm\frac{1}{\sqrt{n}}$.

Find the margin of error for each sample proportion. Then find an interval that is likely to contain the true population proportion.

14. 90% of 400 people asked

15. 35% of 175 teens questioned

16. 68% of 900 households surveyed

17. 12% of 269 pets observed

Binomial Distributions   11-6

A **binomial experiment** has (1) repeated trials, (2) trials that each have two possible outcomes, and (3) probability of success that is constant.

In a binomial experiment with probability of success p and of failure q (with $p + q = 1$), the probability of x successes in n trials is $_nC_x p^x q^{n-x}$.

Use the binomial expansion of $(p + q)^n$ to calculate each binomial probability.

18. $x = 1, n = 4, p = 0.25$ **19.** $x = 3, n = 5, p = 0.7$ **20.** $x = 4, n = 6, p = 0.6$

Normal Distributions   11-7

The **standard normal curve** is a bell-shaped curve centered on the y-axis. The mean is 0, and the standard deviation is 1.

When a data set follows the normal curve, about 68% of the data fall within one standard deviation of the mean. About 95% of the data fall within two standard deviations of the mean.

A set of data with $\bar{x} = 45$ and $\sigma = 4.1$ is normally distributed. Find each value.

21. -1 standard deviation from the mean

22. $+2$ standard deviations from the mean

23. -2 standard deviations from the mean

24. $+3$ standard deviations from the mean

25. Sketch a normal distribution with mean 25 and standard deviation 2. Label the x-axis at one and two standard deviations from the mean.

Getting Ready for ....▸ CHAPTER 12

Find the next two numbers. Then write a rule describing each pattern.

26. $1, 3, 5, 7, 9, 11, \ldots$

27. $-2, -4, -6, -8, -10, -12, \ldots$

28. $0.2, 1, 5, 25, 125, 625, \ldots$

29. $50, 45, 40, 35, 30, 25, \ldots$

30. $512, 256, 128, 64, 32, 16, \ldots$

31. $2, 5, 8, 11, 14, 17, \ldots$

You roll two number cubes. Find the probability distribution for each sample space.

1. {both cubes show the same number, the cubes show different numbers}

2. {the sum of the two cubes is a prime number, the sum is a composite number}

3. **Writing** Describe how a situation can have more than one sample space. Include an example.

Use the results of the survey below to find each probability.

How Many Current Music Groups Can You Name?

Age of Respondent	Number of Groups	
	0 – 4	5 or more
< 30	7	18
≥ 30	13	12

4. $P(5$ or more$)$

5. $P(0\text{–}4$ and age $\geq 30)$

6. $P(5$ or more $\mid$ age $< 30)$

7. $P(\text{age} \geq 30 \mid 0\text{–}4)$

Find the mean, median, and standard deviation of each set of data.

8. 8 9 11 12 13 15 16 18 20

9. 36 36 48 65 75 82 92 101

10. 102 126 156 197 204 253 291

11. **Open-ended** Write a data set that has a range of 10, a mean of 86, and a mode of 85.

Find the margin of error for each sample size. Then find an interval that is likely to contain the true population proportion.

12. 15% of 457 teachers

13. 47% of 296 teens

14. 56% of 87 musicians

15. 23% of 100 bakers

A newspaper wants to take a poll about which candidate voters prefer for President. Identify any bias in each sampling method.

16. The newspaper interviews people at a political debate.

17. The newspaper publishes a number for people to call and express their opinion.

18. The newspaper calls people selected randomly from the local telephone book.

Find the probability of x successes in n trials for the given probability of success p on each trial.

19. $x = 4, n = 10, p = 0.2$

20. $x = 3, n = 8, p = 0.6$

21. $x = 5, n = 10, p = 0.7$

22. **Standardized Test Prep** You are guessing the answers to a multiple-choice quiz with 10 questions. Each question has five possible choices. Which probability is greatest?
    A. $P(1$ of 10 correct$)$ B. $P(2$ of 10 correct$)$
    C. $P(4$ of 10 correct$)$ D. $P(5$ of 10 correct$)$
    E. $P(10$ of 10 correct$)$

23. At a particular high school, 30% of the students buy class rings. You randomly select five students from this school. Find $P(\text{exactly 2 buy rings})$ and $P(\text{at least 2 buy rings})$.

A set of data with $\bar{x} = 29$ and $\sigma = 4$ is normally distributed. Find the percent of data within each interval.

24. between 25 and 33

25. between 21 and 25

26. between 29 and 37

27. less than 21

28. A data set is normally distributed with a mean of 37 and a standard deviation of 8.1. Draw a normal curve to represent the distribution of the data set. Identify and label each standard deviation.

For Exercises 1–9, choose the correct letter.

1. Which is a probability distribution?
   A. $P(2) = 0.4$, $P(3) = 0.7$, $P(4) = -0.1$
   B. $P(\text{red}) = \frac{4}{10}$, $P(\text{blue}) = \frac{2}{10}$, $P(\text{gray}) = \frac{4}{10}$
   C. $P(-1) = 0.3$, $P(-5) = 0.8$
   D. $P(4) = 0.1$, $P(7) = 0.6$, $P(11) = 0.4$
   E. $P(W) = 1$, $P(R) = 0.2$, $P(S) = 0.3$

2. Which is greatest for the data set below?
   9 10 10 10 11 12 12 13 15
   A. mean B. median C. range
   D. mode E. standard deviation

3. Find the product: $\frac{x^2(x-2)}{x+4} \cdot \frac{2(2x+8)}{x^3-x^2}$.

   A. $\dfrac{x^4(x-1)(x-2) + 4(x+4)^2}{x^2(x-1)(x+4)}$

   B. $\dfrac{x^4(x-1)(x-2)}{4(x+4)^2}$

   C. $\dfrac{x^4(x-1)(x-2) - 4(x+4)^2}{x^2(x-1)(x+4)}$

   D. $\dfrac{12x^4 + 14x^3 - 32x^2}{x^4 + 2x^3 - 4x^2}$

   E. $\dfrac{4(x-2)}{x-1}$

4. Which events are complementary for one roll of a number cube?
   A. rolling a 5 or rolling a 2
   B. rolling an even or rolling an odd
   C. rolling a prime or rolling a composite
   D. rolling a factor of 6 or rolling a 3
   E. rolling a 4 or rolling a 1

5. Which function has the graph below?

   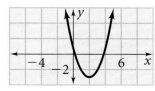

   A. $y = \sin\theta$ B. $y = x^2 - 4x + 1$
   C. $y = |x + 4|$ D. $y = x^3 + x^2 - 4$
   E. $y = x^2 - 4$

6. What are the quartiles of the data set below?
   18 19 20 20 22 23 25 28 32
   A. first: 19.5; second: 22; third: 26.5
   B. first: 20; second: 21; third: 26.5
   C. first: 20; second: 22; third: 25
   D. first: 19; second: 22.5; third: 28
   E. first: 19; second: 22; third: 28

7. Which conic section is the graph of the function $y = (x - 4)^2$?
   A. circle   B. ellipse   C. parabola
   D. hyperbola   E. It is not a conic section.

Compare the boxed quantity in Column A with the boxed quantity in Column B. Choose the best answer.

A. The quantity in Column A is greater.
B. The quantity in Column B is greater.
C. The two quantities are equal.
D. The relationship cannot be determined on the basis of the information supplied.

	Column A	Column B
8.	$P(A) = \frac{1}{2}$, $P(A \text{ and } B) = \frac{1}{3}$	
	$P(A)$	$P(B\mid A)$
9.	for $\bar{x} = 18$ and $\sigma = 2.8$, $\bar{x} + 3\sigma$	for $\bar{x} = 27$ and $\sigma = 1.5$, $\bar{x} - 2\sigma$

Find each answer.

10. **Open-ended** Describe two sample spaces for the outcomes when you roll two number cubes.

11. **Money** You put $600 into an account earning 5% annual interest, compounded continuously. How much will you have after 18 months?

12. **Writing** Explain the difference between a biased and a random sample.

Relating to the Real World

Sequences and series describe patterns such as the number of leaves on a plant or flower, the arc lengths of a pendulum or swing, the number of matches in a chess tournament, or the number of cross-stitches in an embroidery pattern. Sequences and series allow people to make predictions about these patterns.

GET THE PICTURE

When a book such as your mathematics book is being created, artists, designers, and photographers work with writers and editors to make the pages visually attractive by the time it reaches the printer. These professionals often work with patterns including arithmetic and geometric sequences.

As you work through the chapter, you will see how perspective affects length. You will use grids to change the size of drawings. You will also learn how a designer crops a photo and then enlarges or reduces it.

To help you complete the project:

Geometric Series

12-5

Exploring Area Under a Curve

12-6

559

What You'll Learn

- Writing the rule for a given sequence
- Finding the *n*th term in a sequence

...And Why

To predict the height of a ball after a given number of bounces

12-1 **M**athematical Patterns

WORK TOGETHER

What is the least number of phone calls needed for each student in your math class to have a conversation with every other member of the class?

Instead of making the actual phone calls, you can represent phone connections by drawing diagrams like the ones at the left.

Work in a group and record your results in a table similar to the one below.

Number in Group	1	2	3	4	5
Number of Calls	■	■	■	■	■

1. How many calls are necessary for two people to have a conversation?

2. How many calls are necessary for a group of three people to talk to everyone else? a group of four people?

3. Use a diagram to find the number of calls needed for a group of five.

4. **Patterns** Which of the following formulas can you use to find the pattern in the table?
   I. $2n - 3$ **II.** $n(n - 1) - 5$ **III.** $\dfrac{n(n - 1)}{2}$

5. How many calls would be needed for the group of students in the pictures?

6. How many calls would be needed for your class?

Using Recursive Formulas

In the Work Together, you discovered a pattern by recording data about numbers of phone calls. Sometimes steps in a process form a pattern.

Example 1

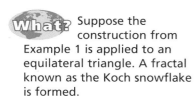

Suppose the construction from Example 1 is applied to an equilateral triangle. A fractal known as the Koch snowflake is formed.

Fractal Geometry To create the Koch snowflake, replace each _____ with _⋀_ . Draw the first four figures of the pattern described.

7. Count the number of segments in each figure above. What pattern do you notice?

A **sequence** is an ordered list of numbers. Each number in a sequence is called a **term.**

8. **a.** Write the first four terms in the sequence in Question 7.
   b. Predict the next term of the sequence. Explain.

Sometimes you can find the next term in a sequence by using a pattern from the terms that come before it.

Example 2   **Relating to the Real World**

Physics A handball is dropped from a height of 10 ft. After the ball hits the floor, it rebounds to 85% of its previous height. How high will the ball rebound after its fourth bounce?

← Original height of ball: 10 ft

← After 1st bounce: 85% of 10 = 0.85(10) = 8.5 ft

← After 2nd bounce: 0.85(8.5) = 7.225 ft

← After 3rd bounce: 0.85(7.225) ≈ 6.141 ft

← After 4th bounce: 0.85(6.141) ≈ 5.220 ft

The ball will rebound to about 5.2 ft after the fourth bounce.

You can use a variable such as *a* with positive integer subscripts to represent the terms in a sequence.

$$a_n \leftarrow \text{subscript}$$

2	4	6	8	10	...	nth term	$n+1$ term	...
↓	↓	↓	↓	↓		↓	↓	
a_1	a_2	a_3	a_4	a_5 ...		a_n	a_{n+1}	...

9. **a.** Describe the pattern that allows you to find the next term in the sequence above.
   b. Find the sixth and seventh terms in the sequence.
   c. Find the value of term a_9 in the sequence above.

10. What subscript would you use for the term before the *n*th term?

A **recursive formula** defines the terms in a sequence by relating each term to the ones before it. If you know the first term in a sequence, a_1, and the recursive formula, then you can find other terms. The pattern in Example 2 was a recursive relationship because the height of the ball after each bounce was 85% of its previous height. The recursive formula that describes this is $a_n = 0.85a_{n-1}$, where $a_1 = 10$.

Using Explicit Formulas

Sometimes you can find the value of a term of a sequence without knowing its preceding term. Instead, you can calculate the term by using the number of the term.

QUICK REVIEW

The *perimeter p* of a square equals four times the length of a side. The *area A* of a square equals the length of a side squared.

$$p = 4s$$
$$A = s^2$$

Example 3

Geometry The spreadsheet below shows the perimeters of squares having sides measuring from one to six units. The numbers in each row form a sequence. For each sequence, find the next term (a_7) and the twenty-fifth term (a_{25}).

	A	B	C	D	E	F	G	H
1		a1	a2	a3	a4	a5	a6	...
2	Length of a Side	1	2	3	4	5	6	...
3	Perimeter	4	8	12	16	20	24	...

In the sequence in row 2, each term is the same as its subscript. Therefore, $a_7 = 7$ and $a_{25} = 25$.

In the sequence in row 3, each term is 4 times its subscript. Therefore, $a_7 = 4(7) = 28$ and $a_{25} = 4(25) = 100$.

11. **Try This** Write the first six terms in the sequence showing the areas of the squares in Example 3. Then find the twentieth term.

Many explicit formulas are proved by mathematical induction (page 630.)

A formula that expresses the nth term in a sequence in terms of n is called an **explicit formula.** The explicit formula for the sequence in row 2 of the spreadsheet is $a_n = n$. In row 3 it is $a_n = 4n$.

12. Write an explicit formula for the sequence in Question 11.

13. Given the recursive formula $a_n = a_{n-1} + 3$, can you find the fourth term in the sequence? Explain.

Exercises ON YOUR OWN

Describe the pattern formed. Find the next three terms.

1. 80, 77, 74, 71, 68, . . .

2. 4, 8, 16, 32, 64, . . .

3. 0, 3, 7, 12, 18, . . .

4. 1, 4, 7, 10, 13, . . .

5. $\frac{1}{2}, \frac{1}{4}, \frac{1}{8}, \frac{1}{16}, \frac{1}{32}, \ldots$

6. 100, 10, 1, 0.1, 0.01

7. 4, −8, 16, −32, 64, . . .

8. 1, 2, 6, 24, 120, . . .

9. $0, 1, 0, \frac{1}{3}, 0, \frac{1}{5}, \ldots$

10. *Critical Thinking* Can the subscript of a term in a sequence be a fraction? Explain.

11. *Geometry* Suppose you are stacking boxes in levels that form squares. The numbers of boxes in each level form a sequence. The figure at the right shows the top four levels of a stack of boxes as viewed from above. How many boxes of equal size would be needed to add three more levels?

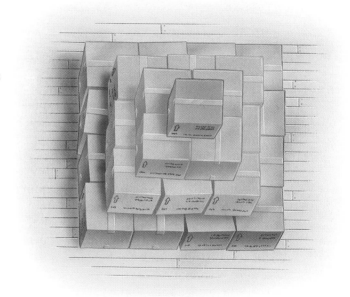

Fractal Geometry **Draw the first four figures of the sequence described.**

12.  ⎯⎯⎯ is replaced by ⎯�⎯ .

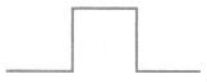

13. 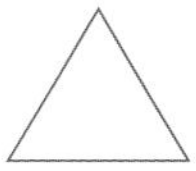 △ is replaced by △△ .

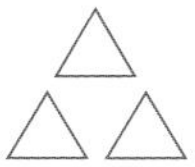

Write a recursive formula for each sequence. Then find the next term.

14. 1, 3, 9, 27, 81, . . .

15. 2, 4, 8, 16, 32, . . .

16. 56, 58, 60, 62, 64, . . .

17. −2, −1, 0, 1, 2, . . .

18. 43, 41, 39, 37, 35, . . .

19. $40, 20, 10, 5, \frac{5}{2}, \ldots$

20. 6, 1, −4, −9, . . .

21. $144, 36, 9, \frac{9}{4}, \ldots$

22. $\frac{1}{2}, \frac{1}{4}, \frac{1}{8}, \frac{1}{16}, \frac{1}{32}, \ldots$

Write an explicit formula for each sequence. Then find a_{12}.

23. 3, 6, 9, 12, 15, . . .

24. 4, 7, 10, 13, 16, . . .

25. 4, 8, 12, 16, 20, . . .

26. 3, 7, 11, 15, 19, . . .

27. $\frac{1}{2}, \frac{1}{3}, \frac{1}{4}, \frac{1}{5}, \frac{1}{6}, \ldots$

28. 4, 5, 6, 7, 8, . . .

29. 9, 14, 19, 24, 29, . . .

30. $-2\frac{1}{2}, -2, -1\frac{1}{2}, -1, -\frac{1}{2}, \ldots$

31. 2, 5, 10, 17, 26, . . .

Decide whether each formula is explicit or recursive. Then find the first five terms of each sequence.

32. $a_n = 5n$

33. $a_1 = 3; a_n = 2a_{n-1} + 3$

34. $a_n = \frac{1}{2}(n)(n-1)$

35. $a_n = 2n^2 + 1$

36. $a_1 = \frac{1}{2}; a_n = a_{n-1} + \frac{1}{n}$

37. $a_1 = 4; a_n = a_{n-1} - 4$

38. $a_n = -4n^2 - 2$

39. $(n-5)(n+5) = a_n$

40. $a_1 = -2; a_n = -3a_{n-1}$

41. **Geometry** The diagram at the right represents the first three *triangular numbers* 1, 3, and 6.
   a. Find the fifth and sixth triangular numbers.
   b. Write a recursive formula for the nth triangular number.
   c. Is the explicit formula $a_n = \frac{1}{2}(n^2 + n)$ a correct formula for this sequence? How do you know?

$n = 1 \qquad n = 2 \qquad n = 3$

Find the next two terms in each sequence. Write a formula for the nth term. Identify each formula as explicit or recursive.

42. 5, 8, 11, 14, 17, . . .

43. 3, 6, 12, 24, 48, . . .

44. 1, 3, 5, 7, 9, . . .

45. 4, 6, 8, 10, 12, . . .

46. 1, 8, 27, 64, 125, . . .

47. 3, 6, 11, 18, 27, . . .

48. −1, 1, −1, 1, −1, 1, . . .

49. 4, 16, 64, 256, 1024, . . .

50. 36, 49, 64, 81, 100, 121, . . .

51. **Finance** Suppose you start a savings account at Mun E. Bank.
   a. Write both a recursive formula and an explicit formula for how much money you would have in the bank at the end of any week.
   b. How much money would you have in the bank after four weeks?
   c. Assume the bank pays you interest every four weeks. To calculate your interest, multiply the amount of money in the bank by 0.005. Then add that much to your account on the last day of the four-week period. Write a recursive formula for how much money you have after each interest payment.
   d. What is the bank's annual interest rate?

52. **Patterns** You are building a tower of cards with levels as displayed below. Complete the table, assuming the pattern continues.

Levels	1	2	3	4	5
Cards Needed	2	7	▇	▇	▇

53. Construction Complete the table showing the number of beige and blue tiles needed to tile part of your rectangular kitchen floor. (All blue tiles should be collinear in the direction of the arrows.)

Number of Blue Tiles	1	2	3	4	5
Number of Beige Tiles	6	10	■	■	■

54. Suppose the cartoon shown included one sheep to the left and another sheep to the right of the three shown. What "names" would you give these sheep?

55. Writing Explain the difference between a recursive formula and an explicit formula.

56. a. Open-ended Write four terms of a sequence of numbers that you can describe both recursively and explicitly.
   b. Write a recursive formula and an explicit formula for your sequence.
   c. Find the 20th term of the sequence by evaluating one of your formulas. Use the other formula to check your work.

WHEN MATHEMATICIANS CAN'T SLEEP

Exercises   **MIXED REVIEW**

Simplify each expression.

57. $16 + 4 \cdot 2 \div 10$

58. $25 - 10^2 + 150 \div 3$

59. $1.25 \div 0.5 + 7.5 - 115$

60. $9 - (8 - 3)^2 \div 2$

61. $5 + \left(\frac{3}{4}\right)^2 \cdot \frac{8}{15} - 2$

62. $12 + ((-6)^2 - 4^2)^2 - 7$

63. $\frac{(4 - 12)}{3} + 6 \cdot 2$

64. $(0.5)^2 (0.4) \div 0.1$

65. $\frac{(-2)^3}{(-1)^3} + 9 \div 4$

66. Economics In one month, the number of help-wanted advertisements rose from 126 to 131. Find the percent increase.

Getting Ready for Lesson 12-2

Describe the pattern in each sequence. Use at least one of the words *add*, *subtract*, or *difference*.

67. $10, 8, 6, 4, 2, 0, \ldots$

68. $100, 117, 134, 151, 168, \ldots$

69. $\frac{5}{7}, \frac{8}{7}, \frac{11}{7}, 2, \ldots$

70. $-\frac{1}{4}, -\frac{1}{2}, -\frac{3}{4}, -1, -\frac{5}{4}, -\frac{3}{2}, \ldots$

FOR YOUR JOURNAL

Give an example each of a recursive formula and an explicit formula. What clues in a problem help you decide which type to use?

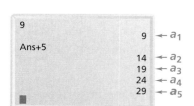
What You'll Learn

- Identifying and generating arithmetic sequences
- Finding the *n*th term of an arithmetic sequence
- Finding an arithmetic mean

...And Why

To make predictions about real-world patterns like fundraising

What You'll Need

- graphing calculator

12-2 **A**rithmetic Sequences

WORK TOGETHER

Work with a partner. Use the sequence at the right.

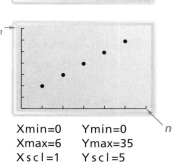

1. **a.** Find the sixth term in the sequence, a_6.
   b. Write a formula for a_6 in terms of a_5.
   c. **Generalize** your formula from part (b) by writing a formula for a_n.

2. **a.** **Open-ended** Generate two sequences by adding or subtracting a constant as shown. Write each sequence.
   b. Write a recursive formula for a_n for each sequence.
   c. What do these formulas and the formula for a_n from Question 1 have in common?
   d. **Graphing Calculator** Graph each sequence as shown.
   e. Compare all three graphs. Write a description to **generalize** the shape of graphs of sequences that add or subtract a constant.

Xmin=0   Ymin=0
Xmax=6   Ymax=35
Xscl=1   Yscl=5

 GRAPHING CALCULATOR HINT

Use the LIST and STAT features to graph each sequence.

THINK AND DISCUSS

In an **arithmetic sequence,** the difference between consecutive terms is constant. This difference is called the **common difference.**

Example 1

Is the given sequence arithmetic?

a. golf ball pattern at the left   **b.** 2, 4, 8, 16, . . .

a.
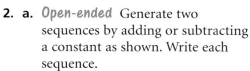
$$6, \underset{12 - 6 = 6}{\overset{+6}{\longrightarrow}} 12, \underset{18 - 12 = 6}{\overset{+6}{\longrightarrow}} 18, \underset{24 - 18 = 6}{\overset{+6}{\longrightarrow}} 24, \ldots$$

There is a common difference of $+6$. This is an arithmetic sequence.

b.

$$2, \underset{4 - 2 = 2}{\overset{+2}{\longrightarrow}} 4, \underset{8 - 4 = 4}{\overset{+4}{\longrightarrow}} 8, \underset{16 - 8 = 8}{\overset{+8}{\longrightarrow}} 16, \ldots$$

There is no common difference. This is *not* an arithmetic sequence.

When the terms of a sequence decrease in value, the common difference of the sequence is a negative number.

3. **Try This** Is the given sequence arithmetic? If so, identify the common difference.
   a. $2, 5, 7, 12, \ldots$
   b. $48, 45, 42, 39, \ldots$

4. Are the sequences in the Work Together arithmetic? If so, identify the common differences.

5. a. Write the first fifteen terms of the arithmetic sequence in Example 1.
   b. How did you find the fifteenth term in the sequence, a_{15}?

Arithmetic Sequence Formulas

Recursive Formula	**Explicit Formula**
$a_1 = $ a given value; $a_n = a_{n-1} + d$	$a_n = a_1 + (n-1)d$

In these formulas, a_n is the nth term, a_1 is the first term, n is the number of the term, and d is the common difference.

You can use an explicit formula to find the value of the nth term when the previous term is unknown.

| **Example 2** | **Relating to the Real World** |

Fund-raising You volunteer to participate in a bike-a-thon for a local charity. The charity starts with $1100 from business donations. Suppose each participant must raise $35 in pledges. What is the amount of money raised if there are 75 participants?

You must find the 76th term of the sequence $1100, 1135, 1170, \ldots$.

$$a_n = a_1 + (n-1)d \quad \longleftarrow \text{Use the explicit formula.}$$
$$a_{76} = 1100 + (76-1)(35) \quad \longleftarrow \text{Substitute } a_1 = 1100, n = 76,$$
$$= 1100 + (75)(35) \qquad\qquad \text{and } d = 35.$$
$$= 1100 + 2625$$
$$= 3725$$

From 75 participants, the bike-a-thon will raise at least $3725.

6. **Critical Thinking** In Example 2, why did you look for the value of the 76th term, not the 75th term?

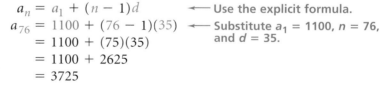

7. **Try This** Find the 25th term in each sequence.
   a. $5, 11, 17, 23, 29, \ldots$ **b.** $20, 17, 14, 11, 8, \ldots$

Graphs of arithmetic sequences are linear.

You can find the **arithmetic mean** of any two numbers by finding the average of the two numbers. You can use the arithmetic mean to find a missing term of an arithmetic sequence.

$$\text{arithmetic mean} = \frac{\text{sum of two numbers}}{2}$$

Two terms of an arithmetic sequence and their arithmetic mean lie on the same line.

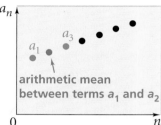

arithmetic mean between terms a_1 and a_2

> ### Example 3
>
> Find the missing term of the arithmetic sequence $84, \blacksquare, 110$.
> $$\text{arithmetic mean} = \frac{84 + 110}{2}$$
> $$= \frac{194}{2}$$
> $$= 97$$
>
> The missing term is 97.

8. **Try This** Find the missing term of the arithmetic sequence $24, \blacksquare, 57$.

9. Find the arithmetic mean of a_1 and a_2.

Exercises   ON YOUR OWN

Write the next three terms in each arithmetic sequence. Then write a recursive formula for a_n.

1. $3, 6, 9, 12, \ldots$
2. $5, 10, 15, 20, \ldots$
3. $-12, -7, -2, 3, \ldots$
4. $0.00234, 0.00261, 0.00288, \ldots$
5. $-34.56, -34.794, -35.028, \ldots$
6. $\frac{1}{2}, -\frac{1}{4}, -1, \ldots$
7. $5, 1\frac{1}{2}, -2, \ldots$
8. $\frac{1}{2}, \frac{5}{6}, 1\frac{1}{6}, \ldots$
9. $77, 63, 49, \ldots$

10. **a.** Calculator Generate an arithmetic sequence starting at 42 with a common difference of -7. How could you use a calculator to find the sixth term? the eighth term? the twentieth term?
    b. Critical Thinking Explain how your answer to part (a) relates to the explicit formula $a_n = a_1 + (n - 1)d$.

11. Writing List some advantages and some disadvantages of a recursive formula and an explicit formula.

Find the arithmetic mean of the given terms.

12. $a_{n-1} = 8, a_{n+1} = 12$

13. $a_{n-1} = 7, a_{n+1} = 1$

14. $a_{n-1} = 21, a_{n+1} = 5$

15. $a_{n-1} = 4, a_{n+1} = -3$

16. $a_{n-1} = -18, a_{n+1} = -21$

17. $a_{n-1} = 9, a_{n+1} = -11$

18. $a_{n-1} = 100, a_{n+1} = 140$

19. $a_{n-1} = \frac{3}{5}, a_{n+1} = 1$

20. $a_{n-1} = 0.3, a_{n+1} = 1.9$

Is the given sequence arithmetic? If so, identify the common difference.

21. 1, 4, 9, 16, . . .

22. 10, 20, 30, 40, . . .

23. 1, 1, 2, 3, 5, 8, . . .

24. 3, 7, 11, 15, . . .

25. 0, 1, 3, 6, 10, . . .

26. $-21, -18, -15, -12, . . .$

27. 100, 10, 1, 0.1, . . .

28. 97, 86, 75, 64, . . .

29. $\frac{1}{2}, \frac{1}{4}, \frac{1}{8}, \frac{1}{16}, . . .$

30. Gardening Each year you plant two more types of vegetables in your garden. You plant tomatoes, lettuce, carrots, and cucumbers the first year. How many types of vegetables do you have by the seventh year?

31. Savings In February you start a holiday savings account with a deposit of $20. You decide to increase each monthly deposit by five dollars until the end of the year.
   a. Find the amount in the account after each deposit.
   b. Write a recursive formula for the amounts.
   c. How much money will you have saved by the end of the year?

Find the 32nd term of each sequence.

32. 34, 37, 40, 43, . . .

33. $-9, -8.7, -8.4, -8.1, . . .$

34. 0.0023, 0.0025, 0.0027, . . .

35. $3, 1, -1, -3, . . .$

36. 0.1, 0.5, 0.9, 1.3, . . .

37. 23, 30, 37, 44, . . .

38. 101, 105, 109, 113, . . .

39. 213, 201, 189, 177, . . .

40. Standardized Test Prep What is the 30th term of the sequence 7, 16, 25, 34, . . . ?
   A. 261   **B.** 277   **C.** 270
   D. 268   **E.** none of these

Find the missing term(s) of each arithmetic sequence. (*Hint:* The arithmetic mean of the first and fifth terms is the third term.)

41. 5, ▪, 21, . . .

42. 17, ▪, 85, . . .

43. 25, ▪, -10, . . .

44. $\frac{13}{2}$, ▪, $\frac{51}{2}$, . . .

45. 2, ▪, ▪, ▪, -22, . . .

46. -10, ▪, ▪, ▪, -11.6, . . .

47. 1, ▪, ▪, ▪, -35, . . .

48. $\frac{13}{5}$, ▪, ▪, ▪, $\frac{37}{5}$, . . .

49. 101, ▪, -115, . . .

50. -17, ▪, ▪, ▪, 17, . . .

51. 203, ▪, 1117, . . .

52. 660, ▪, ▪, ▪, 744, . . .

Write the explicit and recursive formulas for each sequence.

53. $2, 4, 6, \ldots$

54. $1\frac{1}{3}, 1\frac{2}{3}, 2, \ldots$

55. $-20, -8, 4, \ldots$

56. $\frac{1}{8}, \frac{1}{4}, \frac{3}{8}, \ldots$

57. $11.7, 11.2, 10.7, 10.2, \ldots$

58. $5, 12, 19, 26, \ldots$

59. $15, 3, -9, \ldots$

60. $-3.5, -2, -0.5, \ldots$

61. $0, -3, -6, -9, \ldots$

62. Theater Each time a theater group performs, the director hopes that five more audience members will attend. Seventeen people attended the first performance.
 a. Write a formula you can use to find the nth term of this sequence. Is it recursive or explicit?
 b. How many audience members does the director hope will attend the ninth performance? the fortieth performance?

63. Savings Priya is saving money for post-graduate training. During her freshman year of high school she saved $600. Each year through high school she plans to save $80 more than the previous year. How much money does Priya plan to save her senior year?

Chapter Project **Find Out by Researching**

Research the use of one- and two-point perspective and a vanishing point in art as illustrated by the drawing at the right. Measure the lengths of the objects shown. What do you notice? Create a simple drawing. Then draw three or more similar objects whose lengths could be represented as an arithmetic sequence. Write the arithmetic sequence and a recursive or explicit formula.

Exercises   **MIXED REVIEW**

Find the foci of each ellipse.

64. $\frac{x^2}{4} + \frac{y^2}{9} = 1$

65. $\frac{(x-1)^2}{121} + \frac{y^2}{100} = 1$

66. $\frac{(x+1)^2}{64} + \frac{(y-3)^2}{25} = 1$

67. Geometry The volume V of a sphere with radius r is given by the formula $V = \frac{4}{3}\pi r^3$. Write a formula to find the radius of a sphere given its volume.

Getting Ready for Lesson 12-3

Find the next term in each sequence.

68. $1, 2, 4, 8, \ldots$

69. $336, 168, 84, 42, \ldots$

70. $0.1, 1, 10, 100, \ldots$

71. $900, 300, 100, \ldots$

SELF ASSESSMENT

FOR YOUR JOURNAL

Describe a real-world situation you could model with an arithmetic sequence. Write recursive and explicit formulas for the sequence.

The Fibonacci Sequence

After Lesson 12-2

One famous mathematical sequence is the Fibonacci sequence. You can find each term of the sequence by adding, but the sequence is not arithmetic.

Example

The recursive formula for the Fibonacci sequence is $F_n = F_{n-2} + F_{n-1}$, $F_1 = 1$, $F_2 = 1$. Use the formula to generate the first five terms of the sequence.

$F_1 = 1$
$F_2 = 1$
$F_3 = 1 + 1 = 2$
$F_4 = 1 + 2 = 3$
$F_5 = 2 + 3 = 5$

The first five terms of the Fibonacci sequence are 1, 1, 2, 3, 5.

1. **Nature** The numbers of the Fibonacci sequence are often found in other areas, especially nature. Which term of the Fibonacci sequence does each picture represent?

A.

B.

C.

D.

2. **Research** Leonardo da Pisa (c. 1175–1250) is the person credited with first generating the Fibonacci sequence. What other mathematical discoveries did he make?

3. **Critical Thinking** Study Pascal's Triangle (at the right). How is it similar to the Fibonacci sequence?

```
         1
        1 1
       1 2 1
      1 3 3 1
     1 4 6 4 1
    1 5 10 10 5 1
   1 ■ ■ ■ ■ ■ ■
```

4. **a.** Generate the first ten terms of the Fibonacci sequence.
   b. Calculator Find the sum of the first ten terms of the Fibonacci sequence. Divide the sum by 11. What do you notice?
   c. Open-ended Choose two numbers other than 1 and 1. Generate a Fibonacci-like sequence from them. Write the first ten terms of your sequence, find the sum, and divide the sum by 11. What do you notice?
   d. Writing Make a **conjecture** about the sum of the first ten terms of any Fibonacci-like sequence.

What You'll Learn

- Identifying and generating geometric sequences
- Finding the nth term of a geometric sequence
- Finding a geometric mean

...And Why

To make predictions involving design and physics

What You'll Need

- colored paper
- scissors
- ruler
- protractor

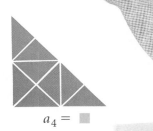

WORK TOGETHER

Work with a partner.

- Make a large right isosceles triangle out of colored paper.

- Cut the triangle into two equal isosceles triangles.

- Layer the triangles on top of each other and repeat the previous step.

Copy and complete the sequence. Each term represents the number of triangles formed.

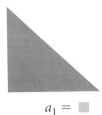  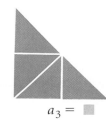

$a_1 = \blacksquare$ $a_2 = \blacksquare$ $a_3 = \blacksquare$ $a_4 = \blacksquare$

1. Is the sequence of triangles arithmetic? Why or why not?

2. a. Find the sixth term a_6 in the sequence.
   b. Write a formula for a_6 in terms of a_5.
   c. **Generalize** your formula from part (b) by writing a formula for a_n in terms of a_{n-1}.

3. a. **Open-ended** Generate two sequences by multiplying by a constant factor. Write each sequence.
   b. Write a recursive formula for each sequence. What do these formulas and the formula for a_n in Question 2 have in common?
   c. **Graphing Calculator** Graph all three sequences. Then sketch each graph. (*Hint:* Place n along the x-axis and a_n along the y-axis.)
   d. Compare all three graphs. Write a description to **generalize** the shape of graphs of sequences with this same pattern.

GRAPHING CALCULATOR HINT

Use the LIST and STAT features to graph each sequence.

THINK AND DISCUSS

In a **geometric sequence**, the ratio between consecutive terms is constant. This ratio is called the **common ratio.** Unlike an arithmetic sequence, the difference between consecutive terms varies.

Example 1

Is the given sequence geometric? If so, identify the common ratio.

a. 5, 15, 45, 135, . . .　　　　　　　　　**b.** 15, 30, 45, 60, . . .

a.

$$5, \xrightarrow[15 \div 5 = 3]{\times 3} 15, \xrightarrow[45 \div 15 = 3]{\times 3} 45, \xrightarrow[135 \div 45 = 3]{\times 3} 135, \ldots$$

There is a common ratio of 3. This is a geometric sequence.

b.

$$15, \xrightarrow[30 \div 15 = 2]{\times 2} 30, \xrightarrow[45 \div 30 = 1\frac{1}{2}]{\times 1\frac{1}{2}} 45, \xrightarrow[60 \div 45 = 1\frac{1}{3}]{\times 1\frac{1}{3}} 60, \ldots$$

There is no common ratio. This is *not* a geometric sequence.

PROBLEM SOLVING

Look Back Is the sequence in part (b) of Example 1 an arithmetic sequence? If so, identify the common difference.

4. Try This Is the given sequence *arithmetic*, *geometric*, or *neither*? Find the next two terms.

a. 6, −24, 96, −384, . . .　　　　　　**b.** 8, 20, 32, 44, . . .

5. a. Write the first ten terms of the geometric sequence in Example 1.
b. How did you find the tenth term in the sequence, a_{10}?

Geometric Sequence Formulas

Recursive Formula　　　　　　　　**Explicit Formula**

$a_1 =$ a given value; $a_n = a_{n-1} \cdot r$　　　$a_n = a_1 \cdot r^{n-1}$

In these formulas, a_n is the nth term, a_1 is the first term, n is the number of the term, and r is the common ratio.

As with arithmetic sequences, you can use an explicit formula to find the value of the nth term when the previous term is unknown.

Example 2　Relating to the Real World

Design Suppose you want a reduced copy of a team logo. The actual length of the logo is 10 in. The maximum reduction the copier can make is 64%. Find the length of the logo after six reductions at 64%.

You need to find the 7th term of the geometric sequence 10, 6.4, . . .

$a_n = a_1 \cdot r^{n-1}$　　←— Use the explicit formula.

$a_7 = 10 \cdot 0.64^{7-1}$　　←— Substitute $a_1 = 10$, $n = 7$, and $r = 0.64$.

　　$= 10 \cdot 0.64^6$

　　≈ 0.687194767　　←— Use a calculator.

After six reductions at 64%, the image has a length of about 0.7 in.

6. Try This Find the 19th term in each sequence.

    a. 11, 33, 99, 297, . . .   **b.** 20, 17, 14, 11, 8, . . .

Arithmetic and geometric graphs have different shapes.

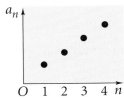

Arithmetic graphs are linear.

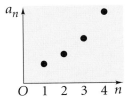

Geometric graphs are exponential.

You can find the **geometric mean** of any two positive numbers by taking the positive square root of the product of the two numbers.

$$\text{geometric mean} = \sqrt{\text{product of the two numbers}}$$

You can use the geometric mean to find a missing term of a geometric sequence.

Example 3   **Relating to the Real World**

Physics Because of air resistance, when a child swings without being pushed, the length of the arc decreases geometrically. Find the missing arc length.

8 ft

■ ft

$6\frac{1}{8}$ ft

Find the geometric mean of the two arc lengths.

$$\text{geometric mean} = \sqrt{8 \cdot 6\frac{1}{8}}$$
$$= \sqrt{49}$$
$$= 7$$

On the second swing, the length of the arc is 7 ft.

7. Try This Find the missing term of each geometric sequence.

    a. 20, ■, 80   **b.** 3, ■, 18.75   **c.** 28, ■, 5103

Is the given sequence geometric? If so, identify the common ratio.

1. 1, 2, 4, 8, . . .

2. 1, 2, 3, 4, . . .

3. 1, −2, 4, −8, . . .

4. −1, 1, −1, 1, . . .

5. 10, 4, 1.6, 0.64, . . .

6. 1, $\frac{1}{2}$, $\frac{1}{3}$, $\frac{1}{4}$, . . .

7. 18, −6, 2, −$\frac{2}{3}$, . . .

8. 10, 15, 22.5, 33.75, . . .

9. Write the formula you would use to find the nth term of a geometric sequence. Define each variable.

10. Sports Each of Brian's putts misses the hole and continues past it for half the distance, as shown.
   a. Write a sequence that represents his distance from the hole before each of his first six putts.
   b. Is this sequence geometric? Explain your reasoning.
   c. Write a recursive formula for the sequence.

11. Is the sequence of triangles from the Work Together a geometric sequence? If so, identify the common ratio.

Identify the sequence as *arithmetic*, *geometric*, or *neither*. Find the next two terms.

12. 45, 90, 180, 360, . . .

13. 25, 50, 75, 100, . . .

14. 30, 35, 40, 45, . . .

15. −5, 10, −20, 40, . . .

16. 2, 1, 0.5, 0.25, . . .

17. 5, 6, 8, 11, 15, . . .

18. 2, 2, 2, 2, . . .

19. 1, 4, 9, 16, . . .

20. Standardized Test Prep Find the geometric mean of 13 and 117.
   A. 65
   B. $\sqrt{130}$
   C. $\frac{13 \cdot 117}{2}$
   D. 39
   E. none of these

21. Critical Thinking How are the formulas for a geometric sequence similar to the formulas for an arithmetic sequence?

22. Open-ended Choose two numbers. Find their geometric mean. Then find the common ratio for a geometric sequence that includes those three terms in that order.

For the geometric sequence 3, 12, 48, 192, . . . , find the indicated term.

23. 5th term

24. 10th term

25. 15th term

26. 14th term

27. 7th term

28. 9th term

Generate the first five terms of each geometric sequence.

29. $a_1 = 5, r = -3$

30. $a_1 = 0.0237, r = 10$

31. $a_1 = \frac{1}{2}, r = \frac{2}{3}$

32. $a_1 = 1, r = 0.5$

33. $a_1 = 100, r = -20$

34. $a_1 = 7, r = 1$

35. $a_1 = 1024, r = 0.5$

36. $a_1 = 4, r = 0.1$

Find the missing term(s) of each geometric sequence. (*Hint:* The geometric mean of the first and fifth terms is the third term.)

37. 5, ▬, 911.25, . . .

38. 9180, ▬, 255, . . .

39. $\frac{2}{5}$, ▬, $\frac{8}{45}$, . . .

40. 19,683, ▬, ▬, ▬, 243

41. 2.5, ▬, ▬, ▬, 202.5, . . .

42. 12.5, ▬, ▬, ▬, 5.12, . . .

43. Suppose a balloon loses one fourth of its helium each day. The balloon starts with a volume of 5000 cm³.

    a. Write the geometric sequence that shows the amount of air in the balloon at the start of each day for five days.

    b. What is the common ratio of the sequence?

    c. How much air will be left in the balloon at the start of the tenth day?

    d. **Graphing Calculator** Graph the sequence. Then sketch the graph.

    e. **Critical Thinking** How does the common ratio relate to the shape of the graph?

44. **Writing** Describe the similarities and differences between a *common difference* and a *common ratio*.

45. **Banking** Copy and complete the table. Use the geometric mean. Assume compound interest is earned and no withdrawals are made.

Period 1	$140.00	$600.00	$25.00	$57.50	$100.00	$250.00
Period 2	▨	▨	▨	▨	▨	▨
Period 3	$145.64	$627.49	$32.76	$60.37	$111.98	$276.55

Chapter Project

Find Out by Creating

Designers or artists must often change the size of their original sketches to fit the space left on the page after the amount of copy is determined. One way to do this is to use graph paper of different sizes. Another way is to change dimensions proportionally. Draw a design and then reduce or enlarge it. Use a ratio to compare the dimensions of your two designs. What would the dimensions be if you used the same ratio to reduce or enlarge the design again? Write a geometric sequence to represent the changes in dimension. Write a recursive or explicit formula for the sequence.

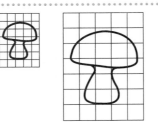

Exercises   MIXED REVIEW

Graph each function.

46. $y = 4 \cos \theta$

47. $y = -3 \sin 2\theta$

48. $y = 2 \sin \pi\theta$

49. **Data Analysis** You take a survey of how long it takes students at your school to get home. The results of the survey are at the right.

    a. What are the mean and the standard deviation of the data?

    b. You surveyed the track and volleyball teams. Explain whether this sampling method gives you a representative sample. If not, how could you have chosen a representative sample?

Number of Minutes to Get Home

45	30	25	60	70	10	15
20	35	45	5	60	75	30
25	20	35	50	55	15	65
55	10	25	40	15	20	45

Find each sum.

50. $4 + 6 + 8 + 10 + 12$ **51.** $1 + 4 + 7 + 10 + 13 + 16$ **52.** $2 + 3.5 + 5 + 6.5 + 8$

Exercises   CHECKPOINT

Identify each sequence as *arithmetic* or *geometric*. Then find the common difference or common ratio.

1. $15, 30, 45, 60, \ldots$ **2.** $2, 6, 18, 54, \ldots$ **3.** $37, 34, 31, 28, 25, \ldots$

4. $700, 350, 175, 87.5, \ldots$ **5.** $8, -4, 2, -1, 0.5, \ldots$ **6.** $4, 2, 0, -2, -4, \ldots$

Find the fifth term of each sequence.

7. $a_n = \frac{1}{2}a_{n-1}; a_1 = 100$ **8.** $a_n = 3a_{n-1} - 2; a_1 = 2$ **9.** $a_n = -n + 6$

10. Writing Explain how to compute the arithmetic mean and the geometric mean of two terms of a sequence.

11. Standardized Test Prep What is the explicit formula for the sequence $-5, -2, 1, 4, \ldots$?

A. $a_n = a_{n-1} + 3; a_1 = -5$ **B.** $a_n = 3(n - 1) - 5$ **C.** $a_n = a_{n-1} - 3; a_1 = -5$

D. $a_n = -3(n - 1) - 5$ **E.** $a_n = 3a_{n-1}; a_1 = -5$

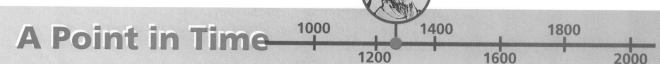

A Point in Time
1000   1200   1400   1600   1800   2000

Patterns of the Sun

The sun reaches its highest and lowest noontime positions on the summer and winter *solstices*, the longest and shortest days of the year. Both days are important for agricultural societies.

In 1276, the Chinese astronomer Guo Shou jing built a clever device for marking the solstices. A hole in the tower of his observatory faced due south. At noon, a horizontal pole in the tower cast a shadow on a low wall that extended north from the building. The sun's rise and fall created a geometric pattern of shadows on the wall. Guo Shou jing learned about the sun's movements through the sky by studying the shadows.

What You'll Learn

- Writing a series from a sequence
- Finding the sum of a given number of terms of a series

...And Why

To solve problems that involve counting objects or people

12-4 Arithmetic Series

WORK TOGETHER

Work in a small group. Use the sequence 1, 2, 3, 4, . . . , 97, 98, 99, 100 to answer the questions.

1. Is the sequence *finite* or *infinite?* Is it *arithmetic, geometric,* or *neither?* **Justify** your reasoning.

2. **a.** Add the first and last terms of the sequence and write down the answer. Then add the second and next-to-last terms. Continue adding terms until you get to the middle of the sequence.
   b. Patterns What patterns did you notice in your answers to part (a)?

3. Use your answer to Question 2 to find the sum of the terms of the sequence.

4. **a.** Describe a short method for finding the following sum.
   $$5 + 10 + 15 + 20 + 25 + 30 + 35 + 40 + 45 + 50$$
   b. Find the sum.

THINK AND DISCUSS

Writing and Evaluating Arithmetic Series

A **series** is the expression for the sum of the terms of a sequence. A series can be *finite* or *infinite,* depending on whether the sequence is finite or infinite.

sequence	series
6, 9, 12, 15, 18	6 + 9 + 12 + 15 + 18

Example 1

Use the finite sequence 2, 11, 20, 29, 38, 47. Write the related series. Then evaluate the series.

related series ⌐ ⌐Add to evaluate.
$$2 + 11 + 20 + 29 + 38 + 47 = 147$$

The sum of the terms of the sequence is 147.

5. **Try This** Write the related series for each finite sequence. Then evaluate each series.
   a. 6, 17, 28, 39, 50, 61, 72
   b. 0.3, 0.6, 0.9, 1.2, 1.5, 1.8, 2.1, 2.4, 2.7, 3.0
   c. 100, 125, 150, 175, 200, 225

When a sequence has many terms, or when you know only the first and last terms of the sequence, you can use a formula to evaluate the related series quickly.

Sum of a Finite Arithmetic Series

The general formula for the sum of a finite **arithmetic series** $a_1 + a_2 + a_3 + \ldots + a_n$ is

$$S_n = \frac{n}{2}(a_1 + a_n).$$

In the formula, S_n is the sum of the series, a_1 is the first term, a_n is the nth term, and n is the number of terms.

6. a. How many terms are in the finite arithmetic series
$10 + 13 + 16 + \ldots + 31$? Explain.
  b. Use the formula above to find the sum of the series.

| **Example 2** | **Relating to the Real World** 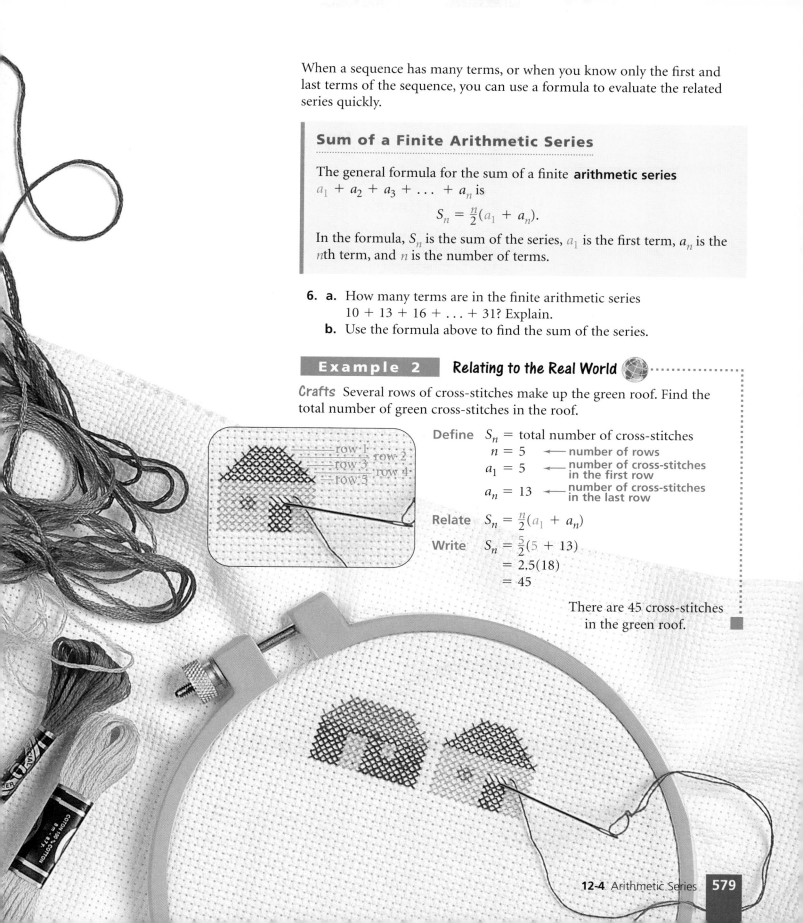 |

Crafts Several rows of cross-stitches make up the green roof. Find the total number of green cross-stitches in the roof.

row 1
row 2
row 3
row 4
row 5

Define S_n = total number of cross-stitches
$n = 5$ ← number of rows
$a_1 = 5$ ← number of cross-stitches in the first row
$a_n = 13$ ← number of cross-stitches in the last row

Relate $S_n = \frac{n}{2}(a_1 + a_n)$

Write $S_n = \frac{5}{2}(5 + 13)$
$= 2.5(18)$
$= 45$

There are 45 cross-stitches in the green roof.

7. Suppose the pattern from Example 2 extends to 14 rows of cross-stitches.
   a. Find the 14th term of the sequence.
   b. **Try This** Use the formula to find the sum of the series.

8. Each sequence has eight terms. Find the sum of each related series.
   a. $\frac{1}{2}, \frac{3}{2}, \frac{5}{2}, \ldots \frac{15}{2}$
   b. $1, -1, -3, \ldots -13$

Using Summation Notation

You can use a summation symbol, Σ, to write a series. Then you can use limits to tell people how many terms you are adding. **Limits** are the least and greatest integral values of n.

upper limit, greatest value of n ——————

explicit formula for the sequence

$$\sum_{n=1}^{3} (5n + 1)$$

lower limit, least value of n ——————

To expand a series from summation notation, you can substitute each value of n into the explicit formula and add the results.

Example 3

Find the sum of the series $\displaystyle\sum_{n=1}^{3} (5n + 1)$.

$$\sum_{n=1}^{3} (5n + 1) = (5(1) + 1) + (5(2) + 1) + (5(3) + 1)$$
$$= 6 + 11 + 16$$
$$= 33$$

The sum of the series is 33.

9. **Try This** For each sum, find the number of terms, the first term, and the last term. Then evaluate each sum.
   a. $\displaystyle\sum_{n=1}^{10} (n - 3)$
   b. $\displaystyle\sum_{n=1}^{4} \frac{1}{2}n + 1$
   c. $\displaystyle\sum_{n=2}^{5} n^2$

Exercises   ON YOUR OWN

Tell whether each list is a *sequence* or a *series*. Then tell whether it is *finite* or *infinite*.

1. $1, 2, 4, 8, 16, 32, \ldots$
2. $5 + 10 + \ldots + 25$
3. $1, 0.5, 0.25, 0.125, 0.0625$
4. $-0.5 - 0.25 - 0.125 - \ldots$
5. $\frac{4}{3}, \frac{7}{3}, \frac{10}{3}, \frac{13}{3}, \frac{16}{3}, \ldots$
6. $2.3 + 4.6 + 9.2 + 18.4$

Write the related series for each finite sequence. Then evaluate each series.

7. 21, 18, 15, 12, 9, 6, 3

8. $-5, -15, -25, -35, -45$

9. $100, 99, 98, \ldots, 95$

10. $4.5, 5.6, 6.7, \ldots, 11.1$

11. $0.5, 0.25, 0, \ldots, -0.75$

12. $17.3, 19.6, 21.9, 24.2, 26.5$

13. Education Luis has taken three math tests so far this semester. The spreadsheet shows his grades.
  a. Suppose his test grades continue to improve at the same rate. What will his grade be on the fifth (and last) test?
  b. What will his test average be for this grading period? (Assume each test is worth 100 points.)

	A	B	C	D
1	Student Name	Test 1	Test 2	Test 3
2	Luis Ortez	75	79	83
3	Marie Bova	78	85	84
4	Lasheha Brown	87	82	91

14. Technology A school committee has decided to spend a large portion of its annual technology budget on graphing calculators. This year, the technology coordinator bought 75 calculators. She plans to buy 25 new calculators each year after that.
  a. Suppose the school committee has decided that each student in the school should have access to a graphing calculator within seven years. The school population is 500. Will the technology coordinator meet this goal? Explain.
  b. Writing What are some pros and cons of buying calculators in this manner? If you could change the plan, would you? If so, how would you do it?

For each sum, find the number of terms, the first term, and the last term. Then evaluate each sum.

15. $\displaystyle\sum_{n=1}^{5} (2n - 1)$

16. $\displaystyle\sum_{n=1}^{5} (-2n - 1)$

17. $\displaystyle\sum_{n=3}^{8} (7 - n)$

18. $\displaystyle\sum_{n=1}^{5} (0.2n - 0.2)$

19. $\displaystyle\sum_{n=2}^{10} \frac{4n}{3}$

20. Standardized Test Prep Which expression defines the series $14 + 20 + 26 + 32 + 38 + 44 + 50$?

A. $\displaystyle\sum_{n=3}^{8} (6n - 4)$
B. $\displaystyle\sum_{n=8}^{14} (n + 6)$
C. $\displaystyle\sum_{n=2}^{8} (7n - 1)$
D. $\displaystyle\sum_{n=3}^{9} (6n - 4)$
E. $\displaystyle\sum_{n=2}^{8} 7n$

21. Theater Design A 20-row theater has two aisles. The two side sections have 4 chairs in the first row and one more chair in each successive row. The middle section has 10 chairs in the first row and one more chair in each successive row.
  a. Find the total number of chairs in each section. Then find the total seating capacity of the theater.
  b. Write an arithmetic series to represent each section.
  c. Every five rows the ticket price goes down $5. Front row tickets cost $60.00. What is the total income generated by a full house?

22. **a.** A supermarket displays cans in a triangle. Write an explicit formula for the sequence of cans.
    b. Use summation notation to write the related series for a triangle with 10 cans in the bottom row.
    c. Suppose the triangle had 17 rows. How many cans would be in the 17th row?
    d. *Critical Thinking* Could the triangle have 110 cans? 140 cans? **Justify** your reasoning.

23. **a.** *Open-ended* Write two explicit formulas for arithmetic sequences.
    b. Write the first five terms of each related series.
    c. Use summation notation to rewrite each series.
    d. Evaluate each sum.

Find the sum of each series to the given term.

24. $2 + 4 + 6 + 8 + \ldots$; 10th term

25. $1 + 3 + 5 + 7 + \ldots$; 20th term

26. $-5 - 25 - 45 - 65 \ldots$; 9th term

27. $12.5 + 15 + 17.5 + 20 + 22.5 + \ldots$; 7th term

28. $2 + 3 + 4 + 5 + \ldots$; 100th term

29. $1500 + 1499 + 1498 + 1497 + \ldots$; 1000th term

30. $\frac{5}{2} + 1 - \frac{1}{2} - 2 - \ldots$; 8th term

31. $0.17 + 0.13 + 0.09 + 0.05 + \ldots$; 12th term

Exercises   M I X E D   R E V I E W

Find the mean and standard deviation for each data set.

32. $5, 2, 1, 7, 4, 3, 5, 6, 6, 5, 7$

33. $10, 11, 11, 13, 10, 9, 10, 11$

34. $1.2, 1.1, 1.0, 1.3, 1.1, 0.9, 2.1$

35. $-10, 3, 42, -5, 22, 0, -10$

Probability **Use the survey results at the right.**

36. Name two mutually exclusive events.

37. Find each probability.
    a. $P(\text{male} \mid 3 \text{ or } 4 \text{ movies})$
    b. $P(5 \text{ or more movies} \mid \text{female})$
    c. $P(2 \text{ or fewer movies} \mid \text{male})$
    d. $P(\text{female} \mid 5 \text{ or more movies})$
    e. $P(2 \text{ or fewer movies})$
    f. $P(5 \text{ or more movies})$

How many movies have you seen in the last month?

	0–2	3–4	5 or more
Male	6	10	7
Female	8	11	3

Getting Ready for Lesson 12-5
Find each sum or difference.

38. $3 + 9 + 27 + 81$

39. $100 + 50 + 25 + \frac{25}{2} + \frac{25}{4}$

40. $-2 + 4 - 8 + 16 - 32$

Evaluating Series

After Lesson 12-4

You can use a graphing calculator to evaluate series with limits.

Example 1

Find the sum of the terms of the sequence 15, 30, 45, 60, 75, 90, 105.

Step 1: Enter the sequence into a list. Press **2nd** Quit to exit.

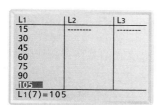

Step 2: Press **2nd** List ▶ **5** to access the sum feature.

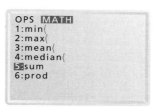

Step 3: Enter the list number. Press **ENTER**.

```
sum L1
                    420
```

The sum of the series $15 + 30 + 45 + \ldots + 105$ is 420.

Example 2

Use your graphing calculator to evaluate $\sum_{n=1}^{5} \frac{n^2}{2}$.

Step 1: Press **2nd** List ▶ **5** to access the sum feature.

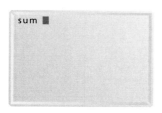

Step 2: Press **2nd** List **5** to access the sequence feature.

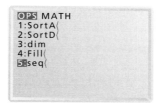

Step 3: Enter the explicit formula, n, the lower limit, the upper limit, and 1 (because n increases by 1 each time). Press **ENTER**.

```
sum seq ( N2 / 2 , N , 1
, 5 , 1 )
                   27.5
```

The value of $\sum_{n=1}^{5} \frac{n^2}{2}$ is 27.5.

Evaluate each series.

1. $595 + 495 + 395 + 295$

2. $3 + 9 + 27 + 81$

3. $\sum_{n=1}^{5} -\sqrt{n^2}$

4. $\sum_{n=1}^{5} (2n^2 - 5)$

5. $\sum_{x=1}^{5} 2^x$

6. $4 + 2 + 1 + \ldots + \frac{1}{8}$

7. **Writing** Compare the methods used in the examples. When would you use the method from Example 1? from Example 2? Explain.

What You'll Learn

- Finding the sum of a finite geometric series
- Finding the sum of an infinite geometric series

...And Why

To find the size of a chambered nautilus shell

12-5 Geometric Series

Work in a group.

Suppose 32 teams participate in a chess tournament. In the first round of play, 16 matches are held. The winners advance to the next round.

1. **a.** Make a tree diagram to determine the chess champion.
   b. How many matches are held in the second round? How many matches are held in the third round?

2. **a.** Write a series to represent the total number of matches played in the first three rounds.
   b. Do consecutive terms of your series show a *constant difference*, a *constant ratio*, or *neither*?

3. Continue the series to represent all the matches played in the tournament. Then find the total number of matches played.

THINK AND DISCUSS

Finding the Sum of a Finite Geometric Series

A **geometric series** is the expression for the sum of the terms of a geometric sequence. As with arithmetic series, you can use a formula to find the sum of a geometric series.

> ### Sum of a Finite Geometric Series
>
> The sum S_n of a finite geometric series is
>
> $$S_n = \frac{a_1(1 - r^n)}{1 - r},$$
>
> where a_1 is the first term, r is the common ratio, and n is the number of terms.

For more practice with ratios, see Skills Handbook page 664.

4. **a.** Identify a_1, r, and n for the series $3 + 6 + 12 + 24 + 48 + 96$.
   b. Use the formula above to evaluate the series.

5. **Verify** the total number of chess matches in the Work Together. First, identify the values of a_1, r, and n. Then use the formula for the sum of a geometric series.

Example 1 Relating to the Real World

Financial Planning In March, the Floyd family starts saving for a vacation to Virginia in August. The Floyds expect the vacation to cost $1375. They start with $125. Each month they plan to deposit 20% more than the previous month. Will they have enough money for their trip?

Define S_n = total amount saved

$a_1 = 125$ ←——— initial amount

$r = 1.2$ ←——— common ratio

$n = 6$ ←——— number of months (March through August)

Relate $S_n = \dfrac{a_1(1 - r^n)}{1 - r}$

Write $S_6 = \dfrac{125(1 - 1.2^6)}{1 - 1.2}$ ←——— Substitute.

$= 1241.24$ ←——— Use a calculator.

PROBLEM SOLVING

Look Back Explain how the common ratio 1.2 was found.

The balance will be $1241.24. So, the Floyds will *not* have enough money for their trip in August.

6. **a.** Suppose each month the Floyds deposit 25% more than the previous month. Describe how this changes the problem.
   b. At this rate of saving, will they have enough money for their trip? **Justify** your answer.

7. **Try This** Find the sum of the eight terms of each series.
   a. $\dfrac{1}{2} + \dfrac{1}{4} + \dfrac{1}{8} + \ldots + \dfrac{1}{256}$ **b.** $1 - 3 + 9 - 27 + \ldots - 2187$

12-5 Geometric Series **585**

Finding the Sum of an Infinite Geometric Series

An **infinite series** has infinitely many terms.

8. Identify each series as *finite* or *infinite*. Explain how you know.

   a. $6 + 3 + 1\frac{1}{2} + \ldots$ **b.** $\frac{1}{2} + 1 + 2 + \ldots + 64$

Surprisingly, it is sometimes possible to find the sum of an infinite series.

9. You can write the sum of the series $0.3 + 0.03 + 0.003 + \ldots$ as $0.333 \ldots$ or $0.\overline{3}$.

   a. Find the values of a_1 and r for this series.

   b. Find the ratio $\frac{a_1}{1 - r}$. How does this ratio relate to the sum of the series?

The series $0.3 + 0.03 + 0.003 + \ldots$ has the following features.

- Each successive term of the series is closer to zero.

- If you stop adding the terms at any point, the sum will be close to $\frac{1}{3}$, but not equal to $\frac{1}{3}$.

- Each successive sum will be closer to $\frac{1}{3}$ than the previous sum.

Similar features are found in any infinite geometric series with $|r| < 1$. When $|r| < 1$, the series **converges,** or gets closer and closer, to the sum S.

Sum of an Infinite Geometric Series

An infinite geometric series with $|r| < 1$ converges to the sum S given by the following formula

$$S = \frac{a_1}{1 - r}.$$

Example: $0.54 + 0.0054 + 0.000054 + \ldots$

$a_1 = 0.54, r = 0.01$

$S = \frac{0.54}{1 - 0.01}$

$= \frac{0.54}{0.99}$

$= \frac{6}{11}$

---

10. Find the sum of each infinite geometric series.

    a. $1 + \frac{1}{2} + \frac{1}{4} + \frac{1}{8} + \ldots$ **b.** $3 - \frac{3}{2} + \frac{3}{4} - \frac{3}{8} + \ldots$

11. **a. Critical Thinking** A classmate uses the formula above to find the sum of the series $1 + 1.1 + 1.21 + 1.331 + \ldots$ and gets a sum of -10. Is this a reasonable answer? Explain.

    b. What did this classmate fail to check before using the formula?

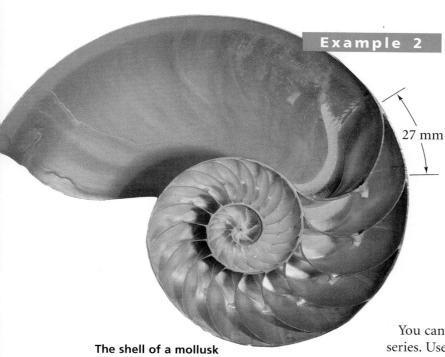

The shell of a mollusk expands as the mollusk grows. This chambered nautilus shell was the home of a mollusk that lived about 35 years.

Example 2

Relating to the Real World

Biology The length of the outside shell of each closed chamber of a chambered nautilus is 0.9 times the length of the larger chamber next to it. Estimate the total length of the outside shell for the enclosed chambers.

27 mm

The outside edge of the largest chamber is 27 mm long, so $a_1 = 27$.

$$S = \frac{a_1}{1 - r}$$ ← To estimate, use the formula for an infinite series.

$$= \frac{27}{1 - 0.9}$$ ← Substitute.

$$= 270$$ ← Simplify.

The total length of the outside shell for the enclosed chambers is about 270 mm.

You can use the summation symbol Σ to write an infinite series. Use the symbol for infinity, ∞, for the upper limit.

12. Try This Find the first term and the common ratio of each infinite geometric series. Then find the sum.

a. $\displaystyle\sum_{n=1}^{\infty} \frac{1}{3^n}$ **b.** $\displaystyle\sum_{n=1}^{\infty} 8\left(\frac{2}{3}\right)^{n-1}$

Exercises   O N   Y O U R   O W N

Find the sum of each geometric series.

1. $\frac{1}{3} + \frac{1}{9} + \frac{1}{27} + \frac{1}{81}$ **2.** $15 - 45 + 135 - 405 + 1215 - 3645$

Find the sum of the eight terms of each geometric series.

3. $3 + 6 + 12 + \ldots + 384$ **4.** $1 + \frac{1}{2} + \frac{1}{4} + \ldots + \frac{1}{128}$ **5.** $2 - 1 + \frac{1}{2} - \ldots - \frac{1}{64}$

6. $20 - 10 + 5 - \ldots - \frac{5}{32}$ **7.** $2 + 6 + 18 + \ldots + 4374$ **8.** $-16 - 8 - 4 - \ldots - \frac{1}{8}$

9. $5 + 0.5 + 0.05 + \ldots + 0.0000005$ **10.** $0.001 + 0.01 + 0.1 + \ldots + 10{,}000$

11. Communications Many companies use a telephone chain to notify employees of a closing due to bad weather. Suppose the first person in the chain calls four employees. Then each of these people calls four others, and so on.
  a. Make a tree diagram to show the first three stages in the telephone chain. How many calls are made at each stage?
  b. Write the series that represents the total number of calls made through the first six stages.
  c. How many employees have been notified after stage six?

Determine whether each series is *arithmetic* or *geometric*. Then find the sum to the given term.

12. $2 + 4 + 8 + 16 + \ldots$; 10th term

13. $2 + 4 + 6 + 8 + \ldots$; 20th term

14. $-5 + 25 - 125 + 625 - \ldots$; 9th term

15. $6.4 + 8 + 10 + 12.5 + \ldots$; 7th term

16. $1 + 2 + 3 + 4 + \ldots$; 1000th term

17. $81 + 27 + 9 + 3 + \ldots$; 200th term

18. Technology Create a spreadsheet to find the sum of the first n terms of each series. Determine whether each infinite series converges to a sum. If so, estimate the sum.

a. $\displaystyle\sum_{n=1}^{\infty} \frac{1}{2^n}$ **b.** $\displaystyle\sum_{n=1}^{\infty} \frac{1}{n}$ **c.** $\displaystyle\sum_{n=1}^{\infty} \frac{1}{(n-1)!}$

	A	B	C
1	term position	term value	sum of first n terms
2	1	0.5	0.5
3	2	0.25	0.75
4	3	0.125	0.875

19. a. Show that the infinite geometric series $0.142\,857 + 0.000\,000\,142\,857 + \ldots$ has a sum of $\frac{1}{7}$.
   b. Find the fraction form of the repeating decimal $0.428\,571\,428\,571\ldots$.

Find the fraction form for each repeating decimal.

20. $0.4444\ldots$

21. $0.010\,101\ldots$

22. $0.003\,636\,36\ldots$

23. $5.666\,66\ldots$

24. $0.144\,144\ldots$

25. $0.252\,525\ldots$

26. $0.074\,074\ldots$

27. $2.011\,11\ldots$

28. Graphing Calculator The graph shows the sum of the first n terms in the series with $a_1 = 20$ and $r = 0.9$.
   a. Write the first four terms of the series.
   b. From the graph, what is the sum of the first 47 terms?
   c. Write and evaluate the formula for the sum of the series.
   d. Graph the sum using the window values shown. Use the graph to **verify** your answer to part (c).

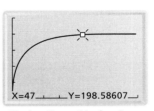

X=47 Y=198.58607

Xmin=0 Ymin=0
Xmax=94 Ymax=250
Xscl=10 Yscl=50

29. Writing Suppose you are to receive an allowance each week for the next 26 weeks. Would it be more beneficial to receive (a) $1000 per week or (b) 2¢ the first week, 4¢ the second week, 8¢ the third week, and so on for the 26 weeks? **Justify** your answer.

Find the sum of each infinite geometric series.

30. $1 - \frac{1}{5} + \frac{1}{25} - \frac{1}{125} + \ldots$

31. $3 + 1 + \frac{1}{3} + \frac{1}{9} + \ldots$

32. $3 + 2 + \frac{4}{3} + \frac{8}{9} + \ldots$

33. $3 - 2 + \frac{4}{3} - \frac{8}{9} + \ldots$

34. $1.1 + 0.11 + 0.011 + 0.0011 + \ldots$

35. $1.1 - 0.11 + 0.011 - 0.0011 + \ldots$

36. Graphing Calculator The function $S(n) = \dfrac{10(1 - 0.8^n)}{0.2}$ represents the sum of the first n terms of an infinite geometric series.
   a. What is the domain of the function?
   b. Find $S(n)$ for $n = 1, 2, 3, \ldots, 10$. Sketch the graph.
   c. Find the sum S of the infinite geometric series.

37. Physics Because of friction, each swing of a pendulum is a little shorter than the previous one. The lengths of the swings form a geometric sequence. Suppose the first swing of a pendulum has a length of 100 cm and the return swing is 99 cm.
   a. On which swing will the arc first have a length less than 50 cm?
   b. Find the total length traveled by the pendulum until it comes to rest.

38. A bouncing ball reaches heights of 16 cm, 12.8 cm, and 10.24 cm on three consecutive bounces.
   a. If the ball started at a height of 25 cm, how many times has it bounced when it reaches a height of 16 cm?
   b. Write a geometric series for the downward distances the ball travels from its release at 25 cm.
   c. Write a geometric series for the upward distances the ball travels from its first bounce.
   d. Find the total distance the ball travels before it comes to rest.

39. Open-ended Write an infinite geometric series that converges to 3.

Exercises   MIXED REVIEW

Probability Suppose a coin is tossed. Find each binomial probability.

40. P(exactly 5 heads in 10 tosses)   **41.** P(exactly 4 heads in 10 tosses)

42. P(at least 4 tails in 6 tosses)   **43.** P(no heads in 12 tosses)

44. Find the measures of the angles of $\triangle ABC$ if $a = 10$, $b = 13$, and $c = 15$. Round your answers to the nearest hundredth.

Getting Ready for Lesson 12-6
Find the area of a rectangle with the given length and width.

45. $\ell = 4$ ft, $w = 1$ ft   **46.** $\ell = 5.5$ m, $w = 0.5$ m

47. $\ell = 6.2$ cm, $w = 0.1$ cm   **48.** $\ell = 9\frac{1}{2}$ in., $w = 3\frac{5}{8}$ in.

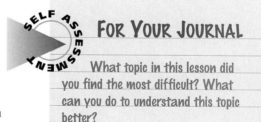

FOR YOUR JOURNAL

What topic in this lesson did you find the most difficult? What can you do to understand this topic better?

Exercises   CHECKPOINT

Determine whether each series is *arithmetic* or *geometric*. Then find the sum to the given term.

1. $1 + 3 + 5 + 7 + \ldots$; 30th term   **2.** $1 + 3 + 9 + 27 + \ldots$; 10th term

3. $-4 - 2 - 1 - 0.5 - \ldots$; 7th term   **4.** $500 + 380 + 260 + 140 + \ldots$; 6th term

5. Open-ended Write a finite geometric series with a sum less than 1.

6. Critical Thinking Can an infinite arithmetic series converge? Explain.

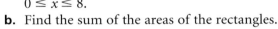

What You'll Learn

- Using rectangles to approximate the area under a curve
- Representing area under a curve as a series
- Using technology to find the area under a curve

...And Why

To solve problems involving populations and inventories

What You'll Need

- graph paper
- graphing calculator

12-6 Exploring Area Under a Curve

WORK TOGETHER

Work with a partner.

1. Draw two coordinate planes with the same scale as the graph at the right. Graph the equation $y = \frac{1}{4}x^2 + 1$ on both coordinate planes.

2. **a.** On one graph, draw four rectangles between the x-axis and the curve. Make each rectangle 2 units wide and as tall as possible without crossing the curve. Use the domain $0 \le x \le 8$.

   b. Find the sum of the areas of the rectangles.

3. **a.** On the other graph, draw eight rectangles between the x-axis and the curve. Make each rectangle 1 unit wide and as tall as possible without crossing the curve. Use the domain $0 \le x \le 8$.

   b. Find the sum of the areas of the rectangles.

4. **Critical Thinking** Which group of rectangles do you think gives the better estimate of the area under the curve? Explain.

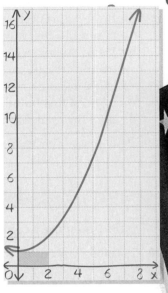

THINK AND DISCUSS

The graph at the right represents a car traveling at a constant speed of 65 mi/h.

5. **a.** What are the dimensions of the shaded rectangle?
   b. Find the area of the shaded rectangle.
   c. Is the area you found exact? Explain.

By applying dimensional analysis to the area of the rectangle, you can determine that the area of the rectangle represents distance in miles.

$$2 \, \cancel{h} \times 65 \, \frac{mi}{\cancel{h}} = 130 \text{ mi}$$

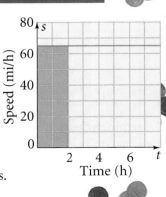

It is easy to calculate the exact area under a line parallel to the *x*-axis, but it is not as easy to calculate the exact area under a curve. The ancient Greeks used rectangles like those in the Work Together to approximate the area under a curve.

Inscribed rectangles:
Approximation is
less than the area.

Circumscribed rectangles:
Approximation is
greater than the area.

Sometimes a smooth curve models real-world data. You can use rectangles to estimate the area under the curve and analyze the data.

Example 1 **Relating to the Real World**

Data Analysis The curve at the left approximates the number of people who immigrated to the United States from 1989 to 1994.

a. What does the area under the curve represent?

b. Use inscribed rectangles 1 unit wide to estimate the area under the curve between 1989 to 1994.

c. Use the answer to part (a) to interpret the answer to part (b).

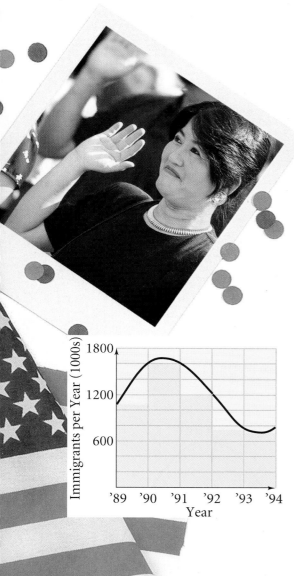

a. $\dfrac{\text{immigrants}}{\text{year}} \cdot \text{years} = \text{immigrants}$ ← **Use dimensional analysis.**

The area under the curve represents the total number of immigrants.

b. Estimate the area of each rectangle. Then add the areas.

$$\begin{aligned}
\text{Rect}_1 &= 1(1050)\\
\text{Rect}_2 &= 1(1600)\\
\text{Rect}_3 &= 1(1200)\\
\text{Rect}_4 &= 1(750)\\
\text{Rect}_5 &= 1(700)\\
\hline
\end{aligned}$$

Total Area $= 5300$

The area under the curve is approximately 5300 units^2.

c. Each unit on the *y*-axis represents 1000 people.

$5300 \cdot 1000 = 5,300,000$

Approximately 5,300,000 immigrants were admitted to the United States between 1989 and 1994. The estimate is low because inscribed rectangles were used.

6. The graph at the right shows the curve from Example 1, but it shows circumscribed rectangles.
  a. Estimate the area using the circumscribed rectangles. How does your answer differ from the solution to Example 1?
  b. Find the mean of the solution to Example 1 and your answer to part (a). Of the three answers, which is the most accurate?

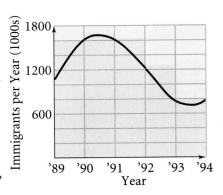

You can use summation notation to represent the area of a series of rectangles and to approximate the area under the curve $f(x)$. Let a_n represent a point on the base of the nth rectangle.

$$A = \sum_{n=1}^{b} (w) f(a_n)$$

number of rectangles ⟵ b

width of each rectangle ⟶ w

function value at a_n ⟶ $f(a_n)$

The expression $f(a_n)$ gives the height of the nth rectangle.

Example 2

Estimate the area under the curve $f(x) = -x^2 + 5$ for the domain $0 \le x \le 2$ by evaluating

$$A = \sum_{n=1}^{4} (0.5) f(a_n).$$

Evaluate the function at the right side of each rectangle.

$a_1 = 0.5, a_2 = 1, a_3 = 1.5, a_4 = 2$ ⟵ Use right-hand endpoints on the x-axis for each rectangle.

$A = 0.5\, f(0.5) + 0.5\, f(1) + 0.5\, f(1.5) + 0.5\, f(2)$
$= 0.5(4.75 + 4 + 2.75 + 1)$ ⟵ total area = width of each rectangle times the sum of the heights
$= 0.5(12.5)$
$= 6.25$

The indicated area is about 6.25 units^2.

7. a. Sketch the graph from Example 2 and draw circumscribed rectangles for the domain $0 \le x \le 2$.
  b. *Critical Thinking* To find the area using these rectangles, you should evaluate the function at the left side of each rectangle. Why?
  c. Use the circumscribed rectangles to evaluate a sum that approximates the area under the curve for the domain $0 \le x \le 2$. Compare your answer to the solution found in Example 2.

8. Try This Approximate the area under the curve $f(x) = x^2$ for the interval $0 \leq x \leq 4$ by evaluating each sum. Use inscribed rectangles.

a. $\displaystyle\sum_{n=1}^{8} (0.5)f(a_n)$

b. $\displaystyle\sum_{n=1}^{4} (1)f(a_n)$

You can use a graphing calculator to find the exact area under a curve.

Example 3

Graphing Calculator Graph the function $f(x) = -2x^2 + 5$. Find the area under the curve for the domain $-1 \leq x \leq 1.5$.

Step 1: Input the equation. Adjust the window values.

Step 2: Press **2nd** CALC **7** to access the $\int f(x)\,dx$ feature.

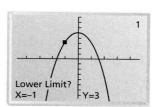

Lower Limit?
X=-1   Y=3

Xmin=-4.7 Ymin=-7
Xmax=4.7   Ymax=8
Xscl=1   Yscl=1

Step 3: Move the cursor until the lower limit is $x = -1$. Press **ENTER**.

Step 4: Move the cursor until the upper limit is $x = 1.5$. Press **ENTER**.

GRAPHING CALCULATOR HINT

To move the cursor by tenths along the *x*-axis, set your *x* window values to multiples of 4.7.

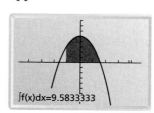

$\int f(x)dx=9.5833333$

The area under the curve between $x = -1$ and $x = 1.5$ is $9.58\overline{3}$ units^2.

9. Graphing Calculator Use the equation from Example 2. Find the area under the curve for each domain.

a. $0 \leq x \leq 1$ **b.** $-1 \leq x \leq 1$ **c.** $-1.5 \leq x \leq 0$

10. Try This Use your graphing calculator to find the area under each curve for the domain $0 \leq x \leq 1$.

a. $y = -x^2 + 2$ **b.** $f(x) = x + 2$ **c.** $y = x^3$

Exercises   ON YOUR OWN

Given each set of axes, what does the area under the curve represent?

1. *y*-axis: meters per second; *x*-axis: seconds

2. *y*-axis: miles per gallon; *x*-axis: gallons

3. *y*-axis: production rate; *x*-axis: time

4. *y*-axis: rate of growth; *x*-axis: time

5. *y*-axis: distance traveled per year; *x*-axis: years

6. *y*-axis: price per pound of gold; *x*-axis: pounds of gold

Use the given rectangles to estimate each area.

7.

8.

9.

Graph each curve. Use inscribed rectangles to approximate the area under the curve for the given domain and rectangle width.

10. $y = x^2 + 1; 1 \le x \le 3; 0.5$ **11.** $y = 3x^2 + 2; 2 \le x \le 4; 1$ **12.** $y = x^2; 3 \le x \le 5; 0.5$

13. $y = 2x^2; 3 \le x \le 5; 1$ **14.** $y = x^3; 1 \le x \le 3; 0.25$ **15.** $y = x^2 + 4; -2 \le x \le 2; 0.5$

16. a. Graph the curve $y = \frac{1}{3}x^3$.
 b. Use inscribed rectangles to approximate the area under the curve for the interval $0 \le x \le 3$ and rectangle width of 1 unit.
 c. Repeat part (b) using circumscribed rectangles.
 d. Find the average of the areas you found in parts (b) and (c). Of the three estimates, which best approximates the area for the interval? **Justify** your reasoning.

 Graphing Calculator Evaluate the area under each curve for $-1 \le x \le 2$.

17. $f(x) = -x^2 + 4$ **18.** $y = (x - 0.5)^2 + 1.75$ **19.** $g(x) = 2 + 3 \cos x$ **20.** $y = 1 + \sin x$

21. $g(x) = 2^x + 1$ **22.** $y = x^3 + 2$ **23.** $y = -(x - 1)^2 + 4\frac{1}{3}$ **24.** $h(x) = \sqrt{x^2}$

25. a. The function $f(t) = 20t + 50$ approximates the number of attendees at a powwow, where t is the number of times the powwow is held. Graph the function.
 b. Use rectangles 0.5 units wide to estimate the total number of people who attended the first six powwows.
 c. Writing How does your choice of inscribed or circumscribed rectangles in part (b) affect your area estimate?

 26. a. Graphing Calculator Graph the functions $y = \frac{1}{4}x^3 + 1$ and $y = 1$ over the domain $-4.7 \le x \le 4.7$.
 b. Critical Thinking Evaluate the area under each curve for the interval $-1.5 \le x \le 1.5$. What do you notice? Explain.

27. Graphing Calculator Use your graphing calculator to find the area of the triangle with vertices $(-4, 0)$, $(-1, 3)$, and $(2, 0)$. (*Hint:* First find the function whose graph makes a peak at $(-1, 3)$.)

28. Open-ended Write equations for three curves that have positive values for $1 \leq x \leq 3$. Use your graphing calculator to evaluate the area under each curve for this domain.

Evaluate a sum to approximate the area under each curve for the domain $0 \leq x \leq 2$. Use inscribed rectangles 1 unit wide.

29. $f(x) = \frac{1}{2}x^2$ **30.** $y = x^2 + 1$ **31.** $g(x) = -x^2 + 5$ **32.** $y = (x - 2)^2 + 2$

Evaluate a sum to approximate the area under each curve for the domain $0 \leq x \leq 2$. Use circumscribed rectangles 1 unit wide.

33. $y = -x^2 + 3$ **34.** $y = 5x^2$ **35.** $h(x) = \frac{2}{3}x^2 + 5$ **36.** $y = 4 - \frac{1}{4}x^2$

37. a. Write the equation $\frac{x^2}{25} + \frac{y^2}{9} = 1$ in calculator-ready form.
     b. Graphing Calculator Graph the top half of the ellipse. Calculate the area under the curve for the interval $-5 \leq x \leq 5$.
     c. Use symmetry to find the area of the entire ellipse.
     d. Open-ended Find the area of another symmetric shape by graphing part of it. Sketch your graph and show your calculations.

Chapter Project ···· ***Find Out by Analyzing***

Photographs are often *cropped* so that only part of the photograph remains. This rectangle can be reduced or enlarged.

Choose a photograph from this book. Trace its original size. Then mark a rectangular area that you want to show. Draw a diagonal of this rectangle and extend it from one corner as shown. Use the diagonal to write a sequence of several other widths that could be used for the cropped photograph.

Exercises MIXED REVIEW

Determine whether each sequence is *arithmetic*, *geometric*, or *neither*. Then find any common ratio or difference.

38. $-4, -2, 0, 2, 4, \ldots$ **39.** $4, 2, 1, \frac{1}{2}, \frac{1}{4}, \ldots$

40. $-1, 3, -9, 27, \ldots$ **41.** $24, 23, 21, 18, \ldots$

42. A teacher distributes her grades normally. What is the probability that one student will get a grade between the mean and one standard deviation above the mean?

PORTFOLIO

Select one or two items from your work in this chapter. Explain why you have included each selection.

Finishing the Chapter Project

GET THE

PICTURE

Find Out questions on pages 570, 576, and 595 should help you complete your project. Prepare a presentation or demonstration that summarizes how an artist, a designer, or a photographer uses sequences. Present it to your classmates. Then discuss the sequences you created. Do they agree with your choices?

Reflect and Revise

Before giving your presentation, review your summary. Are your drawings clear and correct? Are your sequences accurate? Practice your presentation in front of at least two people before presenting it to the class. Ask for their suggestions for improvement.

Follow Up

Geometric and arithmetic patterns are used in other aspects of design and in other careers. Research other areas where sequences are applied.

For More Information

Clifton, Jack. *Manual of Drawing & Painting*. New York: Watson-Guptill Publications, 1957.

Wood, Phyllis. *Scientific Illustration*. New York: Van Nostrand Reinhold, 1979.

Zaidenberg, Arthur. *Drawing Self-Taught*. New York: Pocket Books, 1954.

Key Terms

arithmetic mean (p. 568)
arithmetic sequence (p. 566)
arithmetic series (p. 579)
common difference (p. 566)
common ratio (p. 572)
converge (p. 586)
explicit formula (p. 563)
geometric mean (p. 574)

geometric sequence (p. 572)
geometric series (p. 584)
infinite series (p. 586)
limit (p. 580)
recursive formula (p. 562)
sequence (p. 561)
series (p. 578)
term (p. 561)

How am I doing?

- State three ideas from this chapter that you think are important. Explain your choices.
  - Explain the difference between an arithmetic and a geometric series.

SELF ASSESSMENT

Mathematical Patterns   12-1

A **sequence** is an ordered list of numbers called **terms**. A **recursive formula** gives the first term and defines the other terms in a sequence by relating each term to the ones before it. An **explicit formula** expresses the nth term in a sequence in terms of n, where n is a positive integer.

Decide whether each formula is *explicit* or *recursive*. Then find the first four terms of each sequence.

1. $a_n = 3n - 2$

2. $a_1 = 5; a_n = 4a_{n-1} + 2$

3. $a_n = 2^n$

4. $a_1 = 1; a_n = -2a_{n-1} - 5$

5. $a_1 = -2; a_n = -\frac{1}{2}a_{n-1} + 6$

6. $a_n = 6n^2 - 30$

7. Writing Choose one of the exercises above. Explain how you decided whether the formula was explicit or recursive.

Arithmetic Sequences   12-2

In an **arithmetic sequence**, the difference between consecutive terms is constant. The difference is the **common difference**.

A **recursive formula** for an arithmetic sequence is $a_n = a_{n-1} + d$, given a_1. An **explicit formula** for an arithmetic sequence is $a_n = a_1 + (n - 1)d$. In both cases, a_n is the nth term, a_1 is the first term, n is the number of the term, and d is the common difference.

The **arithmetic mean** of any two numbers (or terms in a sequence) is the average of the two numbers.

$$\text{arithmetic mean} = \frac{\text{sum of two numbers}}{2}$$

Write the next three terms in each sequence. Then write an explicit and a recursive formula for each sequence.

8. $1, 5, 9, 13, \ldots$

9. $104, 101.5, 99, 96.5, \ldots$

10. $-3.4, -3.7, -4.0, -4.3, \ldots$

Find a_n, the arithmetic mean of the given terms.

11. $a_{n-1} = 7, a_{n+1} = 15$

12. $a_{n-1} = -2, a_{n+1} = 3$

13. $a_{n-1} = 13, a_{n+1} = 9.8$

14. Writing Explain how you can determine if a sequence is arithmetic.

Geometric Sequences   12-3

In a **geometric sequence**, the ratio between consecutive terms is constant. The ratio is the **common ratio**. You can use recursive or explicit formulas to express a geometric sequence.

A **recursive formula** for a geometric sequence is $a_n = a_{n-1} \cdot r$, given a_1. An **explicit formula** for a geometric sequence is $a_n = a_1 \cdot r^{n-1}$. In both cases, a_n is the nth term, a_1 is the first term, n is the number of the term, and r is the common ratio.

You can find the **geometric mean** of two positive numbers by taking the positive square root of the product of the two numbers.

$$\text{geometric mean} = \sqrt{\text{product of the two numbers}}$$

A geometric mean is the middle term of any three consecutive terms in a geometric sequence.

Write an explicit and a recursive formula for each sequence.

15. $3, 6, 12, 24, \ldots$

16. $180, 60, 20, \frac{20}{3}, \ldots$

17. $0.004, 0.04, 0.4, 4, \ldots$

Find a_n, the geometric mean of the given terms.

18. $a_{n-1} = 8, a_{n+1} = 128$

19. $a_{n-1} = 1, a_{n+1} = 4$

20. $a_{n-1} = 10, a_{n+1} = 2.5$

Arithmetic Series   12-4

An **arithmetic series** is the expression for the sum of the terms of an arithmetic sequence. The sum S_n of the first n terms of an arithmetic series is $S_n = \frac{n}{2}(a_1 + a_n)$.

You can use a summation symbol, Σ, and **limits** to write a series.

Evaluate each sum.

21. $\displaystyle\sum_{n=1}^{3} (17n - 25)$

22. $\displaystyle\sum_{n=2}^{10} \left(\frac{1}{2}n + 3\right)$

23. $\displaystyle\sum_{n=5}^{15} -\frac{2}{3}n$

Find each sum to the given term.

24. $10 + 7 + 4 + \ldots$; 5th term

25. $50 + 55 + 60 + \ldots$; 7th term

26. $6 + 7.4 + 8.8 + \ldots$; 11th term

27. $21 + 19 + 17 + \ldots$; 8th term

28. Business Deanna Jones opened a video rental store this year with 400 tapes. She plans to buy 150 new tapes each year from now on.

 a. Write a sequence to represent Deanna's video purchases for the first five years. Then write the related series.

 b. Deanna expects to have 1300 tapes available during her fifth year in business. At her current purchasing rate, will she reach her goal? Explain.

Geometric Series 12-5

A **geometric series** is the sum of the terms of a geometric sequence. The sum S_n of the first n terms of a geometric series is $S_n = \frac{a_1(1 - r^n)}{1 - r}$.

You can find the sum of some infinite geometric series. A geometric series **converges** to $S = \frac{a_1}{1 - r}$ when $|r| < 1$.

Write and evaluate the related series for each finite sequence.

29. 150, 30, 6, 1.2, 0.24

30. 2.2, 2.42, 2.662, ..., 3.22102

31. $\frac{2}{3}, \frac{4}{9}, \frac{8}{27}, \frac{16}{81}$

32. 44, 22, 11, ..., 1.375

33. $-10, -20, -40, ..., -1280$

34. $-\frac{4}{5}, -\frac{8}{5}, -\frac{16}{5}, ..., -\frac{512}{5}$

Find the sum of the first seven terms of each geometric series.

35. $3 + 1 + \frac{1}{3} + \frac{1}{9} + ...$

36. $1 + 2 + 4 + 8 + ...$

37. $80 - 40 + 20 - 10 + ...$

38. Open-ended Write an infinite geometric series that converges. Find its sum.

Exploring Area Under a Curve 12-6

You can approximate the area under a curve by using inscribed or circumscribed rectangles. If you use inscribed rectangles, the approximation is less than the area under the curve. If you use circumscribed rectangles, the approximation is greater than the area under the curve. You can use a graphing calculator to find the exact area under a curve.

You can use summation notation to represent the area of a series of rectangles and the approximate area under a curve $f(x)$.

$$A = \sum_{n=1}^{b} (w)f(a_n)$$

where b is the number of rectangles, w is the width of each rectangle, a_n is a point on the base of the nth rectangle, and $f(a_n)$ is the function value at a_n.

Graph each curve. Use inscribed rectangles to approximate the area under the curve for the given domain and rectangle width.

39. $y = x^2; 1 \leq x \leq 4; 1$

40. $y = x^3 - 1; 2 \leq x \leq 4; 0.5$

41. $y = 3x^2; -1 \leq x \leq 1; 0.25$

42. Standardized Test Prep In which interval is the area under the curve $y = 4x^2 + 1$ greatest?

 A. $0 \leq x \leq 3$ **B.** $1 \leq x \leq 3$ **C.** $1 \leq x \leq 4$ **D.** $2 \leq x \leq 5$ **E.** $-5 \leq x \leq -1$

**State whether each sequence is *arithmetic,
geometric,* or *neither.* Then find the tenth term.**

1. 23, 27, 31, 35, 39, . . .

2. $-12, -5, 2, 9, 16, \ldots$

3. $-5, 15, -45, 135, -405, \ldots$

Find the arithmetic mean of the given terms.

4. $a_{n-1} = 4, a_{n+1} = 12$

5. $a_{n-1} = -11, a_{n+1} = 23$

**Write an explicit and a recursive formula for each
sequence.**

6. 7, 13, 19, 25, 31, 37, . . .

7. 10, 20, 40, 80, 160, 320, . . .

8. Chantrell saved $50 the first month of her new
   job. She decides to save $5 more each month.
   a. Write an explicit formula to model this.
   b. How much will she save in the sixth month?

9. Open-ended Write an arithmetic sequence.
   Then write an explicit formula for it.

**Find the common difference or common ratio of
each sequence.**

10. 1620, 540, 180, 60, 20, . . .

11. 78, 75, 72, 69, 66, 63, 60, . . .

12. $\frac{3}{32}, \frac{3}{16}, \frac{3}{8}, \frac{3}{4}, \frac{3}{2}, 3, 6, \ldots$

13. Standardized Test Prep Which sequence has a
    common difference of 3?
    I. $a_n = a_{n-1} - 3, a_1 = 2$
    II. $a_n = 3(n - 1)$
    III. $a_n = a_{n-1} + 3, a_1 = -7$
    IV. $a_n = n^2 + 3$
    A. I only   B. III only   C. I and III
    D. II and IV   E. III and IV

**Generate the first five terms of each sequence
where *r* is a common ratio and *d* is a common
difference.**

14. $a_1 = 2, r = -2$

15. $a_1 = 3, d = 7$

16. $a_1 = -100, r = \frac{1}{5}$

17. $a_1 = 19, d = -4$

Find the geometric mean of the given terms.

18. $a_{n-1} = 2, a_{n+1} = \frac{1}{2}$

19. $a_{n-1} = 2, a_{n+1} = 8$

**Determine whether each series is *arithmetic* or
geometric. Then find the sum of the first eight terms.**

20. $2 + 7 + 12 + 17 + \ldots$

21. $5000 + 1000 + 200 + 40 + \ldots$

22. Writing Explain how you can tell whether a
    geometric series will converge. Include an
    example of a series that converges and the
    number it converges to.

**Given each set of axes, interpret
the area under the curve.**

23. *y*-axis: miles per hour; *x*-axis: hours

24. *y*-axis: pounds per in.^{2}; *x*-axis: in.^{2}

**Graph each curve. Use inscribed rectangles to find
an approximate area for each domain.**

25. curve: $y = 2x^2$ rectangle width: 1
    domain: $0 \le x \le 2$

26. curve: $y = x^2 + 1$ rectangle width: 0.5
    domain: $-1 \le x \le 2$

27. curve: $y = x^3$ rectangle width: 0.5
    domain: $1 \le x \le 3$

28. Critical Thinking Explain how you could use
    circumscribed and inscribed rectangles to find
    the area under a curve.

For Exercises 1–16, choose the correct letter.

1. Which conic section is an ellipse?
A. $(x - 1)^2 + (y - 2)^2 = 4$
B. $(x + 4)^2 - (y - 3)^2 = 25$
C. $\frac{x^2}{36} + \frac{y^2}{81} = 100$ **D.** $x = 2y^2 + 16$
E. $\frac{x^2}{9} - \frac{y^2}{49} = 121$

2. The lengths of the sides of a triangle are 3 cm, 5 cm, and 6 cm. What is the measure of the largest angle of the triangle to the nearest tenth?
A. $0.5°$ **B.** $60°$ **C.** $86.2°$
D. $82.3°$ **E.** $93.8°$

3. How many solutions does the system
$\begin{cases} y = 3x - 1 \\ y = -x + 4 \end{cases}$ have?
A. 0 **B.** 1 **C.** 2 **D.** 3 **E.** 4

4. In which sequence is a_{25} greatest?
A. $a_n = 2a_{n-1} + 7, a_1 = 5$
B. $a_n = 3n - 10$
C. $a_n = a_{n-1} + 18, a_1 = -7$
D. $a_n = -a_{n-1} - 30, a_1 = -40$
E. $a_n = n^2 - 200$

5. What is the inverse of $y = x^2 + 4$?
A. $y = \frac{1}{2}x - 4$ **B.** $y = \sqrt{x} - 4$
C. $y = \pm\sqrt{x - 4}$ **D.** $y = \sqrt[4]{x} - 2$
E. $y = 4 - \sqrt{x}$

6. Which series converges?
A. $\sum_{n=1}^{\infty} 3n$ **B.** $\sum_{n=1}^{\infty} (n - 1)$ **C.** $\sum_{n=1}^{\infty} \frac{1}{2}n$
D. $\sum_{n=1}^{\infty} (2n - 7)$ **E.** none of the above

7. Which function shifts $y = |x + 1| - 3$ right 4 units and down 7 units?
A. $y = |x - 6| + 1$ **B.** $y = |x - 3| + 4$
C. $y = |x + 5| - 10$ **D.** $y = |x + 8| - 7$
E. $y = |x - 3| - 10$

8. Which system has the solution $(3, 1, 2)$?
A. $\begin{cases} x + y + z = 6 \\ 3x - y + 2z = 12 \\ x - 5y + z = 10 \end{cases}$
B. $\begin{cases} 2x + y + z = 8 \\ -x + y - 4z = -6 \\ 6x + 7y - z = 24 \end{cases}$
C. $\begin{cases} 3x - y + z = 10 \\ x + 4y + z = 11 \\ x - y + 4z = 10 \end{cases}$
D. $\begin{cases} x + 2y - z = 1 \\ 2x - y + 3z = 11 \\ -x + y + 3z = 4 \end{cases}$
E. none of the above

9. Which direct variation includes $(10, 1)$?
A. $y = 10x$ **B.** $y = 0.1x$
C. $xy = 10$ **D.** $y = 0.5x - 4$
E. $x = 4y + 6$

10. Which expression(s) is (are) equivalent to $3 \log x + 2 \log y - \log x$?
I. $2 \log xy$ **II.** $\log x^2 + \log y^2$
III. $2 \log x + 2 \log y$ **IV.** $4 \log x - y$
A. I and II **B.** II and III **C.** I and IV
D. III and IV **E.** I, II, and III

11. Which periodic function is a tangent function?

A.  **B.**

C. 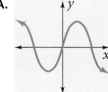 **D.**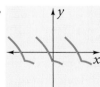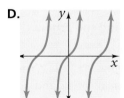

E. none of the above

(continued on next page)

12. Find the solution to the following matrix equation.

$$\begin{bmatrix} 10 & 9 & -5 \\ 3 & 12 & 7 \end{bmatrix} - X = \begin{bmatrix} 4 & -8 & 5 \\ 15 & -3 & 0 \end{bmatrix}$$

A. $\begin{bmatrix} 6 & 17 & -10 \\ -12 & 15 & 7 \end{bmatrix}$ **B.** $\begin{bmatrix} 14 & 1 & 0 \\ 18 & 9 & 7 \end{bmatrix}$

C. $\begin{bmatrix} 15 & 1 & -1 \\ 3 & 9 & 22 \end{bmatrix}$ **D.** $\begin{bmatrix} -6 & -17 & 10 \\ 12 & -15 & -7 \end{bmatrix}$

E. The equation has no solution.

13. What is the distance of $4 - 5i$ from the origin?
A. 9 units **B.** 3 units **C.** -1 unit
D. 1 unit **E.** $\sqrt{41}$ units

14. Which exponential function models successive decreases of 5%?
A. $y = 1.05(1.25)^x$ **B.** $y = 0.95(0.75)^x$
C. $y = 3.1(1.05)^x$ **D.** $y = 6.3(0.95)^x$
E. none of the above

15. Simplify $\dfrac{x^2y^3z}{4x} \div \dfrac{3xy^4z^2}{2z}$.

A. $\dfrac{3x^3y^7z^3}{8xz}$ **B.** $\dfrac{3x^2y^7z^2}{8}$ **C.** $\dfrac{2x^2y^3z^2}{12x^2y^4z^2}$

D. $\dfrac{1}{6y}$ **E.** $\dfrac{x^2y^3z^2 + 6x^2y^4z^2}{4xz}$

16. Which point is in the solution region of the

$$\text{system} \begin{cases} y \le 3x - 2 \\ y < 2x \\ x \ge -1 \\ y \ge -4 \end{cases} ?$$

A. $(0, 7)$ **B.** $(-4, 1)$ **C.** $(3, 1)$
D. $(-1, -5)$ **E.** $(5, -7)$

Find each answer.

17. Graph the function $y = \sin\left(x + \dfrac{\pi}{2}\right)$.

18. $(2x^4 + 4x^3 + 5x^2 + 9x - 2) \div (x + 2)$

19. Find the product $\begin{bmatrix} 2 & 1 \\ -6 & 5 \\ -1 & 3 \end{bmatrix}\begin{bmatrix} 8 & -2 & 0.5 \\ 4 & -7 & 10 \end{bmatrix}$.

20. Open-ended Write a set of numbers with a mean of 37 and a standard deviation of 4.

21. Write the equation of a hyperbola with asymptotes at $y = 4$ and $x = -2$.

22. Simplify $(5 + 2i)(-3 + i)$.

23. Probability You roll three number cubes.
  a. Writing Do the three events {rolling three of the same number, rolling two of the same number, rolling all different numbers} form a probability distribution? Explain.
  b. Find P(all three show the same number).

24. Finance You received $350 for your birthday. You can put the money into an account earning 4.5% annual interest compounded continuously, or into an account earning 5% annual interest compounded monthly. How much would you have in each account after one year? after five years?

25. Open-ended Graph a circle with its center at $(3, 2)$. Write the equation of the circle and find its circumference.

Compare the boxed quantity in Column A with the boxed quantity in Column B. Choose the best answer.

  A. The quantity in Column A is greater.
  B. The quantity in Column B is greater.
  C. The two quantities are equal.
  D. The relationship cannot be determined on the basis of the information supplied.

	Column A	Column B
26.	a_5 when $a_n = 4n - 1$	a_5 when $a_n = 2n^2 - 30$
27.	the degree of the polynomial $2x^5 + 3x - 1$	the number of terms of the polynomial $4x^2y + x^2 - 3y^2 - xy + x$
28.	the third quartile of a given data set	the median of the same data set
29.	the sum of the solutions of $x^2 + 5x + 6 = 0$	the sum of the solutions of $x^2 + 5x + 4 = 0$

Additional Topics in Trigonometry, Polynomials, and Mathematical Induction

You can translate periodic functions horizontally and vertically in the same way as other functions that you have studied.

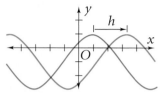

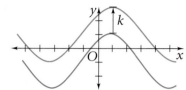

$g(x)$: horizontal translation of $f(x)$
$$g(x) = f(x - h)$$

$h(x)$: vertical translation of $f(x)$
$$h(x) = f(x) + k$$

A horizontal translation of a periodic function is a **phase shift.** When $g(x) = f(x - h)$, the value of h is the amount of the shift. If $h > 0$, the shift is to the right. If $h < 0$, the shift is to the left.

1. What is the value of h in each translation? Describe each phase shift (use a phrase like *3 units to the left*).
   a. $g(x) = f(x - 2)$ **b.** $g(x) = f(x + 4)$

Example 1

Use the graph of $y = \sin x$ at the right. Sketch each translation of the graph in the interval $0 \le x \le 2\pi$.

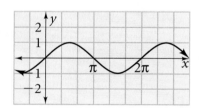

a. $y = \sin x + 3$ **b.** $y = \sin\left(x - \frac{\pi}{2}\right)$ **c.** $y = \sin(x + \pi) - 2$

a.
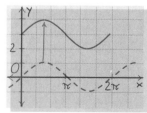

b.
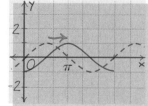

c.
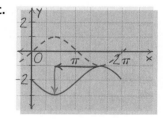

2. Try This The graph of $f(x) = \cos x$ is shown at the right. Sketch each translation. Which one is a phase shift?

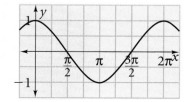

   a. $f(x) + 2$ **b.** $f\left(x - \frac{\pi}{2}\right)$

Translations of Sine and Cosine Functions

$y = a \sin b(x - h) + k$ and $y = a \cos b(x - h) + k$
represent translations of
$y = a \sin bx$ and $y = a \cos bx$.

$|a|$ = amplitude
$\frac{2\pi}{b}$ = period (when x is in radians and $b > 0$)
h = phase shift, or horizontal shift
k = vertical shift

Example 2 — Relating to the Real World

Weather The table gives the normal high temperature in New Orleans, Louisiana, on several days of the year (January 1 = 1, February 1 = 32, and so on). Plot the data in the table. Write a cosine model for the data.

Day of Year	Temperature (°F)
16	62
47	65
75	71
106	79
136	85
167	90
197	91
228	90
259	87
289	79
320	70
350	64

Plot the data.

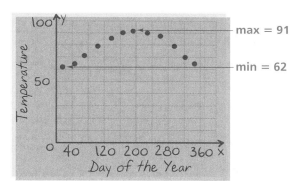

max = 91
min = 62

Use the form $y = a \cos b(x - h) + k$. Find values a, b, h and k.

amplitude $= \frac{1}{2}(\text{max} - \text{min})$
$= \frac{1}{2}(91 - 62)$
$= 14.5$

period $= \frac{2\pi}{b}$

One complete cycle takes 365 days. ⟶ $365 = \frac{2\pi}{b}$

$b = \frac{2\pi}{365}$

So (choosing $a > 0$), $a = 14.5$.

To find the translation values h and k, compare $y = 14.5 \cos \frac{2\pi}{365}x$ with the plot of the data.

phase shift: $h = 197 - 0$
$= 197$

vertical shift: $k = 91 - 14.5$
$= 76.5$

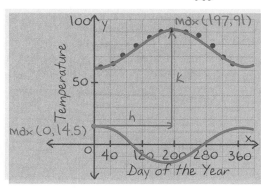

Max (197, 91)
Max (0, 14.5)

The model for the data is $y = 14.5 \cos \frac{2\pi}{365}(x - 197) + 76.5$.

3. **a.** Estimation Use the model in Example 2. Estimate the high temperature in New Orleans on September 1 (day 244).
   b. Graphing Calculator Graph the model on your calculator. Use it to estimate the first day of the year that the high temperature is likely to reach 75°F.

Example 3

Sketch the graph of $y = \sin 2\left(x - \frac{\pi}{3}\right) - \frac{3}{2}$ in the interval from 0 to 2π.

Since $a = 1$ and $b = 2$, the graph is a translation of $y = \sin 2x$.

Step 1: Sketch one cycle of $y = \sin 2x$. Use five points in the pattern *zero - max - zero - min - zero*.

Step 2: Since $h = \frac{\pi}{3}$ and $k = -\frac{3}{2}$, translate the graph $\frac{\pi}{3}$ units to the right and $\frac{3}{2}$ units down. Extend the periodic pattern from 0 to 2π. Sketch the graph.

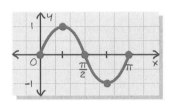

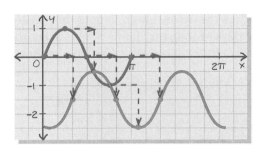

The graph of $y = \sin 2\left(x - \frac{\pi}{3}\right) - \frac{3}{2}$ is shown in red above.

4. Sketch the graph of $y = -3 \sin 2\left(x - \frac{\pi}{3}\right) - \frac{3}{2}$ in the interval from 0 to 2π. How does this graph differ from the graph in Example 3?

5. **Try This** Sketch each graph in the interval from 0 to 2π.
   a. $y = -\sin\left(x + \frac{\pi}{2}\right) + 2$
   b. $y = 2 \cos \frac{\pi}{2}(x + 1) - 3$

6. **a.** Write $y = 3 \sin (2x - 4) + 1$ in the form $y = a \sin b(x - h) + k$. (*Hint:* Factor where possible.)
   b. Find the amplitude and period. Describe any translations.

EXERCISES

1. **a.** Open-ended Sketch your own periodic function. State its amplitude and period. Then sketch a translation of your function 3 units down and 4 units to the left.
   b. Suppose your original function is $f(x)$. Describe your translation using the form $g(x) = f(x - h) + k$.

Use the function $f(x)$ shown at the right. Graph each of the following translations.

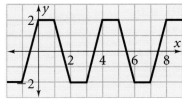

2. $f(x) + 1$

3. $f(x) - 3$

4. $f(x + 2)$

5. $f(x - 1) + 2$

Find the amplitude and period of each function. Describe any phase shift and vertical shift in the graph.

6. $y = 3 \sin x + 1$

7. $y = -\cos (x - \pi) - 3$

8. $y = \cos 2\left(x + \frac{\pi}{2}\right) - 2$

9. $y = -5 \cos \pi(x - 3) + 2$

10. $y = \sin (2x + 6) - 2$

11. $y = 3 \sin \left(\frac{\pi}{2}x - \pi\right)$

Write a cosine function for each graph.

12.
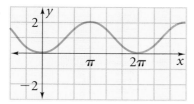

13.
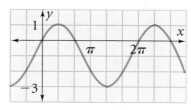

14.
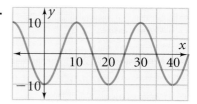

Sketch the graph of each function in the interval from 0 to 2π.

15. $y = \sin x + 3$

16. $y = 3 \sin \frac{1}{2}x$

17. $y = \frac{1}{2} \sin 2x - 1$

18. $y = \sin 3\left(x + \frac{\pi}{3}\right)$

19. $y = -2 \sin \left(x + \frac{\pi}{4}\right)$

20. $y = 2 \sin \left(x - \frac{\pi}{6}\right) + 2$

21. The graphs of $y = \sin x$ and $y = \cos x$ are shown at the right.
  a. What phase shift will translate the cosine function onto the sine function? Write this as an equation in the form $\sin x = \cos (x - h)$.
  b. What phase shift will translate the sine function onto the cosine function? Express your answer in the form $\cos x = \sin (x - h)$.

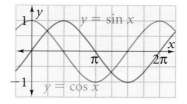

22. The table shows water temperatures at a buoy in the Gulf of Mexico on several days of the year. Plot the data. Then write a cosine model for the data.

Water Temperatures in the Gulf of Mexico

Day of the year	16	47	75	106	136	176	197	228	259	289	320	350
Temperature	71	69	70	73	77	82	85	86	84	82	78	74

Source: *The USA Today Weather Almanac*

23. a. Critical Thinking Use a sine function to model the normal daily high temperature in New Orleans. Use the data given in Example 2 on page 605.
  b. How do the sine and cosine models differ?
  c. Estimation Use your sine model to estimate the high temperature in New Orleans on September 1 (day 244).
  d. Graph your model. Use it to estimate the first day of the year that the high temperature is likely to reach 70°F.

607

In Chapter 9 you studied three trigonometric functions—sine, cosine, and tangent. Three other functions—cosecant, secant, and cotangent—are reciprocals of the three you have used.

Cosecant, Secant, and Cotangent Functions

The cosecant (csc), secant (sec), and cotangent (cot) functions are defined as reciprocals. For all real numbers θ (except those that make a denominator zero):

$$\csc\theta = \frac{1}{\sin\theta} \qquad \sec\theta = \frac{1}{\cos\theta} \qquad \cot\theta = \frac{1}{\tan\theta}$$

1. a. Suppose $\sin\theta = \frac{5}{13}$. Find $\csc\theta$.

   b. Simplify $\frac{1}{\frac{3}{4}}$. What is the reciprocal of $\frac{3}{4}$?

Example 1

Find the value of $\csc 60°$.

Method 1: Use the unit circle to find the exact value of $\sin 60°$. Then write the reciprocal.

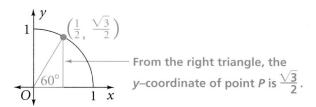

From the right triangle, the y–coordinate of point P is $\frac{\sqrt{3}}{2}$.

Since $\sin 60° = \frac{\sqrt{3}}{2}$, $\csc 60° = \frac{2}{\sqrt{3}}$.

Method 2: Use a calculator. Set it in degree mode.

1/sin 60
         1.154700538

Use the definition.
$\csc 60° = \dfrac{1}{\sin 60°}$

2. Graphing Calculator Evaluate each expression shown below. Which one gives the correct value of $\csc 60°$?
   A. $\sin 60^{-1}$ **B.** $(\sin 60)^{-1}$ **C.** $\sin^{-1} 60$

3. a. In Question 2, which expression represents $\sin\left(\frac{1}{60}\right)°$?
   b. Which expression represents the angle whose sine is 60?

4. Try This Find each value.
   a. $\sec 135°$ **b.** $\cot 30°$ **c.** $\csc(-150°)$

5. Explain why each expression is undefined.
   a. $\csc 180°$ **b.** $\sec 90°$ **c.** $\cot 0°$

You can also evaluate the reciprocal functions in radians.

6. Evaluate each expression. Use radian mode.
   a. $\cot \frac{\pi}{3}$ **b.** $\sec 2$ **c.** $\csc (-1.5)$

Example 2

Sketch the graphs of $y = \sin x$ and $y = \csc x$ in the interval from 0 to 2π.

Method 1:   Make a table of values.

x	0	$\frac{\pi}{6}$	$\frac{\pi}{3}$	$\frac{\pi}{2}$	$\frac{2\pi}{3}$	$\frac{5\pi}{6}$	π	$\frac{7\pi}{6}$	$\frac{4\pi}{3}$	$\frac{3\pi}{2}$	$\frac{5\pi}{3}$	$\frac{11\pi}{6}$	2π
$\sin x$	0	0.5	0.9	1	0.9	0.5	0	−0.5	−0.9	−1	−0.9	−0.5	0
$\csc x$	−	2	−1.2	1	−1.2	2	−	−2	−1.2	−1	−1.2	2	−

Plot the points and sketch the graphs.

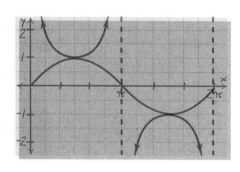

$y = \csc x$ will have a vertical asymptote wherever its denominator ($\sin x$) is 0.

Method 2:   Use a graphing calculator.

Because the graph has vertical asymptotes, select Dot mode.

```
Y1=sinX
Y2=1/sinX
Y3=
Y4=
Y5=
Y6=
Y7=
Y8=
```

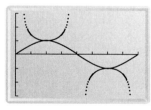

```
Xmin=0
Xmax=2π
Xscl=π/4
Ymin=−3
Ymax=3
Yscl=1
```

7. What are the domain, range, and period of $y = \csc x$?

8. Each branch of $y = \csc x$ has either a relative minimum or a relative maximum.
   a. What is the relative minimum on the interval $0 \leq x \leq \pi$?
   b. What is the relative maximum on the interval $\pi \leq x \leq 2\pi$?

9. Use the relationship $\csc x = \frac{1}{\sin x}$ to explain why each statement is true.
   a. When the graph of $y = \sin x$ is positive, so is the graph of $y = \csc x$.
   b. When the graph of $y = \sin x$ is near a y-value of -1, so is the graph of $y = \csc x$.

You can use the reciprocal functions to solve right triangles. They are often used when it is easier to multiply than to divide. When $\angle A$ is acute, the following equations are equivalent to the ones on page 608.

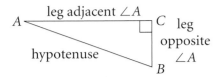

$$\csc A = \frac{\text{hypotenuse}}{\text{leg opposite } \angle A} \quad \sec A = \frac{\text{hypotenuse}}{\text{leg adjacent } \angle A} \quad \cot A = \frac{\text{leg adjacent } \angle A}{\text{leg opposite } \angle A}$$

Example 3

When a crane's boom is elevated to an angle of 70°, it extends to a height of 128 ft. How far is the crane's cab from the point where materials will be dropped?

$$\cot 70° = \frac{d}{128}$$

$$128 \cot 70° = d$$

$$46.6 \approx d$$

The crane's cab should be about 47 ft from the drop point.

128 ft

70°

d

10. a. Suppose you must find the length of the boom in Example 3. Which trigonometric functions could you use? Which one do you think is most convenient? Why?
   b. Find the length of the boom.

EXERCISES

Evaluate each expression. Write your answer in exact form. When appropriate, also state it as a decimal rounded to the nearest hundredth. If the expression is undefined, state this.

1. $\sec 45°$	**2.** $\cot 60°$	**3.** $\cot 90°$	**4.** $\sec 180°$
5. $\csc 0°$	**6.** $\cot 0°$	**7.** $\csc 60°$	**8.** $\cot 30°$
9. $\sec 90°$	**10.** $\csc 30°$	**11.** $\sec 60°$	**12.** $\csc 45°$
13. $\cot (-45°)$	**14.** $\sec (-30°)$	**15.** $\csc (-90°)$	**16.** $\sec (-180°)$

17. a. Radio tower A radio tower has supporting cables attached to it at points 100 ft above the ground. Write a model for the length d of each supporting cable as a function of the angle θ that it makes with the ground.
   b. Find d when $\theta = 60°$ and when $\theta = 50°$.

18. a. Graph $y = \cos x$ and $y = \sec x$ on the same axes.
   b. For each function, state the domain, the range and the period.
   c. For which values of x does $\cos x = \sec x$? **Justify** your answer.
   d. Writing Compare the two graphs. How are they alike? How are they different?
   e. Is the value of $\sec x$ positive when $\cos x$ is positive and negative when $\cos x$ is negative? **Justify** your answer.

100 ft

θ

d

19. Hot-Air Ballooning An observer on the ground at point A watches a hot-air balloon ascend. The observer is 120 ft from the launch point B. As the balloon rises, the distance d from the observer to the balloon increases.
  a. Write a model for $m\angle A$.
  b. Find $m\angle A$ if $d = 150$ ft. Round to the nearest degree.
  c. Find $m\angle A$ if $d = 200$ ft. Round to the nearest degree.

Graph each function in the interval from 0 to 2π.

20. $y = \sin 2\theta$ **21.** $y = \csc 2\theta$

22. $y = \csc 2\left(\theta - \frac{\pi}{2}\right)$ **23.** $y = \cos 2\theta$

24. $y = \sec 2\theta$ **25.** $y = \sec 2\left(\theta + \frac{\pi}{2}\right)$

Solve each equation in the interval from 0 to 2π.

26. $\sec \theta = 2$ **27.** $\csc \theta = -1$ **28.** $\cot \theta = 10$

29. $\csc \theta = 3$ **30.** $\cot \theta = -10$ **31.** $\sec \theta = 1$

32. In $\triangle ABC$, find each value in fraction and in decimal form. Round to the nearest hundredth.
  a. $\sin A$ **b.** $\sec A$ **c.** $\cot A$
  d. $\csc B$ **e.** $\sec B$ **f.** $\tan B$

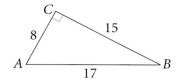

33. In $\triangle PQR$, $\angle R$ is a right angle, $PR = 5$, and $\cot P = \frac{5}{12}$. Draw a sketch. Find the values of the other five trigonometric functions of $\angle P$.

Find each length x. Use a reciprocal trigonometric function and round to the nearest tenth.

34.
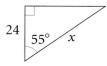

35.
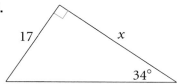

36.

37. a. Graph $y = \tan x$ and $y = \cot x$ on the same axes.
  b. For each function, state the domain, the range, the period, and the asymptotes.
  c. *Writing* Compare the two graphs. How are they alike? How are they different?
  d. *Geometry* The graph of the cotangent function can be reflected about a line to graph the tangent function. Name at least two lines that have this property.

Trigonometric Identities

A trigonometric identity is an equation containing a trigonometric expression. The equation is true for all values except those for which any expression is undefined. Using the Pythagorean Theorem and the unit circle at the right, you can see that $x^2 + y^2 = 1$. If you substitute $\cos \theta$ for x and $\sin \theta$ for y, you find that $\cos^2 \theta + \sin^2 \theta = 1$ for all values of θ.

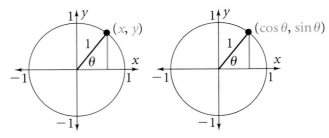

The equation $\cos^2 \theta + \sin^2 \theta = 1$ is a Pythagorean identity. The Pythagorean identities, along with identities you have already studied, are summarized below.

Trigonometric Identities

Tangent and Cotangent Identities

$$\tan \theta = \frac{\sin \theta}{\cos \theta} \qquad \cot \theta = \frac{\cos \theta}{\sin \theta}$$

Reciprocal Identities

$$\csc \theta = \frac{1}{\sin \theta} \qquad \sec \theta = \frac{1}{\cos \theta} \qquad \cot \theta = \frac{1}{\tan \theta}$$

Pythagorean Identities

$$\cos^2 \theta + \sin^2 \theta = 1 \qquad 1 + \tan^2 \theta = \sec^2 \theta \qquad 1 + \cot^2 \theta = \csc^2 \theta$$

One way to simplify a trigonometric expression is to write it in terms of sines and cosines.

Example 1

Simplify the trigonometric expression $\csc \theta \tan \theta$.

$$\csc \theta \tan \theta = \frac{1}{\sin \theta} \cdot \frac{\sin \theta}{\cos \theta} \qquad \longleftarrow \text{Use the reciprocal and tangent identities.}$$

$$= \frac{\sin \theta}{\sin \theta \cos \theta} \qquad \longleftarrow \text{Multiply.}$$

$$= \frac{1}{\cos \theta} \qquad \longleftarrow \text{Simplify.}$$

$$= \sec \theta \qquad \longleftarrow \text{Use the reciprocal identity.}$$

So, $\csc \theta \tan \theta = \sec \theta$.

1. Try This Simplify the trigonometric expression $\sec \theta \cot \theta$.

You can use this skill to verify the other Pythagorean identities.

Example 2

Verify the identity $1 + \tan^2 \theta = \sec^2 \theta$.

$$1 + \tan^2 \theta \overset{?}{=} \sec^2 \theta$$

$$1 + \left(\frac{\sin \theta}{\cos \theta}\right)^2 \overset{?}{=} \frac{1}{\cos^2 \theta} \quad \longleftarrow \text{Write each trigonometric expression in terms of sines and cosines.}$$

$$1 + \frac{\sin^2 \theta}{\cos^2 \theta} \overset{?}{=} \frac{1}{\cos^2 \theta}$$

$$\cos^2 \theta + \sin^2 \theta = 1 \quad \longleftarrow \text{Multiply by } \cos^2 \theta.$$

$$1 = 1 \quad \longleftarrow \text{Simplify.}$$

So, $1 + \tan^2 \theta = \sec^2 \theta$.

You can use the Pythagorean identities in various forms to simplify expressions. For example, another form of $\cos^2 \theta + \sin^2 \theta = 1$ is $\cos^2 \theta = 1 - \sin^2 \theta$. Thus, you can replace $1 - \sin^2 \theta$ with $\cos^2 \theta$.

2. Use a Pythagorean identity to simplify each expression.

    a. $1 - \cos^2 \theta$ **b.** $\sec^2 \theta - 1$ **c.** $1 - \text{cst}^2 \theta$

EXERCISES

Simplify each expression.

1. $\tan \theta \cos \theta$ **2.** $\frac{\tan \theta}{\sin \theta}$ **3.** $1 + \cot^2 \theta$ **4.** $\frac{\tan \theta \cos \theta}{\sin \theta}$

5. $\sec^2 \theta - 1$ **6.** $(\sin \theta + \cos \theta)^2$ **7.** $\frac{\tan^2 \theta}{\sin^2 \theta}$ **8.** $\frac{\tan^2 \theta}{1 - \sec^2 \theta}$

9. $\frac{\cot \theta}{\cos \theta}$ **10.** $\sin \theta \csc \theta$ **11.** $\tan \theta \cot \theta$ **12.** $\frac{\tan^2 \theta}{\sec^2 \theta}$

13. a. Simplify $\frac{\sin^2 \theta}{1 - \cos \theta} \cdot \left(\textit{Hint: Multiply by } \frac{1 + \cos \theta}{1 + \cos \theta}.\right)$

    b. **Writing** Explain why it helps to multiply by $\frac{1 + \cos \theta}{1 + \cos \theta}$.

Verify each identity.

14. $\tan^2 \theta - \sin^2 \theta = \tan^2 \theta \sin^2 \theta$ **15.** $\frac{\cos \theta}{\cot^2 \theta} = \sin \theta \tan \theta$

16. $\cos^2 \theta + \tan^2 \theta \cos^2 \theta = 1$ **17.** $\frac{\sin \theta}{1 + \cos \theta} = \frac{1 - \cos \theta}{\sin \theta}$

18. $\frac{\sin \theta}{\csc \theta} + \frac{\cos \theta}{\sec \theta} = 1$ **19.** $\cos^2 \theta - \sin^2 \theta = 1 - 2 \sin^2 \theta$

20. $(1 + \sec \theta)(1 - \cos \theta) = \tan \theta \sin \theta$ **21.** $\tan^2 \theta \csc \theta = \frac{\sin \theta}{1 - \sin^2 \theta}$

22. **Graphing Calculator** Graph $y = \sec^2 \theta \csc^2 \theta$ and $y = \csc^2 \theta + \sec^2 \theta$ on the same screen. What do you notice?

<table>
<tr><td>Topic</td><td rowspan="2"></td></tr>
<tr><td>4</td></tr>
</table>

Trigonometric Equations

A trigonometric equation is an equation that includes at least one trigonometric function. A solution of a trigonometric equation is any value of the variable for which the equation is true.

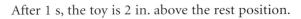

Example 1

Physics The spring at the right is stretched and released. The equation $h = -4 \cos \frac{2\pi}{3} t$ models the toy's height h in inches above or below the rest position as a function of time t in seconds. When will the toy first be 2 in. above the rest position?

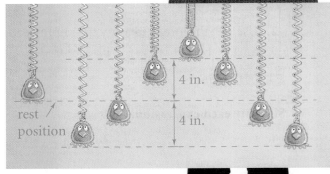

$$h = -4 \cos \frac{2\pi}{3} t$$

$$2 = -4 \cos \frac{2\pi}{3} t \quad \longleftarrow \text{Substitute 2 for } h.$$

$$-\frac{2}{4} = \cos \frac{2\pi}{3} t \quad \longleftarrow \text{Divide by } -4.$$

$$-\frac{1}{2} = \cos \frac{2\pi}{3} t \quad \longleftarrow \text{Simplify.}$$

$$\frac{2\pi}{3} t = \cos^{-1}\left(-\frac{1}{2}\right) \quad \longleftarrow \text{Find the angle whose cosine is } -\frac{1}{2}.$$

$$\frac{2\pi}{3} t = 2.0944 \quad \longleftarrow \text{Use a calculator.}$$

$$t = \frac{3}{2\pi} (2.0944) \quad \longleftarrow \text{Solve for } t.$$

$$= 1$$

After 1 s, the toy is 2 in. above the rest position.

1. How could you use a graphing calculator to solve Example 1?

2. **Try This** When will the toy in Example 1 first be 2 in. below the rest position? 4 in. below the rest position?

3. You found that the toy in Example 1 is 2 in. above the rest position after 1 s. Will it ever be at that same position again? Explain.

The *complete solution* of a trigonometric equation is an expression for all possible real solutions to the equation.

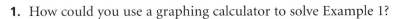

4. Show the angles 30°, 150°, 390°, and 510°, in standard position, on the unit circle. For each angle, what is the y-coordinate of the point at which the terminal side intersects the circle?

5. Use your calculator to evaluate sin 30° and sin 150°. Without your calculator, predict the values of sin 390° and sin 510°.

Angles of θ and $180° - \theta$ have the same sine value. For example, two solutions of $\sin \theta = \frac{1}{2}$ are 30° and 150°. All the angles that are coterminal with 30° and 150° will also be solutions. The complete solution of $\sin \theta = \frac{1}{2}$ is $30° + n \cdot 360°$ and $150° + n \cdot 360°$, where n is any integer.

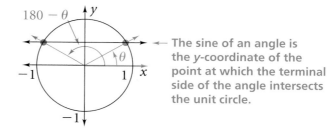

The sine of an angle is the y-coordinate of the point at which the terminal side of the angle intersects the unit circle.

Example 2

Find the complete solution of $2 \cos \theta = 1$.

First solve the equation for θ.

$2 \cos \theta = 1$

$\cos \theta = \frac{1}{2}$

$\theta = \cos^{-1} \frac{1}{2}$

$\quad = 60°$

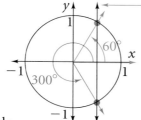

The cosine of an angle is the x-coordinate of the point at which the terminal side of the angle intersects the unit circle.

Show the angle 60° on a unit circle.

Since $\cos 60° = \frac{1}{2}$, draw the line $x = \frac{1}{2}$ on your diagram. The other point on the unit circle at which $x = \frac{1}{2}$ is at the intersection of the terminal side of the angle $360° - 60°$, or 300°.

The complete solution of $2 \cos \theta = 1$ is $60° + n \cdot 360°$ and $300° + n \cdot 360°$.

6. Try This Find the complete solution of $\cos \theta = -\frac{1}{2}$.

Sometimes you can solve equations by factoring.

Example 3

Find the complete solution of $2 \cos \theta \sin \theta + \sin \theta = 0$.

$2 \cos \theta \sin \theta + \sin \theta = 0$

$\sin \theta (2 \cos \theta + 1) = 0$ ← Use the zero-product property.

$\sin \theta = 0$ or $\cos \theta = -\frac{1}{2}$

$\theta = 0°$ and $(180° - 0°)$ $\quad \theta = 120°$ and $(360° - 120°)$

$\theta = 0°$ and $180°$ $\quad\quad\quad \theta = 120°$ and $240°$

$\theta = 0° + n \cdot 360°$, $120° + n \cdot 360°$, $180° + n \cdot 360°$, and $240° + n \cdot 360°$

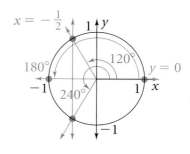

The complete solution of $2 \cos \theta \sin \theta + \sin \theta = 0$ is $0° + n \cdot 360°$, $120° + n \cdot 360°$, $180° + n \cdot 360°$, and $240° + n \cdot 360°$.

7. Try This Find the complete solution of $\sin \theta \cos \theta - \cos \theta = 0$.

EXERCISES

1. Each diagram shows one solution to the equation below it. Find the complete solution of each equation.

a.

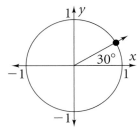

$$5 \sin \theta = 1 + 3 \sin \theta$$

b.

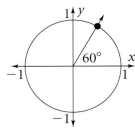

$$6 \cos \theta - 5 = -2$$

c.

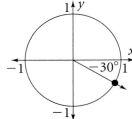

$$4 \sin \theta + 3 = 1$$

Find the complete solution of each equation. Use degrees.

2. $\cos \theta = 0$

3. $2 \sin \theta = 1$

4. $\cos \theta = \dfrac{\sqrt{3}}{2}$

5. $2 \sin \theta = \sqrt{3}$

6. $2 \sin \theta = \sqrt{2}$

7. $\sin^2 \theta - 1 = \cos^2 \theta$

8. $2 \cos \theta = \sqrt{2}$

9. $2 \cos \theta = -\sqrt{3}$

10. $2 \sin \theta = 3$

11. $\sqrt{2} \cos \theta - \sqrt{2} = 0$

12. $2 \sin \theta = -1$

13. $2 \sin \theta = -\sqrt{3}$

Solve each trigonometric equation for θ.

Sample
$$y = 2 \sin 3\theta + 4$$
$$\sin 3\theta = \frac{y - 4}{2}$$
$$3\theta = \sin^{-1}\left(\frac{y - 4}{2}\right)$$
$$\theta = \frac{1}{3} \sin^{-1}\left(\frac{y - 4}{2}\right)$$

14. $y = 2 \sin \theta$

15. $y = \cos 2\theta$

16. $y = 3 \sin (\theta + 2)$

17. $y = -4 \cos 2\pi\theta$

18. $y = \cos \theta + 1$

19. $y = 2 \cos \pi\theta + 1$

20. Writing Describe the similarities and differences in solving the equations $4x + 1 = 3$ and $4 \sin \theta + 1 = 3$.

21. Physics Jonathan and his friend set up a spring experiment similar to the one in Example 1. In their experiment, the toy bobbed up and down 4 cm once every 4 s.
  a. Write an equation for the height h in centimeters of the weight above or below the resting point in terms of time t in seconds.
  b. Solve your equation for t.
  c. Find the times at which the toy is first at a height of 1 cm, 2 cm, and 3 cm above the rest position.

22. Critical Thinking The graphing calculator screen at the right shows a portion of the graphs of $y = \sin \theta$ and $y = 0.5$.
  a. Write the complete solution of $\sin \theta \geq 0.5$.
  b. Write the complete solution of $\sin \theta \leq 0.5$.

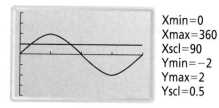

Xmin=0
Xmax=360
Xscl=90
Ymin=-2
Ymax=2
Yscl=0.5

23. Find the complete solution of $\sin^2 \theta + 2 \sin \theta + 1 = 0$.
(*Hint:* How would you solve $x^2 + 2x + 1 = 0$?)

Write the complete solution of the given equation. Express your answer in degrees.

24. $(\sin \theta)(\cos \theta) = 0$

25. $(\sin \theta)(\sin \theta + 1) = 0$

26. $(\cos \theta)(\cos \theta + 1) = 0$

27. $(\cos \theta)(\cos \theta - 1) = 0$

28. $(\sin \theta - 1)(\sin \theta + 1) = 0$

29. $(\cos \theta + 1)(\cos \theta + 1) = 0$

30. $2 \sin^2 \theta + \cos \theta - 1 = 0$

31. $2 \sin^2 \theta - 1 = 0$

32. $2 \sin \theta + 1 = \csc \theta$

33. $\sin^2 \theta + 3 \sin \theta = 0$

34. $\sin \theta = -\sin \theta \cos \theta$

35. $2 \sin^2 \theta - 3 \sin \theta = 2$

36. Geometry A *segment* of a circle is the region formed by an arc of a circle and the line segment joining the endpoints of the arc. (The measure of the arc must be between 0 and 2π.) The expression below gives the area K in square feet of a segment in terms of r, the radius of the circle in feet, and θ, the radian measure of the arc.

$$K = \frac{r^2}{2}(\theta - \sin \theta)$$

50 ft

  a. Suppose a circular park has radius of 50 ft. Write an equation for the area of any segment of the park using $r = 50$.
  b. Use trial and error to approximate the measure of θ that makes the area of the segment 1500 ft^2.

37. Standardized Test Prep Suppose $a > 0$. Under what conditions for a and b will $a \sin \theta = b$ have exactly two solutions in the interval $0 \leq \theta < 2\pi$?
  A. $a = b$ **B.** $b > a$ **C.** $a = -b$ **D.** $a > b > -a$

38. a. Open-ended Write three trigonometric equations whose complete solution is $\pi + 2\pi n$.
  b. Describe how you formed the equations in part (a).

39. Tides One day the tides at a point in Maine could be modeled by $h = 5 \cos \frac{2\pi}{13} t$, where h is the height of the tide in feet above the mean water line and t is the number of hours past midnight.
  a. At what times that day will the tide be 3 ft above the mean water line?
  b. At what times that day will the tide be *at least* 3 ft above the mean water line?

40. Electricity The function $I = 40 \sin 60\pi t$ models the current I (in amps) that an electric generator is producing after t seconds. When is the first time that the current will reach 20 amps? -20 amps?

Applying Trigonometric Identities

The trigonometric identities below combine the measures of two angles, A and B.

Angle Sum Identities

$\sin (A + B) = \sin A \cos B + \cos A \sin B$

$\cos (A + B) = \cos A \cos B - \sin A \sin B$

Example 1

Find the exact value of $\sin 105°$ using the fact that $105° = 60° + 45°$.

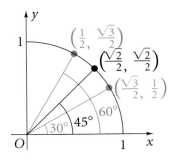

$$\sin (A + B) = \sin A \cos B + \cos A \sin B$$

$$\sin (60° + 45°) = \sin 60° \cos 45° + \cos 60° \sin 45°$$

$$= \frac{\sqrt{3}}{2} \cdot \frac{\sqrt{2}}{2} + \frac{1}{2} \cdot \frac{\sqrt{2}}{2}$$

$$= \frac{\sqrt{6} + \sqrt{2}}{4}$$

Substitute $60°$ for A and $45°$ for B.

So, $\sin 105° = \dfrac{\sqrt{6} + \sqrt{2}}{4}$.

1. **Try This** Find the exact value of $\cos 105°$.

Angle difference identities can be derived from the angle sum identities by replacing B with $-B$. So, we need formulas for $\sin (-\theta)$ and $\cos (-\theta)$.

2. **Open-ended** You know that $\sin 30° = 0.5$ and $\sin (-30°) = -0.5$, so $\sin (-30°) = -\sin 30°$. Choose several other values of θ and show that $\sin (-\theta) = -\sin \theta$ for those values.

3. The graph of $y = \sin \theta$ is symmetric with respect to the origin. Explain how this shows that $\sin (-\theta) = -\sin \theta$.

4. Choose several values of θ and show that $\cos (-\theta) = \cos \theta$ for those values.

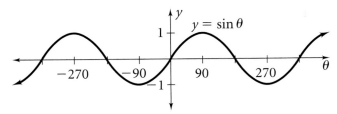

5. Sketch a graph of $y = \cos \theta$ and use it to explain why $\cos (-\theta) = \cos \theta$.

Negative Angle Identities

$\sin (-\theta) = -\sin \theta$ $\qquad$ $\cos (-\theta) = \cos \theta$

Here is a derivation of the angle difference identity for sine.

$$\sin (A + B) = \sin A \cos B + \cos A \sin B \qquad \text{angle sum identity for sine}$$
$$\sin (A + (-B)) = \sin A \cos (-B) + \cos A \sin (-B) \qquad \text{Substitute } -B \text{ for } B.$$
$$\sin (A - B) = \sin A \cos B + \cos A (-\sin B) \qquad \text{Use the negative angle identities.}$$
$$= \sin A \cos B - \cos A \sin B$$

6. Substitute $-B$ for B in the identity for $\cos (A + B)$ to obtain an identity for $\cos (A - B)$.

> ### Angle Difference Identities
> ....
>
> $$\sin (A - B) = \sin A \cos B - \cos A \sin B$$
>
> $$\cos (A - B) = \cos A \cos B + \sin A \sin B$$

Example 2

Find a formula for $\cos (\theta - 90°)$. Use the identity for the cosine of the difference of two angles.

$$\cos (A - B) = \cos A \cos B + \sin A \sin B$$
$$\cos (\theta - 90°) = \cos \theta \cos 90° + \sin \theta \sin 90° \qquad \text{Substitute } \theta \text{ for } A \text{ and } 90° \text{ for } B.$$
$$= (\cos \theta) \cdot 0 + (\sin \theta) \cdot 1 \qquad \cos 90° = 0 \text{ and } \sin 90° = 1$$
$$= \sin \theta$$

The formula $\cos (\theta - 90°) = \sin \theta$ shows that the graph of $y = \cos \theta$ shifted 90° to the right is the graph of $y = \sin \theta$.

7. a. Try This Write a formula for $\sin (\theta - 90°)$.
   b. Graphing Calculator Graph $y = \sin (\theta - 90°)$ and the function defined by your expression from part (a) to check your solution.

If you let $\theta = A = B$ in the sum identities, you can derive the following double angle identities.

> ### Double Angle Identities
> ....
>
> $$\sin 2\theta = 2 \sin \theta \cos \theta \qquad \cos 2\theta = \cos^2 \theta - \sin^2 \theta$$

Example 3

Use a double angle identity to find the exact value of $\cos 120°$.

$$\cos 120° = \cos 2(60°) = \cos^2 60° - \sin^2 60° = \left(\frac{1}{2}\right)^2 - \left(\frac{\sqrt{3}}{2}\right)^2 = -\frac{1}{2}$$

8. Use a double angle identity to **verify** that $\sin 120° = \dfrac{\sqrt{3}}{2}$.

9. Show that $\cos 2x = 2 \cos x$ is not an identity by finding a value of x for which $\cos 2x \neq 2 \cos x$.

Example 4

Find the exact value of $\tan 75°$ by using the angle sum identities for sine and cosine.

$$\tan 75° = \frac{\sin (30° + 45°)}{\cos (30° + 45°)}$$

$$= \frac{\sin 30° \cos 45° + \cos 30° \sin 45°}{\cos 30° \cos 45° - \sin 30° \sin 45°}$$

$$= \frac{\dfrac{1}{2} \cdot \dfrac{\sqrt{2}}{2} + \dfrac{\sqrt{3}}{2} \cdot \dfrac{\sqrt{2}}{2}}{\dfrac{\sqrt{3}}{2} \cdot \dfrac{\sqrt{2}}{2} - \dfrac{1}{2} \cdot \dfrac{\sqrt{2}}{2}} = \frac{\sqrt{2} + \sqrt{6}}{\sqrt{6} - \sqrt{2}}$$

10. Try This Use the angle difference identities for sine and cosine to find the exact value for $\tan (-300°)$.

EXERCISES

Find each exact value. Use a sum or difference identity.

1. $\cos 135°$ **2.** $\sin 15°$ **3.** $\sin 225°$ **4.** $\cos 240°$

5. $\sin (-15°)$ **6.** $\cos (-15°)$ **7.** $\sin 390°$ **8.** $\cos 390°$

9. $\cos 405°$ **10.** $\sin 75°$ **11.** $\cos (-300°)$ **12.** $\sin (-300°)$

Find each exact value. Use the identity $\tan \theta = \dfrac{\sin \theta}{\cos \theta}$ and the sum or difference identities.

13. $\tan 135°$ **14.** $\tan 15°$ **15.** $\tan 105°$ **16.** $\tan 240°$

Write an identity involving only $\sin \theta$ or only $\cos \theta$ for each expression. Use a sum or difference identity.

17. $\cos (180° - \theta)$ **18.** $\cos (90° - \theta)$ **19.** $\sin (\theta - 90°)$

20. $\cos (270° + \theta)$ **21.** $\sin (180° - \theta)$ **22.** $\sin (270° + \theta)$

23. Show that the equation $\sin (A + B) = \sin A + \sin B$ is *not* an identity by finding values for A and B for which the equation is false.

24. a. Graphing Calculator Graph $y = \sin 2x$ and $y = 2 \sin x$ on the same calculator screen.
     b. Does $\sin 2x = 2 \sin x$ for all values of x? Is $\sin 2x = 2 \sin x$ an identity? Explain.
     c. Does $\sin 2x = 2 \sin x$ for any values of x? If so, what are they?

Mental Math Use mental math to find the value of each trigonometric expression.

25. $\cos 50° \cos 40° - \sin 50° \sin 40°$

26. $\sin 80° \cos 35° - \cos 80° \sin 35°$

27. $\sin 100° \cos 170° + \cos 100° \sin 170°$

28. $\cos 183° \cos 93° + \sin 183° \sin 93°$

29. a. Derive the identity for $\sin 2\theta$ using the angle sum identity for sine.
   b. Derive the identity for $\cos 2\theta$ using the angle sum identity for cosine.

30. a. *Critical Thinking* Use the double angle identity for cosine and a Pythagorean identity to **verify** that $\cos 2\theta = 1 - 2 \sin^2 \theta$.
   b. *Critical Thinking* Use the double angle identity for cosine and a Pythagorean identity to **verify** that $\cos 2\theta = 2 \cos^2 \theta - 1$.

Verify each identity using the angle sum and difference identities.

31. $\sin \left(x + \frac{\pi}{3}\right) + \sin \left(x - \frac{\pi}{3}\right) = \sin x$

32. $\sin \left(\frac{3\pi}{2} - x\right) = -\cos x$

Use identities to write each equation in terms of the single angle θ. Then find the complete solution of each equation.

33. $4 \sin 2\theta - 3 \cos \theta = 0$

34. $2 \sin 2\theta - 3 \sin \theta = 0$

35. $\sin (\theta + 60°) + \sin (\theta - 60°) = \frac{1}{2}$

36. $\sin 2\theta \sin \theta = \cos \theta$

37. $\cos 2\theta = -2 \cos^2 \theta$

38. $\cos (\theta + 30°) - \cos (\theta - 30°) = 1$

39. *Standardized Test Prep* Which of the following expressions is not equivalent to $\cos \theta$?
   A. $-\sin (\theta - 90°)$ **B.** $-\cos (-\theta)$ **C.** $\sin (\theta + 90°)$
   D. $-\cos (\theta + 180°)$ **E.** $\sin (90° - \theta)$

40. *Open-ended* Suppose $f(\theta) = \sin \theta$ and $g(\theta) = \sin (\theta + a)$, with $a \neq 0$.
   a. Choose three values for a so that f and g have the same graph.
   b. **Justify** your choices in part (a).

41. *Circular Gears* The diagram at the right shows a gear whose radius is 10 cm. Point A represents a 60° counterclockwise rotation of point $P(10, 0)$. Point B represents a θ-degree rotation of point A. The coordinates of B are $(10 \cos (\theta + 60°), 10 \sin (\theta + 60°))$. Write these coordinates in terms of $\cos \theta$ and $\sin \theta$.

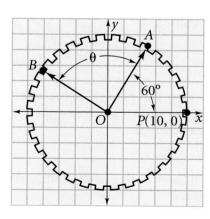

In Lesson 9-7, you applied the Law of Sines and the Law of Cosines to find the missing measures of triangles. The proofs of these laws are shown below.

Proving the Law of Sines

Show that in $\triangle ABC$,

$$\frac{\sin A}{a} = \frac{\sin B}{b} = \frac{\sin C}{c}.$$

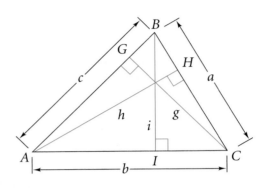

The altitude labeled i forms right $\triangle AIB$. In this triangle, $\sin A = \frac{i}{c}$. So, $i = c \sin A$.

$$\begin{aligned}
\text{area of } \triangle ABC &= \frac{1}{2} \cdot \text{base} \cdot \text{height} \\
&= \frac{1}{2} bi \\
&= \frac{1}{2} bc \sin A
\end{aligned}$$

Similarly, you can use the altitude g to show that

$$\text{area of } \triangle ABC = \frac{1}{2} ac \sin B.$$

Also, using altitude h,

$$\text{area of } \triangle ABC = \frac{1}{2} ab \sin C.$$

These three expressions for the area of $\triangle ABC$ must be equal.

$$\frac{1}{2} bc \sin A = \frac{1}{2} ac \sin B = \frac{1}{2} ab \sin C \qquad \longleftarrow \textbf{Multiply by } \frac{2}{abc}.$$

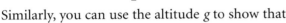

$$\frac{\sin A}{a} = \frac{\sin B}{b} = \frac{\sin C}{c}$$

The length of an altitude of a triangle is also used in the following proof of the Law of Cosines.

Proving the Law of Cosines

Show that in $\triangle ABC$,

$$a^2 = b^2 + c^2 - 2bc \cos A.$$

The altitude labeled h creates two right triangles. Since h and x are not involved in the Law of Cosines, find expressions for h and x that involve the other measures.

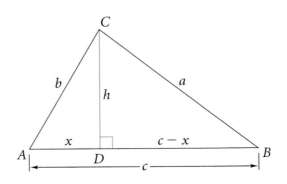

In right $\triangle ACD$, $\cos A = \frac{x}{b}$. So, $x = b \cos A$.

Using the Pythagorean theorem, you can write the square of h in the following two ways:

$$h^2 = b^2 - x^2 \quad \text{and} \quad h^2 = a^2 - (c - x)^2$$

Set these two expressions for h^2 equal to each other.

$$a^2 - (c - x)^2 = b^2 - x^2$$
$$a^2 - c^2 + 2cx - x^2 = b^2 - x^2$$
$$a^2 - c^2 + 2cx = b^2 \qquad \longleftarrow \text{Add } x^2 \text{ to each side.}$$
$$a^2 = b^2 + c^2 - 2cx \qquad \longleftarrow \text{Add } c^2 - 2cx \text{ to each side.}$$
$$a^2 = b^2 + c^2 - 2c\,(b \cos A) \qquad \longleftarrow \text{Substitute } b \cos A \text{ for } x.$$
$$a^2 = b^2 + c^2 - 2bc \cos A \qquad \longleftarrow \text{Simplify.}$$

EXERCISES

Three expressions for the area of a triangle are used in the proof of the Law of Sines. Use the expressions to find the areas of these triangles to the nearest tenth.

1.

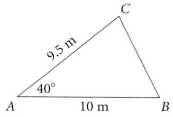

2.

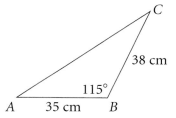

3.

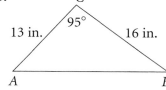

4. Critical Thinking Suppose you could change the size of $\angle C$ in Exercise 3. What size should the angle be to have a triangle with the greatest area?

5. Use the figure at the right to prove the following form of the Law of Cosines.

$$b^2 = a^2 + c^2 - 2ac \cos B$$

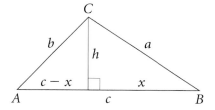

6. Some nylon fabric will be cut to cover the kite frame shown below. Diagonal AC is 29 in. What size should the angles be at A, B, C, and D?

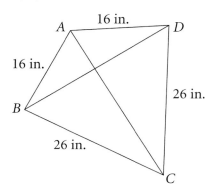

623

Topic 7

The Remainder Theorem

Given the polynomial $P(x) = 3x^3 + 8x^2 - 11x + 21$, you can find $P(2)$ by substituting 2 for x.

$P(2) = 3(2)^3 + 8(2)^2 - 11(2) + 21 = 24 + 32 - 22 + 21 = 55$

There is another way to find $P(2)$. Notice what happens when $P(x)$ is divided by $x - 2$.

$$\begin{array}{r l}
 & \quad 3x^2 + 14x + 17 \leftarrow \text{quotient} \\
\text{divisor} \rightarrow x - 2 & \overline{)3x^3 + 8x^2 - 11x + 21} \\
 & \underline{3x^3 - 6x^2} \\
 & \qquad 14x^2 - 11x \\
 & \qquad \underline{14x^2 - 28x} \\
 & \qquad\qquad 17x + 21 \\
 & \qquad\qquad \underline{17x - 34} \\
 & \qquad\qquad\qquad 55 \leftarrow \text{remainder}
\end{array}$$

The remainder equals $P(2)$. This happens because

$$\begin{aligned}
\text{dividend} &= \text{divisor} \times \text{quotient} + \text{remainder.} \\
P(x) &= (x - 2)(3x^2 + 14x + 17) + 55 \\
P(2) &= (2 - 2)[3(2)^2 + 14(2) + 17] + 55 \\
&= 0[3(2)^2 + 14(2) + 17] + 55 \\
&= 0 + 55 \\
&= 55
\end{aligned}$$

In general, when a polynomial $P(x)$ is divided by $x - a$ to get a quotient $Q(x)$ and a remainder r,

$$\begin{aligned}
P(x) &= (x - a)Q(x) + r \\
P(a) &= (a - a)Q(a) + r \\
&= 0 \cdot Q(a) + r \\
&= 0 + r \\
&= r.
\end{aligned}$$

We have just proved the **remainder theorem.**

Remainder Theorem

If a polynomial $P(x)$ of degree $n \geq 1$ is divided by $(x - a)$, where a is a constant, then the remainder is $P(a)$.

You can use the remainder theorem and synthetic division to find values of polynomials.

Example

Use synthetic division to find $P(-4)$ for the polynomial $P(x) = x^4 - 5x^2 + 4x + 12$.

By the remainder theorem, $P(-4)$ equals the remainder when $P(x)$ is divided by $x - (-4)$.

$-4\rfloor$	1	0	-5	4	12
		-4	16	-44	160
	1	-4	11	-40	172

The remainder is 172, so $P(-4) = 172$.

1. **Try This** Find $P(5)$, $P(-1)$, and $P(2)$ for the polynomial $P(x) = 2x^4 + 6x^3 - 5x^2 - 60$.

2. $x - 3$ is a factor of the polynomial $P(x) = x^3 - 2x^2 - 9x + 18$. What is the remainder when $P(x)$ is divided by $x - 3$? What is $P(3)$?

3. For $P(x) = x^3 - 4x^2 - 3x + 14$, $P(2) = 0$. What is the remainder when $P(x)$ is divided by $x - 2$? Is $x - 2$ a factor of $P(x)$?

You can use the remainder theorem to prove the factor theorem, which you learned about on page 270 and we restate here:

$x - a$ is a factor of a polynomial $P(x)$ if and only if $P(a) = 0$.

Proof: Suppose that $x - a$ is a factor of $P(x)$. Then the remainder when $P(x)$ is divided by $x - a$ is 0. By the remainder theorem, $P(a)$ is also 0.

Suppose, on the other hand, that $P(a) = 0$. The remainder theorem says that this is precisely what you get as remainder when you divide $P(x)$ by $x - a$. This means that $x - a$ divides $P(x)$ "evenly" or that $x - a$ is a factor of $P(x)$.

EXERCISES

Use synthetic division and the remainder theorem to find $P(a)$.

1. $P(x) = x^3 + 4x^2 - 8x - 6$; $a = -2$
2. $P(x) = x^3 + 12x^2 + 47x + 60$; $a = -5$
3. $P(x) = x^3 - 7x^2 + 15x - 9$; $a = 3$
4. $P(x) = 6x^3 - x^2 + 4x + 3$; $a = 3$
5. $P(x) = 2 - 5x + 3x^2 + 2x^3$; $a = -2$
6. $P(x) = x^3 + 4x^2 + 4x$; $a = -2$
7. $P(x) = 2x^4 - 3x^2 + 4x - 1$; $a = 4$
8. $P(x) = 2x^3 - x^2 + 10x + 5$; $a = \frac{1}{2}$

9. For each of Exercises 1–8 for which $P(a) = 0$, write the polynomial as a product of two factors.

The Rational Root Theorem

The equivalent equations

$$x^3 - 5x^2 - 2x + 24 = 0 \text{ and } (x + 2)(x - 3)(x - 4) = 0$$

have -2, 3, and 4 as solutions, or roots. The product of 2, 3, and 4 is 24, so the roots are factors of the constant term, 24.

In general, if the coefficients (including a_0) in the polynomial equation

$$x^n + a_{n-1}x^{n-1} + \dots + a_1x + a_0 = 0$$

are integers, then any integer root of the equation is a factor of the constant term a_0. If the constant term is 6, the possible roots are ± 1, ± 2, ± 3, and ± 6.

1. a. What are the possible integer roots of $x^3 + 5x^2 + x + 5 = 0$?
   b. Use synthetic division to find the integer root(s) of
   $x^3 + 5x^2 + x + 5 = 0$.
   c. Are there roots besides those found in part (b)? Explain.

The equivalent equations

$$24x^3 - 22x^2 - 5x + 6 = 0 \text{ and } (x + \tfrac{1}{2})(x - \tfrac{2}{3})(x - \tfrac{3}{4}) = 0$$

have $-\tfrac{1}{2}$, $\tfrac{2}{3}$, and $\tfrac{3}{4}$ as roots. The numerators 1, 2, and 3 are factors of the constant term, 6. The denominators 2, 3, and 4 are factors of the leading coefficient, 24.

2. Show that $24x^3 - 22x^2 - 5x + 6 = 0$ can be written in the form

$$(x + \tfrac{1}{2})(x - \tfrac{2}{3})(x - \tfrac{3}{4}) = 0.$$

In general, if the coefficients in the polynomial equation

$$a_nx^n + a_{n-1}x^{n-1} + \dots + a_1x + a_0 = 0$$

are integers, then the equation can have a rational root $\frac{p}{q}$. For such a root in simplest form, the integer p must be a factor of the constant a_0 and the integer q must be a factor of the leading coefficient a_n. This idea is key to understanding the **rational root theorem.**

Rational Root Theorem

If $\frac{p}{q}$ in simplest form is a rational root of the polynomial equation $a_nx^n + a_{n-1}x^{n-1} + \dots + a_1x + a_0 = 0$ with integer coefficients, then p must be a factor of a_0 and q must be a factor of a_n.

The rational root theorem can help you find roots of polynomial equations.

Example

Find the roots of $2x^3 - x^2 + 2x - 1 = 0$.

The coefficient of x^3 is 2. The constant term is -1. By the rational root theorem, the only possible rational roots of the equation have the form $\dfrac{\text{factor of } -1}{\text{factor of } 2}$. The factors of -1 are ± 1. The factors of 2 are ± 1 and ± 2. The only possible rational roots are ± 1 and $\pm \frac{1}{2}$.

The values of 1 and -1 are easy to check by substituting for x in $2x^3 - x^2 + 2x - 1$:
$$2(1)^3 - 1^2 + 2(1) - 1 = 2 - 1 + 2 - 1 = 2 \neq 0$$
$$2(-1)^3 - (-1)^2 + 2(-1) - 1 = -2 - 1 - 2 - 1 = -6 \neq 0$$

Use synthetic division to test $\frac{1}{2}$.

$$
\begin{array}{c|cccc}
\frac{1}{2} & 2 & -1 & 2 & -1 \\
 & & 1 & 0 & 1 \\
\hline
 & 2 & 0 & 2 & 0
\end{array}
$$

The quotient is $2x^2 + 2$ and the remainder is 0.

The remainder 0 is the value of $2x^3 - x^2 + 2x - 1$ for $x = \frac{1}{2}$ (by the remainder theorem), so $\frac{1}{2}$ is one root of the equation.

Next, find the roots of $2x^2 + 2 = 0$.
$$2x^2 + 2 = 0$$
$$x^2 + 1 = 0$$
$$x^2 = -1$$
$$x = \pm i$$

The three roots of $2x^3 - x^2 + 2x - 1 = 0$ are $\frac{1}{2}$, i, and $-i$.

3. List the possible rational roots of $2x^4 - 3x^2 + 4x - 10 = 0$.

4. Use the rational root theorem to help solve the equation $2x^3 - 15x^2 + 24x + 16 = 0$.

EXERCISES

Use the rational root theorem to help solve each equation.

1. $12x^3 - 32x^2 + 25x - 6 = 0$

2. $8x^3 - 28x^2 + 14x + 15 = 0$

3. $4x^3 + 16x^2 - 22x - 10 = 0$

4. $6x^4 - 5x^3 - 65x^2 + 85x - 21 = 0$

5. $2x^4 - 5x^3 - 17x^2 + 41x - 21 = 0$

6. $10x^3 - 49x^2 + 68x - 20 = 0$

7. $4x^4 - 37x^2 + 9 = 0$

8. $9x^4 + 3x^3 - 30x^2 + 6x + 12 = 0$

The Fundamental Theorem of Algebra

You have solved polynomial equations and found that their roots are included in the set of complex numbers. That is, the roots have been integers, rational numbers, irrational numbers, and imaginary numbers. But can all polynomial equations be solved by using complex numbers?

In 1799, the German mathmatician Carl Friedrich Gauss (1777–1855) proved that the answer to this question is *yes*; the roots of every polynomial equation, even those with imaginary coefficients, are complex numbers. The answer is so important that his theorem is called the **Fundamental Theorem of Algebra.** Here is one way to state his theorem.

Fundamental Theorem of Algebra

Each *n*th degree polynomial can be factored into *n* linear factors.

For example, the 4th degree polynomial $x^4 - 2x^3 + 2x^2 - 2x + 1$ has the four factors $x - 1$, $x - 1$, $x - i$, and $x + i$. Therefore the roots of the polynomial equation $x^4 - 2x^3 + 2x^2 - 2x + 1 = 0$ are 1, i, and $-i$. Since $x - 1$ repeats as a factor, 1 is a **multiple root** of the equation or a multiple zero of the related polynomial function. (It is a root of *multiplicity* 2.) Using the ideas of roots or zeros, the fundamental theorem can be stated in terms of a polynomial equation or its related polynomial function.

Fundamental Theorem of Algebra

Counting imaginary roots and multiple roots, an *n*th degree polynomial equation has exactly *n* roots; the related polynomial function has exactly *n* zeros.

1. a. Find a polynomial equation whose only root is $1 + \sqrt{2}$.
   b. Find a polynomial equation with root $1 + \sqrt{2}$ of multiplicity 2.
   c. Find c so that $1 + \sqrt{2}$ is a solution of $x^2 - 2x + c = 0$.

2. a. Find the sum of $4 + \sqrt{3}$ and $4 - \sqrt{3}$.
   b. Find the product of $4 + \sqrt{3}$ and $4 - \sqrt{3}$.

The irrational numbers $4 + \sqrt{3}$ and $4 - \sqrt{3}$ are *conjugates* of each other. Their sum and product are both rational numbers. If a polynomial equation has rational coefficients and one of its roots is $4 + \sqrt{3}$, then $4 - \sqrt{3}$ must also be a root. This property can be stated as a theorem.

Irrational Root Theorem

If a and b are rational numbers and $\sqrt{b}$ is an irrational number, and if $a + \sqrt{b}$ is a root of a polynomial equation with rational coefficients, then the conjugate $a - \sqrt{b}$ is also a root.

3. A student states that $2 + \sqrt{3}$ is a root of $x^2 - 2x - (3 + 2\sqrt{3}) = 0$, so by the irrational root theorem $2 - \sqrt{3}$ is another root. What would you say to the student?

The imaginary numbers $5 - 2i$ and $5 + 2i$ are *conjugates* of each other. Their sum and product are both real numbers. If a polynomial equation has real coefficients and one of its roots is $5 - 2i$, then $5 + 2i$ must also be a root.

Imaginary Root Theorem

If the imaginary number $a + bi$ is a root of a polynomial equation with real coefficients, then the conjugate $a - bi$ is also a root.

4. A student claims that $2i$ is the only imaginary root of an equation that has real coefficients. Why must the student be mistaken?

EXERCISES

1. a. If a polynomial equation with real coefficients has $-4i$ and $2 + 3i$ among its roots, what other two roots must it have? Describe the degree of the equation.
  b. What polynomial equation with complex coefficients and no multiple roots has $-4i$ and $2 + 3i$ as its only roots?

Find a fourth-degree polynomial equation with integer coefficients that has the given numbers as roots.

2. -1 (with multiplicity 2) and $-\sqrt{6}$ **3.** $3 + \sqrt{2}$ and $\sqrt{5}$ **4.** $\sqrt{3}$ and $1 - i$

In these equations, r, s, and t represent integers. Tell whether the statement is *sometimes*, *always*, or *never* true. Explain your answers.

5. A root of the equation $3x^3 + rx^2 + sx + 8 = 0$ is 5.

6. A root of the equation $3x^3 + rx^2 + sx + 8 = 0$ is -2.

7. If a is the only root of $x^3 + rx^2 + sx + t = 0$, then a is a root of multiplicity 3.

8. $\sqrt{5}$ and $-\sqrt{5}$ are roots of $x^3 + rx^2 + sx + t = 0$.

9. $2 + i$ and $-2 - i$ are roots of $x^3 + rx^2 + sx + t = 0$.

Consider the pattern in the following statements.

$$1 = 1$$
$$1 + 3 = 4$$
$$1 + 3 + 5 = 9$$
$$1 + 3 + 5 + 7 = 16$$
$$1 + 3 + 5 + 7 + 9 = 25$$

If this pattern continues without end, then the statement
$$1 + 3 + 5 + \ldots + (2n - 1) = n^2$$
is true for all positive integers n.

1. Try This Test the statement to see if it is true for $n = 6, 7$, and 8.

The general statement above is true for the first several values of n. There is, however, no number of examples that would prove it true for *all* positive integers. To prove such a statement true for all positive integers, you can use a method called **mathematical induction.**

Principle of Mathematical Induction

Let S be a statement involving a positive integer n.
Then S is true for all positive integers if the following two conditions hold.

1. S is true for $n = 1$.

2. For any positive integer k, if S is true for k, then S is true for $k + 1$.

The principle of mathematical induction is like a chain reaction in an infinite line of dominoes. Proving that a statement is true for $n = 1$ is like knocking over the first domino. Knowing that if the statement is true for any value of k, then it will be true for $k + 1$, is like knowing that if any domino is knocked over, the one after it will be knocked over also.

Example

Prove that this statement is true for all positive integers n.

$$1 + 3 + 5 + \ldots + (2n - 1) = n^2$$

Proof: First show that the statement is true for $n = 1$.

$$2(1) - 1 = 1^2 \ \checkmark \qquad \longleftarrow \text{True for } n = 1$$

Next, assume that the statement is true for k.

$$1 + 3 + 5 + \ldots + (2k - 1) = k^2$$

From this assumption, prove that the statement is true for $k + 1$.

$$1 + 3 + 5 + \ldots + (2(k + 1) - 1) \overset{?}{=} (k + 1)^2$$

$$
\begin{aligned}
& 1 + 3 + 5 + \ldots + (2(k + 1) - 1) && \longleftarrow \text{Begin with the left side.} \\
= \; & 1 + 3 + 5 + \ldots + (2k + 1) && \longleftarrow \text{Simplify.} \\
= \; & 1 + 3 + 5 + \ldots + (2k - 1) + (2k + 1) && \longleftarrow \text{Rewrite, showing all} \\
& && \quad \text{the odd numbers} \\
& && \quad \text{preceding } 2k + 1. \\
= \; & \qquad\quad k^2 \qquad\qquad\quad + (2k + 1) && \longleftarrow \text{Substitute from the assumption.} \\
= \; & (k + 1)^2 && \longleftarrow \text{Factor.}
\end{aligned}
$$

We have shown that conditions 1 and 2 of the principle of mathematical induction are true. By the principle, then, we conclude that

$$1 + 3 + 5 + \ldots + (2n - 1) = n^2$$

is true for all positive integers, which is what we wanted to prove.

2. **Try This** Complete the mathematical induction steps below to prove that
$$2 + 4 + 6 + \ldots + 2n = n(n + 1)$$
is true for all positive integers n.
   a. Show that the statement is true for $n = 1$.
   b. What statement will you assume to be true?
   c. What statement will you prove true using the assumption from part (b)?
   d. Express the sum in your statement from part (c) in terms of what you assumed. Then substitute and simplify to complete the proof.

EXERCISES

Use mathematical induction to prove that each statement is true for all positive integers n.

1. $\dfrac{1}{1 \cdot 2} + \dfrac{1}{2 \cdot 3} + \dfrac{1}{3 \cdot 4} + \ldots + \dfrac{1}{n(n + 1)} = \dfrac{n}{n + 1}$

2. $1 + 2 + 3 + \ldots + n = \dfrac{n(n + 1)}{2}$

3. $1 + 4 + 7 + \ldots + (3n - 2) = \dfrac{n(3n - 1)}{2}$

4. $\dfrac{1}{2} + \left(\dfrac{1}{2}\right)^2 + \left(\dfrac{1}{2}\right)^3 + \left(\dfrac{1}{2}\right)^4 + \ldots + \left(\dfrac{1}{2}\right)^n = 1 - \left(\dfrac{1}{2}\right)^n$

5. $n^2 + n$ is divisible by 2.

6. $1 \cdot 2 + 2 \cdot 3 + 3 \cdot 4 + \ldots + n(n + 1) = \dfrac{n(n + 1)(n + 2)}{3}$

7. $1^2 + 2^2 + 3^2 + \ldots + n^2 = \dfrac{n(n + 1)(2n + 1)}{6}$

8. $a_1 + a_1 r + a_1 r^2 + a_1 r^3 + \ldots + a_1 r^{n-1} = \dfrac{a_1(1 - r^n)}{1 - r}, r \neq 1$
   (This is the formula for the sum of a finite geometric series, page 584.)

Chapter 1

1-1 When Meg picked up her new car, it had a full tank of gas. The spreadsheet below shows Meg's driving log for the first four times that she filled her car with gas.

	A	B	C	D	E
1	Date	Miles Driven	Gallons Bought	Price per Gallon	Miles per Gallon
2	5/3	223	9.1	$1.099	
3	5/8	250	9.8	$1.079	
4	5/15	187	8.0	$1.119	
5	5/21	202	8.6	$1.119	

a. What formula should Meg write in cell E2 to compute the miles per gallon for her purchase on May 3?

b. What formula should Meg write to compute the average number of miles driven between fill-ups?

c. What formula should Meg write to compute the average price per gallon for the four fill-ups? (*Hint:* Meg purchased different amounts of gasoline at each price.)

1-2 The graph at the top of the next column shows how much the Barra family spent on vacations over the years 1987–1998. On the graph, a trend line has been drawn.

a. Based on the trend line, how much would you predict that the Barras would spend on vacations in 1999?

b. Ignoring the trend line and looking just at the data points, how much would you predict that the Barras would spend on vacations in 1999? Explain any difference between your answer here and in part (a).

Amount Spent on Vacation

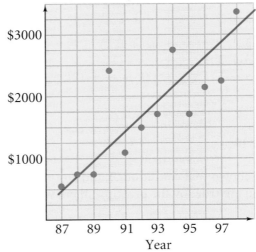

Year

1-3 a. Consider the relations $y = x^2$ and $x = y^2$. Find several ordered pairs (x, y) for each relation. Explain why one of these relations is a function and the other is not.

b. A ball is thrown into the air. Explain why the ball's height is a function of its time aloft, but its time aloft is not a function of its height.

1-4 Find the following compositions of functions. Simplify your answers.
a. $f(f(x))$ for $f(x) = \frac{1}{x}$
b. $f(f(f(x)))$ for $f(x) = \frac{1}{x}$
c. $f(f(f(x)))$ for $f(x) = 1 - \frac{x}{2}$

1-5 Let $f(x) = x^2$. Find equations for five different translations of $f(x)$ in which $f(x)$ is shifted exactly 5 units.

1-6 In the sequence 1!, 2!, 3!, 4!, 5!, 6!, . . . , the first term that ends with a zero is 5!.
a. Explain why 5! and all the terms following 5! end with a zero.
b. Determine the number of zeros with which 100! ends.

1-7 Assume that a, b, and c are integers and $a > 0$.
  a. Prove that the solution of the linear equation $ax + b = c$ must be a rational number.
  b. When are the solutions to $ax^2 + b = c$ rational? Explain.

Chapter 2

2-1 When you find the slope of a nonvertical line, you select any two points (x_1, y_1) and (x_2, y_2) on the line, and then calculate $m = \dfrac{y_2 - y_1}{x_2 - x_1}$. Prove that you will always get the same value for m no matter which two points you choose on the line.

2-2(1) Is each statement true or false? Justify your answer.
  a. The area of a circle varies directly with the radius.
  b. The perimeter of a square varies directly with the length of its side.

2-2(2)a. If x varies directly with y, does y vary directly with x? Explain.
  b. Suppose x varies directly with y, and y varies directly with z. Does x vary directly with z? Explain.
  c. Suppose x varies directly with y and x varies directly with z. Does y vary directly with z? Explain.

2-3 a. The vertices of $\triangle ABC$ have coordinates $A(2, 8)$, $B(4, 2)$, and $C(13, 5)$. Show that $\triangle ABC$ is a right triangle.

  b. The vertices of $\triangle DEF$ have coordinates $D(15, -1)$, $E(11, 11)$, and $F(-7, 5)$. Show that the sides of $\triangle DEF$ are parallel to the sides of $\triangle ABC$.

  c. Show that A, B, and C lie on the lines that contain the sides of $\triangle DEF$.

2-4 A common mistake is thinking that the equation $|-x| = x$ is true for all real numbers x.
  a. Find a value of x for which $|-x| \neq x$.
  b. Find the conditions under which it is true that $|-x| = x$.
  c. Find the conditions under which it is true that $|-x^2| = x^2$.

2-5 Graph $y = |x| + |x + 2|$.

2-6 Bill and Min are playing a game in which a dart is tossed at random at the target shown below. The sides of the square are tangent to the inner circle.

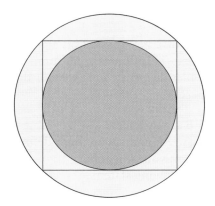

Bill wins if the dart lands in the inner circle; Min wins if the dart lands between the two circles. Who, if anyone, has the greater chance of winning? Justify your answer.

Chapter 3

3-1 The *transpose* of a matrix is found by interchanging its rows and columns. If the original matrix is called A, its transpose is called A^T. For example,

if $A = \begin{bmatrix} 2 & 3 & 1 \\ 4 & 8 & 0 \end{bmatrix}$, then $A^T = \begin{bmatrix} 2 & 4 \\ 3 & 8 \\ 1 & 0 \end{bmatrix}$.

  a. What can you conclude if A and A^T have the same dimensions?
  b. What can you conclude if $A = A^T$? Give an example to support your conclusion.

3-2 A mathematical system consisting of a set of elements G and an operation $*$ is called a *group* if the following properties hold.

- *Closure:* If a and b are elements of G, $a * b$ is an element of G.
- *Associative:* If a, b, and c are elements of G, $(a * b) * c = a * (b * c)$.
- *Identity:* There is an element e of G such that $e * a = a * e = a$.
- *Inverse:* For each element a in G, there exists an element a^{-1} (read "a inverse") in G such that $a * a^{-1} = a^{-1} * a = e$.

  a. The set of integers is a group under the operation addition. Give examples demonstrating each of the properties.

  b. The set of 2×2 matrices is a group under the operation of matrix addition. Give examples demonstrating each of the properties.

3-3(1) A and B are matrices.

  a. Suppose AB and BA are both defined. What can you conclude?

  b. Is the following statement true for *all* matrices A and B, *some* matrices A and B, or *no* matrices A and B? Explain.

  If AB and BA are both defined, then $AB = BA$.

3-3(2) A general $m \times n$ matrix A can be represented by

$$A = \begin{bmatrix} a_{11} & a_{12} & \cdots & a_{1n} \\ a_{21} & a_{22} & \cdots & a_{2n} \\ \vdots & \vdots & & \vdots \\ a_{m1} & a_{m2} & \cdots & a_{mn} \end{bmatrix}$$

where the element in the ith row and jth column is denoted by a_{ij}.

  a. Prove that for any matrix A, and scalars c and d, $(cd)A = c(dA)$.

b. Suppose that A is a general $m \times n$ matrix as shown in the previous column and B is a general $n \times p$ matrix. Copy and complete the following general representation for B.

$$B = \begin{bmatrix} b_{11} & \blacksquare & \cdots & \blacksquare \\ \blacksquare & \blacksquare & \cdots & \blacksquare \\ \vdots & \vdots & & \vdots \\ \blacksquare & \blacksquare & \cdots & \blacksquare \end{bmatrix}$$

  c. For the general $m \times n$ matrix A, and $n \times p$ matrix B described above, the number of columns in A is equal to the number of rows in B, so their product AB is defined. Give a general representation for AB using the elements of A and B and the definition of matrix multiplication.

3-4(1) The number 1 is called the *multiplicative identity* because $1 \cdot x = x \cdot 1 = x$ for all real numbers x.

  a. For the matrix $\begin{bmatrix} 8 & 7 & 2 \\ 6 & 9 & 3 \end{bmatrix}$, show that

  $$\begin{bmatrix} 1 & 0 \\ 0 & 1 \end{bmatrix}\begin{bmatrix} 8 & 7 & 2 \\ 6 & 9 & 3 \end{bmatrix} = \begin{bmatrix} 8 & 7 & 2 \\ 6 & 9 & 3 \end{bmatrix} \text{ and }$$

  $$\begin{bmatrix} 8 & 7 & 2 \\ 6 & 9 & 3 \end{bmatrix}\begin{bmatrix} 1 & 0 & 0 \\ 0 & 1 & 0 \\ 0 & 0 & 1 \end{bmatrix} = \begin{bmatrix} 8 & 7 & 2 \\ 6 & 9 & 3 \end{bmatrix}.$$

  b. Explain how the results of part (a) are similar to and different from the idea that 1 is the multiplicative identity for real numbers.

3-4(2) The matrix $Q = \begin{bmatrix} 1 & 4 & 4 \\ 2 & 2 & 4 \end{bmatrix}$ represents the vertices of a triangle. Each matrix T below represents a transformation. For each matrix T, find the product TQ, graph the triangle and its image (represented by TQ), and describe the transformation.

  a. $\begin{bmatrix} 1 & 0 \\ 0 & -1 \end{bmatrix}$ **b.** $\begin{bmatrix} -1 & 0 \\ 0 & 1 \end{bmatrix}$

  c. $\begin{bmatrix} 0 & 1 \\ 1 & 0 \end{bmatrix}$ **d.** $\begin{bmatrix} -1 & 0 \\ 0 & -1 \end{bmatrix}$

3-5 Suppose that n people gather at a meeting. Everyone shakes hands with everyone else exactly once.

   a. Draw a handshake matrix for $n = 4$ with one row and one column for each person. Let 1 indicate that a person shakes hands with another person and 0 indicate that a person does not shake hands with himself or herself.

   b. Describe the handshake matrix for n people. Write a formula for the number of handshakes that take place. That is, find how many 1's are in the $n \times n$ matrix and divide by 2.

   c. Verify that the formula you found in part (b) works for 5 people.

3-6 $A = \begin{bmatrix} -2 & -2 & 1 \\ 3 & 3 & -1 \end{bmatrix}$ and $B = \begin{bmatrix} 2 & 0 \\ -1 & 1 \\ 3 & 2 \end{bmatrix}$.

   a. Show that $AB = \begin{bmatrix} 1 & 0 \\ 0 & 1 \end{bmatrix}$.

   b. Does $BA = \begin{bmatrix} 1 & 0 \\ 0 & 1 \end{bmatrix}$?

   c. Are A and B inverses? Explain.

Chapter 4

4-1 **a.** Graph the "bowtie" inequality, $|y| \le |x|$.

   b. Write a system of inequalities to describe the graph below.

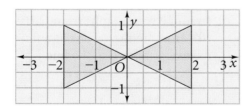

4-2 Barbara works 9 miles from her house. Ordinarily, she walks 20 minutes to the bus stop and then rides a bus for 40 minutes. One day, she just missed her bus and decided to start walking to work since the buses ran infrequently. She walked along the bus route for 40 additional minutes before a bus came by. She then rode the bus for 30 minutes to work. Assuming that she walked at the same average speed both days and that both buses averaged the same speed, what were her speed and the speed of the buses?

4-3 A company manufactures exotic sports cars and boats. The company managers used linear programming to decide how many cars and boats they should manufacture in order to maximize profit. When the managers defined their restrictions, the shaded region shown below was produced. When their objective function was applied to the region, the managers came to the conclusion that there were 4 different ways to maximize profit. What were those 4 ways? Justify your answers.

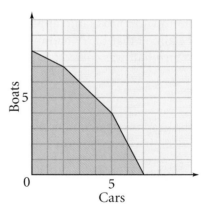

4-4 In three dimensions, the intersection of a plane with any of the xy-, yz-, and xz-planes is a *trace*.

   a. Does every plane have three traces? Explain and give an example.

   b. Must any two traces of a plane intersect? Explain and give an example.

4-5 a. In a *regular polyhedron* all faces are congruent polygons. Use a system of three linear equations to calculate the number of vertices, edges, and faces in the regular polyhedron described below.

> Every face has five edges and every edge is shared by two faces. Every face has five vertices and every vertex is shared by three faces. The sum of the number of vertices and faces is two more than the number of edges. (Euler's formula)

b. Research What regular polyhedron has been described?

4-6 Star student Barry claimed to have solved an enormous system of linear equations. Being well versed in higher mathematics, he decided to express the system using matrices, writing $AX = B$. He explained to his class that he solved the system using the following steps:

$$AX = B$$
$$(AA^{-1})X = BA^{-1}$$
$$X = BA^{-1}$$

Half the class was impressed by the elegance of Barry's solution and broke into applause. The other half claimed that Barry had made a mistake. Which half was correct? Explain.

Chapter 5

5-1 How are the graphs of the functions $y = x^2$ and $y = |x|$ similar? How are they different?

5-2 a. Let $a > 0$. Use algebraic or arithmetic ideas to explain why the lowest point on the graph of $y = a(x - h)^2 + k$ must occur when $x = h$.

b. Suppose in part (a) that the function were $y = a(x - h)^3 + k$. Would your reasoning still be valid? Explain.

5-3 A ball is shot straight up from the ground with a velocity of 80 feet per second. As the ball moves upward, gravity slows the ball and eventually the ball begins to fall back to the ground. The height h of the ball after t seconds in the air is given by the quadratic function $h(t) = -16t^2 + 80t$.

a. How high does the ball go?

b. How many seconds is the ball in the air before it hits the ground again?

5-4 When the point $(3, 5)$ is reflected over the line $y = x$, the image is $(5, 3)$.

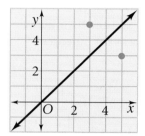

a. Choose one point in each of the quadrants II, III, and IV. Find the image of each point when it is reflected over the line $y = x$.

b. What is the image of point (a, b) when it is reflected over the line $y = x$?

c. On one set of axes, graph the function $y = 2x + 3$ and its inverse. Also graph $y = x$.

d. On another set of axes, draw graphs of the function $y = x^2$ and its inverse. Also graph $y = x$.

e. Examine your graphs from parts (c) and (d). How are the graphs of a function and its inverse related to the line $y = x$?

5-5 The equation $x^2 - 10x + 24 = 0$ can be written in the factored form $(x - 4)(x - 6) = 0$. How can this fact be used to find the vertex of the parabola $y = x^2 - 10x + 24$?

5-6 Complex numbers can be used to generate interesting patterns. Here is a pattern generated by powers of $1 + 3i$.
$(1 + 3i)^1 = 1 + 3i$
and $1^2 + 3^2 = 10$
$(1 + 3i)^2 = -8 + 6i$
and $(-8)^2 + 6^2 = 10^2$
$(1 + 3i)^3 = -26 - 18i$
and $(-26)^2 + (-18)^2 = 10^3$
$(1 + 3i)^4 = 28 - 96i$
and $28^2 + (-96)^2 = 10^4$
Find the powers of $3 + 4i$ through $(3 + 4i)^5$. Generate and verify a similar pattern.

5-7 Solve $x^2 = (6\sqrt{2})x + 7$ by completing the square.

5-8 Use the quadratic formula to prove each of the following.
  a. The sum of the roots of the quadratic equation $ax^2 + bx + c = 0$ is $\frac{-b}{a}$.

  b. The product of the roots of the quadratic equation $ax^2 + bx + c = 0$ is $\frac{c}{a}$.

Chapter 6

6-1 Judge the validity of the following argument. If the argument is correct, give a reason for each step. If the argument is incorrect, explain why it is incorrect.

$$\frac{1}{(1 - \sqrt{2})^2} = (1 - \sqrt{2})^{-2}$$
$$= 1^{-2} - (\sqrt{2})^{-2}$$
$$= \frac{1}{1^2} - \frac{1}{(\sqrt{2})^2}$$
$$= \frac{1}{1} - \frac{1}{2}$$
$$= \frac{1}{2}$$

6-2 The graph of a polynomial function can be described as a connected or unbroken curve.
  a. Is it true that a polynomial function with end behavior ($\swarrow$, $\nearrow$) must have an x-intercept? Explain.

  b. Is it true that a polynomial function with end behavior ($\nwarrow$, $\nearrow$) must have an x-intercept? Explain.

  c. Why can a polynomial function have more than one x-intercept but not have more than one y-intercept?

6-3 Find a fourth-degree polynomial function whose zeros are $1, -1, i,$ and $-i$. Write its equation in standard form.

6-4(1) An enthusiastic student claims that 1, 2, 3, and 4 are the zeros of a cubic polynomial function. Explain why this student is mistaken.

6-4(2) Use these patterns to factor polynomials that are sums and differences of cubes.
$a^3 + b^3 = (a + b)(a^2 - ab + b^2)$
$a^3 - b^3 = (a - b)(a^2 + ab + b^2)$
You can use the acronym SOPPS (Square, Opposite sign, Product, Plus, Square) to help you remember the patterns.
Factor.
  a. $x^3 + 8$
  b. $8x^3 + 27$
  c. $64 - y^3$
  d. $2u^3 + 16v^3$
  e. $d^6 + f^3$
  f. $w^6 - 1$

6-4(3)a. If the sum of two numbers is 6 and the sum of their cubes is 18, what is the sum of their squares? (*Hint:* Factor the sum of the cubes as shown in 6-4(2))
  b. If the product of two positive numbers is 96 and the sum of their squares is 208, what are the two numbers?

6-5 Use synthetic division to find $(x^2 + 4) \div (x - 2i)$. Your answer will contain i.

6-6 a. Show that $_nP_r = r! \cdot {}_nC_r$.
  b. Consider the example of 3 students being selected from a group of 20 students. Use this example to explain why the formula in part (a) makes sense.

6-7 **a.** Show that $(k + 1)! = (k + 1) \cdot k!$

b. Show that $_nC_k + {}_nC_{k+1} = {}_{n+1}C_{k+1}$.

c. Suppose $n = 4$ and $k = 2$. What entries in Pascal's triangle are represented by $_nC_k$, $_nC_{k+1}$, and $_{n+1}C_{k+1}$? Verify that the equation in part (b) is true for these entries.

Chapter 7

7-1 The exponential function is defined using the expression ab^x, where x can be any real number. The properties of exponents hold for such expressions. Use these and other properties to simplify each expression.

a. $(7^{\sqrt{2}})^{\sqrt{2}}$ **b.** $\dfrac{x^{4\pi}}{x^{2\pi}}$ **c.** $5^{2\sqrt{3}} \cdot 25^{-\sqrt{3}}$

d. $9^{\frac{1}{\sqrt{2}}}$ **e.** $\dfrac{x^{\sqrt{4 + 2\sqrt{3}}}}{x}$

f. $(3^{2 + \sqrt{2}})^{2 - \sqrt{2}}$

(*Hint:* For part (e), write $4 + 2\sqrt{3}$ in the form $(a + b\sqrt{3})^2$.

7-2 **a.** A person who invested $10,000 at 5% interest compounded annually was asked when he thought his money would double. "In about 20 years," he answered. He made a common mistake. What was it?

b. You can use the *Rule of 72* to estimate the number of years it takes money to double when earning compound interest. According to the Rule of 72, if money is invested at p% interest compounded annually, the amount of money will double in approximately $\frac{72}{p}$ years. About how long will it take $10,000 to double if invested at 1%, 2%, 3%, 4%, 6%, and 8% interest compounded annually? For each interest rate, find the actual amount you would have at the end of the estimated doubling time.

7-3(1) Evaluate each of the following.

a. $\log_5 5\sqrt{5}$ **b.** $\log_2 \sqrt[3]{16}$

c. $\log_{\sqrt{2}} 2$ **d.** $\log_{\sqrt{x}} x^3$

e. $x^{\log_x 5 - \log_x 4}$ **f.** $(\sqrt{x})^{\log_x 2}$

7-3(2)a. Simplify $\log_{b^n} b^m$.

b. Use part (a) to help you evaluate $\log_2 4 + \log_4 8 + \log_8 16 + \log_{16} 32 + \log_{32} 64 + \log_{64} 128$.

7-4 Prove the change of base formula
$$\log_b M = \frac{\log_c M}{\log_c b}.$$

(*Hint:* Write $\log_b M = \dfrac{\log_b M \cdot \log_c b}{\log_c b}$. Then use the power property in the numerator.)

7-5(1) Suppose an amount of money is invested at 6% interest compounded continuously. Use the formula $A = Pe^{rt}$ to find how long the investment will take to double in value.

7-5(2) What is wrong with each "proof" that $2 = 1$?

a. Let $x = 2$. Then $x^3 = 8$, $4x^2 = 16$, and $5x = 10$.

Thus, $x^3 - 4x^2 + 5x = 8 - 16 + 10$

$x^3 - 4x^2 + 5x = 2$

$x^3 - 4x^2 + 5x - 2 = 0$

$x^3 - 4x^2 + 4x + x - 2 = 0$

$x(x^2 - 4x + 4) + x - 2 = 0$

$x(x - 2)^2 + (x - 2) = 0$

$(x - 2)[x(x - 2) + 1] = 0$

$x(x - 2) + 1 = 0$

$x^2 - 2x + 1 = 0$

$(x - 1)^2 = 0$

$x - 1 = 0$

$x = 1$

Therefore, $2 = x = 1$.

b. $2 = 2^1 = 2^{(2^0)} = (2^2)^0 = 4^0 = 1$

c. $2 = \frac{2}{1} = \dfrac{\log 10^2}{\log 10^1} = \log 10^{2-1} = $

$\log 10^1 = 1$

7-6 The irrational number e can be expressed as a sum of infinitely many terms:
$$e = 1 + 1 + \frac{1}{2!} + \frac{1}{3!} + \frac{1}{4!} + \frac{1}{5!} + \ldots$$

a. Estimate e using the first 10 terms of the sum given above.

b. One student looked at the sum and said, "This can't be! The sum of an infinite number of positive numbers must be infinitely large, and we know that e is less than 3." Where is the student's thinking incorrect? Give an example using a repeating decimal to support your argument.

Chapter 8

8-1 a. Suppose x varies inversely with y, and y varies inversely with z. What relationship, if any, exists between x and z? Justify your answer.

b. Suppose x varies inversely with y, and x varies inversely with z. What relationship, if any, exists between y and z? Justify your answer.

c. Describe variations of x with y and of x with z such that y varies inversely with z. Justify your answer.

8-2 a. Write the equation of the inverse of the function $y = \frac{1}{x-3} + 5$. Describe the asymptotes of the graph of the function. Describe the asymptotes of the graph of the inverse.

b. Write the equation of the inverse of the function $y = \frac{k}{x-b} + c$ where $k \neq 0$. Describe the asymptotes of the graph of the function. Describe the asymptotes of the graph of the inverse.

8-3 How many vertical asymptotes can the graph of a rational function have? Explain your reasoning.

8-4 Simplify.

a. $\dfrac{x^{2n} - 6x^n y^n + 5y^{2n}}{x^{2n} + 2x^n y^n - 3y^{2n}}$

b. $\dfrac{4x^{2n} + 12x^n y^n + 9y^{2n}}{6x^{2n} + 7x^n y^n - 3y^{2n}}$

8-5 The *arithmetic mean* of two numbers is found by adding them together and then dividing by 2. The *harmonic mean* of two numbers is found by adding their reciprocals together, dividing by 2, and then finding the reciprocal of the result. If the two numbers are a and b, then their harmonic mean is $\dfrac{2}{\frac{1}{a} + \frac{1}{b}}$.

a. A man drives to work in the morning, averaging 30 miles per hour. Driving the same distance home in the afternoon, he averages 60 miles per hour. Find his average speed that day. (*Hint:* The answer is not 45 miles per hour.)

b. Find the harmonic mean of 30 and 60.

c. Show that, in general, if a car covers a certain distance at an average speed of r_1 in one direction and r_2 in the opposite direction, then its average speed overall is the harmonic mean of r_1 and r_2.

8-6(1) A number like the unusual one shown below is called a *continued fraction*.

$$x = 1 + \cfrac{1}{1 + \cfrac{1}{1 + \cfrac{1}{1 + \cfrac{1}{1 + \dots}}}}$$

Continued fractions, like nonterminating decimals, go on forever. But you can estimate their values by breaking them off. For example, here are four possible estimates of x:

$$x_1 = 1 \qquad x_2 = 1 + \frac{1}{1} \qquad x_3 = 1 + \cfrac{1}{1 + \frac{1}{1}}$$

$$x_4 = 1 + \cfrac{1}{1 + \cfrac{1}{1 + \frac{1}{1}}}$$

a. Simplify the estimates x_2, x_3, and x_4.

b. Examine the original expression for x again. Explain why $x = 1 + \frac{1}{x}$.

c. Use the result of part (b) to find the exact value of x.

8-6(2) This unusual number is called a *continued radical*.

$$\sqrt{1 + \sqrt{1 + \sqrt{1 + \sqrt{1 + \ldots}}}}$$

   a. Find estimates for the continued radical similar to those found for the continued fraction in 8-6(1).

   b. Find an equation for the continued radical similar to the one in 8-6(1)b.

   c. Use the result of part (b) to find the exact value of the continued radical.

8-7 Three members of a club will be chosen at random to attend a convention. The club has 12 members, 5 of whom are women. What is the probability that those chosen will be all women or all men?

Chapter 9

9-1 Despite the fact that the dates of our calendar year repeat as outputs of a periodic function, your birthday never falls on the same day of the week in consecutive years. Explain why.

9-2 Instead of working with a unit circle, consider the unit square shown below.

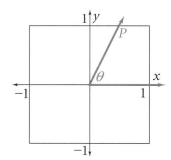

Suppose an angle in standard position has measure θ, and the terminal side of the angle intersects the square at point *P*. Let $c(\theta)$ = the *x*-coordinate of *P*. Find $c(\theta)$ for

$\theta =$ $0°$, $30°$, $45°$, $60°$,
    $90°$, $120°$, $135°$, $150°$,
    $180°$, $210°$, $225°$, $240°$,
    $270°$, $300°$, $315°$, and $330°$.

9-3 A phonograph record spins on a turntable. Calculate how much farther a point on the outside edge of the record travels in one revolution than a point 1 inch closer to the center of the record.

9-4 On the same set of axes, sketch one cycle of $y = \sin\theta$, $y = -\sin\theta$, and $y = \sin(-\theta)$. Use the unit circle to explain any relationships you see among these graphs.

9-5 On the same set of axes, sketch one cycle of $y = \cos\theta$, $y = -\cos\theta$, and $y = \cos(-\theta)$. Use the unit circle to explain any relationships you see among these graphs.

9-6 A spiral of triangles, T_1, T_2, T_3, T_4, . . . , is built around O according to the following rules.
   • T_1 is a right triangle with legs of length 1.
   • T_2 is a right triangle with the hypotenuse of T_1 as one leg and the other leg having length 1.
   • T_n is a right triangle with the hypotenuse of T_{n-1} as one leg and the other leg having length 1.

The first three triangles are shown below.

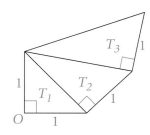

Find the first triangle whose interior overlaps a previous triangle in the spiral.

9-7 **a.** In the diagram, $m\angle A = 30°$, $AB = 10$, and $BC = BD = 6$. Use the Law of Sines to find $m\angle D$.

b. Find $m\angle ABD$ and $m\angle ABC$.

c. Notice that two sides and a nonincluded angle of $\triangle ABC$ are congruent to the corresponding parts of $\triangle ABD$ but the triangles are not congruent. Must $\triangle EFG$ be congruent to $\triangle ABD$ if $EF = 10$, $FG = 6$, and $\angle G \cong \angle D$? Explain.

Chapter 10

10-1(1) Ellipses and hyperbolas do not represent functions. However, you can draw their graphs with a graphing calculator by graphing the "top half" and the "bottom half" on the same set of axes. Write the equations of two functions that can be used to graph each of the following conic sections. Then draw the graph.

a. the ellipse $16x^2 + 25y^2 = 400$

b. the hyperbola $x^2 - 9y^2 = 36$

10-1(2) An "xy" term has an interesting effect on the graph of a conic section. Draw the graph of each conic section given below by the method suggested in 10-1(1). (*Hint:* To solve for y, you will have to complete a square.)

a. $4x^2 + 2xy + y^2 = 9$

b. $4x^2 + 2xy - y^2 = 9$

10-2(1) The directrix of a parabola is the line $y = -2$. The focus is the point $(0, 2)$.

a. Suppose the directrix remains fixed, but the focus is shifted along the y-axis away from the directrix. Explain what happens to the vertex and the shape of the parabola.

b. Suppose the focus moves along the y-axis toward the directrix. Explain what happens to the vertex and the shape of the parabola.

c. What would happen if the focus moved down all the way to the directrix?

10-2(2) Use the definition of a parabola to show that the parabola with vertex (h, k) and focus $(h, k + c)$ has the equation $(x - h)^2 = 4c(y - k)$.

10-3 a. A circle contains the points $(0, 0)$, $(6, 8)$, and $(7, 7)$. Find its equation by solving a system of three equations.

b. Several parabolas contain the three points of part (a), but only one can be described by a quadratic function. Find that function.

10-4 An ellipse and two circles share the same center. The major axis of the ellipse is twice as long as its minor axis. The diameter of the larger circle is the same length as the major axis of the ellipse. The diameter of the smaller circle is the same length as the minor axis of the ellipse.

The area of an ellipse $= \pi$(half the length of the major axis) $\cdot$ (half the length of the minor axis). Compare the areas of the blue and white regions.

10-5 a. Prove that the hyperbola $\frac{y^2}{a^2} - \frac{x^2}{b^2} = 1$ never crosses its asymptotes.

b. Is $\frac{y^2}{16} - \frac{x^2}{9} = 4$ a hyperbola? Explain.

c. Is $\frac{y^2}{16} - \frac{x^2}{9} = -1$ a hyperbola? Explain.

10-6 Consider equations of the form $Ax^2 + By^2 + Cx + Dy + E = 0$.

a. What must be true about A and B if the graph of the equation is a circle? If the graph is an ellipse? If it is a hyperbola? If it is a parabola?

b. Suppose $A = 1$ and $B = 1$. Must the graph be a circle? Explain.

c. Suppose $A = 1$, $B = -1$, and $C = D = E = 0$. Describe the graph.

Chapter 11

11-1 Suppose that three number cubes are rolled.
- **a.** Make a table of the probability distribution for the sample space containing all the possible sums of the three numbers.
- **b.** Describe a set of outcomes that has a 50% chance of occurring.

11-2(1) On a class trip to Washington, D. C., Chris and six classmates are able to meet with one of their state's senators. He offers them the one remaining ticket for a special tour of the White House. The students accept and decide to draw a name from a hat to see who gets the ticket.

They put their names on seven pieces of paper. The senator offers a hat. Chris, wanting to improve his chances of being chosen, slips a second piece of paper with "Chris" on it into the hat. Just as the senator is about to pull a name from the hat, an aide offers another ticket. Now two names will be drawn. What is the probability that Chris's deception will be revealed by "Chris" being drawn twice?

11-2(2) It snows on 20% of the school days in January.
- • When a snowfall is heavy, schools are closed 80% of the time.
- • When a snowfall is light, schools are closed 30% of the time.
- • Snowfalls are light 40% of the time.
- • When there is no snow, schools are closed 1% of the time.
- **a.** Draw a tree diagram for this situation.
- **b.** What is the probability that schools are closed on a school day in January?
- **c.** If there is snow, what is the probability that schools are open?
- **d.** If it snows (S), schools are open (O) or closed (C). If it doesn't snow (N), schools are open or closed. Does it follow that
$$P(O|S) + P(C|S) + P(O|N) + P(C|N) = 1?$$ Explain.

11-3 Twelve family members gather for Thanksgiving dinner. Other than the twins, Kim and Jim, no two people have the same age. Yet the mean, median, and mode of their ages are the same.
- **a.** Create a set of ages that fits this scenario.
- **b.** Suppose the age of a twin is a. Describe the other ten ages.

11-4 Suppose a data set consists of the values $x_1, x_2, x_3, \ldots, x_n$. If each x_i is increased by 20, how are $\bar{x}$ and σ affected? Explain your reasoning.

11-5 You take a sample of your customers and report the results to your boss. She says, "This isn't good enough! The margin of error is twice as great as I'll accept." So you double your sample size, report the new results, and find she is still not satisfied. Explain why.

11-6 A basketball player was successful on 52% of his field goal attempts this season. In the first half of a playoff game, he made only 3 of 15 field goal attempts.
- **a.** According to the formula for binomial probability, how likely is it that this player would make 3 or fewer field goals when 15 are attempted?
- **b.** Explain why the formula used in part (a) may be inappropriate for this situation.

11-7 In a binomial experiment involving n trials in which the probability of success on each trial is p, the mean number of successful trials is np and the standard deviation is $\sqrt{np(1-p)}$. When a binomial experiment involves a large value of n, the normal distribution can be used to approximate the binomial distribution.
- **a.** Suppose you flip a fair coin 500 times. Use a normal distribution to estimate the probability that the number of heads will be between 239 and 261.

b. Increase the bounds on the number of heads in part (a) to represent a 95% probability that they will include the actual number of heads in 500 trials.

c. Suppose you flip a coin 500 times and get 225 heads. Do you think the coin is fair? Explain why or why not.

Chapter 12

12-1 Recursive formulas are given for three sequences. Examine each sequence and then find an equivalent explicit formula.

   a. $a_1 = 10; a_n = a_{n-1} + 8$
   b. $a_1 = 2; a_n = 3a_{n-1}$
   c. $a_1 = 3; a_n = (a_{n-1})^2$

12-2 How many numbers between 60 and 690 are divisible by 13? (*Hint:* Use an arithmetic sequence.)

12-3 (1) Prove that the arithmetic mean of any two positive numbers is greater than or equal to the geometric mean. (*Hint:* The square of any number is greater than or equal to zero. Use the fact that $\left(\sqrt{a} - \sqrt{b}\right)^2 \geq 0$ to show that $\frac{a + b}{2} \geq \sqrt{ab}$ for $a > 0$ and $b > 0$.)

12-3 (2) **Open-ended** Choose any arithmetic sequence $x_1, x_2, x_3, \ldots$. Create a new sequence where each term is of the form $t_n = ab^{x_n}$, where $b > 0$. Show that the new sequence is a geometric sequence.

12-4 a. Each picture illustrates an arithmetic series of odd numbers. Write a formula for the sum of the first n odd numbers.

   b. Prove the formula in part (a).

12-5 To buy a home, many people borrow from a bank and pay back the bank on a monthly basis over 30 years. If the amount borrowed is A, the monthly interest rate is r, and each of the 360 monthly payments is P, then A, r, and P are related by the formula: $A = \dfrac{P}{(1 + r)} +$

$$\dfrac{P}{(1 + r)^2} + \dfrac{P}{(1 + r)^3} + \cdots + \dfrac{P}{(1 + r)^{360}}$$

a. Show that this formula can be solved for P:

$$P = Ar \cdot \left[\dfrac{(1 + r)^{360}}{(1 + r)^{360} - 1}\right]$$

b. Suppose you need to borrow \$100,000 to buy a house. How much more will you pay each month at a bank charging 8.5% annual interest than at a bank charging 8% annual interest? (*Hint:* Remember to use *monthly* interest in the formula.)

12-6 You can approximate the area of a circle by finding the area of a regular inscribed polygon with n sides. The polygon can be divided into n isosceles triangles. See the figure below.

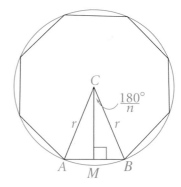

a. In $\triangle CBM$, use trigonometry to express CM and BM in terms of r and n.
b. Use the results of part (a) to write a formula for the area of $\triangle ABC$.
c. Use the formula for the area of $\triangle ABC$ to write a formula for the approximate area of the circle.
d. Use $n = 1000$ to estimate the area of a circle of radius r. How does your estimate compare with the area computed using the standard formula for the area of a circle?

Construct scatter plots to display the data in the tables below. Be sure to label both axes. Describe any correlation. Draw a trend line.

■ Lessons 1-1 and 1-2

1.

x	3	4	5	7	8	9	10
y	5	7	9	10	10	11	13

  a. Predict the value of y if $x = 15$.
  b. If $y = 15$, predict the value of x.

2.

x	6.0	7.0	8.0	9.0	10.0	11.0	12.0
y	15.5	14.0	13.0	12.5	12.0	11.5	10.0

  a. Predict the value of y if $x = 14$.
  b. If $y = 17$, predict the value of x.

Determine whether each relation is a function.

■ Lessons 1-3 and 1-4

3. $\{(0, 1), (1, 0), (2, 1), (3, 1), (4, 2)\}$

4. $\{(7, 4), (4, 9), (-3, 1), (1, 7), (2, 8)\}$

5. $\{(1, 4), (3, -2), (5, 2), (1, -8), (6, 7)\}$

6. $\{(-5, 1), (0, -3), (-2, 1), (-10, 11), (-7, 1)\}$

7. $\{(9, 3), (6, 2), (3, 1), (-3, -1), (-6, -2)\}$

8. $\{(4, 9), (5, 3), (-2, 0), (5, 4), (8, 1)\}$

Suppose $f(x) = 2x + 5$, $g(x) = 3 - x$, and $h(x) = x^2 - x + 2$. Evaluate the following.

9. $f(-5)$

10. $g(1) + h(-3)$

11. $f(6) + 2g(-2)$

12. $h(x) - f(x + 2)$

13. $g(f(3))$

14. $h(g(2))$

15. $f(g(x))$

16. $g(h(1)) - f(1)$

Describe the vertical and/or horizontal translations of $f(x) = x^2$ or $f(x) = |x|$. Then graph each function.

■ Lesson 1-5

17. $f(x) = (x + 4)^2$

18. $f(x) = |x| - 2$

19. $f(x) = x^2 - 3$

20. $f(x) = (x - 1)^2 + 5$

21. $f(x) = |x + 4|$

22. $f(x) = |x + 1| - 5$

23. $f(x) = |x| + 6$

24. $f(x) = (x + 3)^2$

25. $f(x) = |x - 2| - 3$

Evaluate each expression.

■ Lesson 1-6

26. $3!$

27. $7!$

28. $_6P_2$

29. $_5P_3$

30. $_7P_1$

31. $_6P_5$

32. $4!$

33. $_8P_3$

34. $_5P_4$

35. $6!$

36. $_3P_1$

37. $_7P_5$

Solve each equation for x. Simplify your answers. What type of number is each answer?

■ Lesson 1-7

38. $2x - 5 = 10$

39. $3x^2 = 60$

40. $8x + 3 = 19$

41. $4x^2 + 11 = 47$

42. $7x + 1 = -20$

43. $x^2 = 121$

44. $-3x - 10 = -40$

45. $x^2 + 37 = 107$

Find the slope and *y*-intercept of each line. Then find the *x*-intercept if possible. ■ Lesson 2-1

1. $y = 2x - 5$ **2.** $y = -x + 1$ **3.** $y = 4$ **4.** $y = 5x + 10$

5. $y = \frac{1}{3}x - 15$ **6.** $x = -7$ **7.** $y = -6x$ **8.** $y = \frac{-2}{5}x + 20$

Write the equation of each line.

9. $m = 3$; contains $(-1, 4)$ **10.** $m = -1$; contains $(0, 7)$ **11.** $m = \frac{3}{4}$; contains $(2, 8)$

12. $m = \frac{-2}{5}$; contains $(3, -9)$ **13.** $m = \frac{8}{3}$; contains $(-2, 0)$ **14.** $m = -5$; contains $(-3, -12)$

Write the equation of a direct variation that passes through the given point. ■ Lesson 2-2

15. $(3, 7)$ **16.** $(5, -8)$ **17.** $(-4, -10)$ **18.** $(-2, 9)$

19. $(-6, 6)$ **20.** $(6, -3)$ **21.** $(12, 8)$ **22.** $(-15, -1)$

Write each linear equation in standard form. ■ Lesson 2-3

23. $y = 3x + 9$ **24.** $4x = 6y - 9$ **25.** $2y = 8x - 7$ **26.** $y = -x + 1$

27. $0.3x + 1.2y = 2.4$ **28.** $y = \frac{2}{3}x + 15$ **29.** $x = 8 - y$ **30.** $\frac{1}{2}x - \frac{3}{4}y = 1$

Write an equation of the line through the given points.

31. $(0, 2)$ and $(-1, 3)$ **32.** $(1, 2)$ and $(-2, -4)$ **33.** $(11, 4)$ and $(3, 0)$

34. $(-4, -5)$ and $(-1, -8)$ **35.** $(-5, 6)$ and $(3, -10)$ **36.** $(12, 10)$ and $(0, 0)$

Use pencil and paper to solve each equation or inequality. ■ Lesson 2-4

37. $3x - 8 \geq 1$ **38.** $|4m + 2| = 10$ **39.** $7t + 4 \leq 3t$ **40.** $m + 8 = -11$

41. $|9 - 4z| = 53$ **42.** $3v \leq 5v + 18$ **43.** $5 - w = 2w - 1$ **44.** $4a < 2a - 7$

45. $-5r + 2 = 17$ **46.** $|3 - w| < 7$ **47.** $-2s = 3s - 10$ **48.** $|2t + 7| \geq 4$

Graph each equation or inequality on a coordinate plane. ■ Lesson 2-5

49. $y = x - 7$ **50.** $y < -x + 5$ **51.** $4x - y = 8$ **52.** $0.1x + 0.6y \geq 2$

53. $y \leq 3x - 1$ **54.** $y = -x + 4$ **55.** $x + 3y > 12$ **56.** $2x + 5y = 10$

Suppose a number is selected at random from the sample space $\{1, 2, 3, 4, 5, 6, 7, 8, 9, 10\}$. Find each probability. ■ Lesson 2-6

57. P(the number is a multiple of 5)   **58.** P(the number is an integer)

59. P(the number is a factor of 12)   **60.** P(the number is less than or equal to 4)

61. P(the number is greater than 6)   **62.** P(the number is a composite number)

CHAPTER 3

Extra Practice

State the dimension of each matrix. Identify the indicated element. ■ **Lesson 3-1**

1. $\begin{bmatrix} 3 & 1 & -5 \\ 6 & 9 & 10 \end{bmatrix}; a_{21}$

2. $\begin{bmatrix} 0.5 & 6.1 \\ -9.2 & 4.7 \end{bmatrix}; a_{11}$

3. $\begin{bmatrix} 56 & -83 & 12 \\ 101 & -71 & 49 \end{bmatrix}; a_{12}$

Solve each equation for each variable.

4. $\begin{bmatrix} 4 & 2y \\ 5 & 7-t \end{bmatrix} = \begin{bmatrix} m & 8 \\ z+1 & 6t \end{bmatrix}$

5. $\begin{bmatrix} n-4 & 9 \\ 2m+1 & 1 \end{bmatrix} = \begin{bmatrix} -7 & 3w \\ 11 & q-4 \end{bmatrix}$

Find each sum or difference. ■ **Lesson 3-2**

6. $\begin{bmatrix} -8 & 3 \\ 19 & -45 \end{bmatrix} + \begin{bmatrix} 12 & 64 \\ -7 & 63 \end{bmatrix}$

7. $\begin{bmatrix} 3.6 & -9.8 \\ 4.0 & -1.7 \end{bmatrix} - \begin{bmatrix} 0.8 & 3.4 \\ -6.1 & 7.9 \end{bmatrix}$

8. $\begin{bmatrix} 4 & 6 & -3 \\ 8 & -9 & -1 \end{bmatrix} - \begin{bmatrix} 10 & 7 & -3 \\ -9 & 2 & 7 \end{bmatrix}$

9. $\begin{bmatrix} -308 & 651 \\ 912 & -347 \end{bmatrix} + \begin{bmatrix} 105 & 318 \\ -762 & -438 \end{bmatrix}$

Solve each matrix equation for X.

10. $\begin{bmatrix} 25 & -60 \\ 42 & 91 \end{bmatrix} + X = \begin{bmatrix} -37 & 61 \\ 85 & 37 \end{bmatrix}$

11. $\begin{bmatrix} -8 & 3 & 1 \\ -9 & 6 & 7 \end{bmatrix} - X = \begin{bmatrix} 5 & 8 & 3 \\ 4 & 2 & 6 \end{bmatrix}$

12. $X + \begin{bmatrix} 6 & 2 & 9 \\ 1 & 5 & 10 \end{bmatrix} = \begin{bmatrix} 11 & -5 & 16 \\ 3 & 6 & 8 \end{bmatrix}$

13. $X - \begin{bmatrix} 2.3 & 6.5 \\ 9.4 & -8.2 \end{bmatrix} = \begin{bmatrix} -4.7 & 3.6 \\ 9.4 & -5.8 \end{bmatrix}$

Use matrices *A, B, C,* and *D* below. Multiply, if possible. If not possible, ■ **Lesson 3-3**
write *product undefined*.

$A = \begin{bmatrix} 8 & 1 \\ -2 & 5 \end{bmatrix}$

$B = \begin{bmatrix} -3 & 1 & 0 \\ -2 & -1 & 5 \end{bmatrix}$

$C = \begin{bmatrix} 9 & 4 \\ 5 & 1 \\ 2 & 0 \end{bmatrix}$

$D = \begin{bmatrix} 1 & 7 & 3 \\ 8 & 10 & -2 \end{bmatrix}$

14. AB **15.** BD **16.** $2A$ **17.** CD **18.** DA **19.** $-3B$

20. $0.2A$ **21.** BA **22.** $5C$ **23.** CB **24.** $\frac{1}{2}D$ **25.** BC

Use $\triangle ABC$ with coordinates *A*(1, 5), *B*(2, −1), and *C*(4, 3). Find the ■ **Lesson 3-4**
coordinates of the image under each transformation.

26. a dilation 5 times the size

27. a translation 3 units left and 1 unit up

28. a translation 2 units right and 7 units down

29. a dilation one-third the size

For each graph, write a matrix. ■ **Lesson 3-5**

30.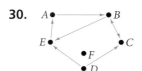

31.

32.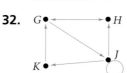

Solve each matrix equation for X. ■ **Lesson 3-6**

33. $\begin{bmatrix} 2 & 1 \\ -1 & 7 \end{bmatrix} X = \begin{bmatrix} 8 & 1 \\ -12 & 41 \end{bmatrix}$

34. $\begin{bmatrix} -1 & 0 \\ 6 & 3 \end{bmatrix} X = \begin{bmatrix} -9 \\ -3 \end{bmatrix}$

35. $\begin{bmatrix} -3 & 5 \\ 1 & 8 \end{bmatrix} X = \begin{bmatrix} 29 \\ 58 \end{bmatrix}$

Extra Practice

Solve each system by graphing.　　　　　　　　　　　　　　　■ **Lesson 4-1**

1. $\begin{cases} y = 2x + 1 \\ y = 4x - 5 \end{cases}$
2. $\begin{cases} y \leq x + 4 \\ y \geq -2x + 3 \end{cases}$
3. $\begin{cases} x < 8 \\ x - y > 2 \end{cases}$

Solve each system. Choose an appropriate method.　　　　　　■ **Lesson 4-2**

4. $\begin{cases} x + y = 5 \\ x - y = -3 \end{cases}$
5. $\begin{cases} y = 3x - 1 \\ 2x + y = 14 \end{cases}$
6. $\begin{cases} 3x + 2y = 12 \\ x + y = 3 \end{cases}$

7. $\begin{cases} x - 4y = 16 \\ x + 2y = 4 \end{cases}$
8. $\begin{cases} y = 2x + 5 \\ y = 4 - x \end{cases}$
9. $\begin{cases} y = 5x - 1 \\ y = 14 \end{cases}$

Use linear programming. Find the values of x and y that maximize or minimize the objective function.　　　　　　　　　　　　　■ **Lesson 4-3**

10. $\begin{cases} x \leq 4 \\ y \leq 3 \\ x \geq 0 \\ y \geq 0 \end{cases}$
Maximum for
$P = 2x + y$

11. $\begin{cases} x + y \leq 5 \\ y \geq x \\ x \geq 0 \end{cases}$
Minimum for
$C = x + y$

12. $\begin{cases} 1 \leq x \leq 6 \\ 2 \leq y \leq 4 \\ x + y \geq 4 \end{cases}$
Maximum for
$P = 3x + 2y$

13. Business A lunch stand makes $.75 profit on each chef's salad and
$1.20 profit on each Caesar salad. On a typical weekday, it sells between
40 and 60 chef's salads and between 35 and 50 Caesar salads. The total
number sold has never exceeded 100 salads. How many of each type
should be prepared to maximize profit?

Graph each point.　　　　　　　　　　　　　　　　　　■ **Lesson 4-4**

14. $(0, 3, 0)$
15. $(4, 0, -2)$
16. $(0, 0, 5)$
17. $(1, 1, 0)$

18. $(0, 4, 2)$
19. $(-1, 2, 2)$
20. $(3, 0, 1)$
21. $(6, 1, 3)$

Graph each plane. Use intercepts and traces.

22. $x - y + z = 4$
23. $2x - y - z = 6$
24. $-x + y + 3z = 9$
25. $x + y + z = 5$

Solve each system or identify it as inconsistent or dependent.　　■ **Lesson 4-5**

26. $\begin{cases} x + y + z = 6 \\ x = 2y \\ z = x + 1 \end{cases}$
27. $\begin{cases} x - 2y + z = 8 \\ y - z = 4 \\ z = 3 \end{cases}$
28. $\begin{cases} 3x + y - z = 15 \\ x - y + 3z = -19 \\ 2x + 2y + z = 4 \end{cases}$

Solve each system. Use an inverse matrix.　　　　　　　　　■ **Lesson 4-6**

29. $\begin{cases} x - y = 3 \\ x + y = 5 \end{cases}$
30. $\begin{cases} x - 2y = 7 \\ x + 3y = 12 \end{cases}$
31. $\begin{cases} 2x + 5y = 10 \\ x + y = 2 \end{cases}$

Extra Practice

Multiply. ■ **Lesson 5-1**

1. $(x - 4)(x + 3)$ **2.** $(3t + 1)(3t - 1)$ **3.** $(b - 2)(b - 2)$ **4.** $(w + 5)(w + 7)$

5. $(r + 5)(r - 5)$ **6.** $(2m + 1)(2m + 4)$ **7.** $(-w + 1)(w - 3)$ **8.** $(4c - 2)(-c - 5)$

Tell whether each function is linear or quadratic.

9. $y = 3x + 4$ **10.** $y = x^2 + 1$ **11.** $y = (x + 1)(x - 1)$ **12.** $3x + 2y = 1$

Sketch the graph of each equation. Label the coordinates of each vertex. ■ **Lesson 5-2**

13. $y = 3x^2$ **14.** $y = (x + 3)^2 + 1$ **15.** $y = 2x^2 + 4$ **16.** $y = \frac{1}{2}(x - 3)^2$

17. $y = x^2 - 9$ **18.** $y = 2(x + 1)^2 - 5$ **19.** $y = (x + 1)^2 - 3$ **20.** $y = (x - 2)^2$

Write the equation of each quadratic function in standard form. ■ **Lesson 5-3**

21. $y = (x + 1)^2$ **22.** $y = 3(x - 2)^2$ **23.** $y = (2x + 1)^2$ **24.** $y = (x - 3)^2 - 5$

25. $y = (x + 2)^2 + 1$ **26.** $y = (-x + 5)^2 + 3$ **27.** $y = (x + 7)^2 - 4$ **28.** $y = (3 - x)^2 + 7$

Write the equation of the inverse of each function. ■ **Lesson 5-4**

29. $y = 3x + 1$ **30.** $y = \frac{1}{5}x$ **31.** $y = (x - 1)^2$ **32.** $y = 2x^2 + 7$

33. $y = 2x^2$ **34.** $y = (x + 3)^2$ **35.** $y = \frac{2}{3}x - 5$ **36.** $y = x^2 + 4$

Solve each equation by finding square roots, graphing, or factoring. When necessary, round your answer to the nearest tenth. ■ **Lesson 5-5**

37. $x^2 + 2x - 1 = 0$ **38.** $4x^2 - 100 = 0$ **39.** $x^2 = -2x + 1$ **40.** $x^2 - 9 = 0$

41. $2x^2 + 4x = 70$ **42.** $x^2 - 30 = 10$ **43.** $x^2 + 4x = 0$ **44.** $x^2 + 3x + 2 = 0$

Simplify each expression. ■ **Lesson 5-6**

45. $(3 - i) + (5 - 2i)$ **46.** $(4 + 2i)(1 - i)$ **47.** $(4 + 2i) - (3 + 5i)$ **48.** $(6 - 7i)(3 - 2i)$

49. $(2 + 5i) - (-6 + i)$ **50.** $(-2 - 3i)(7 - i)$ **51.** $(3 - 9i) + (2 + 10i)$ **52.** $(8 - 3i)(6 + 9i)$

Solve each quadratic equation by completing the square or using the quadratic formula. ■ **Lessons 5-7 and 5-8**

53. $x^2 + 5x + 8 = 4$ **54.** $8x^2 + 64 = 0$ **55.** $2x^2 - 5x + 1 = 0$ **56.** $3x^2 = x - 9$

57. $x^2 + 10 = 4x - 2$ **58.** $x^2 - 7x = 0$ **59.** $x^2 + 4x + 4 = 0$ **60.** $x^2 - 7 = 0$

Evaluate the discriminant of each equation. Tell how many solutions each equation has and whether the solutions are real or imaginary.

61. $x^2 + 4x = 17$ **62.** $2x^2 + 10x - 1 = 0$ **63.** $x^2 - 4x - 2 = 0$ **64.** $2x^2 + 5x = 0$

65. $x^2 - 19 = 1$ **66.** $3x^2 = 8x + 4$ **67.** $-2x^2 + 1 = 7x$ **68.** $4x^2 + 4x = -1$

Extra Practice

Find the inverse of each function.

■ Lesson 6-1

1. $y = 3x^5$

2. $y = 2\sqrt[4]{x}$

3. $y = 10x^2$

4. $y = \sqrt[3]{5x}$

Solve each equation. Discard any extraneous solutions.

5. $\sqrt[3]{x + 4} = 3$

6. $2x^4 + 9 = 530$

7. $\sqrt{3x + 1} = -7$

8. $\sqrt{5x - 2} = \sqrt{3x + 4}$

9. $\sqrt{2x + 3} = x - 4$

10. $x^3 - 4 = 12$

Graph each function. Describe the end behavior and find the x- and y-intercepts. Estimate to the nearest tenth when necessary.

■ Lesson 6-2

11. $y = x^3 - 5x^2 + x$

12. $y = x^4 + x - 3$

13. $y = -2x^3 + x^2 + 4$

14. $y = -x^5 + x^4 + x^3$

15. $y = 4x^3 - x + 8$

16. $y = x^4 + x^2 - 6$

Write a polynomial function in standard form with the given zeros.

■ Lesson 6-3

17. $x = 3, 2, -1$

18. $x = 1, 1, 2$

19. $x = -2, -1, 1$

20. $x = 0, 0, 2, 3$

Solve each equation.

■ Lesson 6-4

21. $t^3 - 3t^2 - 10t = 0$

22. $4m^3 + m^2 - m + 5 = 0$

23. $t^3 - 6t^2 + 12t - 8 = 0$

24. $2c^3 - 7c^2 - 4c = 0$

25. $w^4 - 13w^2 + 36 = 0$

26. $x^3 + 2x^2 - 13x + 10 = 0$

Divide.

■ Lesson 6-5

27. $(x^3 - 3x^2 + 2) \div (x - 1)$

28. $(x^3 - x^2 - 6x) \div (x - 3)$

29. $(2x^3 + 10x^2 + 8x) \div (x + 4)$

30. $(x^4 + x^2 - 6) \div (x^2 + 3)$

31. $(x^2 - 4x + 4) \div (x - 2)$

32. $(x^3 + 11x + 12) \div (x + 3)$

Evaluate each expression.

■ Lesson 6-6

33. $5!$

34. $_6C_2$

35. $_7P_3$

36. $\frac{7!}{4!}$

37. $_8P_5$

38. $_4C_1$

Decide whether each situation is a combination or a permutation. Then solve.

39. How many different orders can you choose to read six of the nine books on the summer reading list?

40. How many ways are there to choose five shirts out of seven to take to camp?

41. How many ways can you choose two out of four kinds of flowers for a bouquet?

Use the binomial theorem to expand each binomial.

■ Lesson 6-7

42. $(x - 1)^3$

43. $(3x + 2)^4$

44. $(4x + 10)^3$

45. $(2x + 5y)^4$

Identify each function as modeling either exponential growth or exponential decay. What is the function's percent increase or decrease? ■ Lesson 7-1

1. $y = 327(0.05)^x$
2. $y = 1.023(0.98)^x$
3. $y = 0.5(1.67)^x$
4. $y = 1.14^x$
5. $y = 8(1.3)^x$
6. $y = 2\left(\frac{9}{10}\right)^x$
7. $y = 4.1(0.72)^x$
8. $y = 9.2(2.3)^x$

Graph each exponential function using a graphing calculator. ■ Lesson 7-2

9. $y = 3^x$
10. $y = 2(4^x)$
11. $y = 2^{-x}$
12. $y = \left(\frac{1}{4}\right)^x$
13. $y = 2^{3x}$
14. $y = 9^{-2x}$
15. $y = -0.1^x$
16. $y = -\left(\frac{1}{2}\right)^x$

Use your calculator to evaluate each expression.

17. e^2
18. $\frac{5}{e}$
19. $2e^3$
20. $\frac{1}{e^4}$
21. $\frac{1}{5}e^5$
22. $6e^{10}$
23. $\frac{3}{e^2}$
24. $\frac{12}{e}$

Write each equation in logarithmic form. ■ Lesson 7-3

25. $9^3 = 729$
26. $64 = 4^3$
27. $\left(\frac{1}{2}\right)^4 = \frac{1}{16}$
28. $49^{\frac{1}{2}} = 7$
29. $\left(\frac{1}{3}\right)^{-3} = 27$
30. $625^{\frac{1}{4}} = 5$
31. $2^{-5} = \frac{1}{32}$
32. $6^2 = 36$

Write each equation in exponential form.

33. $\log_3 27 = 3$
34. $\log_{64} 2 = \frac{1}{6}$
35. $\log_5 25 = 2$
36. $\log_7 7 = 1$
37. $\log_{11} 1 = 0$
38. $\log 1000 = 3$
39. $\log_2 \frac{1}{32} = -5$
40. $\log_4 16 = 2$

Evaluate each logarithm.

41. $\log_2 128$
42. $\log 0.001$
43. $\log_{25} 5$
44. $\log_2 16$

Graph each logarithmic function.

45. $y = 2 \log x$
46. $y = \log_8 x$
47. $y = \log_4 (x + 1)$
48. $y = 3 + \log x$
49. $y = -1 + \log_2 x$
50. $y = \log (x - 2)$
51. $y = \log (x + 2)$
52. $y = \log (x - 5)$

Write each logarithmic expression as a single logarithm. ■ Lesson 7-4

53. $\log 8 + \log 3$
54. $4(\log_2 x + \log_2 3)$
55. $3 \log x + 4 \log x$
56. $\log 4 + \log 2 - \log 5$
57. $\log r - \log t + 2 \log s$
58. $2 \log x - 4 \log y$

Solve and check each equation. ■ Lessons 7-5 and 7-6

59. $\sqrt[3]{y^2} = 4$
60. $2 - 4^x = -62$
61. $\log x + \log 2 = 5$
62. $\log_3 (x + 1) = 4$
63. $e^x = 5$
64. $\ln 3x = 2$
65. $\ln x - \ln 4 = 7$
66. $\log 4x = -1$
67. $\log 4 - \log x = -2$
68. $\ln 2 + \ln x = 4$
69. $4 + 5^x = 29$
70. $e^{3x} = 20$

Each set of data varies inversely. Write the equation of the inverse variation and find the missing value.

■ **Lesson 8-1**

1. $(3, 2)$ and $(1, y)$

2. $(4, -1)$ and $(x, 2)$

3. $(5, 8)$ and $(4, y)$

4. $(-6, -2)$ and $(x, 3)$

5. $(-8, 3)$ and $(12, y)$

6. $(10, 15)$ and $(x, 5)$

7. $(21, 7)$ and $(-14, y)$

8. $(5, 4)$ and $(1, y)$

Sketch the graph of each function. Include any asymptotes.

■ **Lessons 8-2 and 8-3**

9. $y = \dfrac{x + 1}{x - 2}$

10. $y = \dfrac{x - 3}{(x + 1)^2}$

11. $y = \dfrac{3x}{2x + 1}$

12. $y = \dfrac{8 - x}{x}$

13. $y = \dfrac{x - 4}{x^2}$

14. $y = \dfrac{2x + 1}{2x - 1}$

15. $y = \dfrac{x}{x + 3}$

16. $y = \dfrac{x + 2}{x - 4}$

Classify each function as continuous or discontinuous. If discontinuous, give the value(s) of x for which the function is undefined.

17. $y = \dfrac{3x^2 + 2x}{x}$

18. $y = \dfrac{x^2 - 16}{x^2 + 4}$

19. $y = \dfrac{(x + 2)(x - 1)}{(x + 2)^2(x - 1)}$

20. $y = \dfrac{4}{x - 6}$

21. $y = \dfrac{9x}{3x^3 - 6x}$

22. $y = \dfrac{x^2 + 7x + 12}{x + 4}$

23. $y = \dfrac{x - 7}{x - 7}$

24. $y = \dfrac{x^2 - 3x + 2}{x - 1}$

Simplify each rational expression.

■ **Lesson 8-4**

25. $\dfrac{x^2 + 9x + 18}{x + 6}$

26. $\dfrac{x^2 + 3x + 2}{x - 1} \cdot \dfrac{1 - x}{x + 2}$

27. $\dfrac{x^2 - 2x - 8}{x + 3} \div \dfrac{x - 4}{x + 3}$

28. $\dfrac{2x^2 + 5x - 3}{x^2 - 4x} \cdot \dfrac{2x^3 - 8x^2}{x^2 + 6x + 9}$

29. $\dfrac{3x + 1}{x^2 - x - 6} \div \dfrac{6x^2 + 11x + 3}{x^2 + 4x + 4}$

30. $\dfrac{3x^4 - x^3 + 2x^2}{6x^2 - 2x + 4}$

31. $\dfrac{x^4 + 3x^3 + 2x^2}{x^2 + 7x + 12} \div \dfrac{x^2 + 2x}{x^2 + 8x + 16}$

32. $\dfrac{x^3 + 4x^2 + 4x}{-x^2 - x + 6}$

33. $\dfrac{x^2 + 2x - 15}{x + 2} \cdot \dfrac{2x + 4}{x^2 + 7x + 10}$

Add or subtract. Simplify if possible.

■ **Lesson 8-5**

34. $\dfrac{6x + 1}{x + 2} + \dfrac{2x - 5}{2x + 4}$

35. $\dfrac{8}{x^2 - 25} + \dfrac{9}{x - 5}$

36. $\dfrac{x - 3}{x^2 + 3x} + \dfrac{7}{x + 3}$

37. $\dfrac{3x}{x^2 + 5x + 6} - \dfrac{2x}{x^2 + 6x + 9}$

38. $\dfrac{2}{x^2 - 1} - 3$

39. $\dfrac{2x}{x - 5} - \dfrac{x}{x + 7}$

Solve each equation. Check your solution.

■ **Lesson 8-6**

40. $\dfrac{x}{4} = \dfrac{x + 1}{3}$

41. $\dfrac{2}{x^2 - 1} = \dfrac{4}{x + 1}$

42. $\dfrac{3x}{5} + \dfrac{4}{x} = \dfrac{4x + 1}{5}$

43. $\dfrac{3x}{x - 2} = 4 + \dfrac{x}{5}$

44. $x + \dfrac{x}{4} - \dfrac{x}{5} = 21$

45. $\dfrac{3}{x + 4} + \dfrac{5}{4} = \dfrac{18}{x + 4}$

State whether the events are independent or dependent.

■ **Lesson 8-7**

46. $A = $ a main dish is selected
$B = $ a type of salad is selected

47. $A = $ a department is selected
$B = $ a class in that department is selected

48. $A = $ a volleyball team is selected from the league
$B = $ one of the remaining teams is selected

49. $A = $ a color of house paint is selected
$B = $ a type of stove is selected

Extra Practice

State the period and amplitude of each periodic function.   ■ **Lesson 9-1**

1.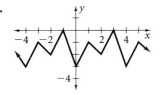

2.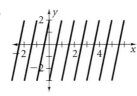

3.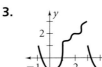

Sketch each angle in standard position.   ■ **Lesson 9-2**

4. $15°$ **5.** $-230°$ **6.** $400°$ **7.** $-145°$ **8.** $280°$ **9.** $-750°$

Write each measure in radians. Express your answers in terms of π.   ■ **Lesson 9-3**

10. $100°$ **11.** $270°$ **12.** $-45°$ **13.** $-550°$ **14.** $425°$ **15.** $10°$

Write each measure in degrees. Round your answers to the nearest degree, if necessary.

16. 5π **17.** -2 radians   **18.** $\dfrac{5\pi}{6}$ **19.** -3π **20.** $-\dfrac{13\pi}{10}$ **21.** 9 radians

Identify the amplitude or asymptotes, and period for each function.   ■ **Lessons 9-4 and 9-5**

22. $y = 4 \sin 3x$ **23.** $y = \cos 4x$ **24.** $y = \frac{1}{3} \tan \pi x$

25. $y = 2 \cos \frac{x}{4}$ **26.** $y = 3 \tan x$ **27.** $y = \frac{1}{9} \sin 5x$

Sketch the graph of each function from 0 to 2π.

28. $y = 2 \cos x$ **29.** $y = 3 \sin 2x$ **30.** $y = \tan \frac{x}{2}$

31. $y = -\sin 3x$ **32.** $y = -2 \tan \pi x$ **33.** $y = \cos 4x$

In $\triangle ABC$, $\angle C$ is a right angle. Two measures are given. Find the remaining sides and angles. Round to the nearest tenth.   ■ **Lesson 9-6**

34. $m\angle A = 29°, b = 8$ **35.** $a = 7, c = 9$ **36.** $m\angle B = 52°, b = 10$

37. $a = 2, b = 4$ **38.** $m\angle A = 37°, c = 12$ **39.** $b = 5, c = 8$

Use the Law of Sines or the Law of Cosines. Find the measure x to the nearest tenth.   ■ **Lesson 9-7**

40. 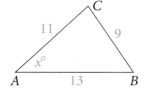   **41.** 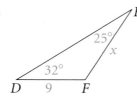   **42.** 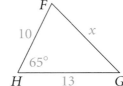   **43.**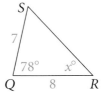

Extra Practice

Graph each equation. Describe each graph and its lines of symmetry. Give the domain and range for each graph. ■ **Lesson 10-1**

1. $x^2 + y^2 = 4$

2. $x^2 - 16y^2 = 64$

3. $4x^2 + 9y^2 = 36$

4. $8x^2 - 16y^2 = 32$

5. $9x^2 + 9y^2 - 36 = 0$

6. $25x^2 + 4y^2 = 100$

Identify the focus and directrix of each parabola. Then graph the parabola. ■ **Lesson 10-2**

7. $y = 4x^2$

8. $x = \frac{1}{16}y^2$

9. $-y = 10x^2$

10. $y^2 - 8x = 0$

11. $x^2 = 6y$

12. $y^2 = 20x$

13. $x^2 + 4y = 0$

14. $x^2 = -2y$

Write the equation of each parabola with its vertex at the origin.

15. focus at $(0, 3)$

16. directrix at $x = 4$

17. focus at $(0, -2)$

18. directrix at $y = 1$

19. directrix at $x = 2$

20. focus at $(0, 1)$

21. directrix at $y = 3$

22. focus at $(0, -5)$

Write an equation of each circle with the given center and radius. Then graph the circle. ■ **Lesson 10-3**

23. center $(0, 0)$; radius 8

24. center $(-4, -6)$; radius 2

25. center $(-5, 1)$; radius 3

Find the radius and center of each circle.

26. $(x + 1)^2 + (y - 3)^2 = 4$

27. $(x - 2)^2 + (y + 4)^2 = 16$

28. $(x + 6)^2 + (y + 9)^2 = 144$

29. $(x - 7)^2 + (y - 2)^2 = 81$

30. $(x - 3)^2 + (y + 10)^2 = 25$

31. $(x + 8)^2 + (y - 1)^2 = 100$

Find the foci of each ellipse whose equation is given. Graph each ellipse. ■ **Lesson 10-4**

32. $\frac{x^2}{9} + \frac{y^2}{25} = 1$

33. $\frac{x^2}{36} + \frac{y^2}{4} = 1$

34. $\frac{x^2}{100} + \frac{y^2}{121} = 1$

35. $\frac{x^2}{81} + \frac{y^2}{64} = 1$

36. $\frac{x^2}{49} + \frac{y^2}{144} = 1$

37. $\frac{x^2}{4} + y^2 = 1$

Write each hyperbola in standard form. Sketch the graph. ■ **Lesson 10-5**

38. $4x^2 - 25y^2 = 100$

39. $81x^2 - 16y^2 = 1296$

40. $4x^2 - y^2 = 36$

41. $12x^2 - 3y^2 = 432$

42. $9x^2 - 121y^2 = 1089$

43. $x^2 - 64y^2 = 64$

Identify each quadratic relation as a parabola, a circle, an ellipse, or a hyperbola. ■ **Lesson 10-6**

44. $(x + 1)^2 + (y - 2)^2 = 7$

45. $\frac{x^2}{89} + \frac{y^2}{62} = 1$

46. $\frac{x^2}{73} - \frac{y^2}{19} = 1$

47. $x + y^2 - 3y + 4 = 0$

48. $x^2 + y^2 + 16x - 6y = 11$

49. $3x^2 - 6x + y - 10 = 0$

Suppose you roll two number cubes. Find the probability distribution for each sample space.

■ **Lesson 11-1**

1. {the product of the two cubes is an even number, the product is an odd number}

2. {the sum of the two cubes is a prime number, the sum is a composite number}

Suppose a counselor is chosen at random. Find each probability.

■ **Lesson 11-2**

3. P(counselor is a junior)

4. P(counselor is female)

5. P(counselor is a senior and male)

6. P(counselor is a junior | counselor is female)

7. P(counselor is male | counselor is a senior)

Characteristics of Camp Counselors

Year		male	female
in high school	Junior	18	21
	Senior	25	16

Find the mean, median, and mode for each data set.

■ **Lesson 11-3**

8. 3 2 6 4 5 3 4 2 7 5 3

9. 16 62 24 13 21 35 24 17 20

10. 125 135 126 138 137 135 121

11. 6.1 9.5 3.8 4.6 6.1 2.3 3.7 2.1

Find the mean, range, interquartile range, and standard deviation for each set of data.

■ **Lesson 11-4**

12. 6 8 5 2 7 3 5 6 7

13. 25 29 21 19 30 26 28

14. 12 9 10 11 13 9 20

15. 100 98 101 100 102 97 100

Find the margin of error for the sample proportion, given a sample of size n.

■ **Lesson 11-5**

16. $n = 90$
17. $n = 300$
18. $n = 125$
19. $n = 900$
20. $n = 1000$
21. $n = 5000$

Find the probability of x successes in n trials for the given probability of success p on each trial.

■ **Lesson 11-6**

22. $x = 2, n = 6, p = 0.7$
23. $x = 3, n = 8, p = 0.4$
24. $x = 9, n = 10, p = 0.3$

Use the expansion of $(p + q)^n$ to graph each binomial distribution.

25. $n = 5, p = 0.2$
26. $n = 6, p = 0.4$
27. $n = 5, p = 0.7$

Sketch a normal curve for each distribution. Label the x-axis values at one, two, and three standard deviations from the mean.

■ **Lesson 11-7**

28. mean = 30; standard deviation = 4

29. mean = 45; standard deviation = 11

Decide whether each formula is *explicit* or *recursive*. Then find the first five terms of the sequence. ■ Lesson 12-1

1. $a_n = 3n + 2$

2. $a_1 = 4; a_n = a_{n-1} + 7$

3. $a_n = 5n(n + 2)$

Write the next three terms in each arithmetic sequence. Then write the explicit and recursive formula for the sequence. ■ Lesson 12-2

4. $3, 5, 7, \ldots$

5. $19, 15, 11, \ldots$

6. $-12, -10.5, -9, \ldots$

7. $0.2, 0.5, 0.8, \ldots$

8. $-23, -36, -49, \ldots$

9. $25, 37.5, 50, \ldots$

Find the arithmetic mean of the given terms.

10. $a_{n-1} = 10, a_{n+1} = 20$

11. $a_{n-1} = 7, a_{n+1} = 19$

12. $a_{n-1} = -2, a_{n+1} = -7$

Generate the first five terms of each geometric sequence. ■ Lesson 12-3

13. $a_1 = 6, r = 2$

14. $a_1 = -27, r = \frac{1}{3}$

15. $a_1 = 1900, r = 0.1$

16. $a_1 = -5, r = 3$

17. $a_1 = 1, r = 4$

18. $a_1 = 500, r = 0.2$

Write the related series for each finite sequence. Then evaluate each series. ■ Lesson 12-4

19. $21, 19, 17, 15, \ldots; 8$ terms

20. $4, 7, 10, 13, 16, 19, \ldots; 10$ terms

21. $-35, -28, -21, -14, \ldots; 7$ terms

22. $97, 96, 95, 94, 93, \ldots; 20$ terms

For each sum, find the number of terms, the first term, and the last term. Then evaluate each sum.

23. $\displaystyle\sum_{n=1}^{5} (2n + 3)$

24. $\displaystyle\sum_{n=2}^{7} (4 - n)$

25. $\displaystyle\sum_{n=1}^{5} (n + 1)$

26. $\displaystyle\sum_{n=3}^{10} (3n - 5)$

Determine whether each series is *arithmetic* or *geometric*. Then find the sum to the given term. ■ Lesson 12-5

27. $3 + 6 + 9 + 12 + 15 + \ldots; 10$th term

28. $3 + 6 + 12 + 24 + 48 + \ldots; 10$th term

29. $-1000 + 500 + -250 + 125 + \ldots; 7$th term

30. $87 + 72 + 57 + 42 + \ldots; 20$th term

Find the sum of each infinite geometric series.

31. $4 + 2 + 1 + \frac{1}{2} + \frac{1}{4} + \ldots$

32. $3 - 1 + \frac{1}{3} - \frac{1}{9} + \ldots$

33. $2.2 - 0.22 + 0.022 + \ldots$

34. $0.9 + 0.09 + 0.009 + \ldots$

35. $5 - \frac{5}{2} + \frac{5}{4} - \frac{5}{8} + \ldots$

36. $1 + 0.1 + 0.01 + \ldots$

Evaluate a sum to approximate the area under each curve for the domain $0 \le x \le 3$. Use inscribed rectangles 1 unit wide. ■ Lesson 12-6

37. $f(x) = 2x^2$

38. $y = x^3$

39. $g(x) = 2x + 3$

40. $h(x) = |x + 3|$

Extra Practice

Problem Solving Strategies

You may find these strategies helpful when solving word problems.

STRATEGY	WHEN TO USE IT
Draw a Diagram	The problem describes a picture or diagram.
Guess and Test	The needed information seems to be missing.
Look for a Pattern	The problem describes a relationship.
Make a Table	The problem has data that need to be organized.
Solve a Simpler Problem	The problem is complex or has numbers that are too cumbersome to use at first.
Use Logical Reasoning	You need to reach a conclusion using given information.
Work Backward	You need to find the number that led to the result in the problem.

Problem Solving: Draw a Diagram

■**Example** **Two students leave school at the same time and travel in opposite directions along the same road. One walks at a rate of 3 mi/h. The other bikes at a rate of 8.5 mi/h. How far apart are the students after two hours?**

Draw a diagram:

walking 3 mi/h • 2h   biking 8.5 mi/h • 2h

6   3   School   8.5   17

After two hours, the students will be 6 + 17, or 23, mi apart.

EXERCISES

1. A bug starts at point $P(0, 0)$. Each time it moves, it crawls one half the distance traveled in the previous move. It travels east, north, west, south, east, north, and so on, in order. Its first move is east 16 units. Where is the bug after six moves?

2. Draw a graph to check this statement: "The graph of $y = 2(x - 3) + 1$ is the graph of $y = 2x + 1$ shifted to the right 3 units."

3. Suppose you have four metal rods with lengths 2 in., 5 in., 7 in., and 9 in. How could you use all four rods to measure a length of 1 in.?

4. Two cars leave Los Angeles at the same time and follow the same route toward the Grand Canyon. The first car averages 55 mi/h. The second car averages 65 mi/h. How far apart are the two cars after five hours?

Problem Solving: Guess and Test

When you are not sure how to start solving a problem, guess an answer and then test it. In the process of testing a guess, you may see a way to revise your guess to get closer to the answer or to get the answer.

■Example　**The automatic leg-counter at the Brazinski farm counted 114 legs as the pigs and ducks swarmed through the gate at feeding time. A total of 40 animals passed through the gate. How many pigs and how many ducks passed through the gate?**

Guess:　20 pigs　　Test:　$20 \cdot 4 =$　　　80 legs
　　　　20 ducks　　　　　$20 \cdot 2 =$　+ 40 legs
　　　　　　　　　　　　　　　　　120 legs

Revise your guess. You need fewer pigs to bring the total number of legs down.

Guess:　18 pigs　　Test:　$18 \cdot 4 =$　　　72 legs
　　　　22 ducks　　　　　$22 \cdot 2 =$　+ 44 legs
　　　　　　　　　　　　　　　　　116 legs

The number is still too high.

Guess:　17 pigs　　Test:　$17 \cdot 4 =$　　　68 legs
　　　　23 ducks　　　　　$23 \cdot 2 =$　+ 46 legs
　　　　　　　　　　　　　　　　　114 legs

Seventeen pigs and 23 ducks passed through the gate.

EXERCISES

1. Suppose the automatic leg-counter at the Brazinski farm counted 126 legs, but there were still a total of 40 animals. How many pigs and how many ducks passed through the gate?

2. Marika biked a total of 110 mi during three days of training for a bicycle race. On the second day of her training session, she biked 15 mi more than on the first day but 5 mi less than on the third day. How many miles did she bike on the third day?

3. Use each of the integers from 1 to 9 once to fill the circles so that the sums along the spokes are equal. (Each spoke contains three numbers.)

4. Find a and b such that $x^2 - x - 72 = (x + a)(x + b)$.

5. Approximate $\sqrt{385}$ to the nearest tenth.

6. The Hoerners spent $45.50 last month watching 11 movies. If movie videos cost $3, movie matinees cost $4.50, and evening movies cost $7, how many of each type of movie did they see?

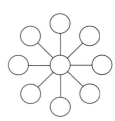

Problem Solving: Look for a Pattern and Make a Table

Some problems describe relationships that involve regular sequences of numbers or other things. To solve the problem you need to be able to recognize and describe the *pattern* that shows the relationship among the numbers or things. One way to organize the information is to *make a table*.

■Example   **After scrounging around in the couch cushions, your father tells you he has found $2.40 in equal numbers of quarters, dimes, and nickels. He says you can have the money if you can tell him how many of each coin he has.**

Make a table to help find a pattern.

Number of Nickels	1	2	3	4	5	6
Number of Dimes	1	2	3	4	5	6
Number of Quarters	1	2	3	4	5	6
Total Value	$.40	$.80	$1.20	$1.60	$2.00	$2.40

Your father has six of each type of coin.

EXERCISES

1. A college radio station sponsors a contest once a week. One resident from a dormitory calls in and tries to answer ten questions correctly. Each correct answer earns the dorm $50, but each incorrect answer reduces the winnings by $25. Last week's contestant earned $350. How many answers were correct?

2. **a.** Make a table to show the perimeters and areas of rectangles whose lengths are 1, 2, 3, 4, 5, 6, and 7 units and whose widths are 1, 2, 3, 4, 5, 6, and 7 units.

   b. Use the table to find out whether there is a rectangle whose area and perimeter are numerically the same.

3. Lisa's school uniform is any combination of a white or light blue shirt, a dark blue skirt or a dark blue pair of pants, and a plaid blazer. How many different outfits can she make?

4. How many different ways are there to make $.50 in change without using pennies?

5. How many ways can you roll two standard number cubes and get a sum of 7?

6. Suppose you have five 32¢ stamps and three 20¢ stamps. How many different amounts of postage could you use to mail a package?

Problem Solving: Solve a Simpler Problem

By solving one or more simpler problems, you can often find a pattern that will help solve a more complicated problem.

█Example   **One thousand snap-together cubes make up a large cube measuring 10 units along each edge. The large cube is painted red and then taken apart. How many of the snap-together cubes are painted red on two sides?**

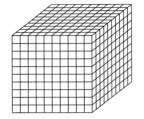

Begin with one snap-together cube, then add cubes to make a larger cube. Find out whether there is a pattern.

Length of edge	1	2	3	4	5	...
Number of snap-together cubes	1	8	27	64	125	...
Number of cubes with two sides painted	0	0	12	24	36	...
Pattern			$12 \cdot 1$	$12 \cdot 2$	$12 \cdot 3$	...

The pattern is that there are $12 \cdot (n - 2)$ snap-together cubes painted red on two sides.

$12 \cdot (10 - 2) = 12 \cdot 8$ ◀——Substitute 10 for n.

$$= 12 \cdot 8$$
$$= 96$$

There are 96 cubes that are painted red on two sides.

EXERCISES

1. Find the number of two-digit whole numbers that contain the digit 7 in at least one place in the number.

2. **a.** Find each sum at right.
   b. Describe a relationship between the number of addends and the sum of each addition in part (a).
   c. Evaluate $1 + 3 + 5 + \ldots + 997 + 999$.

$1 + 3 = $ ▓
$1 + 3 + 5 = $ ▓
$1 + 3 + 5 + 7 = $ ▓
$1 + 3 + 5 + 7 + 9 = $ ▓

3. Find the total number of squares of all sizes on a standard checkerboard, a board with eight units on a side.

4. Suppose your heart beats 68 times per minute.
   a. How many times had your heart beaten by your 15th birthday?
   b. If you live to be 87 years old, how many times will your heart have beaten?

5. **a.** The Steuben County Regional Soccer League has ten teams. During a season, each team plays every other team twice, once at home and once away. How many games are played in one season?
   b. Suppose there are s teams in the league. How many games are played in one season?

Problem Solving: Use Logical Reasoning

Some problems can be solved without using numbers. They can be solved by *logical reasoning*, given some information.

■Example **Four pigs and their owners went home happy after winning prizes at the county fair. None of the pigs have the same first initial as their owners. Juan's pig is not Tina. LaShawn's pig got her name because she was born during a blizzard.**

Make a table to organize what you know.

	Julie	Snowball	Ladybug	Tina
Juan	X	X		X
Suzanne		X		
LaShawn	X	✔	X	X
Trevor		X		X

Juan's pig is not Tina, so put an X in that box.

LaShawn's pig must be Snowball.

Since the pigs and their owners have different first initials, put an X in each box along the main diagonal.

Use *logical reasoning* to complete the table.

	Julie	Snowball	Ladybug	Tina
Juan	X	X	✔	X
Suzanne	X	X	X	✔
LaShawn	X	✔	X	X
Trevor	X	X	X	X

Juan must own Ladybug.

The only possible pig for Suzanne is Tina.

Juan owns Ladybug, Suzanne owns Tina, LaShawn owns Snowball, and Trevor owns Julie.

EXERCISES

1. The junior class is selling mugs with the school logo as part of a school-wide fundraising campaign. The top four salespeople in the class are Pat, Andy, Leon, and Shana. Pat sold more mugs than Andy but fewer than Leon. Shana also sold more than Andy, but she sold fewer than Pat. Andy sold the fewest mugs. Who sold the most mugs in the junior class?

2. Gregor has the same number of brothers as sisters. His sister Delores has twice as many brothers as sisters. How many children are in Gregor and Delores' family?

3. Which expression(s) will be positive for all positive integers n?
   A. $2^n - n$ **B.** $n - 2^n$ **C.** $(n + 1) - 2^n$ **D.** $2^n - (n - 1)$ **E.** $2^n + n$

4. Four people, Luis, Marisa, Neil, and Ophelia, were on a bus. The florist sat next to Marisa. Luis and the surgeon are married to each other. The caterer, the editor, and Neil don't know each other. The surgeon was sitting behind Ophelia. Luis doesn't make bread. Which person does which work?

Problem Solving: Work Backward

To solve some problems you need to start with the end result and work backward to the beginning.

■Example　**A ball bounced four times, reaching one half its previous height with each bounce. After the fourth bounce, the ball reached a height of 2 ft. How high was the ball when it was dropped?**

Each successive bounce reaches one half of the height, so each prior bounce reached two times the height. Multiply each height by 2.

Bounce	4	3	2	1
Height	2 ft	4 ft	8 ft	16 ft

After the first bounce, the ball reached a height of 16 ft, so it must have been dropped from a height of 2(16) or 32 ft.

EXERCISES

1. On Friday, Kamiko deposited $475 in her account. On Sunday, she withdrew $150. On Tuesday she deposited $25 and withdrew $50. On Wednesday she wrote a check for $127.50. She now has $627.45 in her account. How much was in Kamiko's account before she made Friday's deposit?

2. The diagram at the right shows the final resting place of a ball on a billiard table. Suppose the ball bounced off the walls of the table four times. Show where the ball was when it was originally set in motion. (*Hint:* The ball makes equal angles with the side when it rebounds.)

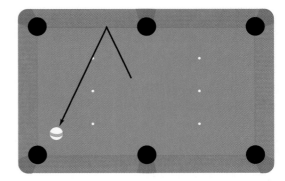

3. Suppose you start with a number. You multiply the number by 3, add 7, divide by $\frac{1}{2}$, subtract 5, and then divide by 12. The result is 5. What number did you start with?

4. Derwood decided to sell a box of pencils. On Monday he sold half the pencils. On Tuesday he sold another 40 pencils. On Wednesday he sold half the pencils that were left. On Thursday he sold the remaining 25 pencils. How many pencils were in the box originally?

5. Tian rented a car to drive from his town to Chicago. The rental company charges $53 per day plus $.27 per mile. When Tian dropped the car off in Chicago three days later, his bill from the rental company was $453.57, which included 5% sales tax. How far from Chicago does Tian live?

Percents and Percent Applications

Percent means *per hundred*. Find fraction, decimal, and percent equivalents by replacing one symbol for *hundredths* with another.

■ Example 1   Write each number as a percent.

a. $0.082 = 8.2\%$ **b.** $1.20 = 120\%$ **c.** $\frac{3}{5} = \frac{60}{100} = 60\%$ **d.** $1\frac{1}{6} = \frac{7}{6}$
$= 1.166\overline{6}$
$= 116.\overline{6}\%$

Move the decimal point two places to the right and write a percent sign.

Write the fraction as hundredths. Then replace hundredths with a percent sign.

First, use $7 \div 6$ to write $1\frac{1}{6}$ as a decimal.

■ Example 2   Write each percent as a decimal.

a. $50\% = 0.50 = 0.5$ **b.** $\frac{1}{2}\% = 0.5\% = 00.5\% = 0.005$

Move the decimal point two places to the left and drop the percent sign.

To model a percent problem with an equation, express each percent as a decimal. There are three basic kinds of percent problems.

■ Example 3   Use an equation to solve each percent problem.

a. What is 30% of 12?

$n = 0.3 \times 12$
$n = 3.6$

b. 18 is 0.3% of what?

$18 = 0.003 \times n$
$\frac{18}{0.003} = \frac{0.003n}{0.003}$
$6000 = n$

c. What percent of 60 is 9?

$n \times 60 = 9$
$60n = 9$
$n = \frac{9}{60} = 0.15 = 15\%$

EXERCISES

Write each number as a percent.

1. 0.46   **2.** 0.3   **3.** 0.294   **4.** 1.03   **5.** 0.007   **6.** 1.506

7. $\frac{1}{4}$ **8.** $\frac{3}{8}$ **9.** $\frac{2}{3}$ **10.** $\frac{4}{9}$ **11.** $1\frac{3}{20}$ **12.** $\frac{1}{200}$

Write each percent as a decimal.

13. 40%   **14.** 8%   **15.** 150%   **16.** 0.7%   **17.** 103.5%   **18.** 3.3%

Use an equation to solve each percent problem.

19. What is 25% of 50?   **20.** What percent of 58 is 37?   **21.** 120% of what is 90?

22. 8 is what percent of 40?   **23.** 15 is 75% of what?   **24.** 80% of 58 is what?

25. In Louisiana the state sales tax is 4%. If you buy a $15,000 car in Louisiana, how much tax will you pay?

26. The Mississippi River drains about 1,247,300 mi^2, which is 13.3% of the land area of North America. Estimate the total area of North America.

Operations with Fractions

To add or subtract fractions, use a common denominator. The common denominator will be the least common multiple of the denominators.

■Example 1   Simplify $\frac{2}{3} + \frac{3}{5}$.

$\frac{2}{3} + \frac{3}{5} = \frac{10}{15} + \frac{9}{15}$ ⟵ For 3 and 5, the least common multiple is 15.
Write $\frac{2}{3}$ and $\frac{3}{5}$ as equivalent fractions with denominators of 15.

$\qquad = \frac{19}{15}$ or $1\frac{4}{15}$ ⟵ Add the numerators.

■Example 2   Simplify $5\frac{1}{4} - 3\frac{2}{3}$.

$5\frac{1}{4} - 3\frac{2}{3} = 5\frac{3}{12} - 3\frac{8}{12}$ ⟵ Write equivalent fractions.

$\qquad = 4\frac{15}{12} - 3\frac{8}{12}$ ⟵ Write $5\frac{1}{4}$ as $4\frac{15}{12}$ so you can subtract the fractions.

$\qquad = 1\frac{7}{12}$ ⟵ Subtract the fractions. Then subtract the whole numbers.

To multiply fractions, multiply the numerators and multiply the denominators. You can simplify by using a greatest common factor.

■Example 3   Simplify $\frac{3}{4} \cdot \frac{8}{11}$.

Method 1: $\frac{3}{4} \cdot \frac{8}{11} = \frac{24}{44} = \frac{24 \div 4}{44 \div 4} = \frac{6}{11}$ **Method 2:** $\frac{3}{\underset{1}{4}} \cdot \frac{\overset{2}{8}}{11} = \frac{6}{11}$

Divide 24 and 44 by 4, their greatest common factor.   Divide 4 and 8 by 4, their greatest common factor.

To divide fractions, use a reciprocal to change the problem to multiplication.

■Example 4   Simplify $3\frac{1}{5} \div 1\frac{1}{2}$.

$3\frac{1}{5} \div 1\frac{1}{2} = \frac{16}{5} \div \frac{3}{2}$ ⟵ Write mixed numbers as improper fractions.

$\qquad = \frac{16}{5} \cdot \frac{2}{3}$ ⟵ Multiply by the reciprocal of the divisor.

$\qquad = \frac{32}{15}$ or $2\frac{2}{15}$ ⟵ Simplify.

EXERCISES

Perform the indicated operation.

1. $\frac{3}{5} + \frac{4}{5}$

2. $\frac{3}{7} + \frac{2}{3}$

3. $4\frac{1}{2} + 2\frac{1}{3}$

4. $6\frac{4}{5} + 1\frac{1}{9}$

5. $5\frac{3}{4} + 4\frac{2}{5}$

6. $\frac{4}{5} - \frac{1}{5}$

7. $\frac{2}{3} - \frac{3}{7}$

8. $5\frac{1}{2} - 3\frac{2}{5}$

9. $8\frac{2}{5} - 1\frac{1}{10}$

10. $7\frac{3}{4} - 4\frac{4}{5}$

11. $\frac{3}{4} \cdot \frac{1}{2}$

12. $\frac{9}{2} \cdot \frac{6}{7}$

13. $3\frac{4}{5} \cdot 10$

14. $2\frac{1}{2} \cdot 3\frac{1}{5}$

15. $6\frac{3}{4} \cdot 5\frac{2}{3}$

16. $\frac{1}{2} \div \frac{1}{3}$

17. $\frac{6}{5} \div \frac{3}{5}$

18. $8\frac{1}{2} \div 4\frac{1}{4}$

19. $5\frac{5}{6} \div 2\frac{1}{3}$

20. $3\frac{1}{6} \div 1\frac{3}{4}$

21. $7\frac{1}{2} + 3\frac{3}{4}$

22. $3\frac{2}{3} \div \frac{1}{2}$

23. $\frac{8}{9} - \frac{2}{3}$

24. $7\frac{2}{7} \div 2\frac{3}{7}$

25. $\frac{7}{8} \cdot 5\frac{1}{2}$

26. $2\frac{3}{4} \cdot \frac{5}{8}$

27. $8 - 5\frac{5}{6}$

28. $14\frac{1}{4} - 5\frac{2}{3}$

29. $4\frac{2}{3} + 1\frac{6}{11}$

30. $5\frac{1}{4} \cdot 8$

Ratios and Proportions

A *ratio* is a comparison of two quantities by division. You can write *equal ratios* by multiplying or dividing each term by the same nonzero number.

Ways to Write a Ratio

$a:b$ a to b $\frac{a}{b}$ $(b \neq 0)$

■Example 1   Write $3\frac{1}{3} : \frac{1}{2}$ as a ratio in simplest form.

$$3\frac{1}{3} : \frac{1}{2} \longrightarrow \frac{3\frac{1}{3}}{\frac{1}{2}} = \frac{20}{3} \text{ or } 20:3$$

In simplest form, both terms should be integers. Multiply by the common denominator, 6.

A *rate* is a ratio that compares different types of quantities. In simplest form for a rate, the second quantity is one unit.

■Example 2   Write 247 mi in 5.2 h as a rate in simplest form.

$$\frac{247 \text{ mi}}{5.2 \text{ h}} = \frac{47.5 \text{ mi}}{1 \text{ h}} \text{ or } 47.5 \text{ mi/h}$$

←Divide by 5.2 to make the second quantity one unit.

A *proportion* is a statement that two ratios are equal. You can find a missing term in a proportion by using the *cross products*.

Cross Products of a Proportion

$\frac{a}{b} = \frac{c}{d} \Rightarrow ad = bc$

■Example 3   Write a proportion. Then solve.

The Copy Center charges $2.52 for 63 copies. At that rate, how much will the Copy Center charge for 140 copies?

$$\begin{aligned}\text{cost} &\longrightarrow \frac{2.52}{63} = \frac{c}{140} & \longleftarrow\text{Write each ratio as } cost : copies.\\\text{copies} &\longrightarrow \\2.52 \cdot 140 &= 63c & \longleftarrow\text{Use cross products.}\\c &= \frac{2.52 \cdot 140}{63} & \longleftarrow\text{Solve for } c.\\&= 5.6 \text{ or } \$5.60\end{aligned}$$

EXERCISES

Write each ratio or rate in simplest form.

1. 15 to 20   **2.** $85:34$ **3.** 38 g in 4 oz   **4.** 375 mi in 4.3 h   **5.** $\frac{84}{30}$

Solve each proportion.

6. $\frac{a}{5} = \frac{12}{15}$ **7.** $\frac{21}{12} = \frac{14}{x}$ **8.** $8:15 = n:25$ **9.** $2.4 : c = 4:3$ **10.** $\frac{17}{8} = \frac{n}{20}$

11. $\frac{13}{n} = \frac{20}{3}$ **12.** $5:7 = y:5$ **13.** $\frac{0.4}{3.5} = \frac{5.2}{x}$ **14.** $\frac{4}{x} = \frac{7}{6}$ **15.** $4:n = n:9$

16. A canary's heart beats 130 times in 12 s. Use a proportion to find how many times its heart beats in 50 s.

17. According to the label, there are 65 calories in 4 fl oz of pineapple juice. How many calories are in 14 oz of the juice?

Simplifying Expressions with Integers

To add two numbers with the same sign, *add* their absolute values. The sum has the same sign as the numbers. To add two numbers with different signs, find the *difference* between their absolute values. The sum has the same sign as the number with the greater absolute value.

■Example 1   **Add.**

a. $-8 + (-5) = -13$ **b.** $-8 + 5 = -3$ **c.** $8 + (-5) = 3$

To subtract a number, add its opposite.

■Example 2   **Subtract.**

a. $4 - 7 = 4 + (-7)$ **b.** $-4 - (-7) = -4 + 7$ **c.** $-4 - 7 = -4 + (-7)$
        $= -3$ $= 3$ $= -11$

The product or quotient of two numbers with the same sign is positive. The product or quotient of two numbers with different signs is negative.

■Example 3   **Multiply or divide.**

a. $(-3)(-5) = 15$ **b.** $-35 \div 7 = -5$ **c.** $24 \div (-6) = -4$

■Example 4   **Simplify $2^2 - 3(4 - 6) + 12$.**

Use the order of operations shown at the right.

$$
\begin{aligned}
2^2 - 3(4 - 6) - 12 &= 2^2 - 3(-2) - 12 \\
&= 4 - 3(-2) - 12 \\
&= 4 - (-6) - 12 \\
&= 4 + 6 - 12 \\
&= 10 - 12 = -2
\end{aligned}
$$

Order of Operations

1. Perform any operation(s) inside grouping symbols.
2. Simplify any terms with exponents.
3. Multiply and divide in order from left to right.
4. Add and subtract in order from left to right.

EXERCISES

Simplify each expression.

1. $-4 + 5$ **2.** $12 - 12$ **3.** $-15 + (-23)$ **4.** $4 - 17$ **5.** $-5 - 12$

6. $17 + (-18)$ **7.** $3 - (-5)$ **8.** $-8 - (-12)$ **9.** $-19 + 5$ **10.** $-8 + (-8)$

11. $(-7)(-4)$ **12.** $-120 \div 30$ **13.** $(-3)(4)$ **14.** $75 \div (-3)$ **15.** $(-6)(15)$

16. $(18)(-4)$ **17.** $-84 \div (-7)$ **18.** $(-13)(-3)$ **19.** $(-225) \div (-15)$ **20.** $-16 \div 8$

21. $-2(1 + 5) + (-3)(2)$ **22.** $-4(-2 - 5) + 3(1 - 4)$ **23.** $20 - (3)(12) + 4^2$

24. $\frac{-15}{-5} - \frac{36}{-12} + \frac{-12}{-4}$ **25.** $5^2 - 6(5 - 9)$ **26.** $4\left[(12)(3) - \frac{12}{3}\right]$

27. $(-3 + 2^3)\left(4 + \frac{-42}{7}\right)$ **28.** $(3 - 10)^2 + 3(-10)$ **29.** $(7 + 7)(7 - 7) - \frac{7}{-7}$

30. $5 - (-4)(-3) + 3^2$ **31.** $\left(\frac{-15}{5}\right)^2 + (7 - 4)^2$ **32.** $[4(-3)]^2 + 4(-3)^2$

Evaluating Formulas and Solving Literal Equations

To evaluate a formula, first substitute the known values for the variables. Then perform the indicated operations.

■Example 1   **Find the volume of a cone that has a radius of 5 in. and a height of 10 in. Use the formula $V = \frac{1}{3}\pi r^2 h$.**

$V = \frac{1}{3}\pi r^2 h$

$\quad = \frac{1}{3}(3.14)(5)^2(10)$ ⟵ Replace π with 3.14, r with 5, and h with 10.

$\quad \approx 262$ in.^{3} ⟵ Round your answer.

Sometimes you do not know values for the variables in a formula, so you cannot substitute. To solve a formula or a literal equation for one of the variables in it, use properties of equality.

■Example 2   **Solve $P = 2(\ell + w)$ for w.**

$P = 2(\ell + w)$

$\frac{P}{2} = \ell + w$ ⟵ Divide each side by 2.

$\frac{P}{2} - \ell = w$ ⟵ Subtract ℓ from each side.

Thus, $w = \frac{P}{2} - \ell$.

EXERCISES

Evaluate each formula. Give decimal answers to the nearest tenth.

1. $P = 2(\ell + w); \ell = 3.2, w = 4$ **2.** $c = 0.5q + 0.5n; q = 3, n = 5$ **3.** $d = rt; r = 35, t = 2.4$

4. $y = 3.5x + 2; x = 1.5$ **5.** $y = (x + 2)(x - 2); x = 5$ **6.** $A = s^2; s = 10.5$

7. $a = \sqrt{c^2 - b^2}; c = 5.5, b = 3$ **8.** $d = 0.5gt^2; g = -32, t = 4.5$

9. $y = 2x^2 - 3x + 1; x = 6$ **10.** $A = \frac{1}{2}(b_1 + b_2)h; b_1 = 13, b_2 = 9, h = 8$

11. $V = \pi r^2 h; r = 4.3, h = 9.1$ **12.** $A = \frac{1}{2}bh; b = 13.7, h = 8.5$

Solve each equation for the given variable.

13. $P = 2(\ell + w); \ell$ **14.** $d = rt; r$ **15.** $2a + b = c; b$ **16.** $I = Prt; P$

17. $\frac{1}{2}x = y; x$ **18.** $2(x + a) = c; a$ **19.** $m + n + p = q; m$ **20.** $\frac{c + d}{2} = a; c$

21. $mnp = q; m$ **22.** $y = mx + b; m$ **23.** $2r + 3s = 1; r$ **24.** $3a = 2b; b$

25. $A = \frac{1}{2}bh; b$ **26.** $V = \ell wh; h$ **27.** $c^2 = a^2 + b^2; b$ **28.** $m = \frac{a + b + c}{3}; b$

29. The formula $V = \frac{1}{2}\ell(A_1 + A_2)$ relates the volume V of a log to its length ℓ and the area of each end A_1 and A_2. Find the length of a log that has a volume of 23 ft^3 and end areas of 0.32 ft^2 and 1.58 ft^2.

Area and Volume

The *area* of a plane figure is the number of square units contained in the figure. The *volume* of a space figure is the number of cubic units contained in the figure. Formulas for area and volume are listed on page 666.

■Example 1 Find the area of each figure.

a.

$A = bh$
$= 3.2 \cdot 1.8$
$= 5.76 \approx 5.8 \text{ cm}^2$

b.

$A = \pi r^2$
$\approx \frac{22}{7} \cdot \left(\frac{21}{10}\right)^2$
$= \frac{693}{50} \approx 13\frac{43}{50} \text{ in.}^2$

c.

$A = \frac{1}{2}(b_1 + b_2)h$
$= \frac{1}{2}(19 + 23) \cdot 8.5$
$= 178.5 \text{ mm}^2$

■Example 2 Find the volume of each figure.

a.

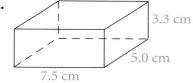

$V = \ell wh$
$= 7.5 \cdot 5.0 \cdot 3.3$
$= 123.75 \approx 124.8 \text{ cm}^3$

b.

$V = \frac{1}{3}Bh$
$= \frac{1}{3}(37^2) \cdot 24$
$= 10{,}952 \text{ ft}^3$

c.

$V = \frac{4}{3}\pi r^3$
$\approx \frac{4}{3} \cdot 3.14 \cdot 2.7^3$
$= 82.406\ 16 \approx 82.4 \text{ m}^3$

EXERCISES

Find the area of each figure.

1.

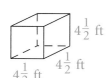

2.

3.

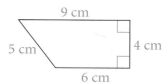

4.

Find the volume of each figure.

5.

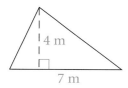

6.

7.

8.

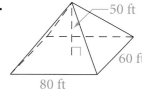

9. Find the area of a triangle with a base of 17 in. and a height of 13 in.

10. Find the volume of a box 64 cm long, 48 cm wide, and 58 cm high.

The Coordinate Plane and Slope of a Line

The *coordinate plane* is formed when two number lines intersect at right angles. The ordered pair $(-2, 4)$ identifies the location of a point on the plane. From the origin, move 2 units to the left and 4 units up.

■**Example 1**   **In which quadrant would you find each point?**

a. $(3, -4)$ Move 3 units right and 4 units down. The point is in Quadrant IV.

b. $(-2, -5)$ Move 2 units left and 5 units down. The point is in Quadrant III.

To find the slope of a line on the coordinate plane, choose two points on the line and use the slope formula.

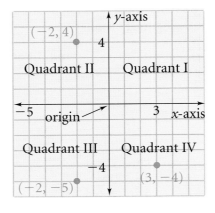

■**Example 2**   **Find the slope of each line.**

a.
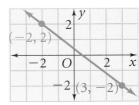

$$m = \frac{y_2 - y_1}{x_2 - x_1}$$
$$= \frac{2 - (-2)}{-2 - 3}$$
$$= \frac{4}{-5} \text{ or } -\frac{4}{5}$$

b.
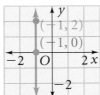

$$m = \frac{y_2 - y_1}{x_2 - x_1}$$
$$= \frac{2 - 0}{-1 - (-1)}$$
$$= \frac{2}{0} \quad \longleftarrow \text{undefined}$$

Since you cannot divide by zero, this line has an undefined slope.

EXERCISES

Name the point with the given coordinates in the graph at the right.

1. $(3, 2)$ **2.** $(-4, 3)$ **3.** $(0, -3)$ **4.** $(4, -2)$

Name the coordinates of each point in the graph at the right.

5. F **6.** A **7.** G **8.** E

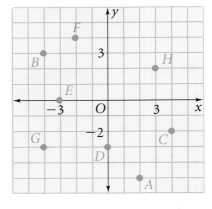

Graph each point on a coordinate plane.

9. $(4, 0)$ **10.** $(-3, 5)$ **11.** $(4, -3)$ **12.** $(-5, -2)$

13. $(0, -2)$ **14.** $(-4, 5)$ **15.** $(4, -5)$ **16.** $(3, -3)$

Find the slope of each line.

17.
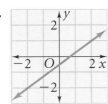

18.
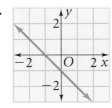

19.
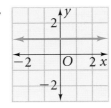

20.
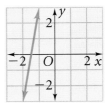

21. the line containing $(-3, 4)$ and $(2, -6)$.

22. the line containing $(25, 40)$ and $(100, 55)$

Solving Linear Equations and Inequalities

To solve a linear equation having one variable, use inverse operations and properties of equality to get the variable alone on one side of the equals sign.

■Example 1   Solve each equation.

a.
$$3x - 11 = -5$$
$$3x - 11 + 11 = -5 + 11 \quad \longleftarrow \text{ Add 11 to each side.}$$
$$\frac{3x}{3} = \frac{6}{3} \quad \longleftarrow \text{ Divide each side by 3.}$$
$$x = 2$$

b.
$$\tfrac{2}{3}x + 1 = -5$$
$$\tfrac{2}{3}x + 1 - 1 = -5 - 1 \quad \longleftarrow \begin{array}{l}\text{Subtract 1 from}\\\text{each side.}\end{array}$$
$$\tfrac{3}{2} \cdot \tfrac{2}{3}x = \tfrac{3}{2} \cdot -6 \quad \longleftarrow \begin{array}{l}\text{Multiply each}\\\text{side by } \tfrac{3}{2}.\end{array}$$
$$x = -9$$

Sometimes you can use the distributive property to simplify an equation.

■Example 2   Solve each equation.

a.
$$2(x + 8) - 5 = 7$$
$$2x + 16 - 5 = 7 \quad \longleftarrow \begin{array}{l}\text{Distribute to remove}\\\text{parentheses.}\end{array}$$
$$2x = -4$$
$$x = -2$$

b.
$$2x + 9 = 6x \quad \quad \quad \begin{array}{l}\text{Subtract}\end{array}$$
$$2x - 2x + 9 = 6x - 2x \quad \longleftarrow \begin{array}{l}2x \text{ from}\\\text{each side.}\end{array}$$
$$9 = 4x$$
$$\tfrac{9}{4} = x \, (\text{or } x = 2.25)$$

In solving an inequality, you must reverse the order of the inequality when you multiply or divide each side by a negative number.

■Example 3   Solve and graph each inequality.

a.
$$\tfrac{x}{3} - 2 > -4$$
$$\tfrac{x}{3} - 2 + 2 > -4 + 2$$
$$3 \cdot \tfrac{x}{3} > 3(-2)$$
$$x > -6$$

b.
$$2x \geq 5x - 9$$
$$2x - 5x \geq 5x - 5x - 9 \quad \begin{array}{l}\text{Divide each side}\\\text{by } -3 \text{ and}\end{array}$$
$$\tfrac{-3x}{-3} \leq \tfrac{-9}{-3} \quad \longleftarrow \begin{array}{l}\text{reverse the order}\\\text{of the inequality.}\end{array}$$
$$x \leq 3$$

EXERCISES

Solve each equation.

1. $x + 4 = 3$

2. $3c - 7 = -13$

3. $8y - 3 + y = 51$

4. $6a = -48$

5. $\tfrac{1}{2}(s - 6) = 17$

6. $\tfrac{d}{3} = -8$

7. $\tfrac{4}{9}h = \tfrac{2}{3}$

8. $\tfrac{2}{3}r + 9 = 75$

9. $4(t + 5) = -36$

10. $7g - 3g + 2 = 6$

11. $3(x - 4) = 2x + 1$

12. $q + 4.5 = 3q - 2.7$

Solve and graph each inequality.

13. $9 + x \leq 15$

14. $-g < 5$

15. $7y + 2 \geq -12$

16. $9h > -18$

17. $\tfrac{s}{5} \geq 7$

18. $4 - a \leq 9$

19. $-\tfrac{c}{4} < 7$

20. $-\tfrac{3v}{5} > -\tfrac{9}{10}$

21. $t - 5.3 < -3.3$

22. $4y - 9y > -55$

23. $-5w > 2w - 21$

24. $\tfrac{3c}{7} \leq -\tfrac{2}{3}$

Absolute-Value Equations and Inequalities

To solve an absolute-value equation, get the absolute value by itself on one side of the equation. Then use the definition of absolute value to write two equations.

■**Example 1**   **Solve** $|x| + 3 = 11$.

$|x| + 3 = 11$ ⟵ Subtract 3 from each side.
$\quad\ |x| = 8$ ⟵ The value of x is either 8 or -8.
$x = 8$ or $x = -8$

■**Example 2**   **Solve** $|p - 20| = 4$.

$|p - 20| = 4$ ⟵ The value of the expression $p - 20$ is 4 or -4.
$\ p - 20 = 4$ or $p - 20 = -4$ ⟵ Write two equations.
$\qquad p = 24$ or $\qquad p = 16$ ⟵ Solve for p.

To solve an absolute-value inequality, write two inequalities. Join the inequalities with *and* when $|x| < c$. Join them with *or* when $|x| > c$.

■**Example 3**   **Solve** $|x - 3| < 5$. **Graph the solution.**

$|x - 3| < 5$
$\ x - 3 < 5$ and $x - 3 > -5$ ⟵ Write two inequalities joined by *and*.
$\qquad x < 8$ and $\qquad x > -2$ ⟵ The solutions are all numbers less than 8 *and* greater than -2.

■**Example 4**   **Solve** $|x + 2| \geq 4$. **Graph the solution.**

$|x + 2| \geq 4$
$\ x + 2 \geq 4$ or $x + 2 \leq -4$ ⟵ Write two inequalities joined by *or*.
$\qquad x \geq 2$ or $\qquad x \leq -6$ ⟵ The solutions are all numbers less than or equal
$\qquad\qquad\qquad\qquad\qquad\qquad$ to -6 *or* greater than or equal to 2.

EXERCISES

Solve each equation.

1. $|y| = 8$ **2.** $|a| + 4 = 7$ **3.** $|c + 4| = 9$ **4.** $3|r| = 18$

5. $|5x| = 35$ **6.** $-7|p| + 4 = -17$ **7.** $|w - 8| = 7$ **8.** $|3t - 2| = 8$

9. $\frac{|v|}{4} = 5$ **10.** $\left|h + \frac{1}{2}\right| = 5\frac{1}{2}$ **11.** $|n - 7| = 0$ **12.** $8|z + 3| = 24$

Solve each inequality. Graph the solution.

13. $|x - 6| \leq 9$ **14.** $|a + 3| > 7$ **15.** $|r| \geq 7$ **16.** $|3y| > 39$

17. $|5p| \leq 12$ **18.** $4|k| + 3 \leq 5$ **19.** $|7x + 4| < 10$ **20.** $7|w - 5| \geq 21$

Graphing Two-Variable Equations and Inequalities

An equation in the form $Ax + By = C$ represents a line. To graph the line, first find the x-intercept and the y-intercept.

■ Example 1   **Graph $2x - 4y = 16$.**

$2x - 4y = 16$
$2x - 4(0) = 16$ ← To find the x-intercept,
$2x = 16$ replace y with 0.
$x = 8$ ← Solve for x.

$2x - 4y = 16$
$2(0) - 4y = 16$ ← To find the y-intercept,
$-4y = 16$ replace x with 0.
$y = -4$ ← Solve for y.

The x-intercept occurs at $(8, 0)$.

The y-intercept occurs at $(0, -4)$.

Plot the points $(8, 0)$ and $(0, -4)$. Then draw a line through the points.

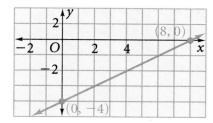

The equation $x = -3$ does not have a y-intercept. In this case, use *any* two points that lie on the line. For example, use $(-3, 1)$ and $(-3, 3)$.

A linear inequality describes a region of the coordinate plane that has a boundary line. Draw a dashed line when the inequality uses $<$ or $>$. Draw a solid line when the inequality uses $\leq$ or $\geq$.

■ Example 2   **Graph $2x + y > 5$.**

First, graph the boundary line $2x + y = 5$. Use the x-intercept $(2.5, 0)$ and the y-intercept $(0, 5)$. Since the inequality uses $>$, draw a dashed line.

Next, test a point. Use $(0, 0)$. $2x + y > 5$
$2(0) + 0 > 5$
$0 > 5$ False

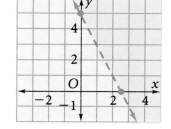

The inequality is *false* for $(0, 0)$. Shade the region that does *not* contain $(0, 0)$.

EXERCISES

Graph each equation or inequality.

1. $x + y = 6$

2. $2x + y = -4$

3. $x = 6$

4. $y = -3$

5. $3x - 2y = 12$

6. $x - 3y = -6$

7. $x - y = -3$

8. $y = x - 4$

9. $3x + 5y = 30$

10. $y = -4x + 5$

11. $2x - 5y = 20$

12. $4x + 7y = -21$

13. $y \geq -2$

14. $x + 2y < 8$

15. $4x - 4y > 8$

16. $x + 3y \leq 12$

17. $x - 5 < 0$

18. $7x - 4y > 12$

19. $y - 3x \leq 6$

20. $5x + 4y \geq 0$

21. $x + 5y \geq -8$

22. $y = \frac{2}{3}x + 2$

23. $\frac{2}{5}x - \frac{1}{2}y > 10$

24. $3y - x \leq 0$

Operations with Exponents

An exponent indicates how many times a number is used as a factor.

Example 1   **Write using exponents.**

a. $3 \cdot 3 \cdot 3 \cdot 3 \cdot 3 = 3^5$

      ↑
  five factors of 3

b. $a \cdot a \cdot b \cdot b \cdot b \cdot b = a^2 b^4$

    ↑   ↑
two factors of a; four factors of b

The patterns shown at the right indicate that $a^0 = 1$ and that $a^{-n} = \frac{1}{a^n}$.

$2^n = \blacksquare$	$10^n = \blacksquare$
$2^2 = 4$	$10^2 = 100$
$2^1 = 2$	$10^1 = 10$
$2^0 = 1$	$10^0 = 1$
$2^{-1} = \frac{1}{2}$	$10^{-1} = \frac{1}{10}$
$2^{-2} = \frac{1}{4}$	$10^{-2} = \frac{1}{100}$

Example 2   **Write each expression so that all exponents are positive.**

a. $a^{-2}b^3 = \frac{1}{a^2} \cdot b^3 = \frac{b^3}{a^2}$

b. $x^3 y^0 z^{-1} = x^3 \cdot 1 \cdot \frac{1}{z} = \frac{x^3}{z}$

You can simplify expressions that contain powers with the same base.

Example 3   **Simplify each expression.**

a. $b^5 \cdot b^3 = b^{5+3}$ ← Add exponents to multiply
       $= b^8$ powers with the same base.

b. $\frac{x^5}{x^7} = x^{5-7}$ ← Subtract exponents
    $= x^{-2} = \frac{1}{x^2}$ to divide powers
          with the same base.

You can simplify expressions that contain parentheses and exponents.

Example 4   **Simplify each expression.**

a. $\left(\frac{ab}{n}\right)^3 = \frac{a^3 b^3}{n^3}$ ← Raise each factor in the
              parentheses to the third power.

b. $(c^2)^4 = c^{2 \cdot 4} = c^8$ ← Multiply exponents to
               raise a power to a power.

EXERCISES

Write each expression using exponents.

1. $x \cdot x \cdot x$

2. $x \cdot x \cdot x \cdot y \cdot y$

3. $a \cdot a \cdot a \cdot a \cdot b$

4. $\frac{a \cdot a \cdot a \cdot a}{b \cdot b}$

Write each expression so that all exponents are positive.

5. c^{-4}

6. $m^{-2}n^0$

7. $x^5 y^{-7} z^{-3}$

8. $ab^{-1}c^2$

Simplify each expression. Use positive exponents.

9. $d^2 d^6$

10. $n^4 n$

11. $r^3 \cdot r^2 \cdot s^7 \cdot s$

12. $x^5 y^3 \cdot xy^2 z^6$

13. $\frac{a^5}{a^2}$

14. $\frac{c^7}{c}$

15. $\frac{n^3}{n^6}$

16. $\frac{a^5 b^3}{ab^8}$

17. $(rt)^3$

18. $(3x)^2$

19. $\left(\frac{a}{b}\right)^4$

20. $\left(\frac{xz}{y}\right)^6$

21. $(c^3)^4$

22. $\left(\frac{x^2}{y^5}\right)^3$

23. $(u^4 v^2)^3$

24. $(p^5)^{-2}$

25. $\frac{(2a^4)(3a^2)}{6a^3}$

26. $(x^{-2})^3$

27. $(4a^2 b)^3 (ab)^2$

28. $(mg^3)^{-1}$

29. $g^{-3} g^{-1}$

30. $\frac{x^2 y^3 z^{-1}}{x^5 y z^3}$

31. $\frac{(3a^3)^2}{18a}$

32. $\frac{c^3 d^7}{c^{-3} d^{-1}}$

Factoring and Operations with Polynomials

When the terms of a polynomial are in descending order by degree and all like terms have been combined, the polynomial is in standard form.

■Example 1 Perform each operation. Write in standard form.

a. $(3y^2 - 4y + 5) + (y^2 + 9y) = (3y^2 + y^2) + (-4y + 9y) + 5$ ◄— To add, group like terms.
$$= 4y^2 + 5y + 5$$ ◄— Write in standard form.

b. $8a^2(3a^2 - 5a - 2) = 8a^2(3a^2) + 8a^2(-5a) + 8a^2(-2)$ ◄— To multiply, distribute $8a^2$.
$$= 24a^4 - 40a^3 - 16a^2$$

c. $(n + 4)(n - 3) = n(n) + n(-3) + 4(n) + 4(-3)$ ◄— Distribute n and 4.
$$= n^2 - 3n + 4n - 12$$
$$= n^2 + n - 12$$

To factor a polynomial, first find the greatest common factor (GCF) of the terms. Then use the distributive property to factor out the GCF.

■Example 2 Factor $6x^3 - 12x^2 + 18x$.

$6x^3 = 6 \cdot x \cdot x \cdot x; -12x^2 = 6 \cdot (-2) \cdot x \cdot x; 18x = 6 \cdot 3 \cdot x$ ◄— List the factors of each term. The GCF is $6x$.

$6x^3 - 12x^2 + 18x = 6x(x^2) + 6x(-2x) + 6x(3)$ ◄— Use the distributive property to factor out $6x$.
$$= 6x(x^2 - 2x + 3)$$

When a polynomial is the product of two binomials, you can work backward to find the factors.

$x^2 + bx + c = (x + \square)(x + \square)$ ⌐ The *sum* of the numbers you use here must equal *b*.
└ The *product* of the numbers you use here must equal *c*.

■Example 3 Factor $x^2 - 13x + 36$.

Choose numbers that are factors of 36. Look for a pair with the sum -13. The numbers -4 and -9 have a product of 36 and a sum of -13. The factors are $(x - 4)$ and $(x - 9)$. So, $x^2 - 13x + 36 = (x - 4)(x - 9)$.

factors	sum
-6×-6	-12
-4×-9	-13

EXERCISES

Perform the indicated operations. Write each answer in standard form.

1. $(x^2 + 3x - 1) + (7x - 4)$ **2.** $(a^3 - 7a) + (3a^3 + 4a)$ **3.** $(8n - 3) + (-3n - 2)$

4. $(5y^2 + 7y) - (3y^2 + 9y - 8)$ **5.** $(c^2 - c + 5) - (c^2 + c - 2)$ **6.** $4x^2(3x^2 - 5x + 9)$

7. $-5d(13d^2 - 7d + 8)$ **8.** $(x - 5)(x + 3)$ **9.** $(n - 7)(n - 2)$

Factor each polynomial.

10. $a^2 - 8a + 12$ **11.** $b^3 + 6b^2$ **12.** $n^2 - 2n - 8$ **13.** $x^2 + 5x + 4$

14. $3m^2 - 9$ **15.** $y^2 + 5y - 24$ **16.** $s^3 + 6s^2 + 11s$ **17.** $2x^3 + 4x^2 - 8x$

18. $y^2 - 10y + 25$ **19.** $3r^2 - 48$ **20.** $2x^2 + 5x - 12$ **21.** $4w^2 - 9$

Scientific Notation and Significant Digits

In *scientific notation*, a number has the form $a \times 10^n$, where n is an integer and $1 \leq |a| < 10$.

■**Example 1** Write 5.59×10^6 in standard form.

$5.59 \times 10^6 = 5\,590\,000$ ⟵ A positive exponent indicates a value greater than 1.
$\qquad\qquad = 5{,}590{,}000$ Move the decimal point six places to the right.

■**Example 2** Write 0.000 031 8 in scientific notation.

$0.0000318 = 3.18 \times 10^{-5}$ ⟵ Move the decimal point to create a number between 1 and 10 (five places to the right). Since the original number is less than 1, use a negative exponent.

When a measurement is in scientific notation, all the digits of the number between 1 and 10 are *significant digits*. When you multiply or divide measurements, your answer should have as many significant digits as the least number of significant digits in any of the numbers involved.

■**Example 3** Multiply $(6.75 \times 10^8 \text{ mi/h})$ and $(3.8 \times 10^4 \text{ h})$.

$(6.75 \times 10^8 \text{ mi/h})(3.8 \times 10^4 \text{ h}) = (6.75 \cdot 3.8)(10^8 \cdot 10^4)$ ⟵Rearrange factors.
$\qquad\qquad\qquad\qquad\qquad\qquad = 25.65 \times 10^{12}$ ⟵Add exponents when multiplying powers of 10.
$\qquad\qquad\qquad\qquad\qquad\qquad = 2.565 \times 10^{13}$ ⟵Write in scientific notation.
$\qquad\qquad\qquad\qquad\qquad\qquad \approx 2.6 \times 10^{13} \text{ mi}$ ⟵Round to two significant digits.

three significant digits   two significant digits

■**Example 4** Simplify $\dfrac{6.332 \times 10^5}{1.6 \times 10^{-2}}$.

$\dfrac{6.332 \times 10^5}{1.6 \times 10^{-2}} = \dfrac{6.332}{1.6} \times 10^{5-(-2)}$ ⟵Subtract exponents when dividing powers of 10.
$\qquad\qquad = 3.9575 \times 10^7$ ⟵Simplify.
$\qquad\qquad \approx 4.0 \times 10^7$ ⟵Round to two significant digits.

EXERCISES

Change each number to scientific notation or to standard form.

1. 1,340,000 **2.** 6.88×10^{-2} **3.** 0.000 775 **4.** 0.0072 **5.** 1.113×10^5

6. 8.0×10^{-4} **7.** 1895 **8.** 2.3×10^3 **9.** 123,400 **10.** 7.985×10^4

Write each product or quotient in scientific notation. Round to the appropriate number of significant digits.

11. $(1.6 \times 10^2)(4.0 \times 10^3)$ **12.** $(2.5 \times 10^{-3})(1.2 \times 10^4)$ **13.** $(4.237 \times 10^4)(2.01 \times 10^{-2})$

14. $\dfrac{7.0 \times 10^5}{2.89 \times 10^3}$ **15.** $\dfrac{1.4 \times 10^4}{8.0 \times 10^2}$ **16.** $\dfrac{6.48 \times 10^6}{3.2 \times 10^5}$

17. $(1.78 \times 10^{-7})(5.03 \times 10^{-5})$ **18.** $(7.2 \times 10^{11})(5 \times 10^6)$ **19.** $(8.90 \times 10^8) \div (2.36 \times 10^{-2})$

20. $(3.95 \times 10^4) \div (6.8 \times 10^8)$ **21.** $(4.9 \times 10^{-8}) \div (2.7 \times 10^{-2})$ **22.** $(3.972 \times 10^{-5})(4.7 \times 10^{-4})$

Operations with Radicals

To simplify a radical, remove all perfect square factors from the radicand.

Example 1 **Simplify $\sqrt{75}$.**

$\sqrt{75} = \sqrt{25 \cdot 3} = \sqrt{25} \cdot \sqrt{3} = 5\sqrt{3}$ ←— Use the property $\sqrt{ab} = \sqrt{a} \cdot \sqrt{b}$.

Example 2 **Simplify $\sqrt{18} - \sqrt{50} + \sqrt{27}$.**

$$\sqrt{18} - \sqrt{50} + \sqrt{27} = \sqrt{9 \cdot 2} - \sqrt{25 \cdot 2} + \sqrt{9 \cdot 3} \quad \text{←— Simplify each radical.}$$
$$= 3\sqrt{2} - 5\sqrt{2} + 3\sqrt{3} \quad \text{←— Use the distributive property}$$
$$= (3 - 5)\sqrt{2} + 3\sqrt{3} \quad \text{to combine like terms.}$$
$$= -2\sqrt{2} + 3\sqrt{3}$$

To remove a radical from the denominator of a fraction, you *rationalize* the denominator. Make the denominator rational by multiplying by a form of 1.

Example 3 **Simplify each expression**

a. $\dfrac{5}{\sqrt{3}} = \dfrac{5}{\sqrt{3}} \cdot \dfrac{\sqrt{3}}{\sqrt{3}}$ ←— Multiply the fraction by $\dfrac{\sqrt{3}}{\sqrt{3}}$ to make the denominator a rational number.

$= \dfrac{5\sqrt{3}}{\sqrt{9}} = \dfrac{5\sqrt{3}}{3}$

b. $\dfrac{2}{\sqrt{3}} \cdot \sqrt{\dfrac{5}{6}} = \dfrac{2}{\sqrt{3}} \cdot \dfrac{\sqrt{5}}{\sqrt{6}}$ ←— Use the property $\sqrt{\dfrac{a}{b}} = \dfrac{\sqrt{a}}{\sqrt{b}}$.

$= \dfrac{2\sqrt{5}}{\sqrt{18}}$ ←— Multiply radicals.

$= \dfrac{2\sqrt{5}\sqrt{2}}{\sqrt{18}\sqrt{2}}$ ←— Multiply by $\dfrac{\sqrt{2}}{\sqrt{2}}$ to make the denominator a rational number.

$= \dfrac{2\sqrt{10}}{\sqrt{36}}$

$= \dfrac{2\sqrt{10}}{6} = \dfrac{\sqrt{10}}{3}$

EXERCISES

Simplify each radical expression.

1. $\sqrt{36}$ 2. $\sqrt{72}$ 3. $\sqrt{18}$ 4. $\sqrt{108}$ 5. $\sqrt{54}$ 6. $\sqrt{60}$

7. $\sqrt{300}$ 8. $\sqrt{\dfrac{1}{2}}$ 9. $\dfrac{2}{\sqrt{3}}$ 10. $\dfrac{3}{\sqrt{5}}$ 11. $\dfrac{\sqrt{2}}{\sqrt{5}}$ 12. $\dfrac{\sqrt{3}}{\sqrt{8}}$

13. $\dfrac{1}{\sqrt{2}} \cdot \dfrac{\sqrt{3}}{\sqrt{2}}$ 14. $\sqrt{\dfrac{2}{3}} \cdot \sqrt{\dfrac{5}{6}}$ 15. $\dfrac{\sqrt{2}}{3} \cdot \sqrt{\dfrac{8}{5}}$ 16. $\sqrt{\dfrac{2}{7}} \cdot \sqrt{\dfrac{8}{7}}$ 17. $\dfrac{2}{\sqrt{2}} \cdot \sqrt{\dfrac{5}{3}}$ 18. $\sqrt{2} + \sqrt{2}$

19. $3\sqrt{5} + 2\sqrt{5}$ 20. $7\sqrt{7} - \sqrt{7}$ 21. $4\sqrt{3} - 3\sqrt{3}$ 22. $\sqrt{18} + \sqrt{98}$

23. $\sqrt{8} - \sqrt{50}$ 24. $\sqrt{6} + \sqrt{24}$ 25. $\sqrt{40} + \sqrt{90}$ 26. $\sqrt{27} + \sqrt{75} - \sqrt{12}$

27. $\sqrt{45} + \sqrt{20} + \sqrt{5}$ 28. $\sqrt{3} - \sqrt{75} + \sqrt{18}$ 29. $\sqrt{98} + \sqrt{50} - \sqrt{5}$ 30. $\sqrt{5} + \sqrt{3} - \sqrt{180}$

The Pythagorean Theorem and the Distance Formula

In a right triangle, the sum of the squares of the lengths of the legs is equal to the square of the length of the hypotenuse. Use this relationship, known as the Pythagorean theorem, to find the length of a side of a right triangle.

The Pythagorean Theorem

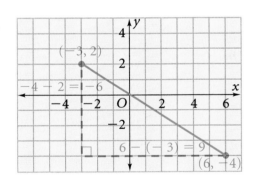

$$a^2 + b^2 = c^2$$

■Example 1   Find m in the triangle below to the nearest tenth.

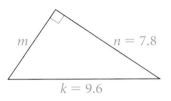

$$m^2 + n^2 = k^2$$
$$m^2 + 7.8^2 = 9.6^2$$
$$m^2 = 9.6^2 - 7.8^2$$
$$m^2 = 31.32$$
$$m = \sqrt{31.32}$$
$$\approx 5.6$$

Thus, m is about 5.6 units.

To find the distance between two points on the coordinate plane, use the distance formula.

The distance d between any two points (x_1, y_1) and (x_2, y_2) is
$$d = \sqrt{(x_2 - x_1)^2 + (y_2 - y_1)^2}.$$

■Example 2   Find the distance between $(-3, 2)$ and $(6, -4)$.

$$d = \sqrt{(6 - (-3))^2 + (-4 - 2)^2}$$
$$= \sqrt{9^2 + (-6)^2}$$
$$= \sqrt{81 + 36}$$
$$= \sqrt{117}$$
$$\approx 10.8$$

Thus, d is about 10.8 units.

EXERCISES

In each problem, a and b are the lengths of the legs of a right triangle and c is the length of the hypotenuse. Find each missing length.

1. c if $a = 6$ and $b = 8$

2. a if $b = 12$ and $c = 13$

3. b if $a = 8$ and $c = 17$

4. c if $a = 10$ and $b = 3$

5. a if $b = 7$ and $c = 25$

6. b if $a = 24$ and $c = 40$

7. a if $b = 100$ and $c = 114$

8. b if $a = 12.0$ and $c = 30.1$

9. c if $a = 8.3$ and $b = 3.3$

Find the distance between each pair of points to the nearest tenth.

10. $(0, 0), (4, -3)$

11. $(-5, -5), (1, 3)$

12. $(-1, 0), (4, 12)$

13. $(0, 15), (17, 0)$

14. $(-4, 2), (4, -2)$

15. $(-8, -8), (8, 8)$

16. $(-1, 1), (1, -1)$

17. $(-2, 9), (0, 0)$

18. $(-5, 3), (4, 3)$

19. $(-2, 1), (3, 4)$

20. $(3, -2), (3, 5)$

21. $(5, 4), (-3, 1)$

Bar and Circle Graphs

Sometimes you can draw different graphs to represent the same data, depending on the information you want to share. A *bar graph* is useful for comparing amounts; a *circle graph* is useful for comparing percents.

■ Example   **Display the 1993 data on immigration to the United States in a bar graph and a circle graph.**

To make a bar graph, place the categories along the bottom axis. For this bar graph, the categories are the places of origin of the immigrants.

Decide on a scale for the side axis. Since the data range from 27.8 to 358.0, an appropriate scale would be 0–400, marked in intervals of 50. For each data item, draw a bar whose height is equal to the data value.

Immigration to the United States, 1993

Place of Origin	Immigrants (1000's)
Africa	27.8
Asia	358.0
Europe	158.3
North America	301.4
South America	53.9

Source: *U.S. Immigration and Nationalization Service*

To make a circle graph, first find the *percent* of the data in each category. Then express each percent as a decimal and multiply by 360° to find the size of each *central angle.*

Africa ⟶ $\dfrac{27.8}{899.4} \approx 0.03$ or 3%
total ⟶
$0.03 \times 360° \approx 11°$

Draw a circle and use a protractor to draw each central angle.

Immigration to the United States, 1993

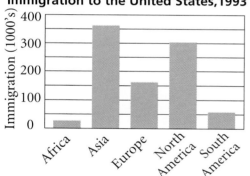

Immigration to the United States, 1993

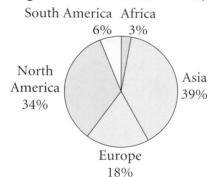

EXERCISES

Display the data from each table in a bar graph and a circle graph.

1.

NASA Space Shuttle Expenses, 1995

Operation	Millions of dollars
Orbiter and external tank	672.4
System integration	190.5
Main engine, solid rocket, and booster	662.4
Launch and landing operations	596.4
Mission and crew operations	298.4

Source: *U.S. National Aeronautics and Space Administration*

2.

Cable TV Revenue, 1993

	Millions of dollars
Advertising and programs	7094
Basic Service	13,609
Pay-per-view and other services	4314
Installation	400
Other	1022

Source: *U.S. Bureau of the Census*

Descriptive Statistics and Histograms

For numerical data, you can find the *mean*, the *median*, and the *mode*.

Mean: The sum of the data values in a data set divided by the number of data values

Median: The middle value of a data set that has been arranged in increasing or decreasing order. If the data set has an even number of values, the median is the mean of the middle two values.

Mode: The most frequently occurring value in a data set

■**Example 1** Find the mean, median, and mode for the following data set.

$$5 \quad 7 \quad 6 \quad 3 \quad 1 \quad 7 \quad 9 \quad 5 \quad 10 \quad 7$$

Mean $\quad \dfrac{5 + 7 + 6 + 3 + 1 + 7 + 9 + 5 + 10 + 7}{10} = 6$

Median $\quad$ 5, 7, 6, 3, 1, 7, 9, 5, 10, 7 $\quad \longleftarrow$ Rearrange the numbers from least to greatest.

$\qquad$ 1, 3, 5, 5, 6, 7, 7, 7, 9, 10 $\quad \longleftarrow$ The median is the mean of the two middle numbers, 6 and 7.

$\qquad$ The median is $\dfrac{6 + 7}{2} = 6.5$.

Mode $\quad$ The most frequently occurring data value is 7.

The frequency of a data value is the number of times it occurs in a data set. A *histogram* is a bar graph that shows the frequency of each data value.

■**Example 2** Use the survey results to make a histogram for the cost of a movie ticket at various theaters.

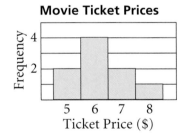
Movie Ticket Prices

Survey of Movie Ticket Prices								
$5	$6	$5	$7	$6	$7	$6	$8	$6

EXERCISES

Find the mean, the median, and the mode of each data set.

1. −3 4 5 5 −2 7 1 8 9

2. 0 0 1 1 2 3 3 5 3 8 7

3. 2.4 2.4 2.3 2.3 2.4 12.0

4. 1 1 1 1 2 2 2 3 3 4

5. 1.2 1.3 1.4 1.5 1.6 1.7 1.8

6. −4 −3 −2 −1 0 1 2 3 4

Make a histogram for each data set.

7. 7 4 8 6 6 8 7 7 5 7

8. 73 75 76 75 74 75 76 74 76 75

Operations with Rational Expressions

A *rational expression* is an expression that can be written in the form $\frac{\text{polynomial}}{\text{polynomial}}$, where a variable is in the denominator. A rational expression is in simplest form if the numerator and denominator have no common factors except 1.

Example 1 Write the expression $\frac{4x + 8}{x + 2}$ in simplest form.

$$\frac{4x + 8}{x + 2} = \frac{4(x + 2)}{x + 2} \quad \longleftarrow \text{Factor the numerator.}$$
$$= 4 \quad \longleftarrow \text{Divide out the common factor } x + 2.$$

To add or subtract two rational expressions, use a common denominator.

Example 2 Simplify $\frac{x}{2y} + \frac{x}{3y}$.

$$\frac{x}{2y} + \frac{x}{3y} = \frac{x}{2y} \cdot \frac{3}{3} + \frac{x}{3y} \cdot \frac{2}{2} \quad \longleftarrow \text{The common denominator of 3y and 2y is 6y.}$$
$$= \frac{3x}{6y} + \frac{2x}{6y}$$
$$= \frac{5x}{6y} \quad \longleftarrow \text{Add the numerators. Place the sum over the common denominator.}$$

To multiply rational expressions, first find and divide out any common factors in the numerators and the denominators. Then multiply the remaining numerators and denominators. To divide rational expressions, first use a reciprocal to change the problem to multiplication.

Example 3 Simplify $\frac{40x^2}{21} \div \frac{5x}{14}$.

$$\frac{40x^2}{21} \div \frac{5x}{14} = \frac{40x^2}{21} \cdot \frac{14}{5x} \quad \longleftarrow \text{Change dividing by } \frac{5x}{14} \text{ to multiplying by the reciprocal, } \frac{14}{5x}.$$
$$= \frac{\overset{8}{\cancel{40x^2}}\,^{1}}{3\,\cancel{21}} \times \frac{\cancel{14}\,^{2}}{1\,\cancel{5x}} \quad \longleftarrow \text{Divide out the common factors of 5, } x, \text{ and 7.}$$
$$= \frac{16x}{3} \quad \longleftarrow \text{Multiply the numerators (8}x \cdot 2\text{). Multiply the denominators (3} \cdot 1\text{).}$$

EXERCISES

Write each expression in simplest form.

1. $\frac{4a^2b}{12ab^3}$ 　　 **2.** $\frac{5n + 15}{n + 3}$ 　　 **3.** $\frac{x - 7}{2x - 14}$ 　　 **4.** $\frac{28c^2(d - 3)}{35c(d - 3)}$

Perform the indicated operation.

5. $\frac{3x}{2} + \frac{5x}{2}$ 　　 **6.** $\frac{3x}{8} + \frac{5x}{8}$ 　　 **7.** $\frac{5}{h} - \frac{3}{h}$ 　　 **8.** $\frac{6}{11p} - \frac{9}{11p}$

9. $\frac{3x}{5} - \frac{x}{2}$ 　　 **10.** $\frac{13}{2x} - \frac{13}{3x}$ 　　 **11.** $\frac{7x}{5} + \frac{5x}{7}$ 　　 **12.** $\frac{5a}{b} + \frac{3a}{5b}$

13. $\frac{7x}{8} \cdot \frac{32x}{35}$ 　　 **14.** $\frac{3x^2}{2} \cdot \frac{6}{x}$ 　　 **15.** $\frac{8x^2}{5} \cdot \frac{10}{x^3}$ 　　 **16.** $\frac{7x}{8} \cdot \frac{64}{14x}$

17. $\frac{16}{3x} \div \frac{5}{3x}$ 　　 **18.** $\frac{4x}{5} \div \frac{16}{15x}$ 　　 **19.** $\frac{x^3}{8} \div \frac{x^2}{16}$ 　　 **20.** $\frac{3}{n^2} \div 9n^4$

Tables

Measures

United States Customary	Metric

Length

United States Customary	Metric
12 inches (in.) = 1 foot (ft)	10 millimeters (mm) = 1 centimeter (cm)
36 in. = 1 yard (yd)	100 cm = 1 meter (m)
3 ft = 1 yard	1000 mm = 1 meter
5280 ft = 1 mile (mi)	1000 m = 1 kilometer (km)
1760 yd = 1 mile	

Area

United States Customary	Metric
144 square inches (in.^{2}) = 1 square foot (ft^2)	100 square millimeters (mm^2) = 1 square centimeter (cm^2)
9 ft^2 = 1 square yard (yd^2)	10,000 cm^2 = 1 square meter (m^2)
43,560 ft^2 = 1 acre (a)	10,000 m^2 = 1 hectare (ha)
4840 yd^2 = 1 acre	

Volume

United States Customary	Metric
1728 cubic inches (in.^{3}) = 1 cubic foot (ft^3)	1000 cubic millimeters (mm^3) = 1 cubic centimeter (cm^3)
27 ft^3 = 1 cubic yard (yd^3)	1,000,000 cm^3 = 1 cubic meter (m^3)

Liquid Capacity

United States Customary	Metric
8 fluid ounces (fl oz) = 1 cup (c)	1000 milliliters (mL) = 1 liter (L)
2 c = 1 pint (pt)	1000 L = 1 kiloliter (kL)
2 pt = 1 quart (qt)	
4 qt = 1 gallon (gal)	

Mass

United States Customary	Metric
16 ounces (oz) = 1 pound (lb)	1000 milligrams (mg) = 1 gram (g)
2000 pounds = 1 ton (t)	1000 g = 1 kilogram (kg)
	1000 kg = 1 metric ton (t)

Temperature

United States Customary	Metric
32°F = freezing point of water	0°C = freezing point of water
98.6°F = normal body temperature	37°C = normal body temperature
212°F = boiling point of water	100°C = boiling point of water

Time

60 seconds (s) = 1 minute (min)	365 days = 1 year (yr)
60 minutes = 1 hour (h)	52 weeks (approx.) = 1 year
24 hours = 1 day (da)	12 months = 1 year
7 days = 1 week (wk)	10 years = 1 decade
4 weeks (approx.) = 1 month (mo)	100 years = 1 century

Symbols

Symbol	Meaning	Page
$=$	equals	p. 6
$\begin{bmatrix} 1 & 2 \\ 3 & 4 \end{bmatrix}$	matrix	p. 7
a_{mn}	element in the mth row and nth column	p. 8
$\%$	percent	p. 8
$\cdot$	multiplication sign, times ($\times$)	p. 10
$(\ )$	parentheses for grouping	p. 10
$\overline{AB}$	segment with endpoints A and B	p. 11
(x, y)	ordered pair	p. 11
x_1, x_2, etc.	specific values of the variable x	p. 11
y_1, y_2, etc.	specific values of the variable y	p. 11
AB	length of $\overline{AB}$; distance between points A and B	p. 11
m	slope of a linear function	p. 11
$\{\ \}$	set braces	p. 20
$f(x)$	f of x; the function value at x	p. 22
$\wedge$	raised to a power (in a spreadsheet formula)	p. 30
$*$	multiply (in a spreadsheet formula)	p. 30
$|a|$	absolute value of a	p. 32
$n!$	n factorial	p. 39
$_nP_r$	permutations of n things taken r at a time	p. 41
$\sqrt{x}$	nonnegative square root of x	p. 44
$\ldots$	and so on	p. 45
π	pi, an irrational number, approximately equal to 3.14	p. 45
$\pm$	plus or minus	p. 47
$\approx$	is approximately equal to	p. 47
$^\circ$	degree(s)	p. 49
b	y-intercept of a linear function	p. 60
$a : b$	ratio of a to b	p. 68
$[x]$	greatest integer	p. 74
$>$	is greater than	p. 75
$\leq$	is less than or equal to	p. 75
$\geq$	is greater than or equal to	p. 75
$<$	is less than	p. 75
$\neq$	is not equal to	p. 75

Symbol	Meaning	Page
$\overset{?}{=}$	is the statement true?	p. 76
$P(\text{event})$	probability of the event	p. 87
$[\ ]$	brackets for grouping	p. 93
A'	A prime	p. 113
$\triangle ABC$	triangle ABC	p. 125
$\begin{vmatrix} a & b \\ c & d \end{vmatrix}$	determinant of matrix A	p. 134
$\det A$	determinant of matrix A	p. 134
A^{-1}	inverse of matrix A	p. 135
$\{x \mid x > 0\}$	the set of all x, such that x is greater than zero	p. 153
$\Rightarrow$	implies	p. 165
i	the imaginary number $\sqrt{-1}$	p. 229
a^n	nth power of a	p. 254
$\frac{1}{a}$	reciprocal of a	p. 254
a^{-n}	$\frac{1}{a^n}, a \neq 0$	p. 254
$_nC_r$	combinations of n things taken r at a time	p. 286
e	the number $2.71828\ldots$	p. 315
$\log_b x$	logarithm of x, base b	p. 318
∞	infinity	p. 357
θ	measure of an angle	p. 410
$\cos \theta$	cosine of θ	p. 411
$\sin \theta$	sine of θ	p. 411
$\angle A$	angle A	p. 417
$\tan \theta$	tangent of θ	p. 432
$\sin^{-1} x$	the angle whose sine is x	p. 439
$\tan^{-1} x$	the angle whose tangent is x	p. 439
$m\angle A$	measure of angle A	p. 439
$\cos^{-1} x$	the angle whose cosine is x	p. 441
$P(A \mid B)$	probability of event A, given event B	p. 512
$\overline{x}$	mean of data values of x	p. 519
σ	sigma	p. 527
$\displaystyle\sum_{n=1}^{5}$	summation	p. 580
$\csc \theta$	cosecant of θ	p. 608
$\sec \theta$	secant of θ	p. 608
$\cot \theta$	cotangent of θ	p. 608

Properties and Formulas of Advanced Algebra

Closure: For all real numbers a and b, $a + b$ and $a \cdot b$ are real numbers.

Associative: For all real numbers a, b, and c:
$$(a + b) + c = a + (b + c)$$
$$(a \cdot b) \cdot c = a \cdot (b \cdot c)$$

Commutative: For all real numbers a and b:
$$a + b = b + a \text{ and } a \cdot b = b \cdot a$$

Identity: For every real number a:
$$a + 0 = a \text{ and } 0 + a = a$$
$$a \cdot 1 = a \text{ and } 1 \cdot a = a$$

Inverse: For every real number a:
$$a + (-a) = 0 \text{ and } a \cdot \frac{1}{a} = 1 \, (a \neq 0)$$

(a and $-a$ are opposites, a and $\frac{1}{a}$ are reciprocals.)

Distributive: For all real numbers a, b, and c:
$$a(b + c) = ab + ac; \, (b + c)a = ba + ca$$
$$a(b - c) = ab - ac; \, (b - c)a = ba - ca$$

Properties of Equality

For all real numbers a, b, and c:

Reflexive: $a = a$

Symmetric: If $a = b$, then $b = a$.

Transitive: If $a = b$ and $b = c$, then $a = c$.

Addition: If $a = b$, then $a + c = b + c$.

Subtraction: If $a = b$, then $a - c = b - c$.

Multiplication: If $a = b$, then $a \cdot c = b \cdot c$.

Division: If $a = b$, and $c \neq 0$, then $\frac{a}{c} = \frac{b}{c}$.

Properties of Inequality

For all real numbers a, b, and c:

Addition: If $a > b$, then $a + c > b + c$.
If $a < b$, then $a + c < b + c$.

Subtraction: If $a > b$, then $a - c > b - c$.
If $a < b$, then $a - c < b - c$.

Multiplication: $c > 0$: If $a > b$, then $ac > bc$.
If $a < b$, then $ac < bc$.

$c < 0$: If $a > b$, then $ac < bc$.
If $a < b$, then $ac > bc$.

Division: $c > 0$: If $a < b$, then $\frac{a}{c} < \frac{b}{c}$.
If $a > b$, then $\frac{a}{c} > \frac{b}{c}$.

$c < 0$: If $a < b$, then $\frac{a}{c} > \frac{b}{c}$.
If $a > b$, then $\frac{a}{c} < \frac{b}{c}$.

Order of Operations

1. Perform any operation(s) inside grouping symbols.
2. Simplify any terms with exponents.
3. Multiply and divide in order from left to right.
4. Add and subtract in order from left to right.

Properties of Exponents

For any nonzero real number a and any integers m and n:

$$a^0 = 1 \qquad a^m \cdot a^n = a^{m+n}$$
$$\frac{a^m}{a^n} = a^{m-n} \qquad (a^m)^n = a^{mn}$$
$$a^{-n} = \frac{1}{a^n} \qquad a^{\frac{1}{n}} = \sqrt[n]{a}$$
$$(ab)^n = a^n b^n \qquad \left(\frac{a}{b}\right)^n = \frac{a^n}{b^n}$$

Properties of Square Roots

For any real numbers $a \geq 0$ and $b \geq 0$,
$$\sqrt{ab} = \sqrt{a} \cdot \sqrt{b}.$$

For any real numbers $a \geq 0$ and $b > 0$,
$$\sqrt{\frac{a}{b}} = \frac{\sqrt{a}}{\sqrt{b}}.$$

The Pythagorean Theorem

In a right triangle, the sum of the squares of the lengths of the legs is equal to the square of the length of the hypotenuse.

The Converse of the Pythagorean Theorem

If a triangle has sides of lengths a, b, and c, and $a^2 + b^2 = c^2$, then the triangle is a right triangle with hypotenuse of length c.

The Distance Formula

The distance d between any two points (x_1, y_1) and (x_2, y_2) is $d = \sqrt{(x_2 - x_1)^2 + (y_2 - y_1)^2}$.

The Midpoint Formula

The midpoint M of a line segment with endpoints $A(x_1, y_1)$ and $B(x_2, y_2)$ is

$$\left(\frac{x_1 + x_2}{2}, \frac{y_1 + y_2}{2} \right).$$

Trigonometric Ratios

sine of $\angle A = \dfrac{\text{length of side opposite } \angle A}{\text{length of hypotenuse}}$

cosine of $\angle A = \dfrac{\text{length of side adjacent to } \angle A}{\text{length of hypotenuse}}$

tangent of $\angle A = \dfrac{\text{length of side opposite } \angle A}{\text{length of side adjacent to } \angle A}$

Factoring Special Cases

For all real numbers a and b:
$$a^2 - b^2 = (a + b)(a - b)$$
$$a^2 + 2ab + b^2 = (a + b)(a + b) = (a + b)^2$$
$$a^2 - 2ab + b^2 = (a - b)(a - b) = (a - b)^2$$
$$a^3 + b^3 = (a + b)(a^2 - ab + b^2)$$
$$a^3 - b^3 = (a - b)(a^2 + ab + b^2)$$

CHAPTER 1

Summary of Vertical and Horizontal Translations

If k and h are positive numbers and $f(x)$ is a function, then

$f(x) + k$ shifts $f(x)$ up k units;

$f(x) - k$ shifts $f(x)$ down k units;

$f(x + h)$ shifts $f(x)$ left h units;

$f(x - h)$ shifts $f(x)$ right h units.

Multiplication Counting Principle

If there are m ways to make a first selection and n ways to make a second selection, there are $m \times n$ ways to make the two selections.

Number of Permutations

The number of permutations of n items of a set arranged r items at a time is

$$_n\mathrm{P}_r = \frac{n!}{(n - r)!} \text{ for } 1 \le r \le n.$$

CHAPTER 2

Slope-Intercept Form

The slope-intercept form of a linear equation is $y = mx + b$, where m is the slope and b is the y-intercept.

Experimental Probability

$$P(\text{event}) = \frac{\text{number of times an event happens}}{\text{number of times the experiment is done}}$$

Theoretical Probability

If a sample space has n equally likely outcomes, and an event A occurs in m of these outcomes, then the **theoretical probability** $P(A) = \frac{m}{n}$.

CHAPTER 3

Matrix Multiplication

If matrix A is an $m \times n$ matrix and matrix B is an $n \times p$ matrix, then the product matrix AB is an $m \times p$ matrix.

The Multiplicative Inverse of a 2 × 2 Matrix

If $A = \begin{bmatrix} a & b \\ c & d \end{bmatrix}$ and $ad - bc \ne 0$, then A has an inverse.

$$A^{-1} = \frac{1}{ad - bc} \begin{bmatrix} d & -b \\ -c & a \end{bmatrix}$$

CHAPTER 5

Parabolas Written in Vertex Form

An equation of the form $y = a(x - h)^2 + k$ is a parabola written in **vertex form**.

The vertex is (h, k) and the axis of symmetry is the line $x = h$. The parabola opens up when a is positive and opens down when a is negative.

If $|a| < 1$, the graph will be wider than the graph of $y = x^2$; if $|a| > 1$, the graph will be narrower.

Zero Product Property

For all real numbers a and b, if $ab = 0$, then $a = 0$, $b = 0$, or both $a = 0$ and $b = 0$.

Perfect-Square Trinomial

A **perfect-square trinomial** is a trinomial formed by squaring a binomial.

Perfect-Square Trinomial	**Binomial Square**
$x^2 + 2kx + k^2$	$= (x + k)^2$

Quadratic Formula

If $ax^2 + bx + c = 0$ for real numbers a, b, c with $a \neq 0$, then

$$x = \frac{-b \pm \sqrt{b^2 - 4ac}}{2a}$$

The Discriminant

The **discriminant** is the value of the expression $b^2 - 4ac$.

$$b^2 - 4ac > 0 \Rightarrow \text{two real solutions}$$
$$b^2 - 4ac = 0 \Rightarrow \text{one real solution}$$
$$b^2 - 4ac < 0 \Rightarrow \text{two imaginary solutions}$$

CHAPTER 6

The Factor Theorem

The expression $x - a$ is a linear factor of a polynomial if and only if the value a is a zero of the polynomial function.

Number of Combinations

The number of combinations of n objects of a set chosen r objects at a time is given by the following formula.

$$_nC_r = \frac{n!}{r!(n - r)!} \text{ for } 0 \leq r \leq n$$

Binomial Theorem

For every positive integer n:
$$(a + b)^n = {_nC_0}a^n + {_nC_1}a^{n-1}b^1 +$$
$$_nC_2 a^{n-2}b^2 + \ldots + {_nC_{n-1}}ab^{n-1} + {_nC_n}b^n.$$

CHAPTER 7

Properties of Logarithms

For any positive numbers, M, N, and b, $b \neq 1$:

$\log_b MN = \log_b M + \log_b N$	**Product Property**
$\log_b \frac{M}{N} = \log_b M - \log_b N$	**Quotient Property**
$\log_b M^x = x \log_b M$	**Power Property**

Change of Base Formula

For any positive numbers M, b, and c, with $b \neq 1$ and $c \neq 1$:

$$\log_b M = \frac{\log_c M}{\log_c b}.$$

CHAPTER 8

Translations of $y = \frac{k}{x}$

The graph of the function $f(x) = \frac{k}{x - b} + c$ is the graph of $y = \frac{k}{x}$ shifted b units horizontally and c units vertically.

Properties of Rational Functions

- The function $f(x) = \frac{g(x)}{h(x)}$ is discontinuous if $h(x) = 0$.
- If $g(x)$ and $h(x)$ have no common factors, then $f(x)$ has a vertical asymptote when $h(x) = 0$.
- $f(x)$ has, at most, one horizontal asymptote.

The Probability of A *or* B

If A and B are mutually exclusive, then $P(A \text{ or } B) = P(A) + P(B)$.

If A and B are not mutually exclusive and $A \cap B$ represents the events common to A and B, then $P(A \text{ or } B) = P(A) + P(B) - P(A \cap B)$.

The Probability of A *and* B

If A and B are independent events, then $P(A \text{ and } B) = P(A) \cdot P(B)$.

CHAPTER 9

Sine Function

If $y = a \sin b\theta$, with $a \neq 0$ and $b > 0$, then

- $|a|$ is the amplitude of the curve
- b is the number of periods from 0 to 2π
- $\frac{2\pi}{b}$ is the period of the curve.

Cosine Function

If $y = a \cos b\theta$, where $a \neq 0$ and $b > 0$, then

- $|a|$ is the amplitude
- b is the number of periods from 0 to 2π
- $\frac{2\pi}{b}$ is the period of the function.

Tangent Function

If $y = \tan b\theta$, with $b > 0$, then

- $\frac{\pi}{b}$ is the period of the function
- one cycle occurs in the interval from $-\frac{\pi}{2b}$ to $\frac{\pi}{2b}$
- there are vertical asymptotes at each end of the cycle.

Law of Cosines

In $\triangle ABC$, let a, b, and c represent the lengths of the sides opposite $\angle A$, $\angle B$, and $\angle C$, respectively.

$$c^2 = a^2 + b^2 - 2ab \cos C$$

Law of Sines

In $\triangle ABC$, let a, b, and c represent the lengths of the sides opposite $\angle A$, $\angle B$, and $\angle C$, respectively.

$$\frac{\sin A}{a} = \frac{\sin B}{b} = \frac{\sin C}{c}$$

CHAPTER 10

Conic Section	Form of Equation
Parabola	vertex (h, k) $y = a(x - h)^2 + k$ $x = a(y - k)^2 + h$
Circle	center (h, k) $(x - h)^2 + (y - k)^2 = r^2$
Ellipse	center (h, k) $\frac{(x - h)^2}{a^2} + \frac{(y - k)^2}{b^2} = 1$ $\frac{(x - h)^2}{b^2} + \frac{(y - k)^2}{a^2} = 1$
Hyperbola	center (h, k) $\frac{(x - h)^2}{a^2} - \frac{(y - k)^2}{b^2} = 1$ $\frac{(y - k)^2}{a^2} - \frac{(x - h)^2}{b^2} = 1$

CHAPTER 11

Conditional Probability Formula

For any two events A and B from a sample space:

$$P(B \mid A) = \frac{P(A \text{ and } B)}{P(A)}.$$

Margin of Error Formula

When a random sample of size n is taken from a large population, the sample proportion has a margin of error of approximately $\pm\frac{1}{\sqrt{n}}$.

Binomial Probability

For repeated independent trials, each with a probability of success p and a probability of failure q (with $p + q = 1$), the probability of x successes in n trials is ${}_nC_x p^x q^{n-x}$.

CHAPTER 12

Arithmetic Sequence Formulas

$a_n = a_{n-1} + d$	**Recursive Formula**
$a_n = a_1 + (n - 1)d$	**Explicit formula**

Geometric Sequence Formulas

$a_1 = $ any value;

$a_n = a_{n-1} \cdot r$	**Recursive Formula**
$a_n = a_1 \cdot r^{n-1}$	**Explicit Formula**

Sum of a Finite Arithmetic Series

The general formula for the sum of a finite arithmetic series $a_1 + a_2 + a_3 + \ldots + a_n$ is $S_n = \frac{n}{2}(a_1 + a_n)$, where S_n is the sum of the series, a_1 is the first term, a_n is the nth term, and n is the number of terms.

Sum of a Geometric Series

The sum S_n of the first n terms of a geometric series is $S_n = \frac{a_1(1 - r^n)}{1 - r}$, where a_1 is the first term, r is the common ratio, and n is the number of terms.

Sum of an Infinite Geometric Series

An infinite geometric series with $|r| < 1$ converges to the sum S given by the following formula.

$$S = \frac{a_1}{1 - r}$$

Formulas from Geometry

You will use a number of geometric formulas as you work through your advanced algebra book. Here are some perimeter, area, and volume formulas.

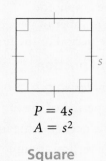

$$P = 2\ell + 2w$$
$$A = lw$$

Rectangle

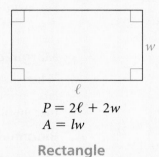

$$P = 4s$$
$$A = s^2$$

Square

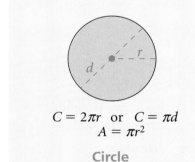

$$C = 2\pi r \quad \text{or} \quad C = \pi d$$
$$A = \pi r^2$$

Circle

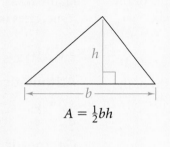

$$A = \tfrac{1}{2}bh$$

Triangle

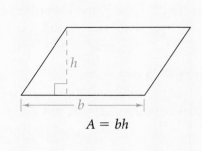

$$A = bh$$

Parallelogram

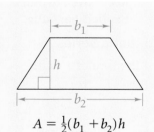

$$A = \tfrac{1}{2}(b_1 + b_2)h$$

Trapezoid

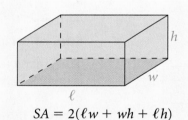

$$SA = 2(\ell w + wh + \ell h)$$
$$V = Bh$$
$$V = \ell wh$$

Rectangular Prism

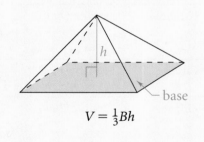

$$V = \tfrac{1}{3}Bh$$

Pyramid

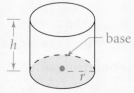

$$SA = 2\pi r(r + h)$$
$$V = Bh$$
$$V = \pi r^2 h$$

Cylinder

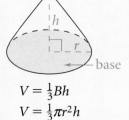

$$V = \tfrac{1}{3}Bh$$
$$V = \tfrac{1}{3}\pi r^2 h$$

Cone

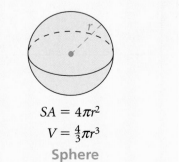

$$SA = 4\pi r^2$$
$$V = \tfrac{4}{3}\pi r^3$$

Sphere

Squares and Square Roots

Number n	Square n^2	Positive Square Root $\sqrt{n}$	Number n	Square n^2	Positive Square Root $\sqrt{n}$	Number n	Square n^2	Positive Square Root $\sqrt{n}$
1	1	1.000	51	2601	7.141	101	10,201	10.050
2	4	1.414	52	2704	7.211	102	10,404	10.100
3	9	1.732	53	2809	7.280	103	10,609	10.149
4	16	2.000	54	2916	7.348	104	10,816	10.198
5	25	2.236	55	3025	7.416	105	11,025	10.247
6	36	2.449	56	3136	7.483	106	11,236	10.296
7	49	2.646	57	3249	7.550	107	11,449	10.344
8	64	2.828	58	3364	7.616	108	11,664	10.392
9	81	3.000	59	3481	7.681	109	11,881	10.440
10	100	3.162	60	3600	7.746	110	12,100	10.488
11	121	3.317	61	3721	7.810	111	12,321	10.536
12	144	3.464	62	3844	7.874	112	12,544	10.583
13	169	3.606	63	3969	7.937	113	12,769	10.630
14	196	3.742	64	4096	8.000	114	12,996	10.677
15	225	3.873	65	4225	8.062	115	13,225	10.724
16	256	4.000	66	4356	8.124	116	13,456	10.770
17	289	4.123	67	4489	8.185	117	13,689	10.817
18	324	4.243	68	4624	8.246	118	13,924	10.863
19	361	4.359	69	4761	8.307	119	14,161	10.909
20	400	4.472	70	4900	8.367	120	14,400	10.954
21	441	4.583	71	5041	8.426	121	14,641	11.000
22	484	4.690	72	5184	8.485	122	14,884	11.045
23	529	4.796	73	5329	8.544	123	15,129	11.091
24	576	4.899	74	5476	8.602	124	15,376	11.136
25	625	5.000	75	5625	8.660	125	15,625	11.180
26	676	5.099	76	5776	8.718	126	15,876	11.225
27	729	5.196	77	5929	8.775	127	16,129	11.269
28	784	5.292	78	6084	8.832	128	16,384	11.314
29	841	5.385	79	6241	8.888	129	16,641	11.358
30	900	5.477	80	6400	8.944	130	16,900	11.402
31	961	5.568	81	6561	9.000	131	17,161	11.446
32	1024	5.657	82	6724	9.055	132	17,424	11.489
33	1089	5.745	83	6889	9.110	133	17,689	11.533
34	1156	5.831	84	7056	9.165	134	17,956	11.576
35	1225	5.916	85	7225	9.220	135	18,225	11.619
36	1296	6.000	86	7396	9.274	136	18,496	11.662
37	1369	6.083	87	7569	9.327	137	18,769	11.705
38	1444	6.164	88	7744	9.381	138	19,044	11.747
39	1521	6.245	89	7921	9.434	139	19,321	11.790
40	1600	6.325	90	8100	9.487	140	19,600	11.832
41	1681	6.403	91	8281	9.539	141	19,881	11.874
42	1764	6.481	92	8464	9.592	142	20,164	11.916
43	1849	6.557	93	8649	9.644	143	20,449	11.958
44	1936	6.633	94	8836	9.695	144	20,736	12.000
45	2025	6.708	95	9025	9.747	145	21,025	12.042
46	2116	6.782	96	9216	9.798	146	21,316	12.083
47	2209	6.856	97	9409	9.849	147	21,609	12.124
48	2304	6.928	98	9604	9.899	148	21,904	12.166
49	2401	7.000	99	9801	9.950	149	22,201	12.207
50	2500	7.071	100	10,000	10.000	150	22,500	12.247

Tables

Trigonometric Ratios

Angle	Sine	Cosine	Tangent	Angle	Sine	Cosine	Tangent
1°	0.0175	0.9998	0.0175	46°	0.7193	0.6947	1.0355
2°	0.0349	0.9994	0.0349	47°	0.7314	0.6820	1.0724
3°	0.0523	0.9986	0.0524	48°	0.7431	0.6691	1.1106
4°	0.0698	0.9976	0.0699	49°	0.7547	0.6561	1.1504
5°	0.0872	0.9962	0.0875	50°	0.7660	0.6428	1.1918
6°	0.1045	0.9945	0.1051	51°	0.7771	0.6293	1.2349
7°	0.1219	0.9925	0.1228	52°	0.7880	0.6157	1.2799
8°	0.1392	0.9903	0.1405	53°	0.7986	0.6018	1.3270
9°	0.1564	0.9877	0.1584	54°	0.8090	0.5878	1.3764
10°	0.1736	0.9848	0.1763	55°	0.8192	0.5736	1.4281
11°	0.1908	0.9816	0.1944	56°	0.8290	0.5592	1.4826
12°	0.2079	0.9781	0.2126	57°	0.8387	0.5446	1.5399
13°	0.2250	0.9744	0.2309	58°	0.8480	0.5299	1.6003
14°	0.2419	0.9703	0.2493	59°	0.8572	0.5150	1.6643
15°	0.2588	0.9659	0.2679	60°	0.8660	0.5000	1.7321
16°	0.2756	0.9613	0.2867	61°	0.8746	0.4848	1.8040
17°	0.2924	0.9563	0.3057	62°	0.8829	0.4695	1.8807
18°	0.3090	0.9511	0.3249	63°	0.8910	0.4540	1.9626
19°	0.3256	0.9455	0.3443	64°	0.8988	0.4384	2.0503
20°	0.3420	0.9397	0.3640	65°	0.9063	0.4226	2.1445
21°	0.3584	0.9336	0.3839	66°	0.9135	0.4067	2.2460
22°	0.3746	0.9272	0.4040	67°	0.9205	0.3907	2.3559
23°	0.3907	0.9205	0.4245	68°	0.9272	0.3746	2.4751
24°	0.4067	0.9135	0.4452	69°	0.9336	0.3584	2.6051
25°	0.4226	0.9063	0.4663	70°	0.9397	0.3420	2.7475
26°	0.4384	0.8988	0.4877	71°	0.9455	0.3256	2.9042
27°	0.4540	0.8910	0.5095	72°	0.9511	0.3090	3.0777
28°	0.4695	0.8829	0.5317	73°	0.9563	0.2924	3.2709
29°	0.4848	0.8746	0.5543	74°	0.9613	0.2756	3.4874
30°	0.5000	0.8660	0.5774	75°	0.9659	0.2588	3.7321
31°	0.5150	0.8572	0.6009	76°	0.9703	0.2419	4.0108
32°	0.5299	0.8480	0.6249	77°	0.9744	0.2250	4.3315
33°	0.5446	0.8387	0.6494	78°	0.9781	0.2079	4.7046
34°	0.5592	0.8290	0.6745	79°	0.9816	0.1908	5.1446
35°	0.5736	0.8192	0.7002	80°	0.9848	0.1736	5.6713
36°	0.5878	0.8090	0.7265	81°	0.9877	0.1564	6.3138
37°	0.6018	0.7986	0.7536	82°	0.9903	0.1392	7.1154
38°	0.6157	0.7880	0.7813	83°	0.9925	0.1219	8.1443
39°	0.6293	0.7771	0.8098	84°	0.9945	0.1045	9.5144
40°	0.6428	0.7660	0.8391	85°	0.9962	0.0872	11.4301
41°	0.6561	0.7547	0.8693	86°	0.9976	0.0698	14.3007
42°	0.6691	0.7431	0.9004	87°	0.9986	0.0523	19.0811
43°	0.6820	0.7314	0.9325	88°	0.9994	0.0349	28.6363
44°	0.6947	0.7193	0.9657	89°	0.9998	0.0175	57.2900
45°	0.7071	0.7071	1.0000	90°	1.0000	0.0000	

Random Numbers

71133	15379	62220	83119	33872	80881	54263	35427
50631	71600	00133	22447	76212	94621	91026	89499
92641	47157	49324	27674	04501	30142	49180	17909
06747	85629	84240	41917	84067	44264	40953	20516
10967	26366	60323	55523	09686	47962	59778	99479
08945	67385	60015	91676	72694	49757	86540	32359
22437	77933	00815	21862	25049	30840	01760	60655
78658	17681	63881	99741	74067	35810	11989	68048
23006	64650	50777	06226	64703	73487	34815	35296
67218	66215	14219	61908	18165	17261	45017	29303
03020	75784	91506	02237	88056	15027	04040	96770
94965	75820	50994	31050	67304	16730	29373	96700
07845	69584	70548	52973	72302	97594	92241	15204
42665	29990	57260	75846	01152	30141	35982	96088
04003	36893	51639	65625	28426	90634	32979	05449
32959	06776	72420	55622	81422	67587	93193	67479
29041	35939	80920	31801	38638	87905	37617	53135
63364	20495	50868	54130	32625	30799	94255	03514
27838	19139	82031	46143	93922	32001	05378	42457
94248	29387	32682	86235	35805	66529	00886	25875
40156	92636	95648	79767	16307	71133	15714	44142
44293	19195	30569	41277	01417	34656	80207	33362
71878	31767	40056	52582	30766	70264	86253	07179
24757	57502	51033	16551	66731	87844	41420	10084
55529	68560	50069	50652	76104	42086	48720	96632
39724	50318	91370	68016	06222	26806	86726	52832
80950	27135	14110	92292	17049	60257	01638	04460
21694	79570	74409	95087	75424	57042	27349	16229
06930	85441	37191	75134	12845	67868	51500	97761
18740	35448	56096	37910	35485	19640	07689	31027
40657	14875	70695	92569	40703	69318	95070	01541
52249	56515	59058	34509	35791	22150	56558	75286
86570	07303	40560	57856	22009	67712	19435	90250
62962	66253	93288	01838	68388	55481	00336	19271
78066	09117	62350	58972	80778	46458	83677	16125
89106	30219	30068	54030	49295	48985	01624	72881
88310	18172	89450	04987	02781	37935	76222	93595
20942	90911	57643	34009	20728	88785	81212	08214
93926	66687	58252	18674	18501	22362	37319	33201
88294	55814	67443	77285	36229	26886	66782	89931
29751	08485	49910	83844	56013	26596	20875	34568
11169	15529	33241	83594	01727	86595	65723	82322
06062	54400	80649	70749	50395	48993	77447	24862
87445	17139	43278	55031	79971	18515	61850	49101
39283	22821	44330	82225	53534	77235	42973	60190

Tables

A

Examples

Absolute value (p. 32)   The absolute value of a number is its distance from 0 on the number line. $|a| = a$ if $a \geq 0$; $|a| = -a$ if $a < 0$

$|3| = 3; |-3| = 3$

Absolute value of a complex number (p. 230)   The absolute value of a complex number is its distance from the origin in the complex number plane. In general, $|a + bi| = \sqrt{a^2 + b^2}$

$|3 + 4i| = \sqrt{3^2 + 4^2} = 5$

Additive inverse of a complex number (p. 230)   If the sum of two complex numbers is 0, then each number is the additive inverse of the other.

$3 - 4i$ and $-3 + 4i$ are additive inverses.

Amplitude of a periodic function (p. 404)   The amplitude of a periodic function is half the difference between the maximum and minimum values of the function.

The maximum and minimum values of $y = 4 \sin x$ are 4 and -4, respectively.
Amplitude $= \frac{4 - (-4)}{2} = 4$

Arithmetic mean (p. 568)   The arithmetic mean of any two numbers is their sum divided by two.

The arithmetic mean of 12 and 15 is $\frac{12 + 15}{2} = 13.5$.

Arithmetic sequence (p. 566)   In an arithmetic sequence, the difference between consecutive terms is constant. The constant is called the common difference.

The arithmetic sequence 1, 5, 9, 13, . . . has a common difference of 4.

Arithmetic series (p. 579)   An arithmetic series is a series whose terms form an arithmetic sequence.

$1 + 5 + 9 + 13 + 17 + 21$ is an arithmetic series with six terms.

Asymptote (p. 357)   An asymptote of a graph is a line the graph approaches as it moves farther from the origin. A graph may cross its asymptote, as the graph of $y = \frac{\sin x}{x}$ does.

Example: The function $y = \frac{x + 2}{x - 2}$ has $x = 2$ as a vertical zasymptote and $y = 1$ as a horizontal asymptote.

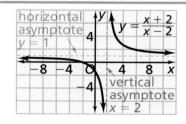

Augmented matrix (p. 182)   An augmented matrix contains the coefficients and constants from a system of equations. Each row of the matrix represents one equation.

linear system
$\begin{cases} x + 4y = 6 \\ -2x + 5y = 7 \end{cases}$

augmented matrix
$\begin{bmatrix} 1 & 4 & | & 6 \\ -2 & 5 & | & 7 \end{bmatrix}$

Axis of symmetry (p. 205)   The vertical line through the vertex of a parabola that opens up or down is its axis of symmetry. The horizontal line through the vertex of a parabola that opens left or right is its axis of symmetry.
Example: $y = x^2 + 2x - 1$

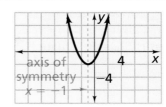

B

Binomial experiment (pp. 538, 540)   A binomial experiment is one in which the situation involves repeated trials. Each trial has two possible outcomes (success or failure), and the probability of success is constant throughout the trials. In a binomial experiment with probability of success p and probability of failure q, the probability of x successes in n trials is given by $_nC_x p^x q^{n-x}$.

Suppose you roll a standard number cube and that you call rolling a 1 a success. Then $p = \frac{1}{6}$ and $q = \frac{5}{6}$. The probability of rolling nine 1's in twenty rolls is
$_{20}C_9\left(\frac{1}{6}\right)^9\left(\frac{5}{6}\right)^{11} \approx 0.0022$.

Binomial theorem (p. 293)   The expansion of $(a + b)^n$, where n is a positive integer, is $(a + b)^n = {_nC_0}a^n + {_nC_1}a^{n-1}b^1 + \ldots + {_nC_{n-1}}a^1 b^{n-1} + {_nC_n}b^n$.

$(x - 3)^3$
$= {_3C_0}(2x)^3 + {_3C_1}(2x)^2(-3)^1$
$\quad + {_3C_2}(2x)^1(-3)^2 + {_3C_3}(-3)^3$
$= 8x^3 - 36x^2 + 54x - 27$

Box-and-whisker plot (p. 521)   A box-and-whisker plot uses quartiles to form the center box and the whiskers.

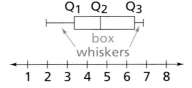

Branch (p. 357)   Each piece of a discontinuous graph is called a branch.

Example: $y = \frac{x + 2}{x - 2}$

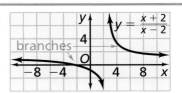

C

Center of a circle (p. 471)   The center of a circle is the point in the plane of the circle that is the same distance from each point of the circle.

Change of base formula (p. 332) $\log_b M = \frac{\log_c M}{\log_c b}$, where M, b, and c are positive numbers and $b \neq 1$ and $c \neq 1$.

$\log_3 8 = \frac{\log 8}{\log 3} \approx 1.8928$

Circle (pp. 471, 492)   A circle is the set of all points in a plane at a distance r from a given point. A circle whose center is (h, k) and whose radius is r has the equation
$$(x - h)^2 + (y - k)^2 = r^2.$$

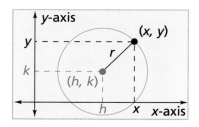

Coefficient matrix (p. 183)   In the matrix equation $AX = B$, matrix A is the coefficient matrix.

$$A \cdot X = B$$
$$\begin{bmatrix} 1 & 2 \\ 3 & 5 \end{bmatrix}\begin{bmatrix} x \\ y \end{bmatrix} = \begin{bmatrix} 5 \\ 14 \end{bmatrix}$$

Combination (pp. 285–286)   Any unordered selection of r objects from a larger set of n objects is a combination. The number of combinations of n objects taken r at a time is $_nC_r = \dfrac{n!}{r!(n - r)!}$ for $0 \le r \le n$.

The number of combinations of seven items taken four at a time is
$$_7C_4 = \frac{7!}{4!(7 - 4)!} = 35.$$
There are 35 ways to choose four items from seven items without regard to order.

Common difference (p. 566)   The common difference is the difference between consecutive terms of an arithmetic sequence.

The arithmetic sequence 1, 5, 9, 13, . . . has a common difference of 4.

Common logarithm (p. 319)   The logarithmic function $x = \log_{10} y$ is the common logarithm. You can write the common logarithm of y as log y.

log 1 = 0; log 10 = 1;
log 50 = 1.698 970 004 . . .

Common ratio (p. 572)   The common ratio is the ratio of consecutive terms of a geometric sequence.

The geometric sequence 2.5, 5, 10, 20, . . . has a common ratio of 2.

Completing the square (pp. 234–235)   By completing the square, you can write a quadratic expression $ax^2 + bx + c$ as the sum of a perfect square and a constant.

$x^2 + 6x - 5 =$
$x^2 + 6x + 9 - 5 - 9 =$
$(x + 3)^2 - 14$

Complex conjugates (pp. 233, 375, 629)   The complex numbers $a + bi$ and $a - bi$ are complex conjugates. The product of two complex conjugates is a real number.

The complex numbers $2 - 3i$ and $2 + 3i$ are complex conjugates.

Complex number (p. 229)   A complex number is any expression of the form $a + bi$, where a and b are real numbers and $i = \sqrt{-1}$. The real part is a and the imaginary part is b. Two complex numbers are equal if their real parts are equal and their imaginary parts are equal.

The complex number $2 - 3i$ has real part 2 and imaginary part -3.

Composite of two functions (p. 27)   Given two functions, their composite uses the output from the first function as the input of the second function.

$f(x) = 2x + 1$ $g(x) = x^2$
$g(f(x)) = g(2x + 1)$ $f(g(x)) = f(x^2)$
$\quad = (2x + 1)^2$ $\quad = 2x^2 + 1$
$\quad = 4x^2 + 4x + 1$

Compound interest formula (p. 312)   The compound interest formula for the amount *A* in an account is given below.

$$A = P\left(1 + \frac{r}{n}\right)nt$$

rate of interest
← time in years

principal

number of times per year the interest is compounded

Suppose that $P = \$1200$, $r = 0.05$, $n = 2$, and $t = 3$. Then
$$A = 1200\left(1 + \frac{0.05}{2}\right)^{2 \cdot 3}$$
$$= 1200(1.025)^6$$
$$\approx 1391.63$$

Conditional probability (pp. 512, 514)   When a probability contains a condition that may limit the sample space, it is called a conditional probability. The notation $P(B \mid A)$ is read "the probability of event *B*, given event *A*." For any two events *A* and *B* in the sample space, $P(B \mid A) = \frac{P(A \text{ and } B)}{P(A)}$.

Suppose that 83% of an airline's flights depart on schedule. Suppose also that 75% of its flights depart and arrive on schedule.

P(arrives on time | departs on time)
$$= \frac{P(\text{arrives and departs on time})}{P(\text{departs on time})}$$
$$= \frac{0.75}{0.83}$$
$$\approx 0.9$$

Conic section (pp. 459, 492)   The intersection of a plane and a double cone forms a conic section.

Examples: If a plane intersects only the top or bottom part of a double cone, the intersection is a circle, an ellipse, or a parabola. If the plane intersects both parts, the intersection is a hyperbola.

ellipse   hyperbola

Conjugates (pp. 375, 628)   The numbers $a + b\sqrt{c}$ and $a - b\sqrt{c}$, where *a*, *b*, and *c* are rational numbers, are conjugates of each other. The product of two conjugates is a rational number.

$5 + 3\sqrt{2}$ and $5 - 3\sqrt{2}$ are conjugates.

Constant matrix (p. 183)   In the matrix equation $AX = B$, matrix *B* is the constant matrix.

$$A \cdot X = B$$
$$\begin{bmatrix} 1 & 2 \\ 3 & 5 \end{bmatrix}\begin{bmatrix} x \\ y \end{bmatrix} = \begin{bmatrix} 5 \\ 14 \end{bmatrix}$$

Constant of variation (pp. 64, 351)   The constant of variation is the value of *k* in the direct variation $y = kx$ or the value of *k* in the inverse variation $xy = k$.

In $y = 3.5x$, the constant of variation *k* is 3.5. In $xy = 5$, the constant of variation *k* is 5.

Continuous function (curve) (p. 364)   A continuous function is a function whose graph is an unbroken curve.

Example: $y = x^2 + 2x - 1$

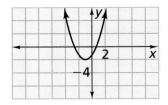

Glossary/Study Guide

Examples

Continuously compounded interest (p. 315)   The formula for continuously compounded interest is $A = Pe^{rt}$.

Suppose that $P = \$1200$, $r = 0.05$, and $t = 3$. Then
$$A = 1200e^{0.05 \cdot 3} = 1200(2.718\ldots)^{0.15}$$
$$\approx 1394.20$$

Converge (p. 586)   An infinite series $\sum\limits_{n=1}^{\infty} A_n$ converges to S if $\sum\limits_{n=1}^{t} A_n$ gets closer and closer to S as the upper limit t increases.

The infinite series $\sum\limits_{n=1}^{\infty} \frac{1}{2^n}$ converges to 1.

Cosine function (p. 429)   The periodic function $y = a \cos bx$, with $a \neq 0$ and $b > 0$, has amplitude $|a|$, period $\frac{2\pi}{b}$ radians, and completes b cycles over the interval from 0 to 2π.

Example: $y = 2 \cos (2x)$ has amplitude 2, period π radians, and completes two cycles over the interval from 0 to 2π.

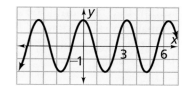

Cosine of an angle (p. 411)   The cosine of an angle in standard position is the x-coordinate of the point where the terminal side of the angle intersects the unit circle.

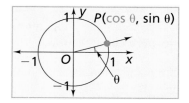

Coterminal angles (p. 410)   Two angles in standard position are coterminal if they have the same terminal side.

Example: Angles that have measures $135°$ and $-225°$ are coterminal.

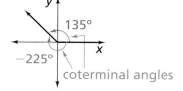

Co-vertices of an ellipse (p. 478)   The two points where an ellipse intersects its minor axis are the co-vertices of the ellipse.

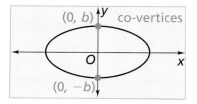

Cramer's rule (p. 189)   Cramer's rule uses determinants to solve a system of linear equations. Form the determinants D_x and D_y by replacing one column of the determinant with the constant terms from the system.

Example: $\begin{cases} x + 2y = 6 \\ -x + y = -6 \end{cases}$ $D = \begin{vmatrix} 1 & 2 \\ -1 & 1 \end{vmatrix} = 3$

$D_x = \begin{vmatrix} 6 & 2 \\ -6 & 1 \end{vmatrix} = 18$; $D_y = \begin{vmatrix} 1 & 6 \\ -1 & -6 \end{vmatrix} = 0$

$x = \frac{D_x}{D} = 6$

$y = \frac{D_y}{D} = 0$

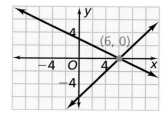

Cycle (p. 403)   The cycle of a periodic function is one complete pattern of *y*-values.

Decay factor (p. 305)   In an exponential decay function of the form $y = ab^x$, with $a > 0$ and $0 < b < 1$, *b* is the decay factor.

In the equation $y = 0.5^x$, 0.5 is the decay factor.

Degree of a term (p. 261)   The exponent in a term of a polynomial determines the degree of the term.

x^2 ←—degree 2
$3y^3$ ←—degree 3
$-4a^{12}$ ←—degree 12

Dependent equations (p. 160)   In a system of equations, if equations simplify to an equation that is always true, the equations are dependent.

$$\begin{cases} 2x + y = 3 \\ 4x + 2y = 6 \end{cases}$$

Dependent events (p. 388)   When the occurrence of one event affects the probability of a second event, the two events are dependent.

Suppose two apples and two oranges are in the refrigerator. Two people each choose one piece of fruit randomly. The outcome of the second choice depends on the outcome of the first choice. The second choice is a dependent event.

Determinant (pp. 134, 189)   The determinant of a square matrix $\begin{bmatrix} a & b \\ c & d \end{bmatrix}$ is the real number $ad - bc$.

The determinant of $\begin{bmatrix} 3 & -2 \\ 5 & 6 \end{bmatrix}$ is $3(6) - 5(-2) = 28$.

Difference of perfect squares (p. 223)   For all real numbers *a* and *b*, $a^2 - b^2 = (a + b)(a - b)$

$25a^2 - 4 = (5a + 2)(5a - 2)$
$m^6 - 1 = (m^3 + 1)(m^3 - 1)$

Dilation (pp. 121, 124)   A dilation enlarges or shrinks a figure by a given scale factor.

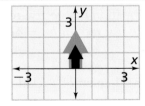

Dimensions of a matrix (p. 7)   The number of rows and columns of a matrix determine its dimensions.

$A = \begin{bmatrix} 1 & -2 & 0 & 10 \\ 9 & 7 & -3 & 8 \\ 2 & -10 & 1 & -6 \end{bmatrix}$

Example: Matrix *A* is a 3 × 4 matrix.

Glossary/Study Guide

Direct variation (p. 64)   A direct variation is modeled by the equation $y = kx$, $k \neq 0$. The graph is a line with slope k that passes through the origin.

$y = 3.5x$, $y = 7x$, $y = -\frac{1}{2}x$

Directed graph (p. 129)   A directed graph is a finite graph that indicates the direction of the paths.

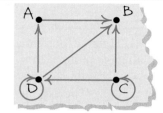

Directrix (p. 466)   The directrix of a parabola is the fixed line used to define a parabola. Each point of the parabola is the same distance from the focus and the directrix.

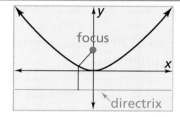

Discontinuous function (curve) (p. 364)   The graph of a discontinuous function has jumps, breaks, or holes in it.

Example: $y = \dfrac{x - 2}{x^2 - 9}$

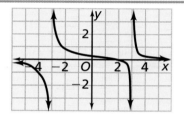

Discriminant (pp. 242)   The discriminant of a quadratic equation in the form $ax^2 + bx + c = 0$ (where a, b, and c are real numbers) is $b^2 - 4ac$. The value of the discriminant determines the number of real roots the equation has. If $b^2 - 4ac < 0$, the equation has no real roots; if $b^2 - 4ac = 0$, the equation has one real root; if $b^2 - 4ac > 0$, the equation has two real roots.

$3x^2 - 6x + 1$

discriminant $= (-6)^2 - 4(3)(1)$
$= 36 - 12 = 24$

The equation has two real roots.

Domain (p. 20)   The domain of a relation is the set of all possible input values.

In the relation {(0, 1), (0, 2), (0, 3), (0, 4), (1, 3), (1, 4), (2, 1)}, the domain is {0, 1, 2}. In the function $f(x) = x^2 - 10$, the domain is all real numbers.

E

Element of a matrix (p. 8)   Every item in a matrix is an element. An element is identified by its position in the matrix.

Example: Element a_{21} is 9, the element in the second row and first column.

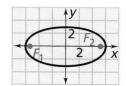

$$A = \begin{bmatrix} 1 & -2 & 0 & 10 \\ 9 & 7 & -3 & 8 \\ 2 & -10 & 1 & -6 \end{bmatrix}$$

Ellipse (pp. 478, 492)   An ellipse is the set of points P in a plane such that the sum of the distances from P to two fixed points F_1 and F_2 is a given constant k. An ellipse with its center at the origin has the equation $\dfrac{x^2}{a^2} + \dfrac{y^2}{b^2} = 1$ if the major axis is horizontal and $\dfrac{x^2}{b^2} + \dfrac{y^2}{b^2} = 1$ if the major axis is vertical. In both cases, $a > b$.

Example: $\dfrac{x^2}{36} + \dfrac{y^2}{9} = 1, F_1 = (-3\sqrt{3}, 0), F_2 = (3\sqrt{3}, 0)$

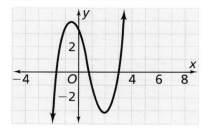

End behavior (p. 262)   The end behavior of a graph describes the far left and far right portions of the graph, that is, the behavior of the function for large values of $|x|$.

Example: For the polynomial function $P(x) = x^3 - 2x^2 - 3x + 3$, the end behavior is ($\nearrow$, $\nearrow$).

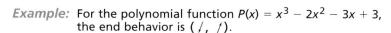

Equal matrices (p. 104)   Two matrices are equal if and only if they have the same dimensions and their corresponding elements are equal.

Matrices A and B are equal.

$$A = \begin{bmatrix} 2 & 6 \\ \frac{9}{3} & 1 \end{bmatrix} \qquad B = \begin{bmatrix} \frac{6}{3} & 6 \\ 3 & \frac{-13}{-13} \end{bmatrix}$$

Even function (p. 256)   The graph of an even function has the y-axis as an axis of symmetry.

Example: $y = 0.5x^2$

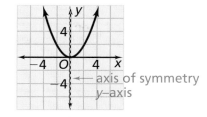

Expanding a binomial (p. 291)   You expand a binomial by multiplying and writing the resulting polynomial in standard form. To expand a binomial raised to an integer power, you can use Pascal's triangle in conjunction with the binomial theorem.

$(x + 4)^3$
$= (x + 4)(x + 4)^2$
$= (x + 4)(x^2 + 8x + 16)$
$= x^3 + 8x^2 + 16x + 4x^2 + 32x + 64$
$= x^3 + 12x^2 + 48x + 64$

Examples

Experimental probability (p. 88) The experimental probability of an event is the ratio $\dfrac{\text{number of times an event happens}}{\text{number of times the experiment is done}}$.

Suppose a basketball player has scored 19 times from the floor in 28 attempts at a basket. The probability of the player's scoring is $P(\text{score}) = \dfrac{19}{28} \approx 0.68$, or 68%.

Explicit formula (p. 563) An explicit formula for a sequence defines each term a_n in terms of its place n in the sequence.

Let $a_n = 2n + 5$ for positive integers n. If $n = 7$, then $a_7 = 2(7) + 5 = 19$.

Exponential equation (p. 332) An equation of the form $a = b^{cx}$, where the exponent includes a variable, is called an exponential equation. You can solve exponential equations by taking the logarithm of each side.

$$5^{2x} = 270$$
$$\log_5 5^{2x} = \log_5 270$$
$$2x = \frac{\log 270}{\log 5}$$
$$2x \approx 3.4785$$
$$x \approx 1.7392$$

Exponential function (p. 305) The standard form of an exponential function is $y = ab^x$, where a is a constant, $a \neq 0$, b is the base, $b \neq 1$, and x is a real number. When $a > 0$ and $b > 1$, the function models exponential growth with growth factor b. When $a > 0$ and $0 < b < 1$, the function models exponential decay with decay factor b.

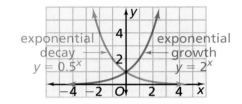

Examples: $y = 2^x$; $y = 0.5^x$; $y = 5 \cdot 10^x$

Extraneous solution (p. 258) An extraneous solution of an equation is a number that satisfies later solution steps, but not the given equation.

$$\sqrt{x - 3} = x - 5$$
$$x - 3 = x^2 - 10x + 25$$
$$0 = x^2 - 11x + 28$$
$$0 = (x - 4)(x - 7)$$
$$x = 4 \text{ or } 7$$

The number 4 is an extraneous solution, since $\sqrt{4 - 3} \neq 4 - 5$.

F

Factor theorem (p. 270) The expression $x - a$ is a linear factor of a polynomial if and only if a is a zero of the related polynomial function.

The value of $f(x) = x^2 + 2x - 8$ is zero for $x = 2$, so $x - 2$ is a factor of $x^2 + 2x - 8$.

Factored form of a polynomial (p. 268) A polynomial written as the product of polynomials of lower degree is in factored form. If the polynomial has a factor whose degree is 1, it has a linear factor.

expanded form   factored form
$x^2 + x - 56$ $(x + 8)(x - 7)$

Finite graph (p. 128) A finite graph is a finite set of points called vertices. Paths connect pairs of vertices.

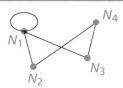

Focus (plural: foci) (pp. 466, 478, 487)   The focus of a conic section is a point in a plane used to define a conic section.

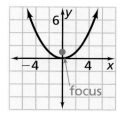 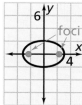 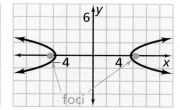

A parabola is the set of all points that are the same distance from its focus and its directrix. An ellipse is the set of all points P such that the sum of the distances from each point P to the two foci is a constant. A hyperbola is the set of all points P such that the difference of the distances from each point P to the two foci is a constant.

Frequency table (p. 506)   A frequency table can be used to list each outcome in a sample space and the number of times in an experiment that each outcome occurs.

Example: Suppose that you roll a standard number cube 40 times and that each number occurs as often as shown in the table. The table is a frequency table and the diagram to its right is a frequency diagram, or histogram.

Roll	Freq.
1	5
2	9
3	7
4	8
5	8
6	3

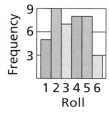

Fundamental Theorem of Algebra (pp. 281, 628)   A polynomial function of degree n has exactly n zeros. Or, equivalently: Counting imaginary roots and multiple roots, an nth-degree polynomial equation has exactly n roots. Or, equivalently: Each nth degree polynomial can be factored into n linear factors.

$p(x) = x^3 - 2x^2 + 4x - 8$ is of degree 3 and so it has 3 zeros (2, $2i$, and $-2i$). The third degree equation $x^3 - 2x^2 + 4x - 8 = 0$ has exactly three roots (2, $2i$, and $-2i$), and you can factor the third degree polynomial $x^3 - 2x^2 + 4x - 8$ into 3 linear factors: $x^3 - 2x^2 + 4x - 8 = (x - 2)(x - 2i)(x + 2i)$.

Function (p. 21)   A function is a relation that assigns exactly one value of the range to each value of the domain. To write a rule in function notation, use $f(x)$ in place of y.

The relation $y = 3x^3 - 2x + 3$ is a function. $f(x) = 3x^3 - 2x + 3$ is the same relation written in function notation.

G

Geometric mean (p. 574)   The geometric mean of two positive numbers a and b is $\sqrt{ab}$.

The geometric mean of 12 and 18 is $\sqrt{12 \times 18} \approx 14.6969$.

Geometric sequence (p. 572)   In a geometric sequence, the ratio of consecutive terms is constant. The constant is called the common ratio.

The geometric sequence 2.5, 5, 10, 20, 40, . . . has a common ratio of 2.

Geometric series (p. 584)   A geometric series is the expression for the sum of terms in a geometric sequence.

The geometric series 2.5 + 5 + 10 + 20 + 40 has five terms.

Growth factor (p. 305)   In an exponential growth function of the form $y = ab^x$, with $b > 1$, b is the growth factor.

In the exponential equation $y = 2^x$, 2 is the growth factor.

Glossary/Study Guide

H

	Examples
Half-life (p. 314) The half-life of a substance is the time it takes for half the material to break down or decompose.	A 60-mg supply of Technetium-99*m* has a half-life of 6 hours. Find the amount left after 48 h. Let *y* represent the amount after *x* half-lives. Then $y = 60(0.5)^x$. $x = 48 \div 6 = 8$ $y = 60(0.5)^8 = 0.234$

Hyperbola (pp. 485, 492) A hyperbola is a set of points *P* in a plane such that the difference between the distances from *P* to the foci F_1 and F_2 is a given constant *k*.

Example: $9x^2 - 25y^2 = 225$, $F_1 = (-\sqrt{34}, 0)$, $F_2 = (\sqrt{34}, 0)$

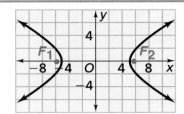

I

Identity matrix (p. 135) The square $n \times n$ matrix with 1's along its main diagonal and 0's elsewhere is the identity matrix for multiplication.

$$I_{2 \times 2} = \begin{bmatrix} 1 & 0 \\ 0 & 1 \end{bmatrix} \qquad I_{3 \times 3} = \begin{bmatrix} 1 & 0 & 0 \\ 0 & 1 & 0 \\ 0 & 0 & 1 \end{bmatrix}$$

Image (p. 123) The image is a figure after a transformation.

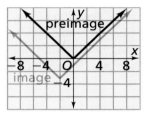

Imaginary number (p. 229) An imaginary number has the form $a + bi$ where $b \neq 0$. $i = \sqrt{-1}$ and $i^2 = -1$.	$3i, -7i, i, 4 + 5i$
Imaginary root theorem (p. 629) If the imaginary number $a + bi$ is a root of a polynomial equation with real coefficients, then the conjugate $a - bi$ is also a root.	$2 + 3i$ is a root of $x^2 - 4x + 13 = 0$, so $2 - 3i$ is also a root.
Inconsistent equations (p. 160) If a system of equations has no solutions, the equations are inconsistent.	$\begin{cases} x + 2y = 3 \\ x + 2y = 5 \end{cases}$
Independent events (p. 388) When the occurrence of one event does not affect the probability of a second event, the two events are independent events. If *A* and *B* are independent events, then $P(A \text{ and } B) = P(A) \cdot P(B)$.	The results of two rolls of a number cube are independent. Getting a 5 on the first roll does not change the probability of getting a 5 on the second roll.

Index (p. 256) With a radical sign, the index indicates what kind of root you want. The index 2 for a square root is usually omitted.

index 2   index 3   index 4
$\sqrt{16}$ $\sqrt[3]{16}$ $\sqrt[4]{16}$

Infinite series (p. 586) An infinite series has infinitely many terms.

$1 + 0.5 + 0.25 + 0.125 + \ldots$

Initial side of an angle (p. 409) When an angle is in standard position on a coordinate plane, the side along the positive x-axis is the initial side of the angle.

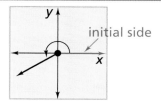

Intercept of a plane (p. 172) An intercept of a plane is a point where the plane intersects an axis of the coordinate system.

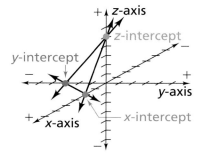

Interquartile range (p. 526) The interquartile range of a set of data is the difference between the third quartile and the first quartile.

The first and third quartiles of the data set {2, 3, 4, 5, 5, 6, 7, 7} are 3.5 and 6.5. The interquartile range is $6.5 - 3.5 = 3$.

Inverse of a function (p. 217) If a function contains the ordered pairs (a, b), then its inverse contains the ordered pairs (b, a). The graphs of a function and its inverse are reflections of each other over the line $y = x$.

Example: The linear functions $y = \frac{2}{3}x + 1$ and $y = \frac{3}{2}x - \frac{3}{2}$ are inverses of one another.

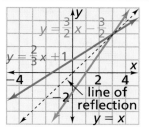

Inverse of a matrix (p. 135) If a square matrix A has an inverse A^{-1}, then $AA^{-1} = A^{-1}A = I$ where I is the identity matrix for multiplication. If $A = \begin{bmatrix} a & b \\ c & d \end{bmatrix}$ and $ad - bc \neq 0$, then

$A^{-1} = \frac{1}{ad - bc}\begin{bmatrix} d & -b \\ -c & a \end{bmatrix}$. You can use the inverse of matrix A to solve the equation $AX = B$ for X. $X = A^{-1}B$.

$A = \begin{bmatrix} 2 & 1 \\ 4 & 0 \end{bmatrix}$

$ad - bc = (2)(0) - (1)(4) = -4$

$A^{-1} = \frac{1}{-4}\begin{bmatrix} 0 & -1 \\ -4 & 2 \end{bmatrix} = \begin{bmatrix} 0 & \frac{1}{4} \\ 1 & -\frac{1}{2} \end{bmatrix}$

Glossary/Study Guide

Inverse variation (p. 351) An equation of the form $y = \frac{k}{x}$ or $xy = k$, where $k \neq 0$, is an inverse variation with constant of variation k.

Example: $xy = 5$, or $y = \frac{5}{x}$

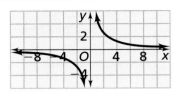

Irrational number (p. 44) Any number that cannot be written as the ratio of two integers is an irrational number.

$\sqrt{2}$, π, $\sqrt[3]{10}$

Irrational root theorem (p. 629) If a and b are rational numbers and $\sqrt{b}$ is an irrational number, and if $a + \sqrt{b}$ is a root ot a polynomial equation with rational coefficients, then the conjugate $a - \sqrt{b}$ is also a root.

$2 + \sqrt{3}$ is a root of $x^2 - 4x + 1 = 0$, so $2 - \sqrt{3}$ is also a root.

Law of Cosines (p. 443) In $\triangle ABC$, let a, b, and c represent the lengths of the sides opposite $\angle A$, $\angle B$, and $\angle C$, respectively. Then

$a^2 = b^2 + c^2 - 2bc \cos A$
$b^2 = a^2 + c^2 - 2ac \cos B$
$c^2 = a^2 + b^2 - 2ab \cos C$.

Given $KL = 11.41$, $KM = 8.72$, and $m\angle K = 18°$,
$LM^2 = 11.41^2 + 8.72^2$
$\qquad - 2(11.41)(8.72) \cos 18°$
$LM^2 = 16.9754$
$LM = 4.12$

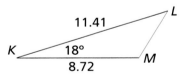

Law of Sines (p. 445) In $\triangle ABC$, let a, b, and c represent the lengths of the sides opposite $\angle A$, $\angle B$, and $\angle C$, respectively. Then $\frac{\sin A}{a} = \frac{\sin B}{b} = \frac{\sin C}{c}$ or $\frac{a}{\sin A} = \frac{b}{\sin B} = \frac{c}{\sin C}$.

Example: Given $KM = 8.72$, $m\angle K = 18°$, and $m\angle M = 120°$,
$m\angle L = 180 - (120 + 18) = 42°$; $\frac{KL}{\sin 120°} = \frac{8.72}{\sin 42°}$;
$KL = \frac{8.72 \sin 120°}{\sin 42°}$
$\qquad \approx 11.29$

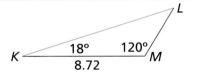

Limits (p. 580) Limits in summation notation are the least and greatest integer values of n.

limits $\displaystyle\sum_{n=1}^{3} 3n + 5$

Line of best fit (p. 19)   The line of best fit is the line that most closely fits a set of data.

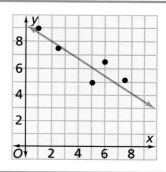

Linear equation (p. 58)   In the coordinate plane, an equation whose graph is a line is a linear equation.

$y = 2x + 1$

Linear function (p. 61)   A function whose graph forms a straight line is a linear function.

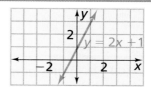

Linear inequality (p. 81)   The graph of a linear inequality describes a region of the coordinate plane that has a boundary line. A sign of ≤ or ≥ indicates that the boundary is included in the solution, shown by a solid boundary line. A sign of < or > indicates that the boundary is not included in the solution, shown by a dashed boundary line.

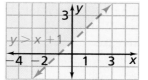

Linear programming (p. 164)   Linear programming identifies conditions that make a quantity as large or as small as possible. This quantity is expressed as the objective function. Limits on the variables in the function are called restrictions.

Example: Restrictions: $x \geq 0$, $y \geq 0$, $x + y \leq 7$, and $y \leq -2x + 8$
Objective function: $B = 2x + 4y$
Graph the restrictions and find the coordinates of each vertex: $(0, 0)$, $(0, 7)$, $(1, 6)$, $(4, 0)$
Evaluate $B = 2x + 4y$ at each vertex:
$2(0) + 4(0) = 0$ $2(0) + 4(7) = 28$
$2(1) + 4(6) = 26$ $2(4) + 4(0) = 8$
The minimum value of B occurs when $x = 0$ and $y = 0$.
The maximum value of B occurs when $x = 0$ and $y = 7$.

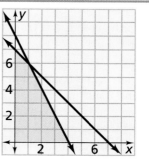

Linear system (p. 150)   In a linear system of equations, the graph of each equation is a line.

Example: $\begin{cases} 2x - 3y = -13 \\ 4x + 5y = 7 \end{cases}$

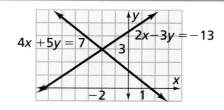

Glossary/Study Guide

Logarithmic function (p. 319) The logarithmic function with base b is the inverse of the exponential function with base b. If $y = b^x$, then $x = \log_b y$. When $b = 10$, the logarithmic function is called the common logarithmic function and the logarithms are called common logarithms.

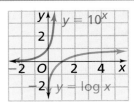

M

Major axis of an ellipse (p. 478) The major axis of an ellipse is the segment that contains the foci and has its endpoints on the ellipse. These endpoints are vertices of the ellipse.

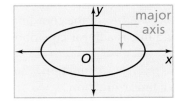

Margin of error (p. 534) A sample proportion may be reported as being in an interval containing the true proportion. The error estimate is called the margin of error. When a random sample of size n is taken from a large population, the sample proportion has a margin of error of about $\pm\frac{1}{\sqrt{n}}$.

A set of 500 items is taken from a population for sampling. The margin of error for a sample proportion is about $\pm\frac{1}{\sqrt{500}} = \pm0.045$.

Mathematical induction, principle of (p. 630) Let S be a statement involving a positive integer n. Then S is true for all positive integers if the following two conditions hold.

1. S is true for $n = 1$.

2. For any positive integer k, if S is true for k, then S is true for $k + 1$.

It can be proved by mathematical induction that
$$1 + 2 + 3 + \ldots + n = \frac{n(n + 1)}{2}$$
for all positive integers n.

Matrix (p. 7) A matrix is a rectangular array of numbers arranged in rows and columns.

$$A = \begin{bmatrix} 1 & -2 & 0 & 10 \\ 9 & 7 & -3 & 8 \\ 2 & -10 & 1 & -6 \end{bmatrix}$$

Matrix addition (p. 108) You add two matrices with the same dimensions by adding their corresponding elements.

$$\begin{bmatrix} 2 & -3 \\ 0 & 4 \end{bmatrix} + \begin{bmatrix} -1 & 0 \\ 5 & -6 \end{bmatrix}$$
$$= \begin{bmatrix} 2 + (-1) & -3 + 0 \\ 0 + 5 & 4 + (-6) \end{bmatrix} = \begin{bmatrix} 1 & -3 \\ 5 & -2 \end{bmatrix}$$

Matrix equation (p. 110) A matrix equation is an equation in which the variable is a matrix.

$$X + \begin{bmatrix} 3 & -2 \\ 5 & 1 \end{bmatrix} = \begin{bmatrix} 4 & 0 \\ 0 & 3 \end{bmatrix}$$
$$X = \begin{bmatrix} 4 & 0 \\ 0 & 3 \end{bmatrix} - \begin{bmatrix} 3 & -2 \\ 5 & 1 \end{bmatrix} = \begin{bmatrix} 1 & 2 \\ -5 & 2 \end{bmatrix}$$

Matrix multiplication (p. 115)   If A is an $m \times n$ matrix and B is an $n \times p$ matrix, then the product matrix AB is an $m \times p$ matrix.

Example: A is a 3×2 matrix and B is a 2×2 matrix. The product matrix AB is a 3×2 matrix.

$$\begin{bmatrix} 1 & 1 \\ 2 & 3 \\ 0 & 2 \end{bmatrix} \begin{bmatrix} 4 & 2 \\ 5 & 6 \end{bmatrix}$$

$$= \begin{bmatrix} (1)(4) + (1)(5) & (1)(2) + (1)(6) \\ (2)(4) + (3)(5) & (2)(2) + (3)(6) \\ (0)(4) + (2)(5) & (0)(2) + (2)(6) \end{bmatrix}$$

$$= \begin{bmatrix} 9 & 8 \\ 23 & 22 \\ 10 & 12 \end{bmatrix}$$

Mean (p. 519)   The sum of the data values divided by the number of data values is the mean.

$\{1, 2, 3, 3, 6, 6\}$

$\text{mean} = \dfrac{1 + 2 + 3 + 3 + 6 + 6}{6}$

$= \dfrac{21}{6} = 3.5$

Measures of central tendency (p. 519)   The mean, the median, and the mode are central values that help describe a set of data. They are called measures of central tendency.

$\{1, 2, 3, 3, 4, 5, 6, 6\}$

mean $= 3.75$; median $= 3.5$; mode $= 3$ and 6

Measures of variation (p. 526)   Measures of variation, such as the range, the interquartile range, and the standard deviation, describe how the data in a data set are spread out.

Median (p. 519)   The median is the middle value in a data set. If the data set contains an even number of values, the median is the mean of the two middle values.

$\{1, 2, 3, 3, 4, 5, 6, 6\}$

$\text{median} = \dfrac{3 + 4}{2}$

$= \dfrac{7}{2} = 3.5$

Minor axis of an ellipse (p. 478)   The minor axis of an ellipse is the segment perpendicular to its major axis at its midpoint. The endpoints of the minor axis are on the ellipse and are the co-vertices of the ellipse.

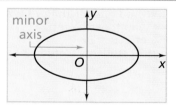

Mode (p. 519)   The mode is the most frequently occurring value in a set of data.

$\{1, 2, 3, 3, 4, 5, 6, 6\}$

mode $= 3$ and 6

Multiple zeros (p. 271)   When a linear factor in a polynomial is repeated, the zero related to that factor is a multiple zero.

The zeros of $p(x) = 2x(x - 3)^2(x + 1)$ are 0, 3, and -1. Since $(x - 3)$ occurs twice as a factor, 3 is a multiple zero.

Multiplication counting principle (p. 38)   If there are m ways to make a first selection and n ways to make a second selection, there are $m \times n$ ways to make the two selections.

There are 13 ways to select a block from one box and 12 ways to select a ball from a second box. There are $13 \times 12 = 156$ ways to select a block and a ball from the two boxes.

Glossary/Study Guide

Multiplicity (p. 271)   The multiplicity of a zero of a polynomial function is the number of times the related linear factor is repeated in the factored form of the polynomial.

The zeros of $p(x) = 2x(x - 3)^2(x + 1)$ are 0, 3, and -1. Since $(x - 3)$ occurs twice as a factor, the zero 3 has multiplicity 2.

Mutually exclusive events (p. 390)   When two events cannot happen at the same time, the events are mutually exclusive. If A and B are mutually exclusive events, then $P(A$ or $B) = P(A) + P(B)$. If A and B are not mutually exclusive, then $P(A$ or $B) = P(A) + P(B) - P(A$ and $B)$.

Rolling an even number E and rolling a multiple of three M on a standard number cube are not mutually exclusive.
$$P(E \text{ or } M) = P(E) + P(M) - P(E \text{ and } M)$$
$$= \tfrac{3}{6} + \tfrac{2}{6} - \tfrac{1}{6}$$
$$= \tfrac{4}{6} = \tfrac{2}{3}$$

N

Natural logarithmic function (p. 337)   The function $y = \ln x$ is the natural logarithmic function. It is the inverse of $y = e^x$.

Examples: $\ln e^3 = 3$
$\ln 10 \approx 2.3026$
$\ln 36 \approx 3.5835$

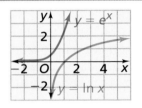

Normal distribution (p. 546)   A normal distribution is a frequency distribution of data that vary randomly from the mean. The graph of the distribution approximates a bell-shaped curve.

Example: In a class of 200 students, the scores on a test were normally distributed. The mean score was 66.5, and the standard deviation was 6.5. The number of students who scored greater than 73 is about 13.5% + 2.5% of those who took the test.
16% of 200 = 32
About 32 students scored 73 or higher on the test.

Distribution of Test Scores

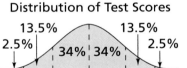

O

Objective function (p. 164)   In a linear programming model, the objective function is the quantity that you want to make as large or as small as possible. (*See* Linear programming.)

Odd function (p. 256)   The graph of an odd function has the origin as a point of symmetry.

Example: $y = 0.5x^3$

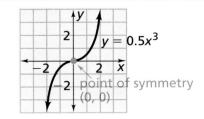

Outlier (p. 522) An outlier is an item of data with a substantially different value from the rest of the items in the data set.

The outlier in the data set {56, 64, 73, 59, 98, 65, 59} is 98.

P

Parabola (pp. 199, 466, 492) A parabola is the set of all points *P* in a plane that are the same distance from a fixed point *F* and a line *d*. Point *F* is the focus and line *d* is the directrix. The graphs of all quadratic functions are parabolas.

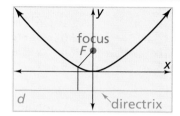

Parametric equations (p. 86) Parametric equations can be used to express horizontal distance *x* and vertical distance *y* in terms of time *t*.

Example: The equations $x(t) = 2t - 1$ and $y(t) = t + 3$ are parametric equations. Their graph is a line. When $t = 0.5$, $x = 0$ and $y = 3.5$.

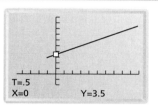

Tmin=0   Xmin=−4.7   Ymin=−2
Tmax=47   Xmax=9.4   Ymax=9.4
Tstep=.1   Xscl=1   Yscl=1

Pascal's triangle (pp. 290, 291) Pascal's triangle is a pattern for finding the coefficients of the terms of a binomial expansion.

Pascal's Triangle

```
              1
            1   1
          1   2   1
        1   3   3   1
      1   4   6   4   1
    1   5  10  10   5   1
```

Perfect-square trinomial (p. 234) A perfect-square trinomial is a trinomial that can be written as the square of a binomial.

perfect-square   binomial
trinomial   square
$16x^2 - 24x + 9 = (4x - 3)^2$

Period of a function (p. 403) The period of a periodic function is the horizontal length of one cycle.

Example: The periodic function $y = \sin x$ has period 2π.

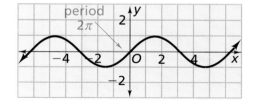

Periodic function (p. 403) A periodic function repeats a pattern of *y*-values at regular intervals or in cycles.

Example: $y = \sin x$

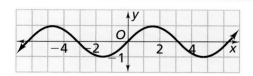

Glossary/Study Guide

Permutation (pp. 39, 41) A permutation is an arrangement of items in a particular order. The number of permutations of n objects taken r at a time is $_nP_r = \dfrac{n!}{(n - r)!}$ for $1 \le r \le n$.

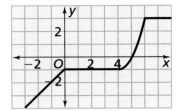

$$_8P_5 = \frac{8!}{(8 - 5)!} = \frac{8 \cdot 7 \cdot 6 \cdot 5 \cdot 4 \cdot 3!}{3!}$$
$$= 8 \cdot 7 \cdot 6 \cdot 5 \cdot 4 = 6720$$

Piecewise function (p. 74) A piecewise function has different rules for different parts of its domain.

Example: $y = \begin{cases} x - 1 & \text{if } x \le 0 \\ -1 & \text{if } 0 < x \le 4 \\ (x - 4)^2 - 1 & \text{if } 4 < x \le 6 \\ 3 & \text{if } 6 < x \end{cases}$

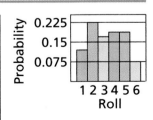

Polynomial function (p. 261) A polynomial function is any sum or difference of power functions and constants. It is in standard form when the terms are written in descending order.

$$P(x) = \overbrace{2x^3 - 5x^2 - 2x + 5}^{\text{polynomial}}$$

leading coefficient | cubic term | quadratic term | linear term | constant term

---

Power function (p. 255) A power function is a function of the form $y = ax^n$, with $a \neq 0$ and n a positive integer.

$y = 0.25x^2; \; y = x^3; \; y = 2x^4$

Preimage (p. 123) The preimage is a figure before a transformation.

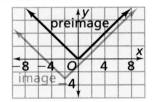

Principal root (p. 256) The principal root of a real number that has multiple roots is the positive root.

The number 25 has two square roots, 5 and -5. The principal square root, 5, is indicated by the symbols $\sqrt{25}$ or $25^{\frac{1}{2}}$.

Probability distribution (p. 507) A probability distribution is a function that tells the probability of each outcome in a sample space.

Example: The table and graph both show the experimental probability distribution for the outcomes of 40 rolls of a standard number cube.

Roll	Fr.	Prob.
1	5	.125
2	9	.225
3	7	.175
4	8	.2
5	8	.2
6	3	.075

Properties of logarithms (p. 325)
Product Property: $\log_b MN = \log_b M + \log_b N$

Quotient Property: $\log_b\left(\dfrac{M}{N}\right) = \log_b M - \log_b N$

Power Property: $\log_b M^x = x \log_b M$

$$\log \dfrac{r^3 s^4}{t^2} = \log(r^3 s^4) - \log t^2$$
$$= \log r^3 + \log s^4 - \log t^2$$
$$= 3 \log r + 4 \log s - 2 \log t$$

Quadratic equation (pp. 224–226)   Any equation that can be written in the form $ax^2 + bx + c = 0$, where $a \neq 0$, is a quadratic equation.

$x^2 - 2x - 63 = 0$
$a = 1$, $b = -2$, $c = -63$

Quadratic formula (p. 240)   Any quadratic equation $ax^2 + bx + c = 0$, $a \neq 0$, can be solved using the quadratic formula.

$$x = \dfrac{-b \pm \sqrt{b^2 - 4ac}}{2a}$$

If $-x^2 + 3x + 2 = 0$, then
$$x = \dfrac{-3 \pm \sqrt{(3)^2 - 4(-1)(2)}}{2(-1)}$$
$$= \dfrac{-3 \pm \sqrt{17}}{-2}$$
$$= \dfrac{3 \pm \sqrt{17}}{2}$$

Quadratic function (p. 199)   A quadratic function can be written in the form $f(x) = ax^2 + bx + c$, where $a \neq 0$. Its graph is a parabola.

Example: $y = x^2 + 2x - 1$

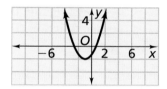

Quartiles (p. 521)   Quartiles separate a finite data set into four equal parts. The second quartile (Q_2) is the median of the data. The first and third quartiles (Q_1 and Q_3) are the medians of the lower half and upper half of the data, respectively.

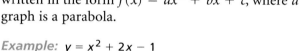

Radian (p. 415)   A radian is the measure of a central angle that intercepts an arc equal in length to the radius of a circle. You can use a proportion to convert an angle measure from one unit of measure to the other.

$$\dfrac{\text{degree measure}}{360} = \dfrac{\text{radian measure}}{2\pi}$$

$60° \longrightarrow$ $\dfrac{60}{360} = \dfrac{x}{2\pi}$
$$x = \dfrac{60(2\pi)}{360} = \dfrac{\pi}{3}$$
Thus, $60° = \dfrac{\pi}{3}$ radians

Radical equation (p. 330)   A radical equation has a variable inside a radicand. It may also be written in the form $x^a = b$ where a is a rational number.

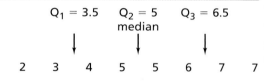

Examples

Radius (p. 471) The radius, r, of a circle is the distance between the center of a circle and each point on the circle.

Random sample (pp. 532, 554) In a random sample, each member of a population is equally likely to be chosen.

Let the set of all females between the ages of 19 and 34 be the population. A random selection of 900 females between those ages would be a random sample of the population.

Range of a relation (p. 20) The range of a relation is the set of all possible output values.

In the relation {(0, 1), (0, 2), (0, 3), (0, 4), (1, 3), (1, 4), (2, 1)}, the range is {1, 2, 3, 4}. In the function $f(x) = |x - 3|$, the range is the set of real numbers greater than or equal to 0.

Range of a set of data (p. 526) The range of a set of data is the difference between the greatest data value and the least data value.

The range of the set {3.2, 4.1, 2.2, 3.4, 3.8, 4.0, 4.2, 2.8} is $4.2 - 2.2 = 2$.

Rational function (p. 363) A function that is the quotient of two polynomials is a rational function. The graph of a rational function may be discontinuous.

Example: The function $y = \dfrac{x - 2}{x^2 - 9}$ is a rational function with three branches separated by asymptotes $x = -3$ and $x = 3$.

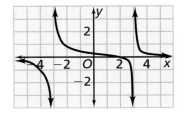

Rational number (p. 44) Any number that can be expressed as the ratio of two integers is a rational number.

$\dfrac{1}{2}, \dfrac{-3}{5}, \dfrac{16}{-7}, \dfrac{100}{10{,}000}, \dfrac{-25}{-17}, -\dfrac{1}{3}$

Rational root theorem (p. 626) If $\dfrac{p}{q}$ in simplest form is a rational root of the polynomial equation $a_nx^n + a_{n-1}x^{n-1} + \ldots + a_1x + a_0 = 0$ with integer coefficients, then p must be a factor of a_0 and q must be a factor of a_n.

The polynomial equation $40x^3 + 26x^2 - 11x - 6 = 0$ has leading coefficient 40 (with factors $\pm1, \pm2, \pm4, \pm5, \pm8, \pm10, \pm20, \pm40$) and constant term -6 (with factors $\pm1, \pm2, \pm3, \pm6$). Its only possible rational roots are

$\pm1, \pm2, \pm3, \pm6, \pm\dfrac{1}{2}, \pm\dfrac{3}{2}, \pm\dfrac{1}{4}, \pm\dfrac{3}{4},$
$\pm\dfrac{1}{5}, \pm\dfrac{2}{5}, \pm\dfrac{3}{5}, \pm\dfrac{6}{5}, \pm\dfrac{1}{8}, \pm\dfrac{3}{8}, \pm\dfrac{1}{10}, \pm\dfrac{3}{10},$
$\pm\dfrac{1}{20}, \pm\dfrac{3}{20}, \pm\dfrac{1}{40}, \pm\dfrac{3}{40}.$

Real numbers (pp. 44–45)   The set of real numbers is the set of all numbers that can be assigned to points on the number line. The diagram shows the relationships among real, rational, irrational, integer, whole, and natural numbers.

Real Numbers

Rational Numbers $\frac{1}{2}$, 0.3, 5, $2\frac{2}{3}$		Irrational Numbers
Integers ... −2, −1, 0, 1, 2, ...		$\sqrt{2}, \pi, \sqrt[3]{6}$
Whole Numbers 0, 1, 2, 3, ...		
Natural Numbers 1, 2, 3, ...		

Recursive formula (p. 562)   A recursive formula defines each term of a sequence in relation to the one(s) before it.

Let $a_n = 2.5a_{n-1} + 3a_{n-2}$
If $a_5 = 3$ and $a_4 = 7.5$, then
$a_6 = 2.5(3) + 3(7.5) = 30$.

Reflection (p. 121)   A reflection flips a figure over the line of reflection.

Relation (p. 20)   A relation is any set of ordered pairs.

{(0, 1), (0, 2), (0, 3), (0, 4), (1, 3)}

Relative maximum (minimum) (p. 269)   The *y*-value of a point on the graph of a function that is higher (lower) than the nearby points of the graph is a relative maximum (minimum).

Example: $y = x^3 - x^2 - x - 1$
The relative maximum occurs at $x = -\frac{1}{3}$.
The relative minimum occurs at $x = 1$.

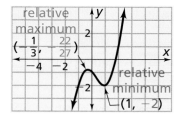

Remainder theorem (p. 624)   If a polynomial $P(x)$ of degree $n \geq 1$ is divided by $(x - a)$, where a is a constant, then the remainder is $P(a)$.

If $P(x) = x^3 - 4x^2 + x + 6$ is divided by $x - 3$, then the remainder is $P(3) = 3^3 - 4(3)^2 + 3 + 6 = 0$ (which means that $x - 3$ is a factor of $P(x)$).

Removable discontinuity (p. 366)   A rational function that has a common linear factor in its numerator and denominator has a removable discontinuity, or hole, at the value of *x* related to this factor.

The graph of $y = \frac{(x + 2)(x - 1)}{(x - 1)}$ is identical to the graph of $y = x + 2$, except it has a hole at $x = 1$.

Restrictions for a linear programming model (p. 164)   Limits on the variables in a linear programming model are called restrictions. (*See* Linear programming.)

Glossary/Study Guide

Rotation (p. 121)   A rotation turns a figure through a given angle about a point called its center.

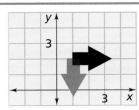

S

Sample (p. 532)   A sample contains information from only part of a population.

Let the set of all males between the ages of 19 and 34 be the population. A random selection of 900 males between those ages would be a sample of the population.

Sample proportion (p. 532)   If an event occurs x times in a sample space of size n, the sample proportion is $\frac{x}{n}$.

For a random selection of 900 males, 350 preferred red shirts to green shirts. The sample proportion would be $\frac{350}{900} = \frac{7}{18}$.

Sample space (p. 90)   The sample space is the set of all possible outcomes of an event.

When tossing two coins, the sample space is (H, H), (H, T), (T, H), (T, T).

Scalar (p. 114)   A scalar is a number that multiplies a matrix. To perform scalar multiplication, multiply each element in the matrix by the scalar.

$$2.5\begin{bmatrix} 1 & 0 \\ -2 & 3 \end{bmatrix} = \begin{bmatrix} 2.5(1) & 2.5(0) \\ 2.5(-2) & 2.5(3) \end{bmatrix}$$
$$= \begin{bmatrix} 2.5 & 0 \\ -5 & 7.5 \end{bmatrix}$$

Scatter plot (p. 5)   A scatter plot is a graph of data involving two variables.

Example: The data and the graph compare the amount (in dollars) spent on TV, radio, and sound equipment and the amount (in dollars) spent on reading material for several years.
{(371, 141), (371, 140), (379, 142), (416, 150), (429, 157), (454, 153), (468, 163), (492, 162), (590, 166)}
Source: U.S. Bureau of Labor Statistics

Per Capita Dollars Spent on Entertainment

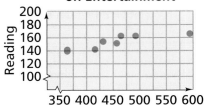

Sequence (p. 561)   A sequence is an ordered list of numbers.

1, 4, 7, 10, . . .

Series (p. 578)   A series is the expression for the sum of the terms of a sequence. The series is finite (infinite) if the corresponding sequence is finite (infinite).

The series 3 + 6 + 9 + 12 + 15 corresponds to the sequence 3, 6, 9, 12, 15. The sum of the series is 45.

Simplest form of a rational expression (p. 371) A rational expression is in simplest form when its numerator and denominator are polynomials that have no common factors.

$$\frac{x^2 - 7x + 12}{x^2 - 9} = \frac{(x - 4)(x - 3)}{(x + 3)(x - 3)}$$

$$= \frac{x - 4}{x + 3} \text{ where } x \neq 3 \text{ or } -3$$

Simulation (p. 88) When actual trials are difficult to conduct, you can find experimental probability by using a simulation, or model.

Suppose a weather forecaster predicts a 50% chance of rain for the next three days. You can use three coins landing heads up to simulate three days in a row of rain.

Sine function (pp. 424) The periodic function $y = a \sin bx$, with $a \neq 0$ and $b > 0$, has amplitude $|a|$, period $\frac{2\pi}{b}$ radians, and completes b cycles over the interval from 0 to 2π.

Example: The function $y = \sin x$ has amplitude 1, period 2π radians, and completes 1 cycle over the interval 0 to 2π.

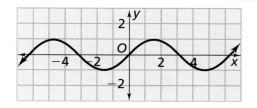

Sine of an angle (p. 411) The sine of an angle in standard position is the y-coordinate of the point where the terminal side of the angle intersects the unit circle.

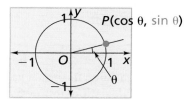

Slope of a line or segment (pp. 11, 58) Slope is a measure of the steepness of a line. The slope of a nonvertical line through $P_1(x_1, y_1)$ and $P_2(x_2, y_2)$ is the ratio of the vertical change to the horizontal change. The slope of a vertical line is undefined.
$$\text{Slope} = \frac{\text{vertical change}}{\text{horizontal change}} = \frac{y_2 - y_1}{x_2 - x_1}, \text{ where } x_2 - x_1 \neq 0$$

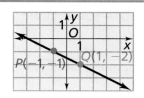

$$\text{Slope} = \frac{y_2 - y_1}{x_2 - x_1}$$
$$= \frac{-2 - (-1)}{1 - (-1)}$$
$$= \frac{-1}{2}$$
$$= -\frac{1}{2}$$

Slope-intercept form (p. 60) The slope-intercept form of a linear equation is $y = mx + b$, where m is the slope and b is the y-intercept.

$y = 8x + 2$
$y = -x + 1$
$y = -\frac{1}{2}x - 14$

Solution of a system of equations (p. 150) A solution of a system is a set of values for the variables that makes each equation true. You can solve a system by graphing, substitution, elimination, or by using a matrix.

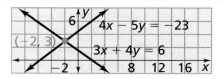

Glossary/Study Guide

Examples

Solution of an equation or inequality (p. 75)   A solution of an equation or inequality is any value of the variable(s) for which the equation or inequality is true.

The solution of $2x - 7 = -12$ is $x = -2.5$.

The solution of $2x - 7 \geq -12$ is $x \geq -2.5$.

Square matrix (p. 134)   A square matrix has the same number of columns as rows.

$$A = \begin{bmatrix} 1 & 2 & 0 \\ -1 & 0 & -2 \\ 1 & 2 & 3 \end{bmatrix}$$

Square root function (p. 219)   A square root function is any function of the form $y = a\sqrt{x - h} + k$.

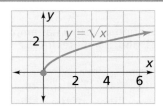

Standard deviation (pp. 526–527)   The standard deviation reflects how each data value in the set varies from the mean, $\bar{x}$. To find the standard deviation, follow five steps.
• Find the mean of the data set.
• Find the difference between each data value and the mean.
• Square each difference.
• Find the mean of the squares.
• Take the square root of the mean of the squares. This is the standard deviation.

$\{0, 2, 3, 4, 6, 7, 8, 9, 10, 11\}$
$\bar{x} = 6$
standard deviation $= \sqrt{12} \approx 3.46$

Standard form of a polynomial (p. 261)   A polynomial is in standard form when its terms are written in descending order.

$3x^2 - 2x + 10$
$2x^4 - x^2$

Standard form of an equation of a line (p. 70)   The standard form of an equation of a line is $ax + by = c$.

In standard form, the equation $y = \frac{4}{3}x - 1$ is $4x + -3y = 3$.

Standard form of the equation of a circle (p. 472)   The standard form (or center-radius form) of the equation of the circle with center (h, k) and radius r is $(x - h)^2 + (y - k)^2 = r^2$.

$(x - 3)^2 + (y - 4)^2 = 2^2$

Standard normal curve (p. 548)   The standard normal curve is a normal distribution centered on the y-axis with a mean of 0 and a standard deviation of 1.

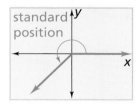

Standard position of an angle (p. 409)   An angle is in standard position when its vertex is at the origin of a coordinate system and its initial side lies along the positive x-axis.

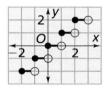

Statistics (p. 519)   Statistics is the study of data analysis and interpretation.

Step functions (p. 74)   Step functions are discontinuous piecewise functions whose graphs look like the steps of a staircase.

Example: The greatest integer function, denoted $y = [x]$, assigns to each real number the greatest integer less than or equal to the number.

Sum of a finite arithmetic series (p. 579)   The sum S_n of a finite arithmetic series $a_1 + a_2 + a_3 + \ldots + a_n$ is $S_n = \frac{n}{2}(a_1 + a_n)$.

The series $3 + 6 + 9 + 12 + 15$ is an arithmetic series with five terms. Its sum is $S_5 = \frac{5}{2}(18) = 5 \cdot 9 = 45$.

Sum of a finite geometric series (p. 584)   The sum S_n of a geometric series $a_1 + a_2 + \ldots + a_n$ with common ratio r is $\frac{a_1(1 - r^n)}{1 - r}$.

The series $2.5 + 5 + 10 + 20 + 40$ is a geometric series with five terms. Its sum is $S_5 = \frac{2.5(1 - 2^5)}{1 - 2} = 77.5$.

Sum of an infinite geometric series (p. 586)   An infinite geometric series with $|r| < 1$ converges to the sum $S = \frac{a_1}{1 - r}$.

$0.5 + 0.05 + 0.005 + \ldots$
$a_1 = 0.5, r = 0.1$
$S = \frac{0.5}{1 - 0.1} = \frac{0.5}{0.9} = \frac{5}{9}$

Synthetic division (p. 280)   In synthetic division, you omit all variables and exponents and perform the division on the list of coefficients. You also reverse the sign of the divisor so that you can add throughout the process, rather than subtract.

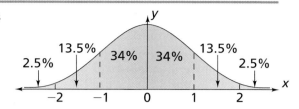

Example: Divide $2x^4 + 5x^3 - 2x - 8$ by $x + 3$.
$2x^4 + 5x^3 - 2x - 8$ divided by $x + 3$ gives
$2x^3 - x^2 + 3x - 11$ as quotient and 25 as remainder.

Glossary/Study Guide

System of equations (p. 150) A system of equations is a set of two or more equations using the same variables.

$$\begin{cases} 2x - 3y = -13 \\ 4x + 5y = 7 \end{cases}$$

System of linear inequalities (p. 152) A system of linear inequalities in x and y is a set of linear inequalities whose solution is the set of all ordered pairs satisfying all the inequalities in the set.

Example: $\begin{cases} y \le x + 4 \\ y \le -x + 2 \end{cases}$

The point $P(-1, 0)$ is a solution since $\begin{cases} 0 \le -1 + 4 \\ 0 \le -(-1) + 2. \end{cases}$

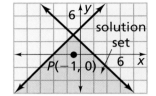

T

Tangent function (p. 433) The periodic function $y = \tan bx$, with $b > 0$, has period $\frac{\pi}{b}$ radians and completes b cycles over the interval from 0 to π.

Example: The function $y = \tan \frac{x}{2}$ has period 2π radians and completes one half cycle over the interval from 0 to π.

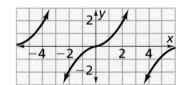

Tangent of an angle (p. 432) Given the unit circle and its tangent line $x = 1$, the tangent of an angle θ is the y-coordinate of the point where the line containing the terminal side of θ and the tangent line intersect.

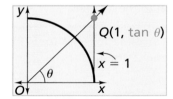

Term of a sequence (p. 561) Each number in a sequence is a term.

1, 4, 7, 10, . . .
The second term is 4.

Terminal side of an angle (p. 409) When an angle is in standard position, the initial side is on the x-axis. The other side is the terminal side of the angle.

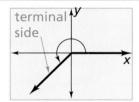

Theoretical probability (p. 90) If a sample space has n outcomes, each of which is equally likely to happen, and an event A occurs in m of these outcomes, then the theoretical probability $P(A) = \frac{m}{n}$.

Use the set {1, 4, 9, 16, 25, 36, 49, 64, 81, 100}. The probability that a randomly selected number is greater than 25 is $P(A) = \frac{5}{10} = 0.5$.

Trace (p. 172) In a three-dimensional coordinate system, a trace of a plane is the intersection of the plane with the xy-plane, the yz-plane, or the zx-plane.

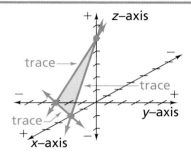

Transformation (pp. 121, 123) A transformation is a change made to a figure. There are four common types of transformations: translations, rotations, reflections, and dilations.

Translation (pp. 32, 121) A translation slides a figure a given distance in a given direction. The graph of $y = f(x - h) + k$ is a translation of the graph of $y = f(x)$ horizontally $|h|$ units and vertically $|k|$ units.

Example: When the graph of the function $y = |x|$ is translated 2 units left and 3 units down, it becomes the graph of $y = |x + 2| - 3$.
You can use a matrix to translate a figure.

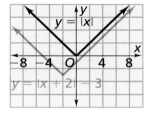

$$\underset{\text{triangle}}{\begin{bmatrix} 1 & 2 & 3 \\ 4 & 5 & 6 \end{bmatrix}} + \underset{\text{translation}}{\begin{bmatrix} 1 & 1 & 1 \\ -1 & -1 & -1 \end{bmatrix}} = \underset{\text{image}}{\begin{bmatrix} 2 & 3 & 4 \\ 3 & 4 & 5 \end{bmatrix}}$$

Transverse axis of a hyperbola (p. 485) The transverse axis is the segment that lies on the line containing the foci and has endpoints on the hyperbola. The endpoints are the vertices of the hyperbola.

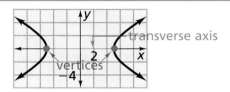

Trigonometric ratios (p. 437) In a right triangle that has an acute angle θ, the three primary trigonometric ratios are sine, cosine, and tangent.

$$\sin \theta = \frac{\text{length of side opposite } \angle \theta}{\text{length of hypotenuse}},$$

$$\cos \theta = \frac{\text{length of side adjacent } \angle \theta}{\text{length of hypotenuse}},$$

$$\tan \theta = \frac{\text{length of side opposite } \angle \theta}{\text{length of side adjacent to } \angle \theta}.$$

$\sin \theta = \frac{4}{5}$

$\cos \theta = \frac{3}{5}$

$\tan \theta = \frac{4}{3}$

U

Unit circle (p. 411) The unit circle has a radius of 1 unit and its center at the origin. An equation for the unit circle is $2x^2 + y^2 = 1$.

V

Variable matrix (p. 183) In the matrix equation $AX = B$, matrix X is the variable matrix.

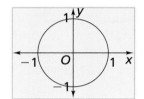

$A \cdot X = B$

$$\begin{bmatrix} 1 & 2 \\ 3 & 5 \end{bmatrix} \begin{bmatrix} x \\ y \end{bmatrix} = \begin{bmatrix} 5 \\ 14 \end{bmatrix}$$

Vertex form of a quadratic function (p. 207) A quadratic function written in the form $y = a(x - h)^2 + k$ is written in vertex form. The coordinates of the vertex are (h, k).

$y = x^2 + 2x - 1 = (x + 1)^2 - 2$
The vertex is $(-1, -2)$.

Vertex of a parabola (p. 205) The intersection of a parabola with its axis of symmetry is its vertex.

Example: The vertex of the quadratic function $y = x^2 + 2x - 1$ is $(-1, -2)$.

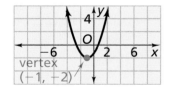

Vertices of a finite graph (p. 128) The vertices of a finite graph are the points of the graph connected by paths.

Example: N_1, N_2, N_3, and N_4 are the vertices of the finite graph.

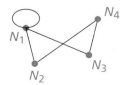

Vertices of a hyperbola (p. 485)   The points at which a hyperbola intersects its transverse axis are its vertices.

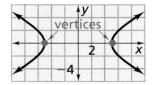

Vertices of an ellipse (p. 478)   The two points where an ellipse intersects its major axis are the vertices of the ellipse.

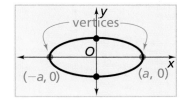

X-Y

***x*- and *y*-intercepts (p. 60)**   A point at which the graph of an equation crosses the *x*-axis (or the *x*-coordinate of that point) is an *x*-intercept. A point at which the graph of an equation crosses the *y*-axis (or the *y*-coordinate of that point) is a *y*-intercept.

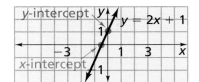

Example: The *x*-intercept of $y = 2x + 1$ is $\left(-\frac{1}{2}, 0\right)$ or $-\frac{1}{2}$.
The *y*-intercept of $y = 2x + 1$ is $(0, 1)$ or 1.

Z

Zero of a function (p. 225)   A zero of a function is any value of the variable for which the function is 0. On the graph of a function, each *x*-intercept represents a zero.

Example: The zeros of the function $p(x) = x(x - 3)^2(x + 1)$ are 0, 3, and -1.

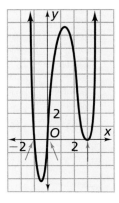

Zero product property (p. 224)   If *a* and *b* are real numbers and $ab = 0$, then either $a = 0$, or $b = 0$, or both $a = 0$ and $b = 0$.

$x(x - 3) = 0$
$x = 0$ or $x - 3 = 0$
$x = 0$ or $x = 3$

Glossary/Study Guide

CHAPTER 1

ON YOUR OWN **1.** positive, weak **3.** no correlation
5. An $m \times n$ matrix has m rows and n columns.
7a. Answers may vary. Sample: weak, positive correlation
7b. You can record substitution times for all players in a match and find out the number of points they scored.
7c. Use a scatter plot.
9.

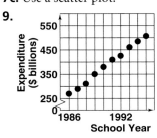

strong, positive correlation

11a. $\begin{bmatrix} 5 & 95 \\ 15 & 90 \end{bmatrix}; \begin{bmatrix} 35 & 65 \\ 30 & 55 \end{bmatrix}; \begin{bmatrix} 65 & 35 \\ 75 & 30 \end{bmatrix}; \begin{bmatrix} 70 & 25 \\ 65 & 45 \end{bmatrix}$
11b. 175 males **11c.** 185 females **11d.** about 51.4%
13. Answers may vary. Sample: You can see the relationship between the variables in a scatter plot more easily than in a table. A table shows the exact values for the data, but it is hard to find the correlation and tell whether it is weak or strong.

MIXED REVIEW **15.** 16.8 **17.** -105 **19.** 3.3
21. 72%
23a–b. Trend lines may vary. Sample:

The data points are very close to a line. There is a strong, positive correlation.
23b. Answers may vary. Sample: $1.25; $12.50; $3.75

1. $\frac{1}{2}$ **3.** $-\frac{8}{5}$ **5.** 7 **7.** $-\frac{2}{3}$ **9.** –3 **11.** 4

ON YOUR OWN **1, 3.** Answers may vary. Samples are given.

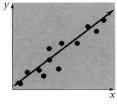 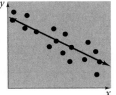

5a.

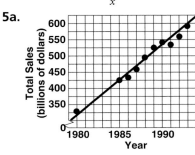

5b. Yes; there is a strong, positive correlation for the data.
5c. Check students' work. Sample:
1998—$706 billion;
1999—$728 billion; 2000—$750 billion;
2001—$772 billion

7a. Trend line may vary. Sample:

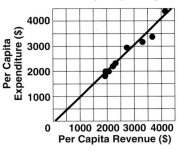

7b. Answers may vary. For sample in part (a), about $2000
7c. Answers may vary. For sample in part (a), about $2300
7d. Answers may vary. For sample in part (a), the expenditure is about $2000 lower than predicted.

9a. strong, positive correlation **9b.** yes
9c. Answers may vary. Sample: 5,100,000; any number between 5,000,000 and 5,400,000 is a reasonable estimate.

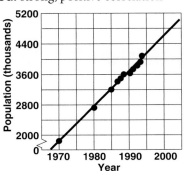

11. Answers may vary. Sample: about 170 min

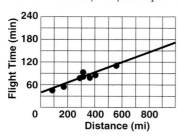

MIXED REVIEW **15.** 14.3% decrease **17.** 20% increase
19. 3220 motorcycles; 167,440 motorcycles

21, 23, 25.

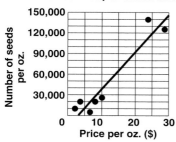

CHECKPOINT **1a, c.** Trend lines may vary. Sample:

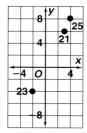

1b. strong, positive
1d. about 60,000 seeds
2. 8 **3.** 2 **4.** Sample:
the number of shrimp
per lb and cost per lb;
latitude North and
length of daylight in
December

Toolbox page 19

1.

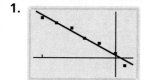

3. Answers may vary. Sample:
The calculator computes the
equation of the line of best fit
automatically and without
guessing.

Lesson 1-3 pages 20–25

ON YOUR OWN **1.** yes **3.** yes **5.** yes **7.** no **9.** yes
11. No; there are two values in the range assigned to one
in the domain. **13.** s^2 **15.** $6s^2$ **17.** -5 **19.** -3
21. -20 **23.** 8 **25.** 39 **27.** $3t + 13$ **29.** $-3x + 5$

MIXED REVIEW **35.** 5% increase **37.** 66.6% decrease
39. 50% increase **41a.** voting-age population, year
41b.

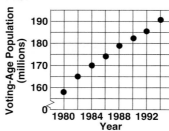

41c. strong, positive
43. -8 **45.** 8
47. about $\frac{1}{2}$

Lesson 1-4 pages 26–31

ON YOUR OWN **1.** 9; -1; $2x + 3$ **3.** 8 **5.** 20
7. 8 **9.** 40 **11.** 58 **13.** -2 **15.** 1 **17.** -3
19. 9.25 **21.** $\frac{25}{4}$ **23.** $\frac{49}{4}$ **25.** $c^2 - 3$
27. $a^2 - 3$ **29a.** $f(x) = 0.9x$ **29b.** $g(x) = x - 2000$
29c. $14,200 **31.** 1 **33.** 0 **35.** -3 **37.** a **39.** $-b$
41a. $h(x) =$ weekly sales over $5000 for total sales $x;
$g(x) =$ bonus on amount x
41b. $g(h(x))$; the bonus is applied after $5000 is subtracted
from the total. **43a.** $f(x)$; $g(x)$ **43b.** 0; 15; 30; 3; 28; 103
43c. $3x^2 + 9$ **43d.** 9; 84; 309 **43e.** $g(f(x)) = 9x^2 + 3$
43f. 3; 228; 903 **45.** $9x^2$; $3x^2$ **47.** $6x^2 + 4$; $12x^2 + 2$
49. $-4x - 28$; $-4x - 7$ **51.** 15 **53.** 8 **55.** $\frac{4}{5}$
57. $8x + 20$ **59.** $x^2 - 5x - 3$ **61.** $-x^2 + 5x + 13$
63a. Answers may vary. Sample: saving 10%; $f(x) = 0.1x$
63b. Answers may vary. Sample: $7 per hour; $g(h) = 7h$
63c. For samples in parts (a) and (b): $f(g(h)) = 0.7h$

MIXED REVIEW **65.** yes **67.** no **69.** yes

Lesson 1-5 pages 32–37

ON YOUR OWN

1.

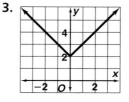

3.

15. white and red rectangle: right 2 or down 1 right 1;
other shape: right 1 and down 1

---

19. 5 units right

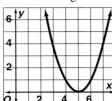

21. 5 units right and 3 units up

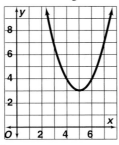

31. $y = x - 3$ **33.** $y = x^2 + 3$ **35.** $y = (x + 3)^2 - 2$
37. Subtracting 1977 from each x-value translates the line to the left and allows the use of smaller numbers. Condensing the scale on the y-axis rotates the line and allows the graph to fit in a smaller space.

39a.

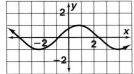

MIXED REVIEW
41. Sample graph:

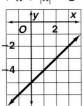

strong, positive

43. Sample graph:

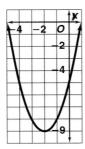

weak, negative

45. 1680
47. 720

CHECKPOINT   **1.** 21   **2.** 11   **3.** 16   **4.** $-2x + 11$
5. -9 **6.** -20 **7.** 304   **8.** $(x + 9)^2 - 3(x + 9)$
9. Answers may vary. Sample: Combine like terms.
$f(x) = x^2 + x - 3$, $g(x) = 3x^2 + |x| + 1$; $f(x) + g(x) = 4x^2 + x + |x| - 2$

10.

11.

12.

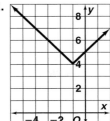

13.

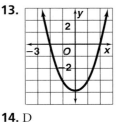

14. D

Lesson 1-6   pages 38–43

ON YOUR OWN   **1.** 120   **3.** 1   **5.** 8   **7.** 336   **9.** 6
11. 60,480   **13.** 12   **15.** 10,897,286,400   **17.** 60
19. True; Sample: Factorials are performed first and then the numbers are added. Addition is commutative.
21. False; sample: $(3 + 4)! \neq 3! + 4!$ because $7! = 5040$ and $3! + 4! = 6 + 24 = 30$; $5040 \neq 30$.
23. False; sample: $(3!)! \neq (3!)^2$ because $(3!)! = (6)! = 720$ and $(3!)^2 = (6)^2 = 36$; $720 \neq 36$.
25. 2; Sample: The ordering in the pair denotes its position on the coordinate plane.   **27a.** Answers may vary. Sample: 99!   **27b.** Answers may vary. Sample: 69!
29a. 2048   **29b.** Answers may vary. Sample: No, because there are too many possible solutions.

MIXED REVIEW   **31.** yes   **33.** no
35. 38   **37.** 3 and -3

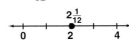

39. 10.5   **41.** $2\frac{1}{12}$

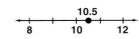

Lesson 1-7   pages 44–49

ON YOUR OWN   **1.** rational   **3.** irrational   **5.** irrational
7. rational   **9.** irrational   **11.** irrational   **13.** 0.9 s
15a. Height increases as time increases.   **15b.** time; height; real; real   **17.** $50\sqrt{7}$ **19.** 10; natural
21. $-6, 6$; integer   **23.** 3; natural   **25.** $-5, 5$; integer
27. -1; integer   **29.** $-4\sqrt{2}, 4\sqrt{2}$; irrational   **33.** V; t; real; real   **35.** m; y; natural; rational   **37.** Answers may vary. Sample: A number is rational if it can be expressed as a ratio of two integers.
39. D

MIXED REVIEW

41.

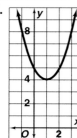

43.

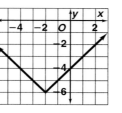

1. 226 points   **2.** 50   **3.** about 9%

4a, c. Trend lines may vary. Sample:

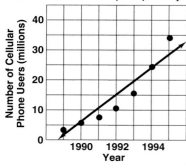

4b. strong, positive
4d. Answers may vary. For sample in part (c), ≈ 80 million users.
5. function
6. function
7. not a function
8. function
9. B
10. −3   **11.** 7
12. −20   **13.** 9

14. 44   **15.** $(-t + 3)^2 - 2$

16. $-4t + 13$ **17.** 7

18. 2 units left

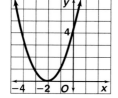

19. 7 units left and 4 units down

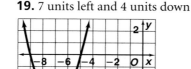

20. 8 units down

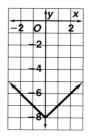

21. 5 units right

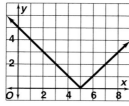

22. 1 unit up

23. 3 units right and 3 units up

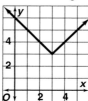

24. Answers may vary. Sample: $y = |x|$; $y = |x - 5| - 2$
25. 720   **26.** 5   **27.** 40,320   **28.** 72   **29.** 120   **30.** 12
31. When n objects are taken one at a time,
$_nP_1 = \dfrac{n!}{(n-1)!} = n.$ **32.** rational   **33.** rational
34. irrational   **35.** irrational   **36.** rational   **37.** rational
38. rational   **39.** rational   **40.** rational   **41.** irrational
42. irrational   **43.** rational   **44.** $56\sqrt{7}$ **45.** -30
46. $40\sqrt{3}$ **47.** $-30\sqrt{3}$ **48.** $6\sqrt{15}$ **49.** $18\sqrt{2}$
50. 0, 1, 2, 3, 4, 5, 6, 7, 8, 9   **51.** 1, 2, 3, 4, 5, 6
52. Sunday, Monday, Tuesday, Wednesday, Thursday,
Friday, Saturday   **53.** heads, tails   **54.** $\frac{1}{6}$ **55.** $\frac{1}{2}$ **56.** 10
57. $\frac{3}{10}$ **58.** $\frac{3}{4}$ **59.** $-\frac{1}{2}$

1. D   **3.** E   **5.** C   **7.** A   **9.** A   **11.** A vertical line describes all the points with the same x-coordinate. If a vertical line crosses the graph at more than one point, the graph has two y-coordinates corresponding to the same x-coordinate.

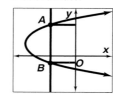

Points A and B have the same x-coordinate but different y-coordinates. The graph cannot be a function.

CHAPTER 2

ON YOUR OWN   **1.** $\frac{4}{3}$ **3.** 3   **5.** -2 **7.** $\frac{2}{3}$; 4; -6

9. 0; 7; no x-intercept   **11.** $-\frac{5}{2}$; 8.5; 3.4   **13.** $-\frac{3}{5}$; -2.4; -4

15. Start with the given point and use the slope to find another point. Then draw the line.

a.

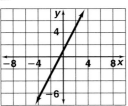

b.

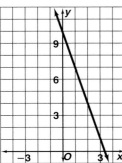

c.

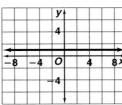

17. $y = -\frac{1}{2}x + 2$ **19.** $y = 2x + 7$ **21.** $y = -4x + 13$
23. $y = 2x + 14$ **25.** $y = -2x + 4$
27a–b.   **b.** $y = 3x + 4$

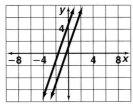

29. $y = 2x + 1$ **31.** $y = -\frac{3}{5}x + 3\frac{4}{5}$

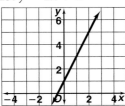 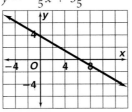

MIXED REVIEW   **39.** 39   **41.** 67   **43.** 7   **45.** $y = \frac{5}{12}x$
47. $y = 30x$

Lesson 2-2   pages 64–68

ON YOUR OWN   **1.** 5   **3.** 7   **5.** 10   **7.** $\frac{3}{4}$

9a. $m = \frac{392}{14}g$ or $m = 28g$ **b.** 103.6 mi   **c.** ≈ 417.9 gal

d. $\approx \$0.05$ **11.** $c = 2.7w$; 311 calories   **17.** $y = \frac{7}{3}x$

19. $y = -500x$ **21a.** $\frac{13}{36}$ **b.** $S = \frac{13}{36}h$ **c.** ≈ 23 ft 1 in.

---

23. 60 ft   **25.** 0.00004 km   **27.** 80.66 ft/s   **29a.** $\frac{1}{2}$
b. 32   **c.** Answers may vary. Sample: $z = k_1 xy$, $x = k_2 w$, so $z = k_1 k_2 wy$ and z varies jointly with w and y.

MIXED REVIEW   **31.** 40,320   **33.** 479,001,600   **35.** 24
37.

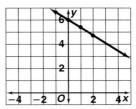

$\{4.2, 3.6, 3\}$

Lesson 2-3   pages 69–73

On Your Own   **1.** $6x - y = 5$ **3.** $x - 5y = -4$
5. $x - y = -6$ **7.** $x - 2y = -2$
9. $y = -5x + 28$ **11.** $y = 0.6x - 4.6$

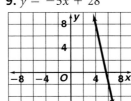 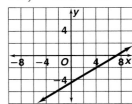

19a.

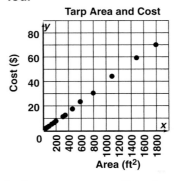

Tarp Area and Cost

; area

b. Answers may vary. Sample: $y = 0.04x$ **c.** Answers may vary. Sample: The model seems reasonable because the prices are very close to the model prices.   **d.** Sample: no; According to the model, the price should be $6.00.
e. Sample: 6 ft $\times$ 8 ft; model is $.07 lower.

Selected Answers

21. $y = -0.125x + 1.75$ **23.** $y = -3x + 20$
25. $y = 3.5x + 8.5$ **27.** $y = 3x + 12$
29. $y = -\frac{10}{11}x + \frac{28}{11}$ **31.** $y = \frac{1}{2}x - 10$

MIXED REVIEW   **37.** $\{-7, -3, -1, 2, 7\}$
39. $\{-3.5, -2.5, -2, -1.25, 0\}$ **41a.** ≈ 20.66 ft/s;
≈ 2066 ft   **b.** $d = 20.66t$ **c.** ≈ 14 mi/h
43. -8 **45.** 7.25

CHECKPOINT   **1.** $9; -3$ **2.** $-\frac{5}{7}; 5$ **3.** $0; 0$ **4.** $-\frac{5}{2}; 10$

5. $y = 2x - 9$ **6.** $y = 4x - 2$ **7.** $y = \frac{3}{5}x - 2$

8. $y = -\frac{2}{3}x + 2$ **9a.** $c = 7f$ **b.** slope $= 7$;
y-intercept $= 0$ **c.** No; no; the number of friends can be
neither negative nor a fraction.   **10.** A

Toolbox   **page 74**

1.   **3.**

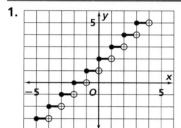 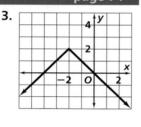

5. $f(x) = \begin{cases} -3x - 10, & \text{if } x \leq -2 \\ \frac{1}{2}x - 3, & \text{if } -2 < x \leq 2 \\ 2x - 6, & \text{if } x > 2 \end{cases}$

Lesson 2-4   **pages 75–80**

ON YOUR OWN   **1.** $x < 12$ **3.** $t \leq 3.2$ **5.** 2.3
7. 10.7 **9.** \$950   **13.** $1540 - w \geq 920; w \leq 620$
15. $s \geq 6$ **17.** $x = 28.75$ **19.** $x \leq -16$ **21.** $x = 2$

23. $x < -9$ or $x > 41$

25. $x > 7$ or $x < -\frac{7}{3}$

27. $-\frac{4}{3} \leq x \leq -1$

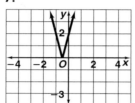

29a. $24.95 + 0.39m \leq 40$ **c.** 26 min; if he uses his
phone for fewer than 14 min each month
31. $-1 \leq x \leq 2$ **33.** $|x| > 1$
35a. $(-\infty, 2); [-1, 2]; [-2, \infty); (-\infty, -1)$ and $(1, \infty)$
b. I. $(2, 5)$ **II.** $[2, 8]$ **III.** $(0, 1)$ **IV.** $(-\infty, -4), (-2, \infty)$
c. I. $[-4, 0]$ **II.** $(-\infty, -1), (5, \infty)$ **III.** $(-\infty, \frac{1}{4}), (\frac{11}{4}, \infty)$
IV. $(1, 4)$

MIXED REVIEW   **37.** -63; rational   **39.** $18\sqrt{10}$;
irrational   **41.** $x = 3$ **43.** $x = 2.5$ **45.** $y = -5$

Lesson 2-5   **pages 81–85**

ON YOUR OWN   **1.** $y < -x - 2$ **3.** $x > -3$
7.   **9.**

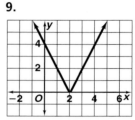

27a. $c + s$ **b.** $c + s \leq 200$
c.

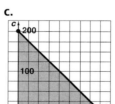

; yes

d. the maximum number of sundaes possible if 60 cones
are sold

MIXED REVIEW   **31.** 7   **33.** 7   **35.** 17   **37.** $e = 8h$;
linear   **39.** TTT, TTH, THT, HTT, HHT, HTH, THH,
HHH   **41.** 1, 2, 3, 4, 5, 6

CHECKPOINT   **1.** $x = 3$ **2.** $t \leq 5.5$ **3.** $m = 3$
4. $c < 1$

5.

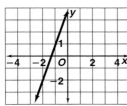

6.

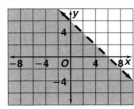

7.

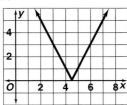

8.

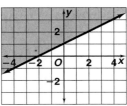

9. $y \geq 300x$; Sample: $x \geq 0$, y an integer ≥ 0
10. Answers may vary. Sample: $|x| = 8$ **11.** When there is one variable, use a number line; if there are two variables, use a coordinate plane.

Toolbox   page 86

1.

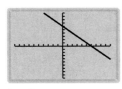

(3, 3)

3.

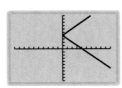

(1, 5)

Lesson 2-6   pages 87–93

ON YOUR OWN   **1.** $\frac{1}{3}$ **3.** $\frac{4}{9}$ **5.** $\frac{4}{85}$ **7a.** 1   **b.** 0
9. $\frac{1}{6}$ **11.** $\frac{1}{9}$ **13.** $\frac{11}{36}$ **15.** 1   **17.** 62.5%   **19.** $\frac{1}{4} = 25\%$
21. Sample: $\frac{2}{3}$ **23a.** 0.54   **b.** 0.04   **c.** 0.03

MIXED REVIEW   **27.** $y = (x - 6)^2 + 2$
29. $y = |x + 1| + 3$ **31.** -105 **33.** 405   **35.** Yes; you save more if the discount is taken first.

Wrap Up   pages 95–97

1. $3; \frac{8}{3} -8$;   **2.** $-1; 5; 5$ **3.** $1; 0; 0$ **4.** undefined; 4; no
y-intercept   **5.** $y = 2x + 1$ **6.** $y = -3x + 12$
7. $y = 0.5x + 4.5$ **8.** Answers may vary. Sample: $x = 3$; $y = 3$ **9.** E   **10.** 4   **11.** 0.5   **12.** 2   **13.** -0.65
14. $y = \frac{5}{3}x$ **15.** $y = -6x$ **16.** $y = -\frac{3}{7}x$ **17.** $y = 2x$
18. Answers may vary. Sample: A function that varies

directly passes through the point (0, 0); $y = 4x$ varies directly; $y = 4x + 2$ does not.   **19.** $3x - y = -1$
20. $2x - y = -4$ **21.** $x - y = \frac{3}{4}$ **22.** $2x - y = 1$
23. $\frac{5}{3}x + y = 10$ **24.** $-x + y = 5$ **25.** $x = 11$
26. $x < \frac{56}{3}$ **27.** $x \geq 19$ **28.** $x = 5$ **29.** $x = 10$
30. $x \leq 5$ **31.** $x \approx 3.64$ **32.** $x < -8$ **33.** 18

34.

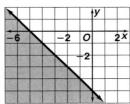

35.

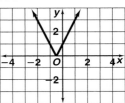

36.

37.

38. Answers may vary. Sample: $y \leq -1$ **39.** $\frac{1}{2}$ **40.** $\frac{5}{8}$
41. $\frac{1}{2}$ **42.** $\frac{1}{8}$ **43.** $\frac{1}{2}$ **44.** $\frac{3}{8}$ **45.** $\frac{1}{8}$ **46.** 2×3
47. 4×4 **48.** 4×2 **49.** Answers may vary. Sample:
$\begin{bmatrix} 1 & 2 & 3 & 4 \end{bmatrix}$

Cumulative Review   page 99

1. A   **3.** E   **5.** C   **7.** D   **9.** C   **11.** C   **14a.** $\frac{1}{2}$ **b.** $\frac{3}{8}$ **c.** $\frac{1}{8}$

CHAPTER 3

Lesson 3-1   pages 102–106

ON YOUR OWN   **1.** 3×3 **3.** 1×2 **5.** not equal; different dimensions   **7.** not equal; different dimensions
9. 2×3; 1   **11.**

	'80	'82	'84	'87	'90	'93
Color	82	85	88	93	96	98
B&W	51	47	43	36	31	20

43, millions of households with B&W televisions in 1984

13. 2×6; 6×2

17. $x = 8.5, t = -4.5$ **19.** $x = 2, t = 0.6$

21. $a = 2, b = 2.25, c = -1, d = 0, e = -4, f = 0.5$

23a. Estimates may vary. Sample:

Type of CDs	Wk 1	Wk 2	Wk 3	Wk 4
Rock	165	150	200	180
R & B	100	94	110	98
Rap	96	90	110	100
Classical	98	97	97	102

b.
$$\begin{array}{c} \text{Rock} \\ \text{R\&B} \\ \text{Rap} \\ \text{Classical} \end{array} \begin{bmatrix} 165 & 150 & 200 & 180 \\ 100 & 94 & 110 & 98 \\ 96 & 90 & 110 & 100 \\ 98 & 97 & 97 & 102 \end{bmatrix}$$

$\qquad$ Wk 1 $\quad$ Wk 2 $\quad$ Wk 3 $\quad$ Wk 4

25. Answers may vary. Sample: Each row and column should indicate the entries and also mention the units.

MIXED REVIEW **27.** -7 **29.** $\frac{5}{3}$ **31.** $-\frac{1}{3}$

33. $\begin{bmatrix} 4 & 13 \\ -2 & 12 \end{bmatrix}$

Toolbox
page 107

1. $\begin{bmatrix} 0 & 5 \\ -3 & -7 \end{bmatrix}$ **3.** $\begin{bmatrix} 3 & 5 \end{bmatrix}$ **5.** $\begin{bmatrix} 3 \\ 5 \\ -8 \end{bmatrix}$ **7.** $\begin{bmatrix} 8 & 4 & -3 \end{bmatrix}$

9. Sample: The dimensions have been interchanged.

Lesson 3-2
pages 108–113

ON YOUR OWN **1.** $\begin{bmatrix} 2 & -3 & 4 \\ 5 & 6 & -7 \end{bmatrix}$ **3.** $\begin{bmatrix} 0 & -2 & 0 \\ -2 & 0 & -2 \end{bmatrix}$

5. $\begin{bmatrix} 1 & 3 \\ 4 & 0 \end{bmatrix}$ **7a.**

$\qquad\qquad$ **Plant 1** $\qquad\qquad$ **Plant 2**

$\qquad\qquad$ Plastic Rubber $\quad$ Plastic Rubber

$\begin{array}{c} \text{1-color} \\ \text{3-color} \end{array} \begin{bmatrix} 1000 & 1400 \\ 2600 & 3800 \end{bmatrix} \begin{bmatrix} 1200 & 3600 \\ 1800 & 4800 \end{bmatrix}$

b. $\qquad$ **Plant 1 − Plant 2**

$\qquad\qquad$ Plastic $\quad$ Rubber

$\begin{array}{c} \text{1-color} \\ \text{3-color} \end{array} \begin{bmatrix} -200 & -2200 \\ 800 & -1000 \end{bmatrix}$; Plant 1; Plant 2

9. $\begin{bmatrix} -6 & -6 \\ 5 & -6 \end{bmatrix}$ **11.** $\begin{bmatrix} 3 & 0 & 1 \\ 1 & 6 & -6 \end{bmatrix}$ **13.** $\begin{bmatrix} -1 & -2 & 6 \\ 2 & -4 & 5 \end{bmatrix}$

17. $\begin{bmatrix} -1 & 1 & 10 \\ 0 & -6 & -2 \\ 0 & 0 & 2 \end{bmatrix}$ **19.** $\begin{bmatrix} 0 & -2 \\ 0 & -1 \\ -2 & 0 \end{bmatrix}$

21. $\begin{bmatrix} -3 & -4.5 & -3.125 & 0.5 \\ 1 & 1.4 & -9 & -9.90 \end{bmatrix}$

23. $\begin{bmatrix} -2 & -46 \\ -0.67 & 4 \\ -21 & -23.15 \end{bmatrix}$ **25.** Not possible. Dimensions are different.

27. $\begin{bmatrix} 4 & 42 \\ 1.33 & 4 \\ 7 & 23.45 \end{bmatrix}$ **29.** Not possible. C has different dimensions than A and D.

31. $\begin{bmatrix} 4 & -1 & 11 \\ -8 & -1 & 2 \end{bmatrix}$ **33.** $\begin{bmatrix} 9 & 62 \\ 125 & -11 \end{bmatrix}$ **35.** $\begin{bmatrix} 2 & 14 \\ 6 & -4 \\ 0 & 2 \end{bmatrix}$

37. $\begin{bmatrix} 2 & 15 \\ -22 & -28 \\ 6 & -21 \end{bmatrix}$ **39a.** Add or subtract the corresponding elements.

b. Reverse the sign of every element of A.

MIXED REVIEW **41.** $\frac{2}{3}, 2$ **43.** $5, 0$ **45.** $\begin{bmatrix} 9 & 15 \\ 6 & 24 \end{bmatrix}$

Lesson 3-3
pages 114–120

ON YOUR OWN

1. $\begin{bmatrix} -1 & 0 \\ 0 & 1 \end{bmatrix}$ **3.** $\begin{bmatrix} 1 & 0 & -1 \\ 0 & 1 & -1 \end{bmatrix}$ **5.** $\begin{bmatrix} -18 & 9 \\ 21 & -12 \end{bmatrix}$

7. 2×3; $\begin{bmatrix} 2 & -1 & 33 \\ 4 & 4 & -50 \end{bmatrix}$

9. 2×2; $\begin{bmatrix} 9w + 3x & -7w + x \\ 9y + 3z & -7y + z \end{bmatrix}$

11. 4×4; $\begin{bmatrix} a & 0 & b & 0 \\ a - 2e & 0 & b & -2f \\ 2e & 0 & 0 & 2f \\ -a + e & 0 & -b & f \end{bmatrix}$

13. $\begin{bmatrix} 8 & 16 & -8 \\ 0 & 40 & 16 \\ 0 & 4 & -28 \end{bmatrix}$ **15.** $\begin{bmatrix} 1.5 & 7 \\ 3.5 & -2 \end{bmatrix}$

17. $\begin{bmatrix} -30 & 6 & 0 \\ -12 & -12 & 6 \\ -42 & 0 & -30 \\ 6 & -24 & 0 \end{bmatrix}$ **19a.** $\begin{bmatrix} 1 & 0 \\ 0 & 1 \end{bmatrix}$

b. $\begin{bmatrix} 2 & -3 \\ 4 & 5 \end{bmatrix}$; $\begin{bmatrix} -3 & 3 \\ 3 & -3 \end{bmatrix}$; $\begin{bmatrix} 10 & 2 \\ -1 & 9 \end{bmatrix}$

c. Sample: The product is the same as one of its factors; the multiplicative identity.

21a. $\begin{bmatrix} 54 & -168 \\ 76 & -210 \end{bmatrix}; \begin{bmatrix} 54 & -168 \\ 76 & -210 \end{bmatrix}$

b. Yes; Multiplication is associative.

Sample: $A = \begin{bmatrix} 1 & 2 \\ 3 & 4 \end{bmatrix}$; $B = \begin{bmatrix} 1 & 3 \\ -3 & 5 \end{bmatrix}$; $C = \begin{bmatrix} 3 & 0 \\ 7 & -2 \end{bmatrix}$.

$A(BC) = (AB)C = \begin{bmatrix} 76 & -26 \\ 176 & -58 \end{bmatrix}$ **23.** Answers may vary.

Sample: $A = \begin{bmatrix} 1 & 2 \\ 3 & 4 \\ 5 & 6 \end{bmatrix}$; $B = \begin{bmatrix} 1 & 2 & 3 \\ 4 & 5 & 6 \end{bmatrix}$

25.

	Thur	Fri	Sat
Income	$2100	$1950	$2570

27. $x = 2, y = 5$
29. $x = -1, y = 3$ **31.** product undefined
33. product undefined **35.** product undefined

37. $\begin{bmatrix} 1.4 & 2.2 & -5.4 \\ -6 & 11 & -11.4 \\ 2 & 0 & -2.4 \\ -4.5 & 4.3 & 3.6 \end{bmatrix}$ **39.** C **41.** $\begin{bmatrix} -9 & 0 \\ -3 & -21 \\ -12 & -6 \end{bmatrix}$

43. $\begin{bmatrix} -10.5 & -12 & -22.5 \\ -4.5 & -7.5 & 9 \end{bmatrix}$ **45.** $\begin{bmatrix} -17 & -10 & -111 \\ -28 & -32 & -60 \\ -16 & -23 & 3 \end{bmatrix}$

47. $\begin{bmatrix} 50 & 53 \\ 11 & -6 \\ 6 & 42 \end{bmatrix}$ **49.** product undefined
51. product undefined

MIXED REVIEW

53.

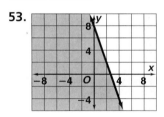

55a. 1 : 2 **b.** $\frac{1}{3}$

c. ≈ 0.11

57.

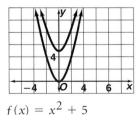

$f(x) = x^2 + 5$

59.

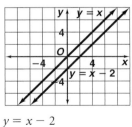

$y = x - 2$

CHECKPOINT

1. $3 \times 2; 1$ **2.** $2 \times 3; -2$ **3.** $3 \times 3; 5$ **4.** $\begin{bmatrix} -2 & 4 \\ 6 & 16 \end{bmatrix}$

5. $\begin{bmatrix} 1 & 5 \\ -4 & -7 \end{bmatrix}$ **6.** $\begin{bmatrix} 4.5 & 6 \\ 27 & -18 \end{bmatrix}$ **7.** $\begin{bmatrix} 19.5 & -28 \\ 82.5 & -52 \end{bmatrix}$

8. $\begin{bmatrix} 42 & 46 \\ 3 & 1 \end{bmatrix}$ **9.** $\begin{bmatrix} 50 & 117 \\ 278 & 495 \end{bmatrix}$ **10.** The numbers of columns of the first matrix should equal the number of rows of the second. **11.** Answers may vary. Sample:

$X - \begin{bmatrix} -3 & 3 & -3 & 6 \\ 2 & 4 & -5 & 1 \end{bmatrix} = \begin{bmatrix} 15 & 4 & 0 & 2 \\ 7 & -4 & -6 & 0 \end{bmatrix}$

Toolbox page 121

1. dilation **3.** reflection or rotation **5a.** Answers may vary. Sample: translation $\left(1, \frac{1}{2}\right), \left(1, \frac{3}{2}\right), \left(2, \frac{3}{2}\right), \left(2, \frac{7}{4}\right), \left(\frac{7}{2}, 1\right), \left(2, \frac{1}{4}\right), \left(2, \frac{1}{2}\right); \left(-2, -\frac{3}{2}\right),$
$\left(-2, -\frac{1}{2}\right), \left(-1, -\frac{1}{2}\right), \left(-1, -\frac{1}{4}\right),$
$\left(\frac{1}{2}, -1\right), \left(-1, -\frac{7}{4}\right), \left(-1, -\frac{3}{2}\right)$ **b.** Answers may vary.
Sample: In a translation, both coordinates are changed by fixed amounts.

Lesson 3–4 pages 122–126

ON YOUR OWN 1. $\begin{bmatrix} 1 & 1 & 5 & 5 \\ -3 & 1 & 1 & -3 \end{bmatrix}$

3. $\begin{bmatrix} -10 & -16 & 12 \\ 2 & a & -5 \end{bmatrix}$ **5.** $\begin{bmatrix} 5 & 1 & 4 & x & 6 \\ -y & 9 & y & 0 & 7 \end{bmatrix}$

7. $\begin{bmatrix} -8 & -8 & -3 & -3 \\ -1 & -3 & -1 & -3 \end{bmatrix}$ **9.** $\begin{bmatrix} -8 & -5 & -2 & -5 \\ -8 & -5 & -8 & -11 \end{bmatrix}$

11. $(-5, -2), (-1, -1), (-3, 1)$

13. $(-2, 8), (2, 9), (0, 11)$

19. $f: \begin{bmatrix} 1 & 2 & 4 & 5 & 2 \\ 2 & 1 & 2 & 5 & 4 \end{bmatrix}, g: \begin{bmatrix} 2 & 4 & 8 & 10 & 4 \\ 4 & 2 & 4 & 10 & 8 \end{bmatrix}$

23a.

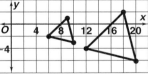

b. Sample: It enlarges or shrinks a figure and moves it farther from or closer to the original.

25.

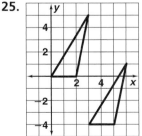

27.

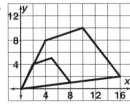

29.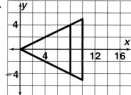

MIXED REVIEW

33a.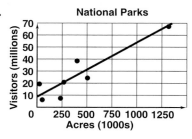

b. The greater the number of park acres, the more visitors there are.
c. See graph.
d. 21 million

35. $2x^2 + 7$ **37.** $4x^2 + 10$ **39.** $|-2x + 4| - 4x^2$

41. $2x^2 + 7 - |-2x + 4|$ **43.** $\begin{bmatrix} 2 & 1 & 1 \\ 1 & 1 & 1 \\ 0 & 0 & 1 \end{bmatrix}$

Lesson 3–5 — pages 128–133

ON YOUR OWN

1.
	N_1	N_2	N_3	N_4
N_1	0	1	0	1
N_2	1	0	1	1
N_3	0	1	0	1
N_4	1	1	1	0

3.
	V_1	V_2	V_3	V_4	V_5
V_1	0	1	0	0	0
V_2	1	0	1	0	0
V_3	0	1	0	1	1
V_4	0	0	1	0	1
V_5	0	0	1	1	0

5.

7.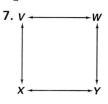

9.
	R	S	T	U	V
R	0	1	0	1	0
S	1	0	1	0	1
T	0	1	0	1	0
U	1	0	1	0	0
V	0	1	0	0	0

11.
	A	B	C	D
A	0	1	0	0
B	0	0	0	0
C	0	1	1	1
D	1	1	0	1

13.
	U	V	W	X
U	1	0	0	1
V	1	0	0	1
W	0	1	0	1
X	0	1	1	0

15a. IV **b.** II **c.** I **d.** III

17.
	C	E	V
C	0	1	0
E	1	0	1
V	1	1	0

MIXED REVIEW

21a. $18 **b.** $y = 4.5h$; linear **c.** $13\frac{1}{3}$ h **23.** 0 or ± 13

25. $1\frac{19}{23}$ **27.** -5 **29.** -0.5

CHECKPOINT

1. $(15, 20), (25, -10), (-5, -5)$ **2.** $(5, 1), (7, -5), (1, -4)$

3. $(1.5, 2), (2.5, -1), (-0.5, -0.5)$

4.
	A	B	C	D	E
A	0	1	0	0	0
B	1	0	1	0	0
C	0	0	0	1	0
D	1	0	1	0	1
E	1	1	0	0	0

5.
	K	L	M	N	O
K	0	1	0	0	0
L	0	0	1	0	0
M	1	1	0	0	0
N	0	0	1	0	1
O	0	0	0	1	0

6.
	T	V	W	X
T	0	1	1	0
V	1	0	1	0
W	1	1	0	0
X	0	0	0	0

7.
	F	G	H	I
F	0	1	0	1
G	1	0	0	0
H	0	1	1	0
I	1	0	1	0

8. A

Toolbox — page 134

1. 5 **3.** $a^2 - b^2$ **5.** 1 **7.** -1087 **9.** 24, 24; does not matter if b and c are interchanged

Lesson 3–6 — pages 135–141

ON YOUR OWN **1.** $\begin{bmatrix} 0 & 1 \\ -1 & 2 \end{bmatrix}$ **3.** $\begin{bmatrix} 2 & -1.5 \\ -1 & 1 \end{bmatrix}$

5. no inverse **7.** $\begin{bmatrix} 0.07 & 0.44 \\ 0.37 & 0.22 \end{bmatrix}$ **9.** $\begin{bmatrix} -0.025 & 0.15 \\ 0.175 & -0.05 \end{bmatrix}$

11. $\begin{bmatrix} 0.133 & 0.2 \\ 0.6 & 0.4 \end{bmatrix}$ **13.** $\begin{bmatrix} 10 \\ 15 \end{bmatrix}$ **15.** $\begin{bmatrix} 3 \\ -8 \end{bmatrix}$ **17.** $\begin{bmatrix} 1 & -3 \\ 0 & 1 \end{bmatrix}$

19. $\begin{bmatrix} 12.5 & -11.5 \\ -13 & 12 \end{bmatrix}$; RAILROAD CROSSING

21. $\begin{bmatrix} \frac{4}{3} & -1 \\ -1 & 1 \end{bmatrix}$; REDUCE SPEED NOW   **23a.** cannot be used; $ad - bc = 0$ **b.** can be used; $ad - bc = 6$ **c.** can be used; $ad - bc = 1$ **d.** can be used; $ad - bc = -1$

27. $\begin{bmatrix} 3 & 3 & -1 \\ -5 & -4 & 2 \\ -2 & -2 & 1 \end{bmatrix}$ **29.** $\begin{bmatrix} 0.4 & 0.4 & 0.2 \\ -0.6 & -0.6 & 0.2 \\ -0.2 & 0.8 & 0.4 \end{bmatrix}$

31. no inverse   **33.** $\begin{bmatrix} 10 \\ -2 \\ 8 \end{bmatrix}$ **35.** $\begin{bmatrix} 5 \\ 8 \\ 2 \end{bmatrix}$

37a. $\begin{bmatrix} -1 \\ 2 \end{bmatrix}$; P_4 **b.** $\begin{bmatrix} -3 \\ 5 \end{bmatrix}$; P_5 **c.** $\begin{bmatrix} 2 & 1 \\ 1 & 1 \end{bmatrix}$ **d.** $\begin{bmatrix} 3 \\ 2 \end{bmatrix}$; P_1

41. $a = \pm 1$, $d = \pm 1$, $b = c = 0$

MIXED REVIEW   **43.** $\frac{3}{5}$ **45.** $\begin{bmatrix} 32 \\ 15 \end{bmatrix}\begin{bmatrix} 82 \\ 32 \end{bmatrix}\begin{bmatrix} 42 \\ 17 \end{bmatrix}\begin{bmatrix} 116 \\ 39 \end{bmatrix}\begin{bmatrix} 130 \\ 45 \end{bmatrix}$ $\begin{bmatrix} 144 \\ 54 \end{bmatrix}\begin{bmatrix} 58 \\ 20 \end{bmatrix}\begin{bmatrix} 82 \\ 29 \end{bmatrix}\begin{bmatrix} 136 \\ 48 \end{bmatrix}\begin{bmatrix} 82 \\ 32 \end{bmatrix}\begin{bmatrix} 82 \\ 34 \end{bmatrix}\begin{bmatrix} 136 \\ 53 \end{bmatrix}\begin{bmatrix} 44 \\ 21 \end{bmatrix}\begin{bmatrix} 130 \\ 45 \end{bmatrix}$

Wrap Up   pages 143–145

1. 2×3; -7 **2.** 3×2; -5 **3.** 3×3; 12
4. 2×2; 54 **5.** $x = -2$; $w = 8$; $r = 4$; $t = -1$

6. $t = -4$; $y = 11$; $r = 4$; $w = 5$ **7.** $\begin{bmatrix} -3 & 10 \\ -3 & 3 \end{bmatrix}$

8. $\begin{bmatrix} -50 & 71 \\ 7 & 16 \end{bmatrix}$ **9.** $\begin{bmatrix} 2 & 8 & 13 \\ 33 & 0 & -7 \end{bmatrix}$ **10.** $\begin{bmatrix} -8.8 & -3.5 \\ 7 & -15.6 \end{bmatrix}$

11. $\begin{bmatrix} 30 & 5 & 0 & 40 \\ -20 & 15 & 35 & 55 \end{bmatrix}$ **12.** $\begin{bmatrix} -5 & 16 \\ -20 & 31 \end{bmatrix}$

13. $\begin{bmatrix} -24 & -1 \\ -36 & -8 \end{bmatrix}$ **14.** E   **15.** $\begin{bmatrix} 1 & 8 & 5 & 2 & 0 \\ 0 & -1 & 3 & 7 & 1 \end{bmatrix}$

16. $\begin{bmatrix} -2 & -4 & -3 & 0 \\ -3 & 0 & 8 & 7 \end{bmatrix}$ **17.** $(-2, 3), (-7, 2), (-4, 7)$

18. $(15, 5), (-10, 0), (5, 25)$ **19.** $(5, -3), (0, -4), (3, 1)$

20.

	A	B	C	D	E
A	0	1	1	1	0
B	1	0	0	0	0
C	1	0	0	0	0
D	1	0	0	0	1
E	0	0	0	1	0

21.

	T	U	V	W	X
T	0	1	0	0	0
U	1	0	1	0	0
V	1	0	0	1	0
W	0	0	1	0	1
X	0	1	0	1	0

22.

	K	L	M	N	O	P
K	0	0	0	1	0	0
L	0	0	0	1	1	1
M	0	0	0	0	0	1
N	1	1	0	0	1	0
O	0	1	0	1	0	0
P	0	1	1	0	0	0

23.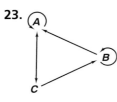

24. 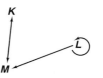   **25.**

26. $\begin{bmatrix} 0.167 & -0.042 \\ 0 & 0.25 \end{bmatrix}$ **27.** no inverse

28. $\begin{bmatrix} 0.12 & -0.02 \\ -0.19 & 0.24 \end{bmatrix}$ **29.** $\begin{bmatrix} 0.33 & -0.67 & 0 \\ -0.16 & 0.33 & -0.5 \\ 0.33 & 0.33 & 0 \end{bmatrix}$

30. $\begin{bmatrix} 1 & 2 \\ -1 & 0 \end{bmatrix}$ **31.** $\begin{bmatrix} 2 & 1 \\ 3 & 2 \end{bmatrix}$ **32.** $\begin{bmatrix} 3.579 & -1 \\ 4.895 & -2 \end{bmatrix}$

33. Answers may vary. Sample: $\begin{bmatrix} 1 & 2 & 3 \\ 4 & 5 & 6 \end{bmatrix}$; no inverse

34. 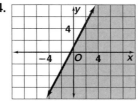   **35.**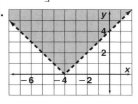

36. 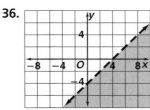   **37.**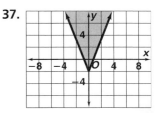

38. 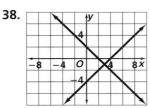   **39.**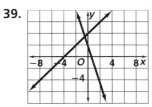

40.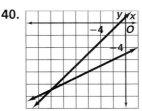

Preparing for Standardized Tests page 147

1. D   **3.** E   **5.** E   **7.** E   **9.** C

CHAPTER 4

Lesson 4-1 — pages 150–155

ON YOUR OWN **1.** two intersecting lines; one solution
3. parallel lines; no solution **5a.** Sample (using LinReg with $x = 1$ for January): $y = 3000x + 2200$ (income); $y = -900x + 36,600$ (expenses) **b.** For the sample given, income first exceeds expenses in September (month 9).

7. $(3, 1)$ **9.** $(2, 1)$

 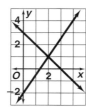

19. after 10 more minutes **21.** Sample: $5x + 2y = 8$
23. Sample: $y = -4x$ **25.** Sample: $-3x + 2y = -1$
27. A and B **29.** A and C **31.** A and C **33.** Sample: $y \le -|x| + 2, y \ge |x| - 2$ **35.** Sample: $y \le 2x, y \ge 2x - 8, 0 \le y \le 4$ **37.** D

MIXED REVIEW **39.** $\begin{bmatrix} -8 \\ -24 \end{bmatrix}$ **41.** *The New York Times* Sunday edition: about 3.33 lb; *USA Today:* about 0.37 lb
43. $y = 3x - 4$ **45.** $y = \frac{5}{2}x + 3$ **47.** $y = \frac{5}{8}x - \frac{70}{8}$

Toolbox — page 156

1a. month 17 **b.** 41 months **c.** $187.74 **d.** 7 payments **e.** B3 + (B3 · 0.018) − (B3 · 0.05) or 0.968(B3) **3.** Answers may vary. Sample: You will pay much more than the price of the item.

Lesson 4-2 — pages 157–162

ON YOUR OWN **1.** $(-2, 4)$ **3.** $\left(\frac{3}{4}, \frac{5}{2}\right)$ **5.** $(10, -1)$

7. $(-6, -9)$ **9.** $x =$ number of 25¢ comic books, $y =$ number of 40¢ comic books; $25x + 40y = 470$, $y = x + 2$; 6 25¢ comic books, 8 40¢ comic books
11. $(2, 4)$; consistent, independent **13.** $(4, 1)$; consistent, independent **15.** no solution; inconsistent, independent
17. $(5, 4)$; consistent, independent
19. Answers may vary. Sample: $2x + 3y = 14$, $4x - 3y = -8$. Solution: $(1, 4)$
21a. $c = 9.95 + 2.25t, c = 2.95t$ **b.** 14.2 h **c.** Answers may vary. Sample: Internet Action because it would cost $4.05 less per month **23.** $(50, 750)$ **25.** $(-300, 400)$
27. $(-6, 30)$ **29.** $\left(\frac{1}{2}, \frac{3}{4}\right)$ **31.** $(300, 150)$ **33.** $\left(1, -\frac{2}{3}\right)$

35. yes; $-40°F$ and $-40°C$

MIXED REVIEW **37.** -4 **39.** 4

41. 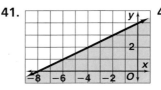 **43.**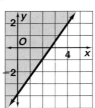

Lesson 4-3 — pages 163–169

ON YOUR OWN **1.** $(4, 2)$ **3.** $(6, 8)$ **5.** Sample: For linear programming, it is necessary to solve systems of equations to find the vertices of the graph of the system of restrictions.

9. 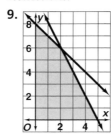 **11.**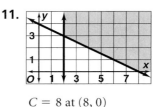

$C = 8$ at $(8, 0)$

$N = 500$ at $(5, 0)$

15a. 15 experienced, 0 training; none; 7500 **b.** 11 experienced, 8 training; 7100 **17.** Any of the following will maximize profit: 36 art, 8 sonnet; 37 art, 6 sonnet; 38 art, 4 sonnet; 39 art, 2 sonnet; 40 art, 0 sonnet. **19.** 70 spruce trees, 0 maple trees

MIXED REVIEW **21.** $\frac{1}{10}$ **23.** $\frac{1}{2}$

25a.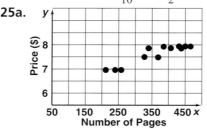
b. Answers may vary. For the scatter plot shown, x-values from 50 to 500 are shown, with 1 unit = 50 pages; y-values from $5.50 to $9.50 are shown, with 1 unit = $.50. **c.** positive **d.** $y = 0.0046x + 5.99$ where $x =$ number of pages, $y =$ price in dollars **e.** Answers may vary. Sample: Using the equation from part (d), $6.45. **27.** 18; 4 **29.** 10; -8

CHECKPOINT **1.** $(4, -3)$ **2.** $(7, 0)$ **3.** $\left(3, \frac{1}{2}\right)$
4. $(2, -4)$ **6a.** In 4.78 yr (about 4 yr, 9 mo) **b.** The energy-saving model; after 12 yr this model should cost $1331, the other $1497. **7.** C **8.** 300 acres of corn, 100 acres of soybeans

Lesson 4-4 — pages 170–174

ON YOUR OWN **1.** $(0, 0, 0)$ **3.** $(0, 40, 0)$
5. $(0, 80, 100)$ **7.** 1 unit back, 5 units right **9.** 2 units forward, 5 units up

11.

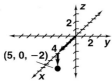

(5, 0, −2)

19. D **21a.** x = number of balloons, y = number of streamers, z = number of noisemakers;
$5x + 25y + 40z = 2000$

b. Answers may vary. Sample: (100 balloons, 20 streamers, 25 noisemakers) and (200 balloons, 40 streamers, 0 noisemakers)

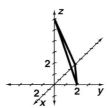

For clarity, traces are shown as segments and shading is omitted.

23.

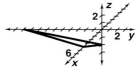

25.

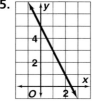

29. Mt. Tahat **31.** Cape Verde

MIXED REVIEW

33.

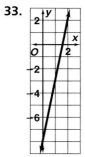

35.

Lesson 4-5 — pages 175–181

ON YOUR OWN **1.** $(2, 1, -5)$ **3.** $(q, r, s) = \left(\frac{1}{2}, -3, 1\right)$

5. $(6, 1.5, 3.2)$ **7.** A: 24,500 seats; B: 14,400 seats; C: 10,100 seats **9.** $(8, -4, 2)$ **11.** inconsistent
13. $(r, s, t) = (-2, -1, -3)$ **15.** $(-2, -1, -3)$
17. $x + 2y = 180, y + z = 180, 5z = 540, (36°, 72°, 108°)$
19. infinitely many **21.** none **23.** 75 apples, 25 pears

MIXED REVIEW **25.** 113 **27.** -62

29. $\begin{bmatrix} 8 & -3 \\ -5 & 2 \end{bmatrix}$ **31.** $\begin{bmatrix} -0.2 & -0.8 \\ 0.4 & 0.6 \end{bmatrix}$

CHECKPOINT

1.

2.

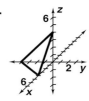

3.

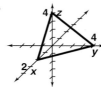

4.

5. $(3, 2, 5)$ **6.** $(0, 6, 3)$ **7.** $(3, -3, 9)$

Toolbox — page 182

1. $(-15, 5)$ **3.** $(3, 1)$

Lesson 4-6 — pages 183–188

ON YOUR OWN **1.** $\begin{bmatrix} 1 & 1 \\ 1 & -2 \end{bmatrix} \begin{bmatrix} x \\ y \end{bmatrix} = \begin{bmatrix} 5 \\ -4 \end{bmatrix}$

3. $\begin{bmatrix} 3 & 5 \\ 1 & 1 \end{bmatrix} \begin{bmatrix} a \\ b \end{bmatrix} = \begin{bmatrix} 0 \\ 2 \end{bmatrix}$ **5.** $\begin{bmatrix} 6 \\ 2 \end{bmatrix}$ **7.** $\begin{bmatrix} 16 \\ -22 \end{bmatrix}$ **9.** $\begin{bmatrix} -7 \\ 8 \end{bmatrix}$

11a. 14 **13.** $(2, 1)$ **15.** $(0.5, 20)$ **17.** $(1, 2, 9)$ **19.** tea 126°F, milk 36°F **21.** grade 10: 425 students; grade 11: 400 students; grade 12: 380 students **23.** $(5.4, 7.4)$
25. $(6, 1)$
27. $(-3, -2, 18)$ **29.** after 40 sold-out performances

MIXED REVIEW

31. $\begin{bmatrix} 9 & -3 \\ -5 & 12 \end{bmatrix}$ **33.** $\begin{bmatrix} 59 & 46 \\ 33 & 22 \end{bmatrix}$

Toolbox — page 189

1. 7 **3.** 17 **5.** $(1, 2)$ **7.** $(2, 0)$

Wrap Up — pages 191–193

1. $(2, 4)$

2.

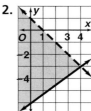

3. $(3, 6)$ **4.**

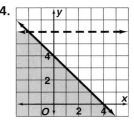

6. $(10, -4)$ **7.** $(3, 7)$ **8.** $(0, 4)$ **9.** $(1, 9)$

10.

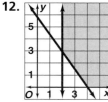

$C = 0$ at $(0, 0)$

11.

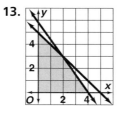

$P = 32$ at $(8, 4)$

12.

$C = 11$ at $(2, 3)$

13.

$P = 25$ at $(0, 5)$

15. 2 units right   **16.** 2 units forward, 3 units right

(0, 2, 0)

(2, 3, 0)

17. 1 unit forward, 4 units up

18. 1 unit forward, 3 units right, 1 unit down

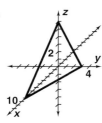

(1, 0, 4)

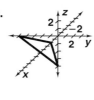

(1, 3, −1)

19.

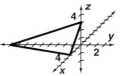

20.

21.

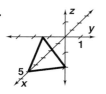

22.

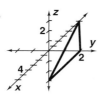

23.

24.

25. D   **26.** $(-1, 3, -4)$ **27.** $(4, -2, 1)$ **28.** $(0, 2, -3)$
29. $(2, 5, 3)$ **30.** inconsistent   **31.** $(6, 0, -2)$
32. 2 five-person canoes, 3 four-person canoes

33. $(-4, -7)$ **34.** $(2, 2)$ **35.** $\left(-\frac{1}{3}, 1\frac{2}{3}\right)$ **36.** $(2, -3)$

37. $\{(x, y) \mid x + 2y = 15\}$ **38.** $(4, -7)$

39.

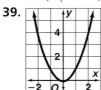

40.

41.

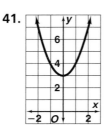

42.

43.

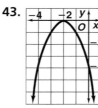

44.

45.

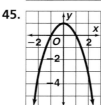

46.

47. $8, 0, 18, 50$ **48.** $-2, 0, -12, -30$ **49.** $-3, -3, 12, 32$
50. $20, 2, 35, 97$

Cumulative Review   page 195

1. C   **3.** B   **5.** A   **7.** C   **9.** D   **11.** A

CHAPTER 5

Lesson 5-1   pages 198–203

ON YOUR OWN   **1.** yes   **3.** no   **5.** $x^2 - 3x - 28$
7. $x^2 + 6x + 9$ **9.** $6t^2 + 23t + 10$
11. $4w^2 - 36w + 81$ **13.** $56x^2 - bx - b^2$

15. $w^3 - 6w^2 + 8w$ **17.** $x =$ elapsed time in seconds; $y =$ water level in millimeters   **a.** $y = -1.55x + 115.75$ **b.** $y = 0.009x^2 - 2.1x + 120.3$ **c.** the quadratic model

21. quadratic   **23.** quadratic   **25.** quadratic   **27.** quadratic   **29.** linear   **31.** quadratic

33a. Table 1

x	0	1	2	3	4	5
y = 2x	0	2	4	6	8	10
Difference		2	2	2	2	2

Table 2

x	0	1	2	3	4	5
y = 2x²	0	2	8	18	32	50
Difference		2	6	10	14	18

b. $y = 2x^2$
c. All of the differences are 2; the differences increase by 4 from cell to cell.
d. $y = -x + 4$

x	0	1	2	3	4	5
y = -x + 4	4	3	2	1	0	-1
Difference		-1	-1	-1	-1	-1

$y = -x^2 + 4$

x	0	1	2	3	4	5
y = -x² + 4	4	3	0	-5	-12	-21
Difference		-1	-3	-5	-7	-9

The patterns are similar but not identical to those in part (c).   **35.** 3   **37.** $f(x) = x^2 + 2x$

MIXED REVIEW   **41.** $\frac{8}{3}$ **43.** 26   **45.** 3 right   **47.** 9 up

Toolbox   page 204

1. quadratic model; Sample: The quadratic residuals are closer to 0 than the linear residuals.   **2.** linear model

Lesson 5-2   pages 205–210

ON YOUR OWN   **1.** $y = \frac{2}{9}x^2$; up   **3.** $y = -\frac{1}{4}x^2$; down
5. $y = \frac{1}{9}x^2$; up   **7.** $y = -\frac{3}{16}x^2$; down   **9.** $y = -x^2 + 4$
11. $y = -2x^2$ **13.** $y = -(x + 2)^2$ **15.** $y = 2(x + 1)^2$
17. $y = 6(x + 3)^2 - 2$

19.

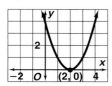

21.

33a. $x = 4, x = 2.5$ **c.** $y = -4(x - 4)^2 + 1$;
$y = 4(x - 2.5)^2 + 1$ **35a.** $y = -\frac{1}{20}x^2 + 5$ **b.** Yes;
the equation can be written as $y = -\frac{1}{20}(x - 0)^2 + 5$.

39.

$y = \frac{5}{2}x^2$

41.

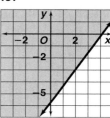

$y = -\frac{4}{9}(x - 3)^2 + 6$

MIXED REVIEW

47.

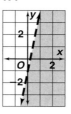

49.

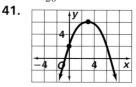

55a. 30 ft   **b.** $67 \le T \le 73$ **57.** $y = 2x^2 - 20x + 50$
59. $y = -3x^2 + 42x - 147$ **61.** $y = x^2 - 12x + 46$
63. $y = -x^2 - 8x - 6$

Lesson 5-3   pages 211–215

ON YOUR OWN   **1.** B   **3.** A   **7.** $y = (x - 2)^2 + 2$
9. in vertex form   **11.** in vertex form
13. $y = 4\left(x + \frac{7}{8}\right)^2 - \frac{49}{16}$ **15.** $y = -3\left(x + \frac{1}{3}\right)^2 + \frac{4}{3}$
17. in vertex form   **19.** 25 ft by 50 ft
21. $y = x^2 - 2x + 3$ **23.** $f(x) = 2x^2 - 8x + 13$
25. $f(x) = -x^2 + 14x - 39$
27. $y = 25x^2 + 60x + 27$ **29.** $y = -2x^2 - 6x$

31.

33.

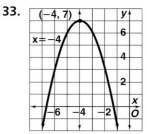

37a. $20   **b.** $6050   **39.** 5

MIXED REVIEW   **41a.** Sample: $y = 2.87x + 22$, where 1980 is $x = 0$
b. Sample: $y = -0.154x^2 + 5.18x + 17.76$, where 1980 is $x = 0$

43. $y = -\frac{6}{5}x + \frac{13}{5}$

45.

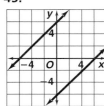

47.

1. $-1, 7$ **3.** $-1.24, 3.24$ **5.** $-1.65, 3.65$

Lesson 5-4   pages 217–222

ON YOUR OWN

1.

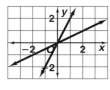

$y = 2x$

3.

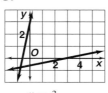

$y = \frac{x-3}{5}$

5. $y = \frac{x}{3}$ **7.** $y = 3x - 5$ **9.** $y = \pm\sqrt{3x}$

11. $y = \pm\sqrt{x-3} + 2$

13a.

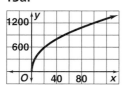

b. ≈ 745 ft; ≈ 1050 ft; ≈ 1340 ft

15. 4.3 s; 6.1 s

17. $x \geq 2; y \geq 0$

19. $x \geq 0; y \geq 3$

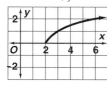

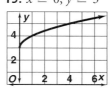

25a. $f(x) = 0.8x$ **b.** $g(x) = 1.25x$ **c.** finding the original price given the sale price

27.

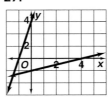

$y = 4x + 4; y = \frac{1}{4}x - 1$

29.

$y = (x+1)^2; y = \pm\sqrt{x} - 1$

MIXED REVIEW   **31.** $(-3, 9)$ **33.** $(9, -4)$

35. $x^2 + 10x + 25$ **37.** $x^2 - 144$ **39.** $x^2 - 2x - 63$

41. $x^2 - 16x + 60$

CHECKPOINT   **1.** quadratic   **2.** linear   **3.** quadratic

4. linear

5.

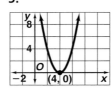

6.

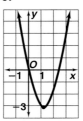

7.

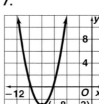

8.

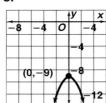

10. $y = \frac{1}{3}x + \frac{7}{3}$ **11.** $y = \pm\sqrt{x+4}$ **12.** $y = 2x - 1$

13. $y = -3 \pm \sqrt{x+4}$

1. $(x+2)^2$ **3.** $(2x-5)(x+3)$ **5.** $(4x-3)(x-3)$

7. $(5x-12)(5x+12)$ **9.** $(3x-2)^2$

11. $2(2x+3)(2x-3)$

Lesson 5-5   pages 224–228

ON YOUR OWN   **1.** $-4, -2$ **3.** $3, -1$ **5.** $-1, -2$

7a. about 6.6 s   **b.** about 6.9 s   **9.** $3, 4$ **11.** -1.5,

-1.7 **13.** $-0.9, 2.3$ **15.** $-1, 0.3$ **17.** $4, -4$

19. $3, 8$ **21.** $3.6, -3.6$ **23.** $3, -0.5$ **25.** $-1.5, -0.7$

27. $7, 1$ **31.** $(0, -2), (2, 2)$ **35.** $x = 4, y = 1$ or

$x = -4, y = 9$ **37a.** $y = (x+3)^2 + 5$ **b.** $-1.3, -4.7$

39. $x^2 - 8x + 15 = 0$ **41.** $x^2 + 7x + 6 = 0$ **43.** C

MIXED REVIEW **45.** $y = -5x + 2$ **47.** $y = -\frac{1}{2}x + 1$
49. 5 **51.** 13 **53.** $\sqrt{130}$ **55.** $|x|\sqrt{2}$

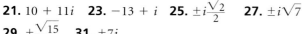

Lesson 5-6   pages 229–233

ON YOUR OWN **1.** -1 **3.** 1 **5.** -1 **7.** As the
exponent keeps increasing by 1, the pattern $i, -1, -i, 1$
keeps repeating. **9.** $4\sqrt{2}i$ or $4i\sqrt{2}$ **11.** $-10i$
13a. $A: -5, 5; B: 3 + 2i, \sqrt{13}; C: 2 - i, \sqrt{5}; D: 3i, 3;$
$E: -6 - 4i, 2\sqrt{13}; F: -1 + 5i, \sqrt{26}$
13b. $A: 5; B: -3 - 2i; C: -2 + i; D: -3i; E: 6 + 4i;$
$F: 1 - 5i$ **15.** $10 - 4i$ **17.** $288i$ **19.** $6 + 10i$
21. $10 + 11i$ **23.** $-13 + i$ **25.** $\pm i\frac{\sqrt{2}}{2}$ **27.** $\pm i\sqrt{7}$
29. $\pm\frac{\sqrt{15}}{5}$ **31.** $\pm 7i$
33a. The quadrilateral is a parallelogram.
35. $-1, 0, -1$ **39.** $x = -7, y = 3$

MIXED REVIEW
43.   **45.**

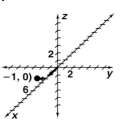 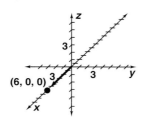

49. $x^2 + 2x + 1$ **51.** $x^2 + 12x + 36$

Lesson 5-7   pages 234–239

ON YOUR OWN **1.** $81; (n + 9)^2$ **3.** $144; (x - 12)^2$
5. $\frac{9}{4}; \left(m - \frac{3}{2}\right)^2$ **9.** $7, -4$ **11.** $1 + \sqrt{5}, 1 - \sqrt{5}$
13. $-3 + 4i\sqrt{2}, -3 - 4i\sqrt{2}$ **15.** $-1, 9$
17. $\frac{3 + i\sqrt{31}}{2}, \frac{3 - i\sqrt{31}}{2}$
19. $-3 + i\sqrt{13}, -3 - i\sqrt{13}$ **21.** E
23a. $(60, 5000)$ **b.** $5000 **c.** $60
25. $y = -(x - 2)^2 + 3$

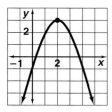

33.

Width	1	2	3	4	5	6	7	8	9
Length	49	48	47	46	45	44	43	42	41
Area	49	96	141	184	225	264	301	336	369

MIXED REVIEW **35a.** profit; income will be $100,
expenses will be $55. **b.** 3 T-shirts **37.** $\begin{bmatrix} -6 & 47 \\ 12 & -19 \end{bmatrix}$
39. $\begin{bmatrix} 3 & -7 & -11 \\ 4 & 32 & 8 \end{bmatrix}$ **41.** 84 **43.** 89

CHECKPOINT **1.** $-8, 3$ **2.** 1 **3.** $-2, \frac{3}{2}$ **4.** $-4, 0$

5.   **6.**

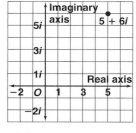

$\sqrt{29}$ $\sqrt{61}$

7.   **8.**

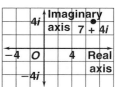

$\sqrt{82}$ $\sqrt{65}$

9. C **10.** $y = \left(x + \frac{1}{2}\right)^2 - \frac{13}{4}$ **11.** $y = -(x - 1)^2$
12. $y = \frac{1}{2}(x + 5)^2 - \frac{17}{2}$ **13.** $y = \left(x + \frac{7}{2}\right)^2 - \frac{41}{4}$
14. The x-coordinate is $-\frac{b}{2a}$. Substitute this value into the
equation and solve for y to find the y-coordinate.

Selected Answers

ON YOUR OWN **1.** $-2 + i\sqrt{2}, -2 - i\sqrt{2}$

3. $\frac{5}{2} + i\frac{\sqrt{3}}{2}, \frac{5}{2} - i\frac{\sqrt{3}}{2}$ **5.** $\frac{3}{2} + \frac{\sqrt{5}}{2}, \frac{3}{2} - \frac{\sqrt{5}}{2}$

7. $-1\frac{2}{3}, \frac{1}{3}$ **9.** $3 + i\sqrt{2}, 3 - i\sqrt{2}$

11. $1 + i\sqrt{2}, 1 - i\sqrt{2}$ **13a.** $x^2 - 18x + 36 = 0$;
2.3 in. and 15.7 in. **b.** 15.7 in. and 2.3 in. **15.** -4;
two imaginary solutions **17.** 0; one real solution
19. 169; two real solutions **21.** 1; two real solutions
23. 0; one real solution

25a. yes

b. 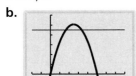 **c.** $0 \le t \le 5$ (assuming
everything occurs on level
ground) **27.** 2 **29.** 0
31. 2 **33.** 0 **35.** 0
37a. II **b.** III **c.** I

39a. Graph the related function
$y = 0.09x^2 - 4.1x + 115.96 - 100$. Then find the
x-intercept. **b.** Solve $0 = 0.09x^2 - 4.1x + 15.96$ for x.
41. 1, 10 **43** 0.5, -1.5 **45.** $1 + i, 1 - i$ **47.** 7, -7
49. $3 + i\sqrt{2}, 3 - i\sqrt{2}$

MIXED REVIEW

51. 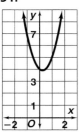 **53.** 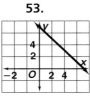 **55.**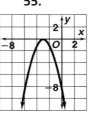

1a. Sample: $y = 48.7x^2 - 661.2x + 4454.9$ (using
quadratic regression where $x = 0$ represents 1980)
1b. 1994 or 1995

2. 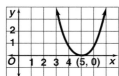 **3.**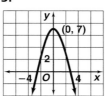

4. 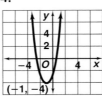 **5.**

6. $(-0.5, -12.25); y = \left(x - \frac{1}{2}\right)^2 + 12\frac{1}{4}$

7. $(0, 5); y = -\frac{1}{2}x^2 + 5$ **8.** $(-2, -11)$;
$y = 2(x + 2)^2 - 11$ **9.** $(1, 3); y = -(x - 1)^2 + 3$
10. $y = \frac{1}{3}x + \frac{2}{3}$ **11.** $y = \pm\sqrt{x + 7}$
12. $y = \pm\frac{1}{2}\sqrt{2x - 12}$ **13.** $y = \pm 2\sqrt{2x - 2}$
14. $-4, 2$ **15.** $-1, 4$ **16.** $\frac{2}{3}, 4$ **17.** 0, 7
19. $-4 + 6i; 4 - 6i; 2\sqrt{13}$ **20.** $51 + 21i$;
$-51 - 21i; 39\sqrt{2}$ **21.** $8 + 6i; -8 - 6i; 10$
22. $2 + 16i; -2 - 16i; 2\sqrt{65}$ **23.** B **24.** $-\frac{3}{2} + \frac{i\sqrt{91}}{2}$,
$-\frac{3}{2} - \frac{i\sqrt{91}}{2}$ **25.** $1 + i\sqrt{3}, 1 - i\sqrt{3}$ **26.** $\frac{1}{2} + \frac{3i\sqrt{3}}{2}$,
$\frac{1}{2} - \frac{3i\sqrt{3}}{2}$ **27.** $-\frac{3}{4} + \frac{\sqrt{73}}{4}, -\frac{3}{4} - \frac{\sqrt{73}}{4}$ **28.** $-\frac{3}{4}, 1$
29. $3 + \sqrt{7}, 3 - \sqrt{7}$ **30.** $\frac{7}{4} + \frac{i\sqrt{31}}{4}, \frac{7}{4} - \frac{i\sqrt{31}}{4}$
31. $3 + \sqrt{5}, 3 - \sqrt{5}$ **33.** 72 **34.** 20 **35.** 10
36. -31 **37.** 400 **38.** 51,000 **39.** 60
40. 8,050,000

1. C **3.** A **5.** E **7.** A **9.** B **13.** $\begin{bmatrix} \frac{6}{25} & \frac{7}{25} \\ -\frac{1}{25} & \frac{3}{25} \end{bmatrix}$

CHAPTER 6

1. $12a^8$ **3.** $16x^6y^{10}$ **5.** $4a^3$ **7.** $\frac{1}{2xy^5}$ **9.** $-18m^3n^3$

11. $\frac{r}{8s^5}$ **13.** x^7 **15.** $4p^4q^4$ **17.** $\frac{1}{p^4q^2}$ **19.** $\frac{t^8}{s}$

21. s^7t^4 **23.** 1

ON YOUR OWN **1.** 2 **3.** 5 **5.** -1 **7.** 3 **9.** -5
11. 1 **13a.** $5^3 = 125$ **15.** 2 **17.** 8 **19.** 32 **21.** 25
23. 3 **25.** 125 **27.** x **29.** 10 **31.** 0

33.

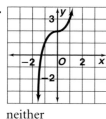

neither

45. $y = \pm\sqrt[4]{\dfrac{x}{2}}$

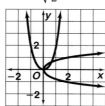

53a. about 64 oz   **b.** $C = 5\sqrt[3]{w}$; the circumference of a cantaloupe having weight w ounces   **c.** about 18.3 in.
55a. $V = 2\pi^2(3r)r^2 = 6\pi^2 r^3$ ✔   **b.** 7.4 in.^{3}, 199.9 in.^{3}, 1598.9 in.^{3} **c.** $R - r > 0$ **57.** 3.16   **59.** 1.78
61. 1.26   **63.** 0.71   **65.** 0.84   **67.** 0.93   **69.** 9   **71.** no solution (6.5 is extraneous.)   **73.** 5   **75.** ± 2 **77.** no solution (16 is extraneous.)   **79.** 2   **81a.** Graph opens upward with y-axis as line of symmetry; even function. Samples: $y = x^2$, $y = 4x^4$ **b.** Graph opens downward; even function. Samples: $y = -x^2$, $y = -4x^4$ **c.** Graph extends into quadrants I and III; odd function. Samples: $y = x$, $y = 4x^5$ **d.** Graph extends into quadrants II and IV; odd function. Samples: $y = -x$, $y = -4x^5$

MIXED REVIEW   **83.** 1.4, -2.4 **85.** Make 12 small pizzas.

Lesson 6-2   pages 261–267

ON YOUR OWN   **1.** $y = 10x + 5$; binomial; 1
3. $n = 2m^2 + 7m - 3$; trinomial; 2   **5.** $q = 2p^2 - p$; binomial; 2   **7.** $f(x) = -2x^3$; monomial; 3
9. $g(x) = -x^4 + 3x^3$; binomial; 4   **11.** D   **13.** A
15. C   **17.** C   **19.** 6   **21.** 2
23. ($\searrow$, $\searrow$); -1.4, 1.4, 3; -6

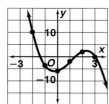

25. A   **27.** ($\nearrow$, $\nearrow$); -6, -1, 1; -6 **29.** ($\nearrow$, $\searrow$); 2; -4
31. ($\nearrow$, $\nearrow$); -3, 0, 4; 0   **33.** ($\searrow$, $\nearrow$); -1, 1; -16
35. ($\nearrow$, $\nearrow$); 2; -8 **37.** ($\nearrow$, $\nearrow$); -0.3, 3.3, 1; 1
39. a. $10\pi r^2$ b. $\frac{2}{3}\pi r^3$ c. $10\pi r^2 + \frac{2}{3}\pi r^3$
43. Odd; the graph is symmetric about the origin.

MIXED REVIEW   **45.** 56   **47.** 6   **49.** 3024
51. $6x^4 - 12x^3$ **53.** $x^2 - x - 6$

CHECKPOINT

CHECKPOINT

1. $y = \pm\sqrt[4]{\dfrac{x}{5}}$

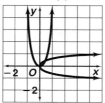

2. $y = \left(\dfrac{x}{2}\right)^3$

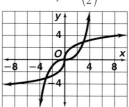

3. $y = \sqrt[3]{x} - 1$

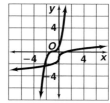

4. $y = \pm\sqrt[4]{\dfrac{x+6}{2}}$

5. $n = 6m^4 + 4m^2 - m$; trinomial; 4
6. $f(t) = 5t^3 + 2t - 9$; trinomial; 3
7. $f(r) = r^2 + 7r + 10$; trinomial; 2   **9.** A

Lesson 6-3   pages 268–273

ON YOUR OWN   **1.** 2 x^3 blocks, 15 x^2 blocks, 31 x blocks, and 12 unit blocks   **3.** $x + 2a$ **5.** -2 (multiplicity 2), 9   **7.** 0, 1 (multiplicity 3)   **9.** 0 (multiplicity 3)

11.

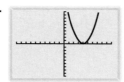

4 (multiplicity 2)
19. $y = x^3 + 12x^2 + 47x + 60$
21. $y = x^3 + 4x^2 + 4x$ **23.** $y = x^3 - x$
27a. $2x^3 + 15x^2 + 31x + 12$; $2x^3 + 7x^2 + 7x + 2$
b. $8x^2 + 24x + 10$ **29.** $x = $ length, $V = x(x-1)(x-2)$;

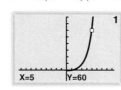

When the volume is 60 m^3, the length is 5 m.

31. $x =$ increase in each dimension, $V = (5 + x)(4 + x)(3 + x)$. The original volume is $60\ \text{ft}^3$, so the new volume must be $120\ \text{ft}^3$.

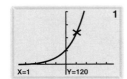
X=1   Y=120

The volume will be doubled when each dimension increases by 1 ft.

33. $y = x^3 - 3x^2 + 2x$
35. $y = x^3 - 4x^2 + 4x$
37. $y = x^3 + x^2 - 2x$
39. $y = x^3 - 9x^2 + 27x - 27$

MIXED REVIEW   41. $\begin{bmatrix} 12 & 24 \\ 36 & 48 \end{bmatrix}$ **45.** Sample: $f(t) = 41 - w$ **47.** $(x + 6)(x - 3)$
49. $x(x + 2)(x - 2)$

Lesson 6-4   pages 274–278

ON YOUR OWN   1. $0, 3, 1$ **3.** $0, 1$ **5.** $0, 2\frac{1}{2}$

7. $0, \frac{3}{2}, -\frac{1}{2}$ **9.** $7, 1$ **11.** $0, -1, -2$ **13.** $0, 4, -1\frac{1}{2}$
15. $0, 1, 6$ **17.** D   **19.** F   **21.** C   **25.** 4.82%
29. $-1, 3$ **31.** $-2, 1, 5$ **33.** $0.8, 1.7$
35. $\frac{1}{2}, 2; (2x - 1)(x - 2)$

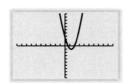

MIXED REVIEW   41a. $n = \dfrac{-4 \pm 3i}{5}$ **b.** $n = \pm 6i$

c. $n = -\dfrac{25}{3}$ **d.** $n = 3\frac{2}{5}, 2\frac{3}{5}$ **43.** $7x^3$

Lesson 6-5   pages 279–284

ON YOUR OWN   1. $x - 8$ **3.** $x^2 + 4x + 3, \text{R } 5$
5. $3x^2 - 7x + 2$ **9.** $x^2 - 2x + 2$ **11.** $x^2 + 2x + 5$
13. $2x^3 + 5x - 15$ **15.** $-2x^2 + 9x - 19, \text{R } 40$
17a. $x^2 - x + 1$ **b.** $x^4 - x^3 + x^2 - x + 1$
c. $x^6 - x^5 + x^4 - x^3 + x^2 - x + 1$ **d.** $(x + 1) \cdot$
$(x^8 - x^7 + x^6 - x^5 + x^4 - x^3 + x^2 - x + 1)$
19. $0, 3$ **21.** $\dfrac{3 \pm \sqrt{13}}{2}$ **23.** $\dfrac{1 \pm i\sqrt{7}}{4}$
25.

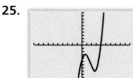
4

31. $P(a) = 0; x - a$ is a factor of $P(x)$.
33. $x - 2$

---

35. 2

39.
$\begin{bmatrix} 0 & 0 & 1 & 0 \\ 1 & 0 & 0 & 0 \\ 1 & 1 & 0 & 1 \\ 0 & 0 & 1 & 0 \end{bmatrix}$

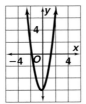

41. 5040   **43.** 120   **45.** 24

CHECKPOINT

1. 2 (multiplicity 2), -1 **2.** $-\frac{1}{2}, 4$ **3.** 3, 0 (multiplicity 3), -1 (multiplicity 2)   **4.** $0, \frac{3}{2}, -1$ **5.** $-2, -1, 1, 2$
6. $0, \frac{1}{2} + i, \frac{1}{2} - i,$ **7.** $x^2 + 2x + 1$ **8.** $2x^2 - 3x + 1$

Lesson 6-6   pages 285–289

ON YOUR OWN   1. permutation   **3.** combination
5. 40,320   **7.** 665,280   **9.** 120   **11.** 56   **13.** 24   **15.** 15
17. 181,440   **19.** 35   **21.** $\frac{5}{18}$ **23a.** 56   **b.** 56   **25a.** 21
b. 35   **c.** 35   **d.** 21   **27.** combination, 4368
29. combination, 21
33. 84   **35.** 5   **37.** 330,791,175   **39.** 5

MIXED REVIEW

41.

45. $x = \frac{3}{2}, -4$ **47.** $x = -\frac{6a}{7}$
49. a little less than 5 wk, a little more than 5 wk
51. $9x^2 + 30xy + 25y^2$

Toolbox   page 290

1. from $A1$ to $B1$ to $B2$ or from $A1$ to $A2$ to $B2$

3.

	A	B	C	D	E	F	G	H	I	J	K
1	1	1	1	1	1	1	1	1	1	1	1
2	1	2	3	4	5	6	7	8	9	10	
3	1	3	6	10	15	21	28	36	45		
4	1	4	10	20	35	56	84	120			
5	1	5	15	35	70	126	210				
6	1	6	21	56	126	252					
7	1	7	28	84	210						
8	1	8	36	120							
9	1	9	45								
10	1	10									
11	1										

Lesson 6-7
pages 291–295

ON YOUR OWN **1.** $13; d^{12}; 12d^{11}e$ **3.** $5; a^4; 4a^3b$

5. $4; a^3; 3a^2b$

7. $a^6 - 6a^5b + 15a^4b^2 - 20a^3b^3 + 15a^2b^4 - 6ab^5 + b^6$

9. $x^3 - 9x^2 + 27x - 27$ **11a.** 6 **b.** 84

13. $n = 7; 7r^6s$ **15.** $s^2 - 2st + t^2$

17. $x^6 - 6x^5 + 15x^4 - 20x^3 + 15x^2 - 6x + 1$

19. $x^4 - 4x^3y + 6x^2y^2 - 4xy^3 + y^4$

21. $x^4 + 2x^2y^2 + y^4$

23. $x^7 + 7x^6y + 21x^5y^2 + 35x^4y^3 + 35x^3y^4 + 21x^2y^5 + 7xy^6 + y^7$

25. $(-1 + \sqrt{3}i)^3 = -1 + 3i\sqrt{3} + 9 - 3i\sqrt{3} = 8$ ✔

27. 41% **31a.** $(s + 0.5)^3$

b. $s^3 + 1.5s^2 + 0.75s + 0.125$

MIXED REVIEW

32. $-0.9, 0.9$ **37.** D

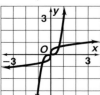

Wrap Up
pages 297–299

1. 10 **2.** 1 **3.** 343 **4.** 9 **5.** 4 **6.** a

7. $y = \pm\sqrt[4]{x}$ **8.** $y = \left(\frac{x}{3}\right)^4$

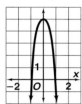 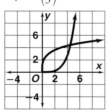

9. $y = \sqrt[3]{\dfrac{x}{3.1}}$ **10.** -66

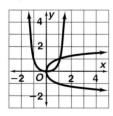

11. 8 (5 is extraneous.) **12.** 9 **13.** Answers may vary. Sample: The origin is the point of symmetry.

14a. 268.08 in.^{3} **b.** $r = \sqrt[3]{\dfrac{3V}{4\pi}}$ **c.** 2.88 in.

15. 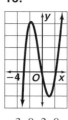 **16.** 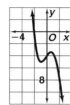 **17.**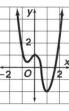

$-2; -4$ $\qquad$ $-3, 0, 2; 0$ $\qquad$ $0.7, 1.9; 1$

18. C **19.** 1, -3 (multiplicity 2) **20.** 0 (multiplicity 3), $-7, 2$ **21.** 5 (multiplicity 2), -1 **22.** $y = x^2 + x - 6$

23. $y = x^3 - 3x^2 - 10x$

24. $y = x^3 - 10x^2 + 32x - 32$ **25.** 0, 4, 1

26. $0, 0.5, -0.5$ **27.** $-1, 3.6, 1.4$ **28.** $-2, 0, 4$

29. $-3, 0, 3$ **30.** $-1.4, 0, 3.4$ **31.** $x^2 - 3x$

32. $x^3 + 2x + 1$ **33.** $2x^3 + 3x^2 - 2$

34. $3x^2 - x + 5$ **35.** 10 **36.** 10 **37.** 9 **38.** 11

39. 70 **40.** 21 **41.** 4368 **42.** $x^3 - 3x^2y + 3xy^2 - y^3$

43. $q^5 + 5q^4 + 10q^3 + 10q^2 + 5q + 1$

44. $4x^2 + 4xy + y^2$

45. $t^3 - 9t^2w + 27tw^2 - 27w^3$

47. 8 **48.** 16 **49.** 2

50. 9 **51.** 1 **52.** $\frac{1}{4}$

Cumulative Review
page 301

1. A **3.** D **5.** D **7.** A **9.** A **11.** B

13a. combination, since order does not matter **b.** 27,405

CHAPTER 7

Lesson 7-1   pages 304–310

ON YOUR OWN

1. growth; 63%   **3.** decay; 35%   **5.** growth; 70%
7. decay; 75%

9a. $y = 26,518,000(1.014)^x$, $y = 16,271,000(1.003)^x$,
     $y = 16,110,000(1.02)^x$, $y = 15,525,000(1.007)^x$

b. 30,473,000; 16,766,000; 19,638,000; 16,647,000; yes

11. about $4833   **17.** 8 years   **19.** $y = 250(1.22)^x$; 676

21. $y = 17,500(0.89)^x$; 9772   **23a.** 56   **b.** 47 years
25. B

MIXED REVIEW   **29.** $-2, 7, 2$

31a.

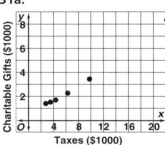

b. yes; strong, positive
c. $y = 0.37x + 153.09$; about $2558   **33.** $33

Toolbox   page 311

1. $y = 6.25(0.5)^x$

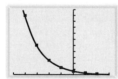

```
WINDOW FORMAT
Xmin=-5
Xmax=3
Xscl=1
Ymin=0
Ymax=110
Yscl=10
```

5. The coffee has reached room temperature and will not get any cooler.

Lesson 7-2   pages 312–317

ON YOUR OWN

1.

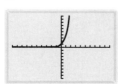

17. $y = 5(0.6)^x$ **19.** $y = \frac{1}{2}(2)^x$
21. 20.0855   **23.** 3289.8995
25. 0.0067   **27.** 0.5518
29. 15.1543   **31.** $\approx$ $42,140
33. 0   **35.** 8.66 yr
37a. $y = 5.63 \cdot (1.02)^x$ **b.** It doubles.   **c.** It increases by less than half.   **39a.** 5.64%
b. 0.0028%

MIXED REVIEW   **41.** 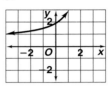   **43.** ($\diagdown$, $\diagdown$)
45.

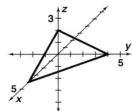

$(4, 0, 0)$; $(0, 4, 0)$; $(0, 0, 2)$

CHECKPOINT   **1.** growth; 45%   **2.** decay; 1%
3. growth; 70%   **4.** decay; 20%

5.

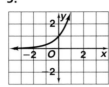

6.

7.

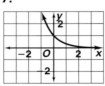

8.

10. $y = 100(0.5)^x$; 9.92 mg

Lesson 7-3   pages 318–323

ON YOUR OWN   **1.** $\log_3 9 = 2$ **3.** $\log_8 64 = 2$

5. $\log_6 1296 = 4$ **7.** $\log_{\frac{1}{2}} 4 = -2$ **9.** $\log_{\frac{1}{3}} \left(\frac{1}{27}\right) = 3$

11. $\log_6 6\sqrt{6} = \frac{3}{2}$ **17.** $3^8 = 6561$ **19.** $7^5 = 16,807$

21. $2^3 = 8$ **23.** $10^{-4} = 0.0001$ **25.** $2^{-3} = \frac{1}{8}$

27. $3^{-5} = \frac{1}{243}$ **29.** 2   **31.** 2   **33.** 2   **35.** 5   **37.** $\frac{1}{2}$

39. $-\frac{1}{2}$ **41a.** 3   **b.** $\frac{1}{32}$ **43.** 7.7

45.

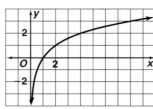

49. 100, 70, 60, 20, 10

MIXED REVIEW   **55.** 5   **57.** $\frac{2}{3}$

1a. III   **b.** II   **c.** I
3.

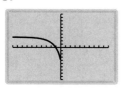

Lesson 7-4   pages 325–329

ON YOUR OWN   **1.** product   **3.** quotient
5. quotient, power   **7.** power, quotient   **9.** quotient
11. 15%   **13.** $\log_2 3$ **15.** $\log 972$ **17.** $\log (ab^3)$

19. $\log_7 \dfrac{\sqrt{xy}}{z^3}$ **21.** $\log \dfrac{r^7 t}{s}$ **23.** $\log_6 \sqrt[4]{5x}$

25. $3 \log x + 5 \log y$ **27.** $2 \log a + 3 \log b - 4 \log c$
29. $\log_4 5 + \frac{1}{2} \log_4 x$ **31.** $3 \log 2 + 3 \log(x + 1)$

33. $5 + 5 \log_4 m + 5 \log_4 n$ **35.** $\frac{1}{2}(\log 2 + \log x - \log y)$
37. 102.2 decibels   **39.** -2 **41.** 2   **43.** 2   **45.** 1
47. 1.301   **49.** 1.204   **51.** 0.097   **53.** 2.097
55. -1.556 **57.** 1.556   **61.** false   **63.** false
65. false   **67.** false   **69.** A

MIXED REVIEW   **71.** $y = \dfrac{x - 7}{5}$ **73.** $y = \pm\sqrt{5 - x}$
75. 2   **77.** 3   **79.** 0.04

Lesson 7-5   pages 330–336

ON YOUR OWN   **1.** 2   **3.** 50   **5.** 3   **7.** 125   **9.** It
increases by a factor of $2\sqrt{2}$.   **11.** 125   **13.** 5792.6
15. 4.33   **17.** 0.222   **19.** 0.03 kg   **21.** 4913
23. 47.17   **25.** 3   **27.** 2.846   **29.** 0.358   **31.** 0.272
33. 1.207 mm   **35a.** cello, viola, violin, harp, guitar,
bassoon   **b.** bass, cello, harp, guitar, bassoon   **c.** violin,
harp   **d.** violin, harp   **37.** 0.316   **39.** 300,000,000
41. 1357.209   **43.** 3.874   **45.** 0.0792   **47a.** 18.966
b. 18.966   **49.** 5 yr   **51.** 1.287   **53.** 14.489
55. 0.210   **57.** 0.823   **59.** 4.524   **61.** 0.463

MIXED REVIEW   **63.** 120   **65.** 35   **67.** 126
69. ≈ 148.4 **71.** ≈ 0.135 **73.** ≈ 3.695

CHECKPOINT

1. 4   **2.** 2   **3.** $\frac{1}{2}$ **4.** -3
5. $2 \log_2 x + 5 \log_2 y$ **6.** $3 \log s - \log 5$
7. $2(\log_5 3 + \log_5 x + \log_5 y)$ **8.** $\log_6 4 + \frac{1}{2} \log_6 x$

9. 512   **10.** 20   **11.** 3   **12.** 1000   **13.** $\dfrac{\log_3 10}{\log_3 2}$ **14.** D

Lesson 7-6   pages 337–341

ON YOUR OWN   **1.** 1.105   **3.** 439,600,000   **5.** 2.401
7. 5.493   **9.** 1.242   **11.** 2   **13.** 100   **17.** 294 days
19. 1.157   **21.** 3.393   **23.** 4.59   **25a.** 43.11 min

b. $t = -24.39 \ln \dfrac{T(t) - 72}{164}$

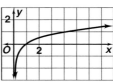 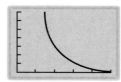

c. 1.69, 6.04, 11.34, 18.13, 27.55, 43.11, 97.59

MIXED REVIEW

27. ≈ 15 in.

29.

	A	B	C	D
A	0	0	1	1
B	1	0	0	1
C	1	1	0	0
D	0	0	0	0

31.

	M	N	O	P
M	0	1	1	0
N	1	0	1	0
O	1	1	0	1
P	0	0	1	0

Wrap Up   pages 343–345

1. growth; 45%   **2.** decay; 88%   **3.** growth; 280%
4. decay; 60%   **5.** $150{,}000(1.01)^x$; 157,651.51
6. $12{,}500(0.91)^x$; 7800.40   **7.** $50(1.03)^x$; 57.96
8. $y = 3^x$ **9.** $y = \frac{1}{8}(8)^x$ **10.** $y = 4(2)^x$

11. $\log_6 36 = 2$ **12.** $\log_2 \frac{1}{8} = -3$ **13.** $\log_3 27 = 3$
14. $\log_{10} 0.001 = -3$ **15.** $2^6 = 64$ **16.** $3^{-2} = \frac{1}{9}$
17. $10^{-5} = 0.00001$ **18.** $2^0 = 1$
19.   **20.**

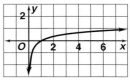

21.   **22.**

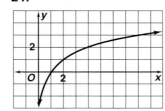 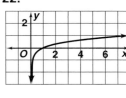

23. 15   **24.** D   **25.** $\log 24$ **26.** $\log_2 \frac{5}{3}$ **27.** $\log_3 7x^4$
28. $\log \frac{z}{y}$ **29.** $2 \log_4 x + 3 \log_4 y$

30. $\log 4 + 4 \log s + \log t$ **31.** $\log_3 2 + \frac{1}{2} \log_3 x$

32. $2 \log x - \log 9$ **34.** No; they have different bases.

35. 81   **36.** 1.5   **37.** 2.173   **38.** 1   **39.** 3.33   **40.** 8

41. 14.142   **42.** 7.63×10^{12} **44.** 9.5 mi   **45.** 0.828

46. 2.264   **47.** 4.307   **48.** 1.816×10^{-4} **49.** 3.773

50. 6.031   **52.** 3   **53.** $\frac{1}{2}$ **54.** 0.56   **55.** -2

56. $(x + 2)(x + 1)$ **57.** $(x - 3)(x - 2)$

58. $x(x^2 - 2x - 1)$ **59.** $(x - 3)(x + 3)$ **60.** $\frac{5}{4}$

61. $\frac{1}{15}$ **62.** $\frac{2}{3}$ **63.** 4

Preparing for Standardized Tests   page 347

1. A   **3.** A   **5.** A   **7.** D   **9.** A

CHAPTER 8

Lesson 8-1   pages 350–355

ON YOUR OWN

1.

x	y
6	1
5	1.2
3	2
1.5	4
2.4	2.5

3.

x	y
2	16
5	6.4
4	8
32	1
0.2	160

5. 18   **7.** 3.6   **9.** 2.1
11. $tn = 36$ **13.** inverse variation; $xy = 42$
15. direct variation; $y = 2x$
17. D   **19.** $xy = 1300$
21. $xy = 56$ **23.** $xy = 84$

25. $xy = 12.6$ **27.** $xy = 250$ **31.** 7200 rpm

33. 2.625   **35.** 8

MIXED REVIEW   **37.** 14   **39.** 8   **41.** $-0.5, -0.67, -1,$ -2, undefined, 2, 1, 0.67, 0.5   **43.** $-0.33, -0.4, -0.5,$ $-0.67, -1, -2$, undefined, 2, 1

Toolbox   page 356

1. 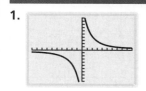   **3.**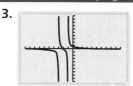

13a.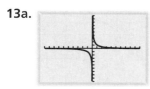

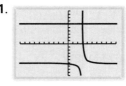

Lesson 8-2   pages 357–362

ON YOUR OWN   **1.** $x = 0; y = 0$ **3.** $x = -3; y = -4$

5. 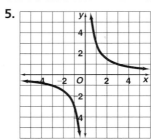   **7.**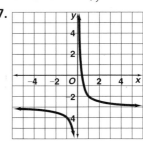

13a.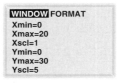

b. Vinson Massif: 12.58 in. of Hg; Mt. Kilimanjaro: 11.59 in. of Hg; Sahara Desert: 26.74 in. of Hg; Kalahari Desert: 29.32 in. of Hg

15. $y = \frac{4}{x + 3} - 1$ **17.** $y = \frac{4}{x - 1} - 1$

19. [graph] $(3, 6)$ **21.** [graph] $(3.08, 6.2)$

23. $(3.8, 4.2)$ **25.** up 2.5 units
27. left 4 units, down 3 units
29. $y = -\frac{5}{x + 2} + 3$ **33.** D

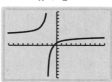

MIXED REVIEW   **35.** $y = 2(x - 0.25)^2 + 6.875$
37. $y = -(x + 2.5)^2 + 6.25$ **39.** $x = 0$ **41.** $x = 5$

Lesson 8-3   pages 363–369

ON YOUR OWN   **1.** discontinuous; -2
3. continuous   **5.** discontinuous; $-\frac{3}{2}, 1$
7. discontinuous; 2   **9.** discontinuous; 0, 2
11. discontinuous; 2   **13a.** $P(n) = 4n^2$ **b.** $B(n) = 4n + 1$
c. $y = \frac{4n^2}{4n + 1}; \frac{64}{17}$ **15.** $x = -3; x = 3$ **17.** none
21. $x = -3$ **23.** $x = 2$ **25.** $x = \sqrt{2}, x = -\sqrt{2}$

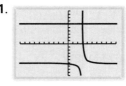

27. 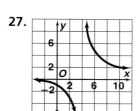　**29.**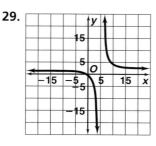

35a. $f(x) = \dfrac{20{,}000x + 200{,}000}{x + 1}$

b.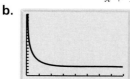

```
WINDOW FORMAT
Xmin=0
Xmax=40
Xscl=4
Ymin=0
Ymax=200000
Yscl=10000
```

MIXED REVIEW　37. growth; 2　**39.** decay; $\frac{1}{2}$　**41.** $\frac{2}{7}$
43. $\frac{9}{40}$

CHECKPOINT

1. $xy = 12$　**2.** $xy = 8$　**3.** $xy = 20$　**4.** $xy = 4$
5. $xy = 7$　**6.** $xy = \frac{3}{32}$

7. 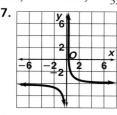　**8.**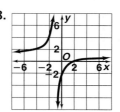

9. 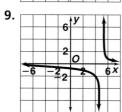　**10.**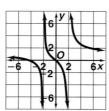

12. D

Lesson 8-4　　　　　　　　pages 370–374

ON YOUR OWN　1. $\dfrac{1}{2x - 1}$　**3.** $b + 1$　**5.** $\dfrac{x}{2x - 1}$
7. $\dfrac{y + 7}{y - 7}$　**9.** $\dfrac{x - 8}{x - 10}$　**11.** $(t - 3)(t + 3)$

13a. $\dfrac{\pi t^2 + \frac{1}{2}(4\pi t^2)}{\frac{1}{2}\left(\frac{4}{3}\pi t^3\right)} = \dfrac{4.5}{t}$　**b.** $\dfrac{2\pi t^2 + 2\pi t(2t)}{\pi t^2(2t)} = \dfrac{3}{t}$

c. cylinder　**17a.** 3 m/s; 6 m/s; 2 s　**b.** $\dfrac{6 - 3}{2} = 1.5$ m/s^2

c. 2.68 m/s^2　**19a.** $\dfrac{1}{8\left(\frac{1}{x}\right)} = \dfrac{x}{8}$　**b.** $\dfrac{1}{8\left(\frac{1}{x + 1}\right)} = \dfrac{x + 1}{8}$

21. 2　**23.** $\dfrac{18x}{(x + 9)(x + 3)}$　**25.** $\dfrac{x + 1}{x - 1}$　**27.** $-\frac{3}{4}a^2b^2$
29. $\dfrac{15}{4n^2}$

MIXED REVIEW　31. 9　**33.** $\frac{3}{7}$　**35.** $\frac{17}{12}$　**37.** $\frac{9}{8}$　**39.** $-\frac{1}{9}$

Toolbox　　　　　　　　　　　page 375

1. $\dfrac{6 - 2\sqrt{2}}{7}$　**3.** $\dfrac{3 - i}{10}$　**5.** $\dfrac{\sqrt{2} + i\sqrt{2}}{2}$　**7.** $\dfrac{3 - i}{2}$
9. $\dfrac{4i - 2}{5}$　**13.** 2.825; 2.825

Lesson 8-5　　　　　　　　pages 376–380

ON YOUR OWN　1. $\frac{1}{x}$　**3.** $\dfrac{2c + 2}{c^2}$　**5.** 1

7. $(2x - 3)(x + 1)(x + 2)$　**9.** $(x + 1)(x - 1)$
11. $10(x - 2)(x + 3)^2$　**13.** $5(y - 4)(y + 4)$
15. $15t^2$　**17.** $3h^3$　**19.** $(y + 2)(y - 1)$
21. $(k + 2)(k - 2)$　**23.** $\dfrac{3x - 8}{4x^2}$　**25.** $\dfrac{2x^3 - x^2 + 1}{x^2(x^2 - 1)}$
27. $\dfrac{x^2 + 9x - 1}{(x - 1)(2x + 1)}$　**29.** $\dfrac{4x - 1}{(2x - 1)2x}$
33a. $\dfrac{R_1R_2R_3}{R_2R_3 + R_1R_3 + R_1R_2}$　**b.** 0.88 ohms　**35.** D

MIXED REVIEW　37. $\begin{bmatrix} -20 & -6 \\ -33 & 3 \end{bmatrix}$　**39a.** $f(n) = 12^n$
b. 2　**41.** $7\frac{1}{2}$　**43.** 14

Lesson 8-6　　　　　　　　pages 381–387

ON YOUR OWN　1. 5　**3.** $\frac{8}{5}$　**5.** $-5, 2$　**7.** no real
solution　**9.** $4, -\frac{5}{2}$　**11.** 3　**13a.** $L = \dfrac{24(R - r)}{T}$
b. 32 in.; 28.2 in.; 25.3 in.　**15.** $\dfrac{1 \pm \sqrt{241}}{10}$　**17.** $-2, -3$
19. no solution　**21.** 30　**23.** $\frac{38}{21}$　**25.** -4
27. $E = \dfrac{mV^2}{2}$　**29.** $F = ma$　**31.** $T = \pm 2\pi\sqrt{\dfrac{\ell}{g}}$
35. 2.4 days　**37a.** $c(x) = \dfrac{60 + 5.5x}{x}$
b. 14 students　**39a.** \$937.50　**b.** $\dfrac{22{,}500}{24 + x}$
c. $937.50 - \dfrac{22{,}500}{24 + x}$　**d.** 30 mi/gal

MIXED REVIEW　43. $y = 3 \pm \sqrt{\dfrac{x}{5}}$
45. $y = \log_5(x - 2)$　**47.** $\frac{1}{6}$　**49.** $\frac{1}{2}$

Selected Answers

CHECKPOINT

1. $\frac{3x}{x+3}$ **2.** $2x+5$ **3.** $\frac{-(2x+5)}{(x+2)(x+1)}$ **4.** $2x(3x+1)$

5. $x = -1, \frac{3}{4}$ **6.** $x = -4$ **7.** $x = 32$ **8.** $x = 2.5$

Lesson 8-7   pages 388–393

ON YOUR OWN   1. independent   **3.** dependent

5. $\frac{1}{6}$ **7.** $\frac{6}{7}$ **9.** 0.14 **11.** 0.96 **15.** yes; $\frac{1}{6}; \frac{1}{2}; \frac{2}{3}$ **17.** $\frac{3}{4}$

19. $\frac{2}{5}$ **21a.** $\frac{1}{4}$ **b.** $\frac{1}{64}$ **23.** $\frac{9}{25}$ **25.** 0.05 **27.** 0.114

MIXED REVIEW

29. $\begin{bmatrix} 0.077 & 0.231 & -0.077 \\ 0.077 & 0.231 & 0.923 \\ -0.154 & 0.538 & 0.154 \end{bmatrix}$ **31.** $\begin{bmatrix} -0.05 & 0.42 \\ 0.16 & -0.26 \end{bmatrix}$

Wrap Up   pages 395–397

1. 4 **2.** $\frac{7}{2}$ **3.** 54 **4.** 24 **5.** 0.8 **6a.** $c \cdot v = 200, c =$ cost per visit and $v =$ number of visits **b.** 21 times in

one year **7.** $y = \frac{4}{x} + 3$ **8.** $y = \frac{4}{x+1}$

9. $y = \frac{4}{x-2} + 2$ **10.** $y = \frac{4}{x+3} - 4$

11.
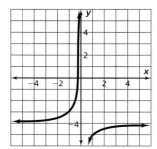

12.
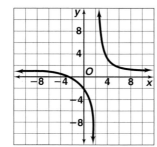

13.
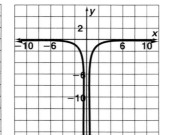

14.

15. discontinuous; -7 **16.** discontinuous; $-2; 1$

17. discontinuous; $0; 1$

18.
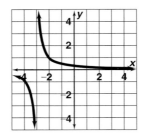

19.
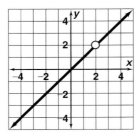

20.
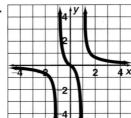

21. C **22.** $\frac{x+5}{x+3}$

23. $\frac{(x-1)(x+1)}{x+3}$

24. $\frac{(2x-1)(x+1)}{(x+4)}$

26. $\frac{2x+9}{3x^2}$

27. $\frac{-x^2 - 9x + 11}{(x+2)(x-3)}$

28. $\frac{3(3x-4)}{(x-2)(x+2)}$ **29.** $\frac{-x+4}{(x+1)(x-1)(x+2)}$

30. $\frac{5x-6}{3(x-2)(x-3)}$ **31.** $\frac{1}{2x+4}$

32. -1 **33.** no solution **34.** $-12, 9$ **35.** $3, -2$

36. $\frac{1}{3}$ **37.** $\frac{2}{3}$ **38.** $\frac{5}{6}$ **39.** $\frac{1}{18}$ **40.** $\frac{1}{6}$ **41.** $\frac{1}{18}$

43. 18.44 cm **44.** 13.23 in. **45.** 9.95 ft **46.** 15.81 m

Cumulative Review   page 399

1. A **3.** C **5.** A **7.** D **9.** E **11.** C

13. ≈ 1.77 **15.** $\begin{bmatrix} 0.075 & 0.05 \\ -0.275 & 0.15 \end{bmatrix}$

CHAPTER 9

Lesson 9-1   pages 402–408

ON YOUR OWN   1. 4; 1 **3.** 5; 3 **5.** 8; 4.5 **7.** C

11a. 67 **b.** 70 **c.** 70 **d.** 67 **13.** No; the population has been increasing for the past 50 yr.

15. 60 beats per minute

17a.

b. 5 s; 1 ft
c. about 2 s
19. 5; 0; 8

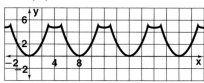

21. 1 year   **23.** 3 months   **25.** 1 day   **27a.** C meets 3 times; the others meet 2 times each.

MIXED REVIEW

29.

31.

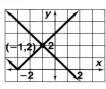

(−1, 2)

33.

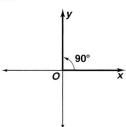

90°

35.

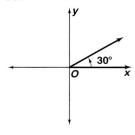

30°

Lesson 9-2   pages 409–414

ON YOUR OWN

1.

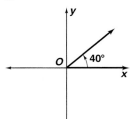

40°

3.

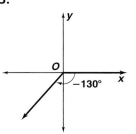

−130°

11. $\left(\frac{1}{2}, \frac{\sqrt{3}}{2}\right)$ **13.** $\left(\frac{\sqrt{3}}{2}, -\frac{1}{2}\right)$

15.

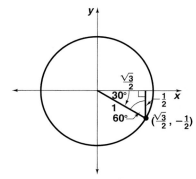

$\left(\frac{\sqrt{3}}{2}, -\frac{1}{2}\right)$

$$\cos(-30°) = \frac{\sqrt{3}}{2}, \sin(-30°) = -\frac{1}{2}$$

21. 140°   **23.** 55°   **25.** 1°   **27.** 405°; −315°
29. 45°; −315°

31.

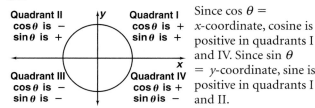

Quadrant II	Quadrant I
cos θ is −	cos θ is +
sin θ is +	sin θ is +
Quadrant III	Quadrant IV
cos θ is −	cos θ is +
sin θ is −	sin θ is −

Since cos θ = x-coordinate, cosine is positive in quadrants I and IV. Since sin θ = y-coordinate, sine is positive in quadrants I and II.

33a. 0.766; 0.766; 0.766   **b.** The angles are coterminal.
37. (0.98, 0.17)   **39.** (0.87, 0.5)   **41.** (0.64, 0.77)
43. (0.34, 0.94)   **45.** (0, 1)
47. (0.17, 0.98)

MIXED REVIEW   **49.** −2

51a.

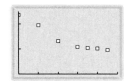

WINDOW FORMAT
Xmin=0
Xmax=50
Xscl=10
Ymin=0
Ymax=25000
Yscl=10000

b. quadratic   **c.** $y = 7.6x^2 - 667.65x + 24301$
d. 9,900,000   **53.** 439.8 m   **55.** 21.4 ft

ON YOUR OWN

1.

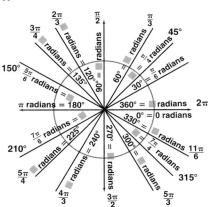

3. $\frac{5}{6}\pi$ radians; 2.62 radians   **5.** $-\frac{1}{2}\pi$ radians; -1.57
radians   **7.** $\frac{1}{9}\pi$ radians; 0.35 radians   **9.** 198°

11. $-172°$ **13.** 270°   **17a.** ≈ 0.5017962;
≈ 0.4999646; the first four terms

b. $1 - \frac{x^2}{2!} + \frac{x^4}{4!} - \frac{x^6}{6!} + \frac{x^8}{8!} - \cdots$

c. ≈ 0.951; 18   **19.** 32 ft

21.   **23.**

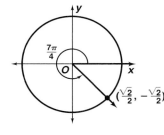
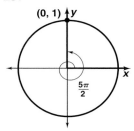

27. $-0.81; 0.59$ **29.** $0.81; -0.59$

31a–b.

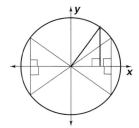

c. yes   **33a.** 15°; $\frac{\pi}{12}$ radians
b. about 1037 mi
c. about 414 mi
35. ≈ 42.2 in.
MIXED REVIEW   **37.** 0.9
39. $x + 3y = 11$ or
$y = -\frac{1}{3}x + \frac{11}{3}$
41. all real numbers
43. $-1 \le y \le 1$

CHECKPOINT   **1.** 10; 4.1   **2.** 4; 2   **3.** 2.5; 1   **4.** $\frac{\pi}{6}$

5. $-\pi$ **6.** $\frac{\pi}{5}$ **7.** 60°   **8.** $-135°$ **9.** 22.5°   **10.** 1; 0

11. $-\frac{\sqrt{2}}{2}; \frac{\sqrt{2}}{2}$ **12.** $-\frac{1}{2}; -\frac{\sqrt{3}}{2}$ **13.** $0; -1$

14. $\frac{\sqrt{2}}{2}, \frac{-\sqrt{2}}{2}$ **15.** $-\frac{\sqrt{3}}{2}; -\frac{1}{2}$ **17.** D

1. 2π radians; 360°; 0   **3.** $\frac{2}{3}\pi$ radians; 120°; -1

ON YOUR OWN   **1.** $3; 2; \frac{2\pi}{3}$ **3.** $2; 3; \pi$ **5.** $5; 1; \frac{2\pi}{5}$
7. $1; 3; 2\pi$ **9.** $2\pi; 5; 1$ **11.** $y = 2\sin\theta$
13. $y = 2.5\sin 2\theta$ **15.** $y = -\sin 2x$

17. $y = \sin 3\theta$ **19.** $y = 4\sin\frac{1}{2}\theta$

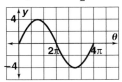

23. 0.64, 2.50   **25.** 0.5, 2.5, 4.5   **27.** 0.68, 5.60
29a. A: 4, 2π; B: 4, 2π; C: 4, 2π **b.** $y = 4\sin\theta$

31.   **33.**

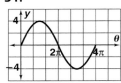

39a.

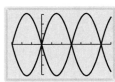

They reflect each other over the
θ-axis and over the
y-axis.

b.

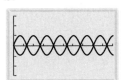

They reflect each other over both
axes.
41. $y = \sin 60\pi\theta$
43. $y = \sin 240{,}000\pi\theta$

MIXED REVIEW

47. $\frac{x^2 + x}{2x - 2}$ **49.** e^{4x+4} **51.** 1   **53.** -1

ON YOUR OWN   **1.** 2π; 3   **3.** 4π; 2   **5.** 6π; 3

7. 2; 0.7   **9.** $\frac{\pi}{5}$; $\pm\frac{\pi}{10}$ **11.** $\frac{\pi}{4}$; $\pm\frac{\pi}{8}$

13. 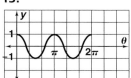   **15.**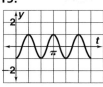

21a. 4 s; 6 ft   **b.** $y = -6\cos\frac{\pi}{2}t$

c. 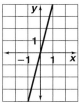   **d.** $-6\cos\frac{\pi}{2}t = 3$

23. 1.98, 4.30   **25.** 0.55, 1.45, 2.55, 3.45, 4.55, 5.45   **27.** 2.03, 5.18

29. 0   **31.** $y = \tan\frac{x}{2}$

33. $y = 5\cos\frac{2}{3}\theta$ **35.** $y = \pi\cos\pi\theta$

37a. 5.5 ft; 1.5 ft   **b.** 12 h 22 min   **c.** $y = 1.5\cos\frac{2\pi t}{742}$

d. 12:17 A.M.–7:49 A.M., 12:39 P.M.–8:11 P.M.   **39.** For any value of $a \neq 0$; the pattern is asymptote, $-a$, 0, a, asymptote.

MIXED REVIEW

41. 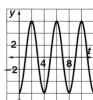   **43.**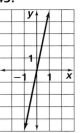

direct

45. $\frac{10}{13}$ **47.** $\frac{9}{14}$ direct

ON YOUR OWN   **1.** 0.6   **3.** 0.6   **5.** 36.9°   **7.** 9

9. 45°   **11.** 48.6°   **13.** 19.6°   **15.** 74.3°

17. 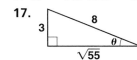 $\cos\theta = \frac{\sqrt{55}}{8}$; $\tan\theta = \frac{3\sqrt{55}}{55}$

19. 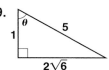 $\sin\theta = \frac{2\sqrt{6}}{5}$ $\tan\theta = 2\sqrt{6}$

21. 8472 ft

23. $c = 12.2$, $m\angle A = 35°$, $m\angle B = 55.1°$, $m\angle C = 90°$

25. $a = 15$, $m\angle A = 61.9°$, $m\angle B = 28.1°$, $m\angle C = 90°$

27. $a = 19.8$, $b = 2.9$, $m\angle A = 81.7°$, $m\angle C = 90°$

31a. 72°   **b.** 19 cm   **c.** 54°; 11.7 cm

MIXED REVIEW

33.   **35.**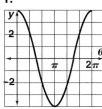

37. 0.83   **39.** −0.42

CHECKPOINT

1. 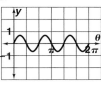   **2.**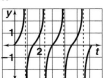

3. 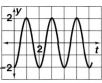   **4.**

5. $y = \frac{3}{2}\sin\theta$ **6.** $y = 0.8\sin 8\theta$ **7.** $y = \sin\pi\theta$

8. $\frac{12}{13}$; $\frac{5}{13}$; 67.4°

ON YOUR OWN   **1.** 47.3°   **3.** 27.0°   **5.** 7.4

7. 9.2   **9.** $b^2 = a^2 + c^2 - 2ac\cos B$

11. $\frac{\sin A}{a} = \frac{\sin B}{b}$ **13.** 42.6 ft   **15.** 7.5 mi from first tower; 7.9 mi from second tower.   **17.** $AC = 34.7$; $m\angle A = 26.7°$; $m\angle C = 33.3°$ **19.** $m\angle A = 50.1°$; $m\angle B = 56.3°$; $m\angle C = 73.6°$ **21.** $m\angle B = 85°$; $AB = 8.7$; $AC = 11.3$ **23.** $m\angle C = 40°$; $AC = 10$; $AB = 6.8$ **25a.** 45.4 mi   **b.** 14.4°; 4.4° west of north

27. no   **29.** yes

MIXED REVIEW

31.

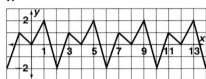

$y = x^2 - 4; 2, -2; -4$
33. 15 tomatoes and 10 squash

Toolbox   **Page 449**

1. $70°, 48°$ or $110°, 8°$ **3.** $87°, 45°$ or $93°, 39°$ **5.** $44.0°,$
$112.4°$ or $136.0°, 20.4°$

Wrap Up   **Pages 451–453**

1.

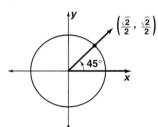

2. 4; 2   **3.** 1, 5, 9

4.

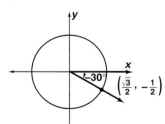

5.

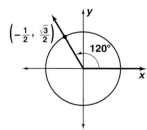

6.

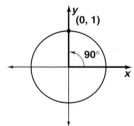

7.

8.

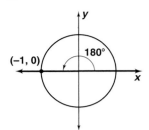

9.

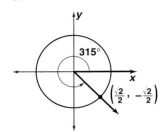

10. $\frac{\pi}{3}$ **11.** $-\frac{\pi}{4}$ **12.** π **13.** -1.5π **14.** 2.5π
15. -4π **16.** $360°$ **17.** $150°$ **18.** $-135°$
19. $432°$ **20.** $-600°$ **21.** $-540°$ **22.** D

23.

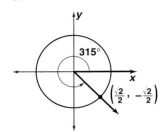

24.

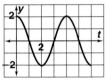

25.

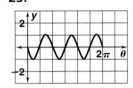

26.

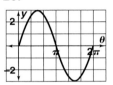

27. $2.35, 3.94$ **28.** 2.50 **29.** $0.24, 2.76, 6.24$
30. $0.97, 1.39, 2.54, 2.96, 4.11, 4.53, 5.68, 6.10$
31. $y = 4\sin 4\theta$ **32.** $c = 5; m\angle A = 53.1°; m\angle B = 36.9°; m\angle C = 90°$ **33.** $a = 6.7; b = 9.9; m\angle B = 56°; m\angle C = 90°$ **34.** $a = 7.3; c = 16.7; m\angle A = 26°; m\angle C = 90°$ **36.** $a = 9.54; m\angle B = 65.21°; m\angle C = 54.79°$ **37.** $b = 1.28; c = 2.56; m\angle A = 97°$

39.

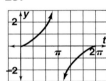

40.

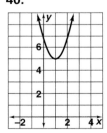

41.

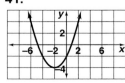

42. $(-2, -5)$ **43.** $(2.4, 6.6)$
44. $(2.4, -0.4)$

1. C   **3.** C   **5.** C   **7.** E   **9.** A   **11.** 42 in.

CHAPTER 10

Lesson 10-1   page 458–463

ON YOUR OWN   1. center: $(0, 0)$; x-intercepts: $-3, 3$;
y-intercepts: $-2, 2$; domain: -3 to 3; range: -2 to 2
3. center: $(0, 0)$; x-intercepts: $-3, 3$; y-intercepts: $-5, 5$;
domain: -3 to 3; range: -5 to 5 **5.** center: $(0, 0)$;
x-intercepts: $-3, 3$; y-intercepts: none; domain: $-\infty$ to -3
and 3 to ∞; range: all real y

7.

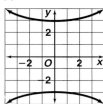

hyperbola; center $(0, 0)$; x- and
y-axes

domain: all real numbers; range:
$-\infty$ to -3 and 3 to ∞

9.

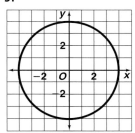

circle; center $(0, 0)$; x- and
y-axes and all lines through
the origin
domain: -4 to 4; range: -4 to
4

11. ellipse; center $(0, 0)$; x- and y-axes
domain: -5 to 5; range: -2 to 2

13. hyperbola; center $(0, 0)$; x- and y-axes
domain: all real x; range: $-\infty$ to $-\sqrt{3}$ and $\sqrt{3}$ to ∞

15. hyperbola; center $(0, 0)$; x- and y-axes
domain: $-\infty$ to -2 and 2 to ∞; range: all real y

17.   **19.**

$x^2 + y^2 = \frac{1}{4}$ $x^2 + y^2 = 1.5625$

23a. All of the axes pass through the center.   **31.** The
curve is a hyperbola. The sharpened portion represents a
cone; each painted side represents a plane. Each plane
intersects the cone in a hyperbola.

MIXED REVIEW   33. 2, 1   **35.** 64
37.   **39.**

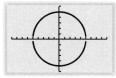   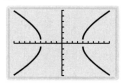

Toolbox   page 464

1.   **3.**

5.   **7.**

9a.   **b.** ±4.5   **c.** ±4.5   **e.** circle

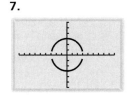

11. Graph the functions $Y1 = x + 3$ and $Y2 = -x + 3$
for $x \geq 0$.

Lesson 10-2   pages 465–470

ON YOUR OWN   1. up   **3.** down   **5.** The light
produced by the bulb will reflect off the parabolic mirror
and will be emitted in parallel rays.   **7.** $x = -\frac{1}{8}y^2$
9. $x = y^2$

11. focus: $(6, 0)$; directrix: $x = -6$

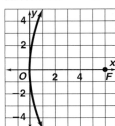

13. focus: $(-2, 0)$; directrix: $x = 2$

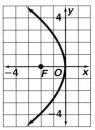

19. $y = -\dfrac{1}{16}x^2$

21. $y = -\dfrac{1}{20}x^2$

23.

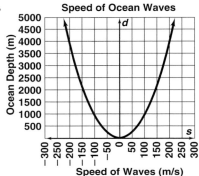

Speed of Ocean Waves

25.

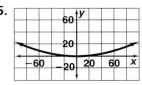

MIXED REVIEW **27.** 2 **29.** 0 **31.** \$757.49
33. $(3, 3), (-7, 3), (-2, 8)$ **35.** $(6, -5), (-14, -5), (-4, 5)$

Lesson 10-3　　pages 471–476

ON YOUR OWN

1. $(x + 3)^2 + (y - 4)^2 = 9$
3. $(x + 4)^2 + (y + 4)^2 = 25$
5. $(x + 4)^2 + (y + 6)^2 = 49$

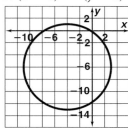

7. $(x + 6)^2 + (y - 10)^2 = 1$

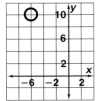

13. $(x - 24)^2 + (y - 22)^2 = 100$ **15.** E **17.** $(-3, 5)$; $\sqrt{38}$ **19.** $(0, 4)$; $\sqrt{11}$ **21.** $(6, 0)$; 8 **23.** $(-3, 9)$; 7

25.

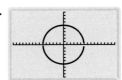

27.

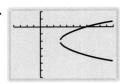

circle; $x^2 + y^2 = 36$　　　parabola; $x - (y + 2)^2 = 3$

29a. The radius would be zero so it cannot be a circle.
b. a point

31b. Earth: $x^2 + y^2 = 15,705,369$
Mars: $x^2 + y^2 = 4,456,321$
Mercury: $x^2 + y^2 = 2,296,740.25$
Pluto: $x^2 + y^2 = 511,225$
33. $(x - 4)^2 + (y - 2)^2 = 121$
35. $(x - 5)^2 + (y + 3)^2 = 25$
37. $(x + 1)^2 + (y + 7)^2 = 36$

MIXED REVIEW

39.

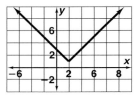

41.

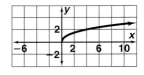

43. 20 **45.** 14

CHECKPOINT

1. focus: $\left(0, \dfrac{1}{12}\right)$; directrix: $y = -\dfrac{1}{12}$

2. focus: $\left(\dfrac{1}{2}, 0\right)$; directrix: $x = -\dfrac{1}{2}$

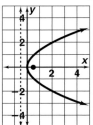

3. focus: $\left(\frac{1}{12}, 0\right)$;
directrix: $x = -\frac{1}{12}$

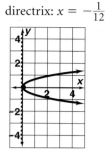

4. focus: $\left(0, -\frac{3}{2}\right)$;
directrix: $y = \frac{3}{2}$

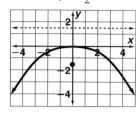

5. $x^2 + y^2 = 25$ **6.** $(x - 1)^2 + (y - 3)^2 = 4$
7. $(x + 6)^2 + (y + 3)^2 = 64$
8. $(x - 2)^2 + (y + 5)^2 = 49$ **10.** circle; ellipse

Toolbox   page 477

1.   **3.**

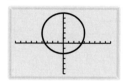

5.

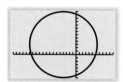

Lesson 10-4   pages 478–483

ON YOUR OWN **1.** $\frac{x^2}{64} + \frac{y^2}{256} = 1$ **3.** $\frac{x^2}{12.25} + \frac{y^2}{25} = 1$
5. $x^2 + \frac{y^2}{16} = 1$ **7.** $\frac{x^2}{900} + \frac{y^2}{400} = 1$ **9.** $\frac{x^2}{729} + \frac{y^2}{2916} = 1$
11. $(\pm 28.98, 0)$
13. $(\pm 8, 0)$ **15.** $(\pm 4\sqrt{2}, 0)$

   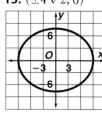

23. $\frac{x^2}{100} + \frac{y^2}{64} = 1$ **25.** $\frac{x^2}{89} + \frac{y^2}{64} = 1$
27. $\frac{x^2}{245} + \frac{y^2}{49} = 1$ **29.** $\frac{x^2}{4} + y^2 = 1$
31. $\frac{x^2}{16} + y^2 = 1$ **33.** $x^2 + \frac{y^2}{9} = 1$ **35a.** 3×10^6 mi
b. 0.016 **c.** $\dfrac{x^2}{8.649 \times 10^{15}} + \dfrac{y^2}{8.647 \times 10^{15}} = 1$
37. $\frac{x^2}{20.25} + \frac{y^2}{4} = 1$ **39.** about 282.67 ft

MIXED REVIEW **41.** $-1, -4$ **43.** 2.26
45.   **47.**

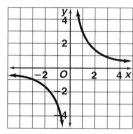   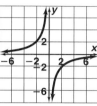

Lesson 10-5   pages 484–490

ON YOUR OWN
1.   **3.**

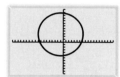

5. $(0, \pm\sqrt{97})$ **7.** $(\pm\sqrt{265}, 0)$

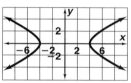   

11. $y = \pm\sqrt{x^2 - 1}$ **13.** $y = \pm\sqrt{2x^2 + 8}$

$(\pm 1, 0)$ $(0, \pm 2.83)$

17. $\frac{y^2}{20.25} - \frac{x^2}{4} = 1$

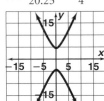

19. $\frac{x^2}{32} - \frac{y^2}{64} = 1$

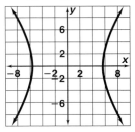

21. $\frac{x^2}{36} - \frac{y^2}{64} = 1$

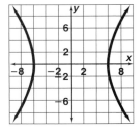

23. $\frac{y^2}{25} - \frac{x^2}{144} = 1$

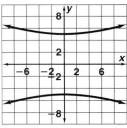

27a. "$ERROR$" appears for the values of x such that $x^2 - 9$ is negative. **b.** As x increases, $x - y$ becomes smaller. **d.** The asymptotes are the lines $y = \pm x$.

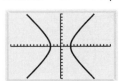

MIXED REVIEW **29.** $\begin{bmatrix} -1 & 4 & -16 \\ -5 & 2 & 5 \end{bmatrix}$ **31.** $\frac{1}{18}$

33. 1 unit left **35.** 2 units right and 1 unit up

CHECKPOINT **1.** $\frac{x^2}{25} + \frac{y^2}{16} = 1$ **2.** $\frac{x^2}{25} + \frac{y^2}{29} = 1$

3. $\frac{x^2}{100} + \frac{y^2}{149} = 1$

4. $(\pm\sqrt{65}, 0)$

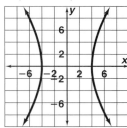

5. $(0, \pm\sqrt{89})$

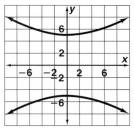

6. $(\pm\sqrt{85}, 0)$

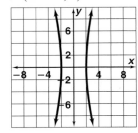

7. $(0, \pm 2\sqrt{34})$

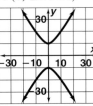

8. Place the center at $(3, -5)$. **9.** E

Lesson 10-6   pages 491–496

ON YOUR OWN **1.** parabola **3.** ellipse **5.** hyperbola

7. $x^2 + (y + 7)^2 = 36$

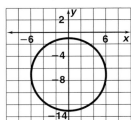

9. $\frac{(x + 2)^2}{9} + \frac{(y - 3)^2}{4} = 1$

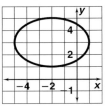

13. They will be translated similarly.

15. $\frac{(x - 3)^2}{36} + \frac{(y - 2)^2}{9} = 1$

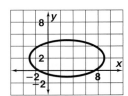

17. $\frac{(y + 3)^2}{4} - \frac{(x - 6)^2}{5} = 1$

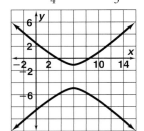

19. $\frac{(x-6)^2}{64} + \frac{(y-2)^2}{36} = 1$ **21.** C

23. ellipse; $\frac{x^2}{9} + \frac{y^2}{36} = 1$ **25.** hyperbola; $\frac{y^2}{36} - \frac{x^2}{9} = 1$

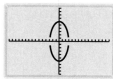

31. $\frac{(x-1)^2}{9} + \frac{(y+1)^2}{16} = 1$

33. $x = (y+3)^2 + 1$

MIXED REVIEW   **35.** $\begin{bmatrix} 2 & 0 & 4 \\ 0 & 2 & -6 \end{bmatrix}$

37. $\begin{bmatrix} 0 & 1.5 & 0 \\ -1.5 & 0 & 6 \end{bmatrix}$

Toolbox   page 497

1.

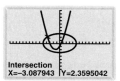

Intersection
X=−3.087943 Y=2.3595042

$(-3.09, 2.36)$,
$(1.22, 2.91)$

3.

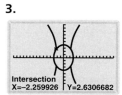

Intersection
X=−2.259926 Y=2.6306682

$(-2.26, 2.63)$,
$(-2.26, -2.63)$.
$(2.26, 2.63)$,
$(2.26, -2.63)$,

7. The lines will not intersect.

Wrap Up   pages 499–501

1.

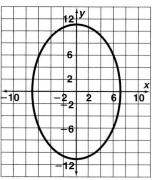

ellipse; $x = \pm7$, $y = \pm11$;
domain: -7 to 7, range:
-11 to 11

2.

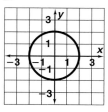

circle; $x = \pm2$, $y = \pm2$; domain:
-2 to 2, range: -2 to 2

3.

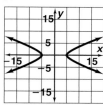

hyperbola; $x = \pm5$;
domain: $-\infty$ to -5
and 5 to ∞, range: all
real numbers

4.

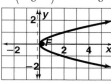

parabola; $x = 5$;
domain: 5 to ∞,
range: $-\infty$ to ∞

5. $\left(0, \frac{1}{20}\right)$; $y = -\frac{1}{20}$

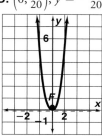

6. $\left(-\frac{1}{8}, 0\right)$; $x = -\frac{1}{8}$

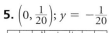

7. $\left(0, -\frac{1}{4}\right)$; $y = \frac{1}{4}$

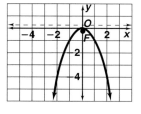

8. $\left(-2, 0\right)$; $x = 2$

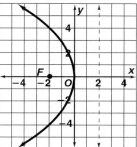

10. $x^2 + y^2 = 16$

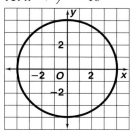

11. $(x-8)^2 + (y-1)^2 = 25$

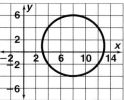

12. $(x + 3)^2 + (y - 2)^2 = 100$

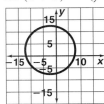

13. The center is the point (h, k) and the circumference is $2\pi r$. Find r and substitute h, k, and r into the equation $(x - h)^2 + (y - k)^2 = r^2$.

14. $\frac{x^2}{17} + \frac{y^2}{16} = 1$ **15.** $\frac{x^2}{25} + \frac{y^2}{29} = 1$ **16.** $\frac{x^2}{9} + \frac{y^2}{10} = 1$

17. $\frac{x^2}{40} + \frac{y^2}{36} = 1$ **18.** $\frac{x^2}{64} + \frac{y^2}{16} = 1$ **19.** B

20. $(\pm 16.2, 0)$ **21.** $(0, \pm 23.9)$

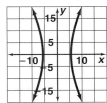

22. $(\pm 14.2, 0)$ **23.** $(0, \pm 10.4)$

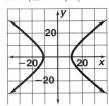

24. $\frac{x^2}{64} - \frac{y^2}{25} = 1$ **25.** hyperbola   **26.** circle

27. hyperbola   **28.** ellipse   **30.** $\frac{1}{18}$ **31.** $\frac{1}{4}$ **32.** $\frac{1}{18}$
33. 1   **34.** 0 0 0 1 1 1 1 1 2 2 3; 1; 1   **35.** 11 11 12 14 18 19 19 19 20; 18; 19   **36.** 27 28 29 30 31 31 32 33 35; 31; 31   **37.** 1 1 2 3 3 3 4 5 5 5 6 7 8; 4; 3 and 5

Cumulative Review   page 503

1. A   **3.** A   **5.** B   **7.** D   **9.** A   **11.** D   **15.** $780.61; $916.05

CHAPTER 11

Lesson 11-1   pages 506–511

ON YOUR OWN   **1.** Yes; probabilities add to 1 and all outcomes are used once.   **3.** No; 2 is used twice, since 2 is both even and prime.   **5.** 0.47   **7.** 0.11   **9.** 0.89   **11.** B

17.
Probability Distribution

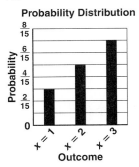

21.

Outcome	Probability
Both even	0.25
Both odd	0.25
One even, one odd	0.5

MIXED REVIEW   **25.** 30°, 150°   **27.** 1.58   **29.** $\frac{1}{16}$
31. $\frac{9}{16}$

Lesson 11-2   pages 512–517

ON YOUR OWN   **1.** $\frac{81}{90}$ or 0.9   **3.** $\frac{54}{90}$ or 0.6   **5.** $\frac{5}{9}$ or 0.56
7a. 0.556   **b.** 0.546   **c.** 0.296   **d.** 0.542   **e.** 0.461
f. 0.220   **9a.** 0.15   **b.** 0.6   **c.** They are equal.

MIXED REVIEW   **15.** $x^4 - 2x^3 - 3x^2$
17. $x^4 + 10x^3 + 33x^2 + 36x$ **19.** 0.2, 0.3, 0.6, 0.7, 0.8, 0.9, 1.2; 0.7

Toolbox   page 518

1a. 0.402   **b.** 0.01   **c.** 0.0002   **3.** 0.64   **5.** 0.7   **7.** 0.16

Lesson 11-3   pages 519–525

ON YOUR OWN   **1.** 90.2; 95; 95   **3.** 441.4; 422; none
5. 1113.4; 1103; none   **7.** $\approx$ 14.7; 15; 15 and 17
9. 17.275; 17.05; 16.3 and 19.1   **11a.** 0%   **b.** No; if there are an even number of items in a data set, the median may lie between data values.   **c.** No; 50% of a data set will always lie at or below the median.

13.   **15.**

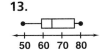 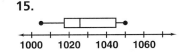

17. 9.8; it raises the mean by 0.7625.   **19a.** 80.3; 83.5
b. Median; it is least affected by the outlier.

21a.   **b.** 34;

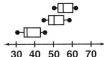 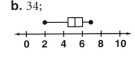

23a.

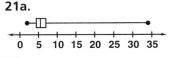

MIXED REVIEW **25.** $y = \log_3 x$ **27.** $y = \pm\sqrt{\dfrac{8}{x}}$ **29.** 7

CHECKPOINT **1.** No; the function values add to more than 1. **2.** Yes; the function values add to 1. **3.** 0.21 **4.** 0.625 **5.** 0.535 **6.** 0.66 **7.** 5.69; 5; 4 **8.** 3.82; 2.85; no mode

Lesson 11-4   pages 526–531

ON YOUR OWN **1.** 5.7; 5; 2.5 **3.** 37.5; 25; 15 **5.** 1648; 486; 288 **7.** 228.33 **9.** 6.93 **11.** 5.98 **13.** 16.33; 72.69; the bird speeds are more spread out. **15a.** 1.92 **b.** 2.12 **17a.** union: $561.83, $352; nonunion: $393.50, $360 **b.** $119.95; $125.18 **c.** 1; 2

MIXED REVIEW **23.** $1 - 6i$ **25.** $-4 + 3i$ **27.** 2 **29.** x **31.** 3 **33.** x **35.** $\dfrac{1}{2}$ **37.** $\dfrac{1}{6}$ **39.** $\dfrac{\sqrt{2}}{10}$

Lesson 11-5   pages 532–537

ON YOUR OWN **1.** 72.8% **3.** 91.7% **5.** ±5% **7.** ±3.2% **9.** Greeting card shoppers will be overrepresented; interview at store entrance. **11.** Bus riders will be overrepresented; select random classrooms. **13.** 100 **15.** 400 **17.** 2500 **19.** 10.7%; ±3.3% **21.** 40%; ±6.3% **23.** E **27a.** Yes; range is 48–64% so she may only have 48% or 49% of the total votes. **b.** More confident; new range is 51–59%. **29.** 92%; ±4.5%; 87.5–96.5% **31.** 67%; ±4.9%; 62.1–71.9%

MIXED REVIEW **37.** $x^3 + 6x^2 + 12x + 8$ **39.** $m^3 + 3m^2n + 3mn^2 + n^3$

CHECKPOINT **1.** 33.83; 34; 34; 20; 6.2 **2.** 11; 10.5; 10; 5; 1.63 **3.** 2.375; 2; 1; 4; 1.41 **4.** 34%; ±3.8%; 30.2–37.8% **5.** E

Lesson 11-6   pages 538–544

ON YOUR OWN **1.** A question is a trial, and a success is a correct guess; 5; 0.5; 0.3125. **3.** A shift is a trial, and a success is no breakdown; 3; 0.9; 0.729. **5.** 0.375 **7.** 0.234 **9.** 0.016 **11.** 0.136 **13.** 0.246 **15.** 0.001 **17a. i.** 28% **ii.** 66% **iii.** 34% **b.** No; probability of that is 34% even when the claim is true. **21a.** symmetric around $x = 3$

c. no

23.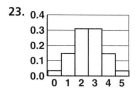

25a. 5 or more correct would be rare; with $n = 10$ and $p = 0.2$, $P(x \geq 5) \approx 0.026 + 0.005 + 0.001 = 3.2\%$.

MIXED REVIEW **29.** 0, 9 **31.** 7, −1 **33.** $2 \pm \dfrac{\sqrt{15}}{3}$ **35.** 0, −5 **37.** 14, 16, 10, 8 **39.** 18.4, 19.3, 16.6, 15.7

Toolbox   page 545

1. 0.68 **3.** 0.38 **5.** 0.48 **7.** 0.28 **9a.** 0.48, 0.48 **b.** The graph is symmetric around $x = 0$.

Lesson 11-7   pages 546–551

ON YOUR OWN **1.** 67.7 **3.** 79.1

5. 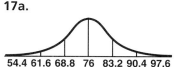 **7.** yes **9.** 68% **11.** 84% **13.** 81.5%

15a. 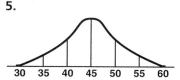 **b.** No; the distribution is not symmetric and has too great a concentration around the mean.

17a. 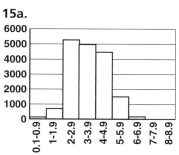 **b.** 81.5%

MIXED REVIEW **21.** $y = \dfrac{2}{x}$

23a. $y = 30 + 3.5x$

b. when you see 8 or fewer movies per month

Wrap Up   pages 553–555

1. No, probability cannot be negative. **2.** Yes, the sum of the probabilities is 1. **4.** 0.6 **5.** 0.9 **6.** 0.76 **7.** 0.2 **8.** 13.4; 12.5; 12 **9.** 4.96; 5; none **11.** 7.5; 7; 3; 2.06 **12.** 268.5; 376; 352; 163.88 **13.** D **14.** ±5%; 85–95% **15.** ±7.6%; 27.4–42.6% **16.** ±3.3%; 64.7–71.3% **17.** ±6.1%; 5.9–18.1%

18. 0.422 **19.** 0.309 **20.** 0.311 **21.** 40.9 **22.** 53.2
23. 36.8 **24.** 57.3

25.

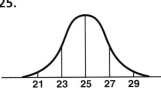

26. 13, 15; each number is 2 greater than the previous one, beginning with 1.

27. −14, −16; each number is 2 less than the previous one, starting with −2. **28.** 3125, 15,625; each number is 5 times the previous one, beginning with 0.2. **29.** 20, 15; each number is 5 less than the previous one, beginning with 50. **30.** 8, 4; each number is half the previous one, beginning with 512. **31.** 20, 23; each number is 3 greater than the previous one, beginning with 2.

Preparing for Standardized Tests page 557

1. B **3.** E **5.** B **7.** C **9.** A **11.** $646.73

CHAPTER 12

Lesson 12-1 pages 560–565

ON YOUR OWN **1.** Add −3 to the nth term; 65, 62, 59.
3. Add $n + 2$ to the nth term; 25, 33, 42. **5.** Multiply the nth term by $\frac{1}{2}$; $\frac{1}{64}$, $\frac{1}{128}$, $\frac{1}{256}$. **7.** Multiply the nth term by −2; −128, 256, −512. **9.** Odd terms are zero, even terms have denominators that increase by 2; 0, $\frac{1}{7}$, 0.
11. 110 boxes

13.

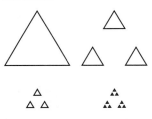

15. $a_n = 2a_{n-1}, a_1 = 2$; 64 **17.** $a_n = a_{n-1} + 1$, $a_1 = -2$; 3 **19.** $a_n = \frac{1}{2}a_{n-1}, a_1 = 40; \frac{5}{4}$

21. $a_n = \frac{1}{4}a_{n-1}, a_1 = 144; \frac{9}{16}$

23. $a_n = 3n; 36$ **25.** $a_n = 4n; 48$ **27.** $a_n = \frac{1}{n+1}; \frac{1}{13}$

29. $a_n = 5n + 4; 64$ **31.** $a_n = n^2 + 1; 145$

33. recursive; 3, 9, 21, 45, 93 **35.** explicit; 3, 9, 19, 33, 51

37. recursive; 4, 0, −4, −8, −12 **39.** explicit: −24, −21, −16, −9, 0 **41a.** 15, 21 **b.** $a_n = a_{n-1} + n$ **c.** Yes; the first six terms fit the formula. **43.** 96, 192; $a_n = 3 \cdot 2^{n-1}$ or $a_1 = 3, a_n = 2a_{n-1}$ **45.** 14, 16; $a_n = 2n + 2$ or $a_1 = 4, a_n = a_{n-1} + 2$ **47.** 38, 51; $a_n = n^2 + 2$ or $a_1 = 3, a_n = a_{n-1} + 2n - 1$ **49.** 4096, 16,384; $a_n = 4^n$ or $a_n = 4a_{n-1}, a_1 = 4$
51a. $a_1 = 25, a_n = a_{n-1} + 5; a_n = 5n + 20$
b. $40 **c.** $a_n = 1.005(a_{n-1} + 20), a_1 = 40.20 **d.** 6.5%
53. 14; 18; 22 **55.** A recursive formula lets you find each term from the one before it. An explicit formula lets you find each term from its position in the sequence.

MIXED REVIEW 57. 16.8 **59.** −105 **61.** 3.3
63. 9.33 **65.** 10.25 **67.** Start at 10 and add −2.

69. Start at $\frac{5}{7}$ and add $\frac{3}{7}$.

Lesson 12-2 pages 566–570

ON YOUR OWN **1.** 15, 18, 21; $a_n = a_{n-1} + 3, a_1 = 3$

3. 8, 13, 18; $a_n = a_{n-1} + 5, a_1 = -12$ **5.** −35.262, −35.496, −35.73; $a_n = a_{n-1} - 0.234, a_1 = -34.56$

7. $-5\frac{1}{2}, -9, -12\frac{1}{2}; a_n = a_{n-1} - 3\frac{1}{2}, a_1 = 5$ **9.** 35, 21, 7; $a_n = a_{n-1} - 14, a_1 = 77$ **13.** 4 **15.** $\frac{1}{2}$ **17.** −1

19. $\frac{4}{5}$ **21.** no **23.** no **25.** no **27.** no **29.** no
31a. 20, 45, 75, 110, 150, 195, 245, 300, 360, 425, 495
b. $a_n = a_{n-1} + (20 + 5(n - 1)); a_1 = 20$ **c.** $495
33. 0.3 **35.** −59 **37.** 240 **39.** −159 **41.** 13 **43.** 7.5
45. −4, −10, −16 **47.** −8, −17, −26 **49.** −7
51. 660 **53.** $a_n = 2 + (n - 1)2; a_n = a_{n-1} + 2, a_1 = 2$
55. $a_n = -20 + (n - 1)12; a_n = a_{n-1} + 12, a_1 = -20$
57. $a_n = 11.7 - 0.5(n - 1); a_n = a_{n-1} - 0.5, a_1 = 11.7$
59. $a_n = 15 + (n - 1)(-12); a_n = a_{n-1} - 12, a_1 = 15$
61. $a_n = (n - 1)(-3); a_n = a_{n-1} - 3, a_1 = 0$
63. $840 **65.** $(1 + \sqrt{21}, 0), (1 - \sqrt{21}, 0)$

67. $r = \sqrt[3]{V \cdot \dfrac{3}{4\pi}}$ **69.** 21 **71.** $33\frac{1}{3}$

Toolbox page 571

1. fifth, seventh, sixth, fourth